OF ENGLAN

YEAR BOOK

129TH EDITION

MarketPlace	: AUK
Order Number	: 203-5868943-5272330
Ship Method	: Standard
Order Date	: 2014-11-27
Email	: bqmcxb4dhcnjy27@marketplace.amazon.co.uk

Items : 1

Qty	**Item**	**Locator**
1	The Church of England Yearbook 2013 ISBN : 0715110594	MUL-7-UD-119-08-12 RY

RCode:

We hope that you are completely satisfied with your purchase and ask you to leave positive feedback accordingly.

However, if you are unsatisfied with your order, please contact us by telephone or email. We will do whatever it takes to resolve the issue.

Mulberry House, Woods Way, Goring By Sea, West Sussex, BN12 4QY. Tel:+44(0)1903 507544
Email: sales@worldofbooks.com | Twitter: @WorldofBooksltd | Web: www.worldofbooks.com

Contents

INDEX TO ADVERTISEMENTS

Advertisements can be found on the following pages

The inclusion of an advertisement is for the purposes of information and is not to be taken as implying acceptance of the objects of the advertiser by the publisher.

Church House Publishing, Church House, Great Smith Street, London SW1P 3AZ

ISBN 978–0–7151–1059–1
ISSN 0069 3987

Typeset by RefineCatch Ltd, Bungay, Suffolk

Printed and bound by CPI Group (UK) Ltd, Croydon, CR0 4YY

The Church of England Year Book
The official Year Book of the Church of England

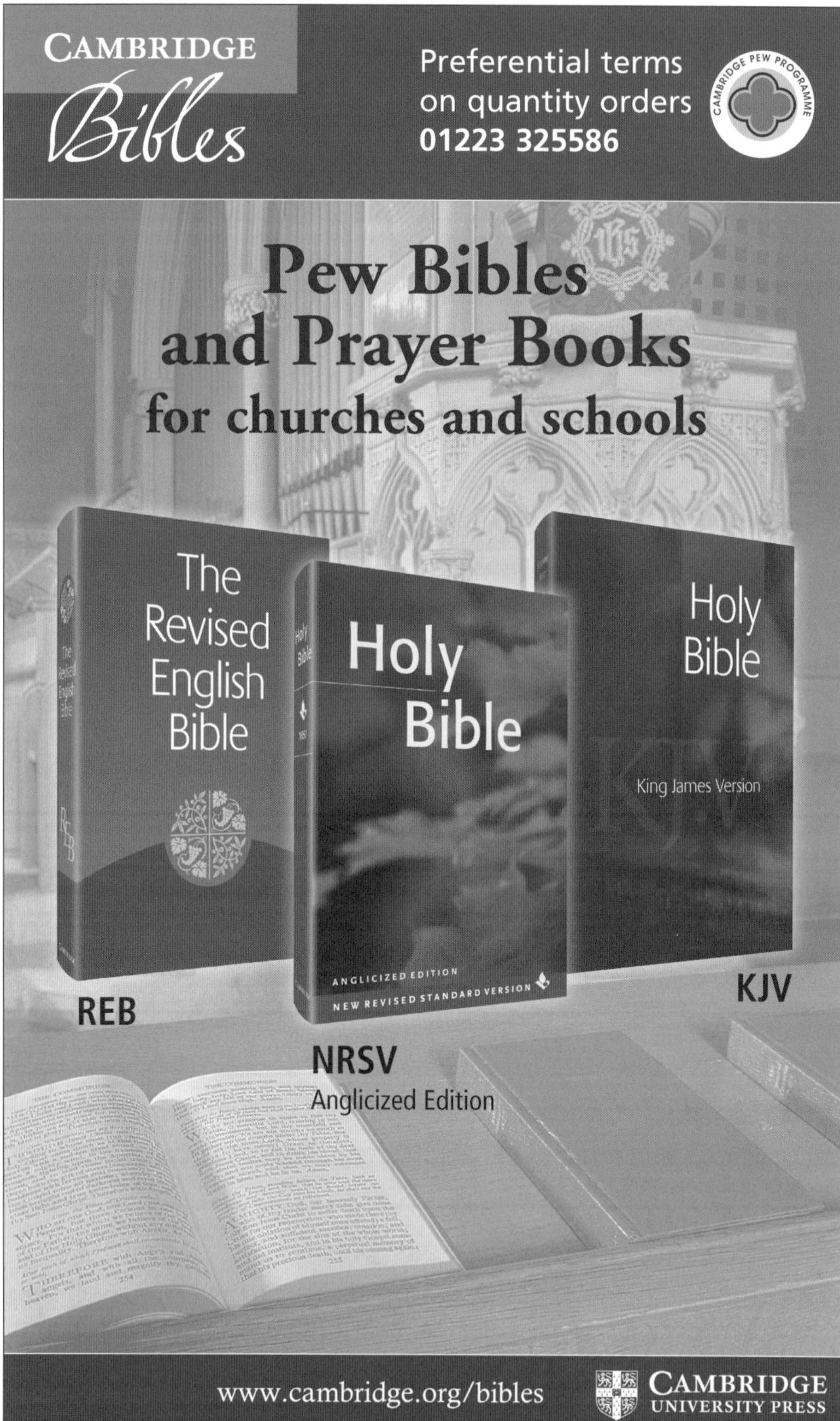
CAMBRIDGE
Bibles
Preferential terms
on quantity orders
01223 325586
CAMBRIDGE PEW PROGRAMME
Pew Bibles
and Prayer Books
for churches and schools
The Revised English Bible
REB
Holy Bible
ANGLICIZED EDITION
NEW REVISED STANDARD VERSION
NRSV
Anglicized Edition
Holy Bible
King James Version
KJV
www.cambridge.org/bibles
CAMBRIDGE
UNIVERSITY PRESS

A YEAR IN REVIEW 2011–12

NOVEMBER

The month opened with St Paul's Cathedral still affected by the Occupy protest. The Mission and Public Affairs Council (MPA) published *Reflections and Resources on the Church and capitalism*, compiled in light of events there.

The two Archbishops questioned the rationale for a wholly or mainly elected House of Lords in their submission to the Parliamentary Joint Committee on the Government's Draft Bill and White Paper, with Dr Williams later giving evidence to the Committee in person.

The Archbishop of Canterbury spoke at a British Academy event examining the historical origins of the Authorized (King James) Bible and its literary and cultural influences. Later in the month he preached at a Thanksgiving Service for the 400th anniversary of the 1611 translation attended by HM The Queen.

The Archbishop joined other faith leaders on a tour of the London 2012 Olympic Park. Dr Williams and Sri Shruti Dharma Das Ji launched the Hindu Christian Forum at Lambeth Palace; to mark National Prisons Week, Dr Williams also hosted a lecture by Crispin Blunt MP on *Restorative Justice*.

The Archbishop of York welcomed the High Pay Commission's report examining executive pay across the UK, calling for an end to corrosive pay deals across all sectors. The Dioceses Commission began formal consultations on its proposals for the Yorkshire dioceses following consideration of the written responses to its initial vision.

The Archbishop of Canterbury released a statement for the World Day of Prayer and Action for Children, and visited The Children's Society's *Safe in the City* project in Birmingham to support the charity's *Make Runaways Safe* campaign. Dr Williams also released video messages of support at a multi-faith rally and concert in Durban, held on the eve of the UN Climate Change Conference; and for World AIDS Day, in which he spoke about the part sexual violence played in the spread of HIV.

The Archbishop wrote his customary Advent letter to the Primates of the Anglican Communion and Moderators of the United Churches. Following a visit to the Diocese of Egypt in 2010, the Archbishop of York launched an Advent Appeal to raise funds for building a new Community Centre for the Deaf in Cairo.

The Rt Hon Eric Pickles MP launched *Near Neighbours* – a £5 million programme created by the Church Urban Fund and Archbishops' Council following the grant by the Department for Communities and Local Government in February 2011. The Council and the Church Commissioners distributed £1 million as part of a nationwide move to help develop successful church growth projects in deprived areas where existing activity had a proven record of growth. The funds were part of a wider research and development programme, a key aim of which was to ensure projects were evaluated to provide evidence of what was proving effective.

MPA published its Response to the Discussion Paper from the Commission on a UK Bill of Rights, giving a clear 'no' to the proposals.

DECEMBER

In his Christmas Letter to the heads of other Churches, the Archbishop of Canterbury urged Christian leaders to overcome suspicion and fear. On BBC Radio's *Pause for Thought*, Dr Williams reassured listeners that however imperfect or 'messy' their Christmasses, God would still be there for them. The Archbishop of York's online Advent Calendar enabled visitors to follow his personal journey towards Christmas.

The Archbishop of Canterbury and the Joint Presidents of the Council of Christians and Jews visited the day centre for the homeless at the Dellow Centre in the City of London. The Archbishop of York called for an urgent new 'social covenant' for funding care for older people in England. The C of E welcomed the Government's announcement of a new £10 million Local Energy Assessment Fund which gave community groups, including churches, a chance to bid for money.

With the support of the Bishop of Chichester, the Archbishop of Canterbury announced an enquiry into child protection issues in that diocese, appointing Bishop John Gladwin and Chancellor Rupert Bursell QC to advise him on any steps needed to ensure the highest possible standards of safeguarding there.

The families of soldiers from Yorkshire killed or seriously injured in Afghanistan joined the Archbishop of York at a service of remembrance and thanksgiving in the chapel at Bishopthorpe Palace. The Bishop of Wakefield called on the international community to chart a new course of action in Afghanistan.

The Times published an article by the Archbishop of Canterbury on Christmas Eve with the message that 'In Congo or in Croydon, God is there for us: whether we are damaged by war, the riots, illness or depression, the Christmas message helps us recover.'

New ethical investment policies on pornography and high interest rate lending were adopted by the Church's national investing bodies following advice from the Church's Ethical Investment Advisory Group (EIAG).

In a submission to the consultation on the BBC *Delivering Quality First* review, the Bishop of Norwich warned that the importance of local radio to the community must not be ignored. Many consulted were convinced that local radio was one of the BBC's 'Crown Jewels' but one which tended to be seriously undervalued.

Appointments Canon Jonathan Draper, Residentiary Canon of York Minster, was appointed Dean of Exeter. The House of Bishops appointed the Rt Revd Robert Paterson, Bishop of Sodor and Man, to chair the Group established to advise the House on reviewing its Pastoral Statement on civil partnerships.

JANUARY

In his BBC New Year message, the Archbishop of Canterbury reflected on the importance that Christianity bestows on young people and challenged us actively to support local youth facilities as a crucial part in a healthy society. The Archbishop of York wrote a special New Year message for *The Yorkshire Post*.

The Archbishop of Cape Town responded to Dr Williams' Advent Letter to the Anglican Primates. In his letter, Dr Makgoba reflected on the Anglican Covenant as 'necessary' for Anglicans 'in recalling us to ourselves'. At Lambeth Palace, Palestinian Authority President, Mahmoud Abbas, met representatives of UK Churches, led by the Archbishop of Canterbury, to discuss the plight of Christians in the Holy Land and the political situation affecting the peace process.

Jamaica welcomed the Archbishop of York to help celebrate the 50th Anniversary of Independence. Closer to home, Dr Sentamu spent two days in the Diocese of Chester, the visit beginning at the ecumenical Cre8 Youth and Community Programme in Macclesfield. The Archbishop of Canterbury visited the Prison Radio Association at HMP Brixton, discussing with prisoners their training and work in prison radio.

Dr Williams joined the other Presidents of Churches Together in England in heralding 2012 as a 'year of celebrations in England', praising the central role of churches in celebrating the Olympic and Paralympic Torch Relays, the Diamond Jubilee and the 30th Olympiad.

The Children's Society called for a radical new approach to childhood as landmark research in *The Good Childhood Report 2012*, launched by the Archbishop of York, revealed that half a million children across the UK were unhappy with their lives. A new funding focus to support bridge-building church community projects was approved by the Church and Community Fund for an initial three years starting in January 2012.

MPA responded to the report of the self-appointed 'Commission on Assisted Dying', which had excluded from its membership anyone with a known objection to assisted suicide. It had failed to demonstrate that vulnerable people would not be placed at greater risk under its proposals than under present legislation, which struck an excellent balance between safeguarding hundreds of thousands of vulnerable people and treating with fairness and compassion those few people who had assisted a loved one to die.

The Church encouraged its 13,000 parishes and their communities to celebrate the Diamond Jubilee, and announced its participation in two national initiatives – *The Big Jubilee Lunch* and *The Big Thank You*. In addition, ChurchCare – the online resource caring for the C of E's 16,000 church buildings – started collecting stories about the regal links between churches, cathedrals and the monarchy. These individual histories were to be woven together to create a 'Royal Trail' around England's places of worship, celebrating the unique links between churches and the Crown.

The Church Buildings Council (CBC) announced a £10,000 prize, funded by The Jerusalem Trust, for commissioning new art for parish churches. CBC also welcomed Home Secretary Theresa May's announcement that paying cash for scrap metal would be outlawed.

Provisional attendance figures for 2010 showed that marriages were up 4 per cent, and national 'mapping' identified at least 1,000 'fresh expressions of church'. Latest attendance figures also showed that approaching 1.7 million people continued to attend C of E services each month, and around 1.1 million attended one of the Church's 16,000 churches as part of a typical week.

A new C of E website developed by the Parish Buying Service was opened, offering parishes savings on £200 million worth of services each year.

Appointment Sir Joseph Pilling was appointed Chair of the Group to advise the House of Bishops on human sexuality.

FEBRUARY

In addition to women bishops, General Synod's agenda included debates on assisted dying, health care, House of Lords reform, and Eucharistic Prayers for use when children were present. It was this Synod's first opportunity to engage with the process designed to make it possible for women to be bishops while also making provision for those who would not be able to receive their ministry. The Archbishop of Canterbury highlighted the Queen's Christian faith as the Synod agreed a Loyal Address on her Diamond Jubilee. In a debate on recent violence in Nigeria, Dr Williams warned Synod that the country was under threat of 'disintegration' at the hands of extremist Islamist group Boko Haram.

The United Reformed Church and the C of E participated in a Service of Reconciliation, Healing of Memories and Mutual Commitment at Westminster Abbey, marking the 350th anniversary of 'the Great Ejectment' following the 1662 Act of Uniformity. The historic service marked a significant step forward in the development of closer relationships between the two Churches.

How to serve your community's needs without reinventing the wheel in every parish was the challenge posed by a new project launched by the Archbishop of York at the Synod. Dr Sentamu emphasized how the nation faced a prolonged economic downturn in which every community would be affected and the need to build up social bonds had rarely been stronger.

Sir Anthony Kenny chaired a dialogue at Oxford University between the Archbishop of Canterbury and Professor Richard Dawkins on the subject of *The nature of human beings and the question of their ultimate origin*.

The Archbishop made a personal pilgrimage to the Holy Land, visiting religious sites associated with Jesus' ministry and describing the pilgrimage as an opportunity for renewal and spiritual refreshment. In meetings with religious leaders Dr Williams commented on the good personal relationships between the leaders of the different faiths and expressed his appreciation of the warm welcome he had received.

Dr Williams welcomed HM The Queen and HRH The Duke of Edinburgh to a multi-faith event at Lambeth Palace, presenting leading representatives of the historic Faith Communities in the UK to Her Majesty and His Royal Highness, including representatives of the eight non-Christian religions as well as Christianity.

With other Church leaders, the Archbishop and the Bishop of London, chair of *Shrinking the Footprint*, signed the Ash Wednesday Declaration, launched by Operation Noah, calling on the Church to care for God's creation and challenging it to realize that concern about climate change was foundational to the Gospel; the Declaration called for repentance over the prevailing 'shrug-culture' towards climate change.

The Archbishop of York repeated his 2009 opposition to a Private Member's Bill in Uganda which sought to prosecute homosexuals. Church leaders in Wakefield secured Foreign Office funding to bring a delegation from Pakistan on a peace mission to Britain to share good practice and help heal rifts between Muslims and Christians.

On BBC Radio's *Sunday Worship*, the Archbishop of Canterbury drew on the life of Dietrich Bonhoeffer as he preached on the theme of freedom – what it meant to be free and how we can achieve the true freedom 'to be what we most deeply are'. In Geneva to meet the World Council of Churches and UN agencies, the Archbishop engaged in high-level dialogue on ecumenical and development-related issues. Dr Williams contributed to a round-table discussion on the unity of the Christian Church, and delivered a lecture on *Human Rights and Religious Faith* at the World Council of Churches Ecumenical Centre.

Student protests and the debate around Higher Education funding prompted the theme for Education Sunday 2012, *Learning and serving*, which issued a strong challenge about responsibility to others and asked what education was for – answering that it should prompt people to use their newly-acquired skills for others, not just themselves.

The Bishop of Carlisle supported a petition, set up by Age UK, calling on the Government to reform the care system for older and disabled people so that everyone received the care they needed to live with respect and dignity.

Appointments The Revd Jonathan Clark, Rector of Stoke Newington St Mary and Vicar of Brownswood Park, was appointed Bishop of Croydon; and the Ven Dr Michael Ipgrave, Archdeacon of Southwark, was appointed Bishop of Woolwich. The Revd Mark Beach, Rector of Rugby, was appointed Dean of Rochester.

MARCH

The Archbishop of Canterbury announced his intention to step down at the end of December 2012 to become Master of Magdalene College, Cambridge. The Archbishop of York expressed his sadness at the news, describing their partnership in the gospel over the previous six years as the most creative period of his ministry.

The Archbishop of Canterbury and Pope Benedict XVI led evening prayer together at the Church of San Gregorio Magno al Celio, as part of the Archbishop's visit to Rome. After a private meeting, the Archbishop and the Pope joined the resident monastic Community for Vespers. Dr Williams met Buddhist leaders at The Buddhist Society's London headquarters to affirm dialogue between the Christian and Buddhist communities.

Dr and Mrs Williams attended a special Eucharist to affirm the achievements of women, timed to mark both International Women's Day and Mothering Sunday, and arranged by the Anglican Alliance in conjunction with the Mothers' Union. The Archbishop preached to a packed cathedral in the city of St David's, a site of worship and pilgrimage for hundreds of years. In his sermon, he spoke on the theme of sainthood and martyrdom, referring to figures such as St David and Oscar Romero.

Dr Williams expressed his sorrow on learning of the death of His Holiness Pope Shenouda III, 'an exemplary and outstanding Christian leader both within Egypt and far beyond its boundaries', whose long ministry had seen the most extraordinary revival in the Coptic Orthodox Church.

The Archbishop of York and BBC Radio presenter the Revd Richard Coles wrote special prayers for the media, featured on the Church and Media Network's website alongside other resources to encourage churches and individual Christians to pray for the media. Dr Sentamu also paid tribute to the work of the BBC World Service on its 80th anniversary. The Archbishop, a long-term supporter and advocate, described it as 'the gold standard for international affairs coverage'.

The Archbishop spoke about the importance of affordable care for older people as he visited Scarborough. Dr Sentamu joined human rights activist Ben Freeth from Zimbabwe and Pastor Paul Negrut from Romania to deliver The Royal Geographical Society Lecture on *Fighting Injustice Under Dictatorship*. The three told their inspirational stories, giving insights into living under dictatorships.

The Chancellor unexpectedly announced in his Budget that zero-rated alterations to listed buildings would in future be charged at the standard rate of 20 per cent, costing the Church up to £20 million per annum. CBC created an e-petition calling on the Chancellor to bring back zero-rate VAT to alterations to the Church's 12,500 listed churches. A coalition of national Churches and charities, including the C of E, welcomed reports that the Government planned to enforce a minimum unit price on alcohol sales, warning, however, that a long delay on implementation could cost lives.

The English group working for unity between Anglicans and Roman Catholics began a new stage of its life. Meeting at Canterbury Cathedral in a context of prayer and worship, the newly configured English Anglican–Roman Catholic Committee set in train a work programme for the next five years.

Church schools were at the heart of the nation and should robustly assert their Christian ethos and foundation, according to recommendations included in a groundbreaking report *The Church School of the Future*.

Appointments The Ven Richard Atkinson, Archdeacon of Leicester, was appointed Bishop of Bedford. The Very Revd Dr David Ison, Dean of Bradford, was appointed Dean of St Paul's; and Canon Dr Peter Wilcox, Residentiary Canon of Lichfield Cathedral, was appointed Dean of Liverpool. The Rt Revd Dr Christopher Cocksworth, Bishop of Coventry, was appointed Chair of the Faith and Order Commission.

APRIL

In his Easter Sermon, the Archbishop of Canterbury said that the ultimate test of the Christian religion was not whether it was useful, beneficial or helpful to the human race but whether its central claim – the resurrection of Christ – actually happened. The Archbishop of York recorded three video messages in preparation for Easter which included short reflections for Good Friday, Holy Saturday and Easter Sunday.

Dr Williams chaired the 11th Annual Building Bridges Seminar in London and Canterbury, titled *Death, Resurrection and Human Destiny: Christian and Muslim Perspectives*. As in previous such seminars, a number of texts from the Christian and Islamic traditions were used as the basis for discussion in a programme that included public lectures and private sessions.

To commemorate the 1,000th anniversary of the martyrdom of St Alfege, Archbishop of Canterbury from 1005 to 1012, Dr Williams joined the Millennium Pilgrimage from Southwark to Greenwich before delivering the sermon at a service of commemoration in St Alfege's Church, Greenwich, the site of his predecessor's martyrdom.

The Archbishop of York, the Roman Catholic Bishop of Middlesbrough and the Chair of the York and Hull District led a special service at York Minster to explore the Christian response to climate change.

The Archbishop of Canterbury urged governments to continue to invest in treatment programmes in his message for World Malaria Day 2012, praising the significant progress that local churches and grassroots organizations had made in the fight, while also cautioning against complacency.

The Archbishop of York addressed the Church Urban Fund's 2012 Conference on how Churches can have a long-term positive impact on poverty at a national and regional level. The Archbishop backed The Children's Society's report *Fair and Square* in its calls to make sure that all children living in poverty get a free school meal. Dr Sentamu also gave the keynote address *Christian Citizenship Today* at a conference at Belfast City Hall; and at Bishopthorpe Palace he addressed 50 headteachers from schools and academies across the North of England, speaking of the importance of Religious Education in schools.

Dr and Mrs Sentamu met 52 people from dioceses in the North of England to discuss relief, development and advocacy work. The Archbishop was joined at the seminar by the Bishop of Durham and the Rt Revd Moses Masamba Nthukah of the Mbeere Diocese in Kenya.

According to the latest statistics, attendance levels at regular weekly services in cathedrals had steadily increased by 30 per cent since the turn of the millennium, a growth of about 3 per cent on average each year.

Following the success of a similar Christmas website, a new website offered local churches opportunity to highlight the wide range of community and parish events being organized for the Queen's Diamond Jubilee weekend, offering the facility to add details of celebration events. MPA worked with HOPE and Biblica to produce a Diamond Jubilee edition of the New Testament, of which some 750,000 copies were given away. One hundred days before the 2012 Games, the Church released details of hundreds of its parishes preparing to serve communities via Games-themed events, hospitality, chaplaincy, sports fixtures, prayer and exhibitions.

The Church of England and a group of charities joined together to urge investors to vote during the 2012 AGM season against excessive executive remuneration packages.

Appointments Rt Hon the Lord Luce KG, GCVO was appointed Chairman of the Crown Nominations Commission for its selection of the next Archbishop of

Canterbury. Canon Mark Bonney, Residentiary Canon of Salisbury Cathedral, was appointed Dean of Ely. The Revd Arun Arora was appointed Director of Communications at Church House, Westminster.

MAY

The Archbishop and Mrs Williams welcomed HRH Prince Charles to open a new exhibition at Lambeth Palace Library, *Royal Devotion: Monarchy and the Book of Common Prayer*, tracing the close relationship between royalty and religion from medieval to modern times, in particular telling the story of the Book of Common Prayer and its importance in national life.

Dr Williams co-hosted the fifth multi-faith dialogue on international development at Lambeth Palace. Participants from more than 30 UK faith-based organizations explored how the values and beliefs contained in different faith traditions can offer fresh perspectives and innovative responses to development.

The Archbishop awarded Lambeth PhDs to Canon Leslie Oglesby and Canon Robert Reiss, the first two such PhDs awarded through the MPhil/PhD research degrees programme launched in 2007 by the Archbishop's Examination in Theology.

Dr Williams visited the diocese of Coventry, including an imaginative new café and drop-in parenting project which was changing the lives of many young families. A *Spirit of the Countryside* gathering was the final event in the Archbishop's visit, and was, said the Bishop of Warwick, 'a wonderful affirmation of rural life'. Nearly 1,500 people gathered at Stoneleigh Park on Pentecost Sunday for a service at which the Archbishop preached, followed by a picnic lunch and live music. The Archbishop of York and the Bishop of Whitby were joined at Whitby Abbey by 1,500 people to celebrate Pentecost. Dr Sentamu also visited the Isle of Man, and preached at a celebration service praising the significant contribution of the Church Urban Fund to social action in the North of England.

The Archbishop of Canterbury contributed to Lord Sacks' debate in the House of Lords to affirm how our modern political and legal settlement owed much to 'a long conversation with the Jewish and Christian intellectual world, with the ethics and theology of the human responsibility characteristic of that world'. He also praised the Department for International Development for their work on partnership with faith organizations in the field of aid and development.

On BBC Radio's *Pause for Thought*, Dr Williams expressed his hope that the Diamond Jubilee would give people the 'chance to get in touch with the background of their lives, the big context, the things that make this the sort of world it is and give us the sort of values we have'.

Prayers composed by young children at an inner city C of E primary school were used across the country as part of the Jubilee celebrations. Two new prayers were released to 'accompany' the Olympic Torch Relay on its tour of England. The Archbishop of York wrote a prayer thanking God for those journalists 'who risk their security and even their lives to expose injustice'.

The Church Commissioners announced a 2.9 per cent total return on their investments during 2011, confirming the fund's strong long-term performance. The EIAG and the rural affairs team welcomed the Groceries Code Adjudicator Bill included in the Queen's Speech, saying 'supermarkets operating ethically and appropriately with their farmer and other suppliers will have nothing to fear from this welcome piece of legislation'.

CBC welcomed the agreement with the Government over the future funding of alterations and repairs to 12,500 listed church buildings, to provide extra funding of £30 million a year in addition to the Listed Places of Worship Grant Scheme.

Appointment The Rt Revd Martin Warner, Bishop of Whitby, was appointed Bishop of Chichester.

JUNE

The Archbishop of Canterbury visited a Hindu Temple in Waltham Forest, north-east London, to learn about the local projects taking place as part of the government-funded *Near Neighbours* programme. Dr Williams was joined by the Secretary of State for Communities and Local Government to celebrate the work of the programme in fostering links between religions.

At a reception at Lambeth Palace to launch the new Christian Aid strategy paper *Partnership for Change*, the Archbishop challenged the 'myths' around international development and praised the overseas aid budget for its remarkable value for money. Lambeth Palace also hosted a launch of the Department for International Development's *Faith Partnership Principles* by the Secretary of State. The document had been produced in consultation with a working group from faith-based development organizations and set out principles to guide DfID's relationship with faith groups, to build greater common understanding, mutual respect and cooperation.

The Archbishop welcomed around 80 students aged between 15 and 18 to Lambeth Palace for a day of sharing and discussion, reflection and worship. The theme of the day ('Help, my friends think I'm mad!') looked at what it meant to be a Christian in an increasingly secular environment.

Churches across the country celebrated the Queen's Diamond Jubilee over the Bank Holiday weekend. Church services gave thanks to God for the Queen's reign, and churches joined with the cities, towns and villages they served for celebration events. In a short film produced by Lambeth Palace, the Archbishop of Canterbury spoke about the Jubilee celebrations and the significance of the 60-year reign 'in which nationally and internationally so much has shifted'. The Archbishop of York opened Bishopthorpe Palace Gardens to the public for a local gala, revealing a unique Jubilee Planting Scheme. He also held a *Party at the Palace* in the evening for 1,000 people to celebrate the Jubilee.

In its submission to the Government consultation on same-sex marriage, the Church stated it could not support the proposal to enable 'all couples, regardless of their gender, to have a civil marriage ceremony'.

On the eve of the UN Rio+20 Conference, Church leaders called for action on sustainable development now to protect future generations.

The C of E and Durham University announced a new partnership to provide validation for the education of ministers.

The Dioceses Commission considered submissions made on the draft Reorganization Scheme for the dioceses of Bradford, Ripon & Leeds and Wakefield. It also heard oral evidence from representatives of the diocesan synods of the three dioceses.

Speaking in the House of Lords in response to the publication of the Government's House of Lords Reform Bill, the Bishop of Leicester, Convenor of the Lords Spiritual, recognized the need for some reform of the House and welcomed the opportunity that the Bill would give for thorough debate about the future of Parliament.

CBC welcomed the announcement from HM Revenue and Customs that transitional arrangements for zero-rated VAT for alterations to cathedral and church buildings would be extended to cover all schemes which had already applied for a faculty or approval under the Care of Cathedrals Measure.

Appointments Canon Edward Condry, Residentiary Canon of Canterbury Cathedral and Diocesan Director of Education, was appointed Bishop of Ramsbury. The Ven Roger Bush, Archdeacon of Cornwall, was appointed Dean of Truro.

JULY

The women bishops legislation was at the centre of the General Synod's agenda at York University. It also included world mission, church growth, the August 2011 riots, manifesting faith in public life, church schools, and Palestine and Israel. The draft legislation was approved, by simple majorities, by the House of Laity and by both Houses of each Convocation. That opened the way for it to be presented for final approval by the whole Synod, but Synod approved a motion of the Steering Committee for the draft legislation to adjourn the Final Approval debate to enable the House of Bishops to reconsider its amendment to clause 5 of the draft Measure. The Archbishops announced that, following reconsideration by the House of Bishops in September, the General Synod would meet in November in London to resume the Final Approval debate.

The Archbishop of Canterbury contributed to BBC Radio's *The Voice of God*, in which priest and broadcaster the Revd Richard Coles explored the different ways that God is depicted as speaking in literature, theatre, music, film and within sacred texts. The Archbishop also took part in a public conversation with the Rt Hon Tony Blair and writer and former *Daily Telegraph* editor Charles Moore on the subject of *Religion in Public Life*.

The Archbishop of Canterbury called for urgent humanitarian assistance in conflict areas of South Sudan and renewed efforts to resolve outstanding differences between it and Sudan. The Archbishop met a group of young people from around the world, gathered for The Peacebuilders' Exchange, organized by the Anglican Alliance in collaboration with the Community of the Cross of Nails in Coventry.

At a gathering for Anglican Communion guests at Lambeth Palace, Dr Williams expressed gratitude for the rich contribution to church life in England made by those from other parts of the worldwide Anglican Communion. This followed his intervention at General Synod in the debate on World-shaped Mission in which he highlighted the value of collaborating with and learning from the global church 'on our own doorstep'.

The Archbishop of York welcomed and gave a blessing at a Service of Thanksgiving for the Yorkshire Regiment held at York Minster on their homecoming from Afghanistan. The Archbishop presented 190 badges and certificates to Year 8 students from Manor C of E Academy who had completed the Young Leaders Award run by his Youth Trust. Thirty-five secondary schools had signed up to the Awards with around 4,000 young people taking part. Dr Sentamu boarded Noah's Ark on the huge stage of York Mystery Plays 2012, of which he is a patron.

As the Archbishop of Canterbury attended the Opening Ceremony of the London 2012 Olympic Games, churches up and down the country got into the Olympic spirit. 'I think it's fantastic that we can celebrate the great sporting talent we have in this country and welcome the best athletes from across the world to compete on the biggest stage. We should celebrate our Team GB with pride,' said the Archbishop of York as the Games began.

The Anglican–Jewish Commission of the Archbishop of Canterbury and the Chief Rabbinate of Israel met in Oxford. The Commission's mandate provides for the Archbishop of Canterbury and the two Chief Rabbis (from the Ashkenazi and Sephardi communities) to meet each year alternately in England and Jerusalem.

The Archbishop of York called for British farmers to be paid a fair price for their produce, contending that supermarkets were not valuing the contribution the agricultural sector made to national life. Dr Sentamu said British consumers, aided and abetted by supermarkets, were paying too little for their food and claimed that cheap imports were making it difficult for the country's farmers to earn a decent living.

The key to unlock the transformation of Auckland Castle was turned, with the ownership of Auckland Castle and the Zurbaran paintings being transferred from the Church Commissioners to new trusts.

The Bishop of Norwich highlighted a scheme in his diocese giving broadband access to remote rural communities as an example of best practice in a report from the Lords Communications Select Committee which said the Government's broadband strategy must not leave communities behind.

AUGUST

The Archbishop of Canterbury's commissaries, Bishop John Gladwin and Chancellor Rupert Bursell QC, published the interim report of their enquiry into the operation of diocesan child protection policies in the Diocese of Chichester.

The Church Commissioners and the Church of England Pensions Board announced the sale of £1.9 million of shares in News Corporation on the advice of the EIAG. As a result, none of the Church's three national investing bodies hold shares in the company.

The Archbishop of Canterbury sent his annual greetings to Muslim communities for Eid Al-Fitr, marking the end of Ramadan. The Archbishop expressed his sorrow at the death of His Holiness Abune Paulos, since 1992 Patriarch of the Ethiopian Orthodox Tewahedo Church. He had played a unique role in reviving and strengthening his Church after a period of prolonged crisis and suffering.

The Archbishop of York visited a WaterAid project in Uganda, touring the Kalerwe community north of Kampala, and saw the facilities constructed with WaterAid's support. Acts 435, the Archbishop of York's online giving charity, was featured in BBC's *Songs of Praise*.

The Bishop of Chelmsford praised the vital legacy of the London Games, describing how in his own diocese – home to the Olympic Park and Village – and beyond, the Games were having an important impact on community life. A new prayer was added to a website section designed to resource churches engaging with the Paralympic Games, and the Archbishop of York tweeted about his excitement at the privilege of attending the opening ceremony.

Churchgoers who had made new friends through local events for the Diamond Jubilee and London 2012 Games were encouraged to invite them back for Back to Church Sunday.

Appointment Canon Glyn Webster, Residentiary Canon of York Minster, was appointed Bishop of Beverley.

SEPTEMBER

The House of Bishops settled the text of the legislation to enable women to become bishops, after its Standing Committee had considered the submissions received from General Synod members and other interested groups. The House made clear its desire for the draft legislation to be passed by the Synod in November.

A letter thanking HM The Queen for 60 years of service was delivered to Buckingham Palace. *The Big Jubilee Thank You*, coordinated by the C of E and HOPE Together, contained thousands of signatures gathered throughout the year in churches and cathedrals all over the country.

The Archbishop of Canterbury hosted a conference on *Education for Children Affected by Armed Conflict*. Later in the month, Dr Williams welcomed the launch in New York of *Education First* by the UN Secretary General, Ban Ki-Moon. The Archbishop of York visited St Peter's School, York, marking 150 years of the school chapel and meeting pupils who had completed the Young Leaders Award. The Bishop of Oxford, Chairman of the Board of Education, wrote to the Secretary of State for Education about how the marking of GCSE English had caused 'great distress to some of our most vulnerable pupils'.

The Archbishop of Canterbury's visit to the Paralympic Games was hosted by the Head of Multi-faith Chaplaincy Services, beginning at the Athletes' Village, where Dr Williams was greeted by London 2012 volunteers. The chaplaincy team, serving those of all faiths and none, had been inspired by the example of the 200,000 staff and volunteers, as well as of the athletes.

The Bishop of Manchester published a prayer following the deaths of PCs Fiona Bone and Nicola Hughes for use by churches across Greater Manchester and nationally. York Minster marked the ninth National Police Memorial Day, honouring police officers throughout the United Kingdom who had lost their lives in the line of duty.

Around two-thirds of children living in parts of Manchester, Liverpool and Newcastle were born into poverty, according to findings from the Church Urban Fund, with life expectancy up to 15 years lower than in the least deprived communities. At Bishopthorpe Palace, the York Fairness Commission, sponsored by the Archbishop, presented seven headline recommendations to York City Council, on tackling inequality and unfairness across York in the face of a difficult national economic situation.

Two new Eucharistic Prayers for school and church use were published, composed to capture children's imaginations in the preparation and celebration of Holy Communion, and with accompanying practical guidance from the Liturgical Commission to help celebrants turn a schoolroom into an exciting place of worship.

More couples explored the option of a church wedding, as visits to the Church of England's 'one-stop' weddings website increased by nearly 50 per cent in 2011, with this extra interest also reflected at the C of E stand at wedding shows around the country. And England's 12,500 parishes gained an improved Church Care website to call on to help maintain their buildings: this central hub of information for managing a church building had received a 'makeover' supported by specialist insurer Ecclesiastical.

The Dioceses Commission completed its consideration of all the submissions made to it on the draft Reorganization Scheme for the dioceses of Bradford, Ripon & Leeds and Wakefield, deciding unanimously to proceed with a draft scheme bringing all three dioceses together.

Dr Williams sent a greeting to Jewish communities on the occasion of Rosh Hashanah, the start of the Jewish New Year. In his final such message as Archbishop, he reflected on the relationship between Christian and Jewish communities over the previous 10 years.

Appointment Canon John Witcombe, Residentiary Canon of Gloucester Cathedral and Diocesan Director of Discipleship and Ministry, was appointed Dean of Coventry.

OCTOBER

The Archbishop of Canterbury launched his *Enough Waiting* campaign to persuade General Synod members to back the new women bishops legislation when it returned for debate in November. In the first address by an Archbishop of Canterbury to the Synod of Bishops in Rome, Dr Williams spoke about the profound connection between contemplation and the task of evangelization, saying it 'must be rooted in a profound confidence that we have a distinctive human destiny to show and share with the world'. The Archbishop launched the first collection of his lectures to be translated for Islamic audiences, into Urdu and Bangla in advance of further translations into Arabic, Hausa and Swahili.

The Archbishop of York presented badges and certificates to students from Archbishop Sentamu Academy who had completed his Youth Trust's Young Leaders Award. Dr Sentamu also visited the new Network Young People's Centre in West Hull, where he unveiled a plaque and planted a tree to mark the special relationship between St John the Baptist, Newington and the Hessle Road Network, a local community organization.

Because of the operational risks involved in transferring functions from the Human Fertilisation and Embryology Authority and the Human Tissue Authority, MPA criticised proposals to absorb both specialist watchdogs into the Care Quality Commission. Churches across the country supported vital foodbanks for their local communities as part of their traditional harvest festivals.

Marking the beginning of Hate Crime Awareness Week, the Archbishop of Canterbury spoke about how hate crime 'should have no possible place in a society that respects the dignity of all'. Dr Williams also expressed his shock and sadness at the violent attack on Malala Yousafzai and two other schoolgirls in Pakistan.

A website was launched to support the work of the Church Growth Research Programme, a national academic research project exploring factors related to spiritual and numerical church growth. The research is paid for through money set aside by the Church Commissioners and Archbishops' Council for research and development.

The Archbishop of York visited the diocese of Pretoria, South Africa, spending time in Pretoria East, Magaliesberg and Rustenburg District, and praying for peace and healing at Marikana, where miners had been shot dead by police. The Archbishop of Canterbury urged help for Sudanese people caught up in conflict, expressing his fear for some 850,000 people displaced from their homes by fighting in South Kordofan and Blue Nile. Dr Williams urged that attention be given to the plight of the affected population, Muslim and Christian alike.

The Archbishop hosted a conference on Pilgrimage to the Holy Land – for dioceses, tour operators and Christian organizations. The conference aimed to help deepen the pilgrimage experience, seeking to foster pilgrimages by using the resources and landmarks of the past to engage with the present, and encountering the present to transform understanding of the Bible. Dr Williams launched the *Lambeth Giving Fund*, a fundraising scheme providing much-needed help to some of the London Borough's inspiring charities and community projects, encouraging local businesses and residents to support local charities making a difference in their own area.

The Bishop of Oxford wrote a special prayer for Parents' Week encouraging parents to slow down and take more time with children in their care, following the Week's theme: *Make a Moment*.

Sir Stuart Bell, MP for Middlesbrough since 1983 and the longest-serving Second Church Estates Commissioner since the post was created in 1850, died at the age of 74.

Appointments The Rt Revd Jonathan Baker, Bishop of Ebbsfleet, was appointed Bishop of Fulham; Prebendary Nicholas McKinnel, Rector of Plymouth St Andrew and Stonehouse, was appointed Bishop of Crediton; and the Revd Philip North, Rector of Old Saint Pancras, was appointed Bishop of Whitby.

CALENDAR 2013–14

According to the Calendar, Lectionary and Collects authorized pursuant to Canon B 2 of the Canons of the Church of England for use from 30 November 1997 until further resolution of the General Synod of the Church of England.

Key
BOLD UPPER CASE – Principal Feasts and other Principal Holy Days
Bold Roman – Sundays and Festivals
Roman – Lesser Festivals
Small Italic – Commemorations
Italic – Other Observances

JANUARY (Year C)
1 **The Naming and Circumcision of Jesus**
2 Basil the Great and Gregory of Nazianzus, bishops, teachers of the faith, 379 and 389
Seraphim, monk, spiritual guide, 1833
Vedanayagam Samuel Azariah, bishop, evangelist, 1945
6 **THE EPIPHANY**
10 *William Laud, archbishop, 1645*
11 *Mary Slessor, missionary, 1915*
12 Aelred of Hexham, Abbot of Rievaulx, 1167
Benedict Biscop, Abbot of Wearmouth, scholar, 689
13 **THE BAPTISM OF CHRIST** – *The Second Sunday of Epiphany*
17 Antony of Egypt, hermit, abbot, 356
Charles Gore, bishop, founder of the Community of the Resurrection, 1932
18–25 Week of Prayer for Christian Unity
18 *Amy Carmichael, spiritual writer, 1951*
19 Wulfstan, Bishop of Worcester, 1095
20 **The Third Sunday of Epiphany**
21 Agnes, child martyr at Rome, 304
22 *Vincent of Saragossa, deacon, martyr, 304*
24 Francis de Sales, bishop, teacher of the faith, 1622
25 **The Conversion of Paul**
26 Timothy and Titus, companions of Paul
27 **The Fourth Sunday of Epiphany**
28 Thomas Aquinas, priest, philosopher, teacher of the faith, 1274
30 Charles, king and martyr, 1649
31 *John Bosco, priest, founder of the Salesian Teaching Order, 1888*

FEBRUARY
1 *Brigid, abbess, c. 525*
2 **THE PRESENTATION OF CHRIST IN THE TEMPLE** (Candlemas)
3 **The Second Sunday before Lent**
4 *Gilbert of Sempringham, founder of the Gilbertine Order, 1189*
6 *Martyrs of Japan, 1597*
Accession of Queen Elizabeth II, 1952
10 **The Sunday next before Lent**
13 **ASH WEDNESDAY**
14 Cyril and Methodius, missionaries, 869 and 885
Valentine, martyr at Rome, c.269
15 *Sigfrid, Bishop, 1045*
Thomas Bray, priest, founder of SPCK and SPG, 1730
17 **The First Sunday of Lent**
23 Polycarp, Bishop of Smyrna, martyr, c.155
24 **The Second Sunday of Lent**
27 George Herbert, priest, poet

MARCH
1 David, bishop, patron of Wales, c.601
2 Chad, Bishop of Lichfield, missionary, 672
3 **The Third Sunday of Lent**
7 Perpetua, Felicity and companions, martyrs, 203
8 Edward King, bishop. 1910
Felix, bishop, 647
Geoffrey Studdert Kennedy, priest, poet, 1929
10 **The Fourth Sunday of Lent** – *Mothering Sunday*
17 **The Fifth Sunday of Lent**
18 *Cyril, bishop, teacher of the faith, 386*
19 **Joseph of Nazareth**
20 Cuthbert, bishop, missionary, 687
21 Thomas Cranmer, archbishop, Reformation martyr, 1556
24 **Palm Sunday**
25 Monday of Holy Week
26 Tuesday of Holy Week
27 Wednesday of Holy Week
28 **Maundy Thursday**
29 **Good Friday**
30 Easter Eve
31 **EASTER DAY**

APRIL
1 Monday of Easter Week
2 Tuesday of Easter Week
3 Wednesday of Easter Week
4 Thursday of Easter Week
5 Friday of Easter Week
6 Saturday of Easter Week
7 **The Second Sunday of Easter**
8 **THE ANNUNCIATION OF OUR LORD TO THE BLESSED VIRGIN MARY**

9 *Dietrich Bonhoeffer, Lutheran pastor, martyr, 1945*
10 William Law, priest, spiritual writer, 1761
William of Ockham, friar, philosopher, teacher of the faith, 1347
11 *George Selwyn, bishop, 1878*
14 **The Third Sunday of Easter**
16 *Isabella Gilmore, deaconess, 1923*
19 Alphege, archbishop, martyr, 1012
21 **The Fourth Sunday of Easter**
23 George, martyr, patron of England, c.304
24 *Mellitus, bishop, 624*
Seven Martyrs of the Melanesian Brotherhood, 2003
25 **Mark the Evangelist**
27 *Christina Rossetti, poet, 1894*
28 **The Fifth Sunday of Easter**
29 **Catherine of Siena, teacher of the faith, 1380**
30 *Pandita Mary Ramabai, translator, 1922*

MAY
1 **Philip and James, Apostles**
2 Athanasius, bishop, teacher of the faith, 373
4 English saints and martyrs of the Reformation Era
5 **The Sixth Sunday of Easter**
8 Julian of Norwich, spiritual writer, c.1417
9 **ASCENSION DAY**
12 **The Seventh Sunday of Easter**
14 **Matthias the Apostle**
16 *Caroline Chisholm, social reformer, 1877*
19 **PENTECOST**
20 **Alcuin, deacon, abbot, 804**
21 *Helena, protector of the Holy Places, 330*
24 John and Charles Wesley, evangelists, hymn writers 1791 and 1788
25 The Venerable Bede, monk at Jarrow, scholar, historian, 735
Aldhelm, bishop 709
26 **TRINITY SUNDAY**
28 *Lanfranc, Prior of Le Bec, Archbishop of Canterbury, scholar, 1089*
30 **Day of Thanksgiving for the Institution of the Holy Communion (Corpus Christi)**
31 **The Visit of the Blessed Virgin Mary to Elizabeth**

JUNE
1 Justin, martyr, c.165
2 **The First Sunday after Trinity**
3 *Martyrs of Uganda, 1885–7, 1977*
4 *Petroc, Abbot of Padstow, 6th century*
5 Boniface (Wynfrith), bishop, martyr, 754
6 *Ini Kapuria, founder of the Melanesian Brotherhood, 1945*
8 Thomas Ken, Bishop of Bath and Wells, non-juror, hymn writer, 1711
9 **The Second Sunday after Trinity**
11 **Barnabas the Apostle**
14 *Richard Baxter, puritan divine, 1691*
15 *Evelyn Underhill, spiritual writer, 1941*
16 **The Third Sunday after Trinity**
17 *Samuel and Henrietta Barnett, social reformers, 193 and 1936*
18 *Bernard Mizeki, apostle of the MaShona, martyr, 1896*
19 *Sundar Singh, sadhu (holy man), evangelist, teacher of the faith, 1929*
22 Alban, first martyr of Britain, c.250
23 **The Fourth Sunday after Trinity**
24 **The Birth of John the Baptist** – *The Third Sunday after Trinity*
27 *Cyril, bishop, teacher of the faith, 444*
28 Irenaeus, bishop, teacher of the faith, c.200
29 **Peter and Paul, Apostles** *or* **Peter the Apostle**
30 **The Fifth Sunday after Trinity**

JULY
1 *Henry, John, and Henry Venn, priests, evangelical divines, 1797, 1813, 1873*
3 **Thomas the Apostle**
6 *Thomas More, scholar, and John Fisher, Bishop of Rochester, Reformation martyrs, 1535*
7 **The Sixth Sunday after Trinity**
11 Benedict, abbot, c.550
14 **The Seventh Sunday after Trinity**
15 Swithun, bishop, c.862
Bonaventure, friar, bishop, teacher of the faith, 1274
16 *Osmund, Bishop of Salisbury, 1099*
18 *Elizabeth Ferard, deaconess, founder of the Community of St Andrew, 1883*
19 Gregory, bishop and his sister Macrina, deaconess, teachers of the faith, c.394 and c.379
20 *Margaret of Antioch, martyr, 4th century*
Bartolomé de las Casas, apostle to the Indies, 1566
21 **The Eighth Sunday after Trinity**
22 **Mary Magdalene**
23 *Bridget of Sweden, Abbess of Vadstena, 1373*
25 **James the Apostle**
26 Anne and Joachim, parents of the Blessed Virgin Mary
27 *Brooke Foss Westcott, Bishop of Durham, teacher of the faith, 1901*
28 **The Ninth Sunday after Trinity**
29 Mary, Martha and Lazarus, companions of Our Lord
30 William Wilberforce, social reformer, Olaudah Equiano and Thomas Clarkson, anti-slavery campaigners, 1833, 1797 and 1846
31 *Ignatius Loyola, founder of the Society of Jesus, 1556*

AUGUST
4 **The Tenth Sunday after Trinity**
5 Oswald, king, martyr, 642
6 **The Transfiguration of Our Lord**
7 *John Mason Neale, priest, hymn writer, 1866*
8 Dominic, priest, founder of the Order of Preachers, 1221
9 Mary Sumner, founder of the Mothers' Union, 1921
10 Laurence, deacon at Rome, martyr, 258
11 **The Eleventh Sunday after Trinity**
13 Jeremy Taylor, Bishop of Down and Connor, teacher of the faith, 1667
Florence Nightingale, nurse, social reformer, 1910
Octavia Hill, social reformer, 1912
14 *Maximilian Kolbe, friar, martyr, 1941*
15 **The Blessed Virgin Mary**
18 **The Twelfth Sunday after Trinity**

20 Bernard, Abbot of Clairvaux, teacher of the faith, 1153
William and Catherine Booth, founders of the Salvation Army, 1912 and 1890
24 **Bartholomew the Apostle**
25 **The Thirteenth Sunday after Trinity**
27 Monica, mother of Augustine of Hippo, 387
28 Augustine, bishop, teacher of the faith, 430
29 Beheading of John the Baptist
30 John Bunyan, spiritual writer, 1688
31 Aidan, Bishop of Lindisfarne, missionary, 651

SEPTEMBER
1 **The Fourteenth Sunday after Trinity**
2 *Martyrs of Papua New Guinea, 1901, 1942*
3 Gregory the Great, Bishop of Rome, teacher of the faith, 604
4 *Birinus, bishop, 650*
6 *Allen Gardiner, missionary, founder of the South American Missionary Society, 1851*
8 **The Fifteenth Sunday after Trinity**
9 *Charles Fuge Lowder, priest, 1880*
13 John Chrysostom, bishop, teacher of the faith, 407
14 **Holy Cross Day**
15 **The Sixteenth Sunday after Trinity**
16 Ninian, bishop, c.432
Edward Bouverie Pusey, priest, 1882
17 Hildegard, Abbess of Bingen, visionary, 1179
19 *Theodore, archbishop, 690*
20 John Coleridge Patteson, bishop and companions, martyrs, 1871
21 **Matthew, Apostle and Evangelist**
22 **The Seventeenth Sunday after Trinity**
25 Launcelot Andrewes, bishop, spiritual writer, 1626
Sergei of Radonezh, monastic reformer, teacher of the faith, 1392
26 *Wilson Carlile, founder of the Church Army, 1942*
27 Vincent de Paul, founder of the Lazarists, 1660
29 **Michael and All Angels** – *The Eighteenth Sunday after Trinity*
30 *Jerome, translator, teacher of the faith, 420*

OCTOBER
1 *Remigius, Bishop of Rheims, apostle of the Franks, 533*
Anthony Ashley Cooper, Earl of Shaftesbury, social reformer, 1885
3 *George Bell, bishop, ecumenist, peacemaker, 1958*
4 Francis of Assisi, friar, deacon, 1226
6 **The Nineteenth Sunday after Trinity**
9 *Denys, bishop, and companions, martyrs, c.250*
Robert Grosseteste, bishop, philosopher, scientist, 1253
10 Paulinus, bishop, missionary, 644
Thomas Traherne, poet, spiritual writer, 1674
11 *Ethelburga, abbess, 675*
James the Deacon, companion of Paulinus, 7th cent.
12 Wilfrid of Ripon, bishop, missionary, 709
Elizabeth Fry, prison reformer, 1845
Edith Cavell, nurse, 1915
13 **The Twentieth Sunday after Trinity**
15 Teresa of Avila, teacher of the faith, 1582
16 *Nicholas Ridley and Hugh Latimer, bishops, martyrs, 1555*
17 Ignatius, bishop, martyr, c.107
18 **Luke the Evangelist**
19 Henry Martyn, translator of the Scriptures, missionary in India and Persia, 1812
20 **The Twenty-first Sunday after Trinity**
25 *Crispin and Crispian, martyrs, c.287*
26 Alfred, king, scholar, 899
Cedd, abbot, bishop, 664
27 **The Last Sunday after Trinity** – *Bible Sunday*
28 **Simon and Jude, Apostles**
29 James Hannington, Bishop of Eastern Equatorial Africa, martyr in Uganda, 1885
31 *Martin Luther, reformer, 1546*

NOVEMBER
1 **ALL SAINTS' DAY**
2 Commemoration of the Faithful Departed (All Souls' Day)
3 **The Fourth Sunday before Advent**
6 *Leonard, hermit, 6th cent.*
William Temple, archbishop, teacher of the faith, 1944
7 Willibrord, bishop, 739
8 Saints and martyrs of England
9 *Margery Kempe, mystic, c.1440*
10 **The Third Sunday before Advent** – *Remembrance Sunday*
11 Martin, bishop, c.397
13 Charles Simeon, priest, evangelical divine, 1836
14 *Samuel Seabury, bishop, 1796*
16 Margaret, Queen of Scotland, philanthropist, reformer of the Church, 1093
Edmund Rich of Abingdon, Archbishop of Canterbury, 1240
17 **The Second Sunday before Advent**
18 Elizabeth, princess, philanthropist, 1231
19 Hilda, Abbess of Whitby, 680
Mechtild, béguine of Magdeburg, mystic, 1280
20 Edmund, king, martyr, 870
Priscilla Lydia Sellon, a restorer of the religious life in the Church of England, 1876
22 *Cecilia, martyr, c.230*
23 Clement, bishop, martyr, c.100
24 **Christ the King** – *The Sunday next before Advent*
25 *Catherine, martyr, 4th cent.*
Isaac Watts, hymn writer, 1748
29 *Day of Intercession and Thanksgiving for the Missionary Work of the Church*
30 **Andrew the Apostle**

DECEMBER
1 **The First Sunday of Advent**
3 *Francis Xavier, missionary, apostle of the Indies, 1552*
4 *John of Damascus, monk, teacher of the faith, c.749*
Nicholas Ferrar, deacon, founder of the Little Gidding Community, 1637
6 Nicholas, bishop, c.326
7 Ambrose, Bishop of Milan, teacher of the faith, 397
8 **The Second Sunday of Advent**
13 Lucy, martyr, 304
Samuel Johnson, moralist, 1784

14 John of the Cross, poet, teacher of the faith, 1591
15 **The Third Sunday of Advent**
17 *O Sapientia*
Eglantyne Jebb, social reformer, founder of 'Save the Children', 1928
22 **The Fourth Sunday of Advent**
24 Christmas Eve
25 **CHRISTMAS DAY**
26 **Stephen, deacon, first martyr**
27 **John, Apostle and Evangelist**
28 **The Holy Innocents**
29 **The First Sunday of Christmas**
31 *John Wyclif, reformer, 1384*

JANUARY 2014
1 **The Naming and Circumcision of Jesus**
2 Basil the Great and Gregory of Nazianzus, bishops, teachers of the faith, 379 and 389
5 **The Second Sunday of Christmas**
6 **THE EPIPHANY**
10 *William Laud, Archbishop of Canterbury, 1645*
11 *Mary Slessor, Missionary in West Africa, 1915*
12 **THE BAPTISM OF CHRIST** – *The First Sunday of Epiphany*
13 Hilary, bishop, teacher of the faith, 367
Kentigern (Mungo), missionary bishop, 603
George Fox, founder of the Society of Friends (Quakers), 1691
17 Anthony of Egypt, hermit, abbot, 356
Charles Gore, bishop, founder of the Community of the Resurrection, 1932
18 *Amy Carmichael, spiritual writer, 1951*
18–25 *Week of Prayer for Christian Unity*
19 **The Second Sunday of Epiphany**
21 Agnes, child martyr at Rome, 304
22 *Vincent of Saragassa, deacon, martyr, 304*
24 Francis de Sales, Bishop of Geneva, teacher of the Faith, 1662
25 **The Conversion of Paul**
26 **The Third Sunday of Epiphany**
28 Thomas Aquinas, priest, philosopher, teacher of the faith, 1274
31 *John Bosco, Priest, Founder of the Salesian Teaching Order, 1888*

Other dates

27 January	Education Sunday
4 February	General Synod meets until 8 February
6 February	Accession Day
10 February	Unemployment Sunday
12 May	Christian Aid Week until 18th
30 June	Day of Prayer for Vocations to Religious Life
5 July	General Synod meets in York until 9th
14 July	Sea Sunday
8 September	Racial Justice Sunday
6 October	Animal Welfare Sunday
13 October	Hospital Sunday
24 October	United Nations Day
17 November	Prisoners Sunday
18 November	General Synod meets until 20th (if required)
1 December	World AIDS Day
8 December	Human Rights Day

SELECTED CHURCH STATISTICS

The Church of England today

The Church of England plays a vital role in the life of the nation, proclaiming the Christian gospel in words and actions and providing services of Christian worship and praise.

Its network of parishes covers the country, bringing a vital Christian dimension to the nation as well as strengthening community life in numerous urban, suburban and rural settings. Its cathedrals are centres of spirituality and service, and its network of chaplaincies across continental Europe meets important local needs.

The Church of England plays an active role in national life with its members involved in a wide range of public bodies. Twenty-six bishops are members of the House of Lords and are engaged in debates about legislation and national and international affairs.

The Church of England is part of the worldwide Anglican Communion.

There are a number of interviews relating to the Church of England on Premier Christian Radio, under the title 'Work in Progress'.

Key facts about the Church of England

Church attendance and visits

- **1.6 million** people take part in a Church of England service each month, a level that has reduced slightly since the turn of the millennium. Around one million participate each Sunday.
- Approximately **2.4 million** participate in a Church of England service on Christmas Day or Christmas Eve. **Thirty-three per cent** of the population attend a church service around Christmas, including 22 per cent among those of non-Christian faiths and 13 per cent of those with no religious alignment.
- In 2011, **70 per cent** of adults attended a church or place of worship for a baptism, wedding, or funeral service for someone who has died and **18 per cent** were seeking a quiet space.
- **Eighty-five per cent** of the population visit a church or place of worship in the course of a year, for reasons ranging from participating in worship to attending social events or simply wanting a quiet space.
- Every year, around **12 million** people visit Church of England cathedrals, including almost **300,000** pupils on school visits. Three of England's top five historic 'visitor attractions' are St Paul's Cathedral, London, Canterbury Cathedral and Westminster Abbey.

Education

- **Seven in ten** (70 per cent) of the population agree that Church of England schools have a positive role in educating the nation's children.
- **One in four** primary schools and **one in 16** secondary schools in England are Church of England schools. Approaching **one million pupils** are educated in more than 4,600 Church of England schools.

Ministers

- At the end of 2010, there were **18,500** ministers licensed by Church of England dioceses, including clergy, Readers and Church Army officers: one minister for every 2,600 people in England. The total does not include almost **1,600** chaplains to prisons, hospitals, the armed forces and in education, nor over **6,000** retired ministers with permission to officiate.

Community involvement

- **More people do unpaid work for church organizations than any other organization.** Eight per cent of adults undertake voluntary work for church organizations while 16 per cent belong to religious or church organizations.
- A quarter of regular churchgoers (among both Anglicans and other Christians separately) are involved in voluntary community service outside the church. Churchgoers overall contribute **23.2 million hours** voluntary service each month in their local communities outside the church.

- The Church of England provides activities outside church worship in the local community for over **500,000 children and young people** (aged up to 25 years). **More than 120,000 volunteers** run children/young people activity groups sponsored by the Church of England outside church worship.

Church buildings

- **Nearly half the population** (46 per cent) think that central taxation, local taxation, the National Lottery or English Heritage should be 'primarily' responsible for providing money to maintain churches and chapels. In fact, these churches and cathedrals are largely supported by the efforts and financial support of local communities. Often, they are the focus of community life and service.
- There are 14,500 places of worship in England listed for their special architectural or historic interest, **85 per cent of which belong to and are maintained by the Church of England.**
- Necessary repairs to all listed places of worship in England have been valued at £925 million over the next five years, or £185 million a year.

Sources: *Church Statistics* 2010/11.
Opinion Research Business national polls 2011.
English Heritage and Church of England Cathedral and Church Buildings Division joint research.

Tables

The following pages contain a selection of tables as available at the Church of England website, www.churchofengland.org

Table K
Consistent measures of church attendance have been employed from 2000.

Average weekly attendance – the average number of attenders at church services throughout the week typically over a four-week period in October.

Average Sunday attendance – the average number of attenders at Sunday church services typically over a four-week period in October.

Tables N to S
The following definitions apply:

Income

Unrestricted income	income that may be used by the PCC for general church expenses.
Restricted income	income which may not be used for any purpose other than as specified by the donor. (Income which a PCC designates for a specified purpose is considered to be unrestricted, since the PCC and not the donor is determining how it is to be used.)
Recurring income	includes direct giving, other voluntary income and any other recurring income. It may be unrestricted or restricted.
One-off income	includes non-recurring grants, legacies, special appeals, insurance claims and the sale of fixed assets. It may be unrestricted or restricted.
Total voluntary income	direct giving plus income tax on gift aid plus other voluntary income.
Total direct giving	planned giving plus church collections and boxes.
Other voluntary income	all other voluntary income for ordinary expenditure excluding direct giving and income tax on gift aid, e.g. fund-raising events, net profit on magazine/bookstall, sundry donations.

Expenditure
Total charitable donations includes payments to: the recognized missionary societies, or other overseas missions, diocesan associations, Diocesan Mission Councils; Christian organizations primarily concerned with relief and development; home missions and other Church societies and organizations (including the Church Urban Fund); other charities – payments to other charities which are secularly based.

Recurring expenditure	includes donations to charities, parish share/quota, clergy expenses, church running costs, costs relating to trading, salaries and support costs.
Capital expenditure	includes major repairs, redecoration and new building work.

Notes on tables N to S
1. Figures for cathedrals are not included.
2. *i.e. adjusted by the Retail Price Index to reflect 2010 purchasing power.
3. The Diocese in Europe is not included in these tables.

Please also note that:

1. Whilst many figures in these tables have been rounded, totals, percentages and averages were calculated before rounding. Hence row and column totals will not always agree exactly with the sum of the stated amounts.
2. Among the 13,000 parishes of the Church of England there are around 600 Local Ecumenical Projects in roughly half of which there is a congregation and a ministry shared between the Church of England and certain other churches. In such circumstances it is not always possible (or indeed desirable) to isolate the Anglican component of the congregation. The parochial statistics will therefore include a small element which may appear also in the statistics of other churches.
3. Where figures are not available for any reason, 'N/A' appears in these tables.

A Church of England Licensed Ministries 2011

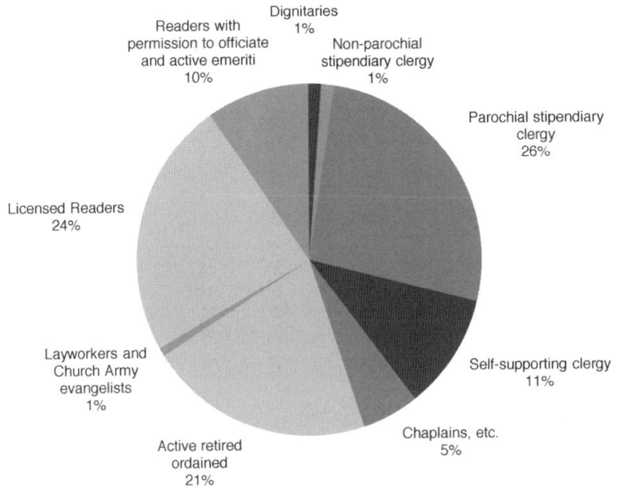

Licensed stipendiary clergy	8,361
Licensed self-supporting clergy	3,074
Chaplains and other ministries	1,556
Licensed layworkers and lay Church Army evangelists	228
Active retired ordained	6,103
Licensed Readers	6,856
Readers with permission to officiate and active emeriti	2,763
Totals CHURCH OF ENGLAND	28,955

The figures for stipendiary clergy (full-time, part-time and including those outside the clergy share system) and for lay workers above are based on statistics derived from the central Church payroll. Details of chaplains and other ministers working outside the parish framework, and of non-stipendiary clergy, are based on statistics derived from the database used to compile *Crockford's Clerical Directory*. Where possible, they have been cross-referenced with material produced by organizing bodies (Church Army, the Home Office for prison chaplains, and the Hospital Chaplaincies Council for hospital chaplains).

The figure shown for active retired ordained clergy is an estimate of the number of licensed retired clergy who take an active part in ministry. It is based on the number of retired clergy known to have either permission to officiate, licence to officiate or actual appointments. Pension Board records indicated a total of 8884 retired stipendiary clergy in 2010.

B Summary of Diocesan Licensed Ministers 2011

Provinces of Canterbury and York (including Europe)

Diocese		Full-time stipendiary clergy			Part-time stipendiary clergy			Self-supporting clergy, except ordained local ministers		
		male	female	Total	male	female	Total	male	female	Total
1 Bath & Wells	C	149	52	201	6	9	15	32	27	59
2 Birmingham	C	119	44	163	2	3	5	16	22	38
3 Blackburn	Y	148	17	165	5	6	11	29	20	49
4 Bradford	Y	79	17	96	4	7	11	15	22	37
5 Bristol	C	97	21	118	3	3	6	12	25	37
6 Canterbury	C	114	24	138	3	2	5	26	34	60
7 Carlisle	Y	98	25	123	1	4	5	24	24	48
8 Chelmsford	C	277	88	365	3	5	8	49	54	103
9 Chester	Y	184	54	238	13	11	24	22	41	63
10 Chichester	C	260	23	283	12	6	18	54	42	96
11 Coventry	C	97	18	115	5	4	9	10	19	29
12 Derby	C	104	42	146	1	1	2	29	31	60
13 Durham	Y	130	32	162	6	6	12	13	19	32
14 Ely	C	87	43	130	3	7	10	27	24	51
15 Exeter	C	169	40	209	12	6	18	25	25	50
16 Gloucester	C	96	33	129	3	6	9	43	45	88
17 Guildford	C	139	32	171	5	12	17	24	42	66
18 Hereford	C	61	29	90	0	2	2	11	24	35
19 Leicester	C	101	41	142	4	3	7	15	21	36
20 Lichfield	C	248	52	300	7	10	17	35	37	72
21 Lincoln	C	114	38	152	3	1	4	17	24	41
22 Liverpool	Y	154	54	208	0	2	2	15	20	35
23 London	C	456	74	530	2	9	11	98	51	149
24 Manchester	Y	172	65	237	5	2	7	23	14	37
25 Newcastle	Y	93	33	126	3	3	6	11	20	31
26 Norwich	C	147	39	186	6	7	13	14	14	28
27 Oxford	C	291	88	379	5	4	9	99	101	200
28 Peterborough	C	96	33	129	4	0	4	20	19	39
29 Portsmouth	C	80	23	103	3	4	7	15	34	49
30 Ripon & Leeds	Y	85	35	120	0	1	1	21	21	42
31 Rochester	C	161	37	198	2	6	8	19	31	50
32 St. Albans	C	167	73	240	7	9	16	32	42	74
33 St. Edms & Ipswich	C	104	39	143	4	5	9	15	22	37
34 Salisbury	C	155	46	201	4	2	6	32	57	89
35 Sheffield	Y	106	36	142	3	6	9	13	11	24
36 Sodor & Man	Y	15	1	16	0	0	0	5	3	8
37 Southwark	C	262	88	350	3	4	7	81	92	173
38 Southwell & Nottingham	Y	96	42	138	4	6	10	13	19	32
39 Truro	C	77	20	97	9	2	11	14	24	38
40 Wakefield	Y	102	34	136	3	3	6	25	22	47
41 Winchester	C	168	28	196	3	2	5	48	46	94
42 Worcester	C	92	29	121	1	0	1	10	24	34
43 York	Y	171	38	209	6	4	10	39	36	75
44 Europe	C	116	14	130	0	0	0	21	10	31
Totals Province of Canterbury	**C**	**4,604**	**1,251**	**5,855**	**125**	**134**	**259**	**943**	**1,063**	**2,006**
Totals Province of York	**Y**	**1,633**	**483**	**2,116**	**53**	**61**	**114**	**268**	**292**	**560**
Totals CHURCH OF ENGLAND		**6,237**	**1,734**	**7,971**	**178**	**195**	**373**	**1,211**	**1,355**	**2,566**

Notes:

1 The above figures include only those ministers who were working within the diocesan framework as at 31 December 2011.

2 The Archbishop of Canterbury and ordained members of his staff at Lambeth Palace are classed as extra-diocesan and are not included in these figures.

B continued

Ordained local ministers among self-supporting clergy: male	female	Total	Total clergy (stipendiary and self supporting)	Readers and Church Army	Total clergy, readers and Church Army	Dio Ref No
0	0	0	275	237	512	1
0	0	0	206	161	367	2
0	0	0	225	141	366	3
0	0	0	144	89	233	4
7	12	19	180	173	353	5
6	6	12	215	94	309	6
0	1	1	177	99	276	7
1	2	3	479	278	757	8
0	0	0	325	287	612	9
0	0	0	397	154	551	10
4	9	13	166	144	310	11
0	0	0	208	268	476	12
1	4	5	211	141	352	13
0	0	0	191	127	318	14
0	0	0	277	191	468	15
3	3	6	232	158	390	16
24	22	46	300	125	425	17
2	6	8	135	68	203	18
0	0	0	185	130	315	19
28	28	56	445	316	761	20
16	22	38	235	132	367	21
10	18	28	273	286	559	22
0	0	0	690	216	906	23
34	43	77	358	147	505	24
8	8	16	179	82	261	25
23	22	45	272	162	434	26
18	25	43	631	201	832	27
0	0	0	172	151	323	28
0	0	0	159	95	254	29
0	0	0	163	101	264	30
0	0	0	256	233	489	31
0	1	1	331	177	508	32
11	22	33	222	108	330	33
12	22	34	330	102	432	34
0	0	0	175	193	368	35
2	0	2	26	19	45	36
0	0	0	530	176	706	37
0	0	0	180	275	455	38
2	2	4	150	76	226	39
5	12	17	206	118	324	40
0	0	0	295	192	487	41
0	0	0	156	136	292	42
0	1	1	295	209	504	43
0	0	0	161	65	226	
157	**204**	**361**	**8,481**	**4,846**	**13,327**	
60	**87**	**147**	**2,937**	**2,187**	**5,124**	
217	**291**	**508**	**11,418**	**7,033**	**18,451**	

3 Reader and Church Army figures do not include Readers with PTO or emeriti, or ordained Church Army evangelists.

C Licensed Readers and Church Army 2011

Provinces of Canterbury and York (including Europe)

Licensed Readers and Church Army: male (m) and female (f)

	Diocese		Reader admissions during year		Licensed Readers at 31 Dec 2011				Readers in training		Church Army (lay evangelists)	
			m	f	m		f		m	f	m	f
1	Bath & Wells	C	6	4	102	(69)	132	(38)	5	7	3	0
2	Birmingham	C	3	5	74	(22)	86	(26)	15	16	1	0
3	Blackburn	Y	1	1	59	(34)	81	(17)	6	18	1	0
4	Bradford	Y	1	5	36	(26)	47	(19)	9	10	5	1
5	Bristol	C	3	8	69	(27)	104	(31)	3	8	0	0
6	Canterbury	C	1	2	35	(30)	52	(22)	10	8	6	1
7	Carlisle	Y	2	6	47	(33)	52	(26)	9	8	0	0
8	Chelmsford	C	2	6	113	(54)	157	(37)	3	10	4	4
9	Chester	Y	7	10	142	(124)	141	(45)	18	24	2	2
10	Chichester	C	0	0	96	(70)	54	(41)	9	17	3	1
11	Coventry	C	3	7	70	(26)	68	(20)	2	5	4	2
12	Derby	C	1	2	126	(30)	140	(27)	3	9	2	0
13	Durham	Y	1	3	62	(9)	76	(8)	5	11	1	2
14	Ely	C	0	4	63	(25)	62	(20)	5	8	2	0
15	Exeter	C	8	9	96	(52)	91	(50)	12	11	4	0
16	Gloucester	C	0	4	84	(17)	73	(10)	9	15	0	1
17	Guildford	C	3	2	73	(35)	46	(21)	5	4	4	2
18	Hereford	C	1	1	34	(11)	31	(8)	5	7	2	1
19	Leicester	C	1	1	60	(25)	68	(14)	10	6	1	1
20	Lichfield	C	3	20	144	(70)	162	(52)	7	13	7	3
21	Lincoln	C	2	0	50	(28)	80	(15)	16	32	2	0
22	Liverpool	Y	10	7	140	(38)	139	(22)	17	19	4	3
23	London	C	13	13	109	(27)	101	(28)	6	24	4	2
24	Manchester (2008 data)	Y	2	3	69	(47)	72	(22)	5	13	4	2
25	Newcastle	Y	2	2	28	(26)	49	(19)	5	13	2	3
26	Norwich	C	1	7	68	(61)	91	(47)	3	9	2	1
27	Oxford	C	3	4	103	(44)	94	(37)	9	17	1	3
28	Peterborough	C	4	8	76	(27)	70	(13)	13	16	3	2
29	Portsmouth	C	3	3	47	(21)	48	(25)	3	2	0	0
30	Ripon & Leeds	Y	2	7	50	(18)	47	(28)	1	11	2	2
31	Rochester	C	2	5	118	(76)	113	(39)	17	12	0	2
32	St. Albans	C	4	6	88	(48)	85	(44)	21	26	4	0
33	St. Edms & Ipswich	C	2	5	60	(38)	44	(33)	5	10	3	1
34	Salisbury	C	0	3	56	(65)	46	(36)	6	8	0	0
35	Sheffield	Y	4	5	90	(18)	84	(15)	15	11	11	8
36	Sodor & Man	Y	1	0	12	(7)	7	(2)	0	2	0	0
37	Southwark	C	6	8	86	(58)	84	(35)	17	22	3	3
38	Southwell & Nottingham	Y	2	10	122	(32)	147	(25)	4	4	4	2
39	Truro	C	0	3	38	(28)	36	(14)	7	9	2	0
40	Wakefield	Y	4	5	57	(13)	58	(14)	9	6	3	0
41	Winchester	C	4	3	91	(51)	95	(16)	14	10	5	1
42	Worcester	C	3	5	54	(27)	78	(14)	3	10	3	1
43	York	Y	3	10	103	(40)	100	(25)	9	14	3	3
44	Europe	C	3	0	40	(25)	25	(11)	19	15	0	0
	Totals Province of Canterbury	**C**	**85**	**148**	**2,323**	**(1,187)**	**2,416**	**(824)**	**262**	**366**	**75**	**32**
	Totals Province of York	**Y**	**42**	**74**	**1,017**	**(465)**	**1,100**	**(287)**	**112**	**164**	**42**	**28**
	Totals CHURCH OF ENGLAND		**127**	**222**	**3,340**	**(1,652)**	**3,516**	**(1,111)**	**374**	**530**	**117**	**60**
	Comparable figures for 2010:											
	Totals Province of Canterbury	**C**	**93**	**154**	**2,514**	**(1,175)**	**2,469**	**(773)**	**290**	**386**	**75**	**35**
	Totals Province of York	**Y**	**45**	**52**	**1,059**	**(455)**	**1,130**	**(310)**	**105**	**180**	**46**	**27**
	Totals CHURCH OF ENGLAND		**138**	**206**	**3,573**	**(1,630)**	**3,599**	**(1,083)**	**395**	**566**	**121**	**62**

1 Readers figures in brackets refer to the additional number of Readers with Permission to Officiate and active Emeriti. These figures have been revised since the publication of the Annual Report of the Central Readers Council of the Church of England 2011.

Notes

There are a further seven Church Army evangelists who are nationally deployed. Ordained Church Army evangelists are counted in the 'Chaplaincy and other ministries' table.

D Ordinations and Reader Admissions 1995 to 2011

	Stipendiary			Self-supporting				
	m	f	Total	m	f	Total	Total stipendiary and self-supporting	Readers
1995	245	65	310	30	42	72	382	661
1996	201	67	268	46	59	105	373	586
1997	186	57	243	69	67	136	379	593
1998	174	67	241	100	127	227	468	608
1999	199	78	277	101	103	204	481	566
2000	223	90	313	106	150	256	569	544
2001	190	105	295	92	109	201	496	494
2002	199	112	311	101	128	229	540	494
2003	181	120	301	79	113	192	493	472
2004	143	92	235	94	140	234	469	487
2005	158	103	261	112	139	251	512	435
2006	128	98	226	106	149	255	481	425
2007	163	104	267	128	160	288	555	435
2008	197	124	321	103	150	253	574	375
2009	193	116	309	105	150	255	564	358
2010	173	111	284	100	179	279	563	344
2011	170	94	264	89	151	240	504	349

Ordination and Reader admissions 1995 - 2011

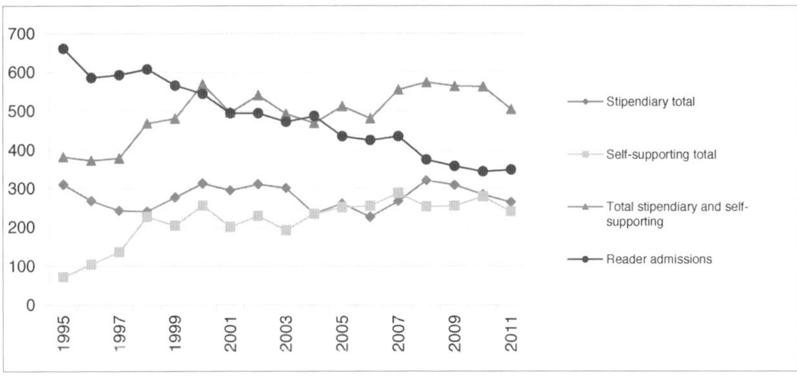

Proportion of ordinations by gender

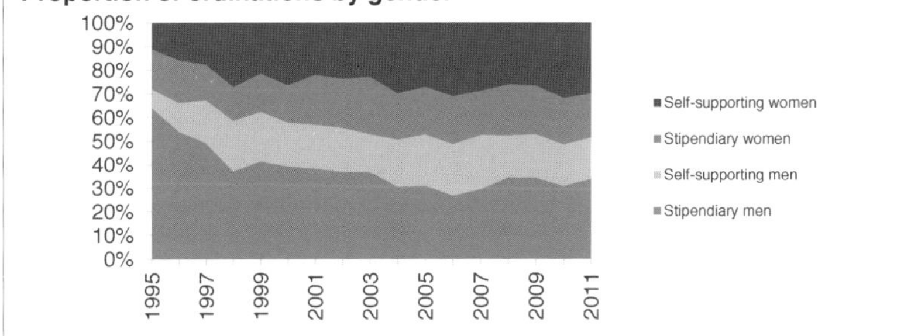

E Ages of Candidates Recommended for Ordination Training 1999 to 2011

	20-29	30-39	40-49	50-59	60 or over	Total
1999	99	140	154	127	28	548
2000	9	146	148	123	14	537
2001	73	126	160	109	18	486
2002	71	103	149	125	27	475
2003	78	118	159	124	26	505
2004	71	117	166	157	53	564
2005	86	123	173	161	35	578
2006	90	149	174	144	37	594
2007	88	155	174	132	46	595
2008	82	117	133	117	41	490
2009	74	112	136	126	43	491
2010	108	94	140	117	56	515
2011	77	126	138	91	32	464

2001 (486)

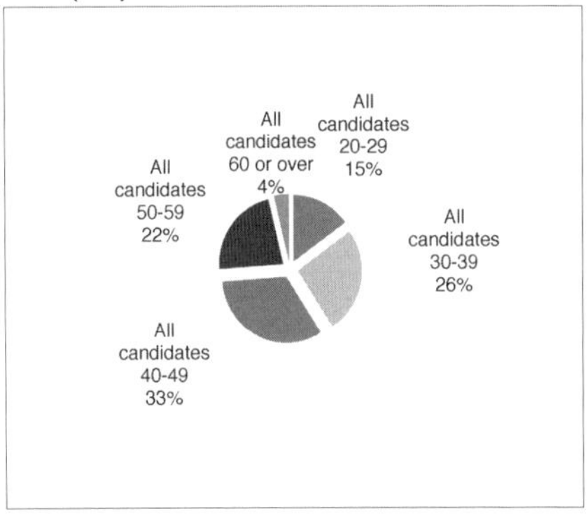

2006 (594)

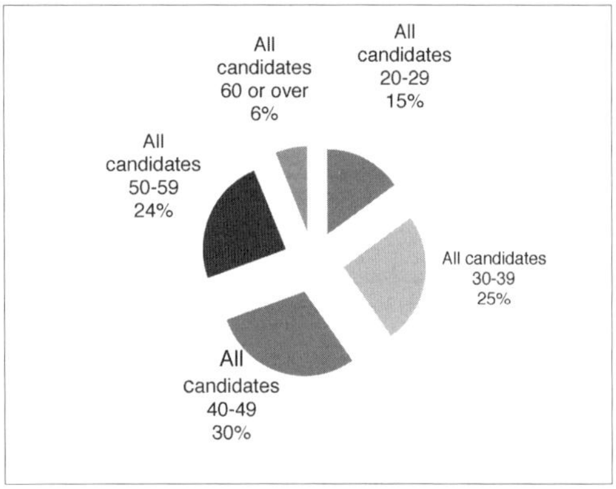

2011 (464)

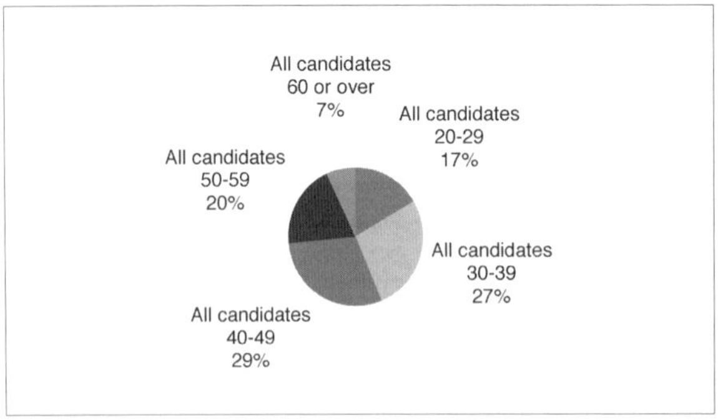

F Parochial Baptisms and Thanksgivings 2010

Provinces of Canterbury and York (including Europe and Cathedrals)

Diocese		Live births	Baptisms: Infants under one year	Baptisms: Infant baptisms per 1,000 live births	Baptisms: Children aged 1 to 12 years	Baptisms: All other persons	Thanksgivings: Infants	Thanksgivings: Child	Baptisms and Thanks-givings Total
1 Bath & Wells	C	9,900	1,790	180	920	230	70	40	3,050
2 Birmingham	C	22,500	1,280	57	840	240	70	20	2,450
3 Blackburn	Y	16,200	2,590	160	1,250	200	50	10	4,110
4 Bradford	Y	10,700	810	76	300	70	70	40	1,280
5 Bristol	C	13,300	1,150	86	550	150	40	20	1,900
6 Canterbury	C	10,700	1,600	150	1,070	260	30	30	2,990
7 Carlisle	Y	5,000	1,560	311	340	70	20	10	2,000
8 Chelmsford	C	43,200	2,660	62	2,040	650	190	110	5,640
9 Chester	Y	18,900	3,290	174	1,390	310	230	70	5,290
10 Chichester	C	17,700	2,130	120	1,410	350	120	60	4,070
11 Coventry	C	10,600	1,100	104	670	160	70	50	2,040
12 Derby	C	12,000	1,580	131	810	180	110	20	2,690
13 Durham	Y	17,400	3,750	215	1,320	310	170	10	5,560
14 Ely	C	9,100	1,280	142	760	260	60	40	2,410
15 Exeter	C	12,000	1,950	162	1,000	290	30	20	3,290
16 Gloucester	C	7,300	1,510	207	690	330	40	20	2,590
17 Guildford	C	12,700	1,680	132	1,050	190	60	40	3,020
18 Hereford	C	3,000	860	286	340	70	10	10	1,290
19 Leicester	C	12,400	1,050	85	600	150	20	40	1,870
20 Lichfield	C	25,700	3,840	150	1,860	420	260	100	6,490
21 Lincoln	C	11,600	2,930	252	1,070	250	70	30	4,350
22 Liverpool	Y	18,700	2,930	157	1,660	250	100	50	4,990
23 London	C	63,800	2,300	36	1,960	660	90	30	5,040
24 Manchester	Y	30,100	3,430	114	1,920	400	250	120	6,120
25 Newcastle	Y	9,000	1,570	175	610	130	20	10	2,340
26 Norwich	C	9,400	1,530	163	650	200	40	30	2,450
27 Oxford	C	31,100	3,570	115	2,060	500	150	40	6,320
28 Peterborough	C	11,800	1,290	109	690	190	40	20	2,230
29 Portsmouth	C	8,600	1,120	131	600	150	20	20	1,900
30 Ripon & Leeds	Y	10,600	1,290	123	620	170	50	30	2,160
31 Rochester	C	16,500	1,670	101	1,290	330	230	140	3,660
32 St. Albans	C	24,900	2,210	89	1,410	350	110	50	4,130
33 St. Edms & Ipswich	C	7,300	1,030	141	550	150	40	10	1,780
34 Salisbury	C	9,900	1,920	195	1,080	310	70	30	3,420
35 Sheffield	Y	15,100	2,210	146	990	370	310	100	3,980
36 Sodor & Man	Y	1,000	230	222	90	30	0	0	350
37 Southwark	C	43,700	2,220	51	1,910	470	90	60	4,750
38 Southwell & Nottingham	Y	13,600	1,420	104	700	280	90	20	2,520
39 Truro	C	5,600	1,110	199	520	150	30	10	1,810
40 Wakefield	Y	15,100	1,980	131	880	270	180	50	3,360
41 Winchester	C	15,700	2,500	160	1,290	200	130	30	4,160
42 Worcester	C	10,000	1,710	171	750	140	140	50	2,790
43 York	Y	16,300	3,290	202	1,140	260	170	60	4,920
44 Europe	C		310		210	80	20	10	640
Totals Province of Canterbury	**C**	**491,900**	52,890	**108**	30,640	8,040	2,470	1,180	95,210
Totals Province of York	**Y**	**197,800**	30,370	**154**	13,210	3,120	1,720	560	48,990
Totals CHURCH OF ENGLAND		**689,800**	83,260	**121**	43,850	11,160	4,190	1,740	144,200
Comparable figures for 2009:									
Totals Province of Canterbury	**C**	**479,900**	53,460	**111**	30,310	7,810	2,490	1,280	95,350
Totals Province of York	**Y**	**194,000**	30,360	**156**	13,170	3,200	1,700	500	48,930
Totals CHURCH OF ENGLAND		**673,900**	83,820	**124**	43,470	11,010	4,190	1,790	144,280

1 Live births per diocese are estimates based on statistics obtained from the Office for National Statistics (ONS).

G Parochial Marriages and Funerals 2010

Provinces of Canterbury and York (including Europe and Cathedrals)

Diocese		Marriages: Marriages	Marriages: Blessings and civil marriages	Marriages: Total	Funerals: Held in church	Funerals: Held in crematoria/ cemeteries	Funerals: Total	Number of deaths	Per cent with C-of-E funeral
1 Bath & Wells	C	1,490	90	1,580	2,380	1,620	4,000	9,500	42%
2 Birmingham	C	1,000	30	1,040	1,280	2,880	4,160	12,200	34%
3 Blackburn	Y	1,090	60	1,150	2,320	1,870	4,190	13,200	32%
4 Bradford	Y	670	30	690	810	790	1,600	6,000	27%
5 Bristol	C	890	40	930	1,070	1,240	2,310	7,500	31%
6 Canterbury	C	1,240	130	1,370	1,340	2,320	3,660	9,000	41%
7 Carlisle	Y	780	50	830	1,730	980	2,710	5,400	50%
8 Chelmsford	C	2,700	120	2,820	2,870	4,180	7,050	23,900	29%
9 Chester	Y	1,640	50	1,690	3,550	2,750	6,300	15,400	41%
10 Chichester	C	1,850	170	2,020	2,220	2,950	5,170	17,000	30%
11 Coventry	C	920	50	980	1,600	950	2,550	7,000	36%
12 Derby	C	1,110	80	1,190	2,510	1,650	4,170	9,600	44%
13 Durham	Y	1,230	80	1,310	3,630	2,380	6,010	14,700	41%
14 Ely	C	1,110	240	1,350	1,660	1,060	2,720	5,800	47%
15 Exeter	C	1,570	140	1,710	2,870	1,640	4,520	12,100	37%
16 Gloucester	C	1,140	80	1,220	1,720	1,320	3,040	5,800	53%
17 Guildford	C	1,210	70	1,290	1,300	1,800	3,100	8,100	38%
18 Hereford	C	660	40	700	1,450	660	2,110	3,200	67%
19 Leicester	C	1,010	60	1,070	1,580	1,070	2,650	8,200	32%
20 Lichfield	C	2,240	110	2,340	5,230	3,960	9,190	19,500	47%
21 Lincoln	C	1,520	90	1,610	2,510	2,030	4,540	10,400	44%
22 Liverpool	Y	1,040	60	1,100	3,460	1,960	5,420	15,400	35%
23 London	C	1,590	160	1,750	1,430	2,190	3,610	22,200	16%
24 Manchester (2008 data)	Y	1,210	60	1,270	2,320	2,430	4,750	18,100	26%
25 Newcastle	Y	710	50	760	1,330	1,490	2,820	8,000	35%
26 Norwich	C	1,230	80	1,310	2,390	2,340	4,730	9,200	51%
27 Oxford	C	2,830	180	3,020	3,380	3,190	6,570	16,300	40%
28 Peterborough	C	1,070	70	1,150	1,480	830	2,320	7,100	33%
29 Portsmouth	C	930	70	1,000	1,170	1,450	2,620	7,300	36%
30 Ripon & Leeds	Y	820	50	880	1,330	920	2,250	7,200	31%
31 Rochester	C	1,160	80	1,240	1,390	3,480	4,870	10,400	47%
32 St. Albans	C	1,680	110	1,790	2,570	2,730	5,300	14,100	38%
33 St. Edms & Ipswich	C	990	60	1,050	1,870	1,110	2,980	6,200	48%
34 Salisbury	C	1,490	120	1,600	2,280	1,720	4,000	9,300	43%
35 Sheffield	Y	1,090	70	1,160	2,390	2,510	4,900	11,500	42%
36 Sodor & Man	Y	120	20	140	270	230	510	800	62%
37 Southwark	C	1,720	90	1,810	1,110	2,890	4,010	16,500	24%
38 Southwell & Nottingham	Y	1,220	60	1,290	2,260	1,930	4,190	10,000	42%
39 Truro	C	1,010	110	1,120	1,560	790	2,350	5,700	41%
40 Wakefield	Y	960	60	1,020	2,010	1,820	3,830	10,500	36%
41 Winchester	C	1,980	120	2,100	2,270	1,750	4,020	11,800	34%
42 Worcester	C	1,090	50	1,150	1,840	1,580	3,420	8,300	41%
43 York	Y	1,580	70	1,650	2,930	2,380	5,300	13,800	38%
44 Europe	C	90	390	490	230	660	890		
Total Province of Canterbury	**C**	40,550	3,230	43,780	58,570	58,060	116,640	313,100	37%
Totals Province of York	**Y**	14,160	790	14,950	30,340	24,440	54,780	150,100	37%
Totals CHURCH OF ENGLAND		54,710	4,020	58,730	88,910	82,510	171,420	463,100	37%
Comparable figures for 2009									
Total Province of Canterbury	**C**	38,930	3,120	42,050	60,270	61,070	121,340	311,300	39%
Totals Province of York	**Y**	13,800	820	14,630	30,780	24,540	55,320	150,200	37%
Totals CHURCH OF ENGLAND		52,730	3,940	56,680	91,060	85,610	176,660	461,500	38%

1 The number of deaths are estimates based on statistics obtained from the Office for National Statistics (ONS).

H Confirmations 2010

Provinces of Canterbury and York (including Europe)

Diocese		Males	Females	Total	Number of services
1 Bath & Wells	C	144	220	364	27
2 Birmingham	C	142	228	370	64
3 Blackburn	Y	541	723	1,264	83
4 Bradford	Y	82	123	205	29
5 Bristol	C	123	156	279	20
6 Canterbury	C	181	345	526	37
7 Carlisle	Y	111	234	345	56
8 Chelmsford	C	388	605	993	80
9 Chester	Y	282	417	699	96
10 Chichester	C	328	414	742	68
11 Coventry	C	98	160	258	69
12 Derby	C	69	132	201	25
13 Durham	Y	166	267	433	39
14 Ely	C	142	198	340	37
15 Exeter	C	212	343	555	43
16 Gloucester	C	102	222	324	32
17 Guildford	C	206	302	508	39
18 Hereford	C	108	112	220	30
19 Leicester	C	131	181	312	26
20 Lichfield	C	366	591	957	104
21 Lincoln	C	185	216	401	45
22 Liverpool	Y	309	497	806	65
23 London	C	630	934	1,564	177
24 Manchester	Y	382	576	958	77
25 Newcastle	Y	72	97	169	22
26 Norwich	C	98	158	256	37
27 Oxford	C	638	712	1,350	110
28 Peterborough	C	179	244	423	26
29 Portsmouth	C	74	96	170	11
30 Ripon & Leeds	Y	186	283	469	53
31 Rochester*	C	204	321	525	57
32 St. Albans	C	302	472	774	70
33 St. Edms & Ipswich	C	136	189	325	37
34 Salisbury	C	184	400	584	27
35 Sheffield	Y	131	210	341	32
36 Sodor & Man	Y	10	20	30	7
37 Southwark	C	347	669	1,016	74
38 Southwell & Nottingham	Y	135	248	383	27
39 Truro	C	70	117	187	43
40 Wakefield	Y	117	166	283	50
41 Winchester	C	143	239	382	48
42 Worcester	C	121	215	336	39
43 York	Y	182	284	466	65
44 Europe	C	110	146	256	35
Totals Province of Canterbury	**C**	**6,161**	**9,337**	**15,498**	**1,537**
Totals Province of York	**Y**	**2,706**	**4,145**	**6,851**	**701**
Totals CHURCH OF ENGLAND		**8,867**	**13,482**	**22,349**	**2,238**
Comparable figures for 2009:					
Totals Province of Canterbury	**C**	**6,719**	**10,662**	**17,381**	**1,943**
Totals Province of York	**Y**	**3,080**	**4,567**	**7,647**	**765**
Totals CHURCH OF ENGLAND		**9,799**	**15,229**	**25,025**	**2,708**

1 Confirmations in the Armed Forces are not included.

I Parochial Church Electoral Rolls 2010 and Selected Years

Provinces of Canterbury and York (including Europe and including Cathedrals from 2002 onwards)

Diocese		2010	2009	2007	2002	1996
1 Bath & Wells	C	36,100	36,200	36,000	38,000	42,700
2 Birmingham	C	17,000	17,200	17,500	18,200	19,300
3 Blackburn	Y	32,800	32,500	34,700	34,300	37,400
4 Bradford	Y	11,600	11,700	11,300	12,300	12,700
5 Bristol	C	15,800	15,800	15,400	16,600	19,000
6 Canterbury	C	20,800	20,700	20,600	21,000	21,000
7 Carlisle	Y	20,400	20,400	20,400	21,600	24,900
8 Chelmsford	C	47,000	46,500	45,300	48,600	50,800
9 Chester	Y	45,800	44,900	42,600	45,700	48,600
10 Chichester	C	53,400	52,200	54,100	51,800	58,200
11 Coventry	C	17,100	16,800	17,300	16,300	17,700
12 Derby	C	18,200	18,300	17,800	20,700	20,100
13 Durham	Y	23,000	23,200	22,800	24,000	27,400
14 Ely	C	19,100	18,900	18,300	19,100	20,900
15 Exeter	C	30,800	30,900	30,800	30,500	33,900
16 Gloucester	C	23,700	23,600	22,100	23,600	26,300
17 Guildford	C	29,900	29,500	28,100	29,500	30,600
18 Hereford	C	18,400	17,500	17,600	18,100	18,900
19 Leicester	C	17,000	16,800	16,400	17,000	16,100
20 Lichfield	C	44,600	43,700	44,600	45,000	52,200
21 Lincoln	C	25,900	25,800	28,400	27,800	31,300
22 Liverpool	Y	28,400	28,000	26,800	28,800	32,500
23 London	C	75,800	74,100	64,400	59,600	52,500
24 Manchester	Y	33,100	32,400	32,600	34,500	38,000
25 Newcastle	Y	16,100	16,000	16,000	16,700	17,500
26 Norwich	C	19,200	19,300	19,800	23,900	25,900
27 Oxford	C	56,200	54,500	52,700	54,600	60,600
28 Peterborough	C	19,400	19,400	18,300	18,000	19,500
29 Portsmouth	C	18,100	17,000	16,400	17,500	18,000
30 Ripon & Leeds	Y	16,700	16,500	15,300	17,600	19,300
31 Rochester	C	30,200	30,100	28,500	29,900	31,300
32 St. Albans	C	38,600	37,600	36,900	39,400	43,100
33 St. Edms & Ipswich	C	23,700	23,100	23,300	24,100	25,300
34 Salisbury	C	41,200	41,400	40,700	42,500	45,900
35 Sheffield	Y	18,200	17,900	17,400	18,600	20,700
36 Sodor & Man	Y	2,500	2,500	2,700	2,400	2,800
37 Southwark	C	49,500	47,600	44,800	44,200	45,400
38 Southwell & Nottingham	Y	20,200	18,900	18,800	18,300	18,700
39 Truro	C	15,800	15,600	15,700	16,900	17,600
40 Wakefield	Y	19,000	19,300	19,800	20,300	23,200
41 Winchester	C	38,800	38,000	37,000	38,500	42,100
42 Worcester	C	18,400	19,200	19,200	20,300	22,400
43 York	Y	35,000	33,900	33,600	35,000	38,200
44 Europe	C	11,500	10,900	10,300	9,300	
Totals Province of Canterbury	**C**	**891,100**	**878,400**	**858,300**	**880,500**	**928,600**
Totals Province of York	**Y**	**323,000**	**318,300**	**314,800**	**330,100**	**361,900**
Totals CHURCH OF ENGLAND		**1,214,100**	**1,196,600**	**1,173,100**	**1,210,600**	**1,290,500**

1 National electoral roll totals for 1996 do not include the Diocese of Europe and do not include Cathedrals.

Notes:

Electoral Rolls are revised annually and new rolls are compiled every six years. Thus in 1996 and 2002 and 2007 new electoral rolls were compiled.

J Average Weekly Attendances 2010
Adults, Children and Young People

Provinces of Canterbury and York (including Europe and Cathedrals)

			Average weekly		Average Sunday		Usual Sunday	
	Diocese		Adults	Children and young people	Adults	Children and young people	Adults	Children and young people
1	Bath & Wells	C	21,700	4,500	20,000	2,600	17,800	2,300
2	Birmingham	C	14,100	3,800	12,400	2,400	11,600	2,100
3	Blackburn	Y	22,100	6,700	19,500	4,900	17,500	3,900
4	Bradford	Y	9,100	2,300	8,100	1,300	7,400	1,100
5	Bristol	C	14,200	3,500	12,500	2,400	10,800	1,900
6	Canterbury	C	21,300	5,900	15,100	3,800	14,000	3,000
7	Carlisle	Y	13,100	2,400	11,900	1,400	9,800	1,100
8	Chelmsford	C	33,300	8,700	29,700	6,000	26,500	5,200
9	Chester	Y	30,800	7,300	27,000	4,800	23,800	3,900
10	Chichester	C	37,300	9,100	31,800	5,600	29,200	4,800
11	Coventry	C	13,500	2,700	11,900	2,100	11,000	1,800
12	Derby	C	14,900	2,800	13,300	2,100	11,400	1,600
13	Durham	Y	18,800	4,100	15,400	2,400	12,300	2,000
14	Ely	C	15,800	4,000	14,400	2,300	12,500	2,100
15	Exeter	C	23,500	3,700	21,700	2,600	18,700	2,200
16	Gloucester	C	17,800	4,000	15,000	2,300	12,800	1,800
17	Guildford	C	21,400	6,500	19,200	4,500	17,700	3,600
18	Hereford	C	11,300	2,000	10,100	1,000	7,300	800
19	Leicester	C	13,400	2,900	11,900	1,800	10,800	1,700
20	Lichfield	C	28,800	7,800	25,000	4,000	22,700	3,500
21	Lincoln	C	18,400	4,900	16,300	2,000	13,300	1,400
22	Liverpool	Y	21,800	6,000	18,800	4,000	16,000	3,100
23	London	C	59,800	16,000	48,200	10,300	45,700	10,000
24	Manchester	Y	25,300	8,400	22,300	5,800	19,100	5,200
25	Newcastle	Y	13,000	2,400	11,100	1,500	9,900	1,200
26	Norwich	C	17,800	2,100	16,600	1,400	14,100	1,100
27	Oxford	C	45,000	10,600	40,400	7,600	36,200	6,700
28	Peterborough	C	15,500	3,500	13,600	2,600	11,800	2,100
29	Portsmouth	C	12,300	2,900	10,900	1,700	9,800	1,400
30	Ripon & Leeds	Y	12,200	2,900	10,800	1,900	9,600	1,600
31	Rochester	C	22,900	6,400	20,600	4,600	18,700	4,200
32	St. Albans	C	29,000	9,400	24,400	5,000	21,100	4,000
33	St. Edms & Ipswich	C	16,800	2,700	15,300	1,900	12,700	1,900
34	Salisbury	C	26,100	5,000	23,200	3,000	20,300	2,700
35	Sheffield	Y	15,800	4,300	13,400	2,500	11,900	1,900
36	Sodor & Man	Y	1,900	400	1,700	300	1,400	300
37	Southwark	C	34,400	11,200	31,400	8,400	27,000	6,900
38	Southwell & Nottingham	Y	13,700	3,100	12,100	1,900	11,800	1,600
39	Truro	C	11,400	1,800	10,100	1,000	8,500	900
40	Wakefield	Y	13,500	3,100	11,400	1,800	10,100	1,400
41	Winchester	C	26,900	7,000	23,700	4,100	21,600	3,800
42	Worcester	C	12,400	2,300	10,800	1,400	9,800	1,100
43	York	Y	24,800	6,000	21,400	3,300	18,000	2,400
44	Europe	C	10,600	1,600	10,000	1,600	9,300	1,600
	Totals Province of Canterbury	**C**	661,600	159,200	579,400	101,700	514,700	87,900
	Totals Province of York	**Y**	235,900	59,400	204,900	37,700	178,600	30,800
	Totals CHURCH OF ENGLAND		897,500	218,600	784,300	139,400	693,300	118,700
	Comparable figures for 2009							
	Totals Province of Canterbury	**C**	665,900	160,700	590,500	104,100	522,800	90,100
	Totals Province of York	**Y**	241,700	62,200	210,200	39,600	181,700	31,500
	Totals CHURCH OF ENGLAND		907,600	223,000	800,700	143,800	704,500	121,600

1. Children and young people are for the majority of dioceses defined as under the age of 16 years.

Parochial Church Attendance 2000 to 2010

K Weekly Church Attendance

Provinces of Canterbury and York (including Europe and Cathedrals)

Weekly attendance										Monthly
	Adult weekly attendance			Children and young people weekly attendance			All age weekly attendance			All age
Year	Highest (000s)	Average (000s)	Lowest (000s)	Highest (000s)	Average (000s)	Lowest (000s)	Highest (000s)	Average (000s)	Lowest (000s)	(000s)
2000*	1,451	1,031	742	455	243	120	1,855	1,274	885	1,855
2001	1,332	976	727	416	229	113	1,708	1,205	862	1,708
2002	1,296	941	693	424	229	111	1,682	1,170	825	1,682
2003	1,312	957	714	430	230	110	1,704	1,187	844	1,704
2004	1,308	951	706	437	235	111	1,707	1,186	839	1,707
2005	1,302	942	696	444	232	107	1,706	1,174	823	1,706
2006	1,294	937	690	442	228	103	1,694	1,163	812	1,694
2007	1,303	940	691	424	219	99	1,690	1,160	811	1,690
2008	1,267	919	679	438	225	100	1,667	1,145	800	1,667
2009	1,252	908	671	436	223	95	1,651	1,131	786	1,651
2010	1,243	898	661	438	219	89	1,645	1,116	768	1,645

L Sunday Church Attendance

Sunday attendance										Christmas
	Adult Sunday attendance			Children and young people Sunday attendance			All age Sunday attendance			All age
Year	Highest (000s)	Average (000s)	Lowest (000s)	Highest (000s)	Average (000s)	Lowest (000s)	Highest (000s)	Average (000s)	Lowest (000s)	(000s)
2000	1,191	878	660	300	180	103	1,464	1,058	781	2,851
2001	1,170	868	657	285	173	99	1,425	1,041	774	2,608
2002	1,143	838	623	278	167	94	1,395	1,005	733	2,600
2003	1,156	853	645	272	164	92	1,401	1,017	755	2,652
2004	1,147	846	638	272	164	91	1,394	1,010	746	2,629
2005	1,136	836	629	264	158	87	1,374	993	733	2,786
2006	1,123	828	622	262	155	84	1,361	983	722	2,994
2007	1,129	830	622	252	148	79	1,357	978	718	2,657
2008	1,099	812	611	249	148	80	1,322	960	707	2,647
2009	1,085	801	603	244	144	77	1,305	944	695	2,421
2010	1,065	784	590	240	139	73	1,283	924	677	2,298

Notes

1. Children and young people are under 16 years of age while adults are 16 years of age or over.
2. From 2000 church attendance figures are calculated typically from a four-week count in October.
3. *In 2000 attendance at midweek weddings and funerals was included.
4. An approximation to monthly attendance can be taken from the highest weekly attendance counted over a typical month.
5. Highest Sunday/weekly attendance = the sum of the highest Sunday (weekly) attendance over the four-week period.
6. Lowest Sunday/weekly attendance = the sum of the lowest Sunday (weekly) attendances over the four-week period.
7. Attendance figures have only been included where local churches held at least one church-based service (which included adult presence) during the week under examination.

M All Age Church Attendance 2000 to 2010

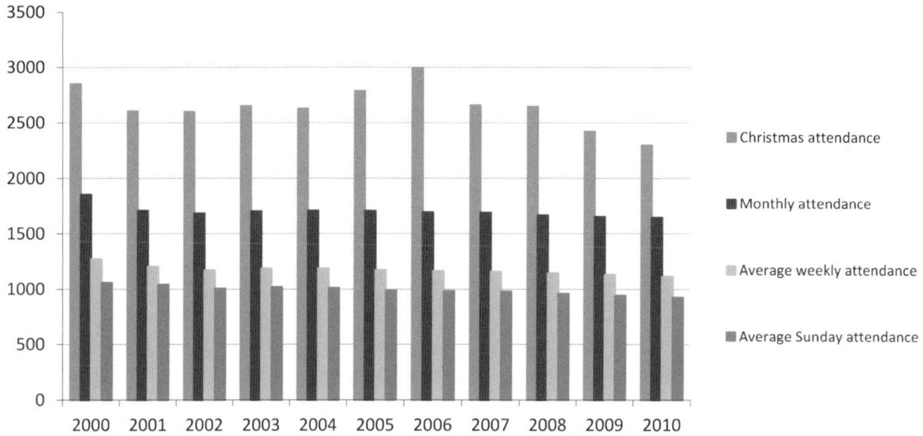

M continued

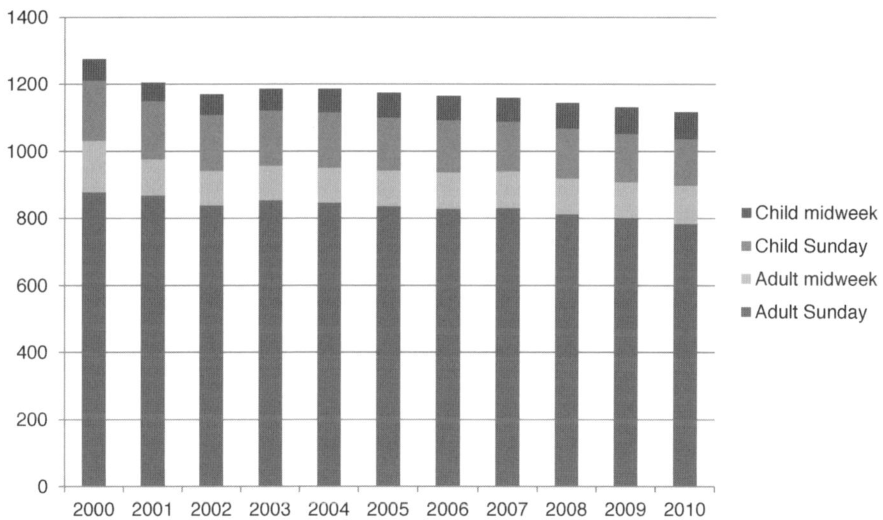

Selected Financial Comparisons 1964 to 2010

N Total Income of Parochial Church Councils 1964 to 2010

Excluding Europe and Cathedrals

Year	Tax-efficient planned giving				Total unrestricted direct giving			
	Net (£ 000s)		Weekly average per subscriber, £		(£ 000s)		Weekly average per Electoral Roll member, £	
	Actual	Real terms	Actual	Real terms	Actual	Real terms	Actual	Real terms
1964	2,113	33,272	0.32	5.08	14,961	235,583	0.11	1.65
1970	3,325	40,188	0.38	4.60	15,847	191,535	0.12	1.44
1980	17,692	59,132	0.94	3.14	51,521	172,199	0.55	1.82
1991	77,902	130,479	3.72	6.23	152,549	255,505	2.04	3.42
1992	86,617	139,838	4.13	6.67	164,854	266,147	2.17	3.51
1993	95,301	151,452	4.53	7.19	175,898	279,537	2.29	3.65
1994	103,745	160,981	4.93	7.64	187,468	290,894	2.44	3.78
1995	111,045	166,530	5.29	7.93	197,163	295,678	2.58	3.87
1996	118,111	172,951	5.62	8.23	205,417	300,794	3.06	4.48
1997	124,439	176,664	5.97	8.47	215,599	306,082	3.15	4.47
1998	132,114	181,342	6.37	8.74	244,338	335,384	3.51	4.82
1999	145,752	197,038	6.80	9.20	253,000	342,024	3.59	4.85
2000	157,922	207,348	6.73	8.84	268,541	352,588	3.78	4.96
2001	179,669	231,684	7.04	9.07	282,244	363,955	3.98	5.14
2002	189,904	240,991	7.25	9.20	296,382	376,113	4.75	6.02
2003	201,272	248,232	7.55	9.31	306,667	378,217	4.81	5.94
2004	215,085	257,595	8.00	9.58	323,403	387,321	5.00	5.99
2005	224,636	261,607	8.26	9.62	335,095	390,246	5.12	5.96
2006	236,625	267,084	8.63	9.75	348,716	393,604	5.34	6.03
2007	247,822	268,214	9.27	10.03	368,713	399,052	6.10	6.60
2008	261,354	272,061	9.77	10.17	383,862	399,588	6.32	6.58
2009	267,013	279,404	10.06	10.53	386,652	404,596	6.27	6.56
2010	271,416	271,416	10.41	10.41	389,393	389,393	6.23	6.23

1 Figures in 'Real terms' have been adjusted by the Retail Price Index to reflect 2010 purchasing power.
2 "Total voluntary income" = "direct giving" plus "other voluntary income" (see notes and definitions).
3 "Total recurring income" = "total voluntary income" plus "other recurring income" (see notes and definitions).
4 Tax-efficient planned giving includes regular Gift Aid donations.

O Giving 2000 to 2010

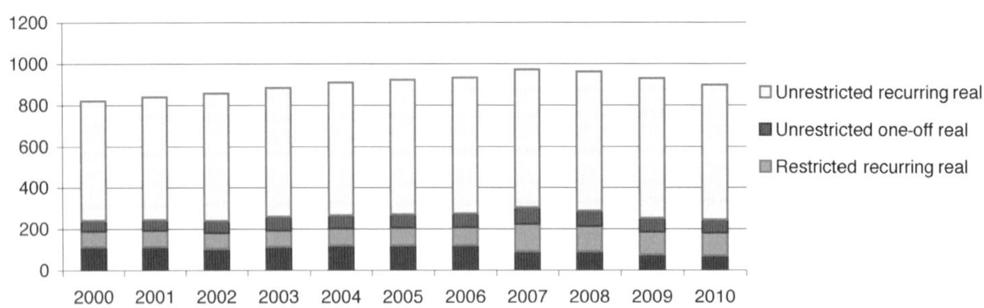

N continued

Total unrestricted voluntary income				Unrestricted			Restricted		Total income		
(£ 000s)		Weekly average per Electoral Roll member, £		recurring income (£m)		one off (£m)	recurring income (£m)	one off (£m)	recurring income (£m)	one off (£m)	Total (£m)
Actual	Real terms	Actual	Real terms	Actual	Real terms	Actual	Actual	Actual	Actual	Actual	Actual
20,033	315,449	0.14	2.21	22	348	-	-	-	-	-	-
22,110	267,232	0.17	2.01	26	319	-	-	-	-	-	-
72,798	243,313	0.77	2.58	86	287	-	-	-	-	-	-
212,974	356,712	2.85	4.77	257	430	-	-	-	-	-	-
230,005	371,329	3.03	4.89	274	442	-	-	-	-	-	-
246,050	391,022	3.21	5.10	287	457	-	-	-	-	-	-
262,886	407,920	3.42	5.30	308	477	-	-	-	-	-	-
275,388	412,990	3.61	5.41	328	491	-	-	-	-	-	-
288,358	422,245	4.30	6.29	345	505	-	-	-	-	-	-
305,345	433,493	4.46	6.34	374	531	-	-	-	-	-	-
314,933	432,284	4.53	6.21	404	554	36	54	63	457	100	557
326,377	441,221	4.63	6.25	419	566	37	55	69	473	106	579
346,856	455,414	4.88	6.40	442	581	39	57	86	499	126	625
365,851	471,766	5.16	6.66	463	597	40	61	88	523	128	652
385,861	489,663	6.18	7.84	487	617	46	61	81	547	128	675
401,600	495,299	6.30	7.77	507	625	54	63	92	570	146	716
423,452	507,144	6.55	7.84	538	644	53	67	101	605	154	759
440,574	513,085	6.73	7.84	561	653	55	73	103	634	158	792
459,800	518,987	7.04	7.95	585	661	59	75	107	660	166	826
485,131	525,050	8.02	8.68	619	670	73	122	84	741	157	898
504,818	525,500	8.31	8.65	651	678	70	117	87	768	157	925
511,720	535,468	8.30	8.68	648	678	65	104	72	752	137	889
515,727	515,727	8.25	8.25	654	654	64	109	70	763	134	897

5 Unrestricted income is income that may be used by the PCC for general church expenses. Restricted income is income which may not be used for any purpose other than as specified by the donor. (Income which a PCC designates for a specified purpose is considered to be unrestricted, since the PCC and not the donor is determining how it is to be used.)

P Weekly Average Tax-efficient Planned Giving per Subscriber

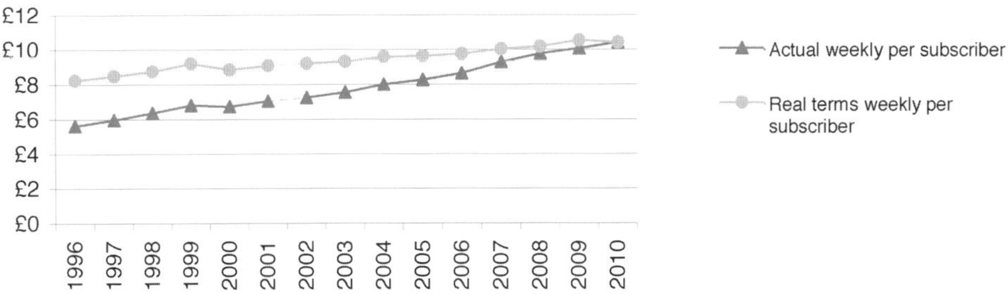

Q Charitable Giving and Total Expenditure 1964 to 2010

Excluding Europe and Cathedrals

Year	Total charitable donations (£m)		Total recurring expenditure (£m)		Capital expenditure (£m)	Total expenditure (£m)
	Actual	Real terms	Actual	Real terms	Actual	Actual
1964	2.17	34.22	21.71	341.87	-	-
1970	2.59	31.34	28.04	338.88	-	-
1980	8.48	28.34	77.85	260.19	-	-
1991	25.95	43.46	250.70	419.91	-	-
1992	26.37	42.57	270.37	436.49	-	-
1993	24.99	39.71	289.45	459.99	-	-
1994	25.81	40.06	307.70	477.46	-	-
1995	25.15	37.72	320.20	480.19	-	-
1996	25.36	37.14	338.67	495.92	-	-
1997	26.87	38.15	365.43	518.80	-	-
1998	35.30	48.46	415.20	569.91	103	518
1999	36.95	49.96	437.05	590.84	127	564
2000	37.46	49.19	458.34	601.79	145	603
2001	41.42	53.41	483.12	622.99	145	628
2002	44.40	56.34	513.85	652.08	149	663
2003	41.95	51.73	534.98	659.80	162	697
2004	45.31	54.26	567.93	680.18	159	727
2005	50.80	59.16	600.76	699.64	178	779
2006	46.55	52.54	617.71	697.22	175	793
2007	50.51	54.66	654.13	707.96	184	838
2008	51.72	53.84	694.28	722.73	194	888
2009	48.77	51.03	714.61	747.77	187	902
2010	48.82	48.82	721.38	721.38	197	918

1 Figures in 'Real terms' have been adjusted by the Retail Price Index to reflect 2010 purchasing power.

2 Total recurring expenditure = the total of ALL expenditure (including charitable giving) for the ordinary purposes of the PCC i.e. excluding only non-recurring items of capital expenditure and non-revenue items.

3 "Recurring expenditure" includes donations to charities, parish share/quota, clergy expenses, church running costs, costs relating to trading, salaries and support costs. "Capital expenditure" includes major repairs, redecoration and new building work.

R Growth in Income and Expenditure

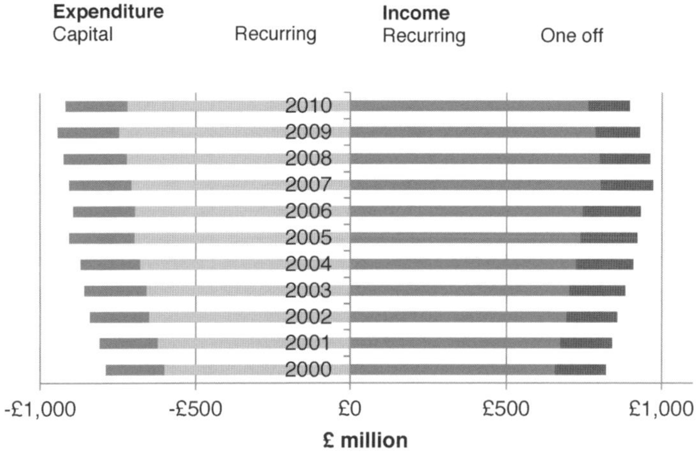

S Income and Expenditure 2005 and 2010

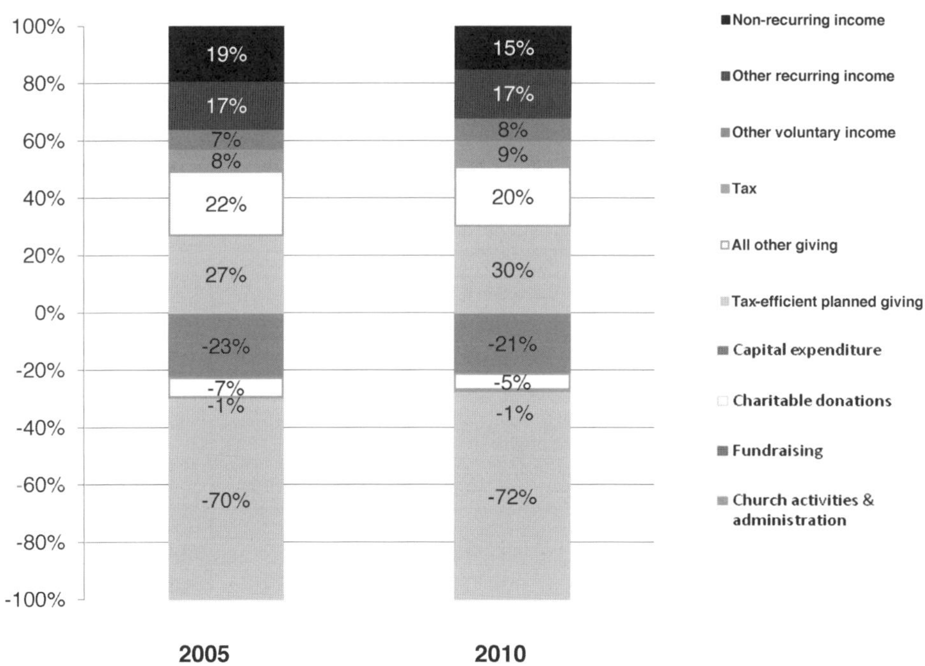

TABLE OF PAROCHIAL FEES from 1 January 2013 *Note: This table sets out the fees prescribed by the Parochial Fees Order 2012 (a Statutory Instrument) and summarizes other relevant information. For legal purposes reference should be made to the Order itself.*	Fee Payable towards Diocesan Board of Finance	Fee Payable to Parochial Church Council	**Total Fee payable**
BAPTISMS	£	£	**£**
Certificate issued at time of baptism (See Note 1)	—	11.00	**11.00**
Short certificate of baptism given under section 2, Baptismal Registers Measure 1961	—	11.00	**11.00**
MARRIAGES			
Publication of banns of marriage	—	21.00	**21.00**
Certificate of banns issued at time of publication	—	13.00	**13.00**
Marriage Service (See Note 5. For Marriage certificate see Note 6)	175.00	206.00	**381.00**
FUNERALS AND BURIALS OF PERSON AGED 16 YEARS OR MORE (See Note 3(i))			
Service in Church			
Funeral service in church, whether taking place before or after burial or cremation (See Note 5)	88.00	72.00	**160.00**
Burial in churchyard immediately preceding or following on from service in church	10.00	250.00	**260.00**
Burial in cemetery or cremation immediately preceding or following on from service in church	26.00	—	**26.00**
Burial of body in churchyard on separate occasion (See Note 3(ii))	36.00	250.00	**286.00**
Burial of cremated remains in churchyard or other lawful disposal of remains on separate occasion (See Note 3(ii))	36.00	102.00	**138.00**
Burial in cemetery on separate occasion (See Note 3(ii))	46.00	10.00	**56.00**
No Service in Church			
Service at graveside	98.00	72.00	**170.00**
Service at crematorium or cemetery	139.00	21.00	**160.00**
Burial of body in churchyard	36.00	250.00	**286.00**
Burial of cremated remains in churchyard or other lawful disposal of cremated remains	36.00	102.00	**138.00**
Certificate issued at time of burial (See Note 3(iii))	—	10.00	**10.00**
MONUMENTS IN CHURCHYARDS			
Permitted in accordance with rules, regulations or directions made by the Chancellor of the diocese, including those relating to a particular churchyard or part of a churchyard (but excluding a monument authorized by a particular faculty, the fee for which is set by the Chancellor)			
Small cross of wood	10.00	26.00	**36.00**
Small vase not exceeding 305mm × 203mm × 203mm (12" × 8" × 8") or tablet, plaque or other marker commemorating a person whose remains have been cremated	11.00	51.00	**62.00**
Any other monument (the above fees include the approval of the original inscription by the incumbent)	10.00	107.00	**117.00**
Additional inscription on existing monument	10.00	10.00	**20.00**
SEARCHES IN CHURCH REGISTERS			
Searching registers of marriages for period before 1 July 1837 (See Note 4) (for up to one hour)	—	21.00	**21.00**
for each subsequent hour or part of an hour	—	21.00	**21.00**
Searching registers of baptism or burials (See Note 4) (including the provision of one copy of any entry therein) for up to one hour	—	21.00	**21.00**
for each subsequent hour or part of an hour	—	21.00	**21.00**
Each additional copy of an entry in a register of baptism or burials	—	10.00	**10.00**
Inspection of instrument of apportionment or agreement for exchange of land for tithes deposited under the Tithe Act 1836	—	—	—
Furnishing copies of above (for every 72 words)	—	10.00	**10.00**
EXTRAS **The fees shown in this table are the statutory fees payable. It is stressed that the figures do not include any charges for extras such as heating, the services of a verger, music (e.g. organist, choir), bells, and flowers, which are fixed by the Parochial Church Council.**	**Published by The Archbishops' Council Church House, Great Smith Street, London. SW1P 3AZ**		

NOTES

1. CERTIFICATES OF BAPTISM

The fee for a certificate issued at the time of baptism is for a certified copy of the entry in the register book of baptisms giving the particulars required in Form No 1 in Schedule 1 to the Parochial Registers and Records Measure 1978. The fees payable for a certified copy of the full entry issued at any other time are the fees prescribed for searching registers of baptisms and burials and, if applicable, for each additional copy of an entry in such a register.

2. DEFINITIONS etc.

'Burial' includes deposit in a vault or brick grave and the interment or deposit of cremated remains.

'Churchyard' includes the curtilage of a church and a burial ground of a church whether or not immediately adjoining such church.

(NOTE: This includes any area used for the interment of cremated remains within such a curtilage or burial ground, whether consecrated or not.)

'Cemetery' means a burial ground maintained by a burial authority.

'Monument' includes headstone, cross, kerb, border, vase, chain, railing, tablet, plaque, marker, flatstone, tombstone or monument or tomb of any other kind.

'immediately preceding or following on from service in church' includes the day before and the day after the service in church.

Where " — " appears in the table no fee is payable to the body indicated.

3. FUNERALS AND BURIALS

i) No fee is payable in respect of a burial of a still-born infant, or for the funeral or burial of a person dying within sixteen years after birth.

ii) The fee for a burial in a churchyard on a separate occasion applies when burial does not take place on the same day as, or on the day before or the day after, a service in church.

iii) The certificate issued at the time of burial is a certified copy of the entry in the register book of burials kept under the Parochial Registers and Records Measure 1978.

4. SEARCHES IN CHURCH REGISTERS

The search fee relates to a particular search where the approximate date of the baptism, marriage or burial is known. The fee for a more general search of a church register is negotiable.

5. COSTS AND EXPENSES

In the case of a marriage service or a funeral service in church, any costs and expenses incurred in respect of routine administration (including arranging dates and times and the making of entries in registers), making the church available and lighting it are included in the fee prescribed as payable to the Parochial Church Council.

6. FEE FOR MARRIAGE CERTIFICATE

The following fees are currently payable to the Parochial Church Council under the Registration of Births, Deaths and Marriages (Fees) (Amendment) Order 2012: certified copy of entry of marriage register at time of registration £4.00; subsequently £10.00. (The fees in Note 6 may be increased from 1 April 2013.)

Dioceses

PART 1

PART 1 CONTENTS

Every effort has been made to ensure that all details are accurate at the time of going to press.

Provinces of Canterbury and York

The dioceses in the respective Provinces of Canterbury and York are as below:

The Province of Canterbury Bath and Wells, Birmingham, Bristol, Canterbury, Chelmsford, Chichester, Coventry, Derby, Ely, Europe, Exeter, Gloucester, Guildford, Hereford, Leicester, Lichfield, Lincoln, London, Norwich, Oxford, Peterborough, Portsmouth, Rochester, St Albans, St Edmundsbury and Ipswich, Salisbury, Southwark, Truro, Winchester, Worcester.

The Province of York Blackburn, Bradford, Carlisle, Chester, Durham, Liverpool, Manchester, Newcastle, Ripon and Leeds, Sheffield, Sodor and Man, Southwell and Nottingham, Wakefield, York.

The entry for each diocese is preceded by a territorial description and a few vital statistics:

Population Derived from the 2010 mid-year estimates published by the Office for National Statistics (source: ONS website www.statistics.gov.uk). Calculations are based on diocesan proportions of Ward and Civil Parish populations.

Area in square miles, as calculated from material supplied by the Office of National Statistics and the Church Commissioners.

Stipendiary clergy Full-time parochial clergy, men and women, working within the diocesan framework in parishes as at 31 December 2011 and counted under the current deployment formula.

Benefices Figures as at December 2011, compiled from information provided by the Church Commissioners. The figure does not include cathedrals or conventional districts.

Parishes, **Churches** are listed in the Parish Register maintained by the Research and Statistics Department of the Archbishops' Council as at 31 December 2011.

In most cases, the Diocesan Secretary/Chief Executive is also the Secretary of the Diocesan Synod.

PROVINCIAL LAY OFFICERS

Canterbury
Dean of the Court of Arches Rt Worshipful Charles George QC

Vicar-General Rt Worshipful Timothy Briden

Registrar Canon John Rees, 16 Beaumont St, Oxford OX1 2LZ *Tel:* 01865 297200
Fax: 01865 726274
email: jrees@wslaw.co.uk

York
Official Principal and Auditor of Chancery Court of York Rt Worshipful Charles George QC

Vicar-General of the Province and Official Principal of the Consistory Court Rt Worshipful Peter Collier QC

Registrar Mr Lionel Lennox, Provincial Registry, Stamford House, Piccadilly, York YO1 9PP
Tel: 01904 623487
Fax: 01904 561470
email: lpml@denisontill.com

Joint Registrar (Provincial Elections) Mr Stephen Slack, The Legal Office, Church House, Great Smith St, London SW1P 3AZ *Tel:* 020 7898 1366
email: stephen.slack@churchofengland.org

Archbishop of Canterbury's Personal Staff

Lambeth Palace, London SE1 7JU
Tel: 020 7898 1200 *Fax:* 020 7401 9886
Web: www.archbishopofcanterbury.org

CHIEF OF STAFF
Mr Christopher Smith

Archbishop's Personal Assistant
Mrs Mary Whitticase

Secretary for Public Affairs and Deputy Chief of Staff
Mrs Kay Brock

Deputy Secretary for Public Affairs
Revd Helen Dawes

Press Secretary
Ms Marie Papworth

Press Officer
Mr David Brownlie-Marshall

Patronage Secretary
Mr Derek Fullarton

Premises and Administration Secretary
Mr Andrew Nunn

Secretary for Anglican Communion Affairs
Revd Canon Joanna Udal

Anglican Communion Liaison Officer
Miss Fiona Millican

Secretary for Anglican Relations
Revd Canon Flora Winfield

Secretary for International Development
Revd Rachel Carnegie

Director of Programmes and Advocacy
Miss Helen Stawski

Ecumenical Officer and Personal Chaplain
Revd Canon Jonathan Goodall

Deputy Secretary for Ecumenism
Revd Dr Leslie Nathaniel

Chaplain
Revd Canon Michael Camp

Secretary for Inter Religious Affairs
Revd Dr Toby Howarth

Archbishops' Missioner and Team Leader of Fresh Expressions
Rt Revd Graham Cray

Steward
Colonel Malcolm Croft

Finance Officer
Miss Rebecca Pashley

Archbishop of York's Personal Staff

Bishopthorpe Palace, Bishopthorpe, York YO23 2GE
Tel: 01904 707021 *Fax:* 01904 709204
email: office@archbishopofyork.org
Web: www.archbishopofyork.org

Chief of Staff
Revd Malcolm Macnaughton
email: malcolm.macnaughton@archbishopofyork.org

Chaplain/Researcher to the Archbishop
Revd Dr Daphne Green
email: daphne.green@archbishopofyork.org

Executive Officer/Researcher
Mrs Margaret Pattinson
email: margaret.pattinson@archbishopofyork.org

Director of Communications
Mr Kerron Cross
email: kerron.cross@archbishopofyork.org

Domestic Chaplain to the Archbishop
Revd Richard Carew
email: richard.carew@archbishopofyork.org

Palace and Events Manager
Mrs Sandy Reynard
email: sandy.reynard@archbishopofyork.org

Senior Secretary
Miss Alison Cundiff
email: alison.cundiff@archbishopofyork.org

DIOCESE OF BATH AND WELLS

Founded in 909. Somerset; north Somerset; Bath; north-east Somerset; a few parishes in Dorset.

Population 915,000 Area 1,614 sq m
Full-time Stipendiary Parochial Clergy 187 Benefices 186
Parishes 469 Churches 564
www. bathandwells.org.uk
Overseas link dioceses: Luapula, Lusaka, Central Zambia, Northern Zambia and Eastern Zambia.

BISHOP (78th)
Rt Revd Peter Price, The Palace, Wells BA5 2PD [2002] *Tel:* 01749 672341
Fax: 01749 679355
email: bishop@bathwells.anglican.org

SUFFRAGAN BISHOP
TAUNTON Rt Revd Peter Maurice, The Palace, Wells BA5 2PD (*Office*) [2006] *Tel:* 01749 672341
Fax: 01749 679355
email: bishop.taunton@bathwells.anglican.org
Bishops' Senior Chaplain and Adviser Preb Stephen Lynas (*same address, tel and fax nos*)
email: chaplain@bathwells.anglican.org
Bishop's Domestic Chaplain Revd Julia Hedley (*same address, tel and fax nos*)
email: julia.hedley@bathwells.anglican.org

ASSISTANT BISHOPS
Rt Revd Richard Third, 25 Church Close, Martock, Yeovil TA12 6DS *Tel:* 01935 825519
Rt Revd William Persson, Ryalls Cottage, Burton St, Marnhull, Sturminster Newton DT10 1PS
Tel: 01258 820452
Rt Revd Paul Barber, Hillside, 41 Somerton Rd, Street BA16 0DR *Tel:* 01458 442916
Rt Revd Barry Rogerson, Flat 2, 30 Albert Rd, Clevedon BS21 7RR *Tel:* 01275 541964
email: barry.rogerson@blueyonder.co.uk
Rt Revd Roger Sainsbury, Abbey Lodge, Battery Lane, Portishead BS20 7JD *Tel:* 01275 847082
email: bishoproger@talktalk.net
Rt Revd John Perry, 8 The Firs, Combe Down, Bath BA2 5ED **Tel:** 01225 833987
email: jperry9391@aol.com
Rt Revd George Cassidy, Darch House, 17 St Andrew Road, Stogursey, Bridgwater TA5 1TE
Tel: 01278 732625
email: georgecassidy123@btinternet.com

CATHEDRAL CHURCH OF ST ANDREW IN WELLS
Dean of Wells Very Revd John Clarke, The Dean's Lodging, 25 The Liberty, Wells BA5 2SZ [2004]
Tel: 01749 670278
email: thedeanofwells@googlemail.com
Cathedral Offices Chain Gate, Cathedral Green, Wells BA5 2UE *Tel:* 01749 674483
Fax: 01749 832210
email: office@wellscathedral.uk.net
Web: www.wellscathedral.org.uk
Canons Residentiary
Chancellor Canon Andrew Featherstone, 8 The Liberty, Wells BA5 2SU [2005] *Tel:* 01749 679587
email: chancellorofwellscathedral@gmail.com
Precentor Vacancy
Treasurer Canon Dr Graham Dodds, 2 The Liberty, Wells BA5 2SU [2010] *Tel:* 01749 670607
email: Graham.Dodds@bathwells.anglican.org
Archdeacon Ven Nicola Sullivan, 6 The Liberty, Wells BA5 2SU [2007] *Tel:* 01749 685147
email: adwells@bathwells.anglican.org
Lay Members
Cathedral Administrator Dr Paul Richards, Cathedral Offices
email: administrator@wellscathedral.uk.net
Preb Adrian I'Anson, Cathedral Offices
Preb Barbara Bates, Cathedral Offices
Preb Gill Hawkings, Cathedral Offices
Registrar Preb Mr Tim Berry, Diocesan Registry, 14 Market Place, Wells BA5 2RE
Tel: 01749 674747
Fax: 01749 834060
email: tim.berry@harris-harris.co.uk
Cathedral Organist Mr Matthew Owens (*based at Cathedral Offices*)
email: musicoffice@wellscathedral.uk.net

ARCHDEACONS
WELLS Ven Nicola Sullivan, 6 The Liberty, Wells BA5 2SU [2007] *Tel:* 01749 685147
Fax: 01749 679755
email: adwells@bathwells.anglican.org
BATH Ven Andy Piggott, 56 Grange Rd, Saltford, Bristol BS31 3AG [2005] *Tel:* 01225 873609
Fax: 01225 874110
email: adbath@bathwells.anglican.org
TAUNTON Ven John Reed, 2 Monkton Heights, West Monkton, Taunton TA2 8LU [1999]
Tel: 01823 413315
Fax: 01823 413384
email: adtaunton@bathwells.anglican.org

CONVOCATION (MEMBERS OF THE HOUSE OF CLERGY OF THE GENERAL SYNOD)

Proctors for Clergy
Ven Andy Piggott
Preb Stephen Lynas
Revd James Dudley-Smith
Revd Sue Rose

MEMBERS OF THE HOUSE OF LAITY OF THE GENERAL SYNOD

Mr Edward Armitstead
Mr Tim Hind
Mrs Jenny Humphreys
Dr Cherida Stobart
Miss Fay Wilson Rudd

DIOCESAN OFFICERS

Dioc Secretary Mr Nicholas Denison, Dioc Office, The Old Deanery, Wells BA5 2UG *Tel:* 01749 670777 *Fax:* 01749 674240 *email:* nick.denison@bathwells.anglican.org
Chancellor of Diocese The Worshipful Timothy Briden, 1 Temple Gardens, Temple, London EC4Y 9BB
Registrar of Diocese and Bishop's Legal Secretary Preb Mr Tim Berry, Diocesan Registry, 14 Market Place, Wells BA5 2RE *Tel:* 01749 674747 *Fax:* 01749 834060 *email:* tim.berry@harris-harris.co.uk

DIOCESAN ORGANIZATIONS

Diocesan Office The Old Deanery, Wells BA5 2UG *Tel:* 01749 670777 *Fax:* 01749 674240 *email:* general@bathwells.anglican.org

ADMINISTRATION

Dioc Synod (Chairman, House of Clergy) Tbc
(Chairman, House of Laity) Tbc
(Secretary) Mr Nicholas Denison, Dioc Office (*as above*)
Board of Finance (Chairman) Mr Harry Musselwhite, Highfields, 207 Bailbrook Lane, Bath BA1 7AB *Tel:* 01225 858913 *email:* harry.musselwhite@btopenworld.com
(Secretary) Mr Nicholas Denison, Dioc Office
Finance Group Mr Nicholas Denison (*as above*)
Board of Patronage Mrs Isobel Chapman, Dioc Office *email:* isobel.chapman@bathwells.anglican.org
Mission and Pastoral Committee Mrs Isobel Chapman (*as above*)
Designated Officer Mrs Isobel Chapman (*as above*)
Assistant Dioc Secretary Mrs Isobel Chapman (*as above*)
Accountant Mr Nick May, Dioc Office *email:* nick.may@bathwells.anglican.org
Property Officer Mrs Alison Walker, Dioc Office *email:* alison.walker@bathwells.anglican.org
Dioc Surveyor Mr Paul Toseland, Dioc Office *email:* paul.toseland@bathwells.anglican.org

CHURCHES

Advisory Committee for the Care of Churches (Chairman) Mr Chris Hyldon, Mill Stream Barn, Martin Street, Baltonsborough, Glastonbury BA6 8QT *Tel:* 01458 851641 *email:* chrishyldon@hotmail.com
(Secretary) Preb Mr Tim Berry, Dioc Registry, 14 Market Place, Wells BA5 2RE *Tel:* 01749 674747 *Fax:* 01749 834060 *email:* tim.berry@harris-harris.co.uk
(Assistant Secretary) Mrs Sarah Davis, Dioc Registry (*as above*) *email:* sarah.davis@harris-harris.co.uk
Association of Change Ringers Revd Tim Hawkings, The Rectory, Cheddar Rd, Axbridge BS26 2DL *Tel:* 01934 732261 *email:* revhawkings@googlemail.com

EDUCATION

Board of Education Diocesan Office, The Old Deanery, Wells BA5 2UG *Tel:* 01749 670777 *Fax:* 01749 674240 *email:* education@bathwells.anglican.org
Dioc Director of Education Mrs Theresa Gale, Dioc Office *email:* theresa.gale@bathwells.anglican.org
School Improvement Advisers
Mrs Pauline Dodds, Dioc Office *email:* pauline.dodds@bathwells.anglican.org
Mr David Williams, Dioc Office *email:* david.williams@bathwells.anglican.org
School Development Advisers
Mr Malcolm Barton, Dioc Office *email:* malcolm.barton@bathwells.anglican.org
Mrs Suzanne McDonald, Dioc Office *email:* suzanne.mcdonald@bathwells.anglican.org
Parish Adviser for Young People Mr Tony Cook, Dioc Office *email:* tony.cook@bathwells.anglican.org
Parish Adviser for Children Mrs Jane Tibbs, Dioc Office *email:* jane.tibbs@bathwells.anglican.org
Safeguarding Adviser Mr Nigel Liddiard, Dioc Office *email:* nigel.liddiard@bathwells.anglican.org

MINISTRY FORUM

Chairman The Bishop of Taunton
Principal of the School of Formation Preb Dr Graham Dodds, Dioc Office *email:* graham.dodds@bathwells.anglican.org
Director of Continuing Ministerial Development Revd Simon Hill, Dioc Office *email:* simon.hill@bathwells.anglican.org
Education for Discipleship Officer Revd Jennifer Cole, Dioc Office *email:* jennifer.cole@bathwells.anglican.org
Diocesan Director of Vocations Preb Dr Catherine Wright, The Rectory, West Monkton, Taunton TA2 8QT *Tel:* 01823 413380 *email:* catherine.wright@bathwells.anglican.org

Adviser in Prayer and Spirituality Revd Jane Eastell, Meadowside, Wild Oak Lane, Trull, Taunton TA3 7JT *Tel:* 01823 321069
email: jane.eastell@bathwells.anglican.org
Adviser in Care and Counselling of the Clergy and their Families Mr John Careswell, The Coach House, Cork Street, Frome BA11 1BL
Tel: 01373 471317
email: john.careswell@fromecounselling.co.uk
Chaplain to the Deaf Mrs Pamela Grottick, 9 Chestnut Close, Baltonsborough, Glastonbury BA6 8PH *Tel:* 01458 851401
email: pamg@wpci.org.uk
Warden of Readers Ven John Reed, 2 Monkton Heights, West Monkton, Taunton TA2 8LU
Tel: 01823 413315
email: adtaunton@bathwells.anglican.org
Director of Reader Studies Preb Dr Graham Dodds (as above)
Dean of Women Clergy Preb Dr Catherine Wright (as above)

MISSION FORUM
Chairman The Archdeacon of Bath
Executive Officer/Diocesan Missioner Canon Roger Medley, Dioc Office
email: roger.medley@bathwells.anglican.org
Social Justice and Environment Adviser Mr David Maggs, Dioc Office
email: david.maggs@bathwells.anglican.org
World Mission Adviser & Exec Sec Zambia Link Mrs Jenny Humphreys, Dioc Office
email: jenny.humphreys@bathwells.anglican.org
Rural Life Adviser Vacancy
Healing Adviser Revd Matthew Thomson, The Vicarage, Station Road, Congresbury, Bristol BS49 5DX *Tel:* 01934 833126
email: revmattthomson@hotmail.com
Renewal Adviser Revd Keith Powell, Homefields House, Paynes Lane, Othery, Bridgwater TA7 0QB *Tel:* 01823 698619
email: jill.powell3@googlemail.com

STEWARDSHIP GROUP
Chairman The Archdeacon of Bath
Stewardship Adviser Mr Andrew Rainsford, Dioc Office
email: andrew.rainsford@bathwells.anglican.org

BISHOP'S LITURGY GROUP
Chairman Revd Robin Lodge, St Andrew's Vicarage, 118 Kingston Road, Taunton TA2 7SR
Tel: 01823 352471
email: robin.lodge1@btinternet.com

PRESS AND PUBLICATIONS
Diocesan Communications Manager Miss Gillian Buzzard, Dioc Office *Mobile:* 07848 028798
email: gillian.buzzard@bathwells.anglican.org
Diocesan Communications Officer Mr James Butterworth, Dioc Office *Mobile:* 07436 090658
email: james.butterworth@bathwells.anglican.org
Diocesan Communications Officer Mrs Helen Hawthorne, Dioc Office *Mobile:* 07436 090256
email: helen.hawthorne@bathwells.anglican.org
Editor of Directory/Database Manager Mrs Gill Davey, Dioc Office
email: gill.davey@bathwells.anglican.org

WIDOWS' OFFICER
Revd Dan Richards, 1 Quaperlake St, Bruton BA10 0HA *Tel:* 01749 812386
email: revdanrich@btinternet.com

RETREAT HOUSE
Abbey House, Glastonbury (*Warden* Liz Pearson)
Tel: 01458 831112
Fax: 01458 831893
email: info@abbeyhouse.org

DIOCESAN RECORD OFFICE
Somerset County Record Office, Somerset Heritage Centre, Brunel Way, Langford Mead, Norton Fitzwarren, Taunton TA2 6SF *Tel:* 01823 278805
Fax: 01823 325402
email: archives@somerset.gov.uk

DIOCESAN RESOURCE CENTRE
Old Deanery, Wells BA5 2UG *Tel:* 01749 685129
Fax: 01749 674240
email: resourcecentre@bathwells.anglican.org

RURAL DEANS

ARCHDEACONRY OF WELLS
Axbridge Revd Tim Hawkings, The Rectory, Cheddar Rd, Axbridge BS26 2DL
Tel: 01934 732261
email: revhawkings@googlemail.com
Bruton and Cary Preb Rose Hoskins, Springfields, Weston Bampfylde, Yeovil BA22 7HZ
Tel: 01963 440026
email: revroseanne@gmail.com
Frome Revd Colin Alsbury, St John's Vicarage, Vicarage Close, Christchurch Street East, Frome BA11 1QL *Tel:* 01373 472853
email: colin.alsbury@btinternet.com
Glastonbury Revd David MacGeoch, The Vicarage, 24 Wells Road, Glastonbury BA6 9DJ
Tel: 01458 834281
email: vicarabbeyparish@btinternet.com
Ivelchester Revd Peter Thomas, Rectory, Cat St, Chiselborough, Stoke-sub-Hamdon TA14 6TT
Tel: 01935 881202
email: PThomas5@aol.com
Yeovil Revd Anthony Perris, St James Vicarage, 1 Old School Close, Yeovil BA21 3UB
Tel: 01935 429398
email: antonyperris@yahoo.com
Shepton Mallet Revd Preb Alastair Wheeler, 3 Orchard Lea, Wells BA5 2LZ *Tel:* 01749 677810
email: AQHW@aol.com

ARCHDEACONRY OF BATH

Bath Revd Martin Lloyd Williams, 71 Priory Close, Combe Down, Bath BA2 5AP
Tel: 01225 835490
email: daftblackdog@yahoo.co.uk

Chew Magna Preb Jan Knott, Rectory, Church Lane, Fanrborough, Bath BA3 1AN
Tel: 01761 479311
email: jpknott@btinternet.com

Locking Revd Richard Taylor, The Rectory, Cecil Rd, Weston Super Mare BS23 2NF
Tel: 01934 623399
email: revrjtaylor@hotmail.com

Midsomer Norton Revd Chris North, The Rectory, The Street, Chilcompton BA3 4HN
Tel: 01761 232219
email: c.north123@btinternet.com

Portishead Revd Noel Hector, The Rectory, All Saints Lane, Clevedon BS21 6AU
Tel: 01275 873257
email: eastcleveub@blueyonder.co.uk

ARCHDEACONRY OF TAUNTON

Crewkerne Revd Jonathan Morris, The Rectory, New Street, North Perrott TA18 7ST
Tel: 01460 72356
email: jonbea@cooptel.net

Ilminster Revd Andrew Tatham, Rectory, Broadway, Ilminster TA19 9RE *Tel:* 01460 52559
email: aftatham@ukonline.co.uk

Exmoor Revd Stephen Stuckes, The Vicarage, Manor Road, Alcombe, Minehead TA24 6EJ
Tel: 01643 703285
email: sstuckes24@btinternet.com

Quantock Revd Stephen Campbell, Hodderscombe Lodge, Holford, Bridgwater TA5 1SA *Tel:* 01278 741329
email: campbell1sa@btinternet.com

Taunton Revd Geoff Boucher, The Rectory, West Monkton, Taunton TA2 8QT *Tel:* 01823 412226
email: geoffboucher@btinternet.com

Tone Revd Christopher Rowley, Vicarage, 62 Rockwell Green, Wellington TA21 9BX
Tel: 01823 662742
email: christopherrowley@uwclub.net

Sedgemoor Revd Chris Keys, The Vicarage, Church Lane, Westonzoyland TA7 0EP
Tel: 01278 691098
email: chris.keys@me.com

DIOCESE OF BIRMINGHAM

Founded in 1905. Birmingham; Sandwell, except for an area in the north (LICHFIELD); Solihull, except for an area in the east (COVENTRY); an area of Warwickshire; a few parishes in Worcestershire.

Population 1,457,000 Area 292 sq m
Full-time Stipendiary Parochial Clergy 147 Benefices 141
Parishes 149 Churches 191
www.birmingham.anglican.org
Overseas link dioceses: Lake Malawi, Southern Malawi, Northern Malawi (Malawi).

BISHOP (9th)

Rt Revd David Andrew Urquhart, Bishop's Croft, Old Church Rd, Harborne, Birmingham, B17 0BG [2006] *Tel:* 0121 427 1163
Fax: 0121 426 1322
email: bishop@birmingham.anglican.org

Domestic Chaplain Revd Kate Stowe, East Wing, Bishop's Croft, Old Church Rd, Birmingham B17 0BE *Tel:* 0121 427 2295 (Home)
0121 427 1163 (Office)
email: bishopschaplain@birmingham.anglican.org

SUFFRAGAN BISHOP

ASTON Rt Revd Andrew Watson [2008], 18 Widney Lane, Solihull B91 3LS
Tel: 0121 426 0448 (Office)
Fax: 0121 428 1114
email: bishopofaston@birmingham.anglican.org

HONORARY ASSISTANT BISHOPS

Rt Revd Michael Humphrey Dickens Whinney, 3 Moor Green Lane, Moseley, Birmingham B13 8NE [1989] *Tel:* 0121 249 2856

Rt Revd Peter Hall, 27 Jacey Rd, Edgbaston, Birmingham B16 0LL [1998] *Tel:* 0121 455 9240

Rt Revd Maurice Walker Sinclair, 55 Selly Wick Drive, Selly Park, Birmingham B29 7JQ [2002]
Tel: 0121 4712617
email: mauricewsinclair@blueyonder.co.uk

Rt Revd Mark Santer, 81 Clarence Rd, Moseley, Birmingham B13 9UH [2003]

Rt Revd Iraj Mottadeheh, 2 Highland Rd, Newport TF10 7AE [2005] *Tel:* 01952 813615

CATHEDRAL CHURCH OF ST PHILIP

Dean Very Revd Catherine Ogle, 38 Goodby Road, Moseley, Birmingham B13 8NJ
Tel: 0121 262 1840
email: dean@birminghamcathedral.com

Cathedral Office Birmingham Cathedral, Colmore Row, Birmingham B3 2QB *Tel:* 0121 262 1840
Fax: 0121 262 1860
email: enquiries@birminghamcathedral.com

Canons Residentiary

Canon Missioner Canon Nigel Hand, 12 Nursery Drive, Handsworth, Birmingham B20 2SW [2008]
Tel: 0121 262 1840
email: canonmissioner@birminghamcathedral.com

Canon Liturgist Revd Canon Janet Chapman, 4 Nursery Drive, Handsworth, Birmingham B20 2SW *Tel:* 0121 262 1840
email: canonliturgist@birminghamcathedral.com

Director of Operations Ruth Harvey, Cathedral Office *Tel:* 0121 262 1847
email: administrator@birminghamcathedral.com

Director of Music Canon Marcus Huxley, Cathedral Office *Tel:* 0121 262 1846
email: music@birminghamcathedral.com

ARCHDEACONS

ASTON Ven Dr Brian Russell, c/o Dioc Office [2005] *Tel:* 0121 426 0437
Fax: 0121 428 1114
email: archdeaconofaston@birmingham.anglican.org

BIRMINGHAM Ven Hayward Osborne, c/o Dioc Office [2001] *Tel:* 0121 426 0441
Fax: 0121 428 1114
email: archdeaconofbham@birmingham.anglican.org

CONVOCATION (MEMBERS OF THE HOUSE OF CLERGY OF THE GENERAL SYNOD)

Proctors for Clergy
Revd Catherine Grylls
Revd Canon Nigel Hand
Ven Hayward Osborne

MEMBERS OF THE HOUSE OF LAITY OF THE GENERAL SYNOD

Canon Dr Paula Gooder
Dr Rachel Jepson
Mr Robert Holgate

DIOCESAN OFFICERS

Dioc Secretary Mr Andrew Halstead, The Church of England, 1 Colmore Row, Birmingham B3 2BJ
Tel: 0121 426 0402
Fax: 0121 428 1114
email: andrew@birmingham.anglican.org

Chancellor of Diocese Vacancy c/o Diocesan Registrar, SGH Martineau, No. 1 Colmore Square, Birmingham B4 6AA

Registrar of Diocese and Bishop's Legal Secretary Mr Hugh Carslake, SGH Martineau, No. 1 Colmore Square, Birmingham B4 6AA
Tel: 0800 763 1000
Fax: 0800 763 1001
email: lawyers@sghmartineau.com
Web: www.sghmartineau.com

Dioc Surveyor Mr Alan Broadway, Dioc Office
Tel: 0121 426 0409
email: a.broadway@birmingham.anglican.org

DIOCESAN ORGANIZATIONS

Diocesan Office The Church of England, 1 Colmore Row, Birmingham B3 2BJ *Tel:* 0121 426 0400
Fax: 0121 428 1114
Web: www.birmingham.anglican.org

ADMINISTRATION

Dioc Synod (*Chair, House of Clergy*) Revd Martin Stephenson, 33 Paradise Lane, Hall Green, Birmingham B28 0DY *Tel:* 0121 777 1935
email: martin.stephenson@cantab.net

(*Chair, House of Laity*) Mr Stephen Fraser, 47 Wroxton Rd, Yardley, Birmingham B26 1SH
email: stevef_bham@sky.com

(*Secretary*) Mr Andrew Halstead, Dioc Office

Board of Finance (*Chair*) Mr Phil Nunnerley (*Secretary*) Mr Andrew Halstead (*as above*)

Parsonages Committee Mr Andrew Halstead (*as above*)

Dioc Trustees (*Secretary*) Mr Andrew Halstead (*as above*)

Pastoral Committee Mr Andrew Halstead (*as above*)

Designated Officer Mr Hugh Carslake, SGH Martineau (*as above*) *Tel:* 0800 763 1000
Fax: 0800 763 1001
email: lawyers@martineau-uk.com

CHURCHES

Advisory Committee for the Care of Churches (*Chair*) Dr Jim Berrow, c/o Dioc Office; (*Secretary*) Mr Adrian Mann, Dioc Office
email: a.mann@birmingham.anglican.org

EDUCATION

Dioc Director of Education Revd Jackie Hughes, Dioc Office
email: j.hughes@birmingham.anglican.org

Schools Support Officer Revd Peter French, Dioc Office
email: p.french@birmingham.anglican.org

RE Adviser Mrs Jill Stolberg, Dioc Office
email: j.stolberg@birmingham.anglican.org

MINISTRY

Director of Ordinands and Women's Ministry Canon Faith Claringbull, Dioc Office
email: f.claringbull@birmingham.anglican.org

MINISTRIES

Chair Ven Dr Brian Russell, Dioc Office

Bishop's Adviser for Continuing Clergy Ministerial Education Revd Mark Pryce, Dioc Office
email: m.pryce@birmingham.anglican.org

Bishop's Adviser for Lay Adult Education and Training Revd Liz Howlett, Dioc Office
email: l.howlett@birmingham.anglican.org

Bishop's Adviser for Minority Ethnic Anglicans Revd Joycelyn Lewis-Gregory, Dioc Office
email: revjoycelyn@gmail.com

Bishop's Adviser for Children's Ministry Ms Claire Wesley, Dioc Office
email: claire@birmingham.anglican.org

Bishop's Adviser for Youth Ministry Miss Helen Tomblin, Dioc Office
email: helen@birmingham.anglican.org

Assistant Adviser for Youth Ministry/Digital Youth Adviser Mr Craig Gilman, Dioc Office
email: craig@birmingham.anglican.org

Dioc Music Adviser Mr Mick Perrier, c/o Dioc Office *email:* mick@mperrier.freeserve.co.uk

Readers' Board (*Secretary*) Mr Michael Lynch, 57 Fairholme Rd, Hodge Hill, Birmingham B36 8HN
Tel: 0121 242 0534
email: mike4jeannie@blueyonder.co.uk

LITURGICAL

Bishop's Liturgical Advisory Committee Chair Revd Peter Babington, Parish Office, St Francis Centre, Sycamore Rd, Bournville, Birmingham B30 2AA
Tel: 0121 472 7215
email: pgbabington@gmail.com

MISSION AND EVANGELISM

Chair The Bishop of Aston

Transforming Church Co-ordinator Revd Rhiannon Jones, 23 Hallewell Road, Edgbaston, Birmingham B16 0LP *Tel:* 0121 454 5040
07595 880584 (Mobile)
email: rhiannon@birmingham.anglican.org

Bishop's Ecumenical Adviser Revd Nick Parker, Vicarage, High Street, Coleshill B46 3BP
Tel: 01675 462188
email: nickthevicparker@btinternet.com

Bishop's Adviser for the Environment Revd Patrick Gerard, Rectory, Church Lane, Lapworth, Solihull B94 5NX *Tel:* 01564 782098
email: Patrick@gerard.net

Bishop's Adviser for New Religious Movements Revd Paul Cudby, Vicarage, Vicarage Hill, Tanworth-in-Arden, Solihull B94 5EB
Tel: 01564 742565
email: paul@logos.myzen.co.uk

Bishop's Rural Adviser Revd Stephen Banks, Vicarage, 132 Main Road, Austrey, Atherstone CV9 3EB *Tel:* 01827 839022
email: stephen@avicarage.plus.com

Malawi Partnership Officer Revd Richard Tucker, 280 Chester Road North, Sutton Coldfield B73 6RR *Tel:* 0121 354 5873
email: malawiofficer@birmingham.anglican.org

HEALTHCARE CHAPLAINCIES

Bishop's Adviser Ven Hayward Osborne, Dioc Office

PRESS AND PUBLICATIONS

Bishop's Director of Communications Mr Steve Squires, Dioc Office *Tel:* 0121 426 0438 (Office) 07973 173195 (Mobile) *email:* steves@birmingham.anglican.org

Editor of Dioc Newsletter Mr Steve Squires

Editor of Dioc Directory Mr Steve Squires

Assistant to the Director of Communications Mrs Cara Butowski *Tel:* 0121 426 0439 *email:* cara@birmingham.anglican.org

CHURCHES AND INDUSTRY GROUP BIRMINGHAM

Industrial Chaplain (CIGB) Revd Peter Sellick, Dioc Office *Tel:* 0121 426 0425 *email:* peters@birmingham.anglican.org

DIOCESAN RECORD OFFICES

Birmingham Archives and Heritage, Central Library, Chamberlain Square, Birmingham B3 3HQ, Archives Dept, *Tel:* 0121 303 4549 (*For parish records in the City and Diocese of Birmingham*) *email:* archives.heritage@birmingham.gov.uk

Warwick County Record Office, Priory Park, Cape Rd, Warwick CV34 4JS, *Archive and Historic Environment Manager* Mrs Sam Collenette *Tel:* 01926 738959 (*For parish records in the Metropolitan Borough of Solihull, together with those still in the County of Warwick*) *email:* recordoffice@warwickshire.gov.uk

Sandwell Council Community History and Archives Service, Smethwick Library, High St, Smethwick, Warley, W Midlands B66 1AA *Borough Archivist* Sarah Chubb, *Tel:* 0121 558 2561 (*For parish records in the Warley deanery*) *email:* archives_service@sandwell.gov.uk

CHRISTIAN STEWARDSHIP

Stewardship and Income Generation Officer Mrs Jayne Grunnill, Dioc Office *Tel:* 0121 426 0424 *email:* jayne@birmingham.anglican.org

COMMUNITY REGENERATION

Director Fred Rattley, Faithful Neighbourhoods Centre, 10 Court Rd, Sparkhill, Birmingham B11 4LX *Tel:* 0121 426 0442 *email:* f.rattley@birmingham.anglican.org

COMMUNITY PROJECTS COMMITTEE

Chair Revd Nigel Traynor

AREA DEANS

ARCHDEACONRY OF ASTON

Aston Revd Nigel Traynor, 1162 Tyburn Rd, Pype Hayes, Birmingham B24 0TB *Tel:* 0121 373 3534 *email:* revnigel@yahoo.co.uk

Coleshill Revd Brian Castle, Vicarage, Haywood Rd, Tile Cross, Birmingham B33 0LH *Tel:* 0121 779 2739 *email:* revbcastle@aol.com

Polesworth Revd Michael Harris, Vicarage, 224 Tamworth Rd, Amington, Tamworth B77 3DE *Tel:* 01827 62573 *email:* mikeharassed@gmail.com

Solihull Canon Tim Pilkington, Rectory, St Alphege Close, Church Hill Rd, Solihull B91 3RQ *Tel:* 0121 705 0069 *email:* rector@solihullparish.org.uk

Sutton Coldfield Revd Dr Matthew Rhodes, The Vicarage, Maney Hill Road, Sutton Coldfield B72 1JJ *Tel:* 0121 354 2426 *email:* vicarofmaney@gmail.com

Yardley and Bordesley Revd Andrew Bullock, 34 Dudley Park Rd, Acocks Green, Birmingham B27 6QR *Tel:* 0121 706 9264 *email:* andrewbullock2@blueyonder.co.uk

ARCHDEACONRY OF BIRMINGHAM

Central Birmingham Revd Ian Harper, St John's Vicarage, Darnley Rd, Ladywood, Birmingham B16 8TF *Tel:* 0121 454 0973 *email:* harper-i1@sky.com

Edgbaston Revd Priscilla White, 115 Balden Road, Harborne, Birmingham B32 2EL *Tel:* 0121 427 2410 *email:* priscillawhite.harborne@btinternet.com

Handsworth Revd Edmund Newey, The Vicarage, 55 Laurel Road, Handsworth, Birmingham B21 9PB *Tel:* 0121 551 2097 *email:* ejnewey@phonecoop.coop

King's Norton Revd Melusi Sibanda, Vicarage, Edgewood Rd, Rednal, Birmingham B45 8SG *Tel:* 0121 453 3347 *email:* melusi.sibanda@googlemail.com

Moseley Revd Peter Babington, Parish Office, St Francis Centre, Sycamore Rd, Bournville, Birmingham B30 2AA *Tel:* 0121 472 7215 (Office) *Tel:* 0121 472 1209 (Home) *email:* pgbabington@gmail.com

Shirley Revd Duncan Hill-Brown, 54 Glendon Way, Dorridge, Solihull B93 8SY *Tel:* 01564 772472 *email:* Duncan@stphilipsandstjames.org

Warley Revd Anthony Perry, Vicarage, 27 Poplar Ave, Edgbaston, Birmingham B17 8EG *Tel:* 0121 429 2165 *email:* trinity20@hotmail.co.uk

DIOCESE OF BLACKBURN

Founded in 1926. Lancashire, except for areas in the east (BRADFORD) and in the south (LIVERPOOL, MANCHESTER); a few parishes in Wigan.

Population 1,303,000 Area 878 sq m
Full-time Stipendiary Parochial Clergy 154 Benefices 186
Parishes 224 Churches 278
www.blackburn.anglican.org
Overseas link dioceses: Free State (South Africa), Braunschweig (Germany) (Evangelical Lutheran Landeskirche).

BISHOP (8th)
Vacancy, Bishop's House, Ribchester Rd, Clayton-le-Dale, Blackburn BB1 9EF
Tel: 01254 248234
Fax: 01254 246668
email: bishop@bishopofblackburn.org.uk
Domestic Chaplain Revd Toby Webber, Bishop's House
email: chaplain@bishopofblackburn.org.uk
Bishop's Secretary Mrs Sue Taylor, Bishop's House
email: secretary@bishopofblackburn.org.uk
Assistant Secretary Mrs Hilary Wilby, Bishop's House
email: asstsecretary@bishopofblackburn.org.uk

SUFFRAGAN BISHOPS
LANCASTER Rt Revd Geoffrey S. Pearson, Shireshead Vicarage, Whinney Brow, Forton, Preston PR3 0AE [2006] *Tel:* 01524 799900
Fax: 01524 799901
email: bishoplancaster@gmail.com
BURNLEY Rt Revd John Goddard, Church House, Cathedral Close, Blackburn BB1 5AA
Tel: 01254 503070
email: bishop.burnley@blackburn.anglican.org

HONORARY ASSISTANT BISHOPS
Rt Revd Gordon Bates, Caedman House, 2 Loyne Park, Whittington, Carnforth LA6 2NX
Tel: 01524 848492
Rt Revd Michael Vickers, 2 Collingham Park, Lancaster LA1 4PD *Tel:* 01524 848492
Rt Revd and Rt Hon Lord Hope of Thornes, 2 Aspinall Rise, Hellifield, Skipton BD23 4JT

CATHEDRAL CHURCH OF ST MARY THE VIRGIN
Dean Very Revd Christopher Armstrong, The Deanery, Preston New Rd, Blackburn BB2 6PS [2001] *Tel:* 01254 52502 (Home)
email: dean@blackburncathedral.co.uk.
Cathedral Office Cathedral Close, Blackburn BB1 5AA *Tel:* 01254 503090 (Office)
Fax: 01254 689666
email: cathedral@blackburncathedral.co.uk.

Canons Residentiary
Sacrist Revd Canon Andrew Hindley, 22 Billinge Ave, Blackburn BB2 6SD [1996]
Tel: 01254 261152 (Home)
01254 503099 (Office)
email: andrew.hindley@blackburncathedral.co.uk.
Chancellor Revd Canon Ian Stockton, St Francis Vicarage, 1, St Francis Road, Blackburn BB2 2TZ [2011] *Tel:* 01254 200720 (Home)
01254 503 090 (Office)
email: ian.stockton@blackburncathedral.co.uk
Community Canon Revd Canon Shannon Ledbetter, 20 Buncer Lane, Blackburn BB2 2SE [2011] *Tel:* 01254 503090 (Office)
email: shannon.ledbetter@blackburncathedral.co.uk
Diocesan Directory of Ministry Revd Canon Dr Susan Penfold, The Vicarage, Church Lane, Great Harwood BB6 7PU [2008]
Tel: 01254 884039 (Home)
01254 503090 ext. 245 (Office)
email: sue.penfold@blackburn.anglican.org
Administrator Vacancy
Director of Music Mr Samuel Hudson, 15 Williams Drive, Blackburn BB2 3WT
Tel: 01254 503090 ext. 251 (Office)
email: samuel.hudson@blackburncathedral.co.uk

ARCHDEACONS
BLACKBURN Ven John Hawley, 19 Clarence Park, Blackburn BB2 7FA [2002] *Tel:* 01254 262571
Fax: 01254 263394
email: john.hawley@blackburn.anglican.org
LANCASTER Ven Michael Everitt, 6 Eton Park, Fulwood, Preston PR2 9NL *Tel:* 01772 700337
email: michael.everitt@blackburn.anglican.org

CONVOCATION (MEMBERS OF THE HOUSE OF CLERGY OF THE GENERAL SYNOD)
Proctors for Clergy
Revd Canon Dr Susan Penfold
Revd Paul Benfield
Revd Canon Dr Simon Cox
Revd Peter Law-Jones

MEMBERS OF THE HOUSE OF LAITY OF THE GENERAL SYNOD
Mrs Rosemary Lyon
Mr Gerald Burrows

Mrs Susan Witts
Mrs Vivienne Goddard
Prof Helen Leathard
Mrs Alison Wynne

DIOCESAN OFFICERS

Dioc Secretary Canon Graeme Pollard, Church House, Cathedral Close, Blackburn BB1 5AA
Tel: 01254 503070
Fax: 01254 693052
email: graeme.pollard@blackburn.anglican.org
Chancellor of Diocese His Honour Judge John Bullimore, Rectory, 5 Snowgate Head, Norn Lane, New Mill Nr Huddersfield HD9 7HD
Tel: 01484 521025
Registrar of Diocese and Bishop's Legal Secretary Mr Stephen Crossley, Roebucks, 7 & 12 Richmond Terrace, Blackburn BB1 7BG *Tel:* 01254 274000
email: registry@blackburn.anglican.org

DIOCESAN ORGANIZATIONS

Diocesan Office Church House, Cathedral Close, Blackburn BB1 5AA *Tel:* 01254 503070
Fax: 01254 693052
email: diocese@blackburn.anglican.org

ADMINISTRATION

Dioc Synod (Chairman, House of Clergy) Revd Canon John Hall, The Vicarage, 49 Mount Road, Fleetwood FY7 6QZ *email:* johnbloem@aol.com
(Chairman, House of Laity) Mr Jeff Warburton, 6 Chapel Street, Longridge, Preston PR3 3JH
email: jeffpne@aol.com
(Secretary) Canon Graeme Pollard, Church House (*as above*)
Board of Finance (Chairman) Canon John Dell, 66 Moseley Rd, Burnley BB11 2RF
(Secretary) Canon Graeme Pollard (*as above*)
Property Committee (Chairman) Revd Canon Andrew Sage; *(Secretary)* Canon Graeme Pollard (*as above*)
Mission and Pastoral Committee Canon Graeme Pollard (*as above*)
Designated Officer Mr Stephen Crossley (*as above*)

CHURCHES

Advisory Committee for the Care of Churches (Chairman) Mr John Tillotson, Bonds Farm, Horns Lane, Goosnargh, Preston PR3 2NE
Tel: 01772 783436
(Secretary) Canon Graeme Pollard (*as above*)

EDUCATION

Board of Education (Acting Director) Canon Fred Kershaw, Church House
email: fred.kershaw@blackburn.anglican.org
Schools' Adviser Miss Lisa Fenton, Church House
email: lisa.fenton@blackburn.anglican.org
Diocesan Youth Officer Miss Kat Witham, Church House
email: kat.witham@blackburn.anglican.org
Children's Work Adviser Mrs Susan Witts, Church House
email: susan.witts@blackburn.anglican.org

DISCIPLESHIP AND MINISTRY

Director of Ordinands Revd Dr John Darch, 24 Bosburn Drive, Mellor Brook, Blackburn BB2 7PA *Tel:* 01254 813544
Director of Ministry Revd Canon Dr Susan Penfold, Church House
email: sue.penfold@blackburn.anglican.org
Director of IME 1–4 Revd Dr John Darch (*as above*)
Adviser in Women's Ministry Revd Canon Fleur Green, The Rectory, 2 St Peter's Close, Darwen BB3 2EA *Tel:* 01254 702411
email: chauntry1@live.co.uk
Mothers' Union Mrs Beverley Laycock, St Stephen's Vicarage, 154 Todmorden Road, Burnley BB11 3ER *Tel:* 01282 424733
Warden of Readers and Pastoral Assistants Revd Sue Williams, St Leonard's House, Potter Lane, Samlesbury PR5 0UE *Tel:* 01772 877930
email: sue.williams@blackburn.anglican.org

LITURGICAL

Chairman Very Revd Christopher Armstrong (*as above*)
Secretary Revd Michael Gisbourne, St Thomas' Vicarage, Church St, Garstang, Preston PR3 1PA
Tel: 01995 602162
email: michael.gisbourne@phonecoop.coop

ECUMENICAL

Ecumenical Officer Revd Mike Hartley, Vicarage, Church Rd, Warton, Preston PR4 1BD
Tel: 01772 632227
email: blackburndeo@googlemail.com

PRESS AND PUBLICATIONS

Dioc Communications Officer Vacancy – contact Revd Toby Webber (*as above*)

DIOCESAN RECORD OFFICES

Diocesan Registry, Cathedral Close, Blackburn BB1 5AB *Tel:* 01254 503070
Lancashire Record Office, Bow Lane, Preston PR1 8ND *Tel:* 01772 254868

PARISH MISSION SUPPORT

Department Leader Revd David Banbury, St Mary's House, Cathedral Close, Blackburn BB1 5AA
Tel: 01254 503070
email: david.banbury@blackburn.anglican.org
Social Responsibility Lead Officer Revd Canon Ed Saville, St Mary's House, Cathedral Close, Blackburn BB1 5AA *Tel:* 01254 503070
email: ed.saville@blackburn.anglican.org
Parish Development Officer Revd Tim Horobin, The Vicarage, Stopes Brow, Lower Darwen BB3 0QP *Tel:* 01254 53898
email: timhorobin@aol.com
Officer for People with Sensory, Physical and Learning Difficulties Vacancy, St Mary's House

Rural and Environmental Officer Revd Chris Halliwell, Starch Hall Farm, Gallows Lane, Ribchester, Preston PR3 3XX *Tel:* 01772 653283
email: chris.halliwell@blackburn.anglican.org
Urban Areas Officer The Archdeacon of Blackburn (*as above*)

AREA DEANS

ARCHDEACONRY OF BLACKBURN

Accrington Vacancy
Blackburn with Darwen Revd Canon Andrew Raynes, Christ Church with St Matthew's Vicarage, Brandy House Brow, Blackburn BB2 3EY *Tel:* 01254 56292
email: andrewraynes@btopenworld.com
Burnley Revd Mark Jones, Vicarage, 1 Arbory Drive, Padiham, Burnley BB12 8JS
Tel: 01282 772442
email: jones.padiham@btinternet.co.uk
Chorley Revd Tim Wilby, St George's Vicarage, Letchworth Place, Chorley PR7 2HJ
Tel: 01257 263064
email: stgeorgeschorley@aol.com
Leyland Revd Alistair McHaffie, St John's Vicarage, Leyland Lane, Leyland PR25 1XB
Tel: 01772 621646
email: alistair@mchaffie.com
Pendle Revd Tony Rindl, The Vicarage, Skipton Rd, Foulridge, Colne BB8 7NP
Tel: 01282 870959
email: tony.rindl@googlemail.com
Whalley Revd Michael Woods, The Vicarage, Somerset Road, Rishton, Blackburn BB1 4BP
Tel: 01254 886191
email: mwoods4@supanet.com

ARCHDEACONRY OF LANCASTER

Blackpool Revd Canon Dr Simon Cox, All Hallows Rectory, 86 All Hallows Rd, Bispham, Blackpool FY2 0AY *Tel:* 01253 351886
email: drsjcox@yahoo.co.uk
Garstang Revd Andrew Wilkinson, Vicarage, Vicarage Lane, Churchtown, Garstang, Preston PR3 0HW *Tel and Fax:* 01995 602294
email: a.wilkinson703@btinternet.com
Kirkham Revd Peter Law-Jones, Vicarage, St Thomas Rd, Lytham St Annes
Tel: 01253 722725
email: peterlaw-jones@hotmail.co.uk
Lancaster Revd Mike Peatman, Rectory, Church Walk, Morecambe LA4 5PR *Tel:* 01524 410941
email: mikepeat@sky.com
Poulton Revd Martin Keighley, Vicarage, 7 Vicarage Rd, Poulton-le-Fylde FY6 3NA
Tel: 01253 883086
email: martinkeighley@btconnect.com
Preston Revd Canon Timothy Lipscomb, Rectory, 13 Ribblesdale Place, Preston PR1 3NA
Tel: 01772 252528
email: lavish@ermine2.fsnet.co.uk
Tunstall Revd Canon Paul Warren, Vicarage, St John's Grove, Silverdale, Carnforth LA5 0RH
Tel: 01524 701268
email: paulk.warren@btinternet.com

DIOCESE OF BRADFORD

Founded in 1919. Bradford; the western quarter of North Yorkshire; areas of east Lancashire, south-east Cumbria and Leeds.

Population 696,000 Area 920 sq m
Full-time Stipendiary Parochial Clergy 83 Benefices 103
Parishes 125 Churches 164
www.bradford.anglican.org
Overseas link dioceses: South Western Virginia, Khartoum and other northern dioceses (Sudan), Erfurt (Germany).

BISHOP (9th)
Rt Revd Nicholas Baines, Bishopscroft, Ashwell Road, Bradford BD9 4AU *Tel:* 01274 545414
email: bishop.nick@bradford.anglican.org/ lyndsay.horsman@bradford.anglican.org
Bishop's Chaplain Canon Denise Poole, Bishopscroft, Ashwell Rd, Bradford BD9 4AU
Tel: 01274 545414
Fax: 01274 544831
email: denise.poole@bradford.anglican.org

HONORARY ASSISTANT BISHOP
Rt Revd Dr Colin Buchanan, 21 The Drive, Alwoodley, Leeds LS17 7QB [2004]
Tel: 0113 267 7721
Rt Revd and Rt Hon Dr David M. Hope, 35 Hammerton Drive, Hellifield BD23 4LZ [2005]

CATHEDRAL CHURCH OF ST PETER
Dean Vacancy, The Deanery, 1 Cathedral Close, Bradford BD1 4EG [2005]
Tel: 01274 777722 (Office)
01274 777727 (Home)
Fax: 01274 777730
email: dean@bradfordcathedral.org
Canons Residentiary
Canon Samuel Corley, 3 Cathedral Close, Bradford BD1 4EG [2010] *Tel:* 01274 777731
Fax: 01274 777730
email: sam.corley@bradfordcathedral.org
Acting Dean Canon Andrew Williams, 2 Cathedral Close, Bradford BD1 4EG [2006]
Tel: 01274 777721 (Office)
01274 735707 (Home)
Fax: 01274 777730
email: andy.williams@bradfordcathedral.org
Cathedral Office Bradford Cathedral, Stott Hill, Bradford BD1 4EH *Tel:* 01274 777720
Fax: 01274 777730
email: julie.bowyer@bradfordcathedral.org
Administrator Mr Chris Aldred, Bradford Cathedral, Stott Hill, Bradford BD1 4EH
Tel: 01274 777726
Fax: 01274 777730
*email:*chris.aldred@bradfordcathedral.org
Education Officer Mrs Gillian Davis, Bradford Cathedral, Stott Hill, Bradford BD1 4EH
Tel: 01274 777734
Fax: 01274 777730
email: gillian.davis@bradfordcathedral.org
Director of Music Mr Alexander Woodrow, Bradford Cathedral, Stott Hill, Bradford BD1 4EH
Tel: 01274 777720
Fax: 01274 777730
email: alex.woodrow@bradfordcathedral.org
Cathedral Organist Mr Paul Bowen, Bradford Cathedral, Stott Hill, Bradford BD1 4EH
Tel: 01274 777720
Fax: 01274 777730
email: paul.bowen@bradfordcathedral.org
Head Verger Mr Jon Howard, Bradford Cathedral, Stott Hill, Bradford BD1 4EH
Tel: 01274 777724
Fax: 01274 777730
email: jon.howard@bradfordcathedral.org
PA to the Dean and Cathedral Administrator Mrs Sandra Howard, Bradford Cathedral, Stott Hill, Bradford BD1 4EH *Tel:* 01274 777723
Fax: 01274 777730
email: sandra.howard@bradfordcathedral.org

ARCHDEACONS
CRAVEN Ven Paul Slater, Woodlands, Netherghyll Lane, Cononley, Keighley BD20 8PB [2005]
Tel: 01535 635113 (Home)
01535 650533 (Office)
email: paul.slater@bradford.anglican.org
BRADFORD Ven Dr David Lee, 47 Kirkgate, Shipley, West Yorkshire BD18 3EH [2004]
Tel: 01274 200698
Fax: 01274 200698
email: david.lee@bradford.anglican.org

CONVOCATION (MEMBERS OF THE HOUSE OF CLERGY OF THE GENERAL SYNOD)
Proctors for Clergy
Revd Paul Ayers
Revd Ruth Yeoman

MEMBERS OF THE HOUSE OF LAITY OF THE GENERAL SYNOD
Mr Malcolm Halliday
Mr Ian Fletcher
Mrs Zahida Mallard

DIOCESAN OFFICERS

Dioc Secretary Mrs Debbie Child, Kadugli House, Elmsley St, Steeton, Keighley BD20 6SE
Tel: 01535 650555
Fax: 01535 650550
email: debbie@kadugli.org.uk

Human Resources Manager Mrs Debbie Child, Kadugli House *Tel:* 01535 650521
Fax: 01535 650550
email: debbie@kadugli.org.uk

Chancellor of Diocese His Honour John de G. Walford, c/o Diocesan Registry, Forward House, 8 Duke St, Bradford BD1 3QX

Registrar of Diocese and Bishop's Legal Secretary Mr Peter William Foskett, Diocesan Registry, Forward House, 8 Duke St, Bradford BD1 3QX
Tel: 01274 202132
Fax: 01274 202107
email: peter.foskett@gordonsllp.com

Dioc Insurance Adviser Ms Sandra Thurlow, Towergate Risk Solutions Leeds Airport West, Towergate House, 5 Airport West, Lancaster Way, Yeadon, Leeds LS19 7ZA
Tel: 0113 391 9316
07725 574837 (mobile)
email: sandra.thurlow@towergate.co.uk

Safeguarding Adviser Mrs Jenny Price, Church House, 1 South Parade, Wakefield WF1 1LP
Tel: 01924 371802
email: jenny.price@bradford.anglican.org

DIOCESAN ORGANIZATIONS

Diocesan Office Kadugli House, Elmsley St Steeton, Keighley BD20 6SE *Tel:* 01535 650555
Fax: 01535 650550
email: office@kadugli.org.uk

ADMINISTRATION

Dioc Synod (*Chairman, House of Clergy*) Canon John Nowell, The Vicarage, Church Hill, Baildon, Shipley BD17 6NE *Tel* and *Fax:* 01274 594941
email: john.nowell@bradford.anglican.org

(*Chairman, House of Laity*) Tbc

(*Secretary*) Mrs Debbie Child, Dioc Office

Board of Finance (*Chairman*) Mrs Sharron Arnold, 42 Effingham Rd, Harden, Bingley BD16 1LQ
Tel: 01535 272894
email: sharron.arnold@talktalk.net

(*Secretary*) Mrs Debbie Child (*as above*)

(*Accountant*) Mr Shaun Birch, Dioc Office
Tel: 01535 650526
email: shaun@kadugli.org.uk

Property Committee (*Chairman*) Mr David Nelson, Old Gledstone, West Marton, Skipton BD23 3JR
Tel: 01282 843476
Fax: 01282 843554

Property Officer Mr David Meadows, Dioc Office
Tel: 01535 650524
email: david@kadugli.org.uk

Pastoral Committee (*Chairman*) Mr Raymond Edwards, Crosslands, Stanbury, Keighley BD22 0HB *Tel:* 01535 642883

Designated Officer Mrs Debbie Child (*as above*)

Diocesan Advisory Committee (*Chairman*) Vacancy

(*Secretary*) Mrs Sylvia Johnson, Dioc Office
Tel: 01535 650523
email: sylvia.johnson@bradford.anglican.org

CHURCH IN THE WORLD

Bishop's Officer Vacancy

Interfaith Adviser Dr Philip Lewis, 9 Garden Lane, Heaton, Bradford BD9 5QJ
Tel: 01274 543891

Ecumenical Officer Revd Peter Mott, Rectory, 13 Westview Grove, Keighley BD20 6JJ
Tel: 01535 601499
email: peter.mott@bradford.anglican.org

World Church Links

Northern Sudan Ven Dr David Lee (*as above*)

Southwestern Virginia Mrs Jill Wright, 15 Walker Close, Glusburn, Keighley BD20 8PW
Tel: 01535 634526
email: jill.wright@bradford.anglican.org

Erfurt Mrs Rosie Tudge, St John's Vicarage, 9 St John's Avenue, Farsley, Pudsey LS28 5DN
Tel: 0113 2570059

COMMUNICATIONS

Communications Officer Ms Alison Bogle, 59 Hookstone Drive, Harrogate HG2 8PR
Tel: 01423 812995
07768 110175 (Mobile)
email: communications@bradford.anglican.org

Dioc News/Diocesan Office (*as above*)

EDUCATION

Chairman Mrs Diana Chambers, Romille Lodge, 4 Ridgeway, Skipton BD23 1LX
Tel: 01756 798389

Director of Education Revd Clive Sedgewick, Windsor House, Cornwall Rd, Harrogate HG1 2PW *Tel:* 01423 817553
Fax: 01423 817051
07903 326053 (Mobile)
email: clives@brleducationteam.org.uk

MINISTRY AND MISSION

Bishop's Officer Ven Paul Slater (*as above*)

Administrator Mrs Judy Mason, Dioc Office
Tel: 01535 650532
email: judy@kadugli.org.uk

Director of In-Service Training see Bishop's Officer

Director of Post-Ordination Training Vacancy

Director of Ordinands Canon Ann Turner, The Rectory, 7 Roundell Drive, Dairy Meadow, West Marton, Skipton BD23 3UL
Tel: 01282 842332
email: ann.turner@bradford.anglican.org

Associate Director of Ordinands Revd Michael Burley, The Vicarage, 21 Southfield Rd, Burley-in-Wharfedale, Ilkley LS29 7PB
Tel: 01943 863216
email: michael.burley@btinternet.com

Stewardship for Parishes Revd Uell Kennedy, Dioc Office *Tel:* 01535 650531
email: uell@kadugli.org.uk

Ministry Development Officer Revd Louise Taylor-Kenyon, The Vicarage, 21 Shires Lane, Embsay, Skipton BD23 6SB *Tel:* 01756 798057 *email:* louise.taylor-kenyon@bradford.anglican.org

Adult Education Canon Steve Allen, 1 Hawkstone Avenue, Guiseley, Leeds LS20 8ET *Tel:* 01943 510653 *email:* steve.allen@bradford.anglican.org

Training Canon Steve Allen (*Lay*); Bishop's Officer Ven Paul Slater (*Clergy*)

Diocesan Evangelist Revd Robin Gamble, The Vicarage, 470 Leeds Rd, Thackley, Bradford BD10 9AA *Tel:* 01274 615411 *email:* robinp.gamble@blueyonder.co.uk

Evangelism Adviser Revd Sue Hope, 31 South Edge, Moorhead, Shipley BD18 4RA *Tel:* 01274 583652 *email:* shope12443@aol.com

Warden of Readers Revd Christine Shedd, Holy Trinity Vicarage, Park House Road, Low Moor, Bradford BD12 0HR *Tel:* 01274 678859 *email:* c.shedd@btinternet.com

Retired Clergy, Widows and Dependents Officer (Bradford Archdeaconry) Canon Chris Hayward, 12 Ron Lawton Crescent, Burley-in-Wharfedale, Ilkley LS29 7ST *Tel:* 01943 865261
(*Craven Archdeaconry*) Canon David Bruno, Pond House, 5 Twine Walk, Burton-in-Lonsdale, Carnforth LA6 3LR *Tel:* 01524 261616

Children's Work Mr Steve Grasham, Dioc Office *Tel:* 01535 650535

Healing Advisers Revd Gill Mack, The Vicarage, Shire Lane, Hurst Green, Clitheroe BB7 9QR *Tel:* 01254 826686 *email:* gfmack@tiscali.co.uk
Revd Canon Andrew Williams, 2 Cathedral Close, Bradford BD1 4EG *Tel:* 01274 777721 *email:* andy.williams@bradfordcathedral.org

DIOCESAN RECORD OFFICES

Diocesan Records Officers (*Craven Archdeaconry*) Mrs Mary Creaser, Rose Cottage, Austwick, Lancaster LA2 8BH *Tel:* 01524 251536 *email:* mary.creaser@bradford.anglican.org
(*Bradford Archdeaconry*) Mrs Margaret Barker, 2 Farnham Close, Baildon, Shipley BD17 6SF *Tel:* 01274 595750

West Yorkshire Archives Service, Bradford Central Library, Princes Way, Bradford BD1 1NN *Archivist* Mr Anthony Hughes, *Tel:* 01274 435099 (*For parishes in Bradford Metropolitan District*)

Archives Dept, Central Library, Northgate House, Halifax HX1 1UN *Archivist* Mr Daniel Sudron, *Tel:* 01422 392636 (*For parishes in Calderdale Metropolitan District*)

Record Office, County Offices, Kendal LA9 4RQ *County Archivist* Ms A. Rowe, *Tel:* 01539 713540 (*For parishes in the County of Cumbria*)

County Record Office, Bow Lane, Preston PR1 2RE *County Archivist* Mrs Jacquie Crosby, *Tel:* 01772 533039 (*For parishes in the County of Lancashire*)

Archives Dept, WYAS Leeds, *email:* leeds@wyjs.org.uk *Archivist* Victoria Grindrod (*For parishes in Leeds Metropolitan District*)

County Record Office, Malpas Rd, Northallerton DL7 8AF *County Archivist* Mr M. K. Sweetmore, *Tel:* 01609 777585 (*For parishes in the County of North Yorkshire*)

RURAL DEANS

ARCHDEACONRY OF BRADFORD

Airedale Revd Gary Hodgson, St Michael's Vicarage, 81 Littlelands, Cottingley, Bingley BD16 1AL *Tel:* 01274 560761 *email:* gshodgson@sky.com

Bowling and Horton Canon Paul Bilton, St Wilfrid's Vicarage, St Wilfrid's Rd, Lidget Green, Bradford BD7 2LU *Tel:* 01274 572504 *email:* paul.bilton@bradford.anglican.org

Calverley Revd Paul Tudge, St John's Vicarage, 9 St John's Avenue, Farsley, Pudsey LS28 5DN *Tel:* 0113 257 0059 *email:* paul.tudge@bradford.anglican.org

Otley Revd Cayte Norman, The Vicarage, Layton Avenue, Rawdon, Leeds LS19 6QQ *Tel:* 0113 2503263 *email:* cayte.norman@bradford.anglican.org

ARCHDEACONRY OF CRAVEN

Bowland Revd Roger Wood, The Vicarage, Stainforth, Settle BD24 9PG *Tel:* 01729 823010 *email:* roger.wood@bradford.anglican.org

Ewecross Revd Ian Greenhalgh, The Vicarage, Austwick, Lancaster LA2 8BE *Tel:* 01524 251313 *email:* ian.greenhalgh@bradford.anglican.org

Skipton Canon Ann Turner, The Rectory, 7 Roundell Drive, West Marton, Skipton BD23 3UL *Tel:* 01282 842332 *email*: ann.turner@bradford.anglican.org

South Craven Revd Susan Griffiths, The Vicarage, Briggate, Silsden, Keighley BD20 9JS *Tel*: 01535 652204 *email*: susan.griffiths@bradford.anglican.org

DIOCESE OF BRISTOL

Founded in 1542. Bristol; the southern two-thirds of South Gloucestershire; the northern quarter of Wiltshire, except for two parishes in the north (GLOUCESTER); Swindon, except for a few parishes in the north (GLOUCESTER) and in the south (SALISBURY); a few parishes in Gloucestershire.

Population 972,000 Area 474 sq m
Full-time Stipendiary Parochial Clergy 103 Benefices 110
Parishes 163 Churches 205
www.bristol.anglican.org
Overseas link province: Uganda.

BISHOP (55th)

Rt Revd Michael Hill, 58a High St, Winterbourne, Bristol BS36 1JQ [2003] *Tel:* 01454 777728
Fax: 01454 777814
email: bishop@bristoldiocese.org

SUFFRAGAN BISHOP

SWINDON Rt Revd Dr Lee Rayfield, Mark House, Field Rise, Swindon SN1 4HP [2005]
Tel: 01793 538654
Fax: 01793 525181
email: bishop.swindon@bristoldiocese.org

CATHEDRAL CHURCH OF THE HOLY AND UNDIVIDED TRINITY

Dean Very Revd Dr David Michael Hoyle, The Deanery, 20 Charlotte Street, Bristol BS1 5PZ [2010] *Tel:* 0117 926 2443
email: dean@bristol-cathedral.co.uk

Cathedral Office Bristol Cathedral, Abbey Gatehouse, College Green, Bristol BS1 5TJ
Tel: 0117 926 4879
Fax: 0117 925 3678
email: dean@bristol-cathedral.co.uk

Canons Residentiary
Theologian Vacancy
City Canon Canon Timothy Higgins, City Rectory, Apt 8, 10 Unity St, Bristol BS1 5HH [2006]
Tel: 0117 927 7977
email: canon@bristol-cathedral.co.uk
Precentor Canon Wendy Wilby, 55 Salisbury Rd, Redland, Bristol BS6 7AS [2007]
Tel: 0117 904 6903
email: precentor@bristol-cathedral.co.uk
Canon Pastor Canon Robert Bull, 41 Salisbury Road, Bristol BS6 7AR [2011] *Tel:* 0117 909 8910
email: canon.pastor@bristol-catherdral.co.uk
Canon Jon Canon, Canon Tim Harle, Canon Richard Outhwaite, Canon Sue Topalian
Minor Canons
Revd Catherine Coster
Chapter Clerk Miss Wendy Matthews, Cathedral Office *Tel:* 0117 946 8172
email: wendy.matthews@bristol-cathedral.co.uk
Cathedral Organist Mr Mark Lee, Cathedral Office
Tel: 0117 946 8177
email: organist@bristol-cathedral.co.uk

ARCHDEACONS

MALMESBURY Ven Christine Froude, Diocesan Office, 1st Floor, Hillside House, 1500 Parkway North, Newbrick Road, Stoke Gifford, Bristol BS34 8YU [2011] *Tel:* 0117 906 0100
email: christine.froude@bristoldiocese.org

CONVOCATION (MEMBERS OF THE HOUSE OF CLERGY OF THE GENERAL SYNOD)

Proctors for Clergy
Revd Christopher Dobson
Revd Dr Emma Ineson
Revd Canon Mark Pilgrim

MEMBERS OF THE HOUSE OF LAITY OF THE GENERAL SYNOD

Prof Glynn Harrison
Vacancy
Canon David Froude

DIOCESAN OFFICERS

Dioc Secretary Mrs Lesley Farrall, Diocesan Office, 1st Floor, Hillside House, 1500 Parkway North, Newbrick Road, Stoke Gifford, Bristol BS34 8YU *Tel:* 0117 906 0100
email: lesley.farrall@bristoldiocese.org
Chancellor of Diocese Revd Justin Gau, 3 Pump Court, Temple, EC4Y 7AJ *Tel:* 020 7353 0711
Registrar of Diocese and Bishop's Legal Secretary Mr Tim Berry, Harris and Harris, 14 Market Place, Wells BA5 2RE *Tel:* 01749 674747
Fax: 01749 676585
email: tim.berry@harris-harris.co.uk

DIOCESAN ORGANIZATIONS

Diocesan Office 1st Floor, Hillside House, 1500 Parkway North, Newbrick Road, Stoke Gifford, Bristol BS34 8YU *Tel:* 0117 906 0100
email: any.name@bristoldiocese.org

ADMINISTRATION

Assistant Dioc Secretary Mrs Sally Moody, Diocesan Office
Dioc Synod (*Chairman, House of Clergy*) TBA
(*Chairman, House of Laity*) TBA

Board of Finance (*Chairman*) Mr Andrew Lucas, c/o Dioc Church House; (*Secretary*) Mrs Lesley Farrall, Dioc Church House
Finance Manager Mr David Hargrave, Diocesan Office
Mission and Pastoral Committee (*Secretary*) Mrs Lesley Farrall (*as above*)
Dioc Electoral Registration Officer Ms Lynette Cox (*as above*)
Designated Officer Mr Tim Berry, Harris and Harris, 14 Market Place, Wells BA5 2RE
Tel: 01749 674747
Fax: 01749 676585
Child Protection Officer Canon Carolyn Buckeridge
Tel: 0844 892 0104
Safeguarding Vulnerable Adults Officer Mrs Jeanette Plumb *Tel:* 07866 495802
0117 906 0100

CHURCHES
Advisory Committee for the Care of Churches (*Chairman*) Revd James Wilson, St Gregory's Vicarage, Filton Rd, Horfield, Bristol BS7 0PD
Tel: 0117 969 2839
email: revjameswilson@aol.com
(*Secretary*) Mr Tim Berry
(*Asst Secretary*) c/o Harris and Harris, 14 Market Place, Wells BA5 2RE
Tel: 01749 674747
Fax: 01749 676585

EDUCATION
Board of Education (*Interim Director*) Mr John Swainston, Diocesan Office *Tel:* 0117 906 0100
email: john.swainston@bristoldiocese.org

DIOCESAN LAY MINISTERS' COUNCIL
Secretary Mrs Susan Farrance, 102 Jersey Avenue, Brislington, Bristol, BS4 4QZ *Tel:* 0117 971 1629

DIOCESAN ECUMENICAL AND GLOBAL DEVELOPMENT OFFICER
Revd Chris Dobson, Diocesan Office

MINISTRY DEVELOPMENT
Adviser for Ministry Development (*DDO*) Canon Revd Derek Chedzey, Diocesan Office
Adviser for Licensed Ministry (*DDO*) Revd Samantha Rushton, Diocesan Office
Asst Adviser for Licensed Ministry (*DDO*) Canon Ray Brazier *Tel:* 0117 952 3209
email: rayvb@tiscali.co.uk
Administrators Miss Rachel Williams, Mrs Hannah Barker, Diocesan Office

STRATEGY SUPPORT
Director of Strategy Support Revd Canon Douglas Holt, Diocesan Office
Leadership Development Adviser Mr George Rendell, Diocesan Office
Leadership Development Adviser Mrs Melanie Griffiths, Diocesan Office
Adviser on Growth Revd Paul Rush, 5 Gold View, Rushy Platt, Swindon SN5 8ZG
Tel: 01793 872 853
email: rev.paul.rush@ntlworld.com
Department Administrator Miss Clare Franklin, Diocesan Office

ADVISER FOR MINISTERIAL SUPPORT
Revd Ian Tomkins, Diocesan Office

DEAN OF WOMEN'S MINISTRY
Canon Wendy Wilby, 55 Salisbury Road, Redland, Bristol, BS6 7AS *Tel:* 0117 904 6903
email: precentor@bristol-cathedral.co.uk

BISHOP'S ADVISORY GROUP ON HEALING
Chairman Revd Ros Wilson, 10 Druid Stoke Avenue, Stoke Bishop, Bristol BS9 1DD
Tel: 0117 330 1610
email: rosw@another.com

DIOCESAN WORSHIP AND LITURGY COMMITTEE
Chairman Canon Gill Behenna, 1 Saxon Way, Bradley Stoke, Bristol BS32 9AR
Tel: 01454 202483
email: gill@signsofgod.org

PRESS, PUBLICITY AND PUBLICATIONS
Communications Officer and Press Officer Mr Oliver Home *Tel:* 01454 777728
email: oliver.home@bristoldiocese.org
Editor of Dioc Directory Ms Lynette Cox, Diocesan Office

DIOCESAN RECORD OFFICES
Bristol Record Office, 'B' Bond, Smeaton Rd, Bristol BS1 6XN *County Archivist* Mr J. S. Williams, *Tel:* 0117 922 4224 (*For parish records in the archdeaconry of Bristol*)
Wiltshire and Swindon History Centre, Cocklebury Rd, Chippenham SN15 3QN *County Archivist* Mr John Darcy, *Tel:* 01249 705500 (*For parish records in the archdeaconry of Malmesbury*)

DIOCESAN RESOURCE CENTRE
All Saints Centre, 1 All Saints Court, Bristol BS1 1JN *Tel:* 0117 906 0100
Fax: 0117 925 0404
email: allsaints@bristoldiocese.org

THE CHURCHES' COUNCIL FOR INDUSTRY AND SOCIAL RESPONSIBILITY
Director Revd Jon Doble, 162 Pennywell Rd, Bristol BS5 0TX *Tel:* 0117 955 7430
Fax: 0117 955 7436
email: jon@ccisr.org.uk
Administrators Mrs Alison Paginton, Mrs Vena Prater (part-time)

Chaplain for Economic Life Revd Angela Overton-Benge
Social Responsibility Officer (Swindon and Wiltshire) Revd Dr Simon Topping (part-time)
Social Responsibility Officer (Bristol) Dr Simon Bale (part-time)
Church Urban Fund Officer Revd Jon Doble
Senior Chaplain Avon and Somerset Constabulary Pastor Andy Paget (part-time)
Senior Chaplain Wiltshire Constabulary Revd Dr Richard Armitage (part-time)
Chaplain to the City Centre (Bristol) Canon Timothy Higgins (part-time)
Marriage and Family Life Adviser Mrs Alison Paginton
Community Ministry Adviser Mrs Sandra O'Shea
Major Emergency Plan Administrator Mrs Vena Prater (part-time)

AREA DEANS

ARCHDEACONRY OF BRISTOL

Bristol South Canon Gwyn Owen, Vicarage, Goslet Rd, Stockwood, Bristol BS14 8SP
Tel: 01275 831138
email: christtheservant@blueyonder.co.uk

Bristol West Canon Mark Pilgrim, St Peter's Vicarage, 17 The Drive, Henleaze, Bristol BS9 4LD *Tel:* 0117 962 0636
email: markpilgrimis@aol.com

City Revd Mat Ineson, St Matthew's Vicarage, 11 Glentworth Road, Redland, Bristol BS6 7EG
Tel: 0117 942 4186
email: mat.ineson@bristol.anglican.org

ARCHDEACONRY OF MALMESBURY

Chippenham Canon Simon Tyndall, The Rectory, 9 Greenway Park, Chippenham SN15 1QG
Tel and *Fax:* 01249 657216
email: simon@tyndall.plus.com

Kingswood and South Gloucestershire Revd Simon Jones, 119 North Road, Stoke Gifford, Bristol, BS34 8PE *Tel:* 0117 979 1656
email: simon@st-michaels-church.org.uk
email: djaadams@surfaid.org

North Wiltshire Revd Neill Archer, Abbey Vicarage, Holloway, Malmesbury SN16 9BA
Tel: 01666 823126
email: neill@malmesburyabbey.com

Swindon Revd Simon Stevenette, The Vicarage, 26 Cricklade Street, Swindon, SN1 3HG
Tel: 01793 529166
email: simonstevenette@tiscali.co.uk

DIOCESE OF CANTERBURY

Founded in 597. Kent east of the Medway, excluding the Medway Towns (ROCHESTER).

Population 890,000 Area 970 sq m
Full-time Stipendiary Parochial Clergy 118 Benefices 147
Parishes 261 Churches 328
www.canterburydiocese.org
Overseas link dioceses: Antananarivo, Antsiranana, Toamasina, Mahajanga (Madagascar), Arras (Pas-de-Calais), Basel.

ARCHBISHOP (105th)
Most Revd and Rt Hon Justin Portal Welby, *Primate of all England and Metropolitan,* Lambeth Palace, London SE1 7JU *Tel:* 020 7898 1200; *Fax:* 020 7261 9836 and Old Palace, Canterbury, Kent CT1 2EE *Tel:* 01227 459382; *Fax:* 01227 784985 [2013]
[Justin Cantuar:]
Dioc Chaplain Revd Matthew Rushton

Matters relating to the Diocese of Canterbury should be referred to the **Bishop of Dover** *(see below)*
For the **Archbishop of Canterbury's Personal Staff** *see page* 4

BISHOP OF DOVER
Rt Revd Trevor Willmott, Old Palace, Canterbury, Kent CT1 2EE, *Tel:* 01227 459382, *Fax:* 01227 784985 [2010]
PA Mrs Anne Neal (*same address, tel and fax nos*)
Secretary Mrs Sue Bowles (*same address, tel and fax nos*)
Chaplain Revd Matthew Rushton, Old Palace, Canterbury, Kent CT1 2EE, *Tel:* 01227 459382, *Fax:* 01227 784985
Hon Chaplains Canon Alan Duke, Roundways, Derringstone Hill, Barham, Canterbury CT4 6QD, *Tel:* 01227 831812, *email:* mail@alanaduke.com
Canon Roger Martin, 'Kwetu', 23 Tanners Hill Gardens, Hythe CT21 5HY *Tel:* 01303 237204, *email:* rogmartin@btinternet.com
Ven John Barton, Glebe House, Military Road, Canterbury CT1 1PA *Tel:* 01227 379688 *email:* johnbarton@greenbee.net
Revd David Maple, 1 Mount Pleasant, Blean, Canterbury CT2 9EU *Tel:* 01227 459044 *email:* dmaple@btinternet.com

PROVINCIAL EPISCOPAL VISITORS
EBBSFLEET Vacancy
RICHBOROUGH Rt Revd Norman Banks, Parkside House, Abbey Mill Lane, St Albans AL3 4HE *Tel:* 01727 836358 *email:* bishop@richborough.org.uk

HONORARY ASSISTANT BISHOPS
Rt Revd Graham Cray, Rectory, Church Rd, Harrietsham, Maidstone ME17 1AP *Tel:* 01622 851170 *email:* grahamcray@btconnect.com
Rt Revd Michael Gear, 10 Acott Fields, Yalding, Maidstone ME18 6DQ *Tel:* 01622 817388 *email:* bp_mikegear@yahoo.com
Rt Revd Richard Llewellin, 193 Ashford Rd, Thanington, Canterbury CT1 3XS *Tel:* 01227 789515 *email:* rllewellin@clara.co.uk
Rt Revd Anthony Michael Turnbull, 67 Strand St, Sandwich CT13 9HN *Tel:* 01304 611389 *email:* bstmt@btopenworld.com

CATHEDRAL AND METROPOLITICAL CHURCH OF CHRIST
Dean Very Revd Dr Robert Willis, The Deanery, The Precincts, Canterbury CT1 2EP [2001] *Tel:* 01227 865200 (Office) *email:* dean@canterbury-cathedral.org
Cathedral Office Cathedral House, 11 The Precincts, Canterbury CT1 2EH *Tel:* 01227 762862 *Fax:* 01227 865222
Canons Residentiary
Canon Treasurer Vacancy
Canon Librarian Canon Christopher Irvine, 19 The Precincts, Canterbury CT1 2EP [2007] *Tel:* 01227 865226 *email:* canon.irvine@canterbury-cathedral.org
Canon Pastor Canon Clare Edwards, 22 The Precincts, Canterbury CT1 2EP [2004] *Tel:* 01227 865227 *email:* canonclare@canterbury-cathedral.org
Archdeacon Ven Sheila Watson, 29 The Precincts, Canterbury CT1 2EP [2007] *Tel:* 01227 865238 *Fax:* 01227 785209 *email:* archdeacon@canterbury-cathedral.org
Precentor and Sacrist David Mackenzie Mills, 2 Starrs House, Canterbury CT1 2EH *Tel:* 01227 876225 *email:* david.mackenzie-mills@canterbury-cathedral.org
Receiver General Brigadier M. J. Meardon, Cathedral House *Tel:* 01227 865212 *email:* ReceiverGeneral@canterbury-cathedral.org

Cathedral organist Dr David Flood, 6 The Precincts, Canterbury CT1 2EE *Tel:* 01227 865242
email: david.flood@canterbury-cathedral.org

ARCHDEACONS

CANTERBURY Ven Sheila Watson, 29 The Precincts, Canterbury CT1 2EP [2007] *Tel:* 01227 865238
Fax: 01227 785209
email: archdeacon@canterbury-cathedral.org

MAIDSTONE Ven Stephen Taylor, The Archdeaconry, 4 Redcliffe Lane, Penenden Heath, Maidstone ME14 2AG [2011] *Tel:* 01622 209153
email: staylor@archdeaconmaid.org

ASHFORD Ven Philip Down, The Archdeaconry, Pett Lane, Charing, Ashford TN27 0DL [2011]
Tel and fax: 01233 712649
email: pdown@archdeacashford.org

CONVOCATION (MEMBERS OF THE HOUSE OF CLERGY OF THE GENERAL SYNOD)

Dignitaries in Convocation
The Dean of Canterbury
Proctors for Clergy
Revd Canon Clare Edwards
Ven Philip Down
Canon Mark Roberts

MEMBERS OF THE HOUSE OF LAITY OF THE GENERAL SYNOD

Mr David Kemp
Ms Sally Muggeridge
Mrs Caroline Spencer

DIOCESAN OFFICERS

Diocesan House, Lady Wootton's Green, Canterbury CT1 1NQ *Tel:* 01227 459401
Fax: 01227 450964

Please note that individual Diocesan Officers may be emailed on initialsurname@diocant.org (e.g. jhills@diocant.org)

Dioc Secretary Mr Julian Hills *Fax:* 01227 787073
email: jhills@diocant.org

Commissary General Miss Morag Ellis QC c/o The Registry, Minerva House, 5 Montague Close, London SE1 9BB *Tel:* 020 7593 5000

Dioc Registrar and Legal Adviser to the Diocese Mr Owen Carew-Jones, Minerva House, 5 Montague Close, London SE1 9BB
Tel: 020 7593 5110

DIOCESAN ORGANIZATIONS

Diocesan House, Lady Wootton's Green, Canterbury CT1 1NQ *Tel:* 01227 459401
Fax: 01227 450964
email: reception@diocant.org

ADMINISTRATION (RESOURCE MANAGEMENT AND COMPLIANCE)

Dioc Synod (Chairman, House of Clergy) Canon Mark Roberts, Rectory, Knightrider St, Sandwich CT13 9ER *Tel:* 01304 613138
email: revdmarkroberts@supanet.com

(Chairman, House of Laity) Mrs Caroline Spencer, Little Eggarton, Godmersham, Canterbury CT4 7DY *Tel:* 01227 731170
email: caroline@eggarton.eclipse.co.uk

(Secretary) Mr Julian Hills, Dioc House

Board of Finance (Chairman) Mr Raymond Harris
(Secretary) Mr Julian Hills *(as above)*

Designated Officer Tbc

Director of Finance Mr Mark Spraggins, Dioc House

Director of Property Services Mr Philip Bell, Old Palace, The Precincts, Canterbury CT1 2EE
Tel: 01227 478390
email: pbell@diocant.org

COMMUNICATONS

Communications Director and Deputy Diocesan Secretary Mrs Emily Shepherd, Dioc House

IT Manager Mark Binns, Dioc House

Editor of Diocesan Directory Online Marilyn Haddock, Dioc House

HR Adviser Miss Sarah Carruthers, Dioc House

CHURCHES

Diocesan Advisory Committee for the Care of Churches (Secretary) Mr Ian Dodd, Old Palace, The Precincts, Canterbury CT1 2EE
Tel: 01227 478390
email: idodd@diocant.org

Chairman Dr Richard Morrice, 3 Stafford Rd, Tunbridge Wells TN25 4QZ

CHILDREN, SCHOOLS AND YOUNG PEOPLE (including the Board of Education)

Chairman Professor Michael Wright CBE

Director of Education Quentin Roper, Dioc House

Assistant Director of Education (School Effectiveness) Mrs Tricia Martin, Dioc House

Assistant Director of Education (Schools Organisation) Revd Simon Foulkes, Dioc House

Children and Young People's (ChYPs) Ministry Adviser Mr Murray Wilkinson, Dioc House

LICENSED MINISTRY

Chair Mrs Caroline Spencer see *Chairman, House of Laity*

Director of Licensed Ministry Canon Rob Mackintosh, Dioc House

Director of Ordinands Revd Clive Todd, Dioc House

Assistant Directors of Ordinands
Revd Marian Bond *Tel:* 01622 858251
email: mnhbond@googlemail.com
Revd Philip Brown *Tel:* 01227 730141
email: filbrown@btinternet.com
Revd Sheila Cox *Tel:* 01233 501193
email: sheila.m.cox@btopenworld.com
Revd Jackie Cray *Tel:* 01622 851822
email: jackiecray@hotmail.co.uk
Revd Richard King *Tel:* 01233 623334
email: richarddking@hotmail.com
Revd Cathy Sigrist *Tel:* 01304 37395
email: catherine.sigrist@btinternet.com

Revd Joss Walker *Tel:* 01622 676282
email: jocelyn.walker@hotmail.co.uk
Ministry Development Officer Mr Neville Emslie, Dioc House
Association of Readers (*Warden*) Revd Canon Rob Mackintosh, Dioc House
Deputy Wardens of Readers Mrs Pat Tatchell
Tel: 01795 471 956
email: tatch@blueyonder.co.uk
Canon Rosemary Walters *Tel:* 01227 768891
email: rosemary.walters@canterbury.ac.uk
(*Hon Secretary*) Mr Nigel Collins, 79 Alfred Rd, Dover CT16 2AD *Tel:* 01304 204737
email: nigelcollins@cross-links.org.uk
Clergy Retirement and Registration Officers
Ashford Archdeaconry, Canon Gilbert Spencer
Tel: 01233 501774
email: gilbert_spencer@hotmail.com
Canterbury Archdeaconery, Revd Grahame Whittlesea *Tel:* 01227 472536
email: gandawhittlesea@tiscali.co.uk
Maidstone Archdeaconery, Revd Ron Gamble
email: r-gamble@sky.com

LOCAL CHURCH DEVELOPMENT

Chairman Miss Judith Rigby *Tel:* 01843 220809
email: judithrigby@sky.com
Mission and Growth Adviser Canon Kerry Thorpe, Dioc House
Mission and Ministry Executive Officer Mrs Emma Siyyer, Dioc House
Local Ministries Officer Revd Peter Ingrams, Dioc House
Children's Missioner Captain Graham Nunn, CA
Tel: 01622 672088
email: gnunn@diocant.org
Stewardship Adviser Ms Liz Mullins, Dioc House
Part-time Stewardship Adviser Mrs Jenny Hunt, Dioc House

COMMUNITY AND PARTNERSHIPS

Chairman Mr Anthony Beattie *Tel:* 01580 240973
email: benendenparishmagazine@gmail.com
Community and Partnership Exec Officer and Rural Life Adviser Canon Caroline Pinchbeck, Dioc House

DIOCESAN RECORD OFFICES

Cathedral Archives and Library, The Precincts, Canterbury CT1 2EH (*For parish records in the archdeaconry of Canterbury*) *Tel:* 01227 865330
Kent History Services, Kent History and Library Centre, James Whatman Way, Maidstone ME14 1LQ (*For parish records in the archdeaconries of Maidstone and Ashford*)
Tel: 08458 247200
email: historyandlibrarycentre@kent.gov.uk

AREA DEANS

ARCHDEACONRY OF ASHFORD

Ashford Canon Timothy Wilson, The Rectory, Great Chart, Ashford, TN23 3AY
Tel: 01233 620371
email: tandcwilson@lineone.net
Dover Revd Sue White, The Vicarage, 20 Alexandra Road, Capel le Ferne, Folkestone CT18 7LD *Tel:* 01304 240539
email: suewhite712@hotmail.com
Elham Revd Mark Hayton, The Vicarage, 21 Manor Road, Folkestone CT20 2SA
Tel: 01303 253831
email: hayton664@btinternet.com
Sandwich Revd Seth Cooper, Elizabeth House, 32 St Marys Road, Walmer CT14 7QA
Tel: 01304 375340
email: sethandjen@tinyworld.co.uk
Romney and Tenterden Revd Jacques Desrosiers, The Vicarage, Rolvenden, Cranbrook TN17 4ND
Tel: 01580 241235
email: vicarage1965@btinternet.com

ARCHDEACONRY OF CANTERBURY

Canterbury Revd Mark Ball, 83 St Peters Lane, Canterbury CT1 2B *Tel:* 01227 472557
email: mark@canterburycityparish.org.uk
Canterbury Revd Peter Cornish, The Rectory, 2 The Hamels, Church Lane, Sturry, Canterbury CT2 0BL *Tel:* 01227 710320
email: rector@sturrychurch.org.uk
East Bridge Revd Stephen Hardy, The Rectory, The Street, Barham, Canterbury CT4 6PA
Tel: 01227 831340
email: stephenhardy1@mac.com
Reculver Revd Anthony Everett, Christ Church Vicarage, 38 Beltinge Road, Herne Bay CT6 5BU
Tel: 01227 374906
email: vicar@cchb.org.uk
Reculver Revd Elaine Richardson, The New Vicarage, Herne Street, Herne CT6 7HE
Tel: 01227 370256
email: elaine.longview@virgin.net
Reculver Revd Canon Steve Coneys, The Vicarage, 11 Kimberley Grove, Seasalter, Whitstable CT5 4AY *Tel:* 01227 276795
email: steveconeys@btinternet.com
Thanet Revd Paul Worledge, St Luke's Vicarage, St Luke's Avenue, Ramsgate CT11 7JX
Tel: 01843 592562
email: adthanet@btinternet.com
West Bridge Revd Stephen Hardy, The Rectory, The Street, Barham, Canterbury CT4 6PA
Tel: 01227 831340
email: stephenhardy1@mac.com

ARCHDEACONRY OF MAIDSTONE

Maidstone Revd Andrew Sewell, St Paul's Vicarage, 130 Boxley Road, Maidstone ME14 2AH
Tel: 01622 691926
email: andrew@asewell@plus.com
North Downs Revd Susan Hollins, Vicarage, The Street, Boxley, Maidstone ME14 3DX
Tel: 01622 600440
email: s.hollins540@btinternet.com
Ospringe Revd Steve Lillicrap, The Vicarage, 76 Station Road, Teynham ME9 9SN
Tel: 01795 522510
email: steve.lillicrap@btopenworld.com

Sittingbourne Revd John Lewis, Vicarage, School Lane, Borden, Sittingbourne ME9 8JS
Tel: 01795 472986
email: fr.johnlewis@tiscali.co.uk

The Weald Revd Richard Williams
Tel: 01580 712150
email: revrwilliams@btinternet.com

DIOCESE OF CARLISLE

Founded in 1133. Cumbria, except for small areas in the east (NEWCASTLE, BRADFORD).

Population 489,000 Area 2,477 sq m
Full-time Stipendiary Parochial Clergy 116 Benefices 120
Parishes 263 Churches 338
www.carlislediocese.org.uk
Overseas link dioceses: Madras (CSI), Zululand (South Africa), Stavanger (Norway), Northern Argentina.

BISHOP (67th)
Rt Revd James Newcome, Bishop's House, Ambleside Road, Keswick, CA12 4DD[2009]
Tel: 01768 773430
email: bishop.carlisle@carlislediocese.org.uk
[James Carliol]
Bishop's Chaplain and Chief of Staff Ven George Howe, Bishop's House (*as above*)
Tel: 01768 773430 (office)
01768 779168 (home)
email: george.howe@carlislediocese.org.uk

SUFFRAGAN BISHOP
PENRITH Rt Revd Robert Freeman, Holm Croft, 13 Castle Road, Kendal LA9 7AU [2011]
Tel: 01539 727836
email: bishop.penrith@carlislediocese.org.uk

HONORARY ASSISTANT BISHOPS
Rt Revd Ian Macdonald Griggs, Rookings, Patterdale, Penrith CA11 0NP [1994]
Tel: 01768 482064
email: ian.griggs@virgin.net
Rt Revd George Lanyon Hacker, Keld House, Milburn, Penrith CA10 1TW [1994]
Tel: 01768 361506
email: bishhack@mypostoffice.co.uk
Rt Revd Andrew Alexander Kenny Graham, Fell End, Butterwick, Penrith CA10 2QQ [1997]
Tel: 01931 713147
Rt Revd Hewlett Thompson, Low Broomrigg, Warcop, Appleby CA16 6PT [2000]
Tel: 01768 341281
Rt Revd Robert Hardy, Carleton House, Back Lane, Langwathby, Penrith CA10 1NB [2002]
Tel: 01768 881210
Rt Revd John Richardson, The Old Rectory, Bewcastle, Carlisle CA6 6PS [2003]
Tel: 01697 748389
Rt Revd Richard Henderson [2011]

CATHEDRAL CHURCH OF THE HOLY AND UNDIVIDED TRINITY
Dean Very Revd Mark Boyling, The Deanery, Carlisle CA3 8TZ [2004] *Tel:* 01228 523335
Fax: 01228 547049
email: dean@carlislecathedral.org.uk
Cathedral Office 7 The Abbey, Carlisle CA3 8TZ
Tel: 01228 548151
Fax: 01228 547049
email: office@carlislecathedral.org.uk
Web: www.carlislecathedral.org.uk

Canons Residentiary
Canon Brian Roy McConnell, 3 The Abbey, Carlisle CA3 8TZ [2006] *Tel:* 01228 521834
email: canonwarden@carlislecathedral.org.uk
Ven Kevin Thomas Roberts, 2 The Abbey, Carlisle, CA3 8TZ [2009] *Tel:* 01228 523026
email: archdeacon.north@carlislediocese.org.uk
Canon Michael Alan Manley, 1 The Abbey, Carlisle CA3 8TZ [2007] *Tel:* 01228 542790
email: canonmissioner@carlislecathedral.org.uk

Lay Canons
Canon Dr Philip Herrick, Fircroft, Houghton, Carlisle CA6 4HZ [2001]
Canon James Westoll, Kirkandrews Tower, Longtown, Carlisle CA6 6NF [2011]
Canon Alex Barbour, Castlehow Scar, via Shap, Penrith CA10 3LG [2012]
Bursar and Chapter Clerk Mr Ian Burns, Cathedral Office
Commercial and Administration Co-ordinator Mrs Wendy Murrell, Cathedral Office
Cathedral Organist Mr Jeremy Suter, 6 The Abbey, Carlisle CA3 8TZ *Tel:* 01228 526646
Fax: 01228 547049
email: jeremysuter@hotmail.com

ARCHDEACONS
CARLISLE Ven Kevin Roberts, 2 The Abbey, Carlisle CA3 8TZ [2009] *Tel:* 01228 523026
email: archdeacon.north@carlislediocese.org.uk
WEST CUMBERLAND Ven Richard Pratt, 50 Stainburn Rd, Workington CA14 1SN [2009]
Tel: 01900 66190
email: archdeacon.west@carlislediocese.org.uk
WESTMORLAND AND FURNESS Ven Penny Driver, The Vicarage, Windermere Road, Lindale in Cartmel, Grange over Sands LA11 6LB [2012]
Tel: 015395 34717
email: archdeacon.south@carlislediocese.org.uk

CONVOCATION (MEMBERS OF THE HOUSE OF CLERGY OF THE GENERAL SYNOD)
Proctors for Clergy
Revd Ferial Etherington
Ven George Howe
Canon Nigel Davies
Revd Simon Austen

MEMBERS OF THE HOUSE OF LAITY OF THE GENERAL SYNOD
Dr Christopher Angus
Dr Charles Hanson
Mr Geoffrey Hine
Mr David Mills

DIOCESAN OFFICERS
Dioc Secretary Mr Derek Hurton, Church House, West Walls, Carlisle CA3 8UE *Tel:* 01228 522573
01228 815402 (Direct Line)
Fax: 01228 815400
email: diocesan.secretary@carlislediocese.org.uk
Chancellor of Diocese Mr Geoffrey Tattersall, 2 The Woodlands, Lostock, Bolton BL6 4JD
Registrar of Diocese and Bishop's Legal Secretary Mrs Jane Lowdon, Sintons Solicitors, The Cube, Barrack Rd, Newcastle-upon-Tyne NE4 6DB
Tel: 0191 226 7878
Fax: 0191 226 7852
email: j.lowdon@sintons.co.uk

DIOCESAN ORGANIZATIONS
Diocesan Office Church House, West Walls, Carlisle CA3 8UE *Tel:* 01228 522573
Fax: 01228 815400
email: enquiries@carlislediocese.org.uk
Web: www.carlislediocese.org.uk

ADMINISTRATION
Dioc Synod (*Chairman, House of Clergy*) Revd Dr Peter Tiplady, Meadow Croft, Wetheral, Carlisle CA4 8JG *Tel:* 01228 561611
email: peter.tiplady@me.com
(*Chairman, House of Laity*) Mr Michael Bonner, 1 Fell View, Branthwaite, Workington CA14 4SY
Tel: 01900 605536
email: mimbonner@talktalk.net
(*Secretary*) Mr Derek Hurton, Dioc Office
Board of Finance (*Chairman*) Mr John Lee, Millersholme, Lanercost, Brampton CA8 2HL
Tel: 016977 2515
(*Secretary*) Mr Derek Hurton (*as above*)
Assistant Dioc Secretary (*Finance*) Mr Neil Barrett, Dioc Office *Tel:* 01228 815404
Property Manager Mr Neal Andrews, Dioc Office
Tel: 01228 815403
Finance Resources Officer Mr Geoffrey Hine, Dioc Office *Tel:* 01228 815401
Pastoral Committee Mr Derek Hurton, Dioc Office
Tel: 01228 815408
Designated Officer Mrs Jane Lowdon (*as above*)

CHURCHES
Advisory Committee for the Care of Churches (*Chairman*) Lord Hothfield, Drybeck Hall, Appleby in Westmorland CA16 6TF; (*Secretary*) Mr Derek Hurton, Dioc Office

EDUCATION
Board of Education, Church House, West Walls, Carlisle CA3 8UE *Tel:* 01228 522573
Fax: 01228 815400
email: education@carlislediocese.org.uk
Director of Education Mr Michael Mill, Dioc Office
Deputy Director of Education Revd Bert Thomas, Dioc Office
Church in Schools Officers Mrs Sarah Hulme and Mrs Emma Richardson, Dioc Office

MINISTRY AND TRAINING
Ministry Development Adviser Canon Amiel Osmaston, Dioc Office *Tel:* 01228 815406
email: ministry.dev@carlislediocese.org.uk
Principal Lancashire and Cumbria Theological Partnership and Adviser for Ministry and Training Canon Tim Herbert, Dioc Office
Tel: 01228 815405
email: admin@lctp.co.uk
Adviser for Clergy Training Revd Ruth Crossley, Vicarage, Levens, Kendal LA8 8PY
Tel: 01539 560233
email: cme@carlislediocese.org.uk
Director of Ordinands Ven George Howe, Bishop's House (*as above*) *Tel:* 01768 773430 (office)
01768 779168 (home)
email: george.howe@carlislediocese.org.uk
Adviser for Women's Ministry Revd Gill Hart, The Vicarage, Church Terrace, Netherton, Maryport CA15 7PS *Tel:* 01900 819886
email: hart.gill@btopenworld.com

SOCIAL RESPONSIBILITY
Churches Social Action Network Ven Richard Pratt, 50 Stainburn Road, Workington CA14 1SN
Tel: 01900 66190
email: archdeacon.west@carlislediocese.org.uk
Industrial Mission Ven Richard Pratt (*as above*)

ECUMENICAL AFFAIRS
Diocesan Ecumenical Officer Revd Cameron Butland, The Rectory, Grasmere, Ambleside LA22 9QD *Tel:* 015394 35326
email: cameronbutland@btinternet.com
Churches Together in Cumbria (*Ecumenical Development Officer*) Revd Ruth Harvey, Croslands, Beacon Street, Penrith CA11 7TZ
Tel: 07882 259631
email: rctic@phonecoop.coop
Rural Officer Revd Sarah Lunn, Rectory, Long Marton, Appleby in Westmorland CA16 6BN
Tel: 01768 361269
email: sarahlunn@care4free.net

PARTNERSHIP IN WORLD MISSION
Officer Mrs Lynne Tembey, Holm Cultram Vicarage, Abbeytown, Wigton CA7 4SP
Tel: 01697 361246
email: lynnetembey@btinternet.com

PRESS AND PUBLICATIONS
Communications Officer Mrs Hannah Horton
Tel: 07809 613531
email: communications@carlislediocese.org.uk
Editor of Dioc News Mrs Hannah Horton
Dioc Directory Mrs Jean Hardman, Dioc Office
Tel: 01228 815408
email: jean.hardman@carlislediocese.org.uk

DIOCESAN ARCHIVIST
County Archivist Ms A. Rowe *Tel:* 01228 226477

DIOCESAN RECORD OFFICES
Cumbria Archive Centre, Lady Gillford's House, Petteril Bank Road, Carlisle CA1 3AJ
Tel: 01228 227285
email: carlisle.archives@cumbria.gov.uk
Cumbria Archive Centre, County Offices, Kendal LA9 4RQ *Tel:* 01539 713540
email: kendal.archives@cumbria.gov.uk
Cumbria Archive Centre and Local Studies Library, 140 Duke St, Barrow-in-Furness LA14 1XW *Tel:* 01229 407377
email: barrow.archives@cumbria.gov.uk
Cumbria Archive Centre and Local Studies Library, Scotch St, Whitehaven CA28 7NL
Tel: 01946 506420
email: whitehaven.archives@cumbria.gov.uk

RURAL DEANS

ARCHDEACONRY OF CARLISLE
Appleby Canon Carole Marsden, Fairfield, Faraday Road, Kirkby Stephen CA17 4QL
Tel: 017683 71279
email: carole.sam@hotmail.co.uk
Brampton Revd Rod Allon-Smith, The Vicarage, Lanercost, Brampton CA8 2HQ
Tel: 016977 2478
email: lanercostrod@bigfoot.com
Carlisle Canon Michael Manley, 1 The Abbey, Carlisle CA3 8TZ *Tel:* 01228 542790
email: ruraldean@carlisledeanery.org.uk
Penrith Canon Richard Moatt, Vicarage, 1 Low Farm, Langwathby, Penrith CA10 1NH
Tel: 01768 881212
email: moatt@btinternet.com

ARCHDEACONRY OF WESTMORLAND AND FURNESS
Barrow Revd Gary Cregeen, The Rectory, 98 Roose Road, Barrow in Furness LA13 9RL
Tel: 01229 877367
email: GMCregeen@btinternet.com
Furness Canon Gary Wemyss, Vicarage, Penny Bridge, Ulverston LA12 7RQ *Tel:* 01229 861285
email: gwemyss@clara.co.uk
Kendal Vacancy
email: ruraldean_kendal@hotmail.com
Windermere Revd James Richards, Rectory, Longlands, Bowness on Windermere LA23 3AS
Tel: 01539 443063
email: rector@stmartin.org.uk

ARCHDEACONRY OF WEST CUMBERLAND
Calder Revd Stephen Griffiths, The Rectory, Low Moresby, Whitehaven CA28 6RR
Tel: 01946 693970
email: steph78griffiths@hotmail.com
Derwent Canon Wendy Sanders, Rectory, Lorton Road, Cockermouth CA13 9DU
Tel: 01900 823269
email: wendy@cateam.org.uk
Solway Canon Bryan Rowe, St Michael's Rectory, Dora Crescent, Workington CA14 2EZ
Tel: 01900 602311
email: bryan.rowe50@yahoo.com

DIOCESE OF CHELMSFORD

Founded in 1914. Essex, except for a few parishes in the north (ELY, ST EDMUNDSBURY AND IPSWICH); five East London boroughs north of the Thames; three parishes in south Cambridgeshire.

Population 2,890,000 Area 1,531 sq m
Full-time Stipendiary Parochial Clergy 342 Benefices 319
Parishes 461 Churches 598
www.chelmsford.anglican.org

Overseas link dioceses: Embu, Mbeere, Kirinyaga, Meru (Kenya); Trinidad and Tobago; Karlstad; Iasi (Romania)

BISHOP

Rt Revd Stephen Cottrell, Bishopscourt, Margaretting, Ingatestone CM4 0HD
Tel: 01277 352001
Fax: 01277 355374
email: bishopscourt@chelmsford.anglican.org

Bishop's Chaplain Chantal Mason (*same address*)
Tel: 01277 352001
Fax: 01277 355374
email: cmason@chelmsford.anglican.org

Director of Communications and Bishop's Press Officer Ralph Meloy *Tel:* 01245 294424 (Office)
07654 382674 (Pager)
email: rmeloy@chelmsford.anglican.org

AREA BISHOPS

BARKING Rt Revd David John Leader Hawkins, Barking Lodge, Verulam Ave, London E17 8ES [2003] *Tel:* 020 8509 7377
email: b.barking@chelmsford.anglican.org

BRADWELL Rt Revd John Wraw, Bishop's House, Orsett Rd, Horndon-on-the-Hill SS17 8NS [from February 2012] *Tel:* 01375 673806
Fax: 01375 674222
email: b.bradwell@chelmsford.anglican.org

COLCHESTER Rt Revd Christopher Heudebourck Morgan, 1 Fitzwalter Rd, Lexden, Colchester CO3 3SS [2001] *Tel:* 01206 576648
Fax: 01206 763868
email: b.colchester@chelmsford.anglican.org

ASSISTANT BISHOPS

Rt Revd Charles Derek Bond, 52 Horn Brook, Saffron Walden, Essex CB11 3JW
Tel: 01799 521308
email: bondd@aol.com

Rt Revd John Martin Ball, 5 Hillview Rd, Chelmsford CM1 7RS *Tel:* 01245 268296
email: ball_john@onetel.com

ASSISTANT BISHOP AND PROVINCIAL EPISCOPAL VISITOR

Rt Revd Norman Banks, Parkside House, Abbey Mill Lane, St Albans AL3 4HE *Tel:* 01727 836358
email: bishop@richborough.org.uk

CATHEDRAL CHURCH OF ST MARY THE VIRGIN, ST PETER AND ST CEDD

Dean Very Revd Peter Judd, The Dean's House, 3 Harlings Grove, Chelmsford CM1 1YQ [1997]
Tel: 01245 354318 (Home)
01245 294492 (Office)
email: peter.judd@chelmsfordcathedral.org.uk

Cathedral Office 53 New St, Chelmsford CM1 1TY
Tel: 01245 294489
Fax: 01245 294499
Web: www.chelmsfordcathedral.org.uk

Canons Residentiary

Vice-Dean Canon Ivor Moody, 4 Bishopscourt Gardens, Springfield, Chelmsford CM2 6AZ
Tel: 01245 294493 (Office)
01245 267773 (Home)
email: ivor.moody@chelmsfordcathedral.org.uk

Canon Theologian Revd Canon Edward Carter, 2 Harlings Grove, Chelmsford CM1 1YQ
Tel: 01245 294486
email: edward.carter@chelmsfordcathedral.org.uk

Canon Precentor Canon Simon Pothen, 1a Harlings Grove, Chelmsford CM1 1YQ [2007]
Tel: 01245 491599 (Home)
Tel: 01245 294482 (Office)
email: simon.pothen@chelmsfordcathedral.org.uk

Hon Associate Chaplain Revd Katy Hacker Hughes, I Swiss Avenue, Chelmsford CM1 2LY
Tel: 01245 600969
email: katyhh@lineone.net

Hon Associate Chaplain and Bishop's Chaplain Chantal Mason, Bishopscourt, Margaretting, Ingatestone CM4 0HD *Tel:* 01277 352001
Fax: 01277 355374

Hon Associate Chaplain and Diocesan Director of Ordinands Canon Richard More, 25 Roxwell Rd, Chelmsford CM1 2LY *Tel:* 01245 264187
email: ddo@chelmsford.anglican.org

Administrator Revd Philip Tarris, Cathedral Office *Tel:* 01245 294488
email: philip.tarris@chelmsfordcathedral.org.uk

Director of Music Mr James Davy, 1 Harlings Grove, Chelmsford CM1 1YQ
Tel: 01245 252429 (Office)
email: james.davy@chelmsfordcathedral.org.uk
Assistant Director of Music Mr Oliver Waterer
Tel: 01245 252429
email: oliver.waterer@chelmsfordcathedral.org.uk
Music Secretary Mrs Angela Palotai
Tel: 01245 294498 (Office)
email: angela.palotai@chelmsfordcathedral.org.uk
Youth Minister Mr Tim Leeson
Tel: 01245 294483 (Office)
email: tim.leeson@chelmsfordcathedral.org.uk
Corporate Events Manager Mrs Julie Brown
Tel: 01245 294480 (Office)
email: julie.brown@chelmsfordcathedral.org.uk
Communications Manager Mrs Amanda Wright
Tel: 01245 294484 (Office)
email: amanda.wright@chelmsfordcathedral.org.uk

ARCHDEACONS

COLCHESTER Ven Annette Cooper, 63 Powers Hall End, Witham CM8 1NH [2004]
Tel: 01376 513130
Fax: 01376 500789
email: a.colchester@chelmsford.anglican.org

HARLOW Ven Martin Webster, Glebe House, Church Lane, Sheering CM22 7NR [2009]
Tel: 01279 734524
Fax: 01279 734426
email: a.harlow@chelmsford.anglican.org

SOUTHEND Ven David Lowman, The Archdeacon's Lodge, 136 Broomfield Road, Chelmsford CM1 1RN [2001] *Tel:* 01245 258257
Fax: 01245 250845
email: a.southend@chelmsford.anglican.org

WEST HAM Ven Elwin Cockett, 86 Aldersbrook Rd, Manor Park, London E12 5DH [2007]
Tel: 020 8989 8557
Fax: 020 8530 1311
email: a.westham@chelmsford.anglican.org

CONVOCATION (MEMBERS OF THE HOUSE OF CLERGY OF THE GENERAL SYNOD)

Proctors for Clergy
Ven Annette Cooper
Revd John Dunnett
Revd Tim Bull
Revd Canon Martin Wood
Revd David Banting
Revd Jenny Tomlinson

MEMBERS OF THE HOUSE OF LAITY OF THE GENERAL SYNOD

Mrs Isabel Adcock
Mr Robert Hammond
Mrs Mary Durlacher
Ms Kathleen Playle
Mr David G Llewelyn Morgan
Mrs Ruth Whitworth
Mr Robin Stevens

DIOCESAN OFFICERS

Chief Executive and Diocesan Secretary John Ball, Diocesan Office, 53 New St, Chelmsford CM1 1AT *Tel:* 01245 294400
Chancellor of Diocese Chancellor George Pulman QC, Diocesan Registry, 53 New St, Chelmsford CM1 1NE *Tel:* 01245 259470
Registrar of Diocese and Bishop's Legal Secretary Mr Aiden Hargreaves-Smith, Diocesan Registry, 5 Montague Close, London SE1 9BB
Tel: 020 7593 5127
Legal Advisers to the Board of Finance Minerva House, 5 Montague Close, London SE1 9BB
Tel: 020 7593 5000

DIOCESAN ORGANIZATIONS

Diocesan Office 53 New St, Chelmsford CM1 1AT
Tel: 01245 294400
Fax: 01245 294477
email: mail@chelmsford.anglican.org

ADMINISTRATION

Dioc Synod (*Chairman, House of Clergy*) Canon Martin Wood, *Tel:* 01992 672115; (*Chairman, House of Laity*) Canon Dr Susan Atkin, *Tel:* 01206 854976; (*Secretary*) John Ball, Dioc Office *Tel:* 01245 294400
Board of Finance (*Chairman*) Canon John Spence OBE (*Company Secretary*) John Ball, Dioc Office
Tel: 01245 294400
email: jball@chelmsford.anglican.org
Senior Property Manager Richard Smith, Dioc Office *Tel:* 01245 294420
Designated Officer Mr Aiden Hargreaves-Smith, Diocesan Registry, 5 Montague Close, London SE1 9BB *Tel:* 020 7593 5127
Dioc Mission and Pastoral Committee (*Chairman*) Rt Revd Stephen Cottrell, Bishopscourt, Margaretting, Ingatestone CM4 0HD; (*Secretary*) Mr Nathan Whitehead, Dioc Office
email: nwhitehead@chelmsford.anglican.org

CHURCHES

Advisory Committee for the Care of Churches (*Chairman*) Dr James Bettley, The Old Vicarage, Church Rd, Maldon CM9 8NP *Tel:* 01612 892450; (*Secretary*) Mrs Sandra Turner, Dioc Office
email: sturner@chelmsford.anglican.org
Redundant Churches Committee (*Secretary*) Kevin Quinlan, Dioc Office
Essex Association of Change Ringers Mary Bone, 11 Bullfields, Sawbridgeworth, Herts CM21 9BD
Tel: 01279 726159

CHILD PROTECTION

Child Protection Adviser Vacancy
Tel: 01245 294457

EDUCATION

Director of Education Tim Elbourne, Dioc Office
Tel: 01245 294440
email: telbourne@chelmsford.anglican.org
Early Years Adviser Vacancy, Dioc Office
Tel: 01245 294440

RE Adviser Mrs Alison Seaman, Dioc Office *Tel:* 01245 294440 *email:* aseaman@chelmsford.anglican.org
School and RE Advisers Ann Bard, Revd Lyn Hillier, Jeff Graham, Dioc Office *email:* abard@chelmsford.anglican.org lhillier@chelmsford.anglican.org jgraham@chelmsford.anglican.org
Children's Work Adviser Mr Stephen Kersys, Dioc Office *email:* skersys@chelmsford.anglican.org

MISSION AND MINISTRY

Dioc Director of Ordinands and NSM Officer Canon Richard More, 25 Roxwell Rd, Chelmsford CM1 2LY *Tel:* 01245 264187 *Fax:* 01245 348789 *email:* ddo@chelmsford.anglican.org
Dean of Mission and Ministry Canon Roger Matthews, Dioc Office *Tel:* 01245 294455 *email:* rmatthews@chelmsford.anglican.org
Lay Development Adviser Elizabeth Jordan, Dioc Office *Tel:* 01245 294449 *email:* ejordan@chelmsford.anglican.org
Adviser for Women's Ministry Revd Canon Jenny Tomlinson, 17 Borough Lane, Saffron Waldon CB11 4AG *Tel:* 01799 500947
Interfaith Adviser Ven Elwin Cockett, 86 Aldersbrook Rd, Manor Park, London E12 5DH *Tel:* 020 8989 8557 *Fax:* 020 8530 1311 *email:* a.westham@chelmsford.anglican.org

COMMUNICATIONS

Communications Director Ralph Meloy, Dioc Office *Tel:* 01245 294424 07654 382674 (Pager) *email:* rmeloy@chelmsford.anglican.org

OTHER COMMITTEES

Readers' Committee Rt Revd Christopher Heudebourck Morgan, 1 Fitzwalter Rd, Lexden, Colchester CO3 3SS [2001] *Tel:* 01206 576648 *Fax:* 01206 763868 *email:* b.colchester@chelmsford.anglican.org
Liturgical Committee (*Chairman*) Ven Elwin Cockett, 86 Aldersbrook Rd, Manor Park, London E12 5DH *Tel:* 020 8989 8557 *email:* a.westham@chelmsford.anglican.org

DIOCESAN RECORD OFFICE

Essex Records Office, Wharf Rd, Chelmsford CM2 6YT *Tel:* 01245 244644 *email:* ero.enquiry@essexcc.gov.uk

DIOCESAN HOUSE OF RETREAT

Pleshey, Chelmsford CM3 1HA (*Warden* Revd Sheila Coughtrey) *Tel:* 01245 237251 *Fax:* 01245 237594 *email:* retreathouse.pleshey@virgin.net *Web:* www.retreathousepleshey.com

RURAL DEANS

ARCHDEACONRY OF WEST HAM

Barking and Dagenham Revd Roger Gayler, St Mark's Vicarage, 187 Rose Lane, Marks Gate, Romford RM6 5NR *Tel:* 020 8599 0414
Havering Revd David Marshall, St James's Vicarage, 24 Lower Bedfords Rd, Romford RM1 4DG *Tel:* 01708 746614 *email:* revdave@dsl.pipex.com
Newham Canon Dave Wade, Vicarage, 16a Ruscoe Rd, Canning Town, London E16 1JB *Tel:* 020 7476 2076 *email:* davenicky@hotmail.com
Redbridge Revd Paul Harcourt, All Saints Vicarage, 4 Inmans Row, Woodford Green IG8 0NH *Tel:* 020 8504 0266 *email:* paul@asww.org.uk
Waltham Forest Revd Steven Saxby, 121 Forest Rise, Walthamstow, London E17 3PW *Tel:* 020 8520 3854 *email:* stevensaxby@btinternet.com

ARCHDEACONRY OF HARLOW

Epping Forest Dr Joyce Smith, St Lawrence House, 46 Mallion Court, Ninefields, Waltham Abbey EN9 3EQ *Tel:* 01992 767916 *email:* joyce.smith@stclarehospice.org.uk
Harlow Revd Martin Harris, 43 Upper Park, Harlow CM20 1TW *Tel:* 01279 411100 *email:* martin.harris@messages.co.uk
Ongar Revd Toni Smith, Vicarage, Church Street, Ingatestone, Essex CM4 0RN *Tel:* 01277 821464 *email:* reverend@tonismith.freeserve.co.uk

ARCHDEACONRY OF SOUTHEND

Brentwood Revd Dr Ian Herbert Jorysz, The Vicarage, Wigley Bush Lane, Brentwood CM14 5QP *Tel:* 01277 212054 *email:* ian@jorysz.com
Basildon Revd Margaret Shaw, St Andrew's Vicarage, 3 The Fremnells, Basildon, Essex SS14 2QX *Tel:* 01268 520516 *email:* sh.ma@btinternet.com
Chelmsford North Canon Carla I Hampton, The New Vicarage, 1 Glebe Meadow, Chelmsford CM3 1EX *Tel:* 01245 364081 *email:* carla@hamptonc.freeserve.co.uk
Chelmsford South Revd Andrew T Griffiths, 450 Beehive Lane, Chelmsford CM2 8RN *Tel:* 01245 353922 *email:* andy.griffiths@yahoo.co.uk
Hadleigh Revd David Tudor, St Nicholas' House, Canvey Island SS8 0JR *Tel:* 01268 682586 *email:* dstudor@tiscali.co.uk
Maldon and Dengie Revd Sandra Ellen Manley, The Vicarage, Fambridge Road, Althorne, Chelmsford CM3 6BZ *Tel:* 01621 772300 *email:* sandra.manley@btinternet.com
Rochford Revd Mike Lodge, Rectory, Hockley Rd, Rayleigh SS6 8BA *Tel:* 01268 742151 *email:* mike.lodge@parishofrayleigh.org.uk

Southend Canon Stephen Burdett, Southend Rectory, 144 Alexandra Road, Southend-on-Sea SS1 1HB *Tel:* 01702 342687
email: stephen@burdett436.orangehome.co.uk
Thurrock Revd Darren Barlow, The Rectory, 10 High View Avenue, Grays RM17 6RU
Tel: 01375 377379
email: revbarlow@talktalk.net

ARCHDEACONRY OF COLCHESTER

Braintree Very Revd Canon Philip Need, The Deanery, Bocking, Braintree CM7 5SR
Tel: 01376 324887
email: thedeanofbocking@tiscali.co.uk
Colchester Revd Ian A Hilton, The Rectory, New Town Rd, Colchester CO1 2EF *Tel:* 01206 530320
email: ian.hilton@talktalk.net
Dunmow Revd Cilla Hawkes, Greenfields, Felstead, Dunmow CM6 3LF *Tel:* 01371 856480
email: cilla@hawkesfarming.co.uk
Harwich Revd Peter Mann, Rectory, 51 Highfield Avenue, Dovercourt, Harwich CO12 4DR
Tel: 01255 502033
email: cookbird@gmail.com
Hinckford Revd Laurie Bond, Vicarage, Queen St, Castle Hedingham, Halstead CO9 3EZ
Tel: 01787 460274
email: revlbond@hotmail.com
Saffron Walden Revd David R. Tomlinson, St John's Vicarage, 8a Victoria Avenue, Grays RM16 2RP *Tel:* 01375 372101
email: rector.saffronwalden@ntlworld.com
St Osyth Revd Guy Douglas A. Thorburn, St John's Vicarage, Valley Avenue, Great Clacton CO15 4AR *Tel:* 01255 423435
*email:*revguy.thorburn@virgin.net
Witham Revd Geoff Bayliss, The Vicarage, 37 Church Street, Tolleshunt D'arcy, Maldon CM9 8TS *Tel:* 01621 869895
email: g.bayliss41@btinternet.com

DIOCESE OF CHESTER

Founded in 1541. Cheshire; Wirral; Halton, south of the Mersey; Warrington, south of the Mersey; Trafford, except for an area in the north (MANCHESTER); Stockport, except for a few parishes in the north (MANCHESTER) and in the east (DERBY); the eastern half of Tameside; a few parishes in Derbyshire; a few parishes in Manchester; a few parishes in Flintshire.

Population 1,573,000 Area 1,017 sq m
Full-time Stipendiary Parochial Clergy 224 Benefices 225
Parishes 272 Churches 366
www.chester.anglican.org
Overseas link province: Aru and Boga Congo, Melanesia.

BISHOP (40th)
Rt Revd Dr Peter Robert Forster, Bishop's House, Abbey Square, Chester CH1 2JD [1996]
Tel: 01244 350864
Fax: 01244 314187
email: bpchester@chester.anglican.org
[Peter Cestr:]

SUFFRAGAN BISHOPS
BIRKENHEAD Rt Revd (Gordon) Keith Sinclair, Bishop's Lodge, 67 Bidston Rd, Prenton CH43 6TR [2007] *Tel:* 0151 652 2741
Fax: 0151 651 2330
email: bpbirkenhead@chester.anglican.org
STOCKPORT Rt Revd Robert Atwell, Bishop's Lodge, Back Lane, Dunham Town, Altrincham WA14 4SG [2008] *Tel:* 0161 928 5611
Fax: 0161 929 0692
email: bpstockport@chester.anglican.org

HONORARY ASSISTANT BISHOPS
Rt Revd William Alaha Pwaisiho, Rectory, Church Lane, Gawsworth, Macclesfield, SK11 9RJ *Tel:* 01260 223201
Rt Revd Colin Frederick Bazley, 121 Brackenwood Rd, Higher Bebington, Wirral CH63 2LU
Tel: 0151 608 1193
Rt Revd Geoffrey Turner, 23 Lang Lane, West Kirby, Wirral CH48 5HG *Tel:* 0151 625 8504
Rt Revd John Hayden, 45 Birkenhead Rd, Hoylake, Wirral CH47 5AF *Tel:* 0151 632 0448
Rt Revd Graham Dow, 34 Kimberley Ave, Romiley SK6 4AB *Tel:* 0161 494 9148

CATHEDRAL CHURCH OF CHRIST AND THE BLESSED VIRGIN MARY
Dean Very Revd Professor Gordon Ferguson McPhate, Deanery, 7 Abbey St, Chester CH1 2JF [2002] *Tel:* 01244 500971
email: dean@chestercathedral.com
Cathedral Office 12 Abbey Square, Chester CH1 2HU *Tel:* 01244 324756
email: office@chestercathedral.com
Web: www.chestercathedral.com
Vice-Dean
Canon Peter Howell-Jones, 12 Abbey Street, Chester CH1 2HU [2011] *Tel:* 01244 500968
email: vicedean@chestercathedral.com
Canon Precentor
Canon Christopher Humphries, 9 Abbey St, Chester CH1 2JF [2005] *Tel:* 01244 500967
Canon Chancellor Canon Jane Brooke, 12 Abbey Square, Chester CH1 2HU [2010]
Tel: 01244 324756
Canon Residentiary
Canon Dr Peter Jenner, 11 Abbey Street, Chester CH1 2JF
email: peter.jenner@chestercathedral.com
Priest Pastor
Revd Christine Bull, 12 Abbey Square, Chester CH1 2HU
Chief Executive, Administrator and Chapter Clerk
Vacancy *Tel:* 01244 500962
email: chief.executive@chestercathedral.com
Director of Music Mr Philip Rushforth, Cathedral Office *Tel:* 01244 500974
email: philip.rushforth@chestercathedral.com
Cathedral Architect Mr James Sanderson, Cathedral Office

ARCHDEACONS
CHESTER Ven Michael Gilbertson, Church House, Lower Lane, Aldford, Chester CH3 6HP [2010]
Tel: 01244 681937 ext 253
Fax: 01244 620456
email: michael.gilbertson@chester.anglican.org
MACCLESFIELD Ven Ian Bishop, 57a Sandbach Road, Congleton CW12 4LH *Tel:* 01260 272875
email: ian.bishop@chester.anglican.org

CONVOCATION (MEMBERS OF THE HOUSE OF CLERGY OF THE GENERAL SYNOD)
Proctors for Clergy
Revd Ian Bishop
Canon David Felix
Revd Robert Munro
Revd Alison Cox
Revd Dr Jonathan Gibbs
Revd Charles Razzall

MEMBERS OF THE HOUSE OF LAITY OF THE GENERAL SYNOD
Prof Tony Berry
Mr Peter Hart

Dr Graham Campbell
Mrs Jenny Dunlop
Mr John Freeman
Mrs Lois Haslam
Dr John Mason
Canon Elizabeth Renshaw MBE

DIOCESAN OFFICERS

Dioc Secretary Mr George Colville, Church House, Lower Lane, Aldford, Chester CH3 6HP *Tel:* 01244 681973 *email:* george.colville@chester.anglican.org
Chancellor of Diocese His Honour Judge David Turner, c/o Friars, White Friars, Chester CH1 1XS
Registrar of Diocese and Bishop's Legal Secretary Mrs Helen McFall, Friars, White Friars, Chester CH1 1XS *Tel:* 01244 321066 *Fax:* 01244 312582 *email:* helen.mcfall@cullimoredutton.co.uk

DIOCESAN ORGANIZATIONS

Diocesan Office Church House, Lower Lane, Aldford, Chester CH3 6HP *Tel:* 01244 681973 *email:* churchhouse@chester.anglican.org

ADMINISTRATION

Dioc Synod (*Vice-President, House of Clergy*) Revd Dr Jonathan Gibbs
(*Vice-President, House of Laity*) Vacancy
(*Secretary*) George Colville, Church House
Board of Finance (*Chairman*) Canon Elizabeth Renshaw MBE
(*Secretary*) George Colville (*as above*)
Diocesan Surveyor Mr Peter Gowrley, Church House
Head of Finance Mr Nigel Strange, Church House
Designated Officer and Director of HR Liz Geddes, Church House

CHURCHES

Advisory Committee for the Care of Churches (*Chairman*) Prof Robert Munn; (*DAC Sec*) Mr Paul Broadhurst, Church House

EDUCATION

Director of Education Mr Jeff Turnbull, Church House
Children Mr David Bell, Church House
Youth Revd Mark Montgomery, Church House

MISSION AND MINISTRY

Director of Ministry Canon Dr Christopher Burkett, Church House *email:* christopher.burkett@chester.anglican.org
Director of Ordinands Revd Ray Samuels, Bishop's House, Abbey Square, Chester CH1 2JD *Tel:* 01244 346945 *email:* ray.samuels@chester.anglican.org
Assistant Director of Ordinands Revd John Lees, 110 Grove Park, Knutsford WA16 8QB *Tel:* 01565 654755 *email:* johnlees@dslpipex.com
Director of Studies for Ordinands Revd Gary O'Neill, 10 Neston Close, Helsby WA6 0FH *Tel:* 01928 723327 *email:* gary.oneill@chester.anglican.org
Bishop's Officer for NSMs Canon Prof Roger Yates, 3 Racecourse Park, Wilmslow SK9 5LU *Tel:* 01625 520246
Diocesan Dean of Women in Ministry Revd Libby Lane, St Peter's Vicarage, 1 Harrop Rd, Hale, Antrincham WA15 9BU *Tel:* 0161 928 4182
Director of Studies for Readers Liz Shercliff, Church House *email:* liz.shercliff@chester.anglican.org
Warden of Readers Revd John Knowles, 15 Clare Avenue, Handforth, Wilmslow SK9 3EQ *Tel:* 01625 520622 *email:* john.knowles@chester.anglican.org
Clergy Development Officer Revd Canon David Herbert, Church House *email:* david.herbert@chester.anglican.org
Warden of Pastoral Workers Revd Vivien Gisby, 1 Fearndown Way, Tytherington, Macclesfield SK10 2UF *Tel:* 01244 671216 *email:* viviengisby@btinternet.com
Pastoral Worker Training Officer Revd Maureen Pickering, Curzon Cottage, 2A Curzon Park South, Chester CH4 8AB *Tel:* 01244 677352 *email:* mapickering@btinternet.com

PARISH DEVELOPMENT TEAM

Parish Development Officers Revd Richard Burton, Church House *email:* richard.burton@chester.anglican.org
Revd Ian Rumsey *email:* ian.rumsey@chester.anglican.org
Adviser in Christian Giving Mr Martin Smith, Church House *email:* martin.smith@chester.anglican.org
Diocesan Worship Adviser Revd Colin Randall *email:* colinrandall@mac.com

MISSIONARY AND ECUMENICAL

Partners in World Mission Mr John Freeman, Stable Court, 20A Leigh Way, Weaverham, Northwich CW8 3PR *Tel:* 01606 852872
County Ecumenical Development Officer Revd David Betts, 3 Oakmoore, Sandymoor, Runcorn, Cheshire WA7 1NR *Tel:* 01928 579466 *email:* ceo.ctic@googlemail.com
Dioc Ecumenical Officer Canon Mike Lowe, 4 Greenway Rd, Heald Green, Cheadle SK8 3NR *Tel:* 0161 419 5889 *email:* mike.lowe@chester.anglican.org

PRESS AND PUBLICATIONS

Dioc Director of Communications Mr Stephen Regan, Church House or 07764 615069 (Mobile) *email:* stephen.regan@chester.anglican.org
Design and Communications Officer Mr Stephen Freeman *email:* stephen.freeman@chester.anglican.org

DIOCESAN RECORD OFFICE
Cheshire Records Office, Duke St, Chester CH1 2DN *Tel:* 01244 603391

SOCIAL RESPONSIBILITY
Director of Social Responsibility
Mrs Janice Mason, Church House
email: janice.mason@chester.anglican.org

RURAL DEANS

ARCHDEACONRY OF CHESTER

Birkenhead Revd Dallas Ayling, 10 Cavendish Road, Claughton, Birkenhead CH41 8AX
Tel: 0151 653 6092
email: revddallasayling@yahoo.co.uk

Chester Revd Dr Mark Hart, Vicarage, Wicker Lane, Guilden Sutton, Chester CH3 7EL
Tel: 01244 300306
email: markhart61@googlemail.com

Frodsham Revd Peter Rugen, The Vicarage, Pike Lane, Kingsley, Frodsham WA6 8EH
Tel: 01928 787180
email: p.rugen@btinternet.com

Great Budworth Revd Alec Brown, The Vicarage, Great Budworth, Northwich CW9 6HF
Tel: 01606 891324
email: alec-brown@tiscali.co.uk

Malpas Revd Keith Hine, The Rectory, The High Street, Tarporley CW6 0AG
Tel: 01829 732491
email: kehine@btinternet.com

Middlewich Revd Simon Drew, The Rectory, Poplar Fell, Nantwich Road, Middlewich CW10 9HG *Tel:* 01606 833440
email: simon.drew@middlewichparishchurch.org.uk

Wallasey Revd Canon Graham Cousins, The Rectory, Dawpool Drive, Moreton, Wirral CH46 0PH *Tel:* 0151 604 0049
email: rector@christchurchmoreton.org.uk

Wirral North Revd Gillian Rossiter, St John's Vicarage, 142 Birkenhead Rd, Meols, Wirral CH47 0LF *Tel:* 0151 632 1661
email: johnsthebaptistchurch@btinternet.com

Wirral South Revd David Fisher, The Vicarage, 1 Church Lane, Great Sutton, Ellesmere Port, CH66 4RE *Tel:* 0151 339 9916
email: daifisher@aol.com

ARCHDEACONRY OF MACCLESFIELD

Bowdon Revd Julian Heaton, St Anne's Vicarage, Church Road West, Sale M33 3GD
Tel: 0161 973 4145
email: julian.heaton@talktalk.net

Chadkirk Revd Janet Parker, 35 Martlet Avenue, Disley, Stockport SK12 2JH *Tel:* 01663 764519
email: janetparker1@homecall.co.uk

Cheadle Revd Rob McLaren, Vicarage, 41 London Road North, Poynton, Stockport SK12 1AF
Tel: 01625 856877

Congleton Canon David Taylor, Mossley Vicarage, 2 Hartley Gardens, Congleton CW12 3WA
Tel: 01260 273182
email: revdtaylor@hotmail.com

Knutsford Canon Prof Roger Yates, 3 Racecourse Park, Wilmslow SK9 5LU *Tel:* 01625 520246
email: raycandoc@yahoo.co.uk

Macclesfield Revd Vereena Breed, The Vicarage, Wincle, Macclesfield SK11 0QH
Tel: 01260 227234
email: verenabreed@talktalk.net

Mottram Revd Richard Lamey, St Mary's Vicarage, 39 Bradley Green Rd, Newton, Hyde SK14 4NA *Tel:* 0161 368 1489
email: richardlamey@btinternet.com

Nantwich Canon Bill Baker, Vicarage, 14 Dane Bank Ave, Crewe CW2 8AA *Tel:* 01270 569000
email: canonbillbaker@uwclub.net

Stockport Revd Canon Diane Cookson, St Saviour's Vicarage, 22 St Saviour's Road, Great Moor, Stockport SK2 2QE *Tel:* 0161 483 2633
email: st.saviours@virgin.net

DIOCESE OF CHICHESTER

Founded in 1070, formerly called Selsey (AD 681). West Sussex, except for one parish in the north (GUILDFORD); East Sussex, except for one parish in the north (ROCHESTER); one parish in Kent.

Population 1,573,000 Area 1,459 sq m
Full-time Stipendiary Parochial Clergy 266 Benefices 291
Parishes 363 Churches 491
www.chichester.anglican.org
Overseas link dioceses: IDWAL (Inter-Diocesan West Africa Link) – Ghana, Sierra Leone, Cameroon, Guinea (West Africa).

BISHOP (103rd)
Rt Revd Dr Martin Warner, The Palace, Chichester PO19 1PY [2012] *Tel:* 01243 782161
Fax: 01243 531332
email: bishop.chichester@chichester.anglican.org
[Martin Cicestr:]
Senior Chaplain and Episcopal Vicar for Ministry Canon Ian Gibson, The Palace (*as above*)
email: ian.gibson@chichester.anglican.org

AREA BISHOPS
HORSHAM Rt Revd Mark Sowerby, Bishop's House, 21 Guildford Rd, Horsham RH12 1LU [2009] *Tel:* 01403 211139
Fax: 01403 217349
email: bishop.horsham@chichester.anglican.org
Chaplain Revd David Swyer, The Rectory, 5 The Twitten, Albourne, Hassocks BN6 9DF
Tel: 01273 832129
email: david.swyer@chichester.anglican.org
LEWES Vacancy
Chaplain Revd David Charles, Christ Church Vicarage, 18 Addingham Rd, Eastbourne, East Sussex BN22 7DY
email: david.charles@chichester.anglican.org

HONORARY ASSISTANT BISHOPS
Rt Revd Norman Banks, Parkside House, Abbey Mill Lane, St Albans AL3 4HE
Tel: 01727 836358
Rt Revd Kenneth Barham OBE, Rosewood, Canadia Road, Battle TN33 0LR
Tel: 01424 773073
Rt Revd Alan Chesters, The College of St Barnabas, Blackberry Lane, Lingfield RH7 6NJ
Tel: 01342 872861
Rt Revd Ralph Farrer, The Vicarage, 26 Maltravers Street, Arundel BN18 9BA
Tel: 01903 885209
Rt Revd Dr Laurence Green, 86 Belle Hill, Bexhill-on-Sea TN40 2AP *Tel:*01424 217872
Rt Revd Christopher Herbert, 1 Beacon Close, Wrecclesham, Farnham GU10 4PA
Tel: 01252 795600
Rt Revd Michael Manktelow, 14 Little London, Chichester, PO19 1NZ *Tel:* 01243 531096
Rt Revd Michael Marshall, 53 Oakley Gardens, London SW3 5QQ *Tel:* 020 7351 0928
Rt Revd Michael Scott-Joynt, Easter House, Funtington, Chichester PO18 9LJ
Tel: 01243 575762
Rt Revd Henry Scriven, 16 East St Helen Street, Abingdon OX14 5EA *Tel:* 01235 536607
Rt Revd Lindsay Urwin, Baverstock House, Bridewell Street, Walsingham NR22 6EE
Tel: 01328 820323
Rt Revd David Wilcox, 4 The Court, Hoo Gardens, Willingdon, Eastbourne BN20 9AX
Tel: 01323 506108

CATHEDRAL CHURCH OF THE HOLY TRINITY
Dean Very Revd Nicholas Frayling, The Deanery, Canon Lane, Chichester PO19 1PX [2002]
Tel: 01243 812484 (Office)
01243 812494 (Home)
Fax: 01243 812499
email: dean@chichestercathedral.org.uk
Cathedral Office The Royal Chantry, Cathedral Cloisters, Chichester PO19 1PX
Tel: 01243 782595
Fax: 01243 812499
email: enquiry@chichestercathedral.org.uk
Precentor Canon Timothy Schofield, 4 Vicars' Close, Chichester PO19 1PT [2006]
Tel: 01243 813589
Fax: 01243 812499
email: precentor@chichestercathedral.org.uk
Chancellor Canon Dr Anthony Cane, The Residentiary, 2 Canon Lane, Chichester PO19 1PX [2007] *Tel:* 01243 813594
Fax: 01243 812499
email: chancellor@chichestercathedral.org.uk
Treasurer Canon Ian Gibson, Caigers Cottage, Woodgate, Chichester PO20 3SQ [2009]
Tel: 01243 782161
Fax: 01243 812499
email: ian.gibson@chichester.anglican.org
Priest-Vicar Canon David Nason, 1 St Richard's Walk, Chichester PO19 1QA *Tel:* 01243 775615
Fax: 01243 812499

Communar Colonel Andrew Maynard RM, Cathedral Office *Tel:* 01243 812489
Fax: 01243 812499
email: communar@chichestercathedral.org.uk
Cathedral Organist and Master of the Choristers Miss Sarah Baldock, 2 St Richard's Walk, Chichester PO19 1QA *Tel:* 01243 812486
Fax: 01243 812499
email: organist@chichestercathedral.org.uk

ARCHDEACONS

CHICHESTER Ven Douglas McKittrick, 2 Yorklands, Dyke Rd Ave, Hove BN3 6RW [2002]
Tel: 01273 505330
Fax: 01273 421041
email: archchichester@chichester.anglican.org
HORSHAM Ven Roger Combes, 3 Danehurst Crescent, Horsham RH13 5HS [2003]
Tel: 01403 262710
Fax: 01403 210778
email: archhorsham@chichester.anglican.org
LEWES AND HASTINGS Ven Philip Hugh Jones, 27 The Avenue, Lewes BN7 1QT [2005]
Tel: 01273 479530
Fax: 01273 476529
email: archlandh@chichester.anglican.org

CONVOCATION (MEMBERS OF THE HOUSE OF CLERGY OF THE GENERAL SYNOD)

Proctors for Clergy
Revd Alastair Cutting
Revd Canon Rebecca Swyer
Revd Jonathan Frais
Revd Richard Jackson
Ven Douglas McKittrick

MEMBERS OF THE HOUSE OF LAITY OF THE GENERAL SYNOD

Mr John Ashwin
Mrs Lorna Ashworth
Mr John Booth
Mr Justin Brett
Mrs Mary Nagel
Miss Joy Gilliver
Ms Andrea Williams
Mr Jacob Vince

DIOCESAN OFFICERS

Diocesan Secretary Ms Angela Sibson OBE, Diocesan Church House, 211 New Church Rd, Hove BN3 4ED *Tel:* 01273 421021
Fax: 01273 421041
email:
Diocesan.Secretary@chichester.anglican.org
Chancellor of Diocese Chancellor Mark Hill, Francis Taylor Building, Inner Temple, London EC4Y 7BY
Registrar of Diocese and Bishop's Legal Secretary Mr John Stapleton, Thomas Eggar, The Corn Exchange, Baffins Lane, Chichester PO19 4GE
Tel: 01243 813238
Fax: 01243 775640
email: john.stapleton@thomaseggar.com

DIOCESAN ORGANIZATIONS

Diocesan Office Diocesan Church House, 211 New Church Rd, Hove BN3 4ED *Tel:* 01273 421021
Fax: 01273 421041
email: enquiry@chichester.anglican.org

ADMINISTRATION

Dioc Synod (Chairman, House of Clergy) Revd Alastair Cutting
(Chairman, House of Laity) Dr B. Hanson
Dioc Fund and Board of Finance (Incorporated) (Chairman) Mr Jeremy Kaye; *(Secretary)* Ms Angela Sibson OBE *(as above)*
Central Services and IT Mr David Mason, Dioc Church House *Tel:* 01273 425794
email: david.mason@chichester.anglican.org
Human Resources (Adviser) Mr Steven Sleight, Dioc Church House *Tel:* 01273 425689
email: steven.sleight@chichester.anglican.org
Parsonages Committee (Property Director) Mr Andrew Craft, Dioc Church House
Tel: 01273 425683
email: andrew.craft@chichester.anglican.org

SAFEGUARDING

Safeguarding Advisor Colin Perkins, Dioc Church House *Tel:* 01273 425792
email: colin.perkins@chichester.anglican.org

PASTORAL AND CHURCH BUILDINGS

Advisory Committee for the Care of Churches (Chairman) Dr Alan Thurlow, c/o Dioc Church House; *(Secretary)* Miss Beth Hale *(as above)*
email: beth.hale@chichester.anglican.org
Pastoral Committee (Secretary) Mr Steven Sleight, Dioc Church House

CHURCH IN SOCIETY

Adviser Revd David Farey, Dioc Church House
email: david.farey@chichester.anglican.org
Association for Family Support Work Central Office, c/o Dioc Church House
email: admin@familysupportwork.org.uk

PRESS AND PUBLICATIONS

Communications Officer Mrs Lisa Williamson, Dioc Church House *Tel:* 01273 425691
Out of Hours *Tel:* 07775 022461
email: communications@chichester.anglican.org

EDUCATION AND TRAINING

Schools
Director of Education Vacancy
Schools Support Mr Martin Lloyd, Mrs Susan Thompson, Mrs Rosie Black, Mr Nigel Sarjudeen, Dioc Church House
Children and Young People
Adviser for Work with Children and Youth Mr Alistair Campbell, Dioc Church House
Tel: 01273 425694
Youth Officer Mr Steve Tennant, Dioc Church House
Children's Officer Mrs Irene Smale, Dioc Church House

DISCIPLESHIP AND MINISTRY

Ministry Development Officer Revd Canon Rebecca Swyer, Dioc Church House
email: rebecca.swyer@chichester.anglican.org
Programme Co-ordinator, Initial Ministerial Education 4–7 Revd Canon Rebecca Swyer (*as above*)
Adult Education and Training Officer Ruth Sowerby, Dioc Church House
email: ruth.sowerby@chichester.anglican.org
Diocesan Director of Ordinands Canon Dr Philip Bourne, 6 Patcham Grange, Brighton BN1 8UR
Tel: 01273 564057
email: philip.bourne@chichester.anglican.org
Vocations Officer Vacancy
Episcopal Vicar for Ministry (Clergy Terms of Service) Canon Ian Gibson
Readers Committee (Hon Secretary) Mr Simon Quail

MISSION AND RENEWAL

Adviser Revd Richard Jackson, Dioc Church House
Diocesan Evangelist Captain Gordon Banks, Dioc Church House
Parish Resources Officers Mr John Sherlock and Mr Tony Cox, Dioc Church House
World Mission Officer Revd Canon Ian Hutchinson-Cervantes

ECUMENICAL

European Ecumenical Committee (Chairman) The Dean of Chichester
(Secretary) Mr Jeffrey Stanbridge
Tel: 01243 789305
Dioc Ecumenical Co-ordinator Mr Ian Chisnall
Tel: 07976 811654 (Mobile)
email: ianpchisnall@aol.com

LITURGICAL

Liturgy Consultant Revd Ian Forrester, c/o Dioc Church House
Music Consultant Revd Ian Forrester (*as above*)

DIOCESAN RECORD OFFICES

East Sussex Mrs Elizabeth Hughes, *County Archivist*, The Maltings, Castle Precincts, Lewes BN7 1YT *Tel:* 01273 482356
West Sussex Mr R. Childs *County Archivist*, County Records Office, County Hall, Chichester PO19 1RN *Tel:* 01243 533911

RURAL DEANS

ARCHDEACONRY OF CHICHESTER

Arundel and Bognor Canon Mark Standen, Rectory, Rectory Lane, Angmering BN16 4JU
Tel: 01903 784979
email: standens@angmering.org.uk
Brighton Revd Andrew Manson-Brailsford, St George's House, 6 Sussex Mews, Kemp Town, Brighton BN2 1GZ *Tel:* 01273 625538
email: revmanson-brailsford@hotmail.co.uk
Chichester Revd Mark Gilbert, St Wilfrid's House, 7 Durnford Close, Chichester PO19 3AG
Tel: 01243 783853
email: frmarkssc@msn.com
Hove Revd Canon Keith Richards, St Barnabas Vicarage, 88 Sackville Road, Hove BN3 3HE
Tel: 01273 933526
email: keithdrichards@tiscali.co.uk
Worthing Revd Colin Kassell, Park House, 3 Madeira Avenue, Worthing BN11 2AT
Tel: 01903 526571
email: c.kassell@virginmedia.com

ARCHDEACONRY OF HORSHAM

Cuckfield Revd Gary Simmons
East Grinstead Canon Julia Peaty, 15 Overton Shaw, East Grinstead RH19 2HN
Tel: 01342 322386
email: julia@peaty.net
Horsham Canon Guy Bridgewater, Vicarage, Causeway, Horsham RH12 1HE
Tel: 01403 272919
email: bridgewaters@tiscali.co.uk
Hurst Revd Kevin O'Brien, St. John's Rectory, 68a Park Road, Burgess Hill RH15 8HG
Tel: 01444 232582
email: frkevinobrien@me.com
Midhurst Revd Derek Welsman, The Priory, Easebourne, Midhurst GU29 0AJ
Tel: 01730 812655
email: derekwelsman@btinternet.com
Petworth Revd David Twinley, Vicarage, Church Lane, Bury, Pulborough RH20 1PB
Tel: 01798 839057
email: frdavid@twinley.me.uk
Storrington Revd David Beal, The Rectory, East Street, West Chiltington RH20 2JY
Tel: 01798 813117
email: dm.beal@btconnect.com
Westbourne Revd Clive Jenkins, The Vicarage, 271 Main Road, Southbourne PO10 8JE
Tel: 01243 372436
email: candmjenkins@hotmail.com

ARCHDEACONRY OF LEWES AND HASTINGS

Battle and Bexhill Revd Canon Dr Edward Bryant, 14 Highwater View, St Leonards on Sea TN38 8EL *Tel:* 01424 853687
email: invenietis@gmx.com
Dallington Revd Stan Tomalin, 1 Barn Close, Hailsham, BN27 1TL *Tel:* 01323 846680
email: stantomalin@googlemail.com
Eastbourne Very Revd Jeffery Gunn, Vicarage, Spencer Road, Eastbourne BN21 4PA
Tel: 01323 722317
email: jtgunn@tiscali.co.uk

Hastings Revd Chris H. Key, 23 Ore Place, Hastings TN34 2RL *Tel:* 01424 751099
email: revchriskey@gmail.com
Lewes and Seaford Revd Geoffrey Daw, The Rectory, 14 Lockitt Way, Lewes Kingston BN7 3LG *Tel:* 01273 473665
email: Geoffrey.Daw@btinternet.com

Rotherfield Revd Jeremy James, Vicarage, High St, Wadhurst TN5 6AA *Tel:* 01892 782083
email: jeremy@jrjames.freeserve.co.uk

Rye Revd Canon David Frost, The Rectory, Gungarden, Rye TN31 7HH *Tel:* 01797 222430
email: david@drfrost.org.uk

Uckfield Vacancy

DIOCESE OF COVENTRY

Re-founded in 1918. Coventry; Warwickshire, except for small areas in the north (BIRMINGHAM) and south-west (GLOUCESTER) and one parish in the south (OXFORD); an area of Solihull.

Population 809,000 Area 686 sq m
Full-time Stipendiary Parochial Clergy 105 Benefices 129
Parishes 198 Churches 242
www.coventry.anglican.org

BISHOP

Rt Revd Dr Christopher John Cocksworth, Bishop's House, 23 Davenport Rd, Coventry CV5 6PW [2008] *Tel:* 024 7667 2244
Fax: 024 7671 3271
email: bishcov@btconnect.com
Personal Assistant Christine Camfield (*same address*)
email: christine.camfield@btconnect.com
Secretary Mrs Elizabeth Egan (*same address*)
email: elizabeth.egan1@btconnect.com

SUFFRAGAN BISHOP

WARWICK Rt Revd John Ronald Angus Stroyan, Warwick House, 139 Kenilworth Rd, Coventry CV4 7AP [2005] *Tel:* 024 7641 2627
Fax: 024 7641 5254
email: Bishop.Warwick@covcofe.org
Personal Assistant Mrs Kerry Vanston-Rumney
email: kerry.rumney@covcofe.org

CATHEDRAL CHURCH OF ST MICHAEL

Dean Very Revd John Witcombe
Tel: 024 7652 1227
email: john.witcombe@coventrycathedral.org.uk
Cathedral Offices 1 Hill Top, Coventry CV1 5AB
Tel: 024 7652 1200
Fax: 024 7652 1220
Web: www.coventrycathedral.org.uk
Canons Residentiary and Senior Staff
Sub Dean and Canon Pastor Revd Canon Timothy John Pullen (*same address*) [2008]
Tel: 024 7652 1223
email: tim.pullen@coventrycathedral.org.uk
Canon Precentor Revd Canon Dr David Stone (*same address*) [2010] *Tel:* 024 7652 1212
email: david.stone@coventrycathedral.org.uk
Canon Director of Reconciliation Ministry Canon David Porter (*same address*) [2008]
Tel: 024 7652 1262
email: david.porter@coventrycathedral.org.uk
Canons Theologian
Revd Canon Professor Ben Quash, Department of Theology and Religious Studies, King's College London, The Strand, London WC2R 2LS [2004]
Tel: 020 7848 2339/2073
Canon Professor Richard Farnell
Tel: 024 7652 1200
Canon John Mumford *Tel:* 024 7652 1200
Clerk to the College of Canons Mr Roger Pascall, 1 The Quadrant, Coventry CV1 2DW
Tel: 024 7663 1212
Director of Music Mr Kerry Beaumont (*same address*) *Tel:* 024 7652 1219
email: kerry.beaumont@coventrycathedral.org.uk

ARCHDEACONS

Archdeacon Pastor: Vacancy
Tel: 024 7652 1337 (Office)
Archdeacon Missioner Ven Morris Rodham, Cathedral and Diocesan Offices *Tel:* 024 7652 1337
email: morris.rodham@covcofe.org
Dean of Women's Ministry Canon Katrina Scott, Willenhall Vicarage, Robin Hood Rd, Coventry CV3 3AY *Tel:* 024 7630 3266
email: krgscott@hotmail.com
Dean of Self Supporting Ministry: Revd Dr Jill Tucker, The Old House, Oxhill, Warwick CV35 0QN *Tel:* 01295 680663
email: revjill.tucker@tiscali.co.uk

CONVOCATION (MEMBERS OF THE HOUSE OF CLERGY OF THE GENERAL SYNOD)

Proctors for Clergy
Revd Canon Martin Saxby
Revd Ruth Walker
Revd Martin Gorrick

MEMBERS OF THE HOUSE OF LAITY OF THE GENERAL SYNOD

Mrs Kay Dyer
Mr Samuel Margrave
Dr Yvonne Warren

DIOCESAN OFFICERS

Diocesan Secretary Canon Simon Lloyd, Cathedral and Diocesan Offices, 1 Hill Top, Coventry CV1 5AB *Tel:* 024 7652 1307
Fax: 024 7652 1330
email: simon.lloyd@covcofe.org
Chancellor of Diocese Chancellor Stephen Eyre, St Phillip's Chambers, 55 Temple Row, Birmingham B2 5LS
Deputy Chancellor Glyn Samuel (*same address*)
Registrar of Diocese and Bishop's Legal Secretary Mrs Mary Allanson, Rotherham & Co, 8 The Quadrant, Coventry CV1 2EL *Tel:* 024 7622 7331

DIOCESAN ORGANIZATIONS

Diocesan Office Cathedral and Diocesan Offices, 1 Hill Top, Coventry CV1 5AB *Tel:* 024 7652 1200
Fax: 024 7652 1330
Web: www.coventry.anglican.org

ADMINISTRATION

Diocesan Synod (*Chairman, House of Clergy*) Revd Ruth Walker
(*Chairman, House of Laity*) Mr Graham Wright
Diocesan Secretary Canon Simon Lloyd, Cathedral and Diocesan Offices
Board of Finance (*Chairman*) Canon Ian Francis, The Firs, Main St, Frankton, Rugby CV23 9NZ
Tel: 01926 632918
email: ian@frankton.org
Systems Development Manager Mr Phil Ash
email: phil.ash@covlec.org
Director of Finance and Administration Mr David Oglethorpe
email: david.oglethorpe@covcofe.org
Senior Property Manager Mrs Nicky Caunt, Cathedral and Diocesan Offices
email: nicky.caunt@covlec.org
Diocesan Projects and Communication Officer Revd Graeme Pringle, Cathedral and Diocesan Offices
Tel: 024 7652 1336
email: graeme.pringle@covcofe.org
Diocesan Trustees David Dumbleton MBE, Rotherham & Co, 8 The Quadrant, Coventry CV1 2EL *Tel:* 024 7622 7331
Diocesan Mission and Pastoral Committee Matt Jermyn
Designated Officer Christine Camfield (*as above*)
Diocesan Directory Editor Revd Graeme Pringle (*as above*)

CHURCHES

Advisory Committee for the Care of Churches Dr Claire Strachan, Cathedral and Diocesan Offices *email:* claire.strachan@covcofe.org

EDUCATION

Diocesan Director Mrs Linda Wainscot, The Benn Education Centre, Claremont Road, Rugby CV21 3LU *email:* linda.wainscot@covcofe.org

MINISTRY

Principal of the Diocesan Training Partnership Canon Dr Richard Cooke, Cathedral and Diocesan Offices *Tel:* 024 7652 1316
email: richard.cooke@covcofe.org
Diocesan Director of Ordinands Canon Dr Richard Cooke Cathedral and Diocesan Offices
Tel: 024 7652 1316
Learning Adviser (*Ministerial Development*) Revd Naomi Nixon, Cathedral and Diocesan Offices
Tel: 024 7652 1304
email: naomi.nixon@covcofe.org
Learning Adviser (Adult Discipleship Development) Revd Martin Kirkbride, Cathedral and Diocesan Offices *Tel:* 024 7652 1316
email: martin.kirkbride@covcofe.org
Warden of Readers Mrs Heidi Cartledge
Tel: 01926 641751
email: hcartledge@fightingclose.freeserve.co.uk
Readers (*Hon Registrar*) Mr Paul Mileham
Tel: 01926 426250
email: paul@mileham.net

STEWARDSHIP

Diocesan Adviser Mr Graham Wright, 1 Mayfield Drive, Kenilworth CV8 2SW *Tel:* 01926 864991
email: grahampjw@aol.com

DIOCESAN RECORD OFFICE

Warwickshire County Record Office, Priory Park, Cape Rd, Warwick CV34 4JS
Archives and Historic Environment Manager Ms Sam Collenette *Tel:* 01926 738959
Fax: 01926 738969
email: recordoffice@warwickshire.gov.uk

AREA DEANS

ARCHDEACONRY OF COVENTRY

Coventry North Revd Robin Trew, Allesley Rectory, Rectory Lane, Coventry CV5 9EQ
Tel: 024 7640 25006
email: robintrew@googlemail.com
Coventry South Revd Stephen Burch, St James Vicarage, 395 Tile Hill Lane, Coventry CV4 9DP
Tel: 024 7646 6262
email: stephenburch59@gmail.com
Coventry East Revd Malcolm Tyler, Walsgrave Vicarage, 4 Faber Rd, Coventry CV2 2BG
Tel: 024 7661 5152
email: stmaryssowe@aol.com
Kenilworth Revd Canon Roy Brown 3 Margetts Close, Kenilworth CV8 1EN *Tel:* 01926 850638
email: brownphilips5@sky.com
Nuneaton Revd Dr Richard Hare, The Rectory, 1 Linden Lea, Bedworth CV12 8UD
Tel: 024 7631 0219
email: thehares@ic24.net
Rugby Revd Canon Martin Saxby, St Matthew's Vicarage, 7 Vicarage Rd, Rugby CV22 7AJ
Tel: 01788 330442
email: martin@m2o.org.uk

ARCHDEACONRY OF WARWICK

Alcester Revd Terry Mason, The Vicarage, Stratford Road, Wootton Wawen, Henley in Arden B95 6BD *Tel:* 01564 7938
email: terrymason@churchesofarden.org.uk
Fosse Revd Kate Mier, The Vicarage, Church Street, Wellesbourne, Warwick CV35 9LS
Tel: 01789 840262
email: kate.mier1@gmail.com
Shipston Revd Dr Jill Tucker, The Old House, Oxhill, Warwick CV35 0QN *Tel:* 01295 688193
email: revjill.tucker@tiscali.co.uk

Southam Revd Craig Groocock, The Rectory, 2 Vicarage Lane, Harbury, Leamington Spa CV33 9HA *Tel:* 01926 612377
email: kankudai43@aol.co.uk

Warwick and Leamington Revd Paul Manuel, St Mark's Vicarage, 2 St Mark's Road, Leamington Spa CV32 6DL *Tel:* 01926 421004
email: paul.manuel4@ntlworld.con

DIOCESE OF DERBY

Founded in 1927. Derbyshire, except for a small area in the north (CHESTER); a small area of Stockport; a few parishes in Staffordshire.

Population 1,017,000 Area 997 sq m
Full-time Stipendiary Parochial Clergy 136 Benefices 151
Parishes 253 Churches 330
www.derby.anglican.org
Overseas link of Derbyshire Churches (Baptist, Methodist, URC and Anglican): Church of North India.

BISHOP (7th)
Rt Revd Dr Alastair Redfern, The Bishop's House, 6 King St, Duffield, Derby DE56 4EU [2005]
Tel: 01332 840132
Fax: 01332 840397
email: bishop@bishopofderby.org
[Alastair Derby]

SUFFRAGAN BISHOP
REPTON Rt Revd Humphrey Southern, Repton House, Lea, Matlock DE4 5JP [2007]
Tel: 01629 534644
Fax: 01629 534003
email: bishop@repton.free-online.co.uk

HONORARY ASSISTANT BISHOPS
Rt Revd Robert Beak OBE, Ashcroft Cottage, Butts Rd, Ashover, Chesterfield S45 0AX [1991]
Tel: 01246 590048
Rt Revd Richard Inwood, 43 Whitecotes Park, Chesterfield S40 3RT [2012] *Tel:* 01246 766288
email: richardinwood@btconnect.com
Rt Revd Jack Nicholls, 75 Rowton Grange Rd, Chapel-en-le-Frith, High Peak SK23 0LD
Tel: 01298 938249
email: jnseraphim@gmx.com

CATHEDRAL CHURCH OF ALL SAINTS
Dean Very Revd Dr John Davies DL, Derby Cathedral Centre, 18–19 Iron Gate, Derby DE1 3GP *Tel:* 01332 341201
Fax: 01332 203991
email: dean@derbycathedral.org
Cathedral Office Derby Cathedral Centre, 18–19 Iron Gate, Derby DE1 3GP
email: office@derbycathedral.org
Canons Residentiary
Canon Precentor Canon David Perkins, Derby Cathedral Centre, 18–19 Iron Gate, Derby DE1 3GP *Tel:* 01332 341201
Fax: 01332 203991
email: precentor@derbycathedral.org
Canon Pastor Canon Elaine Jones, Derby Cathedral Centre, 18–19 Iron Gate, Derby DE1 3GP *Tel:* 01332 341201
Fax: 01332 203991
email: elainejones@derbycathedral.org
Canon Chancellor Canon Dr Simon Taylor, Derby Church House, Full Street, Derby DE1 3DR
Tel: 01332 388650
Fax: 01332 292969
email: simon.taylor@derby.anglican.org
Chaplains Revd Richenda Leigh, University of Derby, Kedleston Rd, Derby DE22 1GB
Tel: 01332 591878 (University)
email: chaplaincy@derby.ac.uk
Lay Chapter Members Mr David Legh, Mr Brian Dollamore, Canon Judi Haywood, Mr Mark Titterton
Cathedral Administrator and Chapter Clerk Mrs Jackie Croft, Cathedral Office
email: Jackie@derbycathedral.org
Finance Officer Mr Peter Holdridge, Cathedral Office *email:* peterh@derbycathedral.org
Visitors' Officer Mr John Armitage, Cathedral Office *Tel:* 01322 341201
email: visitors@derbycathedral.org
Master of Music and Organist Canon Peter Gould, Cathedral Office *Tel:* 01322 202231
email: pdgould@derbycathedral.org
Asssistant Organist Mr Tom Corfield, Cathedral Office *Tel:* 01332 202231

ARCHDEACONS
CHESTERFIELD Ven Christine Wilson, The Old Vicarage, Church St, Baslow, Derby DE45 1RY
Tel: 01246 583023
email: archchesterfield@derby.anglican.org

DERBY Ven Christopher Cunliffe, Derby Church House, Full St, Derby DE1 3DR [2006]
Tel: 01332 388676 (Office)
Fax: 01332 292969
email: archderby@derby.anglican.org

CONVOCATION (MEMBERS OF THE HOUSE OF CLERGY OF THE GENERAL SYNOD)
Proctors for Clergy
Revd Neil Barber
Ven Christine Wilson

MEMBERS OF THE HOUSE OF LAITY OF THE GENERAL SYNOD
Mrs Madelaine Goddard
Canon (Mrs) Christine McMullen
Mr Peter Collard

DIOCESAN OFFICERS
Dioc Secretary Mr Bob Carey, Derby Church House, 1 Full St, Derby DE1 3DR
Tel: 01332 388650
Fax: 01332 292969
email: finance@derby.anglican.org
Chancellor of Diocese His Honour Judge John W. M. Bullimore, 5 Snowgate Head, Horn Lane, New Mill, Holmfirth HD9 7DH
Registrar of Diocese and Bishop's Legal Secretary Mrs Nadine Waldron, Eddowes Waldron Solicitors, 12 St Peter's Churchyard, Derby DE1 1TZ *Tel:* 01332 348484
email: glenis.edwards@btconnect.com

DIOCESAN ORGANIZATIONS
Diocesan Office Derby Church House, 1 Full St, Derby DE1 3DR *Tel:* 01332 388650
Fax: 01332 292969
email: finance@derby.anglican.org
Web: www.derby.anglican.org

ADMINISTRATION
Dioc Synod (Chairman, House of Clergy) Revd Paul Sandford, St Stephen's Vicarage, 313 Sinfin Lane, Sinfin, Derby DE24 9GP
email: prsandford@ntlworld.com
(Chairman, House of Laity) Canon (Mrs) Christine McMullen, Montpelier Farm Cottage, Montpelier Place, Waterswallows Road, Buxton SK17 7EJ
Tel: 01298 73997
(Secretary) Mr Bob Carey, Derby Church House
Board of Finance (Chairman) Mr Brian Dollamore, Castle House, Castle Square, Melbourne, Derby DE73 8DY
(Secretary) Mr Bob Carey *(as above)*
Parsonages Secretary Nigel Sherratt, Derby Church House *Tel:* 01332 388650
Dioc Surveyors
Derby Archdeaconry Bob Spencer, Sir William Baird & Partners, St Michael's House, Queen St, Derby DE1 3DT *Tel:* 01332 347203
Fax: 01332 347708
email: mail@sirwilliambaird.co.uk
Chesterfield Archdeaconry Mr G. Steel, Barlow & Associates Ltd, 7 Vernon St, Derby DE1 1FR
Tel: 01332 603000
email: gary@barlow-associates.co.uk
Mission and Pastoral Committee (Secretary) Revd Ian Price, Derby Church House
Designated Officer Mrs Nadine Waldron *(as above)*

CHURCHES
Advisory Committee for the Care of Churches (Chairman) Mrs Janet Spencer
(Secretary) Mrs Helen Powell, Derby Church House *Tel:* 01332 388683
Fax: 01332 292969

EDUCATION
Dioc Education Office Derby Church House, 1 Full St, Derby DE1 3DR *Tel:* 01332 388660
Fax: 01332 381909
email: nettarussell@ddbe.org
Director David Channon
email: davidchannon@ddbe.org
Deputy Director and Schools Adviser Mrs Alison Brown *email:* alisonbrown@ddbe.org
Finance Officer Mrs Lizzie Walker
Tel: 01332 388662
email: lizziewalker@ddbe.org
Children's Work Adviser Sara Brown
email: sarabrown@ddbe.org
Youth Adviser Mr Alistair Langton
email: alistairlangton@ddbe.org
Warden, Peak Centre Champion House Mr Chris Offord, Champion House, Edale, Hope Valley S33 7ZA *Tel:* 01433 670254
email: warden@peakcentre.org.uk

MISSION AND MINISTRY
Director of Mission and Ministry Revd Canon Andy Broom *Tel:* 01332 388693
email: andy.broom@derby.anglican.org
CMD Officer Revd Canon Dr Simon Taylor
Tel: 01332 388671
email: simon.taylor@derby.anglican.org
Church Growth Officers Mrs Maureen Cole
Tel: 01332 388691
email: maureen.cole@derby.anglican.org
Revd Lee Townend *Tel:* 01332 388668
email: lee.townend@derby.anglican.org
Community Action Officers
Canon Joy Bates *Tel:* 01322 3886868
email: joy.bates@derby.anglican.org
Ms Stella Collishaw *Tel:* 01322 388685
email: stella.collishaw@derby.anglican.org
Lay Ministry Officer/Warden of Readers Dr Esther Elliott *Tel:* 01322 388674
email: esther.elliot@derby.anglican.org
Mission Officer Revd Lakshmi Jeffreys
Tel: 01332 388687
email: lakshmi.jeffreys@derby.anglican.org
Leadership Development Officer Revd Alison Maddocks *Tel:* 01332 288675
email: alison.maddocks@derby.anglican.org

PORTFOLIO HOLDERS AND ADVISERS
Christian Giving/Stewardship
Revd Carole Lloyd *Tel:* 01773 607947
email: carole.lloyd@amnos.co.uk
Mr Mike Warner *Tel:* 01335 346504
email: mike@warnerclan.fsnet.co.uk
Churches Together in Derbyshire Revd Marcus Nolan *email:* derbyshirecuf@gmail.com
Clergy Wellbeing Mrs Jackie Croft
Tel: 07799 644589
email: jackie.croft@derby.anglican.org
Disability
Revd Katie Tupling *Tel:* 01433 650215
email: revtup@tup-house.freeserve.co.uk
Captain Sean Andrews *Tel:* 01332 549212
email: captainsean@btinternet.com
Ecumenical
Revd Kevin Ball *Tel:* 01246 462192
email: k.h.ball@tinyworld.co.uk

Revd Judy Henderson-Smith *Tel:* 01159 460395
email: jhhs91@hotmail.com
Elderly Revd Robert Parker *Tel:* 01691 610628
email: rgparker@tedsmorehall.co.uk
Emergency Mr Alan Winfield *Tel:* 01332 765368
email: winfieldalan28@yahoo.co.uk
Environmental Revd Terry Thake
Tel: 01773 821404
email: terry.thake@btinternet.com
Fresh Expressions Revd Michael Mitton
Tel: 01322 552448
email: michaelmitton@btinternet.com
Interfaith Vacancy
MSE Officer Revd Peter Owen Jones
Tel: 01159 320764
email: ipoj@talktalk.net
NSM Convenor Vacancy
New Religious Movements Revd William Bates
Tel: 01332 550224
*email:*williambates@btconnect.com
Prayer and Worship Revd Alan Harper
Tel: 01332 825667
email: revd.alan8@btinternet.com
Rural Mr Graham Hinds *Tel:* 01322 602124
email: grahamhinds@hotmail.com
Science Revd Dr David de Pomerai
Tel: 01283 711350
email: ddepomerai@aol.com
Spirituality Mrs Glenis Page *Tel:* 01332 781617
email: glenis@consettina.freeserve.co.uk
Tourism Revd Garrie Griffiths *Tel:* 01629 630409
email: ggriffiths787@btinternet.com
Working Agreements Revd Andy Larkin
Tel: 07758 704452
email: andy@larkin.me.uk
World Mission Dr Richard Henderson Smith
Tel: 01159 460395
email: r_smith07@btinternet.com
Worship Advisory Group Revd Karen Padley
Tel: 01773 712097
email: revpadley@fsmail.net
Director of Ordinands Revd Canon Geraldine Pond *Tel:* 01335 343129
email: geraldine@geraldinepond.com
Assistant Directors of Ordinands Revd Philip Waller *Tel:* 01159 734819
email: philipstjohn@tiscali.co.uk
Revd John Baines *Tel:* 01663 743225
email: vicar@newmillschurch.co.uk
Vocations Adviser Revd Canon Geraldine Pond
Tel: 01335 343129
email: geraldine@geraldinepond.com

PRESS AND COMMUNICATIONS

Office Derby Church House, Full St, Derby DE1 3DR *Tel:* 01332 388680
Fax: 01332 292969
Communications Officer Revd Rob Marshall, Derby Church House *Tel:* 01332 388680
email: communications@derby.anglican.org
Communications Co-ordinator Lucy Greensmith

DIOCESAN RECORD OFFICE

Derbyshire Record Office, County Offices, Matlock DE4 3AG *County Archivist* Mrs Sarah Chubb *Tel:* 0845 605 8058
email: record.office@derbyshire.gov.uk

RURAL DEANS

ARCHDEACONRY OF DERBY

Ashbourne Revd Andy Larkin, The Vicarage, Smithy Lane, Parwich, Ashbourne DE6 1QD
Tel: 07758 704452
email: andy@peakfive.org
Derby North Revd Julian Hollywell, St Werburghs Vicarage, Gascoigne Drive, Spondon, Derby DE21 76L *Tel:* 01332 673573
email: fatherjulian@btinternet.com
Derby South Vacancy
Duffield Revd Jonathan Page, Christ Church Vicarage, Bridge Street, Belper DE21 4JU
Tel: 01773 824974
email: vicar@christchurchbelper.org.uk
Erewash Revd Peter Owen-Jones, Bridge Cottage, 63 Derby Road, Stanley, Ilkeston DE7 6EX
Tel: 0115 932 0764
email: peterOJ@talktalk.net
Heanor Revd Terry Williams, The Vicarage, Church Street, Horsley, Derby DE21 5BR
Tel: 01332 880284
email: wterry774@btinternet.com
Longford Revd Andy Murphie, Vicarage, 28 Back Lane, Hilton, Derby DE65 5GJ
Tel: 01283 733433
email: andymurphie@btinternet.com
Melbourne Revd Tony Luke, Rectory, Rectory Gardens, Aston-on-Trent, Derby DE72 2AZ
Tel: 01332 792658
email: tonyluketenor@aol.com
Repton Revd David Perrett, The Vicarage, 120 Church Street, Church Gresley, Swadlincote DE11 9NR *Tel:* 01283 222966
email: DTP@dperrett.freeserve.co.uk

ARCHDEACONRY OF CHESTERFIELD

Alfreton Revd Philip Brooks, Vicarage, 19 Coasthill, Crich, Matlock DE4 5DS
Tel: 01773 852449
email: philipdbro@aol.com
Bakewell and Eyam Revd Canon Tony Kaunhoven, The Vicarage, Bakewell DE45 1FD
Tel: 01629 814462
email: jazzyrector@aol.com
Bolsover and Staveley Revd Canon Helen Guest, The Rectory, Sheepcote Road, Killamarsh, Sheffield S21 1DU *Tel:* 0114 248 2769
email: revsguest@btinternet.com
Buxton Revd John Hudghton, The Rectory, 7 Lismore Park, Buxton SK17 9AU
Tel: 01298 77856
email: Rectorofbuxton@hotmail.com
Chesterfield Revd Matt Barnes, 674 Chatsworth Road, Chesterfield S40 3NU *Tel:* 01246 567634
email: rector@st-thomas-brampton.org

Glossop Revd John Baines, St George's Vicarage, Church Lane, New Mills, High Peak SK22 4NP
Tel: 01663 743225
email: vicar@newmillschurch.co.uk

Wirksworth Canon David Truby, Rectory, Coldwell St, Wirksworth, Matlock DE4 4FB
Tel: 01629 822858
email: david.truby@btinternet.com

DIOCESE OF DURHAM

Founded in 635. Durham, except for an area in the south-west (RIPON AND LEEDS), and four parishes in the north (NEWCASTLE); Gateshead; South Tyneside; Sunderland; Hartlepool; Darlington; Stockton-on-Tees, north of the Tees.

Population 1,464,000 Area 987 sq m
Full-time Stipendiary Parochial Clergy 148 Benefices 187
Parishes 227 Churches 273
www.durham.anglican.org
Overseas link diocese: Lesotho.

BISHOP (73nd)

Vacancy, Auckland Castle, Bishop Auckland DL14 7NR *Tel:* 01388 602576
Fax: 01388 605264
email: bishop.of.durham@durham.anglican.org
Office Manager and Senior PA for the Bishop of Durham Joanne Scott (*same address*)
email: joanne.scott@durham.anglican.org

SUFFRAGAN BISHOP

JARROW Rt Revd Mark Watts Bryant, Bishop's House, 25 Ivy Lane, Low Fell, Gateshead, NE9 6QD [2007] *Tel:* 0191 491 0917
Fax: 0191 491 5116
email: bishop.of.jarrow@durham.anglican.org

HONORARY ASSISTANT BISHOPS

Rt Revd Martyn William Jarrett, 3 North Lane, Roundhay, Leeds LS8 2QJ [2000]
Tel: 0113 265 4280
Fax: 0113 265 4281

Rt Revd Prof Stephen Whitefield Sykes, Ingleside, Whinney Hill, Durham DH1 3BE [1999]
Tel: 0191 384 6465
email: S.W.Sykes@durham.ac.uk

CATHEDRAL CHURCH OF CHRIST, BLESSED MARY THE VIRGIN AND ST CUTHBERT OF DURHAM

Dean Very Revd Michael Sadgrove MA FRSA DL, The Deanery, Durham DH1 3EQ [2003]
Tel: 0191 384 7500 (Office)
email: michael.sadgrove@durhamcathedral.co.uk

Canons Residentiary

Canon Dr David Kennedy, 7 The College, Durham DH1 3EQ [2001] *Tel:* 0191 375 0242
email: canon.precentor@durhamcathedral.co.uk

Canon Rosalind Brown, 6a The College, Durham DH1 3EQ [2005] *Tel:* 0191 384 2415
email: rosalind.brown@durhamcathedral.co.uk

Canon Dr Stephen Cherry, Carter House, Pelaw Leazes Lane, Durham DH1 1TB [2006]
Tel: 0191 374 6012
email: stephen.cherry@durham.anglican.org

Ven Ian Jagger, 15 The College, Durham DH1 3EQ [2006] *Tel:* 0191 384 7534
Fax: 0191 386 6915
email:
archdeacon.of.durham@durham.anglican.org

Canon Prof Mark McIntosh [2009], 14 The College, Durham DH1 3EQ *Tel:* 0191 386 4657
email: mark.mcintosh@durham.ac.uk

Lay Members

Mrs Carolyn Roberts (*Chapter Office*) [2010]
Mr Adrian Beney (*Chapter Office*) [2007]

Chapter Clerk Mr Philip Davies [2009], Chapter Office, The College, Durham DH1 3EH
Tel: 0191 374 4064
Fax: 0191 386 4267
email: philip.davies@durhamcathedral.co.uk

Cathedral Organist (Lay Canon) Canon James Lancelot, 6 The College, Durham DH1 3EQ
Tel: 0191 386 4766
email: organist@durhamcathedral.co.uk

ARCHDEACONS

DURHAM Ven Ian Jagger, 15 The College, Durham DH1 3EQ [2006] *Tel:* 0191 384 7534
Fax: 0191 386 6915
email:
archdeacon.of.durham@durham.anglican.org

AUCKLAND Ven Nick Barker, Vicarage, 45 Milbank Rd, Darlington DL3 9NL [2007]
Tel: 01325 480444
Fax: 01325 354027
email:
archdeacon.of.auckland@durham.anglican.org

SUNDERLAND Ven Stuart Bain, St Nicholas Vicarage, Hedworth Lane, Boldon Colliery NE35 9JA [2002] *Tel:* 0191 536 2300
Fax: 0191 519 3369
email:
archdeacon.of.sunderland@durham.anglican.org

CONVOCATION (MEMBERS OF THE HOUSE OF CLERGY OF THE GENERAL SYNOD)

Dignitaries in Convocation

The Dean of Durham

Proctors in Convocation

Revd David Brooke
Revd Graeme Buttery

Revd Dr Margaret Gilley
Ven Ian Jagger

MEMBERS OF THE HOUSE OF LAITY OF THE GENERAL SYNOD
Dr Richard Goudie
Mrs Frances Wood
Dr James Harrison
Sister Anne Williams

DIOCESAN OFFICERS
Dioc Secretary Mr Ian Boothroyd, Dioc Office, Auckland Castle, Bishop Auckland DL14 7QJ *Tel:* 01388 660010 *Fax:* 01388 603695 *email:* Diocesan.Secretary@durham.anglican.org
Chancellor of Diocese The Worshipful the Revd Canon Rupert Bursell, Diocesan Registry, Messrs Smith Roddam, 56 North Bondgate, Bishop Auckland DL14 7PG *Tel:* 01388 603073 *Fax:* 01388 450483
Deputy Chancellor Mr J. D. C. Harte, The Law School, Newcastle University, 21–24 Windsor Terrace, Newcastle-upon-Tyne NE1 7RU *Tel:* 0191 222 7614 *or* 222 7624
Registrar of Diocese and Bishop's Legal Secretary Ms H. Monckton-Milnes, Dioc Registry (*as above*)
Deputy Registrar Mr D. Harris, Dioc Registry
Property Manager, Dioc Surveyor and Secretary to Houses Committee Mr M. Galley, Dioc Office *Tel:* 01388 660006 *email:* mike.galley@durham.anglican.org

DIOCESAN ORGANIZATIONS
Diocesan Office Auckland Castle, Bishop Auckland DL14 7QJ *Tel:* 01388 604515 *Fax:* 01388 603695 *email:* diocesan.office@durham.anglican.org

ADMINISTRATION
Dioc Synod (*Chairman, House of Clergy*) Canon John Dobson, Vicarage, 104 Blackwell Lane, Darlington DL3 8QQ *Tel:* 01325 354503 *email:* john.dobson@durham.anglican.org
(*Chairman, House of Laity*) Dr Jamie Harrison, 5 Dunelm Court, South Street, Durham DH1 4QX *Tel:* 0191 384 8643
(*Secretary*) Mr Ian Boothroyd [until April 2013], Dioc Office *email:* ian.boothroyd@durham.anglican.org
Board of Finance (*Chairman*) [until April 2013], Dr Julian Chadwick, 31 Wearside Drive, The Sands, Durham DH1 1LE *Tel:* 0191 384 3135 *email:* julian.chadwick@btinternet.com
(*Secretary*) Mr Ian Boothroyd (*as above*)
Glebe Committee (*Chairman*) Dr Julian Chadwick (*as above*); (*Secretary*) Mr Paul Stringer, Dioc Office *Tel:* 01388 660002
Houses Committee (*Chairman*) Revd S Pinnington OBE, Rectory, 5 Lingfield, Houghton le Spring DH5 8QA *Tel:* 0191 584 3487 *email:* rectorstmichaels@btinternet.com
(*Secretary*) Mr M. Galley, Dioc Office
Mission and Pastoral Committee (*Chairman*) Ven Ian Jagger; (*Secretary*) Mr Paul Stringer, Dioc Office *Tel:* 01388 660002 (Direct line) *email:* paul.stringer@durham.anglican.org
Church Buildings Committee (*Chairman*) Mr Geoff Taylor, 14 Academy Gardens, Gainford, Darlington DL2 3EN *Tel:* 01325 730379 *email:* geoffandsue@academygardens.fsnet.co.uk
(*Secretary*) Mr Bill Heslop, Dioc Office *Tel:* 01388 660001 (Direct line) *email:* bill.heslop@durham.anglican.org
Closed Churches Uses Committee (*Chairman*) Mr W. Grant, 6 Sunniside Terrace, Cleadon, Sunderland SR6 7XE *Tel:* 0191 536 4140 *email:* wgrant@talktalk.net
(*Secretary*) Mr Bill Heslop, Dioc Office (*as above*)
Designated Officer Mr Paul Stringer, Dioc Office (*as above*)
Administrative Secretary Mr Paul Stringer, Dioc Office (*as above*)
Officer Manager Mrs Mandy Blackett, Dioc Office *Tel:* 01388 660010 *email:* mandy.blackett@durham.anglican.org
Pensions Officer Canon Keith Woodhouse, 85 Baulkham Hills, Penshaw, Houghton le Spring DH4 7RZ *Tel:* and *Fax:* 0191 584 3977 *email:* keith.woodhouse@durham.anglican.org
Adviser in Women's Ministry Revd Jennifer Bradshaw, Rectory, 2A Park Avenue, Sunderland SR6 9PU *Tel:* 0191 548 6607 *email:* jennifer.bradshaw@durham.anglican.org

CHURCHES
Advisory Committee for the Care of Churches (*Chairman*) Ven Nick Barker (*as above*)
(*Secretary*) Mr G. W. Heslop, Dioc Office (*as above*) *Tel:* 01388 660001

EDUCATION
Director of Education for Durham and Newcastle Mr Jeremy Fitt, Church House, St John's Terrace, North Shields NE29 6HS *Tel:* 0191 270 4163 *email:* jeremy.fitt@drmnewcanglican.org
Assistant Director (Primary) Mr Brian Hedley (*address as above*) *Tel:* 0191 270 4135 *email:* brian.hedley@drmnewcanglican.org
Assistant Director (Secondary and FE) Mr Mike Davison (*address as above*) *Tel:* 0191 270 4162 *email:* mike.davison@drmnewcanglican.org
Bursar Mrs Eileen Bell (*address as above*) *Tel:* 0191 270 4141 *email:* eileen.bell@drmnewcanglican.org

DIOCESAN RESOURCE TEAM
Director of Ministerial Development and Parish Support Canon Dr Stephen Cherry, Carter House, Pelaw Leazes Lane, Durham DH1 1TB *Tel:* 0191 374 6004 *email:* stephen.cherry@durham.anglican.org
Director of Ordinands Revd Richard Collins, Carter House, Pelaw Leazes Lane, Durham DH1 1TB *Tel:* 0191 374 6015 *email:* ddo@durham.anglican.org

Adviser in Pastoral Care and Counselling Mrs Alison Moore, Carter House, Pelaw Leazes Lane, Durham DH1 1TB *Tel:* 0191 374 6021
email: alison.moore@durham.anglican.org
Youth Ministry Adviser Mr Nicholas Rowark, Carter House, Pelaw Leazes Lane, Durham DH1 1TB *Tel:* 0191 374 6008
email: nick.rowark@durham.anglican.org
Children's Ministry Adviser Mrs Sharon Pritchard, Carter House, Pelaw Leazes Lane, Durham DH1 1TB *Tel:* 0191 374 6019
email: sharon.pritchard@ddemt.co.uk
Continuing Ministerial Education Officer Canon Dr Stephen Cherry (address as above)
Ecumenism Resources Officer Revd Sheelagh Aston, 37 Brancepeth Road, Oxclose, Washington NE38 0LA *Tel:* 0191 415 9468
email: sheelaghaston@yahoo.co.uk
Inspired North East Development Officer (Supporting Church Buildings) Mr Peter Biggers, Carter House, Pelaw Leazes Lane, Durham DH1 1TB *Tel:* 0191 374 6018
email: peter.biggers@durham.anglican.org
Liturgical Committee Chairman Canon David Kennedy, 7 The College, Durham DH1 3EQ *Tel:* 0191 375 0242
email: canon.precentor@durhamcathedral.co.uk
Local Church Growth and Development Adviser (Missioner) Canon Judy Hirst, Carter House, Pelaw Leazes Lane, Durham DH1 1TB *Tel:* 0191 374 6014
email: judy.hirst@durham.anglican.org
Social Responsibility Officer Vacant
Stewardship Development Officer Mr Alistair Jenkins, Carter House, Pelaw Leazes Lane, Durham DH1 1TB *Tel:* 0191 374 6016
email: alistair.jenkins@ddemt.co.uk
Warden of Reader Ministry, Bishop of Jarrow, Bishop's House, 25 Ivy Lane, Low Fell, Gateshead. NE9 6QD *Tel:* 0191 491 0917
email: bishop.of.jarrow@durham.anglican.org
Archdeaconry Sub-wardens of Reader Ministry (Sunderland Archdeaconry) Mr David Talbot, 66 Wheatall Drive, Whitburn, Sunderland SR6 7HQ *Tel:* 0191 529 2265
email: talbot886@btinternet.com
(Durham Archdeaconry)
Revd Kevin Dunne, Shincliffe House, Sherburn Hospital, Durham DH1 2SE *Tel:* 0191 372 4993
email: revdunne@btopenworld.com
(Auckland Archdeaconry)
Mrs Hylda Hopper, 3 Dorchester Court, Marlborough Drive, Darlington DL1 5YD
Tel: 01325 460999
email: hyldahopper@aol.com

LINDISFARNE REGIONAL TRAINING PARTNERSHIP

Principal Revd Canon Cathy Rowling, Church House, St John's Terrace, North Shields NE29 6HS *Tel:* 0191 270 4143
email: cathyrowling@lindisfarnertp.org
Director of Studies and Tutor for Ordinands Revd Dr David Bryan, Church House, St John's Terrace, North Shields NE29 6HS *Tel:* 0191 270 4150
email: davidbryan@lindisfarnertp.org
Developing Discipleship Officer Revd Alastair Macnaughton, Church House, St John's Terrace, North Shields NE29 6HS
Tel: 0191 270 4138 or 0191 276 5005
email: alastairmacnaughton@lindisfarnertp.org
IME 4–7 Director Revd Rick Simpson, The Rectory, Brancepeth, Durham DH7 8EL
Tel: 0191 380 0440
email: ricksimpson@lindisfarnertp.org
Tutor for Reader Training Revd Dr Michael Beck, Church House, St John's Terrace, North Shields NE29 6HS *Tel:* 0191 270 4138
email: michaelbeck@lindisfarnertp.org
Administrator Jenny Burton, Church House, St John's Terrace, North Shields NE29 6HS
Tel: 0191 270 4144
email: jennyburton@lindisfarnertp.org

PARTNERSHIP BODIES

DFW Adoption (*Chairman*) Ven Stuart Bain (*as above*); (*Director*) Ms Margaret Bell, Agriculture House, Stonebridge, Durham DH1 3RY
Tel: 0191 386 3719
email: office@dfw.org.uk
Durham-Lesotho Link Executive Officers Revds Rob and Margaret Bianchi, 8 Lindisfarne, Biddick, Washington NE38 7JR *Tel:* 0191 417 0852
email: dleo.bianchi@tiscali.co.uk
Northumbrian Industrial Mission (*Chairman*) Mr Paul Southgate, NIM Office, Sunderland Minster Church, High St West, Sunderland SR1 3ET
Tel: 0191 373 5453
email: director@vip-gb.org
(*Secretary*) Mrs Joan Smith, 64 Cornmoor Rd, Whickham, Newcastle-upon-Tyne NE16 4PY
Tel: 0191 420 1238
Tees Valley Ministry (*Chairman*) Tony Sacco c/o Churches Regional Commission in the North-East, St James' URC, Northumberland Road, Newcastle upon Tyne NE1 8JF
email: tony.sacco@intrainsolutions.co.uk
(*Secretary*) Mr P. Etwell (*same address*)
Tel: 01287 632852
email: peteretwell@sky.com
Chaplaincy to the Arts and Recreation (*Chairman*) Canon Dr J P Cassidy, St Chad's College, University of Durham, 18 North Bailey, Durham DH1 3RH *Tel:* 0191 334 3345
email: j.p.cassidy@dur.ac.uk
Secretary Mr Gary Cox, St Chad's College, University of Durham, 18 North Bailey, Durham DH1 3RH *email:* gary.cox@dur.ac.uk

PRESS AND PUBLICATIONS

Editor of Dioc Directory Mr Ian Boothroyd (*as above*)
Communications Adviser Mr Keith Blundy, Aegies Associates *Tel:* 01325 301220
email: pr@aegies.com or communications@durham.anglican.org

DIOCESAN RECORD OFFICE

Archives and Special Collections, University Library (Palace Green Section), University of Durham, Palace Green, Durham DH1 3RN
Archivist Mr Andrew Gray *Tel:* 0191 334 2972
email: pg.library@durham.ac.uk
(*For diocesan records*)

County Record Office, County Hall, Durham DH1 5UL *Tel:* 0191 383 3253
email: record.office@ durham.gov.uk
(*For parochial records for the whole diocese*)

AREA DEANS

ARCHDEACONRY OF SUNDERLAND

Chester-le-Street Revd David Glover, 27 Wroxton, Biddick, Washington NE38 7NU
Tel: 0191 418 7911
email: htcwashington@tiscali.co.uk

Gateshead Revd Alan Raine, St Andrew's Vicarage, Whinbrooke, Gateshead NE10 8HR
Tel: 0191 469 3257
email: alanraine@virginmedia.com

Gateshead West Revd Tom Jamieson, Barmoor House, 64 Main Road, Ryton NE40 3AJ
Tel: 0191 413 4592
email: tomjamieson@hotmail.com

Houghton-le-Spring (*Acting*) Revd E. Wilkinson, The Vicarage, Front St. Newbottle, Houghton le Spring DH4 4EP *Tel:* 0191 584 3244
email: wilkinson.edward.rev@googlemail.com

Jarrow (*Acting*) *Canon Raymond Dick, Harton Vicarage, 182 Sunderland Road, South Shields NE34 6AH* *Tel:* 0191 427 5538
email: raymonddick@btinternet.com

Wearmouth Revd Dick Bradshaw, Rectory, 2A Park Avenue, Sunderland SR5 9PU
Tel: 0191 548 6607
email: rbradshawbradshaw@btinternet.com

ARCHDEACONRY OF DURHAM

Durham Revd Canon Robert Lawrance, St Cuthbert's Vicarage, 1 Aykley Court, Durham DH1 4NW *Tel:* 0191 384 7825
email: durhamnorthteam@gmail.com

Easington Revd Alan Milne, Vicarage, Church Lane, Murton, Seaham SR7 9RD
Tel and *Fax:* 0191 526 2410
email: revalan17@yahoo.co.uk

Hartlepool Revd Chris Collison, St Hilda's Rectory, Church Close, Hartlepool TS24 0PW
Tel: 01429 267030
email: revchris@hartlepool-sthilda.org.uk

Lanchester Revd Gary Birchall, Vicarage, Front St, Burnopfield, Newcastle-upon-Tyne NE16 6HQ
Tel: 01207 270261
email: gary.birchall@dsl.pipex.com

Sedgefield Revd Keith Lumsdon, St Luke's Vicarage, Church Lane, Ferryhill DL17 8LT
Tel: 01740 651438
email: keithlumsdon@hotmail.com

ARCHDEACONRY OF AUCKLAND

Auckland Canon Neville Vine, 4 Conway Grove, Bishop Auckland DL14 6AF *Tel:* 01388 604397
email: neville.vine@btinternet.com

Barnard Castle Revd Alec Harding, Vicarage, Parsons Lonnen, Newgate, Barnard Castle DL12 8ST *Tel:* 01833 637018
email: alec.harding@durham.anglican.org

Darlington Canon John Dobson, Vicarage, 104 Blackwell Lane, Darlington DL3 8QQ
Tel and *Fax:* 01325 354503
email: john.dobson@durham.anglican.org

Stanhope Revd Vince Fenton, Rectory, 14 Hartside Close, Crook DL15 9NH
Tel: 01388 760939
email: vincent.fenton@durham.anglican.org

Stockton Revd David Brooke, Rectory, Church Lane, Redmarshall, Stockton-on-Tees TS21 1ES
Tel: 01740 630810
email: revdbrooke@stocktonsix.org.uk

DIOCESE OF ELY

Founded in 1109. Cambridgeshire, except for an area in the north-west (PETERBOROUGH) and three parishes in the south (CHELMSFORD); the western quarter of Norfolk; one parish in Bedfordshire.

Population 719,000 Area 1,507 sq m
Full-time Stipendiary Parochial Clergy 115 Benefices 178
Parishes 306 Churches 334
www.ely.anglican.org
Overseas link dioceses: Vellore (Church of South India) (Ecumenical), Church of North Elbe.

BISHOP (68th)

Rt Revd Stephen Conway, The Bishop's House, Ely CB7 4DW *Tel:* 01353 662749
email: bishop@ely.anglican.org

Bishop's Lay Chaplain Dr Bridget Nichols (*same address and tel. no.*)
email: bridget.nichols@ely.anglican.org

Bishop's Personal Assistant (*same address and tel. no.*) Mrs Jane Sansom
email: janemsansom@ely.anglican.org

Bishop's Secretary Mrs Debbie Swinton (*same address and tel. no.*)
email: debbie.swinton@ely.anglican.org

SUFFRAGAN BISHOP

HUNTINGDON Rt Revd Dr David Thomson, 14 Lynn Rd, Ely CB6 1DA [2008] *Tel:* 01353 662137
Fax: 01353 669357
email: suffragan@ely.anglican.org

Bishop's Secretary Mrs Jane Baker (*same address, tel. no. and email*)

CATHEDRAL CHURCH OF THE HOLY AND UNDIVIDED TRINITY

Dean Very Revd Dr Mark Bonney, The Chapter Office, The College, Ely CB7 4DL [2012]
Tel: 01353 667735

Canon Pastor Canon David Pritchard, The Chapter Office, The College, Ely CB7 4DL [2004]
Tel: 01353 660302

Canon Missioner Canon Dr Alan Hargrave, The Chapter House, The College, Ely CB7 4DL [2004]
Tel: 01353 660304

Canon Precentor Canon Dr James Garrard, The Chapter House, The College, Ely CB7 4DL [2008]
Tel: 01353 660335

Administrator Mr John Harrison, The Chapter House, The College, Ely CB7 4DL
Tel: 01353 667735

Director of Music Mr Paul Trepte, The Chapter House, The College, Ely CB7 4DL
Tel: 01353 660336

ARCHDEACONS

CAMBRIDGE Ven John Stuart Beer, St Botolph's Rectory, 1a Summerfield, Cambridge CB3 9HE [2004] *Tel* 01223 350424
Fax: 01223 360929
email: archdeacon.cambridge@ely.anglican.org

HUNTINGDON AND WISBECH Ven Hugh Kyle McCurdy, Whitgift House, The College, Ely CB7 4DL [2005] *Tel:* 01353 658404 (Home)
Tel: 01353 652709 (Office)
Fax: 01353 652745
email: archdeacon.handw@ely.anglican.org

CONVOCATION (MEMBERS OF THE HOUSE OF CLERGY OF THE GENERAL SYNOD)

Proctors for Clergy
Canon Timothy Alban Jones
Revd Michael Booker
Ven Hugh McCurdy

MEMBERS OF THE HOUSE OF LAITY OF THE GENERAL SYNOD

Mrs Janet Perrett
Mr Stephen Tooke
Dr Elaine Storkey

DIOCESAN OFFICERS

Dioc Secretary Graham Shorter, Bishop Woodford House, Barton Rd, Ely CB7 4DX
Tel: 01353 652701
01353 652702 (Direct Line)
Fax: 01353 652745
email: graham.shorter@ely.anglican.org

Chancellor of Diocese The Hon Judge Leonard QC

Registrar of Diocese Mr Peter Beesley, 1 The Sanctuary, London SW1P 3JT *Tel:* 020 7222 5381

DIOCESAN ORGANIZATIONS

Diocesan Office Bishop Woodford House, Barton Rd, Ely CB7 4DX *Tel:* 01353 652701
Fax: 01353 652745
email: office@ely.anglican.org

ADMINISTRATION

Dioc Synod (*Chairman, House of Clergy*) Canon Jonathan Young, Rectory, Parsons Drive, Ellington, Huntingdon PE28 0AU
Tel: 01480 891695

(*Chairman, House of Laity*) Mrs Janet Perrett, 38 Beachampstead Road, Great Staughton PE19 5DX *email:* jrperrett@talktalk.net

(Secretary) Mr Graham Shorter, Dioc Office
Assistant Secretary (Pastoral) Miss Jane Logan, Dioc Office
Finance Committee (Chairman) Mr Hugh Duberly; *(Secretary)* Mr Graham Shorter *(as above)*
Accounts Administrator Vacancy
Dioc Surveyor Mr Stephen Layton, Dioc Office
Board of Patronage (Secretary) Miss Jane Logan, Dioc Office
Designated Officer Mr Graham Shorter *(as above)*

CHURCHES

Advisory Committee for the Care of Churches (Secretary) Miss Jane Logan, Dioc Office
Archdeaconry of Cambridge Church Music Society (Secretary) Mrs. S. Barton, 239 Lichfield Road, Cambridge CB1 3SH *Tel:* 01223 505764 *email:* suzanne_barton@yahoo.com
Ely RSCM Committee (Secretary) Mr K. Diffey, 1 The Maltings, Godmanchester, Cambs PE29 2JR *Tel:* 01480 458846 *email:* diffey@homecall.co.uk

EDUCATION AND TRAINING

email: ed&t@office.ely.anglican.org
web: www.ely.anglican.org/education
Dioc Board of Education and Training (Secretary) Canon Tim Elbourne, Dioc Office
Director of Education and Training Canon Tim Elbourne *(as above)*
Children's Adviser Mrs Julia Chamberlin
Youth Officer Capt David Waters
RE Adviser (Schools) Dr Shirley Hall, Dioc Office
Schools Buildings and Finance Officer Mr David Hicks
Director of Ministry Vacancy
Ministry Officer Revd Christine Worsley
Reader Ministry Contact The Bishop of Huntingdon

MINISTRY

Diocesan Director of Ordinands Revd Anna Matthews *Tel:* 01353 652730 *Fax:* 01353 652745
Readers' Board (Chair) Mr Stephen Mashford, 7a Haggis Gap, Fulbourn, Cambridge CB21 5HD *Tel:* 01223 882163 *email:* sandjmashford@aol.com
Warden Canon Timothy Alban Jones

LITURGICAL COMMITTEE

Secretary Mr Simon Kershaw, 5 Sharp Close, St Ives, Cambs PE27 6UN *Tel:* 01480 381471 *email:* simon@kershaw.org.uk

MISSIONARY AND ECUMENICAL

Council for Mission and Ministry (Chair) The Bishop of Huntingdon *Tel:* 01353 662137
Ecumenical Officer Vacancy

PRESS AND PUBLICATIONS

Bishop's Press Officer Vacancy
Communications Officer Ms Sarah Williams, Dioc Office *Tel:* 01353 652728
Editor of Dioc Directory Mrs Jackie Cox, Dioc Office

DIOCESAN RECORD OFFICES

Dioc Archivist P. M. Meadows, c/o University Library, West Rd, Cambridge CB3 9DR *Tel:* 01223 333141
Cambridgeshire Archives, Shire Hall, Castle Hill, Cambridge CB3 0AP *Principal Archivist* Mr P. C. Saunders *Tel:* 01223 699487/ 699399 *(For parishes in the archdeaconry of Cambridge and the deaneries of Ely and March)*
Huntingdonshire Archives, Grammar School Walk, Huntingdon PE29 3LF *Senior Archivist* Mrs L. S. Akeroyd *Tel:* 01480 375842 *(For parishes in the former archdeaconry of Huntingdon)*
Cambridge Record Office, Shire Hall, Cambridge *(see above) (For parishes in the deaneries of Ely and March)*
Norfolk Record Office, Central Library, Norwich NR2 1NJ *City and County Archivist* Dr John Alban *Tel:* 01603 22233 *(For parishes in the deaneries of Feltwell and Fincham)*
Wisbech and Fenland Museum, Museum Square, Wisbech PE13 1ES *Assistant Curator* Mr J. R. Bell *Tel:* 01945 583817 *(For parishes in the deanery of Wisbech Lynn Marshland)*

DIOCESAN RESOURCE CENTRE

Contact Dioc Resource Centre, Dioc Office

SOCIAL RESPONSIBILITY

Board for Church in Society (Chairman) Canon Alan Hargrave *(see above)*
(Secretary) Dr Hilary Lavis, Dioc Office *Tel:* 01353 652720
Cambridgeshire Deaf Association (Ely Dioc Association for the Deaf) c/o Ms S. Watt, 8 Romsey Terrace, Cambridge
Mothers' Union (President) Mrs Joan Cameron, 5 St Catherine's, Ely CB6 1AP *Tel:* 01353 614467

RURAL AND AREA DEANS

ARCHDEACONRY OF CAMBRIDGE

Bourn Revd Michael Matthews, Vicarage, Broad Lane, Haslingfield, Cambs CB23 1JF *Tel:* 01223 870285
Cambridge North Revd Nick Moir, 10 Lynfield Lane, Chesterton, Cambridge CB4 1DR *Tel:* 01223 303469
Cambridge South Revd Prof Huw Jones, 17 Barrow Road, Cambridge CB2 8AP *Tel:* 01223 358458
Fordham and Quy Canon Timothy Alban Jones, The Vicarage, Cross Green, Soham, Ely, Cambs CB7 5DU *Tel:* 01353 720423
North Stowe Revd James Blandford-Baker, St Andrew's Vicarage, Church St, Histon CB4 9EP *Tel:* 01223 233456

Granta Revd Dr Julie Norris, The Vicarage, 23 Church Lane, Little Abington, Cambridge CB21 6BQ *Tel:* 01223 891350

Shingay Canon Shamus Williams, Vicarage, Church St, Guilden Morden, Royston SG8 0JP *Tel:* 01763 853067

ARCHDEACONRY OF HUNTINGDON AND WISBECH

Ely Revd Peter Taylor, Gravel Head Farm, Downham Common, Lt Downham, Ely CB6 2TY *Tel:* 01353 698714

Fincham and Feltwell Revd Barbara Burton, The Rectory, High Street, Fincham, King's Lynn PE33 9EL *Tel:* 01366 348079

Huntingdon Canon Brian Atling, Blue Cedars, Common Lane, Hemingford Abbots, Huntingdon PE28 9AW *Tel:* 01480 493975

March Revd Nigel Whitehouse, Rectory, 9a St Mary's St, Whittlesey, Peterborough PE7 1BG *Tel:* 01733 203676

St Ives Revd Canon Fred Kilner, The Old White Lion, 125 High Street, Somersham PE28 3EN *Tel:* 01487 842864

St Neots Revd Annette Reed, Vicarage, 24 St James Rd, Little Paxton, Huntingdon PE19 6QW *Tel:* 01480 211048

Wisbech Lynn Marshland Revd Matthew Bradbury, The Vicarage, Church, Wisbech St Mary, Cambs PE13 4RN *Tel:* 01945 410814

Yaxley Canon Malcolm Griffith, 40 Chisenhale, Orton, Waterville, Peterborough PE2 5FP *Tel:* 01753 686042

DIOCESE IN EUROPE

Founded 1980 by union of the Diocese of Gibraltar (founded 1842) and the (Fulham) Jurisdiction of North and Central Europe. Area, Europe, except Great Britain and Ireland; Morocco; Turkey; the Asian countries of the former Soviet Union.

Licensed Clergy 143 Churches and Congregations 295
www.europe.anglican.org

BISHOP OF GIBRALTAR IN EUROPE (3rd)
Rt Revd Dr (Douglas) Geoffrey Rowell, Bishop's Lodge, Church Rd, Worth, Crawley, W Sussex RH10 7RT [2001] *Tel:* 01293 883051
Fax: 01293 884479
email: bishop@europe@churchofengland.org
Bishop's Chaplain Revd Canon Meurig Williams
Bishop's Personal Assistant Mrs Margaret Gibson

SUFFRAGAN BISHOP
IN EUROPE Rt Revd Dr David Hamid, 14 Tufton St, London SW1P 3QZ [2002] *Tel:* 020 7898 1160
Fax: 020 7898 1166
email: david.hamid@churchofengland.org
Bishop's Chaplain and PA Revd Deacon Frances Hiller

HONORARY ASSISTANT BISHOPS
Rt Revd Eric Devenport, 6 Damocles Court, Pottergate, Norwich NR2 1HN [1993]
Tel: 01603 664121
email: eric@edevenport.orangehome.co.uk
Rt Revd John Flack, The Vicarage, 34 Station Road, Nassington, Peterborough PE8 6QB [2003]
Tel: 01780 782271 / 00 44 (0)7810 714056
email: johnrobertflack@hotmail.com
Rt Revd Richard Garrard, 26 Carol Close, Stoke Holy Cross, Norwich NR14 8NN [2001]
Tel: 01508 494165
email: garrard.r.a@btinternet.com
Rt Revd Patrick Harris, Apartment B, Ireton House, Pavillion Gardens, The Park, Cheltenham GL50 2SP [1999] *Tel:* 01242 231376
email: pandvharris@blueyonder.co.uk
Rt Revd Edward Holland, 37 Palfrey St, London W6 9EW [2002] *Tel:* 020 8746 3636
email: ed.holland@btopenworld.com
Rt Revd Michael Manktelow, 14 Little London, Chichester, W Sussex PO19 1NZ [1994]
Tel: 01243 531096
Rt Revd Fernando Soares, Centro Diocesano, Rua de Afonso Albuquerque No 86, Apartado 392, 4431–905 Vila Nova de Gaia, Portugal [1995]
Tel: 00 351 223 754018
Fax: 00 351 223 752016
email: bisposoares@igreja-lusitana.org
Rt Revd David Stancliffe, 15 The Butts, Stanhope, Bishop Auckland, Durham DL13 2UQ
Tel: 01388 526912
email: d.s.stancliffe@durham.ac.uk
Rt Revd John Taylor, 22 Conduit Head Rd, Cambridge CB3 0EY [1998] *Tel:* 01223 313783
email: john.taylor6529@ntlworld.com
Rt Revd David Smith, 34 Cedar Glade, Dunnington, York YO19 5QZ [2002] *Tel:* 01904 481225
email: david@djmhs.force9.co.uk
Rt Revd Dr Stephen Venner, 83 Hathaway Court, Esplanade, Rochester ME1 1QY
Tel: 01634 83878
email: stephen@venner.org.uk
Rt Revd Pierre Whalon, American Cathedral, 23 Avenue George V, 75008 Paris, France [2001]
Tel: 00 33 1 53 23 84 00 (Cathedral)
Fax: 00 33 1 47 23 95 30 (Cathedral)
Tel: 00 33 1 47 20 02 23 (Direct)
Fax: 00 33 1 40 27 03 53 (Home)
email: office@tec-europe.org
Rt Revd Michael Scott-Joynt, Easter House, Funtington, Chichester P018 9LJ [2011]
Tel: 01243 575762
email: michael.scottjoynt1@gmail.com
Rt Revd Michael Turnbull, 67 Strand St, Sandwich CT13 9HN [2003] *Tel:* 01304 611389
email: bstmt@btopenworld.com

CATHEDRAL CHURCH OF THE HOLY TRINITY, GIBRALTAR
Dean Very Revd Dr John Paddock, 41 Jumpers Buildings, Rosia Road, Gibraltar [2008]
Tel: 00 350 200 78377 (Deanery)
Fax: 00 350 200 78463
email: deangib@gibraltar.gi

PRO-CATHEDRAL OF ST PAUL, VALLETTA, MALTA
Chancellor Canon Simon Godfrey, Chancellor's Lodge, St Paul's Anglican Pro-Cathedral, Independence Square, Valletta VLT12, Malta [2009] *Tel:* 00 356 21 22 57 14
Fax: 00 356 21 22 58 67
email: anglican@onvol.net / simonhmgodfrey@googlemail.com

PRO-CATHEDRAL OF THE HOLY TRINITY, BRUSSELS, BELGIUM

Chancellor Canon Dr Robert Innes, Pro-Cathedral of the Holy Trinity, 29 rue Capitaine Crespel, 1050 Brussels [2005] *Tel:* 00 32 2 511 71 83
Fax: 00 32 2 511 10 28
email: chaplain@holytrinity.be

ARCHDEACONS

THE EASTERN ARCHDEACONRY Ven Patrick Curran, c/o British Embassy, Jaurèsgasse 12, 1030 Vienna, Austria [2002] *Tel:* 00 43 1 718 5902 (Home)
Tel: and *Fax:* 00 43 1 714 8900 (Office)
email: office@christchurchvienna.org

NORTH WEST EUROPE (Acting Archdeacon), Revd Canon Meurig Williams, Bishop's Lodge, Church Road, Worth, Crawley, West Sussex RH10 7RN [2012] *Tel:* 01293 883051
Fax: 01293 884479
email: meurig.williams@churchofengland.org

FRANCE (Acting Archdeacon), Revd Ian Naylor, 3 bis rue Pasteur, 64000 Pau, France [2012]
Tel: 00 33 5 59 30 91 84/+33 (0)7885 50980
email: if.naylor@orange.fr

GIBRALTAR Ven David Sutch, St Andrew, Oficina 1, Edificio Jupiter, Avenida Nuestro Padre Jesus Cautivo 74, Los Boliches, 29640 Fuengirola (Malaga), Spain [2008]
Tel: 00 34 952 580 600 (Office)
+34 952 472 140 (Home)
Fax: 00 34 952 580 600 (Office)
email: frdavid@standrews-cofe-spain.com

ITALY AND MALTA Ven Jonathan Boardman, All Saint's Church, Via del Babuino 153, 00187 Rome, Italy [2009] *Tel and Fax:* 39 06 3600 1881
email: j.boardman@allsaintsrome.org (Personal)
office@allsaintsrome.org (Office)

GERMANY AND NORTHERN EUROPE Ven Jonathan LLoyd, Tuborgvej 82, 2900 Hellerup, Copenhagen, Denmark [2010]
Tel: 00 45 39 62 77 36 (Home)
+45 33 11 85 18 (Church)
+45 29 79 40 36 (Mobile)
email: adjonathan@live.com

SWITZERLAND Ven Peter Potter, Jubiläumsplatz 2, CH-3005 Berne, Switzerland [2009]
Tel: 41 31 351 03 43 (Home)
41 31 352 85 67 (Office)
Fax: 41 31 351 05 48
email: peshar@bluewin.ch

CONVOCATION (MEMBER OF THE HOUSE OF CLERGY OF THE GENERAL SYNOD)

Canon Debbie Flach

MEMBERS OF THE HOUSE OF LAITY OF THE GENERAL SYNOD

Lay Canon Mrs Ann Turner
Mrs Madeleine Holmes

DIOCESAN OFFICERS

Dioc Secretary Mr Adrian Mumford, Dioc Office
Chancellor of Diocese The Worshipful Mark Hill, 3 Pump Court, Temple, London EC4Y 7AJ (contact via Dioc Office)
Registrar of Diocese and Bishop's Legal Secretary Mr Aiden Hargreaves-Smith, Winkworth Sherwood, 5 Montague Close, London SE1 9BB *(contact via the Diocesan Office)*
Tel: 020 7898 1155
Fax: 020 7898 1166
email: bron.panter@churchofengland.org

DIOCESAN ORGANIZATIONS

Diocesan Office 14 Tufton St, London SW1P 3QZ
Tel: 020 7898 1155
Fax: 020 7898 1166
email: bron.panter@churchofengland.org

ADMINISTRATION

Dioc Synod Vacancy
(*Lay Vice-President*) Vacancy
(*Secretary*) Mr Adrian Mumford, Dioc Office
Board of Finance (*Chairman*) Mr Michael Hart, c/o Dioc Office; (*Secretary*) Mr Adrian Mumford, Dioc Office

CHURCHES

Faculty Committee (*Secretary*) Mr Adrian Mumford (*as above*)

MINISTRY AND TRAINING

Warden of Readers Rt Revd Dr David Hamid, Dioc Office
Director of Ordinands Revd William Gulliford, Dioc Office
email: william.gulliford@churchofengland.org
or william.gulliford@london.anglican.org
Director of Training Revd Ulla Monberg, Borgmester Jensens Allé 9, 2th, Copenhagen, Denmark *Tel:* 00 45 3526 0660
email: ullamonberg@msn.com *or* ulla.monberg@churchofengland.org

LITURGY

Enquiries to Revd Prof Paul Bradshaw, Notre Dame London Centre, 1 Suffolk Street, London SW1Y 4HG *Tel:* 020 7484 7811
020 7484 7853
email: bradshaw.1@nd.edu

MEDITERRANEAN MISSIONS TO SEAMEN

Administrator Mr Adrian Mumford (*as above*)

PRESS AND PUBLICATIONS

Press and Communications Officer Revd Paul Needle, Dioc Office
Tel: 07712 463806 (Mobile)
email: paul.needle@churchofengland.org
Editor of 'The European Anglican' Revd Paul Needle (*as above*)

DIOCESAN RECORD OFFICE

London Metropolitan Archives, 40 Northampton Road, London EC1R 0HB *Tel:* 020 7332 3820
email: ask.lma@cityoflondon.gov.uk

ARCHBISHOP'S APOKRISARIOI AND REPRESENTATIVES

To the Holy See Very Revd David Richardson, Palazzo Doria Pamphilj, Piazza dei Collegio Romano 2 – Int 7, 00186 Rome, Italy
Tel: 39 06 678 0302
Fax: 39 06 678 0674
email: director@anglicancentre.it

To the Patriarch of Romania, and the Patriarch of Bulgaria Revd Patrick Irwin, British Embassy – Bucharest, Strada Jules Michelet, Nr 22–24, Sector 1, 70154 Bucharest, Romania
Tel: 00 44 740 243789
email: resurrectionbucharest@gmail.com

To the Archbishop of Athens and All Greece Canon Malcolm Bradshaw, c/o British Embassy, Ploutarchou 1, Athens 106 75
Tel and *Fax:* 00 30 210 721 4906 (Home)
email: anglican@otenet.gr

To the Patriarch of Moscow and All Russia Canon Dr Simon Stephens, British Embassy Moscow, Sofiiskaya Naberezhnaya, Moscow 109702
Tel and *Fax:* 007 495 629 0990
email: chaplain@standrewsmoscow.org

To the Patriarch of Serbia Revd Robin Fox, St Mary's Anglican Church, Visegradska 23, 11000 Belgrade, Serbia *Tel:* 00 381 11 3232 948
email: robin.fox@sbb.co.rs

DEANERIES

The archdeaconry of Germany and Northern Europe has Deanery Synods rather than a single Archdeaconry Synod. The names and addresses of the officers are available from the Diocesan Office.

DIOCESE OF EXETER

Transferred to Exeter in 1050, formerly at Crediton in 909. Devon, except for one parish in the south-east (SALISBURY) and one parish in the west (TRURO); Plymouth; Torbay.

Population 1,141,000 Area 2,575 sq m
Full-time Stipendiary Parochial Clergy 194 Benefices 183
Parishes 489 Churches 615
www.exeter.anglican.org
Overseas link diocese: Cyprus and the Gulf; Thika (Kenya).

BISHOP (70th)
Rt Revd Michael Laurence Langrish, The Palace, Exeter EX1 1HY [2000] *Tel:* 01392 272362
Fax: 01392 430923
email: bishop.of.exeter@exeter.anglican.org
[Michael Exon:]
Episcopal Vicar and Chaplain Revd Dr Adrian Hough (*same address*)
email: adrian.hough@exeter.anglican.org
Personal Assistant Ms Sarah Johnson
email: sarah.johnson@exeter.anglican.org
Administrative Secretary Vacancy

SUFFRAGAN BISHOPS
CREDITON Rt Revd Nicholas McKinnel, 32 The Aveue, Tiverton, Devon EX16 4HW [2012]
Tel: 01884 250002
email: bishop.of.crediton@exeter.anglican.org
PLYMOUTH Rt Revd John Ford, 31 Riverside Walk, Tamerton Foliot, Plymouth PL5 4AQ [2006]
Tel: 01752 769836
email: bishop.of.plymouth@exeter.anglican.org

HONORARY ASSISTANT BISHOPS
Rt Revd Ivor Colin Docker, Braemar, Bradley Rd, Bovey Tracey, Newton Abbot TQ13 9EU [1991]
Tel: 01626 832468
Rt Revd Richard Hawkins, 3 Westbrook Close, Whipton, Exeter EX4 8BS [2005] *Tel:* 01392 462622
Rt Revd James Philip Mason, St Maurice's Rectory, 31 Wain Park, Plympton, Plymouth PL7 2HX [2006] *Tel:* 01752 346114
Rt Revd Martin Shaw, 11 Russell Terrace, Exeter EX4 4HX [2010] *Tel:* 01392 663511
*email:*amartinshaw@gmail.com
Rt Revd Alan Winstanley, The Rectory, Shirwell, Barnstaple EX31 4JU [2012] *Tel:* 01271 840436
email: alan.winstanley123@btinternet.com

CATHEDRAL CHURCH OF ST PETER
Dean Very Rev'd Dr Jonathan Draper, The Deanery, 10 Cathedral Close, Exeter EX1 1EZ [2012] *Tel:* 01392 273509 (Office)
Tel: 01392 431266 (Home)
email: dean@exeter-cathedral.org.uk
Canons Residentiary
Precentor Canon Carl Turner, 6 Cathedral Close, Exeter EX1 1EZ [2001] *Tel:* 01392 285976 (Office)
Tel: 01392 272498 (Home)
email: precentor@exeter-cathedral.org.uk
Missioner Canon Anna Norman-Walker, The Old Deanery, The Cloisters, Exeter EX1 1HS [2011]
Tel: 01392 272686 (Office)
Tel: 01392 435526 (Home)
email: missioner@exeter.anglican.org
Chancellor Canon Andrew Godsall, 12 Cathedral Close, Exeter EX1 1EZ [2006]
Tel: 01392 294902 (Office)
Tel: 01392 275756 (Home)
email: andrew.godsall@exeter.anglican.org
Treasurer and Pastor Canon Ian Morter, 9 Cathedral Close, Exeter EX1 1EZ [2010]
Tel: 01392 285987 (Office)
Tel: 01392 758172 (Home)
email: pastor@exeter-cathedral.org.uk
Chapter Canons Mrs Hannah Foster, Mr Jonathan Harris, The Venerable Canon Clive Cohen
Priest Vicars Revd Alison Turner, Revd Philip Darby, Revd Patrick Parks
Cathedral Deacon Revd Andrew Johnson
Head Virger Mr Michael Greaves, 6A Cathedral Close, Exeter EX1 1EZ
Tel: 01392 274779 (Office)
Tel: 01392 479237 (Home)
email: virgers@exeter-cathedral.org.uk
Cathedral Offices 1 The Cloisters, Exeter EX1 1HS
Tel: 01392 255573
Fax: 01392 285986
email: reception@exeter-cathedral.org.uk
Web: www.exeter-cathedral.org.uk
Administrator Mr Paul Snell
Tel: 01392 285973
email: prs@exeter-cathedral.org.uk
Clerk of Works Mr Damian Lawrence
Tel: 01392 285971
email: clerkofworks@exeter-cathedral.org.uk
Liturgy and Music Dept *Tel:* 01392 285984
email: liturgy@exeter-cathedral.org.uk
Director of Music Mr Andrew Millington, 11 Cathedral Close, Exeter EX1 1EZ
Tel: 01392 285985 (Office)
Tel: 01392 277521 (Home)
email: music@exeter-cathedral.org.uk
Assistant Director of Music Mr David Davies, Flat 4 Closter Garth, Exeter EX1 1JS
Tel: 01392 270761 (Office)
Tel: 01392 270877 (Home)
email: adom@exeter-cathedral.org.uk

Third Millennium Campaign Director Mrs Jill Taylor, Cathedral Campaign Office
Tel: 01392 285974
email: campaigndirector@exeter-cathedral.org.uk
Head of Visitor Services Mrs Catherine Escott
Tel: 01392 285983
email: visitors@exeter-cathedral.org.uk

ARCHDEACONS

EXETER Ven Christopher Futcher, Emmanuel House, Station Road, Ide, Exeter EX2 9RS [2012]
Tel: 01392 425577
email: archdeacon.of.exeter@exeter.anglican.org

TOTNES Ven John Rawlings, Blue Hills, Bradley Rd, Bovey Tracey, Newton Abbot TQ13 9EU [2006]
Tel: 01626 832064
Fax: 01626 834947
email: archdeacon.of.totnes@exeter.anglican.org

BARNSTAPLE Ven David Gunn-Johnson, Stage Cross, Sanders Lane, Bishop's Tawton, Barnstaple EX32 0BE [2003]
Tel: 01271 375475
Fax: 01271 377934
email: archdeacon.of.barnstaple@exeter.anglican.org

PLYMOUTH Ven Ian Chandler, St Mark's House, 46a Cambridge Road, Ford, Plymouth PL2 1PU
Tel: 01752 202401
email: archdeacon.of.plymouth@exeter.anglican.org

CONVOCATION (MEMBERS OF THE HOUSE OF CLERGY OF THE GENERAL SYNOD)

Proctors for Clergy
Preb Samuel Philpott
Revd Roderick Thomas
Revd Preb Douglas Dettmer
Revd Canon Andrew Godsall

MEMBERS OF THE HOUSE OF LAITY OF THE GENERAL SYNOD

Mrs Anneliese Barrell
Mr Jack Shelley
Miss Emma Forward
Mrs Anne Foreman
Mr Charles Hodgson

Dioc Synod (*Chairman, House of Clergy*) Revd Preb Douglas Dettmer, Rectory, Thorverton, Exeter EX5 5NR
Tel: 01392 860332
(*Secretary, House of Clergy*) Revd Gilly Maude, Vicarage, 17 Seafields, Dartmouth Road, Goodrington, Paignton TQ4 6NY *Tel:* 01803 846335
email: gillian.maude@btinternet.com
(*Chairman, House of Laity*) Mr Charles Hodgson, The Smithy, East Worlington, Crediton EX17 4SY
Tel: 01884 861571
email: catherine-charles.hodgson@virgin.net
(*Secretary, House of Laity*) Mr Graham Lea, 2 Thornyville Close, Oreston, Plymouth PL9 7LE
Tel: 01752 403392
Synod Secretary Mr Mark Beedell, The Old Deanery

DIOCESAN OFFICERS

Dioc Secretary Mr Mark Beedell, The Old Deanery, The Cloisters, Exeter EX1 1HS
Tel: 01392 272686
Fax: 01392 499594
email: mark.beedell@exeter.anglican.org
Chancellor of Diocese Hon Sir Andrew McFarlane, Royal Courts of Justice, Strand, London WC2A 2LL *Tel:* 020 7947 6008
Deputy Chancellor of Diocese Mr Gregory Percy Jones, Francis Taylor Building, Inner Temple, London EC4Y 7BY *Tel:* 020 7353 8415
Registrar of Diocese and Bishop's Legal Secretary Mr Martin Follett, Michelmores, Woodwater House, Pynes Hill, Exeter EX2 5WR *Tel:* 01392 687421
email: mjf@michelmores.com
Deputy Registrar Mr Christopher Butcher, Michelmores *Tel:* 01392 687419
email: cnb@michelmores.com

THE DEPARTMENT FOR SUPPORT SERVICES

Director and Dioc Secretary Mr Mark Beedell (*as above*)
Asst Dioc Secretary Dr Ed Moffatt, The Old Deanery *Tel:* 01392 294928
Fax: 01392 499594
email: ed.moffatt@exeter.anglican.org
Diocesan Office The Old Deanery, The Cloisters, Exeter EX1 1HS *Tel:* 01392 272686
Fax: 01392 499594
email: admin@exeter.anglican.org

ADMINISTRATION

Board of Finance (*Chairman*) David Cain, Venn Farm, Kingsnympton, Umberleigh EX37 9TR
Tel: 01769 572448
email: twelvetwentyfive@msn.com
(*Secretary*) Mr Mark Beedell (*as above*)
Parsonages Committee (*Secretary*) Mr Graham Davies, The Old Deanery *Tel:* 01392 294954
Fax: 01392 499594
email: graham.davies@exeter.anglican.org
Dioc Surveyors Mr Peter Stanton and Mr Mark Lewis, The Old Deanery *Tel:* 01392 294952
Fax: 01392 499594
email: peter.stanton@exeter.anglican.org *or* mark.lewis@exeter.anglican.org
Smith & Dunn, Alliance House, Cross St, Barnstaple EX31 1BA (*for Barnstaple Archdeaconry*)
Tel: 01271 327878
Fax: 01271 328288
Mission and Pastoral Committee (*Secretary*) Mr Alistair Sutherland *Tel:* 01392 294910
email: alistair.sutherland@exeter.anglican.org
Board of Patronage (*Chairman*) Mrs Shirley-Ann Williams, 2 Katherine's Lane, Ridgeway, Ottery St Mary EX11 1FB *Tel:* 01404 811064
Trusts Mrs Jane Scriven, The Old Deanery
Tel: 01392 294913
email: jane.scriven@exeter.anglican.org
Designated Officer Mr Alistair Sutherland (*as above*)

SAFEGUARDING UNIT
Mrs Sue Chamberlain, The Old Deanery
Tel: 01392 294912
email: sue.chamberlain@exeter.anglican.org

CHURCHES
Dioc Advisory Committee for the Care and Maintenance of Churches (*Chairman*) Revd Nigel Freathy; (*Secretary*) Mrs Louise Bartlett, The Old Deanery, *Tel:* 01392 294944, *email:* louise.bartlett@exeter.anglican.org
Church Buildings Strategy Committee (*Secretary*) Miss Eve Van der Steen
email: eve@exeter.anglican.org

COMMUNICATIONS
Director of Communications Mrs Rebecca Paveley
Publications Officer Mrs Karen Brookes-Ferrari
The Church of England, Devon (Diocesan News)
Tel: 01392 294905
07812 110636 (Mobile)
email: communications@exeter.anglican.org
Web: www.exeter.anglican.org

THE COUNCIL FOR WORK WITH CHILDREN AND YOUNG PEOPLE
Diocesan Director of Education Mr Philip Mantell, The Old Deanery *Tel:* 01392 294950
Fax: 01392 294966
email: philip.mantell@exeter.anglican.org
Executive Assistant Vacancy
Diocesan Education Officer Mrs Tatiana Wilson
Tel: 01392 294941
email: tatiana.wilson@exeter.anglican.org
Revd Richard Maudsley *Tel:* 01392 294961
email: richard.maudsley@exeter.anglican.org
Mrs Penny Burnside *Tel:* 01392 294942
email: penny.burnside@exeter.anglican.org
Dioc Church Schools Liaison Officer Mrs Christina Mabin *Tel:* 01392 294939
Children's Work Adviser Miss Katherine Lyddon
Tel: 01392 294936
email: katherine.lyddon@exeter.anglican.org
Dioc Youth Work Adviser Mr Paul Reisbach, The Old Deanery *Tel:* 01392 294932
email: paul.reisbach@exeter.anglican.org
Dioc Youth Church Adviser Revd James Grier
Tel: 01392 294934
email: james.grier@exeter.anglican.org
Church Schools Surveyors Richard Power and Jason Down *Tel:* 01392 294952
Fax: 01392 294967
email: school.premises@exeter.anglican.org *or* richard.power@exeter.anglican.org *or* jason.down@exeter.anglican.org
Church Schools Funding Adviser Raymond Twohig
Tel: 01392 294952
email: raymond.twohig@exeter.anglican.org

THE COUNCIL FOR WORSHIP AND MINISTRY
Director, Officer for Non-Stipendiary Ministry and Continuing Ministerial Education Canon Andrew Godsall, The Old Deanery *Tel:* 01392 294902
Council Administrator Mrs Justine Tear
Tel: 01392 294920
email: justine.tear@exeter.anglican.org
Director of Ordinands, Adviser for Vocations Revd Becky Totterdell, The Palace, Exeter EX1 1HY
Tel: 01392 477702
email: ddo@exeter.anglican.org
Administrator Miss Louise Spencer, The Palace, Exeter EX1 1HY *Tel:* 01392 477702
email: louise.spencer@exeter.anglican.org
Adviser for Women's Ministry Revd Canon Jane Wilson, 17 Ashleigh Park, Bampton, Tiverton EX16 9LF *Tel:* 01884 332135
email: janeoffwell@aol.com
Local Stewardship Adviser, North Devon Mr Paul Mason *Tel:* 01409 281548
email: paulgidcott@aol.com
Local Stewardship Adviser, South Devon Preb Mark Bate *Tel:* 01392 833485
email: morleybate@freeuk.com
Board of Readers (*Secretary*) Mr Ronald Edinborough, The Old Deanery
Tel: 01392 294907
email: ron.edinborough@exeter.anglican.org
Adult Education Adviser Vacancy
Warden of Readers Ven David Gunn-Johnson, Stage Cross, Sanders Lane, Bishop's Tawton, Barnstaple EX32 0BE *Tel:* 01271 375475
Fax: 01271 377934
email: archdeacon.of.barnstaple@exeter.anglican.org
Co-ordinator Spiritual Direction Revd Helen Bays, 14 Stockton Hill, Dawlish EX7 9LP
Tel: 07722 106632
email: hbays@talktalk.net
Mission Community Teams Adviser Vacancy
Local Ministry Teams Adviser Vacancy
Dioc Consultant for Worship and Music Mr Andrew Maries *Tel:* 01884 34389
email: maries@keynotetrust.org.uk
Web: www.exeterdlc.org.uk

THE COUNCIL FOR MISSION AND UNITY
Director and Diocesan Missioner Revd Canon Anna Norman-Walker, The Old Deanery
Tel: 01392 294903
email: missioner@exeter.anglican.org
Administrator Mrs Justine Tear, The Old Deanery
Tel: 01392 294920
email: justine.tear@exeter.anglican.org
Chaplain with Deaf People Revd Catherine Carlyon, The Old Deanery
Tel: 01392 294909 (voice and text)
Fax: 01392 294965
07855 098953 (Mobile)
email: catherinecarlyon@btopenworld.com
Ministry of Healing and Deliverance The Archdeacon of Totnes
County Ecumenical Officer Revd Sabrina Groeschel, 1 Furze Road, Woodbury, Exeter EX5 1PF
Tel: 01395 579795
email: sabrina.groeschel@churchestogetherdevon.co.uk

Cyprus and the Gulf Link (*Chairman*) Revd Charles Deacon, The Old Deanery *Tel:* 01392 294962
email: charles.deacon@exeter.anglican.org
Thika Link Mrs Jane Inwood (parish links)
Tel: 01647 252519
email: thika.link@exeter.anglican.org
World Development Adviser Vacancy

COUNCIL FOR CHURCH AND SOCIETY

Director Mr Martyn Goss, The Old Deanery
Tel: 01392 294924
Fax: 01392 499594
email: martyn@exeter.anglican.org
Social Responsibility Officer Miss Sally Farrant, The Old Deanery *Tel:* 01392 294918
email: sally.farrant@exeter.anglican.org
Family Life and Marriage Education Coordinator Vacancy
Rural Officer Mrs Sue Tucker, Quither Farm, Quither, Milton Abbot, Tavistock PL19 0PZ
Tel: 01822 860177 (Work)
01392 294921 (Office)
email: sue.tucker@exeter.anglican.org

MISCELLANEOUS ORGANIZATIONS

Widows and Dependants Revd Tony Mortimer, 97 Egremont Road, Exmouth EX8 1SA
Tel: 01395 271390
(Exeter Archdeaconry except Kenn Deanery)
*email:*tpmortimer@googlemail.com
Vacancy (Barnstaple, Plymouth and Totnes Archdeaconries and Kenn Deanery)

DIOCESAN RECORD OFFICE

Devon Record Office, Great Moor House, Bittern Rd, Sowton Industrial Estate, Exeter EX2 7NL
Archivist Mr John Draisey *Tel:* 01392 384253
email: devrc@devon.gov.uk

RURAL DEANS

ARCHDEACONRY OF EXETER

Aylesbeare Revd Canon David Price, 14 The Broadway, Exmouth EX8 2NW
Tel: 01395 269811
email: rea@14broadway.eclipse.co.uk
Cadbury Revd Preb Douglas Dettmer, Rectory, Thorverton, Exeter EX5 5NR *Tel:* 01392 860332
Christianity Revd Robin Eastoe, The Rectory, 10 Victoria Park Road, Exeter EX2 4NT
Tel: 01392 677150
email: theeastoes@btinternet.com
Cullompton Revd Barry Dugmore, The Vicarage, Bakers Hill, Tiverton EX16 5NE
Tel: 01884 252526
email: vicar@tivertonchurch.org
Honiton Revd Alastair McCollum, The Vicarage, Kilmington, Axminster EX13 7RF
Tel: 01297 33156
email: alastair.mccollum@btinternet.com
Kenn Revd Martin Wood, The Rectory, Church Lane, Cheriton Bishop, Exeter EX6 6HY
Tel: 01647 24119
email: revwood@btinternet.com
Ottery Revd Roger Trumper, All Saints Vicarage, All Saints Road, Sidmouth EX10 8ES
Tel: 01395 515963
email: roger.thetrumpers@virgin.net
Tiverton Revd Barry Dugmore, The Vicarage, Bakers Hill, Tiverton EX16 5NE *Tel:* 01884 252526
email: vicar@tivertonchurch.org

ARCHDEACONRY OF TOTNES

Moreton Revd David Sherwood, The Rectory, Copperwood Close, Ashburton, Newton Abbot TQ13 7JQ *Tel:* 01364 652968
email: revdcs@yahoo.co.uk
Newton Abbot and Ipplepen Revd Mark Smith, The Vicarage, Daws Meadow, Kingsteignton, Newton Abbot TQ12 3UA *Tel:* 01626 355127
email: marksmith487@btinternet.com
Okehampton Revd Dr Ruth Hansford, The Rectory, Hatherleigh, Okehampton EX20 3JY
Tel: 01837 810314
email: maggiethecat@waitrose.com
Torbay Revd Gillian Maude, Vicarage, 17 Seafields, Dartmouth Road, Paignton TQ4 6NY
Tel: 01803 846335
email: gillian.maude@btinternet.com
Totnes Revd Julian Ould, The Rectory, Northgate Castle Hill, Totnes TQ9 5NX *Tel:* 01803 865615
email: julian@totnesrectory.co.uk
Woodleigh Revd Daniel French, The Vicarage, Devon Road, Salcombe TQ8 8HJ
Tel: 01548 842853
email: cybervicar@gmail.com

ARCHDEACONRY OF BARNSTAPLE

Barnstaple Revd Giles King-Smith, The Vicarage, Springfield Road, Woolacombe EX34 7BX
Tel: 01271 870467
email: clareandgiles@aol.com
Hartland Revd Shirley Henderson, Vicarage, North Road, Hartland, Bideford EX39 6BP
Tel: 01237 440229
email: shirely.1949@hotmail.co.uk
Holsworthy Revd Kathy Roberts, The Rectory, Black Torrington, Beaworthy EX21 5PU
Tel: 01409 231279
email: robertskm8@aol.com
Shirwell Revd Shaun O'Rourke, The Rectory, Barnstaple Hill, Swimbridge, Barnstaple EX32 0PH *Tel:* 01271 830590
email: revd.shaun@googlemail.com
South Molton Revd Preb David Rudman, The Rectory, Kingsnympton, Umberleigh EX37 9ST
Tel: 01769 580457
email: rudman1064@gmail.com
Torrington Revd Lawrence MacLean, The Vicarage, Calf Street, Torrington EX38 8EA
Tel: 01805 622166
email: lm61@live.co.uk

ARCHDEACONRY OF PLYMOUTH

Ivybridge Revd Freddie Denman, The Vicarage, Sparkwell, Plymouth PL7 5DB
Tel: 01752 837218
email: freddy.sparkwell@hotmail.co.uk

Devonport Revd Stephen Beach, Vicarage, Agaton Road, St Budeaux, Plymouth PL5 2EW
Tel: 01752 361019
email: stephenbeach@btinternet.com

Moorside Revd David Gill, Vicarage, 53 Whitsoncross Lane, Tamerton Foliot, Plymouth PL5 4NT *Tel:* 01752 771033
email: dbmgill@tiscali.co.uk

Sutton Revd Karl Freeman, Rectory, 9 Seymour Drive, Mannamead, Plymouth PL3 5BG
Tel: 01752 248601
email: karldesk@blueyonder.co.uk

Tavistock Revd Nicholas Law, The Rectory, Bere Alston, Yelverton PL20 7HQ *Tel:* 01822 840229
email: nicklaw2@tiscali.co.uk

DIOCESE OF GLOUCESTER

Founded in 1541. Gloucestershire except for a few parishes in the north (WORCESTER); a few parishes in the south (BRISTOL) and one parish in the east (OXFORD); the northern third of South Gloucestershire; two parishes in Wiltshire; a small area in south-west Warwickshire; a few parishes in the southern part of Worcestershire.

Population 631,000 Area 1,140 sq m
Full-time Stipendiary Parochial Clergy 117 Benefices 110
Parishes 304 Churches 388
www.gloucester.anglican.org

BISHOP (40th)
Rt Revd Michael Francis Perham, The Bishop of Gloucester's Office, 2 College Green, Gloucester GL1 2LR [2004] *Tel:* 01452 410022 ext. 270
Fax: 01452 308324
email: bshpglos@glosdioc.org.uk
Home address: Bishopscourt, Pitt St, Gloucester GL1 2BQ *Tel:* 01452 524598
[Michael Gloucester]
Bishop's Chaplain Revd John Paul Hoskins (*same address and fax no.; tel. no. as above, ext. 268*)
email: jphoskins@glosdioc.org.uk
Bishop's Secretary Mrs Diane Best (*same address and tel. no.*) *email:* dbest@glosdioc.org.uk

SUFFRAGAN BISHOP
TEWKESBURY Rt Revd John Stewart Went, 2 College Green, Gloucester GL1 2LR [1995]
Tel: 01452 410022 ext 228
Fax: 01452 308324
email: bshptewk@star.co.uk
Home address: Bishop's House, Staverton, Cheltenham GL51 0TW *Tel:* 01242 680188
Fax: 01242 680233

HONORARY ASSISTANT BISHOPS
Rt Revd Humphrey Taylor, 10 High St, Honeybourne, Evesham WR11 7PQ [2003]
Tel: 01386 834846
Rt Revd David Jennings, Laurel Cottage, East End, Northleach, Cheltenham GL54 3ET
Tel: 01451 860743

CATHEDRAL CHURCH OF ST PETER AND THE HOLY AND INDIVISIBLE TRINITY
Dean Very Revd Stephen Lake, The Deanery, 1 Miller's Green, Gloucester GL1 2BP [2011]
Tel: 01452 524167
email: dean@gloucestercathedral.org.uk
Dean's Secretary Mrs Fiona Price, The Cathedral Office, 12 College Green, Gloucester GL1 2LX
Tel: 01452 508217
email: fiona@gloucestercathedral.org.uk
The Cathedral Office, 12 College Green, Gloucester GL1 2LX *Tel:* 01452 528095
Fax: 01452 300469
Web: www.gloucestercathedral.org.uk

Canons Residentiary
Precentor Canon Neil Heavisides, 7 College Green, Gloucester GL1 2LX [1993]
Tel: 01452 523987
email: nheavisides@gloucestercathedral.org.uk
Canon Pastor Canon Celia Thomson, 3 Miller's Green, Gloucester GL1 2BN [2003]
Tel: 01452 415824
email: cthomson@gloucestercathedral.org.uk
Ven Jackie Searle, 2 College Green, Gloucester GL1 2LR [2012] *Tel:* 01452 835594
Fax: 01452 308324
email: archdglos@glosdioc.org.uk
Canon Nikki Arthy, The Rectory, Hempsted, Gloucester GL2 5LW *Tel:* 01452 523808
email: nikkiarthy@btinternet.com
Chapter Steward Mr Mark Beckett, The Cathedral Office (*as above*) *Tel:* 01452 508216
email: mbeckett@gloucestercathedral.org.uk
Director of Music Mr Adrian Partington, 7 Miller's Green, Gloucester GL1 2BN
Tel: 01452 508212
email: a.partington@gloucestercathedral.org.uk
Assistant Director of Music Mr Anthony Gowing, 14 College Green, Gloucester GL1 2LX
Tel: 01452 508212
email: anthony@gloucestercathedral.org.uk
Music and Liturgy Administrator Mrs Helen Sims, The Cathedral Office (*as above*) *Tel:* 01452 508212
email: helen@gloucestercathedral.org.uk

ARCHDEACONS
GLOUCESTER Ven Jackie Searle, 2 College Green, Gloucester GL1 2LR [2012] *Tel:* 01452 835594
Fax: 01452 308324
email: archdglos@glosdioc.org.uk
CHELTENHAM Ven Robert Springett, 2 College Green, Gloucester GL1 2LY [2010]
Tel: 01452 835594
Fax: 01452 308324
email: archdchelt@glosdioc.org.uk

CONVOCATION (MEMBERS OF THE HOUSE OF CLERGY OF THE GENERAL SYNOD)
Proctors for Clergy
Revd Dr Sandra Millar
Revd Canon Dr Michael Parsons
Revd Canon Celia Thomson

MEMBERS OF THE HOUSE OF LAITY OF THE GENERAL SYNOD
Dr William Belcher
Mr Graham Smith
Prof Jenny Tann

DIOCESAN OFFICERS
Dioc Secretary Dr Kevin Brown, Church House, College Green, Gloucester GL1 2LY
Tel: 01452 410022 ext. 223
Fax: 01452 308324
email: kbrown@glosdioc.org.uk
Executive Assistant Ms Andrea Goodman (same address) *Tel:* 01452 410022 ext. 223
email: agoodman@glosdioc.org.uk
Chancellor of Diocese Chancellor June Rodgers, 2 Harcourt Buildings, The Temple, London EC4Y 9DB
Registrar of Diocese and Bishop's Legal Secretary Vacancy

DIOCESAN ORGANIZATIONS
Diocesan Office Church House, College Green, Gloucester GL1 2LY *Tel:* 01452 410022
Fax: 01452 308324
email: church.house@glosdioc.org.uk
Web: www.gloucester.anglican.org

ADMINISTRATION
Dioc Synod (*Vice President, House of Clergy*) Revd Canon Richard Mitchell. The Vicarage, School Lane, Shurdington, Cheltenham GL51 4TF
Tel: 0242 702911
email: richard.mitchell@talk21.com
(*Vice-President, House of Laity*) Canon Ian Marsh, Mynd House, The Highlands, Painswick GL6 6SL
Tel: 01452 812829
email: ian@marshfamily.eclipse.co.uk
(*Secretary*) Dr Kevin Brown, Church House
Board of Finance (*Chairman*) Mrs Mary Adlard, The Pippins, Gambles Lane, Woodmancote, Cheltenham GL52 9PU *Tel:* 01684 850033
email: madlard@w-h-r.co.uk
(*Secretary*) Dr Kevin Brown (*as above*)
(*Assistant Secretary*) Canon Jonathan MacKechnie-Jarvis, Church House
Director of Finance Mr Benjamin Preece-Smith, Church House
Houses Committee (*Secretary*) Ms Juliet Weston, Church House
Pastoral Committee (*Secretary*) Dr Kevin Brown (*as above*)
Board of Patronage (*Secretary*) Canon Jonathan MacKechnie-Jarvis (*as above*)
Designated Officer Dr Kevin Brown (*as above*)
Trust (*Secretary*) Canon Jonathan MacKechnie-Jarvis (*as above*)
Glebe Committee (*Secretary*) Ms Juliet Weston (*as above*)
HR Manager Mrs Judith Knight, Church House

CHURCHES
Advisory Committee for the Care of Churches (*Chairman*) Mr Henry Russell, Ley Mary Farmhouse, Windrush, Burford, Oxon OX18 4TS
Tel: 01451 844397
(*Secretary*) Canon Jonathan MacKechnie-Jarvis (*as above*)

CHILDREN AND YOUNG PEOPLE DEPARTMENT
Director of Children and Young People Department Canon Helena Arnold, 4 College Green, Gloucester GL1 2LR *Tel:* 01452 410022 ext. 272
email: harnold@glosdioc.org.uk
Advisers to Schools Mrs Shahne Vickery (*same address*) *Tel:* 01452 410022 ext. 259
email: svickery@glosdioc.org.uk
Adviser to Governors Mrs Linda Olijnyk (*same address*) *Tel:* 01452 410022 ext. 239
email: lolijnyk@glosdioc.org.uk
Buildings and Admissions Adviser Mr Rob Stephens (*same address*) *Tel:* 01452 410022 ext. 242
email: rstephens@glosdioc.org.uk
Dioc Youth Officer Revd Steve Jarvis (*same address*)
Tel: 01452 410022 ext. 282
email: sjarvis@glosdioc.org.uk
Dioc Children's Officer Revd Dr Sandra Millar (*same address*) *Tel:* 01452 410022 ext. 246
email: smillar@glosdioc.org.uk

MINISTRY
Director of Discipleship and Ministry Vacancy
Director of Lay Ministry and Parish Development Canon Kathy Lawrence, 4 College Green, Gloucester GL1 2LR *Tel:* 01452 410022 ext. 263
email: klawrence@glosdioc.org.uk
Director of Ordinands Revd Ian Bussell (*same address*) *Tel:* 01452 410022 ext. 292
Dean of Women Clergy Revd Robbin Clark, 36 Larkhay Road, Gloucester GL3 3NR
Tel: 01452 547469
email: rclark@glosdioc.org.uk
NSM Officer Vacancy
Chaplain for Deaf and Hard of Hearing People Revd Steve Morris, The Vicarage, 27a Barnwood Avenue, Gloucester GL4 3AB *Tel:* 01452 619531
email: spadework@fsmail.net
Warden of Readers Revd Stephen Ware, 4 College Green, Gloucester GL1 2LR
Tel: 01452 410022 ext. 261
email: sware@glosdioc.org.uk
Registrar of Readers Revd Gillian Williams (*same address*) *Tel:* 01452 410022 ext 260
email: gwilliams@glosdioc.org.uk
Discipleship and Ministry Development Officers
Canon Kathy Lawrence (*as above*)
Revd Brian Parfitt (*same address*)
Tel: 01452 410022 ext. 238
email: bparfitt@glosdioc.org.uk
Diocesan Ecumenical Officer Vacancy

Diocesan Worship Officer Revd David Deboys (*same address*) *Tel:* 01452 410022 ext 280
email: ddeboys@glosdioc.org.uk

BISHOP'S WORSHIP, PRAYER AND SPIRITUALITY GROUP

Chair Revd Susan Bailey, 28 Burleigh Way, Wickwar, Wotton-under-Edge GL12 8LR
Tel: 01454 294112
email: susan.m.bailey@gmail.com
Secretary Vacancy

PRESS AND PUBLICATIONS

Communications Officer Mrs Lucy Taylor, Church House *Tel:* 01452 410022 ext. 250
07811 174125 (Mobile)
email: ltaylor@glosdioc.org.uk

DIOCESAN RECORD OFFICE

Gloucestershire Records Office, Clarence Row, Gloucester GL1 3DW *Dioc Archivist* Ms Heather Forbes *Tel:* 01452 425295
email: records@gloscc.gov.uk (Office)
email: heather.forbes@gloucestershire.gov.uk

DIOCESAN RESOURCE CENTRE

Manager SIAS Mrs Hannah Hauxwell, 9 College Green, Gloucester GL1 2LX
Tel: 01452 410022 ext 277
email: hhauxwell@glosdioc.org.uk

SOCIAL RESPONSIBILITY

Director of Social Responsibility Vacancy
Assistant Dioc Officer for Social Responsibility Mrs Fran Tolond, 1 Mickle Mead, Highnam, Gloucester GL2 8NF *Tel:* 01452 383441
email: glosasro@star.co.uk
County Ecumenical Officer Revd Dr Alison Evans, Elm Farm House, High St, Kings Stanley, Stonehouse GL10 3JF *Tel:* 01453 824034
email: malcolm.alison@btinternet.com
Accord Mrs Deborah Curram, Windyridge, Amberley, Stroud GL5 5AA *Tel:* 01453 872546
email: deborahcurram@googlemail.com

Rural and Environmental Officer Revd Simon Topping, St Peter's House, 2 College Street, Gloucester GL1 2NE *Tel:* 01452 521438
Ecumenical Adviser Vacancy Church House
Tel: 01452 410022

AREA DEANS

ARCHDEACONRY OF CHELTENHAM

Cheltenham Revd Dr Tudor Griffiths, 38 Sydenham Villas Road, Cheltenham GL52 6DZ
Tel: 01242 234470
email: tudorg@stmstm.org.uk
Cirencester Canon Leonard Doolan, The Vicarage, 1 Dollar Street, Cirencester GL7 2AJ
Tel: 01285 659317
email: vicarcirencester@hotmail.com
North Cotswolds Canon Veronica James, Rectory, Copse Hill Road, Lower Slaughter, Cheltenham GL54 2HY *Tel:* 01451 821777
email: flojoefred@hotmail.com
Tewkesbury and Winchcombe Canon Paul Williams, Abbey House, Abbey Precinct, Church Street, Tewkesbury GL20 5SR *Tel:* 01684 856144
email: vicar@tewkesburyabbey.org.uk

ARCHDEACONRY OF GLOUCESTER

Forest South Canon Philippa Brunt, Tidenham Vicarage, Gloucester Rd, Tutshill, Chepstow, Monmouthshire NP16 7DH *Tel:* 01594 562828
email: pabrunt@btinternet.com
Gloucester City Revd David Smith, St George's Vicarage, Grange Road, Tuffley, Gloucester GL4 0PE *Tel* and *Fax:* 01452 520851
email: draesmith@blueyonder.co.uk
Severn Vale Canon Richard Mitchell, Vicarage, School Lane, Shurdington, Cheltenham GL51 4TF
Tel: 01242 702911
email: richard.mitchell@talk21.com
Stroud Revd Dr Chris Collingwood, The Rectory, Butt Street, Minchinhampton, Stroud GL6 9JP
Tel: 01453 882289
email: rector@minchchurch.org.uk
Wotton Revd Rob Axford, Vicarage, Culverhay, Wotton-Under-Edge GL12 7LS
Tel: 01453 842175
email: rob.axford@metronet.co.uk

DIOCESE OF GUILDFORD

Founded in 1927. The western two-thirds of Surrey south of the Thames, except for a small area in the north-east (SOUTHWARK); areas of north-east Hampshire; a few parishes in Greater London; one parish in West Sussex.

Population 1,011,000 Area 538 sq m
Full-time Stipendiary Parochial Clergy 162 Benefices 139
Parishes 164 Churches 217
www.cofeguildford.org.uk
Overseas link diocese: IDWAL (Inter-Diocesan West Africa Link) – Nigeria.

BISHOP (9th)
Rt Revd Christopher Hill, Willow Grange, Woking Rd, Guildford GU4 7QS [2004]
Tel: 01483 590500
Fax: 01483 590501
Bishop's Chaplain Revd Mark Heather
email: mark.heather@cofeguildford.org.uk
Bishop's Personal Assistant Mary Morris
email: mary.morris@cofeguildford.org.uk

SUFFRAGAN BISHOP
DORKING Rt Revd Ian James Brackley, Dayspring, 13 Pilgrim's Way, Guildford GU4 8AD [1996]
Tel: 01483 570829
Fax: 01483 567268
email: bishop.ian@cofeguildford.org.uk
Bishop's Personal Assistant Muriel Mulvany
email: muriel.mulvany@cofeguildford.org.uk

CATHEDRAL CHURCH OF THE HOLY SPIRIT
Dean Vacancy *Tel:* 01483 547861 (Office)
email: dean@guildford-cathedral.org
Dean's Personal Assistant Mrs Cathy Mansell
Tel: 01483 547862 (Office)
email: cathy@guildford-cathedral.org
Cathedral Office Guildford Cathedral, Stag Hill, Guildford, Surrey GU2 7UP *Tel:* 01483 547860
Fax: 01483 303350
email: reception@guildford-cathedral.org
Canons Residentiary
Sub-Dean and Precentor Revd Canon Dr Nicholas Thistlethwaite, 3 Cathedral Close, Guildford GU2 7TL [1999] *Tel:* 01483 547865
email: precentor@guildford-cathedral.org
Canon Residentiary and University Chaplain Revd Canon Andrew Bishop, 6 Cathedral Close, Guildford GU2 7TL *Tel:* 07891 994069
email: a.bishop@surrey.ac.uk
Canon Residentiary Revd Canon Dr Julie Gittoes, 4 Cathedral Close, Guildford GU2 7TL
Tel: 07702 151173
email: julie@guildford-cathedral.org
Canon Residentiary Ven Stuart Beake, Diocesan House, Quarry Street, Guildford GU1 3XG
Tel: 01483 790352
email: stuart.beake@cofeguildford.org.uk
Director of Operations Mrs Tina Grear
Tel: 01483 547864
email: administrator@guildford-cathedral.org
Cathedral Organist and Master of the Choristers Mrs Katherine Dienes-Williams, 5 Cathedral Close, Guildford GU2 7TL *Tel:* 01483 547866
email: organist@guildford-cathedral.org

ARCHDEACONS
SURREY Ven Stuart Beake, Diocesan House, Quarry St, Guildford GU1 3XG [2005]
Tel: 01483 790352
email: stuart.beake@cofeguildford.org.uk
DORKING Ven Julian Henderson, Diocesan House, Quarry Street, Guildford GU1 3XG [2005]
Tel: 01483 790352
email: julian.henderson@cofeguildford.org.uk

CONVOCATION (MEMBERS OF THE HOUSE OF CLERGY OF THE GENERAL SYNOD)
Dignitaries in Convocation
The Bishop of Guildford
Proctors for Clergy
Revd Robert Cotton
Ven Julian Henderson
Revd Barbara Messham
Revd Philip Plyming
Canon Dr Hazel Whitehead

MEMBERS OF THE HOUSE OF LAITY OF THE GENERAL SYNOD
Canon Peter Bruinvels
Mr Keith Malcouronne
Anne Martin
Mr Adrian Vincent

DIOCESAN OFFICERS
Diocesan Secretary Mr Stephen Marriott, Diocesan House, Quarry St, Guildford GU1 3XG
Tel: 01483 790300
Fax: 01483 790333
Chancellor of Diocese Mr Andrew Jordan, 11 Fairlawn Avenue, Chiswick, London W4 5EF
Registrar of Diocese and Bishop's Legal Secretary Mr Peter Beesley, 1 The Sanctuary, London SW1P 3JT *Tel:* 020 7222 5381
Fax: 020 7222 7502
Deputy Registrars Mr Howard Dellar and Lee Coley

DIOCESAN ORGANIZATIONS

Diocesan Office Diocesan House, Quarry St, Guildford GU1 3XG *Tel:* 01483 790300
Fax: 01483 790333

ADMINISTRATION

President The Bishop of Guildford
Dioc Synod (*Vice-President, House of Clergy*) Revd Canon Nick Whitehead, The Rectory, 5 Spinning Walk, Shere GU5 9HN *Tel:* 01483 202394
(*Vice-President, House of Laity*) Canon Peter Bruinvels, 14 High Meadow Close, St Paul's Rd West, Dorking RH4 2LC *Tel:* 01306 887082
(*Secretary*) Mr Stephen Marriott, Diocesan House
email: diocesan.secretary@cofeguildford.org.uk
Deputy Secretary Mr Colin Harbidge, Diocesan House
email: colin.harbidge@cofeguildford.org.uk
Board of Finance (*Chairman*) Mr Nigel Lewis, Diocesan House
Accountant Mr Stephen Collyer
Pastoral Committee Mr Colin Harbidge (*as above*)
Designated Officer Mr Peter Beesley, 1 The Sanctuary, London SW1P 3JT *Tel:* 020 7222 5381
Fax: 020 7222 7502

CHURCHES

Advisory Committee for the Care of Churches (*Chairman*) Mr John Alpass, Three Kings Cottage, Ruxley Crescent, Claygate, Surrey, KT10 0TZ; (*Secretary*) Mrs Wendy Harris, Diocesan House
email: wendy.harris@cofeguildford.org.uk

EDUCATION

Education Centre Diocesan Education Centre, Stag Hill, Guildford GU2 7UP
Tel: 01483 450423
Fax: 01483 450424
Director of Education and Secretary Dioc Board of Education Mr Derek Holbird
email: derek.holbird@cofeguildford.org.uk
Schools Officer Mrs Heather Henderson
Education Officer Mr David Hallam
Youth Adviser Mr David Welch
Children's Work Adviser Mrs Alison Hendy
Adult Education Adviser Mrs Joanna Walker
Further Education Adviser Mr Bob Linnell
Centre Manager/PA to Director Mrs Jane Baker
Deputy Director of Education – Schools Mr Michael Hall

MINISTRY

Director of Ministerial Training and Co-Chair South Central Regional Training Partnership Revd Canon Dr Hazel Whitehead, Diocesan House
Tel: 01483 790307
email: hazel.whitehead@cofeguildford.org.uk
Director of Ordinands and IME 4–7 Revd William Challis, Diocesan House *Tel:* 01483 790322
email: william.challis@cofeguildford.org.uk
Local Ministry Programme (*Principal*) Revd Dr Steve Summers, Diocesan House
Tel: 01483 790319
email: steve.summers@cofeguildford.co.uk
Warden of Licensed Lay Ministers Mrs Gertrud Sollars, 6 Overbrook, Godalming, Surrey GU7 1LX gertrud.sollars@btinternet.com
Senior Tutor for Pastoral Assistants' Foundation Training Mrs Sue Lawrence, Diocesan House
Tel: 01483 790321
email: sue.lawrence@cofeguildford.org.uk
CMD Tutor for Pastoral Assistants Revd Lynne Bowden *Tel:* 01483 790300
email: lynne.bowden@cofeguildford.org.uk
Vocations Officer Revd Laurence Gamlen
Tel: 01483 790300
email: laurence.gamlen@cofeguildford.org.uk
Assessing the End of Curacy Officer Revd Bev Hunt
Tel: 01483 790300
email: bev.hunt@cofeguildford.org.uk
Readers' Board (*Registrar*) Dr Anthony Metcalfe, Peterstone, 15 The Mead, Ashtead KT21 2LZ
Tel: 01372 274162
email: ar_metcalfe@yahoo.co.uk

MISSION, EVANGELISM AND PARISH DEVELOPMENT

Director Vacancy
Parish Resources Adviser Mrs Juliet Evans, Diocesan House *Tel:* 01483 790329
email: juliet.evans@cofeguildford.org.uk
Local Mission Adviser Revd Stephen Cox, Diocesan House *Tel:* 01483 790330
email: stephen.cox@cofeguildford.org.uk
Spirituality Adviser Revd Alan Elkins
email: alan-elkins@lineone.net
Spiritual Direction Co-ordinator Revd Gill Welford
email: gill.welford@myzen.co.uk
Bishop's Adviser on Hospital Chaplaincy Revd Chris Vallins *email:* chrisvallins@yahoo.com
Healing Adviser Revd Elizabeth Knifton
email: eknifton@acornchristian.org
World Mission Adviser Revd Andrew Wheeler
email: andrew.wheeler@st-saviours.org.uk
Nigeria Link Officer Revd David Minns
email: dkminns@btinternet.com
Sports Ministry Adviser Revd Clive Potter
email: milfordvicarage@gmail.com

PRESS AND PUBLICATIONS

Director of Communications Revd Mark Rudall, Diocesan House *Tel:* 01483 790310
07779 654975 (Mobile)
email: mark.rudall@cofeguildford.org.uk
Communications Officer Mr Nick Edmonds, Diocesan House *Tel:* 01483 790316
email: nick.edmonds@cofeguildford.org.uk
Media Officers Mrs Emma Nutbrown, David Green *Tel:* 01483 790345
Editors of Diocesan Newspaper Mrs Emma Nutbrown, David Green (*as above*)
Tel: 01483 790347
email: editorial@cofeguildford.org.uk
Information and Web Administrator Mrs Mary Peters *Tel:* 01483 790355
email: mary.peters@cofeguildford.org

DIOCESAN RECORD OFFICE

Surrey History Centre, 130 Goldsworth Rd, Woking GU2 1ND *Team Leader, Heritage Public Services* Dr Patricia Reynolds; *Special Collections Archivist* Diana Stiff *Tel:* 01483 518737

SOCIAL RESPONSIBILITY

Director Canon Chris Rich, Diocesan House *Tel:* 01483 790353 *email:* chris.rich@cofeguildford.org.uk

Church's Community Care Adviser Tony Oakden, Diocesan House *Tel:* 01483 790325 *email:* tony.oakden@cofeguildford.org.uk

Health and Wellbeing Adviser Suzette Jones, Diocesan House *Tel:* 01483 790335 *email:* suzette.jones@cofeguildford.org.uk

Deaf and Inclusion Coordinator Tracey Wade, Diocesan House *Tel:* 01483 790327 *email:* tracey.wade@cofeguildford.org.uk

Surrey Faith Links Kauser Akhtar, Diocesan House *Tel:* 01483 790327 *email:* kauser.akhtar@cofeguildford.org.uk

RURAL DEANS

ARCHDEACONRY OF SURREY

Aldershot Revd George Newton, 2 Cranmore Lane, Aldershot GU11 3AS *Tel:* 01252 320618 *email:* g@gjsk.prestel.co.uk

Cranleigh Revd John Bundock, Vicarage, Birtley Rise, Bramley, Guildford GU5 0HZ *Tel:* 01483 892109 *email:* jnebundock@tiscali.co.uk

Farnham Revd Anne Gell, Vicarage, 2 Kings Lane, Wrecclesham GU10 4QB *Tel:* 01252 716431 *email:* annegell@lineone.net

Godalming Revd Clive Potter, The Vicarage, Milford Heath Road, Milford GU8 5BX *Tel:* 01483 414710 *email:* milfordvicarage@gmail.com

Guildford Revd Frank Scammell, Stoughton Vicarage, 3 Shepherds Lane, Guildford GU2 9SJ *Tel:* 01483 560560 *email:* barbaramessham@googlemail.com

Surrey Heath Revd Bob Peck, The Vicarage, Hampshire Road, Old Dean, Camberley GU15 4DW *Tel:* 01276 23958 *email:* vicar@stmartinolddean.com

ARCHDEACONRY OF DORKING

Dorking Revd Paul Bryer, St Paul's Vicarage, 7 South Terrace, Dorking RH4 2AB *Tel:* 01306 881998 *email:* paul@stpaulsdorking.org.uk

Emly Vacancy

Epsom Revd Stuart Thomas, The Minister's House, 71 Ruxley Lane, Ewell KT19 9FF *Tel:* 020 8311 127 *email:* revstuart.thomas@btinternet.com

Leatherhead Revd Robert Jenkins, Vicarage, St Andrew's Walk, Cobham, Surrey KT11 3EQ *Tel:* 01932 862109 *email:* er.jenkins@btinternet.com

Runnymede Revd Tim Hillier, Vicarage, London St, Chertsey KT16 8AA *Tel:* 01932 563141 *email:* tim.hillier@o2.co.uk

Woking Revd Cathy Blair, St Paul's Vicarage, Pembroke Road, Woking GU22 7ED *Tel:* 01483 850489 *email:* cathy@stpaulswoking.org.uk

DIOCESE OF HEREFORD

Founded *c* 676. Herefordshire; the southern half of Shropshire; a few parishes in Powys and Monmouthshire.

Population 306,000 Area 1,660 sq m
Full-time Stipendiary Parochial Clergy 83 Benefices 107
Parishes 342 Churches 416
www.hereford.anglican.org
Overseas link dioceses: Masasi and Tanga with Zanzibar, Dar es Salaam (Tanzania), Kirchenkreis of Nurnberg.

BISHOP (104th)
Rt Revd Anthony Priddis, The Bishop's House, Hereford HR4 9BN [2004] *Tel:* 01432 271355
Fax: 01432 373346
email: bishop@hereford.anglican.org

SUFFRAGAN BISHOP
LUDLOW Rt Revd Alistair J. Magowan, Bishop's House, Corvedale Rd, Craven Arms, Shropshire SY7 9BT [2009] *Tel* and *Fax:* 01588 673571
email: bishopofludlow@btinternet.com

CATHEDRAL CHURCH OF THE BLESSED VIRGIN MARY AND ST ETHELBERT
Dean Very Revd Michael Tavinor, The Deanery, College Cloisters, Hereford HR1 2NG [2002]
Tel: 01432 374203
email: dean@herefordcathedral.org
Cathedral Office 5 College Cloisters, Hereford HR1 2NG *Tel:* 01432 374200
Fax: 01432 374220
email: office@herefordcathedral.org
Web: www.herefordcathedral.org
Canons Residentiary
Chancellor Canon Christopher Pullin, 2 Cathedral Close, Hereford HR1 2NG [2008]
Tel: 01432 374273
chancellor@herefordcathedral.org
Precentor Canon Andrew Piper, 1 Cathedral Close, Hereford HR1 2NG [2003] *Tel:* 01432 374271
email: precentor@herefordcathedral.org
Cathedral Chaplain Preb Kay Garlick, c/o Cathedral Office *Tel:* 01432 374214
email: kay.garlick@herefordcathedral.org

Additional Members
Canon Sandra Elliott, c/o Cathedral Office
Canon Richard Price, c/o Cathedral Office
Administrator and Chapter Clerk Group Captain Julian Andrews, Cathedral Office
Tel: 01432 374201
email: julian.andrews@herefordcathedral.org
Director of Music Mr Geraint Bowen, 7 College Cloisters, Hereford HR1 2NG *Tel:* 01432 374238
email: organist@herefordcathedral.org
Assistant Director of Music Mr Peter Dyke, 1a Cathedral Close, Hereford HR1 2NG
Tel: 01432 353843
email: peter.dyke@herefordcathedral.org

ARCHDEACONS
HEREFORD Ven Paddy Benson, Dioc Office
Tel: 01432 373316
email: archdeacon@hereford.anglican.org
LUDLOW Rt Revd Alistair J. Magowan, Bishop's House, Corvedale Rd, Craven Arms, Shropshire SY7 9BT *Tel* and *Fax:* 01588 673571
email: bishopofludlow@btinternet.com

CONVOCATION (MEMBERS OF THE HOUSE OF CLERGY OF THE GENERAL SYNOD)
Proctors for Clergy
Preb Brian Chave
Revd Simon Cawdell
Revd Neil Patterson

MEMBERS OF THE HOUSE OF LAITY OF THE GENERAL SYNOD
Dr John Dinnen
Dr Martin Elcock
Canon Rosemary Lording

DIOCESAN OFFICERS
Dioc Secretary Mr John Clark, Diocesan Office, The Palace, Hereford HR4 9BL
Tel: 01432 373300
Fax: 01432 352952
email: diosec@hereford.anglican.org
Chancellor of Diocese Chancellor R. Kaye, Leeds Combined Court Centre, The Court House, 1 Oxford Row, Leeds LS1 3BG *Tel:* 0113 306 2800
Registrar of Diocese and Bishop's Legal Secretary Mr Peter Beesley, Dioc Registry, 1 The Sanctuary, Westminster, London SW1P 3JT
Tel: 020 7222 5381
Dioc Surveyors Hook Mason Partnership, 41 Widemarch St, Hereford HR4 9EA *Tel:* 01432 352299

DIOCESAN ORGANIZATIONS
Dioc Office The Palace, Hereford HR4 9BL
Tel: 01432 373300
Fax: 01432 352952
email: diooffice@hereford.anglican.org
Bishop's Office The Palace, Hereford HR4 9BN
Tel: 01432 271355
Fax: 01432 373346

ADMINISTRATION

Dioc Synod (*Chairman, House of Clergy*) Preb B. Chave, Vicarage, Vowles Close, Hereford HR4 0DF *Tel:* 01432 273086

(*Chairman, House of Laity*) Canon Rosemary Lording, 93 Kings Acre Road, Hereford HR4 0RQ *Tel:* 01432 340050

(*Secretary*) Mr John Clark, Dioc Office

Board of Finance (*Chairman*) Mr Charles Hunter, Upper Grange, Bacton, Hereford HR2 0AR *Tel:* 01981 240561

(*Secretary*) Mr John Clark (*as above*)

Financial Secretary Mr Gordon Powell, Dioc Office

Benefice Buildings Committee Mr John Clark (*as above*)

Glebe Committee Mr Stephen Challenger, Dioc Office

Board of Patronage Mr John Clark, Dioc Office

Designated Officer Mr Peter Beesley, 1 The Sanctuary, Westminster, London SW1P 3JT *Tel:* 020 7222 5381

Trusts Mr John Clark (*as above*)

CHURCHES

Advisory Committee for the Care of Churches (*Chairman*) The Archdeacon of Hereford (*as above*)

(*Secretary*) Mr Stephen Challenger (*as above*)

EDUCATION

Director of Education Mr Philip Sell, Dioc Office (Ludlow), Units 8 & 9, The Business Quarter, Ludlow Eco Park, Sheet Rd, Ludlow, Shropshire SY88 1FD *Tel:* 01584 871080 *email:* p.sell@hereford.anglican.org

Schools Officer Mrs Sally McCamley *Tel:* 01584 871077 *email:* s.mccamley@hereford.anglican.org

Young Peoples Officer Miss Esther Gregory *Tel:* 01584 871078 *email:* e.gregory@hereford.anglican.org

LUDLOW CONFERENCE CENTRE

Tel: 01584 873882
Fax: 01584 877945

MINISTRY AND TRAINING

Director of Ordinands Revd Preb Mary Lou Toop, Vicarage, Minsterley, Shropshire SY5 0AA *Tel:* 01743 790399 *email:* maryloutoop@lineone.net

Continuing Ministerial Development Officer Revd Nicholas Helm, c/o Dioc Office (Ludlow)

Lay Development Officer Revd Caroline Pascoe, c/o Dioc Office (Ludlow)

Local Ministry Officer Revd Dr John Daniels, c/o Dioc Office (Ludlow) *Tel:* 01584 871081

Advisers for Non-Stipendiary Ministry Revd M. D. Vockins, Birchwood Lodge, Storridge, Malvern WR13 5EZ *Tel:* 01886 884366

Revd J. Edwards, 2 Madeley Wood View, Madeley, Telford TF7 5TF *Tel:* 01952 583254

Adviser on Women in Ministry Preb Kay Garlick c/o Cathedral Office *Tel:* 01432 374213

Readers' Association (*Warden*) Preb Andrew Talbot-Ponsonby, The Old Barn Cleeve Lane, Ross-on-Wye, Herefordshire HR9 7TB *Tel:* 01989 565003 *email:* andrew@talbot-ponsonby.org

Widows and Dependants (*Hereford Diocese Clerical Charity*) Mr John Clark (*as above*)

WORSHIP

Chairman Canon Andrew Piper (*as above*)

Secretary Vacancy

MISSIONARY AND ECUMENICAL

Ecumenical Committee (*Chairman*) Very Revd Michael Tavinor

Council for World Partnership and Development (*Chairman*) Mrs Hazel Gould

Evangelism Committee (*Chairman*) The Bishop of Ludlow

AGRICULTURE

Chaplain Vacancy

PRESS, PUBLICITY AND PUBLICATIONS

Dioc Communications Officer Ms Anni Holden, The Palace, Hereford HR4 9BL *Tel:* 01432 373342 *email:* a.holden@hereford.anglican.org

Editor of Dioc Newspaper Mr R. Calver, The Palace (*as above*)

DIOCESAN RECORD OFFICE

Hereford Records Office, The Old Barracks, Harold St, Hereford HR1 2QX *Tel:* 01432 260750 (*For diocesan records and parish records for Hereford Archdeaconry*)

Shrewsbury Records and Research Centre, Castle Gates, Shrewsbury SY1 2AQ *Tel:* 01743 255350

Head of Records and Research Mary McKenzie (*For parish records for Ludlow Archdeaconry*)

SOCIAL RESPONSIBILITY

Social Responsibility Officer Miss Jackie Boys, The Gateway Office (*as above*) *Tel:* 01432 373311 *email:* j.boys@hereford.anglican.org

Council for Social Responsibility (*Chairman*) Vacancy

(*Secretary*) Miss Jackie Boys (*as above*)

STEWARDSHIP

Community Partnership and Funding Officer Mrs Wendy Coombey, Dioc Office *Tel:* 01432 373313 *email:* w.coombey@hereford.anglican.org

RURAL DEANS

ARCHDEACONRY OF HEREFORD

Abbeydore Revd A. F. Evans, Rectory, Ewyas Harold, Herefordshire HR2 0EZ *Tel:* 01981 871088

Bromyard Revd A. Seabrook, Penhope House, Balhurst, Bromyard HR7 4EF *Tel:* 01885 482184

Hereford Preb P. Towner, The Vicarage, 102 Green St, Hereford HR1 2QW *Tel:* 01432 273676

Kington and Weobley Preb S. Hollinghurst, The Rectory, Presteigne, Powys LD8 2BP *Tel:* 01544 267777

Ledbury Revd M. D. Vockins, Birchwood Lodge, Storridge, Malvern WR13 5EZ *Tel:* 01886 884366

Leominster Preb M. C. Cluett, Vicarage, Brookside, Caon Pyon, Hereford HR4 8NY *Tel:* 01432 830802

Ross and Archenfield Revd E. C. Goddard, The Vicarage, St Weonards, Herefordshire HR2 8NN *Tel:* 01981 580307

ARCHDEACONRY OF LUDLOW

Bridgnorth Revd S. H. Cawdell, Vicarage, Lodge Park, Claverley, Nr Wolverhampton WV5 7DP *Tel:* 01746 710268

Clun Forest Revd N. Morris, Rectory, Wentnor, Bishop's Castle, Shropshire SY9 5EE *Tel:* 01588 650244

Condover Revd R. Hill, Rectory, Carding Mill Valley, Church Stretton, Shropshire SY6 6JF *Tel:* 01694 722585

Ludlow Revd C. Lording, The Vicarage, Church Street, Tenbury Wells, Worcestershire WR15 8BP *Tel:* 01584 810811

Pontesbury Revd M. G. Whittock, Rectory, Longden, Shrewsbury, Shropshire SY5 8ET *Tel:* 01743 861003

Telford Severn Gorge
Revd M. Lefroy, Woodside Vicarage, Park Lane, Madeley, Telford TF7 5HN *Tel:* 01952 588958

DIOCESE OF LEICESTER

Restored in 1926, Leicestershire; one parish in Northamptonshire; one parish partly in Derbyshire; one parish partly in Warwickshire.

Population 961,000 Area 835 sq m
Full-time Stipendiary Parochial Clergy 123 Benefices 108
Parishes 236 Churches 313
www.leicester.anglican.org
Overseas link dioceses: Yokohama, Mount Kilimanjaro (Tanzania) and Trichy, Tanjore (India).

BISHOP (6th)
Rt Revd Timothy John Stevens, Bishop's Lodge Annexe, 12 Springfield Rd, Leicester LE2 3BD [1999] *Tel:* 0116 270 8985
Fax: 0116 270 3288
[Timothy Leicester]
Bishop's PA Mrs Melanie Freeman *(same address)*
email: melanie.freeman@leccofe.org
Bishop's Policy Advisor and Chaplain Revd Michael Smith (*same address*) *Tel:* 0116 270 3390
Fax: 0116 270 3288
email: mike.smith@leccofe.org
Executive Assistant to the Bishop Mrs Rachel Radford *(same address)* *Tel:* 0116 270 8985
email: rachel.radford@leccofe.org
Bishop's Press Officer Ms Liz Hudson-Oliff, St Martin's House, 7 Peacock Lane, Leicester LE1 5PZ *Tel:* 0116 261 5302
07967 388861 (Mobile)
email: liz.hudson-oliff@leccofe.org

CATHEDRAL CHURCH OF ST MARTIN
St Martin's House, 7 Peacock Lane, Leicester LE1 5PZ *Tel:* 0116 261 5200
Fax: 0116 261 5220
email: LeicesterCathedral@LecCofE.org
Dean Vacancy
Canons Residentiary
Canon Chancellor Canon David Monteith [2009]
Tel: 0116 261 5363
email: David.Monteith@LecCofE.org
Precentor Canon Dr Johannes Arens [2011]
Tel: 0116 261 55371
email: Johannes Arens@LecCofE.org
Urban Canon Canon Barry Naylor
Tel: 0116 261 5371
email: Barry.Naylor@LecCofE.org
Canon Paul Hackwood (NSM) [2007]
Tel: 01530 223265
email: Paul.Hackwood@me.com
Cathedral Administrator Mr Francis Brown
Tel: 0116 261 5359
email: Francis.Brown@LecCofE.org
Marketing and Development Officer Ms Claire Recordon *Tel:* 0116 261 5368
email: Claire.Recordon@LecCofE.org
Director of Music Dr Christopher Johns [2011]
Tel: 0116 261 5374
email: Chris.Johns@LecCofE.org
Assistant Director of Music Mr Simon Headley *email:* Simon.Headley@LecCofE.org
Cathedral Solicitor Mr Trevor Kirkman, Latham & Co., Charnwood House, 2/4 Forest Rd, Loughborough LE11 3NP *Tel:* 01509 238822

ARCHDEACONS
LEICESTER Ven Timothy Stratford, St Martin's House, 7 Peacock Lane, Leicester LE1 5PZ [2002]
Tel: 0116 261 5319
Fax: 0116 261 5220
email: tim.stratford@leccofe.org
LOUGHBOROUGH Ven David Newman, St Martin's House, 7 Peacock Lane, Leicester LE1 5PZ [2009]
Tel: 0116 261 5321
Fax: 0116 261 5220
email: David.Newman@leccofe.org

CONVOCATION (MEMBERS OF THE HOUSE OF CLERGY OF THE GENERAL SYNOD)
Proctors for Clergy
Revd John Plant
Revd Amanda Ford
Revd John McGinley

MEMBERS OF THE HOUSE OF LAITY OF THE GENERAL SYNOD
Mr Stephen Barney
Yvonne Shayne Ardron
Anne Bloor

DIOCESAN OFFICERS
Dioc Secretary Mr Jonathan Kerry, St Martin's House, 7 Peacock Lane, Leicester LE1 5PZ
Tel: 0116 261 5326
Fax: 0116 261 5220
email: jonathan.kerry@leccofe.org
Assistant Dioc Secretary Mr Andrew Brockbank
Tel: 0116 261 5312
Fax: 0116 261 5220
email: andrew.brockbank@leccofe.org
PA to Dioc Secretary Mrs Carol Gibbons
Tel: 0116 261 5326
Chancellor of Diocese Mark Blackett-Ord, 5 Stone Buildings, Lincoln's Inn, London WC2A 3XT
Tel: 020 7421 7510
Fax: 020 7831 8102

Registrar of Diocese and Bishop's Legal Secretary Mr Trevor Kirkman, Latham and Co., Charnwood House, 2 Forest Rd, Loughborough LE11 3NP *Tel:* 01509 238822 *Fax:* 01509 238833 *email:* TrevorKirkman@lathamlawyers.co.uk

DIOCESAN ORGANIZATIONS

Diocesan Office St Martin's House, 7 Peacock Lane, Leicester LE1 5PZ *Tel:* 0116 261 5200 *Fax:* 0116 261 5220

ADMINISTRATION

Director of Finance Mr John Orridge, Dioc Office *email:* john.orridge@leccofe.org

Management Accountant Miss Caroline Wademan, Dioc Office *email:* caroline.wademan@covlec.org

Finance Officer Mr Paul Wilson, Dioc Office *email:* paul.wilson@covlec.org

Accounts Assistant Mrs Karen Issitt, Dioc Office *email:* karen.issitt@leccofe.org

Senior Property Manager Mrs Nicky Caunt, Dioc Office *email:* nicky.caunt@covlec.org

Clergy Housing Officer Mrs Dinta Chauhan, Dioc Office *email:* dinta.chauhan@covlec.org

Property Officer Miss Lesley Whitwell, Dioc Office *email:* lesley.whitwell@covlec.org

IT Manager Mr Phil Ash, Dioc Office *email:* phil.ash@covlec.org

Dioc Synod (Chair, House of Clergy) Tbc

Dioc Synod (Chair, House of Laity) Tbc

Dioc Synod and Bishop's Council (Secretary) Dioc Secretary, Dioc Office

Mission and Pastoral Committee Dioc Secretary (*as above*)

Stipends Officer Mrs Jill Benn, Coventry Cathedral and Diocesan Offices, 1 Hill Top, Coventry CV1 5AB *Tel:* 024 7652 1200 *Fax:* 024 7652 1330 *email:* jill.benn@covlec.org

Board of Finance (Chair) Mr Stephen Barney, 77 Brook St, Wymeswold, Loughborough LE12 6TT *Tel:* 01509 881160 *email:* stephen4747@live.co.uk

Board of Finance (Secretary) Dioc Secretary (*as above*)

Finance Committee Dioc Secretary (*as above*)

Property and Glebe Committee Assistant Dioc Secretary (*as above*)

Designated Officer Mr Jonathan Kerry (*as above*)

Director of Parish Funding and Fundraising Mr Andrew Nutter, Dioc Office *Tel:* 0116 261 5322 *email:* andrew.nutter@leccofe.org

Parish Funding Director Mrs Maxine Johnson, Brook House, Stonton Rd, Church Langton, Market Harborough LE16 7SZ *Tel:* 01858 545745 *email:* mjohnson@resort-solutions.co.uk

Child Protection Officer Mr Andrew Brockbank (*as above*)

CHURCHES

Advisory Committee for the Care of Churches (Chair) Revd Richard Curtis, Vicarage, Oakham Road, Tilton on the Hill LE7 9LB *Tel:* 07855 746041

Advisory Committee for the Care of Churches (Secretary) Mr Rupert Allen, Dioc Office *Tel:* 0116 261 5332 *Fax:* 0116 261 5220 *email:* rupert.allen@leccofe.org

EDUCATION

Diocesan Board of Education St Martin's House, 7 Peacock Lane, Leicester LE1 5PZ *Tel:* 0116 261 5350 *Fax:* 0116 261 5351

Director Mrs Mary Lawson (*same address*) *email:* mary.lawson@leccofe.org

PA to the Director Emma Cottis (*same address*) *email:* emma.cottis@leccofe.org

Chair Ven David Newman (*as above*)

Religious Education Adviser for Schools Mrs Janet Ingram (*as above*) *email:* janet.ingram@leccofe.org

School Inspections and Conference/Training Manager Mrs Helen Van Roose, Dioc Office *email:* helen.vanroose@leccofe.org

School Support Officer Mrs Kerry Miller (*same address*) *email:* kerry.miller@leccofe.org

Senior Education Officer – School Effectiveness Mr Stephen Gleave, Dioc Office *email:* stephen.gleave@leccofe.org

INTERFAITH

Director of Interfaith Relations and of the St Philip's Centre for Study and Engagement in a Multi Faith Society Canon Dr John Hall, St Philip's House, 2a Stoughton Drive North, Leicester LE5 5UB *Tel:* 0116 273 3459 *email:* john.hall@stphilipscentre.co.uk

MINISTRY

Director of Mission and Ministry Canon Dr Mike Harrison, Dioc Office *Tel:* 0116 261 5328 *Fax:* 0116 261 5220 *email:* mike.harrison@leccofe.org

Head of the School for Ministry Revd Dr Stuart Burns, Dioc Office *Tel:* 0116 248 7417 *email:* stuart.burns@leccofe.org

Mission Enabler Revd Barry Hill, Dioc Office *Tel:* 0116 261 5335 *email:* barry.hill@leccofe.org

Youth Ministry Officer Mads Morgan *Tel:* 0116 261 5342 *email:* mads.morgan@leccofe.org

Dioc Director of Ordinands Canon Sue Field, 134 Valley Rd, Loughborough LE11 3QA *Tel:* 01509 234472 *email:* sue.field1@tesco.net

Children's and Families Officer Louise Warner (*as above*) *Tel:* 0116 261 5200 *email:* louise.warner@leccofe.org

Officer for Non-Stipendary Ministry Revd Rachel Ross, The Rectory, 60 Westfield Drive, Loughborough LE11 3QL ***Tel:*** 01509 217029
Warden of Evangelists Mr Ivan Bennett, 102 Dumbleton Avenue, Rowley, Leicester LE3 2EH *Tel:* 0116 223 9730 *email:* thebennetts@ntlworld.com
Warden of Readers Revd Dr Tony Edmonds, The Rectory, Presents Lane, Belton, Loughborough LE12 9UN *Tel:* 01530 223 447 *email:* email: t.e.edmonds@btconnect.com
Reader Training Officer Revd Dr Stuart Burns (*as above*)
Pastoral Assistants Adviser Revd Liz Rawlings, 2 Cransley Close, Hamilton, Leicester LE5 1QQ *Tel:* 0116 274 2088 *email:* lizrawlings@btinternet.com
Director of Post-Ordination Training Revd Canon Jane Curtis, Vicarage, Oakham Road, Tilton on the Hill LE7 9LB *Tel:* 0116 2597244 *email:* jcurtis@leicester.anglican.org
Director of Women's Ministry Revd Sharon Constable, 26 Firwood Road, Melton Mowbray LE13 1SA *Tel:* 01664 481 793 *email:* sharonconstable@msn.com
Retired Clergy and Widows Officer Anthony Wessel Esq, The Old Forge, 16 High St, Desford, Leicester LE9 9JF *Tel:* 01455 822404 *Fax:* 01455 823545 *email:* anthony.wessel@dial.pipex.com

LITURGICAL

Chairman Revd Richard Curtis *(as above)*
Secretary Revd Alison Booker, The Vicarage, Gaulby Road, Billesdon, Leicester LE7 9AG *Tel:* 0116 259 6321 *email:* abooker@leicester.anglican.org

PRESS AND COMMUNICATIONS

Communications Officer Ms Liz Hudson-Oliff, Dioc Office *Tel:* 0116 261 5302 07943 387265 (Mobile) *email:* liz.hudson-oliff@leccofe.org
Editor of Dioc Directory Ms Liz Hudson-Oliff (*as above*)
Editor of 'In Shape' Ms Liz Hudson-Oliff (*as above*)

SOCIAL RESPONSIBILITY

Church and Society Project Officer Revd Canon David Jennings, Dioc Office *email:* davidjennings@leccofe.org
Rural Officer Revd Dr Peter Hooper, 23 Ferndale Drive, Ratby, Leicester LE6 0LH *Tel:* 0116 239 4606 *email:* peter@hoopers.orangehome.co.uk
Environment Officer Revd Andrew Quigley, The Vicarage, 49 Ashley Way, Market Harborough, LE16 7XD *Tel:* 01858 410253 *email:* andrew@aquigley.wanadoo.co.uk

ECUMENICAL

Ecumenical Officer Mr Vic Allsop, Clematis Cottage, 14 Church Lane, Hoby, Melton Mowbray, Leics LE14 3DR

DIOCESAN RECORD OFFICE

Leicestershire Records Office, Long Street, Wigston, Leicester LE18 2AH *Tel:* 0116 257 1080 *Fax:* 0116 257 1120

AREA DEANS

ARCHDEACONRY OF LEICESTER

City of Leicester Revd Amanda Ford, 10 Parkside Close, Beaumont Leys, Leicester LE4 1EP *Tel:* 0116 235 2667 *email:* mandyford@btinternet.co
Framland Revd Kevin Ashby, The Rectory, 57 Burton Road, Melton Mowbray LE13 1DL *Tel:* 01664 410 393 *email*: rector@meltonparish.org.uk
Gartree I and Gartree II Canon Michael Rusk, Rectory, 31 Hill Field, Oadby, Leicester LE2 4RW *Tel:* 0116 271 2135 *email:* m.f.rusk@leicester.anglican.org
Goscote Revd Rob Gladstone, Rothley Vicarage, 128 Hallfields Lane, Rothley, Leicester LE7 7NG *Tel:* 0116 230 2241 *email:* rob@rgladstone.wanadoo.co.uk

ARCHDEACONRY OF LOUGHBOROUGH

Akeley East Revd Dr Tony Edmonds, The Rectory, Presents Lane, Belton, Loughborough LE12 9UN *Tel:* 01530 223447 *email:* t.e.edmonds@btconnect.com
North West Leicestershire Revd Canon Vivien Elphick, The Vicarage, High Street, Measham, Swadlincote DE12 7HZ *Tel:* 01530 270354 *email:* vivien.elphick@btinternet.com
Guthlaxton Revd David Hebblewhite, The Vicarage, 102 Station Road, Countesthorpe, Leicester LE8 5TB *Tel:* 0116 278 4442 *email:* davidheb@talktalk.net
Sparkenhoe West Revd Tom Meyrick, Rectory, 6 The Paddock, Newbold Verdon, Leicester LE9 9NW *Tel:* 01455 824986 *email:* meyrick@ekit.com
Sparkenhoe East Revd Dr Peter Hooper, 23 Ferndale Drive, Ratby, Leicester LE6 0LH *Tel:* 0116 239 4606 *email:* peter@hoopers.orangehome.co.uk

DIOCESE OF LICHFIELD

Founded in 664, formerly Mercia (AD 656). Staffordshire, except for a few parishes in the south-east (BIRMINGHAM, DERBY); a few parishes in the south-west (HEREFORD); the northern half of Shropshire; Wolverhampton; Walsall; the northern half of Sandwell.

Population 2,018,000 Area 1,744 sq m
Full-time Stipendiary Parochial Clergy 275 Benefices 268
Parishes 421 Churches 573
www.lichfield.anglican.org
Overseas link dioceses: W. Malaysia, Kuching, Singapore, Qu'Appelle (Canada), Mecklenburg, Matlosane.

BISHOP (98th)

Rt Revd Jonathan Gledhill, Bishop's House, 22 The Close, Lichfield WS13 7LG [2003]
Tel: 01543 306000
Fax: 01543 306009
email: bishop.lichfield@lichfield.anglican.org
Bishop's Chaplain Mr Simon Jones (*same address*)
email: simon.jones@lichfield.anglican.org
Bishop's Press Officer Vacancy

AREA BISHOPS

SHREWSBURY Rt Revd Mark Rylands, 68 London Rd, Shrewsbury SY2 6PG [2009] *Tel:* 01743 235867
*Fax:*01743 243296
email: bishop.shrewsbury@lichfield.anglican.org
STAFFORD Rt Revd Geoff Annas, Ash Garth, Broughton Crescent, Barlaston, Stoke-on-Trent ST12 9DD [2005] *Tel:* 01782 373308
Fax: 01782 373705
email: bishop.stafford@lichfield.anglican.org
WOLVERHAMPTON Rt Revd Clive Gregory, 61 Richmond Rd, Merridale, Wolverhampton WV3 9JH [2007] *Tel:* 01902 824503
Fax: 01902 824504
email: bishop.wolverhampton@lichfield.anglican.org

HONORARY ASSISTANT BISHOPS

Rt Revd David Bentley, 19 Gable Croft, Lichfield, WS14 9RY [2004] *Tel:* 01543 419376
Rt Revd Iraj Mottahedeh, 2 Highland Rd, Newport, TF10 7AE [2005] *Tel:* 01952 813615

CATHEDRAL CHURCH OF ST MARY AND ST CHAD

Dean Very Revd Adrian Dorber, The Deanery, 16 The Close, Lichfield WS13 7LD [2005]
Tel: 01543 306250 (Office)
email: adrian.dorber@lichfield-cathedral.org
Chapter Office 19a The Close, Lichfield WS13 7LD
Tel: 01543 306100
Fax: 01543 306109
email: enquiries@lichfield-cathedral.org
Web: www.lichfield-cathedral.org

Canons Residentiary
Treasurer Ven Christopher Liley, 24 The Close, Lichfield WS13 7LD [2001] *Tel:* 01543 306145
Fax: 01543 306147
email: chris.liley@lichfield.anglican.org
Chancellor Vacancy *Tel:* 01543 306240
Precentor Canon Wealands Bell, 23 The Close, Lichfield WS13 7LD [2007]
Tel: 01543 306101 (Office)
email: wealands.bell@lichfield-cathedral.org
Administrator Mr Chris Nuttall, Chapter Office, 19a The Close, Lichfield WS13 7LD
Tel: 01543 306105 (Office)
email: chris.nuttall@lichfield-cathedral.org

Lay Members of Chapter
Mrs Margaret Harding
Miss Anne Parkhill
Mr Peter Durrant
Mr Bryan Ramsell

Directors of Music Mr Ben Lamb and Mrs Cathy Lamb, 11 The Close, Lichfield WS13 7LD
Tel: 01543 306200
email: music@lichfield-cathedral.org
Organist Mr Martyn Rawles, 10 The Close, Lichfield WS13 7LD *Tel:* 01543 306201
email: martyn.rawles@lichfield-cathedral.org
Director of Fundraising Ms Patricia Collins, Chapter Office, 19a The Close, Lichfield WS13 7LD *Tel:* 01543 306245
email: patricia.collins@lichfield-cathedral.org
Communications and Marketing Officer Mrs Claire Lamplugh, Chapter Office, 19a The Close, Lichfield WS13 7LD *Tel:* 01543 306121
email: claire.lamplugh@lichfield-cathedral.org

Personal Assistants:
to the Dean: Jodie Galley / Bernice Alexander; *Tel:* 01543 306250; *email:* bernice.alexander@lichfield-cathedral.org
to the Treasurer: Catherine Burrows; ***Tel:*** 01543 306145; *email*: catherine.burrows@lichfield.anglican.org
to the Chancellor: Jo Burkinshaw; *Tel:* 01543 306240; *email:* jo.burkinshaw@lichfield-cathedral.org
to the Precentor: Theresa Willmore; *Tel:* 01543 306101; *email:* theresa.willmore@lichfield-cathedral.org

ARCHDEACONS

LICHFIELD Ven Christopher Liley, 24 The Close, Lichfield WS13 7LD [2001] *Tel:* 01543 306145
Fax: 01543 306147
email: archdeacon.lichfield@lichfield.anglican.org

SALOP Ven Paul Thomas, Archdeacon's House, Tong Vicarage, Shifnal TF11 8PW [2011]
Tel: 01902 372622
Fax: 01902 374060
email: archdeacon.salop@lichfield.anglican.org

STOKE-UPON-TRENT Ven Godfrey Stone, 39 The Brackens, Clayton, Newcastle-under-Lyme ST5 4JL [2002] *Tel:* 01782 663066
Fax: 01782 711165
email: archdeacon.stoke@lichfield.anglican.org

WALSALL Ven Christopher Sims, 55b Highgate Rd, Walsall WS1 3JE [2005] *Tel:* 01922 620153
Fax: 01922 445354
email: archdeacon.walsall@lichfield.anglican.org

CONVOCATION (MEMBERS OF THE HOUSE OF CLERGY OF THE GENERAL SYNOD)

Proctors for Clergy
Revd Paul Farthing
Revd Patricia Hawkins
Revd Stephen Pratt
Revd Maureen Hobbs
Revd Mark Ireland
Ven Christopher Sims

MEMBERS OF THE HOUSE OF LAITY OF THE GENERAL SYNOD

Mr David Beswick
Mrs Penelope Allen
Mr Christopher Corbet
Mrs Joanna Monckton
Mr John Shand
Dr Chik Kaw Tan
Mr John Wilson

DIOCESAN OFFICERS

Dioc Synod (*Chairman, House of Clergy*) Revd John Allan, Vicarage, Church Rd, Alrewas, Burton-on-Trent DE13 7BT *Tel:* 01283 790486
email: revdjohnallan@revdjohnallan.plus.com
(*Chairman, House of Laity*) Mr John Wilson, 49 Oakhurst, Lichfield WS14 9AL
Tel: 01543 268678
email: charity.services@btclick.com

Dioc Secretary Mrs Julie Jones, St Mary's House, The Close, Lichfield, Staffs. WS13 7LD
Tel: 01543 306030
Fax: 01543 306039
email: julie.jones@lichfield.anglican.org

Mission and Pastoral Committee (*Secretary*) Revd David Wright, Rectory, 42 Park Road East, Wolverhampton WV1 4QA *Tel:* 01902 423388
email: david.wright@lichfield.anglican.org

Chancellor of Diocese Mr Stephen Eyre, FBC, Manby Bowdler LLP, Routh House, Hall Court, Hall Park Way, Telford TF3 4NJ
Tel: 01952 292129

Diocesan Registrar and Bishop's Legal Secretary Mr Niall Blackie, Manby Bowdler LLP, Routh House, Hall Court, Hall Park Way, Telford, Shropshire TF3 4NJ *Tel:* 01952 292129
Fax: 01952 291716
email: n.blackie@fbcmb.co.uk

DIOCESAN ORGANIZATIONS

Diocesan Office, see individual addresses below

ADMINISTRATION

Chairman Mr Peter Sharpe

Team Leader Mrs Julie Jones, St Mary's House, The Close, Lichfield WS13 7LD *Tel:* 01543 306030
Fax: 01543 306039

Finance Director Mr Jonathan R. L. Hill, St Mary's House

Benefice Buildings and Glebe Committee (*Secretary*) Mr Andrew Mason, St Mary's House

Diocesan Surveyor Mr Charles Glenn, St Mary's House

Trust (*Secretary*) Mrs Diane Holt, St Mary's House

Designated Officer Mr Niall Blackie, St Mary's House

Manager Christian Giving Mr Neil Bradley, 32 Aitken Close, Tamworth B78 3LR
Tel: 01827 704444
email: bradnsj@aol.com

Child Protection Officer Revd Charmian Beech, Rectory, Abbots Way, Hodnet, Market Drayton TF9 3NQ *Tel:* 01630 685491
email: charmian.beech@virgin.net

Head of Internal Communications Mr Ian Law, 19 Lincoln Croft, Shenstone, Lichfield WS14 0ND
Tel: 01543 480308
email: ianl@eclipse.co.uk

Editor of Dioc Newspaper 'Spotlight' Mrs Carol Law, 19 Lincoln Croft, Shenstone, Lichfield WS14 0ND *Tel:* 01543 480308

ECUMENISM

Area Ecumenical Adviser (Black Country) Revd Simon Mansfield, St Gregory's Vicarage, 112 Long Knowle Lane, Wednesfield, Wolverhampton WV11 1JQ *Tel:* 01902 731667
email: smansfield@toucansurf.com

Area Ecumenical Adviser (Shropshire) Mrs Veronica Fletcher, 67 Derwent Drive, Priorslee, Telford TF2 9QR *Tel:* 01952 299318
email: veronica.fletcher@telford.gov.uk

Area Ecumenical Adviser (Staffordshire) Miss Sue Booth, 6 Fairoak Flats, Harrowby Drive, Newcastle-under-Lyme ST5 3JR
Tel: 01782 613855
email: soobooth1@googlemail.com

CHURCHES

Advisory Committee for the Care of Churches (*Chairman*) Mr Kevin Hartley, 8 Hanbury Hill, Stourbridge DY8 1BE *Tel:* 01384 440868; (*Secretary*) Mrs Kristina Williamson, 27 Frederick Road, Sutton Coldfield B73 5QW *Tel:* 07805 772626
email: kristina.williamson@lichfield.anglican.org

EDUCATION

Chair of Board of Education Mrs Elaine Townsend, 2 The Old Rectory, Rectory Drive, Weston-under-Lizard, Shifnal TF11 8QG
Tel: 01952 850534
Fax: 01952 850626
email: e.townsend@btinternet.com

Director of Education and Team Leader Mr Colin Hopkins, St Mary's House
email: colin.hopkins@lichfield.anglican.org

Schools Advisers Mrs Joan Furlong, 46 Gravelly Drive, Newport TF10 7QS
Tel and *Fax:* 01952 404381
email: joan.furlong@lichfield.anglican.org

Mrs Sue Blackmore, 153 Hockley Rd, Wilnecote, Tamworth B77 5EF *Tel:* 01827 707638
email: sue.blackmore@lichfield.anglican.org

Mrs Rosemary Woodward, 151 Porlock Ave, Stafford ST17 0XY *Tel:* 01785 665883
email: rosemary.woodward@lichfield.anglican.org

Diocesan Schools Outreach Adviser, Miss Libby Leech, St Mary's House
email: libby.leech@lichfield.anglican.org

Warden of Diocesan Youth Centre Revd Arthur Hack, Dovedale House, Ilam, Ashbourne DE6 2AZ *Tel:* 01335 350365
Fax: 01335 350441
email: warden@dovedale-house.org.uk

MINISTRY MISSION AND TRANSFORMING COMMUNITIES

MINISTRY

Director of Ministry Revd Lesley Bentley, St Mary's House, Lichfield
Tel: 01889 508066 (Home)
01543 306227 (Office)
email: lesley.bentley@lichfield.anglican.org

Ministry Development Dept PA Mrs Janet Wallis
Tel: 01653 306227
email: janet.wallis@lichfield.anglican.org

Ministry Development Dept Administrator (with responsibility for Ministry Development Review Mrs Jane Instone
Tel: 01543 306228
email: jane.instone@lichfield.anglican.org

Director of Ordinands Revd David Newsome, St Mary's House, Lichfield
Tel: 01543 306192 (Home)
01543 306220 (Office)
email: david.newsome@lichfield.anglican.org

PA to the Director of Ordinands and Vocations Dept Mrs Angela Bruno *Tel:* 01543 306220 (Office)
email: angela.bruno@lichfield.anglican.org

Vocational Education Officer Revd Deborah Sheridan, 45 High Grange, Lichfield WS13 7DU
Tel: 01543 264363
email: d.sheridan@postman.org.uk

Vocations and Ministry Development Officer for Minority Ethnic Anglicans, Wolverhampton Revd Pamela Daniel, 33 Reform Street, West Bromwich B70 7PF *Tel:* 0121 525 1985
email: pamdaniel@hotmail.com

Director of Lay Development Dr Lindsey Hall, St Mary's House *Tel:* 01543 306225 (Office)
email: lindsey.hall@lichfeld.anglican.org

Lichfield Director of Reader Training / OLM Tutor, The Queen's Foundation, Birmingham Revd Pauline Shelton, Dray Cottage, Cheadle Road, Draycott in the Moors, Stoke on Trent ST11 9RQ (home) St
Tel: 01782 388834 (Home)
01543 306224 (Office)
email: pauline.shelton@lichfield.anglican.org

Local Ministry Scheme Administrator Mrs Sheila Walker *Tel:* 01543 306223 (Office)
email: sheila.walker@lichfield.anglican.org

Warden of Readers Mr John Maddison, 19 Woodland Avenue, Wolstanton, Newcastle-under-Lyme ST5 8AZ *Tel:* 01782 853169
email: john.maddison@lichfield.anglican.org

Chaplain to Deaf People Revd Dr Leonie Wheeler, St Andrew's Rectory, 7 Wallshead Way, Church Aston, Newport TF10 9JG *Tel:* 01952 810942
email: leonie.wheeler@btinternet.com

Bishop's Adviser in Pastoral Care and Counselling Revd Dr Jeff Leonardi, The New Rectory, Bellamour Way, Colton, Rugeley WS14 3JW
Tel: and *Fax:* 01889 570897
email: jeff.leonardi@btinternet.com

MISSION

Director of Parish Mission Revd George Fisher, The Parish Mission Office, The Small Street Centre, 1a Small Street, Walsall WS1 3PR
Tel: 01922 650063 (Home)
01922 707863 (Office)
email: george.fisher@lichfield.anglican.org

Director of World Mission Revd Philip Swan, The World Mission Office, The Small Street Centre, 1a Small Street, Walsall WS1 3PR
Tel: 01902 621148 (Home)
01922 707860 (Office)
email: philip.swan@lichfield.anglican.org

Parish Mission Research Assistant Mr Richard Barrett, The Parish Mission Office, The Small Street, Centre, 1a Small Street, Walsall WS1 3PR
Tel: 01922 707863 (Office)
email: richard.barrett@lichfield.anglican.org

PA to the Director of World Mission Miss Clare Spooner, The World Mission Office, The Small Street Centre, 1a Small Street, Walsall WS1 3PR
Tel: 01922 707861 (Office)
email: worldmission@lichfield.anglican.org

Youth and Children's Adviser Mr Mark Hatcher, Hillcroft, Stoney Lane, Endon, Stoke-on-Trent, ST9 9BX *Tel:* 01782 502822
email: mark.hatcher@lichfield.anglican.org

Spiritual Companions Co-ordinator Revd Christine Polhill, Little Hayes, Beaudesert Park, Cannock Wood, Rugeley WS5 4JJ *Tel:* 01543 674474
email: christine@refectiongardens.org.uk

TRANSFORMING COMMUNITIES

Transforming Communities Director Revd David Primrose, Hill House, Vicarage Lane, Bednall, Stafford ST17 0SE *Tel:* 01785 748976

Transforming Communities Assistant Revd Ruth Brooker, The Small Street Centre, 1a Small Street, Walsall, WS1 3PR *Tel:* 01922 707864
email: ruth.brooker@lichfield.anglican.org

DIOCESAN RECORD OFFICES

Staffordshire Record Office, Eastgate St, Stafford ST16 2LZ *Tel:* 01785 278379, *email:* staffordshire.record.office@staffordshire.gov.uk (*For parishes in the archdeaconries of Lichfield and Stoke-on-Trent*)

Lichfield Record Office, The Library, The Friary, Lichfield WS13 6QG *Tel:* 01543 510720, *email:* lichfield.record.office@staffordshire.gov.uk (*For diocesan records and parishes within the City of Lichfield*)

Shropshire Archives, Castle Gates, Shrewsbury SY1 2AQ *Tel:* 01743 255350, *email:* archives@shropshire.gov.uk (*For parishes in the archdeaconry of Salop*)

RURAL DEANS

ARCHDEACONRY OF LICHFIELD

Lichfield Revd John Allan, Vicarage, Church Rd, Alrewas, Burton-on-Trent DE13 7BT
Tel: 01283 790486
email: revdjohnallan@revdjohnallan.plus.com

Penkridge Revd Simon Witcombe, Codsall Vicarage, 48 Church Road, Codsall, Wolverhampton WV8 1EH *Tel:* 01902 842168
email: simonwitcombe50@gmail.com

Rugeley Preb Michael Newman, Rugeley Rectory, 20 Church St, Rugeley WS15 2AB
Tel: 01889 582149
email: eileennewman20@aol.com

Tamworth Revd Jim Trood, 6 Bamforth St, Glascote, Tamworth B77 2AS *Tel:* 01827 305313
email: jimtrood@btinternet.com

ARCHDEACONRY OF STOKE-ON-TRENT

Alstonfield Revd Revd James Forrester, The Vicarage, Gauledge Lane, Longnor, Buxton SK17 0PA *Tel:* 01298 83742
email: james@longnorvic.plus.com

Cheadle Revd Steve Osbourne, Vicarage, 8 Vicarage Crescent, Caverswall, Stoke-on-Trent ST11 9EW *Tel:* 01782 388037
email: steve.osbourne@btopenworld.com

Eccleshall Revd Nigel Clemas, Whitmore Rectory, Snape Hall Rd, Whitmore Heath, Newcastle-under-Lyme ST5 5HZ
Tel: 01782 680258
email: nclemas@hotmail.com

Leek Revd Matthew Parker, St Edward's Vicarage, 6 Church St, Leek ST13 6AB
Tel: 01538 382515
email: matpark01@aol.com

Newcastle-under-Lyme Revd Terry Bloor, 211 Basford Park Road, Basford Park, Newcastle-under-Lyme ST5 0PG *Tel:* 01782 623668
email: terry.bloor@btinternet.com

Stafford Revd John Davis, Stockton Croft, 87 Weeping Cross Stafford ST17 0DQ
Tel: 01785 661382
email: email: john_davis19@sky.com

Stoke (North) Revd Rod Clark, Christchurch Vicarage, 10 Emery St, Cobridge, Stoke-on-Trent ST6 2JT *Tel:* 01782 212639
email: revrod@tiscali.co.uk

Stoke-upon-Trent Preb David Lingwood, Stoke Rectory, 172 Smithpool Rd, Stoke-on-Trent ST4 4PP *Tel:* 01782 747737
email: dp.lingwood@btinternet.com

Stone Revd Peter Dakin, 20 Tudor Hollow, Fulford, Stoke-on-Trent ST11 9NP
Tel: 01782 397073
email: pdakin@waitrose.com

Tutbury Revd Michael Freeman, St John's Vicarage, 14 Rolleston Road Burton-on-Trent DE13 0JZ *Tel:* 01283 568613
email: email: freeman.burton@googlemail.com

Uttoxeter Revd Brian Leathers, The New Vicarage, Lime Kiln Lane, Alton, Stoke-on-Trent ST10 4AR *Tel:* 01538 702469
*email:*briantopsey@googlemail.com

ARCHDEACONRY OF SALOP

Edgmond and Shifnal Revd Keith Hodson, Rectory, Beckbury, Shifnal TF11 9DG
Tel: 01952 750774
email: keithhodson@talk21.com

Ellesmere Revd Philip Edge, The Vicarage, Church Hill, Ellesmere SY12 0HB *Tel:* 01691 622571
email: philipedge@talktalk.net

Hodnet Revd Charmian Beech, The Rectory, Abbots Way, Hodnet, Market Drayton TF9 3NQ
Tel: 01630 685491
email: charmian.beech@virgin.net

Oswestry Revd Adrian Bailey, Vicarage, Old Chirk Road, Gobowen, Oswestry SY11 3LL
Tel: 01691 661226
email: arb2@totalise.co.uk

Shrewsbury Revd Mark Thomas, 25 The Crescent, Town Walls, Shrewsbury SY1 1TH
Tel: 01743 343761
email: vicar@stchadschurchshrewsbury.com

Telford Revd Andrew Smith, St Matthew's Vicarage, St George's Road, Donnington, Telford TF2 7NJ *Tel:* 01952 291904
email: andysmith@telfordchristiancouncil.co.uk

Wem and Whitchurch Revd Rob Haarhoff, Vicarage, Shrewsbury Rd, Hadnall, Shrewsbury SY4 4AG *Tel:* 01939 210241
email: rob.haarhoff@gmail.com

Wrockwardine Preb David Chantrey, The Rectory, Wrockwardine, Telford TF6 5DD
Tel: 01952 251857
email: david.chantrey@surefish.co.uk

ARCHDEACONRY OF WALSALL

Trysull Revd Maureen Hobbs, Vicarage, 20 Dartmouth Avenue, Pattingham, Wolverhampton WV6 7DP *Tel:* 01902 700257
email: hobbsmaureen@yahoo.co.uk

Walsall Revd Martin Rutter, St Margaret's Vicarage, Chapel Lane, Great Barr, Birmingham B43 7BD *Tel:* 0121 357 5813
email: mcrutter@tesco.net

Wednesbury Revd Clive Howard, St Matthew's Vicarage, 107a Dudley Road, Tipton DY4 8DJ
Tel: 0121 557 1929
email: clive@stmatt.wanadoo.co.uk

West Bromwich Revd Andrew Smith, All Saints Vicarage, 90 Hall Green Rd, West Bromwich B71 3LB *Tel:* 01215 883698
email: vicar.allsaintswestbrom@googlemail.com

DIOCESE OF LINCOLN

Founded in 1072, formerly Dorchester (AD 886), formerly Leicester (AD 680), originally Lindine (AD 678). Lincolnshire; North East Lincolnshire; North Lincolnshire, except for an area in the west (SHEFFIELD).

Population 1,020,000 Area 2,673 sq m
Full-time Stipendiary Parochial Clergy 139 Benefices 211
Parishes 492 Churches 637
www.lincoln.anglican.org
Overseas link dioceses: RC Diocese of Brugge, Härnösands (Sweden), Tirunelveli (CSI), Tuticorin-Nazareth (CSI).

BISHOP (72nd)
Rt Revd Christopher Lowson, The Old Palace, Lincoln LN2 1PU [2011]
Tel: 01522 504090
Fax: 01522 504051
email: bishop.lincoln@lincoln.anglican.org
[Christopher Lincoln]
Bishop's Chaplain Revd Sal McDougall (*same address*)
email: bishops.chaplain@lincoln.anglican.org

SUFFRAGAN BISHOPS
GRIMSBY Vacancy
GRANTHAM Rt Revd Dr Timothy William Ellis, Saxonwell Vicarage, Church St, Long Bennington, Newark NG23 5ES [2006]
Tel: 01400 283344
Fax: 01400 283321
email: bishop.grantham@lincoln.anglican.org

HONORARY ASSISTANT BISHOPS
Rt Revd Donald Snelgrove, Kingston House, 8 Park View, Barton-on-Humber DN18 6AX [1994]
Rt Revd David Tustin, The Ashes, Tunnel Rd, Wrawby, Brigg DN20 8SF [2001]
Tel: 01652 655584

CATHEDRAL CHURCH OF THE BLESSED VIRGIN MARY
Dean Very Revd Philip Buckler, The Deanery, 11 Minster Yard, Lincoln LN12 1PJ [2007]
Tel: 01522 561611
email: dean@lincolncathedral.com
Communications Office (main switchboard)
Tel: 01522 561600
Fax: 01522 561634
Web: www.lincolncathedral.com
Canons Residentiary
Precentor Canon Gavin Kirk, The Precentory, 16 Minster Yard, Lincoln LN2 1PX [2003]
Tel: 01522 561633
email: precentor@lincolncathedral.com
Chancellor Canon Mark Hocknull, The Chancery, 12 Eastgate, Lincoln LN2 1QG [2009]
Tel: 01522 561633
email: chancellor@lincolncathedral.com
Subdean Canon John Patrick, The Subdeanery, 18 Minster Yard, Lincoln LN2 1PY [2011]
Tel: 01522 561626
email: subdean@lincolncathedral.com
Chapter Clerk and Chief Executive Mr Phil Hamlyn Williams, Chapter Office, 4 Priorygate, Lincoln LN2 1PL *Tel:* 01522 561604
Fax: 01522 561603
email: chiefexecutive@lincolncathedral.com
Director of Music and Organist and Master of the Choristers Mr Aric Prentice, Lincoln Minster School, Prior Building, Upper Lindum St, Lincoln LN2 5RW *Tel:* 01522 551300
email: aric.prentice@church-schools.com
Assistant Director of Music and Sub-Organist Mr Charles Harrison, 2a Vicars' Court, Minster Yard, Lincoln LN2 1PT *Tel:* 01522 561647
email: suborganist.lincoln@gmx.co.uk
Organist Laureate Mr Colin Walsh, Graveley Place, 12 Minster Yard, Lincoln LN2 1PJ
Tel: 01522 561646
email: colinwalsh1@btinternet.com

ARCHDEACONS
LINCOLN Ven Timothy Barker, Archdeacon's House, 1a Northfield Rd, Quarrington, Sleaford NG34 8RT [2009] *Tel:* 01529 304348
email: archdeacon.lincoln@lincoln.anglican.org
STOW and LINDSEY Ven Jane Sinclair, Sanderlings, Willingham Rd, Market Rasen, Lincoln LN8 3RE [2007] *Tel:* 01673 849896
email:
archdeacon.stowlindsey@lincoln.anglican.org

CONVOCATION (MEMBERS OF THE HOUSE OF CLERGY OF THE GENERAL SYNOD)
Revd Christopher Lilley
Canon Gavin Kirk
Ven Timothy Barker

MEMBERS OF THE HOUSE OF LAITY OF THE GENERAL SYNOD
Miss Rachel Beck
Mrs Sylvia Pounds
Mrs Susan Slater
Mrs Carol Ticehurst

DIOCESAN OFFICERS

Interim Diocesan Secretary Revd Canon Richard Bowett, Edward King House, Minster Yard, Lincoln LN2 1PU *Tel:* 01522 504030
Fax: 01522 504051
email: diocesan.secretary@lincoln.anglican.org
Chancellor of Diocese HHJ Revd Mark Bishop QC, c/o Diocesan Registry
Registrar of Diocese and Bishop's Legal Secretary Miss Caroline Mockford, The Diocesan Registry, Chattertons, Low Moor Rd, Doddington Rd, Lincoln LN6 3JY *Tel:* 01522 814600
Fax: 01522 814601
email: caroline.mockford@chattertons.com

DIOCESAN ORGANIZATIONS

Diocesan Office Edward King House, Minster Yard, Lincoln LN2 1PU *Tel:* 01522 504050
Fax: 01522 504051
email: reception@lincoln.anglican.org
Web: www.lincoln.anglican.org

ADMINISTRATION

Diocesan Synod (Chairman, House of Clergy) Canon John Patrick *Tel:* 01522 504050
(Chairman, House of Laity) Mr Cameron Watt *Tel:* 01522 504050
(Secretary) Mr Will Harrison, Diocesan Office
Diocesan Council (Chairman) Rt Revd Christopher Lowson, Bishop of Lincoln
(Secretary) Mr Will Harrison *(as above)*
Finance Executive (Chairman) Mr Trevor Bush, Diocesan Office
Trusts Committee Mr Andrew Gosling, Dioc Office
Assets (and Glebe) Committee Mr Peter Gaskell
Property Mr Nicholas Turner, Diocesan Office
Board of Patronage Miss Rachel Beck, Diocesan Office
Designated Officer Miss Caroline Mockford, Chattertons, Low Moor Rd, Doddington Rd, Lincoln LN6 3JY *Tel:* 01522 814600
email: caroline.mockford@chattertons.com
Dioc Electoral Registration Officer Mr Will Harrison, Diocesan Office

CHURCHES

Advisory Committee for the Care of Churches (Chairman) Canon Nick Buck, Dioc Office
(Secretary) Mr Keith Halliday, Diocesan Office
Church Buildings Officer Mr Ben Stoker (Diocesan Office) *Tel:* 01427 617938
Historic Churches Support Officer Miss Rebecca Burrows (Diocesan Office)
Closed Churches Miss Rachel Beck, Diocesan Office

EDUCATION

Director of Education Jacqueline Waters-Dewhurst, Diocesan Office *Tel:* 01522 504010
email: education@lincoln.anglican.org
Diocesan Board of Education (Chair) Prof Muriel Robinson
email: muriel.robinson@lincoln.anglican.org
Deputy Director of Education Mr Paul Thompson, Diocesan Office
Schools and Academies Development Manager Mr Simon Hardy *(same address)*
Schools Adviser Mr David Clements *(same address)*

MINISTRY

Acting Principal of EM3 Revd Sally Myers, Diocesan Office *Tel:* 01522 504021
Discipleship and Lay Ministry Development Officer Revd Andrew Tyler, Diocesan Office
Tel: 01522 504024
Diocesan Director of Ordinands and Vocations Adviser Canon Dr Jeffrey Heskins, Diocesan Office *Tel:* 01522 504029
Adviser on Women's Ministry Canon Kathryn Windslow, Rectory, Vicarage Lane, Wellingore, Lincoln LN5 0JF *Tel:* 01522 810246
email: kathryn.windslow@btinternet.com
Ordinands' Grants Mr Peter Gaskell, Diocesan Office
Warden of Readers Canon Chris Lilley
Tel: 01427 788251
Readers (Secretary) Mr J. Marshall, 73 Sentance Crescent, Kirton, Boston PE20 1XF
Tel: 01205 723097
Clergy Widows Officers Canon and Mrs Michael Boughton, 45 Albion Crescent, Lincoln LN1 1EB
Tel: 01522 569653
Clergy Retirement Officer Ven Geoff Arrand

PRESS, PUBLICITY AND PUBLICATIONS

Director of Communications Mr Will Harrison, Diocesan Office
Editor of Crosslincs and ebulletin Mr Will Harrison, Diocesan Office
Communications Officer Mr Philip Craven, Diocesan Office

LITURGICAL COMMITTEE

Chairman Canon Gavin Kirk *(as above)*

MISSION AND ECUMENICAL CONCERNS

Ecumenical Officer Revd Moira Astin
Churches Together in all Lincolnshire Mr Simon Dean, c/o Diocesan Office *Tel:* 01522 504071
Lincolnshire Chaplaincy Services (Company No. 6491058)
Chair of Board Ven Jane Sinclair
Chaplaincy Director Canon Andrew Vaughan
Tel: 01522 528266
email: andrewvaughan@ntlworld.com
Business Manager Miss Alison McNish, Diocesan Office *Tel:* 01522 504070
Chaplain for Environmental Issues and Sustainable Development Mr Terry Miller, Diocesan Office
Tel: 01522 504072
Agricultural Chaplain Canon Alan Robson, The Manse, 1 Manor Drive, Wragby, Market Rasen LN8 5SL *Tel:* 01673 857871

Work with Young People Capt D. Rose CA, Diocesan Office *Tel:* 01522 504066
Youth Animator Mark Eades-Jones
Parish Support & Youth Project Worker Suzanne Starbuck, Diocesan Office

STEWARDSHIP AND RESOURCES

Director, Resources Consultancy Mr Andrew Wright, Diocesan Office *Tel:* 01522 504060
Resources Consultants Mr Simon Bland, Diocesan Office

DIOCESAN RECORD OFFICE

Lincolnshire Archives Office, St Rumbold St, Lincoln LN2 5AB *Tel:* 01522 526204

AREA DEANS

ARCHDEACONRY OF STOW

North Lincolnshire Revd Moira Astin, The Vicarage, Vicarage Gardens, Frodingham, Scunthorpe DN14 7AZ *Tel:* 01724 334873
email: moira.astin@ntlworld.com

ARCHDEACONRY OF LINDSEY

North East Lincolnshire Revd Andrew Dodd, The Rectory, 49 Park Drive, Grimsby, N E Lincs, DN32 0EG *Tel:* 01472 358610
email: andrew.dodd@grimsbyminster.co.uk

RURAL DEANS

ARCHDEACONRY OF STOW

Isle of Axholme Revd Jonathan Thacker, St George's Vicarage, 87 Ferry Road, Scunthorpe, North Lincolnshire DN15 8LY *Tel:* 01724 843328
Corringham Canon Rhys Prosser, Vicarage, 69 Mill Lane, Saxilby, Lincoln LN1 2HN
Tel: 01522 702427
email: rs.prosser@virgin.net
Lawres Vacancy
Manlake Revd Jonathan Thacker, St George's Vicarage, 87 Ferry Road, Scunthorpe, North Lincolnshire DN15 8LY *Tel:* 01724 843328
email: jon@han195.freeserve.co.uk
West Wold Canon Ian Robinson, The Vicarage, 3 Spa Top, Caistor, Lincoln LN7 6UH
Tel: 01472 851339
email: revianrobinson@tiscali.co.uk
Yarborough Revd David Rowett, The Vicarage, Beck Hill, Barton on Humber, North Lincolnshire DN18 5EY *Tel:* 01652 632202
email: davidrowett@aol.co

ARCHDEACONRY OF LINDSEY

Area Dean for North East Lincolnshire Revd Andrew Dodd
Bolingbroke Canon Peter Coates, The Vicarage, Church St, Spilsby PE23 5DU *Tel:* 01790 752526
email: peter.coates@onetel.net
Calcewaithe and Candleshoe Canon Terry Steele, The Rectory, Glebe Rise, Burgh le Marsh, Skegness PE24 5BL *Tel:* 01754 810216
email: father.terry@btclick.com
Grimsby & Cleethorpes The Revd Peter Vickers, The Rectory, 1A The Avenue, Healing, Grimsby DN41 7NA *Tel:* 01472 885807
email: revd.p.vickers@hotmail.co.uk
Haverstoe The Revd Peter Vickers. The Rectory, 1A The Avenue, Healing, Grimsby DN41 7NA
Tel: 01472 885807
email: revd.p.vickers@hotmail.co.uk
Horncastle The Revd Alyson Buxton, Old Manor House, Main Road, Thimbleby, Horncastle, Lincs LN9 5RE *Tel:* 01507 526769
email: alybux@mac.com
Louthesk Revd Susan Allison, The Rectory, Peppin Lane, Fotherby, Louth LN11 OUW
Tel: 01507 602312
email: susan.333allison@btinternet.com

ARCHDEACONRY OF LINCOLN

Stamford (Formerly Aveland and, Ness with Stamford) Very Revd Mark Warrick, All Saints Vicarage, Casterton Road, Stamford PE9 2YL
Tel: 01780 756942
email: mark.warrick@stamfordallsaints.org.uk
Beltisloe Canon Andrew Hawes, Vicarage, Church Lane, Edenham, Bourne PE10 0LS
Tel: 01778 591358
email: athawes@tiscali.co.uk
Christianity Revd David Osbourne, Rectory, 2A St Helen's Avenue, Boultham, Lincoln LN6 7RA
Tel: 01522 682026
email: davidosbourne@tiscali.co.uk
Elloe East and West Revd Rosamund Seal, Vicarage, 34 Church Lane, Moulton, Spalding PE12 6NP *Tel:* 01406 370791
email: ??????
Graffoe Canon Nicholas Buck, Rectory, 11 Torgate Lane, Bassingham, Lincoln LN5 9HF
Tel: 01522 788383
email: nick_buck@tiscali.co.uk
Grantham Revd Christopher Boland, The Vicarage, Edinburgh Road, Harrowby, Grantham NG31 9QZ *Tel:* 01476 564781
Holland Vacancy
Lafford Revd Christine Pennock, The Rectory, 2 All Saints Close, Manor Street, Ruskington, Sleaford, NG34 9FP *Tel:* 01526 832463
email: revpennock77@btinternet.com
Loveden (acting) Revd Alan Littlewood, The Rectory, 117 Ermine Street, Ancaster, Grantham NG32 3QL *Tel:* 01400 231145
email: ancaster.rectory@btinternet.com

DIOCESE OF LIVERPOOL

Founded in 1880. Liverpool; Sefton; Knowsley; St Helens; Wigan, except for areas in the north (BLACKBURN) and in the east (MANCHESTER); Halton, north of the river Mersey; Warrington, north of the river Mersey; most of West Lancashire.

Population 1,529,000 Area 389 sq m
Full-time Stipendiary Parochial Clergy 196 Benefices 170
Parishes 202 Churches 256
www.liverpool.anglican.org
Overseas link diocese: Akure (Nigeria).

BISHOP (7th)

Rt Revd James Stuart Jones, Bishop's Lodge, Woolton Park, Woolton, Liverpool L25 6DT [1998] *Tel:* 0151 421 0831
[James Liverpool]
Bishop's Personal Assistant Mrs Margaret Funnell *(same address)* *Tel:* 0151 421 0831 (Office)
Fax: 0151 428 3055
email: bishopslodge@liverpool.anglican.org

SUFFRAGAN BISHOP

WARRINGTON Rt Revd Richard Blackburn, St James' House, 20 St James Rd, Liverpool L1 7BY *Tel:* 0151 705 2140
email: bishopofwarrington@liverpool.anglican.org
Bishop's Personal Assistant Mrs Nerys Cooke, St James' House, 20 St James Rd, Liverpool L1 7BY *Tel:* 0151 705 2140
email: nerys.cooke@liverpool.anglican.org

HONORARY ASSISTANT BISHOP

Rt Revd Cyril Ashton, 'Charis', 17c Quernmore Rd, Lancaster LA1 3EB *Tel:* 01524 848684
email: bpcg.ashton@btinternet.com

CATHEDRAL CHURCH OF CHRIST

Dean Very Revd Dr Pete Wilcox
Tel: 0151 702 7220
email: dean@liverpoolcathedral.org.uk
Canons Residentiary
Treasurer Vacancy
Canon Precentor Canon Myles Davies [2008]
Tel: 0151 702 7203 / 0151 228 5252
email: myles.davies@liverpoolcathedral.org.uk
Dwelly Raven Vacancy
Chancellor Canon Cynthia Dowdle [2008]
Tel: 0151 702 7287
email: cynthia.dowdle@liverpoolcathedral.org.uk
Canon for Mission and Evangelism Canon Richard White [2009] *Tel:* 0151 702 7243
email: richard.white@liverpoolcathedral.org.uk
Assistant Curate Revd Tim Watson
Tel: 0151 702 7233
email: tim.watson@liverpoolcathedral.org.uk
Mission Pastor Mike Prescott *Tel:* 0151 702 7235
Director of Operations Mike Eastwood, St James' House, 20 St James Rd, Liverpool L1 7BY
Tel: 0151 709 9722 / 0151 705 2112
email: mike.eastwood@liverpool.anglican.org
Director of Music David Poulter, The Cathedral
Tel: 0151 702 7291 /7240
email: david.poulter@liverpoolcathedral.org.uk
Assistant Director of Music Stephen Mannings
Tel: 0151 702 7234
Organist Titulaire Prof Dr Ian Tracey, The Cathedral
email: ian.tracey@liverpoolcathedral.org.uk

ARCHDEACONS

LIVERPOOL Ven Ricky Panter, St James House, St James Road, Liverpool L1 7BY
Tel: 0151 705 2154
email: rick.panter@liverpool.anglican.org
WARRINGTON Ven Peter Bradley, St James House, St James Road, Liverpool L1 7BY
Tel: 0151 705 2154
email: peter.bradley@liverpool.anglican.org

CONVOCATION (MEMBERS OF THE HOUSE OF CLERGY OF THE GENERAL SYNOD)

Proctors for Clergy
Revd Canon Christopher Cook
Revd Canon Roger Driver
Revd Jacqueline Stober
Canon Peter Spiers
Vacancy

MEMBERS OF THE HOUSE OF LAITY OF THE GENERAL SYNOD

Mr Paul Hancock
Mr Mark Stafford
Mrs Debra Walker
Christopher Pye
Canon Margaret Swinson

DIOCESAN OFFICERS

Dioc Secretary Mike Eastwood, St James' House, 20 St James Rd, Liverpool L1 7BY
Tel: 0151 709 2112
Fax: 0151 709 2885
Chancellor of Diocese Sir Mark Hedley

Registrar of Diocese and Bishop's Legal Secretary Howard Dellar, Lee Bolton Monier-Williams, 1 The Sanctuary, London SW1P 3JT
Tel: 020 7222 5381

DIOCESAN ORGANIZATIONS

Diocesan Office St James' House, 20 St James Rd, Liverpool L1 7BY *Tel:* 0151 709 9722
Fax: 0151 709 2885
Web: www.liverpool.anglican.org

ADMINISTRATION

Dioc Synod (*Chair, House of Clergy*) Revd Canon Nicholas Anderson, The Vicarage, 1 View Rd, Rainhill, Merseyside L35 0LE *Tel:* 0151 426 4666
(*Chair, House of Laity*) Canon Margaret Swinson, 46 Glenmore Ave, Liverpool L18 4QF
Tel: 0151 724 3533
(*Secretary*) Mike Eastwood, Dioc Office
(*Asst Secretary*) Ultan Russell, Dioc Office
Board of Finance (*Chair*) David Greensmith, Dioc Office
(*Secretary*) Mike Eastwood (*as above*)
Mission and Pastoral Committee (*Chair*) Rt Revd Richard Blackburn; (*Secretary*) Sandra Holmes; (*Bishop's Planning Officer*) Revd David Burrows, Dioc Office
email: david.burrows@liverpool.anglican.org
Clergy Housing and Glebe Committee (*Chair*) David Burgess, Dioc Office; (*Surveyor*) Alan Gayner, Dioc Office
Support Claire Evans, Dioc Office
Tel: 0151 705 2129
email: claire.evans@liverpool.anglican.org
Designated Officer Revd David Burrows, Dioc Office

CHURCHES

Advisory Committee for the Care of Churches (*Chair*) Revd Stephen Parish, 1a Fitzherbert St, Warrington WA2 7QG *Tel:* 01925 631781

EDUCATION *Tel:* 0151 705 2190

Chair Bishop of Warrington
Director of Education Jon Richardson, Dioc Office
Asst Director Stuart Harrison, Dioc Office
Senior Diocesan Schools Adviser Joan O'Rourke Dioc Office
Diocesan Schools Adviser Joan Stein, Dioc Office

MINISTRY

Director of Ordinands Revd Canon David Parry, Vicarage, St Michael's Church Rd, Liverpool L17 7BD *Tel:* 0151 286 2422
Dean of Women's Ministries Canon Cynthia Dowdle, Dioc Office *Tel:* 0151 702 7287
email: cynthia.dowdle@liverpool.anglican.org
Readers' Association (Warden) Ms Jean Todd

LEARNING AND STEWARDSHIP

Director Revd Steve Pierce
Learning Managers Suzanne Matthews, Bob Barton
Director of Studies Simon Chesters
Resources Officer Gordon Fath
email: gordon.fath@liverpool.anglican.org

CHURCH GROWTH TEAM *Tel:* 0151 705 2148

email: warren.hartley@liverpool.anglican.org
Director Linda Jones, Dioc Office
Tel: 0151 705 2109
email: linda.jones@liverpool.anglican.org
Youth Missioner Frank Hinds *Tel:* 0151 705 2148
email: frank.hinds@liverpool.anglican.org
Children and Families Missioner Sue Mitchell
Tel: 0151 705 2167
email: sue.mitchell@liverpool.anglican.org
Diocesan Liturgy and Worship Forum (Chair) Rev Jeremy Fagan, 27 Shakespeare Ave, Kirkby L32 9SH *Tel:* 0151 547 2133
Diocesan Ecumenical Adviser Linda Jones, Dioc Office
Director of Pioneer Ministry Canon Philip Potter, Dioc Office

COMMUNICATIONS

Director Stuart Haynes, Dioc Office
Tel: 0151 705 2150
email: stuart.haynes@liverpool.anglican.org
Communications Officer Andrea Young, Dioc Office *Tel:* 0151 705 2131
email: andrea.young@liverpool.anglican.org

DIOCESAN RECORD OFFICE

For further information apply to Mr Howard Dellar, Lee Bolton Monier-Williams, 1 The Sanctuary, London SW1P 3JT *Tel:* 020 7222 5381 *or* The Lancashire Record Office, Bow Lane, Preston PR1 8ND *Archivist* Mr K. Hall *Tel:* 01772 533 039

CHURCH AND SOCIETY

Tel: 0151 705 2130
Fax: 0151 705 2215
email: churchandsociety@liverpool.anglican.org
Director Ultan Russell
email: ultan.russell@liverpool.anglican.org
Departmental Chair Canon Angela White
email: angela.white@seftoncvs.org.uk
Deputy Chair Revd Canon Cynthia Dowdle
email: cynthia.dowdle@liverpool.anglican.org
Disability Awareness and Vulnerable Adults Officer Sister Ruth Reed
email: ruth.reed@liverpool.anglican.org
Child Protection Adviser Su Foster
email: su.foster@liverpool.anglican.org
Chair, Anglican Partnerships and Links Revd Malcolm Rogers
email: malrogers@blueyonder.co.uk
Team Leader, Pastoral Services for the Deaf Community Revd Dr Hannah Lewis
email: hannah.lewis@liverpool.anglican.org

MERSEYSIDE AND REGION CHURCHES ECUMENICAL ASSEMBLY

Ecumenical Development Officer Revd Ian Smith (URC), Quaker Meeting House, 22 School Lane, Liverpool L1 3BT *Tel:* 0151 709 0125

MISSION IN THE ECONOMY (MitE)

Team Coordinator Revd Jean Flood, 22 School Lane, Liverpool L1 3BT *Tel:* 0151 709 6908

AREA DEANS

ARCHDEACONRY OF LIVERPOOL

Bootle Canon Roger Driver, The Vicarage, 70 Merton Rd, Bootle L20 7AT *Tel:* 0151 922 3316
email: rogerdriver@btinternet.com

Huyton Canon John Taylor, Vicarage, Vicarage Place, Prescot L34 1LA *Tel:* 0151 426 6719
email: john.taylor@huytondeanery.org

Liverpool North Canon Henry Corbett, St Peter's Vicarage, Shrewsbury House, Langrove St, Liverpool L5 3PE *Tel:* 0151 207 1948
email: henry-corbett@btinternet.com

Liverpool South – Childwall Canon Christopher John Crooks, Rectory, 67 Church Rd, Woolton, Liverpool L25 6DA *Tel:* 0151 428 1853
email: kipcrooks@blueyonder.co.uk

Sefton Canon Peter Spiers, St Luke's Vicarage, Liverpool Road, Crosby, Liverpool L23 5SE
Tel: 01519 241737
email: pete@spiersfamily.eclipse.co.uk

Toxteth and Wavertree Canon Malcolm Chamberlain, St Mary's Rectory, 1 South Drive, Wavertree, Liverpool L15 8JJ *Tel:* 0151 735 1615
email: malcolm@dream.uk.net

Walton Canon Ray Bridson, St Columba's Vicarage, Pinehurst Ave, Liverpool L4 2TZ
Tel: 0151 474 7231
email: frray@blueyonder.co.uk

West Derby Canon Steve McGanity, St Andrew's Vicarage, 176 Queen's Drive, Liverpool L13 0AL
Tel: 0151 287 2887
email: smcganity@blueyonder.co.uk

ARCHDEACONRY OF WARRINGTON

North Meols Canon Phil Green, Vicarage, Rufford Road, Crossens, Southport PR9 8JH
Tel: 01704 227662
email: revphilgreen@talktalk.net

Ormskirk Canon Nick Wells, Vicarage, 20 Damfield Lane, Maghull, Liverpool L31 6DD
Tel: 0151 531 8972
email: nick.the-vic@blueyonder.co.uk

St Helens Canon Mark Cockayne, St Mark's Vicarage, 2 Stanley Bank Rd, Haydock, St Helens WA11 OUW *Tel:* 01744 602641
email: markcockayne@eplusmail.com

Warrington Canon Stephen Boyd, St Margaret's Vicarage, 2 St Margaret's Ave, Orford, Warrington WA2 8DT *Tel:* 01925 631937
email: stephen.boyd@liverpool.anglican.org

Widnes Canon David Gait, St John's House, 134 Greenway Rd, Widnes WA8 6HA
Tel: 0151 424 3134
email: dave.gait@btinternet.com

Wigan Canon Margaret Sherwin, 3 Green Lane, Hindley Green, Wigan WN2 4HN
Tel: 01942 255833
email: mjsherwin@btinternet.com

Winwick Canon Joan Matthews, 8 The Parchments, Newton-le-Willows WA12 9SR
Tel: 01925 270795
email: revjoan@hotmail.com

DIOCESE OF LONDON

Founded in 314. The City of London; Greater London north of the Thames, except five East London boroughs (CHELMSFORD) and an area in the north (ST ALBANS); Surrey north of the Thames; a small area of southern Hertfordshire.

Population 3,819,000 Area 277 sq m
Full-time Stipendiary Parochial Clergy 481 Benefices 404
Parishes 393 Churches 477
www.london.anglican.org
Overseas link dioceses: Niassa and Lebombo (Mozambique), Angola.

BISHOP (132nd)
Rt Revd and Rt Hon Dr Richard John Carew Chartres KCVO, The Old Deanery, Dean's Court, London EC4V 5AA [1995] *Tel:* 020 7248 6233
Fax: 020 7248 9721
email: bishop@londin.clara.co.uk
[Richard Londin:]
Personal Jurisdiction Cities of London and Westminster (*Archdeaconries of London and Charing Cross*)
Matters relating to the other Areas should be referred to the appropriate Area Bishop
Personal Assistant Janet Laws
Diary Assistant Frances Charlesworth

AREA BISHOPS
STEPNEY Rt Revd Adrian Newman, 63 Coborn Road, London E3 2DB [2011] *Tel:* 020 7932 1140
email: bishop.stepney@london.anglican.org
KENSINGTON Rt Revd Paul Williams, Dial House, Riverside, Twickenham, TW1 3DT [2009]
Tel: 020 7932 1180
email: bishop.kensington@london.anglican.org
EDMONTON Rt Revd Peter Wheatley, 27 Thurlow Rd, London NW3 5PP [1999]
Tel: 020 7435 5890
Fax: 020 7435 6049
email: bishop.edmonton@london.anglican.org
WILLESDEN Rt Revd Peter Broadbent, 173 Willesden Lane, London NW6 7YN [2001]
Tel: 020 8451 0189
07957 144674 (Mobile)
Fax: 020 8451 4606
email: bishop.willesden@btinternet.com

SUFFRAGAN BISHOP
FULHAM Rt Revd Jonathan Baker, c/o London Diocesan House, 36 Causton St, London SW1P 4AU *Tel:* 020 7932 1100
Fax: 020 7932 1112
Assists the Diocesan in all matters not delegated to the Areas and pastoral care of parishes operating under the London Plan.

HONORARY ASSISTANT BISHOPS
Rt Revd Michael Colclough, 2 Amen Court, London EC4M 7BU *Tel:* 020 7236 0199
email: canonpastor@stpaulscathedral.org.uk
Rt Revd Edward Holland, 37 Parfrey St, London W6 9EW *Tel:* 020 8746 3636
email: ed.holland@btopenworld.com
Rt Revd Robert Ladds, Christ Church House, 76 Brent Street, London NW4 2ES
Tel: 020 8202 8123
email: episcopus@ntworld.com
Most Revd Walter Makhulu, 16 Downside, 8–10 St John's Avenue, London SW15 2AE
Tel: 020 8704 1220
email: makhulu@btinternet.com
Rt Revd Michael Marshall, 53 Oakley Gardens, London SW3 5QQ [1984] *Tel:* 020 7351 0928
email: sebastian97@hotmail.co.uk
Rt Revd Preb Sandy Millar, 37 Alde Lane, Aldeburgh IP15 5DZ *Tel:* 01728 452926
email: sandy.millar@techademic.net

CATHEDRAL CHURCH OF ST PAUL
Dean Very Revd Dr David Ison, 9 Amen Court, London EC4M 7BU *Tel:* 020 72367 2827
Fax: 020 7332 0298
email: dean@stpaulscathedral.org.uk
Canons Residentiary
Canon Pastor Rt Revd Michael Colclough, 2 Amen Court, EC4M 7BU [2008] *Tel:* 020 7236 0199
Fax: 020 7489 8579
email: pastor@stpaulscathedral.org.uk
Chancellor Canon Mark Oakley, 6 Amen Court, EC4M 7BU [2012] *Tel:* 020 7248 8572
Fax: 020 7489 8579
email: chancellor@stpaulscathedral.org.uk
Treasurer Vacancy
Precentor Canon Michael Hampel, 1 Amen Court, EC4M 7BU [2011] *Tel:* 020 7248 1817
Fax: 020 7489 8579
email: precentor@stpaulscathedral.org.uk
Lay Canons
Ms Lucrezia Walker, Chapter House, St Paul's Churchyard, London EC4M 8AD
Tel: 020 7246 8350
Fax: 020 7248 3104
email: lucrezia@stpaulscathedral.org.uk

Mr Gavin Ralston, Chapter House, St Paul's Churchyard, London EC4M 8AD
Tel: 020 7246 8350
Fax: 020 7248 3104
email: gavin@stpaulscathedral.org.uk
Professor Peter McCullough, The Chapter House, St Paul's Churchyard, London EC4M 8AD
Tel: 020 7246 8350
Fax: 020 7248 3104
email: peter@stpaulscathedral.org.uk

The College of Minor Canons
Sacrist Revd Jason Rendell, 8a Amen Court, EC4M 7BU [2007] *Tel:* 020 7246 8331
Fax: 020 7246 8336
email: sacrist@stpaulscathedral.org.uk
Succentor Revd Jonathan Coore, 7a Amen Court, London EC4M 7BU [2012] *Tel:* 020 7246 8338
email: succentor@stpaulscathedral.org.uk
Chaplain Revd Sarah Eynstone, 7b Amen Court, London EC4M 7BU [2009] *Tel:* 020 7246 8323
Fax: 020 7246 8336
email: chaplain@stpaulscathedral.org.uk
Headmaster of the School Mr Neil Chippington, St Paul's Cathedral School, New Change, London EC4M 9AD *Tel:* 020 7248 5156
Fax: 020 7329 6568
email: admissions@spcs.london.sch.uk
Registrar Mr Nicholas Cottam, The Chapter House, St Paul's Churchyard, EC4M 8AD
Tel: 020 7246 8311
Fax: 020 7248 3104
email: registrar@stpaulscathedral.org.uk
Dean's Virger Mr Charles Williams, 4b Amen Court, EC4M 7BU *Tel:* 020 7246 8320
Fax: 020 7248 3104
email: deansvirger@stpaulscathedral.org.uk
Solicitor to the Foundation at St Paul's Cathedral Mr Owen Carew-Jones, Winckworth Sherwood, Minerva House, 5 Montague Close, London SE1 9BB *Tel:* 020 7593 5034
Fax: 020 7248 3221
email: ocj@winckworths.co.uk
Surveyor Mr Oliver Caroe, The Chapter House, St Paul's Churchyard, EC4M 8AD
Tel: 020 7236 4128
email: oliver@caroe.com
Director of Music Mr Andrew Carwood, 5 Amen Court, EC4M 7BU *Tel:* 020 7651 0899
Fax: 020 7248 2817
email: andrewc@stpaulscathedral.org.uk
Organist Mr Simon Johnson, 4a Amen Court, EC4M 7BU *Tel:* 020 7236 6883
email: organist@stpaulscathedral.org.uk
Sub-Organist Mr Tim Wakerell, Chapter House, St Paul's Churchyard, EC4M 8AD
Tel: 020 7236 6883
Fax: 020 7248 2871
email: suborganist@stpaulscathedral.org.uk

ARCHDEACONS

LONDON Ven David Meara, The Archdeacon of London's Office, The Old Deanery, Dean's Court, London EC4V 5AA [2009]
Tel: 020 7236 7891
Fax: 020 7248 7455
email: archdeacon.london@london.anglican.org
CHARING CROSS Ven Dr William Jacob, 15A Gower St, London WC1E 6HW [1996]
Tel: 020 7323 1992
Fax: 020 7323 4102
email: archdeacon.charingcross@london.anglican.org
HACKNEY Ven Rachel Treweek, St Andrew's House, 35 St Andrew's Hill, London EC4V 5DE
Tel: 020 7932 1145
email: archdeacon.hackney@london.anglican.org
MIDDLESEX Ven Stephan Welch, 98 Dukes Ave, London W4 2AF [2006] *Tel:* 020 8742 8308
email: archdeacon.middlesex@london.anglican.org
HAMPSTEAD Ven Luke Miller, 39 Bounds Green Road, London N22 8HE *Tel:* 020 7932 1190
email: archdeacon.hampstead@london.anglican.org
NORTHOLT Vacancy
email: archdeacon.northolt@london.anglican.org

CONVOCATION (MEMBERS OF THE HOUSE OF CLERGY OF THE GENERAL SYNOD)

Dignitaries in Convocation
The Bishop of London
The Bishop of Willesden
Revd Prof Richard Burridge
Proctors for Clergy
Preb Philippa Boardman
Revd Christopher Hobbs
Revd Clare Herbert
Revd Jane Morris
Revd Stephen Coles
Preb David Houlding
Revd Preb Charles Marnham
Revd Preb Alan Moses
Ven Rachel Treweek

MEMBERS OF THE HOUSE OF LAITY OF THE GENERAL SYNOD

Mrs Mary Chapman
Ms Susan Cooper
Mrs Sarah Finch
Mr Aiden Hargreaves-Smith
Mrs Mary Johnston
Dr Lindsay Newcombe
Mr Anirban Roy
Mrs Alison Ruoff
Mr Clive Scowen
Mr John Ward
Dr Phillip Rice

DIOCESAN OFFICERS

Dioc Secretary Mr Andy Brookes, London Diocesan House, 36 Causton St, London SW1P 4AU *Tel:* 020 7932 1100 *Fax:* 020 7932 1114

Chancellor of Diocese Chancellor Nigel Seed, Winckworth Sherwood, Minerva House, 5 Montague Close, London SE1 9BB *Tel:* 020 7593 5110 *Fax:* 020 7248 3221

Registrar of Diocese and Bishop's Legal Secretary Mr Paul Morris (*same address*)

Official Principal of the Archdeaconry of Hackney His Honour David Smith QC, Beachcroft, Beach, Bitton, Bristol BS30 6NP

Official Principal of the Archdeaconry of Hampstead Dean Sheila Cameron, 2 Harcourt Bldgs, Temple, London EC4Y 9DB

Official Principal of the Archdeaconry of Northolt Mr Paul Morris (*as above*)

DIOCESAN ORGANIZATIONS

CHAIR

London Dioc Fund (*Dioc Board of Finance*) The Bishop of London

Vice Chair Mr David Loftus and Preb David Houlding

Finance Committee Ven Dr William Jacob

Dioc Synod (*House of Clergy*) Preb David Houlding (*House of Laity*) Mr David Loftus

Dioc Board for Schools Ven Stephan Welch

ADMINISTRATION

Diocesan Office London Diocesan House, 36 Causton St, London SW1P 4AU *Tel:* 020 7932 1100 *Fax:* 020 7932 1112 *Web:* www.london.anglican.org

Director of Finance and Operations Mrs Helen Simmons

Human Resources Manager Ms Paula Bailey

Director of Property Mr Michael Bye

Synodical Secretary Mrs Monica Bolley

Communications Manager Mr Robert Hargrave

Dioc Advisory Committee (*Chair*) Ven Peter Delaney; (*Secretary*) Mr Geoffrey Hunter

EDUCATION

Senior Chaplain for Higher Education Revd Stephen Williams, University Chaplaincy Office, 30B Torrington Square, London WC1E 7JL *Tel:* 020 7580 9812 *Fax:* 020 7631 3219 *email:* chaplaincy@lon.ac.uk

Acting Director of Education Mr Inigo Woolf, London Dioc House *Tel:* 020 7932 1165 *email:* inigo.woolf@london.anglican.org

MINISTRY

Director of Ministry, Dioc Warden of Licensed Lay Ministry Revd Dr Neil Evans, 23 St Albans Avenue, London W4 5LL *Tel:* 020 8987 7332 *email:* neil.evans@london.anglican.org

Vicar General to the London College of Bishops, Dioc Director of Ordinands, Preb Nick Mercer, The Old Deanery, Dean's Court, London EC4V 5AA *Tel:* 020 7489 4274 *email:* nick.mercer@london.anglican.org

Two Cities

Area Director of Training and Development Revd Alan Gyle, St Paul's Vicarage, 32 Wilton Place, London SW1X 8SH *Tel:* 020 7201 9999 *email:* alan.gyle@london.anglican.org

Dean of Women's Ministry Revd Rosemary Lain-Priestley, 13d Hyde Park Mansions, Cabell St, London NW1 5BD *Tel:* 020 7723 5352 *email:* rosemarylainpriestley@btopenworld.com

Stepney

Area Director of Training and Development Revd Irena Edgcumbe, The Centre for Training & Development St. Anne's Community Hall, Hemsworth Street London N1 5LF *Tel:* 020 7033 3446 *email:* irena.edgcumbe@london.anglican.org

Kensington

Area Director of Ministry Revd Martin Breadmore, 207 London Road, Twickenham TW1 1EJ *Tel:* 020 8891 0324 *email:* martin.breadmore@london.anglican.org

Dean of Women's Ministry Revd Anna Brooker, Butterfield House, 63 Church Street, Isleworth TW7 6BE *Tel:* 020 8476 0033 *email:* anna.brooker@allsaints-isleworth.org

Edmonton

Area Director of Training and Development Caulene Herbert, 27 Thurlow Rd, Hampstead, London NW3 5PP *Tel:* 020 7431 6827 *email:* caulene.herbert@london.anglican.org

Willesden

Area Director of Training and Development Revd Neil Evans (*as above*)

MISSION

Children's Ministry Adviser Sam Donoghue, London Dioc House *Tel:* 020 7932 1255 *email:* sam.donoghue@london.anglican.org

Diocesan Community Ministry Adviser Jack Maple *Tel:* 020 7932 1122 *email:* jack.maple@london.anglican.org

LITURGICAL

Chairman Very Revd Dr David Ison

PRESS AND COMMUNICATIONS

Head of Communications Mr Robert Hargrave, London Dioc House *Tel:* 020 7932 1227 *email:* robert.hargrave@london.anglican.org

Press, media and public affairs *Tel:* 020 7618 9106 (24 hours) *email:* dioceseoflondon@luther.co.uk

DIOCESAN RECORD OFFICES

London Metropolitan Archive, 40 Northampton Rd, London EC1R 0HB *Head Archivist* Dr Deborah Jenkins *Tel:* 020 7332 3824 (*All parishes except City and Westminster*)

Guildhall Library, Aldermanbury, London EC2P 2EJ *Archivist* Mr S. G. H. Freeth *Tel:* 020 7606 3030, Ext 1862/3 (*City parishes*)
Westminster Archives Dept, 10 St Ann's St, London SW1P 2XR *Archivist* Mr Jerome Farrell *Tel:* 020 7798 2180 (*Westminster parishes*)

AREA DEANS

ARCHDEACONRY OF LONDON

City Revd Oliver Ross, St Olave's Rectory, 8 Hart St, London EC3R 7NB *Tel:* 020 7488 4318
email: areadeantothecity@gmail.com

ARCHDEACONRY OF CHARING CROSS

Westminster (Paddington) Revd Jeremy Allcock, St Stephen's Vicarage, 25 Talbot Road, London W2 5JF *Tel:* 020 7792 2283
email: jeremyallcock@ststephenschurch.info
Westminster (St Margaret) Revd Philip Chester, St Matthew's House, 20 Great Peter St, London SW1P 2BU *Tel:* 020 7222 3704
email: office@stmw.org
Westminster (St Marylebone) Preb Alan Moses, 7 Margaret St, London W1W 8JG
Tel: 020 7636 1788
email: alanmoses@blackberry.orange.co.uk

ARCHDEACONRY OF HACKNEY

Hackney Revd Julia Porter-Pryce, St Peter's Vicarage, 86 De Beauvoir Rd, London N1 5AT
Tel: 020 7254 5670
email: juliap@freeuk.com
Islington Revd Michael Learmouth, The Rectory, 10 Thornhill Square, London N1 1BQ
Tel: 020 7607 9039
email: michaelwlearmouth@gmail.com
Tower Hamlets Revd Andy Rider, The Rectory, 2 Fournier Street, London E1 6QE
Tel: 020 7247 0790
email: arider@ccspitalfields.org

ARCHDEACONRY OF MIDDLESEX

Hammersmith and Fulham Revd Canon Guy Wilkinson CBE. 31 Lilyville Road, London SW6 5DP *Tel:* 020 7731 4771
email: guy@gwilkinson.org.uk
Hampton Revd Derek Winterburn, Vicarage, 7 Church St, Hampton, Middlesex TW12 2EB *Tel:* 020 8979 3071
email: vicar@winterburn.me.uk
Hounslow Revd Derek Simpson, Rectory, 3 The Butts, Brentford TW8 8BJ
Tel: 020 8568 7442 (Office)
email: derek.simpson@parishofbrentford.org.uk
Kensington Revd David Walsh, 2 Pembroke Road, London W8 6NT *Tel:* 020 7603 4420
email: vicar@specr.org
Chelsea Revd Canon David Reindorp, 2 Old Church Street, London SW3 5DQ
Tel: 020 7352 5627
email: david.reindorp@talk21.com
Spelthorne Revd David McDougall, St Saviour's Vicarage, 205 Vicarage Road, Sunbury on Thames, Middx TW16 7TP
Tel: 01932 782 800 (Office)
email: david@st-saviours-sunbury.org.uk

ARCHDEACONRY OF HAMPSTEAD

Central Barnet Revd Paul Walmsley-McLeod, The Rectory, 147 Friern Barnet Lane, London N20 0NP *Tel:* 020 8445 7844
email: pawm_friernbarnet@hotmail.com
West Barnet Revd Gwyn Clement, The Vicarage, 34 Parson Street, London NW4 1QR
Tel: 020 8203 2884
email: fr.gwyn@btinternet.com
North Camden (Hampstead) Revd Andrew Cain, Ss Mary and James Vicarage, 134a Abbey Rd, London NW6 4SN *Tel* and *Fax:* 020 7624 5434
email: vicaragekilburn@btopenworld.com
South Camden (Holborn and St Pancras) Revd Andrew Meldrum, St Anne's Vicarage, 106 Highgate West Hill, London N6 6AP
Tel and *Fax:* 020 8340 5190
email: javintner@aol.com
Enfield Revd Dr Richard James, Christ Church Vicarage, 2A Chalk Lane, Cockfosters, Herts EN4 9QJ *Tel:* 020 8441 1230
email: richard.j.ccc@btconnect.com
Revd Christopher Mitchell (*Auxiliary Area Dean*), The Vicarage, St Peter's Road, London N9 8JP *Tel:* 020 8807 7431
email: fatherchris@btinternet.com
East Haringey Revd Dr Olubunmi-Fagbemi, Holy Trinity, Vicarage, Philip Lane, London N15 4GZ
Tel: 020 8801 3021
email: bunmif@btinternet.com
West Haringey Revd Philip Goff, St Augustine's Vicarage, Langdon Park Road, London N6 5OG
Tel: 07768 920 506
email: phildress@blueyonder.co.uk

ARCHDEACONRY OF NORTHOLT

Brent Revd Felicity Scroggie, St Andrew's Vicarage, 956 Harrow Road, Wembley HA0 2QA
Tel: 020 8904 4016
email: felicity.scroggie@london.anglican.org
Ealing Revd Christopher Ramsay, 1 Lancaster Road, Southall UB1 1NP *Tel:* 020 8574 1876
email: christopher.ramsay@btinternet.com
Harrow Canon Richard Bartlett, Holy Trinity Vicarage, Gateway Close, Northwood, HA6 2RP
Tel: 01923 825732
email: richard.bartlett@london.anglican.org
Hillingdon Canon Simon Evans, The Vicarage, 13 Eastcote Road, Ruislip HA4 8BE
Tel: 01895 633040
email: frsimon@waitrose.com

DIOCESE OF MANCHESTER

Founded in 1847. Manchester, except for a few parishes in the south (CHESTER); Salford; Bolton; Bury; Rochdale; Oldham; the western half of Tameside; an area of Wigan; an area of Trafford; an area of Stockport; an area of southern Lancashire.

Population 2,027,000 Area 415 sq m
Full-time Stipendiary Parochial Clergy 220 Benefices 203
Parishes 249 Churches 331
www.manchester.anglican.org
Overseas link dioceses: Lahore, Namibia, Tampere.

BISHOP (11th)
Rt Revd Nigel Simeon McCulloch, Bishopscourt, Bury New Rd, Manchester M7 4LE [2002] (until Jan 2013) *Tel:* 0161 792 2096 (Office)
Fax: 0161 792 6826
email:
bishop@bishopscourt.manchester.anglican.org
[Nigel Manchester]
Bishop's Senior Chaplain Revd Canon Dr Christopher Bracegirdle (*same address*)
email:
chaplain@bishopscourt.manchester.anglican.org

SUFFRAGAN BISHOPS
BOLTON Rt Revd Chris Edmonson, Bishop's Lodge, Walkden Rd, Worsley, Manchester M28 2WH [2008] *Tel:* 0161 790 8289
Fax: 0161 703 9157
email: bishopchris@manchester.anglican.org
MIDDLETON Rt Revd Mark Davies, The Hollies, Manchester Rd, Rochdale OL11 3QY [2008]
Tel: 01706 358550
Fax: 01706 354851
email: bishopmark@manchester.anglican.org

CATHEDRAL AND COLLEGIATE CHURCH OF ST MARY, ST DENYS AND ST GEORGE
Dean Very Revd Rogers Govender, Manchester Cathedral, Victoria St, Manchester M3 1SX [2006]
Tel: 0161 833 2220
email: dean@manchestercathedral.org
Cathedral Office Manchester Cathedral, Victoria St, Manchester M3 1SX *Tel:* 0161 833 2220
Fax: 0161 839 6218
email: office@manchestercathedral.org
Web: www.manchestercathedral.org
Canons Residentiary
Sub Dean and Theologian Canon Andrew Shanks, 3 Booth Clibborn Court, Park Lane, Manchester M7 4PJ [2004] *Tel:* 0161 792 8820
Fax: 0161 839 6218
email: canon.shanks@manchestercathedral.org
Canon Evangelist Canon Tony Hardy, 30 Rathen Rd, Withington, Manchester M20 4GH [2009]
Tel: 0161 446 1099
email:
canon.evangelist@manchestercathedral.org

Canon Precentor Vacancy
email: precentor@manchestercathedral.org
Archdeacon of Manchester
Ven Mark Ashcroft 14 Moorgate Avenue, Withington, Manchester M20 1HE
email:
archmanchester@manchester.anglican.org
Cathedral Chaplains
Revd Peter Bellamy-Knights (Retired)
email:
peter.bellamyknights@manchestercathedral.org
Canon Adrian Rhodes
email: office@manchestercathedral.org
Cathedral Curate
Revd Rhiannon Jones, c/o Cathedral Office
email: curate@manchestercathedral.org

Lay Members of Chapter
Canon David Howe
Canon Jennifer Curtis
Canon Barrie Cheshire
Canon Mike Evans
Cathedral Administrator and Chapter Clerk
Vacancy
Education Officer Mrs Pam Elliott, c/o Cathedral Office (tel. ext. 236)
email: pam.elliott@manchestercathedral.org
Organist and Master of the Choristers
Mr Christopher Stokes, c/o Cathedral Office (tel. ext. 225)
email:
christopher.stokes@manchestercathedral.org
Sub-Organist Mr Jeffrey Makinson, c/o Cathedral Office (tel. ext. 225)
email:
jeffrey.makinson@manchestercathedral.org
Dean's PA Mrs Alison Rowland, c/o Cathedral Office (tel. ext. 220)
email:
alison.rowland@manchestercathedral.org
Administrative Secretary: Miss Joanne Hooper, c/o Cathedral Office (tel. ext. 221)
email: joanne.hooper@manchestercathedral.org
Worship and Music Administrator Miss Katy Leese, c/o Cathedral Office (tel. ext. 238)
email:
worship-music.admin@manchestercathedral.org

Office Assistant: Miss Grace Timperley, c/o Cathedral Office (tel. ext. 222)
email: grace.timperley@manchestercathedral.org
Junior Office Assistant Miss Jade Newbury, c/o Cathedral Office (tel. ext. 235)
email: jade.newbury@manchestercathedral.org
Senior Verger Mr Derrick May, c/o Cathedral Office
email: derrick.may@manchestercathedral.org
Cathedral Architect Mr John Prichard, Lloyd Evans Prichard, No 5 The Parsonage, Manchester, M3 2HS *Tel:* 0161 834 6251
email: john.prichard@lep-architects.co.uk
Cathedral Accountant Mr John Atherden, c/o Cathedral Office (tel. ext 234)
accountant@manchestercathedral.org
Finance Assistant Mrs Joanne Hodkin, c/o Cathedral Office (tel. ext. 224)
email: joanne.hodkin@manchestercathedral.org
Director of Fundraising and Development Mr Anthony O'Connor, c/o Cathedral Office (tel. ext. 233)
email: anthony.o'connor@manchestercathedral.org
Logistics Officer and Cathedral Centre Facilities Manager Mr Peter Mellor, c/o Cathedral Office
Tel: 0161 835 4030
email: peter.mellor@manchestercathedral.org
Volunteer Programme Manager Mrs Lauren Bailey-Rhodes, c/o Cathedral Officer (tel. ext. 237)
email: lauren.bailey-rhodes@manchestercathedral.org

ARCHDEACONS

MANCHESTER Ven Mark Ashcroft, 14 Moorgate Avenue, Withington, Manchester M20 1HE
Tel: 0161 448 1976
email: archmanchester@manchester.anglican.org
ROCHDALE Ven Cherry Vann, 57 Melling Rd, Oldham OL4 1PN *Tel:* 0161 678 1454
Fax: 0161 678 1455
email: archrochdale@manchester.anglican.org
SALFORD Ven David Sharples, 2 The Walled Gardens, Ewhurst Avenue, Swinton M7 0FR
Tel: 0161 794 2331 / 0161 708 9366
Fax: 0161 794 2411
email: archsalford@manchester.anglican.org
BOLTON Ven David Bailey, 14 Springside Road, Bury BL9 5JE *Tel:* 0161 761 6117
Fax: 0161 763 7973
email: archbolton@btinternet.com

CONVOCATION (MEMBERS OF THE HOUSE OF CLERGY OF THE GENERAL SYNOD)

Proctors for Clergy
Ven Dr John Applegate
Canon Sarah Bullock
Revd Sharon Jones
Canon Simon Killwick
Revd Canon Andy Salmon
Ven Cherry Vann

MEMBERS OF THE HOUSE OF LAITY OF THE GENERAL SYNOD

Dr Peter Capon
Mr John Barber
Mr Geoffrey Tattersall
Mr Michael Heppleston
Mr James Townsend

DIOCESAN OFFICERS

Diocesan Secretary Canon Martin Miller, Diocesan Office, Church House, 90 Deansgate, Manchester M3 2GH *Tel:* 0161 828 1412
Fax: 0161 828 1480
Chancellor of Diocese The Worshipful Canon G. F. Tattersall QC, Diocesan Registry, Church House, 90 Deansgate, Manchester M3 2GH
Tel: 0161 834 7545
Deputy Chancellor Ms C. Otton-Goulder, Diocesan Registry, Church House, 90 Deansgate, Manchester M3 2GH *Tel:* 0161 834 7545
Registrar of Diocese and Bishop's Legal Secretary Mrs Jane Monks, Diocesan Registry, Church House, 90 Deansgate, Manchester M3 2GH
Tel: 0161 839 0093
Fax: 0161 839 0093
Diocesan Surveyor for Parsonage Houses Mr John Prichard, The Lloyd Evans Partnership, 5 The Parsonage, Manchester M3 2HS
Tel: 0161 834 6251

DIOCESAN ORGANIZATIONS

Diocesan Office Diocesan Church House, 90 Deansgate, Manchester M3 2GH
Tel: 0161 828 1400
Fax: 0161 828 1480

ADMINISTRATION

Diocesan Synod (Chairman, House of Clergy) Revd Canon Andy Salmon
(Chairman, House of Laity) Canon Peter Capon
Board of Finance (Chairman) Canon Phillip Blinkhorn, 1 Blundell Close, Unsworth, Bury BL9 8LH *Tel:* 0161 766 6301
(Secretary) Canon Martin Miller *(Head of Finance and IT)* Mr Richard O'Connell *(Legal Secretary)* Mrs Jane Monks, Diocesan Registry, Church House *Tel:* 0161 834 7545
Property Committee (Property Secretary) Mr Geoff Hutchinson, Diocesan Office *(Chairman)* Ven David Bailey
Mission Pastoral Committee (Secretary) Canon Martin Miller *(Chairman)* Very Revd Rogers Govender
Designated Officer Mrs Jane Monks, Diocesan Registry, Church House *Tel:* 0161 834 7545

CHURCHES

Advisory Committee for the Care of Churches (Chairman) Mr Richard Byrom, 3 Hawkshaw Lane, Hawkshaw, Bury BL8 4JZ *(DAC Secretary)* Mr Alan Simpson, Diocesan Office

EDUCATION

Chairman Rt Revd Mark Davies

Director of Education Canon Maurice Smith, Diocesan Church House, 90 Deansgate, Manchester M3 2GH *Tel:* 0161 828 1400
Fax: 0161 828 1484

Education Officers

Assistant Director of Education and Section 23/RE Mr John Wilson (*same address*)

Assistant Director of Education and School Improvement Mr Malcolm Finney (*same address*)

School Buildings Officer and Office Manager Mr Ian Tomkin (*same address*)

Diocesan Schools Advisor Governor Support Mr Will Leeson

Children's Work Officer Revd Steve Dixon (*same address*)

Youth Work Officer Miss Susie Mapledoram (*same address*)

CHURCH AND SOCIETY

Chairman Rt Revd Mark Davies

Director Mrs Deborah Dalby, Diocesan Office
Tel: 0161 828 1400

Parish Development Officer Vacancy, Diocesan Office

Mission Planning Officer Ms Alison Peacock, Diocesan Office

Parish Resource Officer Canon Dian Leppington, Diocesan Office

DISCIPLESHIP AND MINISTRY TRAINING

Chairman Revd Canon Sarah Bullock

Director of Ministry Training and OLM Principal Revd Peter Reiss, Diocesan Office

Training Officer (*CME and LD*) Revd David Foster, Diocesan Office

Local Ministry Officer Vacancy, Diocesan Office
Tel: 0161 828 1400

Diocesan Director of Ordinands and OLM Officer Ven David Sharples, Bishopscourt, Bury New Rd, Manchester M4 4LE *Tel:* 0161 708 9366

PRESS AND PUBLICATIONS

Director of Communications David Marshall, Diocesan Office *Tel:* 0161 828 1400
07836 224444 (Mobile)
email: dmarshall@manchester.anglican.org

Editor of Diocesan Year Book c/o Diocesan Office

Editor of Diocesan Magazine Mrs Ann Mummery
email: amummery@manchester.anglican.org

DIOCESAN RECORD OFFICE

For further information apply to The Archivist, The Central Library, St Peter's Square, Manchester M2 5PD *Tel:* 0161 234 1980

AREA DEANS

ARCHDEACONRY OF MANCHESTER

Ardwick Revd Ian Gomersall, St Chrysostom's Rectory, 38 Park Range, Manchester M14 5HQ
Tel: 0161 224 6971
Fax: 0161 870 6197
email: ian.gomersall@btinternet.com

Heaton Revd Les Ireland, St Andrew's Rectory, 27 Errwood Rd, Manchester M19 2PN
Tel: 0161 224 5877
email: LesIreland@ntlworld.com

Hulme Revd Canon Sarah Bullock, St Edmund's Rectory, 1 Range Road, Manchester M16 8FS
Tel: 0161 226 1291

North Manchester Revd Mike McGurk, The Rectory, 95 Church Lane, Harpurhey, Manchester M9 5BG *Tel:* 0161 205 4020
email: rev.mikemcgurk@hotmail.co.uk

Stretford Revd John Hughes, St John's Rectory, 1 Lindum Ave, Old Trafford, Manchester M16 9NQ *Tel:* 0161 872 0500
email: john_dhughes@yahoo.co.uk

Withington Vacancy

ARCHDEACONRY OF BOLTON

Bolton Canon Rodger Petch, 101 Cloister St, Bolton BL1 3HA *Tel:* 01204 842627
email: rodgerpetch@yahoo.co.uk

Bury Revd Gordon Joyce, 1a Pimhole Road, Bury BL9 7EY
email: gordonjoyce@gordonjoyce.eclipse.co.uk

Deane Revd T. Clark, Deane Rectory, 234 Wigan Road, Bolton BL3 5QE *Tel:* 01204 61819
email: clark@clark.cc

Radcliffe and Prestwich Revd Canon Debby Plummer, St Margaret's Vicarage, St Margaret's Rd, Prestwich M25 2QB *Tel:* 0161 773 2698
email: prestwichplummers@btinternet.com

Rossendale Revd Susan Davies, Rectory, 539 Newchurch Rd, Rossendale BB4 9HH
Tel and *Fax:* 01706 219708
email: susanannedavies@aol.com

Walmsley Revd Wendy Oliver, Harwood Vicarage, Stitch-mi-Lane, Bolton BL2 4HU
Tel: 01204 525196
email: wendyloliver@googlemail.com

ARCHDEACONRY OF ROCHDALE

Ashton-under-Lyne Revd Roger Farnworth, St James Vicarage, Union St, Ashton-under-Lyne OL6 9NQ *Tel:* 0161 330 2771
email: rogerfarnworth@aol.com

Heywood and Middleton Revd Canon Philip Miller, The Rectory, Wood St, Langley, Middleton M24 5GL *Tel:* 0161 643 5013
email: canonphil@hotmail.co.uk

Rochdale Revd Sharon Jones, St Andrew's Vicarage, Arm Rd, Dearnley, Littleborough OL15 8NJ *Tel:* 01706 378466
email: sharon@dearnleyvicarage.plus.com

Oldham East Revd Alan Butler, St Mary's Vicarage, 18 Rushcroft Road, High Crompton, Shaw OL2 7PP *Tel:* 01706 847455
email: alanbutler@ntlworld.com

Oldham West Revd David Penny, St Matthew's Vicarage, Mill Brow, Chadderton OL1 2RT
Tel: 0161 624 8600
email: revdpenny@btinternet.com

ARCHDEACONRY OF SALFORD

Eccles Revd Dr Jeremy Sheehy, St Peter's Rectory, Vicarage Road, Swinton M27 0WA
Tel: 0161 794 1578
email: paroffsandp@btconnect.com

Salford Revd Canon Andy Salmon, 6 Encombe Place, Salford M3 6FJ *Tel:* 0161 834 2041
email: rev.andy@btinternet.com

Leigh Revd Jonathan Carmyllie, St Stephen's Vicarage, 7 Holbeck, Astley, Manchester M29 7DU *Tel:* 01942 883313
email: j.carmyllie@btinternet.com

DIOCESE OF NEWCASTLE

Founded in 1882. Northumberland; Newcastle upon Tyne; North Tyneside; a small area of eastern Cumbria; four parishes in northern County Durham.

Population 805,000 Area 2,110 sq m
Full-time Stipendiary Parochial Clergy 115 Benefices 133
Parishes 171 Churches 236
www.newcastle.anglican.org
Companion link dioceses: Winchester, More (Norway), Botswana (Africa).

BISHOP (11th)
Rt Revd John Martin Wharton, Bishop's House, 29 Moor Road South, Gosforth, Newcastle upon Tyne NE3 1PA [1998] *Tel:* 0191 285 2220
email: bishop@newcastle.anglican.org
[Martin Newcastle]
Bishop's Chaplain Revd Ian Flintoft, Bishop's House, 29 Moor Road South, Gosforth, Newcastle upon Tyne NE3 1PA *Tel:* 0191 285 2220
email: i.flintoft@newcastle.anglican.org

ASSISTANT BISHOP
Rt Revd Frank White, (Home) The Vicarage, Riding Mill, Northumberland NE44 6AT
Tel: 01434 682120
email: bishopfrank@newcastle.anglican.org
(Office) Bishop's House, 29 Moor Road South, Gosforth, Newcastle upon Tyne NE3 1PA
Tel: 0191 285 2220

HONORARY ASSISTANT BISHOPS
Rt Revd Kenneth Edward Gill, Kingfisher Lodge, 41 Long Cram, Haddington, East Lothian EH41 4NS [1999] *Tel:* 01620 822113
email: k.gill@newcastle.anglican.org
Rt Revd Stephen Pedley, The Blue House, Newbrough NE47 5AN [2005] *Tel:* 01434 674238
Rt Revd John Henry Richardson, Old Rectory, Bewcastle, Carlisle, Cumbria CA6 6PS [2003]
Tel: 01697 748389

CATHEDRAL CHURCH OF ST NICHOLAS
Dean Very Revd Christopher Charles Dalliston, 26 Mitchell Ave, Jesmond, Newcastle upon Tyne NE2 3LA [2003] *Tel:* 0191 281 6554
0191 232 1939
email: dean@stnicnewcastle.co.uk
Chapter Office Cathedral House, 42/44 Mosley Street, Newcastle upon Tyne NE1 1DF
Tel: 0191 232 1939
email: office@stnicnewcastle.co.uk
Canons Residentiary
Ven Geoffrey Vincent Miller, 80 Moorside North, Fenham, Newcastle upon Tyne NE4 9DU [1999]
Tel: 0191 273 8245
Fax: 0191 226 0286
email: g.miller@newcastle.anglican.org
Canon John Robert Sinclair, 16 Towers Ave, Jesmond, Newcastle upon Tyne NE2 3QE [2011]
Tel: 0191 281 0714
email: djelk@tiscali.co.uk
Canon Kevin Hunt, 55 Queens Terrace, Jesmond, Newcastle upon Tyne NE2 2PL [2012]
Tel: 0191 281 0181
email: kevin.hunt@stnicholascathedral.co.uk
Canon Steven Harvey, 2a Holly Avenue, Jesmond, Newcastle upon Tyne NE2 2PY [from April 2013] *Tel:* 0191 281 4329
email: Tbc
Vacancy
Director of Music Mr Michael Stoddart
Tel: 0191 261 4505
email: directorofmusic@stnicnewcastle.co.uk
Director of Girl's Choir Mr James Norris
email: stnicsgirlschoir@btconnect.com
Cathedral Secretary Ms Elspeth Robertson, Cathedral House *Tel:* 0191 232 1939
email: office@stnicnewcastle.co.uk
Cathedral Administrator Mr Julian Haynes, Cathedral House *Tel:* 0191 232 1939
email: julianhaynes@stnicnewcastle.co.uk
Finance Administrator Mr David Dawe, Cathedral House *Tel:* 0191 232 1939
email: d.dawe@stnicnewcastle.co.uk

ARCHDEACONS
NORTHUMBERLAND Ven Geoffrey Vincent Miller, 80 Moorside North, Fenham, Newcastle upon Tyne NE4 9DU [2005] *Tel:* 0191 273 8245
Fax: 0191 226 0286
email: g.miller@newcastle.anglican.org
LINDISFARNE Ven Peter John Alan Robinson, 4 Acomb Close, Stobhill Manor, Morpeth NE61 2YH [2008] *Tel:* 01670 503810
Fax: 01670 503 469
email: p.robinson@newcastle.anglican.org

CONVOCATION (MEMBERS OF THE HOUSE OF CLERGY OF THE GENERAL SYNOD)
Proctors for Clergy
Revd Janet Appleby
Canon John Sinclair
Canon Dr Dagmar Winter

MEMBERS OF THE HOUSE OF LAITY OF THE GENERAL SYNOD
Canon Dr John Bull
Mrs Margaret White
Canon Carol Wolstenholme

DIOCESAN OFFICERS
Dioc Secretary Mr Graham Barnard, Church House, St John's Terrace, North Shields NE29 6HS
Tel: 0191 270 4100
Fax: 0191 270 4101
Chancellor of Diocese His Honour Judge David Hodson, The Law Courts, Quayside, Newcastle upon Tyne NE1 3LA *Tel:* 0191 201 2000
Registrar of Diocese and Bishop's Legal Secretary Mrs Jane Lowdon, Sintons Solicitors, The Cube, Barrack Rd, Newcastle upon Tyne NE4 6DB
Tel: 0191 226 7878
Fax: 0191 226 7850
email: j.lowdon@sintons.co.uk

DIOCESAN ORGANIZATIONS
Diocesan Office Church House, St John's Terrace, North Shields NE29 6HS *Tel:* 0191 270 4100
Fax: 0191 270 4101
email: church_house@newcastle.anglican.org

ADMINISTRATION
Dioc Synod (Chairman, House of Clergy) Canon John Robert Sinclair, 16 Towers Avenue, Jesmond, Newcastle upon Tyne NE2 3QE
Tel: 0191 281 0714
email: johnsinclair247@aol.com
(Chairman, House of Laity) Mr Michael Stoker, 51 Hastings Avenue, Whitley Bay NE26 4AG
Tel: 0191 252 0250
email: mike.stoker@talk21.com
(Secretary) Mr Graham Barnard, Church House
Secretary to the Diocesan Secretary Mrs Heather Boardman, Church House
Finance Board (Chairman) Mr Simon Harper, Church House
(Secretary) Mr Graham Barnard *(as above)*
Director of Finance and IT Mr Kevin Scott
Accountant Mr John Hall, Church House
Property Manager Mr Ian Beswick, Church House
Dioc Society (Trusts) Mr Graham Barnard *(as above)*
Mission and Pastoral Committee Mr Nigel Foxon, Church House

CHURCHES
Advisory Committee for the Care of Churches (Chairman) Canon Dr Geoffrey Purves, Hawthorn House, Kirkwhelpington, Northumberland NE19 2RT *Tel:* 01830 540395
(Secretary) Mr Nigel Foxon *(as above)*
Closed Churches Committee Mr Nigel Foxon *(as above)*

EDUCATION
Director of Education Mr Jeremy Fitt, Church House
Assistant Director of Education Primary Mr Brian Hedley, Church House
Assistant Director of Education Secondary/FE Mr Mike Davison
Bursar Mrs Eileen Bell, Church House
PA to Director Mrs Susie Taylor, Church House
PA to Assistant Directors Mrs Colleen Miller, Church House
Administrator Mrs Ann Adiguzel, Church House
Part Time Finance Administrator Mrs Lisa Padgett, Church House

MINISTRY AND TRAINING
Director of Ordinands Revd Ian Flintoft, Bishop's House, 29 Moor Road South, Gosforth, Newcastle upon Tyne NE3 1PA *Tel:* 0191 285 2220
email: i.flintoft@newcastle.anglican.org
Continuing Ministerial Education Adviser Revd Dr Alan Gregory, Church House
Bishop's Adviser for Women's Ministry Canon Sheila Bamber, Cathedral House
Development Officer for Children's Work Sandra Doore, Church House
Development Officer for Youth Work Team Leader Canon Andrew Shipton, Church House
Lindisfarne Regional Training Partnership Principal Canon Cathy Rowling, Church House
Director of Studies and Formational Tutor for Clergy IME 1–3 Revd Dr David Bryan, Church House
Formational Tutor for Clergy IME 4–7 Revd Rick Simpson, Church House
Formational Tutor for Readers, Revd Dr Michael Beck, Church House
Director of Discipleship Development Revd Alastair Macnaughton, Church House
Administrator Jenny Burton, Church House
Tel: 0191 270 4100
Secretary, Association of Readers Mrs Sue Hart, 73 Monkseaton Drive, Whitley Bay NE26 3DQ
Tel: 0191 2523941
Retreat House Canon George Hepburn, Shepherds Dene Retreat House, Riding Mill, Hexham, Northumberland NE44 6AF *Tel:* 01434 682212
email: enquiry@shepherdsdene.co.uk
Sons of Clergy Society Mrs Gwenda Gofton, 4 Crossfell, Ponteland NE20 9EA
Tel: 01661 820344
Diocesan Widows Officer Mrs Marjorie Craig, 5 Springwell Meadow, Alnwick NE66 2NY
Tel: 01665 602806

LITURGICAL
Chairman Rt Revd Frank White, Bishop's House, 29 Moor Road South, Gosforth, Newcastle upon Tyne NE3 1PA *Tel:* 0191 285 2220
email: bishopfrank@newcastle.anglican.org

MISSION, SOCIAL RESPONSIBILITY AND ECUMENISM
Adviser in Local Evangelism Revd John Sinclair, 16 Towers Avenue, Jesmond, Newcastle upon Tyne NE2 3QE *Tel:* 0191 281 0714
email: johnsinclair247@aol.com

Church and Church Society Revd Dr Nicholas Buxton, The Vicarage, 3 Crossway, Jesmond, Newcastle upon Tyne NE2 3QH
Tel: 0191 212 0181
email: buxton.nicholas@gmail.com

Ecumenical Officer Revd Janet Appleby, The Vicarage, Berwick Drive, Battle Hill, Wallsend NE28 9ED *Tel:* 0191 262 7518
email: janetappleby@yahoo.com

PRESS, PUBLICITY AND PUBLICATIONS

Dioc Communications Officer Mr Martin Sheppard, Church House

Editor of 'Link' (as above)

Editor of Dioc Year Book Mr Graham Barnard (*as above*)

DIOCESAN RECORD OFFICE

For further information apply to Northumberland Collections Service, Woodhorn, Queen Elizabeth II Country Park, Ashington NE63 9YF
Tel: 01670 528080
email: collections@woodhorn.org.uk

DIOCESAN RESOURCE CENTRE

Contact Karenza Passmore, Church House, St John's Terrace, North Shields NE29 6HS
Tel: 0191 270 4161
Fax: 0191 270 4101
email: k.passmore@resourcescentreonline.co.uk

STEWARDSHIP

Parish Giving Officer Mr Richard Gascoyne, Church House *Tel:* 0191 270 3136
email: r.gascoyne@newcastle.anglican.org

AREA DEANS

ARCHDEACONRY OF NORTHUMBERLAND

Bedlington Revd Derry Twomey, 21 Church Lane, Bedlington, Northumberland NE22 5EL
Tel: 01670 823453
email: derrytwomey@aol.com

Newcastle Central Revd Philip Cunningham, 17 Rectory Rd, Gosforth, Newcastle-upon-Tyne NE3 1XR *Tel:* 0191 285 1326
email: philipcunningham@hotmail.com

Newcastle East Revd Martin Lee, The Vicarage, 3 Station Road, Benton, Newcastle upon Tyne NE12 8AN *Tel:* 0191 266 1921
email: martinlee903@btinternet.com

Newcastle West Revd Nick Darby, St James and St Basil Vicarage, Fenham, Newcastle upon Tyne NE4 9EJ *Tel:* 0191 274 5078
email: npdarby@gmail.com

Tynemouth Canon Adrian John Hughes, St George's Vicarage, Beverley Terrace, Cullercoats, North Shields NE30 4NS *Tel:* 0191 252 1817
email: revajh@btinternet.com

ARCHDEACONRY OF LINDISFARNE

Alnwick Canon Jim Robertson, Whittingham Vicarage, Alnwick, Northumberland NE66 4UP
Tel: 01665 574704
email: canjamesrobertson@virginmedia.com

Bamburgh and Glendale Canon Brian Hurst, Vicarage, 7 The Wynding, Bamburgh, Northumberland NE69 7DB *Tel:* 01668 214748
email: brian.hurst1@btopenworld.com

Bellingham Revd Dr Susan Ramsaran, Rectory, Bellingham, Hexham NE48 2JS
Tel: 01434 220019
email: SMRamsaran@aol.com

Corbridge Revd David Hewlett, Vicarage, Greencroft Avenue, Corbridge NE45 5DW
Tel: 01434 632128
email: david.hewlett3@btinternet.com

Hexham Revd Jon Russell, The Rectory, 16 Forster-steads, Allendale, Northumberland NE47 9AS
Tel: 01434 618607
email: jon.russell@allendalechurch.co.uk

Morpeth Canon Dr Dagmar Winter, Vicarage, Kirkwhelpington, Newcastle upon Tyne NE19 2RT *Tel:* 01830 540260
email: dagmar.winter@btinternet.com

Norham Revd Dr George Robert Joseph (Rob) Kelsey, Vicarage, Norham Berwick upon Tweed TD15 2LF *Tel:* 01289 382325
email: Robert@josephkelsey.fsnet.co.uk

DIOCESE OF NORWICH

Founded in 1094, formerly Thetford (AD 1070), originally Dunwich (AD 630) and Elmham (AD 673). Norfolk, except for the western quarter (ELY); an area of north-east Suffolk.

Population 879,000 Area 1,804 sq m
Full-time Stipendiary Parochial Clergy 170 Benefices 185
Parishes 567 Churches 638
www.norwich.anglican.org
Overseas link provinces: Luleå (Sweden), Papua New Guinea.

BISHOP (71st)

Rt Revd Graham Richard James, Bishop's House, Norwich NR3 1SB [1999] *Tel:* 01603 629001
email: bishop@norwich.anglican.org
[Graham Norvic:]

Bishop's Chaplain Revd Simon Ward (*same address*) *Tel:* 01603 614172
email: bishops.chaplain@norwich.anglican.org

Bishop's PA Mrs Coralie Nichols (*same address*)
Tel: 01603 629001
email: coralie.nichols@norwich.anglican.org

SUFFRAGAN BISHOPS

THETFORD Rt Revd Dr Alan Winton, The Red House, 53 Norwich Rd, Stoke Holy Cross, Norwich NR14 8AB [2009] *Tel:* 01508 491014
email: bishop.thetford@norwich.anglican.org

Bishop's Secretary Graham Cossey (*same address*)
email: graham.cossey@norwich.anglican.org

LYNN Rt Revd Jonathan Meyrick, The Old Vicarage, Castle Acre, King's Lynn PE32 2AA (2011)
Tel: 01760 755553
email: bishoplynn@norwich.anglican.org

Bishop's Secretary Mrs Karon Dugdale (*same address*)
email: karon.dugdale@norwich.anglican.org

HONORARY ASSISTANT BISHOPS

Rt Revd N. Banks, Parkside House, Abbey Mill Lane, St Albans AL3 4HE *Tel:* 01727 836358
email: bishop@richborough.org.uk

Rt Revd E. Devenport, 6 Damocles Court, Pottergate, Norwich NR2 1HN [2000]
Tel: 01603 664121
email: eric@edevenport.orangehome.co.uk

Rt Revd A. Foottit, Ivy House, Whitwell St, Reepham NR10 4RA [2004] *Tel:* 01603 870340
email: acfoottit@hotmail.com

Rt Revd P. Fox, Vicarage, Harwood Rd, Norwich NR1 2NG [2008] *Tel:* 01603 625679
email: peterandangiefox@yahoo.co.uk

Rt Revd R. Garrard, 26 Carol Close, Stoke Holy Cross, Norwich NR14 8NN [2003]
Tel: 01508 494165
email: garrard.r.a@btinternet.com

Rt Revd D. Gillett, 10 Burton Close, Diss IP22 4YJ [2008] *Tel:* 01379 640309
email: dkgillett@btinternet.com

Rt Revd D. Leake, The Anchorage, Lower Common, East Runton, Cromer NR27 9PG [2003]
Tel: 01263 513536
email: david@leake8.wanadoo.co.uk

Rt Revd M. Menin, 32c Bracondale, Norwich NR1 2AN [2000] *Tel:* 01603 627987

Rt Revd J. Salt, 5 Common Place, Walsingham NR22 6BW [2011] *email:* jsalt@ogs.net

Rt Revd L. Urwin, The College, Walsingham NR22 6EF [2009] *Tel:* 01328 824204
email: pr.adm@olw-shrine.org.uk

CATHEDRAL CHURCH OF THE HOLY AND UNDIVIDED TRINITY

Dean Very Revd Graham Smith, The Deanery, The Close, Norwich NR1 4EG [2004]
Tel: 01603 218308 (Office)
email: dean@cathedral.org.uk

Cathedral Office 12 The Close, Norwich NR1 4DH
Tel: 01603 218300
email: reception@cathedral.org.uk
Web: www.cathedral.org.uk

Canons Residentiary

Canon Pastor and Custos Canon Richard Capper, 52 The Close, Norwich NR1 4EG [2005]
Tel: 01603 665210 (Home)
01603 218331 (Office)
email: canonpastor@cathedral.org.uk

Precentor and Vice-Dean Canon Jeremy Haselock, 34 The Close, Norwich NR1 4DZ [1998]
Tel: 01603 619169 (Home)
01603 218306 (Office)
email: precentor@cathedral.org.uk

Canon Librarian Canon Dr Peter Doll, 56 The Close, Norwich NR1 4EG [2009]
Tel: 01603 666758 (Home)
01603 218336 (Office)
email: canonlibrarian@cathedral.org.uk

Chapter Steward Mr Neil Parsons, 12 The Close
Tel: 01603 218300
email: chaptersteward@cathedral.org.uk

Master of the Music Mr Ashley Grote, 12 The Close
Tel: 01603 626589
email: masterofmusic@cathedral.org.uk

Sacrist Mr Roger Lee, 12 The Close
Tel: 01603 218325
email: sacrist@cathedral.org.uk

ARCHDEACONS

NORWICH Ven Jan McFarlane, 31 Bracondale, Norwich NR1 2AT [2009] *Tel:* 01603 620007
email: archdeacon.norwich@norwich.anglican.org

LYNN Ven John Ashe, Holly Tree House, Whitwell Rd, Sparham, Norwich NR9 5PN [2009]
Tel: 01362 688032
email: archdeacon.lynn@norwich.anglican.org

NORFOLK Ven Steven Betts, 8 Boulton Rd, Thorpe St Andrew, Norwich NR7 0DF [2012]
Tel: 01603 559199
email: archdeacon.norfolk@norwich.anglican.org

CONVOCATION (MEMBERS OF THE HOUSE OF CLERGY OF THE GENERAL SYNOD)

Proctors for Clergy
Ven Steven Betts
Ven Jan McFarlane
Revd Charles Read
Revd Dr Patrick Richmond

MEMBERS OF THE HOUSE OF LAITY OF THE GENERAL SYNOD

Mr Robin Back
Mrs Susan Johns
Mr Geoff Wortley

DIOCESAN OFFICERS AND ADMINISTRATION

Diocesan Office
Diocesan House, 109 Dereham Rd, Easton, Norwich NR9 5ES *Tel:* 01603 880853
email: diocesan.house@norwich.anglican.org
Dioc Secretary Mr Richard Butler MBE DL, Dioc House *Tel:* 01603 880853
email: richard.butler@norwich.anglican.org
Deputy Dioc Secretary and Director of Operations Mr David Broom, Dioc House *Tel:* 01603 882367
email: david.broom@norwich.anglican.org
Chancellor of Diocese c/o Registrar of the Diocese
Registrar of Diocese and Bishop's Legal Secretary Mr Stuart Jones, Birketts LLP, Kingfisher House, 1 Gilders Way, Norwich NR3 1UB
Tel: 01603 756501
email: stuart.jones@norwich.anglican.org
Diocesan Record Office Norfolk Record Office, Archive Centre, County Hall, Martineau Lane, Norwich NR1 2DO
County Archivist Dr John Alban
Tel: 01603 222599

Diocesan Synod
Chair, House of Clergy The Archdeacon of Norfolk (*as above*)
Chair, House of Laity Mr Geoff Wortley, c/o Dioc House *email:* jamesgwortley@aol.com
Secretary and Dioc Electoral Registration Officer Mr David Broom (*as above*)
Designated Officer Diocesan Secretary (*as above*)
Board of Finance
President The Bishop of Norwich (*as above*)
Chair Mr Bill Husselby, c/o Dioc House
email: bill.husselby@cogent.co.uk
Secretary Diocesan Secretary (*as above*)
Director of Finance Miss Susan Bunting, Dioc House *Tel:* 01603 882377
email: susan.bunting@norwich.anglican.org
Property Committee
Chair Mr David Richardson, c/o Dioc House
email: david.richardson@arnolds.uk.com
Surveyor Mr Michael Marshall, Dioc House
Tel: 01603 882364
email: michael.marshall@norwich.anglican.org

Diocesan Mission and Pastoral Committee
Chair Mrs Sue Johns, c/o Dioc House
email: sue.johns@hse.gsi.gov.uk
Secretary Mr David Broom (*as above*)
Board of Patronage
Chair Canon Stuart Nairn, Rectory, Main Rd, Narborough, King's Lynn PE32 1TE
Tel: 01760 338552
email: nairn.nvgrectory@btinternet.com
Secretary Mrs Jennifer Vere, Southlands, Church Corner, North Lopham, Diss IP22 2LP
Tel: 01379 687679
DAC (*Diocesan Advisory Committee for the Care of Churches*)
Chair Mr Alan Kefford, Dioc House
email: akeff@aol.com
Secretary Mrs Jean Gosling, Dioc House
Tel: 01603 882350
email: jean.gosling@norwich.anglican.org

Board of Education
Chair Canon Peter Hartley, c/o Dioc House
email: peter.hartley49@btinternet.com
Director of Education Mr Andy Mash, Dioc House
Tel: 01603 881352
email: andy.mash@norwich.anglican.org
Schools' Adviser Mrs Gill Hipwell, Dioc House
Tel: 01603 882346
email: gill.hipwell@norwich.anglican.org

Children, Youth and Families
Coordinator Mr Mark Heybourne, Dioc House
Tel: 01603 882362
email: mark.heybourne@norwich.anglican.org
Administrator Mrs Liz Dawes, Dioc House
Tel: 01603 882354
email: liz.dawes@norwich.anglican.org
The Horstead Centre (*Residential Activity Centre*), Rectory Rd, Horstead, Norwich NR12 7EP
Web: www.horsteadcentre.org.uk
Manager Josie Barnett, c/o Horstead Centre
Tel: 01603 737215
email: josie.barnett@norwich.anglican.org

Discipleship and Ministry Forum (and Governing Board of the Ordained Local Ministry Scheme)
Chair The Bishop of Thetford (*as above*)
Emmaus House 65 The Close, Norwich NR1 4DH
Bishop's Officer for Ordinands and Initial Training Revd David Foster *Tel:* 01603 729811
email: david.foster@norwich.anglican.org

Principal of Dioc Ministry Course Revd Dr Sue Woan *Tel:* 01603 729812
email: sue.woan@norwich.anglican.org
Vice-Principal of Dioc Ministry Course and Director of Studies Revd Charles Read *Tel:* 01603 729813
email: charles.read@norwich.anglican.org
Continuing Ministerial Development Officer Revd Tim Dean *Tel:* 01603 729817
email: tim.dean@norwich.anglican.org
Lay Development Co-ordinator Revd Susanna Gunner *Tel:* 01603 729815
email: susanna.gunner@norwich.anglican.org
Dioc Officer for NSMs Revd Roger MacPhee, 8 Lawn Close, Knapton, North Walsham NR28 0SD *Tel:* 01263 720045
email: rmacphee4@aol.com

Readers' Committee
Chair and Warden of Readers) The Archdeacon of Lynn (*as above*)
Hon. Secretary Mr John Pountain, Brambles, Briar Lane, Swainsthorpe, Norwich NR14 8PX
Tel: 01508 470567
County Ecumenical Officer Revd Simon Wilson, Rectory, Guist Rd, Foulsham, Dereham NR20 5RZ *Tel:* 01362 683275
email: simon.wilson@norwich.anglican.org
Diocesan Ecumenical Officer Revd Dale Gingrich, Church Bungalow, Gayton Rd, Gaywood, King's Lynn PE30 4DZ *Tel:* 01508 765167
email: dale.gingrich@norwich.anglican.org
Bishop's Officer for Retired Clergy and Widows Canon Patrick Foreman, Seorah, 7 Mallard's Close, Fakenham NR21 8PU *Tel:* 01328 853691
email: patrick@pandmforeman.eclipse.co.uk
Mission The Archdeacon of Norwich (*as above*)
Liturgical Adviser Canon Jeremy Haselock (*as above*)
Chair of Liturgical Committee Revd Charles Read (*as above*)

Communications
Director of Communications Ven Jan McFarlane (*as above*) *Tel:* 07818 422395 (mobile)
Internal Communications Officer Mr Gordon Darley, Dioc House *Tel:* 01603 882349
email: gordon.darley@norwich.anglican.org
Magazine Editor Revd Barry Furness, Dioc House *Tel:* 01603 882348
email: barry.furness@norwich.anglican.org
Social and Community Concerns
Coordinator Revd Simon Wilson (*as above*)
Urban Affairs and Church Urban Fund Canon Peter Howard, St Francis Vicarage, Rider Haggard Rd, Norwich NR7 9UQ *Tel:* 01603 702799
email: plhoward@btinternet.com
Tourism The Archdeacon of Norfolk (*as above*)

RURAL DEANS

ARCHDEACONRY OF NORWICH

Norwich East Canon Peter Howard, St Francis Vicarage, Rider Haggard Rd, Norwich NR7 9UQ
Tel: 01603 702799
email: plhoward@btinternet.com
Norwich North Revd Paul Mackay, St Catherine's Vicarage, Aylsham Road, Mile Cross, Norwich NR3 2RJ *Tel:* 01603 426767
email: vicar@stcatherinesmilecross.org.uk
Norwich South Canon Alan Strange, Rectory, 17 Essex Street, Norwich NR2 5BL
Tel: 01603 622225
email: rector@trinitynorwich.org

ARCHDEACONRY OF NORFOLK

Blofield Revd Paul Cubitt, The Rectory, 10 Oak Wood, Blofield, Norwich NR13 4JQ
Tel: 01603 713160
email: revp@cubitt.karoo.co.uk
Depwade Revd David Sochon, The Bungalow, Wolfer Green, Shotesham, Norwich NR15 1YP
Tel: 01508 558495
email: davids@tasvalley.org
Great Yarmouth Revd Chris Terry, Ludham House, 55 South Beach Parade, Great Yarmouth NR30 1DJ *Tel:* 01493 842915
email: gyteamrector@btinternet.com
Humbleyard Revd Christopher Davies, Vicarage, 5 Vicar St, Wymondham, NR18 0PL
Tel: 01953 602269
email: vicar@wymondhamabbey.org.uk
Loddon Revd Robert Parsonage, Rectory, Rectory Lane, Poringland, Norwich NR14 7SL
Tel: 01508 492215
email: rector@poringland-benefice.org.uk
Lothingland Canon Ian Bentley, St Mark's Vicarage, 212 Bridge Road, Oulton Broad, Lowestoft NR33 9JX *Tel:* 01502 572563
email: ian@revbentley.freeserve.co.uk
Redenhall Canon Tony Billett, Rectory, 26 Mount St, Diss IP22 3QG *Tel:* 01379 642072
email: disschurch2@btconnect.com
St Benet at Waxham and Tunstead Revd Simon Lawrence, The Rectory, Campingfield Lane, Stalham NR12 9DT *Tel:* 01692 580250
email: simon.stalham@btinternet.com
Thetford and Rockland Revd Matthew Jackson, The Rectory, Surrogate Street, Attleborough NR17 2AW *Tel:* 01953 453185
email: therectory@me.com

ARCHDEACONRY OF LYNN

Breckland Canon Stuart Nairn, Rectory, Main Rd, Narborough, King's Lynn PE32 1TE
Tel: 01760 338552
email: nairn.nvgrectory@btinternet.com
Burnham and Walsingham Revd Canon Peter McCrory, Dane House, The Street, Kettlestone, Fakenham NR31 0AU *Tel:* 01328 878455
email: peter@virgin.net
Dereham in Mitford Canon Sally Theakston, Rectory, Vicarage Meadows, Dereham NR19 1TW
Tel: 01362 693680
email: stheakston@aol.com
Heacham and Rising Revd Steve Davies, The Vicarage, 12b Church Lane, Heacham, King's Lynn PE31 7HJ *Tel:* 01485 570268
email: heacham.vicar@googlemail.com

Holt Revd Jeremy Sykes, The Vicarage, Grange Close, Briston, Melton Constable NR24 2LY
Tel: 01263 860280
email: Jeremy@Sykes-UK.com

Ingworth Revd Brian Faulkner, Rectory, School Road, Erpingham, Norwich NR11 7QX
Tel: 01263 768073
email: brian-faulkner@lineone.net

Lynn Revd Christopher Ivory, St Margaret's Vicarage, St Margaret's Place, King's Lynn PE30 5DL
Tel: 01553 767090
email: vicar@stmargaretskingslynn.org.uk

Repps Revd Canon Dr David Court, The Vicarage, 30 Cromwell Road, Cromer NR27 0BE
Tel: 01263 512000
email: revdavidcourt@btinternet.com

Sparham Revd Selwyn Tillett, The Rectory, Ringland Lane, Weston Longville, Norwich NR9 5JU
Tel: 01603 880563
email: selwyn@tillett.org.uk

DIOCESE OF OXFORD

Founded in 1542. Oxfordshire; Berkshire; Buckinghamshire; one parish in each of Hampshire and Hertfordshire.

Population 2,250,000 Area 2,221 sq m
Full-time Stipendiary Parochial Clergy 358 Benefices 294
Parishes 616 Churches 816
www.oxford.anglican.org
Overseas link dioceses: Vaxjo (Sweden), Kimberley and Kuruman (Southern Africa).

BISHOP (42nd)
Rt Revd John Pritchard, Diocesan Church House, North Hinksey, Oxford OX2 0NB [2007] *Tel:* 01865 208200 (Office) *Fax:* 01865 790470 *email:* bishopoxon@oxford.anglican.org
Bishop's Domestic Chaplain Revd Amanda Bloor (*same address*) *Tel:* 01865 208200 (Office) *Fax:* 01865 790470

AREA BISHOPS
READING Rt Revd Andrew Proud, Bishop's House, Tidmarsh Lane, Tidmarsh, Reading RG8 8HA [2011] *Tel:* 0118 984 1216 *Fax:* 0118 984 1218 *email:* bishopreading@oxford.anglican.org
BUCKINGHAM Rt Revd Dr Alan Wilson, Sheridan, Grimms Hill, Gt Missenden HP16 9BG [2003] *Tel:* 01494 862173 *Fax:* 01494 890508 *email:* bishopbucks@oxford.anglican.org
DORCHESTER Rt Revd Colin Fletcher, Arran House, Sandy Lane, Yarnton, Oxford OX5 1PB [2000] *Tel:* 01865 375541 *Fax:* 01865 379890 *email:* bishopdorchester@oxford.anglican.org

PROVINCIAL EPISCOPAL VISITOR
EBBSFLEET Vacancy

HONORARY ASSISTANT BISHOPS
Rt Revd Keith Arnold, 9 Dinglederry, Olney MK46 5ES [1997] *Tel:* 01234 713044
Rt Revd John Bone, 4 Grove Rd, Henley-on-Thames RG9 1DH [1997] *Tel:* 01491 413482
Rt Revd Anthony Russell, Lye Hill House, Holton, Oxford OX33 1QF [2011] *Tel:* 01865 876415
Rt Revd William Down, 54 Dark Lane, Witney OX28 6LX [2001] *Tel:* 01993 706615
Rt Revd Ronald Gordon, Garden Flat B, St Katherine's House, Ormond Road, Wantage OX12 8EA [1991] *Tel:* 01235 760766
Rt Revd James Johnson, St Helena, 28 Molyneux Drive, Bodicote, Banbury OX15 4AP [2005] *Tel:* 01295 255357
Rt Revd Peter Nott, Westcot House, Westcot, Sparsholt, Wantage OX12 9QA [1999] *Tel:* 01235 751233
Rt Revd Henry Richmond, 39 Hodges Court, Marlborough Rd, Oxford OX1 4NZ [1999] *Tel:* 01865 790466
Rt Revd Henry Scriven, 16 East St Helens St, Abingdon, Oxford, Oxon OX14 5EA *Tel:* 01235 536607

CATHEDRAL CHURCH OF CHRIST
Dean Very Revd Dr Christopher Lewis, The Deanery, Christ Church, Oxford OX1 1DP [2003] *Tel:* 01865 276161 *Fax:* 01865 276238
Dean's PA Miss Rachel Perham (*same address*) *Tel:* 01865 276161 *email:* rachel.perham@chch.ox.ac.uk
Sub-Dean Revd Canon Dr Edmund Newell, Christ Church, Oxford OX1 1DP [2008] *Tel:* 01865 276278 *email:* subdean@chch.ox.ac.uk
Sub-Dean's PA and Education Assistant Miss Hannah Clegg (*same address*) *Tel:* 01865 276278/286829/86003 *Fax:* 01865 276277 *email:* hannah.clegg@chch.ox.ac.uk
Canons Residentiary
Canon Prof. Graham Ward, Christ Church, Oxford OX1 1DP [2012]
Canon Prof. George Pattison, Priory House, Christ Church, Oxford OX1 1DP [2004] *Tel:* 01865 276247 *email:* george.pattison@chch.ox.ac.uk
Canon Prof Sarah Foot, Christ Church, Oxford OX1 1DP [2007] *Tel:* 01865 286078 *email:* sarah.foot@chch.ox.ac.uk
Canon Prof Nigel Biggar, Christ Church, Oxford OX1 1DP [2007] *Tel:* 01865 276219 *email:* nigel.biggar@chch.ox.ac.uk
Canon Angela Tilby, Christ Church, Oxford OX1 1DP [2011] Tel: 01865 208760 *email:* angela.tilby@oxford.anglican.org
Precentor Revd John Paton, Christ Church, Oxford OX1 1DP [2003] *Tel:* 01865 276214 *email:* john.paton@chch.ox.ac.uk/precentor@chch.ox.ac.uk

Liturgy and Publicity Assistant Mr David Bannister, Christ Church, Oxford OX1 1DP
Tel: 01865 276214
email: david.bannister@chch.ox.ac.uk
Cathedral Registrar Mr John Briggs, Christ Church, Oxford OX1 1DP *Tel:* 01865 286846
email: john.briggs@chch.ox.ac.uk
Cathedral Office Manager Mrs Eileen Head, Christ Church, Oxford OX1 1DP *Tel:* 01865 276155
Fax: 01865 276277
email: eileen.head@chch.ox.ac.uk
Cathedral Organist Dr Stephen Darlington, Christ Church, Oxford OX1 1DP *Tel:* 01865 276195
email: stephen.darlington@chch.ox.ac.uk
Organist's Secretary Miss Florence Maskell, Christ Church, Oxford OX1 1DP *Tel:* 01865 276195
email: florence.maskell@chch.ox.ac.uk
Dean's Verger Mr Matthew Power, Christ Church, Oxford OX1 1DP
Tel (Sacristy): 01865 276154/286002
email: matthew.power@chch.ox.ac.uk
Canons' Verger Miss Jessica Hallion, Christ Church, Oxford OX1 1DP
Tel (Sacristy): 01865 276154/286002
email: jessica.hallion@chch.ox.ac.uk
Cathedral Verger Mr Nathan Shipstone, Christ Church, Oxford OX1 1DP
Tel (Sacristy): 01865 276154/286002
email: nathanshipstone@chch.ox.ac.uk
Cathedral Verger Miss Katie McKeogh, Christ Church, Oxford OX1 1DP
Tel (Sacristy): 01865 276154/286002
email: katie.mckeogh@chch.ox.ac.uk
Education and Visitors' Officer/Verger Mr Jim Godfrey, Christ Church, Oxford OX1 1DP
Tel: 01865 276154/286003
email: jim.godfrey@chch.ox.ac.uk

ARCHDEACONS

OXFORD Vacancy *Tel* and *Fax:* 01865 208245
email: archdoxf@oxford.anglican.org
BERKSHIRE Ven Norman Russell, Foxglove House, Love Lane, Donnington, Newbury RG14 2JG [1998] *Tel:* 01635 552820
Fax: 01635 522165
email: archdber@oxford.anglican.org
BUCKINGHAM Ven Karen Gorham, Rectory, Stone, Aylesbury HP17 8RZ [2007] *Tel:* 01865 208264
email: archdbuc@oxford.anglican.org

CONVOCATION (MEMBERS OF THE HOUSE OF CLERGY OF THE GENERAL SYNOD)

Proctors for Clergy
The Bishop of Oxford
Revd Jonathan Beswick
Canon Dr Judith Maltby
Canon Susan Booys
Revd Dr Mark Chapman
Revd Hugh Lee
Revd John Cook
Ven Karen Gorham
Canon Rosie Harper
Canon Christopher Sugden
Canon John Wynburne

MEMBERS OF THE HOUSE OF LAITY OF THE GENERAL SYNOD

Mrs Julie Dziegiel
Mr Robert Hurley
Miss Prudence Dailey
Dr Philip Giddings
Mrs Victoria Russell
Mr Brian Newey
Mr Gavin Oldham
Dr Anna Thomas-Betts

DIOCESAN OFFICERS

Dioc Secretary Canon Rosemary Pearce, Diocesan Church House, North Hinksey Lane, Oxford OX2 0NB *Tel:* 01865 208200
Fax: 01865 790470
email: diosec@oxford.anglican.org
Chancellor of Diocese Revd Dr Rupert Bursell QC, Diocesan Registry, 16 Beaumont St, Oxford OX1 2LZ *Tel:* 01865 297200
Fax: 01865 726274
email: oxford@winckworths.co.uk
Registrar of Diocese and Bishop's Legal Secretary Canon John Rees (*same address*)
Registrar of the Archdeaconries Canon John Rees (*as above*)

DIOCESAN ORGANIZATIONS

Diocesan Office Diocesan Church House, North Hinksey Lane, Oxford OX2 0NB
Tel: 01865 208200
Fax: 01865 790470

ADMINISTRATION

Dioc Synod (*Vice-President, House of Clergy*) Vacancy
(*Vice-President, House of Laity*) Mrs Judith Scott, 4 Crescent Rd, Wokingham RG40 2DB
Tel: 0118 977 1656
email: jscott@bcs.org.uk
(*Secretary*) Canon Rosemary Pearce, Dioc Church House
Board of Finance (*Chairman*) Mr Brian Newey, Chestnut Cottage, The Green South, Warborough, Wallingford OX10 7DN *Tel:* 01865 858322
Fax: 01865 858043
(*Secretary*) Canon Rosemary Pearce (*as above*)
Director of Glebe and Buildings Mr David Mason Dioc Church House *Tel:* 01865 208230
email: david.mason@oxford.anglican.org
Dioc Trustees (Oxford) Ltd Canon Rosemary Pearce (*as above*)
Pastoral Committee (Secretary) and Electoral Roll Officer Mr Howard Cattermole, Dioc Church House *Tel:* 01865 208243
email: howard.cattermole@oxford.anglican.org
Designated Officer Canon John Rees (*as above*)

CHURCHES

Advisory Committee for the Care of Churches (Chairman) Mr Charles Baker *email:* cb@charlesbaker.org
(Secretary) Miss Natalie Merry, Dioc Church House *Tel:* 01865 208229 *email:* natalie.merry@oxford.anglican.org
Sites Advisory Committee (Secretary) Mr Howard Cattermole *(as above)*

MISSION

Director Revd Dr Michael Beasley, Dioc Church House *Tel:* 01865 208251 *email:* michael.beasley@oxford.anglican.org
Parish Development Advisers
Buckingham Mr Andrew Gear, Dioc Church House *Tel:* 01865 208256 *email:* andrew.gear@oxford.anglican.org
Oxford Canon Olivia Graham, Dioc Church House *Tel:* 01865 208246 *email:* olivia.graham@oxford.anglican.org
Berkshire Revd Catharine Morris, Diocesan Church House *Tel:* 01865 208296 *email:* catharine.morris@oxford.anglican.org
Children's Work Mrs Yvonne Morris, Dioc Church House *Tel:* 01865 208255 *email:* yvonne.morris@oxford.anglican.org
Safeguarding Adviser Mr Stephen Barber, Dioc Church House *Tel:* 01865 208290 *email:* stephen.barber@oxford.anglican.org
Christian Giving and Funding Adviser Mr Robin Brunner-Ellis, Dioc Church House *Tel:* 01865 208254 *email:* robin.brunner-ellis@oxford.anglican.org
Director of Local Ministry Training Revd Dr Keith Beech-Gruneberg, Dioc Church House *Tel:* 01865 208282 *email:* keith.gruneberg@oxford.anglican.org
Deputy Warden of Readers and Director of Postgraduate Studies Revd Phillip Tovey, 20 Palmer Place, Abingdon, OX14 5LZ *Tel:* 01865 208212 *email*: phillip.tovey@oxford.anglican.org
Youth Work Mr Ian Macdonald, Dioc Church House *Tel:* 01865 208253 *email:* ian.macdonald@oxford.anglican.org
Director of Initial Ministerial Education (Part 2) Revd Beren Hartless *Tel:* 01865 208258 *email:* beren.hartless@oxford.anglican.org
Diocesan Director of Ordinands Revd Jules Cave Bergquist, Diocesan Church House, North Hinksey Lane, Oxford OX2 0NB *Tel:* 01865 208260
Directors of Ordinands
Oxfordshire and Dorchester Revd Jules Cave Bergquist *(as above)*
Berkshire Revd David Heslop, Dioc Church House *Tel:* 01865 208261
Buckingham Revd Caroline Windley, 1 Cavalry Path, Aylesbury HP19 9RP *Tel* and *Fax:* 01296 432921 *email:* caroline.windley@oxford.anglican.org
Vocation Network Chair Revd Jules Cave Bergquist *(as above)*

EDUCATION

Director of Education Ms Anne Davey, Dioc Church House *Tel:* 01865 208236 *email:* anne.davey@oxford.anglican.org

MISSIONARY AND ECUMENICAL

Partnership in World Mission (Secretary) Vacancy
Ecumenical Officers
Oxford Vacancy
Berkshire Vacancy
Buckingham Canon Tony Dickinson, St Francis' Vicarage, Amersham Rd, Terriers, High Wycombe HP13 5AB *Tel:* 01494 520676 *email:* tony.dickinson@oxford.anglican.org
Milton Keynes Vacancy

COMMUNICATIONS

Director of Communications Ms Sarah Meyrick, Dioc Church House *Tel:* 01865 208224
Editor of Dioc Newspaper 'The Door' Miss Joanne Duckles, Dioc Church House *Tel:* 01865 208227 *email:* joanne.duckles@oxford.anglican.org

DIOCESAN RECORD OFFICES

County Archivist, St Luke's Church, Temple Rd, Cowley, Oxford OX4 2EN *Tel:* 01865 398200 *email:* archives@oxfordshire.gov.uk *(For records of the diocese, and parish records in the archdeaconry of Oxford)*
Berkshire Record Office, 9 Coley Ave, Reading RG1 6AF *Tel:* 0118 901 5132 *(For parish records in the archdeaconry of Berkshire)*
Buckinghamshire Record Office, County Hall, Aylesbury, Bucks. HP20 1UA *Tel:* 01296 382587 *(For parish records in the archdeaconry of Buckingham)*

SOCIAL RESPONSIBILITY

Social Responsibility Adviser (Secretary) Ms Alison Webster, Dioc Church House *Tel:* 01865 208213 *email:* alison.webster@oxford.anglican.org
PACT (Parents and Children Together) Council for Social Work Mrs Jan Fishwick, 7 Southern Court, South St, Reading RG1 4QS *Tel:* 0118 938 7600 *email:* info@pactcharity.org
Council for the Deaf (Chairman) Revd Tim Edge, 27 Burford Road, Witney OX28 6DP *Tel:* 01993 773438 *email:* tim.edge@talk21.com

AREA DEANS

ARCHDEACONRY OF OXFORD

Aston and Cuddesdon Canon Sue Booys, Rectory, Manor Farm Rd, Dorchester OX10 7HZ *Tel:* 01865 340007 *email:* rector@dorchester-abbey.org.uk
Bicester and Islip Revd Charles Masheder, Rectory, Church Walk, Ambrosden, Oxon OX25 2UJ *Tel:* 01869 247813 *email:* chasmash@ic24.net

Chipping Norton Canon Judy French, Vicarage, Church Lane, Charlbury OX7 3PX
Tel: 01608 810286
email: vicar@stmaryscharlbury.co.uk

Cowley Canon Bruce Gillingham, St Clement's Rectory, 58 Rectory Rd, Oxford OX4 1BW
Tel: 01865 246674
email: bruce@stclements.org.uk

Deddington Revd Patricia Freeth, Vicarage, High St, Cropredy, Oxon OX17 1NG
Tel: 01295 750980
email: shiresedge@btinternet.com

Henley Revd Kevin Davies, The Rectory, Checkendon, Reading RG8 0SR *Tel:* 01491 680252
email: revkevdavies-langtree@yahoo.co.uk

Oxford Revd Dr Mark Butchers, 1 Mere Road, Wolvercote ,Oxford OX2 8AN
Tel and *Fax:* 01865 515640
email: mark.butchers@dsl.pipex.com

Witney Revd William Blakey, St John's Rectory, 6 Burford Rd, Caterton, Oxon OX18 3AA
Tel: 01993 846996
email: rector@theblakeys.co.uk

Woodstock Revd Ernest Jones, Rectory, 22 Castle Road, Wootton, Woodstock, OX20 1EG
Tel: 01993 812543
email: three.churches@virgin.net

ARCHDEACONRY OF BERKSHIRE

Abingdon Revd Pam McKellen, Vicarage, Radley, Abingdon OX14 2JN *Tel:* 01235 554739
email: p.mckellen@btinternet.com

Bracknell Canon Nick Parish, 1 Old Lands Hill, Bracknell RG12 2QX *Tel:* 01344 867383
email: nick.parish@ntlworld.com

Bradfield Revd William Watts, The Vicarage, Pangbourne Road, Upper Basildon RG8 8LS
Tel: 01491 671714
email: willwatts@f2s.com

Maidenhead Revd Michael Smith, The Vicarage, Churchgate, Cookham SL6 9SP
Tel: 01628 529661
email: michael_d_smith@btinternet.com

Newbury Canon Rita Ball, Rectory, High Street, Hermitage, Berks RG18 9ST *Tel:* 01635 202967
email: rita.e.ball@btinternet.com

Reading Canon Brian Shenton, Hamelsham, Downshire Square, Reading RG1 6NJ
Tel: 0118 957 1057
Fax: 0118 958 7041
email: stmaryshouserdg@waitrose.com

Sonning Canon David Hodgson, Rectory, 2a Norreys Ave, Wokingham RG40 1TU
Tel: 0118 979 2797
email: david@allsaintswokingham.org.uk

Vale of White Horse Canon Richard Hancock, St Andrew's Vicarage, High St, Shrivenham, Swindon SN6 8AN *Tel:* 01793 780183
email: revdhancock@standrews-shrivenham.fsnet.co.uk

Wallingford Revd Jason St John Nicolle, The Rectory, Church End, Blewbury, OX11 9QH
Tel: 01235 850267
email: office@churnchurches.co.uk

Wantage Vacancy

ARCHDEACONRY OF BUCKINGHAM

Amersham Revd Camilla Walton, 3 St Michael's Green, Beaconsfield HP9 2BN *Tel:* 01494 673464
email: camillawalton@googlemail.com

Aylesbury, Revd Andrew Blyth, The Rectory, 42 Redwood Drive, Aylesbury HP21 9RJ
Tel: 01296 394906
email: andrew.blyth@htaylesbury.org

Buckingham Revd Ron Bundock, 1 Holton Road, Buckingham MK18 1PQ *Tel:* 01280 813887
email: jandrb@bundock.com

Burnham Vacancy

Claydon Revd David Meakin, The Rectory, 1 Greenacres Close, Whitchurch, Aylesbury HP22 4JP *Tel:* 01296 641606
email: d.meakin@btinternet.com

Milton Keynes Revd Tim Norwood, 3 Daubeney Gate, Shenley Church End, Milton Keynes MK5 6EH *Tel:* 01908 505812
email: tim@mkdeanery.org

Mursley Revd Laurence Meering, The Rectory, 1 St Mary's Close, Mursley. MK17 0HP
Tel: 01296 728055
email: laurencemeering@yahoo.co.uk

Newport Canon Christa Pumfrey, New Rectory, 7a Northampton Rd, Lavendon, Olney MK46 4EY
Tel: 01234 240013
email: christa.pumfrey@btinternet.com

Wendover Revd Mark Dearnley, Vicarage, 34a Dobbins Lane, Wendover HP22 6DH
Tel: 01296 622230
email: markdearnley@ntlworld.com

Wycombe Revd Simon Cronk, The Vicarage, Valley Road, Hughenden Valley, Bucks HP14 4PF
Tel: 01494 563439
email: simon.cronk@talktalk.net

DIOCESE OF PETERBOROUGH

Founded in 1541. Northamptonshire, except for one parish in the west (LEICESTER); Rutland; Peterborough, except for an area in the south-east; one parish in Lincolnshire.

Population 847,000 Area 1,149 sq m
Full-time Stipendiary Parochial Clergy 117 Benefices 134
Parishes 343 Churches 378
www.peterborough-diocese.org.uk
Overseas link diocese: Bungoma (Kenya).

BISHOP (37th)
Rt Revd Donald Spargo Allister, Bishop's Lodging, The Palace, Peterborough PE1 1YA
Tel: 01733 562492
Fax: 01733 890077
email: bishop@peterborough-diocese.org.uk
Bishop's Personal Assistant Miss Alex Low (*same address*)
email: alex.low@peterborough-diocese.org.uk
Bishop's Chaplain Revd Canon Julie Hutchinson (*same address*) *Tel:* 01733 887014 (Office)
Fax: 01733 890077 (Office)
email:
julie.hutchinson@peterborough-diocese.org.uk

SUFFRAGAN BISHOP
BRIXWORTH Rt Revd John Holbrook, Orchard Acre, 11 North Street, Mears Ashby, Northampton NN6 0DW [2011] *Tel:* 01604 812328
email:
bishop.brixworth@peterborough-diocese.org.uk

HONORARY ASSISTANT BISHOP
Right Revd Lindsay Urwin, The College, Walsingham, Norfolk NR22 6EF [2011]
Tel: 01328 824204
email: l.urwin@olw-shrine.org.uk

CATHEDRAL CHURCH OF ST PETER, ST PAUL AND ST ANDREW
Dean Very Revd Charles Taylor, The Deanery, Minster Precincts, Peterborough PE1 1XS [2007]
Tel: 01733 562780
Fax: 01733 897874
email: DeanPetOffice@aol.com
Precentor Canon R. Bruce Ruddock, Precentor's Lodging, 14A Minster Precincts, Peterborough PE1 1XX [2004] *Tel:* 01733 355310
email:
bruce.ruddock@peterborough-cathedral.org.uk
Canons Residentiary
Missioner Canon Jonathan Baker, Canonry House, Minster Precincts, Peterborough PE1 1XX [2004]
Tel: 01733 897335 (Home)
01733 355300 (Office)
email:
jonathan.baker@peterborough-cathedral.org.uk
Canon Ian Black, 26 Minster Precincts, Peterborough PE1 1XZ [2012] *Tel:* 01733 566265 (Home)
email: canonianblack@btinternet.com
Lay Members of Chapter
Mr John Henniker-Major, Linden House, Brook Lane, Great Easton, Market Harborough LE16 8SJ *Tel:* 01604 608211 (Office)
01536 770320 (Home)
email: john.henniker-major@carterjonas.co.uk
Hon Treasurer Sir John Parsons, Old Rectory, Eydon, Daventry NN11 3QE *Tel:* 01327 260745
email: jparsoneydon@btopenworld.com
Mr Mike Opperman, Littleworth Mission, Main Rd, Deeping St Nicholas, Spalding, Lincs PE11 3EN *Tel:* 01775 630497
email: jenny@littleworthmission.com
Mrs Sally Trotman, 2 High St, Maxey, Peterborough PE6 9EB *Tel:* 01778 344022
email: sally_trotman@yahoo.co.uk
Chapter Administrator Miss Elizabeth Knight, Cathedral Office, Minster Precincts, Peterborough PE1 1XS *Tel:* 01733 562780
Fax: 01733 897874
email: DeanPetOffice@aol.com
Director of Music Vacancy, Cathedral Office, Minster Precincts, Peterborough PE1 1XX
Tel: 01733 355319

ARCHDEACONS
NORTHAMPTON Ven Christine Allsopp, Westbrook, 11 The Drive, Northampton NN1 4RZ [2005] *Tel:* 01604 714015
Fax: 01604 792016
email: archdeacon.northampton@peterborough-diocese.org.uk
OAKHAM Ven Gordon Steele, The Diocesan Office, The Palace, Peterborough PE1 1YB [2012]
Tel: 01733 887017
Fax: 01733 555271

CONVOCATION (MEMBERS OF THE HOUSE OF CLERGY OF THE GENERAL SYNOD)
Proctors for Clergy
Ven Christine Allsopp
Canon William Croft
Revd Stephen Trott

MEMBERS OF THE HOUSE OF LAITY OF THE GENERAL SYNOD
Mr Dennis Allsopp
Mrs Veronica Heald
Mr Andrew Presland

DIOCESAN OFFICERS

Dioc Secretary Mr Andrew Roberts, Diocesan Office, The Palace, Peterborough PE1 1YB
Tel: 01733 887000
Fax: 01733 555271
email: diosec@peterborough-diocese.org.uk
Deputy Dioc Secretary and Financial Controller Mr Graham Cuthbert, Dioc Office
Tel: 01733 887000
Fax: 01733 555271
email: depsec@peterborough-diocese.org.uk
Chancellor of Diocese Chancellor David Pittaway QC, c/o Diocesan Registrar, 4 Holywell Way, Longthorpe, Peterborough PE3 6SS
Deputy Chancellor Mr George Pulman, c/o Diocesan Registrar (*as above*)
Registrar of Diocese and Bishop's Legal Secretary Revd Raymond Hemingray, 4 Holywell Way (*as above*) *Tel:* 01733 262523
Fax: 01733 330280
email: rh@raymondhemingray.co.uk

DIOCESAN ORGANIZATIONS

Diocesan Office The Palace, Peterborough PE1 1YB
Tel: 01733 887000
Fax: 01733 555271
email: office@peterborough-diocese.org.uk
Web: www.peterborough-diocese.org.uk

ADMINISTRATION

Dioc Synod (*Vice-President, Clergy*) Ven Gordon Steele, 26 Minster Precincts, Peterborough PE1 1XZ *Tel:* 01733 566265
email: gordonsteele@fish.co.uk
(*Vice-President, Laity*) Mrs Anne Toms, The Old Nurseries, 1A Ivydene Terrace, Broughton, Kettering NN14 1NJ *Tel:* 01536 791095
email: acbl@mrc-lmb.cam.ac.uk
(*Secretary*) Mr Andrew Roberts, The Palace, Peterborough PE1 1YB
Board of Finance (*Chairman*) Mr Michael Truman, Diocesan Office, The Palace, Peterborough PE1 1YB *Tel:* 01733 887000
email: m.j.truman@unicombox.co.uk
(*Secretary*) Mr Andrew Roberts (*as above*)
Houses Committee (*Chairman*) Mr Michael Duerden, 21 South Rd, Oundle, Peterborough PE8 4BU *Tel:* 01832 273383
Property Officer Mrs Sandra Allen, Dioc Office
Safeguarding Officer Mr Garry Johnson, Dioc Office
Mission and Pastoral Committee Mr Andrew Roberts (*as above*)
Board of Patronage Mr Andrew Roberts (*as above*)
Designated Officer Revd Raymond Hemingray, 4 Holywell Way, Longthorpe, Peterborough PE3 6SS *Tel:* 01733 262523
Fax: 01733 330280
email: rh@raymondhemingray.co.uk

CHURCHES

Advisory Committee for the Care of Churches (*Chairman*) Mr John White, c/o DAC, Diocesan Office, The Palace, Peterborough PE1 1YB
Tel: 01733 887007
Fax: 01733 555271
email: dac@peterborough-diocese.org.uk

EDUCATION

Board of Education (*Schools*) (*Director of Education* (*Schools*) *and Secretary*) Mrs Miranda Robinson, Bouverie Court, The Lakes, Bedford Rd, Northampton NN4 7YD *Tel:* 01604 887006
Fax: 01604 887077
email: education@peterborough-diocese.org.uk
Deputy Director of Education (*Schools*) Mr Peter Goringe, Bouverie Court, The Lakes, Bedford Rd, Northampton NN4 7YD *Tel:* 01604 887006
email: education@peterborough-diocese.org.uk
Schools Officer Revd Philip Davies, Rectory, 3 Hall Yard, King's Cliffe, Peterborough PE8 6XQ
Tel: 01780 470314
email: P.J.Davies.@tesco.net

MINISTRY

Dioc Vocations Adviser and Director of Ordinands Revd Steve Benoy, Bouverie Court, The Lakes, Bedford Rd, Northampton NN4 7YD
Tel: 01604 887047
Fax: 01604 887077
Coordinator of Adult Education and Training Mrs Liz Holdsworth, Bouverie Court (*as above*)
Tel: 01604 887042
Fax: 01604 887077
email: liz.holdsworth@peterborough-diocese.org.uk
Continuing Ministerial Education Officer and Licensed Lay Minister Officer Revd Quentin Chandler, Bouverie Court (*as above*)
Tel: 01604 887042
Fax: 01604 887077
email: quentin.chandler@peterborough-diocese.org.uk
Continuing Ministerial Education Officer Revd Hannah Jeffery, Bouverie Court (*as above*)
Tel: 01604 887000
Fax: 01604 887077
email: hannah.jeffery@peterborough-diocese.org.uk
Curates' Training Coordinator Revd Guli Francis-Dehqani, The Vicarage, Vicarage Rd, Oakham, Rutland LE15 6EG *Tel:* 01572 722108
or 01604 887054
email: guli.francis-dehqani@peterborough-diocese.org.uk

SELF SUPPORTING MINISTRY OFFICERS

Revd Elizabeth Pelly, Home Farm, Wakefield Lodge, Potterspury, Towcester, Northamptonshire NN12 7QX *Tel:* 01327 811218
Fax: 01327 811326
email: lulu.pelly@farming.co.uk

Revd Jo Saunders, Mellstock, Bourne Road, Essendine, Stamford, Lincolnshire PE9 4LH *Tel:* 01780 480479 *email:* revjosaunders@live.co.uk

Warden of Readers Revd Catherine Ievins, The Rectory, Main Street, Polebrook, Peterborough PE8 5LN *Tel:* 01832 270162 *email:* cievins@yahoo.co.uk

Warden of Pastoral Assistants Revd David Kirby, Rectory, Church Way, Weston Favell, Northampton NN3 3BX *Tel:* 01604 413218 *email:* kirbydg@gmail.com

Warden of Parish Evangelists Revd Melvyn Pereira, 20 Ribble Close, Wellingborough, Northants NN8 5XJ *Tel:* 01933 673437 *email:* melvyn.pereira@gleneagleschurch.co.uk

MISSION

Diocesan Mission Enabler Revd Miles Baker, Bouverie Court, The Lakes, Bedford Rd, Northampton NN4 7YD *Tel:* 01604 887043 *Fax:* 01604 887077 *email:* miles.baker@peterborough-diocese.org.uk

Children's Missioner Mrs Rona Orme, Bouverie Court (*as above*) *Tel:* 01604 887045 *Fax:* 01604 887077 *email:* rona.orme@peterborough-diocese.org.uk

Youth Officer Mr Peter White, Bouverie Court, The Lakes, Bedford Rd, Northampton NN4 7YD *Tel:* 01604 887044 *Fax:* 01604 887077 *email:* peter.white@peterborough-diocese.org.uk

Urban Priority Areas Link Officer and Church Urban Fund Officer Vacancy

Social Responsibility Adviser Revd Robert Hill, Bouverie Court, The Lakes, Bedford Rd, Northampton NN4 7YD *Tel:* 01604 887046 *Fax:* 01604 887077 *email:* robert.hill@peterborough-diocese.org.uk

Ecumenical Officer Revd Giles Godber, Vicarage, 25 West St, Geddington, Kettering NN14 1BD *Tel:* 01536 742200 *email:* ecuman.gilbar@talktalk.net

Hospital Chaplaincy Adviser Canon Lesley McCormack, Barnbrook, Water Lane, Chelveston, Wellingborough NN9 6SP *Tel:* 01933 492609 *email:* lesley.mccormack@kgh.nhs.uk

Rural Officer Vacancy

LITURGICAL

Officer Vacancy

Communications Officer Mrs Liz Hurst (c/o Dioc Office) *Tel:* 01733 887012 *Fax:* 01733 555271 *email:* communications@peterborough-diocese.org.uk

DIOCESAN RECORD OFFICES

Wootton Park, Northampton NN4 9BQ *County Archivist* Miss Sarah Bridges *Tel:* 01604 762129 *email:* archivist@northamptonshire.gov.uk (*For all parishes in Northants. and the former Soke of Peterborough*)

Leicestershire Record Office, Long St, Wigston Magna, Leicester LE18 2AH *County Archivist* Mr Carl Harrison *Tel:* 0116 257 1080 (*For all parishes in Rutland*)

RURAL DEANS

ARCHDEACONRY OF NORTHAMPTON

Brackley Revd Canon M. Roger H. Bellamy, Vicarage, Church Ave, Kings Sutton, Banbury OX17 3RD *Tel:* 01295 811364 *email:* rogerbellamy@hotmail.co.uk

Brixworth Revd Mary Garbutt, Rectory, 35 Main St, Great Oxenden, Market Harborough LE16 8NE *Tel:* 01858 461992 *email:* mary@familygarbutt.plus.com

Daventry Revd Canon Ann Slater, The Rectory, Church Lane, Nether Heyford, Northants NN7 3LQ *Tel:* 01327 342201 *email:* ann.slater@btinternet.com

Northampton Revd Canon David Wiseman, Christ Church Vicarage, 3 Christ Church Rd, Northampton NN3 2LE *Tel:* 01604 633254

Towcester Revd Paul McLeod, St Michael's Vicarage, High Street, Silverstone, Towcester, Northamptonshire NN12 8US *Tel:* 01327 858101 *email:* RevPaulMcLeod@aol.com

Wellingborough Revd Tony Lynett, Vicarage, 154 Midland Rd, Wellingborough NN8 1NF *Tel:* 01933 227101 *email:* tartleknock@aol.com

ARCHDEACONRY OF OAKHAM

Corby Vacancy

Higham Revd Derek Waller, 12 Kensington Close, Rushden, Wellingborough NN10 6RR *Tel:* 01933 356398 *email:* derekwaller@btinternet.com

Kettering Revd Brian Withington, Rectory, Gate Lane, Broughton, Kettering NN14 1ND *Tel:* 01536 791373 *email:* brian.andco@virgin.net

Oundle Revd Canon Richard Ormston, Vicarage, 12 New St, Oundle, Peterborough PE8 4EA *Tel:* 01832 273595 *email:* Ormston4@aol.com

Peterborough Revd Gillian Jessop, The Rectory, 236 Fulbridge Road, Paston, Peterborough PE4 6SN *Tel:* 01733 578228 *email:* rev.gill@tesco.net

Rutland Revd Canon Lee Francis-Dehqani, Vicarage, Vicarage Rd, Oakham, Rutland LE15 6EG *Tel:* 01572 722108 *email:* lee.fd@btinternet.com

DIOCESE OF PORTSMOUTH

Founded in 1927. The south-eastern third of Hampshire; the Isle of Wight.

Population 757,000 Area 408 sq m
Full-time Stipendiary Parochial Clergy 94 Benefices 127
Parishes 142 Churches 173
www.portsmouth.anglican.org
Overseas link diocese: IDWAL (Inter-Diocesan West Africa Link) – Ghana, Gambia, Liberia (West Africa).

BISHOP (8th)
Rt Revd Christopher Foster, Bishopsgrove, 26 Osborn Road, Fareham PO16 7DQ
Tel: 01329 280247
Fax: 01329 231538
email: bishports@portsmouth.anglican.org
Bishop's Chaplain Revd Jenny Gaffin
email: jenny.gaffin@portsmouth.anglican.org
Secretaries Vacancy / Ms Yvonne Collins

HONORARY ASSISTANT BISHOPS
Rt Revd Michael Adie, Greenslade, Froxfield, Petersfield GU32 1EB [2005] *Tel:* 01730 827266
Rt Revd Timothy Bavin, Alton Abbey, Abbey Road, Beech, Alton GU34 4AP *Tel:* 01420 562145
Rt Revd John Hind, 1 Stanley Road, Emsworth, PO10 7BD *Tel:* 01243 430305
email: john@hind.org.uk

CATHEDRAL CHURCH OF ST THOMAS OF CANTERBURY
Dean Very Revd David Brindley, The Deanery, 13 Pembroke Rd, Portsmouth PO1 2NS [2002]
Tel: 023 9282 4400 (Home)
email: david.brindley@portsmouthcathedral.org.uk
Tel: 023 9289 2963 (Personal Assistant)
email: liz.snowball@portsmouthcathedral.org.uk
Cathedral Office Cathedral House, 63–67 St Thomas's St, Old Portsmouth PO1 2HA
Tel: 023 9282 3300
Fax: 023 9289 2964
Web: www.portsmouthcathedral.org.uk
Canons Residentiary
Revd Canon David T. Isaac, 1 Pembroke Close, Old Portsmouth PO1 2NX [1990]
Tel: 023 9289 9654 (Office)
email: david.isaac@portsmouth.anglican.org
Pastor Revd Canon Michael Tristram, 51 High St, Old Portsmouth PO1 2LU [2003]
Tel: 023 9273 1282 (Home)
023 9282 3300 (Office)
email:
michael.tristram@portsmouthcathedral.org.uk
Revd Canon Nick Ralph, 101 St Thomas's Street, Old Portsmouth PO1 2HE [2009]
Tel: 023 9289 9674 (Office)
email: nick.ralph@portsmouth.anglican.org
Precentor Revd Canon Nicholas Jepson-Biddle, 32 Woodville Drive, Pembroke Park, Portsmouth PO1 2TG [2010]
Tel: 023 9282 3300 ext 225 (Office)
Tel: 023 9234 8139 (Home)
email:
nicholas.biddle@portsmouthcathedral.org.uk
Cathedral Administrator, Chapter Clerk and Clerk to Cathedral Council Colonel (Rtd) Jonathan Lloyd MBE *Tel:* 023 9289 2961
email:
jonathan.lloyd@portsmouthcathedral.org.uk
Cathedral Organist and Master of Choristers Dr David Price, Audley House, St James's Street, Southsea PO1 4JA
Tel: 023 9282 3300 ext 228 (Office)
email: david.price@portsmouthcathedral.org.uk
Cathedral Sub-Organist Oliver Hancock, Flat 1, Cathedral House, St Thomas's Street, Old Portsmouth PO1 2EZ *Tel:* 023 9282 3300
email: oliver.hancock@portsmouthcathedral.org.uk

ARCHDEACONS
PORTSDOWN [Vacancy] *Tel:* 023 9243 2693
Fax: 023 9229 8788
email: adportsdown@portsmouth.anglican.org
THE MEON Ven Gavin Collins, Victoria Lodge, 36 Osborn Road, Fareham PO16 7DB
Tel: 01329 608895
email: admeon@portsmouth.anglican.org
ISLE OF WIGHT Ven Peter Sutton, 5 The Boltons, Kite Hill, Wootton Bridge, Isle of Wight PO33 4PB
Tel: 01983 884432
email: adiow@portsmouth.anglican.org

CONVOCATION (MEMBERS OF THE HOUSE OF CLERGY OF THE GENERAL SYNOD)
Proctors for Clergy
Revd Clive Leach
Revd Timothy Jessiman
Revd Canon Bob White

MEMBERS OF THE HOUSE OF LAITY OF THE GENERAL SYNOD
Mrs Lucy Docherty
Canon Susan Rodgers
Canon Deborah Sutton

DIOCESAN OFFICERS

Dioc Secretary Revd Wendy Kennedy, First Floor, Peninsular House, Wharf Rd, Portsmouth PO2 8HB *Tel:* 023 9289 9664
Fax: 023 9289 9651
email: wendy.kennedy@portsmouth.anglican.org

Deputy Dioc Secretary Jenny Hollingsworth
Tel: 023 9282 9664
Fax: 023 9289 9651
email: jenny.hollingsworth@portsmouth.anglican.org

PA to Dioc and Deputy Dioc Secretaries and DAC Secretary Miss Catherine Gray Tel: 023 9282 9664
Fax: 023 9289 9651
email: catherine.gray@portsmouth.anglican.org

Chancellor of Diocese The Worshipful C. Clark QC, Sufree Farm, Probus, Truro TR2 4HL
Tel: 01872 267441
email: cc@3pumpcourt.com

Deputy Chancellor His Honour Judge Keith Cutler, Woodacre, West Gomeldon, Salisbury SP4 6LS *Tel:* 01980 611710

Registrar of Diocese and Bishop's Legal Secretary Miss Hilary Tyler, Messrs Brutton & Co., West End House, 288 West St, Fareham PO16 0AJ
Tel: 01329 236171
Fax: 01329 289915
email: hilary.tyler@brutton.co.uk

Bishop's Council/Board of Finance/Pastoral Committee (Chairman) Rt Revd Christopher Foster (*as above*)
(*Secretary*) Revd Wendy Kennedy (*as above*)

DIOCESAN ORGANIZATION

Diocesan Office First Floor, Peninsular House, Wharf Rd, Portsmouth PO2 8HB
Tel: 023 9289 9650
Fax: 023 9289 9651
email: admin@portsmouth.anglican.org

Dioc Synod (Secretary) Revd Wendy Kennedy (*as above*)

Dioc Synod (Chairman House of Clergy) Revd Canon Bob White, St Mary's Vicarage, Portsmouth PO1 5PA *Tel:* 023 9282 2687 (Home)
023 9282 2990 (Office)
email: revrcwhite@aol.com

(*Chairman, House of Laity*) Mrs Lucy Docherty, 33 Southampton Rd, Fareham PO16 7DZ
Tel: 01329 233602
07952 780108 (Mobile)
email: lucy@docherty1.co.uk

MISSION AND DISCIPLESHIP

Head of Department Revd Canon David Isaac, Dioc Office *Tel:* 023 9289 9654
Fax: 023 9289 9651
email: david.isaac@portsmouth.anglican.org

Dioc Director of Ordinands Canon Robin Coutts, Vicarage, Church Lane, Hambledon, Waterlooville PO7 4RT *Tel:* 023 9263 2717
email: robin.coutts@portsmouth.anglican.org

Dioc IME Ven Peter Sutton, 5 The Boltons, Kite Hill, Wootton Bridge, Isle of Wight PO33 4PB
Tel: 01983 884432
email: adiow@portsmouth.anglican.org

CME adviser Vacancy
email: adiow@portsmouth.anglican.org

Youth and Children's Work Adviser Ben Mizen, Dioc Office *Tel:* 023 9289 9652
email: ben.mizen@portsmouth.anglican.org

Spirituality Adviser Revd Dr Ruth Tuschling, Dioc Office *Tel:* 023 9289 9682
email: ruth.tuschling@portsmouth.anglican.org

Healing Advisor Dr David Pearson, 27 Livingstone Road, Southsea PO5 1RS *Tel:* 023 9275 3260
email: dgrpearson@talk21.com

MISSION AND EDUCATION

Director of Education, Portsmouth and Winchester Mr Tony Blackshaw, Dioc Office
Tel: 023 9289 9658
Fax: 023 9289 9651
email: tony.blackshaw@portsmouth.anglican.org

Head of Department Mr Tony Blackshaw (*as above*)

Assistant Director of Education, Portsmouth and Winchester Miss Emily Fletcher, Dioc Office
Tel: 023 9289 9680
Fax: 023 9289 9651
email: emily.fletcher@portsmouth.anglican.org

Diocesan Further Education Adviser Mr Malcolm Rittman, Dioc Office *Tel:* 023 8289 9658
email: malcolm.rittman@portsmouth.anglican.org

MISSION AND RESOURCES

Head of Department Mrs Jenny Hollingsworth, Dioc Office (*as above*)

Diocesan Property Manager and Surveyor and Secretary to Property Committee Mr Barry Fryer, Dioc Office *Tel:* 023 9289 9663
email: B.Fryer@portsmouth.anglican.org

Synod and Office Support Manager Mrs Jane Dobbs, Dioc Office *Tel:* 023 9289 9661
email: jane.dobbs@portsmouth.anglican.org

Safeguarding Adviser Mr Ian Berry, Dioc Office
Tel: 023 9289 9665
email: ian.berry@portsmouth.anglican.org

Parish Finance Adviser Mr Christopher Malone, Dioc Office *Tel:* 023 9289 9655
email: christopher.malone@portsmouth.anglican.org

MISSION AND SOCIETY

Chair (appointed by the Bishop) Revd Canon Bob White, St Mary's Vicarage, Fratton Road, Portsmouth PO1 5PA *Tel:* 023 9282 2687
email: revrcwhite@aol.com

Head of Mission and Society Section and Social Responsibility Adviser Canon Nick Ralph, First Floor, Peninsular House, Wharf Rd, Portsmouth, Hants PO2 8HB *Tel:* 023 9289 9674
email: nick.ralph@portsmouth.anglican.org

Social Responsibility Co-ordinator Mrs Nicky Pybus, Dioc Office *Tel:* 023 8289 9670
email: nicky.pybus@portsmouth.anglican.org

Chair of the Council for Social Responsibility Steering Group Mrs Lucy Docherty

Chaplain to the Deaf and Hard of Hearing Revd Robert Sanday, The Vicarage, 1 Tangmere Drive, Lord's Hill, Southampton SO16 8GY
Tel: 023 8026 5897
email: robertsanday@aol.com

Church Tourism Adviser Stephen Brett-Hill, 14 Mount Pleasant Road, Newport, Isle of Wight PO30 1EU *Tel:* 01983 526632
email: stevebretthill@yahoo.co.uk

Committee for Minority Ethnic Anglican Concerns (CMEAC) Representative Vacancy

Communications Adviser Mr Neil Pugmire, First Floor, Peninsular House, Wharf Rd, Portsmouth, Hants PO2 8HB *Tel:* 023 9289 9673
email: neil.pugmire@portsmouth.anglican.org

Communications Assistant Vacancy

Disability Adviser Revd Mary Tillman, 3 Fareham Rd, Gosport, Hants PO13 0XL
Tel: 01329 232589
07718 762323 (Mobile)
email: met@tillman.freeserve.co.uk

Environment Adviser Revd Andy Norris, Vicarage, 113 Church Rd, Warsash, Southampton SO31 9GF *Tel:* 01489 570846
email: environment@portsmouth.anglican.org

Ecumenical Adviser Revd Simon Sayers, Rectory, 20 Church Path, Emsworth PO10 7DP
Tel: 01243 372428
email: simonsayers@hotmail.com

Good Neighbours Support Service (Co-Ordinator) Mrs Mary Mitchell GNSS, Peninsular House, Wharf Rd, Portsmouth PO2 8HB
Tel: 023 9289 9671
email: mary.mitchell@goodneighbours.org.uk

(*North Adviser: Local Authority - Basingstoke, Hart, Rushmore, East Hants*) Mrs Elizabeth Foulds (*as above*) *Tel:* 07827 925326 (Mobile)
email: Elizabeth.foulds@neighbourcare.org.uk

(*South West Adviser: Local Authority - New Forest, Test Valley, Eastleigh*) Mrs Angela Smith (*as above*)
Tel: 07827 925327 (Mobile)
email: angela.smith@goodneighbourcare.org.uk

(*South East Adviser: Local Authority - Winchester, Havant, Fareham, Gosport*) Mrs Sandra Osborne (*as above*) *Tel:* 07827 925328 (Mobile)
email: sandra.osborne@goodneighbourcare.org.uk

Interdiocesan West Africa Link (Chair) Revd Canon Terry Louden, Vicarage, East Meon, Petersfield GU32 1NH *Tel:* 01730 823221
email: terrylouden@btinternet.com

Interfaith Adviser Revd Andy Marshall, Oasis Suite, Nuffield Centre, St Michael's Road, University of Portsmouth PO1 2ED
Tel: 023 9284 3030

Mental Health Adviser Revd J. Hair, Fareham and Gosport Adult Mental Health Service, 219 West Street, Fareham PO16 0ET *Tel:* 01329 825231
email: James.Hair@southernhealth.nhs.uk

New Religious Movements Adviser Revd Andy Norris, Vicarage, 113 Church Rd, Warsash, Southampton SO31 9GF *Tel:* 01489 570846

Port Chaplain Revd Philip Hiscock, 36 Gomer Lane, Alverstoke, Gosport, Hants PO12 2SA
Tel: 02392 346881
email: philip.hiscock@ntlworld.com

Porvoo Adviser Vacancy

Diocesan Rural Officer and Rural Affairs Adviser (Mainland) Revd D H Heatley, Vicarage, Hawkley, Liss, Hants GU33 6NF
Tel: 01730 827459
email: dhheatley@aol.com

Rural Affairs Adviser (IOW) Revd Graham Morris, The Vicarage, 14 Argyll Street, Ryde PO33 3BZ *Tel:* 01983 716435
email graham.morris@btinternet.com

Urban Ministry Adviser Revd Canon Bob White, St Mary's Vicarage, Fratton Rd, Portsmouth PO1 5PA *Tel:* 023 9282 2990
email: revrcwhite@aol.com

World Development Adviser Canon Marion Mort, Rivendell, High St, Shirrell Heath, Southampton SO32 3JN *Tel:* 01329 832178
email: marion.mort@portsmouth.anglican.org

Evangelism Canon Deborah Sutton, 2 Taswwell Road, Southsea PO5 2RG *Tel:* 023 9275 6926
email: debtas@hotmail.com

The Mothers' Union Mrs Alison Hubbard, Holmwood, West St, Hambledon PO7 4SN
Tel: 023 9263 2314
email: alisonhubbard1@gmail.com

CHURCHES

Dioc Advisory Committee for the Care of Churches (Chair) Very Revd David Brindley; (*Secretary*) Miss Catherine Gray
email: catherine.gray@portsmouth.anglican.org

Closed Churches for Regular Worship Committee (Chair) Revd Wendy Kennedy (*as above*); (*Secretary*) Mrs Jenny Hollingsworth
email:
jenny.hollingsworth@portsmouth.anglican.org

MINISTRY

Widows Officers (Mainland) Revd Canon Peter Kelly

DIOCESAN RECORD OFFICES

Portsmouth City Records Office, 3 Museum Rd, Portsmouth PO1 2LE *Archivist* Miss Alison Drew
Tel: 023 9282 7261
email: alison.drew@portsmouth.gov.uk
(*For Gosport, Fareham, Havant and Portsmouth deaneries*)

Hampshire Record Office, Sussex St, Winchester SO23 8TH *County Archivist* Miss Janet Smith *Tel:* 01962 846154; *Fax:* 01962 878681; *email:* enquiries.archives@hants.gov.uk (*For Bishop's Waltham and Petersfield deaneries*)

Isle of Wight County Record Office, 26 Hillside, Newport, Isle of Wight PO30 2EB *Archivist* Mr R. Smout *Tel:* 01983 823821
email: record.office @iow.gov.uk
(*For the Isle of Wight deaneries*)

AREA DEANS

ARCHDEACONRY OF THE MEON

Bishop's Waltham Revd Stuart Holt, Rectory, Rectory Lane, Meonstoke S032 3NF
Tel: 01489 877512
email: revstuartholt@btinternet.com

Fareham Revd Canon Stephen Girling, Crofton Vicarage, 40 Vicarage Lane, Stubbington, Fareham PO14 2JX *Tel:* 01329 661154
email: stephengirling@f2s.com

Gosport Revd John Draper, The Rectory, Rowner Lane, Gosport PO13 9SO *Tel:* 023 9258 7934
email: stmrowner174@btinternet.com

Petersfield Revd Will Hughes, The Vicarage, 12 Dragon Street, Petersfield GU31 4AB
Tel: 01730 260213
email: revwillhughes@btinternet.com

ARCHDEACONRY OF PORTSDOWN

Havant Revd Jonathan Jeffrey, The Vicarage, Riders Lane, Leigh Park, Havant PO9 4QT
Tel: 023 9247 5276
email: stfrancis@lineone.net

Portsmouth Revd Canon Bob White, St Mary's Vicarage, Fratton Road, Portsmouth PO1 5PA
Tel: 023 9282 2687
email: revrcwhite@aol.com

ARCHDEACONRY OF THE ISLE OF WIGHT

East Wight Revd Chris Feak, 10 Elmbank Gardens, Sandown, Isle of Wight PO36 9SA
Tel: 01983 402548
email: c.feak123@btinternet.com

West Wight Revd Kath Abbott, The Rectory, Church Road, Wootton, Isle of Wight PO33 4PX
Tel: 01983 882213
email: abbott.kath@googlemail.com

DIOCESE OF RIPON AND LEEDS

Re-constituted in 1836. The central third of North Yorkshire; Leeds, except for an area in the west (BRADFORD), an area in the east (YORK) and an area in the south (WAKEFIELD); an area of south-western County Durham.

Population 861,000 Area 1,359 sq m
Full-time Stipendiary Parochial Clergy 108 Benefices 106
Parishes 165 Churches 256
www.ripon-leeds-diocese.org.uk
Overseas link diocese: Colombo and Kurunagala (Sri Lanka).

BISHOP (12th)
Rt Revd John Richard Packer, Hollins House, Weetwood Avenue, Leeds, LS16 5NG [2000]
Tel: 0113 224 2789
Fax: 0113 230 5471
email: bishop@riponleeds-diocese.org.uk
[John Ripon and Leeds]
Bishop's Personal Assistant Janet Slater (*same address*)

SUFFRAGAN BISHOP
KNARESBOROUGH Rt Revd James Harold Bell, Thistledown, Main St, Exelby, Bedale DL8 2HD [2004] *Tel:* 01677 423525
Fax: 01677 427515
email: bishop.knaresb@btinternet.com
Personal Assistant Mrs Judith Richardson (*same address*)

HONORARY ASSISTANT BISHOPS
Rt Revd David Jenkins, Ashbourne, Cotherstone, Barnard Castle DL12 9PR [1994]
Tel: 01833 650804
Rt Revd Martyn Jarrett, 3 North Lane, Roundhay, Leeds LS8 2QJ [2002] *Tel:* 0113 265 4280
Fax: 0113 265 4281
Rt Revd Clive Handford, Wayside, 1 The Terrace, Kirkby Hill, Boroughbridge YO51 9DQ
Tel: 01423 325406
email: gchandford@gmail.com

CATHEDRAL CHURCH OF ST PETER AND ST WILFRID
Dean Very Revd Keith Jukes, Minster House, Bedern Bank, Ripon HG4 1PE [2007]
Tel: 01765 602609
email: deankeith@riponcathedral.org.uk
Dean's Secretary Mrs Judith Bustard
Cathedral Office Liberty Courthouse, Minster Rd, Ripon HG4 1QS *Tel:* 01765 603462
Fax: 01765 690398
email: postmaster@riponcathedral.org.uk
Web: www.riponcathedral.org.uk
Canon Precentor: Canon Paul Greenwell, St Wilfrid's House, Minster Close, Ripon HG4 1QP
Tel: 01765 600211
email: canonpaul@riponcathedral.org
Canon Residentiary
Canon Keith Punshon, St Peter's House, Minster Close, Ripon HG4 1QR [1996] *Tel:* 01765 604108
email: canonkeith@riponcathedral.org.uk
Cathedral Administrator Lt Col Ian Horsford, Cathedral Office *Tel:* 01765 603462
email: ianhorsford@riponcathedral.org.uk
Director of Music Mr Andrew Bryden, c/o Ripon Cathedral, Ripon HG4 1QT *Tel:* 01765 603496
email: andrewbryden@riponcathedral.org.uk

ARCHDEACONS
LEEDS Ven Paul Hooper, Hollin House, Weetwood Avenue, Leeds, LS16 5NG *Tel:* 0113 2690594
email: paul.hooper@riponleeds-diocese.org.uk
RICHMOND Ven Janet Henderson, Hoppus House, Smith Lane, Hutton Conyers, Ripon HG4 5DX [2007] *Tel:* 01765 601316
email:
janet.henderson@riponleeds-diocese.org.uk

CONVOCATION (MEMBERS OF THE HOUSE OF CLERGY OF THE GENERAL SYNOD)
Proctors for Clergy
Canon Kathryn Fitzsimons
Revd Janet Kearton
Revd Jonathan Clark

MEMBERS OF THE HOUSE OF LAITY OF THE GENERAL SYNOD
Dr John Beal
Mr Nigel Greenwood
Dr Richard Mantle

DIOCESAN OFFICERS
Dioc Secretary Dr Sue Proctor *Tel:* 0113 200 0541
email: sue.proctor@riponleeds-diocese.org.uk
Chancellor of Diocese The Worshipful Simon Grenfell, St John's House, Sharow Lane, Ripon, N Yorks. HG4 5BN
email: simon.grenfell@gmail.com
Joint Registrars of Diocese and Bishop's Legal Secretaries Mr Christopher Tunnard and Mrs Nicola Harding, Ripon and Leeds Diocesan Registry, Cathedral Chambers, 4 Kirkgate, Ripon HG4 1PA *Tel:* 01765 600755
Fax: 01765 690523
email: registry@tunnardsolicitors.com

Dioc Surveyor Mr Michael Lindley, Dioc Office
email: michael.lindley@riponleeds-diocese.org.uk

DIOCESAN ORGANIZATIONS

Diocesan Office Ripon and Leeds Diocesan Office, St Mary's St, Leeds LS9 7DP *Tel:* 0113 200 0540
Fax: 0113 249 1129

ADMINISTRATION

Dioc Synod (Chairman, House of Clergy) Canon Anthony Shepherd, St Peter's Vicarage, 13 Beech Grove, Harrogate HG2 0ET *Tel:* 01423 500901
email: ashepherd@talktalk.net
(Chairman, House of Laity) Mrs Ann Nicholl, 17 Parkland Terrace, Leeds LS6 4PW
Tel: 0113 269 4045
email: anicholl@parkland17.freeserve.co.uk
(Secretary) Dr Sue Proctor, Dioc Office
email: sue.proctor@riponleeds-diocese.org.uk
Board of Finance (Chairman) Mr Simon Baldwin, 4 Boundary Close, Colton, Leeds LS15 9HX
email: s.baldwin@leedsmet.ac.uk
(Secretary) Dr Sue Proctor *(as above)*; *(Administrative and Deputy Secretary)* Mr Peter Mojsa, Dioc Office
email: peter.mojsa@riponleeds-diocese.org.uk
(Financial Secretary) Mr Norman Gardner, Dioc Office
email:
norman.gardner@riponleeds-diocese.org.uk
Parsonages Board Dr Sue Proctor *(as above)*; *(Parsonages Officer)* Mr Michael Lindley, Dioc Office
email: michael.lindley@riponleeds-diocese.org.uk
Pastoral Committee Mr Peter Mojsa *(as above)*
Board of Patronage Mr Peter Mojsa *(as above)*
Designated Officer Dr Sue Proctor *(as above)*
Dioc Electoral Registration Officer Dr Sue Proctor *(as above)*
Widows and Dependants (Widows' Officer) Dr Sue Proctor *(as above)*

CHURCHES

Advisory Committee for the Care of Churches (Chairman) Mr C. Brown, 43 Leeds Rd, Harrogate HG2 8AY *Tel:* 01423 567587
email: coljanbrown@talktalk.net
(Secretary) Mr Peter Mojsa, Dioc Office
Church Buildings Committee Mr Peter Mojsa *(as above)*
Redundant Churches Uses Committee Mr Peter Mojsa *(as above)*

EDUCATION

Director of Education, Bradford, Ripon and Leeds Revd Clive Sedgewick, The Diocesan Education Team, Windsor House, Cornwall St, Harrogate HG1 2PW *Tel:* 01423 817553
Fax: 01423 817051
email: clives@brleducationteam.org.uk
Schools Adviser Fiona Beevers *(same address)*
email: fionab@brleducationteam.org.uk
Buildings Advisers Helen Williams (same address)
email: helenw@brleducationteam.org.uk
Phillip Smith *(same address)*
email: philips@brleducationteam.org.uk
Development Education Worker Vacancy

COUNCIL FOR MISSION

Chair Revd T. Hurren
Director of Mission Resourcing Canon Adrian Alker, Dioc Office *Tel:* 0113 200 0559
email: adrian.alker@riponleeds-diocese.org.uk
Diocesan Director of Lay Training Mrs Liz Williams, Dioc Office *Tel:* 0113 200 0556
email: liz.williams@riponleeds-diocese.org.uk
Diocesan Director of Clergy Training Vacancy
Tel: 0113 200 0557
Director of Ordinands Revd Peter Clement, The Parish House, 16 Orchard Close, Sharow, Ripon HG4 5BE *Tel:* 01765 607017
email: peterc@riponleeds-diocese.org.uk
Adviser for Women's Ministry Canon Alison Montgomery, Washington House, Littlethorpe, Ripon HG4 3LJ *Tel:* 01765 605276
email:
alison.montgomery@holytrinityripon.org.uk
Youth Work Adviser Capt Canon Nic Sheppard, 7 Loxley Grove, Wetherby LS22 7YG
Tel: 01937 585440
email: nic.sheppard@churcharmy.me.uk
Warden of Readers Miss Ann Hemsworth, 12 Kelmscott Grove, Cross Gates, Leeds LS15 8HH
Tel: 0113 293 7494
email: annhemsworth01@btinternet.com
Adviser for Non-Stipendiary Ministry Ven Janet Henderson, Hoppus House, Smith Lane, Hutton Conyers, Ripon HG4 5DX *Tel:* 01765 601316
email:
janet.henderson@riponleeds-diocese.org.uk
Convenor of Advisory Group on Christian Healing Revd Tom Lusty, Sue Ryder Care, Wheatfield Hospice, Grove Rd, Leeds LS6 2AE
Tel: 0113 278 7249
email: tom.lusty@suerydercare.org
World Church Officer Vacancy
Ecumenical Officer Revd Colin Cheeseman, 2a Ryder Gardens, Leeds, LS8 1JS
Tel: 0113 266 9747
email: colin.cheeseman1@ntlworld.com
Social Responsibility Officer Canon Adrian Alker *(as above)*
Community Chaplain for People with Learning Difficulties Vacancy
Racial Justice Officer Vacancy
Rural Ministry Officer Mr Andrew Ryland, 12 Linton Falls, Linton in Craven, Skipton, BD23 6BQ *Tel:* 07771 797073
email: andy.ryland@riponleeds-diocese.org.uk
Urban Ministry Officer Canon Kathryn Fitzsimons, 52 Newton Court, Leeds LS8 2PH
Tel: 0113 248 5011
email: kathrynfitzsimons@hotmail.com

LITURGICAL

Chairman Vacancy

Secretary Revd Stuart Lewis, Rectory, Kirkby Overblow, Harrogate HG3 1HD
Tel: 01423 872314

COMMUNICATIONS

Communications Committee Canon John Carter, 7 Blenheim Court, Harrogate HG2 9DT
Tel: 01423 530369
Fax: 01423 538557
email: jhgcarter@aol.com

Press Officer Canon John Carter (*as above*)

Editor of 'Together' (*monthly*) Canon John Carter (*as above*)

DIOCESAN RECORD OFFICES

County Record Office, County Hall, Northallerton DL7 8DF *Senior Archivist* (*Collections*) Margaret Boustead *Tel:* 01609 777585

West Yorkshire Archive Service, PO Box 30, Nepshaw Lane South, Morley, Leeds LS27 0QP *Head of Archives* Teresa Nixon *Tel:* 0113 3939771

STEWARDSHIP

Stewardship Adviser Mr Paul Winstanley, Dioc Office
email: paul.winstanley@riponleeds-diocese.co.uk

AREA DEANS

ARCHDEACONRY OF RICHMOND

Harrogate Revd Nigel Sinclair, St Robert's Vicarage, 21 Crimple Meadows, Pannal, Harrogate HG3 1EL *Tel:* 01423 870202
email: nigelsinclair@btinternet.com

Richmond Revd John Richards, The Rectory, Barnigham, Richmond DL11 7DW
Tel: 01833 621259
email: johnmr1953@talk21.com

Ripon Revd Matthew Evans, The Vicarage, Dacre Banks, Harrogate HG3 4ED *Tel:* 01423 780262
email: matthew.dhdt@btinternet.com

Wensley Revd Bryan Dixon, The Vicarage, Patrick Brompton, Bedale DL8 1JN
Tel: 01677 450985
email: rev.bryan@virginmedia.com

ARCHDEACONRY OF LEEDS

Allerton Canon Alan Taylor, Vicarage, Elford Place West, Leeds LS8 5QD *Tel:* 0113 248 6992
email: alan.taylor@leeds.gov.uk

Armley Revd Kingsley Dowling, Wortley Vicarage, Dixon Lane Rd, Leeds LS12 4RU

Headingley Revd David Calder, 2 Halcyon Hill, Leeds LS7 3PU *Tel:* 0113 263 8867
email: kingsleydowling@hotmail.co.uk

Headingley Revd Steve Smith, All Hallows Vicarage, 24 Regent Terrace, Leeds LS6 1NP
Tel: 0113 242 2205
email: simeve@ntlworld.com

Whitkirk Revd Mike Benwell, St Luke's Vicarage, Stanks Lane North, Leeds LS14 5AS
Tel: 0113 273 1302
email: Benwell@ndirect.co.uk

DIOCESE OF ROCHESTER

Founded in 604. Kent west of the Medway, except for one parish in the south-west (CHICHESTER); the Medway Towns; the London boroughs of Bromley and Bexley, except for a few parishes (SOUTHWARK); one parish in East Sussex.

Population 1,261,000 Area 542 sq m
Full-time Stipendiary Parochial Clergy 186 Benefices 188
Parishes 215 Churches 265
www.rochester.anglican.org
Overseas link dioceses: Estonia, Harare, Kondoa, Mpwapwa.

BISHOP (106th)

Rt Revd James Langstaff, Bishopscourt, St Margaret's St, Rochester ME1 1TS
Tel: 01634 842471
Fax: 01634 831136
email: bishop.rochester@rochester.anglican.org
Chaplain Canon Alan Vousden *Tel:* 01634 814439
email: bishops.chaplain@rochester.anglican.org

SUFFRAGAN BISHOP

TONBRIDGE Rt Revd Dr Brian Castle, Bishop's Lodge, 48 St Botolph's Rd, Sevenoaks TN13 3AG [2002] *Tel:* 01732 456070
Fax: 01732 741449
email: bishop.tonbridge@rochester.anglican.org

HONORARY ASSISTANT BISHOPS

Rt Revd Graham Cray, The Rectory, Church Road, Harrietsham, Maidstone ME17 1AP
Tel: 01622 851822

Rt Revd Michael Gear, 10 Acott Fields, Yalding, Maidstone ME18 6DQ [1999] *Tel:* 01622 817388
email: mike.gear@rochester.anglican.org

Rt Revd Dr Michael Nazir-Ali, c/o 70 Wimpole Street, London W1G 8AX *Tel:* 020 3327 1130
email: oxtrad@gmail.com

Rt Revd Michael Turnbull, 67 Strand Street, Sandwich CT13 9HN *Tel:* 01304 611389
email: bstmt@btopenworld.com

Rt Revd Stephen Venner, 83 Hathaway Court, Esplanade. Rochester ME1 1QY
Tel: 01634 838787
email: stephen@venner.org.uk

CATHEDRAL CHURCH OF CHRIST AND THE BLESSED VIRGIN MARY

Dean Very Revd Dr Mark Beach [2012]
Chapter Office Garth House, The Precinct, Rochester ME1 1SX *Tel:* 01634 843366
Fax: 01634 401410

Canons Residentiary

Canon Philip Hesketh, East Canonry, The Precinct, Rochester ME1 1TG [2005]
Tel: 01634 202898 (Home)
01634 810073 (Office)
email: canonpastor@rochestercathedral.org

Ven Simon Burton-Jones, The Archdeaconry, The Precinct, Rochester ME1 1TG [2010]
Tel: 01634 813533 (Home)
01634 560000 (Office)
email: archdeacon@rochestercathedral.org

Canon Neil Thompson, Easter Garth, The Precinct, Rochester ME1 1TG [2008]
Tel: 01634 405265 (Home)
01634 810063 (Office)
email: precentor@rochestercathedral.org

Canon Jean Kerr, Prebendal House, King's Orchard, The Precinct, Rochester ME1 1TG [2005]
Tel: 01634 844508 (Home)
email: jean.kerr@rochester.anglican.org

Director of Operations Dr Edwina Bell, Chapter Office *Tel:* 01634 810060 (Office)
email: administrator@rochestercathedral.org

Cathedral Organist and Director of Music Mr Scott Farrell, Chapter Office *Tel:* 01634 810061
email: dom@rochestercathedral.org

ARCHDEACONS

BROMLEY AND BEXLEY Ven Dr Paul Wright, The Archdeaconry, The Glebe, Chislehurst BR7 5PX [2004] *Tel:* 020 8467 8743
email:
archdeacon.bromley@rochester.anglican.org

ROCHESTER Ven Simon Burton-Jones, The Archdeaconry, The Precinct, Rochester ME1 1TG [2010] *Tel:* 01643 560000
email:
archdeacon.rochester@rochester.anglican.org

TONBRIDGE Ven Clive Mansell, 3 The Ridings, Blackhurst Lane, Tunbridge Wells TN2 4RU [2002] *Tel:* 01892 520660
email:
archdeacon.tonbridge@rochester.anglican.org

CONVOCATION (MEMBERS OF THE HOUSE OF CLERGY OF THE GENERAL SYNOD)

Proctors for Clergy
Revd Dr John Perumbalath
Revd Angus MacLeay
Ven Clive Mansell
Canon Gordon Oliver

MEMBERS OF THE HOUSE OF LAITY OF THE GENERAL SYNOD
Mr James Cheeseman
Brig Ian Dobbie
Mr Philip French
Mr Gerald O'Brien
Mrs Angela Scott

DIOCESAN OFFICERS

Diocesan Secretary Canon Louise Gilbert, St Nicholas Church, Boley Hill, Rochester ME1 1SL *Tel:* 01634 560000
email: louise.gilbert@rochester.anglican.org
Chancellor of Diocese Mr John Gallagher, Hardwicke Building, New Square, Lincoln's Inn, London WC2A 3SB *Tel:* 020 7242 2523
Registrar of Diocese and Bishop's Legal Secretary Mr Owen Carew-Jones, Minerva House, 5 Montague Close, London SE1 9BB
Tel: 020 7593 5110
email: a.harrison@wslaw.co.uk

DIOCESAN ORGANIZATIONS

Diocesan Office St Nicholas Church, Boley Hill, Rochester ME1 1SL *Tel:* 01634 560000
email: enquiries@rochester.anglican.org
Web: www.rochester.anglican.org

ADMINISTRATION

Deputy Diocesan Secretary Mr Geoff Marsh, Diocesan Office
email: geoff.marsh@rochester.anglican.org
Diocesan Synod (*Chair, House of Clergy*) Tbc
(*Chair, House of Laity*) Tbc
(*Secretary*) Canon Louise Gilbert, Diocesan Office
Board of Finance (*Chair*) Vacancy
(*Secretary*) Canon Louise Gilbert (*as above*); (*Diocesan Treasurer*) Mr Martyn Burt, Diocesan Office
email: martyn.burt@rochester.anglican.org
Pastoral Committee Mrs Suzanne Rogers, Diocesan Office
email: suzanne.rogers@rochester.anglican.org
Board of Patronage Mrs Suzanne Rogers (*as above*)
Designated Officer Mr Owen Carew-Jones, (*as above*)
Trusts Mr Geoff Marsh (*as above*)
Stewardship Adviser Mr Alan Strachan, Diocesan Office
email: alan.strachan@rochester.anglican.org

CHURCHES

Advisory Committee for the Care of Churches (Chair) Mr Derek Shilling, Ivy Bank, Shoreham Rd, Otford, Sevenoaks TN14 5RP *Tel:* 01959 522059
(*DAC Secretary*) Mrs Sarah Anderson, Diocesan Office
email: sarah.anderson@rochester.anglican.org
Closed Churches Mr Geoff Marsh (*as above*)

EDUCATION

All at Diocesan Office unless otherwise stated
email: education@rochester.anglican.org
Board of Education (*Acting Chair*) Ven Clive Mansell (*as above*)
Secretary and Director Mr Alex Tear
email: alex.tear@rochester.anglican.org
Deputy Director Mr John Constanti
email: john.constanti@rochester.anglican.org
Assistant Director (*Schools*) Mrs Virginia Corbyn
email: virginia.corbyn@rochester.anglican.org
Diocesan Children's Work Adviser Mrs Elaine Stanford-Beale
email:
elaine.stanford-beale@rochester.anglican.org
Diocesan Youth Work Adviser Mrs Cheryl Trice
email: cheryl.trice@rochester.anglican.org

FORMATION AND MINISTRY

Director Canon Christopher Dench, Diocesan Office
email: chris.dench@rochester.anglican.org
Assistant Director Revd Trevor Gerhardt, Diocesan Office
email: trevor.gerhardt@rochester.anglican.org
Training Officer Mrs Alison Callway, Diocesan Office
email: alison.callway@rochester.anglican.or
Directors of Ordinands Revd Glyn Ackerley, Vicarage, Butchers Hill, Shorne, Gravesend DA12 3EB *Tel:* 01474 822239
Canon Elizabeth Walker, Vicarage, Comp Lane, Platt, Sevenoaks TN15 8NR *Tel:* 01732 885482
Warden of Readers Mrs Karen Senior, Diocesan Office *email:* readers@rochester.anglican.org
Warden of Evangelists Canon Jean Kerr (*as above*)
Warden of Pastoral Assistants Revd Bryan Knapp, Vicarage, 169 Maidstone Rd, Paddock Wood, Tonbridge TN12 6DZ *Tel:* 01892 833917
Diocesan Co-ordinator of Spirituality Revd Susanne Carlsson, Sisters of St Andrew, Eden Hall, Stick Hill, Edenbridge TN8 5NN *Tel:* 01342 850388
email: susanne.carlsson@rochester.anglican.org
Diocesan Vocations Adviser Revd Mark Griffin, St Luke's Vicarage, 30 Eardley Road, Sevenoaks TN13 1XT *Tel:* 01732 452462
email: revd.mark.griffin@talk21.com

MISSION AND COMMUNITY ENGAGEMENT

Director Canon Jean Kerr (*as above*)
Interfaith Adviser Ven Dr Paul Wright (*as above*)

PRESS, PUBLICITY AND COMMUNICATIONS

Director and Bishop's Press Secretary Lindy Mackenzie MBE, Diocesan Office
Tel: 01634 560000
07901 670257 (Mobile)
email: lindy.mackenzie@rochester.anglican.org
Communications Assistant Miss Louise Whiffin, Diocesan Office *Tel:* 07827 157330 (Mobile)

DIOCESAN RECORD OFFICES

Kent History and Library Centre, James Whatman Way, Maidstone ME14 1LQ
Tel: 08458 247200

Medway Archives and Local Studies Centre, Civic Centre, Strood, Rochester ME2 4AW
Tel: 01634 732714

Bexley Local Studies and Archive Centre, Central Library, Townley Rd, Bexleyheath DA6 7HJ
Tel: 020 8301 1545

(For the deaneries of Erith and Sidcup in the Archdeaconry of Bromley)

Bromley Local Studies and Archives, Central Library, High St, Bromley, Kent BR1 1EX
Tel: 020 8460 9955

(For the deaneries of Beckenham, Bromley and Orpington in the Archdeaconry of Bromley)

AREA/RURAL DEANS

ARCHDEACONRY OF BROMLEY AND BEXLEY

Beckenham Revd Leon Carberry, The Vicarage, 15 St James' Avenue, Beckenham BR3 4HF
Tel: 020 8650 0420
email: leoncarberry@gmail.com

Bromley Canon Katrina Barnes, St Augustine's Vicarage, Southborough Lane, Bromley BR2 8AT
Tel: 020 8467 1351
email: katrina.barnes@diocese-rochester.org

Erith Canon Antony Lane, Rectory, 1 Claremont Crescent, Dartford DA1 4RJ *Tel:* 020 8301 5086
email: antony.lane@diocese-rochester.org

Orpington Revd Jay Colwill, The Vicarage, 165 Charterhouse Road, Orpington, BR6 9EP
Tel: 01689 870923
email: jay.colwill@diocese-rochester.org

Sidcup Revd Stephen Sealy, St John's Vicarage, 13 Church Avenue, Sidcup DA14 6BU
Tel: 020 8300 0383
email: stephen.sealy@diocese-rochester.org

ARCHDEACONRY OF ROCHESTER

Cobham Revd Hugh Broadbent, The Rectory, 11 St Katherine's Lane, Snodland ME6 5EH
Tel: 01634 240232
email: hughbroadbent@hotmail.com

Dartford Revd Richard Arding, Vicarage, 1 Curate's Walk, Wilmington, Dartford DA2 7BJ *Tel:* 01322 220561

Gillingham Revd Bonnie Appleton, The Rectory, 4 Drewery Drive, Wigmore, Gillingham ME8 0NX
Tel: 01634 231071
email: bonnie@babusinessconsultancy.co.uk

Gravesend Canon Ruth Oates, Vicarage, 57 New House Lane, Gravesend DA11 7HJ
Tel: 01474 740565
email: ruth.oates@diocese-rochester.org

Rochester Revd Alan Smith, St Stephen's Vicarage, 55 Pattens Lane, Chatham ME4 6JR
Tel: 01634 305786
email: revdalansmith@blueyonder.co.uk

Strood Revd David Green, The Vicarage, 3 Central Road, Strood, Rochester ME2 3HF
Tel: 01634 719052
email: revdavidgreen@blueyonder.co.uk

ARCHDEACONRY OF TONBRIDGE

Malling Revd Jim Brown, Vicarage, 2 The Grange, East Malling ME19 6AH
Tel: 01732 843282
email: jim.brown@diocese-rochester.org

Paddock Wood Revd Mandy Carr, The Vicarage, Old Town Hill, Lamberhurst, Tunbridge Wells TN3 8EL *Tel:* 01892 890324
email: mandy.carr@diocese-rochester.org

Sevenoaks Revd Mark Griffin, St Luke's Vicarage, 30 Eardley Road, Sevenoaks TN13 1XT
Tel: 01732 452462
email: revd.mark.griffin@talk21.com

Shoreham Revd Stephen Jones, The Rectory, Bates Hill, Ightham, Sevenoaks TN15 9BG
Tel: 01732 886827
email: srjones49@greenbee.net

Tonbridge Revd Mark Brown, Vicarage, Church St, Tonbridge TN9 1HD *Tel:* 01732 770962
email: mark@tonbridgeparishchurch.org.uk

Tunbridge Wells Revd Brian Senior, St Philip's Vicarage, Birken Rd, Tunbridge Wells TN2 3TE
Tel: 01892 512071
email: brian@bsenior.fsnet.co.uk

DIOCESE OF ST ALBANS

Founded in 1877. Hertfordshire, except for a small area in the south (LONDON) and one parish in the west (OXFORD); Bedfordshire, except for one parish in the north (ELY) and one parish in the west (OXFORD); an area of Greater London.

Population 1,795,000 Area 1,116 sq m
Full-time Stipendiary Parochial Clergy 223 Benefices 201
Parishes 336 Churches 408
www.stalbansdioc.org.uk
Overseas link dioceses: Jamaica, Guyana, NE Caribbean and Aruba (West Indies).

BISHOP (10th)

Rt Revd Dr Alan Gregory Clayton Smith, Abbey Gate House, Abbey Mill Lane, St Albans AL3 4HD *Tel:* 01727 853305
Fax: 01727 846715
email: bishop@stalbans.anglican.org
Chaplain Capt Andrew Crooks, CA
Tel: 01727 853305
email: chaplain@stalbans.anglican.org
Secretaries Mrs Mary Handford, Mrs Rosamund Adlard *email:* bishop@stalbans.anglican.org

SUFFRAGAN BISHOPS

BEDFORD Rt Revd Richard Atkinson, Bishop's Lodge, Bedford Rd, Cardington MK44 3SS [2003]
Tel: 01234 831432
Fax: 01234 831484
email: bishopbedford@stalbans.anglican.org
HERTFORD Rt Revd Paul Bayes, Bishopswood, 3 Stobarts Close, Knebworth SG3 6ND [2010]
email: bishophertford@stalbans.anglican.org

HONORARY ASSISTANT BISHOP

Rt Revd David John Farmbrough, St Michael Mead, 110 Village Rd, Bromham MK43 8HU [1993] *Tel:* 01234 825042
Rt Revd Robin J. N. Smith, 7 Aysgarth Rd, Redbourn, St Albans AL3 7PJ [2002]
Tel: 01582 791964
Rt Revd J. W. Gladwin, The White House, 131A Marford Road, Wheathampstead, St Albans AL4 8NH *Tel:* 01582 834223

CATHEDRAL AND ABBEY CHURCH OF SAINT ALBAN

Dean Very Revd Jeffrey John, The Old Rectory, Sumpter Yard, St Albans AL1 1BY [2004]
Tel: 01727 890202
Fax: 01727 890227
email: dean@stalbanscathedral.org
Cathedral Office The Chapter House, Sumpter Yard, St Albans AL1 1BY *Tel:* 01727 860780
Fax: 01727 850944
email: mail@stalbanscathedral.org
Web: www.stalbanscathedral.org

Canons Residentiary
Canon Richard Watson (*Sub-Dean*), Deanery Barn, Sumpter Yard, St Albans AL1 1BY [2011]
Tel: 01727 890201
email: subdean@stalbanscathedral.org
Canon Kevin Walton (*Canon Chancellor*), 2 Sumpter Yard, St Albans AL1 1BY [2008]
Tel: 01727 890242
email: canon@stalbanscathedral.org
Canon John Kiddle (Officer for Mission and Development), 19 Stanbury Avenue, Watford WD17 3HW [2010] *Tel:* 01923 460083
email: john.kiddle@stalbans.anglican.org
Canon Dennis Stamps (*Ministerial Development Officer*), 7 Corder Close, St Albans AL3 4NH [2002] *Tel:* 01727 841116
email: dstamps@stalbans.anglican.org
Minor Canons
Young People Revd Austin Janes, 2 Dean Moore Close, St Albans AL1 1DW [2011]
Tel: 01727 890206
email: mcyp@stalbanscathedral.org
Precentor Revd Paul Arbuthnot, 1 The Deanery, Sumpter Yard, St Albans AL1 1BY [2006]
Tel: 01727 890207
email: precentor@stalbanscathedral.org
Cathedral Administrator and Clerk to the Chapter Mrs Heather Smith, Cathedral Office
Tel: 01727 890208
email: admin@stalbanscathedral.org
Master of the Music Mr Andrew Lucas, 31 Abbey Mill Lane, St Albans AL3 4HA
Tel: 01727 890245
email: music@stalbanscathedral.org
Assistant Master of the Music and Director of the St Albans Abbey Girls Choir Mr Tom Winpenny, 34 Orchard St, St Albans AL3 4HL
Tel: 01727 890245
email: amom@stalbanscathedral.org
Cathedral Education Officer Steve Clarke, Education Centre, Sumpter Yard, St Albans AL1 1BY *Tel:* 01727 890262
email: education@stalbanscathedral.org
Cathedral Architect Mr Richard Griffiths
Archaeological Consultant Prof Martin Biddle

ARCHDEACONS

ST ALBANS Ven Jonathan Smith, 6 Sopwell Lane, St Albans AL1 1RR [2002] *Tel:* 01727 847212
Fax: 01727 848311
email: archdstalbans@stalbans.anglican.org

BEDFORD Ven Paul Hughes, 17 Lansdowne Rd, Luton LU3 1EE [2003] *Tel:* 01582 730722
Fax: 01582 877354
email: archdbedf@stalbans.anglican.org

HERTFORD Ven Trevor Jones, Glebe House, St Mary's Lane, Hertingfordbury, Hertford SG14 2LE [1997] *Tel:* 01992 581629
Fax: 01992 558745
email: archdhert@stalbans.anglican.org

CONVOCATION (MEMBERS OF THE HOUSE OF CLERGY OF THE GENERAL SYNOD)

Proctors for Clergy
Revd Canon John Kiddle
Revd Richard Hibbert
Ven Jonathan Smith
Revd Anne Hollinghurst
Revd Dr Joan Spreadbury

MEMBERS OF THE HOUSE OF LAITY OF THE GENERAL SYNOD

Mr Samuel Follett
Mr Simon Baynes
Dr Edmund Marshall
Mr William Seddon
Mr Philip McDonough
Mrs Christina Rees

DIOCESAN OFFICERS

Dioc Secretary Miss Susan Pope, Holywell Lodge, 41 Holywell Hill, St Albans AL1 1HE
Tel: 01727 854532
Fax: 01727 844469
email: mail@stalbans.anglican.org

Chancellor of Diocese His Honour the Worshipful Roger G. Kaye QC, Holywell Lodge, 41 Holywell Hill, St Albans AL1 1HD *Tel:* 01727 865765

Registrar of Diocese and Bishop's Legal Secretary Mr Lee Coley LLB (Hons), LLM (Canon Law), 1 The Sanctuary, Westminster, London SW1P 3JT
Tel: 0207 2225371 *Fax:* 0207 799 2781 (day); 0207 222 7502 (night)
email: stalbans.registry@1thesanctuary.com

Surveyor Mr Alastair Woodgate, c/o 41 Holywell Hill, St Albans AL1 1HE
Tel: 01727 854516

DIOCESAN ORGANIZATIONS

Diocesan Office Holywell Lodge, 41 Holywell Hill, St Albans AL1 1HE *Tel:* 01727 854532
Fax: 01727 844469
email: mail@stalbans.anglican.org
Web: www.stalbans.anglican.org

ADMINISTRATION

Dioc Synod (Chairman, House of Clergy) Revd Dr Michael Bowie
(Chairman, House of Laity) Mr John Wallace, 14 Church St, Leighton Buzzard LU7 7BT
Tel: 01525 375133
(Secretary) Miss Susan Pope, Dioc Office
Board of Finance (Chairman) Mr David Nye
(Secretary) Miss Susan Pope (*as above*)
Financial Secretary Mr Martin Bishop, Dioc Office
Estates Secretary Mrs Michèle Manders, Dioc Office
Board of Patronage Mr Jim May, Dioc Office
Designated Officers (Joint) Mr Lee Coley and Miss Susan Pope, Dioc Office
Mission and Pastoral Committee Mr Jim May (*as above*)
Trusts Mr Nigel Benger, Dioc Office

CHURCHES

Advisory Committee for the Care of Churches (Chairman) Dr Christopher Green, Dioc Office; *(Secretary)* Mr Jim May (*as above*)

EDUCATION

Dioc Education and Resources Centre Dioc Office
Tel: 01727 854532
Fax: 01727 844469
Director of Education Mr Jon Reynolds (*as above*)
School Buildings Officer Mrs Julia Creasey (*as above*)
RE Adviser Mrs Jane Chipperton (*as above*)

MINISTRY

Director of Ordinands Revd Susan Groom
Tel: 01727 833777
Ministerial Development Officer/Director of Ministry Vacancy
Parish Development Officer Revd Jeanette Gosney
Tel: 01727 818141
Continuing Ministerial Education Officer Revd Ysmena Pentalow, Dioc Office *Tel:* 01727 818154
Reader Ministry Officer Ms Lauryn Awbrey, Dioc Office *Tel:* 01727 818154
Associate Director of Ordinands Revd Emma Coley
Board of Readers' Work Mrs Margaret Tinsley, 145 The Ridgeway, St Albans AL4 9XA
Tel: 01727 859528
Mr Richard Osborn, 41 Tiverton Rd, Potters Bar EN6 5HX *Tel:* 01707 657491
Youth Officer Mr Dean Pusey, Dioc Office
Children's Work Adviser Revd Ruth Pyke, Dioc Office

MISSIONARY AND ECUMENICAL

Ecumenical Officers
Bedford Archdeaconry Vacancy
Hertford Archdeaconry Revd Paul Seymour
email: revpaulseymour@btinternet.com
St Albans Archdeaconry Vacancy
Board for Church and Society Mr Simon Best *(Chairman)*, The Hollies, Kimpton Rd, Peters Green LU2 9QW
Council for Partnership in World Mission Revd Christopher Briggs, Lawrence Cottage, 2 Hailey Lane, Hertford SG13 7NX *Tel:* 01992 462922

Workplace Matters Revd Dr John Scott, 41 Holywell Hill, St Albans AL1 1HE *Tel:* 01727 869461

PRESS AND PUBLICATIONS

Dioc Communications Officer Mr Arun Kataria, Dioc Office *Tel:* 01727 818110 *Fax:* 01727 844469 *email:* comms@stalbans.anglican.org

Editor of Dioc Directory Miss Susan Pope (*as above*)

Dioc Leaflet Mrs Claudia Brown (*as above*)

DIOCESAN RECORD OFFICES

County Hall, Hertford SG13 8DE *Tel:* 01992 555105 (*For diocesan records and parish records for St Albans and Hertford archdeaconries*)

County Hall, Bedford MK42 9AP *County Archivist* Mr Kevin Ward *Tel:* 01234 63222 Ext 277 (*For parish records for Bedford archdeaconry*)

SOCIAL RESPONSIBILITY

Officer for Mission and Development/Director of Mission Canon John Kiddle, Dioc Office *Tel:* 01727 851748

Social Responsibility Officer Revd Dr Andrew Coleby, Dioc Office *Tel:* 01727 851748

STEWARDSHIP

Stewardship Development Officer Mr Geoff Fletcher, Dioc Office *Tel:* 01727 854532

RURAL DEANS

ARCHDEACONRY OF ST ALBANS

Berkhamsted Revd Dr M Bowie, The Rectory, Rectory Lane, Berkhamsted HP4 2DH *Tel:* 01442 864194

Hemel Hempstead Revd David Lawson, St Mary's Vicarage, 7 Belswain's Lane, Hemel Hempstead HP3 9PN *Tel:* 01442 261610

Hitchin Revd Ann Pollington, The Vicarage, Stevenage Road, St Ippolyts, Hitchin SG4 7PE *Tel:* 01462 457552

Rickmansworth Revd Deborah Snowball, The Vicarage, Bury Lane, Rickmansworth WD3 1ED *Tel:* 01923 772627

St Albans Revd David Ridgeway, St Stephen's Vicarage, 14 Watling Rd, St Albans AL1 2PX *Tel:* 01727 862598

Watford Revd D J Middlebrook, St Luke's Vicarage, Devereux Drive, Watford WD17 3DD *Tel:* 01923 246161

Wheathampstead Revd Will Gibbs, The Vicarage, 49 Church End, Redbourn, St Albans AL3 7DU *Tel:* 01582 791669

ARCHDEACONRY OF BEDFORD

Ampthill and Shefford Revd M. F. J. Bradley, 26 Dew Pond Rd, Flitwick, Bedford MK45 1RT *Tel:* 01525 712369

Bedford Revd Richard Hibbert, Christ Church Vicarage, 115 Denmark Street, Bedford MK40 3TJ *Tel:* 01234 359342

Biggleswade Revd Lindsay Dew *Tel:* 01462 743617

Dunstable Revd R. J. Andrews, Rectory, 8 Furness Avenue, Dunstable LU6 3BN *Tel:* 01582 703271

Luton Vacancy *Tel:* 01582 572737

Sharnbrook Revd R. A. Evens, The Rectory, 81 High Street, Sharnbrook, Bedford MK44 1PE *Tel:* 01234 782000

ARCHDEACONRY OF HERTFORD

Barnet Revd Michael Burns, The Vicarage, 8 Dugdale Hill Lane, Potters Bar EN6 2DW *Tel:* 01707 661266

Bishop's Stortford Vacancy *Tel:* 01279 842609

Buntingford Revd Richard Morgan, The Rectory, Church Lane, Therefield, Royston SG8 9QD *Tel:* 01763 287364

Cheshunt Revd Carol Selby, St Clement's House, 44 Hillview Gardens, Cheshunt EN8 0PE *Tel:* 01992 625098

Welwyn and Hatfield Revd Dr D. Munchin, The Rectory, 2 Ottway Walk, Welwyn AL6 9AS *Tel:* 01438 714150

Hertford and Ware (*Joint Rural Dean*) Canon Pauline Higham, Hertford Hundred House, 1 Little Berkhamsted Lane, Little Berkhamsted Hertford SG13 8LU *Tel:* 01707 875940

Hertford and Ware (*Joint Rural Dean*) Revd N. L. Sharp, Little Amwell Vicarage, 17 Barclay Close, Hertford Heath, Hertford SG13 7RW *Tel:* 01992 589147

Stevenage Revd Duncan Campbell, St Hugh's House, 4 Mobbsbury Way, Chells, Stevenage SG2 0HL *Tel:* 01438 354307

DIOCESE OF ST EDMUNDSBURY AND IPSWICH

Founded in 1914. Suffolk, except for a small area in the north-east (NORWICH); one parish in Essex.

Population 641,000 Area 1,439 sq m
Full-time Stipendiary Parochial Clergy 130 Benefices 129
Parishes 445 Churches 478
www.stedmundsbury.anglican.org
Overseas link dioceses: Hassalt (Belgium), Kagera (Tanzania).

BISHOP (9th)
Rt Revd Nigel Stock, Bishop's House, 4 Park Rd, Ipswich IP1 3ST [2007] *Tel:* 01473 252829
Fax: 01473 232552
email: bishop.nigel@stedmundsbury.anglican.org
[Nigel St Edm and Ipswich]
Bishop's Chaplain Revd Mary Sokanovic (*same address and telephone*)
email: mary@stedmundsbury.anglican.org
Bishop's Secretary Mrs Denise Rudland (*same address and telephone*)
email: denise@stedmundsbury.anglican.org
Assistant Secretary Mrs Julia Venmore-Rowland (*same address and telephone*)
email: julia@stedmundsbury.anglican.org

SUFFRAGAN BISHOP
DUNWICH Rt Revd Clive Young, 28 Westerfield Rd, Ipswich IP4 2UJ [1999] *Tel:* 01473 222276
Fax: 01473 210303
email: bishop.clive@stedmundsbury.anglican.org
Bishop's Secretary Mrs Sheila Burnham (*same address*)
email: sheila@stedmundsbury.anglican.org

CATHEDRAL CHURCH OF ST JAMES AND ST EDMUND, BURY ST EDMUNDS
Dean Very Revd Dr Frances Ward, The Deanery, Bury St Edmunds IP33 1RS [2010]
Tel: 01284 748722
email: dean@stedscathedral.org
Cathedral Office Abbey House, Angel Hill, Bury St Edmunds IP33 1LS *Tel:* 01284 748720
Fax: 01284 768655
email: cathedral.secretary@stedscathedral.org
Canons Residentiary
Precentor Canon Philip Banks, 1 Abbey Precincts, Bury St Edmunds IP33 1RS [2012]
Tel: 01284 748724
email: precentor@stedscathedral.org
Canon Pastor Canon Matthew Vernon, 2 Abbey Precincts, Bury St Edmunds IP33 1RS [2009]
Tel: 01284 701472
email: canon.pastor@stedscathedral.org
Canon Theologian Canon Dr Christopher Burdon, 3 Crown St, Bury St Edmunds IP33 1QX [2007]
Tel: 01284 706813
email: canon.theologian@stedscathedral.org
Administrator Mr Keith Huddart, Cathedral Office *Tel:* 01284 748728
email: cathedral.administrator@stedscathedral.org
Visitor Officer Mrs Margaret Lambeth, Cathedral Office *Tel:* 01284 748721
email: visitor.officer@stedscathedral.org
Public Relations Manager Mrs Sarah Friswell, Cathedral Office *Tel:* 01284 748726
email: pr.manager@stedscathedral.org
Children's Education Officer Mrs Helen Woodroffe, Cathedral Office *Tel:* 01284 747467
email: discoverycentre@stedscathedral.org
Director of Music Mr James Thomas, Cathedral Office *Tel:* 01284 748379
email: dom@stedscathedral.org
Arts Administrator Mrs Sharron Stowe, Cathedral Office *Tel:* 01284 748730
email: art.admin&stedscathedral.org
Assistant Director of Music Mr Dan Soper, Cathedral Office *Tel:* 01284 748737
email: adom@stedscathedral.org
Head Verger Mr Duncan Withers, Cathedral Office
Tel: 01284 748729
email: head.verger@stedscathedral.org

ARCHDEACONS
SUDBURY Ven Dr David Jenkins, Sudbury Lodge, Stanningfield Rd, Great Whelnetham, Bury St Edmunds IP30 0TL [2010]
Tel and *Fax:* 01284 386942
email: archdeacon.david@stedmundsbury.anglican.org
SUFFOLK Ven Ian Morgan, Glebe House, The Street, Ashfield cum Thorpe, Stowmarket IP14 6LX [2012] *Tel:* 01728 685497
Fax: 01728 685969
email: archdeacon.ian@stedmundsbury.anglican.org

CONVOCATION (MEMBERS OF THE HOUSE OF CLERGY OF THE GENERAL SYNOD)
Proctors for Clergy
Revd Canon Jonathan Alderton-Ford
Revd Andrew Dotchin
Revd Tony Redman

MEMBERS OF THE HOUSE OF LAITY OF THE GENERAL SYNOD
Canon Tim Allen
Mrs Margaret Condick
Mr Peter Smith

DIOCESAN OFFICERS
Diocesan Secretary Mr Nicholas Edgell, Diocesan Office, St Nicholas Centre, 4 Cutler St, Ipswich IP1 1UQ *Tel:* 01473 298500
Fax: 01473 298501
email: dbf@stedmundsbury.anglican.org
Chancellor of Diocese Mr David Etherington QC, 20–32 Museum St, Ipswich IP1 1HZ
Deputy Chancellor of Diocese His Honour Judge Anthony Leonard (*as above*)
Registrar of Diocese and Bishop's Legal Secretary Mr James Hall, 20–32 Museum St, Ipswich IP1 1HZ
Tel: 01473 232300
Fax: 01473 230524
email: james-hall@birketts.co.uk
Deputy Registrar Stuart Jones *Tel:* 01603 756501
email: stuart-jones@birketts.co.uk

DIOCESAN ORGANIZATIONS
Diocesan Office St Nicholas Centre, 4 Cutler St, Ipswich IP1 1UQ *Tel:* 01473 298500
Fax: 01473 298501
email: dbf@stedmundsbury.anglican.org

ADMINISTRATION
Diocesan Secretary Mr Nicholas Edgell, Dioc Office
Deputy Diocesan Secretary Ms Nicola Andrews, Dioc Office
Assistant Diocesan Secretaries Mr Gavin Stone, Dioc Office; Canon Graham Hedger, Dioc Office
Pastoral and DAC Secretary Mr James Halsall
Diocesan Accountant Mrs Katy Reade
Diocesan Surveyor Mr Christopher Clarke, Clarke & Simpson, Well Close Square, Framlingham IP13 9DU *Tel:* 01728 724200
Designated Officer Canon Graham Hedger Dioc Office
Diocesan Synod (*Chairman, House of Clergy*) Tbc; (*Chairman, House of Laity*) Tbc; (*Secretary*) Mr Nicholas Edgell, Dioc Office

CHURCHES
Advisory Committee for the Care of Churches (*Chairman*) Canon Tim Allen, Bell House, Quay St, Orford, Woodbridge IP12 2NU *Tel:* 01394 450789
(*Secretary*) Mr James Halsall (*as above*)

COUNSELLING
Adviser in Pastoral Care and Counselling Canon Harry Edwards, Rectory, Marlesford, Woodbridge IP13 0AT *Tel:* 01728 746747
email: harry@psalm23.demon.co.uk
Bishop's Adviser on Exorcism and Deliverance The Bishop of Dunwich

MINISTRY
Accredited Ministry Group (*Chairman*) The Bishop of Dunwich (*as above*)
Vocations Adviser (*Sudbury*) Revd Katharine King, Vicarage, Bures CO8 5AA *Tel:* 01787 227315
email: katharine@rlcking.freeserve.co.uk
Vocations Adviser (*Suffolk*) Revd Betty Mockford, 10 Castle Brooks, Framlingham IP13 9SF
Tel: 01728 724193
Diocesan Director of Ordinands and New Ministers Canon Mark Sanders, Rectory, Woodbridge Rd, Grundisburgh, Woodbridge, IP13 6UF
Tel: 01473 735182
Diocesan Director of Mission Revd Dave Gardner, Dioc Office *Tel:* 01473 298521
email: dave@stedmundsbury.anglican.org
Diocesan Director of Ministry, Education and Training Revd Dr John Parr, Dioc Office
Tel: 01473 298510
email: johnp@stedmundsbury.anglican.org
Adviser for Continuing Ministerial Education Revd Canon Dr Christopher Burdon
Lay Training Officer Revd David Herrick, Dioc Office *Tel:* 01473 298510
email: david@stedmundsbury.anglican.org
Warden of Readers and Licensed Lay Ministers Officer Canon Deirdre Parmenter, Dioc Office
Tel: 01473 298551
email: deidre@stedmundsbury.anglican.org
Diocesan Children's Officer and Cathedral Education Officer Mrs Helen Woodroffe, The Discovery Centre, St Edmundsbury Cathedral, Angel Hill, Bury St Edmunds IP33 1LS
Tel and *Fax:* 01284 748731
email: helen@discoveryc.fsnet.co.uk
Diocesan Widows Officers Revd John and Mrs Helen Elliston, 27 Wyvern Rd, Ravenswood, Ipswich IP3 9TJ *Tel:* 01473 726617
Clergy Retirement Officer Revd Ian Hooper, 26 Drake Close, Stowmarket IP14 1UP
Tel: 01449 770179
email: ianavrilhooper126@btinternet.com

SCHOOLS
Dioc Director of Education and Schools Officer Mrs Jane Sheat, Dioc Office *Tel:* 01473 298570
Dioc Schools Adviser Mrs Helen Matter, Dioc Office

MISSION AND PUBLIC AFFAIRS
Community Affairs Adviser Mrs Kathleen Ben Rabha, Dioc Office
Agricultural Chaplain Canon Sally Fogden, Meadow Farm, Sapiston, Bury St Edmunds IP31 1RX *Tel:* 01359 268923
email: sallyfogden@tiscali.co.uk
Church Buildings & Tourism Officer Ms Marion Welham Dioc Office *Tel:* 01502 578154
email: marion@stedmundsbury.anglican.org
Bishop's Ecumenical Adviser Canon Peter Mortimer, 20 Leggart Drive, Bramford, Ipswich IP8 4ET *Tel:* 01473 747419
email: revpeter@fish.co.uk
Bishop's Inter Faith Adviser Canon Charles Jenkin, The Vicarage, 18 Kingsfield Avenue, Ipswich IP1 3TA *Tel:* 01473 289001
e mail: c.jenkin@tiscali.co.uk

Chaplain to the Deaf Community Vacancy
Parish Resources Adviser Canon Jim Pendorf, Dioc Office *Tel:* 01473 780360
email: jim@stedmundsbury.anglican.org

COMMUNICATIONS

Bishop's Press Officer John Howard, Dioc Office
email: john@stedmundsbury.anglican.org

DIOCESAN RECORD OFFICES

77 Raingate St, Bury St Edmunds IP33 2AR *Tel:* 01284 352352 Ext 2352 (*For parish records for Sudbury archdeaconry and Hadleigh deanery*)
Gatacre Rd, Ipswich IP1 2LQ *Tel:* 01473 264541 (*For parish records for Ipswich and Suffolk archdeaconries*)
The Central Library, Lowestoft NR32 1DR *Tel:* 01502 405357 (*For parish records for NE Suffolk parishes*)

SPIRITUALITY

Diocesan Spiritual Director for Cursillo Revd Mary Sokanovic, Bishop's Office
email: mary@stedmundsbury.anglican.org
Lay Director for Cursillo Mrs Gwen Runnacles, The Bungalow, Church Hill, Burstall, Ipswich IP8 3DU *Tel:* 01473 652494
email: gwen.runnacles@virgin.net

RURAL DEANS

ARCHDEACONRY OF IPSWICH

Bosmere Revd Diane Williams, 10 Meadow View, Needham Market, Ipswich IP6 8RH
Tel: 01449 720316
email: diane.rev@btinternet.com
Colneys Revd Robert Hinsley, The New Vicarage, 54 Princes Road, Felixstowe IP11 7PL
Tel: 01394 286552
email: roberthinsley@tiscali.co.uk
Hadleigh Very Revd Martin Thrower, The Deanery, Church Street, Hadleigh IP7 5DT
Tel: 01473 822218
email: martin.thrower@btinternet.com
Ipswich Canon Charles Jenkin, The Vicarage, 18 Kingsfield Ave, Ipswich IP1 3TA
Tel: 01473 289001
email: c.jenkin@tiscali.co.uk
Samford Revd Brin Singleton, The Rectory, Days Road, Capel St Mary, Ipswich IP9 2LE
Tel: 01473 310759
email: reverend.singleton@tiscali.co.uk
Stowmarket Revd Barbara Bilston, Boy's Hall, Ward Green, Old Newton, Stowmarket IP14 4EY
Tel: 01449 781253
email: b.b.bilston@open.ac.uk
Woodbridge Canon Clare Sanders, The Rectory, Woodbridge Road, Grundisburgh, Woodbridge IP13 6UF *Tel:* 01473 735183
email: revclaresanders@tiscali.co.uk

ARCHDEACONRY OF SUDBURY

Clare Revd Ian Finn, Vicarage, 10 Hopton Rise, Haverhill CB9 7FS *Tel:* 01440 708768
email: ian.finn1@btinternet.com
Ixworth Revd John Fulton, Rectory, Church Lane, Hepworth, Diss IP22 2PU *Tel:* 01359 250285
email: jwfulton@ukonline.co.uk
Lavenham Vacancy
Mildenhall Canon Stephen Mitchell, All Saints Vicarage, The Street, Gazeley, Newmarket CB8 8RB *Tel:* 01638 552630
email: smitch4517@aol.com
Sudbury Canon Robin King, Vicarage, Bures CO8 5AA *Tel:* 01787 227315
email: robin@ricking.freeserve.co.uk
Thingoe Revd Alan Gates, The Vicarage, Church Rd, Great Barton, Bury St Edmunds IP31 2QR
Tel: 01284 787274
email: alan.gates@virgin.net

ARCHDEACONRY OF SUFFOLK

Hartismere Revd Andrew Mitcham, Vicarage, 41 Castle Street, Eye IP23 7AW *Tel:* 01379 870277
email: andrew@redmail.co.uk
Hoxne Canon Fiona Newton, The Vicarage, 15 Noyes Avenue, Laxfield, Woodbridge IP13 8EB
Tel: 01986 798266
email: fionanewton@rmplc.co.uk
Loes Revd Graham Owen, Rectory, Framlingham, Woodbridge IP13 9BJ
Tel: 01728 621082
email: gowen.mowen@talktalk.net
Saxmundham Canon Christine Redgrave, 1 Oakwood Park, Yoxford, Saxmundham IP17 3JU
Tel: 01728 667095
email: redgrave460@btinternet.com
Waveney and Blyth Revd Simon Pitcher, The Vicarage, Gardner Road, Southwold IP18 6HJ
Tel: 01502 725424
email: revsimon@talktalk.net

DIOCESE OF SALISBURY

Founded in 1075, formerly Sherborne (AD 705) and Ramsbury (AD 909). Wiltshire, except for the northern quarter (BRISTOL); Dorset, except for an area in the east (WINCHESTER); a small area of Hampshire; a parish in Devon.

Population 895,000 Area 2,046 sq m
Full-time Stipendiary Parochial Clergy 186 Benefices 147
Parishes 452 Churches 571
www.salisbury.anglican.org
Overseas link provinces and dioceses: Episcopal Church of the Sudan, Evreux (France).

BISHOP (78th)
Rt Revd Nicholas Holtam, South Canonry, 71 The Close, Salisbury SP1 2ER [2011]
Tel: 01722 334031
Fax: 01722 413112
email: bishop.salisbury@salisbury.anglican.org
[Nicholas Sarum]

SUFFRAGAN BISHOPS
SHERBORNE Rt Revd Dr Graham Kings, Sherborne Office, St Nicholas' Church Centre, 30 Wareham Road, Corfe Mullen, Wimborne BH21 3LE [2009]
Tel: 01202 659427
Fax: 01202 691418
email: g.sherborne@salisbury.anglican.org
RAMSBURY Rt Revd Edward Condry, Diocesan Office, Church House, Crane Street, Salisbury, SP1 2QB [2012] *Tel:* 01722 438662
Fax: 01722 411990
email: e.ramsbury@salisbury.anglican.org

CATHEDRAL CHURCH OF THE BLESSED VIRGIN MARY
Dean Very Revd June Osborne, The Deanery, 7 The Close, Salisbury SP1 2EF [2004]
Dean's Office 6 The Close, Salisbury SP1 2EF
Tel: 01722 555110
Fax: 01722 555155
email: thedean@salcath.co.uk
Web: www.salisburycathedral.org.uk
Canons Residentiary
Precentor Canon Tom Clammer, Hungerford Chantry, 54 The Close, Salisbury SP1 2EL [2012]
Office Dept of Liturgy and Music, Ladywell, 33 The Close, Salisbury, SP1 2EJ *Tel:* 01722 555125
Fax: 01722 555117
email: precentor@salcath.co.uk
Chancellor Canon Edward Probert, 24 The Close, Salisbury SP1 2EH [2004] *Tel:* 01722 555193
Office: Chapter Office, 6 The Close, Salisbury SP1 2EF *Tel:* 01722 555189
Fax: 01722 555109
email: chancellor@salcath.co.uk
Treasurer Canon Sarah Mullally, 23 The Close, Salisbury SP1 2EH [2012] *Tel:* 01722 555177
Office: Chapter Office, 6 The Close (*as above*)
Tel: 01722 555186
Fax: 01722 555109
email: treasurer@salcath.co.uk
Vicar of the Close Revd Charles Mitchell-Innes, 32 The Close, Salisbury SP1 2EH *Tel:* 01722 555192
email: voc@salcath.co.uk
Chapter Clerk Mrs Katie Sporle, Chapter Office, 6 The Close, Salisbury SP1 2EF
Tel: 01722 555105
Fax: 01722 555109
email: chapterclerk@salcath.co.uk
Visitors Dept Mr David Coulthard, Ladywell, 33 The Close, Salisbury SP1 2EJ *Tel:* 01722 555120
Fax: 01722 555116
email: d.coulthard@salcath.co.uk
Education Centre Mrs Susan Hayter (*Administrator*), Wren Hall, 56c The Close, Salisbury SP1 2EL *Tel:* 01722 555180
email: wrenhall@salcath.co.uk
Director of Music Mr David Halls, Dept of Liturgy and Music (*as above*) *Tel:* 01722 555127
email: d.halls@salcath.co.uk

ARCHDEACONS
SHERBORNE Ven Paul Taylor, Aldhelm House, West Stafford, Dorchester DT2 8AB [2004]
Tel: 01202 659427
Fax: 01202 691418
email: adsherborne@salisbury.anglican.org
DORSET Ven Stephen Waine, 28 Merriefield Drive, Broadstone, BH18 8BP [2010] *Tel:* 01202 659427
Fax: 01202 691418
email: addorset@salisbury.anglican.org
WILTS Vacancy, c/o Diocesan Office, Church House, Crane Street, Salisbury SP1 2QB
Tel: 01722 438662
Fax: 01722 411990
email: adwilts@salisbury.anglican.org
SARUM Ven Alan Jeans, Herbert House, 118 Lower Rd, Lower Bemerton, Salisbury SP2 9NW [2003]
Tel: 01722 438662
Fax: 01722 411990
email: adsarum@salisbury.anglican.org

CONVOCATION (MEMBERS OF THE HOUSE OF CLERGY OF THE GENERAL SYNOD)
Proctors for Clergy
Canon Jane Charman
Canon Richard Franklin
Canon Nigel LLoyd

Ven Alan Jeans
Revd Christopher Strain

MEMBERS OF THE HOUSE OF LAITY OF THE GENERAL SYNOD
Mr Paul Boyd-Lee
Dr Ian Bromilow
Mrs Christine Corteen
Mr Christopher Fielden
Mr Robert Key
Mrs Deborah Isaac

DIOCESAN OFFICERS
Dioc Secretary Mrs Lucinda Herklots, Church House, Crane St, Salisbury SP1 2QB
Tel: 01722 411922
Fax: 01722 411990
Chancellor of Diocese His Honour Judge Samuel Wiggs, c/o Dioc Office
Registrar of Diocese and Bishop's Legal Secretary Mr Andrew Johnson, Minster Chambers, 42–44 Castle St, Salisbury SP1 3TX
Tel: 01722 411141
Fax: 01722 411566

DIOCESAN ORGANIZATIONS
Diocesan Office Church House, Crane St, Salisbury SP1 2QB *Tel:* 01722 411922
Fax: 01722 411990
email: enquiries@salisbury.anglican.org
Web: www.salisbury.anglican.org

ADMINISTRATION
Dioc Secretary Mrs Lucinda Herklots, Dioc Office
Deputy Dioc Secretary Mr Stephen Dawson, Dioc Office
Dioc Synod (Chairman, House of Clergy) Revd Antony Macrow-Wood, St George's Rectory, 99 Darby's Lane, Oakdale, Poole BH15 3EU
Tel: 01202 660612
(Chairman, House of Laity) Mr Robert Key, 4 Old Street, Salisbury SP2 8JL *Tel:* 01722 326622
(Secretary) Mrs Lucinda Herklots, Dioc Office
Board of Finance (Chairman) Mr Gil Williams, Princes Farm, Ryme Intrinseca, Sherborne DT9 6JX *Tel:* 01935 873580
(Secretary) Mrs Lucinda Herklots, Dioc Office
Diocesan Accountant Mr Phil Musselwhite, Dioc Office *Tel:* 01722 411955
Diocesan Surveyor Mr John Carley, Dioc Office
Tel: 01722 411933
Pastoral Committee (Secretary) Mrs Christine Romano, Dioc Office
Designated Officer Mr Andrew Johnson, Minster Chambers, 42–44 Castle St, Salisbury SP1 3TX
Tel: 01722 411141

CHURCHES
Advisory Committee for the Care of Churches (Chairman) Vacancy; *(Secretary)* Mrs Sue Cannings, Dioc Office *Tel:* 01722 438654
Re-Use of Closed Churches Working Group and Furnishings Officer Mr Simon Ferris, Dioc Office
Tel: 01722 411933
Ringers' Association Mr Anthony Lovell-Wood, 11 Brook Close, Tisbury, Salisbury
Tel: 01747 871121

EDUCATION
Director of Education Mr Chris Shepperd, Diocesan Education Centre, The Avenue, Wilton, Wilts SP2 0AG *Tel:* 01722 428420
Fax: 01722 328010
Board of Education (Chairman) Sir Al Aynsley-Green *(same address)*
Deputy Director of Education Mrs Joy Tubbs *(same address)*
Finance Mrs Jo Brookes *(same address)*
Buildings Officer Mrs Catherine Hannell *(same address)*
Adviser for School Development Mr Mark Stratta *(same address)*
Youth and Children's Officers Youth and Children's Ministry Team *(same address)*
Tel: 01722 428427

MINISTRY
Director of Learning for Discipleship and Ministry Canon Jane Charman, Dioc Office
Tel: 01722 411944
email: ministry@salisbury.anglican.org
Co-ordinator for Vocations and Spirituality, Revd Ian Cowley, Dioc Office
Director of Ordinands/Co-ordinator for Initial Ministerial Education Revd Charlotte Allen, Dioc Office
Co-ordinator for Learning for Discipleship Revd Dr Stella Wood, Dioc Office
Co-ordinator of Locally Deployable Ordained Ministry Vacancy, Dioc Office
Adviser for Women's Ministry Revd Vanda Perrett
Tel: 01672 851746
Warden of Licensed Lay Ministers The Bishop of Sherborne *(as above)*
Lay Pastoral Assistant Officers: (Wilts) Mrs Pip Symonds, *Tel:* 01980 670782; *(Dorset)* Mrs Beth Buchan *Tel:* 01258 450771
Clergy Retirement Officers: (Wilts) Revd Michael Turner *Tel:* 01722 504000; *(Dorset)* Revd Alan Woods *Tel:* 01305 264877

RESOURCE TEAMS
Mission and Stewardship Advisers: (Dorset) Mr Ian Bromilow, The Old School, Hilton, Blandford Forum DT11 0DB *Tel:* 01258 880044; *(Wilts)* Mr John Kilbee, Downs View, Goatacre, Calne SN11 9HY *Tel:* 01249 760776
Social Responsibility (Wilts.) Vacancy *(Dorset)* Mr Colin Brady, 23 Bagber Farm Cottages, Milton Rd, Milborne St Andrew, Blandford Forum DT11 0LB *Tel:* 01258 839140
County Ecumenical Officers (Wiltshire) Vacancy *(Dorset)* Mrs Val Potter, 22 Durbeville Close, Dorchester DT1 2JT *Tel:* 01305 264416

Officers for Rural Areas (*Wiltshire*) Revd Michael McHugh, Vicarage, Wilcot, Pewsey SN9 5NS
Tel: 01672 562676
(*Dorset*) (*also Dioc Environmental Officer*) Revd Dr Jean Coates, Rectory, Main St, Broadmayne, Dorchester CT2 8EB *Tel:* 01305 852435
European Affairs Officer Canon Richard Franklin, Holy Trinity Vicarage, 7 Glebe Close, Weymouth, DT44 9RL *Tel:* 01305 760354
Chaplain to Travelling People Vacancy
International Development and World Mission Canon Ian Woodward, Vicarage, West St, Bere Regis, Wareham BH20 7HQ *Tel:* 01929 471262

PRESS AND PUBLICATIONS

Communications Coordinator Mr Michael Ford, Dioc Office *Tel:* 01722 438650
07770 961629 (Mobile)
email: comms@salisbury.anglican.org
Editor of 'The Sarum Link' Mrs Mary Tapping, Dioc Office *Tel:* 01722 438652
Editor of Dioc Directory Mrs Miriam Darke, Dioc Office *Tel:* 01722 411922

DIOCESAN RECORD OFFICES

Diocesan Record Office and Wiltshire Parochial Records, Wiltshire and Swindon History Centre, Cocklebury Rd, Chippenham SN15 3QN *Tel:* 01249 705500 and ask for the Duty Archivist (*For diocesan records and parishes in the archdeaconries of Wiltshire and Sarum*)
Dorset History Centre, Bridport Rd, Dorchester DT1 1RP *County Archivist* Mr Hugh Jacques *Tel:* 01305 250550 (*For parishes in the County of Dorset*)
Hampshire Record Office, Sussex Street, Winchester SO23 8TH *Tel:* 01962 846154 (*For the few Salisbury diocesan parishes situated in the County of Hampshire*)

RURAL DEANS

ARCHDEACONRY OF SHERBORNE

Dorchester Canon Janet Smith, Vicarage, Mill Lane, Charminster, Dorchester DT2 9QP
Tel: 01305 262477
Lyme Bay Revd Bob Thorn, Rectory, Church Street, Burton Bradstock, Bridport DT6 4QS
Tel: 01308 898799
Sherborne Revd Graham Perryman, The Vicarage, Tollerford Lane, Higher Frome Vauchurch, Dorchester DT2 0AT *Tel:* 01300 320284
Weymouth and Portland Vacancy

ARCHDEACONRY OF DORSET

Blackmore Vale Revd David Seymour, Vicarage, Church St, Sturminster, Newton DT10 1DB
Tel: 01258 471276
Milton and Blandford Revd Simon Everett, Vicarage, Iwerne Minster, Blandford Forum DT11 8NF *Tel:* 01747 811291
Poole Revd Jean de Garis, Vicarage, Lytchett Minster, Poole BH16 6JQ *Tel:* 01202 622253
Purbeck Revd John Wood, Rectory, 12 Church Hill, Swanage BH19 1HU *Tel:* 01929 422916
Wimborne Revd Chris Tebbutt, Rectory, Canford Magna, Wimborne BH21 3AF *Tel:* 01202 883382

ARCHDEACONRY OF SARUM

Alderbury Revd Vanda Perrett, Rectory, High St, Porton, Salisbury SP4 0LH *Tel:* 01980 610305
Chalke Revd Stephen Morgan, The Rectory, Semley, Shaftesbury SP7 9AU *Tel:* 01747 830174
Salisbury Revd David Linaker, Little Bower, Campbell Rd, Salisbury SP1 3BG
Tel: 01722 322537
Stonehenge Revd Mark Zammitt, Rectory, Church Street, Durrington, Salisbury SP4 8AL
Tel: 01980 653953

ARCHDEACONRY OF WILTS

Bradford Revd Andrew Evans, Rectory, Ham Green, Holt, Trowbridge BA14 6PZ
Tel: 01225 782289
Calne Revd Thomas Woodhouse, Vicarage, Glebe Rd, Wootton Bassett SN4 7DU
Tel: 01793 854302
Devizes Revd Jonathan Triffitt, Vicarage, 31 Fruitfields Close, Devizes SN10 5JY
Tel: 01380 721441
Heytesbury Revd John Tomlinson, Rectory, 1 Bests Lane, Sutton Veny, Warminster BA12 7AU
Tel: 01985 840014
Marlborough Revd Andrew Studdert-Kennedy, Rectory, Rawlingswell Lane, Marlborough SN8 1AU *Tel:* 01672 512357
Pewsey Revd Gerald Osborne, Lawn Farm, Milton Lilbourne, Pewsey SN9 5LQ
Tel: 01672 563459

DIOCESE OF SHEFFIELD

Founded in 1914. Sheffield; Rotherham; Doncaster, except for a few parishes in the south-east (SOUTHWELL AND NOTTINGHAM); an area of North Lincolnshire; an area of south-eastern Barnsley; a small area of the East Riding of Yorkshire.

Population 1,226,000 Area 576 sq m
Full-time Stipendiary Parochial Clergy 130 Benefices 149
Parishes 173 Churches 212
www.sheffield.anglican.org
Overseas link dioceses: Argentina, Hattingen Witten (Germany).

BISHOP (7th)

Rt Revd Dr Steven John Lindsey Croft [2009] Bishopscroft, Snaithing Lane, Sheffield S10 3LG *Tel:* 0114 230 2170 *Fax:* 0114 263 0110 *email:* bishop@sheffield.anglican.org

Domestic Chaplain Revd Canon Geoffrey Harbord, Bishopscroft *Tel:* 0114 230 2170 *Fax:* 0114 263 0110 *email:* geoffrey.harbord@sheffield.anglican.org

SUFFRAGAN BISHOP

DONCASTER Rt Revd Peter Burrows, Doncaster House, Church Lane, Fishlake, Doncaster DN7 5JW [2012] *Tel:* 01302 846610 *email:* bishoppeter@bishopofdoncaster.org.uk

PROVINCIAL EPISCOPAL VISITOR

BEVERLEY Rt Revd Glyn Webster, c/o Bishopthorpe Palace, Bishopthorpe, York YO23 2GE *Tel:* 01904 707021/2 *email:* office@archbishopofyork.org

CATHEDRAL CHURCH OF ST PETER AND ST PAUL

Dean Very Revd Peter Bradley, The Cathedral, Church St, Sheffield S1 1HA *Tel:* 0114 263 6063 *email*: dean@sheffield-cathedral.org.uk

Cathedral Office Sheffield Cathedral, Church St, Sheffield S1 1HA *Tel:* 0114 275 3434 *Fax:* 0114 279 7412 *email:* enquiries@sheffield-cathedral.org.uk *Web:* www.sheffieldcathedral.org

Canons Residentiary

Precentor Canon Simon Cowling, The Cathedral [2007] *Tel:* 0114 263 6065 *email:* precentor@sheffield-cathedral.org.uk

Dioc Director of Ordinands and Dean of Women's Ministry Canon Dr Joanne Grenfell, The Cathedral [2006] *Tel:* 0114 263 6074 *email:* joanne.grenfell@sheffield-cathedral.org.uk

Canon for Learning and Development Canon Christopher Burke, The Cathedral [2010] *Tel:* 0114 263 6066 *email:* christopher.burke@sheffield-cathedral.org.uk

General Manager Mr Carl Hutton *Tel:* 0114 275 3434 *email:* carl.hutton@sheffield-cathedral.org.uk

Director of Music Mr Neil Taylor, The Cathedral *Tel:* 0114 263 6069 *email:* musicians@sheffield-cathedral.org.uk

Asst Director of Music Vacancy *Tel:* 0114 263 6070 *email:* musicians@sheffield-cathedral.org.uk

Cathedral Archer Project Manager Tim Renshaw, The Cathedral *Tel:* 0114 321 2314 *email:* cap.reception@sheffield-cathedral.org.uk

ARCHDEACONS

SHEFFIELD AND ROTHERHAM Ven Martyn Snow, 34 Wilson Rd, Sheffield S11 8RN [2010] *Tel:* 07729 104792 *email:* archdeacons.office@sheffield.anglican.org *Office* Diocesan Church House, 95–99 Effingham St, Rotherham S65 1BL *Tel:* 01709 309110 *Fax:* 01709 309107

DONCASTER Ven Stephen Wilcockson, Fairview House, 14 Armthorpe Lane, Doncaster DN2 5LZ *Tel:* 01302 325787 *email:* steve.wilcockson@sheffield.anglican.org *Office* Diocesan Church House, 95–99 Effingham St, Rotherham S65 1BL *Tel:* 01709 309110 *Fax:* 01709 309107

CONVOCATION (MEMBERS OF THE HOUSE OF CLERGY OF THE GENERAL SYNOD)

Proctors for Clergy
Revd Canon Simon Bessant
Revd Canon Geoffrey Harbord
Revd Jeffrey Stokoe

MEMBERS OF THE HOUSE OF LAITY OF THE GENERAL SYNOD

Dr Jacqueline Butcher
Canon Elizabeth Paver
Miss Jane Patterson

DIOCESAN OFFICERS

Dioc Secretary Mr Malcolm Fair, Diocesan Church House, 95–99 Effingham St, Rotherham S65 1BL *Tel:* 01709 309117 *Fax:* 01709 309158 *email:* malcolm.fair@sheffield.anglican.org

Chancellor of Diocese The Worshipful David McClean, Hall House, Ingrams, Sturminster Newton, Dorset DT10 1FR *Tel:* 01258 475 318 *email:* j.d.mcclean@sheffield.ac.uk

Registrar of Diocese and Bishop's Legal Secretary Mr Andrew Vidler, Wake Smith LLP, 68 Clarkehouse Road, Sheffield S10 2LJ
Tel: 0114 266 6660
email: andrew.vidler@wake-smith.com

DIOCESAN ORGANIZATIONS

Diocesan Office Diocesan Church House, 95–99 Effingham St, Rotherham S65 1BL
Tel: 01709 309100
Fax: 01709 512550
email: reception@sheffield.anglican.org
Web: www.sheffield.anglican.org

ADMINISTRATION

Dioc Secretary Mr Malcolm Fair, Dioc Office
Tel: 01709 309117
Deputy Secretary/Finance Officer Mr Roger Pinchbeck, Dioc Office *Tel:* 01709 309142
Property Manager Mr Paul Beckett, Dioc Office
Tel: 01709 309122
Board of Finance (*Chair*) Lay Canon Sandra Newton, 50 Broomgrove Rd, Sheffield S10 2NA
Tel: 0114 266 1079
Diocesan Mission and Pastoral Committee (*Chair*) Rt Revd Dr Steven Croft, Bishopscroft, Snaithing Lane, Sheffield S10 3LG *Tel:* 0114 230 2170
(*Secretary*) Mr Malcolm Fair, Dioc Office
Tel: 01709 309117
Redundant Churches Uses Committee (*Chair*) Ven Martyn Snow (*as above*)
(*Secretary*) Mr Paul Beckett (*as above*)
Board of Patronages (*Chair*) Prof David McClean, Hall House, Ingrams, Sturminster Newton, Dorset DT10 1FR *Tel:* 01258 475 318
(*Secretary*) Mr Malcolm Fair Dioc Office
Tel: 01709 309117
DAC Chair Revd Canon Peter Ingram, The Vicarage, 80 Millhouses Lane, Sheffield S7 2HB
Tel: 0114 236 2838
DAC Secretary Dr Julie Banham, Diocesan Church House, 95–99 Effingham Street, Rotherham S65 1BL *Tel:* 01709 309121
Administration Supervisor Mrs Christine Brocklebank, Dioc Office *Tel:* 01709 309 128
Designated Officer Revd Canon Geoffrey Harbord, Bishopscroft, Snaithing Lane, Sheffield S10 3LG
Tel: 0114 230 2170
Fax: 0114 263 0110
email:
geoffrey.harbord@sheffield.anglican.org.uk
Communications Officer The Revd Rob Marshall, Media 33, 5 Brampton Court, Brough HU15 1DZ
Tel: 01482 562455
email: rob@media33.co.uk

DIOCESAN SYNOD

(*Chair, House of Clergy as at July 2012*) Canon Ian Smith, Warmsworth Rectory, 187 Warmsworth Road, Doncaster DN4 0TW *Tel:* 01302 853324
(*Chair, House of Laity as at July 2012*) Canon Elizabeth Paver, 113 Warning Tongue Lane, Bessacarr, Doncaster DN4 6TB
Tel: 01302 530706
(*Secretary*) Mr Malcolm Fair (*as above*)

CHURCHES

Advisory Committee for the Care of Churches (*Chair*) Canon Peter Ingram, Holy Trinity Vicarage, 80 Millhouses Rd, Sheffield S7 2LL
Tel and Fax: 0114 236 2838
(*Secretary*) Dr Julie Banham, Diocesan Church House, 95–99 Effingham Street, Rotherham S65 1BL *Tel:* 01709 309121

EDUCATION

Dioc Board of Education (*Chair*) Rt Revd Peter Burrows (*as above*); (*Secretary*) Mr Huw Thomas, Dioc Office *Tel:* 01709 309123
Director of Education Mr Huw Thomas, Dioc Office

CHURCH TOURISM

Malcolm Fair, Dioc Office

MINISTRY AND MISSION

Director of Ministry Canon Dr John Thomson, Dioc Office
Director of Mission and Pioneer Ministry Canon Mark Wigglesworth, Dioc Office
Director of Ordinands Canon Dr Joanne Grenfell, The Cathedral Church of St Peter and St Paul, Church St, Sheffield S1 1HA *Tel:* 0114 275 3434
Director of Youth Ministries Mr Mike North, Dioc Office *Tel:* 01709 309146
Children's and Youth Officer Mrs Jenny Lambourne, Dioc Office *Tel:* 01709 309144
Director of IME4–7 Revd Keith Farrow, Christ Church Vicarage, 218 Fox Hill Road, Sheffield S6 1HJ *Tel:* 0114 2311576
Asst POT Officers Revd Lydia Wells, St Peter's Vicarage, 17 Ashland Road, Sheffield S7 1RH (SMs) *Tel:* 0114 2509716
Revd Gary Schofield, The Vicarage, Manor Rd, Wales, Sheffield S26 5PD (SMs)
Tel: 01909 771 111
Revd Jan Foden, The Vicarage, Stainforth Rd, Barnby Dun, Doncaster DN3 1AA (NSM)
Tel: 01302 882 835
Discipleship Development Officer Revd Alan Isaacson, The Rectory, High Bradfield, Sheffield S6 6LG *Tel:* 0114 285 1225
Bishop's Adviser on Women in Ministry Canon Dr Joanne Grenfell, The Cathedral Church of St Peter and St Paul, Church St, Sheffield S1 1HA
Tel: 0114 275 3434
Bishop's Adviser on Music and Worship Revd Helen Bent, The Vicarage, 61 Whitehill Lane, Brinsworth, Rotherham S60 5JR
Tel: 01709 363 850

Bishop's Adviser on Spirituality and Chaplain of Whirlow Grange Conference Centre Revd Philip Roderick, Whirlow Grange Conference Centre, Ecclesall Rd South, Sheffield S11 9PZ
Tel: 0114 235 3704

Bishop's Adviser on Self Supporting Ministry Revd Stephen Hunter, Overhill, Townhead Road, Sheffield S17 3GE *Tel:* 0114 236 9978

Bishop's Adviser on Church Army Ministry Revd Jane Truman, Wilson Carlile College of Evangelism, 50 Cavendish Street, Sheffield S3 7RZ *Tel:* 0114 209 6201

Warden of Readers Canon Richard Parker, 104 Hawshaw Lane, Hoyland, Barnsley S74 0HH
*Tel:*01226 749 231

Readers' Board (Secretary) Miss Joan Robinson, 4 Kelvin Grove, Wombwell, Barnsley S73 0DL

Ecumenical Officer Revd Frances Ecclestone, The Vicarage, 1 Barnfield Road, Crosspool, Sheffield S10 5TD *Tel:* 0114 230 2531

PRESS AND PUBLICATIONS

Director of Communications Revd Rob Marshall, 33rpm public relations, 5 Brampton Court, Brough HU15 1DZ *Tel:* 01482 562455
Fax: 0870 286 3348
email: rob@media.33.co.uk

Editor of Dioc Directory Mrs Christine Brocklebank, Dioc Office *Tel:* 01709 309128

DIOCESAN RECORD OFFICES

Sheffield City Archives, 52 Shoreham St, Sheffield S1 4SP *Tel:* 0114 273 4756
(For parishes in the archdeaconry of Sheffield)

Doncaster Archives, King Edward Rd, Balby, Doncaster DN4 0NA *Tel:* 01302 859811
(For parishes in the archdeaconry of Doncaster)

FAITH AND JUSTICE

Director of Faith and Justice and Secretary Ms Kate Plant, Dioc Office *Tel:* 01709 309136

South Yorkshire Workplace Chaplaincy Capt Christopher Chesters CA, 9 The Copse, Bramley, Rotherham S66 0TP *Tel:* 0114 275 5865
Fax: 0114 272 6767

Office South Yorkshire Workplace Chaplaincy, Cemetery Rd Baptist Church, Napier St Entrance, Sheffield S11 8HA *Tel:* 0114 275 5865

Bishop's Adviser on Black Concerns Mrs Carmen Franklin *Tel:* 0114 245 7160

Bishop's Representative for Child Protection Ms Sue Booth *Tel:* 0113 275 5266

Bishop's Rural Adviser Revd Keith Hale, Tankersley Rectory, 9 Chapel Road, Pilley, Barnsley S75 3AR *Tel:* 01226 744140

STEWARDSHIP

Christian Giving Director Mr Nicholas Hutton, Dioc Office *Tel:* 01709 309151

AREA DEANS

ARCHDEACONRY OF SHEFFIELD

Attercliffe Revd Stephen Willett, Vicarage, 63 Sheffield Rd, Sheffield S12 4LR
Tel: 0114 248 4486

Ecclesall Canon Peter Ingram, Vicarage, 80 Millhouses Lane, Sheffield S7 2HB
Tel: 0114 236 2838

Ecclesfield Revd Rick Stordy, St John's Vicarage, 23 Housley Park, Chapeltown, Sheffield S35 2UE
Tel: 0114 257 0966

Hallam Dr James Grenfell, St John's Vicarage, 389A Fulwood Road, Sheffield S10 3GA
Tel: 0114 2301671

Laughton Revd Gary Schofield, The Vicarage, Manor Road, Wales, Sheffield S26 5PD
Tel :01909 771 111

Rotherham Revd Neil Bowler, The Rectory, Rectory Drive, Whiston, Rotherham S60 4JG
Tel: 01709 364430

ARCHDEACONRY OF DONCASTER

Adwick-le-Street Revd Stephen Gardner, All Saints Vicarage, 9 Great North Road, Woodlands, Doncaster DN6 7RB *Tel:* 01302 700404

Doncaster Revd Jan Foden, The Vicarage, Stainforth Rd, Barnby Dun, Doncaster DN3 1AA
Tel: 01302 882 835

Hickleton Revd W. Jeffrey Stokoe, St Hugh's Vicarage, Levet Road, New Cantley, Doncaster DN4 6JQ *Tel:* 01302 371256

Snaith and Hatfield Revd Paul Wilson, The Vicarage, High Street, Hatfield, Doncaster DN7 6RS *Tel:* 01302 840 280

Tankersley Revd Keith Hale, Tankersley Rectory, 9 Chapel Rd, Pilley, Barnsley S75 3AR
Tel: 01226 744 140

Wath Revd Andrew Brewerton, The Vicarage, Highthorn Road, Kilnhurst, Mexborough S64 5TX *Tel:* 01709 589674

West Doncaster Revd Neil Redeyoff, The Rectory, Rectory Lane, Finningley, Doncaster DN9 3DA
Tel: 01302 770 240

DIOCESE OF SODOR AND MAN

Founded in 447. The Isle of Man.

Population 81,000 Area 221 sq m
Full-time Stipendiary Parochial Clergy 13 Benefices 27
Parishes 28 Churches 45
www.sodorandman.im
Overseas link diocese: Cashel (Ireland).

BISHOP
The Rt Revd Robert M.E. Paterson, Thie Yn Aspick, 4 The Falls, Tromode Rd, Douglas, Isle of Man IM4 4PZ [2008] *Tel:* 01624 622108
email: bishop@sodorandman.im
[+Robert Sodor as Mannin]
Bishop's Chaplain Canon Peter Robinson
email: chaplain@sodorandman.im
Bishop's Secretary Miss Rosemary Bannan
email: secretary@sodorandman.im

CATHEDRAL CHURCH OF ST GERMAN, PEEL
Dean Very Revd Nigel Godfrey, St German's Cathedral Office, Peel, Isle of Man IM5 1HH
Tel: 01624 842608
email: dean@sodorandman.im
Canons
Canon Philip Frear, 37 Hutchinson Square, Douglas, Isle of Man IM2 4HW [2005]
Canon Peter Robinson, Hillcrest Cottage, Minorca Hill, Laxey, Isle of Man IM4 7DP (2012)
Canon Dr Jules Gomes, The Vicarage, Arbory Rd. Castletown, Isle of Man IM9 1ND (2012)
Vacancy

ARCHDEACON
Ven Andrew Brown, St George's Vicarage, 16 Devonshire Rd, Douglas, Isle of Man IM2 3RB [2011] *Tel:* 01624 675430
email: archdeacon@sodorandman.im

YORK CONVOCATION
Proctor for the Clergy Revd Marc Wolverson

(MEMBER OF THE HOUSE OF CLERGY OF THE GENERAL SYNOD)
Proctor for the Clergy Revd Marc Wolverson

MEMBER OF THE HOUSE OF LAITY OF THE GENERAL SYNOD
Miss Laura Davenport

DIOCESAN OFFICERS
Vicar-General and Chancellor of Diocese The Worshipful Clare Faulds, The Lynague, German, IM5 2AQ *Tel:* 01624 842045
Diocesan Registrar and Bishop's Legal Secretary and Bishop's Legal Adviser Mr Kenneth Gumbley, 37 Farmhill Park, Braddan, Isle of Man IM2 2E
Tel: 01624 675091
email: registrar@sodorandman.im
Diocesan Synod Secretary Mrs Sylvia Lawrinson, Apt 8, Hillary Wharf, South Quay, Douglas, Isle of Man IM1 5BL *Tel:* 01624 673477
email: synod@sodorandman.im

CHURCH COMMISSIONERS FOR THE ISLE OF MAN
The Bishop (*Chair*)
The Archdeacon
Mr Peter Cowell
Mr Henry Dawson
Mrs Jacqueline Frear
Mr Stephen Hamer
Revd Margaret Burrow
Revd Canon Duncan Whitworth
(*Secretary*) Mrs Sylvia Lawrinson (*as above*)

DIOCESAN ORGANIZATIONS
DIOCESAN SYNOD
Chairman, House of Clergy Revd Paul Mothersdale
Chairman, House of Laity Vacancy

BOARD OF FINANCE
Chairman The Rt Revd Robert M.E. Paterson
(*Secretary*) Mrs Sylvia Lawrinson (*as above*)
Diocesan Treasurer Mrs Lisa Johnson, 21 Brighton Terrace, Douglas, Isle of Man IM1 4AP
Tel: 01624 677512
email: treasurer@sodorandman.im

CHURCH BUILDINGS
Advisory Committee for the Care of Churches (*Secretary*) Mrs Sylvia Lawrinson (*as above*)
email: secretary@sodorandman.im

SECTOR MINISTERS AND ADVISERS
Contact via the Bishop's Office, Thie yn Aspick, 4 The Falls, Tromode Road, Douglas, Isle of Man IM4 4PZ *Tel:* 01624 622108
Mission Adviser Miss Gillian Poole
email: mission@sodorandman.im
Access & Disability Mr Guy Thompson
Bishop's Visitors Dr Paul and Mrs Barbara Bregazzi

Children's Work Adviser Mrs Nancy Clague
Church School Liaison Revd James McGowan
Youth Work Adviser Vacancy
Christian Giving Adviser Revd Diane Marchment
Media and Communications Officer Revd John Coldwell *Tel:* 01624 621694
email: media@sodorandman.im
Webmaster Vacancy – *via Bishop's Chaplain and Media Officer*
Church and Society Adviser Revd Cyril Rogers
C.M.E.A.C. Link Revd Marc Wolverson
Data Protection Officer Mr Charles Flynn
Ecumenical Adviser Mr Howard Connell
email: ecumenism@sodorandman.im
Environment Advisers Revd Brian and Mrs Mary Evans-Smith
Healing and Deliverance Adviser Revd Canon Philip Frear (*as above*)
Leisure, Sport and Tourism Adviser Miss Marilyn Payne
Director of Vocation & Training (DDO) Very Revd Nigel Godfrey (*as above*)
Director of Ministerial Development (CMD & IME 4–7) Revd Canon Dr Jules Gomes *(as above)*
Director of Studies IME 1–4 Revd Margaret Burrow
Warden of Readers Canon Colin Finney
email: readers@sodorandman.im
Chaplain to P.T.O. Ministers (lay & ordained) Revd Leslie Lawrinson (*as S. Lawrinson above*)
Pastor to Ministers' Widows & Widowers Mrs Brenda Willoughby
Rural Life Adviser Revd Tony Butler
Safeguarding Officer Revd Jo Dudley
Spiritual Life Adviser Revd Canon Peter Robinson (*as above*)
World Mission Co-ordinators Revd Canon Malcolm and Mrs Valerie Convery (*as above*)

CHAPLAINCIES

The Isle of Man College Revd Marc Wolverson
Noble's General Hospital Revd Canon Philip Frear (*as above*)
Hospice Isle of Man Revd Lynda Brady
Ramsey Cottage Hospital Revd Brian Evans-Smith
H.M. Prison, Jurby Revd Brian Evans-Smith (*as above*)

ARCHIVED DIOCESAN RECORDS

Archivist Miss Wendy Thirkettle, The Manx Museum Library, Kingswood Grove, Douglas Isle of Man IM1 3LY *Tel:* 01624 64800

MISSION PARTNERSHIP LEADERS

North Revd Canon Cyril Rogers
South Revd Paul Mothersdale
East Revd Clive Burgess
West Very Revd Nigel Godfrey

DIOCESE OF SOUTHWARK

Founded in 1905. Greater London south of the Thames, except for most of the London Boroughs of Bromley and Bexley (ROCHESTER), and a few parishes in the south-west (GUILDFORD); the eastern third of Surrey.

Population 2,609,000 Area 317 sq m
Full-time Stipendiary Parochial Clergy 326 Benefices 262
Parishes 290 Churches 365
www.southwark.anglican.org
Overseas link dioceses: Manicaland, Central Zimbabwe, Matabeleland, Masvingo (Zimbabwe).

BISHOP

Rt Revd Christopher Chessun, Bishop's House, 38 Tooting Bec Gardens London SW16 1QZ
Tel: 020 8769 3256
Fax: 08432 906894
email: bishop.christopher@southwark.anglican.org
Bishop's Office, Trinity House, 4 Chapel Court, Borough High Street, London SE1 1HW
Tel: 020 7939 9420
Fax: 0843 2906894
Bishop's Chaplain Revd Mark Steadman (Bishop's Office, *same address*)
email: mark.steadman@southwark.anglican.org
Bishop's Personal Assistant Ms Winsome Thomas (Bishop's Office, *same address*)
email: winsome.thomas@southwark.anglican.org
Secretary Mrs Penny Lochead (Bishop's Office, *same address*)
email: penny.lochead@southwark.anglican.org
Bishop's Press Officer Canon Wendy Robins (Bishop's Office, *same address*)
email: wendy.robins@southwark.anglican.org

AREA BISHOPS

CROYDON Rt Revd Jonathan Clark, Croydon Episcopal Area Office, St Matthew's House, 100 George St, Croydon CR0 1PE
Tel: 020 8256 9630
Fax: 020 8256 9631
email: bishop.jonathan@southwark.anglican.org
KINGSTON Rt Revd Dr Richard Cheetham, Kingston Episcopal Area Office, 620 Kingston Rd, Raynes Park, London SW20 8DN [2002]
Tel: 020 8545 2440
Fax: 020 8545 2441
email: bishop.richard@southwark.anglican.org
WOOLWICH Rt Revd Dr Michael Ipgrave OBE, Woolwich Episcopal Area Office, Trinity House, 4 Chapel Court, London SE1 1HW [2012]
Tel: 020 7939 9400
Fax: 020 7939 9465

HONORARY ASSISTANT BISHOPS

Rt Revd Dr David Atkinson, 6 Bynes Road, South Croydon CR2 0PR [2009] *Tel:* 020 8406 0895
email: davidatkinson43@virginmedia.com
Rt Revd Alan Chesters, College of St Barnabas, Blackberry Way, Lingfield, Surrey RH7 6NJ [2011] *Tel:* 01342 872861
email: achesters1937@gmail.com
Rt Revd Michael Doe, 405 West Carriage House, Royal Carriage Mews, London SE18 6GA [2006]
Tel: 020 3259 3841
email: michaeldd@btinternet.com
Rt Revd and Rt Hon Lord Harries of Pentregarth, 41 Melville Road, Barnes, London SW19 9RH [2006] *Tel:* 020 8288 6053
email: richard.d.harries@googlemail.com
Rt Revd Peter Selby, 57 Girton Road, London SE26 5DJ [2011] *email:* peter.selby@onetel.com
Rt Revd S. Mark Wood, College of St Barnabas, Blackberry Lane, Lingfield, Surrey RH7 6NJ [2002] *Tel:* 01342 871556
email: revmarkwood@onetel.com

CATHEDRAL AND COLLEGIATE CHURCH OF ST SAVIOUR AND ST MARY OVERIE

Dean Very Revd Andrew Nunn [2011] (*All correspondence to be addressed to the Cathedral Office*) *Tel:* 020 7367 6727 (Office)
Tel: 020 7928 3336 (Home)
Fax: 020 7367 6725 (Office)
Cathedral Office Montague Chambers, London Bridge, London SE1 9DA *Tel:* 020 7367 6700
Fax: 020 7367 6725/6730
email: cathedral@southwark.anglican.org
Canons Residentiary
Pastor and Sub Dean Canon Bruce Saunders, Cathedral Office [2003]
Tel: 020 7367 6706 (Office)
020 7820 8376 (Home)
email: bruce.saunders@southwark.anglican.org
Precentor Canon Gilly Myers, Cathedral Office [2012] *Tel:* 020 7367 6731 (Office)
020 7735 8322 (Home)
email: gilly.myers@southwark.anglican.org
Chancellor and Theologian Canon Jane Steen, Diocesan Office [2005] *Tel:* 020 7939 9409
email: jane.steen@southwark.anglican.org
Missioner Vacancy
Treasurer and Diocesan Director of Ordinands Canon Leanne Roberts, Diocesan Office [2011]
Tel: 020 7939 9458
email: leanne.roberts@southwark.anglican.org

Succentor Revd Anna Macham, [2007] Cathedral Office *Tel:* 020 7367 6705
email: anna.macham@southwark.anglican.org
Priest Assistant Canon Wendy Robins [2002] *Tel:* 020 7939 9436
email: wendy.robins@southwark.anglican.org
Administrator Mr Matthew Knight, Cathedral Office *Tel:* 020 7367 6726
email: matthew.knight@southwark.anglican.org
Education Officer Ms Alexandra Carton, Cathedral Office *Tel:* 020 7367 6715
email: edcentre@southwark.anglican.org
Visitors' Officer Mr David Payne, Cathedral Office *Tel:* 020 7367 6734
email: david.payne@southwark.anglican.org
Cathedral Organist Mr Peter Wright, Cathedral Office *Tel:* 020 7367 6703
email: peter.wright@southwark.anglican.org

ARCHDEACONS

CROYDON Revd Dr Barry Goodwin (Acting) Croydon Episcopal Area Office, St Matthew's House, 100 George St, Croydon CR0 1PE *Tel:* 020 8256 9630 *Fax:* 020 8256 9631
email: barry.goodwin@southwark.anglican.org
LAMBETH Ven Christopher Skilton, Kingston Episcopal Area Office, 620 Kingston Rd, Raynes Park, London SW20 8DN [2003] *Tel:* 020 8545 2440 *Fax:* 020 8545 2441
email: chris.skilton@southwark.anglican.org
LEWISHAM AND GREENWICH Vacancy
REIGATE Ven Daniel Kajumba, St Matthew's House (*as above*) *Tel:* 020 8256 9630
email: daniel.kajumba@southwark.anglican.org
SOUTHWARK Revd Canon Dianna Gwilliams (Acting), Dioc Office *Tel:* 020 7939 9409
email: dianna.gwilliams@southwark.anglican.org
WANDSWORTH Ven Stephen Roberts, Kingston Episcopal Area Office (*as above*) [2005] *Tel:* 020 8545 2440 *Fax:* 020 8545 2441
email: stephen.roberts@southwark.anglican.org

CONVOCATION (MEMBERS OF THE HOUSE OF CLERGY OF THE GENERAL SYNOD)

Proctors for Clergy
Revd Canon Simon Butler
Revd Canon Giles Goddard
Ven Christine Hardman
Revd Canon Gary Jenkins
Revd Dr Rosemarie Mallett
Very Revd Andrew Nunn
Revd Mark Steadman
Revd Rupert Shelley

MEMBERS OF THE HOUSE OF LAITY OF THE GENERAL SYNOD

Mrs April Alexander
Miss Vasantha Gnanadoss
Mr Adrian Greenwood
Mr Peter Haddock
Mr Robin Hall
Mr Tom Sutcliffe
Mr Brian Wilson

DIOCESAN OFFICERS

Diocesan Secretary Mr Simon J. B. Parton (Lay Canon), Diocesan Office, Trinity House, 4 Chapel Court, Borough High St, London SE1 1HW *Tel:* 020 7939 9400 *Fax:* 020 7939 9468
email: simon.parton@southwark.anglican.org
Deputy Diocesan Secretary Mr Andrew Lane, Diocesan Office (*as above*)
email: andrew.lane@southwark.anglican.org
Chancellor of Diocese Mr Philip Petchey, Francis Taylor Building, Inner Temple, London EC4Y 7BY *Tel:* 020 7353 8415
Registrar of Diocese and Bishop's Legal Secretary Mr Paul Morris, Minerva House, 5 Montague Close, London SE1 9BB *Tel:* 020 7593 5000 *Fax:* 020 7593 5099

DIOCESAN ORGANIZATIONS

Diocesan Office Trinity House, 4 Chapel Court, Borough High St, London SE1 1HW *Tel:* 020 7939 9400 *Fax:* 020 7939 9468
email: trinity@southwark.anglican.org
Web: www. southwark.anglican.org

ADMINISTRATION

Dioc Synod (*Chairman, House of Clergy*) Tbc (*Chairman, House of Laity*) Tbc; (*Secretary*) Mr Simon Parton, Dioc Office
South London Church Fund and Diocesan Board of Finance (*Chairman*) Mr John Kempsell; (*Secretary*) Mr Simon Parton, Dioc Office
Parsonages Board (*Secretary*) Mr Eric Greber, Dioc Office
email: eric.greber@southwark.anglican.org
Mission and Pastoral Committee (*Secretary*) Mr Andrew Lane, Dioc Office
email: andrew.lane@southwark.anglican.org
Redundant Churches Uses Committee (*Secretary*) Mr Eric Greber, Dioc Office
Designated Officer Mr Paul Morris, Minerva House, 5 Montague Close, London SE1 9BB *Tel:* 020 7593 5000 *Fax:* 020 7593 5099

CHURCHES

Advisory Committee for the Care of Churches (*Chairman*) Dr Cyril Young c/o Diocesan Office (*as above*); (*Secretary*) Mr Andrew Lane (*as above*)

ECUMENICAL

Chair of Ecumenical Sub-Group Revd Peter Hart, Vicarage, 70 Marksbury Ave, Richmond TW9 4JF *Tel:* 020 8392 1425
email: Pwhart1@aol.com

EDUCATION

Board of Education (*Director*) Mrs Barbara Lane, 48 Union St, London SE1 1TD *Tel:* 020 7234 9200
email: barbara.lane@southwark.anglican.org

MISSION WORKING GROUP

Acting Chair The Archdeacon of Lambeth (*as above*)
Canon Missioner Vacancy
Spiritual Formation Adviser Mr Chris Chapman, Dioc Office
Inter Faith Relations Co-ordinator Siriol Davies *Tel:* 020 7201 4854 *email:* sirioldavies@yahoo.co.uk
Parish Development Adviser Revd Ruth Worsley *Tel:* 020 7939 9417 *email:* ruth.worsley@southwark.anglican.org
Ecumenical Projects Officer John Richardson *Tel:* 01462 422502 *email:* john@ctslondon.org.uk
Groups Support Worker John Beaumont *Tel:* 020 7939 9414 *Fax:* 020 7939 9467 *email:* john.beaumont @southwark.anglican.org

PUBLIC POLICY GROUP

Bishop of Southwark's Adviser on Urban and Public Policy Terry Drummond CA, Bishop's House, 38 Tooting Bec Gardens, London SW16 1QZ
Chair Revd Stephen Sichel, St Matthew's Vicarage, 5 St Matthew's Road, London SW2 1ND *Tel:* 020 7733 9605 *email:* sichel@tiscali.co.uk
Regeneration Adviser: Revd Andrew Wakefield *Tel:* 020 8542 6566
Groups Support Worker John Beaumont, Dioc Office (*as above*)

CHILDREN AND YOUTH DEVELOPMENT GROUP

Chair Revd Canon Tim Marwood *Tel:* 020 8940 8435 *email:* timmarwood@yahoo.co.uk
Research and Administrative Officer Caroline Gibson *Tel:* 020 7939 9412 *Fax:* 020 7939 9467 *email:* caroline.gibson@southwark.anglican.org

OTHER OFFICERS

Dioc Safeguarding and Child Protection Adviser Jill Sandham, c/o Dioc Office *Tel:* 020 7939 9400 *email:* jill.sandham@southwark.anglican.org
Dean of Women's Ministry Revd Canon Alyson Peberdy *Tel:* 020 8690 2499 *email:* alysonpeberdy@aol.com
Minority Ethnic Anglican Concerns Officer Ms Lola Brown, Dioc Office *Tel:* 020 7939 9418 *email:* lola.brown@southwark.anglican.org
Interfaith Group Chair Siriol Davies *Tel:* 020 7701 4854 *email:* sirioldavies@yahoo.co.uk
Liturgical Committee Revd Dr John Thewlis (*Secretary*), Rectory, 2 Talbot Rd, Carshalton SM5 3BS *Tel:* 020 8647 2366 *email:* rector@jctclerk.demon.co.uk
Retirement Officer Revd Nicky Tredennick *Tel:* 01342 843570 *email:* rev.nicky@btinternet.com
Faith in the Countryside Link Officer Revd Carol Coslett *Tel:* 01737 842102 *email:* ccoslett@btinternet.com
Southwark Dioc WelCare Revd Anne-Marie Garton (*Director*), St John's Community Centre, 19 Frederick Crescent, London SW9 6XN *Tel:* 020 7820 7910 *email:* anne-marie.garton@southwark.anglican.org

MINISTRY AND TRAINING COMMITTEE

Canon Theologian and Director of Ministerial Education Canon Dr Jane Steen, Dioc Office *Tel:* 020 7939 9449 *email:* jane.steen@southwark.anglican.org
Diocesan Director of Ordinands Canon Leanne Roberts *Tel:* 020 7939 9458 *email:* leanne.roberts@southwark.anglican.org
Officer for Reader Training Revd Lu Gale, Dioc Office *Tel:* 020 7939 9473 *email:* lu.gale@southwark.anglican.org
Warden of Readers (*Acting*) Mrs Trot Lavelle, 181 Camberwell Grove, London SE5 8JS *Tel:* 020 7274 1400 *email:* t.lavelle181@btinternet.com
Southwark Pastoral Auxiliary Training Officer Mr Chris Chapman, Dioc Office *Tel:* 020 7939 9474 *email:* chris.chapman@southwark.anglican.org
Officer for Lay Mission and Ministry Revd Lu Gale, Dioc Office (as above)
Southwark Pastoral Auxiliary Co-ordinator Revd Lu Gale, Dioc Office (*as above*)

COMMUNICATIONS

Director of Communications and Resources and Bishop's Press Officer Revd Canon Wendy Robins, Dioc Office *Tel:* 020 7939 9400 (Office) *email:* wendy.s.robins@southwark.anglican.org
Communications Officer Mr Steve Harris, Dioc Office *Tel:* 020 7939 9437 *email:* steve.harris@southwark.anglican.org

DIOCESAN RECORD OFFICES

London Metropolitan Archives, 40 Northampton Rd, London EC1R 0HB *Tel:* 020 7332 3820 *Fax:* 020 7833 9136 (*Parish records for Inner London Boroughs except Lewisham*)
Lewisham Local Studies and Archives Centre, Lewisham Library, 199–201 Lewisham High St, London SE13 6LG *Tel:* 020 8297 0682 *Fax:* 020 8297 1169 (*Parish records for East and West Lewisham deaneries*)
Bexley Local Studies and Archive Centre, Central Library, Townley Road, Bexleyheath DA6 7HJ *Tel:* 020 8301 1545 (*For Parishes in the London Borough of Bexley*)
Surrey History Centre, 130 Goldsworth Rd, Woking GU21 1ND *Tel:* 01483 594594 *Fax:* 01483 594595 (*County of Surrey and Surrey London Boroughs*)
London Borough of Sutton Local Studies Centre, St Nicholas Way, Sutton SM1 1JN *Tel:* 020 8770 5000 (*London Borough of Sutton*)

STEWARDSHIP

Director of Communications and Resources Revd Canon Wendy Robins, Dioc Office *Tel:* 020 7939 9400 *email:* wendy.s.robins@southwark.anglican.org.uk

Stewardship Resources Officer Mrs Jackie Pontin, Dioc Office *Tel:* 020 7939 9461
email: jackie.pontin@southwark.anglican.org

AREA DEANS

ARCHDEACONRY OF SOUTHWARK

Bermondsey (Acting Area Dean) Revd Stewart Hartley, St Anne's Vicarage, 10 Thorburn Square, London SE1 5QH *Tel:* 020 7237 3950
email: stewarthartley@btinternet.com

Camberwell (Acting Area Dean) Revd Ruth Worsley Dioc Office *Tel:* 020 7939 9417

Dulwich Revd Canon Charles Richardson, St John's Vicarage, 62 East Dulwich Road, London SE22 9AU *Tel:* 020 8693 3897
email: stjohnsse22@hotmail.com

Southwark and Newington (Acting Area Dean) Revd Canon Grahame Shaw, St Paul's Vicarage, Lorrimore Square, London SE17 3QU
Tel: 020 7735 2947
email: stpaulspcc@btconnect.com

ARCHDEACONRY OF LAMBETH

Merton Revd Richard Lane, Christ Church Vicarage, 16 Copse Hill, London SW20 0HG
Tel: 020 8946 4491
email: westwimbledon@btinternet.com

Lambeth North Revd Stephen Sichel, St Matthew's Vicarage 5 St Matthew's Road London SW2 1ND
Tel: 020 7733 9605
email: sichel@tiscali.co.uk

Lambeth South Revd Simon P. Gates, Vicarage, 2 Thornton Rd, Balham, London SW12 0JU
Tel: 020 8671 8276
email: simon.gates@stwss.org.uk

ARCHDEACONRY OF REIGATE

Caterham Revd Duncan Swan, The Rectory, 5 Whyteleafe Road, Caterham, Surrey CR3 5EG
Tel: 01883 373083
email: duncpen@hotmail.com

Godstone Revd Peter Moseling, The Rectory, Outwood Lane, Bletchingley, Surrey RH1 4LR
Tel: 01883 743252
email: frp.moseling@tiscali.co.uk

Reigate Revd Canon Gary Jenkins, 4 Carlton Road, Redhill, Surrey RH1 2BX *Tel:* 01737 779917
email: gary@htredhill.com

ARCHDEACONRY OF LEWISHAM AND GREENWICH

Charlton Revd Canon Kim Hitch, St James Rectory, 62 Kidbrooke Park Rd, London SE3 0DU
Tel: 020 8856 3438
email: k.w.hitch@btinternet.com

Deptford Revd Neil Nicholls, St James Vicarage, St James, New Cross, London SE14 6AD
Tel: 020 8691 2167
email: revn@hotmail.co.uk

East Lewisham Revd Richard D. Bainbridge, Vicarage, 47 Handen Rd, London SE12 8NR
Tel: 020 8318 2363
email: revrdb@yahoo.com

Eltham and Mottingham Revd Elaine Cranmer, St Luke's Vicarage, 107 Westmount Rd, Eltham, London SE9 1XX *Tel:* 020 8850 3030
email: rev.elaine@virgin.net

Plumstead Revd Harry Owen, All Saints Vicarage, 106 Herbert Rd, Plumstead, London SE18 3PU *Tel:* 020 8854 2995
email: h.d.owen@talk21.com

West Lewisham Revd Michael Kingston, St Bartholomew's Vicarage, 4 Westwood Hill, Sydenham, London SE26 6QR
Tel: 020 8778 5290
email: michaelkingston@btinternet.com

ARCHDEACONRY OF WANDSWORTH

Battersea Revd Geoffrey Owen, Christ Church Vicarage, Candahar Road, London SW11 2PU
Tel: 020 7228 1225
*email:*geoffrey-owen@o2.co.uk

Kingston Revd Simon Coupland, St Paul's Vicarage, 33 Queen's Road, Kingston-upon-Thames, Surrey KT2 7SF *Tel:* 020 8549 8597
email: simon.coupland@stpaulskingston.org.uk

Richmond and Barnes Revd Canon Tim Marwood, The Vicarage, Bute Avenue, Petersham, Richmond, TW10 7AX *Tel:* 020 8940 8435
email: timmarwood@yahoo.co.uk

Tooting Revd Wilma Roest, St Mary's Vicarage, 218a Balham High Road, London, SW12 9BS
Tel: 020 8673 1188
email: vicar@stmarybalham.org.uk

Wandsworth Revd Heinz Toller, St Paul's Vicarage, 116 Augustus Rd, London SW19 6EW
Tel: 020 8788 2024
email: htoller@gmail.com

ARCHDEACONRY OF CROYDON

Croydon Addington Revd Stephen Knowers, The Vicarage, 49 Shirley Church Road, Shirley, Surrey CR0 5EF *Tel:* 020 8654 1013
email: frstiiv@hotmail.com

Croydon Central Revd Trevor Mapstone, 33 Hurst Way, South Croydon, Surrey CR2 7AP
Tel: 020 8688 6676
email: tmapstone@emmanuelcroydon.org.uk

Croydon North Revd Leonard Marsh, The Vicarage, 49 Chevening Road, London SE13 3TD
Tel: 020 8653 2820
email: leonard.marsh@yahoo.co.uk

Croydon South Revd Christine Spurway, St James' Vicarage, 1b St James' Rd, Purley CR8 2DL *Tel:* 020 8660 5436
email: christinespurway@uwclub.net

Sutton Revd Canon Christopher Wheaton, The Vicarage, 38 Beeches Ave, Carshalton, Surrey SM5 3LW *Tel:* 020 8647 6056
email: good.shepherd432@btinternet.com

CHAPTER OF MINISTERS IN SECULAR EMPLOYMENT

Chapter Dean for Kingston Revd Peter King, 49 Leinster Ave, East Sheen, London SW14 7JW
Tel: 020 8876 8997

DIOCESE OF SOUTHWELL AND NOTTINGHAM

Founded in 1884. Nottinghamshire; a few parishes in South Yorkshire.

Population 1,091,000 Area 847 sq m
Full-time Stipendiary Parochial Clergy 124 Benefices 157
Parishes 256 Churches 306
www.southwell.anglican.org
Overseas link diocese: Natal (South Africa)

BISHOP

Rt Revd Paul Butler, Bishop's Manor, Southwell NG25 0JR [2009] *Tel:* 01636 812112
Fax: 01636 815401
email: bishop@southwell.anglican.org
[Paul Southwell and Nottingham]
Chaplain Revd Lucy Cleland
email: chaplain@southwell.anglican.org
Personal Assistant Mrs Jackie Davies
email: jackie@southwell.anglican.org

SUFFRAGAN BISHOP

SHERWOOD Rt Revd Anthony Porter, Dunham House, 8 Westgate, Southwell NG25 0JL [2006]
Tel: 01636 819133
Fax: 01636 819085
Personal Assistant Miss Jenny Andrews
email: jenny@southwell.anglican.org

PROVINCIAL EPISCOPAL VISITOR

BEVERLEY Rt Revd Glyn Webster, c/o Bishopthorpe Palace, Bishopthorpe, York YO23 2GE
Tel: 01904 707021/2
email: office@archbishopofyork.org

HONORARY ASSISTANT BISHOPS

Rt Revd John Finney, Greenacre, Crow Lane, South Muskham, Newark NG23 6DZ [1998]
Tel: 01636 679791
Rt Revd Ronald Milner, 7 Crafts Way, Southwell NG25 0BL [1994] *Tel:* 01636 816256
Rt Revd Roy Williamson, 30 Sidney Rd, Beeston, Nottingham NG9 1AN [1998] *Tel:* 0115 925 4901
Rt Revd Richard Inwood, 43 Whitecoates Park, Chesterfield, Notts, S40 3RT [2012]
Tel: 01246 766288

CATHEDRAL AND PARISH CHURCH OF THE BLESSED VIRGIN MARY

Dean Very Revd John Arthur Guille, The Residence, 1 Vicars' Court, Southwell NG25 0HP [2007] *Tel:* 01636 812782
email: dean@southwellminster.org.uk
Office The Minster Office, The Minster Centre, Church St, Southwell NG25 0HD
Tel: 01636 812649/817810
Fax: 01636 817284
email: office@southwellminster.org.uk
Web: www.southwellminster.org.uk

Canons Residentiary
Precentor Canon Jacqueline (Jacqui) D. Jones, 2 Vicars' Court, Southwell NG25 0HP [2003]
Tel: 01636 817295
email: jacquijones@southwellminster.org.uk
Canon Pastor Canon Nigel Coates, 3 Vicars' Court, Southwell NG25 0HP [2005]
Tel: 01636 817296
email: nigelcoates@southwellminster.org.uk
Chapter Clerk Mrs Caroline Jarvis, The Minster Office, The Minster Centre, Church St, Southwell NG25 0HD *Tel:* 01636 817285
email: chapterclerk@southwellminster.org.uk
Rector Chori Mr Paul Hale, 4 Vicars' Court, Southwell NG25 0HP *Tel:* 01636 812228/817297
email: RectorChori@diaphone.clara.net
Head Verger Mr Andrew Todd, The Vestry, Southwell Cathedral *Tel:* 01636 817290
email: vergers@southwellminster.org.uk

ARCHDEACONS

NOTTINGHAM Ven Peter Hill, 4 Victoria Crescent, Sherwood, Nottingham NG5 4DA [2007]
Tel: 0115 985 8641 (Home)
01636 817206 (Office)
07771 778182 (Mobile)
Fax: 01636 815084 (Office)
email: archdeacon-nottm@southwell.anglican.org
NEWARK Ven David Picken, 22 Rufford Road, Edwinstowe, Mansfield, Notts NG21 9HY [2012]
Tel: 01636 817206 (Office)
Fax: 01636 815084 (Office)
email:
archdeacon-newark@southwell.anglican.org

CONVOCATION (MEMBERS OF THE HOUSE OF CLERGY OF THE GENERAL SYNOD)

Proctors for Clergy
Ven Peter Hill
Revd Canon Tony Walker
Revd Sally Baylis

MEMBERS OF THE HOUSE OF LAITY OF THE GENERAL SYNOD

Mrs Pamela Bishop
Mr Nick Harding
Mr Colin Slater

DIOCESAN OFFICER

Chief Executive Mr Nigel Spraggins, Dunham House, 8 Westgate, Southwell NG25 0JL
Tel: 01636 817205 (Office)
07887 538682 (Mobile)
01636 816445 (Home)
Fax: 01636 815084
email: ce@southwell.anglican.org

Executive Personal Assistant to the Chief Executive and Archdeacons Miss Jo Delves
Tel: 01636 817206
email: jo.delves@southwell.anglican.org

Chancellor of Diocese The Worshipful Mrs Linda Mary Box, Diocesan Office *Tel:* 01636 817209

Deputy Chancellor Mr Stephen Eyre

Registrar of Diocese and Bishop's Legal Secretary Amanda Redgate *Tel:* 01636 817209

Deputy Registrar Vacancy

DIOCESAN ORGANIZATIONS

Diocesan Office Dunham House, 8 Westgate, Southwell NG25 0JL *Tel:* 01636 817200
Fax: 01636 815084
email: mail@southwell.anglican.org
Web: www.southwell.anglican.org

ADMINISTRATION

Diocesan Synod (*Vice-president and Chair, House of Clergy*) Revd Canon Phil Williams
(*Chair, House of Laity*) Mrs Pam Bishop
(*Secretary*) Mr Nigel Spraggins, Chief Executive
Tel: 01636 817204

FINANCE AND ADMINISTRATION

Director of Finance and Administration Mr David Meredith *Tel:* 01636 817202

PARISH SUPPORT

(*Includes Property, DAC and Stewardship*)
Director of Parish Support and Stewardship Advice Canon Carole Park *Tel:* 01636 817242
*email:*carolepark@southwell.anglican.org

PARISH SUPPORT (PROPERTY)

Building Surveyor Mr Ian Greaves
Tel: 01636 817214

PARISH SUPPORT (STEWARDSHIP)

Director of Funding Canon Carole Park
Tel: 01636 817242
email: carolepark@southwell.anglican.org

CHURCHES

Advisory Committee for the Care of Churches (*Chairman*) Canon Keith Turner, Rectory, Main St, Linby, Nottingham NG15 8AE *Tel:* 0115 963 2346
email: k.h.turner@btopenworld.com
Web: www.southwellchurches.nottingham.ac.uk

DAC Secretary and GIS Manager, Mr Jonathan Pickett *Tel:* 01636 817210
email: jonathan-dac@southwell.anglican.org

EDUCATION

Diocesan Office, Dunham House, 8 Westgate, Southwell NG25 0JL

Director of Education Mrs Claire Meese
Tel: 01636 817238
01636 814504 (General Office)

Diocesan School Advisers Mrs Jane Lewis *and* Mrs Anne Lumb *Tel:* 01636 817236
email: jane.lewis@southwell.anglican.org / anne.lumb@southwell.anglican.org

Youth Ministry Adviser (*Temporary appointment*) Mr Tim Friend *Tel:* 01636 817233
email: youthministryadviser@southwell.anglican.org

Children's Ministry Adviser Mr Nick Harding
Tel: 01636 817234
email: nick@southwell.anglican.org

DEPARTMENT FOR DEVELOPMENT

Diocesan Office, 8 Westgate, Southwell NG25 0JL

Director, Ministry & Mission Canon Dr Nigel Rooms *Tel:* 01636 817231
email: nigel.rooms@southwell.anglican.org

Director, Partnerships & Mission Revd David McCoulough *Tel:* 01636 817987
email: davidmcc@southwell.anglican.org

Vocations Adviser and Diocesan Director of Ordinands Revd Sue Hemsley Halls *Tel:* 01636 817212
email: suehh@southwell.anglican.org

Dean of Women's Ministry Revd Canon Sarah Clark, The Rectory, 569 Farnborough Road, Clifton, Nottingham NG11 9DG
Tel: 0115 878 0541
email: saraheclark@ntlworld.com

Ministry Development Advisers Revd Alison Cox
Tel: 01636 817226
email: alison.cox@southwell.anglican.org

Revd Jackie Johnson
Tel: 01636 817208
email: jackie.johnson@southwell.anglican.org

Warden of Readers and Director of Studies Mr Christopher Perrett, Harvest Barn, Grassthorpe, Newark, Nottingham NG23 5QZ
Tel: 01636 822426
email: chris.perrett@southwell.anglican.org

Sport Ministry
Sport Ambassador Vacancy

Chaplain to Retired Clergy/Clergy Widows Officer Revd David Edinborough *Tel:* 0115 9251066
email: david.edinborough@googlemail.com

Bishop's Adviser on Rural Affairs Vacancy

Workplace Chaplain Revd Rachel Shock

Equality and Diversity Officer and Rainbow Project Leader Ms Dianne Skerritt *Tel:* 0115 948 3658 or 01636 817229
email: dskerritt@southwell.anglican.org

Diocesan Ecumenical Officer Revd Stephen Morris
Tel: 0115 960 4477
email: stephen.morris@nottinghamchurches.org

Natal Link Officer Revd Barbara Holbrook, The Rectory, 1 Eastwood Road, Kimberley, Nottingham NG16 2HX *Tel:* 0115 938 3565
email: bholbrook@btinternet.com

PRESS AND PUBLICATIONS

Director of Communications Mrs Rachel Farmer, Diocesan Office *Tel:* 01636 817218 (Office)
Tel: and *Fax:* 01636 816276 (Home)
07712 196381 (Mobile)
email: rachel@southwell.anglican.org

Editor of Diocesan Magazine 'C' Mrs Rachel Farmer (*as above*)

DIOCESAN RECORDS OFFICE

Nottinghamshire Archives, County House, Castle Meadow Rd, Nottingham NG1 1AG *Principal Archivist* Mr Mark Dorrington
Tel: 0115 950 4524

AREA DEANS

ARCHDEACONRY OF NEWARK

Bassetlaw and Bawtry Revd Jonathan Smithurst, The Rectory, Abbey Road, Mattersey, Doncaster, DN10 5DX *Tel:* 01777 817364
email: j.smithurst@ctmail.co.uk

Mansfield Revd Mark Adams, St John's Vicarage, St John Street, Mansfield NG18 1QH
Tel: 01623 625999
email: vicar@stjohnswithstmarys.org.uk

Newark and Southwell Revd David Milner
Tel: 01636 650063
email: wd.milner55@gmail.com

Newstead Revd Dr Richard Kellett, Vicarage, Mansfield Rd, Skegby, Sutton-in-Ashfield NG17 3ED *Tel:* 01623 558800
email: richard@skegbyparish.org.uk

ARCHDEACONRY OF NOTTINGHAM

East Bingham Canon Jim Wellington, The Rectory, Nottingham Rd, Keyworth, Nottingham NG12 0UB *Tel:* 0115 937 2017
email: jhcwelli@btinternet.com

West Bingham Revd John Bentham, 51 Chatsworth Rd, West Bridgford, Nottingham NG2 7AE
Tel: 0115 846 1054
email: john.bentham@nottingham.ac.uk

Gedling Canon Philip Williams, St James' Vicarage, Marshall Hill Drive, Mapperley, Nottingham NG3 6FY *Tel:* 0115 960 6185
email: phil.stjames@virgin.net

Nottingham North Revd Jerry Lepine, The Rectory, 143 Russell Drive, Nottingham NG8 2BD
Tel: 0115 928 1798
email: jerry.lepine@btopenworld.com

Nottingham South Revd Jonathan MacGillivray, 6 Watcombe Circus, Carrington, Nottingham NG5 2DT *Tel:* 0115 962 1291
email: j j.macg@virgin.net

DIOCESE OF TRURO

Founded in 1877. Cornwall; the Isles of Scilly; one parish in Devon.

Population 538,000 Area 1,390 sq m
Full-time Stipendiary Parochial Clergy 90 Benefices 128
Parishes 219 Churches 307
www.truro.anglican.org
Overseas link diocese: Strängnas, Sweden and Umzimvubu, South Africa.

BISHOP (15th)
Rt Revd Tim Thornton, Lis Escop, Feock, Truro TR3 6QQ [2008] *Tel:* 01872 862657
Fax: 01872 862037
email: bishop@truro.anglican.org
[Timothy Truro]
Domestic Chaplain Revd Jem Thorold
email: chaplain@truro.anglican.org
Bishop's Secretaries Mrs Karen Madeley, Lis Escop
email: office@truro.anglican.org
Mrs Lesley Rogers, Lis Escop
email: office@truro.anglican.org

SUFFRAGAN BISHOP
ST GERMANS Vacancy

CATHEDRAL CHURCH OF THE BLESSED VIRGIN MARY IN TRURO
Dean Very Revd Roger Bush *Tel:* 01872 245006
Cathedral Office 14 St Mary's St, Truro TR1 2AF
Tel: 01872 276782
Fax: 01872 277788
email: dean@trurocathedral.org.uk
Canons Residentiary
Precentor Canon Perran Gay, St Michael's House, 52 Daniell Rd, Truro TR1 2DA [1994]
Tel: 01872 245003
email: perran@trurocathedral.org.uk
Missioner Canon Philip Lambert, Foxhayes, 3 Knights Hill, Kenwyn, Truro TR1 3UY [2006]
Tel: 01872 245018
email: philip@trurocathedral.org.uk
Pastor Canon Lynda Barley, Cathedral Office
Tel: 01872 245016
email: lynda@trurocathedral.org.uk
Chapter Canons
Mr Robert Foulkes [2001]
Mrs Bridget Hugh-Jones [2001]
Chief Executive Mr Alan Wallace
Tel: 01872 245006
email: chiefexecutive@trurocathedral.org.uk
Director of Music Christopher Gray, Cathedral Office *email:* chris@trurocathedral.org.uk

ARCHDEACONS
BODMIN Ven Audrey Elkington, 4 Park Drive, Bodmin PL31 2QF [2011]
Tel and *Fax:* 01208 892811
email: audrey@truro.anglican.org
CORNWALL Vacancy

CONVOCATION (MEMBERS OF THE HOUSE OF CLERGY OF THE GENERAL SYNOD)
Proctors for Clergy
Revd Alan Bashforth
Very Revd Roger Bush
Revd Canon Perran Gay

MEMBERS OF THE HOUSE OF LAITY OF THE GENERAL SYNOD
Mrs Susannah Leafe
Mrs Sheri Sturgess
Gp Capt Paul Terrett

DIOCESAN OFFICERS
Dioc Secretary Mrs Esther Pollard (Acting)
Tel: 01872 274351
email: esther.pollard@truro.anglican.org
Fax: 01872 222510
Web: www.truro.anglican.org
Chancellor of Diocese The Worshipful Timothy Briden, Lamb Chambers, Lamb Building, Temple, London EC4Y 7AS *Tel:* 020 7797 8300
Fax: 020 7707 8308
email: info@lambchambers.co.uk
Registrar of Diocese and Bishop's Legal Secretary Mr Martin Follett, Truro Diocesan Registry, MichelmoresLLP, Woodwater House, Pynes Hill, Exeter EX2 5WR *Tel:* 01392 687415
Fax: 01392 360563
email: mjf@michelmores.com
Dioc Surveyor Mr Matthew Williams, Dioc House, Kenwyn, Truro TR1 1JQ *Tel:* 01872 241507
Fax: 01872 222510
email: matthew.williams@truro.anglican.org

DIOCESAN ORGANIZATIONS
Diocesan Office Diocesan House, Kenwyn, Truro TR1 1JQ *Tel:* 01872 274351
Fax: 01872 222510
email: info@truro.anglican.org

ADMINISTRATION
Dioc Synod and Bishop's Council (Acting Secretary) Mrs Esther Pollard, Dioc Office
Dioc Synod (Chairman, House of Clergy) Revd Alan Bashforth, Vicarage, 6 Penwinnick Parc, St Agnes TR5 0UQ *Tel:* 01872 553391

(*Chairman, House of Laity*) Mrs Sheri Sturgess
Board of Finance (*Chairman*) Mr Roger Caudwell; (*Secretary*) Mrs Esther Pollard (*as above*)
Parsonages Committee Mrs Esther Pollard (*as above*)
Mission & Pastoral Committee Mrs Sue Thorold
Glebe Committee Mrs Clare Jones, Dioc Office
Board of Patronage Vacancy
Designated Officer Mrs Esther Pollard (*as above*)

CHURCHES

Advisory Committee for the Care of Churches (*Chairman*)Dr John Kidman, Trepenal Barn, Blisland, Bodmin PL30 4HS *Tel:* 01208 821525
email: john@tavas.co.uk
(*Secretary*) Mrs Sue Thorold
Truro Diocesan Guild of Ringers (*President*) Mr Michael Wycherley, 34 St Gluvias St, Penryn TR10 8BJ *Tel:* 01326 374119; (*Gen Secretary*) Mr Robert Perry, 11 Trevaylor Close, Truro TR1 1RP, *Tel:* 01872 277117
Churches Uses Committee (*Secretary*) Mrs Sue Thorold (*as above*)

EDUCATION AND TRAINING

Director and Secretary of Education Mrs Sue Green, Dioc Office *Tel:* 01872 247214
email: sue.green@truro.anglican.org
Project Officer Mrs Sarah Welply (*same address*)
email: sarah.welply@truro.anglican.org
Discipleship Project Officer Mrs Shelley Porter, 4 Park Drive, Bodmin PL31 2QF
Tel: 01208 892811
email: shelley.porter@truro.anglican.org

MINISTRY

Director of Ministerial Formation and Development Revd Paul Arthur, Rectory, 16 Trelavour Rd, St Dennis, St Austell PL26 8AH *Tel:* 01726 822317
email: kpaularthur@googlemail.com
Director of Ordinands Revd Jeremy Andrew, The Vicarage, Cocks, Perranporth TR6 0AT
Tel: 01872 573375
email: j.andrew.102@btinternet.com
South-west Ministry Training Course (*Principal*) Revd David Moss, Amory Building, University of Exeter, Rennes Drive, Exeter EX4 4RJ
Tel: 01392 264403
email: principal@swmtc.org.uk
Web: www.swmtc.org.uk
Warden of Readers Ven Audrey Elkington (*as above*)
Deputy Warden of Readers Revd Paul Arthur (*as above*)
Clergy Retirement and Widows Officer Revd Owen Blatchly, 1 Rose Cottages, East Rd, Stithians, Truro TR3 7BD *Tel:* 01209 860845

EVANGELISM AND UNITY

Chairman Revd Angela Butler, 22 Esplanade Road, Pentire, Newquay TR7 1QB
Tel: 01637 859238
email: angelambutler@btinternet.com
Officer for Unity Revd Elizabeth Foot, St Johns in the Fields Vicarage, Hellesvean, St Ives TR26 2HG *Tel:* 01736 794899
email: guenolesenara@hotmail.co.uk
World Church Committee (*Chairman*) Revd Andrew Gough

KINGDOM GROUP

Social Responsibility Officer Revd Andrew Yates, Dioc Office
email: andrew.yates@truro.anglican.org

PRESS AND PUBLICATIONS

Dioc Communications Officer Mr David Watson, Dioc Office *Tel:* 01872 274351
email: david.watson@truro.anglican.org
Editor of Dioc News Leaflet Mr David Watson (*as above*)
Editor of Online Dioc Directory Mrs Clare Jones (*as above*)

DIOCESAN RECORDS

Diocesan Records Officer Mr David Thomas, County Hall, Truro TR1 3AY *Tel:* 01872 323127
email: cro@cornwall.gov.uk
website: cornwall.gov.uk/cro

STEWARDSHIP

Mrs Rebecca Evans, Dioc House
Tel: 01872 274351
email: rebecca.evans@truro.anglican.org

RURAL DEANS

ARCHDEACONRY OF CORNWALL

St Austell Revd Marion Barrett, The Rectory, St Mewan, St Austell PL26 7DP *Tel:* 01726 72679
email: marionstmewan@btinternet.com
Carnmarth North Revd Olive Stevens, Hideaway, The Square, Portreath, Redruth TR16 4LA
Tel: 01209 842372
email: olivestevens@aol.com
Carnmarth South Revd Geoffrey Bennett, The Vicarage, Merry Mit Meadow, Budock Water, Falmouth TR11 5DW *Tel:* 01326 376422
email: rev.bennett@talk21.com
Kerrier Revd Lesley Walker, The Rectory, St Martin, Helston TR12 6BU *Tel:* 01326 231971
email: walker53@btopenworld.com
Penwith Revd Howard Peskett, 7 North Parade, Penzance TR18 4SH *Tel:* 01736 362913
email: howard.peskett@btinternet.com
Powder Revd Alan Bashforth, The Vicarage, 6 Penwinnick Parc, St Agnes, Truro TR5 0UG
Tel: 01872 553391
email: onepaw@btinternet.com
Pydar Revd Christopher Malkinson, The Vicarage, 46 Treverbyn Rd, Padstow PL28 8DN
Tel: 01841 533776
email: chrismalk@hotmail.com

ARCHDEACONRY OF BODMIN

East Wivelshire Revd Michael Goodland, The Vicarage, Millbrook, Torpoint PL10 1BW
Tel: 01752 822264
email: michaelgoodland07@gmail.com

Stratton Revd Robert Thewsey, The Rectory, Boscastle PL35 0DJ *Tel:* 01288 250359
email: robert.thewsey@btinternet.com

Trigg Major Revd David Jasper, East Barton, North Petherwin, Launceston PL15 8LR
Tel: 01566 785996
email: davidjasper5dy@btinternet.com

Trigg Minor and Bodmin Canon Sherry Bryan, The Rectory, Green Briar, Coombe Lane, St Breward PL30 4LT *Tel* and *Fax:* 01208 851829
email: sherrybryan4@aol.com

West Wivelshire Canon Tony Ingleby, The Rectory, Church St, Liskeard PL24 3AQ
Tel: 01579 342178
email: revtonyingleby@gmail.com

DIOCESE OF WAKEFIELD

Founded in 1888. Wakefield; Kirklees; Calderdale; Barnsley, except for an area in the south-east (SHEFFIELD); an area of Leeds; a few parishes in North Yorkshire.

Population 1,130,000 Area 557 sq m
Full-time Stipendiary Parochial Clergy 125 Benefices 145
Parishes 183 Churches 237
Overseas link dioceses: Adelaide (Australia), Faisalabad (Pakistan), Mara, Rorya and Tarime (Tanzania) and Skara (Sweden).

BISHOP (12th)

Rt Revd Stephen Platten, Bishop's Lodge, Woodthorpe Lane, Wakefield WF2 6JL [2003]
Tel: 01924 255349
Fax: 01924 250202
email: bishop@bishopofwakefield.org.uk

Bishop's Domestic Chaplain and Communications Officer Revd Philip Wells, Bishop's Lodge, Woodthorpe Lane, Sandal, Wakefield WF2 6JL
Tel: 01924 255349
Tel: 01924 250574 (Direct Line)
email: pwells@bishopofwakefield.org.uk

SUFFRAGAN BISHOP

PONTEFRACT Rt Revd Anthony Robinson, Pontefract House, 181A Manygates Lane, Sandal Wakefield WF2 7DR [1998] *Tel:* 01924 250781
Fax: 01924 240490
email: bishop.pontefract@wakefield.anglican.org

CATHEDRAL CHURCH OF ALL SAINTS

Cathedral Centre 8–10 Westmorland St, Wakefield WF1 1PJ *Tel:* 01924 373923
Fax: 01924 215054
email: admin@wakefield-cathedral.org.uk
Web: www.wakefield-cathedral.org.uk

Dean Very Revd Jonathan Greener, The Deanery, 1 Cathedral Close, Margaret St, Wakefield WF1 2DP *Tel:* 01924 373923 (Office)
01924 239308 (Home)
email: jonathan.greener@wakefield-cathedral.org.uk

Administrator and Chapter Clerk Mr Ashley Ellis
Tel: 01924 371802
email: diocesan.secretary@wakefield.anglican.org.uk

Dean's PA Mr Neil Holland *Tel:* 01924 373923
email: neil.holland@wakefield-cathedral.org.uk

Cathedral Secretary Mrs Karn Dyson
Tel: 01924 373923
email: karn.dyson@wakefield-cathedral.org.uk

Head Verger Mrs Julie Lovell
Tel: 01924 434486 (Direct Line)

Canons Residentiary

Sub Dean and Canon Pastor Canon Michael Rawson, 3 Cathedral Close, Margaret St, Wakefield WF1 2DP [2007]
Tel: 01924 373923 (Office)
01924 379743 (Home)
email: michael.rawson@wakefield-cathedral.org.uk

Canon Precentor Canon Andrea Hofbauer, 4 Cathedral Close, Margaret St, Wakefield WF1 2DP [2009] *Tel:* 01924 373923 (Office)
01924 200191 (Home)
email: andi.hofbauer@wakefield-cathedral.org.uk

Canon Residentiary Rt Revd Anthony Robinson, Pontefract House, 181A Manygates Lane, Sandal, Wakefield WF2 7DR [2005] *Tel:* 01924 250781
email: bishop.pontefract@wakefield.anglican.org

Canon Librarian Canon Dr John Lawson, 7 Belgravia Rd, St John's, Wakefield WF1 3JP [2005]
Tel: 01924 380182
email: john.lawson@wakefield.anglican.org

Canon Missioner Canon Tony Macpherson, 14 Belgravia Rd, St John's, Wakefield WF1 3JP [2007]
Tel: 01924 275274
email: canontonymac@gmail.com

Honorary Chaplains Revd Prof Roger Grainger, Revd George Midgley, Canon Stuart Ramsden, Revd Derek Birch

Ecumenical Canons Bishop Malhaz Songulashvili (Baptist Church of Georgia) [2006], Bishop Arthur Roche (Roman Catholic Bishop of Leeds) [2006], Revd Dr Elizabeth Smith, Chair, Leeds Methodist District [2011]

Priest Vicar Revd June Lawson
email: jlawson@mirfield.org.uk

Lay Canons
Arthur Mauya, Mrs Linda Box, Dr Keith Judkins, Mrs Celia Kilner, Prof Michael Clarke, Mr Yaqub Masih, Hon Judge John Bullimore, Mr Barry Sheerman MP, Ms Kate Taylor, Mr Paul Whittaker, Mr John McLeod

Clerk to the College of Canons Mrs Linda Box, Bank House, Burton St, Wakefield WF1 2DA
Tel: 01924 373467
Fax: 01924 366234
email: info@dixon-coles-gill.co.uk

Education Officer Ms Ali Bullivent
email: ali.bullivent@wakefield-cathedral.org.uk

Director of Music Mr Tom Moore, Cathedral Office
email: tom.moore@wakefield-cathedral.org.uk
Assistant Director of Music Mr Simon Earl, Cathedral Office
email: simonearl249@btinternet.com

ARCHDEACONS

HALIFAX Ven Dr Anne Dawtry, 2 Vicarage Gardens, Rastrick, Brighouse HD6 3HD
Tel: 01484 714553
email: archdeacon.halifax@wakefield.anglican.org
PONTEFRACT Ven Peter Townley, The Vicarage, Kirkthorpe, Wakefield WF1 5SZ
Tel: 01924 896327
Tel: 01924 434459 (Church House Direct Line)
Fax: 01924 364834 (Church House)
email: archdeacon.pontefract@wakefield.anglican.org

CONVOCATION (MEMBERS OF THE HOUSE OF CLERGY OF THE GENERAL SYNOD)

Proctors for Clergy
Revd Canon Joyce Jones
Revd Canon James Allison
Revd Canon Maggie McLean
Revd Paul Cartwright

MEMBERS OF THE HOUSE OF LAITY OF THE GENERAL SYNOD

Mr David Ashton
Mrs Alison Fisher
Mrs Mary Judkins
Mr Paul Neville

DIOCESAN OFFICERS

Diocesan Secretary Mr Ashley Ellis, Church House, 1 South Parade, Wakefield WF1 1LP
Tel: 01924 371802
Fax: 01924 364834
email: diocesan.secretary@wakefield.anglican.org
Chancellor of Diocese Worshipful Chancellor Mr John Morgans, Octagon House Chambers, 19 Colegate, Norwich NR2 2DH *Tel:* 01603 623186
email: clerks@octagonhouse.co.uk
Joint Registrars of Diocese and Bishop's Legal Secretaries Mr Julian Gill and Mrs Julia Wilding, Bank House, Burton St, Wakefield WF1 2DA
Tel: 01924 373467
Fax: 01924 366234
email: info@dixon-coles-gill.com

DIOCESAN ORGANIZATIONS

Diocesan Office Church House, 1 South Parade, Wakefield WF1 1LP *Tel:* 01924 371802
Fax: 01924 364834
email: church.house@wakefield.anglican.org

ADMINISTRATION

Diocesan Secretary Mr Ashley Ellis, Church House
Finance Manager and Deputy Diocesan Secretary Mr Bryan Lewis, Church House
Diocesan Synod (*Chair, House of Clergy*) Tbc
(*Chair, House of Laity*) Tbc
(*Secretary*) Mr Ashley Ellis (*as above*)
Diocesan Communications Adviser Mrs Jane Bower, Church House *Tel:* 01924 371802
email: jane.bower@wakefield.anglican.org
Board of Finance (*Chairman*) Revd Martin Macdonald, Church House; (*Secretary*) Mr Ashley Ellis (*as above*)
Finance Manager Mr Bryan Lewis, Church House
Diocesan Property Manager Ms Helen Price, Church House
Assistant Property Manager Mr Kevin Smith, Church House
Diocesan Mission and Pastoral Committee (*Secretary*) Mr Ashley Ellis (*as above*)
Diocesan Trust Mr Bryan Lewis (*as above*)
Giving and Resources Adviser Mrs Jo Beacroft-Mitchell, Church House
Board of Patronage Mrs Linda Box, Bank House, Burton St, Wakefield WF1 2DA
Tel: 01924 373467
Fax: 01924 366234
email: info@dixon-coles-gill.com
Designated Officer Mrs Julia Wilding, Bank House (*as above*)

CHURCHES

Diocesan Advisory Committee for the Care of Churches Mrs Julia Wilding (*as above*)

EDUCATION

Director of Education Canon Ian Wildey, Church House
Board of Education (*Chairman*) Ven Peter Townley; (*Secretary*) Revd Canon Ian Wildey

RESOURCING CHILDREN, YOUTH AND FAMILIES TEAM

Team Co-ordinator and 11–18yrs Adviser Mrs Liz Morton, Church House
Under 5yrs Adviser Mrs Ellie Wilson, Church House
5–11yrs Adviser Revd Jenni Honeyman, Church House

MINISTRY

Diocesan Director of Ordinands Revd Stephen Race, St John's Vicarage, Green Rd, Dodworth, Barnsley S75 3R *Tel:* 01226 206276
email: stephen.race@wakefield.anglican.org
Asst Directors of Ordinands Revd Joy Cousans, The Rectory, Church Lane, Clayton West, Huddersfield HD8 9LY *Tel:* 01484 862321
email: joy@daveandjoy.plus.com
Canon Owen Page, Vicarage, 7 Fern Valley Chase, Todmorden OL14 7BB *Tel:* 01706 813180
email: owen@owenpage.plus.com
Diocesan Director of Training Revd Dr John Lawson, Church House
email: john.lawson@wakefield.anglican.org
Warden of Readers Ven Dr Anne Dawtry

Dean of Women's Ministry Revd June Lawson, The Mirfield Centre, Stocks Bank Road, Mirfield WF14 0BW *Tel:* 01484 481911
email: jlawson@mirfield.org.uk
Vocations Officer Revd Matthew Pollard, 1 Vicarage Gardens, Rastrick, Brighouse HD6 3HD *Tel:* 01484 713386
Coordinator for Local Ministry Vacancy
Wakefield Ministry Consultancy Team, Church House
Continuing Ministerial Education Officer Canon Stephen Kelly, Vicarage, Woolley, Wakefield WF4 2JU *Tel:* 01226 382550
email: stephen.kelly@wakefield.anglican.org
Bishop's Adviser for Pastoral Care and Counselling Canon Christine Bullimore, 5 Snowgate Head, Horn Lane, New Mill HD9 7DH
Tel: 01484 521025
email: chrisbullimore@sky.com

SOCIAL RESPONSIBILITY

Development Officer Susan Parker, Church House
Diocesan Rural Officer (Farming) Revd Dennis Handley, Vicarage, Ripponden, Sowerby Bridge HX6 4DF *Tel:* 01422 822239
email: dennis@ntlworld.com
Diocesan Rural Officer (Broader Rural Issues) Revd Hugh Baker, Vicarage, 2 Netherton Hall Gardens, Netherton, Wakefield WF4 4JA
Tel: 01924 278384
email: hughcbaker@googlemail.com
Adviser on Urban Issues Revd David Nicholson, The Vicarage, St John's Road, Cudworth, Barnsley S72 8DE *Tel:* 01226 710279
email: FrNicholson@aol.com
Diocesan Environmental Issues Adviser Vacancy
The Bishop's Advisory Group on Theology and Society (Chair) Revd Roy Clements
Adviser on Disability Vacancy
Canon Missioner Canon Tony Macpherson, 14 Belgravia Road, Wakefield WF1 3JP
Tel: 01924 275274
email: canontonymac@gmail.com

OTHER OFFICERS

Safeguarding and Child Protection Adviser Mrs Jenny Price, Church House
email: jenny.price@wakefield.anglican.org
Bishop's Adviser for Ecumenical Affairs (for West Yorkshire) Revd Glenn Coggins, The Vicarage, 1 Church Lane, East Ardsley, Wakefield WF3 2LJ
Tel: 01924 822184
email: glenn@cogginsg.freeserve.co.uk
Ecumenical Affairs Officer (for South Yorkshire) Vacancy
Minister in the Deaf Community Revd Bob Shrine
Typetalk: 18002 01274 677693
Fax: 01274 889006
email: bob.shrine@btinternet.com
Interfaith Relations Revd Leslie Pinfield, The Vicarage, 17 Cross Church St, Paddock, Huddersfield HD1 4SN *Tel:* 01484 530814
*email:*frleslie@btopenworld.com

Retired Clergy and Widows Officers Revd Norma Webb, 24 High Street, Thornhill Edge WF12 0PS
Tel: 01924463574
email: normafwebb@aol.com
Revd Dick Bradnum, 4 Southlands Drive, Huddersfield HD2 2LT *Tel:* 01484 420721
Tourism Officer Mr Malcolm Warburton

PRESS AND PUBLICATIONS

Diocesan Year Book (Editor) Mr Ashley Ellis, Church House

DIOCESAN RECORD OFFICE

West Yorkshire Archive Service, Registry of Deeds, Newstead Rd, Wakefield WF1 2DE
Tel: 01924 305980
email: wakefield@wyjs.org.uk

DIOCESAN RESOURCES CENTRE

Wakefield Centre Manager: Resourcing Children, Youth and Families Team
Mirfield Centre Manager: Canon John Lawson
Assistant Manager (Wakefield and Mirfield) Mrs Sheila Crosby, Church House

RURAL DEANS

ARCHDEACONRY OF HALIFAX

Almondbury Revd Richard Steel, Rectory, Church Lane, Kirkheaton, Huddersfield HD5 0BH
Tel: 01484 532410
email: rector@kirkheatonchurch.org.uk
Brighouse and Elland Canon David Burrows, All Saints' Vicarage, Charles St, Elland HX5 0JF
Tel: 01422 373184
email: rectorofelland@btinternet.com
Calder Valley Vacancy
Halifax Revd Stephen Bradberry, 129 Paddock Lane, Norton Tower, Halifax HX2 0NT
Tel: 01422 358282
email: sbradberry@tiscali.co.uk
Huddersfield Revd Mary Railton-Crowder, The Vicarage, 4 Brendon Drive, Birkby, Huddersfield HD2 2DF *Tel:* 01484 546966
email: revmrc@yahoo.com
Kirkburton Canon Joyce Jones, Oakfield, 206 Barnsley Road, Denby Dale, Huddersfield HD8 8TS *Tel:* 01484 862350
email: joycerjones@aol.com

ARCHDEACONRY OF PONTEFRACT

Barnsley Revd Stephen Race, St John's Vicarage, Green Road, Dodworth, Barnsley S75 3RT
Tel: 01226 206276
email: stephen.race@wakefield.anglican.org
Birstall Canon Felicity Lawson, St Peter's House, 2a Church Street, Gildersome LS27 7AS
Tel: 0113 253 3339
email: guildsome.pcc@tiscali.co.uk
Dewsbury Revd Paul Maybury, Vicarage, 12 Fearnley Avenue, Ossett WF5 9ET
Tel: 01924 311573
Fax: 0870 137 5994
email: paul@trinityossett.org.uk

Pontefract Canon Bob Cooper, St Giles Vicarage, 9 The Mount, Pontefract WF8 1NE
Tel: 01977 706803
email: Robert_Cooper@msn.com

Wakefield Canon Stephen Kelly, The Vicarage, Woolley, Wakefield WF4 2JU *Tel:* 01226 382550
email: stephen.kelly@wakefield.anglican.org

DIOCESE OF WINCHESTER

Founded in 676. Hampshire, except for the south-eastern quarter (PORTSMOUTH), an area in the north-east (GUILDFORD), a small area in the west (SALISBURY) and one parish in the north (OXFORD); an area of eastern Dorset; the Channel Islands.

Population 1,315,000 Area 1,216 sq m
Full-time Stipendiary Parochial Clergy 184 Benefices 183
Parishes 258 Churches 407
www.winchester.anglican.org
Overseas link provinces: Province of Uganda, Province of Myanmar, Provinces of Rwanda, Burundi and Republic of Congo (formerly Zaïre).

BISHOP

Rt Revd Timothy John Dakin, Wolvesey, Winchester SO23 9ND [2012] *Tel:* 01962 854050
Fax: 01962 897088
Bishop's Chaplain Revd Gavin Foster (*same address*) *Tel:* 01962 897082
email: gavin.foster@winchester.anglican.org
Bishop's Secretary Miss Joyce Cockell (*same address*) *Tel:* 01962 854050
email: joyce.cockell@winchester.anglican.org

SUFFRAGAN BISHOPS

BASINGSTOKE Rt Revd Peter Hancock, Bishop's Lodge, Colden Lane, Old Alfresford SO24 9DH *Tel:* 01962 737330
email: bishop.peter@winchester.anglican.org
SOUTHAMPTON Rt Revd Jonathan Frost, Bishop's House, St Mary's Church Close, Wessex Lane, Southampton SO18 2ST *Tel:* 023 8055 3627
email: bishop.jonathan@winchester.anglican.org

HONORARY ASSISTANT BISHOPS

Rt Revd John Austin Baker, Norman Corner, 4 Mede Villas, Kingsgate Rd, Winchester SO23 9QQ [1994] *Tel:* 01962 861388
Rt Revd Simon Hedley Burrows, 8 Quarry Rd, Winchester, SO23 0JF [1994] *Tel:* 01962 853332
Rt Revd John Dennis, 7 Conifer Close, Winchester SO22 6SH [1999] *Tel:* 01962 868881
Rt Revd John Ellison, The Furrow, Evingar Rd, Whitchurch RG28 7EU [2008] *Tel:* 01256 892126
Rt Revd Christopher Herbert, 1 Beacon Close, Boundstone, Farnham GU10 4PA [2010] *Tel:* 01252 795600

CATHEDRAL CHURCH OF THE HOLY TRINITY, AND OF ST PETER, ST PAUL AND OF ST SWITHUN

Dean Very Revd James Edgar Atwell, Cathedral Office, 9 The Close, Winchester SO23 9LS [2006] *Tel:* 01962 857203
Fax: 01962 857264
email: the.dean@winchester-cathedral.org.uk
Cathedral Office 9 The Close, Winchester SO23 9LS *Tel:* 01962 857200
Fax: 01962 857201
email: cathedral.office@winchester-cathedral.org.uk
Web: www.winchester–cathedral.org.uk

Canons Residentiary
Canon Chancellor Canon Roland Riem, Cathedral Office, 9 The Close, Winchester SO23 9LS [2005] *Tel:* 01962 857216
email: roland.riem@winchester-cathedral.org.uk
Canon Precentor Canon Michael St John-Channell, Cathedral Office, 9 The Close, Winchester SO23 9LS [2006] *Tel:* 01962 857211
email: precentor@winchester-cathedral.org.uk

Lay Canons
Receiver General and Canon Treasurer Mrs Annabelle Boyes, Cathedral Office, 9 The Close, Winchester SO23 9LS *Tel:* 01962 857206
Fax: 01962 857201
email: annabelle.boyes@ winchester-cathedral.org.uk
Professor Lord Raymond Plant, Cathedral Office, 9 The Close, Winchester SO23 9LS *Tel:* 01962 857200
Dr Helen Harvey, Cathedral Office, 9 The Close, Winchester SO23 9LS *Tel:* 01962 857200
Close Vicar Revd Gregory Clifton-Smith, Cathedral Office, 9 The Close, Winchester SO23 9LS *Tel:* 01962 857231
email: gregory.clifton-smith@winchester-cathedral.org.uk
Clerk at Law Mr Julian Hartwell, Martyrwell, Cheriton, Alresford SO24 0QA *Tel:* 01962 857200
Director of Music Mr Andrew Lumsden, Cathedral Office, 9 The Close, Winchester SO23 9LS *Tel:* 01962 857218
email: andrew.lumsden@winchester-cathedral.org.uk
Assistant Director of Music Mr George Castle, Cathedral Office, 9 The Close, Winchester SO23 9LS *Tel:* 01962 857213
email: george.castle@winchester-cathedral.org.uk

ARCHDEACONS

BOURNEMOUTH Ven Dr Peter Rouch, Glebe House, 22 Bellflower Way, Chandlers Ford SO53 4HN [2011] *Tel:* 023 8026 0955
email: peter.rouch@winchester.anglican.org
WINCHESTER Ven Michael Harley, 22 St John's St, Winchester SO23 0HF [2009] *Tel:* 01962 869442
email: michael.harley@winchester.anglican.org

CONVOCATION (MEMBERS OF THE HOUSE OF CLERGY OF THE GENERAL SYNOD)

Dignitaries in Convocation
The Bishop of Winchester
The Bishop of Basingstoke
Proctors for Clergy
Very Revd Bob Key
Revd David Williams
Ven Michael Harley
Canon Clive Hawkins
Revd Rosalind Rutherford

MEMBERS OF THE HOUSE OF LAITY OF THE GENERAL SYNOD

Mr John Davies
Dr Tony Bennett
Mrs Christine Fry
Mr Ken Shorey
Miss Priscilla Hungerford
Channel Islands
Mrs Jane Bisson
Mr David Robilliard

DIOCESAN OFFICERS

Dioc Secretary Mr Andrew Robinson, Old Alresford Place, Alresford SO24 9DH
Tel: 01962 737305
Fax: 01962 737358
email: andrew.robinson@winchester.anglican.org
Chancellor of Diocese Worshipful His Honour Christopher Clark QC, c/o Dioc Office
Registrar of Diocese and Bishop's Legal Secretary Mr Andrew Johnson, Batt Broadbent, Minster Chambers, 42/44 Castle Street, Salisbury SP1 3TX
Tel: 01722 411141
email: aj@battbroadbent.co.uk

DIOCESAN ORGANIZATIONS

Diocesan Office Old Alresford Place, Alresford SO24 9DH *Tel:* 01962 737300
Fax: 01962 737358
Web: www.winchester.anglican.org

ADMINISTRATION

Deputy Dioc Secretary Mr Colin Harbidge, Old Alresford Place *Tel:* 01962 737307
email: colin.harbidge@winchester.anglican.org
Director of Finance Mr Stephen Collyer, Old Alresford Place *Tel:* 01962 737336
email: stephen.collyer@winchester.anglican.org
Dioc Synod (Chairman, House of Clergy) Canon Dr Ian Tomlinson, Rectory, Ragged Appleshaw, Andover SP11 9HX *Tel:* 01264 772414
email: ian@raggedappleshaw.freeserve.co.uk
(Chairman, House of Laity) Mr Ian Newman, Meadow View, 15 Bowerwood Rd, Fordingbridge SP6 1BL *Tel:* 01425 653269
email: ian@innewman.co.uk
(Secretary) Mr Andrew Robinson, *(as above)*
Board of Finance (Chairman) Mr Arthur Binns, Nil-Des, Ashley Lane, New Milton BH25 5AQ
Tel: 01425 611379
email: dustyakjb@aol.com
(Secretary) Mr Andrew Robinson *(as above)*
Director of Property Mr Rolf Hawkins, Old Alresford Place *Tel:* 01962 737330
email: rolf.hawkins@winchester.anglican.org
Mission and Pastoral Committee (Secretary) Canon Simon Baker, Old Alresford Place
Electoral Registration Officer Miss Jayne Tarry, Old Alresford Place *Tel:* 01962 737348
email: jayne.tarry@winchester.anglican.org
Editor of Dioc Directory Miss Jayne Tarry *(as above)*

COMMUNICATIONS

Director of Communications Revd Mark Rudall, Old Alresford Place *Tel:* 01483 790310 *or* 07779 654975 *or* 07500 042769

CHURCHES

Advisory Committee for the Care of Churches (Chairman) Canon Michael Anderson, Old Alresford Place
(Secretary) Mrs Catherine Roberts
Tel: 01962 737306
email: catherine.roberts@winchester.anglican.org

EDUCATION

Director of Education Mr Tony Blackshaw
(Joint working with Diocese of Portsmouth), First Floor, Peninsular House, Wharf Rd, Portsmouth PO2 8HB *Tel:* 023 9289 9681
email: tony.blackshaw@portsmouth.anglican.org

DISCIPLESHIP AND MINISTRY

Director of Discipleship and Ministry Canon Simon Baker *(as above)*
Vocations, Recruitment and Selection Officer (including ordinands) Revd Julia Mourant
Tel: 01962 737316
email: julia.mourant@winchester.anglican.org
Ministry Training Officer (including ordinands) Revd Duncan Strathie *Tel:* 01962 737314
email: duncan.strathie@winchester.anglican.org
Continuing Ministerial Development Officer Revd Norman Boakes *Tel:* 01962 737314
email: norman.boakes@winchester.anglican.org
Adult Discipleship Adviser Revd Phil Dykes, Old Alresford Place *Tel:* 01962 737354
email: mike.powis@winchester.anglican.org
Diocesan Children and Families Adviser Mr Andy Saunders, Old Alresford Place *Tel:* 01962 737321
email: andy.saunders@winchester.anglican.org
Diocesan Youth Officer Mr Pete Maidment
Tel: 01962 737320
email: pete.maidment@winchester.anglican.org

ADVISERS

Stewardship Adviser Mr Gordon Randall, Old Alresford Place *Tel:* 01962 737232
email: gordon.randall@winchester.anglican.org
Clergy HR Adviser Ms Susan Beckett, Old Alresford Place *Tel:* 01962 737353
email: susan.beckett@winchester.anglican.org

DIOCESAN RECORD OFFICES

Hants. Record Office, Sussex St, Winchester SO23 8TH *Archivist* Janet Smith *Tel:* 01962 846154; *email:* enquiries.archives@hants.gov.uk (*For diocesan records and parishes in Hampshire [except Southampton], Bournemouth and Christchurch*)
Southampton City Record Office, Civic Centre, Southampton SO14 7LY *Archivist* Mrs Sue Woolgar *Tel:* 023 8083 2251
email: city.archives@southampton.gov.uk
(*For parishes in Southampton*)
Guernsey Island Archives, St Barnabas, Cornet St, St Peter Port, Guernsey GY1 1LF
Tel: 01481 724512
Fax: 01481 715814
email: archives@gov.gg
Jersey Archive Service, Clarence Rd, St Helier, Jersey JE2 4JY *Archivist* Linda Romeril
Tel: 01534 833300
Fax: 01534 833301
email: archives@jerseyheritagetrust.org

SAFEGUARDING AND INCLUSION

Director for Safeguarding and Inclusion Ms Jane Fisher, Old Alresford Place *Tel:* 01962 737347
email: jane.fisher@winchester.anglican.org

TOURISM

Churches and Tourism Adviser Revd Canon Graham Trasler, Old Alresford Place
email: costadelanton@gmail.com

AREA AND RURAL DEANS

ARCHDEACONRY OF BOURNEMOUTH

Bournemouth Revd Andy McPherson, Vicarage, 53a Holdenhurst Avenue, Iford, Bournemouth BH7 6RB *Tel:* 01202 425978
email: parish.office@stsaviours.f2s.com
Christchurch Vacancy
Eastleigh Canon Peter Vargeson, The Vicarage, School Road, Bursledon, Southampton SO31 8BW *Tel:* 023 8040 2821
email: peter.vargeson@bursledonparish.org
Lyndhurst Revd Dominic Furness, The Vicarage, Lymington Rd, Milford-on-Sea, Lymington SO41 0QN *Tel:* 01590 643289
email: dominic.furness@tiscali.co.uk
Romsey Revd Ron Corne, Broughton Rectory, Rectory Lane, Broughton, Stockbridge SO20 8AB
Tel: 01794 301287
email: cronandrew@aol.com
Southampton Canon Gary Philbrick, The Vicarage, 357 Burgess Rd, Southampton SO16 3BD
Tel: 023 8055 4231
email: gary.philbrick@dsl.pipex.com

ARCHDEACONRY OF WINCHESTER

Alresford Revd Phil Collins, The Rectory, 37 Jacklyns Lane, Alresford SO24 9LF
Tel: 01962 732105
email: nortoncollins@yahoo.co.uk
Alton Revd Howard Wright, The Vicarage, 22 Lymington Bottom, Four Marks, Alton GU34 5AA *Tel:* 01420 563344
email: howardwright@xalt.co.uk
Andover Canon John Harkin, St Mary's Vicarage, Church Close, Andover, SP10 1DP
Tel: 01264 362268
email: harkin12@btinternet.com
Basingstoke Revd Arthur Botham, The Vicarage, 25 Tewkesbury Close, Popley, Basingstoke RG24 9DU *Tel:* 01256 324734
email: arthur.botham@btinternet.com
Odiham Revd Peter Dyson, The Vicarage, Church Street, Upton Grey RG25 2RB *Tel:* 01256 861750
email: pwdyson@onetel.com
Whitchurch Revd Christine Dale, The Rectory, Mount Rd, Woolton Hill, Newbury RG20 9QZ
Tel: 01635 253323
email: cdale001@btinternet.com
Winchester Revd Alan Gordon, The Rectory, 4 Campion Way, King's Worthy, Winchester SO23 7QP *Tel:* 01962 882166
email: rector@worthyparishes.org.uk

CHANNEL ISLANDS

Dean of Jersey Very Revd Bob Key, The Deanery, David Place, St Helier, Jersey, CI JE2 4TE
Tel: 01534 720001
email: robert_f_key@yahoo.com
Dean of Guernsey Very Revd Paul Mellor, The Deanery, Cornet St, St Peter Port, Guernsey, CI GY1 1BZ *Tel:* 01481 720036
Fax: 01481 722948
email: kpaulmellor@cwgsy.net

DIOCESE OF WORCESTER

Founded in 679. Worcestershire, except for a few parishes in the south (GLOUCESTER) and in the north (BIRMINGHAM). Dudley; a few parishes in Wolverhampton, Sandwell and in northern Gloucestershire.

Population 845,000 Area 671 sq m
Full-time Stipendiary Parochial Clergy 108 Benefices 100
Parishes 175 Churches 286
www.cofe-worcester.org.uk
Overseas link diocese: Peru (Province of Southern Cone).

BISHOP (113th)
Rt Revd John Geoffrey Inge, The Bishop's Office, The Old Palace, Deansway, Worcester WR1 2JE [2007] *Tel:* 01905 731599
Fax: 01905 739382
email: bishop.worcester@cofe-worcester.org.uk
[John Wigorn]

SUFFRAGAN BISHOP
DUDLEY Rt Revd David Stuart Walker, Bishop's House, Bishop's Walk, Cradley Heath B64 7RH [2000] *Tel:* 0121 550 3407
Fax: 0121 550 7340
email: bishop.david@cofe-worcester.org.uk

HONORARY ASSISTANT BISHOPS
Rt Revd Michael Hooper, 6 Avon Drive, Eckington, Pershore, Worcs WR10 3BU
Tel: 01386 751589
Rt Revd Christopher Mayfield, Harwood House, 54 Primrose Crescent, St Peter's, Worcester WR5 3HT [2002] *Tel:* 01905 764822
Rt Revd Mark Santer, 81 Clarence Rd, Moseley, Birmingham B13 9UH [2002] *Tel:* 0121 441 2194
Rt Revd Humphrey Taylor, 10 High St, Honeybourne, Evesham WR10 7PQ [2003]
Tel: 01386 934846

CATHEDRAL CHURCH OF CHRIST AND THE BLESSED MARY THE VIRGIN OF WORCESTER
Dean Very Revd Peter Gordon Atkinson, The Deanery, 10 College Green, Worcester WR1 2LH [2007] *Tel:* 01905 732939
Tel: 01905 732909 (Office)
email: PeterAtkinson@worcestercathedral.org.uk
Canons Residentiary
Canon Dr Alvyn Pettersen, 2 College Green, Worcester WR1 2LH [2002] *Tel:* 01905 732942
email: AlvynPettersen@worcestercathedral.org.uk
Canon David Stanton, 15A College Green, Worcester WR1 2LH [2005] *Tel:* 01905 732940
email: DavidStanton@worcestercathedral.org.uk
Canon Dr Georgina Byrne, 15B College Green, Worcester WR1 2LH [2009] *Tel:* 01905 732900
email: GeorginaByrne@worcestercathedral.org.uk
Lay Canons
Mrs Ann Capell, 41 Highclere, Bewdley DY12 2EX *Tel:* 01299 403776
email: anncapell@btinternet.com
Mr Peter Davies, 44 Battenhall Rise, Worcester WR5 2DE *Tel:* 01905 356714
email: peterdaviesworcs@waitrose.com
Dr Janet Harvey, 17 Grayling Close, Worcester WR5 3HY *Tel:* 01905 359490
email: jaharvey@metronet.co.uk
Cathedral Steward Mr Les West, Chapter Office
Tel: 01905 732907
email: LesWest@worcestercathedral.org.uk
Chapter Office 8 College Yard, Worcester WR1 2LA *Tel:* 01905 732900
email: info@worcestercathedral.org.uk
Organist and Director of Music Dr Peter Nardone, 5A College Yard, Worcester WR1 2LA
Tel: 01905 732916
email: PeterNardone@worcestercathedral.org.uk

ARCHDEACONS
WORCESTER Ven Roger Morris, The Archdeacon's House, Walker's Lane, Whittington, Worcester WR5 2RE [2008] *Tel:* 01905 773301
email: jhinds@cofe-worcester.org.uk
DUDLEY Ven Fred Trethewey, 15 Worcester Rd, Droitwich WR9 8AA [2001] *Tel:* 01905 773301
Fax: 0871 813 3256
email: jhinds@cofe-worcester.org.uk

CONVOCATION (MEMBERS OF THE HOUSE OF CLERGY OF THE GENERAL SYNOD)
Dignitaries in Convocation
The Bishop of Dudley
Proctors for Clergy
Revd Canon Stuart Currie
Revd Canon Matthew Baynes
Revd Eva McIntyre

MEMBERS OF THE HOUSE OF LAITY OF THE GENERAL SYNOD
Canon Prof Michael Clarke
Mrs Jennifer Barton
Mr Robin Lunn

DIOCESAN OFFICERS

Dioc Secretary Mr Robert Higham, The Old Palace, Deansway, Worcester WR1 2JE
Tel: 01905 20537

Chancellor of Diocese Mr Charles Mynors, Francis Taylor Building, Inner Temple, London EC4Y 7BD *Tel:* 020 7353 8415

Registrar of Diocese and Bishop's Legal Secretary Mr Michael Huskinson, Messrs Stallard, March & Edwards, 8 Sansome Walk, Worcester WR1 1LN
Tel: 01905 723561
Fax: 01905 723812

Deputy Diocesan Registrar Vacancy, Messrs March & Edwards, 8 Sansome Walk, Worcester WR1 1LN

Dioc Surveyor Mr Mark Wild, Dioc Office
Tel: 01905 20537

DIOCESAN ORGANIZATIONS

Diocesan Office The Old Palace, Deansway, Worcester WR1 2JE *Tel:* 01905 20537
Fax: 01905 612302

ADMINISTRATION

Asst Dioc Secretary (Finance) Mr Stephen Lindner, Dioc Office

DAC Secretary Mr John Dentith, Dioc Office

Dioc Synod (Chairman, House of Clergy) Vacancy
(Chairman, House of Laity) Vacancy, Dioc Office
(Secretary) Mr Robert Higham, Dioc Office

DIOCESAN MISSION, PASTORAL AND RESOURCES COMMITTEE

(being the Diocesan Mission Pastoral Committee)

(Chairman) Mr Alastair Findlay; *(Secretary)* Mr Robert Higham *(as above)*

Parsonages Board (Chairman) Mr Robert Pearce, Dioc Office
(Secretary) Mr Stephen Lindner *(as above)*

Investment and Glebe Committee (Chairman) Mr Peter Seward *(as above)*
(Secretary) Mr Stephen Lindner *(as above)*

Glebe Agent Mr Anthony Champion, Halls, 4 Foregate St, Worcester WR1 1DB
Tel: 01905 611066

Mission & Pastoral Committee Mr Robert Higham *(as above)*

Board of Patronage Mr Robert Higham *(as above)*

Designated Officer Mr Robert Higham *(as above)*

Diocesan Trustees Mr Michael Huskinson, Messrs Stallard, March & Edwards, 8 Sansome Walk, Worcester WR1 1LN *Tel:* 01905 723561
Fax: 01905 723812

CHURCHES

Advisory Committee for the Care of Churches (Chairman) Vacancy Dioc Office; *(Secretary)* Mr John Dentith, Dioc Office

Change Ringers Association Mr D. Andrews

EDUCATION

Board of Education (Chair) Revd Canon Stuart W. Currie, St Stephen's Vicarage, 1 Beech Ave, Worcester WR3 8PZ *Tel:* 01905 452169

Director of Education Mrs Ann Mundy, Dioc Office

Children's Officer Emma Pettifer, Dioc Office

Youth Officer Dr Sarah Brush, Dioc Office

TRAINING AND MINISTRY

Director of Development Canon Robert Jones, Dioc Office *email:* rjones@cofe-worcester.org.uk

Dioc Director of Ordinands Revd Canon Georgina Byrne, Dioc Office

Dean of Women's Ministry Revd Canon Georgina Byrne, Dioc Office

Association of Readers

Secretary Miss E. R. Tomlin, 4 Lambourne Avenue, Malvern Link, Worcestershire WR14 1NL
Tel: 01684 578500

Registrar Dr M. J. Robinson, 5 Park Dingle, Bewdley DY12 2JY *Tel:* 01299 403080
email: mikejrobinson@fsmail.net

Retired Clergy

Dean of Retired Clergy Rt Revd Christopher Mayfield *(as above)*

Non-Stipendiary Ministers/Ministers in Secular Employment

Dean of NSMs/MSEs Revd Canon Jane Fraser *Dioc Office*

LITURGICAL

Secretary Revd D. Chaplin, Vicarage, 29 Old Coach Rd, Droitwich WR9 8BB
Tel: 01905 798929
email: doug.chaplin@gmail.com

MISSION AND UNITY

Ecumenical Officer – Worcestershire Revd David Ryan, Vicarage, 4 Daty Croft, Home Meadow, Warndon, Worcester WR4 0JB
Tel: 01905 616109

Ecumenical Officer – Black Country Churches Engaged Vacancy

SOCIAL RESPONSIBILITY

Commission for Social Responsibility (Chairman) Professor Michael Taylor, Dioc Office

Mission Development Officers Society and World Revd John Paxton, Dioc Office; Miss Margaret Rutter, Dioc Office

Mission Development Office Economic Revd Phillip Jones, 7 Egremont Gardens, Worcester WR4 0QH
Tel and *Fax:* 01905 755037
email: phillipjones@faithatwork.org.uk

Chaplaincy to Agriculture and Rural Life Vacancy

PRESS AND PUBLICATIONS

Dioc Communications Officer and Bishop's Press Office Samantha Setchell, Dioc Office
Tel: 07852 302516

Editor of the Dioc Directory Mrs Alison Vincent

Editor of Dioc News Samantha Setchell

DIOCESAN RECORD OFFICES

County Archivist, The Hive, Sawmill Walk, The Butts, Worcester WR5 3PA *County Archivist* Mr R. Whittaker *Tel:* 01905 766530; *Fax:* 01905 766363 (*For diocesan records and most parish records*)
Dudley Archives and Local History Dept, Mount Pleasant St, Coseley WV14 9JR *Archivist* Mrs K. H. Atkins *Tel:* 01384 812770 (*For parish records for the deaneries of Kingswinford (formerly Himley), Dudley and Stourbridge*)

RURAL DEANS

ARCHDEACONRY OF WORCESTER

Evesham Revd Richard Court, The Vicarage, High Street, Badsey, Evesham WR11 7EJ
Tel: 01386 834550
email: richard.court@btinternet.com

Malvern Revd W. David Nichol, Holy Trinity Vicarage, 2 North Malvern Rd, Malvern WR14 4LR *Tel:* 01684 561126
email: david@trinityandthewest.wanadoo.co.uk

Martley and Worcester West Revd David Sherwin, The Rectory, Martley, Worcester WR6 6QA
Tel: 01886 888664

Pershore Revd Susan Renshaw, The Vicarage, Drakes Bridge Road, Eckington, Pershore WR10 3BN *Tel:* 01386 750203
email: revsusan@btinternet.com

Upton Revd Christopher Moss, Longdon Vicarage, Tewkesbury GL20 6AT
Tel: 01684 833038
email: cmoss.lcbq@gmail.com

Worcester East Revd S. W. Currie, St Stephen's Vicarage, 1 Beech Avenue, Worcester WR3 8PZ
Tel: 01905 452169
email: sw.currie@virgin.net

ARCHDEACONRY OF DUDLEY

Bromsgrove Revd G. E. P. Nathaniel, St Peter's Church Office Ipsley, Church Lane, Redditch, Worcs B98 0AJ *Tel:* 01905 5616351
email: garth_ipsley@btinternet.com

Droitwich Canon Sheila Banyard, Rectory, 205 Worcester Road, Droitwich, Worcs WR9 8AS
Tel: 01905 773134
email: sk.banyard@virgin.net

Dudley Revd Stephen Carter, St Andrew's Vicarage, Highbridge Road, Netherton, Dudley DY2 0HT *Tel:* 01384 257097
email: stevecarter@fastmail.net

Kidderminster Revd Keith James, The Rectory, 57 Park Lane, Bewdley DY12 2HA
Tel: 01299 402275
email: keith.james2@btconnect.com

Kingswinford Revd Colin Jones, The Rectory, 13 Dunsley Drive, Wordsley, Stourbridge DY8 5RA
Tel: 01384 400709
email: paxarana@msn.com

Stourbridge Canon Andrew Hazlewood, The Rectory, Pedmore Lane, Stourbridge DY9 0SW
Tel: 01562 887287
email: andrewhazlewood@gmail.com

Stourport Revd Louise Grace, The Rectory, Lindridge, Tenbury Wells WR15 8JQ
Tel: 01584 881331
email: revgrace@hotmail.co.uk

DIOCESE OF YORK

Founded in 627. York; East Riding of Yorkshire, except for an area in the south-west (SHEFFIELD); Kingston-upon-Hull; Redcar and Cleveland; Middlesbrough; the eastern half of North Yorkshire; Stockton-on-Tees, south of the Tees; an area of Leeds.

Population 1,435,000 Area 2,661 sq m
Full-time Stipendiary Parochial Clergy 189 Benefices 255
Parishes 452 Churches 610
www.dioceseofyork.org.uk
Overseas link dioceses: Cape Town (South Africa), Mechelen-Brussels (Belgium).

ARCHBISHOP (97th)
Most Revd and Rt Hon Dr John Tucker Mugabi Sentamu, *Primate of England and Metropolitan*, Bishopthorpe Palace, Bishopthorpe, York YO23 2GE [2005] *Tel:* 01904 707021/2
Fax: 01904 709204
email: office@archbishopofyork.org
Web: www.bishopthorpepalace.co.uk
[Sentamu Ebor]
Chaplain and Researcher Revd Dr Daphne Green
email: daphne.green@archbishopofyork.org
Domestic Chaplain Revd Richard Carew
email: richard.carew@archbishopofyork.org
Chief of Staff Revd Malcolm Macnaughton
Tel: 01904 772362
email: malcolm.macnaughton@archbishopofyork.org

SUFFRAGAN BISHOPS
SELBY Rt Revd Martin Wallace, Bishop's House, Barton-le-Street, Malton YO17 6PL [2004]
Tel: 01653 627191
Fax: 01653 627193
email: bishselby@clara.net
HULL Rt Revd Richard Frith, Hullen House, Woodfield Lane, Hessle HU13 0ES [1998]
Tel: 01482 649019
Fax: 01482 647449
email: richard@bishop.karoo.co.uk
WHITBY Rt Revd Philip North, c/o Julie Elphee
Tel: 01642 714472
email: julie.elphee@yorkdiocese.org

PROVINCIAL EPISCOPAL VISITOR
BEVERLEY Rt Revd Glyn Webster c/o Bishopthorpe Palace, Bishopthorpe, York YO23 2GE
Tel: 01904 707021/2
email: office@archbishopofyork.org

HONORARY ASSISTANT BISHOPS
Rt Revd Clifford Condor Barker, Flat 29 Dulverton Hall, The Esplanade, Scarborough YO11 2AR [1991] *Tel:* 01723 340129
Rt Revd Gordon Bates, 19 Fernwood Close, Brompton, Northallerton DL6 2UX
Tel: 01609 761586
Rt Revd Graham Cray, The Rectory, Church Road, Harrietsham, Maidstone ME17 1PB
Tel: 01622 851170
email: grahamcray@btconnect.com
Rt Revd Michael Henshall, Brackenfield, 28 Hermitage Way, Eskdaleside, Sleights, Whitby YO22 5HG [1996] *Tel:* 01947 811233
Rt Revd David Charles James, 7 Long Lane, Beverley HU17 0NH *Tel:* 01482 871240
email: david@djmhs.force9.co.uk
Rt Revd David Lunn, Rivendell, 28 Southfield Rd, Wetwang, Driffield YO25 9XX [1997]
Rt Revd David Smith, 34 Cedar Glade, Dunnington, York YO19 5QZ [2002] *Tel:* 01904 481225

CATHEDRAL CHURCH OF ST PETER
Dean Very Revd Vivienne Faull, The Deanery, York YO1 7JQ [2012] *Tel:* 01904 557202 (Office)
Fax: 01904 557204 (Office)
email: dean@yorkminster.org
Dean and Chapter Office Church House, Ogleforth, York YO1 7JN *Tel:* 01904 557200
Fax: 01904 557204
email: reception@yorkminster.org
Canons Residentiary
Chancellor Vacancy
Theologian Vacancy
Precentor Revd Canon Peter Moger, 2 Minster Court, York YO1 7JJ [2010]
Tel: 01904 557265 (Home)
01904 557205 (Office)
Fax: 01904 557204
email: precentor@yorkminster.org
Ven Richard Seed c/o Dean and Chapter Office
Chapter Steward Vacancy, Dean and Chapter Office *Tel:* 01904 557212
Fax: 01904 557204
email: chapter.steward@yorkminster.org
Lay Canons
Canon Dr Andrew Green, Normanby House, Normanby, Sinnington, York YO62 6RH
Tel: 07770 321564
email: andrewgreen@bpipoly.com
Canon Dr Julia Winkley, St Catherine's, 11 Clifton, York *Tel:* 07740 779766
email: juleswinkley@gmail.com
Chapter Clerk Mr Andrew Oates, Dean and Chapter Office *Tel:* 01904 557210
Fax: 01904 557204
email: chapterclerk@yorkminster.org
Head Verger Mr Alex Carberry, York Minster Vestry *Tel:* 01904 557221
email: alexc@yorkminster.org

Director of Music Mr Robert Sharpe, Dean and Chapter Office *Tel:* 01904 557205
Fax: 01904 557204
email: roberts@yorkminster.org
Finance Director Mrs Sue Pace, Dean and Chapter Office *Tel:* 01904 557213
Fax: 01904 557204
email: suep@yorkminster.org
Chamberlain and Director of Development Dr Richard Shephard, Dean and Chapter Office
Tel: 01904 557245
Fax: 01904 557204
email: richards@yorkminster.org
High Steward The Earl of Halifax, Garrowby, York YO41 1QD *Tel:* 01759 368236
Fax: 01759 368154
email: halifax@garrowby.plus.com

ARCHDEACONS

YORK Vacancy
EAST RIDING Ven David Butterfield, Brimley Lodge, 27 Molescroft Rd, Beverley HU17 7DX [2007] *Tel* and *Fax:* 01482 881659
email: archdeacon.of.eastriding@yorkdiocese.org
CLEVELAND Ven Paul Ferguson, 2 Langbaurgh Rd, Hutton Rudby, Yarm TS15 0HL [2001]
Tel: 01642 706095
Fax: 01642 706097
email: archdeacon.of.cleveland@yorkdiocese.org

CONVOCATION (MEMBERS OF THE HOUSE OF CLERGY OF THE GENERAL SYNOD)

Dignitaries in Convocation
The Bishop of Hull
Proctors for Clergy
Revd Jeremy Fletcher
Ven Paul Ferguson
Revd Andrew Howard
Revd Christian Selvaratnam
Canon Suzanne Sheriff

MEMBERS OF THE HOUSE OF LAITY OF THE GENERAL SYNOD

Canon Linda Ali
Mr Martin Dales
Canon Jennifer Reid
Mrs Rosalind Brewer
Mr Richard Brown
Mr Jon Steel

DIOCESAN OFFICERS

Dioc Secretary Canon Peter Warry, Diocesan House, Aviator Court, Clifton Moor, York YO30 4WJ *Tel:* 01904 699500
Fax: 01904 699501
Chancellor of Diocese The Worshipful Peter Collier QC, 12 St Helen's Rd, Dringhouses, York YO24 1HP
Registrar of Diocese and Archbishop's Legal Secretary Mr Lionel Lennox, The Registry, Stamford House, Piccadilly, York YO1 9PP
Tel: 01904 623487
Fax: 01904 611458

DIOCESAN ORGANIZATIONS

Diocesan Office Diocesan House, Aviator Court, Clifton Moor, York YO30 4WJ *Tel:* 01904 699500
Fax: 01904 699501
email: office@yorkdiocese.org
Web: www.dioceseofyork.org.uk

ADMINISTRATION

Dioc Synod (Chairman, House of Clergy) Canon John Harrison, Vicarage, Easingwold, York YO61 3JT *Tel:* 01347 821394
email: vicar.easingwold@hotmail.co.uk
(Chairman, House of Laity) Canon Richard Liversedge, 1 Caledonia Park, Victoria Dock, Hull HU9 1TE *Tel:* 01482 588357
email: r.liversedge@hulldrypool.freeserve.co.uk
(Secretary) Canon Peter Warry, Dioc Office
Assistant Dioc Secretary Ms Shirley Davies, Dioc Office
Board of Finance (Chairman) Mrs Maureen Loffill Dioc Office; *(Secretary)* Mrs Catherine Evans
Finance Manager Mrs Catherine Evans, Dioc Office
Diocesan Surveyor and Estates Manager Mr Graham Andrews, Dioc Office
Pastoral & Mission Committee Ms Shirley Davies *(as above)*
Designated Officer Canon Peter Warry, Dioc Office
Property Sub-Committee Mr Graham Andrews, Dioc Office
Dioc Communications Officer Eleanor Course, Dioc Office

CHURCHES

Advisory Committee for the Care of Churches (Chairman) Canon David Hodgson, The Ascension Vicarage, Penrith Rd, Berwick Hills, Middlesbrough TS3 7JR *Tel:* 01642 244857
(Secretary) Mr Philip Thomas, Dioc Office
Furnishings Officer Mr David Haddon-Reece, Vicarage, Egton, Whitby YO21 1UT
Tel: 01947 895315
Closed Churches Ms Shirley Davies *(as above)*

EDUCATION

Board of Education (Director) Canon Dr R. Ann Lees, Dioc Office
email: ann.lees@yorkdiocese.org
Asst Director of Education Mrs Viv Todd *(Educational Services and Schools Support)*
School Buildings Officer Simon Quartermaine
Religious Education and Collective Worship Mrs Linda Hodson, Mrs Olivia Seymour and Mrs Liz Foster
Adviser for Children and Youth Work (East Riding) Jon Steel, 2 Appin Close, Bransholme, Hull HU7 5BB *Tel:* 01482 828805
07736 378051 (Mobile)
Adviser in Children's and Youth Work (York) Revd Nigel Chapman, Vicarage, Coxwold, York YO61 4AD *Tel:* 01347 868287
email: nigel.chapman@yorkdiocese.org
Children's and Youth Officer (Cleveland) Vacancy

MINISTRY AND MISSION

Training, Mission and Ministry Directory Revd Dr Gavin Wakefield, Dioc Office *Tel:* 01904 699504 *email:* gavin.wakefield@yorkdiocese.org

Diocesan Adviser on Vocations Revd David Mann, 3 Glebe Close, Bolton Percy, York YO23 7HB *Tel:* 01904 744619 *email:* david.mann@yorkdiocese.org

Dean of Self Supporting Ministry Revd Dr Julie Watson, 25 Fox Lane, Thorpe Willoughby, Selby YO8 9NA *Tel:* 01757 703123 julie301watson@btinternet.com

Dean of Women's Ministry Canon Elaine Bielby, St Helen's Vicarage, Welton, Brough HU15 1ND *Tel:* 01482 666677 *email*: ebielby@ebielby.karoo.co.uk

Warden of Readers Ven Paul Ferguson, 2 Langbaurgh Rd, Hutton Rudby, Yarm TS15 0HL *Tel:* 01642 706095 *Fax:* 01642 706097 *email:* archdeacon.of.cleveland@yorkdiocese.org

Ecumenical Advisers

York Archdeaconry Revd Andrew Clements, Vicarage, 80 Osbaldwick Lane, York YO10 3AX *Tel:* 01904 416763 *email:* andrew@ozmurt.freeserve.co.uk

East Riding Archdeaconry Vacancy

Cleveland Archdeaconry Revd Paul Hutchinson, The Rectory, Leven Close, Stokesley, Middlesbrough TS9 5AP *Tel:* 01642 710405 *email:* paul.hutchinson5@btinternet.com

LITURGICAL

York Diocesan Worship and Liturgical Group Canon Peter Moger (*as above*)

PRESS AND PUBLICATIONS

Archbishop's Media Adviser (National) Kerron Cross *Tel:* 01904 707021

Communications Officer (Diocese) Eleanor Course, Dioc Office *Tel:* 01904 699530 07946 748702 (Mobile) *email:* comms@yorkdiocese.org

Diocesan Tourism Group (Chair) Revd Dr Gavin Wakefield (*as above*)

Editor of Dioc Magazine (*as above*)

DIOCESAN RECORD OFFICES

The Borthwick Institute of Historical Research, University of York, Heslington, York YO10 5DD *Director and Diocesan Archivist* Christopher C. Webb *Tel:* 01904 321166 *Web:* www.york.ac.uk/inst/bihr (*For parish records in the Archdeaconry of York*)

East Riding of Yorkshire Archive Office, County Hall, Beverley HU17 9BA *Archivist* Mr Ian Mason *Tel:* 01482 392790 *email:* ian.mason@eastriding.gov *Web:* www.eastriding.gov.uk/learning (*For parish records in the Archdeaconry of the East Riding*)

North Yorkshire County Record Office, Malpas Rd, Northallerton DL7 8PB *Acting County Archivist* Mrs Judith A. Smeaton *Tel:* 01609 777585 (*For parish records in the Archdeaconry of Cleveland**)

*Parishes within the present county boundaries of Cleveland may, if they so wish, deposit their records in the Cleveland County Archives Dept, Exchange House, 6 Marton Rd, Middlesbrough TS1 1DB *Archivist* Mr D. Tyrell *Tel:* 01642 248321

SOCIAL RESPONSIBILITY

Social Responsibility Council Bishop of Whitby (*Chair*) (*as above*)

RURAL DEANS

ARCHDEACONRY OF YORK

Derwent Revd Andrew Clements, The Vicarage, 80 Osbaldwick Lane, York YO10 3AX *Tel:* 01904 416763 *email:* Andrew@ozmurt.freeserve.co.uk

Easingwold Canon John Harrison, Vicarage, Easingwold, York YO61 3JT *Tel:* 01347 821394 *email:* vicar.easingwold@hotmail.co.uk

New Ainsty Canon Chris Coates, The Vicarage, 48 Church Lane, Bishopthorpe, York YO23 2QG *Tel:* 01904 707840 *email:* chriscoates@hotmail.co.uk

Selby Revd Chris Wilton, Vicarage, 2 Sir John's Lane, Sherburn in Elmet, Leeds LS25 6BJ *Tel:* 01977 682122

South Wold Revd Fran Wakefield, The Rectory, 8 Viking Road, Stamford Bridge, York YO41 1BR *Tel:* 01759 371264 *email:* fran.wakefield@btopenworld.com

Southern Ryedale Revd Peter Bowes, The Rectory, Church Street, Amotherby, Malton YO17 6TN *Tel:* 01653 690663 *email:* vicar@stmichaelsmalton.org.uk

York Revd Terence McDonough, Fulford Vicarage, 1 Fulford Park, York YO10 4QE *Tel:* 01904 633261 *email:* tmcd@st-oswalds-fulford.org.uk

ARCHDEACONRY OF THE EAST RIDING

Beverley Canon Angela Bailey, The Rectory, 31 Old Village Rd, Little Weighton Cottingham HU20 3US *Tel:* 01482 843317

Bridlington Revd Glyn Owen, The Vicarage, Rudston, Driffield YO25 4XA *Tel:* 01262 420313 *email:* revglynowen@btinternet.com

Central and North Hull Revd Paul Smith, The Rectory, Hallgate, Cottingham HU16 4DD *Tel:* 01482 847668

Harthill Revd David Fletcher, The Vicarage, Wetwang, Driffield YO25 9XT *Tel:* 01377 236189 *email:* de.fletcher@hotmail.co.uk

Holderness North Revd James Grainger-Smith, The Rectory, 11 Glebe Gardens, Beeford, Driffield YO25 8BF *Tel:* 01262 48804 *email:* j.grainger-smith@sky.com

Holderness South Canon Stephen Cope, The Vicarage, 28 Park Avenue, Withernsea HU19 2JU *Tel:* 01964 611462 *email:* stephenvcope@tiscali.co.uk

Howden Revd James Little, The Minster Rectory, Market Place, Howden DN14 7BL *Tel:* 01430 432056 *email:* RevJLittle@aol.com

Scarborough Revd David Pynn, 6 Stepney Drive, Scarborough YO12 5DH *Tel:* 01723 369687 *email:* Davidpynn12@aol.com

East Hull Revd Mick Fryer, St Aidan's Vicarage, 139 Southcoates Ave, Hull HU9 3HF *Tel:* 01482 374403 *email:* mick@staidans.org.uk

West Hull Revd Tim Boyns, All Saints Vicarage, 4 Chestnut Avenue, Hessle HU13 0RH *Tel:* 01482 648555 *email:* timboyns@timboyns.karoo.co.uk

ARCHDEACONRY OF CLEVELAND

Guisborough Revd Graham Pacey, The Rectory, Church Street, Guisborough TS14 6BS *Tel:* 01287 632588 *email:* g.pacey@ntlworld.com

Middlesbrough Revd Dominic Black. The Vicarage, James Street, North Ormesby, Middlesbrough TS3 6LD *Tel:* 01642 961898 *email:* Dominic.Black@trinitycentre.org

Mowbray Canon Richard Rowling, Rectory, Cemetery Rd, Thirsk YO7 1PR *Tel:* 01845 523183 *email:* rfrowling@aol.com

Northern Ryedale Revd Tim Robinson, The Vicarage, Baxtons Road, Helmsley YO62 5HT *Tel:* 01439 770983 *email:* revtimrobinson@gmail.com

Stokesley Revd John Ford, The Rectory, 6 Westgate, Yarm TS15 9QT *Tel:* 07805 792824 *email:* revjohn.ford@ntlworld.com

Whitby Revd David Cook, The Vicarage, 22 Eskdaleside, Sleights, Whitby YO22 5EP *Tel:* 01947 810349

PART 2

National Structures

PART 2 CONTENTS

Every effort has been made to ensure that all details are accurate at the time of going to press.

THE GENERAL SYNOD OF THE CHURCH OF ENGLAND

Office

Church House, Great Smith St, London SW1P 3AZ
Tel: 020 7898 1000 *Fax:* 020 7898 1369
email: synod@churchofengland.org
Web: www.churchofengland.org

Dates of Sessions

The following periods have been set aside for Groups of Sessions of the General Synod:

2013: 4 February – 8 February
5 July – 9 July
18 November – 20 November (if required)

2014: 10 February – 14 February
11 July – 15 July
17 November – 19 November

Composition of the General Synod

	Canterbury	*York*	*Either*	*Totals*
House of Bishops				
Diocesan Bishops	30	14		44
Suffragan Bishops ... including the Bishop of Dover *ex officio*	6	3		9
	36	17		53
House of Clergy				
Deans	3	2		5
Service Chaplains and Chaplain-General of Prisons	4			4
Elected Proctors and the Dean of Guernsey or Jersey	129	55		184
University Proctors ..	4	2		6
Religious Communities			2	2
Co-opted places (maximum)	3	2		5
	143	61	2	206

	Canterbury	*York*	*Either*	*Totals*
House of Laity				
Elected Laity	136	59		195
Religious Communities			2	2
Lay Armed Services .			3	3
Co-opted places (maximum)........			5	5
Ex officio (First and Second Church Estates Commissioners) ..			2	2
	136	59	12	207
House of Bishops, House of Clergy or House of Laity				
Ex officio (Dean of the Arches, the two Vicars General, the Third Church Estates Commissioner, the Chairman of the Pensions Board and six Appointed Members of the Archbishops' Council)			11	11
Maximum totals	315	137	25	477

The General Synod consists of the Convocations of Canterbury and York, joined together in a House of Bishops and a House of Clergy, and having added to them a House of Laity.

The House of Bishops is made up of the Upper Houses of the Convocations of Canterbury and York. It consists of the archbishops and all other diocesan bishops and the Bishop of Dover as *ex officio* members, four bishops elected by and from the suffragan bishops (and certain other bishops) of the Province of Canterbury (other than the Bishop of Dover), three bishops elected by and from the suffragan bishops (and certain other bishops) of the Province of York, and any other bishops residing in either Province who are members of the Archbishops' Council.

The House of Clergy is made up of the Lower Houses of the Convocations of Canterbury and York. It consists of clergy (other than bishops) who have been elected, appointed or chosen in accordance with Canon H 2 and the rules made under it (including deans, proctors from the dioceses and university constituencies and clerical members of religious communities) together with *ex officio* members.

The House of Laity consists of members from each diocese of the two Provinces elected by lay members of the deanery synods (or annual meetings of the chaplaincies in the case of the Diocese in Europe) or chosen by and from the lay members of religious communities, together with *ex officio* members.

Representatives of other Churches, the Church of England Youth Council, and Deaf Anglicans Together are invited to attend the Synod and under its Standing Orders enjoy speaking but not voting rights.

OFFICERS OF THE GENERAL SYNOD

Presidents
The Archbishop of Canterbury
The Archbishop of York

Prolocutor of the Lower House of the Convocation of Canterbury Ven Christine Hardman

Prolocutor of the Lower House of the Convocation of York Vacancy

Chair of the House of Laity Dr Philip Giddings

Vice-Chair of the House of Laity Mr Tim Hind

Secretary General Mr William Fittall

Clerk to the Synod Dr Colin Podmore (until 31/3/13)

Chief Legal Adviser and *Joint Registrar of the Provinces of Canterbury and York (Registrar of the General Synod)* Mr Stephen Slack

Deputy Legal Adviser Revd Alexander McGregor

Standing Counsel Sir Anthony Hammond

OFFICERS OF THE CONVOCATIONS

Synodical Secretary of the Convocation of Canterbury
Revd Stephen Trott, Rectory, 41 Humfrey Lane, Boughton, Northampton NN28RQ
email: revstrott@btinternet.com

Synodal Secretary of the Convocation of York
Ven Alan Wolstencroft, The Bakehouse, 1 Latham Row, Horwich, Bolton
email: alanchrisw@tiscali.co.uk

NON-DIOCESAN MEMBERS

The following are non-diocesan members of General Synod:

Suffragan Bishops in Convocation

CANTERBURY
The Bishop of Dover (*ex officio*)
The Bishop of Dorchester
The Bishop of Dudley
The Bishop of Grimsby
The Bishop of Willesden

YORK
The Bishop of Burnley
The Bishop of Hull
The Bishop of Knaresborough

Deans in Convocation

CANTERBURY
The Dean of Canterbury
The Dean of Leicester
The Dean of Portsmouth

YORK
The Dean of Sheffield
The Dean of Carlisle

Chaplain-General of Prisons and Archdeacon of Prisons Vacancy

Armed Forces Synod

Ven Martin Poll
Ven Peter Eagles
Ven Ray Pentland
Colonel Peter McAllister
Lt Cdr Philippa Sargent
Mrs Lynn Hayler

University Representatives in Convocation

CANTERBURY
Oxford
Canon Dr Judith Maltby

Cambridge
Revd Duncan Dormor

London
Professor the Revd Dr Richard Burridge

Other Universities (Southern)
Revd Canon Dr Gavin Ashenden

YORK
Durham and Newcastle
Revd Dr Miranda Threlfall-Holmes

Other Universities (Northern)
Revd Dr Kevin Ward

Representatives of Religious Communities in Convocation
CANTERBURY
Revd Sister Rosemary Howorth CHN

YORK
Revd Thomas Seville CR

Lay Representatives of Religious Communities
Sister Anita Smith OHP
Brother Thomas Quin OSB

***Ex officio* Members of the House of Laity**
Dean of the Arches
Rt Worshipful Charles George QC
Vicar-General of the Province of Canterbury
Chancellor Timothy Briden
Vicar-General of the Province of York
His Honour Peter Collier
First Church Estates Commissioner Mr Andreas Whittam Smith

Second Church Estates Commissioner Mr Tony Baldry MP

Third Church Estates Commissioner Mr Timothy Walker

Chairman of the Church of England Pensions Board
Dr Jonathan Spencer

Representatives who have been appointed to the Synod under its Standing Orders with speaking but not voting rights

Ecumenical Representatives
Very Revd Dr Alan McDonald (Church of Scotland)
Very Revd Archimandrite Ephrem Lash (Orthodox Church)
Revd Graham Maskery (United Reformed Church)
Revd Jan Mullin (Moravian Church)
Revd Dr Roger Walton (Methodist Church)
Revd Prof Paul Fiddes (Baptist Union)
Bishop Dr Joe Aldred (Black-led Churches)
Revd Robert Byrne (Roman Catholic Church)
His Grace Bishop Angaelos (Coptic Orthodox Church)

Church of England Youth Council Representatives
Miss Charlotte Cook
Miss Hannah Page
Miss Anita Louise Smith

Deaf Anglicans Together Representatives
Revd Catherine Nightingale
Mrs Patricia Callaghan
Susan Myatt

Appointed Members of the Archbishops' Council
Mr Andrew Britton
Prof John Craven
Mr Philip Fletcher
Mrs Mary Chapman
Revd Dr Rosalyn Murphy
Miss Rebecca Swinson

NATIONAL STRUCTURES

House of Bishops

Chairman The Archbishop of Canterbury

Vice-Chairman The Archbishop of York

Administrative Secretary Mr Ross Gillson
Tel: 020 7898 1375
email: ross.gillson@churchofengland.org

Theological Consultant Dr Martin Davie
Tel: 020 7898 1488
email: martin.davie@churchofengland.org

The House of Bishops meets separately from sessions of the General Synod twice a year, in private session. It has a special responsibility for matters relating to doctrine and liturgy under Article 7 of the Constitution of General Synod. Its agendas nevertheless range more widely, reflecting matters relating to the exercise of *episcope* in the Church. Each year the College of Bishops – consisting of all diocesan and suffragan bishops – also meet, as do diocesan bishops with the archbishops.

The following committees or panels work under the umbrella of the House:

THE STANDING COMMITTEE OF THE HOUSE OF BISHOPS
Chairman Most Revd and Rt Hon John Sentamu (*Archbishop of York*)

Secretary Mr Ross Gillson

The Standing Committee consists of the Archbishops of Canterbury and York and the Bishops of Coventry, Dover, Gloucester, London, Rochester and Sheffield. Its principal role is to prepare the agendas for the House's meetings, but it also deals with other matters on the House's behalf.

CONTINUING MINISTERIAL DEVELOPMENT COMMITTEE
Chairman Rt Revd Stephen Conway (*Bishop of Ely*)

Secretary Ms Christina Hedderly
Tel: 020 7898 1098
email: christina.hedderly@churchofengland.org

House of Clergy

Joint Chairmen The Prolocutors of the Convocations

Secretary Mr Jonathan Neil-Smith
Tel: 020 7898 1373
email: jonathan.neil-smith@churchofengland.org

Membership of the House of Clergy comprises the Lower House of the Convocation of Canterbury and the Lower House of the Convocation of York joined into one House.

The Standing Committee of the House of Clergy consists of the Standing Committee of the Lower House of the Canterbury Convocation (the Prolocutor, Pro-Prolocutors, elected members of the Archbishops' Council, and four elected members) and the Assessors of the York Convocation (the Prolocutor, Deputy Prolocutors, elected members of the Archbishops' Council, and two elected assessors).

House of Laity

Chair Dr Philip Giddings

Vice-Chair Mr Tim Hind

Secretary Mr Nicholas Hills *Tel:* 020 7898 1363
email: nicholas.hills@churchofengland.org

The Standing Committee of the House of Laity consists of the Chair and Vice-Chair and the members elected by the House to the Archbishop's Council (2 members), the Business Committee (3 members) and the Appointments Committee (3 members).

Principal Committees

THE BUSINESS COMMITTEE
Chair Ven Julian Henderson

Secretary Dr Colin Podmore (*Clerk to the Synod until 31/3/13*)
Tel: 020 7898 1385
email: colin.podmore@churchofengland.org

Revd Canon Susan Booys, Revd Canon Simon Butler, Mrs Anne Foreman, Revd Mark Ireland, Mrs Sue Johns, Rt Revd James Langstaff (*Bishop of Rochester*) Mr Gerry O'Brien, Revd Charles Razzall, Mrs Christina Rees.

The Committee is responsible for organizing the business of the Synod, enabling it to fulfil its role as a legislative and deliberative body.

THE LEGISLATIVE COMMITTEE
Ex officio Members
The Archbishop of Canterbury
The Archbishop of York
The Prolocutors of the Convocations
The Chair and Vice-Chair of the House of Laity
The Dean of the Arches
The Second Church Estates Commissioner
Elected Members
Canon Peter Bruinvels, Revd Canon David Felix, Rt Revd James Langstaff (*Bishop of Rochester*), Mr Clive Scowen, Revd Mark Steadman, Mr Geoffrey Tattersall QC

Secretary Mr Stephen Slack *Tel:* 020 7898 1367
email: stephen.slack@churchofengland.org

THE STANDING ORDERS COMMITTEE
Chair Mr Geoffrey Tattersall QC

Ex officio Members
The Prolocutors of the Convocations
The Chair and Vice-Chair of the House of Laity

Appointed Members
Ven Christine Allsopp (*Archdeacon of Northampton*), Revd Canon Sue Booys, Revd Canon Simon Killwick, Canon Elizabeth Paver, Mr Clive Scowen

Secretary Miss Sarah Clemenson
Tel: 020 7898 1371
email: sarah.clemenson@churchofengland.org

PRINCIPAL COMMISSIONS

The Clergy Discipline Commission

Chair Rt Hon Lord Justice Mummery
Deputy Chair His Honour Judge John Bullimore

Secretary Miss Sarah Clemenson

Office Church House, Great Smith St, London SW1P 3AZ
Tel: 020 7898 1371
Fax: 020 7898 1718/1721
email: sarah.clemenson@churchofengland.org

MEMBERS
Mr Niall Blackie, Ven Annette Cooper (*Archdeacon of Colchester*), Revd Alastair Cutting, Revd Canon Cynthia Dowdle, Rt Revd Dr Peter Forster (*Bishop of Chester*), Rt Revd Christopher Hill (*Bishop of Guildford*), Mr David Mills, Mr Michael Sayers, Dr Anna Thomas-Betts, Revd Canon Celia Thomson

The Clergy Discipline Commission is constituted under the Clergy Discipline Measure 2003. Under that Measure the Commission is required to give general advice to disciplinary tribunals, the courts of the Vicars-General, bishops and archbishops as to the penalties which are appropriate in particular circumstances; to issue codes of practice and general policy guidance to persons exercising functions in connection with clergy discipline; and to make annually to the General Synod through the House of Bishops a report on the exercise of its functions during the previous year.

Under the 2003 Measure the Commission is also required to compile and maintain 'provincial panels' of persons available for appointment as members of a disciplinary tribunal or a Vicar-General's Court for the purposes of dealing with cases under it and to formulate guidance for the purposes of the 2003 Measure generally and to promulgate it in a Code of Practice approved by the Dean of the Arches and the General Synod.

The Commission also monitors the exercise of discipline, highlights and encourages best practice, and builds up casework experience in disciplinary matters.

The Crown Nominations Commission

Secretary to the Commission Ms Caroline Boddington, Archbishops' Secretary for Appointments

Office The Wash House, Lambeth Palace, London SE1 7JU
Tel: 020 7898 1876/7
Fax: 020 7898 1899

MEMBERS

Ex officio
The Archbishop of Canterbury
The Archbishop of York
Elected Members

Three members of the House of Clergy
Revd John Dunnett
Revd Canon Judith Maltby
Very Revd Andrew Nunn

Three members of the House of Laity
Mrs April Alexander
Mr Aiden Hargreaves-Smith
Miss Jane Patterson
Six members of the Vacancy-in-See Committee of the diocese whose bishopric is to become, or has become, vacant

Ex officio non-voting members
Sir Paul Britton (*The Prime Minister's Appointments Secretary*)

Ms Caroline Boddington (*Archbishops' Secretary for Appointments*)

The Commission was established by the General Synod in February 1977. Its function is to consider vacancies in diocesan bishoprics in the Provinces of Canterbury and York, and candidates for appointments to them. At each meeting the Chair is taken by the Archbishop in whose Province the vacancy has arisen. The Commission agrees upon two names for nomination to the Prime Minister by the appropriate Archbishop or, in the case of the Archbishopric of Canterbury or York, by the chairman of the Commission. The names submitted are given in an order of preference voted upon by the Commission. The Prime Minister accepts the first name and reverts to the second name should the first be unable to take up the post.

The Dioceses Commission

Chairman Canon Prof Michael Clarke

Vice-Chair Ven Peter Hill (Archdeacon of Nottingham)

Secretary Mr Jonathan Neil-Smith

Office Church House, Great Smith St, London SW1P 3AZ *Tel:* 020 7898 1373
email: jonathan.neil-smith@churchofengland.org

MEMBERS
Revd Canon Jonathan Alderton-Ford (St Edmundsbury & Ipswich), Revd Paul Benfield (Blackburn), Mr Robert Hammond (Chelmsford), Mr Keith Malcouronne (Guildford), Mrs Lucinda Herklots, Revd Canon Sarah Mullally DBE, Canon Prof Hilary Russell, Rt Revd Nigel Stock (*Bishop of St Edmundsbury & Ipswich).*

A Dioceses Commission was set up in 1978 under the Dioceses Measure 1978. In 2008 it was replaced by a new body of the same name, established under the Dioceses, Pastoral and Mission Measure 2007. Part II of that Measure makes provision for such matters as the reorganization of diocesan boundaries, the creation and revival of suffragan sees, and the delegation of episcopal functions by diocesan bishops to suffragan and assistant bishops.

The Commission's duties are laid down by the Measure. Its primary duty is to keep under review the provincial and diocesan structure of the Church of England and in particular the size, boundaries and number of provinces; the size, boundaries and number of dioceses and their distribution between the provinces; the number and distribution of bishops and the arrangements for episcopal oversight. The Commission may make reorganization schemes either of its own volition or in response to proposals from diocesan bishops. Schemes require the approval of the diocesan synods concerned (other than in exceptional circumstances) and that of the General Synod. The Commission also gives advice on good practice regarding diocesan administration and responds to requests for advice on particular issues. It comments on proposals to change the names of episcopal sees. Diocesan bishops are obliged to seek the views of the Commission if they propose to fill a vacant suffragan see.

Further information about the Commission and its work may be found on the Church of England website at www.churchofengland.org/about-us/structure/dioceses-commission

The Fees Advisory Commission

Chair Mr John Alpass

Secretary Miss Sarah Clemenson

Office Church House, Great Smith St, London SW1P 3AZ *Tel:* 020 7898 1371
Fax: 020 7898 1718/1721
email: sarah.clemenson@churchofengland.org

MEMBERS
Rt Revd Colin Fletcher (*Bishop of Dorchester*), Mr Howard Dellar, Mrs Madelaine Goddard, Revd Canon Joyce Jones, Mr Geoffrey Tattersall QC, Canon Elizabeth Renshaw MBE, Revd Canon John Rees, Mr Timothy Walker.

The Fees Advisory Commission is constituted under Part II of the Ecclesiastical Fees Measure 1986, as amended. It makes recommendations as to certain fees to be paid to ecclesiastical judges, legal officers and others, and embodies those recommendations in Orders which are laid before the General Synod for approval. If approved, the Orders take effect unless annulled by either House of Parliament, and are published as Statutory Instruments.

The Legal Advisory Commission

Chair Revd and Worshipful Dr Rupert Bursell QC

Secretary Revd Alexander McGregor
Tel: 020 7898 1748

Administrative Secretary Miss Sarah Clemenson
Tel: 020 7898 1371

Office Church House, Great Smith St, London SW1P 3AZ *Fax:* 020 7898 1718/1721

MEMBERS

Ex officio members

Rt Worshipful Charles George QC (Dean of the Arches and Auditor)
Rt Worshipful Timothy Briden (Vicar-General of Canterbury)
Rt Worshipful Peter Collier QC (Vicar-General of York)
Revd Canon John Rees (Provincial Registrar of Canterbury) (Vice-Chairman of the Commission)
Mr Lionel Lennox (Provincial Registrar of York)
Mr Stephen Slack (Chief Legal Adviser to the Archbishops' Council and Official Solicitor to the Church Commissioners)
Sir Anthony Hammond KCB QC (Standing Counsel to the General Synod)

Appointed and co-opted members

Revd and Worshipful Dr Rupert Bursell QC, Worshipful Professor David McClean CBE QC DCL FBA, Worshipful Mark Hill QC, Worshipful Sir Mark Hedley, Worshipful Dr Charles Mynors, Worshipful Nigel Seed QC, Mr Peter Beesley, Ms Jane Monks, Mr Andrew Johnson, Rt Revd Christopher Hill, Ven Christine Hardman, Revd Canon Gavin Kirk, Revd Mark Steadman, Rt Hon Sir John Mummery, Ms Francesca Quint, Mr Edward Nugee TD QC, Mr Robert Higham, Dr Sheila Cameron CBE QC

The Legal Advisory Commission gives advice on legal matters of general interest to the Church which are referred to it by the Archbishops' Council and its Divisions, Boards, Councils and Commissions, by the General Synod and its Houses and Commissions, by the Church Commissioners and the Church of England Pensions Board, and by diocesan clerical and lay office holders. The Commission cannot accept requests for advice from private individuals or secular bodies. In addition, the Commission cannot normally give opinions on contentious matters, but it may be able to do so (depending on the circumstances) if the facts are agreed by all parties to the dispute, all parties join in referring the matter to the Commission for an opinion and it is not (and is not expected to become) the subject-matter of proceedings in the courts.

The opinions of the Commission and its predecessor, the Legal Board, on matters of general interest are published by Church House Publishing in a loose-leaf form under the title *Legal Opinions Concerning the Church of England*. The 8th edition was published in May 2007. Opinions issued by the Commission since that date can be accessed at http://www.churchofengland.org/about-us/structure/churchlawlegis/guidance

The Legal Aid Commission

Chairman His Honour Judge Andrew Rutherford

Secretary Mr Stephen York

Office Church House, Great Smith St, London SW1P 3AZ *Tel:* 020 7898 1703
Fax: 020 7898 1718/1721

MEMBERS

Mrs Isabel Adcock, Ven Christine Allsopp (*Archdeacon of Northampton*), Revd Paul Benfield, Mrs Rosalind Brewer, Mrs Jennifer Dunlop, Revd Geoffrey Harbord, Mr Aiden Hargreaves-Smith, Revd Canon Joyce Jones, Rt Revd Alistair Magowan (*Bishop of Ludlow*), Ven Clive Mansell (*Archdeacon of Tonbridge*)

The Legal Aid Commission operates under the Church of England (Legal Aid) Measure 1994 and the Church of England (Legal Aid) Rules 1995, and administers the Legal Aid Fund which was originally set up under the Ecclesiastical Jurisdiction Measure 1963 and is continued by the 1994 Measure and the 1995 Rules.

Legal aid under the 1994 Measure may be granted at the discretion of the Commission, subject to various conditions, for certain types of proceedings before Ecclesiastical Courts and tribunals; details of eligibility for legal aid and the Commission's procedures, together with an application form for legal aid, are obtainable from the Secretary, on request, or at www.churchofengland.org/about-us/structure/churchlawlegis/clergydiscipline/legalaid.aspx

The Liturgical Commission

Chair Rt Revd Stephen Platten (*Bishop of Wakefield*)

Secretary and Worship Development Officer Revd Christopher Woods *Tel:* 020 7898 1365
email: christopher.woods@churchofengland.org

Assistant Secretary Sue Moore *Tel:* 020 7898 1376
email: sue.moore@churchofengland.org

Office Church House, Great Smith St, London SW1P 3AZ Tel: 020 7898 1376

MEMBERS
Rt Revd Robert Paterson (*Bishop of Sodor & Man*), Revd Dr Anders Bergquist, Ven Dr Anne Dawtry, Revd Canon Perran Gay (Truro), Revd Mark Earey, Mrs Sarah Finch (London), Revd Canon Christopher Irvine, Revd Dr Simon Jones, Revd Timothy Lomax, Revd Dr Rosemarie Mallett (Southwark), Canon Christine McMullen (Derby), Dr Bridget Nichols, Rt Revd Philip North (*Bishop of Whitby*) (London), Revd Canon Gavin Kirk (Lincoln), Revd Paul Thomas, Revd Gary Waddington

In response to resolutions by the Convocations in October 1954, the Archbishops of Canterbury and York appointed a standing Liturgical Commission 'to consider questions of a liturgical character submitted to them from time to time by the Archbishops of Canterbury and York and to report thereon to the Archbishops'. In 1971 the Commission became a permanent Commission of the General Synod. Its functions are:

1 to prepare forms of service at the request of the House of Bishops for submission to that House in the first instance;
2 to advise on the experimental use of forms of service and the development of liturgy;
3 to exchange information and advice on liturgical matters with other Churches both in the Anglican Communion and elsewhere;
4 to promote the development and understanding of liturgy and its use in the Church.

Further information about the Commission's work and its Transforming Worship initiative may be found on the Transforming Worship website at www.transformingworship.org.uk

General Synod Publications

Printed copies of General Synod publications can be purchased from Church House Bookshop. The *Report of Proceedings* is now only available in electronic format and is available to download, along with the texts of many other papers, on the General Synod section of the Church of England website.

THE CONVOCATIONS OF CANTERBURY AND YORK

CONSTITUTION

Each of the Convocations consists of two Houses, an Upper House and a Lower House. The Upper House consists of all the diocesan bishops in the Province, the Bishop of Dover (in the case of the Convocation of Canterbury), bishops elected by and from amongst suffragan bishops of the Province, and any other bishops residing in the Province who are members of the Archbishops' Council. The Archbishop presides. The Lower House comprises clergy (other than bishops) who have been elected, appointed or chosen in accordance with Canon H 2 and the rules made under it (including deans, proctors from the dioceses and university constituencies and clerical members of religious communities) together with *ex-officio* members. The Prolocutor is the chair and spokesperson of the House.

MEMBERS OF THE CONVOCATIONS

	Canterbury	*York*	*Either Province*
Upper House			
Diocesan Bishops	30	14	
Suffragan Bishops	6	3	
	36	17	
Lower House			
Deans	3	2	
Dean of Jersey or Guernsey	1		
Armed Services	3		
Chaplain-General of Prisons	1		
Elected Proctors	128	55	
University Proctors	4	2	
Religious			2
Co-opted Clergy	0	0	
	140	59	2

OFFICERS

Convocation of Canterbury
President The Archbishop of Canterbury

Prolocutor of the Lower House Ven Christine Hardman (*Archdeacon of Lewisham and Greenwich*)

Other Officers
Pro-Prolocutors
Revd Alastair Cutting, Revd Preb David Houlding

Standing Committee of the Lower House
The Prolocutor
The Pro-Prolocutors
Revd Simon Cawdell, Revd Canon Robert Cotton, Revd Stuart Currie, Revd Mark Ireland, Revd Hugh Lee, Revd Preb Stephen Lynas

Registrar Mr Stephen Slack

Synodical Secretary, Actuary and Editor of the Chronicle of Convocation
Revd Stephen Trott, Rectory, 41 Humfrey Lane, Boughton, Northampton NN2 8RQ
Tel: 01604 845655
email: revstrott@btinternet.com

Ostiarius Mr Clive McCleester, Hospital of St Cross, St Cross Rd, Winchester SO23 9SD

Convocation of York
President The Archbishop of York

Prolocutor of the Lower House Revd Canon Glyn Webster

Other Officers
Deputy Prolocutors
Revd Dr Meg Gilley, Revd Canon Simon Killwick

Assessors (Standing Committee)
Revd Dr Jonathan Gibbs, Revd Canon Suzanne Sheriff

Registrar Mr Lionel Lennox

Synodal Secretary and Treasurer and Editor of the Journal of Convocation
Ven Alan Wolstencroft, The Bakehouse, 1 Latham Row, Horwich, Bolton BL6 6QZ
Tel and *Fax:* 01204 469985
email: alanchrisw@tiscali.co.uk

Apparitor Mr Alex Carberry, Head Verger of York Minster

ACTS AND PROCEEDINGS

For the Acts and Proceedings of the Convocations, readers are referred to *The Chronicle of the Convocation of Canterbury* and to the *York Journal of Convocation*. Back numbers are available from Wm Dawson & Sons Ltd, Cannon House, Folkestone, Kent.

THE ARCHBISHOPS' COUNCIL

The Archbishops' Council
Charity Registration no: 1074857
Tel: 020 7898 1000
Fax: 020 7898 1369

The Turnbull Report
In 1994, a Commission was established by the Archbishops of Canterbury and York 'to review the machinery for central policy and resource direction in the Church of England, and to make recommendations for improving its effectiveness in supporting the ministry and mission of the Church to the nation as a whole'. The following year, the Commission, chaired by the Rt Revd Michael Turnbull, the then Bishop of Durham, produced a report entitled *Working as One Body*.

The need for change
The Commission looked at the constituent parts of the central structures of the Church of England – essentially the Offices of the Archbishops of Canterbury and York, the House of Bishops, the General Synod and its Boards and Councils, the Central Board of Finance, the Church Commissioners and the Church of England Pensions Board. Its conclusion was that more coherence and coordination were needed in order to give the Church an enhanced capacity to consider policy and resource issues together.

The Archbishops' Council
Amongst the Commission's recommendations was the establishment of a new Council to provide a focus for leadership and executive responsibility and a forum for strategic thinking and planning. Within an overall vision for the Church set by the House of Bishops, the Council would propose an ordering of priorities in consultation with the House of Bishops and the General Synod and take an overview of the Church's financial needs and resources. Not all of the details of the Turnbull model were accepted, but the General Synod endorsed the main thrust and agreed to the creation of the Archbishops' Council. It came into being at the beginning of 1999 under the terms of the National Institutions Measure 1998.

Purpose and work
The objects of the Archbishops' Council under the National Institutions Measure 1998 are to *'co-ordinate, promote, aid and further the work and mission of the Church of England'*. It aims to further its statutory object by:

- providing an informed Christian view in public debate;
- promoting the views of the Church of England to parliament and government;
- overseeing the delivery of services and support to dioceses and parishes; and
- ensuring that policy and resources are considered together.

The Archbishops' Council works closely with the Offices of the Archbishops of Canterbury and York, the House of Bishops and the General Synod, the Church Commissioners and the Church of England Pensions Board. It is supported in its wide-ranging brief by the staff and members of its Divisions:

- Education
- Cathedral and Church Buildings – which includes the Church Buildings Council and the Cathedrals Fabric Commission for England
- Central Secretariat – which includes the Council for Christian Unity and Research and Statistics
- Communications – which includes Church House Publishing
- Human Resources
- Legal
- Ministry
- Mission and Public Affairs – which includes the Committee for Minority Ethnic Anglican Concerns

The work of the Council is described in more detail in its annual report. Its mission is to support the Church in her worship of God and her preparation in:

- proclaiming the Good News of the kingdom
- teaching, baptising and nurturing new believers;
- responding to human need by loving service;
- seeking to transform unjust structures in society; and
- striving to safeguard the integrity of creation and sustaining and renewing the life of the earth.

The Council's objectives are:
1. To enhance the Church's mission by
    - promoting spiritual and numerical growth;
    - enabling and supporting the worshipping Church and encouraging and promoting new ways of being Church; and
    - engaging with social justice and environmental stewardship.
2. To sustain and advance the Church's work in education, lifelong learning and discipleship;

3. To enable the Church to select, train and resource the right people, both ordained and lay, to carry out public ministry and to encourage lay people in their vocation to the world; and
4. To encourage the maintenance and development of the inherited fabric of Church buildings for worship and service to the community.

It engages on behalf of the Church with Government on a wide range of issues of concern to the Church of England and its mission to the nation.

Its programme of work for the new quinquennium, in collaboration with the House of Bishops, is set out in GS 1815, *Challenges for the New Quinquennium.* This seeks to build on the following three main themes set out by the Archbishop of Canterbury in his Presidential Address to General Synod in November 2010:

(i) To take forward the spiritual and numerical growth of the Church of England – including the growth of its capacity to serve the whole community of this country;
(ii) To re-shape or reimagine the Church's ministry for the century coming, so as to make sure that there is a growing and sustainable Christian witness in every local community; and
(iii) To further the Common Good.

MEMBERS

Joint Presidents
Most Revd and Rt Hon Dr Rowan Williams, Archbishop of Canterbury
Most Revd and Rt Hon Dr John Sentamu, Archbishop of York

Officers of the General Synod
Ven Christine Hardman, Prolocutor of the Lower House of the Convocation of Canterbury
Revd Canon Glyn Webster, Prolocutor of the Lower House of the Convocation of York
Dr Philip Giddings, Chair of the House of Laity
Mr Tim Hind, Vice-Chair of the House of Laity

Elected by the General Synod:
Rt Revd Dr Steven Croft, Bishop of Sheffield
Rt Revd Trevor Willmott, Bishop of Dover
Revd Canon Robert Cotton
Revd Mark Ireland
Mr Paul Boyd-Lee
Mrs Christina Rees

A Church Estates Commissioner
Mr Andreas Whittam Smith, First Church Estates Commissioner

Appointed by the Archbishops
Mr Andrew Britton, former Director, National Institute of Economic and Social Research
Mrs Mary Chapman, former Chief Executive, the Chartered Institute of Management
Professor John Craven, Vice-Chancellor, University of Portsmouth
Mr Philip Fletcher, Chairman, Water Services Regulation Authority
Revd Dr Rosalyn Murphy, priest-in-charge of St Thomas's Church, Blackpool
Miss Rebecca Swinson, Medical Researcher

Staff
William Fittall, *Secretary General*
Tel: 020 7898 1360
email: william.fittall@churchofengland.org

Revd Janina Ainsworth, *Education/National Society* *Tel:* 020 7898 1500
email: janina.ainsworth@churchofengland.org

Revd Dr Malcolm Brown, *Mission and Public Affairs* *Tel:* 020 7898 1468
email: malcolm.brown@churchofengland.org

Revd Arun Arora, *Communications*
Tel: 020 7898 1462
email: arun.arora@churchofengland.org

Janet Gough, *Cathedral and Church Buildings*
Tel: 020 7898 1887
email: janet.gough@churchofengland.org

Ven Julian Hubbard, *Ministry*
Tel: 020 7898 1390
email: julian.hubbard@churchofengland.org

Su Morgan, *Human Resources* *Tel:* 020 7898 1565
email: su.morgan@churchofengland.org

Stephen Slack, *Legal Adviser* *Tel:* 020 7898 0366
email: stephen.slack@churchofengland.org

Dr Colin Podmore *Clerk to the Synod, Director of Central Secretariat and Ecumenical Relations (until 31/3/13)*
Tel: 020 7898 1559
email: david.williams@churchofengland.org

Nicholas Hills, *Assistant Secretary*
Tel: 020 7898 1363
email: nicholas.hills@churchofengland.org

NATIONAL STRUCTURES

Archbishops' Council: key working relationships

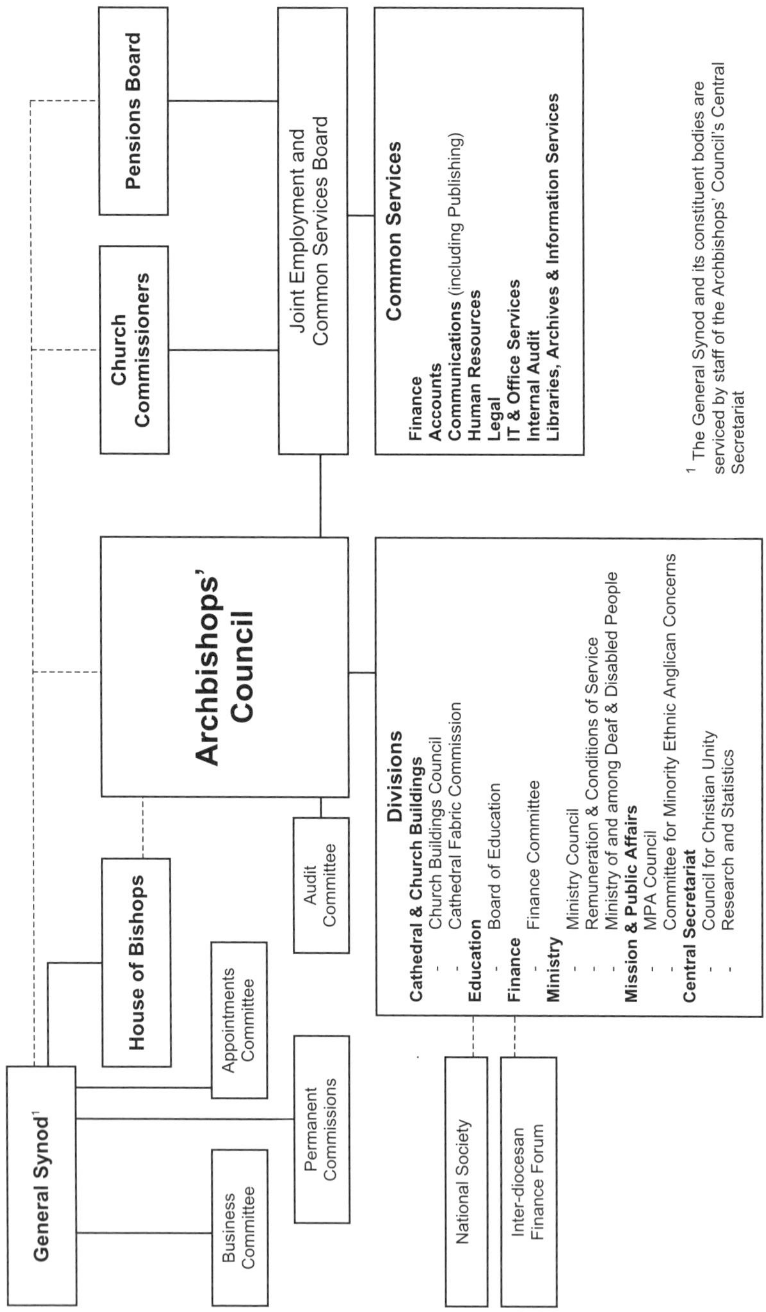

[1] The General Synod and its constituent bodies are serviced by staff of the Archbishops' Council's Central Secretariat

ARCHBISHOPS' COUNCIL BUDGET

The Budget covers five areas, each of which is separately approved by the General Synod annually. These are Training for Ministry, National Church Responsibilities, Grants, Mission agencies pensions support and revenue costs relating to the Church's Housing Assistance for the Retired Ministry (CHARM).

The Vote 1 apportionment for 2013 represents an increase of 1.6 per cent from the previous year, funding a 2.9 per cent net increase in **Training for Ministry** expenditure. The budget for **National Church Responsibilities** covers the costs of work in support of the Church's ministry and mission to the nation that needs to be undertaken, or is most effectively and/or efficiently carried out, at national level. The 2013 Vote 2 apportionment represents an increase of 1.8 per cent against the 2012 level. The **Grants** budget, which mainly funds the Church of England's contributions to the Inter Anglican budget and to ecumenical bodies, shows a decrease of 11.3 per cent on 2012 Vote 3 apportionment due to a further substantial reduction in contribution towards the Council's Legal Costs Fund.

The budget for **Mission Agencies Pensions Contributions** covers payments in respect of the pension contributions of clergy serving with the Partnership for World Mission agencies. Budgeted Vote 4 apportionment in 2013 is 23.4 per cent below 2012 levels due to the use of £120,000 from reserves which continue to be above the Council's target level for this vote.

The final part of the budget comprises the revenue costs relating to the **Church's Housing Assistance for the Retired Ministry** (CHARM), which provides assistance to ensure that all clergy have access to housing upon retirement. The 2013 budget provides for a net expenditure increase of 5.0 per cent. The budgeted Vote 5 apportionment increase of 8.9 per cent funds this increased expenditure and additionally provides £138,785 towards bolstering reserves which are currently below the Council's target for this Vote.

The detailed 2013 budget as agreed by the General Synod in July 2012 (and set out more fully in GS 1872) is summarized in the table overleaf. The overall budget represents an increase in the apportionment of 1.3 per cent.

The Appointments Committee of the Church of England

Chairman Revd Prebendary David Houlding

Secretary Mr Nicholas Hills *Tel:* 020 7898 1363

Four members appointed by the Archbishops' Council
Prof John Craven, Dr Philip Giddings, Ven Christine Hardman, Revd Canon Glyn Webster.

Seven elected Members
Ven Dr John Applegate, Ven Annette Cooper, Ms Susan Cooper, Mrs Sarah Finch, Rt Revd Richard Frith (*Bishop of Hull*), Revd Canon Giles Goddard, Mr Aiden Hargreaves-Smith.

A joint committee of the General Synod and the Archbishops' Council, the Appointments Committee is responsible for making appointments and/or recommendations on appointments to synodical and other bodies as the Archbishops, the Synod or the Archbishops' Council require. It published its guidelines for best practice in the making of such appointments in 2010 as GS Misc 963, copies of which can be obtained from its Secretary.

Audit Committee

MEMBERS
Chair Mary Chapman. Appointed by the Archbishops' Council

Secretary Michael Cole
Membership Keith Malcouronne (elected by General Synod); Paul Boyd-Lee (Archbishops' Council member and appointee); John Neilson (appointed by the Archbishops' Council); Susan Cooper (elected by General Synod); Jonathan Evand OBE (appointed by the Archbishops' Council).

The Committee provides independent oversight of the Archbishops' Council's framework of corporate governance, risk management and internal control. It oversees the discharge of the Council's responsibilities relating to financial statements, external and internal audit and internal control systems, and reports to the Council thereon with recommendations as appropriate.

2013 Budget

	2013	
	£	£
TRAINING FOR MINISTRY (Vote 1)		
Expenditure	12,574,340	**12,574,340**
Financed by:		
Income	(15,000)	
Diocesan apportionment	(12,559,340)	**(12,574,340)**
NATIONAL CHURCH RESPONSIBILITIES (Vote 2)		
Central Secretariat		
(including Christian Unity/Research & Statistics)	1,837,289	
Ministry Division	1,403,813	
Education	749,481	
Mission & Public Affairs	1,285,786	
Cathedral and Church Buildings	844,162	
Projects and Development	102,963	
Church House Publishing	(42,778)	
Communications	453,169	
Human Resources	407,835	
Legal	654,329	
Finance & Resources	880,474	
IT & Office Services	479,861	
Records	204,341	
Internal Audit	76,484	
Accommodation	1,287,554	
Depreciation	161,665	
Contingency	125,000	**10,911,428**
Financed by:		
Income	(275,000)	
Movement from Reserves	(314,728)	
Diocesan apportionment	(10,321,700)	**(10,911,428)**
GRANTS (Vote 3)		
Anglican Communion	492,900	
British ecumenical bodies	260,000	
Conference of European Churches	90,474	
World Council of Churches (including Assembly)	138,000	
Church Urban Fund	203,000	
Legal Costs (including Legal Aid Fund)	50,000	
Other grants and expenses	50,400	**1,284,774**
Financed by:		
Movement from Reserves	(64,000)	
Diocesan apportionment	(1,220,774)	**(1,284,774)**
MISSION AGENCY CLERGY PENSIONS (Vote 4)		
Expenditure	644,986	**644,986**
Financed by:		
Movement from Reserves	(120,000)	
Diocesan apportionment	(524,986)	**(644,986)**
CHARM (Vote 5)		
Expenditure	3,765,615	
Movement to Reserves	138,785	**(3,904,400)**
Financed by:		
Diocesan apportionment	(3,904,400)	**(3,904,400)**
TOTAL EXPENDITURE (net of income)		**28,891,143**
Movement to/(from) reserves		(359,943)
TOTAL DIOCESAN APPOINTMENT		**(28,531,200)**

FINANCE COMMITTEE

MEMBERS
Chair appointed by Archbishops' Council
Mr Andrew Britton

Three members elected by the General Synod:
Revd Stephen France (Chichester), Mr Richard Mantle (Ripon and Leeds), Mrs Sheri Sturgess (Truro)

Three members appointed by the Archbishops' Council on the recommendation of the Appointments Committee:
Rt Revd Donald Allister (*Bishop of Peterborough*), Ven Annette Cooper (*Archdeacon of Colchester*), Canon Sandra Newton (Sheffield)

Three members elected by the Inter-Diocesan Finance Forum:
Canon Michael Arlington (Southwell and Nottingham), Mr Stephen Marriott (Guildford), Mr Brian Newey (Oxford)

Secretary David White *Tel*: 020 7898 1684
email: david.white@churchofengland.org

Terms of reference

1. To advise the Archbishops' Council and the dioceses on all financial aspects of the Archbishops' Council's work, including its investment, stewardship and trustee responsibilities, on the effects of the public financial policy and on the overall financial needs and resources of the Church.
2. To make recommendations to the Archbishops' Council as to its annual budget and on mechanisms for monitoring and controlling the expenditure of the Council.
3. To consult with the dioceses on financial matters, and to make recommendations thereon as appropriate to the Archbishops' Council and the dioceses.
4. To carry out such other work as may be entrusted to it by the Archbishops' Council.

NATIONAL STRUCTURES

INVESTMENT COMMITTEE

MEMBERS
Appointed by the Finance Committee

Canon Michael Arlington (Chair), Mr Andrew Britton, Mr John Booth, Mr Stephen Marriott and Mr Glyn Owen.

Secretary David White *Tel*: 020 7898 1684
email: david.white@churchofengland.org

Summary of Terms of Reference

Responsibility for setting investment policy lies with the Archbishops' Council with advice from its Finance Committee.

Within that policy, the Investment Committee has responsibility for implementing the investment strategy, governed by it constitution and Terms of Reference, and reporting regularly on progress. The Investment Committee's responsibilities include:

1. to select, review, and renew the appointment of or to de-select any of its investment managers;
2. to set the strategy for the Council's investment managers including setting performance objectives, investment guidelines and benchmarks to meet the investment policy set by Council;
3. to decide the most appropriate investment strategy for each of the Council's charitable settlements.

CENTRAL SECRETARIAT

Under the direction of the Clerk to the Synod and Head of Central Secretariat, staff of the Central Secretariat provide the secretariat for the General Synod, its three Houses (House of Bishops, House of Clergy and House of Laity), the Archbishops' Council and the Business and Appointments Committees. Members of staff of the Secretariat serve as secretaries to a number of the Synod's principal commissions and committees and also as secretaries of *ad hoc* committees and working parties as required. They also serve various other groups, such as the Churches' Funerals Group. The Clerk to the Synod acts as Secretary to the Business Committee and provides advice and assistance as necessary to synodical bodies and members of Synod.

The Central Secretariat includes the Council for Christian Unity and Research and Statistics.

Clerk to the Synod and Director Central Secretariat and Ecumenical Relations (until 31/3/13)
Dr Colin Podmore *Tel:* 020 7898 1385
email: colin.podmore@churchofengland.org

Senior Administrative Staff and their teams
Head of Research and Statistics Dr Bev Botting
Tel: 020 7898 1542
email: bev.botting@churchofengland.org
Jonathan Neil-Smith (*Secretary:* Dioceses Commission, House of Clergy, Standing Committee of the House of Clergy) *Tel:* 020 7898 1373
email: jonathan.neil-smith@churchofengland.org
Paul Clarkson (*Assistant Secretary:* Dioceses Commission) *Tel:* 020 7898 1379
email: paul clarkson@churchofengland.org
Revd Christopher Woods
Secretary to the Liturgical Commission and Worship Development Officer *Tel:* 020 7898 1365
email: christopher.woods@churchofengland.org
Sue Moore (*Secretary*: Churches' Funerals Group [www.christianfunerals.org]; *Assistant to Christopher Woods/Jonathan Neil-Smith*)
Tel: 020 7898 1376
email: sue.moore@churchofengland.org

Nicholas Hills (*Secretary*: Appointments Committee, House of Laity, Standing Committee of the House of Laity; *Assistant Secretary*: Archbishops' Council) *Tel:* 020 7898 1363
email: nicholas.hills@churchofengland.org
Andrew Brown (*Head of Synod Support*)
Tel: 020 7898 1374
email: andrewj.brown@churchofengland.org
Ross Gillson (*Administrative Secretary to the House of Bishops*) *Tel:* 020 7898 1375
email: ross.gillson@churchofengland.org
Revd Frances Arnold (*Executive Officer*: House of Bishops) *Tel:* 020 7898 1372
email: frances.arnold@churchofengland.org
Elizabeth Hall (*Safeguarding Adviser – Child and Adult Protection*: Church of England and Methodist Church) *Tel:* 020 7898 1330
email: elizabeth.hall@churchofengland.org

The Council for Christian Unity

Director of Ecumenical Relations (until 31/3/13)
Dr Colin Podmore *Tel:* 020 7898 1385
email: colin.podmore@churchofengland.org

European Secretary Revd Canon Dr Leslie Nathaniel *Tel:* 020 7898 1474
email: leslie.nathaniel@churchofengland.org

National Adviser (Unity-in-Mission) Revd Dr Roger Paul *Tel:* 020 7898 1479
email: roger.paul@churchofengland.org

Assistant Secretary Mr Francis Bassett
Tel: 020 7898 1481
email: francis.bassett@churchofengland.org

Theological Secretary Dr Martin Davie
Tel: 020 7898 1488
email: martin.davie@churchofengland.org

Office Church House, Great Smith St, London SW1P 3AZ *Tel:* 020 7898 1470
Fax: 020 7898 1483
Web: http://www.churchofengland.org/about-us/work-other-churches/ccu.aspx

MEMBERS
Chairman Rt Revd Christopher Hill (*Bishop of Guildford*)

Membership Elected: Revd Janet Appleby, Dr Paula Gooder, Ven George Howe, Canon Elizabeth Paver. Appointed: Revd Dr William Adam, Rt Revd Donald Allister (*Bishop of Peterborough*), Revd Peter Anthony, Mrs Margaret Swinson

The Council was established as an advisory committee of the General Synod on 1 April 1991 to continue and develop the ecumenical work formerly undertaken by the Board for Mission and Unity. That Board, set up on 1 January 1972, had inherited the responsibilities of the Missionary and Ecumenical Council of the Church Assembly (MECCA) and the Church of England Council on Foreign Relations (CFR).

FUNCTIONS OF THE COUNCIL
(*Adapted from the Constitution*)

(*a*) To stimulate and encourage theological reflection in consultation with the Faith and Order Commission and to advise the Archbishops' Council and the General Synod on unity issues and proposals in the light of the Christian understanding of God's purposes for the world.

(*b*) To advise the House of Bishops on matters referred to it by the House.

(*c*) To foster ecumenical work in the Church nationally and in the dioceses.

(*d*) In conjunction with the Archbishops' Council to promote unity and ecumenical concerns in the work of all the Boards, Councils, Divisions, etc.

(*e*) In ecumenical concerns on behalf of the Archbishops' Council to be the principal link between the General Synod and

- (i) The Anglican Consultative Council;
- (ii) individual provinces and dioceses of the Anglican Communion and the United Churches incorporating former Anglican dioceses.

(*f*) On behalf of the Archbishops' Council to be the principal channel of communication between the General Synod and

- (i) The World Council of Churches;
- (ii) The Conference of European Churches;
- (iii) Churches Together in Britain and Ireland;
- (iv) Churches Together in England;
- (v) all other Christian Churches in the British Isles and abroad.

(*g*) To service committees and commissions engaged in ecumenical discussions with other Churches.

THE FAITH AND ORDER COMMISSION
Chairman Rt Revd Christopher Cocksworth (*Bishop of Coventry*)

The Faith and Order Commission consists of not more than sixteen persons appointed by the Archbishops. The Commission advises the Archbishops, House of Bishops and the Council on matters of ecumenical, theological and doctrinal concern.

COMMITTEE FOR ROMAN CATHOLIC RELATIONS
Chairman Rt Revd Tim Thornton (Bishop of Truro)

The Committee for Roman Catholic Relations consists of not more than fifteen persons appointed by the Archbishops after consultation with the Council. This Committee promotes relations between the Church of England and the Roman Catholic Church in this country and it meets twice a year with the equivalent Roman Catholic body. The two bodies form the English Anglican Roman Catholic Committee.

MEISSEN COMMISSION – ANGLICAN COMMITTEE
Chairman Rt Revd Nicholas Baines (*Bishop of Bradford*)
The Meissen Commission (the Sponsoring Body for Church of England EKD Relations) was established in 1991 to oversee the implementation of the Meissen Declaration and encourage relationships with the Evangelical Church in Germany. It comprises Anglican and German committees.

ECUMENICAL INSTRUMENTS
Contact is maintained with the World Council of Churches, the Conference of European Churches, Churches Together in Britain and Ireland, and Churches Together in England, where members and staff represent the Church of England at various levels. The Council is particularly concerned with helping the Church of England to relate effectively at every level to the ecumenical instruments.

PANELS OF THE CCU
The CCU has two subsidiary panels:

Methodist-Anglican Panel for Unity in Mission
Co-Chairman (*Anglican*) Rt Revd Nigel Stock (*Bishop of St Edmundsbury and Ipswich*)
Porvoo Panel
Chairman Rt Revd David Hamid (*Suffragan Bishop in Europe*)

Research and Statistics

Head of Research and Statistics Dr Bev Botting
Tel: 020 7898 1592
Fax: 020 7898 1532
email: statistics.unit@churchofengland.org
Web: www.churchofengland.org/about-us/facts-stats/research-statistics
Office: Church House, Great Smith St, London SW1P 3AZ

While the gathering of parochial statistics for mission and finance statistics remains at the heart of the Research and Statistics department's work, the department has broadened the range of statistics it maintains and diversifies so that it is now providing a statistical and research consultancy service to the central Church, dioceses and beyond. It is also working to develop the department's role as a central resource to colleagues in the National Church Institutions, and with academic institutions. It is based within the Archbishops' Council where it forms part of the Central Secretariat.

The Research and Statistics department is seeking to better understand the needs of users of church statistics and to establish any issues for those (largely volunteers) who provide the data to them. They have recently undertaken two surveys – one for users and one for data providers, and have been overwhelmed by the responses – especially from those who provide the parochial data. Respondents have given so many excellent suggestions for improvements. The results are being interpreted to help improve both what is asked for and how. This is important as the Department is developing a web-based system for parishes to enter their data so our aim is to ensure that the system also helps those in parishes interpret and use their own data. Working closely with the Archbishops' Council, the Mission and Public Affairs Division, and the Church Commissioners Strategy and Development Division, the department continues to develop the annual church attendance and participation statistics. This aims to provide a range of statistics and research resources to be a tool for mission and to monitor progress on the Archbishops' quinquennial objectives. It is also developing an ongoing mechanism for monitoring diversity across the Church. Continued efforts are being made, in conjunction with the Communications Unit, to improve how the research and statistical information is communicated more widely, with planning taking place currently for sharing the 2011 Census data when these become available during the 2012/13 winter.

The department is developing a web-based mapping system which allows dioceses and parishes to visually show particular characteristics of their ecclesiastical area, both demographic and church statistics. Some of the information presently held on the department's database includes social deprivation, diversity, and population profiles. The department maintains strong links with the Cathedral and Church Buildings Division regarding the use of cathedral and church buildings, with the Ministry Division in the preparation and production of *Statistics of Licensed Ministers*, and with the Church Commissioners in the development of the *Crockford* database.

The department provides a professional consultancy service to the NCIs and particular research support for the national Church Wedding project and future development of ministry deployment. It maintains links with other denominations on statistical and research matters and works closely with the Methodist Church to analyse and publish their annual mission statistics. It is developing its role across the Church as a source of reliable research information regarding the place of the Church in modern society.

MINISTRY DIVISION

Chairman of Ministry Division Rt Revd Dr Steven Croft (*Bishop of Sheffield*) *Tel:* 0114 230 2170
email: bishop@sheffield.anglican.org

Director of Ministry Ven Julian Hubbard
Tel: 020 7898 1390
email: julian.hubbard@churchofengland.org

Finance and Administration Mr John Jackson
Tel: 020 7898 1392
email: john.jackson@churchofengland.org

Senior Selection Secretary Revd Stephen Ferns
Tel: 020 7898 1399
email: stephen.ferns@churchofengland.org

Theological Education and Training Dr David Way
Tel: 020 7898 1405
email: david.way@churchofengland.org

Advisers for Ministry of and among Deaf and Disabled People Vacancy – enquiries to Jackie Freestone
email: jackie.freestone@churchofengland.org

Secretary of the Central Readers' Council Dr Alan Wakely *Tel:* 01353 775132
email: crcsec@hallarn.com
Web: www.readers.cofe.anglican.org

Selection Secretaries
Mr Kevin Diamond *Tel:* 020 7898 1402
email: kevin.diamond@churchofengland.org

Dr Carys Walsh *Tel:* 020 7898 1406
email: carys.walsh@churchofengland.org

Revd Catherine Williams (also *Vocations Officer*)
Tel: 020 7898 1395
email: catherine.williams@churchofengland.org

Revd Hilary Ison (also *Adviser on Training Pathways*) *Tel:* 020 7898 1424
email: hilary.ison@churchofengland.org

Revd Liz Boughton (also *Adviser for Young Vocations*) *Tel:* 0207 898 1593
email: liz.boughton@churchofengland.org

Ministry Training Curriculum Project Manager Dr Eeva John *Tel:* 020 7898 1398
email: eeva.john@churchofengland.org
National Continuing Ministerial Education Officer Dr Tim Ling *Tel:* 020 7898 1408
email: tim.ling@churchofengland.org

Grants Officer Dr Mark Hodge *Tel:* 020 7898 1396
email: mark.hodge@churchofengland.org

Quality Assurance Assistance and Policy Adviser Mr David Hanson *Tel:* 020 7898 1413
email: david.hanson@churchofengland.org

National Adviser for Quality in Reader Education Mrs Sue Hart *Tel:* 0191 252 3941
email: harts@sky.com

National Consultant for Reader Selection Mr Nick Daunt *Tel:* 01695 632326
email: nickdaunt@lineone.net

Office Church House, Great Smith St, London SW1P 3AZ *Tel:* 020 7898 1416
Fax: 020 7898 1421

MINISTRY COUNCIL
Chair Rt Revd Dr Steven Croft

Revd Prof Loveday Alexander, Mr Andrew Britton, Mrs Mary Chapman, Mrs Vivienne Goddard, Revd Vanessa Herrick, Revd Canon Dr Judith Maltby, Rt Revd John Packer, Rt Revd Robert Paterson

Support for the ministry of the Church is critical to its mission. The division brings together policy on the selection, training, deployment and remuneration of the Church of England's ministry.

The Ministry Council oversees the work of the Division. The committee meets four times a year under the chairmanship of the Bishop of Sheffield and consists of members appointed by the House of Bishops, the Appointments Committee of the Church of England and elected by the General Synod.

The Ministry Council is supported by panels responsible for Candidates, Research Degrees, Reader Education, Quality in Formation, and Finance. In addition the work of the Remuneration and Conditions of Service Committee and the Committee for Ministry of and Among Deaf and Disabled People is represented on the Council. The Central Readers' Council continues to fulfil its role in enhancing the contribution of Readers to the overall ministry of the Church, and its secretary is an honorary member of staff and attends Council.

QUALITY in FORMATION PANEL
Chair Professor Michael Wright

Revd Dr Ruth Ackroyd, Ven Sheila Watson, Dr Paula Gooder, Revd Paul Goodliff, Mr Sion Evans, Revd Fiona Thomas

Terms of reference
1 To oversee the transition to a single quality framework for inspection, validation, moderation and Reader moderation and to carry out the current processes of inspection, validation, moderation and Reader moderation as required.
2 To provide training and support for reviewers involved in the current and future processes.

NATIONAL STRUCTURES

FINANCE PANEL

Chair Prof John Craven

Mr Tim Allen, Mr John Butler, Mr Richard Finlinson, Mrs Judith Nash

Terms of reference

The responsibility of the Finance Panel is to advise the Ministry Council on all aspects of its financial responsibility regarding the cost of ordinand training funded from Central Church Funds. Specifically:

1 To advise on policy concerning the location, establishment, inspection and financial support of theological colleges and courses;

2 To prepare and administer the Training Budget, and to advise on the financial support of candidates.

CANDIDATES PANEL

Chair Rt Revd Mark Bryant (*Bishop of Jarrow*)

Canon Katrina Barnes, Canon Christine Bullimore, Canon Sam Corley, Revd Dr James Gardom, Miss Caulene Herbert, Mrs Susan Knowles, Revd Preb Dr Brian Leathard, Revd Gary Renison, Sister Edith Margaret CHN, Revd Tim Sledge, Canon James Stewart, Dr Yvonne Warren, Canon Brian Watchom, Mr Hugh Wright

Terms of reference

1 To advise sponsoring bishops on:

(1) the reduction or lengthening of candidates' training

(2) the transferral of candidates from one training institution to another

(3) the return of candidates to training after a break of more than three months

(4) the suitability of candidates for transfer of category of ministry or change of focus of ministry

(5) the suitability of ministers from other denominations to be ministers in the Church of England

(6) candidates' potential to be theological educators

2 To undertake other work in relation to recruitment and selection

RESEARCH DEGREES PANEL

Chair Canon Dr Judith Maltby

Revd Prof William Horbury, Revd Prof Ben Quash, Prof Andrew Wright, Revd Prof Simon Oliver

Terms of reference

1 To give permission to ordinands seen as potential theological educators to study for research degrees (MPhil, PhD etc) outside of Bishops' Regulations for Training as part of pre-ordination training.

2 To allocate its budget to pay for, or contribute to, the additional costs of such training.

DEPLOYMENT

Members of the Ministry Division work with colleagues in advising the Ministry Council on contemporary and future clergy deployment and assist senior staff in dioceses in their workforce planning.

COMMITTEE FOR MINISTRY OF AND AMONG DEAF AND DISABLED PEOPLE

Chair Rt Revd Nicholas Reade (*Bishop of Blackburn*)

Vice Chair Ven Cherry Vann

Mrs Penny Beschizza, Revd Catherine Carlyon, Revd David Huntley, Revd Eva McIntrye, Mrs Gail Robinson, Revd Bob Shrine, Mrs Alison Wynne, Revd Ruth Yeoman

The functions of the Committee include:

1 To monitor and advise on the progress of sector and chaplaincy ministries among deaf and disabled people within the total ministry of the Church, in consultation with those responsible for specific areas.

2 To encourage and strengthen the participation of deaf people in the life and witness of the Church, to represent the views of deaf people to the Church and of the Church to deaf people, and to support the work of the chaplains.

3 To report regularly through the Ministry Council to the Archbishops' Council on the work of the Committee.

4 To advise the Central Bodies and the dioceses on matters related to general disability issues, especially the implementation of the Disability Discrimination Act as it applies to the Church.

Following elections to the General Synod in October 2010, membership of these bodies is uncertain at the time of going to press. Please refer to the Secretary of the body in question for current membership.

RECENT MINISTRY DIVISION PUBLICATIONS

Ministry in the Church of England

In association with The Ecclesiastical Law Society
Canon Law for the Newly Ordained (2nd Ed)
Supporting the Ministry of Retired Clergy

The 38th Report of the Central Stipends Authority
Dignity at Work: Working to reduce incidents of bullying and harassment
Drawn Together: The formation of the Yorkshire Regional Training Partnership

Reader Upbeat: revised report

Opening Doors: Guidelines and introductory DVD – Ministry with people with learning difficulties and people on the autistic spectrum

Clergy Couples Guidance
Criteria for Selection for the Ordained Ministry in the Church of England

BISHOPS' REGULATIONS FOR TRAINING SELECTION FOR ORDAINED MINISTRY

1 Candidates should be commended in the first place by someone who has pastoral responsibility for them to the Diocesan Director of Ordinands. Before being accepted for training, they are required:

i) to have the necessary educational qualifications for or show that they have the potential to benefit from a formal course of training;
ii) to satisfy medical requirements;
iii) to be sponsored by their bishop for attendance at a Bishops' Advisory Panel.

2 Candidates for ordained ministry will be sponsored for a Bishops' Advisory Panel under the single category of 'ordained ministry'.

3 Central Church funds for pre-ordination/licensing training will be available for the pre-ordination phase of training:

(1) to those candidates who have attended a Bishops' Advisory Panel
(2) where the training pathway lies within the parameters of these regulations
(3) where the pathway comprises either (*a*) an approved route or combination of routes approved by the Ministry Division or (*b*) where an individual training plan for a candidate which has been approved by the Ministry Division, through the Candidate's Panel or the Research Degrees Panel.

4 If sponsoring papers envisage an incumbent status post in the future then the candidate's training may include access to college, course or a combination of these. Where candidates can demonstrate a high level of academic aptitude (normally through having a 2.1 in a first degree or equivalent), the pathway can include the departmental theology degrees in theological faculties where these are part of routes approved by the Ministry Division.

5 If an assistant ministry is envisaged then the candidate's training will normally be in course-type training. In addition there will be the option for the negotiation for elements of college-type or OLM-type training where this can be negotiated and financed within the RTP or region.

6 If the envisaged focus of ministry is OLM/locally deployed, then normally the candidate will train on the diocese's OLM scheme or local ministry pathway. In addition there will be an option for the negotiation for elements of college-type or course-type training where this can be negotiated and financed within the RTP or region.

7 The expected levels of attainment are set out in the Learning Outcomes at the point of ordination, on completion of IME and, where appropriate, for those seeking a post of incumbent status or equivalent.

8 In Higher Education terms, the normal minimum level of attainment at the point of ordination is diploma level. In this context 'diploma level' means attainment in both ministerial formation and theological learning. OLM/locally deployed ministry candidates should be working towards or complete Level 2 or equivalent.

9 Two years full-time and three years part-time for formation and education will act as a starting point in terms of expectation about training in the pre-ordination phase.

10 The normal expectation will be that candidates will make the maximum use of both prior learning and IME4–7 to ensure they reach the highest appropriate level of attainment appropriate for them (normal minimum of diploma level but also higher levels as appropriate).

11 This approach to choice of pathways applies to all candidates irrespective of age. However, where candidates are 55 or over at the point of entry into training, the ordaining bishop has discretion over the final form of the training.

12 Access to types and length of training should normally fall within the bands set out in the points system the current version of which is available from the Ministry Division.

13 Where a diocese wishes for a candidate to train outside Bishops' Regulations, it should make a case to the Ministry Division (see 3. (3) above).

GRANTS

Candidates who have been recommended for training are eligible for financial help from Church funds. Details about grants can be obtained from the Grants Officer, Ministry Division, Church House, Great Smith St, London SW1P 3AZ.

For **Theological Colleges** *and* **Regional Courses** *see also* pages 239–240.

The Central Readers' Council

Patron HRH The Duke of Edinburgh

Presidents The Archbishops of Canterbury and York

Chair Rt Revd Robert Paterson (*Bishop of Sodor and Man*)

Vice-Chair Canon Chrysogon Bamber

Secretary Dr Alan Wakely *Tel:* 01353 775132
email: crcsec@hallarn.com

Associate Secretary Jenny Macpherson
Tel: 020 7898 1401
email: jennie.macpherson@churchofengland.org

National Consultant for Quality in Reader Education
Mrs Sue Hart *Tel:* 0191 252 3941
email: harts@sky.com

National Consultant for Reader Selection Mr Nick Daunt *Tel:* 01695 632326
email: nickdaunt@lineone.net

National Consultant for Reader CMD Ms Lynn Comer *Tel:* 01904 656295
*email:*lynncomer@yorkdiocese.org

Editor of 'The Reader' Revd Heather Fenton
Tel: 01490 412169
email: reader.editor@btconnect.com

MEMBERS

The CRC Executive Committee is elected for a five-year term co-terminous with General Synod. In addition to the Chair, Vice-Chair and all the officers listed above, the Committee consists of:

Two Wardens
Ven John Reed, Revd Dr Christopher Bracegirdle
Reader representatives
Dr Marion Gray, Mrs Jennifer Williams, Miss Gloria Cadman, Mr Andy Lie
Treasurer
Mrs Carol Lidgett

The Central Readers' Council (CRC) works to enhance the contribution of Readers to the overall ministry of the Church, particularly to encourage the most effective integration with other forms of ministry, ordained and lay. It works in cooperation with the Ministry Division which moderates and coordinates the training of Reader candidates. CRC arranges national conferences for Readers, provides a forum for the exchange of ideas between dioceses on Reader matters and publishes a quarterly magazine, *The Reader*.

CRC is a registered charity, which derives its income mostly from capitation grants made by diocesan Readers' boards. It has its origins in the revival of Reader ministry in the Church of England in 1866 and particularly in the Central Readers' Board, which was granted a constitution by the Archbishops in 1921. CRC today is the immediate successor to the Central Readers' Conference, under a new constitution adopted in 2002, and revised in 2007 and 2010.

CRC has three representatives from each diocese, including the Warden and Secretary of Readers, and one representative from each of the Armed Forces. Any Reader appointed to a Ministry Division committee is *ex officio* a member of CRC. A non-voting observer is invited from the Deaf Readers and Pastoral Assistants Association, the Church of Ireland, the Scottish Episcopal Church and each of the dioceses of the Church in Wales. The annual general meeting is held in March/April each year.

MISSION AND PUBLIC AFFAIRS DIVISION

Mission and Public Affairs Council

Chairman Mr Philip Fletcher

Vice-Chairs: Rt Revd Michael Hill (*Bishop of Bristol*); Rt Revd Richard Atkinson (*Bishop of Bedford*)

Director Revd Dr Malcolm Brown
Tel: 020 7898 1468
email: malcolm.brown@churchofengland.org

MISSION AND PUBLIC AFFAIRS COUNCIL

FUNCTIONS OF THE COUNCIL
The functions of the Council shall be:

(a) To advise the Archbishops' Council, the General Synod and the House of Bishops on matters within the Council's remit;
(b) To work with dioceses, relevant diocesan networks and the Church's voluntary societies on matters within its remit;
(c) To relate to and cooperate with appropriate bodies within the churches of Britain and Ireland and the ecumenical instruments of CTBI and CTE;
(d) To take lead responsibility in relating to other Churches of the Anglican Communion and the Anglican Consultative Council, its Commissions and Networks, on issues relating to the Church's mission and role in public life;
(e) To relate to government departments and voluntary bodies relevant to its work.

In discharging its functions, the MPA Council shall include within its remit the following areas:

(i) the Church's engagement with social, ethical, political, environmental issues and work for justice and peace at local, national and international levels;
(ii) mission and evangelism; the Church of England's responsibilities for world mission and development; inter faith relations; and theological and missiological reflection on them;
(iii) the Church's mission and ministry (in liaison with Ministry Division) in urban and rural areas;
(iv) the Church's responsibility to confront the reality of racism in its own life and in society;
(v) the support of minority ethnic Christians in the Church of England, and their contribution to its life and witness;
(vi) the work of Hospital Chaplaincy and the Church's relation to the Department of Health, the National Health Service and Trusts and the provision of professional training and Continuing Professional Education for Chaplains.

MEMBERS
The Council is constituted of:

Chair Mr Philip Fletcher
Vice Chairs Rt Revd Richard Atkinson, Rt Revd Michael Hill
General Synod elected members:
Revd Duncan Dormor, Revd Richard Hibbert, Dr Lindsay Newcombe, Mr Clive Scowen, Dr Anna Thomas-Betts, Revd Canon Dr Dagmar Winter
Professor the Revd Nigel Biggar (Appointed), Revd Dr Victoria Johnson (Appointed)
Ven Daniel Kajumba (Chair of CMEAC, Co-opted)

STAFF
Director Revd Dr Malcolm Brown
Tel: 020 7898 1468
email: malcolm.brown@churchofengland.org
Parliamentary Secreatary Mr Richard Chapman
Tel: 020 7898 1438
email: richard.chapman@churchofengland.org

Deputy Parliamentary Secretary Mr Simon Stanley
Tel: 020 7898 1478
email: simon.stanley@churchofengland.org

Home Affairs Vacancy *Tel:* 020 7898 1531

International and Development Affairs Dr Charles Reed *Tel:* 020 7898 1533
email: charles.reed@churchofengland.org

Marriage and Family Policy Jo Winn-Smith
Tel: 020 7898 1535
email: jo.winn-smith@churchofengland.org

Medical Ethics, Health and Social Care Policy Revd Dr Brendan McCarthy *Tel:* 020 7898 1523
*email:*brendan.maccarthy@churchofengland.org

Economic and Social Affairs Tom Sefton
Tel: 020 7898 1446
email: tom.sefton@churchofengland.org

Adviser for Minority Ethnic Anglican Concerns Vacancy *Tel:* 020 7898 1442
Fax: 020 7898 1431

World Mission Policy Adviser Canon Janice Price
Tel: 020 7898 1328
email: janice.price@churchofengland.org

Adviser for Mission Theology, Alternative Spiritualities and New Religious Movements Dr Anne Richards *Tel:* 020 7898 1444
email: anne.richards@churchofengland.org

National Adviser for Mission and Evangelism Dr Rachel Jordan *Tel:* 020 7898 1436
email: rachel.jordan@churchofengland.org

National Inter Faith Relations Adviser Revd Dr Toby Howarth *Tel:* 020 7898 1477
email: toby.howarth@churchofengland.org

National Rural Officer Canon Dr Jill Hopkinson
Tel: 024 7685 3073
Fax: 024 7669 6460
email: jillh@arthurrankcentre.org.uk

Hospital Chaplaincies Administrator Miss Mary Ingledew *Tel:* 020 7898 1895
email: mary.ingledew@churchofengland.org

All staff are based in Church House, Westminster with the following exception: the office of the National Rural Officer is at the Arthur Rank Centre, Stoneleigh Park, Warwickshire CV8 2LZ. The National Inter Faith Relations Adviser is based at Lambeth Palace.

COMMITTEE FOR MINORITY ETHNIC ANGLICAN CONCERNS
Chair Ven Daniel Kajumba
Adviser Vacancy
The principal tasks of the Committee are to monitor and make recommendations about issues which arise or which ought to arise in the context of the work of the Archbishops' Council and its Divisions and of the General Synod itself, as far as they have policy implications for minority ethnic groups within the Church and the wider community; and to assist the Bishops and their dioceses in developing diocesan-wide strategies for combating racial bias within the Church and in society, encouraging them to make the problem of racism a priority concern in their programmes and to circulate the best analyses of racism, including theological analyses.

GROUPS AND PANELS OF THE MPA COUNCIL
The Council currently has the following working groups or panels. Those which are ecumenical or formally constituted with other agencies, are described in greater detail.

CofE: World Mission and Anglican Communion Panel
Chairman Rt Revd Michael Hill (*Bishop of Bristol*)

Secretary Canon Janice Price *Tel:* 020 7898 1328
email: janice.price@churchofengland.org

The CofE: World Mission and Anglican Communion Panel is a partnership between the General Synod and the World Mission Agencies of the Church of England drawing its members from the General Synod, the Mission Agencies, representatives of Diocesan Companion Links, Associate Members and our ecumenical partners. There are eleven full partner Agencies: Church Army, the Church's Ministry among Jewish People (CMJ), Church Mission Society (CMS), Church Pastoral Aid Society (CPAS), Crosslinks, Intercontinental Church Society (ICS), The Mission to Seafarers, The Mothers' Union, the Society for Promoting Christian Knowledge (SPCK) and the United Society for the Propagation of the Gospel (USPG). There are over 20 Associate Members.

Its main tasks are concerned with the Church of England's role in furthering partnership in mission within the Anglican Communion; supporting the work of Diocesan Companion Links; and with coordinating the policies and selected tasks of the Church of England's World Mission Agencies. It has an advisory role in enabling English dioceses and General Synod to see their way more clearly towards their participation in world mission as members of the Anglican Communion and ecumenically.

Mission Theological Advisory Group (MTAG)
Co-Chairman (with Revd Prof John Drane) Rt Revd Dr Brian Castle *(Bishop of Tonbridge)*
Secretary Dr Anne Richards *Tel:* 020 7898 1444
email: anne.richards@churchofengland.org

The ecumenical Mission Theological Advisory Group is composed of nominees from the Mission and Public Affairs Division of the Archbishops' Council and the Global Mission Network (GMN) of Churches Together in Britain and Ireland (CTBI). It is concerned with the theology of mission as a resource for the churches' engagement with the world, and deals with theological issues referred to it by the participating bodies.

Presence and Engagement Task Group
Chairman Rt Revd Tony Robinson (*Bishop of Pontefract*)
Secretary Revd Dr Toby Howarth
Tel: 020 7898 1477
email: toby.howarth@churchofengland.org

Rural Affairs Group
Chair Rt Revd James Bell (*Bishop of Knaresborough*)

Secretary Canon Dr Jill Hopkinson
Office The Arthur Rank Centre, Stoneleigh Park, Warwickshire CV8 2LZ *Tel:* 024 7685 3073
Fax: 024 7669 6460
email: jillh@arthurrankcentre.org.uk

EDUCATION DIVISION

Transforming Church and Community through Education and Learning

THE BOARD OF EDUCATION

The Board of Education's Constitution (as laid down by General Synod) sets out three main functions: to advise the General Synod and the Archbishops' Council on all matters relating to education; to advise the dioceses similarly; to take action in the field of education (in the name of the Church of England, the Archbishops' Council and the General Synod) on such occasion as is required.

The Board of Education meets twice a year, in April and October. Agendas cover the full range of education contexts within which the Church is active, developing policy and strategy and managing ingoing projects and work. Board members, diocesan education staff and Church of England secondary schools and academies receive a regular electronic bulletin about the issues being addressed by the Education Division staff providing regular reports and seeking responses to consultations.

Chair Rt Revd John Pritchard (*Bishop of Oxford*)

EDUCATION DIVISION STAFF

Chief Education Officer and Head of the Education Division Revd Janina Ainsworth
Tel: 020 7898 1500

National Adviser for Higher Education and Chaplaincy Revd Dr Stephen Heap *Tel:* 020 7898 1513
email: stephen.heap@churchofengland.org

National Further Education and post 16 Adviser
Tel: 020 7898 1517

Head of School Effectiveness Mrs Nicola Sylvester
Tel: 020 7898 1490
email: nicola.sylvester@churchofengland.org

Head of School Policy Revd Nigel Genders
Tel: 020 7898 1789
email: nigel.genders@churchofengland.org

National Schools Support Officer Mrs Liz Carter
Tel: 020 7898 1515
email: liz.carter@churchofengland.org

National Going for Growth (Children and Youth) Adviser Ms Mary Hawes Tel: 020 7898 1504
email: mary.hawes@churchofengland.org

National Adult Education and Lay Development Adviser Miss Joanna Cox *Tel:* 020 7898 1511
email: joanna.cox@churchofengland.org

Business and Support Manager Mrs Cheryl Payne
Tel: 020 7898 1501
email: cheryl.payne@churchofengland.org

Office Church House, Great Smith St, London SW1P 3AZ *Tel:* 020 7898 1501
Fax: 020 7898 1520

THE WORK OF THE EDUCATION DIVISION

The work of the Education Division embraces four main aspects which support activity at national, diocesan, parish and school level. The four aspects are:

- **Engaging with national institutions** through ensuring a high profile and working closely with Government and key organizations.
- **Growing the Church's mission** by increasing the opportunities for children, young people and students to encounter the Christian faith. In part this is achieved by increasing the number of designated schools and organizations and developing their Christian distinctiveness.
- **Professional support and nurture** by supporting high professional standards, providing high quality support and advice and achieving the best quality outcomes for the people the Division serves.
- **Research, development and evaluation** through a co-ordinated research programme and maintaining databases which inform the work.

The Division operates in four main areas, with overall leadership provided by the Chief Education Officer.

1. developing the Church's presence and witness in **higher education** by:

- developing, implementing and monitoring policy for the Church of England in relation to higher education
- stimulating and developing practical concern in student and university affairs – a concern both for the life of higher education institutions, their ethical, social, spiritual and religious concerns, and for the individuals who work and study in the sector

- liaison and partnership with national bodies, including the Department for Business, Innovation, and Skills, the Higher Education Funding Council, representative university groups, ecumenical and other faith bodies
- supporting and developing the network of chaplains in higher education by providing training and ongoing communication.

2. In **further education** the key role is strategic thinking and planning with the aim of developing the Church's presence and witness within FE colleges and the wider post-16 sector by:

- engaging with the Government's programme of reform by monitoring policy and contributing to improvement strategies
- increasing the Church's involvement through establishing and supporting chaplaincy and college/faith partnerships
- helping to shape the sector's understanding of spiritual and moral development for staff and students, fostering shared human values and dialogue and promoting a more holistic educational experience for all students
- working with a range of ecumenical and interfaith partners.
- resourcing and supporting the growing number of chaplains in schools.

The Division is involved in the work of the 11 **Universities and university colleges** founded as a direct result of the Church's role as first provider of mass schooling. All are highly diverse organizations which retain a commitment to teacher education alongside a wide portfolio of courses, including (for most) significant departments of theology and religious studies. In 2009 all bar one of the 11 institutions, along with 3 Roman Catholic institutions, signed a Memorandum of Understanding committing them to the outworking of the Christian foundation in the 21st century.

3. Informal learning and nurture of **children, young people** and **adults** is guided by *Going for Growth*, the formally adopted framework now entering the second phase of national work. *Going for Growth* provides three focuses of work at national level:

- working towards every child and young person having a life-enhancing encounter with the Christian faith and the person of Jesus Christ
- working for the transformation of communities, recognizing and enabling the capacity of children and young people to be the agents of change for themselves and for others
- professional support and challenge of all those working with children and young people in the name of the church.

Support and development of the diocesan youth and children's officers is provided through training and ongoing communication, principally through the *Going for Growth* website and the *Child in the Midst* mailing.

The work with **lay discipleship and shared ministry** involves consultancy, support, research and development to enhance the capacity and provision of adult Christian formation and lifelong leaning in the Church. The work seeks to:

- promote the development of theological education for lay people
- provide guidance on developing volunteer, lay and shared ministry, and to resource new diocesan developments in formal lay ministry and patterns of integrated training, in association with the Ministry Division
- improve the quality of adult and lifelong learning through training the trainers, promoting partnerships, researching and disseminating good practice and developing new initiatives encouraging Christian discipleship in the Church and the world.

4. Work with **schools** is carried out by both the Board and the National Society, furthering the development and effectiveness of the Church's 4,800 academies, primary and secondary schools. In 2012 the report *The Church School of the Future* laid out the agenda for church schools in the light of far-reaching changes to the education system in England.

The ongoing work of the Division includes:

- monitoring the impact of legislation, capital programmes and the various programmes for expanding and changing the school system
- increasing the number of Church of England schools especially through the Academies programme
- enabling DBEs to grow their provision through professional support and guidance, releasing and accessing funds for new developments
- support for governors and employers of the school workforce
- supporting the implementation of succession strategies for school leadership and research into the performance and characteristics of church schools
- identifying, disseminating and sharing the best practice within the diverse national family of Anglican schools
- developing and maintaining the Statutory Inspection of Anglican Schools (SIAS) Section 48 framework, training and quality assuring inspectors
- providing training and research for school improvement in church schools
- resourcing high quality Religious Education and collective worship
- developing the whole curriculum for church schools and for the spiritual, moral, social and cultural development and wellbeing of children and young people.

CATHEDRAL AND CHURCH BUILDINGS DIVISION

This area of the Archbishops' Council's responsibilities relates to the Church's concern with cathedral and church buildings and related matters.

Cathedral and Church Buildings Division

Chairman Rt Revd and Rt Hon Dr Richard Chartres KCVO DD FSA

Director Janet Gough

The Cathedral and Church Buildings Division is the Church of England's national resource supporting the conservation and development of the Church of England's 42 cathedrals and 16,000 parish churches for worship, mission and community engagement. The Church of England has responsibility for 12,500 listed buildings (including 45 per cent of England's Grade I buildings), while many churchyards are an important ecological resource.

We provide the secretariat for three statutory bodies: the Church Buildings Council (CBC), the Council's Statutory Advisory Committee (SAC) on Closed and Closing Churches and the Cathedrals Fabric Commission for England (CFCE). The Director of the Division is Secretary to the CBC and CFCE.

We campaign on behalf of cathedral and church buildings, with the Government, Church, English Heritage and heritage bodies to keep church buildings in their vision and to ensure church buildings' interests are taken into account.

We aim to be strategic, to add value to the work of cathedrals, dioceses and parishes where national initiatives can make a significant difference and always to be outward-looking and service-orientated.

Shrinking the Footprint is the Church's national campaign working with the Church's 44 dioceses to reduce their carbon footprint by 80 per cent by 2050 and raise awareness of environmental issues. *Shrinking the Footprint* is a cross-divisional campaign involving Cathedral and Church Buildings Division and Mission and Public Affairs.

ChurchCare, www.ChurchCare.co.uk, is the Division's website. Completely relaunched in 2012 thanks to the generous sponsorship of Ecclesiastical Insurance Group, it is a single resource for churches, cathedrals and *Shrinking the Footprint*. ChurchCare supports all those in parishes, dioceses and cathedrals caring for their buildings today and for the enjoyment of future generations. It is the comprehensive source of information for everyone managing a church building. The ChurchCare E-Bulletin is distributed three times a year, keeping all subscribers up to date on church matters (visit www.ChurchCare.co.uk for a free subscription). The Division participates in many training events supporting church buildings and *Shrinking the Footprint*. In 2012 the Division ran three keynote seminars in response to demand: on *New work in churches and cathedrals* at Lambeth Palace, *Heating without the hot air* – the future of heating in church buildings, hosted at the Mercers' Hall and on Monuments at Risk at Cheyneygates, Westminster Abbey

In 2012, in response to the Chancellor of the Exchequer's introduction of VAT to alterations to listed buildings the Bishop of London, the Second Church Estates Commissioner, the Chair of the Church Buildings Council and the Director of the Division negotiated an additional £30 million for the Listed Places of Worship Grant Scheme to ensure repairs and alterations to all listed church buildings will not be impacted by the VAT change. The Division, led by the Chair of the Church Buildings Council, is campaigning to tighten the legislation to prevent metal theft; this is the biggest single issue facing church buildings and has already affected a third of our buildings. The Division has successfully reduced the impact of the High Speed Rail Link between London and Birmingham on the churches in its vicinity.

The policy underlying all our activities is to keep church buildings open, serving the worshipping community and wider society. In 2012 the Division launched the Open and Sustainable Churches campaign to support and encourage congregations, dioceses and archdeacons in sharing their buildings and engaging with community, cultural, and commercial interests and groups, thereby gaining more financial and social capital to further mission and maintain the Church's priceless heritage. Guidance and tools for achieving this are being developed and can be accessed at www.ChurchCare.co.uk

The Division campaigns for greater financial support for church buildings, in the first instance from public sources. It also raises funds for distribution to cathedrals and church buildings for the conservation of fabric and the nation's ecclesiastical decorative and fine art heritage contained within cathedrals and church buildings. Two new funds, ChurchCare (charity number 114888066) and the English Cathedrals Fund, have been set up as vehicles for charitable donations including from overseas, to support these programmes. Since 2000 we have distributed over £7 million for church buildings projects.

The Division maintains a library of books and other material dedicated solely to ecclesiastical architecture, art, design and liturgy available for readers interested in those areas.

The Church Buildings Council

Chairman Mrs Anne Sloman OBE

MEMBERS
Revd Canon Michael Ainsworth, Mr Tim Allen, Ms Louise Bainbridge, Ven Tim Barker, Dr John Beal, Revd Preb Philippa Boardman MBE, Revd Stephen Brookes, Mr Quinton Carroll, Mr John Coates, Revd Nigel Cooper, Revd Jeremy Fletcher, Mr Geoffrey Hunter, Mrs Sylvia Johnson, Dr Neil Moat, Mrs Valerie Owen, Mrs Sarah Quail, Revd Tony Redman, Miss Anne Riches OBE, Mr Henry Russell OBE, Dr Hilary Taylor and Dr Alan Thurlow.

The Church Buildings Council (CBC) advises diocesan chancellors and Diocesan Advisory Committees on faculty applications, and clergy, churchwardens, architects and others responsible for church buildings and their contents on their care, use and development. We concentrate on proposals that have a high impact on significant buildings, parts of buildings or their contents that are or may become the subject of faculty applications e.g. the construction of church extensions, re-ordering schemes, the sale of church furnishings, the partial demolition of churches, the conservation of significant furnishings and related archaeological work. The CBC offers guidance on preparing Quinquennial Inspections reports and Statements of Significance and Need.

The CBC aims to concentrate on developing policies where value can be added with initiatives from the centre. In the past year these included a policy on treasures to help and encourage churches to keep and celebrate their treasures, detailed negotiations with DEFRA and Natural England on bat mitigation measures, a competition to design a new church chair to emphasise the importance of quality replacements when pews are removed and, following the publication of last year's policy on commissioning new art in churches, a competition with a cash prize for the best conceived commission.

The CBC also advises the Archbishops' Council on all matters relating to the use, care and planning or design of places of worship, their curtilages and contents; acts on the Council's behalf in contacts with government departments and other bodies and in negotiations with professional bodies over church inspection and repair; and assists in the review or revision of legislation relating to church buildings and their contents.

The CBC maintains contact with Diocesan Advisory Committees through regular circulation of information, by an annual meeting for Chairmen, Secretaries and other members and by visits. The Chair of the CBC and Director of the Division have regular meetings with the Dean of the Arches and the Chair of the Ecclesiastical Judges Association and contribute to their biennial conferences.

The CBC's specialist committees offer expert advice on conservation matters. They consist of experts from leading institutions including the V&A, Royal Collection and the British Museum. The CBC administers funds (generously provided by charitable bodies, including the Pilgrim Trust) for the conservation of furnishings and works of art in churches; for example a grant from the Headley Foundation has funded a project to evaluate and conserve the internationally significant collection of East Anglian Rood Screens. The Committees also provide specialist advice to the Heritage Lottery Fund and other grant-making bodies.

Most types of furnishings found in church buildings are eligible for consideration for the grants programme. They include: organs, bells, clocks, textiles, timberwork, monuments, metalwork and plate, historic books and manuscripts, wall paintings, paintings and stained glass. The repair of historic fabric of parish churches and their churchyard structures is also eligible.

In addition, under an agreement reached with the Wolfson Foundation, the Council considers applications for grant aid towards fabric repairs for Grade I and Grade II* Anglican churches in England, Scotland and Wales. More information about these grants and applications can be made online at www.ChurchCare.co.uk

In 2011, 23 churches were closed. The CBC, through its SAC, advises the Church Commissioners and others on the interest, quality and importance of closed and closing churches and their contents, and the alteration and conversion of churches to alternative use, working closely with government and local authorities of Church and State. The CBC provides Diocesan Pastoral Committees with detailed reports about the architectural and historic qualities of churches likely to be closed for regular worship.

The Cathedrals Fabric Commission for England

Chairman Rt Hon Frank Field MP

Vice-Chairman Miss Jennie Page CBE

MEMBERS
Mr Tim Allen, Very Revd James Atwell (*Dean of Winchester*), David Baker OBE, Canon Peter Bruinvels (Guildford), Mr Richard Carr-Archer, Mr John Carter RA Mr Geoffrey Clifton, Prof Paul Crossley, Canon Jeremy Davies, Mrs Mary Durlacher, Revd Canon Perran Gay (Truro), Revd Canon Christopher Irvine (Canterbury), Very Revd Peter Judd (*Dean of Chelmsford*), Mrs Ulrike Knox, Mrs Judith Leigh, Dr William McVicker, Dr Robyn Pender, Rt Revd Stephen Platten (*Bishop of Wakefield*), Mrs Carol Pyrah, Mr Nicholas Rank, Mr Dickon Robinson, Revd Canon Celia Thomson.

The Cathedrals Fabric Commission oversees the Church's own system of controls under the Care of Cathedrals (Measure 2011). Before implementing any proposals which would materially affect the character of a cathedral building, its setting, or archaeological remains within its precinct, or an object of artistic, archaeological, architectural or historic interest owned by the Chapter, in its possession or to the possession of which it is entitled, the Dean and Chapter are required to get approval under the Measure, either from the Fabric Advisory Committee serving the cathedral or from the Commission itself.

The Commission also offers advice on matters relating to the architecture, archaeology, art and history of cathedrals and their precincts, landscape and environment, and publishes a range of guidance and advisory notes (available on www.ChurchCare.co.uk) and also run seminars and conferences for Fabric Advisory Committees and cathedral chapters and their professional advisers.

We run three grants programmes to assist Chapters in the care of their cathedral building and its historic contents:

1. **Major fabric repairs to Church of England cathedrals in England and the Isle of Man:** A partnership between the Cathedrals Fabric Commission, the Wolfson Foundation, the Pilgrim Trust and others, supporting cathedrals in carrying out essential and urgent fabric repair works.
2. **Repair and conservation of artworks and historic furnishings in Anglican cathedrals in England:** Supporting the conservation of monuments, historic timberwork, metalwork, church plate, textiles, stained glass, paintings and wall paintings, bells and bell frames, organs and their decorative cases, clocks, books and manuscripts.
3. **Preservation and improvements to the setting of ancient cathedrals, abbeys and greater churches in England, Wales, Scotland and Northern Ireland:** Cathedrals, abbeys and greater churches that substantially date from before 1714 are eligible for assistance with the preservation and improvement of their visual amenity. In 2011 £743,750 was awarded to 17 cathedral projects.

Details of the grant schemes can be found on www.ChurchCare.co.uk.

Staff of the Cathedral and Church Buildings Division

Director Janet Gough *Tel:* 020 7898 1887
email: janet.gough@churchofengland.org

Senior Cathedrals Officer and Deputy Secretary CFCE
Maggie Goodall *Tel:* 020 7898 1888
email: maggie.goodall@churchofengland.org

Cathedrals Officer Anne Locke
Tel: 020 7898 1862
email: anne.locke@churchofengland.org

Senior Advisor, Closed Churches Dr Jeffrey West
Tel: 020 7898 1872
email: jeffrey.west@churchofengland.org

Casework Officer, Closed Churches Anne McNair
Tel: 020 7898 1871
email: anne.mcnair@churchofengland.org

Casework Officer and *Special Projects*
Catherine Townsend *Tel:* 020 7898 1883
email: catherine.townsend@churchofengland.org

Senior Churches Officer Jonathan Goodchild
Tel: 020 7898 1883
email: jonathan.goodchild@churchofengland.org

Major Project Officer Dr Joseph Elders
Tel: 020 7898 1875
email: joseph.elders@churchofengland.org

Casework Officer Christina Emerson
Tel: 020 7898 1864
email: christina.emerson@churchofengland.org
(*During maternity leave of Jude Johncock*)

Divisional Support Officer Diana Coulter
Tel: 020 7898 1860
email: diana.coulter@churchofengland.org

Senior Conservation Officer – Budget and Training
Dr David Knight *Tel:* 020 7898 1886
email: david.knight@churchofengland.org

Senior Conservation Officer – Grants and Development Dr Pedro Gaspar *Tel:* 020 7898 1889
email: pedro.gaspar@churchofengland.org

Environmental Policy Officer Ruth Knight
Tel: 020 7898 1865
email: ruth.knight@churchofengland.org

ChurchCare Support Officer Ben Greener
Tel: 020 7898 1886
email: ben.greener@churchofengland.org

Shrinking the Footprint Audit Project Manager Kate Symonds *Tel:* 020 7898 1484
email: kate.symonds@churchofengland.org

Diocesan Environment Officers
Blackburn Canon Ed Saville *Tel:* 01254 503275
email: ed.saville@blackburn.anglican.org
Bradford Dr Gerald W. Partridge
Tel: 07768 312466
email: gerald.partridge@bradford.anglican.org
Bath and Wells David Maggs *Tel:* 01749 685119
email: david.maggs@bathwells.anglican.org
Bristol Simon Bale *Tel:* 0117 955 7430
email: simon@ccisr.org.uk
Canterbury Revd Canon Caroline Pinchbeck, Director, Communities and Partnership Network and Rural Life Adviser, Diocesan House, Lady Wootton's Green, Canterbury Kent CT1 1NQ
Tel: 01227 459401
email: cpinchbeck@diocant.org
Carlisle Revd Professor Ian N. James
Tel: 01229 718223
email: dr.i.n.james@btinternet.com
Chester Mrs Elizabeth (Liz) Gentil
email: liz.gentil@hotmail.co.uk
Chichester Revd Barry North, Adviser for Church in Society *Tel:* 01273 421021
email: barry.north@chichester.anglican.org
and Revd Dr Mark Betson, Joint Environment Officer *Tel:* 01403 891367
email: m.betson@clara.co.uk
Ely Revd Nigel Cooper *Tel:* 0845 196 2398
email: nigel.cooper@anglia.ac.uk
Europe Madeleine Holmes
email: madeleine@peladis.plus.com
Exeter Martyn Goss *Tel:* 01392 294924
email: martyn.goss@exeter.anglican.org
Gloucester Revd Dr Simon Topping
Tel: 0117 955 7430
email: simontopping@ccisr.org.uk
Leicester Revd Andrew Quigley
Tel: 01858 410253
email: andrew@aquigley.wanadoo.co.uk
Lichfield Revd Paul Cawthorne
Tel: 01952 510333
email: paulcawthorne@tiscali.co.uk
Lincoln Terry Miller *Tel:* 01522 504072
email: t.miller@lincschaplaincy.org.uk
Liverpool Paul Beardwood *Tel:* 0151 932 1272
email: paul.beardwood@liverpool.anglican.org
London Brian Cuthbertson, Head of Environment and Sustainability *Tel:* 020 7932 1229
email: brian.cuthbertson@london.anglican.org
Oxford Matt Freer *Tel:* 01865 208745
email: environment@oxford.anglican.org
Web: oxford.anglican.org/environment | earthingfaith.org
Peterborough Dr Peter Brotherton
email: peter.brotherton@naturalengland.org.uk
Portsmouth Revd Andy Norris
Tel: 01489 572324
email: Environment@portsmouth.anglican.org
Ripon and Leeds Jemima Parker
Tel: 01423 569121
email: Jemima.parker@riponleedsdiocese.org.uk
Salisbury Canon Jean Coates *Tel:* 01305 852435
email: jean@coates.ctlconnect.co.uk
St Albans Helen Hutchison *Tel:* 01727 869645
email: helenhutchison@btopenworld.com
Southwell Revd David Fudger, Temporary DEO
Tel: 01623 640250 (church office)
email: mail@stpeters-mansfield.org.uk
York Graham Andrews, Archbishop's Advisor for the Environment *Tel:* 01904 699500
email: graham.andrews@yorkdiocese.org

SHARED SERVICES

Finance and Resources

Chief Finance Officer: Mr Ian Theodoreson
Tel: 020 7898 1795
email: ian.theodoreson@ian.theodoreson@churchofengland.org

Finance and Resources is a shared service function providing five levels of support to the NCIs and wider Church generally:

1. The Accounting Services Section is responsible for processing, recording and maintaining the prime books of account, banking, payments, payroll, (including Clergy Pay), management reporting, statutory financial reporting, budgeting and forecasting, securing assets and ensuring the bodies are legally compliant in terms of statutory reporting, tax and charity law.
2. The Financial Policy and Planning section provides financial information to help inform management decisions, including the production of financial policy advice and analysis.
3. The SAP support team is responsible for

managing the use of and controls within the NCIs SAP system.

4. The Strategy and Development Unit advises on resource allocation, evaluating the effectiveness of spending plans and measuring impact.
5. The work of the National Stewardship & Resources Officer involves supporting parishes and dioceses in developing mechanisms for effective giving and looking at better ways to manage expenditure through common working.

Accounting Services

Director of Accounting Services: Mr Paul Burrage
Tel: 020 7898 1677
email: paul.burrage@churchofengland.org

The Accounting Services Section provides accounting services principally for (the three largest NCIs) the Archbishops' Council, the Church Commissioners and the Church of England Pensions Board. It is responsible for payroll (including clergy pay), cash and treasury, processing, tax expertise (principally property and VAT related), and for the largest NCIs provides statutory financial accounting, management accounting, and support for budget setting and forecasts.

Financial Policy and Planning

Head of Financial Policy & Planning: Mr David White
Tel: 020 7898 1684
email: david.white@churchofengland.org

The Financial Policy Section supports the Archbishops' Council, Church Commissioners and Pensions Board in the development of financial policy and analysis, and in the monitoring and management of their finances. It works in close partnership with dioceses as well as departments across the organizations in order to provide financial analysis, advice and other information to help decision-making by trustees/members and senior managers. It calculates and communicates the apportionment of the Council's budget to dioceses.

The section supports the development of spending plans from the Church Commissioners' fund, including liaison with their actuaries. It seeks to ensure that the General Synod (through a Financial Memorandum) is aware of the significant financial implications of proposals before decisions are taken and contributes to the development of policy on financial matters across the Church. It also produces a financial overview of Church finances.

The department provides secretariat support for the Council's Finance Committee which is responsible for the management of the Council's financial business and advice and coordination on financial matters over the Church as a whole, its Investment Committee and the Inter-Diocesan Finance Forum. The latter meets twice a year, comprises three representatives of each diocese and provides an opportunity for consultation on remuneration policy, conditions of service, pensions policy, the Council's budget and apportionment, grants to dioceses for the support of mission and ministry and other issues with a financial perspective.

The section supports the work of the Church Commissioners[1] Assets Committee and staff level Assets Management Group. Key roles include the production of coordinated investment performance statistics and financial forecasts in respect of income, cashflow and longer term actuarial projection. It assists the Pensions Board in the financial management of the CHARM clergy retirement housing scheme.

SAP Support

Service Delivery Manager Sarah Jowett
Tel: 020 7898 1600
email: sarah.jowett@churchofengland.org

The SAP support team is responsible for managing the use of the NCIs SAP system, supporting the core modules of finance, real estate, purchasing, loans management and plant maintenance. The team works to ensure that users obtain maximum benefit from the opportunities SAP provides whilst at the same time maintaining the integrity of controls within the system.

The SAP team provides a helpdesk service for the Archbishops' Council, Church Commissioners and Church of England Pensions Board, dealing with technical changes to the system and user queries in relation to all modules.

Strategy and Development Unit

Head of Unit Mr Philip James
The role of the (Resource) Strategy and Development Unit is to undertake research and strategy development on behalf of the Church in respect of its mission resourcing (principally relating to those resources held at national level). A key part of the role is to ensure that the funds of the Church Commissioners are being used effectively to advance the spiritual and numerical growth of the Church. The Unit is also responsible for administering the Church and Community Fund.

Stewardship and Resources

National Stewardship and Resources Officer
Dr John Preston *Tel:* 020 7898 1540
email: john.preston@churchofengland.org

Through its Christian Stewardship Committee, the Archbishops' Council affirms the principles and practice of Christian stewardship as a part of discipleship. Stewardship advisers encourage church people to respond to God's love and generosity and resource God's mission through the Church by the discovery and use of human and financial resources. This is often focused on the giving of money – regularly, tax-effectively and in proportion to income.

Initiatives are promoted, support given and ideas exchanged between the diocesan members of the Christian stewardship network. There is a particular focus on identifying, documenting and resourcing elements of good practice, so that other dioceses and parishes can benefit from what is proven to be effective.

A national website to resource all those concerned with Christian giving, stewardship and parish finances is available at www.parishresources.org.uk. This contains a wide range of resources for parish-giving officers, treasurers, gift-aid secretaries and those who preach and teach on stewardship and generosity.

Through the Parish Buying initiative, all parts of the church are able to access national contracts which pool the Church's purchasing power. This not only aims to save money, but to save time and enable parishes and others to buy with confidence. This is supervised by a National Procurement Group, and can be accessed at www.parishresources.org.uk.

INTERNAL AUDITING DEPARTMENT

Director of Risk Management and Internal Audit
Mr Michael Cole *Tel:* 020 7898 1658
email: michael.cole@churchofengland.org

The Internal Auditing Department provides internal audit services to the Church Commissioners, the Church of England Pensions Board, the Archbishops' Council and the other National Church Institutions.

The department carries out risk-based internal audit assignments in accordance with the annual internal audit plan, approved by the Audit Committee, and also investigates particular issues that might arise from time to time.

The Internal Auditing Department coordinates and facilitates the risk management process and works with management to update operational and strategic risk registers. In addition it provides consultancy support to managers on matters of governance, risk and internal control.

INFORMATION TECHNOLOGY AND OFFICE SERVICES

Head of Information Technology and Office Services
Andy Budge *Tel:* 020 7898 1640

Office Church House, Great Smith St, London SW1P 3AZ
The Information Technology department provides and maintains the IT and Telecommunications infrastructure for the National Church Institutions, including IT systems implementation, integration and maintenance, as well as all aspects of PC desktop and network support and training. The department also provides central purchasing of IT equipment for the NCIs and some bishops' offices. Office Services includes reprographics, telephony, some central buying facilities across the NCIs and coordinates central meeting room bookings and catering.

LIBRARIES AND ARCHIVES

Director of Libraries, Archives & IT Mr Declan Kelly
Tel: 020 7898 1432

Address Church of England Record Centre, 15 Galleywall Rd, South Bermondsey, London SE16 3PB *Tel:* 020 7898 1030
email: archives@churchofengland.org
Web: www.lambethpalacelibrary.org

The Centre, which is a central service operated by the Church Commissioners, houses the non-current records of the Church Commissioners, the Archbishops' Council, the Church of England Pensions Board, the General Synod and the National Society, together with those of some ecumenical bodies. Its main purpose is to provide records management advice and low-cost off-site storage for the business records of the Central Church Bodies. The Centre also serves as an advisory point for queries concerning the archives of the Church of England. Enquiries are welcome; archive material can be seen at our Reading Room by prior appointment.

THE LEGAL OFFICE

The Legal Office of the National Institutions of the Church of England is responsible for providing legal advice and other services to the National Church Institutions. Its principal functions are:

- responsibility for the legislative programme of the General Synod;
- giving advice to the National Church Institutions and their respective committees and staff; and
- undertaking some transactional work for the National Church Institutions, especially the Church Commissioners and the Pensions Board.

Head of the Legal Office, Chief Legal Adviser to the Archbishops' Council, Registrar and Chief Legal Adviser to the General Synod and Official Solicitor to the Church Commissioners
Mr Stephen Slack *Tel:* 020 7898 1366
email: stephen.slack@churchofengland.org

Secretary Miss Judith Gracias *Tel:* 020 7898 1367
email: judith.gracias@churchofengland.org

Deputy Legal Adviser to the Archbishops' Council and the General Synod Revd Alexander McGregor
Tel: 020 7898 1748
email: alexander.mcgregor@churchofengland.org

Deputy Official Solicitor Ms Saira Salimi
Tel: 020 7898 1717
email: saira.salimi@churchofengland.org

Standing Counsel to the General Synod Sir Anthony Hammond QC *Tel:* 020 7898 1799
email: anthony.hammond@churchofengland.org

Secretary Miss Judith Gracias *Tel:* 020 7898 1367
email: judith.gracias@churchofengland.org
Office Church House, Great Smith St, London, SW1P 3AZ *Fax:* 020 7898 1718/1721
email: legal@churchofengland.org
DX: 148403 WESTMINSTER 5
Web: www.churchofengland.org/about-us/structure/churchlawlegis

COMMUNICATIONS OFFICE

Communication is central to the mission of the Church as *a Christian presence in every community*. The Communications Office serves the Church at every level, seeking to convey the vibrant life of the Church, and its vital role at the heart of society.

The Office serves all the National Church Institutions, General Synod and the House of Bishops, works closely with Lambeth Palace and Bishopthorpe, and supports the activities of diocesan communicators around the country.

Working to a 'mission-shaped communications' agenda, the Office seeks to ensure all its activities are mission-oriented, proactive, professional and integrated.

It works with all sections of the media, issuing information, assisting them in their coverage of the Church and providing a 24-hour media response service throughout the year. It also produces information to improve communications within the Church, including a regular Communications Update available via free email across the Church. Increasingly, the Office is making use of social media such as Twitter and Facebook.

The focus for the Church's role in public discussions involving media policy, the office liaises with the BBC, commercial broadcasters, and various government bodies. It also supports the Church's role in other public affairs issues, ensuring that the Church of England's voice is heard on key issues. In addition, it presents information to Parliament and other audiences on issues of concern, such as the cost of maintaining and extending the use of the Church's listed buildings, embryology laws and climate change. It also promotes the Church's national environmental campaign *Shrinking the Footprint* (www.shrinkingthefootprint.org).

A communications training programme offers a range of skills to equip the Church to communicate using the latest technologies. The full schedule and range of expert tutors can be seen at www.churchcommstraining.org. The Office led the relaunch of the Church of England's popular website, www.churchofengland.org as one of the first 'entry points' for information about the Church.

The Office is increasingly involved in promoting key mission opportunities such as major festivals, life's special occasions, especially weddings, and projects like *Say One for Me and Back to Church Sunday.*

The Communications Office also runs an enquiry service answering questions from the public.

Director of Communications Revd Arun Arora
Tel: 020 7898 1462
email: arun.arora@churchofengland.org

Head of Media Relations Steve Jenkins
Tel: 020 7898 1457
email: steve.jenkins@churchofengland.org

Senior Media Officer Louis Henderson
*Tel:*020 7898 1621
email: lou.henderson@churchofengland.org

Senior Media Officer Rachel Harden
Tel: 020 7898 1464
email: rachel.harden@churchofengland.org

Senior Communications Officer Nick Clarke
Tel: 020 7898 1459
email: nick.clarke@churchofengland.org

Office Church House, Great Smith St, London SW1P 3AZ *Tel:* 020 7898 1326
Fax: 020 7898 1636
Web: www.churchofengland.org

Diocesan Communicators Panel

Chairman Rt Revd Mark Rylands (*Bishop of Shrewsbury)*

Members Canon John Carter, Arun Kataria, Rachel Farmer, Anni Holden, Sarah Meyrick, Revd David Marshall, Marie Papworth, Michael Ford

Church House Publishing

Church House Publishing (CHP) is the official publisher to the Archbishops' Council and the General Synod. In addition to publishing *Common Worship*, CHP publishes resources to further the mission and enhance the reputation of the Church of England. Reference publications include *Crockford's Clerical Directory* and *The Church of England Year Book*. Both these publications are continually updated and you are welcome to send corrections to the addresses below. For up-to-date information visit our online catalogue at www.chpublishing.co.uk

On 30 June 2009, the Archbishops' Council signed an outsourcing agreement with Anglican charity Hymns Ancient & Modern Ltd. Under the agreement, the Council continues to publish a range of titles to support the ministry and mission of the Church under its Church House Publishing imprint, with Hymns Ancient & Modern (HA&M) acting as its production and marketing arm.

Director of Communications Revd Arun Arora
Tel: 020 7898 1462
email: arun.arora@churchofengland.org

Publishing Manager Dr Thomas Allain-Chapman
Tel: 020 7898 1450
email: thomas.allain-chapman@churchofengland.org

General Enquiries *Tel:* 01603 785923
Fax: 01603 785915
email: publishing@churchofengland.org
Web: www.chpublishing.co.uk

The Church of England Year Book
email: yearbook@churchofengland.org

Crockford's Clerical Directory
The Compiler, Crockford, Church House, Great Smith St, London SW1P 3AZ *Tel:* 020 7898 1012
Fax: 020 7898 1769
email: crockford@churchofengland.org

HUMAN RESOURCES DEPARTMENT

What we are here to do

The Human Resources (HR) department aims to facilitate the National Church Institutions (NCIs) and diocesan bishops in achieving their mission and business objectives by delivering efficient and cost-effective HR services, including support for recruitment, in relation to the 478 staff employed by the NCIs and the 140 staff of diocesan bishops. It also contracts with the Corporation of Church House for services in relation to their 40 staff. It works with the Ministry Division, the Legal Office and some dioceses to design, develop and implement the Church's strategy in relation to parochial clergy.

How we do it in relation to the NCIs

- Establishing a partnership culture and collaborative working between the employers and their people
- Creating a high-performance working environment where employees have role clarity and focus on delivery, learning and development
- Sustaining a diverse workforce and a fair and just workplace
- Working together in culturally aligned organizations
- Maximizing opportunities for employees and the organizations through strategic resourcing, succession planning and talent management
- Engaging with our customers to assist their articulation and our understanding of their needs and expectations to facilitate the successful delivery of their service
- Promoting a safe and healthy working environment
- Enabling, with others (particularly diocesan HR Advisers), bishops and dioceses to better support and develop their parochial clergy.

STAFF

Director of Human Resources Ms Su Morgan
Tel: 020 7898 1565
email: su.morgan@churchofengland.org

HR Senior Staff

Mr Peter Cunningham *HR Manager – Operations*
Tel: 020 7898 1182
email: peter.cunningham@churchofengland.org

Miss Leann Dawson *HR Manager – Clergy deployment and remuneration/Secretary to Remuneration and Conditions of Service Committee*
Tel: 020 7898 1751
email: leann.dawson@churchofengland.org

Ms Poli Shajko, *HR Manager/Diocesan Team Leader (based in Oxford Diocese)* *Tel:* 01865 208770
email: poli.shajko@churchofengland.org

Remuneration and Conditions of Service Committee

Chair Rt Revd John Packer (Bishop of Ripon and Leeds)

Rt Revd David Walker, Mrs Lesley Farrall, Revd Mary Gregory, the Venerable Ian Jagger, Mr Brian Newey, Revd Dr Philip Plyming, Mrs Susan Pope, Ms Stephanie Ridge, Mr Nigel Spraggins, Mr Brian Wilson

The Remuneration and Conditions of Service Committee meets four times a year and advises the Archbishops' Council and the House of Bishops on a strategy for ministry, with particular reference to the remuneration and conditions of service of those in authorized ministry. The Committee works in collaboration with dioceses, the Church Commissioners and the Church of England Pensions Board, and with ecumenical partners on the following matters:

(a) To produce, in partnership with dioceses, a framework of national policy for stipends and other related matters, and to advise dioceses as appropriate on such matters.

(b) To develop policy relating to pensions in collaboration with the Church of England Pensions Board and, where appropriate, the Church Commissioners.

(c) To promote, in partnership with dioceses, clear conditions of work for all licensed ministers.

(d) To make recommendations about the scope, structure and level of parochial fees.

(e) To monitor and advise in consultation with interested parties on sector and chaplaincy ministries within the total ministry of the Church.

(f) To work in collaboration with dioceses and, as far as possible, with ecumenical partners in the provision and development of continuing ministerial education for and review of accredited ministers, ordained and lay.

(g) To report regularly to the Archbishops' Council on its work.

THE CHURCH COMMISSIONERS FOR ENGLAND

Office Church House, Great Smith St, London SW1P 3AZ *Tel:* 020 7898 1000
Fax: 020 7898 1131
email: commissioners.enquiry@churchofengland.org

Chairman The Archbishop of Canterbury

Secretary Mr Andrew Brown *Tel:* 020 7898 1134
email: andrew.brown@churchofengland.org

Chief Finance Officer for the National Church Institutions Mr Ian Theodoreson
Tel: 020 7898 1795
email: ian.theodoreson@churchofengland.org

Director of Investments Mr Tom Joy
Tel: 020 7898 1115
email: tom.joy@churchofengland.org

Pastoral and Closed Churches Secretary and Bishoprics and Cathedrals Secretary Mr Paul Lewis (Pastoral reorganization, closed churches, clergy housing and glebe) *Tel:* 020 7898 1741
email: paul.lewis@churchofengland.org

Director of Libraries, Archives and Information Services Mr Declan Kelly *Tel:* 020 7898 1432
email: declan.kelly@churchofengland.org

LEGAL DEPARTMENT
Official Solicitor Mr Stephen Slack
Tel: 020 7898 1704
email: stephen.slack@churchofengland.org
Deputy Official Solicitor Ms Saira Salimi
Tel: 020 7898 1717
email: saira.salimi@churchofengland.org
Web: www.churchofengland.org/about-us/structure/churchlawlegis

MEMBERS
The Archbishops of Canterbury and York

First Church Estates Commissioner Mr Andreas Whittam Smith
Second Church Estates Commissioner Sir Tony Baldry MP

Third Church Estates Commissioner Mr Timothy Walker

Four bishops elected by the House of Bishops of the General Synod Rt Revd and Rt Hon Richard Chartres (*Bishop of London*), Rt Revd David Urquhart (*Bishop of Birmingham*), Rt Revd Michael Hill (*Bishop of Bristol*), Rt Revd Peter Forster (*Bishop of Chester*)

Two deans or provosts elected by all the deans and provosts Very Revd Jonathan Greener (*Dean of Wakefield*), Very Revd John Clarke (*Dean of Wells*)

Three clergy elected by the House of Clergy of the General Synod
Canon Bob Baker, Canon David Stanton, Revd Stephen Trott

Four lay persons elected by the House of Laity of the General Synod
Mrs April Alexander, Canon Peter Bruinvels, Mr Gavin Oldham, Mr Jacob Vince

Three persons nominated by Her Majesty the Queen
Mr Harry Hart, Canon Dr John Spence, Mr John Wythe

Three persons nominated by the Archbishops of Canterbury and of York acting jointly Mr Nicholas Sykes, Mr Jeremy Clack, Mr Peter Harrison QC

Three persons nominated by the Archbishops acting jointly after consultation with others including the Lord Mayors of the cities of London and York and the Vice-Chancellors of Oxford and Cambridge Mr Brian Carroll, Mrs Emma Osborne, Mr Hywel Rees-Jones

Six State Office Holders The First Lord of the Treasury; the Lord President of the Council; the Lord Chancellor; the Speaker of the House of Lords; the Secretary of State for Culture, Media and Sport; and the Speaker of the House of Commons.

FUNCTIONS
The Church Commissioners' main tasks are to manage their assets, and make money available in accordance with the duties laid upon them by Acts of Parliament and Measures of the General Synod and former Church Assembly, and to discharge other administrative duties entrusted to them.

These duties include financial support for mission and ministry in parishes, particularly in areas of need and opportunity, clergy pensions for service before 1998 and other legal commitments such as those in relation to bishops and cathedrals, and the administration of the legal framework for pastoral reorganization and settling the future of churches closed for worship.

CONSTITUTION
The Church Commissioners were formed on 1 April 1948, when Queen Anne's Bounty (1704) and the Ecclesiastical Commissioners (1836) were united.

The full body of Commissioners meets once a year to consider the Report and Accounts and the allocation of available money. The management of the Commissioners' affairs is shared between the Board of Governors, the Assets Committee, the Bishoprics and Cathedrals Committee, the Pastoral Committee, the Church Buildings (Uses and Disposals) Committee and the Audit and Risk Committee.

The National Institutions Measure 1998 created the Archbishops' Council, with consequential amendment to the Church Commissioners' functions and working relationships. The Measure also transferred their former function and powers as Central Stipends Authority to the Council on 1 January 1999.

As from 2010 the Church Commissioners are a registered charity and regulated by the Charity Commission.

NATIONAL STRUCTURES

Functions of the Board of Governors and the Commissioners' Committees

BOARD OF GOVERNORS
The Board is responsible for overall policy matters and there are individual committees covering policy in the following specific areas. All Commissioners are Board Members except for the six Officers of State.

ASSETS COMMITTEE
Chairman Mr Andreas Whittam Smith
Deputy Chairman Mr Nicholas Sykes
Rt Revd Michael Hill (*Bishop of Bristol*), Canon Bob Baker, Mr Brian Carroll, Mr Gavin Oldham, Mrs Emma Osborne, Mr Harry Hart, Mr John Wythe
Secretary Mr Andrew Brown

Exclusive responsibility for managing the Commissioners' assets, for investment policy and for advising the Board on the maximum amount of money available for distribution each year. The Committee is assisted by two sub-groups working on the Commissioners' stock exchange and property portfolios.

AUDIT AND RISK COMMITTEE
Chairman Mr Hywel Rees-Jones
Mrs April Alexander, Mr Stephen East*, Mr George Lynn*, Mr Chris Daykin*, Canon Dr John Spence, Mr Hywel Rees-Jones
Secretary Mr Michael Cole

Responsible for all matters relating to the audit of the Commissioners' accounts and related matters.

BISHOPRICS AND CATHEDRALS COMMITTEE
Chairman Mr Timothy Walker
Deputy Chairman Rt Revd David Rossdale*, Rt Revd David Urquhart (*Bishop of Birmingham*), Very Revd Jonathan Greener (*Dean of Wakefield*), Very Revd John Clarke (*Dean of Wells*), Revd Mary Bide*, Mr Jacob Vince, Revd Canon Jeremy Haselock*, Ms Sallie Bassham*, Mrs Rosemary Butler†
Secretary Mr Paul Lewis

Responsible for the costs of episcopal administration, the provision and management of suitable housing for diocesan bishops, assisting by grants and loans with the housing of suffragan and assistant bishops, and some assistance in respect of cathedral clergy and lay staff.

PASTORAL COMMITTEE
Chairman Mr Timothy Walker
Deputy Chairman Rt Revd Peter Forster (*Bishop of Chester*)
Rt Revd John Pritchard* (*Bishop of Oxford*), Ven Penny Driver* (*Archdeacon of Westmoreland and Furness*), Canon David Stanton, Revd Canon Stephen Evans*, Canon Peter Bruinvels, Mrs Julia Flack*, Mr Peter Harrison QC, Mrs Stephanie Ridge*
Secretary Mr Paul Lewis

Responsible for matters concerning pastoral reorganization, parsonages and glebe property.

CHURCH BUILDINGS (USES AND DISPOSALS) COMMITTEE
Chairman Mr Timothy Walker
Deputy Chairman Revd Stephen Trott
Canon Bob Baker, Revd Canon Peter Cavanagh*, Revd Simon Talbott*, Mr Brian Carroll, Mrs April Alexander, Mr John Steel*, Mr Charles Wilson*
Secretary Mr Paul Lewis

Responsible for the Commissioners' work relating to closed church buildings.

The Commissioners draw no income from the State.

The asterisks in the above lists indicate non-Commissioner committee members.

The dagger symbol (†) in one of the above lists indicates consultant.

CHARITABLE EXPENDITURE IN 2011
The Commissioners' charitable expenditure falls under two main headings:

1 Provision of non-pensions support – £81 million in 2011 – to the Church including parish mission and ministry support of £37.7 million which was mainly targeted towards areas of greatest financial need.
2 Payment of clergy pensions and pensions to their widows – £114.6 million in 2011. The Church of England Pensions Board authorizes pensions, but much of the money is provided and paid by the Church Commissioners. The Commissioners are responsible for pensions earned on service before 1 January 1998 and dioceses and parishes for pensions earned after that date.

MANAGEMENT OF ASSETS

The total return on the Commissioners' assets in 2011 was 2.9 per cent and their return over the twenty years to 2011 averaged 9.5 per cent per annum (industry benchmark 4.5 per cent per annum).

PASTORAL MEASURE RESPONSIBILITIES

The Commissioners are responsible for preparing schemes for pastoral reorganization based on proposals put forward by Bishops under the Pastoral Measure 1983. This includes the consideration of any representations made in response to consultation on draft schemes. Those making representations have the opportunity to address the relevant Commissioners' Committee.

The Commissioners also deal with objections to certain personage and glebe transactions.

CLOSED CHURCH BUILDINGS

The Pastoral Measure 1983 sets out the process for closing a church building which is no longer needed for public worship. The Commissioners will prepare a draft scheme to give effect to the proposals, consult locally and hear any representations received in respect of them.

The Commissioners also determine the future use of closed church buildings. Under the Pastoral Measure, dioceses are charged with the seeking of a suitable use for the buildings and reporting to the Commissioners who will then publish a draft scheme to facilitate that use and its sale for that purpose.

Buildings of high heritage value for which no suitable alternative use can be found may be vested in the Churches Conservation Trust, an independent body jointly funded by the Church and State to care for such closed church buildings.

FURTHER INFORMATION

Further information is available in the Commissioners' Annual Report and Accounts which, together with other information leaflets, is available free of charge from the Commissioners and *via* the Church of England website at http://www.churchofengland.org/about-us/structure/churchcommissioners/annual-and-quarterly-reports.aspx.

THE CHURCH OF ENGLAND PENSIONS BOARD

Office 29 Great Smith Street, London SW1P 3PS
Tel: 020 7898 1806
Fax: 020 7898 1801
email: cepb.enquiries@churchofengland.org

Chairman Dr Jonathan Spencer

Chief Executive Bernadette Kenny
Tel: 020 7898 1806
email: bernadette.kenny@churchofengland.org

Pensions Manager Peter Dickinson
Tel: 020 7898 1810
email: peter.dickinson@churchofengland.org

Housing Manager Loraine Miller
Tel: 020 7898 1852
email: loraine.miller@churchofengland.org

Customer Strategy and Insight Director Linda Ferguson *Tel:* 020 7898 1833
email: linda.ferguson@churchofengland.org

Chief of Staff Lee Marshall *Tel:* 020 7898 1681
email: lee.marshall@churchofengland.org

Executive Assistant Sion Hughes Carew
Tel: 020 7898 1815
email: sion.hughes-carew@churchofengland.org

Investment Officer Pierre Jameson
Tel: 020 7898 1122
email: pierre.jameson@churchofengland.org

MEMBERS

The 20 members of the Board represent a balance of skills and expertise and are drawn from a wide range of constituencies, as specified in the Church of England Pensions Regulations 1997.

Appointed Chair by the Archbishops with the approval of the General Synod
Dr Jonathan Spencer

Appointed by the Archbishops of Canterbury and York after consultation with the representatives of dioceses
Canon David Froude

Appointed by the Archbishops of Canterbury and York
Roger Mountford (*Chairman of the Pensions Committee*)

Elected by the House of Bishops
Rt Revd David Walker (*Vice Chairman; Chairman of the Housing Committee*)

Elected by the House of Clergy
Revd Paul Benfield, Revd Paul Boughton, Revd Nigel Bourne, Revd Canon Ian Gooding

Elected by the House of Laity
James Archer, Simon Baynes, Jane Bisson, Dr Graham Campbell, Alan Fletcher, Brian Wilson

Elected by Members of the Church Workers Pension Fund
Ian Clark, Colin Peters

Elected by Members of the Church Administrators Pension Fund
John Ferguson

Elected by the Employers participating in the Church Workers Pension Fund and Church Administrators Pension Fund
Clive Hawkins (*Deputy Vice Chairman; Chairman of the Investment Committee*), Canon Sandra Newton

Appointed by the Church Commissioners
Jeremy Clack

CO-OPTIONS

The Board has co-opted the following, who bring a particular expertise, to serve on its committees:
Ian Bate (*Housing Committee*);
Debbie Clarke (*Investment Committee*);
Jane Clarke (*Housing Committee*);
Jon Head (*Housing Committee*);
David Hunt (*Audit and Risk Committee*);
Peter Parker (*Investment Committee*);
Mark Powell (*Investment Committee*);
Graham Shorter (*Pension Committee*);
Helen Simmons (*Audit and Risk Committee*)

INTRODUCTION

The Church of England Pensions Board provides retirement services for those who have worked for or served the Church.

It was established in 1926 by the Church Assembly as the Church of England's pensions authority. Subsequently it was given wider powers in respect of discretionary benefits and the provision of retirement accommodation to those retired from the stipendiary ministry and their dependents.

Vision and Values

The Board's vision is to deliver a professional, high-quality and efficient service to our customers, respecting the needs of those who provide us with the money to do this.

In our decision-making and operations we are guided by the following values:

- We are part of the Church of England.
- We understand our customers and their needs.

- We work closely with employers, dioceses and all our partners and take careful account of their views.
- We behave with openness and integrity.
- We take pride in doing a good job.
- We value our people and the contribution they make.

Pensions

The Church of England Funded Pension Scheme (CEFPS) commenced on 1 January 1998 for the purpose of providing pensions and associated benefits for clergy and others in the stipendiary ministry. Pension benefits arising from service prior to 1998 is financed wholly by the Church Commissioners, but administered by the Board. The CEFPS held assets of £784.8 million at the end of 2011. Its next actuarial valuation will be carried out as at 31 December 2012.

The Board is also corporate trustee of the Church Worker's Pension Fund (CWPF) providing pensions for the employees of over 200 organizations associated with the Church of England; and of the Church Administrators Pension Fund (CAPF) for staff employed by the National Church Institutions.

Retirement Housing

At least one in four clergy retiring from the stipendiary ministry seeks our assistance in the provision of retirement housing.

The purpose of the retirement housing scheme – the Church Housing Assistance for the Retired Ministry (CHARM) – is to assist those vacating tied accommodation who have not been able throughout their service and ministry to the Church to make their own provision for somewhere to live in retirement.

CHARM is a discretionary facility. The Board specifies a number of parameters relating to the size and type of property which is available, as well as the form and amount of assistance which is available.

Rental housing is purchased through a loan agreement with Santander Corporate Banking. CHARM is subsidised by the wider Church of England through Vote 5 of the Archbishops' Council's Budget. The total grant for 2011 was £3.4 million.

A shared ownership scheme was introduced in 2008. Properties are purchased by the Board in partnership with the customer who contributes a minimum of 25 per cent of the property cost.

In total, the Board assists around 3,000 retired clergy households with their retirement housing.

Supported Housing, Nursing and Dementia Care

For over 60 years, the Board has been providing supported housing for those retired clergy and their dependants who wish to live as independently as possibly in a caring Christian community with access to a range of comprehensive support services.

The Board maintains seven supported housing schemes and one care home. Each scheme not only provides residents with a self-contained flat but also includes dining facilities, meeting spaces, libraries, a chapel and communal grounds.

A specialist dementia care unit is in operation within the care home. At present this is a seven-bed unit which includes a communal dining area, a specialist bathing facility, and a sensory garden with raised beds to promote interest and stimulation. The Board is currently looking to expand this area of its work.

Publications

Various publications including detailed information about the different pension schemes, the retirement housing and supported living schemes, and how to leave a legacy to the Board, are available to download from www.cepb.org.uk.

The Board's Annual Report and Summary Report for 2011 are also available to download from the same website.

OTHER BOARDS, COUNCILS, COMMISSIONS, ETC. OF THE CHURCH OF ENGLAND

The Advisory Board for Redundant Churches

Function transferred to the Statutory Advisory Committee of the Church Buildings Council.

The Churches Conservation Trust
(formerly the Redundant Churches Fund)

Chief Executive Mr Crispin Truman, 1 West Smithfield, London EC1A 9EE *Tel:* 020 7213 0660
Fax: 020 7213 0678
email: central@tcct.org.uk
Web: www.visitchurches.org.uk

Deputy Chief Executive and Director of Conservation Ms Sarah Robinson

Director, West Mr Colin Shearer

Director, North Ms Rosi Lister

Director, South East Mr Peter Aiers

Director of Income Generation Ms Melanie Knight

Head of Finance, Mr Stuart Popple

Head of Regeneration Mr Matthew McKeague

Head of Resources Ms Tanya Bunney

BOARD OF TRUSTEES
Mr Loyd Grossman OBE FSA (***Chairman***), Mrs Deborah Dance, Very Revd Peter Judd, Revd Brian McHenry CBE, Mr Nick Thompson, Ms Jane Weeks, Mr Duncan Wilson OBE, Mr Christopher Knight, Mr Keith Halstead, Mr Humphrey Welfare

The Churches Conservation Trust is the national charity protecting historic churches at risk. We've saved over 340 unique buildings which attract almost 2 million visitors a year. With our help and your support they are kept open, in use and free to all – living once again at the heart of their communities.

Trust churches host occasional services as well as concerts, exhibitions and lectures. The Trust, which is a registered charity, depends upon statutory funding from the Church Commissioners (21 per cent) and the Department for Culture, Media and Sport (45 per cent) and charitable grants and voluntary donations (34 per cent).

CCLA Investment Management Limited

Registered Office Senator House, 85 Queen Victoria Street, London, EC4V 4ET
Company Registration No 2183088
Authorized and regulated by the Financial Services Authority *Tel:* 0844 561 5000
Fax: 0844 561 5128
Web: www.ccla.co.uk

Executive Directors
Chief Executive Mr Michael Quicke
email: michael.quicke@ccla.co.uk

Chief Investment Officer Mr James Bevan
email: james.bevan@ccla.co.uk

Investment Director Mr Colin Peters
email: colin.peters@ccla.co.uk
Director of Market Development Mr Andrew Robinson *email:* andrew.robinson@ccla.co.uk
Chief Operating Officer Mr Sean Curran
email: sean.curran@ccla.co.uk
Non Executive Directors
Mr James Dawnay (*Chairman*), Mr Richard Fitzalan Howard, Mr Trevor Salmon, Revd John Tattersall, Mr Richard Williams
Company Secretary Mrs Jacqueline Fox

CCLA Investment Management Limited (CCLA) is a specialist investment management company serving charities, churches and local authorities. It is the largest manager of charitable funds in the UK, both by the value of funds managed and the number of individual investing charities. It aims to provide good quality investment management services at reasonable cost. It is the manager, registrar and administrator of the CBF Church of England Funds, the trustee of which is CBF Funds Trustee Limited and to which CCLA is accountable. Six Funds are offered to Church of England investors: the Investment Fund, a mixed fund invested mainly in equities, the UK Equity Fund, the Global Equity Income Fund, the Fixed Interest Securities Fund, the Deposit Fund and the Property Fund. CCLA also manages several segregated charity portfolios. CCLA is owned 60 per cent by the CBF Church of England Investment Fund, 25 per cent by the COIF Charities Investment Fund (part of which is non voting) and 15 per cent by the Local Authorities Mutual Investment Trust. CCLA is authorized and regulated by the Financial Services Authority (FSA) under the Financial Services and Markets Act 2000 (FSMA). Under the FSMA, the CBF, in its role as Trustee, is not considered to be operating the Funds 'by way of business'. In consequence, it is not required to be regulated by the FSA. Deposits taken by the CBF Church of England Deposit Fund are exempted from the FSMA by virtue of the Financial Services and Markets Act (Exemption) Order 2001.

The CBF Church of England Funds

Established under the Church Funds Investment Measure 1958, these open-ended funds aim to meet most of the investment needs of a church trust and are used by diocesan boards of finance and trusts, cathedrals, diocesan boards of education, theological colleges, church schools and educational endowments, church societies and many PCCs.

Investment Fund
The main CBF Church of England Fund for capital that can be invested for the long term. A widely spread portfolio mainly of UK and overseas equities but also including some bond and property investments. Aims to provide steady and rising income and capital growth. Weekly share dealings. The Fund targets an attractive and rising level of income.

UK Equity Fund
This Fund provides church trustees with a means of obtaining investment solely in a specialist UK equity portfolio. Weekly share dealings. The Fund targets an attractive and rising level of income.

Fixed Interest Securities Fund
Invested only in UK fixed interest stocks. Recommended only for a small proportion of long-term capital as it offers little protection from inflation over the longer term. Weekly share dealings.

Deposit Fund
This money Fund is for cash balances which need to be available at short notice and with minimal risk of capital loss. Accounts in the Fund obtain a rate of interest close to money market rates even on small sums. Daily deposit and withdrawal facilities. The Fund is rated AAA/VI by Fitch Ratings.

Property Fund
Invests directly in UK commercial property. Fund is intended primarily for long-term investment by large church trusts. Month end share dealings but periods of notice may be imposed. The Fund provides a high level of income.

Global Equity Income Fund
This fund targets a high and growing income from a portfolio of international shares including the UK. Weekly share dealings.

Risk Warnings: The value of the Investment, UK Equity, Fixed Interest Securities, Global Equity Income and Property Funds and their income can fall as well as rise and an investor may not get back the amount invested. Past performance is no guarantee of future returns. The Funds are intended for long term investment and are not suitable for money liable to be spent in the near future. Guarantees regarding repayment of deposits in the Deposit Fund cannot be given.

Brochures and Reports and Accounts are available from CCLA Investment Management Limited at the address above and on its website, www.ccla.co.uk

31 May 2011	**Investment Fund**	**Fixed Interest Securities Fund**	**Deposit Fund**	**Property Fund**	**UK Equity Fund**	**Global Equity Income Fund**
Value of Fund	£788 million	£76 million	£668 million	£127 million	£40 million	£61 million
Net Asset Value per share	1041.86p	165.23p	–	117.59p	109.74p	120.87p
Income Yield %	4.62	5.33	0.90	7.02	5.01	5.31
Gross Redemption Yield %	–	2.66	–	–	–	–

The Church and Community Fund

Chairman Ven George Howe
Grants Manager Mr Andrew Hawkings

Formerly known as the Central Church Fund, the Church and Community Fund (CCF) aims to grow the Church of England and develop its capacity to engage with the whole community by making grants to the national church and local projects.

The Archbishops' Council (registered charity number 1074857) is trustee of the CCF but has delegated management to a CCF Committee whose members are the administrative trustees of the Fund.

By making grants the CCF assists the Church of England to:

a) develop its capacity to engage with the whole community through supporting innovative use of resources;
b) help transform areas of greatest need and opportunity, and
c) grow spiritually and numerically.

In 2012 to 2014 the CCF will support projects that:

1) significantly expand the Church's engagement with neighbourhood renewal;
2) seek innovative ways of developing established community projects so that they help grow the church, and
3) replicate models of successful community engagement across the wider church.

The CCF awarded around £500,000 to church community projects in 2011. It also gave £280,000 as a direct grant to the Archbishops' Council in support of the national work of the Church.

The CCF welcomes legacies and donations to help increase the number of grants awarded so that more churches can reach out to their communities and respond to real local needs. Please contact the Grants Manager to find out more about how to make a donation, leave a legacy or apply for a grant.

The Church and Community Fund, Church House, Great Smith St, London SW1P 3AZ
Tel: 020 7898 1541
email: ccf@churchofengland.org
Web: www.ccfund.org.uk
Twitter: @CCF_CofE

The Corporation of the Church House

Presidents The Archbishop of Canterbury; The Archbishop of York

Chairman of Council Michael Chamberlain OBE

Treasurer David Barnett

Secretary Chris Palmer CBE *Tel:* 020 7898 1311
email: chris.palmer@churchofengland.org

Office Church House, Great Smith St, London SW1P 3AZ *Tel:* 020 7898 1311
Fax: 020 7898 1321

The Corporation owns and maintains Church House, Westminster which is the administrative headquarters of the national institutions of the Church of England.

The original Church House was built in the early 1890s as the Church's memorial of Queen Victoria's Jubilee, to be the administrative headquarters of the Church of England, and was replaced by the present building to a design by Sir Herbert Baker. The foundation stone was laid in 1937 by Queen Mary and on 10 June 1940 King George VI, accompanied by the Queen, formally opened the new House and attended the first Session of the Church Assembly in the great circular hall. The building was almost immediately requisitioned by the Government and for the rest of the war became the alternative meeting place of both Houses of Parliament; the Lords sat in the Convocation Hall and the Commons in the Hoare Memorial Hall. Oak panels in these halls commemorate this use.

By October 1946 some administrative offices of the Church Assembly returned to Church House and the Church Assembly was able to return for its Autumn Session in 1950. The building is now the headquarters of the Archbishops' Council, the Church Commissioners and the Church of England Pensions Board, as well as being the venue for the General Synod in the spring and (if it meets) in the autumn. A large-scale refurbishment carried out in 2006 has provided sufficient open-plan office space to accommodate nearly all staff of the Central Church Institutions, who moved into Church House during the early part of 2007.

Church House has also become an important national centre for conferences and meetings, the income from which contributes significantly to the maintenance costs of the building.

The business of the Corporation is vested in its Council of 9 (of whom 3 are nominated by the Appointments Committee, 2 are elected by the membership of the Corporation and 4 are co-opted by the Council).

The National Society (Church of England) for Promoting Religious Education

Leading Education with Christian Purpose

Patron Her Majesty The Queen

President The Archbishop of Canterbury

Vice Presidents The Archbishop of York and the Archbishop of Wales

Chairman of the Council Rt Revd Dr John Pritchard (*Bishop of Oxford*)

General Secretary Revd Janina Ainsworth

Treasurer Revd Peter Ballard

Deputy Secretary Mrs Nicola Sylvester
Tel: 020 7898 1490
email: nicola.sylvester@churchofengland.org

Deputy Secretary Revd Nigel Genders
Tel: 020 7898 1789
email: nigel.genders@churchofengland.org

Deputy General Secretary (Wales) Revd Edwin Counsel

National Schools Support Office: Mrs Liz Carter
Tel: 020 7898 1515
email: liz.carter@churchofengland.org

Business and Support Manager Mrs Cheryl Payne
Tel: 020 7898 1501
email: cheryl.payne@churchofengland.org

Executive Assistant Mr Peter Churchill
Tel: 020 7898 1518
email: peter.churchill@churchofengland.org

Executive Assistant Mrs Daniela Longhin
Tel: 020 7898 1491
email: daniela.longhin@churchofengland.org
Web: www.churchofengland.org/education

The National Society celebrated its **bicentenary in 2011** with a programme of events in schools and dioceses, culminating in a Service of Thanksgiving in Westminster Abbey in October. The original purpose of the Society was '*The Promotion of the Education of the Poor in the Principles of the Established Church*'. It works in close association with the Education Division (*see* page 183), sharing the main objectives focused particularly on schools work. Founded in 1811, the Society was chiefly responsible for setting up, in cooperation with local clergy and others, the **nationwide network of Church schools** in England and Wales; it was also, through the Church colleges, a pioneer in teacher education.

The Society was instrumental in the *Church School of the Future Review* which led to the Report published in March 2012. The main areas of recommendation in the Report form the agenda for the work of the Society for the next three years, including supporting and enabling Diocesan Education teams to meet the challenges of the new environment; a renewed focus on church school performance including through skilled and supported leadership; additional resources for church school RE and the development of a distinctive approach to the whole curriculum; streamlining internal organization and developing a new approach to membership.

The Society provides the following services to the Church through its schools:

- support to diocesan education teams in the development of academies
- revision and development of the nationally authorized framework for the denominational inspection of Anglican and Methodist schools
- training and accreditation for inspectors for Church schools under Section 48 of the Education Act 2005 (Statutory Inspection of Anglican Schools)
- sample contracts and application forms and associated policies for appointment of staff in church schools
- funded developmental work in recruitment and training of leaders in church schools

- support for RE and collective worship in dioceses and schools through the work of the RE Development Officer and the Worship Workshop website
- a legal and advisory service for dioceses and schools
- links to courses accredited by the church universities and university colleges
- presentation scrolls available to mark significant anniversaries in the life of Church of England and Church in Wales schools signed by the Archbishop of Canterbury and the General Secretary.

The Society represents the Church of England in planning and promoting Education Sunday, an ecumenical observation that takes place every year on the ninth Sunday before Easter.

Archive material

After nearly two centuries of close association with Church schools and colleges, the National Society has built up an impressive collection of documents in its archives. These include about 15,000 files of correspondence with schools throughout England and Wales founded in association with the National Society and many published works, including the Society's own. Access is available to *bona fide* researchers by appointment at the Church of England Record Centre.

Applications for membership and donations to The National Society from individuals, schools and other bodies wishing to support the Society's work and share its resources are welcomed (*see membership form on the website or contact Cheryl Payne*).

THE ECCLESIASTICAL COURTS

The Ecclesiastical Courts consist of (1) the Diocesan or Consistory Courts, (2) the Provincial Courts, and for both Provinces (3) the Court of Ecclesiastical Causes Reserved and, when required, (4) a Commission of Review. In certain faculty cases an appeal lies from the Provincial Courts to the Judicial Committee of the Privy Council. The jurisdiction of the Archdeacons' Courts is now confined to the visitations of archdeacons. The Ecclesiastical Courts are in the main now regulated by the Ecclesiastical Jurisdiction Measure 1963. The Court of Faculties is the Court of the Archbishop of Canterbury through which the legatine powers transferred to the Archbishop of Canterbury by the Ecclesiastical Licences Act 1533 are exercised.

The personnel of the Diocesan Courts is given in the diocesan lists. The personnel of the Court of Faculties and of the Provincial and some of the other Courts is as follows:

THE COURT OF ARCHES

Dean of the Arches Rt Worshipful Charles George QC

Registrar Canon John Rees
16 Beaumont St, Oxford OX1 2LZ
Tel: 01865 297200
Fax: 01865 726274
email: jrees@wslaw.co.uk

THE COURT OF THE VICAR-GENERAL OF THE PROVINCE OF CANTERBURY

Vicar-General Rt Worshipful Timothy Briden

Registrar Canon John Rees (*as above*)

THE CHANCERY COURT OF YORK

Auditor Rt Worshipful Charles George QC

Registrar Mr Lionel Lennox
The Provincial Registry, Stamford House, Piccadilly, York YO1 9PP
Tel: 01904 623487
Fax: 01904 561470
email: lpml@denisontill.com

THE COURT OF THE VICAR-GENERAL OF THE PROVINCE OF YORK

Vicar-General Rt Worshipful Peter Collier QC

Registrar Mr Lionel Lennox (*as above*)

THE COURT OF ECCLESIASTICAL CAUSES RESERVED

Judges

Rt Revd David Hope
Rt Revd Richard Harries
Rt Revd Thomas Wright
Dame Elizabeth Butler-Sloss
Sir John Mummery

Registrar for the Province of Canterbury Canon John Rees (*as above*)

Registrar for the Province of York Mr Lionel Lennox (*as above*)

THE COURT OF FACULTIES

Master of the Faculties Rt Worshipful Charles George QC

Registrar Mr Peter Beesley
1 The Sanctuary, London SW1P 3JT
Tel: 020 7222 5381
Fax: 020 7222 7502
email: faculty.office@1Thesanctuary.com

Disciplinary Tribunals constituted under the Clergy Discipline Measure 2003

President of Tribunals Rt Hon Lord Justice Mummery

Deputy President of Tribunals His Honour Judge John Bullimore
c/o The Legal Office, Church House, Great Smith St, London SW1P 3AZ

'Legally qualified' members of the provincial panels of Canterbury and York (the same ten are appointed to each panel) from which the chair of a disciplinary tribunal will be appointed by the President of Tribunals if the President or Deputy President is not to chair the tribunal.

Chancellor Linda Box
His Honour Judge Dr Rupert Bursell QC
Mr David Cheetham
His Honour Judge Simon Grenfell
Canon Christopher Hodson
His Honour the Worshipful Roger Kaye QC
His Honour Judge John Lodge
Mr Geoffrey Tattersall QC
His Honour Judge David Turner QC
His Honour Judge Samuel Wiggs

Registrar of Tribunals for the Province of Canterbury Canon John Rees (*as above*)

Registrar of Tribunals for the Province of York Mr Lionel Lennox (*as above*)

Designated Officer Mr Adrian Iles, The Legal Office, Church House, Great Smith St, London SW1P 3AZ

NATIONAL STRUCTURES

Appeal Panels

APPEAL PANEL CONSTITUTED UNDER SCHEDULE 4 MISSION AND PASTORAL MEASURE 2011

(Tribunals to settle compensation claims of clergy dispossessed under a Pastoral Scheme or Order)

Chair The Dean of the Arches

Deputy Chairs
The Vicar-General of Canterbury
The Vicar-General of York

In addition to the Chair, a tribunal comprises three members of the Lower House of the relevant Province and one member of the House of Laity drawn from the following panels:

Convocation of Canterbury, Lower House
Ven Annette Cooper (Chelmsford)
Revd Canon Robert Cotton (Guildford)
Revd Canon Stuart Currie (Worcester)
Revd Maureen Hobbs (Lichfield)
Very Revd Robert Key (Winchester, Channel Islands)
Revd Prebendary Stephen Lynas (Bath and Wells)
Ven Clive Mansell (Rochester)
Revd Prebendary Sam Philpott MBE (Exeter)
Revd Dr Philip Plyming (Guildford)
Revd Mark Steadman (Southwark)
Revd Canon Dr Hazel Whitehead (Guildford)
Ven Christine Wilson (Derby)

Convocation of York, Lower House
Revd Paul Ayers (Bradford)
Revd Ferial Etherington (Carlisle)
Revd Dr Jonathan Gibbs (Chester)
Revd Canon Geoffrey Harbord (Sheffield)
Ven Ian Jagger (Durham)
Revd Canon Joyce Jones (Wakefield)
Revd Canon Susan Penfold (Blackburn)
Revd Canon Suzanne Sheriff (York)
Revd Canon John Sinclair (Newcastle)
Revd Peter Spiers (Liverpool)
Ven Cherry Vann (Manchester)
Revd Canon Tony Walker (Southwell and Nottingham)

House of Laity of the General Synod
Mr Martin Dales (York)
Mrs Jenny Dunlop (Chester)
Ms Mary Johnston (London)
Mrs Mary Judkins (Wakefield)
Mr Aiden Hargreaves-Smith (Europe)
Mr Clive Scowen (London)
Mr Geoffrey Tattersall QC (Manchester)
Mr John Ward (London)
Ms Frances Wood (Durham)
(3 vacancies)

Secretary Vacancy

APPEAL PANEL CONSTITUTED UNDER STANDING ORDER 120(f)(i)

(Tribunals to hear appeals in internal General Synod elections)

House of Bishops
Rt Revd Paul Butler (*Bishop of Southwell and Nottingham*)
Rt Revd Dr Peter Forster (*Bishop of Chester*)
Rt Revd Graham James (*Bishop of Norwich*)
Rt Revd Michael Langrish (*Bishop of Exeter*)
Rt Revd Nigel McCulloch (*Bishop of Manchester*)
(1 vacancy)

House of Clergy
Revd Canon Jonathan Alderton-Ford (St Edmundsbury and Ipswich)
Ven Christine Allsopp (Peterborough)
Revd Preb Philippa Boardman MBE (London)
Ven Annette Cooper (Chelmsford)
Revd Prebendary David Houlding (London)
Ven Clive Mansell (Rochester)
Revd Stephen Trott (Peterborough)
(5 vacancies)

House of Laity
Mr Martin Dales (York)
Miss Prudence Dailey (Oxford)
Mrs Jenny Dunlop (Chester)
Mrs Sarah Finch (London)
Dr Philip Giddings (Oxford)
Mrs Christina Rees (St Albans)
Mrs Caroline Spencer (Canterbury)
Mr Geoffrey Tattersall QC (Manchester)
Dr Anna Thomas-Betts (Oxford)
Mr John Ward (London)
(2 vacancies)

Secretary Vacancy

APPEAL PANEL APPOINTED PURSUANT TO RULE 44(8) OF THE CHURCH REPRESENTATION RULES AS AMENDED BY THE NATIONAL INSTITUTIONS MEASURE 1998 (SCHEDULE 5, PARAGRAPH 2(c))

(Tribunals to hear appeals in elections to the House of Laity of the General Synod)

The Dean of the Arches
The Vicar-General of Canterbury
The Vicar-General of York
Miss Prudence Dailey (Oxford)
Mr Martin Dales (York)
Mrs Jenny Dunlop (Chester)
Mrs Sarah Finch (London)
Dr Philip Giddings (Oxford)
Mrs Christina Rees (St Albans)
Mrs Caroline Spencer (Canterbury)
Mr Geoffrey Tattersall (Manchester)
Dr Anna Thomas-Betts (Oxford)
Mr John Ward (London)
(2 vacancies)

Secretary Vacancy

APPEAL PANEL APPOINTED PURSUANT TO RULE 25(5) OF THE CLERGY REPRESENTATION RULES 1975 TO 2004
(Tribunals to hear appeals in elections to the Convocations)

The Dean of the Arches
The Vicar-General of Canterbury
The Vicar-General of York
Revd Jonathan Alderton-Ford (St Edmundsbury and Ipswich)
Ven Christine Allsopp (Peterborough)
Revd Prebendary Philippa Boardman MBE (London)
Revd Canon Simon Butler (Southwark)
Revd Canon David Felix (Chester)
Revd Prebendary David Houlding (London)
Ven Clive Mansell (Rochester)
(5 vacancies)

Secretary Vacancy

GENERAL SYNOD LEGISLATION, CONSTITUTION AND BUSINESS

Legislation passed 2003–2012 together with commencement dates

Dates in brackets are the dates of legislation coming into force. Items of legislation no longer in force are omitted.

MEASURES

Synodical Government (Amendment) Measure 2003 (1 January 2004)

Church of England (Pensions) Measure 2003 (1 May 2003)

Clergy Discipline Measure 2003 (in force 1 October 2003: sections 3, 39, 45 and 48; in force 1 June 2005: sections 44(3) and (4); in force 8 September 2005: sections 4, 5 and 21; remainder in force 1 January 2006)

Stipends (Cessation of Special Payments) Measure 2005 (1 July and 31 December 2005)

Church of England (Miscellaneous Provisions) Measure 2005 (1 June and 1 September 2005)

Church of England (Miscellaneous Provisions) Measure 2006 (all in force 1 October 2006 except section 1 and Schedule 1; section 1 and schedule 1 in force 1 December 2007)

Dioceses, Pastoral and Mission Measure 2007 (in force 1 January 2008: sections 1, 51, 62(1)–(3), 63(1) (so far as it relates to paragraph 7(b) of Schedule 5), 63(5) and 66 and paragraph 7(b) of Schedule 5; in force 1 February 2008: sections 52, 61, 62(5), 64 and 65 (so far as it relates to the repeals in Schedule 7 coming into force on the same date), Schedules 3 and 6 and the repeals in Schedule 7 of section 1 and Schedules 1 and 5 of the Pastoral Measure 1983, section 11(e) of the Church of England (Miscellaneous Provisions) Measure 1995 and sections 2(4) and (5) of the Synodical Government (Amendment) Measure 2003; in force 31 March 2008: sections 47–50 and 63(4); in force 1 May 2008: sections 13–16, 22, 63(7) and 65 (so far as it relates to the repeals in Schedule 7 coming into force on the same date) and the repeals in Schedule 7 of sections 10–15 of the Dioceses Measure 1978, sections 8 and 10 of the Church of England (Miscellaneous Provisions) Measure 1983, section 11(2) of the Bishops (Retirement) Measure 1986, section 2 of the Clergy (Ordination) Measure 1990 and section 12 of the Church of England (Miscellaneous Provisions) Measure 1995; in force 11 June 2008: sections 23–46, 53–60, 62(4) and (6), 63(1) (so far as it is not already in force), (2) and (3) and 65 (so far as it relates to the repeals in Schedule 7 coming into force on the same date) and Schedules 4 and 5 (so far as it is not already in force) and the repeals in Schedule 7 of section 15 of the Faculty Jurisdiction Measure 1964, sections 2, 41, 45 and 87(1) of and paragraphs 1–4 of Schedule 5 to the Pastoral Measure 1983, section 20(1) of the Care of Cathedrals Measure 1990, section 31(1) of the Care of Churches and Ecclesiastical Jurisdiction Measure 1991, section 1 of the Pastoral (Amendment) Measure 1994, section 6(1) of the Care of Places of Worship Measure 1999, section 2(3) of the Synodical Government (Amendment) Measure 2003 and paragraphs 10 and 13 to Schedule 4 to the Church of England (Miscellaneous Provisions) Measure 2005; in force 1 September 2008: section 2, 3(5) and (6), 4, 5, 6((1)–(2) and (4)–(8), 7–11, 18–21, 63(6) and 65 (so far as it relates to the repeals in Schedule 7 coming into force on the same date) and the repeals in Schedule 7 of the words after "being" to "any other diocese" in rule 34(1)(c) in Schedule 3 to the Synodical Government Measure 1969, sections 1–9, 16–17 and 18(1)(a) and (2)–(4), the words "and the report of the Commission thereon" in sections 18(5) and (7) and sections 19–25 of and the Schedule to the Dioceses Measure 1978, section 6 of the Church of England (Legal Aid and Miscellaneous Provisions) Measure 1988, paragraph 18 of Schedule 3 to the Church of England (Miscellaneous Provisions) Measure 1992, paragraph 7 of Schedule 2 to the Cathedrals Measure 1999 and section 18 of the Church of England (Miscellaneous Provisions) Measure 2000; in force 1 February 2009: sections 3(1) to (4) and section 6(3); the remainder in force 1 January 2011)

Church of England Marriage Measure 2008 (1 October 2008)

Ecclesiastical Offices (Terms of Service) Measure 2009 (in force 1 July 2009: sections 2, 10 and 13; in force 24 November 2009: section 8; in force 31 January 2011: all those provisions which have not previously been brought into force, except paragraphs 6, 10, 12 and 13 of Schedule 2; the remainder to come into force on a date or dates yet to be determined)

Church of England Pensions (Amendment) Measure 2009 (2 April 2009)

Vacancies in Suffragan Sees and Other Ecclesiastical Offices Measure 2010 (in force 1 June 2010: sections 1 and 3; in force 11 June 2010: section 4 (so far as not already in force); in force 1 January 2011: section 2)
Church of England (Miscellaneous Provisions) Measure 2010 (in force 1 July 2010: sections 3, 4, 9, 10(1) and (3), and 13; in force 1 September 2010: all remaining provisions except section 8 (to come into force on a date yet to be determined))
Crown Benefices (Parish Representatives) Measure 2010 (1 January 2011)
Ecclesiastical Fees (Amendment) Measure 2011 (in force 1 July 2011: Part 1, Sections 4, 5(2) and (3) and Schedules 1 and 2; the remainder in force 1 October 2011)
Care of Cathedrals Measure 2011 (1 September 2011)
Mission and Pastoral Measure 2011 (1 July 2012)

STATUTORY INSTRUMENTS
Church Representation Rules (Amendment) Resolution 2004 SI 2004 No. 1889 (1 August 2004, 1 January 2005 and 15 February 2005)
Clergy Discipline Rules 2005 SI 2005 No 2022 (1 January 2006)
Clergy Discipline Appeal Rules 2005 SI 2005 No 3201 (1 January 2006)
Church of England (Legal Aid) (Amendment) Rules 2006 SI 2006 No 1939 (1 August 2006)
Care of Cathedrals Rules 2006 SI 2006 No 1941 (1 January 2008)
Parsonages Measure (Amendment) Rules 2007 SI 2007 No 862 (1 May 2007)
National Institutions of the Church of England (Transfer of Functions) Order 2007 SI 2007 No 1556 (1 January 2008)
Ecclesiastical Offices (Terms of Service) Regulations 2009 SI 2009 No 2108 (1 January 2011)
Church of England Pensions (Amendment) Regulations 2009 SI 2009 No 2109 (1 January 2010)
Church Representation Rules (Amendment) Resolution 2009 SI 2009 No 2129 (1 January 2010)
Ecclesiastical Offices (Terms of Service) Directions 2010 (1 January 2011)
Church of England Pensions (Amendment) Regulations (1 January 2011)
Ecclesiastical Offices (Terms of Service) (Amendment) Regulations 2010 (1 January 2011)
Ecclesiastical Offices (Terms of Service) (Consequential and Transitional Provisions) Order 2010 (31 January 2011)
Ecclesiastical Offices (Terms of Service) (Amendment) (No.2) Regulations 2010 (31 January 2011)
Church of England Pensions (Sodor and Man) (Amendment) Regulations 2011 (10 July 2011)
Payments to the Churches Conservation Trust Order 2011 (1 April 2012)
Ecclesiastical Offices (Terms of Service) (Consequential Provisions) Order 2012 (1 July 2012)
Parochial Fees and Scheduled Matters Amending Order 2012 (1 January 2013)
Legal Officers (Annual Fees) Order 2012 (1 January 2013)
Ecclesiastical Judges, Legal Officers and Others (Fees) Order 2012 (1 January 2013)

Copies of the above legislation as originally enacted may be obtained from TSO (details below) or from the Office of Public Sector Information website: http:www.legislation.gov.uk/ukcm. The consolidated text of the Church Representation Rules (as at 1 January 2011) is published by Church House Publishing (£7.99) and is available on the Church of England website: http://www.churchofengland.org/about-us/structure/churchlawlegis/church-representation-rules.

Further Details
Lists of Church of England Measures which have received the Royal Assent from 1920 onwards and of Statutory Instruments to date which are still in force are available the Legal Office website at: http://www.churchofengland.org/about-us/structure/churchlawlegis/legislation/measures/list. Recently passed Measures and Rules made pursuant to Measures are sold by TSO and may be obtained from (TSO) Orders, PO Box 29, Norwich NR3 1GN (*telephone enquiries:* 0870 600 5522, *email:* customer.services@tso.co.uk *online ordering:* www.tsoshop.co.uk). TSO or the Legal Office will advise on obtaining copies of Measures that are out of print. All requests should quote as a reference the title and year of the Measure. Church of England legislation in up to date form may also be found on the UK Statute Law Database at: www.statutelaw.gov.uk.

Constitution

1 The General Synod shall consist of the Convocations of Canterbury and York joined together in a House of Bishops and a House of Clergy and having added to them a House of Laity.

2 The House of Bishops and the House of Clergy shall accordingly comprise the Upper and the Lower Houses respectively of the said Convocations, and the House of Laity shall be elected and otherwise constituted in accordance with the Church Representation Rules.

3 (1) The General Synod shall meet in sessions at least twice a year, and at such times and places as it may provide, or, in the absence of such provision, as the Joint Presidents of the Synod may direct.

(2) The General Synod shall, on the dissolution of the Convocations, itself be automatically dissolved, and shall come into being on the calling together of the new Convocations.

(3) Business pending at the dissolution of the General Synod shall not abate, but may be resumed by the new Synod at the stage reached before the dissolution, and any Boards, Commissions, Committees or other bodies of the Synod may, so far as may be appropriate and subject to any Standing Orders or any directions of the Synod or of the Archbishops of Canterbury and York, continue their proceedings during the period of the dissolution, and all things may be done by the Archbishops or any such bodies or any officers of the General Synod as may be necessary or expedient for conducting the affairs of the Synod during the period of dissolution and for making arrangements for the resumption of business by the new Synod.

(4) A member of the General Synod may continue to act during the period of the dissolution as a member of any such Board, Commission, Committee or body:

Provided that, if a member of the Synod who is an elected Proctor of the clergy or an elected member of the House of Laity does not stand for re-election or is not re-elected, this paragraph shall cease to apply to him with effect from the date on which the election of his successor is announced by the presiding officer.

4 (1) The Archbishops of Canterbury and York shall be joint Presidents of the General Synod, and they shall determine the occasions on which it is desirable that one of the Presidents shall be the chairman of a meeting of the General Synod, and shall arrange between them which of them is to take the chair on any such occasion:

Provided that one of the Presidents shall be the chairman when any motion is taken for the final approval of a provision to which Article 7 of this Constitution applies and in such other cases as may be provided in Standing Orders.

(2) The Presidents shall, after consultation with the Appointments Committee of the Church of England, appoint from among the members of the Synod a panel of no fewer than three or more than eight chairmen, who shall be chosen for their experience and ability as chairmen of meetings and may be members of any House; and it shall be the duty of one of the chairmen on the panel, in accordance with arrangements approved by the Presidents and subject to any special directions of the Presidents, to take the chair at meetings of the General Synod at which neither of the Presidents takes the chair.

[(3) Under the Synodical Government Measure the Provincial Registrars are Joint Registrars of the General Synod but since 1980 the responsibility has been exercised by the Legal Adviser to the General Synod whom each Archbishop appointed as his Joint Registrar for this purpose.]

5 (1) A motion for the final approval of any Measure or Canon shall not be deemed to be carried unless, on a division by Houses, it receives the assent of the majority of the members of each House present and voting:

Provided that by permission of the chairman and with the leave of the General Synod given in accordance with Standing Orders this requirement may be dispensed with.

(2) All other motions of the General Synod shall, subject as hereinafter provided, be determined by a majority of the members of the Synod present and voting, and the vote may be taken by a show of hands or a division:

Provided that, except in the case of a motion relating solely to the course of business or procedure, any 25 members present may demand a division by Houses and in that case the motion shall not be deemed to be carried unless, on such a division, it receives the assent of the majority of the members of each House present and voting.

(3) This Article shall be subject to any provision of this Constitution or of any Measure with respect to special majorities of the Synod or of each House thereof, and where a special majority of each House is required the vote shall be taken on a division by Houses, and where a special majority of the whole Synod is required, the motion shall, for the purposes of this Article, be one relating solely to procedure.

(4) Where a vote is to be taken on a division by Houses, it may be taken by an actual division or in such other manner as Standing Orders may provide.

6 The functions of the General Synod shall be as follows:

(*a*) to consider matters concerning the Church of England and to make provision in respect thereof –

(1) by Measure intended to be given, in the manner prescribed by the Church of England Assembly (Powers) Act 1919, the force and effect of an Act of Parliament, or

(2) by Canon made, promulged and executed in accordance with the like provisions and subject to the like restrictions and having the like legislative force as Canons heretofore made, promulged and executed by the Convocations of Canterbury and York, or

(3) by such order, regulation or other subordinate instrument as may be

authorized by Measure or Canon, or

(4) by such Act of Synod, regulation or other instrument or proceeding as may be appropriate in cases where provision by or under a Measure or Canon is not required;

(*b*) to consider and express their opinion on any other matters of religious or public interest.

7 (1) A provision touching doctrinal formulae or the services or ceremonies of the Church of England or the administration of the Sacraments or sacred rites thereof shall, before it is finally approved by the General Synod, be referred to the House of Bishops, and shall be submitted for such final approval in terms proposed by the House of Bishops and not otherwise.

(2) A provision touching any of the matters aforesaid shall, if the Convocations or either of them or the House of Laity so require, be referred, in the terms proposed by the House of Bishops for final approval by the General Synod, to the two Convocations sitting separately for their provinces and to the House of Laity; and no provision so referred shall be submitted for final approval by the General Synod unless it has been approved, in the terms so proposed, by each House of the two Convocations sitting as aforesaid and by the House of Laity.

(3) The question whether such a reference is required by a Convocation shall be decided by the President and Prolocutor of the Houses of that Convocation, and the Prolocutor shall consult the Standing Committee of the Lower House of Canterbury or, as the case may be, the Assessors of the Lower House of York, and the decision of the President and Prolocutor shall be conclusive:

Provided that if, before such a decision is taken, either House of a Convocation resolves that the provision concerned shall be so referred or both Houses resolve that it shall not be so referred, the resolution or resolutions shall be a conclusive decision that the reference is or is not required by that Convocation.

(4) The question whether such a reference is required by the House of Laity shall be decided by the Prolocutor and Pro-Prolocutor of that House who shall consult the Standing Committee of that House, and the decision of the Prolocutor and the Pro-Prolocutor shall be conclusive:

Provided that if, before such a decision is taken, the House of Laity resolves that the reference is or is not required, the resolution shall be a conclusive decision of that question.

(5) Standing Orders of the General Synod shall provide for ensuring that a provision which fails to secure approval on a reference under this Article by each of the four Houses of the Convocations or by the House of Laity of the General Synod is not proposed again in the same or a similar form until a new General Synod comes into being, except that, in the case of objection by one House of one Convocation only, provision may be made for a second reference to the Convocations and, in the case of a second objection by one House only, for reference to the Houses of Bishops and Clergy of the General Synod for approval by a two-thirds majority of the members of each House present and voting, in lieu of such approval by the four Houses aforesaid.

(6) If any question arises whether the requirements of this Article or Standing Orders made thereunder apply to any provision, or whether those requirements have been complied with, it shall be conclusively determined by the Presidents and Prolocutors of the Houses of the Convocations and the Prolocutor and Pro-Prolocutor of the House of Laity of the General Synod.

8 (1) A Measure or Canon providing for permanent changes in the Services of Baptism or Holy Communion or in the Ordinal, or a scheme for a constitutional union or a permanent and substantial change of relationship between the Church of England and another Christian body, being a body a substantial number of whose members reside in Great Britain, shall not be finally approved by the General Synod unless, at a stage determined by the Archbishops, the Measure or Canon or scheme, or the substance of the proposals embodied therein, has been approved by a majority of the dioceses at meetings of their Diocesan Synods, or, in the case of the Diocese in Europe, of the Bishop's Council and Standing Committee of that diocese.

(1a) If the Archbishops consider that this Article should apply to a scheme which affects the Church of England and another Christian body but does not fall within paragraph (1) of this Article, they may direct that this Article shall apply to that scheme, and where such a direction is given this Article shall apply accordingly.

(1b) The General Synod may by resolution provide that final approval of any such scheme as aforesaid, being a scheme specified in the resolution, shall require the assent of such special majorities of the members present and voting as may be specified in the resolution, and the resolution may specify a special majority of each House or of the whole Synod or of both, and in the latter case the majorities may be different.

(1c) A motion for the final approval of a Measure providing for permanent changes in any such Service or in the Ordinal shall not be deemed to be carried unless it receives the assent of a majority in each House of the General Synod of not less than two-thirds of those present and voting.

(2) Any question whether this Article applies to any Measure or Canon or scheme, or whether its requirements have been complied with, shall

be conclusively determined by the Archbishops, the Prolocutors of the Lower Houses of the Convocations and the Prolocutor and Pro-Prolocutor of the House of Laity of the General Synod.

9 (1) Standing Orders of the General Synod may provide for separate sittings of any of the three Houses or joint sittings of any two Houses and as to who is to take the chair at any such separate or joint sitting.

(2) The House of Laity shall elect a Chairman and Vice-Chairman of that House who shall also discharge the functions assigned by this Constitution and the Standing Orders and by or under any Measure or Canon to the Prolocutor and Pro-Prolocutor of that House.

10 (1) The General Synod shall appoint a Legislative Committee from members of all three Houses, to whom shall be referred all Measures passed by the General Synod which it is desired should be given, in accordance with the procedure prescribed by the Church of England Assembly (Powers) Act 1919, the force of an Act of Parliament; and it shall be the duty of the Legislative Committee to take such steps with respect to any such Measure as may be so prescribed.

(2) The General Synod may appoint or provide by their Standing Orders for the appointment of such Committees, Commissions and bodies (in addition to the Committees mentioned in Section 10 of the National Institutions Measure 1998), which may include persons who are not members of the Synod, and such officers as they think fit.

(3) Each House may appoint or provide by their Standing Orders for the appointment of such Committees of their members as they think fit.

11 (1) The General Synod may make, amend and revoke Standing Orders providing for any of the matters for which such provision is required or authorized by this Constitution to be made, and consistently with this Constitution, for the meetings, business and procedure of the General Synod.

(1a) Provision may be made by Standing Order that the exercise of any power of the General Synod to suspend the Standing Orders or any of them shall require the assent of such a majority of the members of the whole Synod present and voting as may be specified in the Standing Order.

(2) Each House may make, amend and revoke Standing Orders for the matter referred to in Article 10 (3) hereof and consistently with this Constitution and with any Standing Orders of the General Synod, for the separate sittings, business and procedure of that House.

(3) Subject to this Constitution and to any Standing Orders, the business and procedure at any meeting of the General Synod or any House or Houses thereof shall be regulated by the chairman of the meeting.

12 (1) References to final approval shall, in relation to a Canon or Act of Synod, be construed as referring to the final approval by the General Synod of the contents of the Canon or Act, and not to the formal promulgation thereof:

Provided that the proviso to Article 4 (1) shall apply both to the final approval and to the formal promulgation of a Canon or Act of Synod.

(2) Any question concerning the interpretation of this Constitution, other than questions for the determination of which express provision is otherwise made, shall be referred to and determined by the Archbishops of Canterbury and York.

(3) No proceedings of the General Synod or any House or Houses thereof, or any Board, Commission, Committee or body thereof, shall be invalidated by any vacancy in the membership of the body concerned or by any defect in the qualification, election or appointment of any member thereof.

13 Any functions exercisable under this Constitution by the Archbishops of Canterbury and York, whether described as such or as Presidents of the General Synod, may, during the absence abroad or incapacity through illness of one Archbishop or a vacancy in one of the Sees, be exercised by the other Archbishop alone.

NATIONAL STRUCTURES

General Synod Business

Full details of the General Synod's Sessions can be found at: www.churchofengland.org

FEBRUARY 2012 GROUP OF SESSIONS

PROGRESS OF MEASURES AND STATUTORY INSTRUMENTS

The Archbishop of Canterbury reported that:

- the Care of Cathedrals Measure 2011 had come into force on 1 September 2011;
- the provisions of the Ecclesiastical Fees (Amendment) Measure 2011 which were not previously in force had come into force on 1 October 2011;
- the Ecclesiastical Judges, Legal Officers and Others (Fees) Order 2011 and the Legal Officers (Annual Fees) Order 2011 had come into force on 1 January 2012; and

- the Payments to the Churches Conservation Trust Order 2011 would come into force on 1 April 2012.

LOYAL ADDRESS

The motion 'That this Synod congratulate most warmly Her Majesty Queen Elizabeth II on her Diamond Jubilee and approve the submission to Her Majesty of a Loyal Address along the lines indicated in the Second Notice Paper' was carried.

LEGISLATIVE BUSINESS

DRAFT PAROCHIAL FEES AND SCHEDULED MATTERS AMENDING ORDER 2012

Order made under the Ecclesiastical Fees Measure 1986 for Approval

The Synod having approved the Parochial Fees and Scheduled Matters Amending Order with amendment, the order stood referred to the Archbishops' Council.

DRAFT CLERGY DISCIPLINE (AMENDMENT) MEASURE

Draft Measure for Revision (First Consideration February 2011)

Report by the Revision Committee (GS 1814Y)

The Synod took note of the Report of the Revision Committee, and completed the Revision Stage, for the draft Clergy Discipline (Amendment) Measure. The draft Measure accordingly stood committed to the Steering Committee in respect of its final drafting.

DRAFT DIOCESE IN EUROPE MEASURE (GS 1853)

Draft Measure for First Consideration

The Synod resolved that the draft Diocese in Europe Measure be considered for revision in committee.

THE ECCLESIASTICAL OFFICES (TERMS OF SERVICE) (CONSEQUENTIAL PROVISIONS) ORDER 2012

Order made under section 11 of the Ecclesiastical Offices (Terms of Service) Measure 2009 for approval

The Synod having approved the Ecclesiastical Offices (Terms of Service) (Consequential Provisions) Order 2012 with amendment, the Order stood referred to the Archbishops' Council.

DRAFT BISHOPS AND PRIESTS (CONSECRATION AND ORDINATION OF WOMEN) MEASURE and DRAFT AMENDING CANON NO 30

Draft Measure and draft Amending Canon for Final Drafting (Revision July 2010)

Report by the Steering Committee

The Synod completed the Final Drafting Stage for the draft Bishops and Priests (Consecration and Ordination of Women) Measure and draft Amending Canon No 30.

DIOCESAN SYNOD MOTIONS

WOMEN IN THE EPISCOPATE

The motion 'That this Synod

(a) noting the significant support the draft Bishops and Priests (Consecration and Ordination of Women) Measure has received in the Houses of Bishops, Clergy and Laity of diocesan synods, and
(b) desiring that the draft Measure be returned to the Synod for consideration on the Final Approval Stage substantially unamended so that it can be seen if the proposals embodied in it in the form in which it has been referred to the dioceses can attain the level of support required to achieve Final Approval, request the House of Bishops in the exercise of its power under Standing Order 60(b) not to amend the draft Measure substantially'

was carried.

PRIVATE MEMBERS' MOTIONS

INDEPENDENT COMMISSION ON ASSISTED DYING

The motion 'That this Synod

(a) express its concern that the Independent Commission on Assisted Dying was insufficiently independent to be able to develop proposals which will properly protect the interests of vulnerable and disabled people;
(b) endorse the responses to the Commission on Assisted Dying referred to in paragraphs 7 and 8 of GS 1815B;
(c) affirm the intrinsic value of every human life and express its support for the current law on assisted suicide as a means of contributing to a just and compassionate society in which vulnerable people are protected; and
(d) celebrating the considerable improvement in the quality of care of the dying brought about by the hospice and palliative care movements and by the input of clinicians, clergy and others, encourage the Church's continued involvement in the wider agenda of the care of those approaching the end of their lives and the support of those caring for them'

was carried after a division of the whole Synod. The voting was as follows: *In Favour: 284; Against: 0; Recorded Abstentions: 4.*

REFORM OF THE HOUSE OF LORDS

The motion 'That this Synod, welcoming both the Archbishops' submission to the Joint Parliamentary Committee on the draft Bill on House of Lords Reform and the extension of the Episcopal group on Lords Reform to include members of the other two Houses of Synod invite the extended group to bring to the February 2013 group of sessions

(i) an assessment of the implications for the Church and nation of any Bill to be brought forward by the Government,
(ii) recommendations for changes in custom and practice to accommodate any new requirements of the Church'

was carried.

HEALTH CARE AND THE CHURCH'S MISSION: REPORT FROM THE MISSION AND PUBLIC AFFAIRS COUNCIL
The motion 'That this Synod, mindful of our Lord's ministry of healing and his charge to his disciples to heal the sick in his name:

(a) affirm the ministry of all who promote health and wholeness in body, mind and spirit, and, recognizing in particular the role of chaplains in the NHS as an expression of the Church of England's commitment to minister to all in the community, whether as patients or healthcare workers, call upon Her Majesty's Government to ensure that chaplaincy provision remains part of the core structure of a National Health Service committed to physical, mental and spiritual health;
(b) call upon Her Majesty's Government to apply as the test to any proposed changes to the NHS whether they are best calculated to secure the provision throughout the country of effective and efficient healthcare services provided free at the point of delivery and according to clinical need;
(c) commend the work of mission agencies and the networks of the Anglican Communion in embodying the churches' contribution to health and wholeness and promoting fairer sharing of health resources worldwide.'

was carried after a division of the whole Synod. The voting was as follows: *In Favour: 208; Against: 0; Recorded Abstentions: 0.*

OTHER BUSINESS
RECENT VIOLENCE IN NIGERIA
The motion 'That this Synod, gravely concerned at the desperate plight of Christian communities in parts of Nigeria, as described in GS 1861, request the British Government to do all it can to support those in Nigeria seeking to protect religious minorities of all faiths and enable them to practise their religion without fear' was carried after a division of the whole Synod. The voting was as follows: *In Favour: 344; Against 0; Recorded Abstentions; 1.*

JULY 2012 GROUP OF SESSIONS

PROGRESS OF MEASURES AND STATUTORY INSTRUMENTS
The Archbishop of York reported that:

- the Mission and Pastoral Measure 2011 had come into force on 1 July 2012;
- the Ecclesiastical Offices (Terms of Service) (Consequential Provisions) Order 2012 had come into force on 1 July 2012; and
- the Parochial Fees and Scheduled Matters Amending Order 2012 would come into force on 1 January 2013.

LEGISLATIVE BUSINESS
DRAFT CLERGY DISCIPLINE (AMENDMENT) MEASURE
Draft Measure for Final Drafting and Final Approval (Revision February 2012)
Report by the Steering Committee
The Synod completed the Final Drafting Stage for the draft Clergy Discipline (Amendment) Measure and subsequently gave it Final Approval. The draft Measure accordingly stood committed to the Legislative Committee.

DRAFT DIOCESE IN EUROPE MEASURE
Draft Measure for Revision and Final Approval (First Consideration February 2012)
The Synod completed the Final Drafting Stage for the draft Diocese in Europe Measure and subsequently gave it Final Approval. The draft Measure accordingly stood committed to the Legislative Committee.

DRAFT CHURCH OF ENGLAND (MISCELLANEOUS PROVISIONS) MEASURE
Draft Measure for First Consideration
The Synod resolved that the draft Church of England (Miscellaneous Provisions) Measure be considered for revision in committee.

DRAFT AMENDING CANON NO. 31
Draft Amending Canon for First Consideration
The Synod resolved that draft Amending Canon No. 31 be considered for revision in committee.

THE CHURCH OF ENGLAND FUNDED PENSION SCHEME (AMENDMENT) RULES 2012 (GS 1867)
Rules made under the Pensions Measure 1997 for Approval
The Synod approved the Church of England Funded Pensions Scheme (Amendment) Rules 2012.

DRAFT BISHOPS AND PRIESTS (CONSECRATION AND ORDINATION OF WOMEN) MEASURE and DRAFT AMENDING CANON NO. 30

Draft Measure and Draft Amending Canon for Final Approval (Final Drafting February 2012)

The Archbishop of York reported that the Convocations of Canterbury and York and the House of Laity had approved both the draft Bishops and Priests (Consecration and Ordination of Women) Measure and Draft Amending Canon No.30. The motion 'That the Measure entitled "Bishops and Priests (Consecration and Ordination of Women) Measure" be finally approved' was moved. The motion 'That the debate be now adjourned to enable the new clause 5(1)(c) inserted by the House of Bishops into the draft Measure entitled "Bishops and Priests (Consecration and Ordination of Women) Measure" to be reconsidered by the House of Bishops' was carried after a division of the whole Synod. The voting was as follows: *In Favour: 288; Against: 144; Recorded Abstentions 15.* The draft Bishops and Priests (Consecration and Ordination of Women) Measure accordingly stood referred to the House of Bishops. The motions for the Final Approval of draft Amending Canon No 30 and the adoption of the petition for Her Majesty's Royal Assent and Licence were not moved.

DIOCESAN SYNOD MOTIONS

VACANCY IN SEE COMMITTEES

The motion 'That the Synod resolve that the Vacancy in See Committees Regulation 1993 (as amended in 2003, 2007 and 2008) be amended so as to ensure that Vacancy in See Committees have at least 21 members' was carried.

PRIVATE MEMBERS' MOTIONS

PAROCHIAL CHURCH COUNCILS (POWERS) MEASURE 1956

The motion 'That this Synod call on the Archbishops' Council to bring forward legislation to amend the Parochial Church Councils (Powers) Measure 1956 so as to permit a PCC which is a registered charity to acquire and hold any interest in land and any interest in personal property to be held on permanent trusts, without any requirement for the interest to be vested in the diocesan authority' was carried after a division of the whole Synod. The voting was as follows: *In Favour: 137; Against: 122; Recorded Abstentions 16.*

MANIFESTATION OF FAITH IN PUBLIC LIFE

The motion 'That this Synod express its conviction that it is the calling of Christians to order and govern our lives in accordance with the teaching of Holy Scripture, and to manifest our faith in public life as well as in private, giving expression to our beliefs in the written and spoken word, and in practical acts of service to the local community and to the nation' was carried after a division of the whole Synod. The voting was as follows: *In Favour 263; Against: 25; Recorded Abstentions 52.*

PALESTINE AND ISRAEL

The motion 'That this Synod affirm its support for:

(a) the vital work of the World Council of Churches Ecumenical Accompaniment Programme in Palestine and Israel (EAPPI), encouraging parishioners to volunteer for the programme and asking churches and synods to make use of the experience of returning participants;
(b) mission and other aid agencies working amongst Palestinians in Gaza, the West Bank and elsewhere in the region;
(c) Israelis and Palestinians in all organizations working for justice and peace in the area, such as the Parents Circle – Families Forum; and
(d) Palestinian Christians and organizations that work to ensure their continuing presence in the Holy Land.'

was carried after a division by Houses. The voting was as follows: *In Favour: Bishops 21, Clergy 89, Laity 91; Against: Bishops 3, Clergy 21, Laity 30; Recorded Abstentions: Bishops 14, Clergy 44, Laity 35.*

LITURGICAL BUSINESS

ADDITIONAL EUCHARISTIC PRAYERS

Drafts for Final Approval

The Synod approved the Additional Eucharistic Prayers for a period from 1 September 2012 until further Resolution of the Synod after a division by Houses, a majority of not less than two-thirds of those present and voting in each House being required. The voting was as follows: *In Favour: Bishops 26, Clergy 110, Laity 95; Against: Bishops 0, Clergy 0, Laity 5; Recorded Abstentions: Bishops 0, Clergy 0, Laity 5.*

FINANCIAL BUSINESS

VOTE FOR TRAINING FOR MINISTRY

The Synod approved the Archbishops' Council's expenditure for the year 2013, as shown in its budget, of £12,559,340 (net of income from sources apart from diocesan contributions) in respect of training for ministry.

VOTE FOR NATIONAL SUPPORT

The Synod approved the Archbishops' Council's expenditure for the year 2013, as shown in its budget, of £10,636,428 (net of income from sources apart from diocesan contributions) in respect of national support.

VOTE FOR GRANTS AND PROVISIONS

The Synod approved the Archbishops' Council's expenditure for the year 2013, as shown in its budget, of £1,284,774 (net of income from sources apart from diocesan contributions) in respect of grants and provisions.

VOTE FOR MISSION AGENCIES' CLERGY PENSION CONTRIBUTIONS
The Synod approved the Archbishops' Council's expenditure for the year 2013, as shown in its budget, of £644,986 (net of income from sources apart from diocesan contributions) in respect of mission agencies' clergy pension contributions.

VOTE FOR CHARM
The Synod approved the Archbishops' Council's expenditure for the year 2013, as shown in its budget, of £3,765,615 (net of income from sources apart from diocesan contributions) in respect of the CHARM scheme.

APPORTIONMENT
The Synod approved the Archbishops' Council's proposals for the apportionment amongst the dioceses of the net sum to be provided by them to enable the Council to meet the expected expenditure shown in its budget for the year 2013.

POOLING ADJUSTMENT
The Synod approved the Archbishops' Council's proposals for the pooling adjustment for 2013 in respect of additional maintenance grants for ordinands.

OTHER BUSINESS
WORLD-SHAPED MISSION
The motion 'That this Synod, recognizing the Church of England's historic and continuing participation in world mission as essential to our identity as members of the universal Church, welcome the report entitled *World-Shaped Mission* and commend it to the dioceses, deaneries and parishes of the Church of England for further study;

(a) affirm the ongoing role of the Mission Agencies in resourcing the mission of the Church of England at home and overseas;
(b) affirm the continuing growth, whether through the Diocesan Companion Links, initiatives by parishes or otherwise, in the relationships between the Church of England, the Provinces of the Anglican Communion and the world Church; and
(c) encourage the building of continuing partnership between all involved in Church of England world mission and development relationships.'

was carried.

FRESH EXPRESSIONS AND CHURCH GROWTH: REPORT FROM THE MISSION AND PUBLIC AFFAIRS COUNCIL, to which is appended FRESH EXPRESSIONS IN THE MISSION OF THE CHURCH
The motion 'That this Synod, recognizing fresh expressions as authentic manifestations of Anglican ecclesiology:

(a) express gratitude to the Fresh Expressions team for its leadership, inspiration and effectiveness as catalyst to over 1,000 fresh expressions within the Church of England, and many more ecumenically;
(b) affirm the mixed economy of church as an enduring model for ministry and mission into the future;
(c) affirm that radical social action and comment are essential elements of the Biblical witness and Christian tradition, and therefore of any ecclesiology;
(d) call upon the Archbishops' Council and House of Bishops to ensure that the report *Fresh Expressions in the Mission of the Church* and its recommendations are incorporated into the programme "re-imagine ministry" and are reflected in the future work of the Ministry Division, the Mission and Public Affairs Council and other National Church Institutions; and
(e) request the Archbishops' Council to report to the Synod before July 2014 on how the Fresh Expressions team's legacy is to be secured within the life of the Church.'

was carried.

PART 3

General

PART 3 CONTENTS

GENERAL INFORMATION

Addressing the Clergy

Since the Lambeth Conference of 1968, at which styles of address were debated, there has been a trend towards simpler forms of address. Resolution 14 stated: 'The Conference recommends that the bishops, as leaders and representatives of a servant Church, should radically examine the honours paid to them in the course of divine worship, in titles and customary address, and in style of living, while having the necessary facilities for the efficient carrying on of their work.'

Whereas formerly a bishop would have been addressed as 'My Lord' and a dean as 'Mr Dean', it has become more usual to address a bishop in speech as 'Bishop' and a dean as 'Dean'. There is, however, a correct way to address clergy on an envelope, which is normally as follows:

Archbishop of Canterbury or York	The Most Revd and Rt Hon the Lord Archbishop of
Archbishop of another Province	The Most Revd the Lord Archbishop of
Bishop of London	The Rt Revd and Rt Hon the Lord Bishop of
Diocesan/Suffragan Bishop	*Either* The Rt Revd the Lord Bishop of *or* The Rt Revd the Bishop of
Assistant/Retired Bishop	The Rt Revd J. D. Smith (*or* John Smith)
Dean	The Very Revd the Dean of
Provost	The Very Revd the Provost of
Archdeacon	The Ven the Archdeacon of
Canon	The Revd Canon J. D. Smith (*or* John or Jane Smith)
Prebendary	The Revd Prebendary J. D. Smith (*or* John or Jane Smith)
Rural Dean	No special form of address (The Revd, the Revd Canon, etc.)
Dean of Oxford/Cambridge College	No special form of address
Cleric also Professor	*Either* The Revd Professor J. D. Smith *or* Professor the Revd J. D. Smith
Canon also Professor	*Either* The Revd Canon Professor J. D. Smith *or* Professor the Revd Canon J. D. Smith
Cleric also Doctor	*Either* The Revd Dr J. D. Smith *or* The Revd J. D. Smith (degree)
Canon also Doctor	The Revd Canon J. D. Smith (degree)
Other Clergy/Priest/Deacon	The Revd J. D. Smith (*or* John or Jane Smith)

The following points should be noted particularly:

1 A diocesan or suffragan bishop has a title conferred on him by his consecration or subsequent translation, which he is entitled to hold until he resigns. He then reverts to his personal name, retaining the title 'Right Reverend'.

2 A dean, provost or archdeacon has a territorial title until he resigns. He then reverts to his personal name, and his title is 'Reverend' unless the rank of dean, provost or archdeacon emeritus has been awarded.

3 Retired archbishops properly go back to the status of a bishop but may be given as a courtesy the style of an archbishop.

4 A bishop holding office as a dean or archdeacon is addressed as The Rt Revd the Dean/Archdeacon of.

5 If a cleric's name or initials are unknown, he or she should be addressed as The Revd — Smith or the Revd Mr/Mrs/Miss/Ms Smith. It is never correct to refer to a cleric as 'The Reverend Smith' or 'Revd Smith'.

6 There is no universally accepted way of addressing an envelope to a married couple of whom both are in holy orders. We recommend the style 'The Revd A. B. and the Revd C. D. Smith'.

Archbishops of Canterbury and York

CANTERBURY
597 Augustine
604 Laurentius
619 Mellitus
624 Justus
627 Honorius
655 Deusdedit
668 Theodore
693 Beorhtweald
731 Tatwine
735 Nothelm
740 Cuthbeorht
761 Breguwine
765 Jaenbeorht
793 Æthelheard
805 Wulfred
832 Feologild
833 Ceolnoth
870 Æthelred
890 Plegmund
914 Æthelhelm
923 Wulfhelm
942 Oda
959 Æfsige
959 Beorhthelm
960 Dunstan
*c*988 Athelgar
990 Sigeric Serio
995 Ælfric
1005 Ælfheath
1013 Lyfing
1020 Æthelnoth
1038 Eadsige
1051 Robert of Jumièges
1052 Stigand
1070 Lanfranc
1093 Anselm
1114 Ralph d'Escures
1123 William de Corbeil
1139 Theobald
1162 Thomas Becket
1174 Richard [of Dover]
1185 Baldwin
1193 Hubert Walter
1207 Stephen Langton
1229 Richard le Grant
1234 Edmund Rich
1245 Boniface of Savoy
1273 Robert Kilwardby
1279 John Peckham
1294 Robert Winchelsey
1313 Walter Reynolds
1328 Simon Mepeham
1333 John Stratford
1349 Thomas Bradwardine
1349 Simon Islip
1366 Simon Langham
1368 William Whittlesey
1375 Simon Sudbury
1381 William Courtenay
1396 Thomas Arundel†
1398 Roger Walden
1414 Henry Chichele
1443 John Stafford
1452 John Kemp
1454 Thomas Bourchier
1486 John Morton
1501 Henry Dean
1503 William Warham
1533 Thomas Cranmer
1556 Reginald Pole
1559 Matthew Parker
1576 Edmund Grindal
1583 John Whitgift
1604 Richard Bancroft
1611 George Abbot
1633 William Laud
1660 William Juxon
1663 Gilbert Sheldon
1678 William Sancroft
1691 John Tillotson
1695 Thomas Tenison
1716 William Wake
1737 John Potter
1747 Thomas Herring
1757 Matthew Hutton
1758 Thomas Secker
1768 Frederick Cornwallis
1783 John Moore
1805 Charles Manners Sutton
1828 William Howley
1848 John Bird Sumner
1862 Charles Thomas Longley
1868 Archibald Campbell Tait
1883 Edward White Benson
1896 Frederick Temple
1903 Randall Thomas Davidson
1928 Cosmo Gordon Lang
1942 William Temple
1945 Geoffrey Francis Fisher
1961 Arthur Michael Ramsey
1974 Frederick Donald Coggan
1980 Robert Alexander Kennedy Runcie
1991 George Leonard Carey
2002 Rowan Douglas Williams
2013 Justin Portal Welby

YORK

BISHOPS
625 Paulinus
[vacancy for 30 years]
664 Ceadda
669 Wilfrith I
678 Bosa‡
705 John of Beverley
718 Wilfrith II

ARCHBISHOPS
*c*734 Ecgbeorht
767 Æthelbeorht
780 Eanbald I
796 Eanbald II
*c*812 Wulfsige
837 Wigmund
854 Wulfhere
900 Æthelbeald
*c*928 Hrothweard
931 Wulfstan I
958 Oscytel
971 Edwaldus
972 Osweald
992 Ealdwulf
1003 Wulfstan II
1023 Ælfric Puttoc
1041 Æthelric§
1051 Cynesige
1061 Ealdred
1070 Thomas I
1100 Gerard
1109 Thomas II
1119 Thurstan
1143 William Fitzherbert
1147 Henry Murdac*
1154 Roger of Pont l'Eveque
1191 Geoffrey Plantagenet
1215 Walter de Gray
1256 Sewal de Bovill
1258 Godfrey Ludham
1266 Walter Giffard
1279 William Wickwane
1286 John le Romeyn
1298 Henry Newark
1300 Thomas Corbridge
1306 William Greenfield
1317 William Melton
1342 William Zouche
1352 John Thoresby
1374 Alexander Neville
1388 Thomas Arundel
1396 Robert Waldby
1398 Richard le Scrope
1407 Henry Bowet
1426 John Kemp
1452 William Booth
1465 George Nevill
1476 Lawrence Booth
1480 Thomas Rotherham (or Scot)
1501 Thomas Savage
1508 Christopher Bainbridge
1514 Thomas Wolsey
1531 Edward Lee
1545 Robert Holgate
1555 Nicholas Heath
1561 Thomas Young
1570 Edmund Grindal
1577 Edwin Sandys
1589 John Piers
1595 Matthew Hutton
1606 Tobias Matthew
1628 George Montaigne
1629 Samuel Harsnett
1632 Richard Neile
1641 John Williams
1660 Accepted Frewen
1664 Richard Sterne
1683 John Dolben
1688 Thomas Lamplugh
1691 John Sharp
1714 William Dawes
1724 Lancelot Blackburn
1743 Thomas Herring
1747 Matthew Hutton
1757 John Gilbert
1761 Robert Hay Drummond
1777 William Markham
1808 Edward Venables Vernon Harcourt
1847 Thomas Musgrave
1860 Charles Thomas Longley
1863 William Thomson
1891 William Connor Magee
1891 William Dalrymple Maclagan
1909 Cosmo Gordon Lang
1929 William Temple
1942 Cyril Foster Garbett
1956 Arthur Michael Ramsey
1961 Frederick Donald Coggan
1975 Stuart Yarworth Blanch
1983 John Stapylton Habgood
1995 David Michael Hope
2005 John Tucker Mugabi Sentamu

† On 19 October 1399 Boniface IX annulled Arundel's translation to St Andrews and confirmed him in the see of Canterbury.
‡ Wilfrith was restored to office in 686 and Bosa in 691.
§ Ælfric Puttoc was restored in 1042.
* William Fitzherbert was restored in 1153.

Bishops in the House of Lords

The Archbishops of Canterbury and York and the Bishops of London, Durham and Winchester always have seats in the House of Lords. The twenty-one other seats are filled by diocesan bishops in order of seniority. In the case of bishops awaiting seats, the order of seniority is shown (1), (2), (3), etc.

The Bishop of Sodor and Man and the Bishop of Gibraltar in Europe are not eligible to sit in the House of Lords.

	Election as Diocesan Bishop confirmed	Translated to present See	Entered House of Lords
Canterbury (Most Revd & Rt Hon Justin Portal Welby)	2013	2013	2013
York (Most Revd & Rt Hon J. T. M. Sentamu)	2002	2005	2006
London (Rt Revd & Rt Hon R. J. C. Chartres)	1995		1996
Durham (Rt Revd J. P. Welby)	2011		2011
Winchester (Rt Revd T. J. Dakin)	2012		2012
Bath and Wells (Rt Revd P. B. Price)	2002		2008
Birmingham (Rt Revd D. Urquhart)	2006		2010
Blackburn (Vacant)			(17)
Bradford (Rt Revd N. Baines)	2011		(13)
Bristol (Rt Revd M. Hill)	2003		2009
Carlisle (Rt Revd J. Newcome)	2009		(5)
Chelmsford (Rt Revd S. Cottrell)	2010		(9)
Chester (Rt Revd P. R. Forster)	1996		2001
Chichester (Rt Revd M. Warner)	2012		(16)
Coventry (Rt Revd C. J. Cocksworth)	2008		(1)
Derby (Rt Revd A. L. J. Redfern)	2005		2010
Ely (Rt Revd S. J. Conway)	2010		(11)
Exeter (Rt Revd M. L. Langrish)	2000		2005
Gloucester (Rt Revd M. F. Perham)	2004		2009
Guildford (Rt Revd C. J. Hill)	2004		2010
Hereford (Rt Revd A. M. Priddis)	2004		2009
Leicester (Rt Revd T. J. Stevens)	1999		2003
Lichfield (Rt Revd J. M. Gledhill)	2003		2009
Lincoln (Rt Revd C. Lowson)	2011		(15)
Liverpool (Rt Revd J. S. Jones)	1998		2003
Manchester (Rt Revd N. S. McCulloch)	1992	2002	1997
Newcastle (Rt Revd J. M. Wharton)	1997		2003
Norwich (Rt Revd G. R. James)	1999		2004
Oxford (Rt Revd J. L. Pritchard)	2007		2011
Peterborough (Rt Revd D. Allister)	2010		(7)
Portsmouth (Rt Revd C. Foster)	2010		(8)
Ripon and Leeds (Rt Revd J. R. Packer)	2000		2006
Rochester (Rt Revd J. Langstaff)	2010		(10)
St Albans (Rt Revd A. G. C. Smith)	2009		(4)
St Edmundsbury and Ipswich (Rt Revd W. N. Stock)	2007		2011
Salisbury (Rt Revd N. R. Holtam)	2011		(14)
Sheffield (Rt Revd S. J. L. Croft)	2009		(3)
Southwark (Rt Revd C. T. J. Chessun)	2011		(12)
Southwell and Nottingham (Rt Revd P. Butler)	2009		(6)
Truro (Rt Revd T. M. Thornton)	2008		(2)
Wakefield (Rt Revd S. G. Platten)	2003		2009
Worcester (Rt Revd J. G. Inge)	2008		2012

* As Bishop of Monmouth in the Church in Wales, the bishops of which do not have seats in the House of Lords.

GENERAL

Chaplains

Chaplains in Her Majesty's Services

ROYAL NAVY
Chaplains of all denominations are employed in many parts of the world, ashore and afloat in capital ships, frigates and destroyers, Royal Marine Commando Units, hospitals, Royal Naval Air Stations, HM Naval Bases and Training Establishments. Apart from conducting the customary services in their ships, units or establishments, for which all the necessary facilities are provided, chaplains find numerous opportunities for extending the work of the Church through pastoral contacts with families and dependants, as well as being 'friend and adviser of all on board'. They are given particular opportunity to teach the Christian faith to young people in Training Establishments. In-Service training for all Royal Naval Chaplains is carried out at the Armed Forces Chaplaincy Centre, Amport House, Andover, Hants. SP11 8BG. Christian Leadership Courses for all service personnel are provided at the centre during the year. The Anglican Church in the Royal Navy is served by 45 priests and is very much a part of the Church of England with the Single Service and Tri-Service Synodical structures. The Senior Anglican Chaplain in the Royal Navy is granted the ecclesiastical dignity of Archdeacon by the Archbishop of Canterbury. The Archbishop is the Ordinary for all service chaplains and grants ecclesiastical licences to all Anglican chaplains on the Active List. The Royal Navy is an Equal Opportunities employer and applications for entry from both male and female priests up to the age of 49 are always welcome. Full particulars concerning the entry of Anglican Chaplains can be obtained from DGNCS, Navy Command HQ, MP 1.2, Leach Building, Whale Island, Portsmouth PO2 8BY. *Tel:* 023 9262 5553
Fax: 023 9262 5134
email: lee.foley211@mod.uk

ARMY
Army chaplains serve wherever soldiers serve, including the front line in Afghanistan, providing spiritual, moral and pastoral support to soldiers and their families. Army chaplains are non-combatants and do not bear arms. They are ordained men and women recommended for this ministry by the Sending Churches: Church of England, Church of Scotland, Roman Catholic, Methodist and United Board (United Reformed Church and Baptist), Elim Pentecostal and Assemblies of God. They provide an 'all-souls' ministry to all in their care but ensure that soldiers have access to a chaplain of a particular denomination or faith group when required. Chaplains of all denominations are administered by the Chaplain General. The Chaplain General's post may be filled by a chaplain from any of the Sending Churches. The appointment is currently held by a Baptist Minister, Revd Jonathan Woodhouse CF QHC. The Archdeacon for the Army is Ven Peter Eagles: Ministry of Defence Chaplains (Army), Headquarters Land Forces, Ramillies Building, Marlborough Lines, Monxton Road, Andover SP11 8HJ *Tel:* 01264 381841
Fax: 01264 381824
email: peter.eagles330@mod.uk

ROYAL AIR FORCE
From the foundation of the Royal Air Force, chaplains have been proud to minister to the needs of servicemen and women and their families, in peace and war. The Chaplains' Branch of the Royal Air Force offers a real challenge and a rewarding ministry to young priests who have the necessary qualities, initiative and enthusiasm. The Royal Air Force is a large body of men and women drawn from every corner of Britain and from every stratum of society. There is a continuing need for clergy to minister to these men and women and the Royal Air Force understands and supports this ministry. Chaplains are commissioned by Her Majesty the Queen to provide for the pastoral and spiritual needs of all Service personnel and their families. This care is unlimited, and extends wherever members of the Royal Air Force are called to serve. Clergy may apply for a position in either a full-time or reserve capacity. Further details concerning chaplaincy in the Royal Air Force can be obtained from: Chaplaincy Services (RAF), Valiant Block, RAF High Wycombe HP14 4UE
Tel: 01494 494469
Web: www.raf.mod.uk/chaplains

For a list of **Chaplains to Her Majesty's Services** *see Crockford.*

Forces Synodical Council

President The Archbishop of Canterbury

Senior Vice-President Rt Revd Stephen Venner (*The Archbishop of Canterbury's Episcopal Representative to Her Majesty's Forces*)

Lay Vice-President Lieutenant Commander Philippa Sargent RN

Secretary Revd Martin Gough RN, Naval Chaplaincy Service, Naval Command HQ, MP 1.2, Leach Building, Whale Island, Portsmouth PO2 8BY *email:* martyn.gough656@mod.uk

On the direction of the Secretary of State for Defence and the Archbishop of Canterbury in the 1980s, the Forces Synodical Council (also now known as the Armed Forces Synod) was first convened in 1990 in London. It consists of thirty-six elected members (six clergy and six laity from each of the Royal Navy, Army and Royal Air Force) and up to ten *ex officio* members: the elected Service members of General Synod (currently one clergy and one laity from each Service), the three Service Archdeacons and the Bishop to HM Forces. However, the clergy members of General Synod are currently the three Service Archdeacons.

The Council is chaired by the Bishop to HM Forces but has no fiscal or Armed Service command authority. It gives the Anglican clergy and laity of the whole Armed Services the opportunity to contribute to General Synod, to the Armed Services Chain of Command and to the Ministry of Defence. They can also make decisions pertinent to the life and ministry of the Anglican Church within the Armed Forces, and although members are not drawn exclusively from the Church of England, all ministers hold the Licence of the Archbishop of Canterbury.

Until 2009, each Service was required to convene an Archdeaconry Synod and, below this level, Chaplaincy Councils. Under the new Representation Rules, however, this formal requirement has been dispensed with, although the Army still maintains this structure.

Chaplains in Higher Education

The Church of England supports chaplains in universities and university colleges across the country including the Church Colleges and Universities. The National Adviser for Higher Education, based in the Education Division at Church House, Westminster, is the officer of the Board of Education leading on the Church's policy and ministry in higher education.

The National Adviser advises the Board on policy relating to HE; resources dioceses, universities and colleges and their chaplains, coordinates conferences, induction, and training for HE chaplains (with ecumenical cooperation through the Churches' Higher Education Liaison Group (CHELG)), acts as consultant to chaplains and ecumenical chaplaincy teams, and advises enquirers considering ministry in this sector of education. In general, organized events are open to chaplains throughout Great Britain as well as to ecumenical partners and diocesan staff. The National Adviser and the Board of Education's Higher Education Panel are available to advise the government and Church at all levels when required.

The role of chaplain includes ministry to staff and students, and to institutions as a whole, their leaders and structures. Chaplains are also a point of contact for people of other faiths. The university student experience has changed dramatically in recent years, the sector is undergoing further changes at present, with new funding arrangements having already been agreed and a White Paper, 'students at the heart of the system', proposing yet further change. A key focus for chaplaincy is enlarging an understanding of faith and the Church's ministry in the higher education sector. This is a challenging ministry in the context of mission, in the face of continuing change and increasing student numbers, with all the pressures on people, finance and structures that these bring. It is increasingly carried out in a multi-faith context and is seen as bringing a major contribution to community cohesion. It requires wisdom and understanding. A range of materials reflecting the church's work in Higher Education can be found at: www.churchofengland.org or obtained from the National Adviser for Higher Education, Education Division, Church House, London SW1P 3NZ

Tel: 020 7898 1513

email: stephen.heap@churchofengland.org

For a list of **Educational Chaplains** *see Crockford.*
For **Church Universities and Colleges of Higher Education** *see* page 225.

GENERAL

Chaplains in Further Education

Chaplaincy to Further Education Colleges began in the 1970s and has from the beginning been ecumenical in character and funding. The National Adviser in Further Education is based at Church House, and works closely with the education teams of other bodies, particularly the Methodist Church, and with the National Council on Faiths and Belief in Further Education (fbfe)

Some 200 Further Education chaplaincies are increasingly organised as ecumenical and multi-faith teams, with a mix of ordained and lay members contributing time on a part-time and often voluntary basis to support a regular presence and activities in their local college. Further Education Chaplaincy is concerned with providing for the spiritual and moral welfare of all students, of any faith or none. This is a vital, though challenging mission among today's young people, 43 per cent of whom are educated in further education colleges. This is more than those (40 per cent) who are in schools after the age of 16, and it includes higher proportions of young people from deprived areas, and especially, from ethnic minority backgrounds. As well as full-time chaplains (often combining their role with that of counsellor or tutor), an increasing number of part-time posts mean that over half of colleges have some form of provision and there are many examples of imaginative collaboration between faith groups, colleges and local communities, especially as resources are increasingly constrained in the present economic climate.

Colleges are continuing to adapt to the impact of large-scale curriculum, assessment and funding changes, as well as seeking to embrace the opportunities offered through localism, community engagement and the expansion of Apprenticeships to better serve their learners. In these testing conditions, chaplaincies can offer support to staff and students, as well as their contribution to the wider curriculum and their help with the exploration of values and ethos during a time of such radical change.

At a national level, the Education Division is developing its FE strategy for the next five years, building on the success of the *Pushing Further* programme, which sought to increase the number of colleges which support a chaplaincy, to strengthen existing chaplaincies, especially those where a single local minister is working in isolation, and to contribute to policy making in key areas such as SMSC, inspection, working in multi-faith communities and equality and diversity. In partnership with the All Faiths and None (AFAN) network, an increasing range of curriculum materials are becoming available to support college staff who need to explore sensitive issues of faith and belief in imaginative and fruitful ways.

All who are interested in supporting or learning more about this work may contact:

The National Further Education Adviser, Education Division, Church House, London SW1P 3AZ *Tel:* 020 7898 1517
Web: www.churchofengland.org/education

Chaplains in the Prison Service

The Prison Service Chaplaincy, in partnership with the wider Church, provides chaplains for all HM Prisons in England and Wales. It works within the Prison Service which is part of the National Offender Management Service (NOMS) in the Ministry of Justice. The responsibilities of the Chaplain General and his headquarters colleagues include the giving of advice to ministers and officials about policy decisions with a religious or ethical dimension. In addition, chaplains are recruited, trained, deployed and supported in their work of providing for the religious needs of prisoners, giving opportunities for worship, formation and instruction, and offering a pastoral ministry at times of crisis and opportunity. Chaplains are also involved in enabling the observance of all faith traditions. Their ministry is always available to staff.

All prisons have an Anglican, a Roman Catholic and a Free Church chaplain, with chaplains from many different faiths; the headquarters team includes senior representatives of all three denominations, and the Muslim Adviser. The Chaplain General has responsibility for all faith traditions.

The Bishop to Prisons
Rt Revd James Jones (*Bishop of Liverpool*), Bishop's Lodge, Woolton Park, Liverpool L25 6DT
Tel: 0151 421 0831

Chaplain General
Vacancy

Anglican Adviser to HMPs
Canon Michael Kavanagh Chaplaincy HQ, 3rd Floor – Red Zone, Post Point 3.08, Clive House, 70 Petty France, London SW1H 9EX
Tel: 0300 047 6822
Fax: 0300 047 5182
email: michael.kavanagh@noms.gsi.gov.uk

For a list of **Prison Chaplains** see *Crockford*.

Chaplains to the Police

Apart from a handful of chaplains who are paid full-time or half-time with the Police, the majority of chaplains are ordinary clergy, both men and women working in parishes or local churches and giving their time and energy as volunteers. Most, but not all, chaplains are from the mainstream Christian denominations, but there are a growing number of chaplains of other faiths and belief systems. The services of police chaplains are available to all police officers and staff, and are not dependent upon membership of a faith community. Chaplains can be contacted at local police stations, or privately by telephone or email.

The National Association of Chaplains to the Police advances and supports the work of chaplains to the police in the United Kingdom. Further information is available through the website at www.police-chaplains.org.uk
President Baroness Harris of Richmond
Vice-President Matthew Baggott (*Chief Constable, Police Service in Northern Ireland*)
National Chaplain Revd David Wilbraham (*Force Chaplain, Thames Valley Police*)
Deputy National Chaplain Revd Viv Baldwin (*Volunteer Chaplain, West Midlands Police*)
National Secretary Revd Viv Baldwin, 20 Castle Rd, Woodford Halse, Northants NN11 3RS
email: secretary@police-chaplains.org.uk

GENERAL

Church Universities and University Colleges

Bishop Grosseteste University College, Newport, Lincoln LN1 3DY *Tel:* 01522 527347
Principal Professor Muriel Robinson
Chaplain Revd Dr Peter Green *Tel:* 01522 583607
email: peter.green@bishopg.ac.uk

Canterbury Christ Church University, North Holmes Rd, Canterbury, Kent CT1 1QU
Tel: 01227 767700
Vice Chancellor Dr Robin Baker
Dean of Chapel Revd Dr Jeremy Law
Tel: 01227 782747
email: j.law@canterbury.ac.uk
Chaplains
Revd David Stroud
email: david.stroud@canterbury.ac.uk
Revd Sally Womersley
email: sally.womersley@canterbury.ac.uk

University of Chester, Parkgate Rd, Chester CH1 4BJ *Tel:* 01244 511000
Vice Chancellor Professor Tim Wheeler
Chester Campus
Chaplains
Revd Dr Peter Jenner
email: p.jenner@chester.ac.uk
Revd Dot Gosling
email: d.gosling@chester.ac.uk
Chaplaincy Assistant
Mrs Alison Upton *email:* a.upton@chester.ac.uk
Warrington Campus
Chaplain Fr Ian Delinger *Tel:* 01925 534361
email: i.delinger@chester.ac.uk

University of Chichester, Bishop Otter Campus, College Lane, Chichester PO19 4PE
Tel: 01243 816000
Vice Chancellor Professor Clive Behagg
Chaplain Revd John Dane *Tel:* 01243 816036
email: j.dane@chi.ac.uk

University of Gloucestershire, Francis Close Hall, Swindon Rd, Cheltenham, Gloucestershire GL50 2QF *Tel:* 01242 532700
Vice Chancellor and Principal Mr Stephen Marston
Chaplain Bruce Goodwin *Tel:* 01242 532735
email: bgoodwin@glos.ac.uk

Liverpool Hope University, Hope Park, Liverpool L16 9JD *Tel:* 0151 291 3000
Liverpool Hope is an ecumenical Roman Catholic / Church of England institution.
Vice Chancellor Professor Gerald Pillay
Chaplain Vacancy

University College of St Mark and St John, Plymouth, Derriford Rd, Plymouth PL6 8BH
Tel: 01752 636700
Principal Vacancy *Tel:* 01752 636700 Ext 6528
Chaplain Revd Paul Thompson *Tel:* 01542 384384
email: chaplaincy@marjon.ac.uk

University of Cumbria, Fusehill Street, Carlisle, Cumbria CA1 2HH
Vice Chancellor Prof Peter Strike
Fusehill Street Campus
Chaplain Matthew Firth *Tel:* 01524 385689
email: matthew.firth@cumbria.ac.uk
Lancaster Campus *Tel:* 01524 384260
Chaplain Vacancy
Chaplaincy Assistant Steven Kay
email: steven.kay2@cumbria.ac.uk

Whitelands College, Roehampton University, Parkstead House, Holybourne Avenue, Roehampton, London SW15 4JD *Tel:* 020 8392 3500
Vice Chancellor Professor Paul O'Prey
Principal Dr Mark Garner
Chaplain Revd Dr Daniel Eshun
Tel: 020 8392 3516
email: d.eshun@roehampton.ac.uk

University of Winchester, Sparkford Rd, Winchester SO22 4NR *Tel:* 01962 841515
Vice Chancellor Professor Joy Carter *Tel:* 01962 827063
Chaplain Dr Peter Waddell *Tel:* 01904 624624
email: chaplaincy@winchester.ac.uk

York St John University, Lord Mayor's Walk, York YO3 7EX *Tel:* 01904 624624
Vice Chancellor Professor David Fleming
Chaplain Revd Dr Lukas Njenga
email: L.njenga@yorksj.ac.uk

Church Urban Fund

President
The Archbishop of Canterbury

Chairman of Trustees
Canon Paul Hackwood

Other Trustees
Mr Derek Twine (Deputy Chair), Rt Revd Christopher Chessun, Mr Brian Caroll, Mr Patrick Coldstream CBE, Mr Andrew Dorton, Mr Michael Eastwood, Canon Denise Poole, Rt Revd David Walker, Marnie Woodward FCMA

Office Church House, Great Smith St, London SW1P 3AZ *Tel:* 020 7898 1647
Fax: 020 7898 1601
email: enquiries@cuf.org.uk
Web: www.cuf.org.uk

Church Urban Fund (CUF) raises money to change lives in the poorest communities in England. Working with the Church of England, CUF's mission is to serve people of faith who put their faith into action in the community. Working in collaboration with dioceses and partner organizations, CUF funds faith-based social action in the most economically and socially deprived areas of England, but its support also extends to advocacy and practical advice, working to create sustainable, relevant and local solutions to deep-rooted issues. The projects CUF partners with work in a broad range of areas, including community development, support for vulnerable and marginalized groups, housing and homeless, and interfaith dialogue. CUF is also closely involved in wider debate, both inside and outside the Church, representing faith-based social action and enabling the voices of faith communities and practitioners to be heard at a national level. Our vision is to see all local churches and Christians in England empowered to work to end poverty in their communities.

Established in 1987 following the landmark report *Faith in the City*, CUF has supported nearly 5.500 projects across England. Our experience over the last 23 years has been that a combination of money and capacity building is the best way to sustainably support projects. This explains CUF's shift from an endowed fund towards an active, fundraising foundation model. We are now a development organization that provides advice, money and guidance to local churches and activists who share our passion to see lives changed. This change marks an important stage in the charity's development and maturation.

CUF's work has been made possible by the continuing support of individuals, parishes and dioceses, which have contributed to the Fund's work through time, money and prayers.

CUF is about Christians working together to tackle poverty, transforming the lives of society's poorest and most marginalized in England.

We recognize the inherent worth of all human beings, made, as they are, in the image of God, and believe in an inclusive society that values each and every individual.

We embrace and embody the Church's calling to respond to poverty in England. We want to see all Christians, in every church and every community, tackling the problem together through the giving of time, money, action and prayer.

We believe that the most effective response to poverty happens at the local, personal level, from people working within the community and sensitive to its needs. With an established presence in every community in England, the Church is uniquely placed to deliver such a response, touching areas that other agencies simply cannot reach.

Many Christians, both clergy and lay people, are already building transformative relationships with the poor and vulnerable. Living sacrificially, they achieve miracles but they can often feel isolated in challenging circumstances.

Nurturing them is part of CUF's work, but there is much more to be done. That's why, we are moving from offering short-term funding to developing local partnerships with Anglican dioceses which will provide long-term, sustainable support.

In partnership with dioceses throughout England, we are expanding our networks to reinforce the efforts of those working in deprived areas, by improving their access to resources, in the form of money, information and expertise.

Whilst continuing to educate people about the problem of poverty in England, we need to share the many stories of lives being turned around and the once desperate being given back their future.

We need the solidarity and commitment of Christians everywhere. Then, together, we can really tackle poverty in England.

For further information on the resources available please visit our website, www.cuf.org.uk.

Clergy Appointments Adviser

The adviser has been appointed by the Archbishops of Canterbury and York to assist clergy, in England and from overseas, to find suitable new appointments and to assist patrons and others responsible for making appointments to find suitable candidates. The adviser has a responsibility for beneficed and unbeneficed clergy, together with stipendiary deacons. A list of vacancies for incumbencies, team posts and specialized ministries is available on-line.

For further information please contact: Revd John Lee, Clergy Appointments Adviser, The Wash House, Lambeth Palace, London SE1 7JU

Tel: 020 7898 1898
Fax: 020 7898 1899
email: admin.caa@churchofengland.org
Web: www.churchofengland.org/clergy-office-holders/clergy-appointments-adviser.aspx

Conference Centres and Retreat Houses

CONFERENCE CENTRES

ASHBURNHAM PLACE	Ashburnham Place, Battle, E Sussex TN33 9NF (*Administrator:* Revd Andrew Wooding-Jones) *Tel:* 01424 892244 *Fax:* 01424 894200 *email:* bookings@ashburnham.org.uk *Web:* www.ashburnham.org.uk
BELSEY BRIDGE CONFERENCE CENTRE	Ditchingham, Bungay, Suffolk NR35 2DZ (*Manager:* Erica Strange) *Tel:* 01986 892133 *Fax:* 01986 895765 *email:* belseybridge@cct.org.uk *web:* www.cct.org.uk
HAYES CONFERENCE CENTRE	Hayes Conference Centre, Swanwick, Derbyshire DE55 1AU (*Manager:* Mr Peter Anderson) *Tel:* 01773 526000 *Fax:* 01773 540841 *email:* office@cct.org.uk *Web:* www.cct.org.uk
HIGH LEIGH CONFERENCE CENTRE	High Leigh Conference Centre, Lord St, Hoddesdon, Herts EN11 8SG (*Manager:* Mr Ian Andrews) *Tel:* 01992 463016 *Fax:* 01992 446594 *email:* highleigh@cct.org.uk *Web:* www.cct.org.uk
LEE ABBEY	Lee Abbey Fellowship, Lynton, Devon EX35 6JJ (*Warden:* David Rowe) *Tel:* 0800 389 1189 *Fax:* 01598 752619 *email:* publicity@leeabbey.org.uk *Web:* www.leeabbey.org.uk

RETREAT HOUSES

The following is a list of diocesan conference centres and retreat houses including some run by religious communities. For details of accommodation for individual retreats *see* Religious Communities page 247, or contact the Retreat Association, Kerridge House, 42 Woodside Close, Amersham, Bucks HP6 5EF *Tel:* 01494 433004 *email:* info@retreats.org.uk, *Web:* www.retreats.org.uk

BATH AND WELLS	Abbey House, Chilkwell St, Glastonbury, Som. BA6 8DH (*Retreat House*) (*The Warden*) *Tel:* 01458 831112
BLACKBURN	Whalley Abbey, Whalley, Clitheroe, Lancs. BB7 9SS (*Warden*: Canon Andrew Sage) *Tel:* 01254 828400 *Fax:* 01254 825519
BRADFORD	Parcevall Hall, Appletreewick, Skipton, N Yorks. BD23 6DG *Tel:* 01756 720213 *Fax:* 01756 720656
CARLISLE	Carlisle Diocesan Conference and Retreat Centre, Rydal Hall, Ambleside, Cumbria LA22 9LX (*General Manager:* Jonathan Green) *Tel:* 01539 432050 *Fax:* 01539 434887 *email:* mail@rydalhall.org
CHELMSFORD	Diocesan House of Retreat, Pleshey, Chelmsford, Essex CM3 1HA (*Warden:* Revd Sheila Coughtrey) *Tel:* 01245 237251
CHESTER	Chester Diocesan Conference Centre, Foxhill, Tarvin Road, Frodsham, Cheshire WA6 6XB (*Wardens:* Mr & Mrs Ian Cameron) *Tel:* 01928 733777 *Fax:* 01928 551041 *email:* foxhill@chester.anglican.org *Web:* foxhillconferences. co.uk

CHICHESTER	Monastery of the Holy Trinity, Crawley Down, Crawley, W Sussex RH10 4LH *Tel:* 01342 712074
	St Margaret's Convent, Hooke Hall, 250 High St, Uckfield, East Sussex TN22 1EN *Tel:* 01825 766808
COVENTRY	Offa House (Coventry Diocesan Retreat House), Offchurch, Leamington Spa, War. CV33 9AS (*Warden*: Ruth Godber) *Tel:* 01926 423309
DERBY	Morley Retreat and Conference House, Church Lane, Morley, Derby DE7 6DE *Tel:* 01332 831293
DURHAM	*See* entry for NEWCASTLE
ELY	Bishop Woodford House, Barton Road, Ely, Cambs. CB7 4DX (*Warden*: Peggie Banks) *Tel:* 01353 663039
GLOUCESTER	Glenfall House, Mill Lane, Charlton Kings, Cheltenham, Glos. GL54 4EP (*Warden:* Liz Palin) *Tel:* 01242 583654 *Fax:* 01242 251314
GUILDFORD	St Columba's House, Maybury Hill, Woking, Surrey GU22 8AB (*Director:* Fr Owen Murphy) *Tel:* 01483 766498
	House of Bethany, 7 Nelson Rd, Southsea, Hants. PO5 2AR *Tel:* 023 9283 3498
HEREFORD	Ludlow Conference Centre, Lower Galdeford, Ludlow, Shropshire SY8 1RZ *Tel:* 01584 873882 *Fax:* 01584 877945 *email:* info@ludlowconferencecentre.co.uk
LEICESTER	Launde Abbey, East Norton, Leicestershire LE7 9XB (*Warden*: Revd Tim Blewett) *Tel:* 01572 717254 *Fax:* 01572 717454 *email:* laundeabbey@leicester.anglican.org *Web:* www.launde.org.uk
LICHFIELD	Lichfield Diocesan Retreat and Conference Centre, Shallowford House, Shallowford, Stone, Staffs. ST15 0NZ (*Director*: Simon Hudson) *Tel:* 01785 760233 *Fax:* 01785 760390
LONDON	The Royal Foundation of Saint Katharine, 2 Butcher Row, London E14 8DS (*Master:* Preb David Paton) *Tel:* 0300 111 1147 *Fax:* 020 7702 7603 *email:* info@rfsk.org.uk
NEWCASTLE/DURHAM	Shepherd's Dene, Riding Mill, Northumberland NE44 6AF *Tel:* 01434 682212
NORWICH	Horstead Centre, Norwich NR12 7EP (*Manager:* Mark Heybourne) *Tel:* 01603 737215 (*Office*); 01603 737674 (*Guests*)
	All Hallows Convent, Ditchingham, Bungay NR35 2DT *Tel:* 01986 892840
OXFORD	St Mary's Convent, Wantage OX12 9DJ *Tel:* 01235 763141 / 01235 774075

SALISBURY	Sarum College, 19 The Close, Salisbury SP1 2EE *Tel:* 01722 424800 *Fax:* 01722 338508 *email:* hospitality@sarum.ac.uk
	Society of St Francis, The Friary, Hilfield, Dorchester DT2 7BE *Tel:* 01300 341345
	St Denys Retreat Centre, Ivy House, 2 Church St, Warminster BA12 8PG *Tel:* 01985 214824
SHEFFIELD	Whirlow Grange Conference Centre, Ecclesall Road South, Sheffield, S Yorks. S11 9PZ (*General Manager:* Graham Holland) *Tel:* 0114 236 3173 (*Office*); 236 1183 (*Visitors*) *email:* manager@whirlowgrange.co.uk
SOUTHWARK	Wychcroft, Bletchingley, Redhill, Surrey RH1 4NE *Tel:* 01883 743041
	The Community of Sisters of the Church, St Michael's Convent, 56 Ham Common, Richmond TW10 7JH *Tel:* 020 8940 8711/8948 2502
SOUTHWELL	Sacrista Prebend Retreat House, 4 Westgate, Southwell, Notts NG25 0JH *Tel:* 01636 816 833
TRURO	Epiphany House, Kenwyn, Church Rd, Truro, Cornwall TR1 3DR *Tel:* 01872 272249
WAKEFIELD	Community of the Resurrection, Stocksbank Road, Mirfield, W Yorks. WF14 0BN *Tel:* 01924 483348 *Fax:* 01924 490489 *email:* guests@mirfield.org.uk
	Community of St Peter, Horbury, W Yorks. WF4 6BB *Tel:* 01924 272181 *Fax:* 01924 261225
WINCHESTER	Old Alresford Place, Winchester Retreat and Conference Centre, Old Alresford, Hants. SO24 9DH *Tel:* 01962 737360 *Fax:* 01962 737300 *email:* ian.knight@winchester.anglican.org
	Alton Abbey, King's Hill, Beech, Alton, Hants. GU34 4AP (*Abbot:* Rt Revd Dom Giles Hill OSB) *Tel:* 01420 562145/563575
WORCESTER	Holland House, Cropthorne, nr Pershore, Worcs. WR10 3NB (*Warden:* Ian Spenser) *Tel:* 01386 860330 *email:* enquiries@hollandhouse.org
YORK	Wydale Hall, York Diocesan Retreat and Conference Centre, Brompton-by-Sawdon, Scarborough, N Yorks. YO13 9DG (*The Warden*) *Tel:* 01723 859270 *Fax:* 01723 859702 *email:* admin@wydale.org *Web:* www.wyedale.org
	St Oswald's Pastoral Centre, Woodlands Drive, Sleights, Whitby, N Yorks. YO21 1RY *Tel:* 01947 810496
	Sneaton Castle Centre, Whitby, N Yorks. YO21 3QN (*Centre Manager:* Linda Antill) *Tel:* 01947 600051 *Fax:* 01947 603490 *email:* sneaton@globalnet.co.uk *Web:* www.sneatoncastle.co.uk

Evangelism

The Mission and Public Affairs Division (MPA) seeks to help the Church of England to do its evangelism appropriately, courteously and clearly.

The MPA Council's report *Mission-shaped Church* has had substantial impact on the Church of England. The report was discussed at General Synod in February 2004 and was warmly commended to the Church; Synod then debated a follow up report in 2010 that noted the progress that had been made implementing the original report. Synod is due to debate the report again in 2015. A number of follow-up volumes have also been produced by Church House Publishing, covering practical subjects such as spirituality, the rural church, children and youth as well as exploring in depth the theological questions raised by today's missional initiatives.

Mission-shaped Church encourages dioceses to build an enabling framework for new ways of being church, alongside well-loved and traditional forms. The Dioceses, Pastoral and Mission Measure 2007 offers bishops the opportunity to make clear legal provision for new mission initiatives within the life of their dioceses and so far 13 of these orders have been made. The House of Bishops has also approved guidelines to identify, train and support pioneer ministers, resulting in ordained pioneers working as missionaries in 21st century England, with a further group of pioneers in training. Working alongside its partners MPA offers resource and support to dioceses as they make sense of this enabling framework in their own contexts.

Within MPA Dr Rachel Jordan is responsible for this area. Her work is done in close alliance with a number of partner organizations, in particular Fresh Expressions, the Archbishops' initiative presently led by the Rt Revd Graham Cray and with CMS (Church Missionary Society) and Church Army who have both radically re-worked their organizations to prioritise pioneering and the creation of fresh expressions of church. MPA staff also work in partnership with colleagues in other denominations, the ACC, other Mission Agencies, Churches Together in England and other evangelistic agencies in this country.

The Archbishop of Canterbury's vision is of a mixed economy church, developing a spectrum of inherited and emerging forms of church and deploying these where each is most appropriate. The Mission and Evangelism desk works closely with Diocesan Missioners and Advisers on Evangelism to implement this vision and to identify and share good practice across the Church.

Fresh Expressions

Changing Church for Changing World

Fresh Expressions encourages new forms of church for a fast-changing world, working with Christians from a variety of denominations and traditions. It was initiated by the Archbishops of Canterbury and York with the Methodist Council and now includes the United Reformed Church, Church of Scotland, Congregational Federation, Ground Level Network, Church Army, CMS, ACPI and 24/7 Prayer as formal partners. The initiative has resulted in hundreds of new congregations being formed alongside more traditional churches.

Tel: 0300 3650563
email: contact@freshexpressions.org.uk
Web: www.freshexpressions.org.uk

Archbishops' Missioner and Team Leader of the Fresh Expressions Team Rt Revd Graham Cray, The Rectory, Church Road, Harrietsham, Kent ME17 1AP *Tel:* 01622 851170
email: graham.cray@freshexpressions.org.uk

Names and contact details for other team members can be found on the website.

Faculty Office and Special Marriage Licences

The Faculty Office of the Archbishop of Canterbury, otherwise known as The Court of Faculties, exercises on behalf of the Archbishop the dispensing powers that he has by virtue of the Ecclesiastical Licences Act of 1533. These comprise the appointment of Notaries Public, the granting of degrees, and the granting of marriage licences. The right to grant a Special Licence for marriage at any convenient time or place in England or Wales is unique to the Archbishop, and this jurisdiction is sparingly exercised and good cause must always be shown why a more normal preliminary to Anglican marriage cannot be used. At the time of writing, marriage with any other preliminary must by law be solemnized between 8.00 a.m. and 6.00 p.m., and although a Special Licence could omit this requirement, that will only in practice be done in a case of serious illness.

The more common need for a Special Licence is the parties' desire to marry in a building not normally authorized for Anglican marriage, or in a parish where they do not have a legal qualification. Even in the last case cause must be shown, normally in the form of a real connection with the parish or church in question; the *Special Licence procedure is not intended to enable parties to choose a church building on aesthetic or sentimental grounds.*

More detailed guidance on the grounds that may be considered sufficient for the granting of a Special Licence may always be sought from the Faculty Office by letter or telephone.

Special arrangements may sometimes be made in a genuine emergency. In such cases the clergy or the couple concerned should first contact the Diocesan Registrar, archdeacon, or diocesan or area bishop. If unable to resolve the difficulty himself he will make arrangements for the Faculty Office to be approached.

Orders made by the Master of the Faculties prescribe from time to time fees which are to be charged for applications for Special Licences. The fee is currently £250.00 (until 31 March 2013).

The Faculty Office is open to telephone and personal callers between 10.00 a.m. and 4.00 p.m. Monday to Friday, except on public holidays and certain days around Easter and Christmas.

The Faculty Office 1 The Sanctuary, Westminster, London SW1P 3JT *Tel:* 020 7222 5381 Ext 7162
Fax: 020 7222 7502
email: faculty.office@1thesanctuary.com
Web: www.facultyoffice.org.uk

Hospice Movement

The word 'Hospice' was first used from the fourth century onwards when Christian orders welcomed travellers, the sick and those in need. It was first applied to the care of dying patients by Mme Jeanne Garnier who founded the Dames de Calvaire in Lyon, France in 1842. The modern hospice movement, however, with its twin emphases on medical and psychosocial intervention, dates from the founding of St Christopher's Hospice by Dame Cicely Saunders in 1967. Since 1967, 'hospice' has become a worldwide philosophy adapting to the needs of different cultures and settings – hospital, hospice and community – and is established in six continents.

Hospice and palliative care is the active, total care of patients whose disease no longer responds to curative treatment, and for whom the goal must be the best quality of life for them and their families. Palliative medicine is now a distinct medical speciality in the UK. It focuses on controlling pain and other symptoms, easing suffering and enhancing the life that remains. It integrates the psychological and spiritual aspects of care, to enable patients to live out their lives with dignity. It also offers support to families, both during the patient's illness and their bereavement. It offers a unique combination of care in hospices and at home.

Hospice and palliative care services mostly help people with cancer, although increasingly patients with other life-threatening illnesses may also be supported; this includes HIV/AIDS, motor neurone disease, heart failure and kidney disease. Hospice and palliative care is free of charge to the patient regardless of whether it is provided by an independent charitable hospice, Macmillan Service, Marie Curie Cancer Care, Sue Ryder Palliative Care Centre or by an NHS service. The criteria for admission are based on medical, social and emotional need. Referral to a hospice or palliative care service (including inpatient and home care nursing services) is normally arranged by the patient's own GP or hospital doctor. Further information about hospice care in the UK and overseas, including the facility to find your local hospice and resources for health professionals, is available from The Hospice Information Service (*see below*). This is a partnership between Help the Hospices and St Christopher's Hospice and provides an enquiry service for the public and professionals. Publications include UK and International Directories of Hospice and Palliative Care.

Tel: 020 7520 8222
email: info@helpthehospices.org.uk
Web: www.helpthehospices.org.uk

Together for Short Lives

Together for Short Lives is the only charity working across the UK to help ensure that every child and young person unlikely to reach adulthood, and their family, has the best possible care and support whenever and wherever they need it.

Providing care – often 24 hours a day, seven days a week – can place families under enormous emotional, physical and financial strain. Relationships can suffer; careers may have to be abandoned; well brothers and sisters can feel left out; and normal activities become almost impossible. These are ordinary people leading extraordinary lives.

Many remarkable organizations, including children's hospice services embrace not only the physical, but the emotional, social and spiritual elements of care, focusing on quality of life for the child or young person, and practical support for the family. However, whilst there are some excellent care services, we know that families need so much more.

Together for Short Lives is here to help. We want to see support available from the moment a child is diagnosed, wherever families want it, for as long as it's needed. We:

- help families to know about the range of care support available
- support organizations to continue to offer the highest standards of care
- raise and distribute essential funding to care organisations
- give a powerful voice to children, families and providers, ensuring their views influence Government policy.

Together for Short Lives, Fourth Floor, Bridge House, 48–52 Baldwin St, Bristol BS1 1QB
Tel: 0117 989 7820
Fax: 0117 929 1999
email: info@togetherforshortlives.org.uk
Web: www.info@togetherforshortlives.org.uk

For details of the **Association of Hospice and Palliative Care Chaplains** *see* page 272.

Marriage: Legal Aspects

The comprehensive statement of the law and information on related matters published by the Faculty Office of the Archbishop of Canterbury, *Anglican Marriage in England and Wales – A Guide to the Law for Clergy*, has recently been revised and updated and copies were sent to incumbents and licensed clergy of the Church of England and the Church in Wales in 2010. Further copies are available by post, price £7.50, from: The Faculty Office, 1 The Sanctuary, Westminster, London SW1P 3JT (cheques are to be made payable to 'The Faculty Office').

For details of **Special Marriage Licences** *see* the entry for the Faculty Office, page 231.

Press

CHURCH TIMES

Established 1863. The best-selling, award-winning independent weekly newspaper and website, reporting on the worldwide Christian Church and Anglicanism in particular. As well as its wide news coverage, the paper contains a full comment section on current affairs, general features, reviews of books, music and arts, a comprehensive gazette, and the biggest selection of church job advertisements. Goes to press on Wednesday; published on Friday; advertisements to be placed on Friday for the following week; price £1.80; subscription £70. *Editor* Mr Paul Handley. *Office* 3rd Floor, Invicta House, 108–114 Golden Lane, London EC1Y 0TG
Tel: 020 7776 1089
Fax: 020 7490 7093
Subscriptions: *Tel:* 01603 785911
email: editor@churchtimes.co.uk
Web: www.churchtimes.co.uk

CHURCH OF ENGLAND NEWSPAPER

A weekly newspaper which aims to provide a full, objective and lively coverage of Christian news from Britain and overseas. Contents include general features, book, music, film and art reviews, the latest clergy appointments and an ongoing focus on how the Church can improve its mission. Goes to press on Tuesday; published Friday; deadline for advertisements 10.00am Monday; price £1.35 (annual subscription UK £65, Eur £90, Rest of world £110; Online £25; other rates on application). *Editor* C. M. Blakely. *Office* The Church of England Newspaper, 14 Great College St, London SW1P 3RX *Tel:* 020 7222 8700
email: cen@churchnewspaper.com
Web: www.churchnewspaper.com

ENGLISH CHURCHMAN

Church of England newspaper (established 1843), incorporating *St James's Chronicle* 1761. Protestant and evangelical. News, various features, book reviews, correspondence and church calendar. Published fortnightly, Fridays, price 40p. *Editor* Revd Peter Ratcliff. *Tel:* 020 8417 0875
email: englishchurchman@aol.com
Web: www.englishchurchman.com

Services Authorized and Commended

Public worship in the Church of England is a matter governed by law.

Canon B 2 provides that the General Synod may approve forms of service with or without time limit. Services thus approved are alternative to those of *The Book of Common Prayer*. The power given to General Synod under Canon B 2 derives from the Worship and Doctrine Measure 1974.

Canon B 4 provides that the convocations, the archbishops in their provinces or the bishops in their dioceses may approve forms of service for use on occasions for which *The Book of Common Prayer* or *Authorized Alternative Services* do not provide.

Canon B 5 (paragraph 2) allows discretion to any minister where no other provision has been made under Canons B 1 or B 4, to use other forms of service that are considered suitable. If questions are raised as to whether such forms of service are suitable the decision rests with the bishop.

Authorized Alternative Services are those approved by the General Synod under Canon B 1 (for fuller details *see* below).

Commended Services are those that the bishops corporately have judged to be 'suitable' either for approval under Canon B 4 or for use in the contexts envisaged in Canon B 5 (for fuller details *see* page 235).

AUTHORIZED SERVICES ALTERNATIVE TO THE BOOK OF COMMON PRAYER APPROVED BY THE GENERAL SYNOD PURSUANT TO CANON B 2

As at 1 January 2013

Published in *Common Worship: Services and Prayers for the Church of England* and *Common Worship: Collects and Post Communions*

1 A Service of the Word
2 Schedule of permitted variations to *The Book of Common Prayer* Orders for Morning and Evening Prayer where these occur in *Common Worship*
3 Prayers for Various Occasions
4 The Litany
5 Authorized Forms of Confession and Absolution
6 Creeds and Authorized Affirmations of Faith
7 The Lord's Prayer
8 The Order for the Celebration of Holy Communion also called The Eucharist and The Lord's Supper
9 Collects and Post Communions
10 Rules for Regulating Authorized Forms of Service
11 The Lectionary
12 Opening Canticles at Morning and Evening Prayer; Gospel Canticles; Other Canticles; A Song of Praise (Epiphany); Te Deum Laudamus

Published in *Common Worship: Initiation Services*

13 Holy Baptism
14 Emergency Baptism
15 Holy Baptism and Confirmation
16 Seasonal Provisions and Supplementary Texts
17 Affirmation of Baptismal Faith
18 Reception into the Communion of the Church of England

Published in *Common Worship: Pastoral Services*

19 Wholeness and Healing
20 The Marriage Service with prayers and other resources
21 Thanksgiving for the Gift of a Child
22 The Funeral Service with prayers and other resources
23 Series One Solemnization of Matrimony
24 Series One Burial Services

Published in *Common Worship: Ordination Services*

25 Ordination Services

Published in *Common Worship: Daily Prayer (Fourth Impression 2010)*
26 The Calendar

Published separately
27 Public Worship with Communion by Extension (*NB explicit permission must be obtained from the bishop for the use of this rite.*)
28 Weekday Lectionary
29 An Order of Marriage for Christians from Different Churches
30 Additional Weekday Lectionary
31 Additional Eucharistic Prayers *with guidance for celebrating the Eucharist with children*

The above are all authorized for use until further resolution of the Synod.

Form of Service authorized by the Archbishops of Canterbury and York without time limit for use in their respective Provinces

A Service for Remembrance Sunday (included in *Common Worship: Times and Seasons – see* below)

GENERAL

COMMENDED SERVICES AND RESOURCES
(Material commended by the House of Bishops as being suitable for use by ministers in exercise of their discretion under Canon B 5)
As at 1 January 2012

Published in *Common Worship: Services and Prayers for the Church of England*
1 Introduction to Morning and Evening Prayer on Sunday
2 Introduction to Holy Baptism
3 Short Prefaces for the Sundays before Lent and after Trinity
4 Additional Canticles

Published in the President's Edition of *Common Worship*
5 Additional Blessings

Published in *Common Worship: Christian Initiation*
6 Rites Supporting Disciples on the Way of Christ
7 Admission of the Baptized to Communion
8 Celebration after an Initiation Service outside the Parish
9 Thanksgiving for Holy Baptism
10 A Corporate Service of Penitence
11 The Reconciliation of a Penitent

Published in *Common Worship: Pastoral Services*
6 An Order for Prayer and Dedication after a Civil Marriage
7 Thanksgiving for Marriage
8 Ministry at the Time of Death
9 Receiving the Coffin at Church before the Funeral
10 Funeral of a Child: Outline Orders and Resources
11 At Home after the Funeral
12 Memorial Services: Outline Orders and Sample Services
13 Prayers for Use with the Dying and at Funeral and Memorial Services
14 Canticles for Marriages, Funerals and Memorial Services

Published separately
15 Material contained in *New Patterns for Worship*
16 Material contained in *Common Worship: Times and Seasons*
17 Material contained in *Common Worship: Times and Seasons – President's Edition for Holy Communion*
18 Material contained in *Common Worship: Festivals*
19 *Common Worship: The Admission and Licensing of Readers*
20 Material contained in: *Common Worship: Holy Week and Easter*
21 Material contained in: *Common Worship: A Pastoral Ministry Companion*

SERVICES WHICH COMPLY WITH THE PROVISIONS OF A SERVICE OF THE WORD
(see Authorized Services, no. 2)
As at 1 January 2013

Published in *Common Worship: Services and Prayers for the Church of England*
1 An Order for Morning Prayer on Sunday
2 An Order for Evening Prayer on Sunday
3 An Order for Night Prayer (Compline)
4 An Order for Night Prayer (Compline) in Traditional Language

Published separately
5 Sample services contained in *New Patterns for Worship*
6 Services contained in *Common Worship: Daily Prayer*

PUBLICATIONS

The material is published in the following volumes:
- *Common Worship: Services and Prayers for the Church of England*
- *Common Worship: President's Edition*
- *Common Worship: Collects and Post Communions*
- *Common Worship: Christian Initiation*
- *Common Worship: Pastoral Services*
- *Common Worship: Daily Prayer*
- *Common Worship: Times and Seasons*
- *Common Worship: Festivals*
- *Common Worship: Ordination Services (Study Edition)*
- *Common Worship: Times and Seasons – President's Edition for Holy Communion*
- *Common Worship: Holy Week and Easter*
- *Common Worship: Additional Eucharistic Prayers*
- *Common Worship: A Pastoral Ministry Companion*
- *New Patterns for Worship*
- *Public Worship with Communion by Extension*
- *Common Worship: The Admission and Licensing of Readers*
- *An Order of Marriage for Christians from Different Churches*
- annual editions of the Common Worship Lectionary

It may also be found in the Common Worship area of the Church of England website at www.cofe.anglican.org/worship/liturgy/commonworship/

VERSIONS OF THE BIBLE AND OF THE PSALMS

The following may be used in Book of Common Prayer services (with the permission of the Parochial Church Council) instead of the Authorized Version of the Bible and the Psalter in *The Book of Common Prayer:*

Revised Version
Revised Standard Version
New English Bible
The Revised Psalter
The Liturgical Psalter (The Psalms
in a new translation for worship)
Jerusalem Bible
Good News Bible
(Today's English Version)

Any version of the Bible or Psalter not prohibited by lawful authority may be used with Alternative Services and Commended Services.

A leaflet entitled *A Brief Guide to Liturgical Copyright* deals with the procedures for local reproduction. It provides guidance on preparing local texts and information about copyright requirements. The third edition (2000) is available at £1.50 from Church House Publishing and in the *Common Worship* area of the Church of England website at www.cofe.anglican.org/worship/liturgy/commonworship/copyright/

BBC LOCAL RADIO
Additional weekly content is provided to stations by a senior broadcast journalist for religious affairs, Alex Strangwayes-Booth, and editorial leadership by the editor of religion and ethics for English regions, Ashley Peatfield. There are thirty-nine BBC local radio stations in counties and cities throughout England. Each station has a Sunday religious affairs programme produced locally by a named producer, and seeking to reflect the national and news agenda from a distinctive faith perspective. Most include Christian worship songs and secular music. Some stations have a weekly act of worship, reflective elements or will include worship on special occasions. BBC local radio Sunday shows also work in partnership with national BBC stations on special projects like the annual Lent course.
email: ashley.peatfield@bbc.co.uk

BBC RELIGION AND ETHICS DEPARTMENT
Produces a wide variety of religious programmes for transmission on BBC Television and Network Radio, including the Radio 4 shows *Thought for the Day* and *The Moral Maze*, made out of Salford together with Television shows such as *Songs of Praise*. BBC One's *Sunday Morning Live* is produced in Belfast and a number of shows such as *Island Parish* are made by independent production companies.

The Religion and Ethics Website is part of Knowledge and Learning and is run by BBC Learning in conjunction with the Head of Religion.

For all Radio, TV and Online programme information please contact:
Commissioning Editor Religion and Head of Religion and Ethics Aaqil Ahmed, BBC 1st Floor, Dock House, MediaCityUK, Salford M50 2LH
Assistant to Aaqil Ahmed Barbara Cummins

STANDING CONFERENCE ON RELIGION AND BELIEF
The Standing Conference on Religion and Belief meets biannually to provide a forum for the BBC and its audience to discuss issues of religion and belief. Its membership is drawn from the major Christian traditions, along with other world faiths and humanist groups represented in the United Kingdom. The Standing Conference is chaired by Rt Revd Stephen Cottrell, Bishop of Chelmsford and Dilwar Hussein, and the secretariat is provided by the Church and Media Network. Contact Andrew Graystone
Tel: 07772 710090
email: andrew.graystone1@btinternet.com

CHURCH AND MEDIA NETWORK
The Church and Media Network is an ecumenical body with charitable status. It was formed in 2009, succeeding the Churches' Media Council. The Network aims to build bridges of understanding between the Christian community and the media. The Church and Media Network also runs *theMediaNet*, which encourages vocations to the media and also offers support, encouragement and discipleship to Christians working in the media. *Acting Chair* Revd. Tony Miles *Director* Andrew Graystone *Tel:* 0845 6520027
07772 710090 (Mobile)
email: info@churchandmedia.net
Web: www.churchandmedia.net *or* www.themedianet.org

FOUNDATION FOR CHRISTIAN COMMUNICATION LTD (CTVC)
Major television, radio and new media production company founded by the British film pioneer, Lord Rank, which specializes in making documentaries on religious, ethical and moral issues. CTVC have produced programmes for Channel 4 and ITV as well as radio programmes for BBC Radio 4 and The World Service. Some of Britain's leading presenters, such as Rageh Omaar, John McCarthy and Robert Beckford have presented several of CTVC's programmes. In the last few years CTVC has been awarded the prestigious religious broadcasting award – The Sandford St Martin. CTVC also hosts TrueTube – an interactive website which provides young people with an outlet to express their views on issues that matter to them, from teen crime to gangs to personal relationships, as well as hosting films young people have created. The site has been presented with a Jerusalem Award for best IPTV content. CTVC has one of the largest film and tape archive of any independent production company in Britain, covering the hundreds of films and programmes we have made over the past 80 years. *Chief Executive Officer* Mr Peter Weil, CTVC, 9–10 Copper Row, Tower Bridge Piazza, London SE1 2LH
Tel: 020 7940 8480
Fax: 020 7940 8490
email: info@ctvc.co.uk
Web: www.ctvc.co.uk and www.truetube.co.uk

OFFICE OF COMMUNICATIONS (Ofcom)
Ofcom is the independent regulator and competition authority for the UK communications industries, with responsibilities across television, radio, telecommunications and wireless communications services. *Chairman* Colette Bowe *Deputy Chairman* Philip Graf CBE *Chief Executive* Ed Richards, Ofcom, Riverside House, 2a Southwark Bridge Rd, London SE1 9HA.
Tel: 0300 123 3000
Textphone: 0300 123 2024
Fax: 020 7981 3333
email: contact@ofcom.org.uk
Web: www.ofcom.org.uk

INDEPENDENT CHRISTIAN BROADCASTERS

A range of independent Christian broadcasters operate in the UK, including:

Premier Radio and TV *Web:* www.premier.org.uk
United Christian Broadcasting (UCB) *Web:* www.ucb.co.uk
God TV *Web:* http://uk.god.tv/
Eternal World Television Network *Web:* http://www.ewtn.com/

For a full list of Christian Digital Satellite Channels, visit: http://www.christiantv.org.uk/

SANDFORD ST MARTIN (CHURCH OF ENGLAND) TRUST

The Trust was established in 1978. From the beginning its purpose was to recognize and promote excellence in religious broadcasting, and to encourage Christian involvement in television and radio at both national and local levels. Founded through the generosity and vision of a distinguished Anglican layman, the late Sir David Wills, its origins were Anglican, but it operates ecumenically, seeking to promote high-quality programmes inspired by any of the major world religions as well as all Christian traditions. The Trust's principal activity is making annual awards for outstanding achievement in religious broadcasting. For the first 25 years of its existence awards were made at Lambeth Palace for radio and for television programmes in alternate years. In 1997 the Trust inaugurated a Religious Education award for an outstanding television programme, video or CD-rom in the field of religious education, and further awards were made in 1999, 2001 and 2003. From 2003 both awards for television and radio programmes have been made annually, 2006 saw the Trust sponsoring the first *Radio Times* Readers' Award, which was presented at the annual television awards ceremony at Lambeth Palace.

In 2009, for the first time, the Trust hosted a single Awards Ceremony which combined awards for both radio and television programmes. In 2012 a joint awards ceremony was again held at Lambeth Palace and chaired by the Trust's Chairman, the Bishop of Bradford, Rt Revd Nick Baines. The sixth *Radio Times* Readers' Award was presented to Tommy Nagra by the editor of *Radio Times*, Ben Preston, for the *Songs of Praise* trilogy of programmes celebrating the strand's 50th anniversary.

The Premier Radio Award went to *Resurrection Stories* (BBC Scotland) while the Runner Up was *Faith and 9/11* (LTBI Media for BBC Radio 2). Merit awards were made for *Something Understood – Abraham* (Unique for BBC Radio 4) and *Good Friday Reflection* (Central FM).

In the Television category *The Life of Muhammad – The Seeker* (Crescent Films for BBC2) took the Premier Award while *The King James' Bible – the Book that Changed the World* (BBC Religion for BBC2) was the runner up. Merit Awards were made for *Ian Hislop – When Bankers were Good* (Wingspace for BBC2) and *Wonderland – an Hasidic Guide to Love, Marriage and Finding a Bride.* (BBC Factual for BBC2)

Chairman Rt Revd Nicholas Baines, Bishop of Bradford. *Awards Administrator* Gill Macdonald, *Hon Secretary* Mr David Craig, Room 202, Church House, Great Smith St, London SW1P 3AZ *Tel:* 020 7898 1796
Fax: 020 7898 1797
email: SandfordSMT@churchofengland.org.uk
Web: www.sandfordawards.org.uk

WORLD ASSOCIATION FOR CHRISTIAN COMMUNICATION (WACC)

WACC is an organization of corporate and personal members who wish to give high priority to Christian values in the world's communication and development needs. It is not a council or federation of churches. The majority of members are communication professionals from all walks of life. Others include partners in different communication activities, and representatives of churches and agencies. It funds communication activities that reflect regional interests, and encourages ecumenical unity among communicators. As a professional organization, WACC serves the wider ecumenical movement by offering guidance on communication policies, interpreting developments in communications worldwide, discussing the consequences that such developments have for churches and communities everywhere but especially in the Third World, and assisting the training of Christian communicators. WACC publishes *Media Action*, an on-line newsletter; *Media Development*, a quarterly journal; *Media and Gender Monitor*, a bi-annual bulletin; and occasional books, monographs and brochures. It has 1500 members affiliates in 120 countries. UK members and affiliates include the Anglican Communion Office, Council for World Mission, Feed the Minds, and SPCK. *Gen Secretary* Revd Randy Naylor, 71 Lambeth Walk, London SE11 6DX
Tel: 020 7735 2877
Fax: 020 7735 2877
email: info@waccglobal.org
Web: www.waccglobal.org

Theological Colleges and Regional Courses

Address and Telephone Number	Diocese	Principal or Warden
All Saints Centre for Mission and Ministry (formerly SNWTP), Aiken Hall, University of Chester, Crab Lane, Warrington WA2 0BD *Tel:* 01925 534303 *email:* snwtpprincipal@chester.ac.uk	Chester	Ven Dr John Applegate
Cranmer Hall (St John's College), Durham DH1 3RJ *Tel:* 0191 334 3895 *Fax:* 0191 334 3501 *email:* enquiries@cranmerhall.com	Durham	Revd Mark Tanner
College of the Resurrection, Mirfield, W Yorks. WF14 0BW *Tel:* 01924 490441 *Fax:* 01924 492738 *email:* principal@mirfield.org.uk	Wakefield	Revd Fr Peter Allan
Eastern Region Ministry Course, including Norwich OLM Scheme, Wesley House, Jesus Lane, Cambridge CB5 8BJ *Tel:* 01223 741026 *Fax:* 01223 741027 *email:* mcintosh@ermc.cam.ac.uk	Ely	Revd Dr Ian McIntosh Revd Dr Sue Woan
Lancashire and Cumbria Training Partnership, Church House, West Walls, Carlisle, Cumbria CA3 8UE *Tel:* 01228 815405 *Fax:* 01228 815400 *email:* admin@lctp.co.uk	Carlisle	Revd Canon Dr Tim Herbert
Lincoln School of Theology, University of Lincoln, Chad Varah House, Wordsworth Street, Lincoln LN1 3BP *Tel:* 01522 504025 *email:* sally.myers@lincoln.anglican.org	Lincoln	Revd Sally Myers
Lindisfarne Regional Training Partnership, Church House, St John's Terrace, North Shields NE29 6HS *Tel:* 0191 270 4144 *email:* enquiries@lindisfarnertp.org	Newcastle	Revd Canon Cathy Rowling
Local Ministry Programme: Guildford, Diocesan House, Quarry St, Guildford GU1 3XG *Tel:* 01483 790319 *email:* steve.summers@cofeguildford.org.uk	Guildford	Revd Dr Stephen Summers
Oak Hill Theological College, Chase Side, Southgate, London N14 4PS *Tel:* 020 8449 0467 *Fax:* 020 8441 5996 *email:* mindyc@oakhill.ac.uk	London	Revd Dr Michael Ovey
Oxford Local Ministry Programme, Diocesan Church House, North Hinksey, Oxford OX2 0NB *Tel:* 01865 208282 *email:* keith.beech-gruneberg@oxford.anglican.org	Oxford	Revd Dr Keith Beech-Gruneberg
Queen's Foundation for Ecumenical Theological Education, Somerset Rd, Edgbaston, Birmingham B15 2QH (Ecumenical) *Tel:* 0121 454 1527 *Fax:* 0121 454 8171 *email:* enquire@queens.ac.uk	Birmingham	Revd Dr David Hewlett
Ridley Hall, Ridley Hall Road, Cambridge CB3 9HG *Tel:* 01223 746580 *Fax:* 01223 746581 *email:* ridleypa@hermes.cam.ac.uk	Ely	Revd Andrew Norman
Ripon College, Cuddesdon, Oxford OX44 9EX including Oxford Ministry Course and West of England Ministerial Training Course. *Tel:* 01865 874404 *Fax:* 01865 875431 *email:* enquiries@ripon-cuddesdon.ac.uk	Oxford	Revd Canon Prof Martyn Percy

St John's College, Chilwell Lane, Bramcote, Nottingham NG9 3DS *Tel:* 0115 925 1114 *Fax:* 0115 943 6438 *email:* principal@stjohns-nottm.ac.uk	Southwell	Revd Dr David Hilborn
St Mellitus College , 24 Collingham Road, London SW5 0LX, including NTMTC, *Tel:* 020 7052 0573 *email:* info@stmellituscollege.org.uk	London	Revd Dr Graham Tomlin
St Stephen's House, 16 Marston St, Oxford OX4 1JX *Tel:* 01865 613500 *Fax:* 01865 613513 *email:* enquiries@ssho.ox.ac.uk	Oxford	Revd Canon Dr Robin Ward
South East Institute for Theological Education, Room Hf17, Christ Church Canterbury University, North Holmes Road, Canterbury, Kent CT1 1QU *Tel:* 01634 846683 *email:* administrator@seite.co.uk (*office*); principal@seite.co.uk (*Principal*)	Canterbury	Revd Canon Dr Jeremy Worthen
Southern Theological Education and Training Scheme, 19 The Close, Salisbury, Wilts. SP1 2EE *Tel:* 01722 424820 *Fax:* 01722 424811 *email:* danolgate@stets.ac.uk	Salisbury	Revd Dr David Holgate
South West Ministry Training Course, Amory Building, University of Exeter, Rennes Drive, Exeter EX4 4RJ *Tel:* 01392 264403 *email:* admin@swmtc.org.uk	Exeter	Revd Preb. David Moss
Trinity College, Stoke Hill, Bristol BS9 1JP *Tel:* 0117 968 2803 *Fax:* 0117 968 7470 *email:* principal@trinity-bris.ac.uk	Bristol	Revd Canon George Kovoor
Westcott House, Jesus Lane, Cambridge CB5 8BP *Tel:* 01223 741000 *Fax:* 01223 741002 *email:* general-enquiries@westcott.cam.ac.uk	Ely	Revd Canon Martin Seeley
Wycliffe Hall, Oxford OX2 6PW *Tel:* 01865 274200 *Fax:* 01865 274215 *email:* enquiries@wycliffe.ox.ac.uk	Oxford	Revd Simon Vibert (Acting Principal)
Yorkshire Ministry Course, The Mirfield Centre, Stocks Bank Rd, Mirfield, West Yorkshire WF14 0BW *Tel:* 01924 481 925 *email:* principal@ymc.org.uk	Yorkshire	Dr Christine Gore
Theological Institute of the Scottish Episcopal Church, TISEC General Synod Office, 21 Grosvenor Crescent, Edinburgh EH12 5EE *Tel:* 0131 225 6357 *Fax:* 0131 346 7247 *email:* tisec@scotland.anglican.org	Edinburgh	Revd Canon Dr Michael Fuller
St Michael's College, Llandaff, Cardiff CF5 2YJ *Tel:* 029 2056 3379 *Fax:* 029 2083 8008 *email:* ps@stmichaels.ac.uk	Llandaff	Revd Dr Peter Sedgwick

ROYAL PECULIARS, THE CHAPELS ROYAL, ETC.

Westminster Abbey

Description of Arms. Azure, a cross patonce between five martlets or; on a chief or France and England quarterly on a pale, between two roses, gules, seeded and barbed proper.

COLLEGIATE CHURCH OF ST PETER

The Collegiate Church of St Peter in Westminster, usually called Westminster Abbey, is a Royal Peculiar, and, as such, it is extra-provincial as well as extra-diocesan and comes directly under the personal jurisdiction of Her Majesty The Queen, who is the Visitor.

Throughout medieval times it was the Abbey Church of a great Benedictine Monastery, which was in existence at Westminster before the Norman Conquest. After the dissolution of the monastery in 1540 it became increasingly a great national shrine, where famous writers, poets, statesmen and leaders in the Church and State are buried. It is the Coronation Church, and in it also take place from time to time Royal weddings and many services on great occasions of a National or Commonwealth character. Daily, the Holy Communion is celebrated and Morning and Evening Prayers are said or sung.

THE VISITOR

The Sovereign

DEAN

Very Revd Dr John R. Hall, The Deanery, Westminster SW1P 3PA [2006] *Tel:* 020 7654 4801
Fax: 020 7654 4883
email: john.hall@westminster-abbey.org
Web: www.westminster-abbey.org

CANONS OF WESTMINSTER

Rector of St Margaret's Church, Revd Andrew Tremlett, 5 Little Cloister SW1P 3PL [2010]
Tel: 020 7654 4806
Fax: 020 7654 4811
email: andrew.tremlett@westminster-abbey.org

Canon Theologian Revd Prof Vernon P. White, 3 Little Cloister, London SW1P 3PL [2011]
Tel: 020 7654 4808
Fax: 020 7654 4811
email: vernon.white@westminster-abbey.org

Canon Treasurer and Almoner Revd Dr Robert P. Reiss, 1 Little Cloister, London SW1P 3PL [2005]
Tel: 020 7654 4804
Fax: 020 7654 4811
email: robert.reiss@westminster-abbey.org

Canon Steward Revd Dr Jane B. Hedges, 2 Little Cloister, London SW1P 3PL [2006]
Tel: 020 7654 4815
Fax: 020 7654 4811
email: jane.hedges@westminster-abbey.org

MINOR CANONS

Revd Dr James D. T. Hawkey, 6 Little Cloister, London SW1P 3PL [2010] *Tel:* 020 7654 4850
email: james.hawkey@westminster-abbey.org

Revd Michael D. Macey, 7 Little Cloister, London SW1P 3PL [2008] *Tel:* 020 7654 4855
email: michael.macey@westminster-abbey.org

CHAPLAIN

Sister Judith CSC, 3b Dean's Yard, London SW1P 3NY *Tel:* 020 7654 4800
email: judith.csc@westminster-abbey.org

PRIESTS VICAR

Revd Paul Bagott
Revd Alan Boddy
Revd Laura Burgess
Revd Dr Paul Bradshaw
Revd Philip Chester
Revd Chris Chivers
Revd Dr Alasdair Coles
Revd Dominic Fenton
Revd Ralph Godsall
Revd Jonathan Goodall
Revd Alan Gyle
Revd Dr Sarah Hartley
Revd Rose Hudson-Wilkin
Revd Peter McGeary
Revd Jonathan Osbourne
Revd David Peters
Very Revd Dr Victor Stock
Revd Garry Swinton
Revd Gavin Williams

LAY OFFICERS

Receiver General & Chapter Clerk Sir Stephen Lamport KCVO DL, The Chapter Office, 20 Dean's Yard, London SW1P 3PA *Tel:* 020 7654 4861
Fax: 020 7654 4914
email: stephen.lamport@westminster-abbey.org
Web: www.westminster-abbey.org

Organist and Master of the Choristers Mr James O'Donnell (*same address*) *Tel:* 020 7654 4854
email: music@westminster-abbey.org

Registrar Sir Stephen Lamport KCVO DL (*same address*)

Press and Communications Office (*same address*)
Tel: 020 7654 4923
email: press@westminster-abbey.org

Head of Communications Mr Duncan Jeffery (*same address*) *Tel:* 020 7654 4888
Fax: 020 7654 4891
email: duncan.jeffery@westminster-abbey.org

Surveyor of the Fabric Mr Ptolemy Dean (*same address*)

Head of the Abbey Collections Dr Tony Trowles, The Muniment Room and Library, Westminster Abbey, London SW1P 3PL *Tel:* 020 7654 4829
email: tony.trowles@westminster-abbey.org

Keeper of the Muniments Matthew Payne (*same address*) *Tel:* 020 7654 4829
email: matthew.payne@westminster-abbey.org

Headmaster of the Choir School Mr Jonathan Milton, Dean's Yard, London SW1P 3NY
Tel: 020 7654 4918
email: jonathan.milton@westminster-abbey.org

Legal Secretary Mr Christopher Vyse, The Chapter Office, 20 Dean's Yard, London SW1P 3PA
Tel: 020 7654 4885
email: chris.vyse@westminster-abbey.org

Auditor Mr Andrew McIntyre, Ernst & Young, 1 More London Place, London SE1 2AF
Tel: 020 7951 2068

Windsor

Description of Arms. The shield of St George, argent a cross gules, encircled by the Garter

THE QUEEN'S FREE CHAPEL OF ST GEORGE WITHIN HER CASTLE OF WINDSOR

A ROYAL PECULIAR
Founded by Edward III in 1348 and exempt from diocesan and provincial jurisdictions, the College of St George is a self-governing secular community of priests and laymen, the first duty of which is to celebrate Divine Service daily on behalf of the Sovereign, the Royal House and the Order of the Garter. Its present Chapel was founded by Edward IV in honour of Our Lady, St George and St Edward in 1475 and, with the cloisters and buildings annexed, is vested in the Dean and Canons. In it the Eucharist, Mattins and Evensong are sung or said daily and are open to all.

The Order of the Garter has its stalls and insignia in the Quire, where Knights and Ladies Companions are installed by the Sovereign. Beneath the Quire – the scene of many Royal funerals – are vaults in which lie the bodies of six monarchs. Elsewhere in the Chapel are the tombs of four others.

The College has its own school of 400 children, where it maintains twenty-four choristerships. It also awards an organ scholarship. A house for conferences has been established under the name of St George's House.

THE VISITOR
The Sovereign

DEAN
Rt Revd David Conner KCVO, The Deanery, Windsor Castle, Windsor, Berks. SL4 1NJ [1998]
Tel: 01753 865561

CANONS
Chaplain in the Great Park Canon Martin Poll, Chaplain's Lodge, Windsor Great Park, Windsor, Berks. [Oct 2012]
Tel: 01784 432434

Warden, St George's House and Canon Treasurer Canon Dr Hueston Finlay, 8 The Cloisters, Windsor Castle, Windsor, Berkshire SL4 1NJ [2004] *Tel:* 01753 848887

Steward Canon Dr James Woodward, 6 The Cloisters, Windsor Castle, Windsor, Berkshire SL4 1NJ [2009] *Tel:* 01753 848709

MINOR CANONS
Chaplain to St George's School Revd Andrew Zihni, 24 The Cloisters, Windsor Castle [2006]
Tel: 01753 848710

LAY OFFICERS
Chapter Clerk Miss Charlotte Manley LVO OBE, Chapter Office, 2 The Cloisters, Windsor Castle [2003] *Tel:* 01753 848888

Director of Music Mr Timothy Byram-Wigfield, 23 The Cloisters, Windsor Castle [2004] *Tel:* 01753 848747

Assistant Director of Music Mr Richard Pinel, 3 The Cloisters, Windsor Castle, Windsor, Berkshire SL4 1NJ

Clerk of Accounts Mr Nick Grogan, 2 The Cloisters, Windsor Castle, Windsor, Berkshire SL4 1NJ *Tel:* 01753 848720

Clerk of Works Mr Ian Poole, Clerk of Works Office, The Cloisters *Tel:* 01753 848888

Archivist and Chapter Librarian Dr Clare Rider, The Vicars' Hall Undercroft, Windsor Castle, Windsor, Berkshire SL4 1NJ *Tel:* 01753 848724

Virger Mr Vaughn Wright, 22 Horseshoe Cloister, Windsor Castle *Tel:* 01753 848727

Interim Head Master, St George's School Mr Christopher McDade, St George's School, Windsor Castle, Windsor, Berkshire SL4 1QF *Tel:* 01753 865553

Domestic Chaplains to Her Majesty the Queen

Buckingham Palace Preb William Scott
Windsor Castle The Dean of Windsor
Sandringham Revd Jonathan Riviere

Chapels Royal

The Chapel Royal is the body of Clergy, Singers and Vestry Officers appointed to serve the spiritual needs of the Sovereign – in medieval days on Progresses through the Realm as well as upon the battlefields of Europe, as at Agincourt. Its ancient foundation is first century with the British Church: its latter day choral headquarters have been at St James's Palace since 1702 along with the Court of St James. Since 1312 the Chapel Royal has been governed by the Dean who, as the Ordinary, also exercises, along with the Sub-Dean, jurisdiction over the daughter establishments of Chapels Royal at the Tower of London and at Hampton Court Palace. Members of the public are welcome to attend Sunday and weekday services as advertised.

The Chapel Royal conducts the Service of Remembrance at the Cenotaph in Whitehall, with a Forces Chaplain in company, and combines with the choral establishment of the host abbey or cathedral on the occasion of Royal Maundy, under the governance of the Lord High Almoner and Sub-Almoner. Each Member of the College of thirty-six Chaplains to Her Majesty the Queen, headed by the Clerk and Deputy Clerk of the Closet, is required by Warrant to preach in the Chapel Royal once a year, and is visibly distinguished, along with the Chapel Royal, Forces and Mohawk Chaplains, by the wearing of a royal scarlet cassock.

Dean of the Chapels Royal
The Bishop of London

Sub-Dean
Preb William Scott
Chapel Royal, St James's Palace, London SW1A 1BL *Tel:* 020 7024 5576

CHAPEL ROYAL AND THE QUEEN'S CHAPEL, ST JAMES'S PALACE

Priests in Ordinary
Revd Richard Bolton
Canon Paul Thomas
Revd William Whitcombe

Deputy Priests
Revd Roger Hall
Revd Dennis Mulliner
Canon Mark Oakley
Revd Dr Stephen Young

HAMPTON COURT PALACE
Chapel Royal, Hampton Court, East Molesey, Surrey KT8 9AU *Tel:* 020 3166 6515

Chaplain
Canon Denis Mulliner

HM TOWER OF LONDON
The Chaplain's Residence, London EC3N 4AP *Tel:* 020 3166 6796
(includes the Chapels Royal of St John the Evangelist and St Peter ad Vincula)

Chaplain
Canon Roger Hall

THE ROYAL CHAPEL OF ALL SAINTS, WINDSOR GREAT PARK
This is a Private Chapel and the property of the Crown within the grounds of the Royal Lodge. Attendance is restricted to residents and employees of the Great Park.

Chaplain
Ven Martin Poll, Chaplain's Lodge, Windsor Great Park, Windsor, Berks SL4 2HP *Tel:* 01784 432434

College of Chaplains

The position of Royal Chaplain is a very ancient one. The College of Chaplains, the members of which as such must not be confused with the Priests in Ordinary, preach according to a Rota of Waits in the Chapels Royal. The College comprises the Clerk of the Closet (who presides), the Deputy Clerk of the Closet, and thirty-six Chaplains. When a vacancy in the list of chaplains occurs, the Private Secretary to Her Majesty the Queen asks the Clerk of the Closet to suggest possible names to Her Majesty. The duties of the Clerk of the Closet include the presentation of bishops to Her Majesty when they do homage before taking possession of the revenues of their Sees; and he also examines theological books whose authors desire to present copies to Her Majesty the Queen. He preaches annually in the Chapel Royal, St James's Palace.

CLERK OF THE CLOSET
Rt Revd Christopher Hill (*Bishop of Guildford*)

DEPUTY CLERK OF THE CLOSET
Preb William Scott

CHAPLAINS TO HER MAJESTY THE QUEEN
Canon Christopher Andrews
Canon Gavin Ashenden
Preb Paul Avis
Revd Hugh Bearn
Canon John Byrne
Canon Gillian Calver
Canon Andrew Clitherow
Canon Richard Cooper
Canon Ann Easter
Preb Kathleen Garlick
Canon Roger Hill
Revd Rose Hudson-Wilkin
Canon George Kovoor
Revd John Lee
Revd Edward Lewis
Preb Paul Locket
Canon Bill Matthews
Canon Paul Miller
Canon George Moffat
Ven William Noblett
Canon John Ovenden
Rev Hugh Palmer
Canon Stephen Palmer
Revd Jonathan Riviere
Canon Bruce Ruddock
Canon Anthony Shepherd
Canon Christopher Smith
Preb Pippa Thorneycroft
Rt Revd Glyn Webster
Canon Andrew Wingate
Canon Alison Woodhouse
Revd Ruth Worsley

Extra Chaplains
Canon Anthony Caesar
Canon Gerry Murphy
Revd John Robson

Royal Almonry

The Royal Almonry dispenses the Queen's charitable gifts and is responsible for the Royal Maundy Service each year, at which Her Majesty distributes Maundy money to as many men and as many women pensioners as the years of her own age.

HIGH ALMONER
Rt Revd Nigel McCulloch (*Bishop of Manchester*)

SUB-ALMONER
Preb William Scott
Chapel Royal, St James's Palace, London SW1A 1BL

The Queen's Chapel of the Savoy

Savoy Hill, Strand, London WC2R 0DA
Tel: 020 7379 8088 (Chaplain) *or* 020 7836 7221 (Steward)
email: chapel@duchyoflancaster
web: www.duchyoflancaster.org.uk

CHAPEL OF THE ROYAL VICTORIAN ORDER

The Queen's Chapel of the Savoy was built as the principal chapel of a hospital for 'pouer, nedie people' founded by King Henry VII and finished in 1512 after his death. It is a private Chapel of Her Majesty the Queen in right of her Duchy of Lancaster, and Her Majesty appoints the chaplain. It is, therefore, a 'free' Chapel not falling within any diocese or episcopal jurisdiction.

On the occasion of his Coronation in 1937, King George VI commanded that the chapel of the Savoy should become the chapel of the Royal Victorian Order, an honour in the personal gift of the Sovereign, and the Chaplain of the Queen's Chapel is ex officio Chaplain of the Order. An ante-chapel, chaplain's office and robing room were constructed in 1958 to provide additional accommodation.

A new three-manual Walker organ was presented to the Chapel by Her Majesty the Queen in 1965. Further work in 2011–12 included the creation of a new sunken courtyard on the north side of the ante-chapel, the construction of a new chaplain's study, an extension of the royal robing room, an office for the Steward, the development of new facilities for receptions, and the installation of a new stained glass window to mark the Diamond Jubilee of the Queen's reign.

Members of the public are welcome to attend services which are held on Sundays (11 am) and weekdays (except August and September) with the exception of those for special or official occasions. The Chapel has a particularly fine musical tradition with a choir of men and boys.

CHAPLAIN
Revd Prof Peter Galloway OBE

MASTER OF MUSIC
Mr Philip Berg FRCO, ARCM

STEWARD
Sqn Ldr Thomas Leyland RAF (rtd)

CHAIRMAN OF THE COUNCIL
The Lord Shuttleworth, KCVO

GENERAL

Royal Memorial Chapel Sandhurst

Camberley, Surrey GU15 4PQ *Tel:* 01276 412543
Fax: 01276 412097

The Royal Memorial Chapel Sandhurst is the Chapel of the Royal Military Academy Sandhurst. It is also the Memorial Chapel of the officers of the British Army.

The present building was erected after the First World War as a memorial to those trained at Sandhurst who gave their lives in that conflict. Their names are inscribed on the Chapel's pillars. A memorial book contains the names of all officers of the Commonwealth Armies who died in the Second World War, and a page of this book is turned at the beginning of principal services.

A Book of Remembrance containing the names of all officers who have been killed in service since 1947 is kept in the South Africa Chapel.

The main Sunday service is at 1030. The forms of service include the *Book of Common Prayer, Common Worship*, and special services within the Academy's calendar. Services are open to the public, and passes may be obtained by contacting the Chapel Office.

CHAPLAIN
Canon J. R. B. Gough

ASSISTANT CHAPLAIN
Revd S. J. H. Dunwoody

CHOIRMASTER AND ORGANIST
Mr Peter Beaven

CONSTITUTION OF THE CHAPEL COUNCIL
Maj-Gen P. C. Marriot (*Chairman*); Canon J. R. B. Gough (*Deputy Chairman*); Maj. J. M. Watkinson (*Secretary*); Ven Peter Eagles (*Chaplain General*); Maj-Gen Sir Simon Cooper; Maj Gen R. L. Kirkland; Brig M. Owen

The Royal Foundation of St Katharine

2 Butcher Row, London E14 8DS
Tel: 0300 111 1147
Fax: 020 7702 7603
email: info@rfsk.org.uk
Web: www.rfsk.org.uk

St Katharine's, founded by Queen Matilda in 1147 originally adjacent to the Tower of London, is a charitable conference and retreat house at Limehouse in East London, between the City and Canary Wharf. It serves the Church of England, other churches and charities, offering an attractive setting for day or residential group meetings, seminars or retreats. Individuals from home and overseas are also welcome to stay. There are excellent facilities with residential en suite accommodation for 44 people and a choice of 7 meeting rooms. Daily worship is held in the re-ordered chapel.

Her Majesty Queen Elizabeth II is Patron of the Foundation.

MEMBERS OF THE COURT
Mr Benjamin Hanbury (*Chairman*)
Revd John Tattersall (Treasurer)
The Viscount Churchill
Rt Revd and Rt Hon Richard Chartres (*Bishop of London*)
The Countess of Airlie
Sir Stephen Lamport
Mrs Elizabeth Marshall
Preb David Paton (*Master*)

MASTER
Preb David Paton

Deans of Peculiars

The few present-day Deans of Peculiars are the residue of some 300 such office-holders in the medieval period, when the granting of 'peculiar' status, fully or partially exempting a jurisdiction from episcopal control, was commonly employed by popes and others to advance the interests of a particular institution, or limit the power of the bishops. Unlike the Royal Peculiars, the deaneries had little in common, and the privileges and duties of the individual posts ranged from nominal to significant. Most of the special provisions were brought to an end in the nineteenth century. But each Peculiar has interesting light to throw on a phase of Anglican or national history.

Battle
Very Revd Dr John Edmondson, The Deanery, Caldbec Hill, Battle, E. Sussex TN33 0JY [2005]
Tel and *Fax:* 01424 772693

Bocking
Very Revd Philip Need, The Deanery, Bocking, Braintree, Essex CM7 5SR (Bocking, Essex) [1996]
Tel: 01376 324887
01376 553092 (Office)
email: thedeanofbocking@tiscali.co.uk
Very Revd Martin Thrower, The Deanery, Church St, Hadleigh, Ipswich IP7 5DT (Hadleigh, Suffolk) [2009]
Tel: 01473 822218
email: martin.thrower@btinternet.com

Stamford
Very Revd Mark Warrick (*Priest in Charge of Stamford All Saints with St John the Baptist*)

The Deans of Jersey and Guernsey
The Deans of Jersey and Guernsey are very senior members of insular society. The Dean of Jersey ranks next after the Lieutenant Governor, Bailiff and Deputy-Bailiff and is an ex officio member of the States. The Dean of Guernsey ranks third after the Lieutenant Governor and Bailiff, and though not a member of the States of Deliberation (the Island Parliament) he is a member of the States of Election (which appoints Jurats to the Royal Court). From their respective positions the Deans are expected to offer spiritual and moral leadership.

References to these offices go back to the tenth century in the case of Guernsey and 1135 in the case of Jersey; the names of the Deans of Guernsey since 1295 and almost all the Deans of Jersey since 1180 are known. Since 1495 the Dean of Jersey has been appointed by the Crown. Traditionally Rector of one of the twelve Jersey parishes, since 1875 the Dean of Jersey has always been Rector of St Helier. The Dean of Guernsey has usually been Rector of the Town Church in St Peter Port, but this has not always been the case.

The Channel Islands were formerly part of the Diocese of Coutances, Normandy, but were transferred to Winchester by Papal Bull in 1500. Their annexation to the Diocese of Winchester was confirmed by Queen Elizabeth I in 1568 (they continue to be 'annexed to' rather than being 'part of' that diocese), but, the reformation having reached the islands in an extreme Calvinist Presbyterian form, the authority of Winchester was little regarded until the Restoration in 1660.

The Deans are presidents of their respective Ecclesiastical Courts and have the right to grant marriage licences, including special licences and faculties. The Guernsey Ecclesiastical Court also retains its jurisdiction in matters concerning probate and issues Letters of Administration in matters of personality. As the Bishop's Commissaries, the Deans carry out many of the duties performed in England by suffragan bishops and archdeacons, including instituting and inducting new incumbents.

Jersey
Very Revd Robert Key, The Deanery, David Place, St Helier, Jersey JE2 4TE
Tel: 01534 720001
Fax: 01534 720001
email: robert_f_key@yahoo.com

Guernsey and Dependencies
Very Revd Paul Mellor, The Deanery, Cornet St, St Peter Port, Guernsey GY1 1BZ [2003]
Tel: 01481 720036
Fax: 01481 722948
email: paul@townchurch.org.gg

Preachers at the Inns of Court

THE TEMPLE
Master Revd Robin Griffith-Jones, The Master's House, Temple, London EC4Y 7BB
Tel: 020 7353 8559
email: master@templechurch.com

Reader Revd A. H. Mead, 11 Dungarvan Ave, London SW15 5QU *Tel:* 020 8876 5833

LINCOLN'S INN
Very Revd Derek Watson, 29 The Precincts, Canterbury CT1 2EP *Tel:* 01227 865238

GRAY'S INN
Rt Revd Michael Doe, 405 West Carriage House, Royal Carriage Mews, Royal Arsenal, Woolwich SE18 6GA *Tel:* 020 3259 3841

RELIGIOUS COMMUNITIES

Anglican Religious Communities

The roots of the Religious Life can be traced back to the Early Church in Jerusalem, and the subsequent traditions such as the Benedictines, Franciscans, etc., were flourishing in England until the Reformation when all were suppressed.

Most Anglican Communities were founded in the nineteenth century as a result of the Oxford Movement. There are over forty different Communities in the British Isles and throughout the Anglican Communion. Some are very small. Some have over 80 members.

Religious Communities are formed by men and women who feel called to seek God and live out their baptismal vows in a particular way under vows. There are some 500 Anglican men and women living this life in the United Kingdom.

PRAYER AND WORK

Each Community has its own history and character; some follow one of the traditional Rules, and others those written by more recent founders, but all have one thing in common: their daily life based on the work of prayer and living together centred in their Daily Office and the Eucharist. The work grows from the prayer, depending on the particular Community and the gifts of its members.

Some Communities are 'enclosed'. The members do not normally go out, but remain within the convent or monastery and its grounds, seeking and serving God through silence and prayer, study and work. Other Communities share the basic life of prayer and fellowship and may also be involved in work outside the Community.

HOSPITALITY

Most Community houses offer a place where people can go for a time of Retreat, either alone or with a group, for a day, several days, or occasionally for longer periods of time. They offer a place of quiet to seek God, grow in prayer and find spiritual guidance.

THE CALLING

People who feel called to the Religious Life and who wish to apply to a Community are usually aged between 21 and 45. They normally need to be physically and psychologically robust. Academic qualifications are not essential. There is a training period of about three years before any vows are taken.

Those who are considering a vocation are advised to visit Community houses to experience their particular ethos: further information is available from the houses or general enquiries may be made to Anglican Religious Communities at the address below.

GENERAL

Advisory Council on the Relations of Bishops and Religious Communities

This Council, to serve the two Provinces, is responsible to the Archbishops and the House of Bishops. Its functions are (1) to advise bishops upon (*a*) questions arising about the charters, constitutions and rule of existing Communities, (*b*) the establishment of new Communities, (*c*) matters referred to it by a diocesan bishop; (2) to advise existing Communities or their Visitors in any matters that they refer to it; (3) to give guidance to those who wish to form Communities. The Chairman and Convenor of the Council must be a diocesan bishop appointed by the Archbishops of Canterbury and York. The Council consists of at least 13 members, 3 of whom are nominated by the bishops and 10 elected by the Communities. Up to 5 additional members may be co-opted. The present membership is: *Acting Chair* Rt Revd David Walker (*Bishop of Dudley*); *3 members nominated by the House of Bishops* Rt Revd John Pritchard (*Bishop of Oxford*), Rt Revd Anthony Robinson (*Bishop of Pontefract*), Rt Revd Humphrey Southern (*Bishop of Repton*); *10 members elected by the Communities* Sister Anita CSC, Sister Elizabeth Pio SSB, Sister Joyce CSF, Sister Mary Julian Gough CHC, Sister Mary Stephen OSB, Sister Rosemary CHN, Mother Winsome CSMV, Abbot Stuart Burns OSB, Father Colin Griffiths SSM, Brother Damian SSF; *Co-opted*, Father Peter Allan CR, Rt Revd Dominic Walker OGS (*Bishop of Monmouth*); Revd Canon Christopher Neal CMS; Revd Ian Mobsby; *ARC Representative* Dom Simon Jarratt OSB. *Roman Catholic Observer* Sister Catherine McGovern OSF; *Secretary* Father Colin CSWG.

Correspondence in relation to the Advisory Council should be addressed to: The Bishop of Dudley, Bishop's House, Bishops Walk, Cradley Heath B64 7RH

Tel: 0121 550 3407
email: bishop.david@cofe-worcester.org.uk

Anglican Religious Communities in England

ARC is an umbrella body of all members of Anglican Religious Communities, Monks and Nuns, Brothers and Sisters living in community under vows of poverty, chastity and obedience. The communities range from large monastic houses to small groups of two or three brothers or sisters living and working in urban areas. It acts to support its members by encouraging cooperation and the exchange of ideas and experiences which are relevant to Religious Life. The ARC Committee has members elected from four constituent groups: Leaders, General Synod Representatives, Novice Guardians and Professed Religious. An annual conference is held. Details of Communities may be found in *Anglican Religious Life*, published by Canterbury Press, or, in an abbreviated form, via the following Web address: www.arcie.org.uk

Contact The Secretary, Anglican Religious Communities, c/o Mr Ross Gillson, Church House, Great Smith St, London SW1P 3AZ
email: info@arcie.org.uk
Registered Charity no. 1097586

Communities for Men

BENEDICTINE COMMUNITY OF ST BENEDICT'S PRIORY
19a The Close, Salisbury, SP1 2EB
email: salisburypriory@virginmedia.com

Conventual Prior Dom Simon Jarratt OSB

Visitor Rt Revd Dominic Walker OGS (*Bishop of Monmouth*)

Founded 1914. 1926–87 Nashdom Abbey, 1987–2010 Elmore Abbey, From 2010 St Benedict's Priory, Salisbury. Resident community 4 monks. Oblate confraternity of around 300. It is hoped to receive retreatants and day guests once building alterations at the Priory have been completed.

BENEDICTINE COMMUNITY AT MUCKNELL ABBEY
See **Mixed Communities** page 257.

COMMUNITY OF OUR LADY AND ST JOHN
Alton Abbey, Abbey Road, Alton, Hants. GU34 4AP
Tel: 01420 562145/563575
email: abbey@domghill.mail1.co.uk

Abbot Rt Revd Dom William Hughes OSB

Visitor Rt Revd Michael Scott-Joynt

Founded 1884. A community of Benedictine monks which undertakes retreats. Guest accommodation for 18 people. Other work includes the manufacture of altar wafers and incense. The Seamen's Friendly Society of St Paul is managed from the Abbey. Day conference facilities and residential groups welcome: contact the Guestmaster.

COMMUNITY OF THE GLORIOUS ASCENSION
The Priory, Lamacraft Farm, Start Point, Kingsbridge, Devon TQ7 2NG *Tel:* 01548 511474
email: ascensioncga@fsnet.com

Prior Bro Simon CGA

Visitor Rt Revd Edward Holland

Founded in 1960 – the brothers are based in Devon and continue the monastic pattern of a common-life, prayer and worship; together with their work of hospitality and ministry. They have recently been joined by the sisters of the Community of the Glorious Ascension, who have moved from their previous base in France.

COMMUNITY OF THE RESURRECTION
House of the Resurrection, Mirfield, W Yorks. WF14 0BN *Tel:* 01924 494318
Fax: 01924 490489
email: community@mirfield.org.uk

Superior Fr George Guiver CR *Tel:* 01924 483301

Visitor Rt Revd Graham James (*Bishop of Norwich*)

Founded 1892, it undertakes teaching (theological college), retreats, missions and missionary works.

Theological College College of the Resurrection, Mirfield, W Yorks. WF14 0BW *Tel:* 01924 481900
Fax: 01924 492738
email: registrar@mirfield.org.uk

The Mirfield Centre offers a programme of day and evening events and small conferences as well as offering a meeting place for about 50 people. *Address* Mirfield Centre, College of the Resurrection, Mirfield, W Yorks. WF14 0BW
Tel: 01924 481920
Fax: 01924 492738
email: centre@mirfield.org.uk

COMMUNITY OF THE SERVANTS OF THE WILL OF GOD
See **Mixed Communities** page 257.

COMPANY OF MISSION PRIESTS
Secretary Canon Peter Brown CMP, The Clergy House, Sawmill Lane, Durham DH7 8NS
Tel: 0191 378 0845
email:
peterandbrian@sawmill-lane.freeserve.co.uk

Visitor Bishop Lindsay Urwin OGS

Warden Father Pike CMP

Founded 1940. A society of apostolic life, a dispersed community of male priests of the Anglican Communion who, wishing to consecrate themselves wholly to the Church's mission, keep themselves free from the attachments of marriage and family, and endeavour to encourage and strengthen one another by mutual prayer and fellowship, sharing the vision of St Vincent de Paul of a priesthood dedicated to service, and in association with the whole Vincentian family.

ORATORY OF THE GOOD SHEPHERD
Web: www.ogs.net

Superior Revd Prof Peter Hibbert OGS, 2 Blossom Road, Erdington, Birmingham B24 0UD
email: phibbert@ogs.net

European Provincial Brother Michael Bartlett OGS, 3–5 Park Road, Sandy, Bedfordshire SG19 1JB
email: mbartlett@ogs.net

Founded in 1913 at Cambridge University. The Oratory is a society of celibate priests and laymen of the Anglican Communion who are endeavouring, under the direction of the Rule, to live a life of devotion and service. Members of the Oratory work in four provinces: Europe, Australia, North America and Southern Africa. They are bound together by a common Rule and discipline. They do not normally live together in community but meet for Chapter and are resident regularly for an annual Oratory Retreat and for Provincial Chapter (annual) and General Chapter (triennial). Members include bishops, parish priests, lecturers and missionaries. A two-year period of probation precedes profession, and after ten years of profession, life vows may be taken. The Rule of the Oratory requires celibacy, the daily offices, where possible daily Eucharist, and a regular account of spending and direction of life. In addition, 'Labour of the Mind' is a characteristic of the Oratory and members are expected to spend time in study. Attached to the Oratory are Companions and Associates, lay, ordained, married and single, who keep a Rule of Life and are part of the Oratory family.

THE SOCIETY OF ST FRANCIS
The Society comprises a First Order for men (Society of St Francis) and women (*see* Community of St Francis, page 251), called to the Franciscan life under the vows of poverty, chastity and obedience; a Second Order of enclosed sisters (*see* Community of St Clare, page 251); and the Third Order for ordained and lay people, pledged to the spirit of the vows (*see* Third Order, Society of St Francis, page 257).

The Brothers of the First Order, founded in 1921, live a life of community centred on prayer and engage in active work especially in the areas of the poor and underprivileged. Four Friaries in this province (at Hilfield, Glasshampton, Canterbury and Alnmouth) have a ministry with guests and retreatants. The other centres of work are principally within a city context from which the brothers engage in various active ministries. Some work with educational institutions, conducting retreats and with parishes continues.

There are five Provinces: Europe, Province of the Divine Compassion, Papua New Guinea, the Solomon Islands, and the Americas.

Minister General Brother Clark Berge SSF, Little Portion Friary, PO Box 399, Mt Sinai, NY 11766/0399 *Tel:* (+1) 631 473 0553
email: clarke.berge@s-s-f.org

European Province
Minister Brother Benedict SSF, St Matthias' Vicarage, 45 Mafeking Road, Canning Town, London E16 4NS *Tel:* 020 7511 7848
email: ministerssf@franciscans.org.uk
Web: www.franciscans.org.uk

Assistant Minister Brother Philip Bartholomew SSF (Canning Town)

Bishop Protector Rt Revd Michael Perham (*Bishop of Gloucester*)

Houses
All SSF-UK houses can be emailed using [name of the house] ssf@franciscans.org.uk e.g. hilfieldssf@franciscans.org.uk
Friary of St Francis, *Alnmouth* *Tel:* 01665 830213/830660
Fax: 01665 830580
The Master's Lodge, 58 St Peter's Street, *Canterbury* CT1 2BE *Tel:* 01227 479364
Bentley Vicarage, 3a High Street, Bentley, *Doncaster* DN5 0AA *Tel:* 01302 872240
St Mary at the Cross, *Glasshampton*, Shrawley, Worcester WR6 6TQ *Tel:* 01299 896345
Friary of St Francis, *Hilfield*, Dorchester, Dorset, DT2 7BE *Tel:* 01300 341345
Fax: 01300 341293

GENERAL

25 Karnac Road, *Leeds* LS8 5BL *Tel:* 0113 226 0647
House of the *Divine Compassion*, 42 Balaam Street, Plaistow, London E13 8AQ *Tel:* 020 7476 5189
St Matthias' Vicarage, 45 Mafeking Road, *Canning Town*, London E16 4NS *Tel:* 020 7511 7848

Province of the Divine Compassion
Minister Brother Christopher John SSF. *Houses:* Brisbane (QLD), Stroud (NSW), Kirikiriroa/ Hamilton (NZ), Gangchon (Korea)

Papua New Guinea Province
Minister Brother Oswald Dumbari SSF. Houses: Haruro, Dipoturu, Koki, Popondetta: Ukaka

Province of the Solomon Islands
Minister, Brother Clifton Henry SSF. *Houses:* Auki, Busa, Hautambu: La Verna, Hautambu: Little Portion, Honiara, Kira Kira, Kohimarama, Honiara Temotu

Province of the Americas
Minister Brother Jude SSF. *Houses:* Long Island, Los Angeles, San Francisco, São Paulo (Brazil)

Communities for Women

EDGWARE ABBEY
Anglican Benedictine Community of St Mary at the Cross, 94A Priory Field Drive, Edgware, Middx HA8 9PU
Tel: 020 8958 7868
Fax: 020 8958 1920
email: info@edgwareabbey.org.uk

Abbess Mother Mary Therese Zelent OSB

Visitor Rt Revd Peter Wheatley (*Bishop of Edmonton*)

The Community was founded by Revd Henry Daniel Nihill and Mother Monica Skinner in 1866 in Shoreditch, London. Living under the Rule of St Benedict, the Community's primary objective is prayer at the heart of the Church through the offering of the Divine Office and Eucharist, and through the service of hospitality, especially in caring for the sick and poor as Christ Himself.

From the beginning, under the dedication of St Mary at the Cross, the vocation of the Community has been to stand with Mary, the Mother of Jesus beside those who suffer. The care given in those early days to the sick and poor and disabled children of the local area grew and developed through the years, and continues today in Henry Nihill House in the beautiful grounds of the abbey, providing high-quality care and nursing for disabled people and frail elderly people.

Edgware Abbey is seen as a haven of peace which enfolds many visitors. All are offered Benedictine hospitality with space for rest and renewal. The small comfortable guest wing provides short-stay accommodation and a small centre for Parish Group Quiet Days and Meetings. All visitors are welcome to share in the Community's offering of the Divine Office and Eucharist, which remains central to its life.

Chapel Service times are subject to change: please check with Edgware Abbey.

BENEDICTINE COMMUNITY OF ST MARY'S ABBEY
52 Swan St, West Malling, Kent ME19 6JX
Tel: 01732 843309
Fax: 01732 849016
Web: www.mallingabbey.org

Abbess Sister Mary David Best OSB

Visitor Rt Revd Laurie Green

We are a monastic community of women following the Rule of St Benedict. Our home is a Benedictine Abbey that flourished from c. 1090 to 1538. Our priorities are prayer, community life and hospitality to those who stay at our guest house and who wish to share in our worship and silence.

BENEDICTINE COMMUNITY AT MUCKNELL ABBEY
See **Mixed Communities** page 257.

COMMUNITY OF ALL HALLOWS
All Hallows Convent, Ditchingham, Norfolk

Postal Address Bungay, Suffolk NR35 2DT
Tel: 01986 892749
Fax: 01986 895838
email: allhallowsconvent@btinternet.com

Leaders Sister Elizabeth and Sister Sheila CAH

Visitor Rt Revd Graham James (*Bishop of Norwich*)

Founded 1855. Augustinian Visitation Rule.

Work and Houses at Ditchingham:
The Convent (*as above*)
Lavinia House, Ditchingham
Guests, retreats and spiritual direction
Tel: 01986 892840

All Hallows House, Rouen Rd, Norwich NR1 1QT
Tel: 01603 624738
Guests, retreats and spiritual direction

All Hallows Country Hospital and All Hallows Nursing Home: the hospital and nursing home have now been combined under the management of the All Hallows Health Care Trust.

Ditchingham Day Nursery: the childcare provision has transferred ownership and is now managed by The Benjamin Foundation.

COMMUNITY OF ST ANDREW
40 Homecross House, 21 Fishers Lane, Chiswick W4 1YA
Tel: 020 8747 0001 (Mother Lillian)
Tel: 020 7221 4604 (Sr Teresa)
email: teresajoan@btinternet.com
Superior Revd Mother Lillian CSA
Visitor Rt Revd Richard Chartres (*Bishop of London*)
Founded 1861. Full membership of the Community consists of professed sisters who are Deaconesses or Distinctive Deacons or Priests. Present number is five.

The fundamental ministry is the offering of prayer and worship, evangelism and pastoral work now through retirement ministries.

The Community celebrated its 150th anniversary at St Andrewstide 2011 with the (private) publication of "The Deaconess Community of St Andrew 1861–2011", 225pp and photos (Available from Sr Teresa).

The 150th anniversary of the reception of Deaconess Licence No.1 by Elizabeth Ferard, on 18 July 1862 was celebrated by members of the Deaconess Order of the Church of England at Lambeth Palace in July 2012.

COMMUNITY OF ST CLARE
St Mary's Convent, Freeland, Witney, Oxon. OX29 8AJ
Tel: 01993 881225
Fax: 01993 882434
email: community@oscfreeland.co.uk

Abbess Sister Paula OSC

Bishop Protector Rt Revd Michael Perham (*Bishop of Gloucester*)

Founded 1950. Second Order of Society of St Francis. Contemplative and enclosed.

COMMUNITY OF ST DENYS
Ivy House, 2–3 Church St, Warminster, Wilts. BA12 8PG

Leader Mrs June Watt (oblate)

Visitor Rt Revd Nicholas Holtam (*Bishop of Salisbury*)

Christian mission through the operation of a day and residential Retreat Centre, prayer and intercession, and the award of small charitable grants for religious or educational purposes.
Tel: 01985 214824
email: stdenys@ivyhouse.org

COMMUNITY OF ST FRANCIS
Founded in 1905, the sisters of the First Order of the Society of St Francis, in the European Province (now including a Region in South Korea) and in the Province of the Americas, seek to live the gospel for today through lives of prayer, study and work. Prayer, together and alone, with the Eucharist having a central place, is the heart of each house and each sister's life. Six sisters are priests, and three live the solitary life. Study nurtures each sister's spiritual life and enables and enriches ministries. Work (voluntary or salaried) includes the practical running of the houses and a wide range of ministries, presently including hospitality, prison, hospital and cathedral chaplaincy, spiritual direction, leading retreats and quiet days, parish work and missions, running an after school project for children, speaking and writing, counselling, caring for the homeless, and providing support for families of those with a life-threatening illness. In all this the sisters seek to follow Christ in the footsteps of Francis and Clare of Assisi, and in the spirit of humility, love and joy.

Minister General Sister Helen Julian CSF, Freeland
Tel: 01993 358722
email: ministergeneralcsf@franciscans.org.uk

Minister Provincial, European Sister Sue CSF, Southwark *Tel:* 01993 358722
email: ministercsf@franciscans.org.uk
Web: www.franciscans.org.uk

Bishop Protector Rt Revd Michael Perham (*Bishop of Gloucester*)

Houses St Alphege Clergy House, Pocock St, London SE1 0BJ *Tel:* 020 7898 8912
email: southwarkcsf@franciscans.org.uk

San Damiano, 38 Drury Street, Metheringham, Lincoln LN4 3EZ
Tel: 01526 321115
email: metheringhamcsf@franciscans.org.uk

The Vicarage, 11 St Mary's Rd, Plaistow, London E13 9AE *Tel:* 020 8552 4019
email: stmaryscssf@franciscans.org.uk

St Francis House, 113 Gillott Rd, Birmingham B16 0ET *Tel:* 0121 454 8302
email: birminghamcsf@franciscans.org.uk

St Matthew's House, 25 Kamloops Crescent, Leicester LE1 2HX *Tel:* 0116 253 9158
email: leicestercsf@franciscans.org.uk

Korean Region: Box 1003, Gumi Post Office, Gumi, Gyeongbukdo 730–600, Republic of Korea
Tel: 054 451 2317; *email:* koreanfs@hotmail.com

Deputy Bishop Protector for Korean Region Rt Revd Onesimus Park (*Bishop of Busan*)

Minister Provincial, Province of the Americas Sister Pamela Clare CSF, St Francis House, 3743 Cesar Chavez St, San Francisco CA 94110-4316 USA
email: csfsfo@aol.com
Web: www.communitystfrancis.org

Bishop Protector Rt Revd Bevi Edna (Nedi) Rivera, (*Bishop of Eastern Oregon*)

COMMUNITY OF ST JOHN BAPTIST
Community of St John Baptist, Priory House, 25 Woodstock Road West, Begbroke, Kidlington, Oxon OX5 *Tel:* 01865 855320
email: csjbteam@csjb.org.uk
(shortly moving to Ripon College, Cuddesdon, Oxford OX44 9EX)

Community Leader Sr Ann Verena CJGS

Visitor Rt Revd John Pritchard (*Bishop of Oxford*)

Chaplain Very Revd Lister Tonge (*Dean of Monmouth*)

Founded 1852 to honour and worship Almighty God and to serve him in works of charity. Undertakes mission and parish work, group quiet days, private retreats and spiritual direction.

COMMUNITY OF ST JOHN THE DIVINE
St John's House, 652 Alum Rock Rd, Birmingham, W Midlands B8 3NS *Tel:* 0121 327 4174
email: csjdivine@btinternet.com
Web: www.csjd.org.uk

Leaders of the Community Sister Christine CSJD and Sister Margaret Angela CSJD

Visitor Rt Revd David Urquhart (*Bishop of Birmingham*)

The Community was founded in 1848. The underpinning of our life and work is a spirituality based on St John the Apostle of Love. Today, as we continue to welcome people to test their vocation in the Religious Life, we have considered the challenge of change. The small core group of the Community has become the centre for a growing circle of Associates and Alongsiders who share much of our life. Our vision is to be a centre of prayer within the diocese, to exercise a ministry of hospitality to individuals and groups, to offer a ministry of spiritual accompaniment and to be open to new ways in which God might use us here, for example building friendships with our Muslim neighbours.

COMMUNITY OF ST LAURENCE
Convent of St Laurence, 4a Westgate, Southwell, Nottinghamshire NG25 0JH *Tel:* 01636 815005

Warden Very Revd David Leaning
Founded 1874 in Norwich and moved to Belper in Derbyshire in 1877. Moved to Southwell in September 2001. Accommodation for visitors is available in the Sacrista Prebend Retreat House next door. (*See* **Retreat Houses** page 228.)

COMMUNITY OF ST MARY THE VIRGIN
St Mary's Convent, Challow Rd, Wantage, Oxon. OX12 9DJ *Tel:* 01235 763141
email: conventsisters@csmv.co.uk
guestwing@csmv.co.uk
Web: www.csmvonline.org.uk

Superior Mother Winsome CSMV

Visitor Rt Revd John Pritchard (*Bishop of Oxford*)

The Community of St Mary the Virgin (CSMV) was founded in 1848. We are called to respond to our vocation in the spirit of the Blessed Virgin Mary: 'Behold, I am the handmaid of the Lord. Let it be to me according to your word.' Our common life is centred in the worship of God through the Eucharist, the daily Office and personal prayer, from which all else flows. The strong musical tradition of CSMV continues to enrich our worship. The work of the Community is inspired by Mary's words, 'Whatever He says to you, do it.' It may take the form of outgoing ministry in neighbourhood and parish or in living alongside those in inner city areas. For others, it will be expressed in hospitality, spiritual direction, preaching and retreat giving, or in creative work in studio and press. Sisters also live and work among the elderly at St Katharine's House, a large Care Home for the elderly in Wantage. An extensive new area of mission has opened up for us since the launch of our interactive website in September 2009. In addition to a daily update, we offer weekly meditations and retreats on line. We are able to receive requests for prayer through our website, and we also stream all our Offices live. The Community has had a share in the nurturing and training of a small indigenous Community in Madagascar, and continues to maintain links with the sisters there. The Community also lived and worked in India and South Africa for many years. Involvement with both these countries remains through 'Wantage Overseas'. Our links with South Africa are also maintained by groups of Oblates and Associates living there. There are larger groups of Oblates and Associates in England. At St Mary's Convent there is a Guest Wing for those who wish to spend time in rest, retreat and silence within the setting of a religious community.

366 High St, Smethwick B66 3PD
Tel: 0121 558 0094
email: smethwick.sisters@btinternet.com

116 Seymour Rd, Harringay, London N8 0BG
Tel and *Fax:* 020 8348 3477
email: wanatage-os@fireflyuk.net

St Katharine's House, Ormond Rd, Wantage OX12 8EA (Home for the Elderly)
Tel: 01235 767380
email: sisters.stkatharines@gmail.com

COMMUNITY OF ST PETER
St Columba's House, Maybury Hill, Woking, Surrey GU22 8AB *Tel:* 01483 750739
email: reverendmother@stpetersconvent.co.uk
Web: stcolumbashouse.org.uk

Superior Mother Lucy Clare CSP

Visitor Rt Revd David Walker (*Bishop of Dudley*)

Founded in 1861 for mission work and nursing. The Sisters are dispersed, but meet together at least monthly. Reverend Mother Lucy Clare, our Ordained Sister, and Sister Angela live in Woking and work within St Columba's House, the Sisterhood's retreat and conference centre. Sister Caroline Jane lives in Staines, is a community psychiatric nurse and also works in a local parish in Thorpe. Sister Rosamond and Sister Margaret Paul are at St Mary's Convent and Nursing Home in Chiswick. Sister Georgina Ruth lives in Croydon and works within a local parish.

COMMUNITY OF ST PETER, HORBURY
St Peter's Convent, 14 Spring End Road, Horbury, Wakefield, West Yorkshire WF4 6DB
Tel: 01924 272181
email: stpetersconvent@btconnect.com

Reverend Mother Mother Robina CSPH

Visitor Rt Revd Stephen Platten (*Bishop of Wakefield*)

Benedictine in spirit. Undertakes a variety of pastoral ministries and retreat work.

COMMUNITY OF THE COMPANIONS OF JESUS THE GOOD SHEPHERD
Priory House, 25 Woodstock Road West, Begbroke, Kidlington, Oxon OX5 1RJ
Tel: 01865 855326
email: cjgs@csjb.org.uk

Superior Sister Ann Verena CJGS

Visitor Rt Revd Dominic Walker OGS (*Bishop of Monmouth*)

Founded 1920. Undertakes work with the elderly, lay and ordained ministry training, quiet days and retreats, spiritual direction and visiting HMP Bullingdon.

COMMUNITY OF THE HOLY CROSS
Holy Cross Convent, Highfields, Nottingham Rd, Costock, Nr Loughborough LE12 6XE
Tel: 01509 852761
Fax: 01509 853051
Web: www.holycrosschc.org.uk
email: mother@holycrosschc.org.uk / sisters@holycrosschc.org.uk

Mother Superior Revd Mother Mary Luke CHC

Visitor Rt Revd Dr David Hope

Founded in 1857 for mission work but later adopted the Rule of St Benedict. All the work, centred on the daily celebration of the Divine Office and the Eucharist, is done within the Enclosure.

The Sisters contribute articles on spirituality and Christian unity to various publications and disseminate these via their website. A variety of prayer and greeting cards are also produced by the Sisters. The Community provides for Quiet Days for individuals and groups, and there is limited residential accommodation for those wishing to make longer retreats.

COMMUNITY OF THE HOLY NAME
Convent of the Holy Name, Morley Rd, Oakwood, Derby DE21 4QZ *Tel:* 01332 671716
Fax: 01332 669712
email: bursarsoffice@tiscali.co.uk
web: www.chnderby.org

Superior Sr Monica Jane CHN

Visitor Rt Revd John Inge

Founded 1865. Undertakes mission and retreat work. Guests received.

Branch Houses
Cottage 5, Lambeth Palace, London SE1 7JU
Tel: 020 7928 5407
64 Allexton Gardens, Welland Estate, Peterborough PE1 4UW *Tel:* 01733 352077
St John's Rectory, St John's Rd, Longsight, Manchester M13 0WU *Tel:* 0161 224 4336

Overseas
Lesotho Convent of the Holy Name, PO Box 22, Ficksburg 9730, RSA *Tel:* 00266 22400249

Zululand Convent of the Holy Name, P/B 806, Melmoth 3835, RSA *Tel:* 00273 54502892

COMMUNITY OF THE SACRED PASSION
Mother House: Convent of the Sacred Passion, 22 Buckingham Rd, Shoreham-by-Sea, W Sussex BN43 5UB *Tel:* 01273 453807
email: communitysp@yahoo.co.uk
Superior Mother Philippa CSP

GENERAL

Visitor Rt Revd Ian Brackley (*Bishop of Dorking*)

Founded 1911. An order which combines prayer and mission work in varying forms. In England the sisters continue their life of prayer at the Mother House and a house in Clapham. Their active work is a response to the needs of the people among whom they live and so keeps developing. The Community withdrew from Tanzania in June 1991, leaving behind a community of more than ninety Tanzanian women known as the Community of St Mary. This community is still given support by CSP, as is the Kwamkono Polio Hostel which was founded by CSP.

COMMUNITY OF THE SERVANTS OF THE CROSS
Green Willow Residential Home, 23 Vicarage Lane, East Preston, Littlehampton BN16 2SP
Tel: 01903 868761
Superior Mother Angela CSC
Visitor Rt Revd Martin Warner (*Bishop of Chichester*)
Warden and Chaplain Revd J. Lyon

Augustinian Rule. The sisters are now in retirement.

COMMUNITY OF THE SERVANTS OF THE WILL OF GOD
See **Mixed Communities** page 257.

COMMUNITY OF THE SISTERS OF THE CHURCH
St Michael's Convent, 56 Ham Common, Richmond, Surrey TW10 7JH
Tel: 020 8940 8711 and 020 8948 2502
Fax: 020 8948 5525
email: info@sistersofthechurch.org.uk
Web: www.sistersofthechurch.org.uk

UK Provincial Sister Susan CSC
email: susan@sistersofthechurch.org.uk

Visitor Rt Revd Christopher Chessun (*Bishop of Southwark*)
Founded 1870 and has a modern rule, based on the original, expressing a life rooted in prayer and worship, which flows into an active ministry through hospitality, pastoral and social justice work, spiritual direction and counselling.
Other Houses in the UK
82 Ashley Rd, St Paul's Bristol BS6 5NT
Tel: 0117 941 3268
Fax: 0117 908 6620

112 St Andrew's Rd North, St Annes-on-Sea, Lancs. FY8 2JQ *Tel:* 01253 728016
10 Furness Rd, West Harrow, Middx HA2 0RL
Tel and *Fax:* 020 8423 3780
Well Cottage, Upper Street, Kingsdown, Nr Deal, Kent CT14 8BH *Tel:* 01304 361601
email: wellcottage@sistersofthechurch.org.uk

Novitiate
St Gabriel's, 27a Dial Hill Rd, Clevedon, North Somerset BS21 7HL *Tel:* 01275 544 471

Main Houses of Overseas Provinces
Sister Linda Mary CSC, Mother Superior and Australian Provincial
29 Lika Drive, Kempsey, NSW 2440, Australia
send all correspondence to: PO Box 1105, Glebe, NSW2037, Australia
Sister Margaret CSC, Canadian Provincial
St Michael's House, 1392 Hazelton Boulevard, Burlington, Ontario L7P 4V3, Canada
Sister Phyllis CSC, Solomon Islands Provincial
Tetete ni Kolivuti, Box 510, Honiara, Solomon Islands

COMMUNITY OF THE SISTERS OF THE LOVE OF GOD
Convent of the Incarnation, Fairacres, Parker St, Oxford OX4 1TB *Tel:* 01865 721301
Fax: 01865 250798
email: sisters@slg.org.uk
Guest Sister guests@slg.org.uk
Web: www.slg.org.uk

Reverend Mother Sister Margaret Theresa SLG

Visitor Rt Revd Michael Lewis (*Bishop of Cyprus and the Gulf*)

A contemplative community with a strong monastic tradition founded in 1906, which seeks to witness to the priority of God and to respond to the love of God – God's love for us and our love for God. We believe that we are called to live a substantial degree of withdrawal, in order to give ourselves to a spiritual work of prayer which, beginning and ending in the praise and worship of God, is essential for the peace and well-being of the world. Through offering our lives to God within the Community and through prayer and daily life together, we seek to deepen our relationship with Jesus Christ and one another. The Community has always drawn upon the spirituality of Carmel; life and prayer in silence and solitude is an important dimension in our vocation. The Community also draws from other traditions, and our Rule is not specifically Carmelite. Another important ingredient is an emphasis on the centrality of Divine Office and Eucharist together in choir, inspired partly by the Benedictine way of life.

SLG Press publishes pamphlets on spirituality and prayer.

SLG Press, Convent of the Incarnation, Fairacres, Parker St, Oxford OX4 1TB *Tel:* 01865 241874
Fax: 01865 241889
email: editor@slgpress.co.uk
Web: www.slgpress.co.uk

ORDER OF THE HOLY PARACLETE
St Hilda's Priory, Sneaton Castle, Whitby, N Yorks. YO21 3QN *Tel:* 01947 602079
Fax: 01947 820854
email: ohppriorywhitby@btinternet.com
Web: www.ohpwhitby.org

Superior Sister Dorothy Stella OHP

Visitor Most Revd John Sentamu

Founded in 1915 and based on the Rule of St Benedict. Main undertaking: prayer, pastoral work, retreats, conferences, missions, parish work.

Residential Conference Centre Sneaton Castle Centre, Whitby, N Yorks. YO21 3QN
Tel: 01947 600051
Fax: 01947 603490
email: sneaton@globalnet.co.uk
Web: www.sneatoncastle.co.uk
Accommodation and facilities for large and small groups for parish activities, conferences and educational courses.

Branch Houses
Beach Cliff, 14 North Promenade, Whitby, N Yorks. YO21 3JX *Tel:* 01947 601968
St Oswald's Pastoral Centre, Woodlands Drive, Sleights, Whitby, N Yorks. YO21 1RY
Tel: 01947 810496
Fax: 01947 810759
email: ohpstos@globalnet.co.uk

1A Minster Court, York YO1 7JJ
Tel: 01904 557276
email: sistersohp@googlemail.com
Working in York Minster and Library.

All Saints House, South Avenue, Dormanstown TS10 5II *Tel:* 01642 486424
email: sisteranita@btinternet.com

Parish work
3 Acaster Lane, Bishopthorpe YO23 2SA
Tel: 01904 777294
email: ohpbishopthorpe@archbishopofyork.org

Chaplain Rev Andrew Symonds

Overseas
Convent of the Holy Spirit, PO Box AH 9375, Ahinsan, Kumasi, Ashanti, Ghana
Tel: 00233 242 203 432
email: ohpjac@yahoo.com

Fostering indigenous vocations, undertaking pastoral work and eye clinic ministry.

Anglican Sisters OHP, Resurrection House, PO Box 596, Sunyani, Brong Ahafo Ghana
Tel: 00233 243 7068
email: nyamebekyere2010@yahoo.com
Fostering vocations, Bishop's Secretary, wafer making development work.

PRIORY OF OUR LADY, WALSINGHAM
Priory of Our Lady, Walsingham, Norfolk NR22 6ED *Tel:* 01328 820340 (Reverend Mother); 01328 820901 (Sisters and Guest Sister)

Superior Mother Mary Teresa SSM
email: teresa@prioryofourlady.co.uk

Visitor Rt Revd Peter Wheatley (*Bishop of Edmonton*)

Autonomous house of the Society of St Margaret. Sisters are involved in the ministry of healing and reconciliation in the Shrine, the local parishes and the wider Church. They are also available to pilgrims, visitors and others, and offer spiritual direction. They work in the Shrine, the Shrine Shop and the Welcome Centre, and join in the life of the village and local parishes whenever possible. Short retreats and quiet days can be arranged on request. The Guest House offers periods of rest, relaxation and retreat. All bookings to be made through the Guest Sister.

ST SAVIOUR'S PRIORY
18 Queensbridge Rd, London E2 8NS
Tel: 020 7739 6775 (Guest bookings)
020 7739 9976 (Sisters)
email: ssmpriory@aol.com
Web: www.stsavioursprioryorg.uk

Superior Revd Sr Helen Loder SSM

Visitor Rt Revd Dominic Walker OGS (*Bishop of Monmouth*)

Autonomous convent of the Society of St Margaret, working as staff members (lay or ordained) in various parishes, dance workshops, complementary therapy, with the homeless, etc.; retreats and individual spiritual direction. The Priory has a few guest rooms and facilities for individual private retreats as well as excellent facilities for small group meetings.

SISTERS OF BETHANY
7 Nelson Rd, Southsea, Hants. PO5 2AR
Tel: 023 9283 3498
email: ssb@sistersofbethany.org.uk
Web: www.sistersofbethany.org.uk

Superior Mother Rita-Elizabeth, SSB

Visitor Rt Revd Trevor Willmott (*Bishop of Dover and Bishop in Canterbury*)

Founded 1866 for hospitality, retreat work and prayer for Christian Unity. The Sisters are available for leading quiet days and retreats, as spiritual directors, and also to give talks on prayer. People are welcome to come individually

GENERAL

or as groups to spend time in silence and prayer. It is possible to accommodate a few residential guests, or groups of up to 24 for the day. A reference is required for guests applying to stay for the first time.

SISTERS OF CHARITY
83 Fore Street, Plympton, Plymouth PL7 2HP
Tel: 01752 336112
email: plymptonsisters@gmail.com

Superior Revd Mother Elizabeth Mary SC

Visitor Vacancy

Founded 1869. The Rule is based on that of St Vincent de Paul. We assist as required in parish work and in intercessory prayer, and maintain a nursing home.

Morning Prayer 9 am. Most convenient time to telephone 5.30–7.00 pm.

Branch Houses
St Vincent's Nursing Home, Plympton, Plymouth PL7 1NE *Tel:* 01752 336205
Carmel, 7a Gress, Isle of Lewis HS2 0NB
Tel: 01851 820734

SOCIETY OF ALL SAINTS SISTERS OF THE POOR
All Saints Convent, St Mary's Rd, Oxford OX4 1RU *Tel:* 01865 249127
email: admin@socallss.co.uk
Guests' email: guestsister@socallss.co.uk

Community Leader Sister Jean Raphael ASSP

Visitor Rt Revd Bill Ind

Founded in London 1851. Works of the Society:
St John's Residential Home for the Elderly, St Mary's Rd, Oxford OX4 1QE *Tel:* 01865 247725
email: admin@st-johns-home.org

Guest House (single, twin and double accommodation available). Also conference facilities for groups of up to about 12, weekdays, daytime only. Enquiries regarding visits, private retreats and conferences welcomed. Telephone as shown above for All Saints' Convent.

The Society is associated with:
Helen and Douglas House; The Porch Steppin' Stone Centre; All Saints Embroidery.

SOCIETY OF ST MARGARET
St Margaret's Convent, Hooke Hall, 250 High St, Uckfield RN22 1EN *Tel:* 01825 766808
Fax: 01825 763474
email: egmotherssm@hotmail.com

Superior Sister Cynthia Clare SSM

Visitor Rt Revd John Hind until July 2013, then Rt Revd Martin Warner (*Bishop of Chichester*)

Founded 1855 and undertakes nursing and parish work. Sisters available for spiritual guidance and quiet afternoons.

Branch House St Mary's Convent and Nursing Home, Burlington Lane, Chiswick, London W4 2QE (guest house for elderly ladies and nursing home for geriatric and handicapped ladies)
Tel: 020 8994 4641
Fax: 020 8995 9796

Superior Sister Jennifer Anne SSM

Visitor Rt Revd John Hind until July 2013, then Rt Revd Martin Warner (*Bishop of Chichester*)

A Residential Home for elderly retired ladies; and Nursing Home for those needing full-time nursing care.

Overseas St Margaret's Convent (*semi-autonomous*), 157 St Michael's Rd, Polwatte, Colombo 3, Sri Lanka

A home for the aged, a retreat house and a children's home.

Sister Superior Sister Chandrani SSM
Tel: 00 94 11 2320692
Visitor Rt Revd Dhiloraj Canagasaby (*Bishop of Colombo*)

Branch House
St John's Home, 133 Galle Rd, Moratuwa, Sri Lanka. *Tel:* 00 94 11 2645304

Independent Convents of the Society St Margaret
St Saviour's Priory, 18 Queensbridge Rd, London E2 8NS
Leader Sister Helen SSM *Tel:* 020 7739 6775
email: ssmpriory@aol.com
Priory of Our Lady, Walsingham, Norfolk, NR22 6ED
Superior Mother Mary Teresa SSM
Tel: 01328 820340
email: teresa@prioryofourlady.co.uk
St Margaret's Convent, 17 Highland Park St, Boston, MA 02119, USA
Superior Sister Adele Marie SSM
Tel: 00 1 617 445 8961
Fax: 00 1 617 445 7120
email: ssmconvent@ssmbos.com

SOCIETY OF THE PRECIOUS BLOOD
Burnham Abbey, Lake End Rd, Taplow, Maidenhead, Berks. SL6 0PW *Tel:* 01628 604080
email: burnhamabbey@btinternet.com
Web: www.burnhamabbey.org

Superior The Revd Mother SPB

Visitor Rt Revd Stephen Cottrell (*Bishop of Chelmsford*)

Founded 1905 and based on Rule of St Augustine. Contemplative and exists for the purpose of perpetual intercession for the Church and for the world.

Overseas Independent Daughter House Priory of Our Lady Mother of Mercy, Masite, PO Box MS 7192, Maseru 100, Lesotho

Dependent House of the Overseas House St Monica's House of Prayer, 46 Green St, West End, Kimberley 8301, Cape, RSA

SOCIETY OF THE SACRED CROSS
Tymawr Convent, Lydart, Monmouth, Gwent NP25 4RN *Tel:* 01600 860244
email: tymawrconvent@btinternet.com
Web: www.churchinwales.org.uk/tymawr

Superior Sister Gillian Mary SSC

Visitor Rt Revd Dominic Walker OGS (*Bishop of Monmouth*)

Founded in 1914 at St George's, Chichester; four sisters felt called to the monastic, contemplative life, which was established in Wales in 1923. The community lives a life of prayer based on silence, solitude and learning to live together, under vows of poverty, chastity and obedience, with a modern rule, Cistercian in spirit. It is possible for women and men, married or single, to experience our life of prayer by living alongside the community for periods longer than the usual guest stay. There are facilities for retreatants and small groups. The extended community consists of companions, oblates and associates. The community is dedicated to the crucified and risen Lord as the focus of its life and the source of the power to live it. The setting in the unspoilt rural border country of Wales plays a very real part in the spirituality of the community.

SOCIETY OF THE SACRED MISSION
See **Mixed Communities** page 257.

GENERAL

Mixed Communities

BENEDICTINE COMMUNITY AT MUCKNELL ABBEY
The Community of Benedictine nuns and monks recently relocated from Burford to a new ecologically sustainable monastery in Worcestershire.

Mucknell Abbey, Mucknell Farm Lane, Stoulton, Worcestershire WR7 9RB *Tel:* 01905 345900
email: information@mucknellabbey.org.uk

Abbot Rt Revd Stuart Burns OSB
email: abbot@mucknellabbey.org.uk

Visitor Rt Revd John Inge

By a common life of prayer, manual work and study the Community tries to create an atmosphere of stillness and silence in which the Community and its guests are enabled to be open and receptive to the presence of God.

While the recitation of the Office and celebration of the Eucharist constitute the principal work of the Community, the ministry of hospitality, the care of the grounds (which comprise a large organic kitchen garden in 40 acres of orchard, meadow and woodland), and the income-generating crafts of incense-making, icon writing and block-mounting, and Chinese brush painting provide a variety of manual work for the members of the Community and those guests who wish to share in it.

The monastery seeks to be a place of encounter and reconciliation. The early concern of the Community was to pray for Christian unity, and the Community enjoys links with Baptist, Lutheran, Orthodox and Roman Catholic communities, and is particularly committed to the furthering of the Covenant between the Church of England and the Methodist Church. This ecumenical concern has broadened to include dialogue with people of other faiths, particularly those with a monastic tradition, and those who are seeking a spiritual way, either within or outside an established religious tradition.

COMMUNITY OF THE SERVANTS OF THE WILL OF GOD
Monastery of the Holy Trinity, Crawley Down, Crawley, W Sussex RH10 4LH *Tel:* 01342 712074
email: brother.andrew@cswg.org.uk

Father Superior Revd Fr Colin CSWG

Visitor Rt Revd John Hind

Founded 1953 for men (clerical and lay). Women are now received also. Contemplative. Retreats and conferences. The Community has also founded a charitable trust for promoting the Christian tradition of contemplative life and prayer within the Church.

SOCIETY OF ST FRANCIS, THIRD ORDER
One of the three Orders of the Society of St Francis (see also Communities for Men, page 249; Communities for Women, page 251). The Third Order is made up of women and men, lay and ordained, single and married, seeking to live out

Franciscan ideals in the ordinary walks of life. There are just under 2000 Tertiaries in the European Province; there are four other Provinces: Africa, the Americas, Australia with Papua New Guinea and East Asia and Aotearoa – New Zealand and Polynesia with Melanesia.

Minister General Ken E. Norian TSSF, 45 Malone Street, Hicksville NY 11801 USA
Tel: +1 917 416 9579
email: ken@tssf.org

Minister Provincial European Province Averil E. Swanton, 11, The Grange, Fleming Way, Exeter EX2 4SB *Tel:* 01392 430355
email: ministertssf@tssf.org.uk
Web: www.tssf.org.uk

SOCIETY OF THE SACRED MISSION
Founded 1893. A religious community engaged in educational, pastoral and missionary work. The Society is divided into Provinces:

Province of Europe
Visitor Rt Revd John Pritchard (*Bishop of Oxford*)
Provincial Fr Colin Griffiths SSM
The Well, Newport Rd, Willen MK15 9AA
Tel: 01908 300552
email: cgcolgrif10@gmail.com

Houses
St Antony's Priory, 74 Claypath, Durham DH1 1QT *Tel:* 0191 384 3747
email: durhamstant@aol.com
1 Linford Lane, Milton Keynes, Bucks. MK15 9DL
Tel: 01908 663749
The Well, Newport Rd, Willen MK15 9AA
Tel: 01908 242190

Southern Province
Visitor Most Revd Philip Freier (*Archbishop of Melbourne*)
Provincial Fr Christopher Myers SSM
St John's Priory, 14 St John's Street, Adelaide, South Australia 5000
email: ssm.s.province@esc.net.au
Houses
St John's Priory, 14 St John's St, Adelaide, S Australia 5000
St Michael's Priory, 75 Watsons Rd, Diggers Rest, Victoria, Australia 3427

Southern African Province
Visitor Most Revd Thabo Makgoba (*Archbishop of Cape Town*)
Provincial Fr Michael Lapsley SSM
SSM House, 33 Elgin Rd, Syband Park, Cape Town 7700, RSA *email:* michaelssm@gmail.com
SSM Priory, PO Box 1579, Maseru 100, Lesotho, Southern Africa *email:* ssmaseru@tlmail.co.ls

PART 4

Organizations

Classified List of Organizations Included in this Section

Animal Welfare
Anglican Society for the Welfare of Animals

Art, Architecture
Art and Christianity Enquiry
Art and Sacred Places
Christian Arts
Church Monuments Society
Ecclesiological Society
Friends of Friendless Churches
York Glaziers' Trust

Bell-ringing
Ancient Society of College Youths
Central Council of Church Bell Ringers
Society of Royal Cumberland Youths

Bible Study
BRF
Bible Society
Lord Wharton's Charity
SASRA
Scripture Union
SGM Lifewords (formerly Scripture Gift Mission International)
Vacation Term for Biblical Study

Blind People
Blind People, Royal National Institute for
Guild of Church Braillists
St John's Guild

Church Buildings
Friends of Friendless Churches
Greater Churches Network
Incorporated Church Building Society
Marshall's Charity
Vergers, Church of England Guild of

Church Societies – General
Additional Curates Society
Affirming Catholicism
Association of English Cathedrals
Cathedral and Church Shops Association
Cathedral Libraries and Archives Association
Cathedrals Administration and Finance Association
Catholic Group in General Synod
Church of England Flower Arrangers Association
CPAS (Church Pastoral Aid Society)
Church Society
Church Union
Churches' Advertising Network
Modern Church
Open Synod Group
Parish and People
Society for the Maintenance of the Faith
Society of the Faith (Inc)
Unitas – The Catholic League

Church Societies – Specific
Anglican Fellowship in Scouting and Guiding
Anglican Mainstream
Association of Diocesan Registry Clerks (Southern Province)
Baptismal Integrity
Christian Evidence Society
CHRISM
Church House Deaneries Group
Church of England Record Society
College of Readers
Community of Aidan and Hilda
Day One Christian Ministries
Diocesan Clergy Chairs' Forum
Ecumenical Society of the Blessed Virgin Mary
Forward in Faith
Foundation for Church Leadership
Guild of St Leonard
Guild of Servants of the Sanctuary
Reform
Royal Martyr Church Union
Society of King Charles the Martyr
Society of Mary
Third Province Movement

Clergy Associations
Anglo-Catholic Ordination Candidates' Fund
Association of Black Clergy
Association of Hospice and Palliative Care Chaplains
Association of Ordinands and Candidates for Ministry
College of Health Care Chaplains
English Clergy Association
Federation of Catholic Priests
Fellowship of Word and Spirit
Industrial Mission Association
Retired Clergy Association
School Chaplains' Association
Society of Catholic Priests
Society of Ordained Scientists
Society of the Holy Cross
Unite Clergy and Faith Workers
See also **Professional Groups**

Consultancy
CTBI Christians Abroad
Grubb Institute
Living Stones

Coordinating Bodies
Church of England Evangelical Council
Churches' Funerals Group
Churches' Legislation Advisory Service

Evangelical Alliance
National Association of Diocesan Advisers for Women's Ministry
Religious Education Council of England and Wales
Universities and Colleges Christian Fellowship

Counselling
Anglican Association of Advisers in Pastoral Care and Counselling
Lesbian and Gay Christian Movement
Relate
True Freedom Trust

Deaf People
British Deaf Association
Deaf Anglicans Together
Deaf People, Royal Association for
RNID

Defence, Disarmament, Pacifism
Anglican Pacifist Fellowship
Commonwealth War Graves Commission
Council on Christian Approaches to Defence and Disarmament

Diocesan Associations *see* pages 321–322

Drama
Actors' Church Union
Radius

Ecumenism
Anglican and Eastern Churches Association
Anglican–Lutheran Society
Churches' Funeral Group
Fellowship of St Alban and St Sergius
Fellowship of St Thérèse of Lisieux
International Ecumenical Fellowship
Nikaean Club
Nikaean Ecumenical Trust
Order of Christian Unity
Society of Archbishop Justus Ltd
Society of St Willibrord

Education
Archbishop's Examination in Theology
Association of Church College Trusts
Awareness Foundation
Bloxham Project
Christian Education
Culham Institute
Culham St Gabriel's Trust
Lincoln Theological Institute
Mirfield Centre
North of England Institute for Christian Education
RE Today Services
Religious Education Council of England and Wales
Royal Alexandra and Albert School
Royal Asylum of St Ann's Society
St George's College, Jerusalem
St Hild and St Bede Trust
Scripture Union
United Church Schools Trust
Woodard Corporation, the (Woodard Schools)

Evangelism
Church Army
College of Evangelists

Family
CARE
Family Action
Fellowship of St Nicholas
Mothers' Union
St Michael's Fellowship

Finance
Christian Ethical Investment Group
Ecclesiastical Insurance Office PLC
Ecumenical Council for Corporate Responsibility
Number 1 Trust Fund

Grant-Making Bodies
All Saints Educational Trust
Bristol Clerical Education Society
Church of England Clergy Stipend Trust
Church Pastoral Aid Society Ministers in Training Fund
Cleaver Ordination Candidates' Fund
Culham St Gabriel's Trust
Elland Society Ordination Fund
Foundation of St Matthias
Hockerill Educational Foundation
Keswick Hall Trust Charity
Newton's Trust
Ordination Candidate Funds (General)
Pilgrim Trust
Queen Victoria Clergy Fund
Revd Dr George Richards' Charity
Sarum St Michael Educational Charity
St Christopher's Educational Trust
St Luke's College Foundation
St Mary's College Trust
St Peter's Saltley Trust
See also **Welfare**

Health, Healing and Medicine
Acorn Christian Foundation
Association of Hospice and Palliative Care Chaplains
Burrswood
Cautley House
Christian Healing Mission
Christian Medical Fellowship
College of Health Care Chaplains
Guild of Health
Guild of Pastoral Psychology
Guild of St Raphael
Harnhill Centre of Christian Healing
Pilsdon at Malling Community
Richmond Fellowship
St Luke's Healthcare for the Clergy

Inter Faith, Religions
Council of Christians and Jews
INFORM
Inter Faith Network
World Congress of Faiths

Internet
COIN: Christians on the Internet
Society of Archbishop Justus Ltd

Libraries *see* pages 323–328

Marriage
Anglican Marriage Encounter
Broken Rites
Relate

Ministry
CHRISM
Diaconal Association of the Church of England
Diakonia
Distinctive Diaconate
MODEM

Ministry, Women
Li Tim-Oi Foundation
WATCH

Mission
Aim International
Bible Society
Christian Witness to Israel
CPAS (Church Pastoral Aid Society)
Church's Ministry Among Jewish People
Greenbelt Festivals
London City Mission
Mersey Mission to Seafarers, The
Mission to Seafarers, The
SASRA
Scripture Union
SGM Lifewords (formerly Scripture Gift Mission International)
Society for Promoting Christian Knowledge
Student Christian Movement
Trinitarian Bible Society
Universities and Colleges Christian Fellowship

Mission Overseas
All Nations Christian College
Church Mission Society
Crosslinks
Feed the Minds
Highbury Centre, The
Intercontinental Church Society
Interserve
Korean Mission Partnership
Leprosy Mission
Melanesian Mission
Mid-Africa Ministry
Mozambique and Angola Anglican Association (MANNA)
New England Company
OMF International (UK)
Overseas Bishoprics Fund
Oxford Mission
Papua New Guinea Church Partnership
Reader Missionary Studentship Association
South American Mission Society
Southern Africa Church Development Trust
Tearfund
USPG: Anglicans in World Mission
World Vision

Music
Archbishops' Certificate in Church Music
Choir Benevolent Fund
Choir Schools Association
Church Music Society
Guild of Church Musicians
Hymn Society of Great Britain and Ireland
Jubilate Group
Morse-Boycott Bursary Fund
Plainsong and Medieval Music Society
Royal College of Organists
Royal School of Church Music

Overseas
Christian Aid
CTBI Christians Abroad
Farnham Castle International Briefing and Conference Centre
United Nations Association (UNA–UK)
Womenaid International
World Vision

Patronage Trusts *see* pages 328–330

Prayer, Meditation, Retreats
Archway
Association for Promoting Retreats
Confraternity of the Blessed Sacrament
Friends of Little Gidding
Guild of All Souls
Guild of St Leonard
Julian Meetings, The
Julian of Norwich, Friends of
Pilsdon at Malling Community
Retreat Association
Sarum College
Servants of Christ the King
Society of Retreat Conductors
Women's World Day of Prayer

Professional Groups
Actors' Church Union
Association of Christian Teachers
Association of Christian Writers
Association of Ordinands and Candidates for Ministry
Christian Arts
Christians at Work
Church House Deaneries' Group
Church Schoolmasters' and School Mistresses' Benevolent Institution

Deans' Conference
Deans' Vergers' Conference
Ecclesiastical Law Society
Guild of Pastoral Psychology
Homes for Retired Clergy
Industrial Mission Association
Librarians' Christian Fellowship
National Association of Diocesan Advisers in Women's Ministry
Society of Retreat Conductors
Unite Clergy and Faith Workers
Vergers, Church of England Guild of
See also **Clergy Associations**

Publishing, Print Media
BRF
Book Aid
Feed the Minds
Rebecca Hussey's Book Charity
Scripture Union
Society for Promoting Christian Knowledge
Trinitarian Bible Society

Renewal
Keswick Convention
Sharing of Ministries Abroad (SOMA)

Research
Arthur Rank Centre
CARE
Centre for the Study of Christianity and Sexuality
Christian Research
Churches' Fellowship for Psychical and Spiritual Studies
Culham Institute
Latimer Trust
Rural Theology Association
St George's House, Windsor
Urban Theology Unit
William Temple Foundation

Rural Affairs
Arthur Rank Centre
Rural Theology Association

Scholarship and Science
Alcuin Club
Canterbury and York Society
Christian Evidence Society
Ecclesiastical Law Society
Faith and Thought
Henry Bradshaw Society
Latimer Trust
Liddon Trust
National Archives, The
Philip Usher Memorial Fund
Pusey House
Society for Liturgical Study
Society for Old Testament Study
Society of Ordained Scientists
Vacation Term for Biblical Study

Social Concern
Age UK
Changing Attitude
Christian Socialist Movement
Church Housing Trust
English Churches Housing Group
Lesbian and Gay Christian Movement
Livability
mediawatch–uk
National Council for Social Concern
Order of Christian Unity
Pilsdon at Malling Community
St Pancras and Humanist Housing Association
Samaritans

Training
Anglican Marriage Encounter
Association of Church Fellowships
Bridge Pastoral Foundation
Christian Education
Christians at Work
College of Preachers
Girls Friendly Society in England and Wales
Industrial Christian Fellowship
Paradox Ministries
RE Today Services
Student Christian Movement
William Temple Foundation

Travel, Pilgrimage
Accueil, Rencontre, Communauté UK
British Isles and Eire Airport Chaplains' Network
Cathedrals Plus
Journeying
Walsingham, Shrine of Our Lady of

Welfare
Almshouse Association
Beauchamp Community
Bromley and Sheppard's Colleges
Came's Charity for Clergymen's Widows
Catch 22 (formerly Rainer)
Church of England Soldiers', Sailors' and Airmen's Clubs
Church of England Soldiers', Sailors' and Airmen's Housing Association
Church Schoolmasters' and School Mistresses' Benevolent Institution
Church Welfare Association
College of St Barnabas
Community Housing and Therapy
Compassionate Friends, The
Corporation of the Sons of the Clergy
Diocesan Institutions of Chester, Manchester, Liverpool and Blackburn
Elizabeth Finn Care
Family Action
Frances Ashton's Charity
Friends of the Clergy Corporation
Friends of the Elderly
Homes for Retired Clergy
House of St Barnabas in Soho

Keychange
Livability
Langley House Trust
MACA – (Mental After Care Association)
Pyncombe Charity
Revd Dr George Richards' Charity
St Michael's Fellowship
Samaritans
Seamen's Friendly Society of St Paul
Society for the Assistance of Ladies in Reduced Circumstances
Society for the Relief of Poor Clergymen
Society of Mary and Martha
YMCA
YWCA England and Wales

Worship
Alcuin Club
Praxis
Prayer Book Society

Youth
Accueil, Rencontre, Communauté UK
Barnardo's
Boys' Brigade
Campaigner Ministries
Catch 22 (formerly Rainer)
Children's Society
Church Lads' and Church Girls' Brigade
Fellowship of St Nicholas
Frontier Youth Trust
Girlguiding UK
Girls' Brigade
Girls Friendly Society in England and Wales
Lee Abbey Household Communities
Lee Abbey International Students' Club
St Christopher's Fellowship
Scout Association
Shaftesbury Homes and 'Arethusa'
Urban Saints (formerly Crusaders)
William Temple House

ORGANIZATIONS

The following list of societies and organizations with importance for the Church of England includes many that are specifically Anglican, others that are inter-denominational, and others without religious affiliation.

The inclusion of an organization is for the purposes of information and is not to be taken as implying acceptance of the objects of the organization by the Editor and Publishers of the *Year Book* or by the General Synod.

A classified list of organizations is provided in the preceding pages. **Diocesan Associations** (in support of overseas provinces and dioceses), **Libraries**, and **Patronage Trusts** are grouped together at the end of the section. *See also* Part 3 (General Information).

Accueil, Rencontre, Communaute UK (ARC UK)

ARC UK is a charity that organizes summer projects in which young people from across Europe give guided tours in their native language to visitors to churches. In so doing we seek to turn tourists into pilgrims through devotional tours in which visitors have the chance to engage, question and wonder. Our projects aim to enable churches in their ministry of welcome and education, ecumenical links and youth involvement. ARC UK is part of a network of associated organizations which organizes such projects throughout Europe. We are always interested to hear from those who might like to participate on one of our projects, or churches who might be interested in hosting a project.We are supported in our work by our Patron, the Bishop of Southwark, the Rt Revd Christopher Chessun. *President:* Stephen Stavrou. *Secretary:* Anna Dorofeeva. *Recruitment Officer:* Christa Neudecker. *Treasurer:* Louise Lamb, Westcott House, Jesus Lane, Cambridge, CB5 8BP *Tel:* 07528 930 966 (Mobile)
email: arc_england@yahoo.co.uk
Web: www.encounterarc.org.uk

Acorn Christian Foundation

Founded originally as the Acorn Christian Healing Trust in 1983 by Bishop Morris Maddocks and his wife Anne to see the Church and nation renewed in the service of Christ the Healer, believing that every person has the right to receive the best care and attention that will enable them to grow into wholeness. Acorn offers all Christian churches a variety of teaching and training resources in Christian healing. Many of these are conducted at Whitehill Chase, Acorn's resource centre in Hampshire, where a weekly open day is held every Tuesday (except August) in conjunction with a service of healing. Quiet Days are held bi-monthly, normally on Thursdays, and include three devotional talks and a midday service with the opportunity for personal prayer and reflection. 'Deeper Healing Days' are also run bi-monthly and these are days of prayer for inner healing concluding with a communion service. The well-established Christian Listener courses range from a short introductory unit through to a twelve-session course, taught by trained tutors. There are 500 Acorn trained voluntary tutors throughout the country who teach listening skills to local church members. They in turn offer these resources in their church, home, workplace, local schools and wider community. Acorn has identified priority listening areas for rural and inner city deprived areas, a schools programme for youth, listening to Aids in Africa and reconciliation in Northern Ireland. Whitehill Chase is also available as a retreat centre and for church groups to hold meetings and conferences. Registered Charity no. 1080011. *Patron:* The Archbishop of Canterbury. *Director:* Revd Dr Russ Parker, Whitehill Chase, High St, Bordon, GU35 0AP *Tel:* 01420 478121
Fax: 01420 478122
email: info@acornchristian.org
Web: www.acornchristian.org

Actors' Church Union

Founded 1899, members and associates serve those engaged in the performing arts through their interest, their action – often in association with other related bodies – and their prayers. Additionally, more than two hundred honorary chaplains serve all members of the profession in theatres, studios and schools at home and overseas. As well as spiritual counsel and practical advice, material help is given when possible. Through the Children's Charity, for example, funds are available for theatrical parents facing difficulties with the costs of their children's education. *President:* Rt Revd Jack Nicholls. *Senior Chaplain:* Revd Lindsay Meader, St Paul's Church, Bedford St, Covent Garden, London, WC2E 9ED *Tel and Fax:* 020 7240 0344
email: actorschurchunion@gmail.com
Web: www.actorschurchunion.org

Additional Curates Society

Founded in 1837 to help maintain additional curates in poor and populous parishes and especially in new areas. The Society also fosters vocations to the priesthood. *General Secretary:* Revd Darren Smith. *Chairman:* Canon J. Winston. *Vice*

Chair: Rt Revd A. Robinson. *Treasurer:* Revd M. Lane, Gordon Browning House, 8 Spitfire Rd, Birmingham, B24 9PB *Tel:* 0121 382 5533
Fax: 0121 382 6999
email: info@additionalcurates.co.uk
Web: www.additionalcurates.co.uk

Affirming Catholicism
A movement within the Church of England and the Anglican Communion, formed in 1990. 'The object of the Foundation shall be the advancement of education in the doctrines and the historical development of the Church of England and the Churches of the wider Anglican Communion, as held by those professing to stand within the catholic tradition' (extracted from the Trust Deed). Its purposes are to promote theological thinking about the contemporary implications of Catholic faith and order; to further the spiritual growth and development of clergy and laity; to organize or support lectures, conferences and seminars; to publish or support books, tracts, journals and other educational material; to provide resources for local groups meeting for purposes of study and discussion. *Chair:* Revd Jonathan Clark. *Administrator:* Mark Perrett, St Mary's Parish Office, Stoke Newington Church St, London, N19 9ES *Tel:* 079 9185 1722
email: admin@affirmingcatholicism.org.uk
Web: www.affirmingcatholicism.org.uk

Age UK (Formerly Age Concern England)
Age UK cares about all older people and believes later life should be fulfilling and enjoyable. For too many this is impossible. As the leading charitable movement in the UK concerned with ageing and older people, Age UK finds effective ways to change that situation. Nationally, we take a lead role in campaigning, parliamentary work, policy analysis, research, specialist information and advice provision, publishing and training in the care of older people. Where possible we enable older people to solve problems themselves, providing as much or as little support as they need. Locally, Age UK provides community-based services such as lunch clubs, day centres and home visiting. These services are made possible through the work of many thousands of volunteers. Innovative programmes promote healthier lifestyles and provide older people with opportunities to give the experience of a lifetime back to their communities. Age UK is dependent on donations and legacies. The helpline is open seven days a week from 8 a.m. to 7 p.m. *Director General:* Mr Gordon Lishman CBE, Astral House, 1268 London Rd, London, SW16 4ER
Tel: 0800 169 6565 (Helpline)
020 8765 7200 (Reception)
email: contact@ageuk.org.uk
Web: www.ageuk.org.uk

AIM International
AIM International is an interdenominational evangelical Christian mission agency serving in over 20 countries in Africa and ministering to the African diaspora living around the world. Founded in 1895, it has nearly 1000 mission partners working together to see Christ-centred churches established amongst all Africa's peoples. With a priority for church planting, AIM International is also involved in long and short term ministries of leadership training, education and healthcare. *International Director:* Revd Lanny Arenson. *UK Director:* Revd Andrew Chard MA, AIM International, Halifax Place, Nottingham, NG1 1QN *Tel:* 0115 983 8120
email: uk@aimeurope.net
Web: www.aimint.org/eu/

Alcuin Club
Founded in 1897 to promote the study of liturgy, the Alcuin Club has a long and proud record of publishing both works of scholarship and practical manuals. Publications include collections, tracts and a new series of liturgy guides designed to accompany Common Worship. It also publishes, in conjunction with GROW, a series of Joint Liturgical Studies which has won wide acclaim. Members pay an annual subscription and receive new titles on publication. *President:* Rt Revd Michael Perham. *Chairman:* Canon Donald Gray. *Treasurer:* Mr John Collins. *Secretary:* Revd Gordon Jeanes. *Editorial Secretary:* Revd Dr Ben Gordon Taylor, 5 Saffron St, Royston, Herts, SG8 9TR *Tel:* 01763 248678
email: alcuinclub@gmail.com
Web: www.alcuinclub.org.uk

All Nations Christian College
All Nations came into existence in 1971 following the merger of three Bible colleges. Whilst interdenominational in character, around twenty per cent of its students are members of the Anglican Communion. The College exists to train students primarily for cross-cultural ministries. With up to 120 international students of about 30 nationalities, as well as a respected international team of tutors, the community studying and socializing life is vibrant and challenging. Students can follow a ten-week (en route), one-year or two-year Biblical and Intercultural studies course with a profound missiological emphasis. In addition to the popular Cert HE, Dip HE and BA (Hons) programmes, there are now validated specialist pathways in the Arts, Leadership and Development Studies. The College also offers a thirteen week online programme (en route explore) and a five day short course for groups heading out on to short term mission trips (en route express).This can be accessed as a residential or on line course. The All Nations Masters programme in Contemporary Mission Studies was the first to be taught in the UK and has attracted leaders from around the world. There

are five exit awards to choose from: MA in Contemporary Mission Studies, MA in Development with Mission, MA in Leadership with Mission, MTh in Contextual Theology with Mission, MTh in Messianic Jewish Theology and Intercultural Studies. The College has a good mix of married and single students. There are number of facilities to help such as a crêche on site, wifi access, multi-gym, sports ground and beautiful surroundings to name a few. All Nations, Easneye, Ware, SG12 8LX *Tel:* 01920 443500
Fax: 01920 462997
email: info@allnations.ac.uk
Web: www.allnations.ac.uk

All Saints Educational Trust
Home/EU applicants: personal scholarships for intending teachers in degree-level education and/or professional training, particularly teachers of religious education, home economics and other subjects; those studying dietetics, food and nutrition, and public health promotion. Postgraduate qualifications relevant to continuing professional development may be considered. Financial constraint must in all cases be demonstrated. Not assisted: school pupils, students of counselling, engineering, law, medicine, ordination, social work, commercial hospitality. Overseas applicants: scholarships for full-time, taught postgraduate study in the UK only (taught Master's programmes favoured; doctorates and PGCE programmes will not normally be funded). Corporate awards: given for imaginative new projects that will support the classroom teacher and build up the profession, preference being given to those aimed at enhancing the Church's contribution to education. Member of the Association of Church College Trusts (see separate entry). *Clerk to the Trust:* Mr S. P. Harrow, Suite 8C, First Floor, Royal London House, 22–25 Finsbury Square, London, EC2A 1DX
Tel: 020 7920 6465
email: clerk@aset.org.uk
Web: www.aset.org.uk

Almshouse Association (National Association of Almshouses)
Is concerned with the preservation and extension of over 1,750 member Almshouse Trusts. A number of major almshouses have a resident Anglican chaplain, or appoint Anglican clergy as Master or Custos of the foundation. It advises members on any matters concerning almshouses and the welfare of the elderly and aims to promote improvements in almshouses, to promote study and research into all matters affecting almshouses, and to make grants or loans to members. It also keeps under review existing and proposed legislation affecting almshouses and when necessary takes action, and encourages the provision of almshouses. *Chairman:* Mr Simon Pott. *Director:* Mr Anthony De Ritter. *Deputy Director:* Mr Julian Marczak. *Assistant Director:* Mr T. P. Wild. *Assistant Director:* Mrs S. Turner, Billingbear Lodge, Maidenhead Rd, Wokingham, RG40 5RU
Tel: 01344 452922
Fax: 01344 862062
email: naa@almshouses.org
Web: www.almshouses.org

Ancient Society of College Youths
Established 1637. An international bell-ringing society based in the City of London, the College Youths seeks to recruit leading ringers from any part of the world in which English style change-ringing is practised. Members are active in supporting ringing for church services throughout the world. The Society maintains a charitable fund for the maintenance of bells, fittings and towers of churches where it has a current or historic association. *Secretary:* Mr David E. House, 28 Waldegrave Road, Brighton, Sussex, BN1 6GE
Tel: 01273 507077 07710 085403
email: secretary@ascy.co.uk
Web: www.ascy.org.uk

Anglican and Eastern Churches Association
Founded 1864 to promote mutual understanding of, and closer relations between, the Orthodox, Oriental and Anglican Churches. Patrons: the Archbishop of Canterbury and the Patriarch of Constantinople. *Presidents:* The Lord Bishop of London and Archbishop Gregorios of Thyateira and Great Britain. *Chairman:* Revd Dr William Taylor. *General Secretary:* Ms Janet Laws, c/o The Old Deanery, Dean's Court, London, EC4V 5AA
Tel: 020 7248 6233
email: janet.laws@btopenworld.com

Anglican Association of Advisers in Pastoral Care and Counselling
To support the work of Bishops' and Diocesan Advisers in Pastoral Care and Counselling or their equivalents; to encourage the appointment of an adviser in every diocese; to promote good practice in pastoral care and counselling of those in ministry, within the structures of the Church of England. Full membership is open to Bishops' and Diocesan Advisers or their equivalents. Associate membership is open to those holding similar appointments in other denominations and those interested in furthering the work of the Association. *Chair:* Canon Ian Tomlinson, Rectory, Ragged Appleshaw, Andover, SP11 9HX
Tel: 01264 772414
Web: www.pastoralcare.org.uk

Anglican Fellowship in Scouting and Guiding
Founded in 1983 at the request of Guiders, Scouters and clergy. Its aims are to support

leaders and clergy in the religious aspect of the Promise and Law and other training programmes in Scouting and Guiding, and to maintain links with other Guide/Scout religious guilds and fellowships in order to foster ecumenical understanding. The Anglican Fellowship is a national Scout 'Active Support Unit' and is recognised in a support role by the Guide Association, the Church of England and the Church in Wales. Membership is open to Scout Groups (which do not have to be church sponsored), individuals aged 18 years or over who are members of the Scout or Guiding movement, and others (e.g. clergy) who are sympathetic to the aims of Guiding or Scouting. *Chairman:* Mrs June Davies. *Vice-Chairman:* Vacancy. *Secretary:* Miss Joan Taylor. *Treasurer:* Miss Sandra Bendall, 31 Loseley Rd, Farncombe, Godalming, GU7 3RE
Tel: 01483 428876
email: nanniejune@btinternet.com
Web: www.anglicanfellowship.org.uk

Anglican Mainstream
Anglican Mainstream is a movement of organizations, churches, dioceses and individuals within the Anglican Communion worldwide, dedicated to teaching and preserving the Scriptural truths on which the Anglican Church was founded. It seeks to nurture, support and provide a network for orthodox Anglicans throughout the Communion. It published 'Repair the Tear' as a response to the Windsor Report and 'God, gays and the Church'. Its 'Marriage, Sex and Culture' group seeks, through bi-annual conferences, to support Christian marriage as a calling. It has a website, www.anglican-mainstream.net, as an information resource for orthodox Anglicans. *Convenor:* Dr Philip Giddings. *Executive Secretary:* Canon Dr Chris Sugden, 21 High St, Eynsham, OX29 4HE *Tel:* 01865 883388
email: sugdenmainstream@googlemail.com
Web: www.anglican-mainstream.net

Anglican Marriage Encounter
Anglican Marriage Encounter is a voluntary organization which offers residential and non-residential programmes for married and engaged couples to review and deepen their relationship by developing a compelling vision for their marriage, and providing the communication skills to support this. *Lay Executive Couple:* Harry and Alison Longman, 70 Main Street, Cossington, Leicestershire, LE7 4UW *Tel:* 01509 816063
email: mail@marriageencounter.org.uk
Web: www.marriageencounter.org.uk

Anglican Pacifist Fellowship
Founded 1937. Members pledged to renounce war and all preparation to wage war and to work for the construction of Christian peace in the world. Quarterly newsletter 'The Anglican Peacemaker'. *Chairperson:* Mrs Mary Roe. *Hon Secretary:* Dr Tony Kempster, 11 Weavers End, Hanslope, Milton Keynes, MK19 7PA
Tel: 01908 510642
email: ajkempster@aol.com
Web: www.anglicanpeacemaker.org.uk

Anglican Society for the Welfare of Animals
Founded 1972, for the purpose of including the whole creation in the redemptive love of Christ and especially for prayer, study and action on behalf of animals. Registered Charity no. 1087270. Promotes Animal Welfare Sunday each October and offers a free information pack to all churches. *President:* Rt Revd Dominic Walker OGS. *Chairman:* Rt Revd Richard Llewellin. *Treasurer:* Mrs Jenny White, PO Box 7193, Hook, RG27 8GT *Tel and Fax:* 01252 843093
email: AngSocWelAnimals@aol.com
Web: www.aswa.org.uk

Anglican–Lutheran Society
Founded in 1984 to pray for the unity of the Church and especially the Anglican and Lutheran Communions; to encourage opportunities for common worship, study, friendship and witness; to encourage a wider interest in and knowledge of the Anglican and Lutheran traditions and contemporary developments within them. The Society publishes a newsletter, 'The Window', organizes conferences, lectures and other events. *Co-Presidents:* Very Revd Dr John Arnold, Rt Revd Jürgen Johannesdotter. *Co-Moderators:* Rt Revd Jana Jeruma-Grinberga, Rt Revd Dr Rupert Hoare. *Secretary:* Revd Dr Roy Long, 15 Fishpond Close, Denton, Northants, NN7 1EE *Tel:* 01604 891383 (Secretary)
email: Helen@ccwatford.u-net.com
Web: www.anglican-lutheran-society.org

Anglo-Catholic Ordination Candidates' Fund
Secretary: Revd J. F. H. Shead SSC, 57 Kenworthy Rd, Braintree, CM7 1JJ *Tel:* 01376 321783
email: j.shead@tiscali.co.uk

Archbishop's Examination in Theology
Until 2007 the Archbishop's Examination in Theology comprised the Diploma of Student in Theology (the Lambeth Diploma) and the Degree of Master of Arts (the Lambeth MA). The Lambeth Diploma was instituted in 1905 by Archbishop Randall Davidson. It provided an opportunity for women to study theology, principally so that they could teach religious education in schools and churches. It was then extended to both men and women and the means of study was either by thesis or examination. The Lambeth MA was inaugurated by Dr Runcie in 1990 in order to provide an opportunity for theological study at a more advanced level. In 2007 the Archbishop's Examination in Theology was revised and now offers the Lambeth MPhil research degree, with the opportunity to extend to a Lambeth PhD. (The Lambeth Diploma and Lambeth MA are no

longer options.) *For more information about the MPhil/PhD research degrees please contact:* Executive Assistant: Patronage and Awards, Archbishop's Examination in Theology, Lambeth Palace, London, SE1 7JU
email: ruth.ruse@lambethpalace.org.uk

Archbishops' (Canterbury, Wales and Westminster) Certificate in Church Music
See Guild of Church Musicians, page 294.

Archway
Anglican Retreat and Conference House Wardens' Association. Promotes the use of retreat and conference houses as a vital contribution to the life and development of Church and community. Is available to advise trustees/management committees and diocesan boards on issues concerning the running of retreat houses. *President:* Rt Rev Christopher Edmonson, Bishop of Bolton. *Chairperson:* Mrs Liz Palin. *Secretary:* Ms Eleanor Godber. *Treasurer:* Mr Jeff Witts, Glenfall House, Mill Lane, Charlton Kings, Cheltenham, Glos, GL54 4EP *Tel:* 01242 583654
Fax: 01242 251314
email: liz@glenfallhouse.org
Web: www.archwaywardens.org.uk

Art and Christianity Enquiry (ACE)
ACE is the leading UK organisation in the field of visual arts and religion. ACE offers stimulating educational projects and publications, advice, information and skills. The ACE awards for religious art, architecture and literature are given biennially. The quarterly journal *Art and Christianity* is available by membership; complimentary copy available on request. *Director:* Laura Moffatt. *Art in Churches Officer:* Paul Bayley, All Hallows on the Wall, 83 London Wall, London, EC2M 5ND *Tel and Fax:* 020 7374 0600
email: enquiries@acetrust.org
Web: www.acetrust.org

Art and Sacred Places (ASP)
ASP promotes interaction between religion and art, largely by siting specially commissioned contemporary art in sacred places. It engages new audiences by exploring the relationship between art and spirituality, encouraging debate and understanding. ASP's work is based on the conviction that art and religion share fundamental concerns and explore similar territory, albeit in significantly different ways. ASP's portfolio of projects includes inspirational permanent commissions, innovative temporary commissions and mutually beneficial interfaith projects. ASP was founded under the auspices of Bishop John Gladwin in 1999 and became a charity in 2001. Charity Registration no. 108739. Enquiries welcome. *Project Director:* Angela Peagram, Bakerswell, Meonstoke, Southampton, SO32 3NA
Tel: 01489 878725
Fax: 01489 878737
email: angela@artandsacredplaces.org
Web: www.artandsacredplaces.wordpress.com (blog); www.artandsacredplaces.org

Arthur Rank Centre
The Arthur Rank Centre, established in 1972, is an independent charity supported by the national churches, the Royal Agricultural Society of England and the Rank Foundation. It is an ecumenical body and is recognized as the rural focus and resource centre for the churches in England. The ARC offers training for clergy recently appointed to rural areas and on multi-parish benefices. Members of staff are peripatetic and are available for consultations and conferences at local, diocesan and national levels. The Diocesan Rural Officers meet annually with the Church of England National Rural Officer, who is a member of staff at the ARC and who offers ongoing advice, information and support. The ARC publishes the magazine 'Country Way – life and faith in rural Britain' and a wide range of other resources and publications, including information on rural ministry and mission, worship, evangelism, community engagement and examples of good practice. *Director:* Vacancy. *National Rural Officer, Mission and Public Affairs Division, Archbishops' Counci:* Canon Dr Jill Hopkinson, Arthur Rank Centre, Stoneleigh Park, Warwickshire, CV8 2LG *Tel:* 024 7685 3060
Fax: 024 7641 4808
email: info@arthurrankcentre.org.uk
Web: www.arthurrankcentre.org.uk

Association for Promoting Retreats (APR)
The APR celebrates its centenary year in 2013, having been founded in 1913 to foster the growth of the spiritual life in the Anglican Communion by the practice of retreats. Welcomes as members all Christians in sympathy with this aim. Membership by subscription for individuals, parishes and retreat houses. The APR is one of the retreat groups which form the Retreat Association (see separate entry). *Administrator and Secretary to the Executive Committee:* Mrs Julia Reading, PO Box 10248, Newark, NG24 9LQ *Tel:* 01636 555085
email: promoting.retreats@gmail.com
Web: www.promotingretreats.org

Association of Black Clergy
Founded 1982 to bring together the minority ethnic clergy and lay ministers of the Christian Church in the United Kingdom, to provide support for all minority ethnic clergy and lay ministers, to encourage good practice and challenge racism individually, institutionally and structurally in particular in the Christian Church in the United Kingdom and to promote theological education and training that is relevant to minor-

ity ethnic Christian leadership. *Chairman:* Revd Jennifer Thomas. *Vice-Chair:* Revd Karowei Dorgu. *Facilitators (South):* Revd Yvonne Clarke, Revd Charles Lawrence. *Facilitator (North):* Very Revd Rogers Govender. *Secretary:* Revd Smitha Prasadam, Sherwood Park Vicarage, Sherwood Park Rd, Mitcham, CR4 1NJ *Tel:* 020 8764 1258
Fax: 020 8764 8369
email: theascension@freeuk.com

Association of Christian Teachers
ACT is a non-denominational Christian membership organization which provides professional and spiritual support to Christians engaged in pre-school, primary, middle, secondary, special, college and university education in England. ACT encourages Christians to apply their faith to their work and provides opportunities for them to share together in prayer and fellowship. ACT strives to influence policy makers, politicians, the media and the Church by speaking from a professionally well-informed standpoint with a loving, Christian voice on behalf of Christians working in education. *Director (Strategy):* Mr Clive Ireson. *Office Manager:* Mrs Carol Horne, Suite 7 Rowan House, 23 Billing Road, Northampton, NN1 5AT *Tel:* 01604 632046
email: act@christians-in-education.org.uk
Web: www.christians-in-education.org.uk

Association of Christian Writers
A group of Christians who wish to serve God in the field of writing. Some members are professional writers, others part-time and many are beginners in different areas of writing. Three writers' days a year are held and many local groups meet regularly. Members receive a quarterly magazine, and a manuscript criticism service is available. Applicants are asked to sign a declaration of faith. *Chairman:* Lin Ball. *Vice-Chairs:* Jan Greenough, Jan Clampett. *Treasurer:* Rosamund Rowe. *Company Secretary/Administrator:* Jenn Bratt, Po Box 551, Hounslow, TW3 3DQ
Tel: 020 8572 8349
email: admin@christianwriters.org.uk
Web: www.christianwriters.org.uk

Association of Church College Trusts
In 1979 the Association of Church College Trusts was established as a loosely knit organization to facilitate an exchange of information and cooperation. It meets every six months. The Church College Trusts were formed following the closure of their respective Colleges of Education. They are autonomous, answerable only to the Charity Commission; their financial management policies are such that they are required both to sponsor present work from their income and also to ensure that their capital is maintained at a level that can finance similar levels of work in the future. In the last 30 years they have been involved in helping individual teachers, students and others, sponsoring corporate projects in part or in total, and aiding school, college and church educational activities. The individual Trusts are: All Saints Educational Trust, Culham Educational Foundation, Foundation of St Matthias, Hockerill Educational Foundation, Keswick Hall Charity, St Christopher's College Trust, Culham St Gabriel's Trust, St Hild and St Bede Trust, St Luke's College Foundation, St Mary's College Trust, St Peter's Saltley Trust, Sarum St Michael Educational Charity (see separate entries). Please note that applications have to be made to the individual Trusts concerned and not centrally through the Association. *Secretary:* Revd Dr John Gay, Culham Institute, 15 Norham Gardens, Oxford, OX2 6PY *Tel:* 01865 284885
Fax: 01865 284886
email: enquiries@culham.ac.uk
Web: www.culham.ac.uk

Association of Church Fellowships
Founded 1963. Sponsored by clergy and laity to meet a growing need in this country and overseas to encourage and enable the laity to take their full part in the life and work of the Church in open groups and in cooperation with existing groups. *National Chairman:* Revd Andrew Bullock, 34 Dudley Park Rd, Acocks Green, Birmingham, B27 6QR *Tel:* 0121 706 9764
email: andrewbullock2@blueyonder.co.uk

Association of Diocesan Registry Clerks
The Association was established in 1999 to support and assist clerks and assistant staff in the furtherance of their professional roles in the diocesan and provincial registries and the Faculty Office of the Church of England by encouraging and sharing knowledge of ecclesiastical law, practice and procedures, imparting and exchanging information, and promoting discussion relevant to their roles. A day conference is organized for members, alternating biannually with a two-day residential conference; a lively group email correspondence provides an invaluable resource and a semi-regular newsletter keeps members informed. *President:* The Right Worshipful Charles George QC, Dean of the Arches and Auditor. *Chair:* Mrs Elisabeth Crouch. *Communications Officer:* Gini Stuart, Chattertons 2 Lower Moor Road, off Doddington Road, Lincoln, LN6 3JY *Tel:* 01522 814600
DX: 700679 NORTH HYKEHAM
Fax: 01522 813601
email: gini.stuart@chattertons.com

Association of English Cathedrals
Established in 1990 and authorized by the Administrative Chapters of the Anglican Cathedrals as their representative organization, the AEC deals with governmental agencies, the General Synod and its constituent bodies and the Churches' Legislation Advisory Service on behalf of the English cathedrals, provided only that it cannot commit any individual cathedral chapter

ORGANIZATIONS

to a specific decision. Membership consists of one representative of each Administrative Chapter. *Chairman:* Very Revd Vivienne Faull. *Coordinator:* Mrs Sarah King, PO Box 53506, London, SE19 1ZL *Tel:* 020 8761 5130
email: sarah.king@englishcathedrals.co.uk
Web: www.englishcathedrals.co.uk

Association of Hospice and Palliative Care Chaplains (AHPCC)
The AHPCC exists to promote good standards among Chaplains involved in the pastoral and spiritual care of people (including carers) facing death from a life threatening illness. Hospice and Palliative Care Chaplains seek to: meet spiritual and religious needs in hospice and palliative care units as a part of a multidisciplinary team that meets regularly; be proactive in assessing and addressing the complex spiritual and religious needs of patients and their families/carers that are an integral part of hospice and palliative care; discern, respect and meet the cultural, spiritual and religious needs, traditions and practices of all patients and their families/carers, including those of no faith; ensure that all spiritual and religious care is patient led and focused on the needs of the individual and their family/carers. The aims of the AHPCC are: to identify and promote good practice; to be an agent of professional development; to provide professional support and fellowship; to promote links with the constituency of palliative care; to promote links with relevant church bodies and faith communities. AHPCC offers training and support for clergy and lay people involved (whether on a full-time or part-time basis) by means of advice about appointments, induction, and training courses, keeps members up to date with current information by means of its website, and organises a three day conference/training event in May each year. St Christopher's Hospice, Sydenham, provides courses for chaplains newly appointed, and many hospices offer placements and courses which form part of pre- and post-ordination training. The AHPCC monitors professional developments within the constituency of palliative care, works to his own professional standards, and offers members support through regional groups. It works closely with the College of Health Care Chaplains, the Scottish Association of Chaplains in Healthcare, and the Chaplaincy Academic Accreditation Board to further the professionalism of healthcare chaplaincy throughout the UK. Membership fee is £30, and, in the first instance, prospective members should make contact with the membership secretary. The AHPCC is supported by 'Help the Hospices', and our link is Anne Garley at Help the Hospices, 33–44 Britannia St, London WC1X 9JG. *President:* Revd Judy Davies. *Hon Secretary:* Revd Karen Murphy. *Treasurer:* Revd Judie Horrocks. *Webmaster and Newsletter Editor:* Ms Dawn Tierney, Sue Ryder – Duchess of Kent House, 22 Libenrood Road, Reading, RG30 2DX
email: president@ahpcc.org.uk
Web: www.ahpcc.org.uk

Association of Ordinands and Candidates for Ministry
Founded in 1968, AOCM represents ordinands from the Church of England, Church in Wales, Episcopal Church of Scotland and Church of Ireland as well as trainee Church Army evangelists. AOCM holds regional and national conferences during the year, to which every theological college, course and OLM scheme may send a representative. These conferences allow ordinands to share fellowship, and also for information and questions to pass between AOCM and the Ministry Division. AOCM publishes an annual handbook, *Together in Training*, which is provided free of charge to all ordinands, bishops and DDOs. *Chairman:* Alan Maxwell. *Treasurer:* Ian Robinson. *Secretary:* John Allister
email: secretary@aocm.org.uk
Web: www.aocm.org.uk

Awareness Foundation
The Awareness Foundation is an international ecumenical institution committed to fostering community harmony through education. The Foundation's teaching programme, the Awareness Course, is designed and written by Bishop Michael Marshall and Revd Nadim Nassar to educate Christians for life in the twenty-first century. Each course module is written from a Christian viewpoint, teaching Christians about their own faith and that of their neighbours, so that they can respect the differences and live in a diverse society without fear and without compromising their faith. The Course considers Islamic and Jewish perspectives to build an awareness of 'the other' and to go deeper into the Christian faith. It is designed to be taught in churches, parish halls or any appropriate space, and is suitable for regular or occasional churchgoers, Christians outside the Church, seekers and the undecided. New courses are published each year. *President:* Rt Revd Michael Marshall. *Director:* Revd Nadim Nassar. *Chair of Trustees:* Charles Longbottom. *Chief Executive Officer:* Helen Carey. *Education Director:* St. John Wright, Holy Trinity Church, Sloane St, London, SW1X 9BZ *Tel:* 020 7730 8830 (Office) 020 7259 0619 (Education) *Fax:* 020 7730 9287
email: tfcc@tfccinternational.com
Web: www.tfccinternational.com

Baptismal Integrity (BI)
BI has four aims: to bring to an end the indiscriminate administration of infant baptism; to demonstrate that baptism is the sacrament instituted by Christ for those becoming members of the visible church; to seek the reform of the Canons and rules of the Church of England in

line with the above stated aims; to promote within the Church of England debate and review of the biblical, theological, pastoral and evangelistic aspects of Christian initiation. BI affirms the propriety of baptising the infants of practising Christian believers and also of deferring baptism until later years. It also affirms the relevance and value of the Service of Thanksgiving for the Gift of a Child. BI publishes its magazine 'Update' at intervals. Membership is £10 per annum (or concession) – more information via website or Chairman. *President:* Rt Revd Colin Buchanan. *Acting Chairman:* Revd Stephen Corbett. *Vice-Chairman:* Mr Roger Godin. *Secretary:* Revd John Hartley. *Treasurer:* Ms Sallie Bassham, The Stables, Capland Lane, Hatch Beauchamp, Taunton, LA6 3AT *Tel:* 01823 480606
email: roger.godin@baptism.org.uk
Web: www.baptism.org.uk

Barnardo's
Founded in 1866, Barnardo's is the UK's largest children's charity, whose inspiration and values derive from the Christian faith. It runs more than 400 projects nationwide and each year helps more than 100,000 children, young people and their families to overcome severe disadvantage. Barnardo's believes in children and works with them over the long term to tackle the effects of disadvantage and to ensure they can fulfil their potential. Children are helped to address problems such as abuse, homelessness and poverty and to tackle the challenges of disability. Barnardo's also campaigns for better care for children and their families in the community and champions the rights of every child. The charity no longer runs orphanages and now concentrates on working with children and their families in the community. *Chair of Council:* Geoffrey Barnett. *Chief Executive:* Ann Marie Carrie, Barnardo's, Tanners Lane, Barkingside, Ilford, IG6 1QG
Tel: 020 8550 8822
Fax: 020 8551 6870
email: dorothy.howes@barnardos.org.uk
Web: www.barnardos.org.uk

Beauchamp Community
Homes for retired people, clerical or lay, either sex. Unfurnished, single and double flats available from time to time. Applicants should be aged 60 – 74. Daily Eucharist. Apply to the Chaplain. Newland, Malvern, WR13 5AX
Tel: 01684 562100
email: grevile@aol.com

Bible Reading Fellowship
At the heart of BRF's ministry is the desire to help people of all ages – children, adults and families – to explore Christianity and to grow in faith. We're passionate about helping people to engage with the Bible and prayer, and about resourcing Christian discipleship. These aims are fulfilled through the following ministries and resources: Barnabas in Churches – Visit www.barnabasinchurches.org.uk. Includes free resources to use with under 11s and much more. Barnabas in Schools – Visit www.barnabasinschools.org.uk. Working with primary schools to help children and their teachers explore Christianity creatively. Bible Reading Notes – Visit www. biblereadingnotes. org.uk. Four different series to choose from. Bible Reading Notes Resource Pack – Visit www.biblereadingnotes.org.uk. Discover all you need to know about promoting daily reading notes in church.BRF publishing – Visit www.brfonline.org.uk. Church resources, prayer and spirituality, group study books and more. Church accounts – Receive discount off BRF's books to help you encourage reading in your church. Contact Rebecca Fillis on 01865 319714 to find out more. Faith in Homes – Visit www.faithinhomes.org.uk. Helping churches to support families to develop faith in the home. Free ideas, resources and more. Electronic books – Visit www.brfonline.org/ebooks. New BRF titles available for the Kindle. Foundations21 – Visit www.foundations21.net. BRF's free online discipleship resource for groups and individuals. Messy Church – Visit www.messychurch.org.uk. BRF's dynamic fresh expression of church based around welcome, crafts and art celebration, and eating together. Active in 14 countries. Who Let The Dads Out – *Visit www.wholetthedadsout.org. A way of reaching dads and their young children in your community. BRF is a registered charirty (no. 233280). Chair of Trustees:* Rt Revd Colin Fletcher, Bishop of Dorchester. *Chief Executive:* Mr Richard Fisher. *Deputy Chief Executive:* Mrs Karen Laister, 15 The Chambers, Vineyard, Abingdon, Oxfordshire OX14 3FE *Tel:* 01865 319700
Fax: 01865 319701
email: enquiries@brf.org.uk
Web: www.brf.org.uk

Bible Society
Bible Society is working towards a day when the Bible's life-changing message is shaping lives and communities everywhere. We aim to show how the Bible connects with life. We make Scriptures available where there are none. And we work with the Church to help it live out the Bible's message in its daily life and witness. *Chief Executive:* James Catford. *Deputy Chief Executive:* Philip Poole. *Director of Programme:* Ann Holt. *Executive Director of Services:* Lesley Whelan, Stonehill Green, Westlea, Swindon, SN5 7DG
Tel: 01793 418100
Fax: 01793 418118
email: contactus@biblesociety.org.uk
Web: www.biblesociety.org.uk

Bloxham Project
Founded in 1967, charged with developing an understanding of Christian faith and values in

ORGANIZATIONS

education. Offering a spiritual, inspirational and practical resource for schools and educators, helping to develop spirituality, pastoral care, Christian leadership and ethos and values. Providing a forum for debate and the exchange of best practice. Offers consultancy services and tailor-made training, day events, regional meetings, a termly publication and some other materials. A network of schools across denominations and sectors. A resource for headteachers, leadership teams, chaplains, teaching and pastoral staff. *Chair of Trustees:* Dr Priscilla Chadwick. *Director:* Revd Gordon Parry, Ripon College, Cuddesdon, Oxford, OX44 9EX
Tel: 01865 877417
email: admin@bloxhamproject.org.uk
Web: www.bloxhamproject.org.uk

Book Aid Charitable Trust
Founded in 1988, Book Aid Charitable Trust supplies over one million handpicked new and used Christian books and Bibles to some of the poorest areas of the world each year. All these books and Bibles are donated by Christians in the UK from every denomination and background. The books are distributed mainly to Africa, Asia and the Caribbean, with smaller shipments sent to many other places. Book Aid is manned by volunteer workers and is funded by donations. Registered Charity no. 1039484. *Coordinator:* Ama Bamfo, Bromley House, Kangley Bridge Rd Lower Sydenham, London, SE26 5AQ
Tel: 020 8778 2145
Fax: 020 8778 2265
email: office@book-aid.org
Web: www.book-aid.org

Boys' Brigade
Founded 1883 for the advancement of Christ's kingdom among boys and the promotion of habits of obedience, reverence, discipline, self-respect and all that tends towards a true Christian manliness. *Brigade Secretary:* Steve Dickinson, Felden Lodge, Felden Lane, Hemel Hempstead, HP3 0BL *Tel:* 01442 231681
Fax: 01442 235391
email: enquiries@boys-brigade.org.uk
Web: www.boys-brigade.org.uk

Bridge Pastoral Foundation (formerly the Clinical Theology Association)
Founded in 1962. The core activity of the Association is seminars in pastoral care and pastoral counselling, which are directed by authorized tutors and widely available in the UK. Seminars are designed to promote self-awareness, which is needed for effective pastoral work, and to teach the theory and practice of pastoral counselling with reference to the assumptions, values and meanings of the Christian faith. Further information about Bridge Pastoral Foundation education and training may be obtained from the Administrator. *Administrator:* Angela Ryan, 8 Kingsmead Rd North, Prenton, Birkenhead, CH43 6TB
Tel: 0151 652 0429
email: admin@bridgepastoral.org.uk
Web: www.bridgepastoral.org.uk

Bristol Clerical Education Society
Grants of up to £250 to ordinands and, occasionally, to clergy undertaking CME, for specific and practical needs. *Secretary:* Mrs S. J. Clover, The Croft, Cox's Hill, Ashton Keynes Wiltshire, SN6 6NY *Tel:* 01285 861199
email: sueclover.clover@googlemail.com

British Deaf Association
The British Deaf Association (BDA) is the largest national organization run by Deaf people with Deaf people. We represent the UK's Deaf community and campaign for the official recognition of British Sign Language (BSL). Our vision is 'Deaf people fully participating and contributing as equal and valued citizens in the wider society'. Our Mission is to ensure a world in which the language, culture, community, diversity and heritage of Deaf people in the UK is respected and fully protected, ensuring that Deaf people can participate and contribute as equal and valued citizens in the wider society. This will be achieved through:Improving the quality of life by empowering Deaf individuals and groups Enhancing freedom, equality and diversity Protecting and promoting BSL. *Patron:* HRH The Duke of York. *Chair:* Terry Riley. *Chief Exec:* David Buxyon, BDA Head Office, 18 Leather Lane, London, EC1N 7SU *Tel:* 020 7405 0090
email: admin@bda.org.uk
Web: www.bda.org.uk

British Isles and Eire Airport Chaplains' Network
The British Isles and Eire Airport Chaplains' Network meets twice a year for a day or two-day conference and is working towards seeing airport chaplaincy established at every international or regional airport in the UK and Ireland. In 2005 there were chaplaincies at 35 airports, with others being negotiated. Of these, full-time chaplains or chaplaincy teams are at: Heathrow, Gatwick, Manchester, Luton and East Midlands. All airport chaplains are on call and are pleased to be able to assist those travelling through airports in any way. They can be contacted via the airport information desk. Some airport chaplaincies have web pages on their particular airport web sites; for a list of sites visit the address given below. (See also International Association of Civil Aviation Chaplains.) *Coordinator:* Revd Roy Monks. *General Secretary:* Vacancy, East Midlands Airport Chaplaincy Team, Chaplains' Office, East Midlands Airport, Castle Donington, Derby, DE74 2SA *Tel:* 01332 818407 ext 6407
email: roy.monks@talk21.com
Web: www.aoa.org.uk/ourmem/index.asp

Broken Rites
Formed in 1983, Broken Rites is an interdenominational and independent association for the divorced and separated spouses of Anglican clergy, ministers and Church Army officers living in the United Kingdom, the Republic of Ireland and the geographical area covered by the Diocese in Europe. It welcomes the support of everyone who is in sympathy with its aims: to support one another with compassion, understanding and practical help where possible; to continue to draw the attention of the Churches to the problems of former clergy spouses; and, while affirming the Christian ideal of lifelong marriage, to promote a more vivid awareness among Christian people of the increasing incidence of clergy marriage breakdown and the implications for the witness of the Church and its teaching on marriage. *Hon Secretary:* Sue Atack, 13 Manse Avenue, Wrightington, Wigan, WN6 9RP
Tel: 01257 423893/07967 058114
email: secretary@brokenrites.org
Web: www.brokenrites.org

Bromley and Sheppard's Colleges
Bromley College was founded in 1666 to provide houses for clergy widows and Sheppard's College in 1840 to provide houses for unmarried daughters of clergy widows who had lived with their mothers at Bromley College. Houses in both colleges have been converted into flats and widows/widowers of clergy, retired clergymen and their spouses, divorced and separated spouses of clergy or retired clergy of the Church of England, the Church in Wales, the Scottish Episcopal Church or the Church of Ireland may now be admitted. Contact the Chaplain/Clerk to the Trustees. *Clerk and Chaplain:* Revd Andrew Sangster, Chaplain's Office, Bromley & Sheppard's Colleges, London Rd, Bromley, BR1 1PE
Tel: 020 8460 4712 (Chaplain)
020 8464 3558 (Office)
Fax: 020 8464 3558 *email:* bromcoll@aol.com
Web: www/bromleycollege.org

Burrswood
Burrswood is a Christian hospital and place of healing founded in 1948 by Dorothy Kerin, who received a commission from God to 'heal the sick, comfort the sorrowing and give faith to the faithless'. The Dorothy Kerin Trust is a registered charity, administered by a board of trustees and has a non-surgical hospital with 40 beds for short-term inpatient care supported by an interdisciplinary team of resident doctors, nurses, physiotherapists and counsellors; a church with resident chaplains, which is fully integrated within the hospital and has healing services open to the public twice a week; a guest/retreat house with single and twin rooms, sleeping 9; a physio- and hydrotherapy complex for inpatients and outpatients and a medical and counselling outpatient facility. Additional public facilities include a Christian bookshop and tea room onsite and a charity shop in nearby Crowborough. Profits from these trading operations go into Burrswood's 'Access to Care' bursary fund which assists financially disadvantaged patients to receive care. *Chief Executive Officer:* Dr Gareth Tuckwell . *Senior Chaplain:* Revd Christine Garrard. *Senior Physician:* Dr Paul Worthley, Groombridge, Tunbridge Wells, TN3 9PY
Tel: 01892 863637 (Enquiries)
01892 863818 (Admissions)
Fax: 01892 863623; 01892 862597 (Admissions)
email: enquiries@burrswood.org.uk
Web: www.burrswood.org.uk

Came's Charity for Clergymen's Widows
Founded to provide small annual grants to benefit clergy widows who are wanting. Apply to the Clerk. Worshipful Company of Cordwainers, Dunster Court Mincing Lane, London, EC3R 7AH *Tel:* 020 7929 1121
Fax: 020 7929 1124
email: office@cordwainers.org

Campaigner Ministries
Founded 1922, Campaigner Ministries is a national youth movement working in partnership with local churches. Campaigner Ministries trains and resources local leaders, enabling them to operate an exciting and relevant relational and holistic programme of evangelism and Christian discipleship for boys and girls between 4 and 18. It is recognized by UK government education departments and is a member of the Evangelical Alliance. *Executive Director:* Mr John Radcliffe. *Resources Director:* Mr Tony Etherington, 6 Eaton Court Rd Colmworth Business Park, Eaton Socon, St Neots, PE19 8ER *Tel:* 01480 215622
Fax: 01480 405550
email: info@campaigners.org.uk
Web: www.campaigners.org.uk

Canterbury and York Society
Founded 1904 for the printing of bishops' registers and other ecclesiastical records. *Joint Presidents:* The Archbishops of Canterbury and York. *Chairman:* Dr P. Zutshi. *Secretary:* Dr C. Fonge. *Treasurer:* Dr R. Hayes. *Editor:* Dr P. Hoskin, c/o Borthwick Institute, University of York Heslington, York, YO10 5DD
email: charles.fonge@york.ac.uk
Web: http://www.canterburyandyork.org

CARE (Christian Action Research and Education)
CARE is a registered charity seeking to combine practical caring initiatives, at national and community level, with public policy on social and ethical issues. CARE campaigns, provides resouces, undertakes caring work and helps to bring Christian insight and experience to matters of public policy, education and practical caring

ORGANIZATIONS

initiatives, particularly on the behalf of the needy. *Chairman:* Revd Lyndon Bowring. *Chief Executive:* Mrs Nola Leach. *Director of Parliamentary Affairs:* Dr Dan Boucher. *Operations Manager:* Mrs Bobbie Fasham, 53 Romney St, London, SW1P 3RF *Tel:* 020 7233 0455
08453 100 244 (supporter helpline)
Fax: 020 7233 0983
email: mail@care.org.uk
Web: www.care.org.uk

Catch 22 (formerly Rainer)
A national voluntary organization, founded in 1788, working primarily with young people at risk, through over 60 community-based projects, some in partnership with local authorities and other voluntary organizations. Particular services include leaving care projects and bail support schemes, accommodation and support to young people on release from young offender institutions or who are homeless, youth training and employment schemes. *Chief Exec:* Mrs Joyce Moseley, Churchill House, 142–146 Old Street, London, EC1V 9BW *Tel:* 020 7336 4800
Fax: 020 7336 4801
email: information@catch-22.org.uk
Web: www.catch-22.org.uk

Cathedral and Church Shops Association
The Association provides a forum for the exchange of information, and arranges an annual conference and trade fair for its members. We sponsor meetings of shop staff in several areas of the country each spring, giving advice and assistance for the setting up and running of church shops from experienced shop managers. Membership is open to any cathedral/church-/abbey/religious house which is under sole control, or operated by a trading company for the sole benefit, of its chapter, parochial church council or religious house. *Chairman:* Hugh Fearnall JP. *Hon Secretary:* Ann Waller, Stable Cottage, Aydon, Corbridge Northumberland, NE45 5PL
Tel: 07779 346150
email: hugh_fernall@yahoo.com

Cathedral Libraries and Archives Association
The CLAA supports the work of the cathedral and capitular libraries and archives in the Anglican churches of the United Kingdom and Ireland. It seeks to advance education by the promotion, preservation and protection of those collections and provides a forum for cooperation and the exchange of information among those who care for them. *Chairman:* Very Revd Peter Atkinson. *Hon Secretary:* Mrs Gudrun Warren. *Hon Treasurer:* Mr Jo Wisdom, c/o Norwich Cathedral Library, 12 The Close, Norwich, NR1 4DH
Tel: 01603 218327
Fax: 01603 766032
email: library@cathedral.org.uk
Web: http://www.cofe.anglican.org/about/librariesandarchives/ cathanddioceseslibs/

Cathedrals Administration and Finance Association (CAFA)
In 1975 cathedral administrators and treasurers began, as a body, to exchange information on all matters touching on best practice and the most effective administration of the English Anglican cathedrals. The association now enjoys a valued link with the Association of English Cathedrals for which organization it undertakes research as needed. There is an annual conference and regular regional meetings. *Chairman:* John Morris. *Admin Secretary:* Miss Casey Chick. *Treasurer:* Mrs Caroline Robinson, Church House, Great Smith St, London, SW1P 3NZ *Tel:* 020 7898 1058
email: casey.chick@churchofengland.org

Cathedrals Plus
Founded in 1981, Cathedrals Plus, formerly known as the Pilgrims' Association, provides a forum in which those responsible for the care and welcome of pilgrims, visitors and tourists to our cathedrals, abbeys, churches, shrines and chapels can meet and exchange ideas and experiences. It is now also increasingly involved in bringing together those in cathedrals and churches who deliver education outside the classroom both to schools and adults. Originally a Trust, it is now a fully democratic institution governed by a Council of 15 members elected at the annual general meeting. Membership is both ecumenical and international, consisting of the great majority of Church of England cathedrals, three Roman Catholic cathedrals and several of the most visited parish churches, abbeys, priories and chapels from Anglican, Roman Catholic and Free Church denominations in England, Wales, the Republic of Ireland and Belgium. It operates mainly through an annual conference and periodic newsletters and through its web site. It is consulted regularly by government and VisitBritain on tourism and educational matters relating to cathedrals and churches. *Chairman:* Very Revd Charles Taylor, Dean of Peterborough. *Secretary:* Mrs Judy Davies. *Hon Treasurer:* Barry Palmer, 1 St John's Rd, Queen's Park, Chester, CH4 7AL
Tel: 01244 677991/07767 675540 (Mobile)
Fax: 01244 677991
email: secretary@cathedralsplus.org.uk
Web: www.cathedralsplus.org.uk

Catholic Group in General Synod
The Catholic Group consists of those on General Synod committed to the catholic, traditional and orthodox voice in the Church of England. It seeks to make a positive contribution to all debates and especially where Catholic faith and order are involved. It welcomes both the ARCIC discussions and dialogue with the Orthodox churches. The group maintains that ethical teaching which scripture and tradition have consistently upheld. *Chairman:* Canon Simon Killwick. *Secretary:* Mrs

Mary Nagel, Aldwick Vicarage, 25 Gossamer Lane, Bognor Regis, PO21 3AT
Tel: 01243 262049
email: nagel@aldwick.demon.co.uk

Cautley House
A Christian centre for healing and wholeness, established in 1994. An Anglican foundation which seeks to be a resource for the whole Church. Individuals or groups (up to 24) are welcome to visit for up to two weeks. Daily services are held in the chapel and staff are available for confidential listening and prayer ministry. Non-residents are invited to attend the healing services which are held twice a week. *Director:* Revd Pat Vowles, 95 Seabrook Rd, Hythe, CT21 5QY
Tel: 01303 230762
Fax: 01303 237447
email: susan.evans@cautleyhouse.org.uk
2nd email: admin@cautleyhouse.org.uk
Web: www.cautleyhouse.org.uk

Central Council of Church Bell Ringers
Founded 1891. Its aims are to promote the ringing of church bells, to represent the ringing exercise to the world at large and to provide expert information and advice to ringers, church authorities and the general public on all matters relating to bells and bell-ringing. *President:* Mrs Kate Flavell. *Hon Secretary:* Mrs Mary Bone, 11 Bullfields, Sawbridgeworth, CM21 9DB *Tel:* 01297 726159
email: secretary@cccbr.org.uk
Web: www.cccbr.org.uk

Centre for the Study of Christianity and Sexuality
Launched in 1996, CSCS aims to provide a safe platform to promote objective debate within the Christian Churches on matters concerning human sexuality, with a view to developing the spiritual teaching and doctrines of such Christian Churches. CSCS is associated with the international journal *Theology and Sexuality* and publishes the quarterly *CSCS News*. It also organizes a conference each year. Patrons and Matron: Rt Revd John Gladwin (Bishop of Chelmsford), Revd David Gamble (Co-ordinating Secretary, Legal and Constitutional Practice, Methodist Church), Revd Roberta Rominger (Moderator, N Thames Synod of the URC). *Chair:* Canon Jane Fraser. *Secretary:* Vacancy. *Treasurer:* Mrs Daphne Cook. *Newsletter Editor:* Mr Anthony Woollard, The Campanile, Church Lane, Stoulton, Worcester WR7 4RE *Tel:* 01905 840266/01789 762553/
Fax: 01789 400040
email: cscs@revjane.demon.co.uk
Web: www.cscs.co.uk

Changing Attitude
Working for lesbian, gay, bisexual and transgender affirmation within the Anglican Communion, Changing Attitude is a network of lesbian, gay, bisexual, transgendered and heterosexual members of the Anglican churches of the UK, founded in 1995. Local groups meet regularly in 24 dioceses to offer encouragement and support and provide educational and training resources. We have a network of contacts in over 33 dioceses and supporters in every English diocese. We work alongside Integrity USA and Changing Attitude organizations in Nigeria, Australia, New Zealand, Ireland and Scotland. *Director:* Revd Colin Coward. *Hon Administrator:* Brenda Harrison, 6 Norney Bridge, Mill Rd, Marston, SN10 5SF *Tel:* 01380 724908/07770 844302/
email: info@changingattitude.org
Web: www.changingattitude.org.uk

Children's Society, The
The Children's Society wants to create a society where children can be children. We reach out to young people of all faiths and none, and are committed to helping vulnerable and disadvantaged young people, including children in care and young runaways. We give a voice to disabled children, help young refugees to rebuild their lives and provide relief for young carers. Through our campaigns and research, we seek to influence policy and perceptions, so that young people have a better chance in life. We are inspired by Christian values and work in close partnership with the churches. All we do is driven by the deep conviction that every child deserves to be valued, respected and happy. *Chair of Trustees:* Rt Revd Tim Thornton, Bishop of Truro. *Chief Executive Officer:* Revd Matthew Reed, Edward Rudolf House, 69–85 Margery St, London, WC1X 0JL
Tel: 020 7841 4400 (Switchboard)
0845 300 1128 (Supporter Action Line)
email: supportercare@childrenssociety.org.uk
Web: www.childrenssociety.org.uk

Choir Benevolent Fund
Founded 1851. A registered Friendly Society for subscribing cathedral and collegiate lay clerks and organists. *Trustees:* The Deans of St Paul's, Westminster and Windsor. *Secretary:* Mr Roland Tatnell, Foxearth Cottage, Frittenden, Cranbrook, TN17 2AU *Tel:* 01580 712825

Choir Schools Association
Founded 1919 to promote the welfare of cathedral, collegiate and parish church choir schools. In 1985 it set up a bursary trust to help children from low income families become choristers. *Chairman:* Mr Roger Overend. *Administrator:* Mrs Susan Rees, Wolvesey, College St, Winchester, SO23 9ND *Tel:* 01962 890530
Fax: 01962 869978
email: info@choirschools.org.uk
Web: www.choirschools.org.uk

CHRISM
(CHRistians In Secular Ministry)
Formed in 1984, CHRISM is the national association for all Christians who see their secular

employment as their primary Christian ministry and for those who support that vision. CHRISM welcomes members, both lay and ordained, from all Christian denominations, encourages them to be active within their own faith communities and to champion ministry in and through secular employment. A journal is published quarterly, as well as occasional papers. We hold an open annual conference and also a members' reflective weekend. *Presiding Moderator:* Lyn Page, Willow Bank, Hawkley, Nr Liss, Hants, GU33 6NF
Tel: 01730 827334
email: lynpage@btconnect.com
Web: www.chrism.org.uk

Christian Aid
Christian Aid is an agency of the British and Irish churches and as such is one of the largest church-related international relief and development agencies in Europe. It works largely in the developing world providing support wherever the need is greatest, irrespective of race or religion. A substantial amount of its voluntary income is received through the annual Christian Aid Week collections led by churchgoers. It funds projects in more than 50 countries, standing by poor communities whether they are digging wells or fighting the consequences of debt, unfair trade or climate change, learning to read or articulating human rights abuses, healing the wounds of war or tackling the spread of preventable illnesses. Money spent overseas is passed to local partner organizations as Christian Aid believes that poor communities are best placed to devise and run their own projects and solve their own problems. Channelling money in this way is seen as an effective and respectful way of giving poor people the means to help themselves. Prevention of the causes of poverty is better than cure, but Christian Aid remains active in emergencies, sending immediate help and capacity to cope with emergencies and disaster mitigation including food, shelter, medicine and transport when flood, famine, earthquake or war strike. The agency's charitable work includes campaigning and education work in the UK and Ireland, which accounts for up to eleven per cent of its income. This is because Christian Aid believes it must also tackle the structures and systems that keep people poor. It puts great emphasis on the involvement of individuals to address the root causes of poverty and encourage action by politicians and international institutions that will lead to their removal. *Director:* Loretta Minghella OBE. *Chair of the Board:* Dame Anne Owers, Inter-Church House, 35–41 Lower Marsh, London, SE1 7RL
Tel: 020 7620 4444
Fax: 020 7620 0719
email: info@christian-aid.org.uk
Web: www.christian-aid.org.uk

Christian Arts
An association of artists, architects, designers, craftsmen and women all involved in the arts who are committed Christians and wish to explore and deepen the relationship between their faith and the arts. Its activities include holding exhibitions, study days and an annual conference. An illustrated magazine is published twice a year, with interim newsletters. Many members are available to accept commissions. Application may be made for the Christian Arts Directory of Artists. *Secretary:* Paula Widdicombe, 16 Belcombe Place, Bradford-on-Avon, Wiltshire, BA15 1NA
Tel: 01225 863726
email: widdicombebutton@btinternet.com
Web: www.christianarts.org.uk

Christian Education
(Incorporating International Bible Reading Association and RE Today Services)
Christian Education provides advice, resources and opportunities for teaching and learning in the school, the church and the family group, carrying forward the work of the National Christian Education Council and the Christian Education Movement. *Chief Executive:* Peter Fishpool, 1020 Bristol Rd, Selly Oak, Birmingham, B29 6LB
Tel: 0121 472 4242
Fax: 0121 472 7575
email: admin@christianeducation.org.uk
Web: www.christianeducation.org.uk

Christian Ethical Investment Group
Part of ECCR since 2008. For further details, see Ecumenical Council for Corporate Responsibility (ECCR) or contact info@eccr.org.uk/www.eccr.org.uk.
email: info@eccr.org.uk
Web: www.eccr.org.uk

Christian Evidence Society
Founded in 1870 its principal object is 'to give instruction in evidences of Christianity'. Initially it produced tracts, sponsored lectures and arranged open-air work at Tower Hill and Hyde Park Corner. Later it organised annual Drawbridge Lectures by distinguished names. Nowadays its literature is on its website, available for free download by all and it sponsors broadcasts on Premier Radio. To mark the Darwin anniversary, in 2009 the Revd Professor Alister McGrath delivered a Drawbridge Lecture on 'Belief in God'. *President:* The Archbishop of Canterbury. *Chairman:* Revd Prof Richard Burridge. *Administrator:* Canon Harry Marsh, 5 Vicarage Lane, Great Baddow, Chelmsford, CM2 8HY
Tel: 01245 478038
email: harry.marsh@talktalk.net
Web: www.christianevidencesociety.org.uk

Christian Healing Mission
The Christian Healing Mission (CHM) is a non-residential healing centre in London, dedicated to bringing healing to individuals and encouraging healing in churches. A number of link centres and churches have been established throughout the country. The CHM has four main

aims: to offer a place where people may come to receive prayer for healing; to visit churches to encourage them in the healing ministry; to provide training for individuals and groups wanting to learn more about praying for the sick; and finally to offer a prayer request service whereby people can request prayer for those known to them who are sick. Although rooted in the Church of England, the CHM is keen to work with people and churches of all denominations. The Director is an Anglican priest with many years' experience of parish ministry and is also the Bishop of Kensington's Adviser for Healing. *Director:* Revd John Ryeland. *Chaplain:* Revd Sarah Swift, 8 Cambridge Court, 210 Shepherds Bush Rd, London, W6 7NJ
Tel: 020 7603 8118 (Office)
Fax: 020 7603 5224
email: chm@healingmission.org
Web: www.healingmission.org

Christian Medical Fellowship
CMF aims (1) to unite Christian doctors and medical students in Christ, and to encourage them to deepen their faith, live like Christ, and serve him obediently, particularly through acting competently and with compassion in their medical practice; (2) to encourage Christian doctors and medical students to be witnesses for Christ among all those they meet; (3) to mobilize and support all Christian doctors, medical students and other healthcare professionals, especially members, in serving Christ throughout the world; (4) to promote Christian values, especially in bioethics and healthcare, among doctors and medical students, in the Church and in society. *Chief Executive:* Dr Peter Saunders. *Head of Communications:* Catherine Butcher, 6 Marshalsea Rd, London, SE1 1HL *Tel:* 020 7234 9660
email: mail@cmf.org.uk
Web: www.cmf.org.uk

Christian Research
Using a full range of Qualitative and Quantitative research methodologies, we help organizations identify and maximise opportunities to grow God's kingdom numerically, strategically and in depth. Our ongoing projects include ChurchCheck, Faith Journeys and Religious Trends, and we also conduct bespoke research for clients such as Bible Society, Tearfund, Alpha and Evangelical Alliance. Members receive 'Quadrant', a bi-monthly publication and 'Research Brief', a monthly email digest of trends in church and society. Forums and seminars help leaders apply the findings to their own context. Please ask for details. *Exec Director:* Mrs Benita Hewitt, Stonehill Green, Westlea, Swindon, SN5 7DG
Tel: 01793 418 264
Fax: 01793 418 100
email: admin@christian-research.org.uk
Web: www.christian-research.org.uk

Christian Socialist Movement
The Christian Socialist Movement (CSM) seeks to be the Christian conscience of the Labour Party and a voice to churches on social and political issues. We have a tradition stretching back 150 years, believing that the teachings of Jesus; justice, equality and love for one another; are inextricably linked to the foundations and continuation of the Labour Party. Our magazine *The Common Good* is published twice a year. We also organize events, such as hustings for the leadership of the Labour Party, and have a presence at the Labour Conference; where we run fringe events with other major organisations, well known journalists and prominent political figures. Details of CSM membership rates is available on our web site. *Director:* Dr Andy Flannagan. *Chair:* Rt Hon Alun Michael MP, PO Box 65108, London, SW1P 9PQ
Tel: 020 7783 1590
email: info@thecsm.org.uk
Web: www.thecsm.org.uk

Christian Witness to Israel
To a people of promise – the message of Messiah. Working alongside local churches, Christian Witness to Israel has been sharing the message of Messiah with the Jewish people for over 150 years. It is a non-denominational, international and evangelical organization with workers in seven countries worldwide. We believe that the Jewish people's greatest need is to know Jesus their Messiah. In order to help meet this need, we provide appropriate literature and run an evangelistic website. We also host outreach events and provide training for Christians who wish to share the gospel with their Jewish friends, neighbours and colleagues. *General Secretary:* Mr Mike Moore, 166 Main Rd, Sundridge, Sevenoaks, TN14 6EL *Tel:* 01959 565955
Fax: 01959 565966
email: hq@cwi.org.uk
Web: www.cwi.org.uk

Christians at Work
Christians at Work seeks to encourage, support and equip Christian fellowship, evangelism and witness in the workplace. It does this by seeking to unite Christian men and women at work in order to promote a sense of unity in the gospel. The organization produces resources, fact sheets and Bible study material; organizes conferences and seminars for local churches; and coordinates a network of around 200 workplace groups and around 200 individual members committed to the extension of Christ's kingdom in the working world. It was founded in 1942 to bring together Christians to pray and work for the extension of Christ's kingdom in the world of business and industry; to encourage active evangelism and fellowship; to provide information, literature and other facilities; to help Christians who stand alone in their place of work and to provide a means whereby young Christians starting work

may be strengthened in their faith. *Director:* Revd Brian Allenby, Suite 11 Hubbway House, Bassington Lane, Cramlington Northumberland, NE23 8AD *Tel:* 01670 700809
email: brianallenby@caw.uk.net
Web: www.caw.uk.net

Church Army
Church Army is a mission-focused community of people who are transforming lives and communities through the work of Evangelists, staff and supporters. We are committed to sharing the Christian faith through words and action in a variety of contexts across the United Kingdom and Ireland. We work beyond church buildings with those on the margins of society: the elderly, the homeless, those living on deprived housing estates and many more. We have more than 300 Evangelists who are now trained through a four year mission-based programme in which the trainee is sent to a Centre of Mission. Church Army also runs Xplore, a gap-year progamme for adults aged 18 to 25. For more information and to watch films about our work, please visit www.churcharmy.org.uk *President:* Most Revd Desmond Tutu. *Chief Secretary:* Canon Mark Russell. *Vocations and Volunteering Secretary:* Captain Sean Andrews, Wilson Carlile Centre, Cavendish St, Sheffield, S3 7RZ *Tel:* 0300 123 2113
email: info@churcharmy.org.uk
Web: www.churcharmy.org.uk / http://twitter.com/churcharmy

Church House Deaneries' Group – The National Deaneries Network
The Church House Deaneries' Group – The National Deaneries Network – exists to stimulate local and national consideration of the developing role of the deanery, to encourage an informal network for the exchange of information about deanery thinking and deanery initiatives through its web site and Deanery Exchange, published by Parish and People (see separate entry), and to promote the mission opportunities of deaneries. Every two years since 1988 it has held a national conference about deaneries. It has very close links with Parish and People, which resources deaneries with printed material (see separate entry). *Chairman:* Canon Robin Brown (St Alban's). *Secretary:* Mr David Maxwell (Rochester). *Treasurer:* Mr John Wilson (Lichfield), 14 Honeypot Close, Frindsbury, Rochester, ME2 3DU *Tel:* 01634 722097
email: davel.maxwell@virgin.net

Church Housing Trust
Church Housing Trust is committed to changing the lives of homeless people, providing the help and services they would otherwise be denied. Our principal objective is to raise funds to benefit homeless people and those in housing need, and in particular those cared for by Riverside ECHG (formerly English Churches Housing Group). Our funds support residents in over 80 projects throughout England, including hostels, women's refuges, projects for young people, supported housing for the ex Services, accommodation for vulnerable young parents and children, specialist supported housing for people with drug, alcohol and mental health problems, and projects for ex offenders. Our funds help turn hostels into homes and prepare homeless people for independent living through life skills and education and training programmes. Charity no. 802801. PO Box 50296, London, EC1P 1WF
Tel: 020 7269 1630
Fax: 020 7404 2562
email: info@churchhousingtrust.org.uk
Web: www.churchhousingtrust.org.uk

Church Lads' and Church Girls' Brigade
The Brigade is the Anglican Church's only uniformed youth organisation, welcoming children and young people of all faiths and none, from ages 5 years to 21 years, engaging in 'fun, faith and friendship', equipping them to cope with the demands that society places upon them. The Brigade creates a caring and safe environment in which friendships between young people, children and adults can be established; helping children and young people to grow in confidence, developing their individual skills and abilities to work together, showing concern for others and the environment, exploring their spirituality and developing moral values. Operating in four age groups: 5–7 years, 7–10 years, 10–13 years and 13–21 years, there are appropriate training and activity programmes for all leaders and members to be engaged in. *Patron:* HM The Queen. *President:* The Archbishop of Canterbury. *Governor:* Anthony Baker. *Brigade Chaplain:* Rt Revd Jack Nicholls. *Brigade Secretary:* Alan Millward, National Headquarters, Saint Martin's House, 2 Barnsley Rd, Wath-Upon-Dearne, Rotherham, South Yorkshire S63 6PY *Tel:* 01709 876535
Fax: 01709 878089
email: brigadesecretary@clcgb.org.uk
Web: www.clcgb.org.uk

Church Mission Society
We want the world to know Jesus. CMS is an acknowledged community of the Church of England with over 2,500 members who recognise that they are called to serve, wherever they are, in God's mission. CMS supports people in mission in over 35 countries in Africa, Asia, Europe, the Middle East and Latin America, including many indigenous mission workers. CMS Pioneer Mission Leadership Training is a unique course for pioneer mission leaders working in many contexts, including those training to be ordained pioneer ministers in the Church of England. CMS is committed to working in networks, especially with CMS Africa and AsiaCMS, and is a founder member of the Faith2Share mission movements network. (See also Religious Communities:

Church Mission Society.) Registered Charity no. 1131655. Company no. 6985330. *Patron:* The Archbishop of Canterbury. *Episcopal Visitor:* Rt Revd Dr Christopher Cocksworth, Bishop of Coventry. *Chair of Trustees:* John Ripley. *Executive Leader:* Revd Philip Mountstephen, Watlington Rd, Oxford, OX4 6BZ
Tel: 01865 787 400 (Switchboard)
Fax: 01865 776 375
email: info@cms-uk.org
Web: www.cms-uk.org / www.wearesayingyes.org

Church Monuments Society
Founded in 1979 to encourage the appreciation, study and conservation of monuments. The Society promotes a biennial symposium, excursions, study days, a twice-yearly newsletter and an annual refereed journal. It also offers a programme of visits to locations throughout the country, a series of occasional lectures and an opportunity for people to meet and exchange views on a subject which spans many disciplines. It is the only society to cover all periods and all types of monument, and is the sponsor of the National Ledger Stone Survey. *President:* Dr Phillip G. Lindley. *Secretary:* Dr Amy L. Harris. *Treasurer:* Dr John Brown. *Membership Secretary:* Mr Clive Easter. *Publicity:* Dr John Bromilow, c/o Society of Antiquaries of London, Burlington House, Piccadilly, London, W1J 0BE
Tel: 01752 773634 (Membership)
01837 851483 (Publicity)
Fax: 01837 851483
email: churchmonuments@aol.com
Web: www.churchmonumentssociety.org

Church Music Society
Founded 1906. The society is a leading publisher of all types of Church music, and has consistently served the Church of England by this means. An annual lecture and other events for members pursue further aims of advancing knowledge of the art and science of Church music. Although much of the society's focus is on music specifically for liturgy, CMS publications are also in world-wide use by choirs of all types for concerts, recitals and recordings. 'Te Deum Laudamus', a CD of CMS publications, is now available. Details of membership and activities are available from the Secretary. *President:* The Dean of Hereford. *Chairman:* Mr Timothy Byram-Wigfield. *Hon Secretary:* Dr Simon Lindley. *Hon General Editor:* Mr Richard Lyne, 17 Fulneck, Pudsey, LS28 8NT *Tel and Fax:* 0113 255 6143
email: cms@simonlindley.org.uk
Web: www.church-music.org.uk

Church of England Clergy Stipend Trust
Founded 1952 to augment stipends of parochial clergy, normally through Diocesan Boards of Finance. *Chairman:* Mr J. W. Parkinson FCA, 3 Bunhill Row, London, EC1Y 8YZ
Tel: 020 7423 8000
Fax: 020 7423 8001

Church of England Evangelical Council
Founded 1960 to (1) bring together evangelical leaders of the Church of England for mutual counsel and discussion (2) seek to reach a common mind on the issues of the day and when appropriate to reveal their findings to the Church and nation (3) encourage those societies and individuals in a position to do so to increase the evangelical contribution to the Church of England (4) assist in such work throughout the Anglican Communion. It organizes an occasional National Evangelical Anglican Congress to help further its aims. *President:* Rt Revd Wallace Benn. *Chairman:* Ven Michael Lawson. *Secretary:* Canon Michael Walters. *Treasurer:* Mr John Challen, 27 Alvanley Rise, Northwich, CW9 8AY
Tel: 01606 333126
email: executive.officer@ceec.info
Web: www.ceec.info

Church of England Flower Arrangers Association
The Church of England Flower Arrangers Association (CEFAA) was founded in 1981 to help and encourage all those who tend flowers in churches and link them in fellowship and friendship. It is open to all those baptized in the Christian faith. The aims are to expand interest in church flower arranging, to use talent to enrich places of worship and to support what theology and creation try to teach. CEFAA is a voluntary charity whose constitution covers the work members do in churches, church buildings and at church events. The Association is not sponsored and is non-competitive. Registered Charity no. 514372. *President:* Revd Noel Michell. *Chairman:* Mrs Hillary Brian. *Treasurer:* Mrs Naomi Hadden. *Secretary:* Mr Roger Brown, 25B Church Road, Hale Village, Liverpool, L24 4AY
Tel: 0151 425 2823
email: cefaa@btinternet.com
Web: www.cefaa.org.uk

Church of England Record Society
Founded in 1991 with the object of promoting interest in and knowledge of the history of the Church of England from the sixteenth century onwards, the Society publishes primary material of national significance for Church history. It aims to produce one volume each year, set against an annual subscription of £20 (individuals), and £30 (institutions). *Hon Secretary:* Dr Michael Snape, Dept of Modern History, University of Birmingham, Edgbaston, Birmingham, SE23 3XN *Tel:* BI5 2TT
email: m.f.snape@bham.ac.uk
Web: www.coers.org

Church of England Soldiers', Sailors' and Airmen's Clubs (1891)
A registered charity which, since its foundation in 1891, has maintained clubs at home and abroad for HM Forces and their dependants, whatever their religious denomination. The work of the association now encompasses rented housing for elderly ex-Service people or their widows/widowers. The association also helps other charities to build sheltered housing for ex-Service people, working in parallel with its sister organization, CESSA Housing Association. Donations always welcomed. *General Secretary:* Cdr Martin Marks. *Assistant Secretary:* Cdr Mike Pearce, CESSAC, 1 Shakespeare Terrace, 126 High St, Portsmouth, PO1 2RH *Tel:* 023 9282 9319
Fax: 023 9282 4018
email: martin.marks@ntlbusiness.com

Church of England Soldiers', Sailors' and Airmen's Housing Association Ltd (1972)
A charitable Housing Association, registered with the Tenant Services Authority to provide low cost rented sheltered accommodation for retired ex-Service people and/or their partners of all denominations. Construction costs were provided partly by government grants, but donations are always welcome to help fund modernisation. *Chief Exec:* Cdr Mike Pearce. *Housing Manager:* Chris Wrenn, CESSA H. A., 1 Shakespeare Terrace, 126 High St, Portsmouth, PO1 2RH *Tel:* 023 9282 9319
Fax: 023 9282 4018
email: mike.pearce@cessaha.co.uk
Web: www.cessaha.co.uk

Church Pastoral Aid Society Ministers in Training Fund
The Church Pastoral Aid Society administers the Ministers in Training Fund. This fund gives grants for personal maintenance (not fees) to evangelical men and women, married or single, who are facing financial hardship whilst training for ordained ministry. *Ministers in Training Administrator:* Miss Joanna Coleman, Ministers in Training Fund, CPAS, Sovereign Court One (Unit 3), Sir Williams Lyons Road Coventry, CV4 7EZ *Tel:* 0300 123 0780
Fax: 01926 458459
email: jcoleman@cpas.org.uk
Web: www.cpas.org.uk

Church Schoolmasters and School Mistresses' Benevolent Institution
Founded in 1857 to provide assistance for Church of England teachers in England and Wales in times of temporary affliction or misfortune, or upon retirement or permanent disablement, and assistance towards the maintenance and education of their orphans. The CSSBI runs Glen Arun Care Home which has a strong Christian ethos and is set in a semi-rural location. The home provides residential and nursing care accomodation. It has 35 single rooms where residents can benefit from 24 hour nursing care. *Patron:* HM The Queen. *President:* The Bishop of London. *Chairman:* Miss Diana Bell. *Patient Care Manager:* Mrs Sue Green. *Company Secretary:* Mrs Marie di Cara, Glen Arun, 9 Athelstan Way, Horsham, RH13 6HA *Tel:* 01403 253881 (Admin)
01403 255749 (Nursing Office)
Fax: 01403 254971
email: glenarun@hotmail.com

Church Society
Formed in 1950 by the amalgamation of the Church Association and National Church League, which was founded in 1835, continues to seek to maintain the evangelical and reformed faith of the Church of England, based upon the authority of Holy Scripture (see Canon A 5) and the foundational doctrines of the Thirty-nine Articles and the Book of Common Prayer. Publishes a journal, *Churchman*, and a quarterly broadsheet, *Cross+Way*. The Society publishes books, booklets and leaflets on current issues and organizes conferences and public meetings. Patronage is administered through the Church Society Trust. (See also Patronage Trusts.) *President:* The Viscount Brentford. *Chairman:* Mr James Crabtree, Dean Wace House, 16 Rosslyn Rd, Watford, WD18 0NY *Tel:* 01923 235111
Fax: 01923 800362
email: admin@churchsociety.org
Web: www.churchsociety.org

Church Union
Founded in 1859 at the time of the Oxford Movement, to promote catholic faith and order, it continues this work today by providing support and encouragement to those lay people and priests who wish to see catholic faith, order, morals and spirituality maintained and upheld, and who wish to promote catholic unity. The Union publishes books and tracts and produces an in-house magazine, the *Church Observer*. *President:* Prebendary David Houlding SSC. *Chairman:* Mr David Morgan. *Treasurer:* Revd Owen Higgs. *Membership Secretary:* Mrs Jenny Miller, 2a The Cloisters, Gordon Square, London, WC1H 0AG
Tel: 020 7388 3588 01884 34563 (Membership)
email: secretary@churchunion.co.uk
2nd email: membership@churchunion.co.uk
Web: www.churchunion.co.uk

Church Welfare Association (Incorporated)
(formerly the Church Moral Aid Association)
Founded 1851. Gives financial aid to Church projects assisting and supporting women and children in need of residential care and/or moral support. We can also support Day Care projects designed to assist and support women and children, particularly single-parent families. *Honorary Secretary:* Canon Bridget Trump, 82 St Edmund's Church Street, Salisbury, SP1 1EQ
email: secretary@churchwelfareassociation.org.uk
Web: www.churchwelfareassociation.org.uk

Church's Ministry Among Jewish People
Founded 1809 as London Society for Promoting Christianity Among the Jews, to take the Christian gospel to Jewish people. *President:* Rt Revd David Evans. *Chair:* Mr Ben Salter. *CEO:* Revd Alex Jacob, Eagle Lodge, Hexgreave Hall Business Park, Farnsfield, Notts, NG22 8LS
Tel: 01623 883960
Fax: 01623 884295
email: enquiries@cmj.org.uk
Web: www.cmj.org.uk

Churches Tourism Association
A charitable ecumenical organisation committed to promoting the daily openness of church buildings to visitors and tourists as a contributory component of the Church's mission, and to the significance of church buildings as places of worship, repositories of architectural heritage and locations for community engagement. In addition to its own resources CTA, through its website, signposts organisations which specialise in offering literature and training in ministry to visitors and tourists. A newsletter is published approximately bi-monthly. Charity Registration No. 1101254. *Chair:* Canon John D. Brown. *Administrator:* Mrs Carol Roast, c/o 556 Galleywood Road, Chelmsford, Essex, CM2 8BX
Tel: 01245 358185
email: canonjbrown@mac.com
Web: www.churchestourismassociation.info

Churches' Advertising Network (also known as ChurchAds.Net)
A professional group of Christians from all traditions cooperating to develop the professional use of advertising as part of the Churches' communication and outreach. CAN seeks free or low cost poster space and radio airtime from leading media owners, which it uses on behalf of the Churches. All members give their services free. Charity Registration no. 1096868. *Chair:* Mr F. Goodwin. *Secretary & Treasurer:* Revd Tony Kinch. *Asst Treasurer:* Mrs Karen Gray. *Trustee:* Mr Michael Elms, The Methodist Centre, 24 School St, Wolverhampton, WV1 4LF *Tel:* 01902 422100
Fax: 01902 313301
email: churchads@methodist.fsnet.co.uk
Web: www.churchads.org.uk

Churches' Fellowship for Psychical and Spiritual Studies
Founded 1953 to study the psychic and spiritual and their relevance to Christian faith and life. *President:* Very Revd Alexander Wedderspoon. *Chair:* Mrs Davina Thomas. *General Secretary:* Mr Julian Drewett, The Rural Workshop, South Rd, North Somercotes, Louth, LN11 7PT
Tel and Fax: 01507 358845
email: gensec@churchesfellowship.co.uk
Web: www.churchesfellowship.co.uk

Churches' Funerals Group
The Churches' Group on Funeral Services at Cemeteries and Crematoria was formed as an advisory group in 1980 by the mainstream Churches in England and Wales to co-ordinate their policies in connection with the pastoral and administrative aspects of funeral services at cemeteries and crematoria, and to represent the Churches at national level in joint discussions with public and private organizations on any matters relating to ministry at such funerals. The Group keeps in close touch with the main organizations concerned with funeral provision and bereavement counselling. To reflect its involvement in the wider aspects of all concerned with funerals and death in our society, the Group shortened its working title in 2002 to 'The Churches' Funerals Group'. Publications sponsored by the Group include *The Role of the Minister in Bereavement: Guidelines and Training Suggestions* (Church House Publishing, 1989); *Guidelines for Best Practice of Clergy at Funerals* (Church House Publishing, 1997); and two joint funeral service books (The Canterbury Press, Norwich), one for use in England (1986, 1994, 2001 and 2009), the other for use in Wales (1987). Three previous conference reports have been published: *The Role of a Minister at a Funeral* (1991), *Bereavement and Belief* (1993) and *Clergy and Cremation Today* (1995). An information leaflet entitled *Questions Commonly Asked about Funerals* (2nd edition, 2007) is also available free of charge from the Secretary. *Chairman:* Rt Revd Dr Geoffrey Rowell, Bp of Gibraltar in Europe. *Secretary:* Ms Sue Moore, Church House, Great Smith St, London, SW1P 3AZ *Tel:* 020 7898 1376
Fax: 020 7898 1369
email: enquiries@christianfunerals.org
Web: www.christianfunerals.org

Churches' Legislation Advisory Service
Founded 1941 (as the Churches Main Committee), and first registered as a charity in 1966, CLAS exists to advance the religious and other charitable work of its member Churches by furthering their common interests in those secular issues (such as property matters, finance, tax and charitable status) which help underpin and deliver that work. Registered Charity No. 256303. *Chairman:* Rt Revd Michael Langrish. *Secretary:* Frank Cranmer, Church House, Great Smith St, London, SW1P 3AZ *Tel:* 020 7222 1265
email: frank.cranmer@centrallobby.com
Web: www.clas.org.uk

Cleaver Ordination Candidates' Fund
The Cleaver Ordination Candidates Fund exists for the support and encouragement of Anglo-Catholic ordinands and parish clergy who are committed to a traditional understanding of the priesthood and historic episcopate. Grants are given to ordinands, to clergy pursuing recognized courses of postgraduate study, and to those

clergy wishing to recover the habit of serious theological study. *Clerk to the Cleaver Trustees:* Revd John Hanks, 50 Thames Street, Oxford, OX1 1SU *email:* clerk@cleaver.org.uk
Web: www.cleaver.org.uk

COIN: Christians on the Internet
An interdenominational group of Christians throughout Britain and Ireland working together since 1995 to advise, help and encourage the Church in its use of the Internet. It functions both as a group of individuals able to offer their particular expertise, and also, through email, as a lively online community discussing in depth a wide variety of issues affecting Christians, including specialist lists discussing Church of England issues, and Common Worship. Further details of COIN and its activities can be found on its web site. *Chair:* Revd Karen Spray. *Secretary:* Simon Kershaw. *Treasurer:* Revd Gordon Giles. *Membership Secretary:* Revd Alan Jesson
Tel: 01480 381471
email: secretary@coin.org.uk
2nd email: membership@coin.org.uk
Web: www.coin.org.uk

College of Evangelists
The national College of Evangelists was founded in 1999 to support and give the accreditation of the Archbishops of Canterbury and York to evangelists in the Church of England. To be admitted as a member of the College, evangelists will be involved in active evangelistic ministry (not just training or teaching about evangelism) and will be operating nationally or regionally, beyond their diocesan boundaries. Potential candidates should contact their diocesan bishop in the first instance. *Chairman:* The Bishop of Worcester. *Enquiries to:* Jenny Lowery, The Bishop of Worcester's Office, Old Palace, Deansway, Worcester, WR1 2JE
email: admin@collegeofevangelists.org.uk

College of Health Care Chaplains
Founded in 1992, the College is a multi-faith, interdenominational professional association open to all recognized health care chaplaincy staff, full-time and part-time, including voluntary and support workers, and others with an interest in health care chaplaincy. With around 900 members throughout the United Kingdom, it provides peer support, advice and fellowship for members nationally and in 13 regional branches with a focus for professional development, good practice and training. The College publishes two issues a year of 'The Journal of Health Care Chaplaincy' (available on subscription to non-members). It is an autonomous professional organization within Unite the Union (Britain and Ireland's biggest trade Union with 1.5 million memberships), which negotiates terms and conditions for all chaplains (irrespective of College membership) on a national basis, and members receive professional support on employment issues. *President:* Revd Mark Burleigh. *Vice-President:* Revd Gareth Rowlands. *Registrar:* Revd William Sharpe, Unite Health Sector, 128 Theobald's Rd, London, WC1X 8TN
Tel: 020 3371 2004
Fax: 0870 731 5043
email: william.sharpe@unitetheunion.org
Web: www.healthcarechaplains.org

College of Preachers
An ecumenical network of preachers, ordained and lay, dedicated to preaching which is faithful and fresh, biblical and relevant, and to helping one another to develop preaching skills through seminars, conferences, a journal and guided study. *Chairman:* Revd Dr Leslie Griffiths. *Director:* Mr Paul Johns. *Administrator:* Miss Helen Skinner, 6th Floor, City Gate East, Tollhouse Hill, Nottingham, NG1 5FS *Tel:* 0115 925 2025
Fax: 020 8883 0843
email: administrator@collegeofpreachers.org.uk
Web: www.collegeofpreachers.org.uk

College of Readers
An independent membership organization providing fellowship and support for Readers of the Anglican Communion in the British Isles, especially to those Readers who subscribe to the authority of scripture, the grace of the sacraments and the traditional understanding of the ordained ministry of the bishop, priest and deacon. The College is establishing a network of local circles and chaplains, and publishes a quarterly magazine, *Blue Scarf*, which keeps all members in touch. Distance learning packages are available, as are a series of publications on aspects of Reader ministry. Regional and national meetings are organized each year. *Patron:* Rt Revd Norman Banks. *Chairman:* Mr Barry Barnes. *Registrar/Treasurer:* Mrs Mary E. Snape, 6 The Chase, Penn, High Wycombe, HP10 8BA *Tel:* 01494 813045
email: mary@college-of-readers.org.uk
Web: www.college-of-readers.org.uk

College of St Barnabas
Set in idyllic Surrey countryside, the College is a residential community of retired Anglican clergy, including married couples and widows. Admission is also open to licensed Church Workers and Readers. There are facilities for visitors and guests, and occasional quiet days and private retreats can also be accommodated. Residents lead active, independent lives for as long as possible. There is a Nursing Wing providing residential and full nursing care for those who need it, to which direct admission is possible. This enables most residents to remain members of the College for the rest of their lives. Respite care can occasionally be offered here. Sheltered flats in the Cloisters all have separate sitting rooms, bedrooms and en suite facilities. There are two

chapels, daily Mass and Evensong, three libraries, a well equipped common room and refectory, a snooker table and a nine-hole putting green. The College is easily accessible by road and is also next to Dormans Station on the line from London to East Grinstead. For further details or to arrange a preliminary visit, please see our website or contact the Warden. *Warden:* Fr Howard Such. *Bursar:* Paul G. F. Wilkin, The College of St Barnabas, Blackberry Lane, Lingfield, Surrey RH7 6NJ *Tel:* 01342 870260
Fax: 01342 871672
email: warden@collegeofstbarnabas.com
Web: www.st-barnabas.org.uk

Commonwealth War Graves Commission
Founded 1917. Responsible for marking and maintaining in perpetuity the graves of those of Commonwealth Forces who fell in the 1914–18 and 1939–45 Wars and for commemorating by name on memorials those with no known grave. *President:* HRH The Duke of Kent. *Chairman:* Secretary of State for Defence in the UK. *Enquiries:* Director Legal Services, 2 Marlow Rd, Maidenhead, Berkshire, SL6 7DX *Tel:* 01628 507 138
Fax: 01628 507 134
email: legal@cwgc.org
Web: www.cwgc.org

Community Housing and Therapy
CHT provides group and individual psychotherapy in residential settings to clients who are experiencing mental health and emotional difficulties. The care of each client is planned through an individual Care Plan which is reviewed every three to six months. Reviews are interdisciplinary and CHT therapists with social workers and psychatrists, together with others, review progress and set goals together with the client. These goals focus on key areas in the life of each client, for example, housing needs, relationships, medication and re-training for work. *Chief Exec:* Mr John Gale. *Chief Operating Officer:* Ms Inma Vidana. *Deputy Director, Clinical Services:* Miss Beatriz Sanchez. *Senior Managers:* Mr Terry Saftis, Mrs Yin Ping Leung, 24/5–6 The Coda Centre, 189 Munster Rd, London, SW6 6AW
Tel: 020 7381 5888/0800 018 1261 (Freephone)
Fax: 020 7610 0608
email: co@cht.org.uk
Web: www.cht.org.uk

Community of Aidan and Hilda
A dispersed, ecumenical and international body of Christians who journey with God, and reconnect with the Spirit and the Scriptures, the saints and the streets, the seasons and the soil. The Community seeks to cradle a Christian spirituality for today which renews the Church and brings healing to fragmented people and communities. It welcomes people of all backgrounds and countries who wish to be wholly available to God the Holy Trinity, and to the way of Jesus as revealed in the Bible. In the earthing of that commitment members draw particular inspiration from Celtic saints such as Aidan and Hilda. Members follow a Way of Life based on a rhythm of prayer and study, simplicity, care for creation, and mission, seeking to weave together the separated strands of Christianity. Each shares their journey with a spiritual companion known as a Soul Friend. The work of the Community is the work of each member and can be expressed individually and corporately in many ways, such as through link houses, churches, monastic experiments, and indigenous national branches. Its mother house and spirituality centre is The Open Gate, Holy Island, Berwick-upon-Tweed, TD15 2SD. *Community Soul Friend (Episcopally endorsed visitor):* Canon Godfrey Butland. *International Guardian:* Revd Ray Simpson. *Secretary:* Naomi Ackland. *Retreat House Wardens:* Revd Graham and Dr Ruth Booth, Lindisfarne Retreat, Holy Island, Berwick-upon-Tweed, TD15 2SD
Tel: 01289 389249 (International Office)
01289 389222 (Holy Island Retreat House Bookings)
email: admin@aidanandhilda.org.uk
Web: www.aidanandhilda.org

Compassionate Friends, The
A nationwide charitable organization run by bereaved parents offering support and understanding to parents whose child has died at any age and from any cause. Also support for bereaved grandparents and adult siblings. Local Contacts and Support Groups, quarterly journal, leaflets and publications, postal library, website forum, retreats and a yearly gathering. The national helpline, which is always answered by a bereaved parent, is available for support and information daily from 10.00–16.00 and 19.00–22.00. *Office Manager:* Michael Brown, 53 North St, Bristol, BS3 1EN
Tel: 08451 23 23 04 (Helpline)
0845 120 3785 (Admin)
Fax: 0845 120 3786
email: helpline@tcf.org.uk
Web: www.tcf.org.uk

Confraternity of the Blessed Sacrament
Founded 1862 to honour Jesus Christ our Lord in the Blessed Sacrament; to make mutual eucharistic intercession and to encourage eucharistic devotion. Registered Charity no. 1082897. *Superior-General:* Revd Christopher Pearson. *Secretary General:* Canon Lawson Nagel, Aldwick Vicarage, 25 Gossamer Lane, Bognor Regis, PO21 3AT *Tel:* 01243 262049
email: cbs@confraternity.org.uk
Web: www.confraternity.org.uk

Corporation of the Sons of the Clergy and Friends of the Clergy Corporation
The two charities work together and are able to assist Anglican clergy and their widows/

widowers and dependants in times of financial need or distress. Grants are made for a wide range of purposes including holidays and resettlement, school clothing and school trips, university maintenance for undergraduate children, clerical clothing, heating and home maintenance for the retired, bereavement expenses and some of the expenses arising from separation and divorce. Book grants can be considered for ordinands in training. The Corporation of the Sons of the Clergy also administers the Clergy Orphan Corporation. *Registrar and Secretary:* Robert Welsford, 1 Dean Trench St, Westminster, London, SW1P 3HB *Tel:* 020 7799 3696
Fax: 020 7222 3468
email: enquiries@clergycharities.org.uk
Web: www.clergycharities.org.uk

Council of Christians and Jews
Founded 1942 to combat all forms of religious and racial intolerance, to promote mutual understanding and goodwill between Christians and Jews, and to foster cooperation in educational activities and in social and community service. Forty local branches in the UK. *Patron:* HM The Queen. *Presidents:* Archbishop of Canterbury; Chief Rabbi; Cardinal Archibishop of Westminster; Moderator of the Free Churches; Rabbi Tony Bayfield; Head, Reform Movement; Archbishop of Thyatira and Great Britain; Moderator of the Church of Scotland. *Chair:* Rt Revd Nigel McCulloch, Bishop of Manchester. *Chief Executive:* David Gifford MA, 21 Godliman Street, London, EC4V 5BD *Tel:* 020 7015 5160
Fax: 020 7820 0504
email: cjrelations@ccj.org.uk
Web: www.ccj.org.uk

Council on Christian Approaches to Defence and Disarmament
CCADD was established in 1963 by the Rt Revd Robert Stopford, then Bishop of London, to study problems relating to defence and disarmament within a Christian context. The British Group of CCADD comprises Christians of different traditions, varying vocations and specializations and political views, with a range of responsibilities, governmental and non-governmental. CCADD seeks to bring an ethical viewpoint to bear on disarmament and arms control and related issues and to this end the British Group has always stressed the importance of dialogue between official and non-official bodies. *President:* Rt Revd Richard Harries. *Chairman:* Mr Brian Wicker. *Admin Secretary:* Mrs Liza Hamilton, 5 Cubitts Meadow, Buxton, Norwich, NR10 5EF
Tel and Fax: 01603 279939
email: ccadd@lineone.net
Web: http://website.lineone.net/ccadd

Crosslinks
Crosslinks is an international mission society with its roots in the Bible, working largely within the worldwide Anglican Communion.Our business is making Christ known through the teaching of God's word in the power of the Holy Spirit. We do this by organising gospel partnerships across cultural boundaries. *President:* Mr David Mills. *General Secretary:* Canon Andy Lines. *Chairman:* Revd M. Payne, 251 Lewisham Way, London, SE4 1XF *Tel:* 020 8691 6111
Fax: 020 8694 8023
email: info@crosslinks.org
Web: www.crosslinks.org

CTBI Christians Abroad
CTBI Christians Abroad is a project of the Churches Together in Britain and Ireland. CTBI Christians Abroad provides self-funded opportunities for men and women of any age to work overseas in development or mission in Africa, Asia, South America and the Caribbean for short periods in projects associated with local Christian communities. Using a team of six experienced consultants CTBI Christians Abroad also provides, to national and local churches in Britain and Ireland, support and consultancy services to mission partners working overseas, to the personnel function of the church and to development projects overseas. For further information and travel, health and accident or medical insurance for overseas travellers, visit www.cabroad.org.uk. For Volunteer opportunities contact David Brett, recruit@cabroad.org.uk. For Consultancy services contact Colin South, support@cabroad.org.uk c/o 22 Ebenezer Close, Witham, Essex, CM8 2HX *Tel:* 03000 121 201
email: recruit@cabroad.org.uk
2nd email: support@cabroad.org.uk
Web: www.cabroad.org.u

Culham Institute
This is a research, development and information agency working in the fields of Church schools, Church colleges, RE and collective worship. It has established a national system of networking, collaborative activity and project management. Current collaboration includes work with the Jerusalem Trust, the Culham St Gabriel's Trust, the All Saints Trust and the National Society. It is planning to establish a national Centre for Religious Education in the City of London. The Association of Church College Trusts and RE online have their bases at Culham. *Director:* Revd Dr John Gay, 15 Norham Gardens, Oxford, OX2 6PY *Tel:* 01865 284885
Fax: 01865 284886
email: enquiries@culham.ac.uk
Web: www.culham.ac.uk

Culham St Gabriel's Trust
Culham St Gabriel's is an endowed charitable trust dedicated to educational work in support of religious education (RE). We are committed to excellence in religious education for all learners. We support teachers by helping them to offer the

best, high-quality learning experiences in RE, school worship and spiritual and moral development. We also support work that promotes the links between school ethos, values, leadership and school improvement. Culham St Gabriel's is formed of the union of two church college trusts, Culham Educational Foundation and St Gabriel's Trust, both of which have shared a long-term commitment to supporting religious education. We provide individual and corporate grants to support research, development and innovation in RE in the UK. We run an extensive programme of conferences, professional development opportunities and websites for teachers of RE, supported by our national network of consultants and collaborative projects. Current collaboration includes work with the Jerusalem Trust and the National Society to improve the teaching of Christianity in primary and secondary schools, and work with the Association of Church College Trusts and other partners to redevelop REonline. *Director:* Dr Mark Chater FRSA. *Chair of Trustees:* Dr Priscilla Chadwick FRSA, 15 Norham Gardens, Oxford, OX2 6PY *Tel:* 01865 284885
Fax: 01865 284886
email: enquiries@cstg.org.uk
Web: www.cstg.org.uk

Day One Christian Ministries
Day One Publications produces Christian books and cards, and Day One Prison Ministry works to supply prisons with evangelistic items. We also now do tours to Israel, Egypt, Greece andTurkey, with more places to follow. *President:* Mr John Roberts. *Managing Director:* Mr Mark Roberts, Ryelands Rd, Leominster, HR6 8NZ
Tel: 01568 613740
Fax: 01568 611473
email: sales@dayone.co.uk
Web: www.dayone.co.uk

Deaf Anglicans Together (DAT)
(formerly National Deaf Church Conference)
This is the members' organization for Deaf People in the Church of England, and it welcomes members of other churches and hearing people as well. DAT provides fellowship and training through conferences (twice a year) and other events, and promotes British Sign Language and Deaf Culture by means of workshops and festivals, exploring the use of drama, storytelling. signed hymns and poems. DAT also acts as a forum for exploring relevant issues, and encourages the participation of Deaf people in the structures of the Church. DAT has three representatives on General Synod. *Contact:* Revd Bob Shrine, 7 Russell Hall Lane, Queensbury, Bradford, BD13 2AJ *Fax:* 01274 889006
email: bob.shrine@btinternet.com

Deaf People, Royal Association for
RAD promotes the welfare and interests of deaf people, working with the Deaf Community, Deaf Clubs, deaf individuals and the parents of deaf children. Most of RAD's work is in London, Essex and the south-east of England. RAD is organized around the following services: Deaf Community Development; Advice and Advocacy; Learning Disability; Mental Health; Sign Language Interpreting; Training. *Chief Executive:* Mr Tom Fenton, 18 Westside Centre, London Rd, Stanway, Colchester, CO3 8PH
Tel: 0845 688 2525/0845 688 2527 (Text)
Fax: 0845 688 2526
email: info@royaldeaf.org.uk
Web: www.royaldeaf.org.uk

Deans' Conference
The Deans' Conference is the meeting together (three times annually) of those who preside over their Cathedral Chapters to reflect upon cathedral issues of particular concern to Deans in their public and cathedral roles. *Chairman:* The Dean of Canterbury. *Treasurer:* The Dean of Exeter. *Secretary:* The Dean of St Albans, Cathedral Office, New St, Chelmsford, CM1 1TY
Tel: 01245 294492
Fax: 01245 294499
email: dean@chelmsfordcathedral.org.uk

Deans' Vergers' Conference
Founded in 1989 to bring together Head Vergers who are employed in that capacity by a Dean and Chapter of the Church of England. The Conference enables members to communicate with one another, exchange and discuss ideas of common interest and to have regular contact with the Deans' Conference. The Head Vergers of the forty-two English cathedrals, Westminster Abbey and St George's Windsor are eligible for membership. *Chairman:* Alex Carberry . *Treasurer:* Clive McCleester . *Secretary:* Glynn Usher, Head Verger and Sub-Sacrist, Bristol Cathedral, College Green, Bristol BS1 5TJ *Tel:* 0117 946 8179 (Direct)
0117 926 4879 (Cathedral Office)
Fax: 0117 925 3678
email: glynn.usher@bristol-cathedral.co.uk

Diaconal Association of the Church of England
DACE is a professional association for diaconal ministers (deacons, accredited lay workers and Church Army officers) working in the Church of England, established in 1988 to succeed the Deaconess Committee and the Anglican Accredited Lay Workers Federation. Associate membership is also open to those who support diaconal ministry, and diaconal ministers working in other provinces in the UK. DACE exists to promote the distinctive (permanent) diaconate and other diaconal ministries in the Church of England, support all nationally recognized diaconal ministers, and to consider the theological and practical implications of diaconal ministry within the total ministry of the Christian Church, in partnership with other agencies and denominations. DACE is a member of the Diakonia World Federation of

Diaconal Associations and Diaconal Communities. A registered charity. *President:* Revd David Rogers. *Secretary:* Revd Ann Wren. *Treasurer:* Revd Christopher Wren, St Peter's Bourne, 40 Oakleigh Park South, London, N20 9JN
Tel: 0208 4455 535
email: secretary@dace.org
Web: www.dace.org

Diakonia
Founded in 1947 to link the various European deaconess associations, it is now a 'World Federation of Diaconal Associations'. It concerns itself with the nature and task of 'Diakonia' and encourages deaconesses, deacons, and lay people doing diaconal work. It also furthers ecumenical relations between the diaconal associations in other countries. The Diaconal Association of the Church of England is a member. There is a Diakonia 'UK Liaison Group' which also includes representatives from the Methodist Diaconal Order, the Church of Scotland Diaconate and the Deaconesses of the Presbyterian Church in Ireland. *President, DRAE:* Deacon Jackie Fowler, 82 Empress Road, Derby, DE23 6TE
Tel: 01332 361290
email: jackie.fowler@diakonia-world.org
Web: www.diakonia-world.org

Diocesan Clergy Chairs' Forum
The Forum is a voluntary group, allowing the elected chairs of the houses of clergy in each diocese to share ideas and experience, to address together various issues affecting the Church of England, to offer mutual support, and to develop principles of best practice in fulfilling this role in each diocese. Guidelines for best practice have been agreed with the House of Bishops. *Chair:* Revd Dr Jonathan Gibbs. *Hon. Secretary:* Revd Steve Parish, 1A Fitzherbert St, Warrington, WA2 7QG *Tel:* 01925 631781
email: s.parish17@ntlworld.com

Diocesan Institutions of Chester, Manchester, Liverpool and Blackburn
For the relief of widows and orphans of clergymen who have officiated in their last sphere of duty in the Archdeaconries of Chester, Macclesfield, Manchester, Rochdale, Liverpool, Warrington or Blackburn. *Chair:* Canon Michael S. Finlay, Rectory, Warrington, WA1 2TL
Tel: 01925 635020
email: finlay289@btinternet.com

Distinctive Diaconate
An unofficial Church of England centre which serves to promote the diaconate as one of the historic orders of the Church's ministry with manifold potential for ministry today. From 1981 to 2012 it produced 'Distinctive Diaconate News' and, from 1994–2012, 'Distinctive News of Women in Ministry'. A 'History of the Community of St Andrew: 1861–2011' was produced for its sesquicentennial, 30 November 2012. A commemorative booklet, 'Our 150th', is being prepared for the 150th anniversary of the Deaconess Order of the Church of England which was celebrated at Lambeth Palace in July 2012. Writings on the history of women's diaconate are in preparation. *Editor:* Revd Dr Sr Teresa CSA, St Andrew's House, 16 Tavistock Crescent, Westbourne Park, London, W11 1AP
Tel: 020 7221 4604
email: teresajoan@btinternet.com
Web: www.distinctive-diaconate.org.uk

Ecclesiastical Insurance Office PLC
Ecclesiastical is an independent UK-owned insurer and investment management organization that donates a significant proportion of its profits to charity. Ecclesiastical has been providing a range of personal insurances, financial advice and investment services for the Church and community for more than a century. Today Ecclesiastical provides a range of personal insurances and financial services including home, wedding and travel insurance, savings and investments, independent financial advice, life assurance and protection, mortgage advice, pensions and funeral plans through their partner company. They also offer a specialist commercial insurance for churches, church halls, charities, historic buildings and care sector organizations, plus clerical and church supplies through CPS. *Chairman:* Mr Will Samuel. *Group Chief Executive:* Mr Michael Tripp, Beaufort House, Brunswick Rd, Gloucester, GL1 1JZ *Tel:* 0845 777 3322
Fax: 01452 304818
email: information@ecclesiastical.com
Web: www.ecclesiastical.com

Ecclesiastical Law Society
Founded in 1987 to promote the study of ecclesiastical law, through the education of office bearers and practitioners in the ecclesiastical courts, the enlargement of knowledge of ecclesiastical law among clergy and laity of the Anglican Communion, and assistance in matters of ecclesiastical law to the General Synod, Convocations, bishops and church dignitaries. *President:* Dr Sheila Cameron QC CBE. *Chairman:* The Bishop of Guildford. *Secretary:* Mr Howard Dellar. *Deputy Secretary:* Mr Stephen Borton, 1 The Sanctuary, London, SW1P 3JT
Tel: 020 7222 5381
Fax: 020 7799 2781
email: info@ecclawsoc.org.uk
Web: www.ecclawsoc.org.uk

Ecclesiological Society
For those who love churches. Studies the arts, architecture and liturgy of the Christian Church by meetings, tours and publications. *President:* David Stancliffe. *Chairman of the Council:* Trevor

Cooper. *Honorary Membership Secretary:* Valerie Hitchman, PO Box 287, New Malden, KT3 4YT
Tel: 020 8942 2111/07718 155541
email: admin@ecclsoc.org
Web: www.ecclsoc.org

Ecumenical Council for Corporate Responsibility (ECCR)
ECCR, founded in 1989, is a church-based investor coalition and membership organization working for economic justice, human rights, environmental stewardship, and corporate and investor responsibility. It undertakes research, advocacy and dialogue with companies and investors and seeks to influence company policy and practice and to raise awareness of corporate and investor responsibility issues among the British and Irish churches, the investor community and the general public. It is a Body in Association with Churches Together in Britain and Ireland and a company limited by guarantee, registered in England and Wales. *Researcher:* Suzanne Ismail. *Coordinator:* Miles Litvinoff. *Administrator:* Binia Nightingale. *Church and Membership Relations Officer:* Helen Boothroyd, PO Box 500, Oxford, OX1 1ZL *Tel:* 01865 245 349 (Admin)
075 0393 1172 (Membership)
email: info@eccr.org.uk
Web: www.eccr.org.uk

Ecumenical Society of the Blessed Virgin Mary
Founded in London in 1967, 'to advance the study at various levels of the place of the Blessed Virgin Mary in the Church under Christ and to promote ecumenical devotion'. Patrons: the Archbishop of Canterbury, the Archbishop of Westminster, Archbishop Gregorios of Thyateira, Revd Dr John Newton. *General Secretary:* Fr W. McLoughlin. *Hon Treasurer:* Mr F. O'Brien. *Publications Secretary:* Mr D. Carter. *Constitution Secretary:* Revd V. Cassam. *Secretary:* Mr J. P. Farrelly, 11 Belmont Rd, Wallington, SM6 8TE
Tel: 020 8647 5992
email: gensec@esbvm.org.uk
2nd email: j.farrelly.123@btinternet.com
Web: www.esbvm.org.uk

Elizabeth Finn Care
Elizabeth Finn Care gives grants and support to people struggling to cope with sudden or unexpected changes in their circumstances. We provide a financial and supportive safety net for people from over 120 occupations. Elizabeth Finn Care helps by providing both one-off and ongoing financial help, tailored to individual circumstances, as well as emotional support through our experienced caseworkers and national volunteer network. In 2007 we founded Turn2us, a charity offering website and helpline services designed to help people in financial need, and those who support them, access the welfare benefits and grants available to them. Turn2us and EFC joined together as a single charity with effect from October 2009. *Chief Exec:* Matthew Sykes. *Director of Income Generation and Communications:* Malcolm Tyndall, Hythe House, 200 Shepherds Bush Rd, London, W6 7NL
Tel: 020 8834 9200/0800 413 220 (helpline)
Fax: 020 7396 6739
email: info@elizabethfinn.org.uk
Web: www.elizabethfinncare.org.uk / www.turn2us.org.uk

Elland Society Ordination Fund
Grants are made to applicants who are evangelical in conviction and who are in either residential or non-residential training for ordination in the Church of England. Priority is given to ordinands who are sponsored by dioceses in the Province of York or who intend to serve their title in that Province. Grants are usually to help those with unexpected or special financial needs which were not included in their main Church grant (if any). *Secretary/Treasurer:* Revd Colin Judd, 57 Grosvenor Road, Shipley, BD18 4RB
Tel: 01274 584775
email: thejudds@saltsvillage.wanadoo.co.uk
Web: www.ellandsociety.co.uk

English Churches Housing Group
In 2006 ECMG merged with Riverside Housing to become their specialist provider of sheltered and supported housing services. ECMG has gone on to win national awards for its work and each year provides housing and support for over 10,000 people across 170 local authorities. *Chair:* Mr Philip Raw. *Managing Director:* Derek Caren, 49 Western Boulevard, Leicester, LE2 7HN
Tel: 0845 155 9002 (customers)
0151 295 6518 (customers)
email: enquiries@echg.org.uk
Web: www.echg.org.uk

English Clergy Association
Founded 1938, the Association seeks to sustain in fellowship all Clerks in Holy Orders in their vocation and ministry within the Church of England, promoting in every available way the good of English parish and cathedral life and the welfare of clergy. Related Trustees give discretionary clergy holiday grants upon application to the Hon Almoner. The Association seeks to foster the independence within the Established Church of all clergy whether in freehold office or not, and broadly supports the patronage system. Publishes twice-yearly *Parson and Parish* magazine. Lay members may be admitted. Subscription £10 p.a. (£5 retired/ordinands). *Patron:* The Bishop of London. *Chairman:* Revd John Masding. *Deputy Chairman:* Mrs Margaret Laird. *Vice-Chairman:* Revd Jonathan Redvers Harris, Office Address: The Old School, Norton Hawkfield, Bristol, BS39 4HB *Tel:* 01275 830017/01983 565953/
Fax: 01275 830017
email: benoporto-eca@yahoo.co.uk
Web: www.clergyassoc.co.uk

Evangelical Alliance
Founded in 1846 as a representative body with denominational, congregational, organizational and individual supporters, its vision is to unite evangelicals and to provide an evangelical voice in the public square. Also aims to encourage action among evangelicals leading to spiritual and social transformation in the UK. Operates in England, Northern Ireland, Scotland and Wales. *General Director:* Mr Steve Clifford. *Executive Director – England and Churches in Mission:* Dr Krish Kandiah. *Executive Director – Finance and Operations:* Miss Helen Calder. *Advocacy Director:* Dr David Landrum, Whitefield House, 186 Kennington Park Rd, London, SE11 4BT
Tel: 020 7207 2100
Fax: 020 7210 2150
email: info@eauk.org
Web: www.eauk.org

Faith and Thought
(the operational name of the Victoria Institute or Philosophical Society of Great Britain)
Founded 1865 to enquire into the relationship between the Christian revelation and modern scientific research. Publishes *Faith and Thought new series* in succession to *The Journal of the Transactions of the Victoria Institute* (JTVI); from 1958 *Faith and Thought*; from 1989 *Faith&Thought Bulletin*. Jointly with Christians in Science, since 1989 it sponsors the publication of *Science and Christian Belief*. Charity Registration no. 285871. *President:* Sir John Houghton. *Chairman:* Revd Dr Robert Allaway. *Hon. Treasurer & Membership Secretary:* Revd John Buxton. *Editor & Meetings Secretary:* Reginald S. Luhman, 110 Flemming Avenue, Leigh on Sea, SS9 3AX *Tel:* 01279 422661 (Hon Treasurer & Membership Secretary) 01702 475110 (Editor & Meeting Secretary)
email: drapkerry@gmail.com
Web: www.faithandthought.org.uk

Family Action
Family Action has been the leading provider of services to disadvantaged and socially isolated families since its foundation in 1869. We work with over 45,000 children and families a year by providing practical, emotional and financial support through over 100 services based in communities across England. Family Action works with the whole family and helps to tackle some of the most complex and difficult issues facing families today – including domestic abuse, mental health problems, learning disabilities and severe financial hardship. 501–505 Kingsland Rd, Dalston, London, E8 4AU *Tel:* 020 7241 6251
email: info@family-action.org.uk
Web: www.family-action.org.uk

Farnham Castle International Briefing and Conference Centre
Farnham Castle, the former palace of the bishops of Winchester, offers a unique and special location for church weekend retreats. Several London churches are regular visitors. The castle has 31 en suite bedrooms, including some family rooms, all with television. Facilities include two historic consecrated chapels, a wide choice of conference rooms and five acres of beautifully maintained gardens. Farnham Castle has an excellent dining room and bar. It overlooks the town of Farnham and is only seven minutes by taxi from the railway station. Farnham is 30 miles west of London, with good rail connections to Waterloo station (55 minutes). Special weekend rates are available for groups of over 30 adults. Please contact Teresa Clue, Events Manager, for further information. A video tour is available on the web site. *Chief Executive:* Mr James Twiss. *Director of Marketing & Client Services:* Mr Jeff Toms. *Conference Manager:* Mrs Barbara Milam. *Events Manager:* Teresa Clue, Farnham Castle, Farnham, GU9 0AG
Tel: 01252 721194
email: info@farnhamcastle.com
Web: www.farnhamcastle.com

Federation of Catholic Priests
A federation of priests in communion with the See of Canterbury who have undertaken to live in accordance with Catholic doctrine and practice. It exists for mutual support in propagating, maintaining and defending such doctrine and practice and for the deepening of the spiritual life of members. *Chairman:* Revd Peter Walsh. *Secretary General:* Preb Brian Tubbs, 58 Dorset Avenue, Exeter, EX4 1ND *Tel:* 01392 200506
email: fathertubbs@aol.com
Web: www.priests.org.uk

Feed the Minds
Feed the Minds believes that education saves lives, reduces poverty and builds community. Working in partnership worldwide, Feed the Minds funds a wide variety of innovative, indigenous educational projects. By improving access to knowledge and learning, Feed the Minds helps give people the opportunity to experience life in all its fullness. Registered Charity no. 291333 *President:* Revd David Cornick. *Chair of Trustees:* Dr David Goodbourn. *Director:* Ms Josephine Carlsson, Feed the Minds, Park Place, 12 Lawn Lane, London, SW8 1UD
Tel: 08451 21 21 02/
+44 (0)20 7582 3535 (International)
Fax: +44 (0)20 7735 7617
email: info@feedtheminds.org
Web: www.feedtheminds.org

Fellowship of St Alban and St Sergius
Founded 1928. An unofficial body which fosters understanding and friendship between Eastern Orthodox and Western Christians. *Patron:* The Archbishop of Canterbury. *Presidents:* The Bishop of London and Archbishop Gregorios of Thyateira and Great Britain. *General Secretary:*

Revd Stephen Platt, 1 Canterbury Rd, Oxford, OX2 6LU *Tel:* 01865 552991
email: gensec@sobornost.org
Web: www.sobornost.org

Fellowship of St Nicholas (FSN)
FSN uses its resources to offset the disadvantage, deprivation and abuse of children in need in Sussex. Our current services include 2 centre-based family support and day care services including mobile and outreach, UK on-line centres, youth clubs, nurseries, children's bereavement project and family support. *Chairman:* Mrs Mollie Green. *Chief Executive:* Ms Christine Unsworth, The St Nicholas Centre, 66 London Rd, St Leonards-on-Sea, TN37 6AS *Tel:* 01424 423683/01424 855222
Fax: 01424 460446
email: enquiries@fellowshipofstnicholas.org.uk
Web: www.fsncharity.co.uk

Fellowship of St Therese of Lisieux
Founded in 1997, the centenary year of St Therese's death and in anticipation of her being proclaimed a Doctor of the Church in 1998. Its purpose is to inform members of the Church of England about her teaching and its relevance to Christians of all denominations, and to gain an entry for her in the Anglican calendar of saints. Those who would like to know more about her approach to spirituality and Christian discipleship and share in the interest of others are welcome to join the fellowship. Members commit themselves to learn more about St Therese through reading, study and prayer; pray for other members regularly; take opportunities to spread her message within our churches; meet together once a year for a time of retreat, teaching or pilgrimage; and encourage one another by contact and correspondence as appropriate. *Contact:* Revds Graeme and Sue Parfitt, Brook End, Rectory Gardens, Henbury, Bristol, BS10 7AQ
Tel: 0117 959 0293
email: suegraeme@fish.co.uk
Web: www.geocities.com/fellowship_of_st_therese/

Fellowship of Word and Spirit
Anglican evangelical organization comprising 300 clergy and lay people committed to empowering, equipping and encouraging evangelicals through the development of thoughtful biblical theology for the 21st century using publications, conferences and a network of supportive fellowship. *Honorary President:* Rt Revd Wallace Benn. *Chairman:* Revd Simon Vibert, c/o 86 All Hallows Rd, Bispham, Blackpool, FY2 0AY
email: admin@fows.org
Web: www.fows.org

Forward in Faith
Founded in November 1992, Forward in Faith exists to support all who in conscience are unable to accept the ordination of women to the priesthood or the episcopate. It seeks an ecclesial structure which will continue the orders of bishop and priest as the Church has received them. It offers support to all who need it via a national and local network. It is governed by a council elected by the members of its National Assembly, which meets annually. Through Forward in Faith International, it collaborates with its sister organizations in Australia and North America. It publishes the monthly journal *New Directions*, the quarterly newspaper *Forward/Plus*, the catechetical weekly Pew Sheet *Forward/* and the Sunday School course *Forward Teaching*. *Chairman:* The Bishop of Ebbsfleet. *Director:* Mr Stephen Parkinson, 2A The Cloisters, Gordon Square, London, WC1H 0AG *Tel:* 020 7388 3588
Fax: 020 7387 3539
email: FiF.UK@forwardinfaith.com
Web: www.forwardinfaith.com

Foundation for Church Leadership
The Foundation for Church Leadership (FCL) is an endowed charitable trust: its aims are to facilitate the support and development of emerging and senior church leaders, faith representatives and organizations for the benefit of leadership across the church. The Foundation primarily delivers its objectives through the provision of a series of consultancy and research initiatives. *Chair:* Dame Janet Trotter. *Director:* Julie Farrar, 16 Sycamore Business Park, Copt Hewick, Ripon, HG4 5DF *Tel:* 01765 609167
Fax: 01765 709168
email: director@churchleadershipfoundation.org
Web: www.churchleadershipfoundation.org

Foundation of St Matthias
Considers applications for personal and corporate grants with preference given to higher and further education; applicants from the dioceses of Bath and Wells, Bristol and Gloucester and from former students of the college. This does not preclude applicants from elsewhere. Applications should show how the chosen subject will contribute to the advancement of the Christian religion. Examples of personal study not considered: medicine, veterinary science, engineering, law. Corporate applications should promote projects for the educational training of others and show how the Church's contribution to higher and further education will be enhanced. Closing dates for applications: 31 January, 31 May and 30 September each year. The Trust is a member of the Association of Church College Trusts (see separate entry). *Correspondent:* Miss L. Cox, Diocesan Church House, 23 Great George St, Bristol, BS1 5QZ *Tel:* 0117 906 0100
Fax: 0117 925 0460
email: lynette.cox@bristoldiocese.org
Web: www.stmatthiastrust.org.uk

Frances Ashton's Charity
Supports serving or retired members of the Church of England clergy, or the widows/

widowers thereof, who are in need. The trustees will consider almost any kind of financial hardship; so long as the applicant is a serving or retired member of the Churchof England clergy or the widow/widower thereof. There are only a few exceptions. Where the applicant has an exceptional and urgent need, the trustees will consider applications quickly and at any time. Any urgent applications should be discussed with the adminstrator before applying. Please seek the new applicant form from the administrator. For ordinary applications, the dealine is 1 June annually with decisions in September. *Adminsitrator:* Georgina Fowle, Beech House, Woolston North Cadbury, Somerset, BA22 7BJ
Tel: 07775 717 606
Fax: 03000 123 001
email: francesashton@hotmail.co.uk

Friends of Friendless Churches
Founded 1957 to preserve churches and chapels of architectural or historic interest. Now owns 45 redundant places of worship, half in England and half in Wales. Also administers the Cottam Will Trust, which gives grants for the introduction of works of art into ancient Gothic churches. *President:* The Marquess of Salisbury. *Chairman:* Mr Roger Evans. *Hon Secretary:* Mr John Bowles. *Director:* Mr Matthew Saunders. *Asst Director:* Mrs Alison Du Cane, St Ann's Vestry Hall, 2 Church Entry, London, EC4V 5HB *Tel:* 020 7236 3934
email: office@friendsoffriendlesschurches.org.uk
Web: www.friendsoffriendlesschurches.org.uk

Friends of Julian of Norwich
The cell of Julian of Norwich, a chapel attached to St Julian's Church, Norwich, stands on the site where the 14th-century anchoress wrote her book *Revelations of Divine Love.* The Julian Centre, beside the church, houses a small bookshop and a library of works on Julian and spirituality and welcomes visitors and pilgrims (open Monday to Saturday 10.30 a.m. to 3.30 p.m.). Large parties should book in advance (office hours as above). Accommodation is often available in the small convent beside the church. Quiet days can be arranged. Please contact the Sister in Charge, All Hallows House. The Julian Centre, Rouen Rd, Norwich, NR1 1QT
Tel: 01603 767380 (group bookings)
01603 624738 (accommodation, quiet days)
email: centre@friendsofjulian.org.uk
Web: www.friendsofjulian.org.uk

Friends of Little Gidding, The
Little Gidding is rightly called a 'thin place'. From the seventeenth-century Ferrar family community to T. S. Eliot's visit in 1936 and up to the present time, many have experienced the presence of God at Little Gidding. The Friends (founded in 1947) take a practical and active involvement in the care of the historic church and the old farmhouse – now a retreat centre. It co-ordinates, with the T. S. Eliot Society, an annual Eliot Festival; arranges an annual pilgrimage in May; commemorates Nicholas Ferrar's life on his feast day, 4 December; and supports the provision of accommodation and hospitality for visitors and pilgrims. *Chair:* Simon Kershaw. *Secretary:* Judith Hodgson, c/o Ferrar House, Little Gidding, Huntingdon, PE28 5RJ
Tel: 01832 275343
email: chair@littlegidding.org.uk
Web: www.littlegidding.org.uk

Friends of the Clergy Corporation
See Corporation of the Sons of the Clergy

Friends of the Elderly
Friends of the Elderly has been helping older people since 1905. Our vision is that all older people should retain their independence, dignity and peace of mind. We offer high quality residential and nursing care in 14 care homes, some with dementia units. We support older people to stay living in their own homes with a range of community services including welfare grants for those in financial need, day care, home support, home visiting and telephone befriending. Registered Charity no. 226064 *Patron:* HM The Queen. *Chief Executive:* Richard Furze, 40–42 Ebury St, London, SW1W 0LZ *Tel:* 020 7730 8263
Fax: 020 7259 0154
email: enquiries@fote.co.uk
Web: www.fote.org.uk

Frontier Youth Trust
Founded 1964. Provides training, resources information, support and association for Christians working with disadvantaged young people in the community, whether church-based, unattached or within the youth and community service, particularly in urban/industrial areas. *Chief Executive:* Dr Alastair Jones, Office S15b St George's Community Hub, Great Hampton Row Newtown, Birmingham, B19 3JG
Tel: 0121 687 3505
email: frontier@fyt.org.uk
Web: www.fyt.org.uk

Fulcrum
A network for evangelical clergy and laity. Launched in 2003 at the National Evangelical Anglican Congress in Blackpool, Fulcrum seeks to renew the evangelical centre by giving a voice to a nourishing, generous orthodoxy. It provides support, theological exploration and encouragement for moderate evangelical Anglicans and creates a space in which genuine debate can take place in a spirit of non-defensiveness and gracious disagreement, acknowledging that the clash of ideas can be creative and worthwhile. It has a web site with regularly updated articles from leading evangelical theologians. *President:* Dr Elaine Storkey. *Chair:* Revd Stephen Kuhrt. *Theological Secretary:* Rt Revd Graham Kings.

General Secretary: John Martin, The Rectory, 16 Castle East Street, Bridgnorth Shropshire, WV16 4AL

email: admin@fulcrum-anglican.org.uk
Web: www.fulcrum-anglican.org.uk

Girlguiding UK
Founded 1910. Open to all girls and women between 5 and 65 years regardless of race, faith or any other circumstance. Its purpose is to enable girls to mature into confident, capable and caring women determined, as individuals, to realize their potential in their career, home and personal life, and willing as citizens to contribute to their community and the wider world. Rainbows age 5–7; Brownies age 7–10; Guides age 10–14; Senior Section age 14–25; Leaders age 18 plus. *Chief Guide:* Mrs Liz Burnley. *Chief Executive:* Miss Denise King, 17/19 Buckingham Palace Rd, London, SW1W 0PT *Tel:* 0800 169 5901/020 7834 6242/
Fax: 020 7828 8317
email: join.us@girlguiding.org.uk
Web: www.girlguiding.org.uk

Girls Friendly Society in England and Wales, The
(Campaign name GFS Platform)Established in 1875, GFS Platform works with girls and young women aged 7+. The work focuses on two specific areas, namely four community projects that work with young women between the ages of 14 and 25 who are either pregnant or who have children, and 40 parish-based youth work branches throughout England and Wales that run voluntary youth groups for girls and young women aged 7+. Main activities include reducing social exclusion and building self-esteem by providing social, formal educational and health awareness sessions and generic support in a single gender and non-judgemental environment. GFS Platform offers young women and girls the opportunity to explore their own personal and social development. This enables them to acquire new skills and knowledge, gain confidence, make informed choices and take responsibility for their own lives. *Director:* Joy Lauezzari, Unit 2 Angel Gate, 326 City Rd, London, EC1V 2PT
Tel: 020 7837 9669
Fax: 020 7837 4107
email: annualreport@gfsplatform.org.uk
Web: www.gfsplatform.org.uk

Girls' Brigade England and Wales
An international interdenominational youth organization having as its aim 'to help girls to become followers of the Lord Jesus Christ and through self-control, reverence and sense of responsibility to find true enrichment of life'. *National Director:* Miss Ruth Gilson, PO Box 196, 129 Broadway, Didcot, OX11 8XN
Tel: 01235 510425
Fax: 01235 510429
email: gbco@girlsbrigadeew.org.uk
Web: www.girlsb.org

Greater Churches Network
The Greater Churches Group (now 'Network') was founded in 1991 as an informal association of non-cathedral churches, which, by virtue of their great age, size and of their historical, architectural or ecclesiastical importance, display many of the characteristics of a cathedral and also fulfil a role which is additional to that of a normal parish church. Its aims are to provide help and mutual support in dealing with the special challenges of running a 'cathedral-like' church within the organizational and financial structure of a parish church; to enhance the quality of parish worship in such churches; and to promote wider recognition of the unique position and needs of churches in this category. The group also serves as a channel of communication for other organizations wishing to have contact with churches of this type. *Hon Secretary:* Ms Philippa Shaw, Tewkesbury Abbey Office, Church Street, Tewkesbury, Gloucestershire, GL20 5RZ
Tel: 01684 856141
email: philippa.shaw@tewkesburyabbey.org.uk

Greenbelt Festivals
Greenbelt Festival takes place annually over the August Bank Holiday weekend, gathering together artists, musicians, speakers and performers, alongside 20,000 festivalgoers at Cheltenham Racecourse. Its 40–year history is firmly rooted within a Christian tradition which is politically and culturally engaged. The festival is a family-friendly celebration, inclusive and accepting of all, regardless of ethnicity, gender, sexuality, background or belief. *Chair:* Andy Turner. *Director:* Paul Northup, Greenbelt Festivals Ltd, 1B Snowhill Court, London, EC1A 2EJ
Tel: 020 7374 2755 (office)
020 7874 2760 (ticket line)
email: info@greenbelt.org.uk
Web: www.greenbelt.org.uk

Grubb Institute, The
The Grubb Institute seeks to contribute to the repair, healing and transformation of the world, which we have all contributed to creating both consciously and unconsciously. It enables leaders to work with their experience of human systems, institutions and personal relations in the context of Christ's activity, using insights and concepts developed from the human sciences and Christian theology and values. It provides consultancy, action research and learning events for people of all faiths or of none, from voluntary organizations, education, health, social care, criminal justice agencies, and business. As a Christian foundation, it has worked since 1969 with leaders in churches and dioceses, religious orders and agencies worldwide. *Executive Director:* Bruce Irvine. *Senior Organizational Analysts:* Jean Reed, Colin Quine, John Bazalgette, Vega Roberts. *Organizational Analyst:* Revd Rosy

Fairhurst, The Grubb Institute, Cloudesley Street, London, N1 0HU *Tel:* 020 7278 8061
Fax: 020 7278 0728
email: info@grubb.org.uk
Web: www.grubb.org.uk

Guild of All Souls
Founded 1873 as an intercessory guild, caring for the dying, the dead and the bereaved. Open to members of the Church of England and Churches in communion with her and any who share the objects of the Guild. Chantry chapel at Walsingham and at St Stephen's, Gloucester Rd, London. Patron of 41 livings of the Catholic tradition. *President:* The Bishop of Richborough. *General Secretary:* David Llewelyn Morgan. *Warden:* Louis A. Lewis. *Hon Treasurer:* Revd Paul E. Jones, Royal London House, 22–25 Finsbury Square, London, EC2A 1DX *Tel:* 0207 920 6468/ 01371 830132
Fax: 01371 831430
email: contact@guildofallsouls.org.uk
Web: www.guildofallsouls.org.uk

Guild of Church Braillists
The Guild consists of a group of people who give their services to help blind readers by transcribing a variety of religious literature into Braille. Requests are welcome from individual readers for books, special services, etc. All other productions are sent to the National Library for the Blind or the Library of the RNIB. For further details contact the Secretary. *Secretary:* Mary Hazlewood, Farthings, Pennymoor, Tiverton Devon, EX16 8LF *Tel:* 01727 845183
email: info@gocb.org
Web: www.gocb.org

Guild of Church Musicians
Patrons: The Archbishop of Canterbury; the Archbishop of Westminster. Founded in 1888, but since 1961 has administered the Archbishops' Certificate in Church Music (ACert.CM) on behalf of the Archbishops of Canterbury and Westminster. This Certificate is a minimum qualification for church organists, choir trainers, cantors, choristers and leaders of instrumental groups and is fully ecumenical. The Archbishops' Award in Church Music is available for those who wish to be examined in practical skills only and the Guild's Preliminary Certificate in Church Music is aimed at young people and those starting in church music. Since 2002 the new qualification of Archbishops' Certificate in Public Worship (ACert.PW), for all who lead public worship, both clerical and lay, has been established. There is also a Fellowship examination (FGCM). *General Secretary:* Mr John Ewington OBE. *Warden:* Revd Canon Jeremy Haselock. *President:* Dr Mary Archer. *Chairman Academic Board:* Revd Canon Peter Moger. *Examinations Secretary:* Dr Helen Burrows, St Katharine Cree Church, 86 Leadenhall St, London, EC3A 3DH
Tel: 01883 743168
email: JohnMusicsure@orbixmail.co.uk
Web: www.churchmusicians.org

Guild of Health
The Guild of Health is an ecumenical Christian society serving the Healing Ministry which was founded (in 1904) to bring together doctors and clergy, in the first instance, to work together for health and wellbeing. We have a long history of the practice of meditation and intercessory prayer within the Christian tradition. More than a century later, we are still seeking to offer resources for healing in a variety of settings, through retreats, seminars and prayer groups. We are proud to be supporting the work of three organizations, sympathetic to our mission, who are engaged in specific aspects of healing and health: the Durham Project for Spirituality, Theology and Health; Saint Marylebone Healing and Counselling Centre; and Burrswood Christian Hospital (with particular regard to those suffering from ME). For further information please contact us or visit our website.Further information about the Guild or any of these projects can be obtained from: The Guild of Health at any of the following: *President:* Rt Revd John Pritchard. *Chair:* Revd Roger Hoath. *Membership Secretary:* Mrs Rosie Press, c/o St Marylebone Parish Church, 17 Marylebone Rd, London, NW1 5LT
Tel: 020 7563 1389
email: guildofhealth@stmarylebone.org
2nd email: enquiries@gohealth.org.uk (membership)
Web: www.gohealth.org.uk

Guild of Pastoral Psychology
The Guild offers a meeting ground for all interested in the relationship between religion and depth psychology, particularly the work of C. G. Jung and his followers. Depth psychology has contributed many new insights into the meaning of religion and its symbols and their relevance to everyday life. The Guild has monthly lectures in central London, a day conference in London in the spring and a three-day summer conference at Oxford. Further information and details of membership available from the Administrator. *Secretary:* Robert Macdonald, Flat 5, 75 Hatton St, London, NW8 0PL *Tel:* 020 7724 7282
email: guild@macdonaldmedia.co.uk
Web: www.guildofpastoralpsychology.org.uk

Guild of Servants of the Sanctuary
Founded 1898 to raise the spiritual standard of Servers, to promote friendship among them and to encourage attendance at Holy Communion in addition to times of duty. *Warden:* Revd David Moore. *Secretary General:* Mr Terry Doughty, 7 Church Ave, Leicester, LE3 6AJ
Tel: 0116 262 0308
email: secretary.general@gssonline.org.uk
Web: www.gssonline.org.uk

Guild of St Leonard
The Guild was founded by the Revd John Sankey. Its object is to pray for all prisoners, those on licence or probation and for all who care for them. The Guild publishes a quarterly Intercession Paper. *Warden:* Rt Revd Lloyd Rees. *Secretary:* Revd Andrew Nichols, The Chaplain's Office, HMP Ford, Arundel, BN18 0BX
Tel: 01903 663000

Guild of St Raphael
Founded 1915 to work for the restoration of the Ministry of Healing as part of the normal function of the Church, by preparing the sick for all ministries of healing, by teaching the need of repentance and faith, by making use of the Sacraments of Healing and by Intercession. *Organizing Secretary:* Mrs Hanna Hart. *Warden:* Rt Revd N. Reade. *Sub-Warden:* Canon Paul Nener. *Editor of 'Chrism':* Prof Helen Leathard, 1a Snaetell Ave, Tuebrook, Liverpool, L13 7HA
Tel: 0151 228 3193/0151 228 2023
Fax: 0151 228 3193
email: office@guildofstraphael.org.uk
Web: www.guildofstraphael.org.uk

Harnhill Centre of Christian Healing
A resource centre for the ministry of Christian Healing through counselling, prayer, quiet days, teaching courses and Christian Healing Services. The Centre provides residential accommodation. *Chairman:* Dr David Wells. *Chaplain/Warden:* Revd Paul Springate, Harnhill Manor, Cirencester, GL7 5PX *Tel:* 01285 850283
Fax: 01285 850519
email: office@harnhillcentre.org.uk
Web: www.harnhillcentre.org.uk

Henry Bradshaw Society
Founded 1890 for printing liturgical texts from manuscripts and rare editions of service books, etc. For available texts, please consult the Society's web site. *Secretary:* Dr Nicolas Bell, Music Collections, The British Library, 96 Euston Rd, London, NW1 2OB *email:* nicolas.bell@bl.uk
Web: www.henrybradshawsociety.org

Highbury Centre
Christian guesthouse on quiet private road with ample free on-street parking. Reductions for missionaries/clergy. *Manager:* Mrs S. Scalora, 20–26 Aberdeen Park, Highbury, London, N5 2BJ
Tel: 020 7226 2663
email: enquiries@thehighburycentre.org
Web: www.thehighburycentre.org

Hockerill Educational Foundation
The Foundation makes personal awards to teachers, intending teachers and others in further or higher education, with a priority for the teaching of Religious Education. It does not make awards to those training for ordination, mission, social work or counselling, or to children at school. The Foundation makes corporate grants to support the development of religious education, particularly in the Dioceses of Chelmsford and St Albans. Full details of eligibility for awards can be found on our website at www.hockerillfoundation.org.uk. The applications deadline is 31 March each year. Working with NATRE it provides the Hockerill NATRE Prize for Innovation in the teaching of Religious Education. Available in both the Primary and Secondary sectors, this annual award gives a monetary prize to the school and an educational bursary to the teacher. It is a member of the Association of Church College Trusts (see separate entry), and the RE Council. *Correspondent:* Mr Derek J. Humphrey, 3 The Swallows, Harlow, Essex, CM17 0AR *Tel:* 01279 420855
Fax: 560 3140931
email: info@hockerillfoundation.org.uk
Web: www.hockerillfoundation.org.uk

Holy Rood House, Centre for Health and Pastoral Care
Opened in 1993, the Centre is a friendly house with a residential community. The house offers a gentle and holistic approach in a Christian environment where individuals or groups, of all ages and backgrounds, can work towards their own healing and explore their spiritual journey within an atmosphere of acceptance, love and openness. Professional counsellors and therapists, working closely with the medical profession, offer support at times of bereavement, abuse, addiction, relationship breakdown or illness, and creative arts and stress management play an important role in the healing process. Holy Rood House ministers within an awareness of justice and peace to daily or residential guests, and is also the home of the Centre for the Study of Theology and Health. *Patron:* The Archbishop of Canterbury. *Vice-Patron:* Prof Mary Grey. *Joint Exec Directors:* Revd Stanley and Revd Elizabeth Baxter. *Director,Therapeutic Care:* Jan Younger. *Director, Centre for Study of Theology & Health:* Revd Dr Jan Berry, 10 Sowerby Rd, Sowerby, Thirsk, YO7 1HX *Tel:* 01845 522580/01845 522004
Fax: 01845 527300
email: enquiries@holyroodhouse.org.uk
Web: www.holyroodhouse.freeuk.com

Homes for Retired Clergy
See separate entries for Beauchamp Community and College of St Barnabas.

House of St Barnabas in Soho
Chief Executive: Andy Griffiths, 1 Greek St, Soho, London, W1D 4NQ *Tel:* 020 7437 1894
Fax: 020 7434 1746
email: andy.griffiths@houseofstbarnabas.org.uk
Web: www.houseofstbarnabas.org.uk

Hymn Society of Great Britain and Ireland
Founded in 1936 to encourage study and research into hymns, both words and music; to promote

ORGANIZATIONS

good standards of hymn singing and to encourage the discerning use of hymns and songs in worship. The Society publishes a quarterly magazine and there is a three-day annual conference. Further information and details of membership from the Secretary. *Secretary:* Revd Robert A. Canham, Windrush, Braithwaite, Keswick CA12 5SZ *Tel:* 017 687 78054
email: robcanham.causeypike@gmail.com
Web: www.hymnsocietygbi.org.uk

Incorporated Church Building Society
Founded 1818. The Incorporated Church Building Society is managed by the National Churches Trust. Registered Charity no. 212752. *Patron:* HM The Queen. *Chairman:* Very Revd Henry Stapleton FSA. *Chief Executive:* Andrew Edwards. *Grants Manager:* Alison Pollard, 31 Newbury St, London, EC1A 7HU *Tel:* 020 7600 6090
Fax: 020 7796 2442
email: info@nationalchurchestrust.org
Web: www.nationalchurchestrust.org

Industrial Christian Fellowship
Founded in 1918 as a successor to the Navvy Mission (1877) and incorporating the Christian Social Union, ICF is a nationwide ecumenical network that provides support for Christians who want to apply their faith in fresh and creative ways in the everyday working world. A recent new initiative to make links between the local church and working life is the 'Take your Minister to Work' project. ICF provides resources, including liturgy and prayers for personal and corporate use, reflections and services related to work; a newsletter and occasional papers; and the quarterly journal 'Faith in Business' (in association with the Ridley Hall Foundation). Close links with other groups and agencies involved with faith and work are maintained. Membership is open to individuals and organizations. *Chair:* Revd Phil Jump. *Secretary:* Mrs Ann Wright. *Treasurer:* Revd Jeremy Brown, PO Box 414, Horley, RH6 8WL
Tel: 01293 821322
email: wright@btinternet.com *Web:* www.icf-online.org

Industrial Mission Association
The Industrial Mission Association (IMA) is a national and ecumenical association, mainly, though not exclusively, comprised of chaplains appointed to places of work throughout the UK. *Moderator:* Stephen Hazlett. *Membership Secretary:* Revd Crispin White. *Honorary Treasurer:* Adrian Thomas. *Hon Secretary:* David Wrighton, 34 Chalvington Rd, Chandlers Ford, Eastleigh, SO53 3DX *Tel:* 0238 026 1146 (Secretary)
0190 383 0785 (Membership Secretary)
email: wrigdgshim@aol.com
Web: http://www.industrialmission.org.uk/cms/

INFORM
Inform is an independent charity founded in 1988 with funding from the British Home Office and mainstream Churches with the aim of obtaining and making available accurate, balanced and up-to-date information about alternative spirituality and new religious movements or 'cults'. It has a large collection of data on computer and in various other forms (books, articles, cuttings, videos and cassettes), and is in touch with an international network of scholars and other specialists. People with questions or concerns about new religious movements or alternative spirituality should contact the Inform office, which is based at the London School of Economics, between 10 a.m. and 4.30 p.m., Mondays to Fridays. *Hon Director:* Prof Eileen Barker. *Deputy Director:* Amanda van Eck Duymaer van Twist. *Research Officers:* Sarah Harvey and Suzanne Newcombe. *Assistant Research Officers:* Silke Steidinger, Matthew Francis and Adviya Khan. *Administrative Officer:* Sibyl Macfarlane, LSE, Houghton St, London, WC2A 2AE
Tel: 020 7955 7654 (Information line)
email: INFORM@LSE.ac.uk
Web: www.inform.ac

Inter Faith Network for the UK
Established in 1987 to encourage contact and dialogue between different faith communities in the United Kingdom. It aims to advance public knowledge and mutual understanding of the teaching, traditions and practices of the different faith communities in Britain, including an awareness of their distinctive features and of their common ground, and to promote good relations between persons of different faiths. Its member organizations include representative bodies from the Baha'i, Buddhist, Christian, Hindu, Jain, Jewish, Muslim, Sikh and Zoroastrian communities; national, regional and local inter faith bodies; and academic institutions and educational bodies concerned with inter faith issues. *Director:* Dr Harriet Crabtree. *Co-Chairs:* Rt Revd Dr Alastair Redfern and Dr Manazir Ahsan, 2 Grosvenor Gardens, London, SW1W 0DH *Tel:* 020 7730 0410
Fax: 020 7730 0414
email: ifnet@interfaith.org.uk
Web: www.interfaith.org.uk

Intercontinental Church Society
Founded 1823. ICS makes known the Christ of the Scriptures to people who speak English. It is a patronage society (nominating chaplains for international Anglican churches abroad), owns church buildings, and a mission agency engaged in church planting, growth and outreach to tourists, principally in Europe and around the Mediterranean; and publishes the *Directory of English-speaking Churches Abroad*. *President:* Viscount Brentford. *General Manager:* Mr David Healey,

Unit 11, Ensign Business Centre, Westwood Way, Westwood Business Park, Coventry CV4 8JP
Tel: 024 7646 3940
email: enquiries@ics-uk.org
Web: www.ics-uk.org

International Ecumenical Fellowship – British Region
IEF is a community of Christians both lay and ordained, with regional groups in Belgium, Czech Republic, France, Germany, Great Britain, Hungary, Poland, Romania, Slovak Republic and Spain. It also has individual members in various other countries. Through annual international gatherings and smaller regional groups, Christians from Catholic, Orthodox and Protestant traditions meet to worship, pray, study and enjoy fellowship together. IEF tries to strengthen the spirit of ecumenism and international friendship. IEF practises eucharistic hospitality as far as church discipline and individual conscience permit. *President of British Region:* Vacancy. *Secretary:* Revd C. R. Hardiman. *Treasurer:* Mr G. Morton, 20 Kent Place, South Shields, NE34 6PU *Tel:* 0191 456 1943
email: cyntthiahardiman@blueyonder.co.uk
Web: www.ief-oecumenica.org

Interserve
Interserve is an interdenominational, evangelical mission agency with over 800 full-time Christian professionals working across Asia, the Arab World, and among ethnic groups in England and Wales. Interservers work in many different ministries, seeking to share the love of Christ through everything they say and do. All Christians with a burden to respond to Jesus' commission and make disciples of all nations are welcomed for both long and short term periods of service, with the aim of seeing lives and communities transformed through encounter with Jesus Christ. *Chairman:* Tim Baynes-Clarke. *National Director:* Steve Bell, 5/6 Walker Avenue, Wolverton Mills, Milton Keynes, MK12 5TW *Tel:* 01908 552700
Fax: 01908 552779
email: enquiries@isewi.org
Web: www.interserveonline.org.uk

Journeying
Journeying is an ecumenical oragnization which takes small groups of people on holiday in an informal Christian ambience to the more off-the-beaten-track parts of Britain and Ireland. What we offer is almost certainly unique in Britain. Its origins lie in Celtic spirituality and most of our trips still reflect that approach. Pilgrimage too has been part of our story from the earliest days and that aspect continues to form a thread woven through all that we do. Journeying was founded in 2009 – the organization is a development of Pilgrim Adventure, founded in 1988, *Co-ordinators:* Cate Macfarlane, Paul Heppleston, David Gleed, 1 Westfields, Saffron Walden, Essex, CB11 3DZ *Tel:* 01799 513750
email: info@journeying.co.uk
Web: www.journeying.co.uk

Jubilate Group
An association of authors and musicians formed in 1974 for the purpose of publishing material for contemporary worship: *Hymns for Today's Church, Church Family Worship, Carols for Today, Carol Praise, Let's Praise!* 1 and 2, *Prayers for the People, Psalms for Today, Songs from the Psalms, The Dramatised Bible, The Wedding Book, Hymns for the People, World Praise* 1 and 2 and *Sing Glory. Chairman:* Revd Steve James. *Secretary:* David Peacock. *Copyright Managers:* Mrs M. Williams, Mr P. Williams, 4 Thorne Park Rd, Chelston, Torquay, TQ2 6RX *Tel:* 01803 607754
Fax: 01803 605682
email: copyrightmanager@jubilate.co.uk
Web: www.jubilate.co.uk

Julian Meetings, The
A network of Christian contemplative prayer groups, begun in Britain in 1973. There are now about 350 groups in Great Britain and some in Australia, Canada, Ireland, Southern Africa and the USA. Ecumenical. Magazine three times a year. *Contact:* Deidre Morris, 263 Park Lodge Lane, Wakefield, WF1 4HY *Tel:* 01924 369437
email: gb@julianmeetings.org
Web: www.julianmeetings.org

Keswick Convention
The Keswick Convention is the main event organised annually by Keswick Ministries and has been taking place since 1875. It offers something for everyone – life-changing Bible teaching, uplifting worship and great fellowship combined with the chance to relax and enjoy a holiday in the wonderful setting of the Lake District. *Chairman:* Mr John Risbridger. *General Director:* Mr David Bradley. *Operations Manager:* Mr Simon Overend, Keswick Convention Trust, Skiddaw St, Keswick, CA12 4BY *Tel:* 01768 780075
Fax: 01768 775276
email: info@keswickministries.org
Web: www.keswickministries.org

Keswick Hall Trust Charity
The Trustees' spending gives priority to their own local initiatives, but they also have limited funds and give grants in response to personal or corporate applicants for research or study in religious education. Within this field, they give priority to teachers or student teachers and to work in East Anglia. Member of the Association of Church College Trusts (see separate entry). Applications should be made online only at our website www.keswickhalltrust.org.uk *Executive*

ORGANIZATIONS

Officer: Malcolm Green, Keswick Hall Trust, PO Box 307, Woodbridge, IP13 6WL
Tel: 07760 433 409
email: admin@keswickhalltrust.org.uk
Web: www.keswickhalltrust.org.uk

Keychange Charity
(formerly Christian Alliance)
Established 1920. Offers care, acceptance and Christian community to people in need through the provision of residential care for frail elderly people and supported accommodation for young homeless people. *Chief Executive:* Graham Waters, 5 St George's Mews, 43 Westminster Bridge Rd, London, SE1 7JB *Tel:* 020 7633 0533
Fax: 020 7928 1872
email: info@keychange.org.uk
Web: www.keychange.org.uk

Korean Mission Partnership
Founded in 1889 by Edward White Benson, Archbishop of Canterbury, as the Church of England Mission to Korea, the name was changed in 1993 when the Province of Korea was inaugurated. The name reflects the two-way nature of our mission today. Support goes to Korea by way of prayer, interest and funding. The Province has sent a priest from Seoul to run the Korean Chaplaincy in the Diocese of London, ministering to Korean people who live mainly in and around the Home Counties. *President:* The Primate of Korea . *Chairman:* Revd Luke Lee. *Hon Admin Secretary:* Revd Martin Fletcher. *Hon Treasurer:* Mr Edwin Ward, The Rectory, Rectory Rd, Tiptree, CO5 0SX *Tel:* 01621 815260/01296 423133/
email: luke.gh.lee@googlemail.com
Web: www.koreanmission.org

Langley House Trust
Founded in 1958, the Langley House Trust, a national Christian charity, provides care and rehabilitation for ex-offenders (and those at risk of offending) as they work towards crime-free independence and reintegration into society. The Trust aims to help ex-offenders address their physical, emotional, mental and spiritual needs. It currently runs 16 residential projects and move-on accommodation across the UK (including a drug rehabilitation centre, and women's projects) providing bedspaces for ex-offenders, including those who are hard to place and those who have special needs, such as mental disorders. The Trust bases its services on Christian beliefs and values but is open to men and women of any or no faith. *Chairman:* Anthony Howlett-Bolton. *Chief Exec:* Steve Robinson. *Corporate Operations Director:* Tracy Wild. *Corporate Services Director:* Ken Brown. *Corporate Development Director:* Andrew Lerigo, PO Box 181, Witney, OX28 6WD *Tel:* 01993 774075
Fax: 01993 772425
email: info@langleyhousetrust.org
Web: www.langleyhousetrust.org

Latimer Trust
The Latimer Trust is dedicated to providing a biblical and considered response to the issues facing today's Anglican Communion. Through a range of resources it is continuing and developing the work of Latimer House, founded in Oxford in the 1960s. Reg. Charity no. 1084337. *Chairman of the Council:* Revd Dr Mark Burkill. *Director of Research:* Revd Dr Gerald Bray, c/o Oak Hill College, Chase Side, London, N14 4PS
Tel: 020 8449 0467 ext. 227
email: administrator@latimertrust.org
Web: www.latimertrust.org

Lee Abbey Household Communities
There are two household communities based in Urban Priority Areas in Birmingham and Bristol. Community members live under a common rule of life and seek to be involved in their local community and church. *Contact:* Gill Arbuthnot, 101 Dorridge Rd, Dorridge, Solihull, B93 8BS
Tel: 0121 327 0095/01567 776558/
Web: www.leeabbey.org.uk/households/

Lee Abbey International Students' Club
Founded in 1964 by the Lee Abbey Fellowship as a ministry to students of all nationalities, the Club provides long- and short-term hostel accommodation for students of all faiths or none and is served by a Christian community, which consists of young people from all over the world. Applications are invited from anyone interested in joining the community, residing as a student or staying as a holiday-maker. *Warden:* Canon Trevor Hubble, 57–67 Lexham Gardens, London, W8 6JJ *Tel:* 020 7373 7242
Fax: 020 7244 8702
email: personnel@leeabbeylondon.com
2nd email: accommodation@leeabbeylondon.com
Web: www.leeabbeylondon.com

Leprosy Mission, The
We are an international Christian development organization. Inspired by our Christian values, we work in equal partnership with people affected by leprosy and with other stakeholders. As partners, together we transform lives through advocacy and the enablement of physical, social, economic and spiritual development of individuals and communities affected by leprosy and other disabilities. *National Director:* Peter A. Walker, Goldhay Way, Orton Goldhay, Peterborough, PE2 5GZ *Tel:* 01733 370505
Fax: 01733 404880
email: post@tlmew.org.uk
Web: www.leprosymission.org.uk

Lesbian and Gay Christian Movement
LGCM has four principal aims: to encourage fellowship, friendship and support among lesbian and gay Christians through prayer, study and action; to help the whole Church examine its understanding of human sexuality and to work

for positive acceptance of gay relationships; to encourage members to witness to their Christian faith within the gay community and to their convictions about human sexuality within the Church; to maintain and strengthen links with other lesbian and gay Christian groups both in Britain and elsewhere. An extensive network of local groups exists and a wide range of resources are available. *Chief Executive:* Revd Richard Kirker, Oxford House, Derbyshire St, Bethnal Green, London, E2 6HG
Tel and Fax: 020 7739 1249
email: lgcm@lgcm.org.uk
Web: www.lgcm.org.uk

Li Tim-Oi Foundation
The Foundation was launched on the 50th anniversary of the priesting of the first Anglican woman, Florence Li Tim-Oi, on 25 January 1944. On the centenary of her birth on 5 May 2007 the Foundation was relaunched with the mantra: 'It takes ONE woman'. The Foundation has allocated more than £550,000 in bursaries to empower over 275 Anglican women in the Two-thirds World of the 'South' to become agents for change in church and society. About 50 new requests for help a year, particularly from Africa, continue to outstrip available funds. Thus every donation from parishes and individuals is put to effective use. Several have chosen the Foundation to benefit in lieu of presents at birthdays, weddings, anniversaries, Christmas and priesting, or of funeral flowers. Bequests, especially from women in gratitude for their own priesting, are particularly welcome. *Patrons:* The Archbishop of Canterbury, The Archbishop of Kenya, The Archbishop of the Congo, The Rt Rev Victoria Matthews, Bishop K. H. Ting, Baroness Perry of Southwark and Mrs Jane Williams.. *Chair:* Canon Pamela Wilding MBE. *Secretary:* Canon Christopher Hall, The Knowle, Deddington, Banbury, OX15 0TB
Tel: 01869 338225
Fax: 0871 750 3483
email: achall@globalnet.co.uk
Web: www.ittakesonewoman.org / www.litim-oi.org

Librarians' Christian Fellowship
Constituted 1976 to provide opportunities for Christian librarians to consider issues in librarianship from a Christian standpoint, and to promote opportunities for presenting the Christian faith to people working in libraries of all kinds. *Hon Secretary:* Graham Hedges, 34 Thurlestone Ave, Ilford, IG3 9DU
Tel: 020 8599 1310
email: secretary@librarianscf.org.uk
Web: www.librarianscf.org.uk

Liddon Trust
See Society of the Faith (Incorporated).

Lincoln Theological Institute
Inaugurated in 1997 and now based at the University of Manchester, the Institute's primary aim is to undertake, promote and support theological enquiry into contemporary society and thereby to practise theology in the fullest sense. It focuses on postgraduate and postdoctoral research, working closely with colleagues in the Religions and Theology subject area. Core areas for research include: (1) place, locality, habitation and ecology; (2) global threats and powers; (3) religion and civil society; (4) technology, limits and transformation; (5) power and institutions (including the church); (6) liberation, political, ecologial and public theologies; (7) culture – includng religious cultures – and resources of hope. Students wishing to study under the auspices of the Institute may enrol through the University of Manchester for Master's and Doctoral degree programmes. Formal and informal enquiries from prospective students are encouraged. The Lincoln Theological Institute originated from Lincoln Theological College, founded in 1874 as an ordination training college. Since 2003 the Institute has been a fully integrated research unit within the University of Manchester. For further information please contact the Director. *Director:* Dr Peter M. Scott. *Research Associate:* Dr Susannah M. Cornwall, School of Arts, Histories and Cultures, University of Manchester, Oxford Rd, Manchester, M13 9PL
Tel: 0161 275 3064 0161 275 3736
email: peter.scott@manchester.ac.uk
Web: http://www.lincolntheologicalinstitute.com

Livability
(Formerly know as the Shaftesbury Society)
Livability is a new charity, formed by the merger of the Shaftesbury Society and John Grooms. Livability creates choices for disabled people and brings life to local communities. We offer a wide range of services to around 8,000 disabled people and their families, including residential care, supported living, education and accessible holidays. We also provide community organizations with the resources, advice and confidence to transform their neighbourhoods. *Chief Executive:* Mary Bishop, 50 Scrutton St, London, EC2A 4XQ
Tel: 020 7452 2000
Fax: 020 7452 2001
email: info@livability.org.uk
Web: www.livability.org.uk

Liverpool Seafarers Centre
See Mersey Mission to Seafarers, The.

Living Stones
(formerly Church and Community Trust)
An independent organization that offers guidance and information to local churches concerning the more effective use of their resources – buildings, money, people – for worshipping God and serving the community. *Field Workers:* Roger

Munday, Graham Ball, Quoin House, 11 East Park, Crawley, RH10 6AN
Tel and Fax: 01293 431899
email: info@living-stones.org.uk
Web: www.living-stones.org.uk

London City Mission
For over 175 years, LCM has been working with churches to bring the Christian message to the people of London. Today, in the workplace, out on the streets and in the various communities of London, over 300 workers and volunteers are actively seeking to bring Christian values and hope to those they meet. *Chairman:* Mark Harding. *Chief Executive:* Revd Dr John Nicholls, Nasmith House, 175 Tower Bridge Rd, London, SE1 2AH *Tel:* 020 7407 7585
Fax: 020 7403 6711
email: enquiries@lcm.org.uk
Web: www.lcm.org.uk

Lord Wharton's Charity
Founded 1696 to distribute Bibles and other religious books to children and young people of all denominations in all counties of the United Kingdom and Northern Ireland. *Clerk to the Trustees:* Mrs B. Edwards, Magnolia Cottage, Harrowbeer Lane, Yelverton, PL20 6EA
Tel and Fax: 01822 852636
email: edwardsbobbarbara@btinternet.com

Marshall's Charity
Founded 1627. Makes grants for (1) building, purchasing or modernizing parsonages of the Church of England or the Church in Wales, (2) repairs to churches in Kent, Surrey and Lincolnshire. *Clerk to the Trustees:* Mrs Catherine Dawkins, Marshall House, 66 Newcomen St, London, SE1 1YT *Tel:* 020 7407 2979
Fax: 020 7403 3969
email: grantoffice@marshalls.org.uk
Web: www.marshalls.org.uk

Mediawatch-UK
(Formerly the National Viewers' and Listeners' Association)Mediawatch-UK is a voluntary association which campaigns for family values in the media. We believe that the media we consume inevitably shapes the moral, ethical, social and political values of our culture and we champion the rights of the public to socially responsible broadcasting. Our campaigns include fighting for meaningful protection for children from premature sexualization by the media and from potentially harmful material online. The organization was founded in 1965 by Mary Whitehouse and her associates who were concerned that that television was attacking and undermining family life. Benefits of membership include representation at the highest levels, regular newsletters and updates and assistance to enable members to make theirvoices heard. *Director:* Miss Vivienne Pattison, 3 Willow House, Kennington Rd, Ashford, TN24 0NR
Tel: 01233 633936
Fax: 01233 633836
email: info@mediawatchuk.org
Web: www.mediawatchuk.org

Melanesian Mission
The Melanesian Mission was established in 1854 to buy the first 'Southern Cross' ship for Bishop Selwyn to use for mission work in the islands of Melanesia. Today the Mission supports the Church of Melanesia (including the religious orders) through money, prayer and people – helping the church to fulfil its priorities and work through this vast and isolated region. *Chairman:* Rt Revd Nigel Stock. *Hon. Treasurer:* Mrs Helen Miller. *Executive Officer:* Mrs Katie Drew, 21 The Burlands, Feniton Honiton, Devon, EX14 3UN
email: mission@melanesia.anglican.org
Web: www.melanesia.anglican.org

Mersey Mission to Seafarers, The
Founded 1856 to 'promote the spiritual and temporal welfare of seafarers' from around the world who visit the ports of the River Mersey, Manchester Ship Canal and the Isle of Man. We will also respond to any emergency within the geographical area, Holyhead to Scottish Borders. *Chairman:* Mrs Pamela Brown MBE, JP, DL. *Chief Executive:* John P. Wilson, Liverpool Seafarers Centre, 20 Crosby Rd South, Liverpool, L22 1RQ
Tel: 0300 800 8080 07973 824154 (Mobile)
Fax: 0871 900 3223
email: admin@liverpoolseafarerscentre.org
Web: www.liverpoolseafarerscentre.org

Mid-Africa Ministry (CMS)
Mid-Africa Ministry (MAM), founded in 1921, now forms part of the Church Mission Society. See separate entry for Church Mission Society.

Mirfield Centre
Offers a meeting place for about 60 people. Small residential conferences are possible in the summer vacation. Day and evening events are arranged by the Centre management team. *Director:* Revd June Lawson. *Centre Administrator:* Mrs Rachael Salmon. *Centre Brothers:* Father Oswin Gartside, Father Simon Holden, Father Dennis Berk, The Mirfield Centre, Stocks Bank Road, Mirfield, WF14 0BWW *Tel:* 01924 481920
email: centre@mirfield.org.uk
Web: www.mirfieldcentre.org.uk

Mission to Seafarers, The
World mission agency which supports and links the Anglican Church's ministry to seafarers of all races and creeds in ports throughout the world. It has full-time staff and/or seafarers' centres in over 100 ports, honorary chaplains in over 120 others. In many ports it works in close cooper-

ation with Christian societies of other denominations, and it is a member of the International Christian Maritime Association. *President:* HRH The Princess Royal. *Secretary General:* Revd Tom Heffer. *Director of Justice and Welfare:* Canon Ken Peters. *Director of Chaplaincy:* Vacancy, St Michael Paternoster Royal, College Hill, London, EC4R 2RL *Tel:* 020 7248 5202
Fax: 020 7248 4761
email: general@missiontoseafarers.org
Web: www.missiontoseafarers.org

MODEM

MODEM is a network/association whose mission is to lead and enable authentic dialogue between exponents of Christian leadership, management and organization, and spirituality, theology and ministry. MODEM is an ecumenical membership organization, open to all Christians irrespective of age, gender, race, culture or nationality, and welcoming dialogue with all comers of all faiths. In association with SCM-/Canterbury Press, MODEM has published three ground-breaking books, *Management and Ministry* – appreciating contemporary issues; *Leading, Managing, Ministering* – challenging questions for church and society; and *Creative Church Leadership* – on the challenge of making a difference through leadership, the latter edited by Dr John Adair and John Nelson. The fourth and latest book *How to Become a Creative Leader* was published in February 2008, and is essentially the 'how to' book following the previous three. See web site for further information and details of special introductory membership offer to include some or all of the books. *Chairman:* Revd Elizabeth Welch. *Secretary:* John Nelson. *Contact:* Peter J. Bates, Carselands, Woodmancote, Henfield, BN5 9SS *Tel and Fax:* 01273 493172
email: info@modem-uk.org
2nd email: membership@modem-uk.org
Web: www.modem-uk.org

Modern Church

(formerly Modern Churchpeople's Union)
Modern Church promotes liberal theology and offers Christian debate and discussion on religious issues. It embraces the spirit of freedom and informed enquiry and seeks to involve the Christian faith in an ongoing search for truth by interpreting traditional doctrine in the light of present day understanding. It was founded at the end of the nineteenth century as a Church of England society but now welcomes all who share its ethos. It holds an annual conference on contemporary issues. Membership includes subscription to the journal 'Modern Believing'. *President:* Professor John Barton. *General Secretary:* Revd Jonathan Clatworthy, Modern Church Office, 9 Westward View, Liverpool, L17 7EE
Tel: 0845 345 1909
email: office@modernchurch.org.uk
Web: www.modernchurch.org.uk

Montgomery Trust Lectures

This endowment by Sir Alexander Montgomery of Albury, Surrey supports public lectures particularly for theological societies and religious education teachers on the results of modern scholarship on the Bible, with an emphasis on Christian apologetics. Thirty lectures were provided in 2011–12. Hosts included: University departments; Further Education colleges; organizations providing ministerial support; ordinand and preacher training; theological societies; local groupings of Religious Education teachers; Standing Advisory Councils for Religious Education, churches and cathedrals. Host organizations should contact the Administrator to identify a lecturer/theme. An interactive catalogue is available on our website http://www.montgomerytrust.org.uk/. Printed copies of the catalogue are available by post. The Administrator arranges the booking with an available lecturer. The host organization gathers an audience in excess of 30 people and provides the venue. After the Lecture the host organization completes and returns to the Trust a straight forward report pro forma. Then the Trust provides the Lecturer direct with an honorarium and reimburses their travel expenses. The Advisory committee meets in the summer when amongst other duties they approve new additions to the list of Montgomery Lecturers. Suggestions for new additions to this list are invited to our Administrator Mark Clarke in Birmingham. *Advisers:* Revd Prof Richard Burridge Dean of King's College London, Very Revd David Ison Dean of St Paul's Cathedral and Very Revd Dr John Hall Dean of Westminster. *Administrator:* Mark Clarke, Christian Education, 1020 Bristol Road, Selly Oak, Birmingham, B29 6LB
Tel: 0121 472 4242
Fax: 0121 472 7575
email:
professionalservices@christianeducation.org.uk
Web: http://www.montgomerytrust.org.uk/

Morse-Boycott Bursary Fund

(formerly St Mary-of-the-Angels Song School Trust)
Founded in 1932 originally as a parochial Choir School but from 1935 to 1970 served the Church at large. Now provides financial assistance to the parents of boy choristers at cathedral choir schools throughout the UK. The Fund depends entirely on donations and legacies to build the capital from which bursaries can be provided to the needy. *Trustees:* Dean and Chapter of Chichester. *Administrator:* The Communar, The Royal Chantry, Cathedral Cloisters, Chichester, PO19 1PX
Tel: 01243 782595 01243 812 92
Fax: 01243 812499
email: admin@chichestercathedral.org.uk
Web: www.chichestercathedral.org.uk

Mothers' Union
A Christian organization devoted to promoting marriage and the well-being of families worldwide. The Vision of Mothers' Union is 'A world where God's love is shown through loving, respectful and flourishing relationships'. This means that Mothers' Union invests in relationship. Through programmes, policy work, community outreach, Christian fellowship and prayer, Mothers' Union supports and nurtures relationships in the belief that this brings about stable families and benefits society. To do this, Mothers' Union takes positives steps to encourage marriage and family life. Projects tackle the most urgent needs threatening relationships and communities, and work towards fostering strong families and independent, cohesive communities. Mothers' Union is not a mission-sending organization, or a development charity, although mission and development are strong characteristics of its work. Rather, it is a network of 3.6 million people, each serving Christ in their local community at the grassroots level. It has a subscribers magazine, *Families First* and a magazine for members, Families Worldwide which includes the prayer diary material. Further information and resources are available from the charity's website. *Worldwide President:* Mrs Rosemary Kempnell. *Chief Exec:* Mr Reg Bailey, Mary Sumner House, 24 Tufton St, London, SW1P 3RB *Tel:* 020 7222 5533
Fax: 020 7227 9737
email: mu@themothersunion.org
Web: www.themothersunion.org

Mozambique and Angola Anglican Association (MANNA)
Founded by 1906, MANNA was formed to support the Diocese of Lebombo in southern Mozambique; it has now developed into supporting work within both the former Portuguese Territories, which are among the poorest in the world. While two world wars and lengthy civil wars hindered the work, since peace was established in both countries the church is growing at a great rate, predominantly by indigenous clergy who need support for their work. There are now three dioceses with well over 200 clergy. Registered Charity no. 262818. *Chair:* Ven Christopher Cunliffe, Archdeacon of Derby. *General Secretary:* Mr Ian Gordon, 16 Bayle Court, The Bayle, Folkestone, CT20 1SN *Tel:* 01303 257248
email: n_grdn@yahoo.co.uk
Web: www.newportchurches.com/Manna

National Archives, The
Records of central government and courts of law from the Norman Conquest (Domesday Book) to the recent past (for example, the Suez Campaign). Kew, Richmond-upon-Thames, TW9 4DU *Tel:* 020 8876 3444
email: enquiry@pro.gov.uk
Web: www.nationalarchives.gov.uk

National Association of Diocesan Advisers in Women's Ministry
NADAWM is a national network of diocesan advisers, appointed by their Bishop, for the purpose of advising in relation to the ministry of ordained women in the Church of England. This work involves monitoring the culture in which women clergy exercise their roles, consulitng with those women, supporting them in their work, celebrating their ministry and acting as advocates of ordained women in a wide range of ways and contexts. *Chair:* Revd Rosemary Lain-Priestly. *Treasurer:* Revd Irena Edgcumbe. *Secretary:* Canon Georgina Byrne, 15b College Green, Worcester, WR1 2LH
email: georgina18byrne@hotmail.com

National Churches Trust
The National Churches Trust, launched in 2007, is the successor to the Historic Churches Preservation Trust (HCPT) and administers the Incorporated Church Building Society (ICBS) funds. The National Churches Trust aims to fund, protect and support the built heritage of 47,000 churches, chapels and meeting houses throughout the UK. The Trust offers grants mainly for structural repairs, new facilities and improved access. Registered charity no. 1119845. *Patron:* HM The Queen. *Chairman of Trustees:* Michael Hoare. *Chief Executive:* Claire Walker. *Grants Manager:* Alison Pollard, 31 Newbury St, London, EC1A 7HU
Tel: 020 7600 6090
email: info@nationalchurchestrust.org
Web: www.nationalchurchestrust.org

National Council for Social Concern
(formerly the Church of England National Council for Social Aid, Church of England Temperance Society and Police Court Missionaries)
The charity (also known by the short titles 'Concern' and 'Social Concern') has promoted a wide range of activities in connection with the Church of England, but in recent years has had a particular interest in aspects of the criminal justice system and in issues arising from addictions. It works closely with the Church of England Board for Social Responsibility. Details from the Secretary. *Presidents:* The Archbishops of Canterbury and York. *Chairman:* Rt Revd Colin Docker. *Secretary:* Mr Francis Mac Namara, 3 Vinson Rd, Liss, GU33 7NE *Tel:* 01730 300974/ 07958 425927
email: info@social-concern.org
Web: www.social-concern.org

New England Company
A charity founded 1649. It is the senior English missionary society. *Governor:* Mr T. C. Stephenson. *Treasurer:* D. M. F. Scott. *Secretary:* Nikki Johnson, Flinders Cottage, The Street, Bolney, West Sussex RH17 5QW *Tel:* 01444 882898
email: johnsonnikki@yahoo.co.uk
Web: www.newenglandcompany.org

Newton's Trust
Established to provide assistance to widows, widowers, separated or divorced spouses and unmarried children of deceased clergy and to divorced or separated wives of clergy of the Church of England, the Church in Wales and the Scottish Episcopal Church. Applications are considered by the Trustees, and one-off cash grants are made at their discretion. The Trustees meet four times a year. *Chairman:* Ven George Frost. *Treasurer:* Mr John Allen. *Secretary:* Mr D. E. Wallington, Secretary to Newton's Trust, 1 Tudor Close, Lichfield, Staffordshire WS14 9RX
Tel: 01543 302924 (Evenings)
email: d.wallington@ntlworld.com

Nikaean Club
Founded in 1925 is an association of Anglican clergy and laity. It provides the ecumenical ministry of the Archbishop of Canterbury with a network of ecumenical expertise and the capacity to offer hospitality to visiting Christian leaders, heads of non-Anglican churches and international ecumenical bodies. *Chair:* Dame Rosemary Spencer. *Guestmaster:* Revd Canon Jonathan Goodall. *Hon Secretary:* Mr Christopher Austen. *Hon Treasurer:* Revd Martin Macdonald, Lambeth Palace, London, SE1 7JU *Tel:* 020 7898 1221
Fax: 020 7401 9886
email: christopher.austen@lambethpalace.org.uk

Nikaean Ecumenical Trust
Founded in 1992 and relaunched in 2002, the Trust exists to support ecumenical links between the Church of England and Christian churches overseas. It acts as the charitable wing of the Nikaean Club (see separate entry) and receives support from its members as well as from other Anglican bodies and individuals. It has also acquired the assets of the former Harold Buxton Trust, thanks to the generous co-operation of the SPCK. The Trust's principal activity at present is to provide grants to scholars from needy, non-Anglican Churches overseas (particularly the Orthodox and Oriental Orthodox Churches) who wish to study at colleges in the UK which are specifically Anglican or have strong Anglican connections. As the funds are still relatively modest, donations towards the work of the Trust are welcome. *Chair:* Rt Revd Dr Geoffrey Rowell. *Hon Secretary:* Mrs Margery Roberts, 7 Nunnery Stables, St Albans, AL1 2AS *Tel:* 01727 856626
email: robertssopwellnunnery@btopenworld.com

North of England Institute for Christian Education
Founded in 1981 as an ecumenical foundation managed by a board representing the educational interests of the Churches, universities and other educational institutions in the North East of England. Its primary objective is to create links, at both the theoretical and practical level, between Christian theology and education so as to contribute, mainly by research projects and publications, towards the further education of those with a responsibility for teaching the Christian faith. *Director:* Revd Prof Jeff Astley. *Secretary:* Mrs Evelyn Jackson, 18 North Bailey, Durham City, DH1 3RH *Tel:* 0191 33 43331 (Director)
0191 33 43332 (Secretary)
email: Jeff.Astley@durham.ac.uk
Web: www.durham.ac.uk/neice

Number 1 Trust Fund
Founded 1909 for holding property and investments for the promotion of catholic practice and teaching within the Church of England, reformed by the Fidelity Trust Act 1977, and incorporated by the Charity Commissioners in 1996. One trustee is appointed by each of the Abbot of Elmore, the Superior of the Community of the Resurrection, the President of the Church Union, the President of the Society for the Maintenance of the Faith, the Master of the Guardians of the Shrine at Walsingham, the Principal of Pusey House, Oxford and the Principal of St Stephen's House, Oxford. *Chairman:* Revd Canon R. Ward. *Trustees:* Rt Revd J. M. R. Baker, Revd A. A. Mayoss, Mr J. D. Hebblethwaite, Revd P. J. North, Dr B. J. T, Hanson. *Secretary and Trustee:* Canon P. E. Ursell, Ascot Priory, Priory Rd, Ascot, SL5 8RT
Tel: 01344 885157
email: secretary@numberonetrust.org.uk

OMF International (UK)
(formerly China Inland Mission)
We serve the church and seek to bring the gospel to all the peoples of East Asia. We help place Christians with professional skills in China and other Asian countries, and share the love of Christ with East Asians worldwide. *National Directors:* Peter and Christine Rowan, Station Approach, Borough Green, Sevenoaks, TN15 8BG *Tel:* 01732 887299
Fax: 01732 887224
email: omf@omf.org.uk
Web: www.omf.org.uk

Open Synod Group
The Open Synod Group provides a safe space in which Christians of all persuasions can meet and discuss any issues without fear of censure. The meetings are a mixture of interactive meetings about matters of concern and social events to foster friendships. The magazine attracts articles from a wide range of contributors of all shades of churchmanship. *President:* The Bishop of Ripon and Leeds. *Chairman:* Mr Tim Hind. *Secretary:* Mr Roy Thompson. *Treasurer and Membership Secretary:* Mr John Freeman. *Magazine Secretary:* Shirley-Ann Williams, May Rose Cottage, Sheriff Hutton, York, YO60 6SS *Tel:* 01347 878644/
07779 095273 (Mobile)
email: roythompson2@btinternet.com
Web: www.opensynodgroup.org.uk

Order of Christian Unity/Christian Projects
Christians from all denominations who care about Christian values in the family, medical ethics, Christian education and the media, and run an annual Schools Bible Project for secondary schools across Britain. *Chairman:* Mrs Joanna Bogle. *Treasurer:* Mr Andrew Pollock. *Vice-Chairman:* Lady Elizabeth Benyon, PO Box 44741, London, SW1P 2XA
email: auntiejoanna@yahoo.co.uk
Web: www.christianprojects.org.uk

Ordination Candidate Funds (General)
See separate entries for Anglo-Catholic Ordination Candidates' Fund, Bristol Clerical Education Society, Church Pastoral Aid Society Ministers in Training Fund, Cleaver Ordination Candidates' Fund, Elland Society Ordination Fund, Lady Peel Legacy Trust.

Overseas Bishoprics' Fund
Founded 1841 to assist towards the endowment and maintenance of bishoprics in any part of the world and to act as trustees of episcopal endowment funds. *Chairman:* Mr John Broadley. *Secretary:* Mr Stephen Lyon. *Clerk:* Mr Paul Burrage, Church House, Great Smith St, London, SW1P 3NZ *Tel:* 020 7803 3200
Fax: 020 7633 0185

Oxford Mission
Founded 1880. The Oxford Mission consists of two Religious Communities, the Brotherhood of St Paul and the Christa Sevika Sangha. Has houses in India and Bangladesh. Their work is pastoral, medical and educational and is carried on in the Dioceses of Kolkata and Dhaka. India: Col Subir Ghosh (Administrator); Bangladesh: Father Francis Pande SPB, Sister Superior, Sister Jharna *General Secretary:* Mrs Mary K. Marsh, PO Box 86, Romsey, SO51 8YD
Tel and Fax: 01794 515004
email: oxfordmission@aol.com
Web: www.oxford-mission.org

Papua New Guinea Church Partnership
PNGCP is the voluntary agency through which the Anglican Church of Papua New Guinea and the Church of England relate to each other. In 2007 ACPNG celebrated 30 years as an independent province in the Anglican Communion. Registered as a charity in 1960, the New Guinea Mission was founded in 1891 to give support to the then Diocese of New Guinea in prayer, by sending staff and raising money. In 1977, when the Province was inaugurated with five dioceses, the agency name was changed to Papua New Guinea Church Partnership in order to reflect the reciprocal nature of the work: giving and receiving. ACPNG continues to request people with skills and experience for governmentally approved support posts, mainly in health and administration. There are currently several in the country, including the Bishop of Port Moresby, the Rt Revd Peter Ramsden, for whom PNGCP acts as agent. Most years see a steady trickle of 'gap year' students and medical and nursing electives travelling to PNG to gain never-to-be-forgotten experience in the poorest, most populous Pacific nation. An annual grant goes to the provincial budget, money is raised for provincially approved projects, and audited accounts are sent to the UK. *President:* Rt Revd Dr David M. Hope. *Chairman:* Revd Paul Bagott. *General Secretary:* Miss Louise Ewington
Tel: 020 7313 3918
email: holyredeemerstmark@tiscali.co.uk
Web: www.pngcp.com

Paradox Ministries
Paradox Ministries encourages Christians to understand and pray about the Israeli–Palestinian Conflict, seeing it through the eyes of both people groups involved, and taking the needs, fear and pain of both sides seriously. Its director, who was Rector of a church in the Old City of Jerusalem for a number of years, circulates a free email newsletter, speaks at seminars and encourages support of indigenous reconciliation ministry in Jerusalem. The website contains background material, advice to clergy and regular news updates, together with a blog. *Directors (Chairman):* Revd Tony Higton. *(Executive):* Mrs Patricia Higton, 17 Church View, Marham, King's Lynn, PE33 9HW *Tel:* 01760 338342
email: tony@higton.info
Web: www.prayerforpeace.org.uk

Parish and People
Parish and People was originally founded in 1949 and helped make the Parish Communion popular. P&P continues to promote new life in the Anglican Church, by publishing materials to enable parishes and deaneries to grow from the grass roots into a lively, open, people concerned with mission. The Deanery Resource Unit was launched in 1989. Over 250 deaneries throughout the Church of England now subscribe to its twice-a-year mailing. This includes Deanery Exchange, an A4 sheet sharing ideas and good practice, together with copies of booklets and briefing papers on matters of parish and deanery concern. P&P co-operates with the Church House Deaneries Group and other bodies enlivening deaneries.Our latest project is a campaign to encourage the whole church to take the the Ministry of the Laity more seriously, whilst General Synod is considering 'Re-Imagining Ministry'. *Convenor and Editor of Deanery Exchange:* Peter Bates. *Treasurer:* Revd John Cole . *Orders to:* Canon Christopher Hall, The Knowle, Deddington, Banbury, OX15 OTB. *Secretary:* Revd

Jimmy Hamilton-Brown, April Cottage, West St, Winterborne Stickland, Blandford, DT11 0NT
Tel: 01258 880627 (Secretary)
01869 338225 (Orders)
email: secretary@parishandpeople.org.uk
2nd email: orders@parish&people.org.uk
Web: www.parishandpeople.org.uk

Philip Usher Memorial Fund
Founded 1948. Grants annual scholarships to Anglican priests, deacons or ordinands, preferably under 35 years of age, to study in a predominantly Orthodox country. *Chairman:* Rt Revd Dr Geoffrey Rowell. *Administrator:* Janet Laws, c/o The Old Deanery, Dean's Court, London, EC4V 3AA *Tel:* 020 7248 6233
Fax: 020 7248 9721
email: janet.laws@londin.clara.co.uk

Pilgrim Trust, The
The Pilgrim Trust considers applications from charities and exempt public bodies. The Trust operates two programmes: Social Welfare and Preservation and Scholarship. More details on the programme themes can be found in the Trust's guidelines which are available on the website. The Pilgrim Trust makes large annual block grants to the Church Buildings Council and the National Churches Trust. Church of England churches seeking grants for the conservation of items of church furniture e.g. repairs to bells/organs/monuments etc. should apply directly to the Church Buildings Council. Applications for repairs to the fabric of a building should be directed towards the National Churches Trust. *Director:* Miss Georgina Nayler, Clutha House, 10 Storeys Gate, London, SW1P 3AY
Tel: 020 7222 4723
email: info@thepilgrimtrust.org.uk
Web: www.thepilgrimtrust.org.uk

Pilsdon at Malling Community
The Pilsdon Community established a new community in 2004, taking over the former Ewell Monastery site next to St Mary's Abbey, West Malling, Kent. The community is dedicated to the same ideals of the Christian Gospel as the original community in Dorset, offering community living, sustainable self-sufficient lifestyle and open hospitality, particularly to those who are homeless, recovering from addiction, mental illness or breakdown. The community consists of 7 or 8 community members (leadership) and children and resident volunteers, about 12 long stay resident guests and up to 2 visitors and wayfarers/asylum seekers. The six acres of land and two large glasshouses are used for livestock and horticulture. The 16th-century barn chapel is used for daily offices, and the Eucharist is celebrated daily in either the barn or the Abbey chapel. Enquiries are always welcome. Please see our website for more details and also the Pilsdon Community entry. Registered Charity no. 1123682. Company no. 6218667. *Guardian:* Revd Pam Rink. *Treasurer:* Mr Albert Granville. *Admissions:* The Guardian. *Enquiries:* Any community member, 27 Water Lane, West Malling, ME19 6HH *Tel:* 01732 870279
Fax: 01732 870434
email: pilsdon.malling@tiscali.co.uk
Web: www.pilsdonatmalling.org.uk

Pilsdon Community
The Pilsdon Community is dedicated to the ideals of the Christian gospel in the context of community living and open hospitality. The Community at any one time will comprise between six to eight community members (leadership) and their children, about 20 guests (staying from one month to several years), up to six visitors (staying one day to a week) and up to eight wayfarers (staying up to three days). Many of the guests have experienced a crisis in their lives (e.g. mental breakdown, alcoholism, drug addiction, marital breakdown, abuse, homelessness, prison, dropping out of college, asylum-seeking, etc.). Pilsdon provides an environment of communal living, manual work, creative opportunities (pottery, art, crafts, music, etc.) recreation, worship and pastoral care, to rebuild people's lives, self-respect, confidence and faith. Founded in 1958 by an Anglican priest, the Community occupies an Elizabethan manor house and its outbuildings and smallholding of twelve acres, six miles from the sea near Lyme Regis. The community life is inspired by the monastic tradition and the Little Gidding Community built around families. The worship and spirituality is Anglican and sacramental, but ecumenical in membership, and all faiths and none as well as all races and cultures are welcome. Membership enquiries should be made to the Warden, enquiries from guests in need and visitors should be directed to the Admissions Officer. *Warden:* Revd Adam Dickens. *Administrator:* Alan Frost, Pilsdon Manor, Pilsdon, Bridport, DT6 5NZ *Tel:* 01308 868308
Fax: 01308 868161
email: pilsdon@btconnect.com
Web: www.pilsdon.org.uk

Plainsong and Medieval Music Society
Formed 1888 to promote the study and appreciation of plainsong and medieval music, especially through performance and publications; related journal, *Plainsong and Medieval Music*. *Administrator:* Anna Burson. *Chairman:* Prof John Harper, c/o RSCM, 19 The Close, Salisbury, SP1 2EB *Tel:* 01722 424843
Fax: 01722 424849
email: pmms@rscm.com
Web: www.plainsong.org.uk

Praxis
Founded in 1990, Praxis is sponsored by the Liturgical Commission, the Alcuin Club and the

ORGANIZATIONS

Grove Group for the Renewal of Worship. Its aims are to enrich the practice and understanding of worship in the Church of England; to serve congregations and clergy in their exploration of God's call to worship; and to provide a forum in which different worshipping traditions can meet and interact. Praxis events include day meetings, residential conferences and national consultations. *Chair:* Revd Jo Spreadbury. *Secretary:* Canon Michael Rawson. *Administrator:* Revd Peter Furber, 19 The Close, Salisbury, SP1 2EB *Tel:* 01202 296886
email: praxis@praxisworship.org.uk
Web: www.praxisworship.org.uk

Prayer Book Society
The Prayer Book Society exists to promote the use of the Book of Common Prayer and to defend the worship and doctrine contained therein. Diocesan branches provide members with regular meetings, Prayer Book services and advice on church matters. It runs the yearly Cranmer Awards for young people.It has a popular mail order book company stocking a wide range of religious books and Christmas cards. Donations and memberships are appreciated and needed. Membership form from 011898 42582 or from any Secretary shown on the website. *Patron:* HRH The Prince of Wales. *Ecclesiastical Patron:* The Bishop of London. *Chairman:* Miss Prudence Dailey, The Studio, Copyhold Farm, Goring Heath, RG8 7RT *Tel:* 0118 984 2582
Fax: 0118 984 5220
email: pbs.admin@pbs.org.uk
Web: www.pbs.org.uk

Pusey House, Oxford
Founded 1884 to continue the work of Dr Pusey, academic and pastoral, in Oxford. *Principal:* Vacancy. *Custodian of the Library:* Revd William Davage. *Archivist:* Revd Barry Orford, Pusey House, Oxford, OX1 3LZ *Tel:* 01865 278415/ 01865 288024/
email: chapter@puseyhouse.org.uk
Web: www.puseyhouse.org.uk

Pyncombe Charity
Income about £10,000 p.a. applied to assist needy serving ordained clergy in financial difficulties due to illness, or occasionally other special circumstances, within the immediate family. Applications must be made through the diocesan bishop. *Secretary:* Mrs Rita Butterworth, Wingletye, Hagleys Green Crowcombe, Taunton, TA4 4AL *email:* joeandrita@waitrose.com

Queen Victoria Clergy Fund
Founded 1897 to raise money towards the support of Church of England parochial clergy. All the Fund's income is disbursed annually in block grants to dioceses specifically for the help of the clergy. Requests for assistance should be directed to the diocese. *Chairman:* John Booth. *Secretary:* Chris Palmer CBE, Church House, Great Smith St, London, SW1P 3AZ *Tel:* 020 7898 1311
email: chris.palmer@churchofengland.org

Radius
Radius (The Religious Drama Society of Great Britain). Founded in 1929 to promote drama which throws light on the human condition and to support people who create and use drama as a means of Christian understanding. Organizes training events, publishes a magazine and a small number of plays, offers a playwrights' assessment service and holds a collection of photocopiable typescripts suitable for use in churches and by church groups. *Patrons:* The Archbishop of Canterbury, Dame Judi Dench. *President:* Rt Revd Graeme Knowles. *Magazine/ General Enquiries/Council Vice-Chair:* Margaret Hunt, 7 Lenton Rd, The Park, Nottingham, NG7 1DP *Tel:* 0115 941 3922
email: office@radius.org.uk
Web: www.radius.org.uk

RE Today Services
RE Today Services is wholly owned by the charity Christian Education, and is committed to the teaching of the major world faiths in religious education, and to an accurate and fair representation of their beliefs, values and practices in all its teaching materials. It carries forward the work of the Christian Education Movement (CEM). *Chief Executive:* Peter Fishpool. *Professional Team Director:* Resemary Rivett, 1020 Bristol Rd, Selly Oak, Birmingham, B29 6LB *Tel:* 0121 472 4242
Fax: 0121 472 7575
email: retoday@retoday.org.uk
Web: www.retoday.org.uk

Reader Missionary Studentship Association
Founded 1904 to offer financial assistance to Readers training as priests for service in the Church overseas. *Chairman:* Mr G. E. Crowley. *Hon Treasurer:* Mr Ron Edinborough. *Hon Secretary:* Dr Ann Whitfield, 30 Balmoral Drive, Methley, Leeds, LS26 9LE *Tel:* 01977 602176
email: secretary@rmsa.org.uk
Web: www.rmsa.org.uk

Rebecca Hussey's Book Charity
Established 1714 to give grants of religious and useful books to institutions in the United Kingdom. 425 Bromyard House, Bromyard Avenue, London, W3 7BY *Tel:* 020 8743 0181
email: carolinejdavis@aol.com

Reform
Established in 1993, Reform is a network of individuals and churches within the Church of England. We are committed to reforming the Church of England from within according to the Holy Scriptures. *Chairman:* Rod Thomas.

Administrators: Jonathan and Fiona Lockwood, PO Box 1183, Sheffield, S10 3YA
Tel: 0114 230 9256
email: administrator@reform.org.uk
Web: www.reform.org.uk

Relate

Relate, the country's largest relationship counselling organisation providing help and support for couples, singles, families and in schools. Also the national organisation for sex therapy and a leading source of information and advice online. Help is available at around 600 locations nationwide and by calling 0300 100 1234 or visit the website: www.relate.org.uk *Chief Executive Officer:* Ruth Sutherland, Premier House, Lakeside, Doncaster, DN4 5RA
Tel: 0300 100 1234 (Helpline)
Web: www.relate.org.uk

Religious Education Council of England and Wales

The Religious Education Council of England and Wales seeks to represent the collective interests of a wide variety of organizations and communities in deepening and strengthening provision for religious education in schools and colleges. The Council was formed in 1973 and is open to national organizations which have a special interest in the teaching of religious education. The present membership of more than 45 organizations includes representation from the main Christian denominations, the world faiths, the British Humanist Association and the main educational bodies with professional and academic RE interests. *Chair:* John Keast OBE. *Deputy Chair:* Joyce Miller. *Treasurer:* Dr Trevor Cooling, Voluntary Sector Centres, 76 Shoe Lane, London, EC4A 3JB *Tel:* 020 7842 8514
email: info@religiouseducationcouncil.org.uk
Web: www.religiouseducationcouncil.org.uk

Retired Clergy Association

Founded 1927 to act as a bond of friendship in prayer and mutual help to retired clergy. Membership at 31 July 2012 was 3,389. There are local branches in Aston, Bexhill, Birmingham, Bournemouth, Bristol, Bury St Edmunds, Cambridge, Canterbury, Carlisle, Cheltenham, Chester/Nantwich, Chichester, Craven, Diss, Durham, Eastbourne, Ely, Exeter, Gloucester, Halifax, Harrogate, Hereford, Huntingdon, Isle of Man, Isle of Wight, Lancaster, Leeds, Leigh-on-Sea, Ludlow, Manchester, Newcastle-upon-Tyne, Norwich, Oxford, Pontefract, Richmond, Ripon, Rochester, Rugby, Salisbury, Scarborough/Filey, Southampton, Southport, Whitby, Winchester and Arlesford, Worcester, York. *President:* The Bishop of Gloucester. *Chairman:* Rt Revd David Jennings. *Secretary and Treasurer:* Revd David Phypers, 15 Albert Road, Chaddesden, Derby, DE21 6SL *Tel:* 01332 239134
email: david@phypers.co.uk

Retreat Association

Comprising these Christian retreat groups: Association for Promoting Retreats, Baptist Union Retreat Group, Catholic Network for Retreats and Spirituality, Reflect (Methodists supporting spirituality and retreats)United Reformed Church Retreats Group and Affiliates of the Retreat Association. Offers information and resources about retreats to both would-be and seasoned retreatants, facilitates spiritual direction, promotes the work of retreat houses and coordinates training opportunities and regional activity. 'Retreats', an ecumenical journal listing retreat houses and their programmes in the UK and beyond, is published annually (2012 edition £9.00 incl p+p). Other literature available; send for publications list. *Director:* Alison MacTier, Kerridge House, 42 Woodside Close, Amersham, Bucks, HP6 5EF *Tel:* 01494 433004
Fax: 0871 715 1917
email: info@retreats.org.uk
Web: www.retreats.org.uk

Revd Dr George Richards' Charity

Founded 1837 to provide financial assistance to clergy of the Church of England forced to retire early owing to ill-health. Widows, widowers and dependants can also apply for assistance. *Secretary:* Dr P. D. Simmons, 96 Thomas More House, Barbican, London, EC2Y 8BU
Tel: 020 7588 5583

Richmond Fellowship

Established in 1959, Richmond Fellowship (RF) currently operates over 100 services for people with mental health problems throughout England. These include supported housing, registered care homes and care homes with nursing support, employment and training services, individual self-directed packages of care and community and day services. For further information contact Richmond Fellowship: communications@richmondfellowship.org.uk *Chief Executive:* Derek Caren. *PA to Chief Executive:* Marise Willis, 80 Holloway Rd, London, N7 8JG *Tel:* 020 7697 3300
Fax: 020 7697 3301
email: marise.willis@richmondfellowship.org.uk
Web: www.richmondfellowship.org.uk

RNID

(Formerly known as Royal National Institute for Deaf People)

RNID is the largest charity representing the 9 million deaf and hard of hearing people in the UK. It offers a range of services for deaf and hard of hearing people, and provides information and support on all aspects of deafness, hearing loss and tinnitus. As a membership charity, it aims to achieve a radically better quality of life for deaf and hard of hearing people. RNID's work involves campaigning and lobbying, providing services, training, products and equipment, and

ORGANIZATIONS

undertaking medical and technical research. It works throughout the UK. *Chairman:* Mr James Strachan. *Chief Executive:* Dr John Low, 19–23 Featherstone St, London, EC1Y 8SL

Tel: 0808 808 0123 (Voice)
0808 808 9000 (Textphone)
email: informationline@rnid.org.uk
Web: www.rnid.org.uk

Royal Alexandra and Albert School
Founded in 1758, a voluntary-aided junior and secondary school providing boarding education for boys and girls aged 7–18 who are without one or both parents or who would benefit from boarding education because of home circumstances. Only boarding fees payable and bursaries available. Bursaries for children of clergy are available for two thirds of the fees at this state boarding school where the full fees are only £3,655 per term for full boarding. In exceptional circumstances, further bursary support can be provided. Exceptional facilities. Contact: Headmaster for further details. *Patron:* HM the Queen. *President:* HRH the Duchess of Gloucester. *Headmaster:* Paul D. Spencer Ellis. *Foundation Secretary:* Diana Bromley. *Admissions Secretary:* Sue Harrington, Gatton Park, Reigate, RH2 0TW

Tel: 01737 649000
Fax: 01737 649002
email: headmaster@gatton-park.org.uk
Web: www.gatton-park.org.uk

Royal Asylum of St Ann's Society
The Society, founded in 1702, offers grants towards the expenses of educating children, from the age of 11, at boarding or day schools. Most, but not all, of those aided are children of clergy of the Church of England; however, in the first instance clergy should approach the Corporation of the Sons of the Clergy. The Society welcomes collections, donations and legacies towards this purpose. *President:* The Dean of Westminster. *Chairman:* Mr Peter Ashby. *Secretary:* Mr David Hanson, King Edward's School, Witley, Petworth Rd, Wormley, GU8 5SG

Royal College of Organists
Founded 1864, incorporated by Royal Charter 1893, 'to promote the art of organ-playing and choir training'. Holds lectures, recitals and master-classes nationwide. Examinations for Certificate, Associateship, Fellowship, Licentiateship in Teaching and Diploma in Choral Directing. Holds a large specialist library and archive, and publishes a scholarly journal every year. Membership open to all who take an interest in the work and profession of the organist and in organ music. *Patron:* HM The Queen. *President:* James O'Donnell. *General Manager:* Kim Gilbert, PO Box 56357, London, SE16 7XL

Tel: 05600 767208
email: admin@rco.org.uk
Web: www.rco.org.uk

Royal Martyr Church Union
Founded 1906: (1) Ever to cherish the sacred remembrance of Charles the First, King and Martyr, both in public worship and private devotion, and to this end to promote the restoration of his name to its proper place in the calendar of the worldwide Anglican Communion, and the observance of 30 January, the day of his martyrdom, by suitable services in the Book of Common Prayer and elsewhere. (2) To maintain the principles of faith, loyalty and liberty for which the King died – the faith of the Church, loyalty to the Crown, and the ancient liberties of the people. Holds annual commemorative eucharists in London and Edinburgh. Subscription £15.00 p.a.to include 'Royal Martyr Annual'. *Chairman:* Tom Kerr. *Hon Secretary and Treasurer:* David Roberts, 7 Nunnery Stables, St Albans, AL1 2AS *Tel:* 01727 856626

Royal National Institute of Blind People (RNIB)
Royal National Institute of Blind People (RNIB) is a charity which supports blind and partially sighted people to remain independent by: giving you free advice about your eye condition, the benefits you're entitled to, and the specialist and local support that's available; providing employment services and practical help for children and their families; suggesting ideas on how you can continue to enjoy your hobbies and leisure time; recommending everyday items and gadgets to make your life easier; offering a listening ear. *President:* His Grace the Duke of Westminster. *Chairman:* Lord Low of Dalston CBE. *Chief Executive:* Lesley-Anne Alexander, 105 Judd St, London, WC1H 9NE

Tel: 0845 766 9999 (Helpline) 020 7391 2000
email: helpline@rnib.org.uk
Web: www.rnib.org.uk

Royal School of Church Music
The Royal School of Church Music (RSCM) is the leading organization promoting and supporting church music. It is an educational charity dedicated to raising standards and promoting the best use of music in every style of Christian worship and in every denomination. It is funded through membership subscriptions, publication sales, course fees and the charitable support of individuals and institutions. It provides musical and educational resources to train, develop and inspire clergy, music leaders, musicians, singers and congregations. Its *Voice for Life* programme is a training scheme for singers of all ages that can be used by individual churches and schools, and *Church Music Skills* provides practical training for those leading music in worship. These programmes are complemented by workshops, festivals and short residential courses, and a network of volunteers runs events to meet local needs in the UK and five overseas branches. The

RSCM publishes music through the RSCM Press, including musical resources for *Common Worship*, and RSCM Music Direct provides a fast and efficient mail-order service for music from all publishers. Affiliated churches and schools and individual members receive *Church Music Quarterly*, a highly informative and interesting magazine for all those concerned with church music, and *Sunday by Sunday*, an essential liturgy planner aiding those who plan and lead worship to enhance it through music appropriate to the day. Appointed the official music agency for the Church of England from April 1996. *President:* The Archbishop of Canterbury. *Chairman:* Lord Brian Gill. *Director:* Mr Andrew Reid, 19 The Close, Salisbury, SP1 2EB
Tel: 01722 424848 / 01722 424841 (membership)
Fax: 01722 424849
email: enquiries@rscm.com
Web: www.rscm.com

Rural Theology Association
Founded 1981 to provide a forum for the rural churches and to focus for the Church at large the distinctive ways and needs and contributions of the rural. Its aims are to study the gospel and develop theology in a rural setting, to encourage the development of patterns of ministry and mission appropriate to the countryside today, and to discover ways of living in the countryside which embody a Christian response to the world. It publishes the journal 'Rural Theology' twice yearly. *President:* Revd Prof Leslie Francis. *Chairman:* Rt Revd Mark Rylands. *Secretary:* Canon Stephen Cope. *Treasurer:* Revd Dr Christine Brewster, Vicarage, 28 Park Ave, Withernsea, HU19 2JU *Tel:* 01964 611426
email: secretary@rural-theology.org.uk
Web: www.rural-theology.org.uk

Saint George's Trust
The Trust exists to give grants to individuals to further the work of the Church of England. The Fellowship of Saint John (UK) Trust Association is the sole trustee. The funds at the Trust's disposal do not permit large grants for restoration projects, or any long-term financial support. The wide remit enables it to help a large number of individuals for sabbaticals, gap years and the like to a maximum of £350. All applications should be sent, together with a stamped addressed envelope, to the Trust with as much supporting documentation as possible. St Edward's House, 22 Great College St, London, SW1P 3QA

Samaritans
Samaritans exists to provide confidential emotional support to any person, irrespective of race, creed, age or status who is in emotional distress or at risk of suicide; and to increase public awareness of issues around suicide and depression. *Chief Exec:* Mr Dominic Rudd, The Upper Mill, Kingston Rd, Ewell, Surrey, KT17 2AF *Tel:* 020 8394 8300 (admin)
08457 909090 (helpline)
Fax: 020 8394 8301
email: admin@samaritans.org
Web: www.samaritans.org

Sarum College
Sarum College is an ecumenical study and research centre based in Salisbury's Cathedral Close. The College is housed in a Grade 1 listed building in Salisbury Cathedral Close and offers an extensive and varied programme of short residential and day courses, as well as four postgraduate programmes with options to gain a PG certificate, diploma or master's degree. The College has bedrooms for short or long-term stays and some overlook the Cathedral. There is also a range of meeting and conference rooms, a 19th-century chapel, common room/bar, and a dining room seating up to 120. On-site parking is usually available. Residential conferences, parish groups, training events, board meetings and individual guests are all welcome. The College also houses a fine theological library with more than 35,000 volumes, and Salisbury's only independent theological bookshop, both of which offer postal/mail order services. *Principal:* Canon Keith Lamdin. *Bursar:* Mark Manterfield. *Director of Learning Resources:* Jenny Monds. *Residential Services Manager:* Linda Cooper. *Director of Development and Communications:* Christine Nielsen-Craig, 19 The Close, Salisbury, SP1 2EE *Tel:* 01722 424800
Fax: 01722 338508
email: info@sarum.ac.uk
Web: www.sarum.ac.uk

Sarum St Michael Educational Charity
Personal grants may be awarded for further or higher education, to those who live, work or study within the Salisbury or adjacent dioceses (also to former students of the college). Bursaries may be awarded to those who live or study within the Salisbury diocese or adjacent dioceses, who intend to train to teach RE. Grants may be made to local schools, mainly for RE and worship resources. Grants may be made to parishes within the Salisbury diocese, for work with children and young people. Corporate grants may be made, where funds permit, to certain projects within the Salisbury diocese and adjacent dioceses. The governors meet four times a year to consider applications. Grants are not awarded retrospectively. Please consult our website for closing dates for applications, and to download application forms. Member of the Association of

Church College Trusts (see separate entry). First Floor, 27A Castle St, Salisbury, SP1 1TT
Tel: 01722 422296
Fax: 0870 135 9943
email: clerk@sarumstmichael.org
Web: www.sarumstmichael.org

SASRA
(The Soldiers' and Airmen's Scripture Readers Association)
Founded 1838 to present the claims of Christ to the men and women serving in the Army and later the RAF, to promote interdenominational Christian fellowship among them and to encourage individual serving Christians to witness to their comrades. *Chairman:* Brigadier Ian Dobbie. *General Secretary:* Sqdn Ldr Colin Woodland, Havelock House, Barrack Rd, Aldershot, GU11 3NP
Tel: 01252 310033
Fax: 01252 341804
email: admin@sasra.org.uk
Web: www.sasra.org.uk

School Chaplains' Association
An association for all people, ordained and lay, involved in Christian ministry in state or independent schools. *President:* Rt Revd L. Urwin. *Chairman:* Revd John Thackeray. *Secretary:* Revd Jim Gascoigne. *Administrator:* Revd Robert Easton, c/o Kings's School, Rochester, ME1 1TE
Tel: 01634 888555
email: treasurer@schoolchaplains.org.uk
Web: www.schoolchaplains.org.uk

Scout Association, The
Founded in 1907 to promote the development of young people in achieving their full physical, intellectual, social and spiritual potential, as individuals, as responsible citizens and as members of their local, national and international communites. Membership 475,000. Tel: 0845 300 1818 (8 a.m. to 6 p.m. Mon to Fri) or 020 8433 7100. *Chief Scout:* Lt Cdr (Hons) Bear Grylls RN. *Chief Executive:* Derek Twine CBE, Gilwell Park, Bury Rd, Chingford, London, E4 7QW
Tel: 020 8433 7100
Fax: 020 8433 7103
email: info.centre@scout.org.uk
Web: www.scouts.org.uk

Scripture Union
Scripture Union seeks to make the Christian faith known to children, young people and families and to support the Church through resources, Bible reading and training. SU's work in Britain includes schools work, Bible ministries, digital and conventional publishing, training, evangelism, holidays, missions and family ministry. Scripture Union is active in more than 100 countries. *National Director:* Revd Tim Hastie-Smith. *Development Director:* Mr Terry Clutterham. *Managing Director:* Mr David Thorpe, 207–209 Queensway, Bletchley, Milton Keynes, MK2 2EB
Tel: 01908 856000
Fax: 01908 856111
email: info@scriptureunion.org.uk
Web: www.scriptureunion.org.uk

Seamen's Friendly Society of St Paul
Trust administered by Alton Abbey, able to offer financial assistance to merchant sailors. *Contact:* Rt Revd Dom William Hughes OSB, Alton Abbey, Abbey Rd, Beech, Alton, Hampshire, GU34 4AP
Tel: 01420 562145/01420 563575
email: abbot@altonabbey.org.uk

Servants of Christ the King
Founded 1942 by Canon Roger Lloyd of Winchester. A movement of groups or 'Companies' of Christians who seek to develop a corporate life by praying together in silence, with disciplined discussion. They actively wait upon God to be led by the Holy Spirit, and undertake to do together any work which they are given by him to do. *Enquirers' Correspondent:* Dr Pauline Waters, Swallowfield, Wheelers Lane, Linton, Maidstone, ME17 4BN
Tel: 01622 743392
Web: www.sck.org.uk

SGM Lifewords
(formerly Scripture Gift Mission)
SGM creates Bible resources to help people communicate God's word to today's generation. A new, research-based range uses up-to-date Bible versions and contemporary graphics. SGM publishes materials in over 200 languages for use worldwide. 75 Westminster Bridge Rd, London, SE1 7HS
Tel: 020 7730 2155
Fax: 020 7401 9070
email: uk@sgmlifewords.com
Web: www.sgmlifewords.com

Shaftesbury Homes and 'Arethusa'
Founded 1843 to house and educate homeless children in London, the charity is now the leading voluntary sector provider of residential care for children in London. In London and Suffolk the charity also provides services for young people leaving care, and supported housing for the young homeless. Personal development is promoted through venture activities at the Arethusa Venture Centre on the Medway. *Chairman:* Gerri McAndrew. *Chief Exec:* Karen Wright, The Chapel, Royal Victoria Patriotic Building, Trinity Rd, London, SW18 3SX
Tel: 020 8875 1555 *Fax:* 020 8875 1954
email: info@shaftesbury.org.uk
Web: www.shaftesbury.org.uk

Sharing of Ministries Abroad (SOMA)
Founded in 1978 to serve the renewal of the Church throughout the world, particularly in the Anglican Communion, SOMA has eleven centres across the world. SOMA works for the transformation of individuals and churches, and the

healing of communities and their lands through the renewing power of the Holy Spirit by intercession and sending and receiving teams worldwide on short-term mission across the Anglican Communion. A newsletter, 'Sharing', is published three times a year. *SOMA International Chairman:* The Most Revd Ben Kwashi. *SOMA UK National Director:* Revd Stephen Dinsmore. *SOMA UK Finance Administrator:* Steve Fincher, PO Box 69, Merriott, TA18 9AP

Tel: 01460 279737
email: info@somauk.org
2nd email: facebook SOMA UK twitter somauk
Web: www.somauk.org

Social Responsibility Network, The
The Network (developed from the Anglican Association for Social Responsibility) aims to share good practice, ideas and information on a wide range of issues and provide peer support and encouragement for Christian practitioners in social responsibility and related fields in England and Wales. We do this by meeting together in local and regional groups, holding an annual conference on key issues, making resources available to one another, and sharing ideas, needs and resources via our discussion e-net. Open to all Christian practitioners. *Chair:* Canon Peter Williams. *Treasurer:* Tony Oakden. *Secretary:* Mrs Ann Wright, Faith in Families, 7 Telfaen Road Bonymaen, Swansea, SA1 7HA

Tel: 01792 644106
email: wright@btinternet.com
Web: www.srnet.org.uk

Society for Liturgical Study
Founded 1978. The Society promotes liturgical study and research, particularly amongst younger scholars, through postgraduate study days and a biennial conference, and through its peer-reviewed journal, 'Anaphora', published twice a year. Membership is interdenominational and is open to persons involved in teaching liturgy, or in research in this field, or holding official appointments with responsibility for liturgy and worship. *Secretary:* Mr Harvey Howlett, 88 Gainsborough Road, New Malden, KT3 5NX *email:* secretary@studyliturgy.org.uk
Web: www.studyliturgy.org.uk

Society for Old Testament Study
Founded 1917 as a society for OT/HB scholars in Britain and Ireland. Scholars not resident in the British Isles may also become members. Two meetings to hear and discuss papers are arranged annually. The Society also publishes its annual 'Book List' and is involved in other publishing activities. It maintains links with OT/HB scholars throughout the world, particularly the Dutch-Flemish OT Society with which it holds joint meetings every three years. Candidates for membership must be proficient in biblical Hebrew and be proposed by two existing members. *Hon Secretary:* Dr Francesca Stavrakopoulou, Department of Theology and Religion, University of Exeter, Amory Building, Rennes Drive, Exeter, EX4 4RJ *Tel:* 01392 724290
email: f.stavrakopoulou@exeter.ac.uk
Web: www.sots.ac.uk

Society for Promoting Christian Knowledge
SPCK was founded in 1698 to help people to understand – and to grow in – the Christian faith. It works to support and develop the knowledge of Christians and to interest and inform others. Throughout its history SPCK has been associated with the spread of education and informative literature in all its forms. It is an Anglican foundation but supports a diversity of Christian traditions. The Society has been involved in publishing since its foundation in 1698, and currently publishes around 100 new titles each year. Its output includes Christian books, websites and electronic products across a broad spectrum, from the catholic to the evangelical and from the conservative to the liberal. The range includes liturgy, theology, science and religion, biblical studies and spirituality, academic and student texts as well as stationery and books for a popular market, with resources for clergy, parishes and study groups. The International Study Guides series is aimed particularly at those training for ministry in the developing world, including many for whom English is not a first language. Under the Azure imprint are books for readers who are searching for faith but who might not ordinarily look to Christianity for help or guidance. The Assemblies website (www.assemblies.org.uk) provides teachers with regularly updated materials for school assemblies which they can download free of charge. SPCK Diffusion aims to produce innovative materials to resource a wide audience with information in a form relevant to their interests and experience. SPCK Worldwide supports the distribution of books and educational materials for Christians overseas, including in some of the poorest parts of the world. It depends entirely upon donations from individuals, churches and charitable trusts. *President:* The Archbishop of Canterbury. *Chairman of the Governing Body:* Rt Revd John Pritchard. *General Secretary:* Mr Simon Kingston. *Executive Administrator:* Mrs Pat Phillips, 36 Causton St, London, SW1P 4ST

Tel: 020 7592 3900
Fax: 020 7592 3939
email: spck@spck.org.uk
Web: www.spck.org.uk /
www.assemblies.org.uk

Society for the Assistance of Ladies in Reduced Circumstances
Founded by the late Miss Edith Smallwood in 1886. Assistance is given to ladies living alone in their own home (either owned or rented) on a low income and domiciled in the United

ORGANIZATIONS

Kingdom, irrespective of age or social status. Registered Charity no. 205798. Enquiries welcome on freephone helpline. Donations and legacies gratefully received. *Patron:* HM The Queen. *Apply:* The Secretary, Lancaster House, 25 Hornyold Rd, Malvern, WR14 1QQ

Tel: 01684 574645/
0800 587 4696 (freephone helpline)
Fax: 01684 577212
email: info@salrc.org.uk
Web: www.salrc.org.uk

Society for the Maintenance of the Faith
Founded in 1873, the Society presents, or shares in the presentation of, priests to over 80 benefices. As well as its work as a patronage body the Society aims to promote Catholic teaching and practice in the Church of England at large. *President:* Dr Brian Hanson. *General Secretary:* Rt Revd Jonathan Baker, Pusey House, Oxford, OX1 3LZ *email:* secretary@smftrust.org.uk

Society for the Relief of Poor Clergy (SRPC)
Founded 1788 to aid evangelical Anglican clergy and their dependants in times of financial distress due to sickness, bereavement or other difficulties. *Secretary:* Mrs Pauline Walden, c/o CPAS Sovereign Court One (Unit 3), Sir William Lyons Road, Coventry, CV4 7EZ

Tel: 01926 458458
Fax: 01926 458459
email: secretary@srpc-aid.com
Web: www.srpc-aid.com

Society of Archbishop Justus Ltd
The Society, named after the fourth Archbishop of Canterbury, was formed in 1996 and incorporated in 1997 as a non-profit corporation in New York, USA for the purpose of using the Internet to foster and further unity among Christians, especially Anglicans. It focuses on internet information services: web and email servers that help Anglicans to be one body. Members help install, operate and maintain the computers and networks that enable online communication, and help educate the Anglican public about how best to use those computers. Directors include both Church of England and ECUSA members. The Society sponsors the Anglicans Online web site and, on behalf of the International Anglican Domain Committee, administers the anglican.org internet domain. More information is available on the web site. *Director:* Simon Sarmiento, 22 Rodney Avenue, St Albans, AL1 5SX

email: directors@justus.anglican.org
Web: www.justus.anglican.org/soaj.html

Society of Catholic Priests
Founded in 1994, with around 700 members in the UK and Ireland, an inclusive society of priests who 'believe in one, holy, catholic and apostolic church ordaining men and women to serve as deacons, priests and bishops in the Church of God'. The objects of the Society are to promote the formation and support of priestly spirituality and catholic evangelism. *Patron:* The Archbishop of Canterbury. *Visitor General:* The Bishop of Truro. *Rector General:* Very Revd Andrew Nunn. *Secretary General:* Revd Michael Skinner. *Membership Secretary:* Revd John Joyce, 3 Wolstonbury Road, Hove, West Sussex, BN6 6EJ

Tel: 07798 941095
email: membership@scp.org.uk
Web: www.scp.org.uk

Society of King Charles the Martyr
Founded 1894 to promote observance of January 30, the day of the martyrdom of King Charles I in 1649, and uphold the traditional Anglican Catholic principles for which he died. Publishes various material including the journal *Church and King*. *Chairman:* Mr Robin Davies, 22 Tyning Rd, Winsley, Bradford on Avon, BA15 2JJ

Tel: 01225 862965
email: robinjbdavies@talktalk.net
Web: www.skcm.org

Society of Mary
Founded 1931 to promote devotion to Our Lady. Originally an Anglican Society and now an ecumenical Society welcoming all practising Catholics, and organizes pilgrimages to Marian Shrines, in particular Lourdes and Nettuno. *Superior General:* Rt Revd Robert Ladds. *Chaplain General:* Revd G. C. Rowlands. *Secretary:* Mrs Celia Bush, 169 Humber Doucy Lane, Ipswich, IP4 3PA

Society of Mary and Martha
An independent ecumenical charity run by a mixed lay Community providing confidential support for clergy and/or spouses, especially at times of stress, crisis, burnout or breakdown. Resources exclusively for people in ministry include the famous 12,000-mile Service weeks, Family Holiday week, and Linhay Lodges: well-appointed, self-contained accommodation for private retreats, sabbaticals, safe place, emergency bolt-hole or battery re-charge. Programme events open to everyone include retreat and training resources for personal and spiritual growth. Hen Runs and Pig Pens available for private retreats, open to everyone. The Sheldon Centre is a beautifully converted farm with lovely views across the Teign Valley, just ten miles from the M5 and main line railway at Exeter. £1m upgrade completed in 2011 – all rooms now en-suite. Also available for self-catering hire for groups of 10–50 (cell groups, leadership training, parish retreats, etc.) *Warden:* Carl Lee. *Administrator:* Sarah Horsman, Sheldon, Dunsford, Exeter, EX6 7LE *Tel:* 01647 252752

Fax: 01647 253900
email: smm@sheldon.uk.com
Web: www.sheldon.uk.com

Society of Ordained Scientists
Founded 1987. A dispersed order for ordained scientists, men and women. Members aim to offer to God, in their ordained role, the work of science in the exploration and stewardship of creation, to express the commitment of the Church to the scientific enterprise and their concern for its impact on the world, and to support each other in their vocation. Associate membership is available to those who are not ordained but are interested in the work of the Society. *Visitor:* Rt Revd David Walker, Bishop of Dudley. *Secretary:* Revd Dr Robin G. Harvey. *Warden:* Revd Dr Keith Suckling, 21 St Cadoc House, Temple Street, Bristol, BS31 1HD
email: rgharvey.194@btinternet.com
Web: www.ordainedscientists.org

Society of Retreat Conductors
Founded in 1923 for the training of retreat conductors, the running of retreat houses and the conducting of retreats. *Chairman:* Revd David Sutton. *Company Secretary:* Mrs Kathryn Redington, c/o St Mary Woolnoth Vestry, Lombard St, London, EC3V 9AN *Tel:* 020 7929 0199
email: admin.src@btconnect.com

Society of Royal Cumberland Youths
Bell-ringing society founded in 1747. Its headquarters are at St Martin-in-the-Fields and the Society is responsible for ringing at a number of London churches. The society has a worldwide membership, promoting high standards among proficient change-ringers. *Master:* Mr Peter Harrison. *Secretary:* Ms Penelope Sharpe, 62 Arthurdon Rd, London, SE4 1JU *Tel:* 07734 960808
email: secretary@srcy.org.uk
Web: www.srcy.org.uk

Society of St Willibrord
(The Anglican and Old Catholic Society of St Willibrord)
Founded 1908 to promote friendly relations between the Anglican and Old Catholic Churches, including the fullest use of the full Communion established between them in 1931. Membership of the society is open to members of churches in full communion with Canterbury and/or Utrecht. *President:* Rt Revd Geoffrey Rowell, Bishop of Gibraltar in Europe. *Patrons:* The Archbishops of Canterbury and Utrecht. *Hon Secretary:* Mthr Ariadne van den Hof. *Chairman:* Rt Revd J. Gledhill, Bishop of Lichfield, 1 Craigholm, Shooters Hill, London, SE18 3RR
Tel: 020 8856 5858
email: honsecssw@gmail.com
Web: www.willibrord.org.uk

Society of the Faith (Incorporated)
The objects of the Society are to act as an Association of Christians in communion with the See of Canterbury for mutual assistance in the work of Christ's Church and for the furtherance of charitable undertakings, especially for the popularization of the Catholic Faith. We have occupied Faith House in Westminster since 1935 and formerly ran the Faith Press and Faithcraft. We manage Faith House as a resource for the Church, promote charitable activities, hold the annual Liddon Lecture and sponsor publications which promote the Society's objects. The restricted Liddon Fund provides two or three grants per year for young Anglicans (under 25 years old) who are engaged in advanced theological study, for example for a second degree. *Principal:* Dr Julian Litten. *Vice-principal:* Canon Robert Gage. *Secretary and Treasurer:* Mrs Margery Roberts, Faith House, 7 Tufton St, London, SW1P 3QB
Tel: 01727 856626

Society of the Holy Cross (SSC)
Founded 1855 for priests (1100 members) 'to maintain and extend the Catholic faith and discipline and to form a special bond of union between Catholic clergy'. Provinces: European Union, Australasia, Canada, Africa, USA. *Master General:* Preb Dr David Houlding SSC. *Provincial Master (for England):* Fr Nicolas Spicer SSC. *Secretary General:* Fr Colin Amos SSC. *Treasurer General:* Fr David Lawson SSC. *Registrar:* Fr Trevor Buxton SSC, All Hallows House, 52 Courthope Rd, London, NW3 2LD
Tel: 020 7267 7831 (Home)
020 7263 6317 (Office)
Fax: 020 7267 6317 *email:* sscmaster@lineone.net

South American Mission Society
(Incorporating the Spanish and Portuguese Church Aid Society)
Founded 1844 to make known the gospel of the Lord Jesus Christ to the people of Latin America and the Iberian Peninsula and continuing in active partnership now with the mission priorities of the Anglican churches in these regions. *Mission Director for South America:* Rt Revd Henry Scriven. *Mission Education Officer:* Mr Robert Lunt. *Finance Secretary:* Mr Philip Tadman, Allen Gardiner Cottage, Pembury Rd, Tunbridge Wells, TN2 3QU *Tel:* 01892 538647/0114 269 2070
Fax: 01892 525797
email: finsec@samsgb.org
Web: www.samsgb.org

Southern Africa Church Development Trust
Founded 1960 to inform, encourage concern for and involvement in the Church in Southern Africa. Supports churches, community centres and schools, primary and secondary education through scholarships, clergy and lay training, and medical work. Publishes a quarterly bulletin of information and projects which is sent to all subscribers and supporters. *President:* Mr Martin Kenyon. *Director:* Dr Jack Mulder. *Chairperson:* Canon David Cook. *Hon Treasurer:* Mr Jim Wilkinson. *Secretary to the Board:* Mrs

ORGANIZATIONS

Susan Howden, 51 Heathside, Hinchley Wood, KT10 9TD *Tel:* 020 8398 9638/020 8398 8699
email: jlerm2@hotmail.com
Web: www.sacdt.org

St Christopher's Educational Trust
Small grants to promote Christian religious education by improving practice in teaching, by developing new programmes of education and nurture for adults and young people and by support for individual study or research. The Trustees meet twice a year. Member of the Association of Church College Trusts (see separate entry). *Clerk to the Trustees:* Mrs Lindsey Anderson-Gear, 55 Manston Close, Bicester, Oxon, OX26 4FA
email: stchristopherstrust@hotmail.co.uk
Web: www.churchofengland.org/education

St Christopher's Fellowship
St Christopher's is a charity and housing association providing care, accommodation, education, training and support to children, young people and vulnerable adults. We run children's homes, fostering services, supported housing and hostels, along with education, employment and outreach services. *Chairman:* Mr Anthony Hickinbotham. *Chief Exec:* Mr Jonathan Farrow, 1 Putney High St, London, SW15 1SZ *Tel:* 020 8780 7800
Fax: 020 8780 7801
email: info@stchris.org.uk
Web: www.stchris.org.uk

St George's College, Jerusalem
St George's College is a unique centre of continuing education in the Anglican Communion, offering short-term courses as well as facilities for individual reflection and study. It is open to both clergy and laity. Since its founding in 1962, the College has hosted participants from 92 countries and 96 Christian traditions. Course members engage with a wide range of biblical texts in the context of the land; encounter Jewish, Christian and Muslim faith as it is exercised today; and come to appreciate anew the rich fabric of faith and spirituality that this environment offers to the pilgrim. The College is situated 500 metres north of the Damascus Gate of the Old City of Jerusalem, and set in its own grounds adjacent to the Anglican Cathedral of St George the Martyr. Full details of courses can be obtained from the web site or the Secretary of the British Regional Committee. *Secretary of the British Regional Committee:* Revd Paul Conder, St. George's College Jerusalem, Post Office Box 1248, Jerusalem 91000, Israel *Tel:* 1 972 2 626 4704
Fax: 1 972 2 626 4703
email: registrar@stgeorges.org.il
Web: www.sgcjerusalem.org

St George's House, Windsor Castle
Founded 1966. A residential consultation centre within Windsor Castle, and part of the fourteenth-century College of St George. Apart from ecumenical clergy conferences the House also hosts a range of other consultations. Some are internally organised, while others are instigated by external groups under the guidance of House staff. The range of themes is wide but all share a concern for greater human well-being. Accommodation for up to 33 people. *Chairman, Board of Trustees and Council:* Rt Revd David J. Conner, Dean of Windsor. *Warden:* Canon Dr Hueston Finlay. *Programme Director:* Mr Gary McKeone. *Clergy Consultation Administrator:* Mrs Patricia Birdseye . *Warden's Administrator:* Miss Jenna Tyer, St George's House, Windsor Castle, Windsor, Berkshire SL4 1NJ *Tel:* 01753 848848/
Fax: 01753 848849
email: jenna.tyer@stgeorgeshouse.org
Web: www.stgeorgeshouse.org

St Hild and St Bede Trust
The Trust's annual income is restricted to the advancement of higher and further education in the Dioceses of Durham and Newcastle, and is presently committed to supporting the North East Religious Learning Resources Centre based in the City of Durham and in the Diocese of Newcastle, several lectureships, the chaplaincies of the College of St Hild and St Bede and of the University of Newcastle, scholarships and a Church of England aided school. Member of the Association of Church College Trusts (see separate entry). *Correspondent:* Mr W. Hurworth. *Home:* 16 Tempest Court, Wynyard Park, Billingham TS22 5TD, c/o College of St Hild and St Bede, Pelaw Leazes Lane, Durham, DH1 1SZ
Tel: 01740 644 274
email: w.hurworth@btinternet.com

St John's Guild
Founded in 1919 to assist the spiritual well-being of blind people, as well as to ease the isolation and loneliness in which some of them lived. Since that time both needs and society have changed. St John's Guild has developed to meet those changes. The Guild supports 10 Branches, which are located in different parts of the country and meet to provide worship, fellowship and friendship. Regular publications in Braille and audio are produced and widely distributed. *Chairman:* Mrs Judith Dunk. *Finance Officer:* Mrs Patricia Richards, Guild Office, 8 St Raphael's Court, Avenue Rd, St Albans, AL1 3EH
Tel: 01727 864076
email: stjohnsaccounts@btconnect.com
2nd email: r.mcewan1@btinternet.com
Web: www.stjohnsguild.org

St Luke's College Foundation
The Foundation's object is the advancement of further and higher education in religious education and theology. Grants are awarded to individuals for research and taught postgraduate qualifications in these fields; and to eligible organizations for related initiatives and facilities.

The Foundation does not finance buildings, or provide bursaries for institutions to administer; and it is precluded from the direct support of schools (although it supports teachers who are taking eligible studies). Member of the Association of Church College Trusts (see separate entry). *Director:* Dr David Benzie, 15 St Maryhaye, Tavistock, Devon, PL19 8LR
email: director@st-lukes-foundation.org.uk

St Luke's Healthcare for the Clergy
Providing appropriate physical and psychological healthcare services to the clergy, their spouses, widows, and dependent children, monks and nuns, deaconesses, ordinands, Church Army staff, and overseas missionaries. To find out more or to access these services please contact the Medical Secretary. *President:* The Archbishop of Canterbury. *Chairman:* Mr Bernard Cazenove. *General Secretary:* Mr Neil Stevenson, Room 201, Church House, Great Smith Street, London, SW1P 3AZ *Tel:* 020 7898 1700
email: medical@stlukeshealthcare.org.uk
Web: www.stlukeshealthcare.org.uk

St Mary's College Trust
The Trust's annual income is normally committed to supporting the Welsh National Centre for Religious Education, WNCRE at Gladstone's Library, Hawarden, Flint, and the Anglican Chaplaincy at the University of Wales, Bangor. As a result, grants to individuals and other institutions are only awarded in very exceptional circumstances. Member of the Association of Church College Trusts (see separate entry). *Correspondent and Clerk/Financial Officer:* Mr Dewi W. Williams. *Joint Chairmen:* The Bishops of Bangor and St Asaph, 26 Hampton Road, Caernarfon, BGwynedd, LL55 1BP *Tel:* 01286 674514
email: DEWIWILLIAMS@aol.com

St Michael's Fellowship
Runs four residential family assessment centres in South London working in partnership with parents to enable them to meet the needs of their child. Works with adolescent mothers, one- or two-parent families where parents may have learning disabilities, psychiatric illness, a history of abuse, domestic violence and where there are child protection concerns. Runs one supported housing scheme for vulnerable families, with self-contained flats and low support. Through Sure Start Children's Centres offers community support to teenage parents and young fathers in the Borough of Lambeth. *Director:* Mrs Sue Pettigrew, 136 Streatham High Road, London, SW16 1BW *Tel:* 020 8835 9570
Fax: 020 8677 4883
email: admin@stmichaelsfellowship.org.uk
Web: www.stmichaelsfellowship.org.uk

St Pancras and Humanist Housing Association
Founded 1924 by the Revd Basil Jellicoe, this charitable association provides housing and support for families, single people and those with special needs in nearly 4,500 flats and houses in N London and Hertfordshire. c/o Origin Housing, St Richards, 110 Eversholt St, London, NW1 1BS *Tel:* 020 7209 9287
Fax: 020 7209 9223
email: enquiries@originhousing.org.uk
Web: www.sph.org.uk

St Peter's Saltley Trust
The Trust's annual income is committed to supporting, developing and evaluating creative, innovative, locally-based project work in adult Christian learning and discipleship, the churches' work in further education and religious education in schools. The Trust's area of benefit comprises the region covered by the Anglican dioceses of Birmingham, Coventry, Hereford, Lichfield and Worcester. The Trust does not make grants towards capital projects or ongoing core costs (e.g., to fund building works or subsidise ongoing staff salaries) or to individuals for personal research or continuing education purposes. Member of the Association of Church College Trusts (see separate entry). *Director:* Dr Ian Jones. *Bursar and Clerk to the Trustees:* Mrs Lin Brown, Grays Court, 3 Nursery Rd, Edgbaston, Birmingham, B15 3JX *Tel:* 0121 427 6800
email: director@saltleytrust.oeg.uk
Web: www.saltleytrust.org.uk

Student Christian Movement
SCM is a student led community passionate about faith and justice. We have a long history of bringing students together to explore how to live out a radical faith in today's world. The national network is made up of university links, individual members, friends and subscribers. The movement holds regular conferences and produces a variety of resources, including the termly magazine *Movement*. It is affiliated to the World Student Christian Federation. *National Coordinator:* Hilary Topp. *Links Worker:* Rosie Venner. *Administrator:* Lisa Murphy, 308F The Big Peg, 120 Vyse St, Hockley, Birmingham, B18 6ND
Tel: 0121 200 3355
email: scm@movement.org.uk
Web: www.movement.org.uk

Tearfund
Tearfund is an evangelical Christian relief and development charity working with the local church around the world to bring physical, emotional and spiritual transformation to people living in poverty. Responding to natural disasters and emegencies, engaging in longer-term community development and speaking out to challenge injustice, Tearfund aims to make the fullness of life promised by Christ a reality for people in need. With support from individuals and churches in the UK and Ireland, Tearfund is in active partnership with local Christians in more than 60 countries. *Chief Executive:* Mr

Matthew Frost, 100 Church Rd, Teddington, TW11 8QE *Tel:* 0845 355 8355
Fax: 020 8943 3594
email: enquiry@tearfund.org
Web: www.tearfund.org

Third Province Movement
The object of the Third Province Movement, which was started in November 1992, is to advocate, and eventually secure, the establishment within the Church of England of an autonomous province for all those, whatever their churchmanship, who in conscience cannot accept the ordination of women to the priesthood, the episcopate and other liberal developments. It also advocates a realignment on the same principle within the whole Anglican Communion. *Chairman:* Mrs Margaret Brown, Luckhurst, Mayfield, TN20 6TY *Tel:* 01435 873007
email: thirdprovince@aol.com
Web: www.thirdprovince.org.uk

Together (Mental After Care Association)
(formerly MACA)
Together is a leading national charity providing a wide range of quality community- and hospital-based services for people with mental health needs and their carers, including: advocacy, assertive outreach schemes, community support, employment schemes, forensic services, helplines/information, respite for carers, social clubs, supported accommodation with 24–hour care. *Chief Executive:* Liz Felton, 12 Old Street, London, EC1V 9BE *Tel:* 020 7780 7300
Fax: 020 7780 7301
email: contact-us@together-uk.org
Web: www.together-uk.org

Traditional Choir Trust, The
The Traditional Choir Trust was started in 2002 by Dr John Sanders in Gloucester to: 'Give grants, bursaries and scholarships to boys otherwise unable to attend recognised choir schools. To encourage and financially assist choir schools, cathedrals, Chapels Royal, collegiate churches, university chapels, parish churches and other choral foundations to maintain the ancient tradition of the all male choir.' Upon Dr Sanders' death in 2003, the Trusteeship was handed over to the Dean and Chapter of Chichester Cathedral. The Trust relies solely upon donations and legacies to build capital from which bursaries can be provided. *Trustees:* Dean and Chapter of Chichester. *Patron:* Very Revd Michael Tavinor, Dean of Hereford. *Administrator:* The Communar, The Royal Chantry, Cathedral Cloisters, Chichester. West Sussex, PO19 1PX
Tel: 01243 782595 01243 812492
Fax: 01243 812499
email: admin@chichestercathedral.org.uk
Web: www.chichestercathedral.org.uk

Trinitarian Bible Society
Founded in 1831 for the circulation of Protestant or uncorrupted versions of the Word of God. The Society will only circulate the Authorized Version in English, and foreign language scriptures translated from the same Greek and Hebrew texts with comparable accuracy. *Office Manager:* Mr J. M. Wilson, Tyndale House, Dorset Rd, London, SW19 3NN *Tel:* 020 8543 7857
Fax: 020 8543 6370
email: tbs@trinitarianbiblesociety.org
Web: www.trinitarianbiblesociety.org

True Freedom Trust
An interdenominational support and teaching ministry for people struggling with same-sex attraction and related issues, and for their church leaders, families and friends. It believes that the Bible forbids all sexual practice outside of heterosexual marriage. It supplies resources, speakers and organizes conferences to help the Church overcome fear and prejudice and act with understanding and love in a biblical and Christlike way. *Chairman:* Mr Stefan Cantore. *Director:* Mr Jonathan Berry, PO Box 13, Prenton, Wirral, CH43 6YB *Tel:* 0151 653 0773
email: info@truefreedomtrust.co.uk
Web: www.truefreedomtrust.co.uk

Unitas – The Catholic League
Founded in 1913, the special objects of this ecumenical society are the reunion of all Christians with See of Rome, the spread of the Catholic faith, the promotion of fellowship among Catholics and the deepening of the spiritual life. It is governed by a Priest Director and six elected members. Further details from the Secretary. *The Secretary:* Mr David Chapman, Lower Flat, 293 Ordnance Road, Enfield, EN3 6HB
Tel: 01992 763 893
email: nomadyane@btinternet.com
Web: www.unitas.org.uk

Unite Clergy and Faith Workers
Unite Faith Workers is the union for those who work for religious organizations as ministers, clergy and lay staff. Membership is open to all faiths and denominations. Set up in 1994, it is now part of Unite, which has more than 1.5 million members., following the merger of Amicus with TGWU. Unite Faith Workers provides its members with a professional association of their own, with access to all the facilities and support of a modern union. Unite is recognized by the Church of England for staff in the National Church Institutions, and by some of the largest church-related charities, including Action for Children and The Children's Society. A growing number of diocesan office staff and others working for church organizations and agencies are members. Unite Faith Workers has its own

Executive, and a national network of local representatives providing support for members, and belongs to the specialist Community, Youth Workers and Non-Profit Sector within Unite, in partnership with a number of national agencies, professional associations and charities. It works to bring about fairness and dignity at work for all its members, whatever their situation, and is currently leading the campaign for modern conditions of service for those who serve as ministers. A wide range of benefits is provided for members in good standing, including legal representation and professional advice on many issues affecting work and pensions, equal opportunities, harassment and bullying at work, and much more. *Chair of Church of England Section:* Revd Christopher Elson. *Unite National Officer:* Rachael Maskell. *Communications:* Maureen German, Community, Youth Workers and Not for Profit Sector Unite the Union Unite, House 128 Theobald's Road London, WC1X 8TN
Tel: 020 337 2028
Fax: 0870 731 5043
email: maureen.german@unitetheunion.org
Web: www.unitetheunion.org

United Church Schools Trust
(Formerly Church Schools Company)
Founded as an educational charity in 1883 to create schools that offer pupils a good academic education based on Christian principles with particular reference to the Church of England. The Company's council has developed the concept of offering a broad and challenging education. To achieve this it has invested in the provision of excellent buildings and facilities including extensive ICT at each school. This ideal of strong schools embraces not just academic learning to high standards, but also the development of skills that will be essential throughout life both at work and socially. Teamwork, leadership, an enthusiastic response to challenge and an active concern for others are all attributes which are valued. Schools at Blackpool, Guildford, Surbiton, Caterham, Ashford, Hampshire near Romsey, Hull, Lincoln, Sunderland, Bournemouth and Claygate. Clergy bursaries available. A subsidiary charity, the United Learning Trust, was founded in 2002 to manage a number of City Academies spread across the country. Twenty Academies and one City Technology College are currently open, mainly in inner city areas, with more to be added during the academic year 2011–12. *Chairman:* Rt Revd and Rt Hon The Lord Carey of Clifton. *Acting Chief Executive:* Charlotte Rendle-Short. *Acting Deputy Chief Executive:* James Nicholson, Fairline House, Nene Valley Business Park, Oundle, Peterborough, PE8 4HN *Tel:* 01832 864444
Fax: 01832 734760
email: admin@church-schools.com
Web: www.ucst.org.uk

United Nations Association of Great Britain and Northern Ireland (UNA-UK)
The UN Association of the UK is the UK's leading source of independent information and analysis on the United Nations, and a UK-wide grassroots movement. UNA-UK is committed to a strong, credible and effective UN. We belive that a strengthened UN is in the UK's national interest. We advocate strong government support for the UN, and seek to demonstrate why the UN matters to people everywhere. *Executive Director:* Mr Phil Mulligan. *Administration and Policy Support Officer:* Hayley Richardson, 3 Whitehall Court, London, SW1A 2EL *Tel:* 020 7766 3454
Fax: 020 7930 5893
email: richardson@una.org.uk
Web: www.una.org.uk

Universities and Colleges Christian Fellowship
UCCF: The Christian Unions exists to give every student in Great Britain an opportunity to hear and respond to the gospel of Jesus. We are full time staff, volunteers, supporters and students all working together to make disciples of Christ in the student world. Visit www.uccf.org.uk to find out more. UCCF: The Christian Unions, Blue Boar House 5 Blue Boar Street, Oxford, OX1 4EE *Tel:* 01865 253678
email: email@uccf.org.uk
Web: www.uccf.org.uk

Urban Saints
Since 1906 Urban Saints (formerly known as Crusaders) has been reaching out to children and young people with the good news of Jesus Christ. We are passionate about working with all children and young people, helping them to realise their full God-given potential as they journey from childhood to adulthood. Young people (aged 5 to 18+) connect with the movement in a variety of ways, including weekly youth groups, special events, holidays, community projects and training programmes. These activities are led by thousands of volunteers who are comprehensively trained and supported in order to help them work effectively and achieve the highest possible standards of youth work practice. Whilst much of our work is in the UK and Ireland, increasingly we are helping indigenous churches within countries in the developing world to set up and run outreach work among un-churched children and young people. *Exec Director:* Matt Summerfield. *Volunteers Director:* Mark Arnold. *Marketing and Income Development Director:* Lorne Campbell. *Ministry Development Director:* John Fudge. *HR Manager:* Liz Dore, Kestin House, 45 Crescent Rd, Luton, LU2 0AH
Tel: 01582 589850
Fax: 01582 721702
email: email@urbansaints.org
Web: www.urbansaints.org / www.crusadersreunited.org.uk / www.urbansaints.org/energize

Urban Theology Unit
Ecumenical educational charity offering academic programmes engaging with contextual theology, ministerial practice, and urban realities. Academic programmes include Foundation Degree, MA in Theology and Ministry and MA in Urban Theology (York St John University), and M Phil/Ph D in Contextual, Urban and Liberation Theology and Ministerial Practice (University of Birmingham). There are UTU publications on British Liberation Theology, urban ministry, and contextual Bible readings. *Chairperson:* Revd Eileen Sanderson. *Acting Director:* Revd Dr Ian K Duffield. *Support Services Manager:* Mrs Kate Thompson, 210 Abbeyfield Rd, Sheffield, S4 7AZ *Tel:* 0114 243 5342
Fax: 0114 243 5356
email: office@utusheffield.org.uk
Web: www.utusheffield.org.uk

USPG: Anglicans in World Mission
Founded in 1701 as the Society for the Propagation of the Gospel in Foreign Parts (SPG), we are one of the oldest Anglican mission agencies. In 1965 we merged with the Universities' Mission to Central Africa (UMCA) and then the Cambridge Mission to Delhi to become USPG. The name was supplemented in 2007 to become USPG: Anglicans in World Mission. We work in direct partnership with Anglican churches in over 50 countries. In Africa, Asia and Latin America, we are enabling churches to reach out to poor and marginalized communities in practical and life-changing ways. This means that we are helping churches to run schools, hospitals and clinics, build houses and wells, and provide agricultural training for subsistence farmers. We also support church outreach, theological training and youth work programmes. The vision is of holistic mission, and decision-making is shared in equal partnership with churches according to priorities which belong to the "local" church in the shape of Province or diocese. Where grants are provided, they are given so that churches may plan on a long-term basis for sustainability. We run a range of personnel programmes – recruiting priests, teachers and medical workers in the UK as requested by overseas partners. We also send personnel between churches around the world. Additionally, we provide volunteers – clergy, ordinands and church workers from Britain and Ireland – with experience of the world church by sending them on short-term placements overseas. Churches and individuals in Britain and Ireland can get involved with USPG and world mission through prayer, fundraising (including a large Project Scheme) and speakers. We produce a range of publications including our regular newspaper, 'Transmission' and 'Prayer Diary' and a range of free resources for study and worship at Advent, Lent and Harvest, as well as materials to provide for engagement with individual Projects. *President:* The Archbishop of Canterbury. *Chair:* Lay Canon Linda Ali. *General Secretary:* Janette O'Neill, Harling House, 47–51 Great Suffolk Street, London, SE1 OBS
Tel: 020 7921 2200 0845 273 1701
Fax: 020 7921 2222
email: enquiries@uspg.org.uk
Web: www.uspg.org.uk

Vacation Term for Biblical Study
The Vacation Term for Biblical Study is a residential Summer School which takes place at St Anne's College, Oxford, during the last week in July and the first week in August. It is particularly suitable for theology students and any ordained and lay people with an interest in critical biblical study. Participants can take part for one or both weeks; non-residents are also welcome. Lectures are given by professional biblical scholars, specialising in Old and New Testament studies and related subjects. There is also the opportunity (optional) for tuition in biblical Greek or Hebrew at absolute beginner, intermediate or advanced level. Participants have time to enjoy the attractions of Oxford and the surrounding countryside. A limited number of bursaries towards the cost of accommodation are available. The progamme and application form are available from the website from about mid-January. Contact the Treasurer or Secretary for further details. Registered Charity no. 1125494. *Chairman:* Dr Barbara Spensley. *Secretary:* Miss Gillian Glenn. *Treasurer:* Mr Richard Garner, 45 Souldern Street, Watford, Hertfordshire, WD18 0EU *Tel:* 01923 229306
email: jrmgarner@btinternet.com
Web: www.vtbs.org.uk

Vergers, Church of England Guild of
Founded in 1932 to promote Christian fellowship and spiritual guidance among the vergers of the cathedrals and parish churches of England. The Guild is divided into branches which meet locally every month and nationally several times throughout the year. The Guild provides a comprehensive training course which students can study from home with the help of an area tutor and mentor. The course works alongside the well-established Annual Training Conference. The Guild Diploma is awarded to successful students. Advice concerning appointments, job descriptions and contracts is available through the Welfare Officer. Contact can be made through the General Secretary. *General Secretary:* Stephen Stokes, 20 Benians Court, Cambridge, CB3 0DN *Tel:* 01223 322860
email: cevgensec@gmail.com
Web: www.cofegv.org.uk

Walsingham, Shrine of Our Lady of
Founded in 1061 in response to a vision, destroyed in 1538, restored in 1922 by Revd A. Hope Patten, Vicar of Walsingham. Since 1931, when it was moved from the parish church, the Shrine

has contained the image of Our Lady of Walsingham together with the Holy House, representing the house of the Annunciation and the home in Nazareth of the Holy Family. Nowadays Walsingham is England's premier place of pilgrimage. It is administered by a College of Guardians. Special facilities include accommodation for people of all ages and those with special needs, an Education Department for school visits, and retreat and conference facilities. Information is available from the Administrator. *Administrator:* Rt Revd Lindsay Urwin OGS. *Shrine Priest and Youth Missioner:* Revd S. Gallagher, The College, Walsingham, NR22 6EF *Tel:* 01328 820255
Fax: 01328 824206
email: pr.adm@olw-shrine.org.uk
Web: www.walsingham.org.uk

WATCH (Women and the Church)
Founded in 1996, WATCH promotes the ministry of women in the Church of England. It is based on a vision of the Church as a community of God's people where justice and equality prevail, regardless of gender. WATCH works for an inclusive church in which women will take their place alongside men at every level in the Church of England, including the episcopate. Other priorities shaping our work are to achieve honesty and openness in church appointments and better support for women in ministry, and to challenge barriers which impede the full expression of a woman's vocation and gifts. The ministry of both lay and ordained women is fostered through local diocesan WATCH branches, and members receive the magazine 'Outlook' *Chair:* Revd Rachel Weir. *Secretary:* Revd Kate Stacey, St John's Church, Waterloo Rd, London, SE1 8TY
Tel: 07815 729565 01993 832514
Fax: 01763 848774
email: ifor@womenandthechurc.org
Web: www.womenandthechurch.org

William Temple Foundation
Founded in 1947, as a research and training centre focusing on the links between theology, the economy and urban mission practice. The Foundation's current programme reflects theologically and strategically on the evolving relationship between religion and public space, including the mission and identity of the church in postsecular society, and the contribution of Christianity and other religions to current well-being and happiness agendas, public policy and social welfare. This agenda also encompasses mapping and analysing the ongoing contribution of religion to ethics and economics, including the regulation of business and financial institutions. The Foundation continues its research into the work and identity of faith-based organizations in civil society across the UK, using the concept of religious and spiritual capital, and has just competed a major Leverhulme Trust programme in this area (2007–2010). The Foundation works with a wide variety of partners in this research, including several community and grassroots organization in the UK and across Europe. Emerging from this research, the Foundation is contributing teaching at post-doctoral level at the University of Chester with whom it has recently signed a research partnership, leading to the creation of a new Centre for Faiths and Public Policy (2011). It produces several publications on its research and regularly updates its work on its website. Dept of Theology and Religious Studies, University of Chester, Parkgate Road, Chester, CH1 4BJ *Tel:* 01244 511074
email: temple@wtf.org.uk *Web:* www.wtf.org.uk

William Temple House
William Temple House is a residence for 49/50 students from overseas and the United Kingdom in full-time education. The male and female students are of all faiths and nationalities. The House is under the management of The International Students' Club (C of E) Ltd, a registered charity. Enquiries to the Warden. International Students Club (C of E) Ltd, William Temple House, 29 Trebovir Rd, London, SW5 9NQ
Tel: 020 7373 6962/
Fax: 020 7341 0003
email: office@williamtemplehouse.co.uk
Web: www.williamtemplehouse.co.uk

Women's World Day of Prayer
Founded in America in 1887 (Britain 1930–34) to unite Christian women in prayer by means of services held on the first Friday in March each year, by fostering local interdenominational prayer groups meeting throughout the year and to give financial support to Christian charities throughout the world. *President:* Mrs Jean Hackett. *Chairperson:* Mrs Kathleen Skinner. *Administrator:* Mrs Mary Judd, WWDP, Commercial Rd, Tunbridge Wells, TN1 2RR *Tel:* 01892 541411
Fax: 01892 541745
email: office@wwdp-natcomm.org
Web: www.wwdp-natcomm.org

Womenaid International
A humanitarian aid and development agency run by volunteers in the UK, which provides relief and assistance to women and children suffering distress caused by war, disasters or poverty. It seeks to empower women through education, training, provision of credit, and also campaigns against violations of women's human rights. An implementing partner of the European Community Humanitarian Office (ECHO), the British Government and several UN agencies, it has provided over 30,000 tonnes of food, medical supplies and clothing to more than 1.5 million refugees in the former Yugoslavia, the Caucasus and Central Asia. Development assistance

globally has ranged from building and repairing schools, supporting rescue centres for street children, repairing hospitals and providing medical equipment/supplies to micro-credit support and water/sanitation projects. *Founder:* Ms Pida Ripley, 3 Whitehall Court, London, SW1A 2EL
Tel: 020 7839 1790
Fax: 020 7839 2929
email: womenaid@womenaid.org
Web: www.womenaid.org

Woodard Schools
Founded by Canon Nathaniel Woodard in 1848 to promote education in the doctrines and principles of the Church of England. Woodard now owns some 18 schools and a further 24 schools are linked to Woodard through formal agreements of affiliation or association. Woodard also sponsors four academies. *President:* Rt Revd Dr Anthony Russell. *Senior Provost:* Canon Brendan Clover. *Director of Education:* Mr Christopher Wright. *Director of Finance and Company Secretary:* Mr Michael Corcoran, High St, Abbots Bromley, Rugeley, WS15 3BW *Tel:* 01283 840120
Fax: 01283 840893
email: jillshorthose@woodard.co.uk
Web: www.woodard.co.uk

World Congress of Faiths
Founded in 1936 to promote mutual understanding and a spirit of fellowship between people of different religious traditions. WCF works to explain and reconcile religious conflict and the tensions between the different communities. Conferences and lectures are arranged. The journal 'Interreligious Insight' is published two or three times a year, jointly with the Interreligious Engagement Project, and has its own website. A newsletter, 'One Family', is also published at least four times a year. *President:* Revd Marcus Braybrooke. *Chairman:* Revd Dr Alan Race. *Hon Treasurer:* Pejman Khojasteh. *Editor:* Revd Dr Alan Race. *Secretary:* Revd Feargus O'Connor, London Interfaith Centre, 125 Salusbury Rd, London, NW6 6RG *Tel:* 01935 864055
email: admin@worldfaiths.org
Web: www.worldfaiths.org

World Vision
Formed in London in 1979, World Vision UK is part of the international World Vision partnership and is a major UK relief and development agency. World Vision is at work in over 100 countries in Africa, Asia, Eastern Europe, Latin America and the Middle East. It is involved in partnering churches and other non-governmental organizations in projects which range from relief work in Africa to income generation projects in Bangladesh. *Chief Exec Officer:* Charles Badenoch. *Church Relations Manager:* Alistair Metcalfe, World Vision House, Opal Drive, Fox Milne, Milton Keynes, MK15 0ZR
Tel: 01908 841000
Fax: 01908 841001
email: church@worldvision.org.uk
Web: www.worldvision.org.uk/church

YMCA
Founded 1844 to promote the physical, intellectual and spiritual well-being of young people. *President:* The Archbishop of York. *National Secretary:* Angela Sarkis, National Council of YMCAs, 640 Forest Rd, London, E17 3DZ
Tel: 020 8520 5599
Fax: 020 8509 3190
email: national.secretary@england.ymca.org.uk
Web: www.ymca.org.uk

York Glaziers' Trust
Established 1967 by the Dean and Chapter of York and the Pilgrim Trust (1) to conserve and restore the stained glass of York Minster; (2) to conserve, restore and advise on all stained glass or glazing of historic or artistic importance, in any building whether religious or secular, public or private; (3) to establish and maintain within the City of York a stained glass workshop dedicated to the training and employment of conservators and craftsmen specializing in the preservation of glass of historic and artistic importance; and (4) to encourage public interest in the preservation of stained glass, to collaborate with educational institutions and to assist with scientific and art historical research into stained and painted glass. Advice should always be sought when considering treatment of glass of artistic or historic value. The Trust welcomes enquiries from all sources. It offers a full advisory service and will compile comprehensive condition reports. *Director:* Mrs Sarah E. Brown FSA. *Senior Conservator:* Nick Teed MA. *Business Manager:* Trevor Lawson MRICS, MAPM, 6 Deangate, York, YO1 7JB *Tel:* 01904 557228
email: info@yorkglazierstrust.org
Web: www.yorkglazierstrust.org

YWCA England & Wales
YWCA England & Wales is a force for change for women facing discrimination and inequalities of all kinds. Our principal aims are to enable young women who are experiencing particular disadvantage to identify and realize their full potential, to influence public policy in order to achieve equality and social justice for young women, and to provide opportunities for participation in a worldwide women's movement. Clarendon House, 52 Cornmarket House, Oxford, OX1 3EJ *Tel:* 01865 304200
Fax: 01865 204805
email: info@ywca.org.uk
Web: www.ywca.org.uk

Diocesan Associations

Association of the Dioceses of Singapore and West Malaysia	Mrs Jane Sheard Ivy Cottage 9 Queen Street Kirton-in-Lindsey Gainsborough Lincolnshire DN21 4NS *email:* jane_ivycottage@btinternet.com
Belize Church Association	Mrs Barbara Harris Honeysuckle Cottage 19 Whittall St Kings Sutton Banbury Oxon. OX17 3RD *Tel:* 01295 811310 *email:* bkayharris@googlemail.com
Church of Ceylon Association	Prebendary Brian Leathard The Rectory 64A Flood Street London SW3 5TE *Tel:* 020 7351 7365 *email:* brianleathard@chelseaparish.org
Congo Church Association	Mrs Rosemary Peirce 8 Burwell Meadow Witney Oxford OX28 5JQ *Tel:* 01993 200103 *email:* rosemary.peirce@ntlworld.com
Egypt Diocesan Association	Mrs Elspeth Mackinlay The Horseshoes The Green Gressenhall Dereham Norfolk NR20 4DT *Tel:* 01362 860302 *email:* eda.egypt@googlemail.com
Fellowship of the Maple Leaf *(Provides grants to further mutual learning between the Church in Canada and the UK)*	Preb. David Sceats St John's Rectory Viewfield Park Selkirk TD7 4LH *Tel:* 01750 213164 *email:* d-sceats@sky.com *Web:* www.mapleleaf.org.uk
Friends of the Church in India	Mrs Angela Wingate Secretary 23 Roundhill Road Leicester LE5 5RJ
Friends of the Diocese of Cyprus and the Gulf	Mrs Sally Milner 123 Barnett Wood Lane Ashtead Surrey KT21 2LR *Tel:* 01372 270263 *email:* sallymilner14@gmail.com
Friends of the Diocese of Iran	Mr John Clark 32 Weigall Rd Lee London SE12 8HE *email:* john@mclark32.freeserve.co.uk
Friends of the Diocese of Uruguay	N. J. Roberts 2 Upland Rise Walton Chesterfield S40 2DD *Tel:* 01246 233590 *Mobile:* 07896 162461 *email:* nick.roberts@bcs.org *Web:* www.friends-of-the-diocese-of-uruguay.org.uk
Guyana Diocesan Association	Revd Canon Allan Buik 17 Hermitage Road Higham Rochester Kent ME3 7DB *Tel:* 01474 82382 07703 479715 (mobile) *email:* allanbuik@gmail.com
Jerusalem and the Middle East Church Association	Ms Shirley Eason 1 Hart House The Hart Farnham Surrey GU9 7HJ *Tel and fax:* 01252 726994 *email:* secretary@jmeca.eclipse.co.uk *Web:* www.jmeca.org.uk

Kenya Church Association	*Hon Secretary:* Revd Bryan Wadland 55 Copthall Rd East Ickenham UB10 8SE *Tel:* 01895 613904 *email:* douglas087@btinternet.com
Lesotho Diocesan Association	Sister Jean Mary CHN Convent of the Holy Name Morley Road Oakwood Derby DE21 4QZ *Tel:* 01332 671 716 *email:* chnjmary@yahoo.co.uk
MANNA Mozambique and Angola Anglican Association	*General Secretary:* Ian Gordon 16 Bayle Court The Bayle Folkestone Kent CT20 1SN *Tel:* 01303 257248 *email:* n_grdn@yahoo.co.uk
Nigeria Fellowship	*Chair:* Dr Anne Phillips 33 Cliffe Road Sheffield S6 5DR *Tel:* 0114 233 8529 *email:* annephillips2@hotmail.co.uk
Province of the Indian Ocean Support Association	*Hon. Secretary:* Vacancy *Chair:* Canon Hall Speers The Rectory 38 Manor Rd Barnet EN5 2JJ *Tel:* 020 8449 3894 *email:* hall.speers@talk21.com *Hon. Treasurer:* Revd Hilary C. Jones St Martin's Rectory Horn St Folkestone CT20 3JJ *Tel:* 01303 238509 *email:* revhilaryjones@btinternet.com
St Helena Association	Canon Patricia Ann Turner 7 Roundell Drive West Marton Skipton BD23 3UL *Tel:* 01282 842332 *email:* ann.turner@bradford.anglican.org
Sudan Church Association	Mrs Sara Taffinder 69 Poynders Rd Clapham London SW4 8PL *Tel* and *Fax:* 020 8671 1974
TZABA Trans-Vaal, Zimbabwe and Botswana Association	Mrs Liz Martin 120 Church Lane East Aldershot Hampshire GU11 3SS *Tel* and *Fax:* 01252 320108 *email:* elizmmartin@yahoo.co.uk
Uganda Church Association	Revd Dr Michael Hunter The Vicarage 51 Vicarage Lane Dore Sheffield S17 3GY *Tel:* 0114 236 3480 *email:* mutagwok@aol.com
Zululand Swaziland Association	The Zululand Swaziland Association has ceased to exist as an independent charity. The Zululand Swaziland Trusteeship has now passed to the trustees of USPG, and donations to its ongoing work can be received by cheques made payable to 'USPG', earmarked 'Zululand Swaziland Trust'. USPG: Anglicans in World Mission Harling House 47–51 Great Suffolk Street London SE1 0BS

Libraries

Canterbury

Cathedral Library
The Precincts
Canterbury
Kent CT1 2EH

Cathedral Librarian (acting)
Mrs Karen Brayshaw

Cathedral Archivist
Mrs Cressida Williams

The archives and library at Canterbury are separate departments. Information about the archives is available on the archives pages of the Cathedral website at www.canterbury-cathedral.org/history/archives.aspx or by telephoning 01227 865330. Information about the library can be found at www.canterbury-cathedral.org/history/libraries.aspx or by telephoning 01277 865287.

Tel: 01227 865330 (Archives)
01227 865287 (Library)
Fax: 01227 865222
email: library@canterbury-cathedral.org

Library collections: 52,000 printed volumes, 15th century to present. The Howley-Harrison Collection (16,000 books and pamphlets) includes anti-slavery and Oxford Movement material. Also cathedral printed music, and scores of Canterbury Catch Club. Mendham Collection of Catholic and anti-Catholic writings. Two parish libraries: Elham and Preston-next-Wingham, in a Dr Bray cabinet. The collections include substantial holdings on national and local history, including the English Civil War, travel, botany, English and foreign literature.

Archive collections: large collections of manuscript and archives, including the Cathedral archives; records of the Diocese of Canterbury; parish records; records of the City Council and other organizations, businesses, administrations and individuals in the Canterbury area.

Crowther Library

Crowther Centre for Mission Education
Church Mission Society
Watlington Rd
Oxford
OX4 6BZ

Librarian Ken Osborne

Tel: 01865 787552
Fax: 01865 776375
email: ken.osborne@cms-uk.org
Web: www.cms-uk.org/heritage/default.htm
Open: 0900–1700 hours Mon–Fri
Closed public holidays.

30,000 volumes, 250 current periodicals. Successor to the Partnership House Mission Studies Library that incorporated the post-1945 collections of the former Church Missionary Society and United Society for the Propagation of the Gospel Stock focuses on the work of the Church worldwide, missiology, history of mission, church history, African and Asian Christianity and interfaith relations. Also houses CMS's pre-1945 collection entitled the Max Warren Collection. Reference only.

ORGANIZATIONS

Durham Durham Cathedral Library The College Durham DH1 3EH	*Canon Librarian* Canon Rosalind Brown *Head of Collections* Gabriel Sewell *Tel:* 0191 386 2489 *email:* Library@durhamcathedral.co.uk Open: 0900–16.45 hours Mon–Fri	Chapter Library of 375 medieval manuscripts from the 7th century onwards, including Northumbrian, Norman and scholastic material. 1000 post-medieval manuscripts. Manuscript and printed music 16th cent–early 19th cent. Archival collections include historical collections for County Durham and the NE of England, with much of wider interest, formed by local antiquaries, 17th–20th cent; papers and correspondence of 19th–20th cent. bishops and churchmen. Printed books include 70 incunabula, 11,000 books printed pre-1851 and modern works of church history, local interest and the arts. Archdeacon Sharp Library of modern theology of approx. 10,000 books in English. Meissen Library of theology in German of approx. 20,000 books donated by EKD inaugurated 1998. Catalogue at its website www.meissenlibrarydurham.co.uk.
Exeter Exeter Cathedral Library and Archives West Wing The Palace Palace Gate Exeter EX1 1HX	*Cathedral Librarian* Peter Thomas *Assistant Librarian* Stuart Macwilliam *Cathedral Archivist* Ellie Jones *Tel:* 01392 421423 *email:* library@exeter-cathedral.org.uk archive@exeter-cathedral.org.uk *Web:* http://www.exeter-cathedral.org.uk/Admin/Library/html Open: 1000–1600 hours Mon, Tues, Thur, Fri. Closed on public holidays. (Archives, by appointment only). Closed on public holidays.	20,000 items (Library); 50,000 (Archives), Manuscripts include Exeter Book and Exon Domesday; special collections include cathedral manuscripts and archives, early printed books in medicine and science, Cook Collection (16th–19th c., early linguistics), printed tracts (mainly Civil War period), Harington Collection (16th–19th c., theology, ecclesiastical history, history). Pre-2001 accessions included in online catalogue of Exeter University Library at www.ex.ac.uk/library/. Medical and scientific collections also catalogued in *Medicine and science at Exeter Cathedral Library*, compiled by Peter W. Thomas (University of Exeter Press, 2003). See also *The library and archives of Exeter Cathedral*, by L. J. Lloyd and Audrey M. Erskine, 3rd edn (Exeter 2004).

Gladstone's Library Gladstone's Library Church Lane Hawarden Flintshire CH5 3DF	*Warden* Revd Peter Francis *Tel:* 01244 532350 *Fax:* 01244 520643 *email:* enquiries@ gladlib.org *Web:* www.gladstoneslibrary.org	Extensive holdings in Theology and Religious Studies. Main subject areas include: contextual theologies, Christian doctrine, biblical studies, ethics, spirituality, liturgy, church history plus Islamic Collection, Liberal/ Radical Theology Archive, Bishop Moorman Franciscan Collection and excellent holdings in nineteenth-century history, art and literature. Twenty-six bedrooms, four conference rooms and chapel. Subsidised rates for clergy and students. Bursaries and scholarships available.
Hereford Hereford Cathedral Library and Archives Hereford Cathedral Hereford HR1 2NG	*Canon Chancellor* Canon Christopher Pullin *Archivist* Mrs Rosalind Caird *Librarian* Dr Rosemary Firman *Cataloguer* Tessa Smart *Library and Archives Assistant* Lucy Barrell *Photographer* Gordon Taylor MBE LRPS *Tel:* 01432 374225/6 *email:* library@ herefordcathedral.org *Web:* www.herefordcathedral.org Open: Tues and Thurs 1000–1600 hours. Other times by prior appointment. Closed in January for essential conservation and maintenance work.	The Library cares for the Mappa Mundi (*c.* 1300), Chained Library and All Saints' Chained Library. The collection includes 227 medieval manuscripts from the 8th to the early 16th centuries, over 3,000 pre-1801 printed books including 56 incunabula, 10,000 books published post-1800 (many borrowable) and manuscript and printed music (18th to 20th centuries). There are also 30,000 archives of the Dean and Chapter, dating from the 9th to 21st centuries. Photographic service available.
Lambeth Lambeth Palace Library London SE1 7JU	*Librarian and Archivist* Giles Mandelbrote *Tel:* 020 7898 1400 *email:* archives@ churchofengland.org *Web:* www. lambethpalacelibrary.org Open: 1000–1700 hours Mon–Fri (1030–1700 Wed) Closed public holidays and ten days at Christmas and Easter.	Main library for the history of the Church of England, open for public use since 1610. 200,000 printed books and pamphlets, 4,900 manuscripts 9th–20th centuries. Registers and correspondence of Archbishops of Canterbury 12th–20th centuries. Records of Province of Canterbury, the Faculty Office, Lambeth Conferences up to 1968, Bishops of London, and papers of churchmen, statesmen and organizations within the Church of England. Also holds the manuscripts and printed books earlier than 1850 from Sion College Library.

Pusey House Pusey House Oxford OX1 3LZ	*Principal* Vacancy *Custodian and Archivist* Revd Dr Barry A. Orford *Chaplain* Revd Philip Corbett *Tel:* 01865 278415 *email:* chapter@ puseyhouse.org.uk *Web:* www.puseyhouse.org.uk Open: 0930–1230, 1400–1630 Mon–Fri; 0930–1230 Sat (by appointment only) during full term (weeks 0–8) During vacation the library is open Monday to Friday by appointment only. The library is closed during August and at the beginning of September until after the St Giles' Fair. Contact the Custodian for vacation opening times	80,000 volumes. A theological library specializing in patristics, Church history and liturgy. An extensive archive of Oxford Movement and related material.
St Paul's The Library St Paul's Cathedral London EC4M 8AE	*Librarian* Mr Jo Wisdom *Tel:* 020 7246 8345 *Fax:* 020 7248 3104 *email:* library@ stpaulscathedral.org.uk	Re-established after the Great Fire of 1666, the library is strong in theology, ecclesiastical history, and sermons, especially of 17th and 18th centuries. Special collections include early printed Bibles; St Paul's Cross sermons; 19th-century tracts. The archive of Dean and Chapter is deposited at Guildhall Library, Aldermanbury, London EC2P 2EJ.
Sarum College Sarum College Library 19 The Close Salisbury Wilts. SP1 2EE	*Director of Learning Resources* Jennifer Monds *Librarian* Jayne Downey *Tel:* 01722 424803 *Fax:* 01722 338508 *email:* library@sarum.ac.uk *web:* www.sarum.ac.uk/ library Open: 0900–1700 Mon–Fri and some evenings during term time Fees: £30 per annum for reading rights; £40 per annum for reading and borrowing rights; £5 per day or £10 per week for visitors	Founded 1860. 36,000 volumes mostly on academic theology, church history, ethics and Christian spirituality. Rare book collection including 274 bound volumes of mainly 20th-century tracts, sermons, charges and letters. About 1000 volumes are added each year. Fifty journals are taken, with back numbers available for reference use. Inter-library loan services offered. Internet, word processing facilities and Wi-Fi access available. Archive of the Christian Socialist Movement. Catalogue accessible from the library homepage at the above web address. Accommodation available. Researchers and sabbaticals welcome. Quiet space. Coffee, tea and lunches may be purchased. There is also a bookshop selling academic theology.

Sarum College Bookshop 19 The Close Salisbury Wilts. SP1 2EE	*Director of Learning Resources* Jennifer Monds *Assistant Manager* Emily Button *Tel:* 01722 326899 *email:* bookshop@sarum.ac.uk *web:* www.sarum.ac.uk/bookshop Open: 0900–1645 Mon–Fri, 1000–1600 Sats and Tues. evenings during term time	Excellent selection of new and second-hand academic theology, church history, ethics, Christian spirituality, etc. Mail order facility. Out-of-print and hard to find title search facility. Church supplies and cards for all church events (ordination, confirmation, baptism, etc.)
Sion College	The library has closed. The older books (–1850) were transferred to Lambeth Palace Library. The bulk of the balance of the collection is in the library of King's College, London.	Biblical studies, philosophy, Anglican theology, church history, biography and liturgy. Special collections include Sion College Port Royal Library, Industrial Christian Fellowship Library, and extensive pamphlet collections.
United Society for the Propagation of the Gospel Bodleian Library of Commonwealth and African Studies at Rhodes House South Parks Rd Oxford OX1 3RG	*Archivist* Miss Lucy McCann *Tel:* 01865 270908 *email:* rhodes.house.library@bodleian.ox.ac.uk Bodleian reader's ticket required – details at www.bodleian.ox.ac.uk/bodley/services/admissions.	The Society's library to 1944 and archival material circa 1701–1965. Extensive collections from the 19th century, back holdings of missionary journals.
Westminster Abbey Westminster Abbey Muniment Room and Library London SW1P 3PA	*Librarian* Dr Tony Trowles *Keeper of the Muniments* Mr Matthew Payne *Tel:* 020 7654 4830 *email:* library@westminster-abbey.org *Web:* www.westminster-abbey.org Open: 1000–1300, 1400–1645 hours Mon–Fri; appointments required	Library and archives of the Dean and Chapter of Westminster. Library includes manuscripts, early printed books (16,000), and modern collections (4,000) concerned with the history of Westminster Abbey and associated subjects. Extensive archive of the medieval monastery and its estates together with post-Reformation Abbey records to the present day.
York Minster York Minster Historic Collections The Old Palace Dean's Park York YO1 7JQ	*Librarian* Ms Sarah Griffin *Archivist* Mr Peter Young *Collections Manager* Miss Victoria Harrison *Tel:* 0844 939 0021 ext 2500 (Library), ext 2520 (Archives) ext 2540 (Collections) *email:* Library: library@yorkminster.org Archives: petery@yorkminster.org	Library: 120,000 volumes. Theology; church history, art, architecture and stained glass; extensive collections of pre-1801 books; incunables; special collections of Yorkshire history, Yorkshire topographical prints, and Yorkshire Civil War tracts. Archives: music and photographic collections; archives of Dean and Chapter from medieval times; manuscripts.

	Collections: vickyh@yorkminster.org *Web:* (Library catalogue) http://yorsearch.york.ac.uk/ (Guide to Historic Collections) http://www.yorkminster.org/treasures-and-collections/historic-collections.html Open: 0900–1700 hours Mon–Fri for general use. Archive, Special Collections and artefacts by appointment only Closed on public holidays	Collections: Cathedral and Parish Plate; Textiles; Historic Furnishings inc. ornaments, furniture and adornments; Monuments; Displaced Glass; Worked Stone; Archaeology; Treasures.

See also main Organizations section

Patronage Trusts

Church Pastoral Aid Society Patronage Trust	*Secretary* Revd John Fisher CPAS, Unit 3, Sovereign Court One Sir William Lyons Road Coventry CV4 7EZ *Tel:* 0300 123 0780 extn 4387/4388 *email:* jfisher@ cpas.org.uk / patronage@cpas.org.uk	A Trust holding Rights of Presentation to a number of benefices. Administered by the Church Pastoral Aid Society.
Church Patronage Trust	*Secretary* Canon Roger Salisbury 6 Church Street Widcombe Bath BA2 6AZ *Tel:* 01225 489076 *email:* patronage@btinternet.com *Web:* www.churchpatronagetrust.co.uk	A Trust holding the Rights of Presentation to a number of benefices. Evangelical tradition.
Church Society Trust	*Chairman* Revd Dick Farr Dean Wace House 16 Rosslyn Rd Watford, Herts. WD18 0NY *Tel:* 01923 235111 *Fax:* 01923 800362 *email:* admin@churchsociety.org	Patron of more than 100 livings.
Church Trust Fund Trust	*Secretary* Revd John Fisher CPAS, Unit 3, Sovereign Court One Sir William Lyons Road Coventry CV4 7EZ *Tel:* 0300 123 0780 extn 4387/4388 *email:* jfisher@ cpas.org.uk / patronage@cpas.org.uk	A Trust holding Rights of Presentation to a number of benefices. Administered by the Church Pastoral Aid Society.

Guild of All Souls	*General Secretary* David G. Llewelyn Morgan Guild of All Souls Royal London House 22–25 Finsbury Square London EC2A 1DX *Tel:* 01371 830132 *Web:* www.guildofallsouls.org.uk	Patron of 41 livings of Catholic tradition.
Hulme Trustees	*Secretary* Mr Jonathan Shelmerdine, Butcher and Barlow Solicitors 31 Middlewich Rd Sandbach Cheshire CW11 1HW *Tel:* 01270 762521	A Trust holding the Rights of Presentation to a number of benefices.
Hyndman's (Miss) Trustees	*Executive Officer* Mrs Ann Brown 6 Angerford Ave Sheffield S8 9BG *Tel:* 0114 255 8522 *email:* ann.brown@hyndmans.org.uk	Patronage Trust. Varied churchmanship.
Intercontinental Church Society	Unit 11 Ensign Business Centre Westwood Way Westwood Business Park Coventry CV4 8JA *Tel:* 024 7646 3940 *Fax:* 024 7767 5868 *email:* enquiries@ics-uk.org	ICS is an Anglican mission society which makes known the Christ of the Scriptures to people of any nationality who speak English, mainly in countries where English is not the first language.
Martyrs Memorial and Church of England Trust	*Secretary* Revd John Fisher CPAS, Unit 3, Sovereign Court One Sir William Lyons Road Coventry CV4 7EZ *Tel:* 0300 123 0780 extn 4387/4388 *email:* jfisher@ cpas.org.uk / patronage@cpas.org.uk	A Trust holding Rights of Presentation to a number of benefices. Administered by the Church Pastoral Aid Society.
Peache Trustees	*Secretary* Canon Roger Salisbury 6 Church Street Widcombe Bath BA2 6AZ *Tel:* 01225 489076 *email:* patronage@btinternet.com	A Trust holding the Rights of Presentation to a number of benefices. Evangelical tradition.
Simeon's Trustees	*Executive Officer* Mrs Ann Brown 6 Angerford Ave Sheffield S8 9BG *Tel:* 0114 255 8522 *email:* ann.brown@simeons.org.uk	Holds and administers the patronage of those livings in the Church of England which belong to the Trust on the principles laid down in Charles Simeon's Charge.

ORGANIZATIONS

Society for the Maintenance of the Faith	*President* Dr Brian Hanson *Secretary* Revd Paul Conrad Christ Church Vicarage, 10 Cannon Place, London, NW3 1EJ. *Tel* and *Fax:* 020 7435 6784	Founded in 1873, the Society presents, or shares in the presentation of, priests to over 80 benefices. As well as its work as a patronage body the Society aims to promote Catholic teaching and practice in the Church of England at large.

PART 5

Anglican and Porvoo Communions

PART 5 CONTENTS

THE ANGLICAN COMMUNION

OUR FAITH

Anglican/Episcopal churches uphold and proclaim the Catholic and Apostolic faith, proclaimed in the Scriptures, interpreted in the light of tradition and reason. Following the teachings of Jesus Christ, Anglicans are committed to the proclamation of the good news of the Gospel to all creation. Our faith and ministry have been expressed through the *Book of Common Prayer*, received and adapted by the local churches, in the Services of Ordination (the Ordinal), and in the Chicago-Lambeth Quadrilateral, first expounded at the missionary Conference in Chicago, and revised by the Lambeth Conference of 1888. The Quadrilateral sets out four essential elements of the Christian faith:

1 The Holy Scriptures of the Old and New Testaments as 'containing all things necessary to salvation', and as being the rule and ultimate standard of faith.
2 The Apostles' Creed, as the baptismal symbol; and the Nicene Creed as the sufficient statement of the Christian Faith.
3 The two Sacraments ordained by Christ himself – Baptism and the Supper of the Lord – ministered with unfailing use of Christ's words of institution and of the elements ordained by Him.
4 The Historic Episcopate, locally adapted in the methods of its administration to the varying needs of the nations and peoples called of God into the unity of His Church.

Central to Anglican worship is the celebration of the Holy Eucharist (also called the Holy Communion, the Lord's Supper or the Mass). In this offering of prayer and praise, the life, death, resurrection and ascension of Jesus Christ are made a present reality through the proclamation of the Word and the celebration of the Sacrament. Anglicans celebrate the Sacrament of Baptism with water in the name of the Trinity, as the rite of entry into the Christian Church, and celebrate other Sacramental rites, including Confirmation, Reconciliation, Marriage, Anointing the sick and Ordination.

Common prayer is at the heart of Anglicanism. Its styles may vary from the simple to the elaborate, from evangelical to catholic, charismatic to traditional. The various Books of Common Prayer give expression to a comprehensiveness found within the churches, which seeks to chart a *via media* in relation to other Christian traditions.

OUR CHURCHES

Deriving from the ancient Celtic and Saxon churches of the British Isles, Anglicanism found its distinctive identity in the sixteenth and seventeenth century Reformation, when the separate Church of England came into being, together with the Church of Ireland, and the Scottish Episcopal Church. At the time of the American Revolution, an autonomous Episcopal Church was founded in the United States, and later Anglican or Episcopal churches were founded across the globe as a result of the missionary movements of the eighteenth and nineteenth centuries. Many of these were given autonomy as Provinces in the course of the nineteenth and twentieth centuries. In South Asia, the United Churches, formed between Anglican and several Protestant denominations, also joined the Anglican Communion, as did churches elsewhere such as the Spanish Episcopal Reformed Church and the Lusitanian Church of Portugal.

Today, the Anglican Communion Episcopal family consists of an estimated 78 million Christians, made up of 34 Provinces, 4 United Churches and 6 other Churches, spread across the globe.

THE INSTRUMENTS OF COMMUNION

The Archbishop of Canterbury

The churches are all in communion with the See of Canterbury in the Church of England, and thus the Archbishop of Canterbury, in his person and ministry, is the unique focus of Anglican unity. He calls the Lambeth Conference, and Primates' Meeting, and is President of the Anglican Consultative Council. The 104th Archbishop of Canterbury in succession to St. Augustine, the Most Revd and Rt Hon Rowan Williams, was enthroned in February 2003.

The Primates Meeting

Since 1979, the Archbishop of Canterbury has also invited the primates (the presiding bishop, archbishop or moderator) of each of the 38 Provinces to join him in regular meetings for consultation, prayer and reflection on theological, social and international matters. These meetings take place approximately every eighteen months to two years.

The Anglican Consultative Council

In 1968 the bishops of the Lambeth Conference requested the establishment of a body representative of all sections (bishops, clergy and laity) of the churches, which could co-ordinate aspects of international Anglican ecumenical and mission work. With the consent of the legislative bodies of all the Provinces, the Anglican Consultative Council was established, and has met regularly since.

ACC Meetings:
Limuru, Kenya (1971), Dublin, Eire (1973), Trinidad (1976), London, Ontario, (1979), Newcastle upon Tyne, England (1981), Badagry, Nigeria (1984), Singapore (1987), Lampeter, Wales (1990), Cape Town, South Africa (1993), Panama (1996), Dundee, Scotland (1999), Hong Kong (2002), Nottingham, England (2005), Jamaica (2009).

The Lambeth Conference

The Lambeth Conference is the longest-standing of the Instruments of Communion of the worldwide Anglican Communion. Its origins go back to 1865 when, on 20 September, the Provincial Synod of the Church of Canada unanimously agreed to urge the Archbishop of Canterbury and the Convocation of his Province to find a means by which the bishops consecrated within the Church of England and serving overseas could be brought together for a General Council to discuss issues facing them in North America, and elsewhere. Part of the background for this request was a serious dispute about the interpretation and authority of the Scriptures which had arisen in Southern Africa between Robert Gray, Archbishop of Cape Town, and Bishop Colenso, Bishop of Natal.

Notwithstanding the opposition of a significant number of the bishops in England, Archbishop Longley invited Anglican bishops to their first Conference together at Lambeth Palace on 24 September, 1867 and the three subsequent days. Seventy-six bishops finally accepted the invitation and the Conference was called to order and met in the Chapel of Lambeth Palace. A request to use Westminster Abbey for a service was not granted.

Of the 76 bishops attending the first Lambeth Conference the distribution was the following:

England	18 bishops
Ireland	5 bishops
Scotland	6 bishops
Colonial and Missionary	28 bishops
United States	19 bishops

It was made clear at the outset that the Conference would have no authority of itself as it was not competent to make declarations or lay down definitions on points of doctrine. But the Conference was useful in that it explored many aspects of possible inter-Anglican co-operation and by providing common counsel it inaugurated a practical way in which the unity of the faith of the Church could be maintained. The Conference did not take any effective action regarding the issues raised by Bishop Colenso but its far-reaching impact can be seen in the fact that it was the precursor of the Lambeth Conference that we know today.

Lambeth Conferences:
Lambeth Palace (1878, 1888, 1897, 1908, 1920, 1930, 1948 and 1958), Church House, Westminster (1968), University of Kent, Canterbury (1978, 1988), Canterbury (1998, 2008).

The Lambeth Conference hosted by Archbishop Williams in Canterbury in July 2008 was attended by 650 bishops. The model adopted by the Archbishop of Canterbury (indaba) was not oriented towards the passing of resolutions but rather towards respectful listening and the imperative that all bishops' voices be heard and valued; offering an open space for bishops to express their views knowing that they would be heard. This process generated honest interchange and mutual understanding and assisted bishops to respond to the concerns and mission imperatives of their colleagues across two broad themes: Equipping Bishops for God's Mission and Strengthening Anglican Identity. Reports and reflections can be found on the Lambeth Conference website (www.lambethconference.org)

THE ANGLICAN COMMUNION OFFICE

This is a permanent secretariat based in London under the leadership of the Anglican Communion's Secretary General the Revd Canon Dr Kenneth Kearon. The staff of the Anglican Communion Office (ACO) facilitate all meetings of the conciliar Instruments of Communion, as well as the Commissions and Networks of the Communion. They support the Secretary General in carrying out the decisions and resolutions of the Instruments.

ACO staff also act as guardians of Communion history, information and data; they co-ordinate Communion projects on church growth and evangelism, relief and development and theological studies; and they communicate Communion news and information worldwide. They maintain a presence at the United Nations and also facilitate meetings on ecumenical dialogues, interfaith dialogues and on Unity, Faith and Order issues.

Funding comes from a variety of sources, but mainly from the Inter-Anglican Provincial contributions as supported by all member Churches according to their membership and means. Member Churches are also invited to contribute to special projects, initiatives and emergencies as they arise.

More information and resources about the Communion and the work of the Anglican Communion Office can be found on at www.anglicancommunion.org. These include the official prayer cycle (daily prayer intentions for the dioceses of the Communion), full details of all member Churches, and the latest news from across the Communion via the Anglican Communion News Service (ACNS). ACNS is also available by subscribing online to the free email news service. A selection of Anglican Communion books and reports are also available from the online shop.

PROVINCES OF THE ANGLICAN COMMUNION

The Anglican Church in Aotearoa, New Zealand and Polynesia
The Anglican Church of Australia
The Church of Bangladesh
The Episcopal Anglican Church of Brazil
The Province of the Anglican Church of Burundi
The Anglican Church of Canada
The Church of the Province of Central Africa
The Anglican Church of the Central American Region
The Anglican Church of the Congo
The Church of England
Hong Kong Sheng Kung Hui
The Church of the Province of the Indian Ocean
The Church of Ireland
Nippon So Ko Kai – The Anglican Communion in Japan
The Episcopal Church in Jerusalem and the Middle East
The Anglican Church of Kenya
The Anglican Church of Korea
The Church of the Province of Melanesia
The Anglican Church of Mexico
The Church of the Province of Myanmar (Burma)
The Church of Nigeria (Anglican Communion)
The Church of North India
The Church of Pakistan
The Anglican Church of Papua New Guinea
The Episcopal Church in the Philippines
The Episcopal Church of Rwanda
The Scottish Episcopal Church
The Church of the Province of South East Asia
The Anglican Church of Southern Africa
The Anglican Church of the Southern Cone of America
The Church of South India
The Episcopal Church of the Sudan
The Anglican Church of Tanzania
The Church of the Province of Uganda
The Episcopal Church
Includes overseas dioceses in Taiwan, Haiti, Columbia, Honduras, Dominican Republic and Ecuador
The Church in Wales
The Church of the Province of West Africa
The Church of the Province of the West Indies

EXTRA PROVINCIAL DIOCESES AND OTHER CHURCHES

The Anglican Church of Bermuda
The Anglican Church of Ceylon (Sri Lanka)
The Episcopal Church of Cuba
The Lusitanian Church (Portugal)
The Spanish Reformed Episcopal Church
Falkland Islands

CHURCHES IN COMMUNION

The Mar Thoma Syrian Church
The Old Catholic Churches of the Union of Utrecht
The Philippine Independent Church
The Church in China is a 'post denominational' Church whose formation included Anglicans in the Holy Catholic Church in China.
Anglicans/Episcopalians, in certain parts of the Communion, are in full communion with some Lutheran Churches.

THE ANGLICAN COMMUNION OFFICE

Secretary General Canon Dr Kenneth Kearon, Anglican Communion Office, St Andrew's House, 16 Tavistock Crescent, London, W11 1AP.
Tel: 0207 313 3900
Fax 0207 313 3999
email: aco@anglicancommunion.org
Web: www.anglicancommunion.org

The Anglican Centre in Rome

The Anglican Centre in Rome was established in April 1966, endorsed by the Metropolitans of the Anglican Communion. This followed consultations among representatives of the several Churches of the Anglican Communion on action for the furtherance of Christian unity and the prospects for renewed fellowship and cooperation between Anglicans and Roman Catholics held out by the Second Vatican Council and by the historic visit of the Archbishop of Canterbury to Rome in March 1966. The Anglican Centre celebrated the fortieth anniversary of its foundation in 2006.

The Anglican Centre:

1. Provides a meeting place where clergy and laity, Anglican, Roman Catholic, and those of other Christian denominations, may come together for discussion, worship and prayer for the achievement of Christian unity.
2. Sponsors courses, lectures, seminars and discussions to enable a deeper understanding of the Roman Catholic Church, Anglicanism and the whole Western Christian tradition.
3. Is a welcoming reference point for visitors to Rome from member churches of the Anglican Communion, helping tourists in becoming pilgrims.
4. Holds a growing library of Anglican history, theology and liturgy, and of ecumenism, for the use of students and scholars of all Christian denominations.
5. Offers assistance to visiting Anglican scholars who wish to work in Rome, where possible putting them in touch with resident scholars in their field.
6. Offers a focal point for Anglican collaboration with the various agencies of the Roman Catholic Church and in particular the Pontifical Council for the Promotion of Christian Unity.
7. Supports the official dialogues for promoting unity between the Anglican Communion and the Roman Catholic Church.
8. Publishes a magazine, *CENTRO*, both online and in paper form, twice a year.

At the heart of the Centre's life is the chapel. Here the Eucharist is celebrated weekly on Tuesdays, at which the congregation is a microcosm of Christianity: Anglicans from around the world, Lutherans, Methodists, Roman Catholics and others. Visitors are welcome at the Eucharist and the lunch that follows.

The Centre's library is open from 9 a.m. to 1 p.m. Monday to Friday and by arrangement at other times. The Centre itself is normally open from 9 to 5 Monday to Friday, but it is advisable to ring ahead. It is closed in August and on public holidays. There is a governing body, and a director.

Director and Archbishop of Canterbury's Representative to the Holy See Very Revd Canon David Richardson, The Anglican Centre in Rome, Palazzo Doria Pamphilj, Piazza del Collegio Romano 2, 00186 Rome, Italy *Tel:* 39 06 678 0302
Fax: 39 06 678 0674
director@anglicancentre.it
Web: www.anglicancentreinrome.org

PA to the Director and Course Administrator Jan Hague
email: administrator@anglicancentre.it

Centre Receptionist and Librarian Marcella Menna
email: anglicancentre@anglicancentre.it

Development Officer UK Revd Bill Snelson
email: developmentUK@anglicancentre.it

FRIENDS OF THE ANGLICAN CENTRE IN ROME

Founded in 1984 to enlist support through both prayer and financial assistance for the work of the Centre.

President The Archbishop of Canterbury

Chairman Rt Revd Edward Holland

Chairman, English Friends Rt Revd Edward Holland, 37 Parfrey St, London W6 9EW

Secretary Miss Virginia Johnstone, 127 Cranmer Court, Whiteheads Grove, London SW3 3HE
Tel: 020 7589 0697

CHURCHES AND PROVINCES OF THE ANGLICAN COMMUNION

AUTONOMOUS CHURCHES AND PROVINCES IN COMMUNION WITH THE SEE OF CANTERBURY

Note: In the following directory section most provinces correspond to a specific country. In the postal addresses given, the name of the country is included only if some dioceses in the province are outside the country indicated by the name of the province.

Anglican Church in Aotearoa, New Zealand and Polynesia

Members 564,892
Formerly known as the Church of the Province of New Zealand, the Church covers 106,000 square miles and includes the countries of Aotearoa, New Zealand, Fiji, Tonga, Samoa and the Cook Islands. It was established as an autonomous Church in 1857. A revised constitution adopted in 1992 reflects a commitment to bicultural development that allows freedom and responsibility to implement worship and mission in accordance with the culture and social conditions of the Maori (Tikanga Maori), European (Tikanga Pakeha) and Polynesian (Tikanga Pasefika) membership. The Church has a strong and effective Anglican Missions Board.

Primates/Archbishops
Most Revd William Brown Turei (*Tikanga Maori*), PO Box 568, Gisborne 4040, New Zealand
Tel: 64 6 867 7028
Fax: 64 6 867 8859
email: browntmihi@xtra.co.nz
Web: www.anglican.org.nz

Most Revd Dr Winston Halapua (*Tikanga Pasefika*), PO Box 35, Suva, Fiji Islands *Tel:* 679 330 4716
Fax: 679 330 2152
email: bishoppolynesia@connect.com.fj
Web: www.anglican.org.nz

Most Revd David John Moxon (*Tikanga Pakeha*), PO Box 21, Hamilton 3240, New Zealand
Tel: 64 7 857 0020
Fax: 64 7 856 9975
email: bishop@hn-ang.org.nz
Web: www.anglican.org.nz

General Secretary and *Treasurer* Revd Michael Hughes, PO Box 87188, Meadowbank, Auckland 1742, New Zealand *Tel:* 64 9 521 4439
Fax: 64 9 521 4490
email: gensec@ang.org.nz/gensecpa@ang.org.nz
Web: www.anglican.org.nz

THEOLOGICAL COLLEGES
The College of St John the Evangelist, Private Bag 28–907, Remuera, Auckland 1541, New Zealand (serves both Anglicans and Methodists) *Commissioner* Vacancy; *Tikanga Pakeha* Revd Dr Helen-Ann Hartley; *Tikanga Maori* Dr Jenny Plane-Te Paa; *Tikanga Polynesia* Revd Dr Frank Smith *Tel:* 64 9 521 2725
Fax: 64 9 521 2420
email: stjohnscollege@auckland.ac.nz
Web: www.stjohnscollege.ac.nz

Theology House, PO Box 6728 Upper Riccarton, Christchurch 8442, New Zealand (*Director* Revd Dr Peter Carrell) *Tel:* 64 3 351 1364
Fax: 64 3 355 6140
email: director@theologyhouse.ac.nz
Web: www.theologyhouse.ac.nz

Selwyn College, 560 Castle St, Dunedin 9016, New Zealand (*Warden* Dr Neil Rodgers)
Tel: 64 3 477 3326
Fax: 64 3 477 9926
email: warden.selwyn@otago.ac.nz
Web: www.selwyn.ac.nz

The two last named cater for pre-ordination or post-graduate studies.

AOTEAROA
Bishop of Aotearoa Most Revd William Brown Turei (*Primate/Archbishop*), PO Box 568, Gisborne 4040, New Zealand
Tel: 64 6 867 7028
Fax: 64 6 867 8859
email: browntmihi@xtra.co.nz

Bishop of Te Manawa o Te Wheke Rt Revd Ngarahu Katene, PO Box 146, Rotorua 3040, New Zealand
Tel: 64 7 348 4043
Fax: 64 7 348 4053
email: bishop @motw.org.nz

ANGLICAN AND PORVOO COMMUNIONS

Bishop of Te Tairawhiti Most Revd William Brown Turei, PO Box 568, Gisborne 4040, New Zealand
Tel: 64 6 867 708
Fax: 64 6 867 8859
email: browntmihi@xtra.co.nz

Bishop of Te Tai Tokerau Rt Revd Te Kito Wiremu Pikaahu, PO Box 25 Paihia, Bay of Islands 0247, New Zealand *Tel:* 64 9 402 6788
email: tkwp@xtra.co.nz

Bishop of Te Upoko o Te Ika Rt Revd Muru Walters, 14 Amesbury Drive, Churton Park, Wellington 6037, New Zealand *Tel:* 64 4 478 3549
Fax: 64 4 472 8863
email: muru.walters@xtra.co.nz

Bishop of Te Waipounamu Rt Revd John Robert Kuru Gray, PO Box 10086, Phillipstown, Christchurch 8145, New Zealand
Tel: 64 3 389 1683
Fax: 64 3 389 0912
email: bishopgray@hawaipounamu.co.nz

NEW ZEALAND

Bishop of Auckland Rt Revd Ross Graham Bay, PO Box 37242, Parnell, Auckland, 1151, New Zealand *Tel:* 64 9 302 7201
Fax: 64 9 302 7217
email: bishop@auckanglican.org.nz
Web: www.auckanglican.org.nz

Assistant Bishop of Auckland Rt Revd James White, PO Box 37242, Parnell, Auckland 1151, New Zealand *Tel:* 64 9 302 7201
Fax: 64 9 302 7217
email: jwhite@auckanglican.org.nz
Web: www.auckanglican.org.nz

Bishop of Christchurch Rt Revd Victoria Matthews, PO Box 4438, Christchurch 8140, New Zealand *Tel:* 64 3 348 6957
Fax: 64 3 379 5954
email: bishop@anglicanlife.org.nz
Web: www.anglicanlife.org.nz

Bishop of Dunedin Rt Revd Dr Kelvin Peter Wright, PO Box 13170, Green Island, Dunedin 9052, New Zealand *Tel:* 64 3 488 0820
Fax: 64 3 488 2038
email: bishop@calledsouth.org.nz
Web: www.calledsouth.org.nz

Bishop of Nelson Rt Revd Victor Richard Ellena, PO Box 100, Nelson 7040, New Zealand
Tel: 64 3 548 3124
Fax: 64 3 548 2125
email: bprichard@nelsonanglican.org.nz
Web: www.nelsonanglican.org.nz

Bishop of Waiapu Rt Revd David Rice, PO Box 227, Napier 4140, New Zealand *Tel:* 64 6 835 8230
Fax: 64 6 835 0680
email: bishop@waiapu.com
Web: www.waiapu.com

Bishop of Waikato Most Revd David John Moxon, PO Box 21, Hamilton 3240, New Zealand
Tel: 64 7 857 0020
Fax: 64 7 836 9975
email: bishop@hn-ang.org.nz
Web: www.waikatotaranakianglican.org.nz

Bishop of Taranaki Rt Revd Philip Richardson, PO Box 547, Taranaki Mail Centre, New Plymouth 4340, New Zealand *Tel:* 64 6 759 1178
Fax: 64 6 759 1180
email: bishop@taranakianglican.org.nz
Web: www.waikatotaranakianglican.org.nz

Bishop of Wellington Rt Revd Justin Charles Hopkins Duckworth, PO Box 12046, Wellington 6144, New Zealand
Tel: 64 4 472 1057
Fax: 64 4 449 1360
email: justin@wn.ang.org.nz
Web: www.wn.anglican.org.nz

POLYNESIA

Bishop of Polynesia Most Revd Dr Winston Halapua (*Primate/Archbishop*), PO Box 35, Suva, Fiji Islands *Tel:* 679 330 4716
Fax: 679 330 2152
email: bishoppolynesia@connect.com.fj
Web: www.anglican.org.nz

Bishop in Vanua Levu and Taveuni Rt Revd Apimeleki Nadoki Qiliho, PO Box 29, Labasa, Fiji Islands *Tel* and *Fax:* 679 881 1420
email: minoff@connect.com.fj

Bishop in Viti Levu West Rt Revd Gabriel Mahesh Prasad Sharma, PO Box 117, Lautoka, Fiji Islands
Tel and *Fax:* 679 666 0124
email: gabsharma@yahoo.com

Anglican Church of Australia

Members 3,881,162 (2001)
The Church came to Australia in 1788 with the 'First Fleet', which was made up primarily of convicts and military personnel. Free settlers soon followed. A General Synod held in 1872 formed the Australian Board of Missions. The Church became fully autonomous in 1962 and in 1978 published its first prayer book. A second Anglican prayer book was published in 1995. Women were first ordained to the Diaconate in 1985 and to the Priesthood in 1992. There are 23 dioceses of which 19 ordain women as priests and chaplains. The Anglican Church of Australia is part of the Christian Conference of Asia and of the Council of the Church of East Asia. Links with Churches of New Guinea, Melanesia, and Polynesia are strong especially through the Anglican Board of Mission – Australia.

Primate of the Anglican Church of Australia Most Revd Dr Phillip John Aspinall (*Archbishop of Brisbane*)

General Secretary of the General Synod Mr Martin Drevikovsky

Hon Treasurer Mr John McKenzie

General Synod Office Suite 2, Level 9, 51 Druitt Street, Sydney, NSW 2000 *Tel:* 61 2 8267 2700
Fax: 61 2 8267 2727
email: gsoffice@anglican.org.au
Web: www.anglican.org.au

THE ANGLICAN THEOLOGICAL COLLEGES

Moore Theological College, 1 King St, Newtown, NSW 2042 (*Principal* Revd John Woodhouse)
Tel: 61 2 89577 999
Fax: 61 2 9577 9988
email: info@moore.usyd.edu.au
Web: www.moore.edu.au

Nungalinya College, PO Box 40371, Casuarina, NT 0811 (*Principal* Revd Dr L. Lee Levett-Olson)
Tel: 61 8 8920 7500
Fax: 61 8 8927 2332
email: info@nungalinya.edu.au
Web: www.nungalinya.edu.au

Ridley College, 170 The Avenue, Parkville, VIC 3052 (*Principal* Revd Dr Peter Adam)
Tel: 61 3 9207 4800
Fax: 61 3 9387 5099
email: registrar@ridley.unimelb.edu.au
Web: www.ridley.unimelb.edu.au

St Barnabas Theological College, 34 Lipsett Terrace, Brooklyn Park, SA 5032 (*Principal* Revd Dr M. Anstey) *Fax:* 61 8 8416 8450
email: admin@sbtc.org.au
Web: http://ehlt.flinders.edu.au/theology/information

St Francis Theological College, 233 Milton Rd, PO Box 1261, Milton QLD 4064 (*Principal* The Revd Dr Steve Ogden) *Tel:* 61 7 3514 7411
Fax: 61 7 3369 4691
email: stfran@ministryeducation.org.au
Web: www.stfran.qld.edu.au

St Mark's National Theological Centre, 15 Blackall St, Barton, ACT 2600 (*Director* Professor Tom Frame) *Tel:* 61 2 6272 6252
Fax: 61 2 6273 4067
email: stmarks@csu.edu.au
Web: www.stmarksntc.org.au

Trinity College Theological School, Royal Parade, Parkville, VIC 3052 (*Dean* Revd Dr Andrew McGowan) *Tel:*61 3 9348 7127
Fax: 61 3 9348 7460
email: tcts@trinity.unimelb.edu.au
Web: www.trinity.unimelb.edu.au/theolog

The John Wollaston Theological College, Wollaston Rd, Mt Claremont, WA 6010
Tel: 61 8 9286 0270
Fax: 61 8 9385 3364
email: info@wollastoncollege.com.au
Web: www.wollastoncollege.com.au

CHURCH PAPERS

The Adelaide Church Guardian Monthly newspaper containing wide news coverage from the diocese, province and nationally. *Editorial Offices* 26 King William Road, North Adelaide, SA 5006.
email: communications@adelaide.anglican.com.au

The Melbourne Anglican Large monthly diocesan newspaper contains extensive news, comment locally and from around the world; with colour pictures. *Director/Editor* The Anglican Centre, 209 Flinders Lane, Melbourne, VIC 3000.
email: media@melbourne.anglican.com.au
Web: www.melbourne.anglican.com.au

Anglican Encounter Monthly newspaper of Newcastle Diocese, containing diocesan and Australian news. *Editorial Offices* PO Box 817, Newcastle, NSW 2302.
email: editor@angdon.com
Web: www.angdon.com

Tasmanian Anglican Monthly small newspaper format, from Tasmania Diocese, containing wide comment. *Editorial Offices* PO Box 748, Hobart, TAS 7001. *email:* editor@anglicantas.org.au
Web: www.anglicantas.org.au

Southern Cross Large monthly newspaper of Sydney Diocese, containing diocesan, national, world news and comment, Archbishop's letter in both English and Chinese translation. Extensive use of colour. *Editorial Offices* PO Box W185 Parramatta Westfield NSW 2150.
email: newsroom@anglicanmedia.com.au
Web: www.anglicanmedia.com.au

Anglican Messenger Monthly newspaper of the Anglican Province of Western Australia, includes news from Perth, North West Australia and Bunbury. *Editorial Offices* GPO Box W2067, Perth, WA 6846. *email:* messenger@perth.anglican.org
Web: www.anglicanmessenger.com.au

Market Place A monthly independent Anglican newspaper, includes national and international Anglican news and comment. *Editorial Offices* PO Box 335, Orange, NSW 2800.
email: market@ix.net.au

Focus Monthly newspaper based in Brisbane, containing diocesan and national news. *Editorial Offices* GPO Box 421, Brisbane, QLD 4001.
email: focus@anglicanbrisbane.org.au
Web: www.anglicanbrisbane.org.au

All diocesan newspapers contain a letter from the Archbishop or Bishop of the Diocese. The Dioceses of Armidale, Ballarat, Bathurst, Bendigo, Canberra and Goulburn, Gippsland, Grafton, Murray, Northern Territory, Riverina, Rockhampton, Wangaratta, and Willochra also produce magazines/Bishop's newsletters, with mainly diocesan and parochial news.

PROVINCE OF NEW SOUTH WALES

Metropolitan Most Revd Dr Peter Jensen (*Archbishop of Sydney*)

ARMIDALE

Bishop Rt Revd Dr Peter Robert Brain, PO Box 198, Armidale, NSW 2350 *Tel:* 61 2 6772 4491
Fax: 61 2 6772 9261
email: office@armidaleanglicandiocese.com
Web: www.armidaleanglicandiocese.com

BATHURST

Bishop Rt Revd Richard Hurford OAM, PO Box 23, Bathurst, NSW 2795 *Tel:* 61 2 6331 1722
Fax: 61 2 6332 2772
email: registrar@bathurstanglican.org
Web: www.bathurstanglican.org.au

Assistant Bishop John Stead *Tel:* 61 2 6885 2670
Fax: 61 2 6881 6740
email: mdo@bathurstanglican.org.au

CANBERRA AND GOULBURN

Bishop Rt Revd Stuart Robinson, GPO Box 1981, Canberra, ACT *Tel:* 61 2 6248 0811
Fax: 61 2 6247 6829
Web: www.anglicancg.org.au

Assistant Bishops
Rt Revd Allan B. Ewing, PO Box 8605, Wagga Wagga, NSW 2650 *Tel:* 61 2 6926 4226
Fax: 61 2 6926 4226
email: allan.ewing@anglicancg.com.au

Rt Revd Trevor W. Edwards, 28 McBryde Crescent, Wanniassa, ACT 2903 *Tel:* 61 2 648 0811
Fax: 61 2 6247 6829
email: trevor.edwards@anglicancg.org.au

GRAFTON

Bishop Rt Revd Keith Slater, Bishopsholme, PO Box 4, Grafton, NSW 2460 *Tel:* 61 2 6642 4122
Fax: 61 2 6643 1814
email: angdiog@nor.com.au
Web: www.graftondiocese.org.au

NEWCASTLE

Bishop Rt Revd Brian George Farran, Bishop's Registry, PO Box 817, Newcastle, NSW 2300
Tel: 61 2 4926 3733
Fax: 61 2 4926 1968
email: bishop@angdon.com
Web: www.angdon.com

Assistant Bishop Rt Revd Peter Stuart, PO Box 817, Newcastle, NSW 2300 *Tel:* 61 2 4926 3733
Fax: 02 4926 1968
email: BishopPeter@angdon.com

RIVERINA

Bishop Rt Revd Douglas R. Stephens, PO Box 10, Narrandera, NSW 2700 *Tel:* 61 2 6959 1648
Fax: 61 2 6959 2903
email: rivdio@dragnet.com.au
Web: www.anglicanriverina.com

SYDNEY

Archbishop Most Revd Dr Peter Jensen (*Metropolitan of the Province of NSW*), PO Box Q190, QVB Post Office, NSW 1230
Tel: 61 2 9265 1555
Fax: 61 2 9261 1170
email: registry@sydney.anglican.asn.au
Web: www.sydneyanglicans.net

Assistant Bishops
Vacancy (*Bishop of Liverpool & Georges River Region*) (*same address*) *Tel:* 61 2 9265 1530
Fax: 61 2 9265 1543
Rt Revd Glenn Davies (*Bishop of Northern Region*) (*same address*) *Tel:* 61 2 9265 1533
Fax: 61 2 9265 1543
email: gdavies@sydney.anglican.asn.au
Rt Revd Robert Charles Forsyth (*Bishop of South Sydney*) (*same address*) *Tel:* 61 2 9265 1501
Fax: 61 2 9265 1543
email: robforsyth@sydney.anglican.asn.au

Rt Revd P. L. Hayward (*Bishop of Wollongong*), 74 Church St, Wollongong, NSW 2500
Tel: 61 2 4201 1800
Fax: 61 2 4228 4296
email: phayward@wollongong.anglican.asn.au

Rt Revd Ivan Yin Lee (*Bishop of Western Sydney*), PO Box 129, Parramatta, NSW 2124
Tel: 61 2 8023 6700
Fax: 61 2 9633 3636
email: ilee@westernsydney.anglican.asn.au

PROVINCE OF QUEENSLAND

Metropolitan Most Revd Dr Phillip John Aspinall (*Primate of the Anglican Church of Australia and Archbishop of Brisbane*)

BRISBANE

Archbishop Most Revd Dr Phillip John Aspinall (*Metropolitan of the Province of Queensland and Primate of the Anglican Church of Australia*), GPO Box 421, Brisbane, QLD 4001
Tel: 61 7 3835 2222
Fax: 61 7 3831 1170
email: archbishop@anglicanbrisbane.org.au
Web: www.anglicanbrisbane.org.au

Assistant Bishops

Rt Revd Geoff Smith (*Bishop of the Southern Region*) (*same address*) *Tel:* 61 7 3835 2213
Fax: 61 7 3832 5030

Rt Revd Jonathan Charles Holland (*Bishop of the Northern Region*) (*same address*) *Tel:* 61 7 3835 2213
Fax: 61 7 3832 5030
email: jholland@anglicanbrisbane.org.au

Rt Revd Robert William Nolan (*Bishop of the Western Region*), Box 2600, Toowoomba, QLD 4350
Tel: 61 7 4639 1875
Fax: 61 7 4632 6882
email: nolan@anglicanbrisbane.org.au

NORTH QUEENSLAND

Bishop Rt Revd William James (Bill) Ray, PO Box 1244, Townsville, QLD 4810 *Tel:* 61 7 4771 4175
Fax: 61 7 4721 1756
email: bishopnq@anglicannq.org
Web: www.anglicannq.org

Assistant Bishops

Rt Revd Saibo Mabo (*Assistant Bishop and National Torres Strait Islander Bishop*), PO Box 338, Thursday Island, QLD 4875 *Tel:* 6 1 7 4069 2747
Fax: 61 7 4969 1960
email: bishopti@anglicannq.org

Rt Revd James Randolph Leftwich (*Assistant Bishop and National Aboriginal Bishop*), 14 Village Tce, Redlynch QLD 4870 *Tel:* 61 7 4051 1055
Fax: 61 7 4051 1033
email: bishopleftwich@gmail.com

THE NORTHERN TERRITORY

Bishop Rt Revd Gregory Edwin (Greg) Thompson, PO Box 2950, Darwin, NT 0801
Tel: 61 8 8941 7440
Fax: 61 8 8941 7446
email: ntdiocese@internode.on.net
Web: www.northernterritory.anglican.org

ROCKHAMPTON

Bishop Rt Revd Godfrey Charles Fryar, PO Box 710, Central Queensland Mail Centre, Rockhampton, QLD 4702 *Tel:* 61 7 4927 3188
Fax: 61 7 4927 3188
email: bishop@anglicanrock.org.au
Web: www.anglicanrock.org.au

PROVINCE OF SOUTH AUSTRALIA

Metropolitan Most Reverend Jeffrey William Driver (*Archbishop of Adelaide*)

ADELAIDE

Archbishop Most Reverend Jeffrey William Driver (*Metropolitan of the Province of South Australia*), 18 King William Rd, N Adelaide, SA 5006
Tel: 61 8 8305 9350
Fax: 61 8 8305 9399
email: archbishop@adelaide.anglican.com.au
Web: www.adelaide.anglican.com.au

Assistant Bishop

Bishop Rt Revd Stephen Kim Pickard (*same address*)
email: spickard@adelaide.anglican.com.au

THE MURRAY

Bishop Vacancy *Tel:* 61 8 8532 2270
Fax: 61 8 8532 5760
email: registry@murray.anglican.org
Web: www.murray.anglican.org

WILLOCHRA

Bishop Rt Revd Garry Weatherill, PO Box 96, Gladstone, SA 5473 *Tel:* 61 8 8662 2249
Fax: 61 8 8662 2027
email: bishop@diowillochra.org.au
Web: www.diowillochra.org.au

PROVINCE OF VICTORIA

Metropolitan Most Revd Philip Leslie Freier (*Archbishop of Melbourne*)

BALLARAT

Bishop Vacancy *Tel:* 61 3 5331 1183
Fax: 61 3 5333 2982
email: bpsec@ballaratanglican.org.au
Web: www.ballaratanglican.org.au/

BENDIGO

Bishop Rt Revd Andrew William Curnow, PO Box 2, Bendigo, VIC 3552 *Tel:* 61 3 5443 4711
Fax: 61 3 5441 2173
email: bishop@bendigoanglican.org.au
Web: www.bendigoanglican.org.au

GIPPSLAND
Bishop Rt Revd John Charles McIntyre, PO Box 928, Sale, VIC 3853 *Tel:* 61 3 5144 2044
Fax: 61 3 5144 7183
email: bishop@gippsanglican.org.au
Web: www.gippsanglican.org.au

MELBOURNE
Archbishop Most Revd Philip Leslie Freier (*Metropolitan of the Province of Victoria*), The Anglican Centre, 209 Flinders Lane, Melbourne, VIC 3000 *Tel:* 61 3 9653 4220
Fax: 61 3 9653 4268
email: archbishopsoffice@melbourne.anglican.com.au
Web: www.melbourne.anglican.org.au/

Assistant Bishops
Rt Revd Paul Raymond White (*Bishop of the Southern Region*) (*same address*)
Tel: 61 3 9653 4220
Fax: 61 3 9653 4268
email: sthregbishop@melbourne.anglican.com.au
Rt Revd Philip Huggins (*Bishop of the North-Western Region*) (*same address*)
email: phuggins@melbourne.anglican.com.au
Rt Revd Barbara Darling (*Bishop of the Eastern Region*) (*same address*)
email: estregion@melbourne.anglican.com.au

WANGARATTA
Bishop Rt Revd Anthony John Parkes, Bishop's Registry, PO Box 457, Wangaratta VIC 3676
Tel: 61 3 5721 3484
Fax: 61 3 5722 1427
email: bishop@wangaratta.anglican.org
Web: www.wangaratta.anglican.org

PROVINCE OF WESTERN AUSTRALIA
Metropolitan Most Revd Roger Adrian Herft (*Archbishop of Perth*)

BUNBURY
Bishop Rt Revd Allan Bowers Ewing, PO Box 15, Bunbury, WA 6231 *Tel:* 61 8 9721 2100
Fax: 61 8 9791 2300
email: bishop@bunbury.org.au
Web: www.bunbury.org.au

NORTH WEST AUSTRALIA
Bishop Rt Revd David Mulready, PO Box 2783, Geraldton, WA 6531 *Tel:* 61 8 9921 7277
Fax: 61 8 9964 2220
email: bishop@anglicandnwa.org
Web: www.anglicandnwa.org

PERTH
Archbishop Most Revd Roger Adrian Herft (*Metropolitan of the Province of Western Australia*), GPO Box W2067, Perth, WA 6846
Tel: 61 8 9325 7455
Fax: 61 8 9221 4118
email: archbishop@perth.anglican.org
Web: www.perth.anglican.org

Assistant Bishops
Rt Revd Kay Goldsworthy (*same address*)
Rt Revd Tom Wilmot (*same address*)
email: twilmot@perth.anglican.org

TASMANIA
Bishop Rt Revd John Douglas Harrower, OAM, GPO 748, Hobart, TAS 7001 *Tel:* 61 3 6220 2015
Fax: 61 3 6223 8968
email: bishop@anglicantas.org.au
Web: www.anglicantas.org.au/

DEFENCE FORCE
Bishop Rt Revd Len Eacott AM (*Anglican Bishop to the Australian Defence Force and Bishop Assistant to the Primate*), Department of Defence, DSG-Duntroon, ACT 2600 *Tel:* 61 2 9265 9935
Fax: 61 2 9265 9959
email: dfc@anglican.org.au
Web: www.anglican.org.au/defence

The Episcopal Anglican Church of Brazil

(Igreja Episcopal Anglicana do Brasil)

The Episcopal Anglican Church of Brazil is the 19th Province of the Anglican Communion, and its work began in 1890 as a result of the missionary work of two north American missionaries in Porto Alegre: James Watson Morris and Lucien Lee Kinsolving. Autonomy from the Episcopal Church in the United States was granted in 1965. The Episcopal Church now has more than a hundred thousand baptized members and a team of more than two hundred clergy, among whom are thirty women priests. It has established communities, and educational and social institutions, in the main urban areas of Brazil. The Brazilian province comprises nine dioceses: Southern, Southwestern, Rio de Janeiro, São Paulo, Recife, Brasília, Pelotas, Curitiba and Amazon. It also has one missionary district: Missionary District West.

Primate Most Revd Mauricio José Araújo Andrade (*Bishop of Brazília*)
email: mandrade@ieab.org.br
Web: www.ieab.org.br

Provincial Secretary Revd Arthur Cavalcante

Provincial Offices Praça Olavo Bilac, 63, Campos Elíseos, CEP 01201-050, São Paulo, SP
Tel and *Fax:* 55 11 3 667 8161
email: acavalcante@leab.org.bs

Provincial Treasurer Mrs Silvia Fernandes (*address, etc. as above*)
email: silviaieab@gmail.com

CHURCH PAPER
Estandarte Cristão, a bimonthly church journal in Portuguese, published since 1893, which contains general articles and news about the life of the Church at local, national and international level. This journal is the main channel of the Communication Department of the Church. Revdo Felix Batista Filho *Editorial Offices:* Rua Ferreira Lopez, 401-AP 2302, Casa Amarela, Recife, PE, 52060-02
Tel and *Fax:* 55 81 3267 3926/9488 3194
email: fqbfilho@gmail.com

AMAZON
Bishop Rt Revd Saulo Mauricio de Barros, Av. Sezerdelo Correia, 514, Batista Campos, 66025–240, Belem, PA *Tel* and *Fax:* 55 91 3241 9720
email: saulomauricio@gmail.com

BRASÍLIA
Bishop Most Revd Maurício José Araújo de Andrade (*Primate of the Episcopal Anglican Church of Brazil*), EQS 309/310, sala 1 – Asa Sul, Caixa Postal 093, 70359–970, Brasília, DF
Tel: 55 61 3443 4305
Fax: 55 61 3443 4337
email: mandrade@ieab.org.br
Web: www.dab.ieab.org.br

CURITIBA
Bishop Rt Revd Naudal Alves Gomes, Rua Sete de Setembro, 3927 – Centro, 80250-010 Curitiba, PR
Tel: 55 41 3232 0917
email: naudal@yahoo.com.br

PELOTAS
Bishop Rt Revd Renato da Cruz Raatz, Rua Felix da Cunha, 425 – Centro, Caixa Postal 791, 96001–970 Pelotas, RS *Tel* and *Fax:* 55 53 3227 7120
email: renatoraatz@terra.com.br
Web: www.dap.ieab.org.br

RECIFE
Bishop Rt Revd Sebastião Armando Gameleira Soares, Rua Virgílio Mota, 70, Parnamirim, 52060–582, Recife, PE *Tel:* 55 81 3441 6843
email: sgameleira@gmail.com
Web: www.dar.ieab.org.br

RIO DE JANEIRO
Bishop Rt Revd Filadelfo Oliveira Neto, Rua Fonseca Guimarães, 12 Sta.Teresa, 20240–260, Rio de Janeiro, RJ *Tel:* 55 21 2220 2148
Fax: 55 21 2252 9686
email: oliveira.ieab@gmail.com
Web: www.anglicana.com.br

SÃO PAULO
Bishop Rt Revd Douglas Bird, Rua Borges Lagoa, 172 – Vila Clementino, 04038–030 São Paulo, SP
Tel: 55 11 5549 9086/5579 9011
Fax: 55 11 5083 2619
email: rogerbird@uol.com.br
Web: www.dasp.org.br

SOUTH WESTERN BRAZIL
Bishop Rt Revd Francisco de Assis Silva, Av. Rio Branco, 880/Sub-solo – Centro, Caixa Postal 116, 97010–970 Santa Maria, RS
Tel and *Fax:* 55 55 3221 4328
email: fassis@ieab.org.bs
Web: www.swbrazil.anglican.org

SOUTHERN BRAZIL
Bishop Rt Revd Orlando Santos de Oliveira, Av. Eng. Ludolfo Boehl, 278, Teresópolis, 91720–150, Porto Alegre, RS *Tel* and *Fax:* 55 51 318 6199
email: dmbispo@terra.com.br
Web: www.dm.ieab.org.br

Eglise Anglicane du Burundi

(The Province of the Anglican Church of Burundi)

Members 900,000
There are at least 900,000 Anglicans out of an estimated population of just over 9 million in Burundi. An Anglican presence was established through the work of the CMS in the 1930s and grew rapidly as a result of the East African revival. The former Ruanda Mission (now CMS) set up its first mission stations at Buhiga and Matana in 1935, and Buye in 1936. Activities were mainly focused on evangelism, education and medical work. The first national bishop was consecrated in 1965 and Buye diocese was created, covering the whole country. The Church of the Province of Burundi now consists of six dioceses, and it has been an independent province within the Anglican Communion since 1992. Among the Church's main concerns are peace and reconciliation, repatriation of returnees, community development, literacy, education, and health. It is committed to mission and evangelism with faith in the risen Christ as Lord and Saviour central to its preaching and teaching. It is concerned to

support theological education and training for ministry, based on the authority of Scripture.

Primate Most Revd Bernard Ntahoturi (*Archbishop of Burundi and Bishop of Matana*)

Provincial Secretary Revd Pédaçuli Birakengana, BP 2098, Bujumbura *Tel:* 257 22 224 389
Fax: 257 22 229 129
email: peab@cbinf.com
Provincial Accountant Christine Niyonkuru

THEOLOGICAL COLLEGES
Matana Theological Institute (Provincial)
Canon Warner Memorial College, EAB Buye, BP 94 Ngozi
Kosiya Shalita Bible College, EAB Matana, DS 13, Bujumbura *or* BP 447, Bujumbura
Buhiga College, EAB Gitega, BP 23 Gitega
Makamba College, EAB Makamba, BP 96 Makamba
Bujumbura Bible College, EAB Bujumbura, BP 1300 Bujumbura

BUJUMBURA
Bishop Rt Revd Pie Ntukamazina, BP 1300, Bujumbura *Tel:* 257 22 249 104/5
Fax: 257 22 227 495
email: bishoppie@gmail.com

BUYE
Bishop Rt Revd Sixbert Macumi, BP 94, Ngozi
Tel: 257 22 302 210
Fax: 257 22 302 317
email: buyedioc@yahoo.fr

GITEGA
Bishop Rt Revd Jean Nduwayo, BP 23, Gitega
Tel: 257 22 402 247
email: eab.diocgitega@gmail.com

MAKAMBA
Bishop Rt Revd Martin Blaise Nyaboho, BP 96, Makamba *Tel:* 257 22 508 080
Fax: 257 22 229 129
email: eabdiocmak@yahoo.fr

MATANA
Bishop Most Revd Bernard Ntahoturi (*Archbishop of Burundi*), BP 447, Bujumbura
Tel: 257 79 924 595
Fax: 257 22 229 129
email: ntahober@cbinf.com/ ntahober@yahoo.co.uk

MUYINGA
Bishop Rt Revd Eraste Bigirimana, BP 55, Muyinga
Tel: 257 22 306 019
Fax: 257 22 306 152
email: bigirimanaeraste@yahoo.fr/ eabmuyinga@yahoo.fr

The Anglican Church of Canada

Members 2,035,500 (2001)
The Anglican witness in Canada started in the eighteenth century with the Church Missionary Society and the United Society for the Propagation of the Gospel. The Eucharist was first celebrated in Frobisher Bay (now Iqaluit) in 1578; the first church building was St Paul's, Halifax in 1750. The Church includes a large number of the original inhabitants of Canada (Indians, Inuit, and Metis) and has been a strong advocate of their rights. A book of alternative services was published in 1985. The Church has a strong international role in sustainable development and humanitarian assistance through the Primate's World Relief and Development Fund (PWRDF).

Primate of The Anglican Church of Canada Most Revd Fred J. Hiltz, 80 Hayden St, Toronto, ON, M4Y 3G2 *Tel:* 1 416 924 9192
Fax: 1 416 924 0211
email: primate@national.anglican.ca
Web: www.anglican.ca

General Secretary Ven Dr Michael Thompson
email: mthompson@national.anglican.ca

General Treasurer Vacancy

Offices of the General Synod and of its Departments
80 Hayden St, Toronto ON, M4Y 3G2
Tel: 1 416 924 9192
Fax: 1 416 968 7983

National Indigenous Anglican Bishop Rt Revd Mark L. MacDonald (*same address*)
email: mmacdonald@national.anglican.ca
Web: http://www.anglican.ca/im/

Bishop Ordinary to the Canadian Forces Rt Revd Peter Coffin, 42 Bridle Park Dr., Kanata, ON, K2M 2E2 *Tel:* 1 613 591 7137
Fax: 1 613 232 3995
email: petercoffin@rogers.com

UNIVERSITIES AND COLLEGES OF THE ANGLICAN CHURCH OF CANADA
British Columbia
Vancouver School of Theology*, 6000 Iona Dr, Vancouver, BC, V6T 1L4 (*Principal* Revd Dr Paula Sampson) *email:* possibilities@vst.edu

Manitoba
Henry Budd College for Ministry, Box 2518, The Pas MB, R9A IM3 (*Joint Co-ordinators* Ms Marion Jenkins and Revd Paul Sodtke)
email: hbcm@mts.net

St John's College, 92 Dysart Rd, Winnipeg, MB, R3T 2M5 (*Warden* Dr Christopher Trott)
email: stjohns_college@umanitoba.ca

Newfoundland
Queen's College, 210 Prince Philip Dr (Q3000), St John's NF, A1B 3R6 (*Acting Administrator* Canon Dr Boyd Morgan) *email:* queens@mun.ca

Nova Scotia
Atlantic School of Theology*, 660 Francklyn St, Halifax, NS, B3H 3B5 (*Principal* Canon Dr Eric Beresford)
email: academicoffice@astheology.ns.ca

University of King's College, 6350 Coburg Rd., Halifax, NS B3H 2A1 (*President* Dr William Barker) *email:* admissions@ukings.ns.ca

Nunavut
Arthur Turner Training School *Enquiries to* Diocese of the Arctic, Box 190, Yellowknife, NT X1A 2N2

Ontario
Canterbury College, 2500 University Ave W, Windsor ON, N9B 3Y1 (*Principal* Dr Gordon Drake) *email:* canter@uwindsor.ca

Huron University College, 1349 Western Rd, London, ON, N6G 1H3 (*Principal* Dr Stephen McClatchie) *email:* rlumpkin@uwo.ca

Renison College, 240 Westmount Rd N, Waterloo, ON, N2L 3G4 (*Principal* Dr Glenn Cartwright)
email: glenn.cartwright@renison.uwaterloo.ca

Saint Paul University, Anglican Studies Program, 223 Main St., Ottawa, ON, K1S 1C4 (*Director* Revd Kevin Flynn)

Thorneloe College, 935 Ramsey Lake Rd, Sudbury, ON, P3E 2C6 (*Provost* Revd Dr Robert Derrenbacker)
email: thorneprov@laurentian.ca

Trinity College, 6 Hoskin Ave, Toronto, ON, M5S 1H8 (*Dean of Divinity* Revd Canon Dr David Neelands) *email:* divinity@trinity.utoronto.ca

Wycliffe College, 5 Hoskin Ave, Toronto, ON, M5S 1H7 (*Principal* Canon Dr George Sumner)
email: wycliffe.college@utoronto.ca

Quebec
Bishop's University, PO Box 5000, Lennoxville, QC, J1M 1Z7 (*Registrar Yves Jodoin)*
email: yjodoin@ubishops.ca

*Ecumenical

Montreal Diocesan Theological College, 3473 University St, Montreal, QC, H3A 2A8 (*Principal* Canon Dr John Simons)
email: diocoll@netrover.com

Saskatchewan
College of Emmanuel and St Chad, 1337 College Dr, Saskatoon, SK, S7N OW6 (*Principal* Revd Dr Terry Wiebe)
email: emmanuel.stchad@usask.ca

Centre for Christian Studies (Anglican, United) Maybee, Woodsorth House, 160 Maryland St. Winnipeg, MB R3G 1K7 (*Principal*: Revd Canon Maylanne) *Tel:* 1 866 780 8887
Fax: 1 204 786 3012
email: info@ccsonline.ca

CHURCH PAPERS
Anglican Journal Tabloid format, national church paper with 23 diocesan publications inserted regionally. The paper is under the management of a committee appointed by General Synod.
Editorial Offices: 80 Hayden St, Toronto, ON M4Y 3G2
email: anglican.journal@national.anglican.ca
Web: www.anglicanjournal.com

PROVINCE OF BRITISH COLUMBIA AND YUKON

Metropolitan Most Revd John E. Privett (*Bishop of Kootenay)*

BRITISH COLUMBIA
Bishop Rt Revd James A. J. Cowan, 900 Vancouver St, Victoria, BC, V8V 3V7
Tel: 1 250 386 7781
Fax: 1 250 386 4013
email: jcowan@bc.anglican.ca

CALEDONIA
Bishop Rt Revd William J. Anderson, 201–4716 Lazelle Avenue, Terrace, BC, V8G 1T2
Tel: 1 250 635 6016
Fax: 1 250 635 6026
email: bishopbill@telus.net
Web: www.caledonia.anglican.ca

CENTRAL INTERIOR, ANGLICAN PARISHES OF
Bishop Rt Revd Barbara J. Andrews, 360 Nicola St, Kamloops BC V2C 2P5 *Tel:* 1 778 471 5573
Fax: 1 778 471 5586
email: apcibishop@shaw.ca
Web: www.apcionline.ca

KOOTENAY
Bishop Most Revd John E. Privett, 201–380 Leathead Rd., Kelowna, BC, V1X 2H8
Tel: 1 250 762 3306
Fax: 1 250 762 4150
email: bishop of kootenay@telus.net
Web: www.kootenay.anglican.ca

NEW WESTMINSTER
Bishop Rt Revd Michael C. Ingham, Suite 580, 401 West Georgia St, Vancouver, BC, V6B 5A1
Tel: 1 604 684 6306
Fax: 1 604 684 7017
email: bishop@vancouver.anglican.ca
Web: www.vancouver.anglican.ca

YUKON
Bishop Rt Revd Larry D. Robertson, PO Box 31136, Rpo Main Street, Whitehorse, Yukon Y1A 5P7
Tel: 1 867 667 7746
Fax: 1 867 667 6125
email: synodoffice@klondiker.com
Web: http://anglican.yukon.net

PROVINCE OF CANADA

Metropolitan Most Revd Claude E. W. Miller (*Bishop of Fredericton*)

CENTRAL NEWFOUNDLAND
Bishop Rt Revd F. David Torraville, 34 Fraser Rd, Gander, NL, A1V 2E8
Tel: 1 709 256 2372
Fax: 1 709 256 2396
email: bishopcentral@nfld.net
Web: www.centraldiocese.org

EASTERN NEWFOUNDLAND AND LABRADOR
Bishop Rt Revd Cyrus C. J. Pitman, 19 King's Bridge Rd, St John's, NL, A1C 3K4
Tel: 1 709 576 6697
Fax: 1 709 576 7122
email: cpitman@anglicanenl.nf.net
Web: www.nfol.ca

FREDERICTON
Bishop Most Revd Claude E. W. Miller, 115 Church St, Fredericton, NB, E3B 4C8
Tel: 1 506 459 1801
Fax: 1 506 460 0520
email: claude.miller@anglican.nb.ca
Web: www.anglican.nb.ca

MONTREAL
Bishop Rt Revd Barry B. Clarke, 1444 Union Ave, Montreal, QC, H3A 2B8
Tel: 1 514 634 1965
Fax: 1 514 843 3221
email: bcclarke@montreal.anglican.ca
Web: www.montreal.anglican.ca

NOVA SCOTIA AND PRINCE EDWARD ISLAND
Bishop Rt Revd Susan Moxley, 6017, Quinpool Rd, Halifax, NS, B3K 5J6
Tel: 1 902 420 0717
Fax: 1 902 425 0717
email: smoxley@nspeidiocese.ca
Web: www.nspeidiocese.ca
Suffragan Bishop Rt Revd Ronald W. Cutler (*same address*)

QUEBEC
Bishop Rt Revd Dennis P. Drainville, 31 rue des Jardins, Quebec, QC, G1R 4L6
Tel: 1 418 692 3858
Fax: 1 418 692 3876
email: synodoffice@quebec.anglican.ca
Web: www.quebec.anglican.org

WESTERN NEWFOUNDLAND
Bishop Rt Revd Percy D. Coffin, 25 Main St, Corner Brook, NF, A2H 1C2
Tel: 1 709 639 8712
Fax: 1 709 639 1636
email: dsown@nf.aibn.ca
Web: www.westernnewfoundland.anglican.org

PROVINCE OF ONTARIO

Metropolitan Most Revd Colin R. Johnson (*Archbishop of Toronto*)

ALGOMA
Bishop Rt Revd Stephen Andrews, Box 1168, Sault Ste Marie, ON, P6A 5N7
Tel: 1 705 673 1730
Fax: 1 705 673 4979
email: bishop@dioceseofalgoma.com
Web: www.dioceseofalgoma.com

HURON
Bishop Rt Revd Robert F. Bennett, 190 Queens Ave, London, ON N6A 6H7
Tel: 1 519 434 6893
Fax: 1 519 673 4151
email: bbennett@huron.anglican.org
Web: www.diohuron.org
Suffragan Rt Revd Terrance A. Dance (*same address*) *email:* bishops@huron.anglican.ca

MOOSONEE
Archbishop Rt Revd Thomas A. Corston, 435 Hemlock Ave, Timmins, ON, P4N 6T4
Tel: 1 705 360 1129
Fax: 1 705 360 1120
email: bishop@moosoneeanglican.ca
Web: http://moosonee.anglican.org

NIAGARA
Bishop Rt Revd Michael A. Bird, Cathedral Place, 252 James St North, Hamilton, ON, L8R 2L3
Tel: 1 905 527 1316
Fax: 1 905 527 1281
email: mabird@cgocable.net
Web: www.niagara.anglican.ca

ONTARIO
Bishop Rt Revd Michael D. Oulton, 90 Johnson St, Kingston, ON, K7L 1X7
Tel: 1 613 384 1782
Fax: 1 613 547 3745
email: moulton@ontario.anglican.ca
Web: www.ontario.anglican.ca

OTTAWA
Bishop Rt Revd John H. Chapman, 71 Bronson Ave, Ottawa, ON, K1R 6G6
Tel: 1 613 233 7741
Fax: 1 613 521–6613
email: bishopsoffice@ottawa.anglican.ca
Web: www.ottawa.anglican.ca

TORONTO
Bishop Most Revd Colin R. Johnson, 135 Adelaide St East, Toronto, ON, M5C 1L8
Tel: 1 416 363 6021
Fax: 1 416 363 3683
email: cjohnson@toronto.anglican.ca
Web: www.toronto.anglican.ca

Area Bishops
Rt Revd Linda Nicholls (*Trent-Durham Area*), 965 Dundas St West, Suite 207, Whitby, ON, L1P 1G8
Tel: 1 905 668 1558
Fax: 1 905 688 8216
email: lnicholls@toronto.anglican.ca
Rt Revd M. George H. Elliott (*York-Simcoe Area*), PO Box 233 St. Main, King City, ON L7B 1A5
Tel: 1 905 833 8327
Fax: 1 905 833 8329
email: vsimcoe@@toronto.anglican.ca
Rt Revd Patrick T. Yu (*York-Scarborough Area*), 135 Adelaide St East, Toronto, ON, M5C 1L8
Tel: 1 416 293 5711
Fax: 1 416 363 3683
email: pyu@toronto.anglican.ca
Rt Revd M. Philip Poole (*York Credit Valley*), 135 Adelaide St East, Toronto, ON, M5C 1L8
Tel: 1 416 503 9903
Fax: 1 416 503 8299
email: ppoole@toronto.anglican.ca

PROVINCE OF RUPERT'S LAND

Metropolitan Most Revd David N. Ashdown (*Archbishop of Keewatin*)

THE ARCTIC
Bishop Vacancy *email:* diocese@arcticnet.org
Web: www.arctic.anglican.org

Rt Revd David Parsons, Co-adjutor Bishop , 4910 51st Street, Box 190, Yellowknife, NT X1A 2N2
Rt Revd Darren McCartney, Suffragan Bishop, 4910 51st Street, Box 190, Yellowknife, NT X1A 2N2
Tel: 1 867 873 5432
Fax: 867 873 8478
email: arctic@arcticnet.org

ATHABASCA
Archbishop Rt Revd Fraser W. Lawton, Box 6868, Peace River, AB, T8S 1S6 *Tel:* 1 780 790 1114
Fax: 1 780 624 2365
email: bpath@telusplanet.net
Web: www.dioath.ca

BRANDON
Bishop Rt Revd James D. Njegovan, Box 21009, WEPO, Brandon, MB, R7B 3W8
Tel: 1 204 727 7550
Fax: 1 204 727 4135
email: bishopbdn@mymts.net
Web: www.dioceseofbrandon.org

CALGARY
Bishop Rt Revd Gregory Kerr-Wilson, 180, 1209–59th Ave SE, Calgary, AB, T2H 2P6
Tel: 1 403 243 3673
Fax: 1 403 243 2182
email: synod@calgary.anglican.ca
Web: www.calgary.anglican.ca

EDMONTON
Bishop Rt Revd Jane Alexander, 10035–103 St, Edmonton, AB, T5J 0X5 *Tel:* 1 780 439 7344
Fax: 1 780 962 2103
email: janealexander@shaw.cas
Web: www.edmonton.anglican.org

KEEWATIN
Archbishop Most Revd David N. Ashdown, 915 Ottawa St, PO Box 567, Keewatin, ON, P0X 1C0
Tel: 1 807 547 3353
Fax: 1 807 547 3356
email: keewatinbishop@shaw.ca
Web: www.gokenora.com/~dioceseofkeewatin

Area Bishop for Northern Ontario Region Rt Revd Lydia Mamakwa, Box 65, Kingfisher Lake, ON P0V 1Z0 *Tel:* 1 807 532 2067
Fax: 1 807 532 2063/2344
email: lydiam@kingfisherlake.ca

QU'APPELLE
Bishop Vacancy 1501 College Ave, Regina, SK, S4P 1B8 *Tel:* 1 306 522 1608
Fax: 1 306 352 6808
email: quappelle@sasktel.net
Web: http://diocse.sasktelwebsite.net

RUPERT'S LAND
Bishop Rt Revd Donald D. Phillips, 935 Nesbitt Bay, Winnipeg, MB, R3T 1W6 *Tel:* 1 204 922 4212
Fax: 1 204 922 4219
email: dphillips@rupertsland.anglican.ca
Web: www.rupertsland.ca

SASKATCHEWAN
Bishop Rt Revd Michael W. Hawkins, 1308 5th Ave East, Prince Albert, SK, S6V 2H7
Diocesan Indigenous Bishop-elect Adam Halkett, 1308 5th Ave East, Prince Albert, SK, S6V 2H7
Tel: 1 306 763 2455
Fax: 1 306 764 5172
email: bishopmichael@sasktel.net
Web: www.saskatchewan.anglican.org

SASKATOON
Bishop Rt Revd David M. Irving, 1403 9th Ave N., Saskatoon, SK, S7K 2Z6 *Tel:* 1 306 244 5651
Fax: 1 306 933 4606
email: bishopdavid @sasktel.net
Web: www.saskatoon.anglican.org

The Church of the Province of Central Africa

Members 600,000

The province includes Botswana, Malawi, Zambia and Zimbabwe. The first Anglican missionary to Malawi was Bishop Charles Mackenzie who arrived with David Livingstone in 1861. The province was inaugurated in 1955 and has a movable bishopric. The countries forming the province are very different. Zambia and Botswana suffer the difficulties of rapid industrialization, along with underdevelopment and thinly populated areas. In Malawi 30% of the adult males are away as migrant labourers in other countries at any given time. Zimbabwe is experiencing problems of social adjustment after independence.

Archbishop of the Province Vacancy

Provincial Secretary Vacancy

Provincial Treasurer Mr R. Kanja, CPCA, PO Box 22317, Kitwe, Zambia *Tel:* 260 351 081
260 9719 5368 (Mobile)
Fax: 267 351 668

ANGLICAN THEOLOGICAL COLLEGES

Leonard Kamungu (Anglican) Theological College, PO Box 959, Zomba. Malawi (*Dean* Revd Alinafe Kalemba) *Tel*: 265 1 525 286
265 8 856 410 (Mobile)

National Anglican Theological College of Zimbabwe (Ecumenical Institute of Theology), 11 Thornburg Ave, Groom Bridge, Mount Pleasant, Harare, Zimbabwe

St John's Seminary, Mindolo, PO Box 20369, Kitwe, Zambia (*Rector* Rt Revd John Osmers)
Tel: 260 2 210960
email: josmers@zamnet.zm

CHURCH PAPER

Link Monthly newspaper for the Dioceses of Mashonaland and Matabeleland giving news and views of the dioceses. *Editorial Offices* Link Board of Management, PO Box UA7, Harare City.

BOTSWANA

Bishop Rt Revd Trevor Mwamba, PO Box 679, Gaborone, Botswana *Tel:* 267 395 3779
Fax: 267 391 3015
email: angli_diocese@info.bw / musonda_mwamba@yahoo.com

CENTRAL ZAMBIA

Bishop Rt Revd Derek Gary Kamukwamba, PO Box 70172, Ndola, Zambia *Tel:* 260 2 612 431
email: adcznla@zamnet.zm

CENTRAL ZIMBABWE

Bishop Rt Revd Ishmael Mukuwanda, PO Box 25, Gweru, Zimbabwe *Tel:* 263 54 21 030
Fax: 263 54 21 097
email: diocent@telconet.co.zw / imukuwanda@gmail.com

EASTERN ZAMBIA

Bishop Rt Revd William Muchombo, PO Box 510154, Chipata, Zambia
Tel and *Fax:* 260 216 221 294
email: dioeastzm@zamnet.zm

HARARE

Bishop Rt Revd Chad Gandiya, Monmouth Rd, Avondale, Harare, Zimbabwe
Tel: 263 4 308 042
email: diohrecpca@ecoweb.co.zw

LAKE MALAWI

Bishop Rt Revd Francis Kaulanda, PO Box 30349, Lilongwe 3, Malawi *Tel:* 265 797 858 (Office)
265 794 268 (Home)
Fax: 265 731 966
email: anglama@eomw.net

LUAPULA

Bishop Rt Revd Robert Mumbi, PO Box 710210, Mansa, Luapula, Zambia
emaill: diopula@zamtel.zm

LUSAKA

Bishop Rt Revd David Njovu, Bishop's Lodge, PO Box 30183, Lusaka, Zambia

Tel: 260 211 254 789 (Office)
260 211 252 449 (Home)
Fax: 260 1 254789
email: dnjovu@zamnet.zm

MANICALAND

Bishop Rt Revd Julius Makoni, 115 Herbert Chitepo St, Mutare, Zimbabwe
Tel: 263 20 64 194
Fax: 263 20 63 076
email: diomani@syscom.co.zw

MASVINGO

Bishop Rt Revd Godfrey Tawonezvi, PO Box 1421, Masvingo, Zambia *Tel:* 263 39 362 536
email: bishopgodfreytawonezvi@gmail.com / anglicandiomsv@comone.co.zw

MATABELELAND

Bishop Rt Revd Wilson Sitshebo, PO Box 2422, Bulaweyo, Zimbabwe *Tel:* 263 9 61 370
Fax: 263 9 68 353
email: angdiomat@telconet.co.zw / bishmat@mweb.co.zw

NORTHERN MALAWI

Bishop Rt Revd Leslie Mtekateka, Box 120, Mzuzu, Malawi, Central Africa *Tel:* 265 331 486
Fax: 265 333 805
email: bishopboyle@sdnp.org.mw

NORTHERN ZAMBIA
Bishop Rt Revd Albert Chama, PO Box 20798, Kitwe, Zambia
Tel: 260 2 223 264 (Office) / 260 2 230 082 (Home)
Fax: 260 2 224 778
email: cpca@zamnet.zm

SOUTHERN MALAWI
Bishop Rt Revd James Tengatenga, PO Box 30220, Chichiri, Blantyre, 3, Malawi *Tel:* 265 1 641 218
Tel: 265 1 641 218
Fax: 265 1 641 235
email: angsoma@sdnp.org.mw / jatenga@sdnp.org.mw

SOUTHERN MALAWI – UPPER SHIRE
Bishop Rt Revd Brighton Vitta Malasa, Private Bag 1, Chilema, Zomba, Malawi
Tel and *Fax:* 265 1 539 514
265 9545 609 (Mobile)
email: dionorth@zamnet.zm

The Anglican Church of the Central American Region

(Iglesia Anglicana de la Región Central de América)

Members 15,600
This province of the Anglican Communion is made up of the Dioceses of Guatemala, El Salvador, Nicaragua, Costa Rica and Panama. The Church was introduced by the Society for the Propagation of the Gospel when England administered two colonies in Central America, Belize (1783–1982) and Miskitia (1740–1894). In the later years Afro-Antillean people brought their Anglican Christianity with them. The province is multicultural and multiracial and is committed to evangelization, social outreach, and community development.

Primate Most Revd Martin de Jesus Barahona Pascacio (*Bishop of El Salvador*)

Provincial Secretary Rt Revd Hector Monterroso (*Bishop of Costa Rica*) *Tel:* 506 253 0790
Fax: 506 253 8331
email: iarca@amnet.co.cr

Provincial Treasurer Mr Harold Charles, Apt R, Balboa, Republic of Panama *Tel:* 507 212 0062
Fax: 507 262 2097
email: iarcahch@sinfo.net

COSTA RICA
Bishop Rt Revd Hector Monterroso, Apt 10502, 1000 San José, Costa Rica *Tel:* 506 225 0209/253 0790
Fax: 506 253 8331
email: anglicancr@racsa.co.cr/iarca@amnet.co.cr

EL SALVADOR
Bishop Most Revd Martin de Jesus Barahona Pascacio (*Primate of the Anglican Church of the Central American Region*), 47 Avenida Sur, 723 Col Flor Blanca, Apt Postal (01), 274 San Salvador, El Salvador *Tel:* 503 2223 2252
Fax: 503 2223 7952
email: anglican.sal@integra.com.sv

GUATEMALA
Bishop Rt Revd Armando Román Guerra-Soria, Apt 58A, Avenida La Castellana 40–06, Guatemala City, Guatemala *Tel:* 502 2472 0852
Fax: 502 2472 0764
email: diocesis@terra.com.gt/ diocesis@infovia.com.gt

NICARAGUA
Bishop Rt Revd Sturdie Downs, Apt 1207, Managua, Nicaragua *Tel:* 505 2225 174
Fax: 505 2226 701
email: episcnic@cablenet.com.ni/ episcnic@tmx.com.ni

PANAMA
Bishop Rt Revd Julio Murray, Box R, Balboa, Republic of Panama
Tel: 507 212 0062/507 262 2051
Fax: 507 262 2097
email: iepan@cwpanama.net/anglipan@sinfo.net
Web: www.episcopalpanama.org

The Church of the Province of Congo

Members approximately 500,000

Ugandan evangelist Apolo Kivebulaya established an Anglican presence in the Democratic Republic of Congo (formerly Zaire) in 1896. The Church reached the Katanga (formerly Saba) region in 1955, but evangelization did not progress on a large scale until the 1970s. Following independence, the Church expanded and formed dioceses as part of the Province of Uganda, Burundi, Rwanda, and Boga-Zaire. The new province was inaugurated in 1992 and changed its name in 1997. On 17 September 2002 the then Archbishop Njojo and many other Congolese citizens had to flee to Uganda because of internal tribal warfare.

Archbishop Most Revd Henri Isingoma Kahwa (*Bishop of Kinshasa*) PO Box 16482 Kinshasa 1 DR Congo *Tel:* 243 99 3333 3090
email: peac_isingoma@yahoo.fr

Provincial Secretary Rt Revd Jean Molanga Botola (*Assistant Bishop of Kinshasa*) (*same address*)
email: molanga2k@yahoo.co.uk

Provincial Treasurer and Liaison Office in Kampala Mr Fréderick Ngadjole Badya, PO Box 25586, Kampala, Uganda *Tel:* 256 77264 7495
email: eac-mags@infocom.co.ug

Provincial Coordinator of Evangelism Vacancy

THEOLOGICAL COLLEGE

Anglican University of Congo (Universite Anglicane du Congo 'U.A.C.') PO Box 25586, Kampala, Uganda *Rector* Revd Canon Sabiti Tibafa Daniel
Tel: 243 99 779 1013
email: email: revdsabiti@yahoo.fr

ARU

Bishop Rt Revd Dr Georges Titre Ande, PO Box 226, Arua, Uganda *Tel:* 243 81 039 30 71
email: revdande@yahoo.co.uk

BOGA (*formerly* BOGA-ZAIRE)

Bishop Rt Revd William Bahemuka Mugenyi, PO Box 25586, Kampala, Uganda
Tel: 243 99 0668639
email: mugenyiwilliam@yahoo.com

BUKAVU

Bishop Rt Revd Sylvestre Bahati Bali-Busane, Av. Mgr Ndahura, No. Q/Nyalukemba, C/Ibanda, CAC-Bukavu, BP 2876, Bukavu, Democratic Republic of Congo / PO Box 134, Cyangugu, Rwanda *Tel:* 243 99 401 3647
email: bahati_bali@yahoo.fr

KATANGA

Bishop Rt Revd Corneille Kasima Muno, 1309 Chaussee do Kasenga, Bel-Air, Lubumbashi, PO Box 22037, Kitwe, Zambia
Tel and Fax: 243 81 475 6075
email: kasimamuno@yahoo.fr

KINDU

Bishop Rt Revd Zacharie Masimango Katanda (*Dean of the Province*), PO Box 5, Gisenyi, Rwanda
Tel: 243 99 891 6258
email: angkindu@yahoo.fr

KINSHASA (Missionary diocese)

Bishop Most Revd Henri Isingoma Kahwa (*Archbishop of the Province*), 11 Ave. Basalakala, Quartier Immocongo Commune de Kalamu, Kinshasa 1, PO Box 16482, DR Congo
email: peac_isingoma@yahoo.fr

Assistant Bishop
Rt Revd Jean Molanga Botola, (*Provincial Secretary*), EAC-Kinshasa, BP 16482, Kinshasa 1, DR Congo *Tel:* 243 99 471 3802
email: molanga2k@yahoo.co.uk

KISANGANI

Bishop Rt Revd Lambert Funga Botolome, Av. Bowane, N°10, Quartier des Musiciens, C/Makiso, PO Box 86, Kisangani, DR Congo *or* c/o PO Box 25586, Kampala, Uganda
Tel: 243 997 252 868 (Mobile)
email: lambertfunga@hotmail.com

NORD KIVU

Bishop Rt Revd Adoplh Muhindo Isesomo, PO Box 322, Butembo, DR Congo *or* PO Box 25586 Kampala, Uganda *Tel:* 243 99 8854 8601

KASAIS

Bishop Rt Revd Marcel Kapinga Kayibabu wa Ilunga, PO Box 16482, Kinshasa 1, DRCongo
Tel: 243 99 357 0080
email: anglicanekasai@yahoo.fr

The Church of England

Baptized members 26,000,000
Covering all of England, the Isle of Man and the Channel Islands; Europe except Great Britain and Ireland; Morocco; Turkey; and the Asian countries of the former Soviet Union. The Church of England is the ancient national Church of the land. Its structures emerged from the missionary work of St Augustine, sent from Rome in AD 597, and from the work of Celtic missionaries in the north. Throughout the Middle Ages, the Church was in communion with the See of Rome, but in the sixteenth century it separated from Rome and rejected the authority of the Pope. The Church of England is the established Church, with its administration governed by a General Synod, which meets twice a year.

Hong Kong Sheng Kung Hui

(Hong Kong Anglican Church)

Members 30,000
This dynamic province was inaugurated in 1998. The history of the Church in China dates back to the mid-nineteenth century; missionaries were provided by the American Church, the Church of England, the Church of England in Canada, etc. The Province of Chung Hua Sheng Kung Hui (the Holy Catholic Church in China) was established in 1912 of which the Anglican Church in Hong Kong and Macau was an integral part. Chung Hua Sheng Kung Hui ceased to exist in the 1950s and the diocese of Hong Kong and Macau was associated to other dioceses in South East Asia under the custodianship of the Council of Churches of East Asia, until the recent establishment of the diocese as the 38th province of the Anglican Communion. It has parishes in Hong Kong and Macau, which returned to Chinese sovereignty in 1997 and 1999 respectively. It enjoys autonomy and independence as guaranteed by the Basic Law (the mini constitution governing Hong Kong, the Special Administrative Region of China).

Primate Most Revd Paul Kwong, Provincial Office, 16/F Tung Wai Commercial Building, 109–111 Gloucester Road, Wanchai, Hong Kong SAR
Tel: 852 2526 5355
Fax: 852 2521 2199
email: office1@hkskh.org
Web: www.hkskh.org

Provincial Secretary General Revd Peter Douglas Koon (*same address*)
email: peter.koon@hkskh.org

Bishop of Hong Kong Island Most Revd Paul Kwong, 25/F Wyndham Place, 40–44, Wyndham Street, Central, Hong Kong SAR
Tel: 852 2526 5366
Fax: 852 2523 3344
email: do.dhk@hkskh.org
Web: http://dhk.hkskh.org

Bishop of Eastern Kowloon Rt Revd Louis Tsui, Diocesan Office, 4/F Holy Trinity Bradbury Centre, 139 Ma Tau Chung Rd, Kowloon City, Kowloon, Hong Kong SAR
Tel: 852 2713 9983
Fax: 852 2711 1609
email: ekoffice@ekhkskh.org.hk
Web: ekhkskh.org.hk

Bishop of Western Kowloon Rt Revd Andrew Chan, Diocesan Office, 11 Pak Po Street, Mongkok, Kowloon, Hong Kong SAR
Tel: 852 2783 0811
Fax: 852 2783 0799
email: dwk@hkskh.org
Web: http://dwk.hkskh.org

Bishop of Missionary Area of Macau Most Revd Paul Kwong, 1 andar A, Edf, HuaDu, No. 2 Trav. Do Pato, No. 49–51 Rua do Campo, Macau SAR
Tel: 853 2835 3867
Fax: 853 2832 5314
email: skhmma@macau.ctm.net
Web: www.hkskh.org

The Church of the Province of the Indian Ocean

Members 90,486
The Anglican mission was begun in Mauritius in 1812 by the Revd H. Shepherd, and the first Anglican church in the Seychelles was dedicated in January 1856. The growth of the church was fostered both by the Society for the Propagation of the Gospel and by the Church Missionary Society. The dioceses of Madagascar and Mauritius and Seychelles combined in 1973 to create the province, which now comprises seven dioceses.

Archbishop Most Revd Ian Gerald Ernest (*Bishop of Mauritius*)

Provincial Secretary Revd Samitiana Razafindralamo, Évêché Anglican, 12 rue Rabezavana, Ambodifilao, 101 TNR Antananarivo, Madagascar *Tel:* 261 20 24 39162
Fax: 261 20 226 1331
email: eemtma@hotmail.com / eemdanta@dts.mg

Treasurer Mr Philip Tse Rai (*same address*)

Chancellor of the Province Mrs Hilda Yerriah, 4 rue Commerson, Beau Bassin
Tel: 230 20 80429 (Office)
230 46 75710 (Home)
email: hilda5885@hotmail.com

Dean of the Province Rt Revd Jean-Claude Andrianjafimanana (*Bishop of Mahajanga*)

THEOLOGICAL COLLEGES

St Paul's College, Ambatohararana, Merimandroso, Ambohidratrimo, Madagascar (*Warden* Revd Vincent Rakotoarisoa)

St Paul's College, Rose Hill, Mauritius (*Warden* Vacancy)

St Philip's Theological College, La Misère, Seychelles (*Diocesan Trainer* The Revd Peter Raath)

CHURCH PAPERS

Newsletters of the Province of the Indian Ocean Support Assn. *Editor* The Revd Philip Harbridge, Chaplain, Christ's College, Cambridge CB2 3BY, UK

Seychelles Diocesan Magazine A quarterly newspaper covering diocesan events and containing articles of theological and other interest.

Magazine du Diocèse de Maurice (Le Cordage) A quarterly newspaper covering diocesan events and containing articles of theological and ecumenical interest.

ANTANANARIVO

Bishop Rt Revd Samoela Jaona Ranarivelo, Évêché Anglican, Lot VK57 ter, Ambohimanoro, 101 Antananarivo, Madagascar *Tel:* 261 20 222 0827
Fax: 261 20 226 1331
email: eemdanta@dts.mg

Assistant Bishop Rt Revd Todd MacGregor (*Tulear*) (*same address*)

ANTSIRANANA

Bishop Rt Revd Roger Chung Po Chuen, Évêché Anglican, BP 278, 4 rue Grandidier, 201 Antsiranana, Madagascar *Tel:* 261 20 82 2 2650
email: mgrchungpo@blueline.mg

FIANARANTSOA

Bishop Rt Revd Gilbert Rateloson Rakotondravelo, Évêché Anglican Manantsara, BP 1418 Fianarantsoa, Madagascar
Tel: 261 20 75 51583
261 33 14 043 36 (Mobile)
email: eemdiofianara@yahoo.fr

MAHAJANGA

Bishop Rt Revd Jean-Claude Andrianjafimanana, BP 570, Rue de Temple Ziona, Mahajanga 401, Madagascar *Tel*: 261 62 23611
261 32 04 55143 (Mobile)
email: andrianjajc@yahoo.fr / eemdmaha@dts.mg

MAURITIUS

Bishop Most Revd Ian Gerald Ernest (*Archbishop of the Province*), Bishop's House, Ave. Nallétamby, Phoenix, Mauritius
Tel: 230 686 5158
230 787 8131 (Mobile)
Fax: 230 697 1096
email: dioang@intnet.mu

SEYCHELLES

Bishop Rt Revd James Richard Wong Yin Song, PO Box 44, Victoria, Mahé, Seychelles
Tel: 248 32 1977 / 32 3879
248 52 7770 (Mobile)
Fax: 248 22 4043
email: angdio@seychelles.net
Web: www.seychelles.anglican.org

TOAMASINA

Bishop Rt Revd Jean Paul Solo, Évêché Anglican, Rue James Seth, BP 531, Toamasina 501, Madagascar *Tel:* 261 20 533 1663
261 32 04 55143 (Mobile)
Fax: 261 20 533 1689
email: eemtoam@wanadoo.mg

The Church of Ireland

According to the 2011 Census figures for the Republic of Ireland the Church of Ireland population has increased in the Republic of Ireland. To date we do not have the 2011 Census figures for Northern Irelan;d therefore the Northern Ireland figures are based on the 2001 Census.

Members 392,153

Tracing its origins to St Patrick and his companions in the fifth century, the Irish Church has been marked by strong missionary efforts. In 1537 the English king was declared head of the Church, but most Irish Christians maintained loyalty to Rome. The Irish Church Act of 1869 provided that the statutory union between the Churches of England and Ireland be dissolved and that the Church of Ireland should cease to be established by law. A General Synod of the Church, established in 1871 and consisting of archbishops, bishops, and representatives of the clergy and laity, has legislative and administrative power. Irish Church leaders have played a key role in the work of reconciliation in the Northern Ireland conflict.

The Primate of All Ireland and Metropolitan Most Vacancy (*Archbishop of Armagh*)

The Primate of Ireland and Metropolitan Most Revd Dr Michael Geoffrey, St Aubyn Jackson (*Archbishop of Dublin & Bishop of Glendalough*)

Central Office of the Church of Ireland Church of Ireland House, Church Ave, Rathmines, Dublin 6, Republic of Ireland *Tel:* 353 1 497 8422
Fax: 353 1 497 8821
email: office@rcbdub.org

Chief Officer and Secretary, Representative Church Body Mr Adrian Clements
email: chiefofficer@rcbdub.org

Head of Synod Services and Communications Mrs Janet Maxwell *email:* comms@rcbdub.org

THEOLOGICAL INSTITUTE

The Church of Ireland Theological Institute, Braemor Park, Churchtown, Dublin 14, which conducts courses in conjunction with the School of Hebrew, Biblical and Theological Studies, Trinity College, Dublin, Republic of Ireland (*Director* Revd Dr Maurice Elliott)
Tel: 353 1 492 3506
Fax: 353 1 492 3082
email: admin@theologicalinstitute.ie
web: theologicalinstitute.ie

CHURCH PAPER

Church of Ireland Gazette (weekly) Deals with items of general interest to the Church of Ireland in a national context and also contains news from the various dioceses and parishes together with articles of a more general nature. *Editor/Editorial Offices* 3 Wallace Ave, Lisburn, Co Antrim BT27 4AA *Tel:* 44 28 9267 5743
Fax: 44 28 9266 7580
email: gazette@ireland.anglican.org

PROVINCE OF ARMAGH

ARMAGH

Vacancy (*Primate of the Church of Ireland*), c/o Church House, 46 Abbey Street, Armagh BT61 7DZ *Tel:* 44 28 3752 7144 (Office)
Fax: 44 28 3751 0596
email: archbishop@armagh.anglican.org
Web: http://armagh.anglican.org

CATHEDRAL CHURCH OF ST PATRICK, Armagh
Dean Very Revd Gregory John Orchard Dunstan, The Deanery, Library House, 43 Abbey Street, Armagh BT61 7DY *Tel:* 44 28 3752 3142 (Office)
Tel: 44 28 3751 8447 (Home)
Fax: 44 28 3752 4177
email: dean@armagh.anglican.org

CLOGHER

Bishop Rt Revd Rt Revd Francis John McDowell, The See House, Fivemiletown, Co Tyrone BT75 0QP *Tel* and *Fax:* 44 28 8952 2461
email: bishop@clogher.anglican.org

CATHEDRAL CHURCHES OF ST MACARTAN, Clogher, and ST MACARTIN, Enniskillen
Dean Very Revd Kenneth Robert James Hall, The Deanery, 13 Church Street, Enniskillen, Co Fermanagh BT74 7DW
Tel: 44 28 6632 2917 (Office)
Tel: 44 28 6632 2465 (Home)
email: dean@clogher.anglican.org

CONNOR

Bishop Rt Revd Alan Francis Abernethy, Diocesan Office, Church of Ireland House, 61–67 Donegall Street, Belfast BT1 2QH
Tel: 44 28 9082 8870
email: bishop@connor.anglican.org
Web: connor.anglican.org

CATHEDRAL CHURCH OF ST SAVIOUR, Lisburn
Dean Very Revd John Frederick Augustus Bond, The Rectory, 49 Rectory Gardens, Broughshane, Ballymena, Co Antrim, BT42 4LF
Tel and *Fax:* 44 28 2586 1215
email: skerry@connor.anglican.org

CATHEDRAL CHURCH OF ST ANNE, Belfast
(Cathedral of the United Dioceses of Down and Dromore and the Diocese of Connor)
Dean Very Revd John Owen Mann, The Deanery, 5 Deramore Drive, Belfast BT9 5JQ
Tel: 44 28 9066 0980 (Home)
44 28 9032 8332 (Cathedral)
Fax: 44 28 9023 8855
email: dean@belfastcathedral.org

DERRY AND RAPHOE

Bishop Rt Revd Kenneth Raymond Good, The See House, 112 Culmore Rd, Londonderry, Co Derry BT48 8JF *Tel:* 44 28 7126 2440 (Office)
Fax: 44 28 7135 2554
email: bishop@derry.anglican.org
Web: http://derry.anglican.org

CATHEDRAL CHURCH OF ST COLUMB, Derry
Dean Very Revd William Wright Morton, The Deanery, 30 Bishop St, Londonderry, Co Derry BT48 6PP *Tel:* 44 28 7126 2746
email: dean@derry.anglican.org

CATHEDRAL CHURCH OF ST EUNAN, Raphoe
Dean Very Revd John Hay, The Deanery, Raphoe, Co Donegal *Tel:* 353 74 914 5226

DOWN AND DROMORE
Bishop Rt Revd Harold Creeth Miller, The See House, 32 Knockdene Park South, Belfast BT5 7AB *Tel:* 44 28 9082 8850 (Office)
Fax: 44 28 9023 1902
email: bishop@down.anglican.org
Web: http://down.anglican.org

CATHEDRAL CHURCH OF THE HOLY AND UNDIVIDED TRINITY, Down
Dean Very Revd Thomas Henry Hull, Lecale Rectory, 9 Quoile Road, Downpatrick, Co Down BT30 6SE *Tel:* 44 28 4461 3101
Fax: 44 28 4461 4456

CATHEDRAL CHURCH OF CHRIST THE REDEEMER, Dromore
Dean Very Revd Stephen Harold Lowry, Dromore Cathedral Rectory, 28 Church Street, Dromore, Co Down BT25 1AA
Tel: 44 28 9269 2275 (Home)
44 28 9269 3968 (Office)
email: cathedral@dromore.anglican.org

KILMORE, ELPHIN AND ARDAGH
Bishop Vacancy, 48 Carrickfern, Cavan, Co Cavan, Republic of Ireland *Tel:* 353 49 4372759
email: bishop@kilmore.anglican.org
Web: http://kilmore.anglican.org

CATHEDRAL CHURCH OF ST FETHLIMIDH, Kilmore
Dean Very Revd Wallace Raymond Ferguson, Danesfort, Cavan, Co Cavan, Republic of Ireland
Tel and *Fax:* 353 49 433 1918
email: dean@kilmore.anglican.org

CATHEDRAL CHURCH OF ST MARY THE VIRGIN AND ST JOHN THE BAPTIST, Sligo, Republic of Ireland
Dean Very Revd Arfon Williams, The Deanery, Strandhill Road, Sligo, Co Sligo, Republic of Ireland *Tel:* 353 71 915 7993

TUAM, KILLALA AND ACHONRY
Bishop Rt Revd Rt Revd Patrick William Rooke, 2 Summerfield, Cahergowan, Claregalway, Co Galway, Republic of Ireland *Tel:* 353 91 799359
email: bishop@tuam.anglican.org
Web: http://tuam.anglican.org

CATHEDRAL CHURCH OF ST MARY, Tuam
Dean Very Revd Alistair John Grimason, Deanery Place, Cong, Co Mayo, Republic of Ireland *Tel:* 353 94 954
email: deantuam@yahoo.co.uk

CATHEDRAL CHURCH OF ST PATRICK, Killala
Dean Very Revd Wendy Mary Callan, St Michael's Rectory, Church Road, Ballina, Co Mayo, Republic of Ireland *Tel:* 353 96 77894
email: revwendycallan@googlemail.com

PROVINCE OF DUBLIN

CASHEL, WATERFORD, LISMORE, OSSORY, FERNS AND LEIGHLIN
Bishop Rt Revd Michael Andrew James Burrows, Bishop's House, Troysgate, Kilkenny, Republic of Ireland *Tel:* 353 56 77 86633 (Home)
email: cashelossorybishop@eircom.net
Web: http://cashel.anglican.org

CATHEDRAL CHURCH OF ST JOHN THE BAPTIST AND ST PATRICK'S ROCK, Cashel
Dean Very Revd Philip John Knowles, The Deanery, Cashel, Co Tipperary, Republic of Ireland *Tel:* 353 62 61232 (Home)
353 62 61944 (Office)

CATHEDRAL CHURCH OF THE BLESSED TRINITY (CHRIST CHURCH), Waterford
Dean Very Revd Maria Patricia Jansson, The Deanery, 41 Grange Park Rd, Waterford, Co Waterford, Republic of Ireland
Tel: 353 51 874119
email: dean@waterford.anglican.org

CATHEDRAL CHURCH OF ST CARTHAGE, Lismore
Dean Very Revd Paul Richard Draper, The Deanery, The Mall, Lismore, Co Waterford, Republic of Ireland *Tel:* 353 58 54105

CATHEDRAL CHURCH OF ST CANICE, Kilkenny
Dean Very Revd Katharine Margaret Poulton, The Deanery, Kilkenny, Republic of Ireland
Tel: 353 56 772 1516
email: dean@ossory.anglican.org

CATHEDRAL CHURCH OF ST EDAN, Ferns
Dean Very Revd Paul Gerard Mooney, The Deanery, Ferns, Enniscorthy, Co Wexford, Republic of Ireland *Tel:* 353 53 936 6124
email: dean@ferns.anglican.org

CATHEDRAL CHURCH OF ST LASERIAN, Leighlin
Dean Very Revd Thomas William Gordon, The Deanery, Old Leighlin, Co. Carlow, Republic of Ireland *Tel:* 353 59 9721570
email: dean.leighlin@gmail.com

CORK, CLOYNE AND ROSS
Bishop Rt Revd William Paul Colton, St Nicholas' House, 14 Cove Street, Cork, Republic of Ireland
Tel: 353 21 500 5080 (Office)
email: bishop@ccrd.ie
Web: http://.cork.anglican.org

CATHEDRAL CHURCH OF ST FIN BARRE, Cork
Dean Very Revd Nigel Kenneth Dunne, The Deanery, Gilabbey St, Cork, Republic of Ireland
Tel: 353 21 4318073
email: dean@cork.anglican.org

CATHEDRAL CHURCH OF ST COLMAN, Cloyne
Dean Very Revd Alan Gordon Marley, The Deanery, Midleton, Co Cork, Republic of Ireland
Tel: 353 21 463 1449
email: dean@cloyne.anglican.org

CATHEDRAL CHURCH OF ST FACHTNA, Ross
Dean Very Revd Christopher Lind Peters, The Deanery, Rosscarbery, Co Cork, Republic of Ireland *Tel:* 353 23 48166
email: candjpeters@eircom.net

DUBLIN AND GLENDALOUGH
Archbishop Most Revd Dr Michael Geoffrey St Aubyn Jackson, The See House, 17 Temple Rd, Dartry, Dublin 6, Republic of Ireland
Tel: 353 1 497 7849
Fax: 353 1 497 6355
email: archbishop@dublin.anglican.org
Web: http://dublin.anglican.org

CATHEDRAL CHURCH OF THE HOLY TRINITY (COMMONLY CALLED CHRIST CHURCH)
Cathedral of the United Dioceses of Dublin and Glendalough, Metropolitan Cathedral of the United Provinces of Dublin and Cashel

Dean Very Revd Dermot Patrick Martin Dunne, 19 Mountainview Road, Ranelagh, Dublin 6
Tel: 353 1 677 8099 (Cathedral)
Fax: 353 1 679 8991
email: dean@cccdub.ie

THE NATIONAL CATHEDRAL AND COLLEGIATE CHURCH OF ST PATRICK, Dublin
(The 'National Cathedral of the Church of Ireland having a common relation to all the dioceses of Ireland')
Dean and Ordinary Very Revd Victor George Stacey, The Deanery, Upper Kevin St, Dublin 8, Republic of Ireland
Tel: 353 1 475 5449 (Home)
353 1 475 4817 (Cathedral)
353 1 453 9472 (Office)
Fax: 353 1 454 6374

LIMERICK, ARDFERT, AGHADOE, KILLALOE, KILFENORA, CLONFERT, KILMACDUAGH AND EMLY
Bishop Rt Revd Trevor Russell Williams, Rien Roe, Adare, Co Limerick, Republic of Ireland
Tel: 353 61 396 244
email: bishop@limerick.anglican.org
Web: http://limerick.anglican.org

CATHEDRAL CHURCH OF ST MARY, Limerick
Dean Very Revd Sandra Ann Pragnell, The Deanery, 7 Kilbane, Castletroy, Limerick, Republic of Ireland *Tel* and *Fax:* 353 61 338 697
email: dean@limerick.anglican.org

CATHEDRAL CHURCH OF ST FLANNAN, Killaloe
Dean Vacancy

CATHEDRAL CHURCH OF ST BRENDAN, Clonfert
Dean Vacancy

MEATH AND KILDARE
Bishop Most Revd Dr Richard Lionel Clarke, Bishop's House, Moyglare, Maynooth, Co Kildare, Republic of Ireland
Tel: 353 1 628 9354 (Office)
email: bishop@meath.anglican.org
Web: http://meath.anglican.org

CATHEDRAL CHURCH OF ST PATRICK, Trim
Dean of Clonmacnoise Vacancy

CATHEDRAL OF ST BRIGID, Kildare
Dean Very Revd John Joseph Marsden, The Deanery, Morristown, Newbridge, Co Kildare, Republic of Ireland *Tel:* 353 45 438 158

The Anglican Communion in Japan

(Nippon Sei Ko Kai)

Members 35,000
In 1859 the American Episcopal Church sent two missionaries to Japan, followed some years later by representatives of the Church of England and the Church in Canada. The first Anglican Synod took place in 1887. The first Japanese bishops were consecrated in 1923. The Church remained oppressed during the Second World War and assumed all church leadership after the war.

Primate Most Revd Nathaniel Makoto Uematsu (*Bishop of Hokkaido*)

Provincial Office Nippon Sei Ko Kai, 65–3 Yarai-cho, Shinjuku-ku, Tokyo 162–0805 (Please use this address for all correspondence)
Tel: 81 3 5228 3171
Fax: 81 3 5228 3175
email: province@nskk.org
Web: www.nskk.org

General Secretary Revd John Makito Aizawa
email: general-sec.po@nskk.org

Provincial Treasurer Mr Matthias Shigeo Ozaki

THEOLOGICAL TRAINING

Central Theological College, 1–12–31 Yoga, Setagaya-ku, Tokyo 158–0097, for clergy and lay workers

Bishop Williams Theological School, Shimotachiuri-agaru, Karasuma Dori, Kamikyo-ku, Kyoto 602–8332

CHURCH NEWSPAPERS

Sei Ko Kai Shimbun Published on the twentieth of each month in Japanese. Usually eight pages, tabloid format. Subscription through the Provincial Office. Each diocese also has its own monthly paper.

NSKK News English-language newsletter. Published quarterly. Available through the Provincial Office and also on the web page of Anglican Communion.

CHUBU

Bishop Rt Revd Peter Ichiro Shibusawa, 28–1 Meigetsu-cho, 2-chome, Showa-ku, Nagoya 466–0034 *Tel:* 81 52 858 1007
Fax: 81 52 858 1008
email: office.chubu@nskk.org
Web: www.nskk.org/chubu

HOKKAIDO

Bishop Most Revd Nathaniel Makoto Uematsu (*Archbishop of the Province*), Kita 15 jo, Nishi 5-20, Kita-Ku, Sapporo 001-0015 *Tel:* 81 11 717 8181
Fax: 81 11 736 8377
email: hokkaido@nskk.org
Web: www.nskk.org/hokkaido

KITA KANTO

Bishop Rt Revd Zerubbabel Katsuichi Hirota, 2–172 Sakuragi-cho, Omiya-ku, Saitama-shi, 331–0852 *Tel:* 81 48 642 2680
Fax: 81 48 648 0358
email: kitakanto@nskk.org
Web: www.nskk.org/kitakanto

KOBE

Bishop Rt Revd Andrew Yutaka Nakamura, 5–11–1 Yamatedori, Chuo-ku, Kobe-shi 650–0011
Tel: 81 78 351 5469
Fax: 81 78 382 1095
email: aao52850@syd.odn.ne.jp
Web: www.nskk.org/kobe

KYOTO

Bishop Rt Revd Stephen Takashi Kochi, 380 Okakuencho, Shimotachiuri-agaru, Karasuma-dori, Kamikyo-ku, Kyoto 602–8011
Tel: 81 75 431 7204
Fax: 81 75 441 4238
email: nskk-kyoto@mse.biglobe.ne.jp
Web: www.nskk.org/kyoto

KYUSHU

Bishop Rt Revd Gabriel Shoji Igarashi, 2–9–22 Kusakae, Chuo-ku, Fukuoka 810–0045
Tel: 81 92 771 2050
Fax: 81 92 771 9857
email: d-kyushu@try-net.or.jp
Web: http://www1.bbiq.jp/d-kyushu

OKINAWA

Bishop Rt Revd David Shoji Tani, 3–5–5 Meada, Urasoe-shi, Okinawa 910-2102 *Tel:* 81 98 942 1101
Fax: 81 98 942 1102
email: office.okinawa@nskk.org
Web: http://anglican-okinawa.jp

OSAKA

Bishop Rt Revd Samuel Osamu Ohnishi, 2–1–8 Matsuzaki-cho, Abeno-ku, Osaka 545–0053
Tel: 81 6 6621 2179
Fax: 81 6 6621 3097
email: office.osaka@nskk.org
Web: www.nskk.org/osaka

TOHOKU

Bishop Rt Revd John Hiromichi Kato, 2-13-15 Kokubun-cho, Aoba-ku, Sendai 980-0803
Tel: 81 22 223 2349
Fax: 81 22 223 2387
email: hayashi.tohoku@nskk.org
Web: www.nskk.org/tohoku

TOKYO

Bishop Rt Revd Peter Jintaro Ueda, 3-6-18 Shiba Koen, Minato-ku, Tokyo 105-0011
Tel: 81 3 3433 0987
Fax: 81 3 3433 8678
email: office.tko@nskk.org

YOKOHAMA

Bishop Rt Revd Laurence Yutaka Minabe, 14-57 Mitsuzawa Shimo-cho, Kanagawa-ku, Yokohama 221-0852 *Tel:* 81 45 321 4988
Fax: 81 45 321 4978
email: yokohama.kyouku@nskk.org
Web: anglican.jp/yokohama

The Episcopal Church in Jerusalem and the Middle East

Members 10,000

The Church comprises the dioceses of Jerusalem, Iran, Egypt, Cyprus, and the Gulf. The Jerusalem bishopric was founded in 1841 and became an archbishopric in 1957. Reorganization in January 1976 ended the archbishopric and combined the Diocese of Jordan, Lebanon and Syria with the Jerusalem bishopric after a 19-year separation. Around the same time, the new Diocese of Cyprus and the Gulf was formed and the Diocese of Egypt was revived. The Cathedral Church of St George the Martyr in Jerusalem is known for its ministry to pilgrims. St George's College, Jerusalem is in partnership with the Anglican Communion.

THE CENTRAL SYNOD
President-Bishop Most Revd Mouneer Hanna Anis (*Bishop in Egypt with North Africa and the Horn of Africa)*

Provincial Secretary The Revd Hanna Mansour, PO Box 3, Doha, Qatar
Tel and *Fax:* (Qatar) 974 442 4329
email: tianyoung@hotmail.com

Acting Provincial Treasurer Revd Canon William Schwartz, PO Box 87, Zamalek, Cairo 11211, Egypt *Tel:* 202 738 0829
Fax: 202 735 8941
email: bishopmouneer@link.net

The Jerusalem and the Middle East Church Association acts in support of the Episcopal Church in Jerusalem and the Middle East, the Central Synod and all four dioceses. *Secretary* Mrs Vanessa Wells, 1 Hart House, The Hart, Farnham, Surrey GU9 7HA *Tel:* 01252 726994
Fax: 01252 735558
*email:*secretary@jmeca.eclipse.co.uk

CYPRUS AND THE GULF
Bishop in Rt Revd Michael Augustine Owen Lewis, PO Box 22075, Nicosia 1517, Cyprus
Tel: 357 22 671220
Fax: 357 2 22 674553
email: bishop@spidernet.com.cy/ cygulf@spidernet.com.cy
Web: www.cyprusgulf.anglican.org

EGYPT WITH NORTH AFRICA AND THE HORN OF AFRICA
Bishop in Rt Revd Mouneer Hanna Anis (*President Bishop of the Episcopal Church of Jerusalem and the Middle East*), Diocesan Office, PO Box 87, Zamalek Distribution, 11211, Cairo, Egypt
Tel: 20 2 738 0829
Fax: 20 2 735 8941
email: bishopmouneer@gmail.com
Web: www.dioceseofegypt.org

Suffragan Rt Revd Andrew Proud (*Horn of Africa*) (*same address*)

Assistant Bishop Rt Revd Bill Musk (*North Africa*) (*same address*)
email: billamusk@googlemail.com

IRAN
Bishop in Rt Revd Azad Marshall, St Thomas Center, Raiwind Road, PO Box 688, Lohore, Punjab, 54000, Pakistan *Tel:* 92 42 542 0452
email: bishop@saintthomascenter.org

JERUSALEM
Bishop in Rt Revd Suheil Dawani, St George's Close, PO Box 1278, Jerusalem 91 019, Israel
Tel: 972 2 627 1670
Fax: 972 2 627 3847
email: bishop@j-diocese.com
Web: www.j-diocese.org

ANGLICAN AND PORVOO COMMUNIONS

The Anglican Church of Kenya

Members 3,500,000
Mombasa saw the arrival of Anglican missionaries in 1844, with the first African ordained to the priesthood in 1885. Mass conversions occurred as early as 1910. The first Kenyan bishops were consecrated in 1955. The Church became part of the Province of East Africa, established in 1960, but by 1970 Kenya and Tanzania were divided into separate provinces.

Primate Most Revd Benjamin M. Nzimbi (*Bishop of All Saints Cathedral Diocese*) PO Box 40502, 00100 Nairobi *Tel:* 254 2 714 755
Fax: 254 2 718 442
email: archoffice@swiftkenya.com
Web: www.ackenya.org

Provincial Secretary Rt Revd Lawrence Dena (Assistant Bishop of Mombasa)
Tel: 254 2 271 4752/3/4
Fax: 254 2 271 4750
email: ackenya@insightkenya.com/ psd@akenya.org

Provincial Treasurer Dr William Ogara, Corat Africa, PO Box 42493, 00100 Nairobi
Tel: 254 2 890 165/6
Fax: 254 2 891 900/890 481

THEOLOGICAL COLLEGES
ACK Language School and Orientation School, PO Box 47429, Nairobi *Tel:* 254 2 721893
email: c/o ackenya@insightkenya.com

ACK Guest House, PO Box 56292, Nairobi
Tel: 254 2 723200/2724780
email: ackghouse@insightkenya.com

ACK St Julian's Centre, PO Box 574, Village Market 00621 *Tel:* 254 66 76221
email: ackstjulians@swiftkenya.com

ACK Guest House Mombasa, PO Box 96170, Likoni, Mombasa
email: ackmsaghouse@swiftkenya.com

Carlile College for Theology & Business Studies, PO Box 72584, Nairobi *Tel:* 254 2 558596/253
email: Williams@insightkenya.com

St Andrews College of Theology and Development Kabare, PO Box 6, Kerugoya
Tel: 254 60 21256
email: ackstandrewskabare@swiftkenya.com

Berea Theological College, PO Box 1945, Nakuru
Tel: 254 51 51295
email: berea-tc@africaonline.co.ke

St Paul's Theological College, Kapsabet, PO Box 18, Kapsabet *Tel:* 254 53 2053
email: ackstpaulskapsabet@africaonline.co.ke

St Philip's Theological College Maseno, PO Box 1, Maseno *Tel:* 254 57 51019

Bishop Hannington Institute Mombasa, PO Box 81150, Mombasa *Tel:* 254 41 491396
email: ackbhanning-msa@swiftmombasa.com

Provincial TEE Programme (Trinity College), PO Box 72430, Nairobi *Tel:* 254 2 558655/542607
email: acktrinitycollege@swiftkenya.com

Church Commissioners for Kenya, PO Box 30422, 00100 Nairobi *Tel:* 254 20 717106
email: churchcom@insightkenya.com

Uzima Press, PO Box 48127, Nairobi
Tel: 254 20 220239/216836
email: uzima@nbnet.co.ke

ALL SAINTS CATHEDRAL DIOCESE
Bishop Most Revd Eliud Wabukala (*Archbishop of Kenya*), PO Box 40502, 00100 Nairobi *Tel:* 254 20 714 755
Fax: 254 20 718 442/714 750
email: archoffice@swiftkenya.com

BONDO
Bishop Rt Revd Johannes Otieno Angela, PO Box 240, 40601 Bondo *Tel:* 254 57 5 20415
email: ackbondo@swiftkenya.com

BUNGOMA
Bishop Vacancy, PO Box 2392, 50200 Bungoma
Tel and *Fax:* 254 337 30481
email: ackbungoma@swiftkenya.com

BUTERE
Bishop Rt Revd Michael Sande, PO Box 54, 50101 Butere *Tel:* 254 56 620 412
Fax: 254 56 620 038
email: ackbutere@swiftkenya.com

ELDORET
Bishop Rt Revd Thomas Kogo, PO Box 3404, 30100 Eldoret *Tel:* 254 53 62785
email: ackeldoret@africaonline.co.ke

EMBU
Bishop Rt Revd Henry Tiras Nyaga Kathii, PO Box 189, 60100 Embu *Tel:* 254 68 30614
Fax: 254 68 30468
email: ackembu@swiftkenya.com

KAJIADO
Bishop Rt Revd John Mutua Taama, PO Box 203, 01100 Kajiado *Tel:* 254 301 21201/05
Fax: 254 301 21106
email: ackajiado@swiftkenya.com

KATAKWA
Bishop Rt Revd Zakayo Iteba Epusi, PO Box 68, 50244 Amagoro *Tel:* 254 55 54079
email: ackatakwa@swiftkenya.com

KERICHO
Bishop Rt Revd Jackson Ole Sapit, c/o PO Box 181, Kericho

KIRINYAGA
Bishop Rt Revd Daniel Munene Ngoru, PO Box 95, 10304 Kutus *Tel:* 254 163 44221
Fax: 254 163 44 020
email: ackirinyaga@swiftkenya.com

KITALE
Bishop Rt Revd Stephen Kewasis Nyorsok, PO Box 4176, 30200 Kitale *Tel:* 254 325 31631
email: ack.ktl@africaonline.co.ke

KITUI
Bishop Rt Revd Josephat Mule, PO Box 1054, 90200 Kitui *Tel:* 254 141 22682
Fax: 254 141 22119
email: ackitui@swiftkenya.com

MACHAKOS
Bishop Rt Revd Mutie Kanuku, PO Box 282, 90100 Machakos *Tel:* 254 145 21379
Fax: 254 145 20178
email: ackmachakos@swiftkenya.com

MASENO NORTH
Bishop Rt Revd Simon M. Oketch, PO Box 416, 50100 Kakemega *Tel* and *Fax:* 254 331 30729
email: ackmnorth@swiftkenya.com

MASENO SOUTH
Bishop Rt Revd Francis Mwayi Abiero, PO Box 114, 40100 Kisumu *Tel:* 254 35 21297
Fax: 254 35 21009
email: ackmsouth@swiftkenya.com

MASENO WEST
Bishop Rt Revd Joseph Otieno Wasonga, PO Box 793, 40600 Siaya *Tel:* 254 334 21483
Fax: 254 334 21483
email: ackmwest@swiftkenya.com

MBEERE
Bishop Rt Revd Moses Masambe Nthuka, PO Box 122, 60104 Siakago *Tel:* 254 162 21261
Fax: 254 162 21083
email: ackmbeere@swiftkenya.com

MERU
Bishop Rt Revd Charles Mwendwa, PO Box 427, 60200 Meru *Tel:* 254 164 30719
email: ackmeru@swiftkenya.com

MOMBASA
Bishop Rt Revd Julius R. K. Kalu, PO Box 80072, 80100 Mombasa *Tel:* 254 41 231 1105
Fax: 254 41 231 6361
email: ackmsa@swiftmombasa.com

Assistant Bishop Rt Revd Lawrence Dena (*same address*)

MOUNT KENYA CENTRAL
Bishop Rt Revd Isaac Maina Ng'ang'a, PO Box 121, 10200 Murang'a *Tel:* 254 60 30560/30559
Fax: 254 60 30148
email: ackmkcentral@wananchi.com

Assistant Bishop Rt Revd Allan Waithaka (*same address*)

MOUNT KENYA SOUTH
Bishop Rt Revd Timothy Ranji, PO Box 886, 00900 Kiambu *Tel:* 254 66 22521/22997
Fax: 254 66 22408
email: ackmtksouth@swiftkenya.com

MOUNT KENYA WEST
Bishop Rt Revd Joseph M. Kagunda, PO Box 229, 10100 Nyeri *Tel:* 254 61 203 2281
email: ackmtkwest@wananchi.com

MUMIAS
Bishop Rt Revd Beneah Justin Okumu Salalah, PO Box 213, 50102 Mumias *Tel:* 254 333 41476
Fax: 254 333 41232
email: ackmumias@swiftkenya.com

NAIROBI
Bishop Rt Revd Peter Njagi Njoka, PO Box 40502, 00100 Nairobi *Tel:* 254 2 714 755
Fax: 254 2 226 259
email: acknairobi@swiftkenya.com

NAKURU
Bishop Rt Revd Stephen Njihia Mwangi, PO Box 56, 20100 Nakuru *Tel:* 254 37 212 155/1
Fax: 254 37 44379
email: acknkudioc@net2000ke.com

NAMBALE
Bishop Rt Revd Josiah M. Were, PO Box 4, 50409 Nambale *Tel:* 254 336 24040
Fax: 254 336 24040
email: acknambale@swiftkenya.com

NYAHURURU
Bishop Rt Revd Charles Gaikia Gaita, PO Box 926, 20300 Nyahururu *Tel:* 254 365 32179
email: nyahu_dc@africaonline.co.ke

SOUTHERN NYANZA
Bishop Rt Revd James Kenneth Ochiel, PO Box 65, 40300 Homa Bay *Tel:* 254 385 22127
Fax: 254 385 22056
email: acksnyanza@swiftkenya.com

TAITA TAVETA
Bishop Rt Revd Samson M. Mwaluda, PO Box 75, 80300 Voi *Tel:* 254 147 30096
Fax: 254 147 30364
email: acktaita@swiftmombasa.com

THIKA
Bishop Rt Revd Gideon G. Githiga, PO Box 214, 01000 Thika *Tel:* 254 151 21735/31654
Fax: 254 151 31544
email: ackthika@swiftkenya.com

The Anglican Church of Korea

(Daehan Seong Gong Hoe)

Members 14,558
From the time when Bishop John Corfe arrived in Korea in 1890 until 1965, the Diocese of Korea has had English bishops. In 1993 the Archbishop of Canterbury installed the newly elected Primate and handed jurisdiction to him, making the Anglican Church of Korea a province of the Anglican Communion. There are four religious communities in the country as well as an Anglican university.

Primate Most Revd Paul Keun Sang Kim (*Bishop of Seoul*)

Provincial Offices 3 Jeong-dong, Jung-gu, Seoul 100–120 *Tel:* 82 2 738 8952
Fax: 82 2 737 4210
email: anglicankorea@gmail.com

Secretary-General Revd Abraham Gwang Joon Kim (*same address*) *Tel:* 82 2 738 8952
Fax: 82 2 737 4210
email: abgwk@hanmail.net
Web: www.skh.or.kr

ANGLICAN UNIVERSITY

(*Sungkonghoe University*) 1–1 Hang-dong, Guro-gu, Seoul 152–716 (*President* Revd Augustine Jeong Ku Lee) *Tel:* 82 2610 4100
Fax: 82 2 737 4210
email: ksyang@skhu.ac.kr

CHURCH PAPER

Daehan Seonggonghoesinmun This fortnightly paper of the Anglican Church of Korea is the joint concern of all three dioceses. Tabloid format. Printed in Korean. Contains regular liturgical and doctrinal features as well as local, national and international church news. *Tel:* 82 2 736 6990
Fax: 82 2 738 1208

BUSAN

Bishop Rt Revd Onesimus Dongsin Park, Anglican Diocese of Busan, 18 Daecheong-dong 2ga, Jung-gu, Busan 600–092 *Tel:* 82 51 463 5742
Fax: 82 51 463 5957
email: onesimus63@hanmail.net
Web: skhpusan.onmam.com

DAEJEON

Bishop Rt Revd Michael Hi Yeon Kwon, Anglican Diocese of Daejeon, 87–6 Seonhwa 2-dong, Jung-gu, Daejeon 301–823 *Tel:* 82 42 256 9987
Fax: 82 42 255 8918
email: tdio@unitel.co.kr
Web: www.djdio.or.kr

SEOUL

Bishop Most Revd Paul Keun Sang Kim (*Presiding Bishop of the Province*), Anglican Diocese of Seoul, 3 Jeong-dong, Jung-gu, Seoul 100–120 *Tel:* 82 2 735 6157
Fax: 82 2 723 2640
email: paulkim7@hitel.net
Web: www.skhseoul.or.kr

The Church of the Province of Melanesia

Members 250,000

After 118 years of missionary association with the Church of the Province of New Zealand, the Church of the Province of Melanesia was formed in 1975. The province encompasses the Republic of Vanuatu and the Solomon Islands, both sovereign island nations in the South Pacific, and the French Trust Territory of New Caledonia.

Archbishop of the Province David Vunagi (*Bishop of Central Melanesia*)

General Secretary Mr Abraham Hauriasi (*same address*) *Tel:* 677 20470
email: hauriasi_a @comphq.org.sb

ANGLICAN THEOLOGICAL COLLEGE

Bishop Patteson Theological College, Kohimarama, PO Box 19, Honiara, Solomon Islands (trains students up to degree standard) (*Principal* Revd Anthony Kame) *Tel:* 677 29124
Fax: 677 21098

BANKS AND TORRES

Bishop Rt Revd Nathan Tome, PO Box 19, Sola, Vanualava, Torba Province, Republic of Vanuatu
Tel and *Fax:* 678 38520
email: Nathan.tome.digicelpacific.blackberry.com

CENTRAL MELANESIA

Bishop Most Revd David Vunagi, PO Box 19, Honiara, Solomon Islands *Tel:* 677 26101
Fax: 677 21098
email: dvunagi@comphq.org.sb

CENTRAL SOLOMONS

Bishop Rt Revd Ben Seka, PO Box 52, Tulagi, CIP, Solomon Islands *Tel:* 677 32006
Fax: 677 32113

HANUATO'O

Bishop Rt Revd Alfred Karibongi, PO Box 20, Kira Kira, Makira Province, Solomon Islands
Tel: 677 50012
email: bishophanuatoo@solomon.com.sb

MALAITA

Bishop Rt Revd Samuel Sahu, Bishop's House, PO Box 7, Auki Malaita Province, Solomon Islands *Tel:* 677 40125
email: sam.malaita@gmail.com

TEMOTU

Bishop Rt Revd George Angus Takeli, Bishop's House, Lata, Santa Cruz, Temotu Province, Solomon Islands *Tel:* 677 53080
email: peace.gtakeli@gmail.com

VANUATU

Bishop Rt Revd James Marvin Ligo, Bishop's House, PO Box 238, Luganville, Santo, Republic of Vanuatu *Tel* and *Fax:* 678 37065/36631
email: diocese_of_vanuatu@ecunet.org/ comdov@vanuatu.com.vu

YSABEL

Bishop Rt Revd Richard Naramana, Bishop's House, PO Box 6, Buala, Jejevo, Ysabel Province, Solomon Islands *Tel:* 677 35124
email: episcopal@solomon.com.sb

The Anglican Church of Mexico

Members 21,000
The Mexican Episcopal Church began with the political reform in 1857, which secured freedom of religion, separating the Roman Catholic Church from the government and politics. Some priests organized a National Church and contacted the Episcopal Church in the United States, seeking the ordination of bishops for the new church. They adopted the name 'Mexican Episcopal Church'. The Mexican Church became an autonomous province of the Anglican Communion in 1995 with the name Iglesia Anglicana de Mexico.

Archbishop Rt Revd Carlos Touché-Porter (*Bishop of Mexico*)

Provincial Secretary Revd Canon Habacuc Ramos Huerta, Calle La Otra Banda # 40, Col. San Angel, Delegación Alvaro Obregón, 01000 México
Tel: 52 55 5616 2490/5550 4073
Fax: 52 55 5616 4063
email: ofipam@att.net.mx / habacuc_mx@yahoo.es
Web: www.iglesiaanglicanademexico.org

Provincial Treasurer C. P. Edgar Gómez-González (*same address*) *email:* ofipam@att.net.mx

CUERNAVACA
Bishop Rt Revd James H. Ottley, Calle Minerva No 1, Col. Delicias, CP 62330 Cuernavaca, Morelos, México
Tel: 52 777 315 2870 (Office)
52 777 322 2559 (Home)
email: diocesisdecuernavaca@hotmail.com

MEXICO
Bishop Most Revd Carlos Touché Porter (*Archbishop of the Province*), Ave San Jerónimo 117, Col. San Ángel, Delegación Álvaro Obregón, 01000 México, D.F. *Tel:* 52 55 5616 3193
Fax: 52 55 5616 2205
email: diomex@netvoice.com.mx

NORTHERN MEXICO
Bishop Rt Revd Francisco Manuel Moreno, Acatlán 102 Ote, Col. Mitras Centro, CP 64460, Monterrey, NL *Tel:* 52 81 8333 0992
Fax: 52 81 8348 7362
email: diocesisdelnorte@prodigy.net.mx

SOUTHEASTERN MEXICO
Bishop Rt Revd Benito Juárez-Martínez, Avenida de Las Américas #73, Col. Aguacatal, 91130 Xalapa, Veracruz *Tel:* 52 228 814 6951
Fax: 52 228 814 4387
email: dioste99@aol.com

WESTERN MEXICO
Bishop Rt Revd Lino Rodríguez-Amaro, Torres Quintero #15, Col. Seattle, 45150 Zapopan, Jalisco *Tel:* 52 33 3560 4726
Fax: 52 33 3616 4413
email: iamoccidente@prodigy.net.mx

The Church of the Province of Myanmar (Burma)

Members 63,845
Anglican chaplains and missionaries worked in Burma in the early and mid-nineteenth century. The Province of Myanmar was formed in 1970, nine years after the declaration of Buddhism as the state religion and four years after all foreign missionaries were forced to leave.

Archbishop of the Province Most Revd Stephen Than Myint Oo (*Bishop of Yangon*)

Provincial Secretary Mr Kenneth Saw, PO Box 11191, 140 Pyidaungsu Yeiktha Rd, Dagon, Yangon *Tel:* 95 1 395279
Tel: 95 1 395350
email: cpm.140@mptmail.net.mm

Provincial Treasurer Daw Myint Htwe Ye (*same address*)

Secretary and Treasurer, Yangon Diocesan Trust Association Daw Pin Lone Soe (*same address*)

ANGLICAN THEOLOGICAL COLLEGES
Holy Cross Theological College, 104 Inya Rd, University PO (11041), Yangon (*Principal* Samuel San Myat Shwe)

Emmanuel Theological College, Mohnyin, Kachin State (*Principal* Bishop David Than Lwin)

CHURCH NEWSLETTER
The province publishes a monthly 36-page *Newsletter. Editor and Manager* Mr Saw Peter Aye, PO Box 11191, Bishopscourt, 140 Pyidaungsu Yeiktha Rd, Dagon, Yangon

HPA-AN
Bishop Rt Revd Saw Stylo, No (4) Block, Bishop Gone, Diocesan Office, Hpa-an, Kayin State
Tel: 95 58 21696

MANDALAY
Bishop Rt Revd Noel Nay Lin, Bishopscourt, 22nd St, 'C' Rd (between 85–86 Rd), Mandalay
Tel: 95 2 34110

MYITKYINA
Bishop Rt Revd David Than Lwin, Diocesan Office, Tha Kin Nat Pe Rd, Thida Ya, Myitkyina
Tel: 95 74 23104

SITTWE
Bishop Rt Revd James Min Dein, St John's Church, Paletwa, Southern Chin State, Via Sittwe

TOUNGOO
Bishop Rt Revd Saw (John) Wilme, Diocesan Office, Nat Shin Naung Rd, Toungoo
Tel: 95 54 23 519 (Office)
95 54 24216 (Home)

YANGON
Bishop Most Revd Stephen Than Myint Oo (*Archbishop of the Province*), PO Box 11191, 140 Pyidaungsu-Yeiktha Rd, Dagon, Yangon
Tel: 95 1 395279/395350 (Office)
95 1 381909 (Home)

Assistant Bishop Samuel Htan Oak, 44 Pyi Road, Dagon, Yangon *Tel:* 95 1 372300

The Church of Nigeria

(Anglican Communion)

Members 17,500,000
The rebirth of Christianity began with the arrival of Christian freed slaves in Nigeria in the middle of the nineteenth century. The Church Missionary Society established an evangelistic ministry, particularly in the south. The division of the Province of West Africa in 1979 formed the Province of Nigeria and the Province of West Africa. In the 1990s, nine missionary bishops consecrated themselves to evangelism in northern Nigeria. Membership growth has dictated the need for new dioceses year by year. In 1997 the Church of Nigeria was divided into three provinces to enable more effective management. In 1999 another twelve dioceses were created, and in January 2003 the Church was re-organized into ten provinces. There are currently fourteen provinces.

Metropolitan and Primate of All Nigeria Most Revd Nicholas Okoh (*Archbishop of the Province of Abuja and Bishop of Abuja*)

Provincial Secretary Ven Michael Olurohunbi, Episcopal House, 24 Douala St, Wuse District, Zone 5, PO Box 212, Abuja, ADCP Garki
Tel: 234 9 523 6950
email: mikefarohunbi08@gmail.com
Web: www.anglican-nig.org

Provincial Treasurer Chief O Adekunle, PO Box 78, Lagos *Tel:* 234 1 263 3581

THEOLOGICAL COLLEGES
Vining College, PMB 729, Oke Emeso, Akure, Ondo State (*Principal* Ven Dr Williams Aladekugbe)

Ezekiel College of Theology, Ujoelen, Ekpoma, Edo State (*Principal* Ven Dr Steve Fagbemi)

PROVINCE OF ABA
Archbishop Most Revd Dr Ikechi Nwachukwu Nwosu (*Bishop of Umahia*)

AROCHUKWU-OHAFIA
Bishop Rt Revd Johnson Onuoha, Bishopscourt, PO Box 193, Arochukwa, Abia State
Tel: 234 802 538 6407
email: aroohafia@anglican.ng.org

IKWUANO
Bishop Rt Revd Chigozirim Onyegbule, Bishopscourt, PO Box 5, Ahaba-Oloko, Abia State
Tel: 234 803 085 9319
email: ikwuano@anglican-nig.org

ISIALA NGWA
Bishop Rt Revd Owen N. Azubuike, Bishopscourt, St George's Cathedral Compound, PNB 2033., Mbawsi, Abia State *Tel:* 234 805 467 0528
email: bpowenazubuike@yahoo.com

ISIALA NGWA SOUTH
Bishop Rt Revd Isaac Nwaobia, St Peter's Cathedral, PO Box 15, Owerrinta, Abia State
Tel: 234 803 711 9317
email: isialangwasouth@anglican-nig.org

ISIUKWUATO
(Missionary diocese) *Bishop* Rt Revd Samuel C. Chukuka, Bishopscourt, PO Box 350, Ovim, Abia State *Tel:* 234 803 338 6221
email: isiukwuato@anglican-nig.org

UKWA
Bishop Rt Revd Samuel Kelechi Eze, PO Box 20468, Aba, Abia State *Tel:* 234 803 789 2431
email: kelerem53787@yahoo.com

UMUAHIA
Bishop Most Revd Dr Ikechi Nwachukwu Nwosu (*Archbishop of the Province of Aba*), Bishopscourt, PO Box 96, Umuahia, Abia State
Tel: 234 88 221 037
email: ik_nwosu01@yahoo.com

PROVINCE OF ABUJA
Archbishop Most Revd Nicholas Okoh (*Metropolitan and Primate of All Nigeria and Bishop of Abuja*)

ABUJA
Bishop Most Revd Nicholas Okoh (*Metropolitan and Primate of All Nigeria and Archbishop of the Province of Abuja*), Episcopal House, 24 Douala St, Wuse District, Zone 5, PO Box 212, Abuja, ADCP Garki *Tel:* 234 56 580 682
email: nickorogodo@yahoo.com

BIDA
Bishop Rt Revd Jonah Kolo, Bishop's House, St John's Mission Compound, PO Box 14, Bida
Tel: 234 66 461 694
email: bida@anglican-nig.org

GBOKO
Bishop Rt Revd Emmauel Nyitsse

GWAGWALADA
Bishop Rt Revd Tanimu Samari Aduda, Diocesan Headquarters, Secretariat Road, PO Box 287, Gwagwalada, Abuja *Tel:* 234 9 882 2083
email: anggwag@skannet.com.ng

IDAH
Bishop Rt Revd Joseph N. Musa, Bishopscourt's, PO Box 25, Idah, Kogi State
email: idah@anglican-nig.org

KAFANCHAN
Bishop Rt Revd William Diya, PO Box 29, Kafanchan, Kaduna State *Tel:* 234 61 20 634

KUBWA
Bishop Rt Revd Duke Akamisoko, Bishop's House, PO Box 67, Kubwa, Abuja FCT, Nigeria
Tel: 234 0803 451 9437
email: dukesoko@yahoo.com

KWOI
Bishop Rt Revd Paul Samuel Zamani, Bishop's Residence, Cathedral Compound, Samban Gide, PO Box 173, Kwoi, Kaduna State
Tel: 234 080 651 8160
email: paulzamani@yahoo.com

LAFIA
Bishop Rt Revd Miller Kangdim Maza, PO Box 560, Lafia, Nasarawa State *Tel:* 234 0803 973 5973
email: anglicandioceseoflafia@yahoo.com

MAKURDI
Bishop Rt Revd Nathaniel Inyom, Bishopscourt, PO Box 1, Makurdi, Benue State
Tel: 234 44 533 349
email: makurdi@anglican.skannet.com.ng

OTUKPO
Bishop Rt Revd David K. Bello, Bishopscourt, PO Box 360, Otukpo, Benue State
Tel: 234 0803 309 1778
email: bishopdkbello@yahoo.com

ZAKI-BIAM
Bishop Rt Revd Benjamin Vager, Bishopscourt, PO Box 600, Yam Market Road, Zaki-Biam, Benue State *Tel:* 234 0803 676 0018
email: rubavia@yahoo.com

ZONKWA (Missionary diocese)
Bishop Rt Revd Praises Omole-Ekun, Bishop's Residence, PO Box 26, Zonkwa, Kaduna State 802002 *Tel:* 234 0803 311 0252
email: zonkwa@anglican-nig.org

PROVINCE OF BENDEL
Archbishop Most Revd Friday John Imakhai (*Bishop of Esan*)

AKOKO-EDO
Bishop Rt Revd Jolly Oyekpen, Bishopscourt, PO Box 10, Igarra, Edo State *Tel:* 234 803 470 5941
email: venjollye@yahoo.com

ASABA
Bishop Rt Revd Justus Mogekwu, Bishopscourt, PO Box 216, Cable Point, Asaba, Delta State
Tel: 234 802 819 2980
email: email: justusmogekwu@yahoo.com

BENIN
Bishop Rt Revd Peter O. J. Imasuen, Bishopscourt, PO Box 82, Benin City, Edo State
Tel: 234 52 250 552

ESAN
Bishop Most Revd Friday John Imakhai (*Archbishop of Bendel Province and Bishop of Esan*), Bishopscourt, Ojoelen, PO Box 921, Ekpoma, *email:* Edo State *Tel:* 234 55 981 079
email: bishopimaekhai@hotmail.com

ETSAKO
Bishop Rt Revd Jacob Bada, Bishopscourt, PO Boox 11, Jattu, Auchi, Edo State

IKKA
Bishop Rt Revd Peter Onekpe, St John's Cathedral, PO Box 1063, Agbor, 321001 Delta State *Tel:* 234 55 250-14

NDOKWA
Bishop Rt Revd David Obiosa, Bishopscourt, 151 Old Sapele Road, Obiaruka, Delta Square
Tel: 234 803 776 9464
email: dfao1963@yahoo.com

OLEH
Bishop Rt Revd Jonathan Francis Ekokotu Edewor, Bishopscourt, PO Box 8, Oleh, Delta State *Tel:* 234 53 701 062
email: email: angoleh2000@yahoo.com

SABONGIDDA-ORA
Bishop Rt Revd John Akao, Bishopscourt, PO Box 13, Sabongidda-Ora, Edo State
Tel: 234 57 54 132
email: akaojohn@yahoo.com

SAPELE
Bishop Rt Revd Blessing Erifeta, Bishopscourt, PO Box 52, Sapele, Delta State
Tel: 234 803 662 4282
email: dioceseofsapele@yahoo.com

UGHELLI
Bishop Rt Revd Cyril Odutemu, Bishopscourt, Ovurodawanre, PO Box 760, Ughelli, Delta State
Tel: 234 53 600 403
email: ughellianglican@yahoo.com

WARRI
Bishop Rt Revd Christian Esezi Ideh, Bishopscourt, 17 Mabiaku Rd, GRA, PO Box 4571, Warri, Delta State *Tel:* 234 53 255 857
email: angdioceseofwarri@yahoo.com

WESTERN IZON (Missionary diocese)
Bishop Rt Revd Edafe Emamezi, Bishopscourt, PO Box 5, Patani, Delta State
Tel: 234 822 05 6228
email: anglizon@yahoo.com

PROVINCE OF ENUGU
Archbishop Rt Revd Amos Amankechinelo Madu (*Bishop of Oji River*)

ABAKALIKI
Bishop Rt Revd Benson C. B. Onyeibor, All Saints' Cathedral, PO Box 112, Abakaliki, Ebonyi State
Tel: 234 43 220 762
email: abakaliki@anglican-nig.org

AFIKPO
Bishop Rt Revd Paul Udogu, Bishop's House, Uwana, PO Box 699, Afikpo, Ebonyi State
email: udogupaul@yahoo.com

AWGU-ANINRI
Bishop Rt Revd Emmanuel Ugwu, Bishopscourt, PO Box 305, Awgu, Enugu State
Tel: 234 803 334 9360
email: afamnonye@yahoo.com

EHA-AMUFU
Bishop Rt Revd Daniel Olinya, St Andrew's Cathedral, Bishopscourt, PO box 85, Eh-Amufu, Enugu State *Tel:* 234 803 089 2131
email: dankol@yahoo.com

IKWO
Bishop Rt Revd Kenneth Ifemene, Bishop's Residence, Agubia Ikwo, PO Box 998, Abakaliki, Ebonyi State *Tel:* 234 805 853 4849
email: bishopikwoanglican.@yahoo.com

NGBO
Bishop Rt Revd Christian I. Ebisike, Bishop's House, PO Box 93, Abakaliki, Ebonyi State
Tel: 234 806 779 4899
email: vendchris@yahoo.com

NIKE
Bishop Rt Revd Evans Jonathan Ibeagha, Bishopscourt, Trans-Ekulu, PO Box 2416, Enugu, Enugu State *Tel:* 234 803 324 1387
email: pnibeagha@yahoo.com

NSUKKA
Bishop Rt Revd Aloysius Agbo, St Cypran's Compound, PO Box 516, Nsukka, Enugu State
Tel: 234 803 932 7840
email: nsukka@anglican-nig.org

OJI RIVER
Bishop Rt Revd Amos Amankechinelo Madu (*Archbishop of the Province of Enugu*), PO Box 123, Oji River, Enugu State *Tel:* 234 803 670 4888
email: amosmadu@yahoo.com

PROVINCE OF IBADAN
Archbishop Most Revd Joseph Akinfenwa (*Bishop of Ibadan*)

AJAYI CROWTHER
Bishop Rt Revd Olugbenga Oduntan, Bishopscourt, Iseyin, PO Box 430, Iseyin, Oyo State
Tel: 234 803 719 8182
email: ajayicrowtherdiocese@yahoo.com

ETIKI KWARA
Bishop Rt Revd Andrew Ajayi
Tel: 234 803 470 3522
email: andajayi@yahoo.com

IBADAN
Bishop Most Revd Joseph Akinfenwa (*Archbishop of the Province of Ibadan*), PO Box 3075, Mapo, Ibadan *Tel:* 234 2 810 1400
Fax: 234 2 810 1413
email: ibadan@anglican.skannet.com.ng

IBADAN NORTH
Bishop Rt Revd Dr Segun Okubadejo, Bishopscourt, Moyede, PO Box 28961, Agodi, Ibadan *Tel:* 234 2 8107 482
email: angibn@skannet.com

IBADAN SOUTH
Bishop Rt Revd Jacob Ademola Ajetunmobi, Bishopscourt, PO Box 166, St David's Compound, Kudeti, Ibadan *Tel* and *Fax:* 234 2 231 6464
email: jacajet@skannet.com

IFE
Bishop Rt Revd Oluwole Odubogun, Bishopscourt, PO Box 312, Ife, Osun State
Tel: 234 36 2300 46
email: rantiodubogun@yahoo.com

IFE EAST
Bishop Rt Revd Oluseyi Oyelade, Bishop's House, PMB 505, Modakeke-Ife, Osun State
Tel: 234 802 322 4962
email: seyioyelade@yahoo.com

IJESA NORTH EAST
Bishop Rt Revd Joseph Olusola, PO Box 40, Ipetu Ijesa, Ogun State *Tel:* 234 803 942 8275
email: bpafsola@gmail.com

IJESHA NORTH
Bishop Rt Revd Titus Fajemirokun, Bishopscourt, PO Box 4, Ijebu-Jesa, Osun State
Tel: 234 802 344 0333
email: titusfajemirokun@yahoo.com

ILESA
Bishop Rt Revd Olubayu Sowale, Diocesan headquarters, Muroko Road, PO Box 237, Ilesa, Osun State *Tel:* 234 36 460 138
email: ilesha@anglican-nig.org

ILESA SOUTH WEST
Bishop Rt Revd Samuel Egbebunmi, Bishopscourt, Cathedral of the Holy Trinity, Imo Ilesa, Osun State *Tel:* 234 803 307 1876
email: segbebunmi@yahoo.com

OGBOMOSO (Missionary diocese)
Bishop Rt Revd Dr Matthew Osunade, Bishopscourt, St David's Anglican Cathedral, PO Box 1909, Ogbomoso, Osun State
Tel: 234 805 593 6164
email: maaosunade@yahoo.com

OKE-OGUN
Bishop Rt Revd Solomon Amusan, Bishopscourt, PO Box 30, Saki, Oyo State *Tel:* 234 802 323 3365
email: solomonamusan@yahoo.com

OKE-OSUN
Bishop Rt Revd Abraham Akinlalu, Bishopscourt, PO Box 251, Gbongan, Osun State
Tel: 234 803 771 7194
email: abrahamakinlalu@yahoo.com

OSUN
Bishop Rt Revd James Afolabi Popoola, PO Box 285, Osogbo, Osun State *Tel:* 234 35 240 325
email: folapool@yahoo.com

OSUN NORTH EAST
Bishop Rt Revd Humphery Olumakaiye, Bishopscourt, PO Box 32, Otan Ayegbaju, Osun State
Tel: 234 803 388 2678
email: bamisebi2002@yahoo.co.uk

OYO
Bishop Rt Revd Jacob Ola Fasipe, Bishopscourt, PO Box 23, Oyo, Oyo State *Tel:* 234 38 240 225
email: oyo@anglican-nig.org

PROVINCE OF JOS

Archbishop Most Revd Benjamin A. Kwashi (*Bishop of Jos*)

BAKURU
Bishop Rt Revd Jawn Zhumbes, Bishopscourt, Citrus Estate Sabon Bariki, PO Box 605, Plateau State

BAUCHI
Bishop Rt Revd Musa Tula, Bishop's House, 2 Hospital Rd, PO Box 2450, Bauchi
Tel: 234 77 546 460
email: bauchi@anglican-nig.org

DAMATURU
Bishop Rt Revd Abiodun Ogunyemi, PO Box 312, Damaturu, Yobe State *Tel:* 234 74 522 142
email: damaturu@anglican-nig.org

GOMBE
Bishop Rt Revd Henry C. Ndukuba, Cathedral Church of St Peter, PO Box 39, Gombe
Tel: 234 72 221 212
email: gombe@anglican-nig.org

JALINGO
Bishop Rt Revd Timothy Yahaya, PO Box 4, Magami, Jalingo, Taraba State
Tel and *Fax:* 234 806 594 4694
email: timothyyahaya@yahoo.com

JOS
Bishop Most Revd Benjamin A. Kwashi (*Archbishop of the Province of Jos*), Bishopscourt, PO Box 6283, Jos, 930001, Plateau State
Tel: 234 73 612 2215
email: benkwashi@gmail.com

LANGTANG
Bishop Rt Revd Stanley Fube, 87 Solomon Lar Road, PO Box 38, Langtang, Plateau State
Tel: 234 803 605 8767
email: stanleyfube@gmail.com

MAIDUGURI
Bishop Rt Revd Emmanuel Kana Mani, Bishopscourt, PO Box 1693, Maiduguri, Borno State *Tel* and *Fax:* 234 76 234 010
email: bishope-45@yahoo.com

PANKSHIN
Bishop Rt Revd Olumuyiwa Ajayi, Diocesan Secretariat, PO Box 24, Pankshin, Plateau State
Tel: 234 803 344 7318
email: olumijayi@yahoo.com

YOLA
Bishop Rt Revd Markus A. Ibrahim, PO Box 601, Jimeta-Yola, Adamawa State *Tel:* 234 75 624 303
email: marcusibrahim2002@yahoo.com

PROVINCE OF KADUNA

Archbishop Most Revd Edmund E. Akanya (*Bishop of Kebbi*)

BARI
Bishop Rt Revd Idris Zubairu, Bishopscourt, Gidan Mato Bari, Kano State *Tel:* 234 808 559 7183

DUTSE
Bishop Rt Revd Yesufu Ibrahim Lumu, PO Box 67, Yadi, Dutse, Jigawa State *Tel:* 234 64 721 379
email: dutse@anglican-nig.org

GUSAU
Bishop Rt Revd John Garba, PO Box 64, Gusau, Zamfara State *Tel:* 234 63 204 747
email: gusau@anglican.skannet.com

IKARA
Bishop Rt Revd Yusuf Janfalan, Bishopscourt, PO Box 23, Ikara, Kaduna State *Tel:* 234 803 679 3865
email: ikara@anglican-nig.org

KADUNA
Bishop Rt Revd Josiah Idowu-Fearon, PO Box 72, Kaduna *Tel:* 234 62 240 085
Fax: 234 62 244 408
email: archbishopfearonk@yahoo.com

KANO
Bishop Rt Revd Zakka Lalle Nyam, Bishopscourt, PO Box 362, Kano *Tel* and *Fax:* 234 64 647 816
email: kano@anglican.skannet.com.ng

KATSINA
Bishop Rt Revd Jonathan Bamaiyi, Bishop's Lodge, PO Box 904, Katsina *Tel:* 234 65 432 718
234 803 601 5584 (Mobile)
email: bpjonathanbamaiyi@yahoo.co.uk

KEBBI
Bishop Most Revd Edmund E. Akanya (*Archbishop of the Province of Kaduna*), , Bishop's Residence, PO Box 701, Birnin Kebbi, Kebbi State
Tel and *Fax:* 234 68 321 179
email: eekanya@yahoo.com

SOKOTO
Bishop Rt Revd Augustine Omole, Bishop's Lodge, 68 Shuni Road, PO Box 3489, Sokoto
Tel: 234 60 234 639
email: akin_sok@yahoo.com

WUSASA
Bishop Rt Revd Ali Buba Lamido, PO Box 28, Wusasa, Zaria, Kaduna State *Tel:* 234 69 334 594
email: lamido2sl@aol.co.uk

ZARIA
Bishop Rt Revd Cornelius Bello, Bishopscourt, PO Box 507, Zaria, Kaduna State
Tel: 234 802 708 9555
email: cssbello@hotmail.com

PROVINCE OF KWARA

Archbishop Most Revd Michael Akinyemi (*Bishop of Igbomina*)

IGBOMINA
Bishop Most Revd Michael Akinyemi, Bishopscourt, PO Box 102, Oro, Kwara State
Tel: 234 803 669 1940
email: oluakinyemi2000@yahoo.com

IGBOMINA WEST
Bishop Rt Revd James Akinola, Bishop's House, PO Box 32, Oke Osin, Kwara State
Tel: 234 803 392 3720
email: olaotimuyiwa@yahoo.com

JEBBA
Bishop Rt Revd Timothy Adewole, Bishopscourt, PO Box 2, Jebba, Kwara State
Tel: 234 803 572 5298
email: bishopadewole@yahoo.com

KWARA
Bishop Rt Revd Olusegun Adeyemi, Bishopscourt, Fate Rd, PO Box 1884, Ilorin, Kwara State
Tel: 234 31 220 879
email: bishopolusegun@yahoo.com

NEW BUSA
Bishop Rt Revd Israel Amoo, Bishopscourt, PO Box 208, New Busa, Niger State
Tel: 234 803 677 3839
email: bishopamoo@yahoo.com

OFFA
Bishop Rt Revd Akintunde Popoola, Bishop's House, 78–80 Ibrahim Rd, PO Box 21, Offa, Kwara State *Tel:* 234 805 925 0011
email: tpopoola@anglican-nig.org

OMU-ARAN
Bishop Rt Revd Philip Adeyemo, Bishop's House, PO Box 244, Omu-Aran, Kwara State
Tel: 234 806 592 4891
email: rtrevadeyemo@yahoo.com

PROVINCE OF LAGOS

Archbishop Most Revd Ephraim Adebola Ademowo (*Bishop of Lagos*)

AWORI
Bishop Rt Revd Johnson Akinwamide Atere, Bishopscourt, PO Box 10, Ota, Ogun State
Tel: 234 803 553 7284
email: dioceseofawori@yahoo.com

BADAGRY (Missionary diocese)
Bishop Rt Revd Joseph Adeyemi, Bishopscourt, PO Box 7, Badagry, Lagos State
Tel: 234 1 773 5546
234 803 306 4601 (Mobile)
email: badagry@anglican-nig.org

EGBA
Bishop Rt Revd Emmanuel Adekunle, Bishopscourt, Cathedral of St Peter, PO Box 46, Ile-oluji, Ondo State
email: egba@anglican-nig.org/ mowadayo@yahoo.com

EGBA WEST
Bishop Rt Revd Samuel Ajani, Bishopscourt, Oke-Ata Housing Estate, PO Box 6204, Sapon, Abeokuta *Tel:* 234 805 518 4822
email: samuelajani@yahoo.com

IFO
Bishop Rt Revd Joseph Odejide, Bishopscourt, Trinity House KM1, Ibogun Rd, PO Box 104, Ifo, Ogun State *Tel:* 234 802 778 4377
email: jaodejide@yahoo.com

IJEBU
Bishop Rt Revd Ezekiel Awosoga, Bishopscourt, Ejinrin Rd, PO Box 112, Ijebu-Ode
Tel: 234 37 432 886
email: ijebu@anglican-nig.org/ bishop@ang-ijebudiocese.com

IJEBU NORTH
Bishop Rt Revd Solomon Kuponu, Bishopscourt, PO Box 6, Ijebu-Igbo, Ogun State
Tel: 234 803 457 8506 (Mobile)
email: dioceseofijebunorth@yahoo.com

LAGOS
Bishop Most Revd Ephraim Adebola Ademowo (*Archbishop of the Province of Lagos*), 29 Marina, PO Box 13, Lagos *Tel:* 234 1 263 6026
email: adebolaademowo@dioceseoflagos.org

LAGOS MAINLAND
Bishop Rt Revd Adebayo Akinde, Bishop's House, PO Box 849, Ebute, Lagos
Tel: 234 703 390 5522
email: adakinde@gmail.com

LAGOS WEST
Bishop Rt Revd Peter A. Adebiyi, Vining House 3rd Floor, Archbishop Vining Memorial Cathedral, Oba Akinjobi Road, GRA Ikeja, Nigeria *Tel:* 234 1 493 7333
email: dioceseoflagoswest@yahoo.com

REMO
Bishop Rt Revd Michael O. Fape, Bishopscourt, Ewusi St, PO Box 522, Sagamu, Ogun State
Tel: 234 37 640 598
email: remo@anglican-nig.org

YEWA
Bishop Rt Revd Simeon O. M. Adebola, Bishopscourt, PO Box 484, Ilaro, Ogun State
Tel: 234 39 440 695

PROVINCE OF LOKOJA
Archbishop Most Revd Emmanuel Sokowamju Egbunu (*Bishop of Lokoja*)

DOKO
Bishop Rt Revd Uriah Kolo, PO Box 1513, Bida, Niger State *Tel:* 234 803 590 6327
email: uriahkolo@gmail.com

IJUMA
Bishop Rt Revd Ezekiel Ikupolati, Bishopscourt, PO Box 90, Iyara-Ijumi Kogi State
Tel: 234 807 500 8780
email: efikupolati@yahoo.com

KABBA
Bishop Rt Revd Steven Akobe, Bishopscourt, Obara Way, PO Box 62, Kabba, Kogi State
Tel: 234 58 300 633

KONTAGORA
Bishop Rt Revd Jonah Ibrahim, Bishop's House, GPA PO Box 1, Kontagora, Niger State
Tel: 234 803 625 2032
email: jonahibrahim@yahoo.co.uk

KUTIGI
Bishop Rt Revd Jeremiah Kolo, Bishop's House, St John's Mission Compound, PO Box 14, Bida
Tel: 234 803 625 2032
email: bishopkolo@yahoo.com

LOKOJA
Bishop Most Revd Emmanuel Sokowamju Egbunu (*Archbishop of the Province of Lokoja*) Bishopscourt, PO Box 11, Bethany, Lokoja, Koji State *Tel:* 234 58 220 588
email: emmanuelegbunu@yahoo.co.uk

MINNA
Bishop Rt Revd Daniel Abu Yisa, Bishopscourt, Dutsen Kura, PO Box 2469, Minna
Tel: 234 803 588 6552
email: danyisa2007@yahoo.com

OGORI-MAGONGO
Bishop Rt Revd Festus Davies, Bishop's House, St Peter's Cathedral Ogori, Kogi State
Tel: 234 803 451 0378
email: fessyoladiran@yahoo.com

OKENE
Bishop Rt Revd Emmanuel Bayo Ajulo, Bishopscourt, PO Box 43, Okene, Kogi State
Tel: 234 803 700 0016
email: okenediocese@yahoo.com

PROVINCE OF THE NIGER
Archbishop Most Revd Most Revd Christian Ogochukwo Efobi (*Bishop of Aguata*)

AGUATA
Bishop Most Revd Christian Ogochukwo Efobi (*Archbishop of the Province of the Niger*), Bishopscourt, PO Box 1128, Ekwulobia, Anambra State *Tel:* 234 803 750 1077
email: christianefobi@yahoo.com

AMICHI
Bishop Rt Revd Ephraim Ikeakor, Bishopscourt, PO Box 13, Amichi, Anambra State
Tel: 234 803 317 0916
email: eoikeakor@yahoo.com

AWKA
Bishop Rt Revd Alexander Ibezim, Bishopscourt, PO Box 130, Awka, Anambra State
Tel: 234 48 550 058
email: chioma1560@aol.com

ENUGU
Bishop Rt Revd Dr Emmanuel O. Chukwuma, Bishop's House, PO Box 418, Enugu, Enugu State *Tel:* 234 42 453 804
email: enugu@anglican-nig.org

IHIALA
Bishop Rt Revd Ralph Okafor, Bishopscourt, St Silas Cathedral, PO Box 11, Ihiala, Anambra State *Tel:* 234 803 711 2408
email: raphoka@yahoo.com

MBAMILI
Bishop Rt Revd Henry Okeke, Bishopscourt, PO Box 2653, Onitsha, Anambra State
Tel: 234 803 644 9780
email: bishopokeke@yahoo.com

NIGER WEST
Bishop Rt Revd Anthony O. Nkwoka
Tel: 234 803 384 3339 (Mobile)
email: ankwoka@yahoo.com

NNEWI
Bishop Rt Revd Dr Godwin Izundu Nmezinwa Okpala, Bishopscourt, PO Box 2630, Uruagu-Nnewi, Anambra State *Tel:* 234 803 348 5714
email: okpalagodwin@yahoo.co.uk

OGBARU
Bishop Rt Revd Samuel Ezeofor, Bishopscourt, PO Box 46, Atani, Anambra State
email: ezechukwunyere@yahoo.com

ON THE NIGER
Bishop Rt Revd Owen Chidozie Nwokolo, Bishopscourt, Ozala Rd, Onitsha, Anambra State
Tel: 234 803 726 0548
email: owenelsie@yahoo.com

PROVINCE OF NIGER DELTA

Archbishop Most Revd Ugochuckwu U. Ezuoke (*Bishop of Aba*)

ABA
Bishop Most Revd Ugochuckwu U. Ezuoke, Bishopscourt, 70–72 St Michael's Rd, PO Box 212, Aba, Abia State *Tel:* 234 82 227 666
email: aba@anglican-nig.org

ABA NGWA NORTH
Bishop Rt Revd Nathan C. Kanu, Bishopscourt, All Saints Cathedral, Abayi-Umuocham 1610165, Owerri Road, PO Box 43, Aba, Abia State
Tel: 234 803 822 4623
email: odinathnfe@sbcglobal.net

AHOADA
Bishop Rt Revd Clement Nathan Ekpeye, Bishopscourt, St Paul's Cathedral, PO Box 4, Ahoada East L.G.A., Rivers State
Tel: 234 803 542 2847 (Mobile)
email: ahoada@anglican-nig.org

CALABAR
Bishop Rt Revd Tunde Adeleye, Bishopscourt, PO Box 74, Calabar, Cross River State
Tel: 234 87 232 812
email: calabar@anglican-nig.org

ENUGU NORTH
Bishop Rt Revd Sosthenes Eze, Bishopscourt, St Mary's Cathedral, Ngwo-Enugu
Tel: 234 803 870 9362
email: bishopsieze@yahoo.com

ETCHE
Bishop Rt Revd Okechukwu Precious Nwala, Bishopscourt, PO Box 89, Okehi, Etche Rivers State *Tel*: 234 807 525 2842 (Mobile)
email: etchediocese@yahoo.com/
precious_model5@yahoo.com

EVO
Bishop Rt Revd Innocent Ordu, Bishopscourt, PO Box 3576, Port Harcourt, Rivers State
Tel: 234 803 715 2706
email: innocent-ordu@yahoo.com

IKWERRE
Bishop Rt Revd Blessing Enyindah, Bishopscourt, St Peter's Cathedral, PO Box 14229, Port Harcourt, Rivers State *Tel*: 234 802 321 2824
email: blessingenyindah@yahoo.com

NIGER DELTA
Bishop Rt Revd Ralph Ebirien, PO Box 115, Port Harcourt, Rivers State *Tel:* 234 708 427 9095
email: revpalph_ebirien@yahoo.com

NIGER DELTA NORTH
Bishop Rt Revd Ignatius Kattey, PO Box 53, Diobu, Port Harcourt, Rivers State
Tel: 234 803 309 4331
email: bishopicokattey@yahoo.com

NIGER DELTA WEST
Bishop Rt Revd Emmanuel Oko-Jaja, Bishopscourt, PO Box 10, Yenagoa, Bayelsa State
Tel: 234 803 870 2099
email: niger-delta-west@anglican-nig.org

NORTHERN IZON
Bishop Rt Revd Anga Fred Nyanabo, Bishopscourt, PO Box 705, Yenagoa, Bayelsa State
Tel: 234 803 316 0938
email: fred_nyanabo@yahoo.co.uk

OGBIA
Bishop Rt Revd James Oruwori, Bishop's House, 10 Queens Street, Ogbia town, Bayelsea State
Tel: 234 803 73 4746
email: jaoruwori@yahoo.com

OGONI (Missionary diocese)
Bishop Rt Revd Solomon S. Gberegbara, Bishopscourt, PO Box 73, Bori-Ogoni, Rivers State
Tel: 234 803 339 2545
email: ogoni@anglican-nig.org

OKRIKA
Bishop Rt Revd Tubokosemie Abere, Bishopscourt, PO Box 11, Okrika, Rivers State
Tel: 234 803 312 5226
email: dioceseofokrika@yahoo.com

UYO
Bishop Rt Revd Isaac Orama, Bishopscourt, PO Box 70, Uyo, Akwa Ibom State
Tel: 234 802 916 2305
email: uyo@anglican-nig.org

PROVINCE OF ONDO
Archbishop Most Revd Samuel Adedayo Abe (*Bishop of Ekiti*)

AKOKO
Bishop Rt Revd Gabriel Akinbiyi, PO Box 572, Ikare-Akoko, Ondo State
Tel: 31 801 011
email: bishopgabrielakinbiyi@yahoo.com

AKURE
Bishop Rt Revd Michael O. Ipinmoye, Bishopscourt, PO Box 1622, Akure, Ondo State
Tel and *Fax:* 234 241 572
email: mikeomoipinmoye@yahoo.com

DIOCESE ON THE COAST (FORMERLY IKALE-ILAJE)
Bishop Rt Revd Joshua Ogunele, Bishopscourt, Ikoya Road, PMB 3, Ilutitun-Osooro, Ondo State
Tel: 234 803 467 1879
email: joshuaonthecoast@yahoo.ca

EKITI
Bishop Most Revd Samuel Adedayo Abe (*Archbishop of the Province of Ondo*), Bishopscourt, PO Box 12, Okesa St, Ado-Ekiti, Ekiti State
Tel: 234 30 250 305
email: adedayoekiti@yahoo.com

EKITI OKE
Bishop Rt Revd Isaac O. Olubowale, Bishopscourt, PO Box 207, Usi-Ekiti, Ekiti State
Tel: 234 803 600 9582 (Mobile)
email: ekitioke@anglican-nig.org

EKITI WEST
Bishop Rt Revd Samuel O. Oke, Bishop's Residence, 6 Ifaki St, PO Box 477, Ijero-Ekiti
Tel: 234 30 850 314
email: ekitiwest@anglican-nig.org

IDOANI
Bishop Rt Revd Ezekiel Dahunsi, Bishopscourt, PO Box 100 Idoani, Ondo State
Tel: 234 803 384 4029
email: bolaezek@yahoo.com

ILAJE
Bishop Rt Revd Fredrick Olugbemi, Bishopscourt, PO Box 146, Igbokoda, Ondo State
Tel: 234 806 624 8662
email: forogbemi@yahoo.com

ILE-OLUJI
Bishop Rt Revd Samson Adekunle, Bishopscourt, Cathedral of St peter, PO Box 46, Ile-Oluji, Ondo State
Tel: 234 803 454 1236
email: adkulesamson86@yahoo.co.uk

IRELE-ESEODO
Bishop Rt Revd Felix Akinbuluma, Bishopscourt, Sabomi Road, Ode Irele, Ondo State
Tel: 234 805 671 2653
email: felixgoke@yahoo.com

ONDO
Bishop Rt Revd George L. Lasebikan, Bishopscourt, College Rd, PO Box 265, Ondo
Tel: 234 34 610 718
email: ondoanglican@yahoo.co.uk

OWO
Bishop Rt Revd James Adedayo Oladunjoye, Bishopscourt, PO Box 472, Owo, Ondo State
Tel: 234 51 241 463
email: bishopoladunjoye@yahoo.co.uk

PROVINCE OF OWERRI
Archbishop Most Revd Bennett C. I. Okoro (*Bishop of Orlu*)

EGBU
Bishop Rt Revd Prof Emmanuel U. Iheagwam, All Saints' Cathedral, PO Box 1967, Owerri, Imo State
Tel: 234 83 231 797
email: egbu@anglican-nig.org

IDEATO
Bishop Rt Revd Caleb A. Maduomo, Bishopscourt, PO Box 2, Ndizuogu, Imo State
Tel: 234 803 745 4503 (Mobile)
email: bpomacal@hotmail.com

IKEDURU
Bishop Rt Revd Emmanuel Maduwike, Bishop's House, PO Box 56, Atta, Imo State
Tel: 234 803 704 4686
email: emmamaduwike@yahoo.com

MBAISE
Bishop Rt Chamberlain Chinedu Ogunedo, Bishopscourt, PO Box 10, Ife, Ezinihitte Mbaise, Imo State *Tel:* 234 803 336 9836
email: ogunedochi@yahoo.com

OJAHI-EGBEMA
Bishop Rt Revd Chidi Collins Oparaojiaku, Bishop's House, PO box 8026, New Owerri, Imo State *Tel:* 234 803 312 1063
email: chidioparachiaku@yahoo.com

OKIGWE
Bishop Rt Revd Edward Osuegbu, Bishopscourt, PO Box 156, Okigwe, Imo State
Tel: 234 803 724 6374
email: edchuc@justice.com

OKIGWE NORTH
Bishop Rt Revd Godson Udochukwu Ukanwa, PO Box 127, Anara, Imo State
Tel: 234 803 672 4314
email: venukanwa@yahoo.com

OKIGWE SOUTH
Bishop Rt Revd David Onuoha, Bishopscourt, Ezeoke Nsu, PO Box 235, Nsu, Ehime Mbano LGA, Imo State *email:* okisouth@yahoo.com

ON THE LAKE
Bishop Rt Revd Chijioke Oti, Bishopscourt, PO Box 36, Oguta, Imo State, Nigeria
Tel: 234 802 788 8738
email: chijiokeoti72@yahoo.com

ORLU
Bishop Most Revd Bennett C. I. Okoro (*Archbishop of the Province of Owerri*), Bishopscourt, PO Box 260, Nkwerre, Imo State *Tel:* 234 82 440 538
email: anglicannaorlu@yahoo.com

ORU
Bishop Rt Revd Geoffrey Chukwunenye, PO Box 91, Mgbidi, Imo State *Tel:* 234 803 308 1270
email: geoinlagos@yahoo.com

OWERRI
Bishop Rt Revd Dr Cyril Chukwunonyerem, Okorocha, Bishop's Bourne, PMB 1063, Owerri, Imo State *Tel:* 234 83 230 784
email: owerri_anglican@yahoo.com

The Anglican Church of Papua New Guinea

Members 200,000
The Anglican Church functions mostly in rural areas where mountains and rainforest provide natural barriers to travel. Some 60 per cent of the funding is raised internally; most of the balance comes from grants from Australia, New Zealand, Canada and the UK-based Papua New Guinea Church Partnership. The Church had played an active role in the development of this country, and has a long history of more than a century (120 years, from 1891 to 2011) of providing service throughout its five established Dioceses in PNG (Dogura, Popondota,Port Moresby, Aipo Rongo and New Guinea Islands). The Church's work has expanded over the years into establishing and operating Social Welfare, Education, Health and Economic Development programmes for the most disadvantaged and rural sectors of our communities. The Anglican Church will continue to do this in the years ahead.

Archbishop Most Revd Joseph Kopapa (*Primate of ACPNG*)

General Secretary Mr Richard Rabiafi, PO Box 673, Lae, Morobe Province *Tel:* 675 472 4111
Fax: 675 472 1852
email: richardr@acpng.org.pg

Provincial Cellenger Justice Bernard Sakora, Chamber of Justice, Supreme and National Courts of Justice, PO Box 7018, Boroko, NCD, PNG *Tel:* 675 324 5734

Provincial Registrar Mr Goodwin Poole, PO Box 389, Port Moresby, Level 5 Defence House, Crn Hunter St & Champion Pde, National Capital District *Tel:* 675 308 8300
Digicel: 675 720 88300
Fax: 675 308 8399
Web: www.obriens.com.pg

THEOLOGICAL COLLEGE
Newton Theological College, PO Box 162, Popondetta, Oro Province (*Principal* Revd Peter Moi) *Tel (Digicel):* 675 713 95018
email: fr.petermoi@gmail.com

CHURCH PAPER
Family Magazine. Published three times a year. *Editors* Archbishop Most Revd Joseph Kopapa, PO Box 673,, Lae, Morobe Province 411
Tel: 675 472 4111
Fax: 675 472 1852
email: joekopapa@gmail.com

AIPO RONGO
Bishop Rt Revd Nathan Ingen, PO Box 893, Mt Hagen, Western Highlands Province
Tel: 675 542 1131/3727
Fax: 675 542 1181
email: niacpng@online.net.pg

DOGURA
Bishop Rt Revd Clyde Igara, PO Box 19, Dogura, MBP *Tel:* 675 641 1530
Fax: 675 641 1129

NEW GUINEA ISLANDS
Bishop Rt Revd Allan Migi, Bishop's House, PO Box 806, Kimbe *Tel* and *Fax:* 675 9 835 120
email: migi.allan@gmail.com

POPONDOTA
Bishop Rt Revd Lindsley Ihove, Bishop's House, PO Box 26, Popondetta, Oro Province
Tel: 675 329 7194
Fax: 675 329 7476

PORT MORESBY
Bishop Rt Revd Peter Ramsden, PO Box 6491, Boroko, NCD *Tel:* 675 323 2489
Fax: 675 323 2493
email: acpngpom@global.net.pg/ psramsden.pomanglican@gmail.com
Web: www.portmoresby.anglican.org

The Episcopal Church in the Philippines

Members 170,000
The Philippines is the only Christian nation in Asia. Its 90,000,000 or so population is composed of 75% Roman Catholics while the other 25% are Muslims and other Christian bodies including the Episcopal Church in the Philippines (ECP) which now has six dioceses. The ECP was first established by the Protestant Episcopal Church in the USA (PECUSA) in 1901 and became an autonomous province of the Anglican Communion in 1991. It continues to maintain a close relationship with PECUSA. Its ministry after gaining autonomy is focused not only in the nurture of the faith of the believers and doing evangelism. It is actively involved in community development projects to help eradicate poverty which is hounding the lives of millions of Filipinos today.

National Office The ECP Mission Center, 275 E Rodriguez Sr Ave, 1102 Quezon City

(*Postal address*) PO Box 10321, Broadway Centrum, 1112 Quezon City
Tel: 63 2 722 8478/8481
Fax: 63 2 721 1923
email: ecpnational@yahoo.com.ph

Prime Bishop Most Revd Edward P. Malecdan (*same address*) *email:* edmalecdan@yahoo.com

Provincial Secretary Atty. Floyd P. Lalwet (*same address*) *email:* flaw997@gmail.com

Corporate Secretary Ms Laura S. Ocampo (*same address*) *email:* lbso2@yahoo.com

Administrative Assistant Vacancy

National Finance Officer Ms Bridget T. Lacdao
email: bbalitog@yahoo.com

CENTRAL PHILIPPINES
Bishop Rt Revd Dixie C. Taclobao, 281 E. Rodriguez Sr. Avenue, 1102 Quezon City
Tel: 63 2 412 8561
Fax: 63 2 724 2143
email: dixie_taclobao@yahoo.com.ph

NORTH CENTRAL PHILIPPINES
Bishop Rt Revd Joel A. Pachao, 358 Magsaysay Ave, Baguio City 2600 *Tel:* 63 74 443 7705
email: bpjoelpachao@yahoo.com

NORTHERN LUZON
Bishop Rt Revd Renato M. Abibico, Bulanao, 3800 Tabuk, Kalinga *Tel:* 63 920 271 9999
email: reneabibico@yahoo.com

NORTHERN PHILIPPINES
Bishop Rt Revd Brent Harry W. Alawas, 2616 Bontoc, Mountain Province
Tel: and *Fax:* 63 74 602 1026
email: ednpbrent@yahoo.com

SANTIAGO
Bishop Rt Revd Alexander A. Wandag, Maharlika Highway, 3311 Divisoria Santiago City, Isabela
Tel: 63 78 682 3756
Fax: 63 78 682 1256
email: alexwandageds@yahoo.com

SOUTHERN PHILIPPINES
Bishop Rt Revd Danilo Labacanacruz Bustamante, 186 Sinsuat Ave, Rosario Heights, 9600 Cotabato City *Tel:* 63 64 421 2960
Fax: 63 64 421 1703
email: edsp_ecp@yahoo.com

The Church of the Province of Rwanda

Members 1,200,000
In just over 10,170 square miles there are more than one million Anglicans among a fast-growing population, currently 9.5 million. The former Rwanda Mission (now CMS) established its first station at Gahini in 1925 and grew through the revival of the 1930s and 1940s, with the first Rwandan bishop appointed in 1965. Nine dioceses have up to 306 parishes and 379 clergy, organized in 96 deaconries. Like all strata of Rwandan society, the Church suffered, on many levels, through the genocide, and it is a major priority of the Church to replace clergy through training. The Church has a role as a healing ministry to the many traumatized people in Rwanda and to reconciliation, restoration, and rehabilitation. The Church has also been involved in rural development, medical work, vocational training, and education.

Archbishop Most Revd Emmanuel Mbona Kolini (*Bishop of Kigali*)

Dean of the Province Rt Revd Onesphore Rwaje (*Bishop of Byumba*)

Provincial Secretary Revd Emmanuel Gatera, BP 2487, Kigali *Tel:* 250 514 160
Fax: 250 516 162
email: egapeer@yahoo.com

Provincial Treasurer Vacancy (*same address*)

BUTARE
Bishop Rt Revd Nathan Gasatura, BP 225, Butare *Tel* and *Fax:* 250 530 504
email: rusodilo@yahoo.fr

BYUMBA
Bishop Rt Revd Onesphore Rwaje, BP 17, Byumba *Tel* and *Fax:* 250 64 242
email: eer@rwanda1.com

CYANGUGU
Bishop Rt Revd Geoffrey Rwubusisi, BP 52, Cyangugu *Tel* and *Fax:* 250 53 7878
email: bishoprwubusisi@yahoo.co.uk

GAHINI
Bishop Rt Revd Alexis Bilindabagabo, BP 22, Kigali *Tel* and *Fax:* 250 567 422

KIBUNGO
Bishop Rt Revd Josias Sendegeya, EER Kibungo Diocese, BP 719, Kibungo
Tel and *Fax:* 250 566 194
email: bpjosias@yahoo.fr

KIGALI
Bishop Most Revd Emmanuel M. Kolini (*Archbishop of the Province*), BP 61, Kigali
Tel and *Fax:* 250 573 213
email: ek@terracom.rw

KIGEME
Bishop Rt Revd Augustin Mvunabandi, BP 67, Gikongoro *Tel:* 250 535 086 (Office)
250 535 088 (Secretary)
250 535 087 (Home)
email: dkigeme@rwanda1.com

KIVU
Bishop Rt Revd Augustin Ahimana, BP 166 Gisenyi *Tel*: 250 788 350 119

SHYIRA
Bishop Rt Revd John Rucyahana Kabango, BP 26, Ruhengeri *Tel* and *Fax:* 250 546 449
email: bpjohnr@rwanda1.com

SHYOGWE
Bishop Rt Revd Jered Kalimba, BP 27, Gitarama
Tel: 250 562 460
Tel and *Fax:* 250 562 469
email: dsgwegit@yahoo.com

The Scottish Episcopal Church

Members 34,916
The roots of Scottish Christianity go back to St Ninian in the fourth century and St Columba in the sixth. After the Reformation, the Episcopal Church was the established Church of Scotland. It was however replaced as the established Church by the Presbyterians at the Revolution in 1689. Penal statutes in force from 1746 to 1792 weakened the Church, although many congregations remained and the bishops maintained continuity. In 1784 in Aberdeen, the Scottish Church initiated the world-wide expansion of the Anglican Communion with the consecration of the first bishop of the American Church. There was rapid growth in the nineteenth century influenced by the Tractarian movement.

Primus Most Revd David Chillingworth (*Bishop of St Andrews, Dunkeld & Dunblane*)
email: bishop@standrews.anglican.org
Web: www.standrews.anglican.org

Secretary General Mr John Stuart, 21 Grosvenor Crescent, Edinburgh EH12 5EE
Tel: 0131 225 6357
Fax: 0131 346 7247
email: secgen@scotland.anglican.org
Web: www.scotland.anglican.org

MINISTERIAL TRAINING
The Theological Institute of the Scottish Episcopal Church, 21 Grosvenor Crescent, Edinburgh EH12 5EE *Tel:* 0131 225 6357
Fax: 0131 346 7247
email: tisec@scotland.anglican.org

CHURCH MAGAZINE
Inspires, twenty-eight pages, four issues per year. Magazine format. Produced in-house – contact: *Inspires*, 21 Grosvenor Crescent, Edinburgh, EH12 5EE *email:* inspires@scotland.anglican.org

ABERDEEN AND ORKNEY
Bishop Rt Revd Dr Robert Gillies, Diocesan Office, St Clement's Church House, Mastrick Drive, Aberdeen, AB16 6UF *Tel:* 01224 662247
email: office@aberdeen.anglican.org
Web: www.aberdeen.anglican.org

Dean Very Revd Dr A. E. Nimmo, St Margaret's Clergy House, Gallowgate, Aberdeen AB25 JEA
Tel: 01224 644969
email: alexander306@btinternet.com

ST ANDREW'S CATHEDRAL, Aberdeen
Provost Very Revd Richard Kilgour, St Andrew's Cathedral, 28 King Street, Aberdeen AB24 5AX
Tel: 01224 640119
email: provost@aberdeen.anglican.org

ARGYLL AND THE ISLES
Bishop Rt Revd Kevin Pearson, St Moluag's Diocesan Centre, Croft Avenue, Oban, Argyll, PA34 5JJ *Tel:* 01631 570 870
Fax: 01631 570411
email: office@argyll.anglican.org
Web: www.argyllandtheisles.org.uk

Dean Vacancy *Tel:* 01631 570870
email: office@argyll.anglican.org

ST JOHN THE DIVINE CATHEDRAL, Oban
(The Cathedral of Argyll)
Provost Very Revd Nicola McNelly, The Rectory, Ardconnel Terrace, Oban, PA34 5DJ
Tel: 01631 562323
email: ProvostOban@argyll.anglican.org

COLLEGIATE CHURCH OF THE HOLY SPIRIT, Millport, Cumbrae
(The Cathedral of The Isles)
Warden David Todd *Tel:* 01475 530353
Fax: 01475 531291
email: Cathedral_Cumbrae@btconnect.com
Web: www.island-retreats.org

BRECHIN
Bishop Rt Revd Dr Nigel Peyton, Diocesan Office. Unit 14 Prospect III, Technology Park, Gemini Crescent, Dundee DD2 1SW *Tel:* 01382 562244
email: office@brechin.anglican.org
Web: www.thedioceseofbrechin.org

Dean Vacancy *Tel:* 01382 562244
email: office@brechin.anglican.org

ST PAUL'S CATHEDRAL, Dundee
Provost Very Revd Jeremy Auld, St Paul's Cathedral, Castle Hill, 1 High Street, Dundee DD1 1TD *Tel:* 01382 224486
email: email@stpaulscathedraldundee.org

EDINBURGH
Bishop Rt Revd Dr John Armes, Diocesan Centre, 21a Grosvenor Crescent, Edinburgh, EH12 5EL
Tel: 0131 538 7044
Fax: 0131 538 7088
email: office@edinburgh.anglican.org
Web: www.edinburgh.anglican.org

Dean Very Revd Susan Macdonald, Diocesan Centre, 21a Grsovenor Crescent, Edinburgh EH12 5EL *Tel:* 0131 538 7033
email: Dean@dioceseofedinburgh.org

ST MARY'S CATHEDRAL, Edinburgh
Provost Very Revd Dr Graham John Thomson Forbes, Cathedral Office, Palmerston Place, Edinburgh EH12 5AW *Tel:* 0131 225 6293
Fax: 0131 225 3181
email: provost@cathedral.net

GLASGOW AND GALLOWAY
Bishop Rt Revd Dr Gregor Duncan, Diocesan Centre, 5 St Vincent Place, Glasgow G1 2DH
Tel: 0141 221 6911
email: bishop@glasgow.anglican.org
Web: www.glasgow.anglican.org

Dean Very Revd Ian Barcroft, The Rectory, 4c Auchingramont Road, Hamilton ML3 6JT
Tel: 01698 429895
email: dean@glasgow.anglican.org

ST MARY THE VIRGIN CATHEDRAL, Glasgow
Provost Very Revd Kelvin Holdsworth, St Mary's Cathedral, 300 Great Western Rd, Glasgow G4 9JB *Tel:* 0141 339 6691
Fax: 0141 334 5669
email: provost@thecathedral.org.uk

MORAY, ROSS AND CAITHNESS
Bishop Rt Revd Mark Strange, Bishop's House, St Duthac's Centre, Arpafeelie, North Kessock IV1 3XD *Tel:* 01463 811333
email: bishop@moray.anglican.org
Web: www.moray.anglican.org

Dean Very Revd Clifford J. Piper, St John's Rectory, Victoria Road, Forres, Moray IV36 3BN
Tel: 01309 672856
email: deanofmoray@tiscali.co.uk

ST ANDREW'S CATHEDRAL, Inverness
Provost Very Revd Alex Gordon, 15 Ardross Street, Inverness, IV3 5NS *Tel:* 01463 233 535
email: canonalexgordon@btconnect.com

ST ANDREWS, DUNKELD AND DUNBLANE
Bishop Most Revd David Chillingworth (*Primus*), Diocesan Centre, 28a Balhousie Street, Perth, PH1 5HJ *Tel:* 01738 580426
Fax: 01738 443174
email: bishop@standrews.anglican.org
Web: www.standrews.anglican.org

Dean Very Revd Kenneth Rathband, 10 Rosemount Park, Blairgowrie PH10 6TZ
Tel: 01250 874 583
email: abcsaints@btinternet.com

ST NINIAN'S CATHEDRAL, Perth
Provost Very Revd Hunter Farquharson, St Ninian's Cathedral, North Methven Street, Perth PH1 5PP *Tel:* 01738 632 053
email: provost@perthcathedral.co.uk

The Province of the Anglican Church in South East Asia

Members 224,200
The Anglican Church in South East Asia was originally under the jurisdiction of the Bishop of Calcutta. The first chaplaincy was formed in West Malaysia in 1805; the first bishop was consecrated in 1855. The Diocese of Labuan, Sarawak and Singapore was formed in 1881. A separate Diocese of Singapore was formed in 1909, and in 1962 the Diocese of Jesselton, later renamed Sabah, and the Diocese of Kuching were formed from the former Diocese of Borneo. In 1970 the Diocese of West Malaysia was formed from what had been the Diocese of Malaya and Singapore. Until the inauguration of the Church of the Province of South East Asia, the four dioceses (Kuching, Sabah, Singapore, and West Malaysia) were under the jurisdiction of the Archbishop of Canterbury. Although the province exists under certain social constraints, the Church has experienced much spiritual renewal and has sent out its own mission partners to various parts of the world, especially neighbouring Indonesia, Cambodia, Nepal, Laos, Vietnam and Myanmar.

Primate Most Revd Datuk Bolly Anak Lapok (*Bishop of Kuching*)

Provincial Secretary Mr Leonard David Shim, Messrs. Reddi & Co. Advocates, Lane Building, 29 Lorong Kai Joo, 93000 Kuching, Sarawak, Malaysia *Office:* 60 82 248866
Fax: 60 82 248867
email: anglican@streamyx.com

Provincial Treasurer Mr Keith Chua, 35 Ford Avenue, Singapore 268714, Singapore
Tel: 65 6235 3344
Fax: 65 6736 1201

Provincial Chancellor Mr. Andrew Khoo, Messrs Andrew Khoo & Daniel Lo (Advocates & Solicitors), 34, Jalan SS20/26, Damansara Utama, 47400 Petaling Jaya, Selangor, Malaysia
Tel: 60 37 726496
email: andrew_khoo@akdl.com

Provincial Registrar Dato' Benedict Bujang Tembak, Hardin & Co., Adocates, 25, Jalan Tabuan, PO Box 103, 93700 Kuching, Sarawak, Malaysia *Tel:* 60 82 252599 *Fax:* 60 82 429041
email: hardintembak@gmail.com

THEOLOGICAL COLLEGES
House of the Epiphany, PO Box No 347, 93704 Kuching, Sarawak, Malaysia (*Warden* Revd Canon Michael S. Woods)

Trinity Theological College, 490 Upper Bukit Timah Road, Singapore
678093 (interdenominational)

St Peter's Hall, residential hostel for Anglican students at Trinity Theological College, Singapore (*Warden* Rt Revd Yong Chen Fah)

Seminari Theoloji Malaysia (STM), Lot 3011, Taman South East, Jalan Tampin Lama, Batu 3, Seremban 70100, Negeri Sembilan, Malaysia (*Principal* Revd Dr Ezra Kok)

KUCHING
Bishop Most Revd Datuk Bolly Anak Lapok, Bishop's House, PO Box 347, 93704 Kuching, Sarawak, Malaysia *Tel:* 60 82 240 187
Fax: 60 82 426 488
email: bpofkuching@gmail.com

Assistant Bishop Rt Revd Aeries Sumping Jingan, PO Box 347, 93704 Kuching, Sarawak, Malaysia
Tel: 60 82 429755
Fax: 60 82 426488
email: aersumjin@gmail.com

SABAH
Bishop Rt Revd Datuk Albert Vun Cheong Fui, PO Box 10811, 88809 Kota Kinabalu, Sabah, Malaysia *Tel:* 60 88 245 846
Fax: 60 88 261 422
email: vunalbert@gmail.com

Assistant Bishops
Rt Revd Melter Tais, PO Box 106, 89300 Telupid, Sabah, Malaysi *Tel and Fax:* 60 89 521448
email: mjtais@hotmail.com

Rt. Revd John Yeo, 201, Jalan Dunlop, 91000 Tawau *email:* johnyeo@gmail.com

SINGAPORE
Bishop Rt Revd Rennis Ponniah, St. Andrews Village, No. 1, Francis Thomas Drive, #01–01, Singapore 359340 *Tel:* 65 62 887585
Fax: 65 62 885574
email: rennis@sjsm.org.sg

WEST MALAYSIA
Bishop Rt Revd Datuk Ng Moon Hing, No. 16 Jalan Pudu Lama, 50200 Kuala Lumpur, Malaysia *Tel:* 60 32 031 3213
Fax: 60 2 031 3225
email: anglican@streamyx.com

Assistant Bishops
Rt Revd Andrew Phang See Yin, Church of Our Redeemer, 306, Jalan Bagan Lebai Tahir, Bagan Ajam, 13050 Butterworth, Penang, Malaysia
Tel: 60 4 3231568
Fax: 60 4 3231568
email: bpphang@gmail.com

Rt Revd Jason Selvaraj, Christ Church, 48, Jalan Gereja, 75000 Melaka, Malaysia
Tel: 60 62 848804
Fax: 60 62 848804
email: jasondaphne101@gmail.com

The Anglican Church of Southern Africa

Members 2,600,000
The province is the oldest in Africa. British Anglicans met for worship in Cape Town after 1806, with the first bishop appointed in 1847. The twenty-eight dioceses of the province extend beyond the Republic of South Africa and include the Foreign and Commonwealth Office (St Helena and Tristan da Cunha), Mozambique (Lebombo and Niassa), the Republic of Namibia, the Kingdom of Lesotho, and the Kingdom of Swaziland. This Church and its leaders played a significant role in the abolition of apartheid in South Africa and in peace keeping in Mozambique and Angola. A mission diocese was inaugurated in August 2002 in Angola. The Diocese of Ukhahlamba was inaugurated in October 2009 and the Diocese of Mbashe was inaugurated in July 2010

Primate Most Revd Dr Thabo Makgoba (*Archbishop of Cape Town and Metropolitan of the Anglican Church of Southern Africa*)

Provincial Executive Officer Revd Canon Allan Kannemeyer, 20 Bishopscourt Dr, Bishopscourt, Claremont, Western Cape 7708, South Africa
Tel: 27 21 763 1300
Fax: 27 21 797 1329
email: peo@anglicanchurchsa.org.za
Web: www.anglicanchurchsa.org.za

Provincial Treasurer Mr Rob S. Rogerson, PO Box 53014, Kenilworth, 7745, South Africa
Tel: 27 21 763 1300
Fax: 27 21 797 8319
email: rogerson@anglicanchurchsa.org.za

THEOLOGICAL COLLEGE
The College of the Transfiguration, PO Box 77, Grahamstown 6140 *Tel:* 27 46 622 3332
Fax: 27 46 622 3877
email: office@cott.co.za

ANGOLA (Missionary Diocese)
Bishop Rt Revd Andre Soares, Av. Lenini, Travessa D. Antonia Saldanha N.134, CP 10 341, Luanda, Angola *Tel:* 244 2 395 792
Fax: 244 2 396 794
email: anglicana@ebonet.net/ bispo-Soares@hotmail.com

CAPE TOWN
Archbishop Most Revd Dr Thabo Makgoba (*Metropolitan of Southern Africa*), 20 Bishopscourt Dr, Bishopscourt, Claremont, Cape Town 7708, Western Cape, South Africa *Tel:* 27 21 763 1300
Fax: 27 21 797 1298/761 4193
email: archpa@anglicanchurchsa.org.za
Web: www.anglicanchurchsa.org

Bishop Suffragan
Rt Revd Garth Counsell (*Bishop of Table Bay*), PO Box 1932, Cape Town 8000 *Tel:* 27 21 465 1557
Fax: 27 21 465 1571
email: tablebay@ctdiocese.org.za

CHRIST THE KING
Bishop Rt Revd Peter John Lee, PO Box 1653, Rosettenville 2130, South Africa
Tel: 27 11 435 0097
Fax: 27 11 435 2868
email: bishop@ctkdiocesel.co.za

FALSE BAY
Bishop Rt Revd Merwyn Edwin Castle, PO Box 2804, Somerset West 7129, South Africa
Tel: 27 21 852 5243
Fax: 27 21 852 9430
email: bishopm@falsebaydiocese.org.za

GEORGE
Bishop Rt Revd Brian Melvyn Marajh, PO Box 227, George 6530, Cape Province, South Africa
Tel: 27 44 873 5680
Fax: 27 44 873 5680
email: bishopbrian@george.diocese.co.za

GRAHAMSTOWN
Bishop Rt Revd Ebenezer St Mark Ntlali, PO Box 181, Grahamstown 6140, Cape Province, South Africa *Tel:* 27 46 636 1996
Fax: 27 46 622 5231
email: bpgtn@intekom.co.za

HIGHVELD
Bishop Rt Revd Hugh Bannerman, PO Box 17462, Benoni West 1503, South Africa
Tel: 27 11 422 2231
Fax: 27 11 420 1336
email: bishophveld@iafrica.com

JOHANNESBURG
Bishop Rt Revd Dr Brian Charles Germond, PO Box 1131, Johannesburg 2000, South Africa
Tel: 27 11 486 1014
Fax: 27 11 486 1015
email: brian.germond@anglicanjoburg.org.za

KIMBERLEY AND KURUMAN
Bishop Rt Revd Oswald Peter Patrick Swartz, PO Box 45, Kimberley 8300, South Africa
Tel: 27 53 833 2433
Fax: 27 53 831 2730
email: oppswartz@onetel.com

LEBOMBO
Bishop Rt Revd Dinis Salomâo Sengulane, CP 120, Maputo, Mozambique
Tel: 258 1 404 364/405 885
Fax: 258 1 401 093
email: bispo_sengulane@virconn.com

LESOTHO
Bishop Rt Revd Adam Andrease Mallane Taaso, PO Box 87, Maseru 100, Lesotho
Tel: 266 22 31 1974
Fax: 266 22 31 0161
email: diocese@ilesotho.com

MATLOSANE
Bishop Rt Revd Stephen Molopi Diseko, PO Box 11417, Klerksdorp 2570, South Africa
Tel: 27 18 464 2260
Fax: 27 18 462 4939
email: diocesematlosane@telkomsa.net

MPUMALANGA
Bishop Rt Revd Daniel Malasela Kgomosotho, PO Box 4327, White River 1240 *Tel:* 27 13 751 1960
Fax: 27 13 751 3638
email: diompu@telkomsa.net

MTHATHA
Bishop Rt Revd Dr Sitembele Tobela Mzamane, PO Box 25, Umtata, Transkei 5100, South Africa
Tel: 27 47 532 4450
Fax: 27 47 532 4191
email: anglicbspmthatha@intekom.co.za

NAMIBIA
Bishop Rt Revd Nathaniel Ndxuma Nakwatumbah, PO Box 57, Windhoek, Namibia
Tel: 264 61 238 920
Fax: 264 61 225 903
email: bishop@anglicanchurchnamibia.com

NATAL
Bishop Rt Revd Rubin Phillip, PO Box 47439, Greyville, 4023 South Africa *Tel:* 27 31 309 2066
Fax: 27 31 308 9316
email: bishop@dionatal.org.za

Bishops Suffragan
Rt Revd Dr Hummingfield Charles Nkosinathi Ndwandwe (*Suffragan Bishop of the South Episcopal Area*) (*same address*) *Tel:* 27 33 394 1560
email: bishopndwandwe@dionatal.org.za

Rt Revd Tsietse Edward Seleoane (*Suffragan Bishop of the North West Episcopal Area*), PO Box 463, Ladysmith 3370, South Africa
Tel: 27 36 631 4650
Fax: 27 86 547 1882
email: bishopseleoane@dionatal.org.za

NIASSA
Bishop Rt Revd Mark van Koevering, CP 264, Lichinga, Niassa, Mozambique
Tel and *Fax:* 258 712 0735
email: bishop.niassa@gmail.com

PORT ELIZABETH
Bishop Rt Revd Nceba Bethlehem Nopece, PO Box 7109, Newton Park 6055, South Africa
Tel: 27 41 365 1387
Fax: 27 41 365 2049
email: bpsec@pediocese.org.za

PRETORIA
Bishop Rt Revd Dr Johannes Thomas Seoka, PO Box 1032, Pretoria 0001, South Africa
Tel: 27 12 322 2218
Fax: 27 12 322 9411
email: ptabish@dioceseofpretoria.org

SALDANHA BAY
Bishop The Rt Revd Raphael Bernard Viburt Hess, PO Box 420, Malmesbury 7299, South Africa *Tel:* 27 22 487 3885
Fax: 27 22 487 3886
email: bishop@dioceseofsaldanhabay.org.za

ST HELENA
Bishop Rt Revd Dr Richard David Fenwick, PO Box 62, Island of St Helena, South Atlantic
Tel: 290 4471
Fax: 290 4728
email: richard.d.fenwick@googlemail.com

ST MARK THE EVANGELIST
Bishop Rt Revd Martin Andre Breytenbach, PO Box 643, Polokwane 0700, South Africa
Tel: 27 15 297 3297
Fax: 27 15 297 0408
email: martin@stmark.org.za

SWAZILAND
Bishop Vacancy, Bishop's House, Muir Street, Mbabane, Swaziland *Tel:* 268 404 3624
Fax: 268 404 6759

THE FREE STATE
Bishop Vacancy PO Box 411, Bloemfontein, 9300, South Africa *Tel:* 27 51 447 6053
Fax: 27 51 447 5874
Web: www.cpsa.org.za/bloemfontein

UMZIMVUBU
Bishop Rt Revd Mlibo Mteteleli Ngewu, PO Box 644, Kokstad 4700, South Africa
Tel and *Fax:* 27 39 727 4117
email: mzimvubu@futurenet.co.za

ZULULAND
Bishop Rt Revd Dino Gabriel, PO Box 147, Eshowe 3815, South Africa
Tel and *Fax:* 27 354 742 047
email: bishopdino@netactive.co.za

UKHAHLAMBA
Bishop Rt Revd Mazwi Ernest Tisani, PO Box 1673 Queenstown, 5320 South Africa
Tel: 27 45 858 8673
Fax: 27 45 858 8675
email: ukhahlamba@lantic.net

MBASHE
Bishop Rt Revd Elliot Sebenzile Williams, PO Box 1184, Butterworth, 4960, South Africa
Tel: 27 47 491 8030
Fax: 27 43 740 4766
email: dioceseofmbhashe@telkomsa.net

The Anglican Church of the Southern Cone of America

(Iglesia Anglicana del Cono Sur de América)

Members 22,490
British immigrants brought Anglicanism to South America in the nineteenth century. The South American Missionary Society continues to work effectively among indigenous peoples and today actively supports diocesan initiatives. In 1974 the Archbishop of Canterbury gave over his metropolitical authority for the dioceses of the Southern Cone, and in 1981 the new province was formed. It includes Argentina, Bolivia, Chile, Northern Argentina, Paraguay, Peru and Uruguay.

Presiding Bishop Most Revd Gregory James Venables (*Bishop of Argentina*)
Web: www.anglicanos.net

Provincial Secretary Mrs Leticia Gomez, A. Gallinal 1852, Montevideo, Uruguay
email: lego@adinet.co.uy

Provincial Treasurer Mrs Margarita Cornejo, Iglesia Anglicana, Cochabamba, Bolivia
Tel and *Fax:* 591 7 226 7356
email: margarita_cornejo@hotmail.com

Executive Secretary Mrs Aída Cuenca de Fernandez, Casilla de Correo 187, CP4400, Salta, Argentina *Tel:* 54 387 431 1718
Fax: 54 387 431 26
email: educris@salnet.com.ar

THEOLOGICAL EDUCATION
Planned and carried out by a Theological Education Commission which selects candidates, applies grants and sets courses of study, some of which are led by clergy of the diocese. Some students follow courses of theological training 'by extension' and others attend ecumenical seminaries.

ARGENTINA
Bishop Most Revd Gregory James Venables (*Presiding Bishop of the Province*), Rioja 2995 (1636), Olivos, Provincia de Buenos Aires, Argentina *Tel:* 54 11 4342 4618
Fax: 54 11 4331 0234
email: bpgreg@ciudad.com.ar

BOLIVIA
Bishop Rt Revd Francisco Lyons, Iglesia Anglicana, Casilla 848, Cochabamba, Bolivia
Tel and *Fax:* 591 4 440 1168
email: BpFrank@sams-usa.org
Web: www.bolivia.anglican.org

CHILE
Bishop Rt Revd Héctor Zavala Muñoz, Casilla 50675, Correo Central, Santiago, Chile
Tel: 56 2 638 3009
Fax: 56 2 639 4581
email: tzavala@iach.cl
Web: www.iglesiaanglicana.cl

Assistant Bishop Rt Revd Abelino Manuel Apeleo, Casilla de Correo 26-D, Temuco, Chile
Tel and *Fax:* 56 45 910 484
email: aapeleo@iach.cl

NORTHERN ARGENTINA
Bishop Most Revd Gregory James Venables (*Bishop of Argentina*)

Assistant Bishop Rt Revd Nicholas Drayson, Casilla 19, 3636 Ingeniero Juárez, FCNGB Formosa, Argentina *Tel:* 54 387 431 1718
Fax: 54 387 431 2622
email: diana.epi@salnet.com.ar

PARAGUAY
Bishop Rt Revd John Alexander Ellison, Iglesia Anglicana de Paraguay, Casilla de Correo 1124, Asunción, Paraguay *Tel:* 595 21 200 933
Fax: 595 21 214 328
email: jellison@pla.net.py
Web: www.paraguay.anglican.org

PERU
Bishop Rt Revd Harold William Godfrey, Calle Alcala 336, Urb. La Castellana, Santiago de Surco, Lima 33, Peru *Tel:* 51 1 422 9160
Fax: 51 1 440 8540
email: diocesisperu@anglicanperu.org/ wgodfrey@amauta.rcp.net.pe
Web: www.peru.anglican.org

URUGUAY
Bishop Rt Revd Miguel Tamayo, CC 6108, Montevideo, CP11000, Uruguay
Tel: 598 2 915 9627
Fax: 598 2 916 2519
email: mtamayo@netgate.com.uy
Web: www.uruguay.anglican.org

Suffragan Bishop Rt Revd Gilberto Obdulio Porcal Martinez, Reconquista 522, CC 6108, 11000 Montevideo, Uruguay
Tel: 598 2 915 9627
Fax: 598 2 916 2519
email: anglican@netgate.com.uy

The Church of the Province of the Sudan

Members 5,000,000
The Church Missionary Society began work in 1899 in Omdurman; Christianity spread rapidly among black Africans of the southern region. Until 1974, the diocese of Sudan was part of the Jerusalem archbishopric. It reverted to the jurisdiction of the Archbishop of Canterbury until the new province, consisting of four new dioceses, was established in 1976. In 1986 the number of dioceses increased to 11 and in 1992 to 24 dioceses. The doubling of the number of dioceses by 1992 was partly due to leadership crises in the Church and partly due to church growth. Civil and religious strife and a constant flow of refugees have challenged the Church. Its heroic witness to faith in Christ continues to inspire the Anglican Communion and its people.

Archbishop and Primate Most Revd Dr Daniel Deng Bul (*Bishop of Juba*)
Tel and *Fax:* 249 121212607
email: ecsprovince@hotmail.com
archbishopdanieldeng@yahoo.com
Web: www.sudan.anglican.org

Acting Provincial Secretary John Augustino Lumori, PO Box 604, Khartoum, Sudan
Tel: 249 122232176
email: jlumori@yahoo.com/ ecsprovince@hotmail.com
Honorary Provincial Treasurer Mr Evans Sokiri (*same address*) *email*: sokirik@yahoo.co.uk

THEOLOGICAL COLLEGES
Bishop Gwynne College, PO Box 110, Juba, Sudan (*Acting Principal* Revd David V. Bako)
Tel: 249 9124 54933 (Mobile)
email: davidbako7@hotmail.com

Bishop Alison Theological College, PO Box 1076, Arua, Uganda (*Principal* Dr Oliver Duku)
Tel: 254 77 685 554
email: bat_college@yahoo.com

Shokai Bible Training Institute, PO Box 65, Omdurman, 135 Khartoum, Sudan (*Principal* Revd Musa Elgadi) *Tel:* 249 187 564944
email: sbti70@yahoo.com
Renk Bible School, PO Box 1532, Khartoum North, Sudan (*Acting Principal* Revd Abraham Noon Jiel) *Tel:* 249 918 068 125 (Mobile)
email: joseph_atem@yahoo.com
Bishop Ngalamu Theological College, PO Box 3364, Khartoum, Sudan (*Principal* Revd Paul Issa)
email: leyeonon@hotmail.com

AKOT
Bishop Rt Revd Isaac Dhieu Ater, c/o CMS Office, PO Box 40360, Nairobi, Kenya

BOR
Bishop Rt Revd Nathaniel Garang Anyieth (*Dean of the Province*), c/o NSCC, PO Box 66168, Nairobi, Kenya *Tel:* 254 733 855 521/855 675
email: ecs_dioceseofbor@yahoo.co.uk

Assistant Bishop Rt Revd Ezekel Diing Malaangdit, c/o NSCC, PO Box 66168, Nairobi, Kenya

CUEIBET
Bishop Rt Revd Reuben Maciir Makoi, c/o CEAS, PO Box 40870, Nairobi, Kenya *Fax:* 254 2 570 807
email: eapo@cms-africa.org

EL-OBEID
Bishop Rt Revd Ismail Gibriel, PO Box 211, El-Obeid, Sudan *Tel:* 249 9122 53459 (Mobile)
email: ismailabudigin2007@yahoo.com

EZO
Bishop Rt Revd John Zawo, c/o ECS Support Office, PO Box 7576, Kampala, Uganda
Tel: 256 41 343 497
email: kereborojohn@yahoo.com

IBBA
Bishop Rt Revd Wilson Elisa Kamani, c/o ECS Support Office, PO Box 7576, Kampala, Uganda
Tel and *Fax:* 256 41 343 497
email: ecs_ibbadiocese@hotmail.com/ ecs-kpa@africaonline.co.ug

JUBA
Bishop Most Revd Dr Daniel Deng Bul (*Archbishop and Primate*), PO Box 604, Khartoum, Sudan
Tel: 249 811 820065
email: dioceseofjuba@yahoo.com
Assistant Bishop Rt Revd Joseph Makor Atot, c/o CMS, PO Box 40360, Nairobi, Kenya

KADUGLI AND NUBA MOUNTAINS
Bishop Rt Revd Andudu Adam Elnail, PO Box 35, Kadugli, Sudan *Tel:* 249 631 822898
email: bishandudu@yahoo.com

KAJO-KEJI
Bishop Rt Revd Anthony Poggo, c/o ECS Support Office, PO Box 7576, Kampala, Uganda
Tel: 256 41 343 497
email: bishopkk@gmail.com

KHARTOUM
Bishop Rt Revd Ezekiel Kondo, PO Box 65, Omdurman, 35 Khartoum, Sudan
Tel: 249 187 556931
email: ecs_bishop_Khartoum@kastanet.org

LAINYA
Bishop Rt Revd Peter Amidi, c/o ECS Support Office, PO Box 7576, Kampala, Uganda
Tel and *Fax:* 256 77 658 753
email: petamidi@yahoo.com

LUI
Bishop Rt Revd Bullen A. Dolli, PO Box 60837, Nairobi, Kenya *Tel:* 254 2 720 037/56
Fax: 254 2 714 420
email: bishop@luidiocese.org/ cms-nbi@maf.org.ke

MALAKAL
Bishop Rt Revd Hilary Garang Aweer, PO Box 604, Khartoum, Sudan
email: ecs_malak@hotmail.com

MARIDI
Bishop Rt Revd Justin Badi Arama, ECS Support Office, PO Box 7576, Kampala, Uganda
Tel and *Fax:* 256 41 343 497
email: ecsmaridi@hotmail.com

MUNDRI
Bishop Rt Revd Bismark Monday Avokaya, c/o ECS Support Office, PO Box 7576, Kampala, Uganda *Tel* and *Fax:* 256 41 343 497
email: ecsmundri@yahoo.com

PACONG
Bishop Rt Revd Joseph Maker
email: ecs.pacongdiocese@yahoo.com

PORT SUDAN
Bishop Rt Revd Yousif Abdalla Kuku, PO Box 278, Port Sudan, Sudan
Tel and *Fax:* 249 311 821224
email: ecsprovince@hotmail.com

REJAF
Bishop Rt Revd Michael Sokiri Lugör, PO Box 110, Juba, Sudan *Tel:* 249 1290 76288
email: rejafdioceseecs@yahoo.com

RENK
Bishop Rt Revd Joseph Garang Atem, PO Box 1532, Khartoum North, Sudan
Tel: 249 122 99275 (Mobile)
email: ecs_renk@hotmail.com

ROKON
Bishop Rt Revd Francis Loyo, PO Box 6702, Nairobi 00100 APO, Kenya
Tel: 254 2 568 541/539
Fax: 254 2 560 864
email: bployo@yahoo.co.uk
Web: www.rokon.anglican.org

RUMBEK
Bishop Rt Revd Alapayo Manyang Kuctiel, c/o CMS Nairobi, PO Box 56, Nakuro, Kenya
Tel: 254 37 43186
email: kuctiel@yahoo.com

TEREKEKA
Bishop Rt Revd Micah Dawidi, c/o CMS Nairobi, PO Box 56, Nakuru, Kenya

TORIT
Bishop Rt Revd Bernard Oringa Balmoi, c/o ECS Support Office, PO Box 7576, Kampala, Uganda
Tel: 256 41 343 497
email: ecs_bishop_torit@kastanet.org

WAU
Bishop Rt Revd Henry Cuir Riak, c/o CMS Nairobi, PO Box 56, Nakuro, Kenya
Tel: 254 37 43186
email: riakcuir@yahoo.com / wauvtc@yahoo.com

YAMBIO
Bishop Rt Revd Peter Munde Yacoub, ECS Support Office, PO Box 7576, Kampala, Uganda
Tel and *Fax:* 256 41 343 497
256 77 622 367 (Mobile)
email: yambio2002@yahoo.com/ ecs-kpa@africaonline.co.ug

YEI
Bishop Rt Revd Hilary Luate Adeba, PO Box 588, Arua, Uganda *Tel:* 256 756 561 175
email: hill_sherpherd@yahoo.com/ 72wca@techserve.org

YIROL
Bishop Rt Revd Benjamin Mangar Mamur, c/o St Matthew's Church, PO Box 39, Eldoret, Kenya
email: mamurmangar@yahoo.com/ cms-nbi@maf.or.ke

The Anglican Church of Tanzania

Members over 3,000,000
The Universities Mission to Central Africa and the Church Missionary Society began work in 1863 and 1876 in Zanzibar and at Mpwapwa respectively. The province was inaugurated in 1970 following the division of the Province of East Africa into the Province of Kenya and the Province of Tanzania. The 20 dioceses represent both evangelical and Anglo-Catholic Churches.

Archbishop Most Revd Dr Valentino Mokiwa (*Bishop of Dar-es-Salaam*)

Dean Rt Revd Dr Philip Baji (*Bishop of Tanga*)

Provincial Secretary Dr R. Mwita Akiri, PO Box 899, Dodoma *Tel:* 255 26 232 4574
Fax: 255 26 232 4565
email: akiri@anglican.or.tz
Web: www.anglican.or.tz

Provincial Treasurer Rt Revd Hilkah Omindo Deya (*Bishop of Mara*)

Provincial Registrar Justice Augustino Ramadhani, PO Box 20522, Dar es Salaam
Tel: 255 022 211 5418
email: aslramadhani@yahoo.co.uk

THEOLOGICAL COLLEGES
St Philip's Theological College, PO Box 26, Kongwa (*Principal* Rev John Madinda)
Tel: 255 26 232 0096
email: stphilipstz@yahoo.com

St Mark's Theological College, PO Box 25017, Dar es Salaam (*Principal* Canon John Simalenga)
Tel: 255 22 286 3014
email: st-alban@kicheko.com/ jsimalenga@yahoo.com

CHURCH NEWSLETTER
ACT Forum is issued three times a year (April, August, December) in English containing diocesan, provincial and world church news. *Editor* Vacancy

CENTRAL TANGANYIKA
Bishop Rt Revd Godfrey Mdimi Mhogolo, PO Box 15, Dodoma *Tel:* 255 26 232 1714
Fax: 255 26 232 4518
email: bishop@dct-tz.org/mhogolo@pnc.com.au

Assistant Bishop Rt Revd Ainea Kusenha (*same address*) *email*: ngombe2004@kicheko.com

DAR ES SALAAM
Bishop Most Revd Dr Valentino Mokiwa (*Archbishop*), PO Box 25016, Ilala, Dar-es-Salaam *Tel:* 255 22 286 4426
email: mokiwa_valentine@hotmail.com

KAGERA
Bishop Rt Revd Aaron Kijanjali, PO Box 18, Ngara *Tel:* 255 28 222 3624
Fax: 255 28 222 2518
email: act-kagera@africaonline.co.tz

KITETO
Bishop Rt Revd Isaiah Chambala, PO Box 74, Kibaya, Kiteto *Tel:* 255 27 255 2106
email: dkiteto@iwayafrica.com

KONDOA
Bishop Rt Revd Yohana Zakaria Mkavu, PO Box 7, Kondoa *Tel:* 255 26 236 0312
Fax: 255 26 236 0304/0324
email: d-kondoa@do.ucc.co.tz

LWERU
Bishop Rt Revd Jackton Yeremiah Lugumira, PO Box 12, Muleba *Tel:* 255 713 274 085
email: jlugumira2@juno.com

MARA
Bishop Rt Revd Hilkiah Deya Omindo Deya, PO Box 131, Musoma *Tel:* 255 28 262 2376
Fax: 255 28 262 2414
email: actmara@juasun.net

MASASI
Bishop Rt Revd Patrick Mwachiko, Private Bag, PO Masasi, Mtwara Region *Tel:* 255 23 251 0016
Fax: 255 23 251 0351
email: actmasasi@africaonline.co.tz

MOROGORO
Bishop Rt Revd Dudley Mageni, PO Box 320, Morogoro *Tel* and *Fax:* 255 23 260 4602
email: act-morogoro@africaonline.co.tz

MOUNT KILIMANJARO
Bishop Rt Revd Simon Elilekia Makundi, PO Box 1057, Arusha *Tel:* 255 27 254 8396
Fax: 255 27 254 4187
email: dmk@habari.co.tz

MPWAPWA
Bishop Rt Revd Jacob Chimeledya, PO Box 2, Mpwapwa *Tel:* 255 26 232 0017/0825
Fax: 255 26 232 0063
email: dmp@do.ucc.co.tz

NEWALA
Bishop Rt Revd Oscar Mnunga, c/o Bishop of Masasi

RIFT VALLEY
Bishop Rt Revd John Lupaa, PO Box 16, Manyoni
Tel: 255 26 254 0013
Fax: 255 26 250 3014
email: act-drv@maf.or.tz

RUAHA
Bishop Rt Revd Donald Leo Mtetemela, PO Box 1028, Iringa *Tel:* 255 26 270 1211
Fax: 255 26 270 2479
email: ruaha@anglican.or.tz

RUVUMA
Bishop Rt Revd Dr Maternus Kapinga, PO Box 1357, Songea, Ruvumu *Tel:* 255 25 260 0090
Fax: 255 25 260 2987
email: mkkapinga@yahoo.com

SHINYANGA
Bishop Rt Revd Ngusa Charles Kija, PO Box 421, Shinyanga *Tel:* 255 754 347 746 (Mobile)
email: ckngusa@yahoo.com

SOUTHERN HIGHLANDS
Bishop Rt Revd John Mwela, PO Box 198, Mbeya
Tel: 255 754 266 668 (Mobile)
email: dsh-dev@atma.co.tz

SOUTH-WEST TANGANYIKA
Bishop Vacancy, PO Box 32, Njombe
Tel: 255 26 278 2010
Fax: 255 26 278 2403
email: dswt@africaonline.co.tz

TABORA
Bishop Rt Revd Sadock Makaya, PO Box 1408, Tabora *Tel:* 255 26 260 4124
Fax: 255 26 260 4899
email: smakaya1@yahoo.co.uk

TANGA
Bishop Rt Revd Dr Philip D. Baji, PO Box 35, Korogwe, Tanga *Tel:* 255 27 264 0631
Fax: 255 27 264 0568
email: bajipp@anglican.or.tz

VICTORIA NYANZA
Bishop Rt Revd Boniface Kwangu, PO Box 278, Mwanza *Tel:* 255 28 250 0627
Fax: 255 28 250 0676
email: revkahene1@yahoo.com

WESTERN TANGANYIKA
Bishop Rt Revd Dr Gerard E. Mpango, PO Box 13, Kasulu *Tel:* 255 28 281 0321
Fax: 255 28 281 0706
email: askofugm@yahoo.com

Assistant Bishops
Rt Revd Naftal Bikaka (*Lake Zone Area of Kigoma District*), PO Box 1378, Kigoma
Tel: 255 28 280 3407
email: bpwbikaka@yahoo.co.uk
Rt Revd Marko Badeleya (*Southern Zone Area of Rukwa Region in Sumbawanga*), PO Box 226, Sumbawanga *Tel:* 255 25 280 0287
email: bpbadeleya@yahoo.co.uk

ZANZIBAR
Bishop Vacancy, PO Box 5, Mkunazini, Zanzibar
Tel: 255 24 223 5348
Fax: 255 24 223 6772
email: secactznz@zanlink.com

ANGLICAN AND PORVOO COMMUNIONS

The Church of the Province of Uganda

Members 9,200,000
After its founding in 1877 by the Church Missionary Society, the Church grew through the evangelization of Africa by Africans. The first Ugandan clergy were ordained in 1893 and the Church of Uganda, Rwanda and Burundi became an independent province in 1961. The history of the Church in Uganda has been marked by civil strife and martyrdom. In May 1980 the new Province of Burundi, Rwanda and Zaire was inaugurated; the Province of Uganda has since grown from 17 to 32 dioceses.

Archbishop of the Province Most Revd Henry Luke Orombi (*Bishop of Kampala*)

Primatial and Provincial Secretariat PO Box 14123, Kampala *Tel:* 256 41 270 218
Fax: 256 41 251 925
email: provinceuganda@yahoo.com

Provincial Secretary Canon Aaron Mwesigye Kafundizeki (*same address*)
email: ankundarev@yahoo.com
Tel: 256 772 455 129 (Mobile)

Provincial Treasurer Mr Richard Obura (*same address*) *email:* ricobura57@yahoo.com
Tel: 256 41 270 218
Fax: 256 41 251 925

Bishop in charge of continuing education for clergy in service Rt Revd David Sebuhinja (*same address*)
email: sebuhinjadavid@yahoo.co.uk

THEOLOGICAL COLLEGES

Uganda Christian University, Mukono, PO Box 4, Mukono (*Principal* Revd Prof. Stephen Noll)

Bishop Balya College, PO Box 368, Fort-Portal (*Principal* Revd Y. Kule)

Bishop Barham University College (constituent college of Uganda Christian university, Mukono), PO Box 613, Kabale (*Acting Principal* Canon Jovan Turyamureeba)

Archbishop Janani Luwum Theological College, PO Box 232, Gulu (*Principal* Revd Ayela Okot)

Mityana Theological Training College, PO Box 102, Mityana (*Principal* Revd Mukasa-Mutambuze)

Ngora Diocesan Theological College, PO Box 1, Ngora (*Principal* Revd S. Amuret)

Uganda Martyrs Seminary Namugongo, PO Box 31149, Kampala (*Principal* Canon Dr Henry Segawa)

Aduku Diocesan Theological College, PO Aduku, Lira (*Principal* Revd S. O. Obura)

Kabwohe College, PO Kabwohe, Mbarara (*Principal* Revd Y. R. Buremu)

St Paul's Theological College Ringili, PO Box 358, Arua (*Principal* Canon Dr Milton Anguyo)

Bishop Usher Wilson, Buwalasi, Mbale (*Principal* Revd Naphtah Opwata)

Uganda Bible Institute, Mbarara (*Director* Revd Amos Magezi)

Bishop McAllister College, Kyogyera (*Principal* Revd Paul Jefferees)

ANKOLE
Bishop Rt Revd George Tibeesigwa, PO Box 14, Mbarara, Ankole *Tel:* 256 485 20290

BUKEDI
Bishop Rt Revd Nicodemus Okille, PO Box 170, Tororo *Tel:* 256 772 542 164 (Mobile)

BUNYORO-KITARA
Bishop Rt Revd Nathan Kyamanywa, PO Box 20, Hoima *Tel:* 256 464 40 128
256 772 648 232 (Mobile)
email: bkdioces@infocom.co.ug

BUSOGA
Bishop Rt Revd Dr Michael Kyomya, PO Box 1568, Jinja *Tel:* 256 752 649 102 (Mobile)

CENTRAL BUGANDA
Bishop Rt Revd Jackson Matovu, PO Box 1200, Kinoni-Gomba, Mpigi
Tel: 256 772 475 640 (Mobile)
email: bishopmatovu@yahoo.com

KAMPALA
Bishop Most Revd Henry Luke Orombi (*Archbishop of Uganda*), PO Box 335, Kampala
Tel: 256 414 279 218
256 772 450 178 (Mobile)
Fax: 256 414 251 925
email: kdcou@africaonline.co.ug

Assistant Bishop Rt Revd Dr Zac Niringiye, PO Box 335, Kampala *Tel:* 256 414 290 231
Fax: 256 414 342 601

KARAMOJA
Bishop Rt Revd Joseph Abura, PO Box 44, Moroto
Tel: 256 782 658 502

KIGEZI
Bishop Rt Revd George Katwesigye, PO Box 3, Kabale *Tel:* 256 486 22 003
256 772 446 954 (Mobile)
Fax: 256 486 22 802
email: kigezi@infocom.co.ug

KINKIZI
Bishop Rt Revd John Ntegyereize, PO Box 77, Karuhinda, Rukungiri
Tel: 873 761 604 794/5 (Satellite)
256 772 507 163 (Mobile)
Fax: 875 761 604 796/7 (Satellite)

KITGUM
Bishop Rt Revd Benjamin Ojwang, PO Box 187, Kitgum *Tel:* 256 772 959 924 (Mobile)
email: benojwang2004@yahoo.co.uk

KUMI
Bishop Rt Revd Thomas Edison Irigei, PO Box 18, Kumi *Tel:* 256 772 659 460 (Mobile)
email: coukumidiocese@yahoo.com

LANGO
Bishop Rt Revd John Charles Odurkami, PO Box 6, Lira *Tel:* 256 772 614 000 (Mobile)
email: bishoplango@yahoo.com

LUWERO
Bishop Rt Revd Evans Mukasa Kisekka, PO Box 125, Luwero *Tel:* 256 414 610 048/070
256 772 421 220 (Mobile)
Fax: 256 414 610 132/070
email: kiromas@yahoo.co.uk

MADI / WEST NILE
Bishop Rt Revd Joel Obetia, PO Box 370, Arua
Tel: 256 752 625 414 (Mobile)
email: jobetia@ucu.ac.ug

MASINDI-KITARA
Bishop Rt Revd Stanley Ntagali, PO Box 515, Masindi *Tel:* 256 772 618 822
email: bishopntagali@yahoo.com

MBALE
Bishop Rt Revd Patrick Gidudu, Bishop's House, PO Box 473, Mbale *Tel:* 256 45 33 533
256 772 512 051 (Mobile)

MITYANA
Bishop Rt Revd Stephen Samuel Kaziimba, PO Box 102, Mityana *Tel:* 256 46 2017
email: mtndiocese@hotmail.com

MUHABURA
Bishop Rt Revd Cranmer Mugisha, PO Box 22, Kisoro *Tel:* 256 486 30 014/058
256 712 195 891 (Mobile)
Fax: 256 486 30 059

MUKONO
Bishop Rt Revd Elia Paul Luzinda Kizito, PO Box 39, Mukono *Tel:* 256 41 290 229
256 772 603 348 (Mobile)
email: mukodise@utlonline.co.ug

NAMIREMBE
Bishop Rt Revd Samuel Balagadde Ssekkadde, PO Box 14297, Kampala *Tel:* 256 41 271 682
256 772 500 494 (Mobile)
email: namid@infocom.co.ug

NEBBI
Bishop Rt Revd Alphonse Watho-kudi, PO Box 27, Nebbi *Tel:* 256 772 650 032 (Mobile)
email: bpalphonse@ekk.org

NORTH ANKOLE
Bishop Rt Revd John Muhanguzi, c/o PO Box 14, Rushere-Mbarara, Ankole
Tel: 256 772 369 947 (Mobile)
email: northankole@gmail.com

NORTH KARAMOJA
Bishop Rt Revd James Nasak, PO Box 26, Kotido
Tel: 256 772 660 228

NORTH KIGEZI
Bishop Rt Revd Edward Muhima, PO Box 23, Rukungiri *Tel:* 256 486 42 433
256 772 709 387 (Mobile)
email: northkigezi@infocom.co.ug

NORTH MBALE
Bishop Rt Revd Daniel Gimadu, Bishop's House, PO Box 1837, Mbale *Fax:* 256 752 655 225
email: northmbalediocese@yahoo.com/ petgim2000@yahoo.com

NORTHERN UGANDA
Bishop Rt Revd Nelson Onono-Onweng, PO Box 232, Gulu *Tel:* 256 772 838 193 (Mobile)
email: ononobp@yahoo.co.uk

RUWENZORI
Bishop Rt Revd Benezeri Kisembo, Bishop's House, PO Box 37, Fort Portal
Tel: 256 772 470 671 (Mobile)
email: bishop@biznas.com

SEBEI
Bishop Rt Revd Augusto Arapyona Salimo, PO Box 23, Kapchorwa *Tel:* 256 45 51 072
256 772 550 520 (Mobile)
email: augustinesalimo@yahoo.co.uk

SOROTI
Bishop Rt Revd Charles Bernard Obaikol-Ebitu, PO Box 107, Soroti *Tel:* 256 45 61 795
256 772 557 909 (Mobile)
email: couteddo@infocom.co.ug

SOUTH RUWENZORI
Bishop Rt Revd Jackson T. Nzerebende, PO Box 142, Kasese *Tel:* 256 772 713 736 (Mobile)
Fax: 256 483 44 450
email: bpbende@yahoo.com

WEST ANKOLE
Bishop Rt Revd Yonah Katoneene, PO Box 140, Bushenyi *Tel:* 256 753 377 193 (Mobile)
email: wad@westankolediocese.org

WEST BUGANDA
Bishop Rt Revd Dr Samuel Kefa Kamya, PO Box 242, Masaka *Tel:* 256 772 413 400 (Mobile)
email: wesbug@infocom.co.ug

The Protestant Episcopal Church in the United States of America

(also known as The Episcopal Church)

Members 2,400,000

Anglicanism was brought to the New World by explorers and colonists with the first celebration of the Holy Eucharist in Jamestown, Virginia in 1607. The need for clergy in the colonies was acute and English missionaries provided temporary relief. Though the Bishop of London was responsible for maintaining the church in the colonies, there was no resident bishop for nearly two hundred years, which meant that colonists had to travel to England to be ordained; this caused difficulties when many of the colonial clergy sided with the Crown during the American Revolution. In 1784 the first American bishop (Samuel Seabury of Connecticut) was consecrated in Scotland, and three years later bishops were consecrated in England for the Dioceses of Pennsylvania and New York. In 1785 the first General Convention was held; in 1821 the Domestic and Foreign Missionary Society was formed; and in 1835, by resolution of General Convention, all members of The Episcopal Church were made members of the Missionary Society. The Episcopal Church today maintains 100 dioceses within the United States plus 10 overseas dioceses (Colombia, the Dominican Republic, Central Ecuador, Litoral Ecuador, Haiti, Honduras, Puerto Rico, Taiwan, Venezuela and the Virgin Islands), the Mission Territory of Micronesia (Guam), the Convocation of American Churches in Europe, and, together with the Anglican Church of Canada and the Church in the Province of the West Indies, is a partner in the Metropolitan Council which oversees the Episcopal Church of Cuba; it is governed by the triennial General Convention consisting of a House of Clergy and Lay Deputies, and a House of Bishops, which includes all serving diocesan, suffragan, coadjutor and assisting bishops. Between General Conventions, church affairs are managed by the Executive Council, whose members are elected in part by the two Houses and in part by the nine regional provinces. The Executive Council meets three times each year (except twice during a General Convention year). The province is a strong base of support to the Anglican Communion and has a significant crisis ministry through Episcopal Relief and Development. Episcopalians are also very active in the areas of social justice and ecumenical and interfaith relations, and witness to their faith in all walks of national life.

Presiding Bishop and Primate Most Revd Katharine Jefferts Schori

Offices of the Episcopal Church and its departments Episcopal Church Center, 815 Second Ave, New York, NY 10017, USA *Tel:* 1 212 716 6000
email: via website
Web: www.episcopalchurch.org

President of the House of Deputies Gay Jennings (*same address*) *Tel:* 1 212 922 5183
email: via website

Executive Officer and Secretary of the General Convention Revd Canon Dr Gregory Straub (*same address*) *Tel:* 1 212 922 5184
email: via website

Bishop Suffragan for Armed Services and Federal Ministries 3504 Woodley Road NW, Washington DC, 20016, USA *Tel:* 1 202 459 9998
email: via website

Deputy to the Presiding Bishop for Anglican Communion Relations Rt Revd Herbert A. Donovan Jr, Episcopal Church Center, 815 Second Ave, New York, NY 10017, USA
Tel: 1 212 716 6000
email: via website

Bishop, Office of Pastoral Development Rt Revd F. Clayton Matthews, 2857 Trent Rd, New Bern, NC, 28562, USA *Tel:* 1 252 635 5004
email: via website

Treasurer Mr N. Kurt Barnes Episcopal Church Center, 815 Second Ave, New York, NY 10017, USA *Tel:* 1 212 716 6000
email: via website
Web: www.episcopalchurch.org

THEOLOGICAL SEMINARIES

California
Church Divinity School of the Pacific, 2451 Ridge Rd, Berkeley, CA 94709, USA (*President and Dean* Very Rvd Dr W. Mark Richardson)
Web: www.cdsp.edu

Connecticut
Berkeley Divinity School at Yale University, 409 Prospect St, New Haven, CT 06511, USA (*Dean and President* Very Revd Joseph H. Britton) *Web:* www.berkeleydivinity.net

Illinois
Seabury-Western Theological Seminary, 8785 W. Higgins Road, Chicago, IL 60631, USA (*President* Revd Dr Roger Farlo) *Web:* www.seabury.edu

Massachusetts
Episcopal Divinity School, 99 Brattle St, Cambridge, MA 02138, USA (*President and Dean* Very Revd Dr Katharine Hancock Ragsdale) *Web:* www.eds.edu

Ohio
Bexley Hall Episcopal Seminary, 583 Sheridan Ave, Columbus, OH 43209, (*President* Revd Dr Roger Farlo) *Web:* www.bexley.edu

New York
The General Theological Seminary of The Episcopal Church in the United States, 440 West 21st St, New York, NY 10011, USA (*Dean* Rt Revd Peter Lee) *Web:* www.gts.edu

Pennsylvania
Trinity School for Ministry, 311 Eleventh St, Ambridge, PA 15003, USA (*Dean and President* Very Revd Dr Justyn Terry) *Web:* www.tsm.edu

Tennessee
The School of Theology, The University of the South, 335 Tennesse Ave, Sewanee, TN 37383–0001, USA (*Dean* Rt Revd J. Neil Alexander) *Web:* www.theology.sewanee.edu

Texas
Seminary of the Southwest, 501 East 32nd St, Austin, TX 78768, USA (*Dean* Very Revd Douglas Travis) *Web:* www. ssw.edu

Virginia
Virginia Thelogical, Seminary, 3737 Seminary Rd, Alexandria, VA 22304, USA (*Dean and President* Very Revd Dr Ian S. Markham) *Web:* www.vts.edu

Wisconsin
Nashotah House, 2777 Mission Rd, Nashotah, WI 53058, USA (*Dean* Rt Revd Edward L. Salmon Jr) *Web:* www.nashotah.edu

CHURCH PAPERS

Episcopal Life An independently edited, officially sponsored monthly newspaper published by the Episcopal Church, 815 Second Ave, New York, NY 10017, USA, upon authority of the General Convention of the Protestant Episcopal Church in the USA. Also see *episcopallife online*, our electronic news service *Web:* www.episcopalchurch.org/episcopal_life.htm

The Living Church Weekly magazine. *Editorial and Business Offices* PO Box 514036, Milwaukee, WI 53203, USA. Contains news and features about Christianity in general and the Episcopal Church in particular.

ALABAMA (Province IV)
Bishop Rt Revd John McKee Sloan, Carpenter House, 521 N 20th St, Birmingham, AL 35203, USA *Tel:* 1 205 715 2060
Fax: 1 205 715 2066
email: ksloan@dioala.org
Web: www.dioala.org

ALASKA (Province VIII)
Bishop Rt Revd Mark Lattime, 1205 Denali Way, Fairbanks, Alaska 99701–4178, USA
Tel: 1 907 452 3040
Fax: 1 907 456 6552
email: mlattime@gci.net
Web: www.episcopalak.org

ALBANY (Province II)
Bishop Rt Revd William H. Love, 68 South Swan St, Albany, NY 12210, USA *Tel:* 1 518 465 4737
Fax: 1 518 436 1182
email: via website
Web: www.albanyepiscopaldiocese.org

ARIZONA (Province VIII)
Bishop Rt Revd Kirk Stevan Smith, 114 West Roosevelt St, Phoenix, AZ 85003–1406, USA
Tel: 1 602 254 0976
Fax: 1 602 495 6603
email: bishop@azdiocese.org
Web: www.azdiocese.org

Assisting Bishop William G. Burrill (*same address*)

ARKANSAS (Province VII)
Bishop Rt Revd Larry R. Benfield, PO Box 164668, Little Rock, AR 72216–4668, USA
Tel: 1 501 372 2168
Fax: 1 501 372 2147
email: bishopbenfield@mac.com
Web: www.arkansas.anglican.org

ATLANTA (Province IV)
Bishop Rt Revd John Neil Alexander, 2744 Peachtree Rd, Atlanta, GA 30305, USA
Tel: 1 404 601 5320
Fax: 1 404 601 5330
email: bishop@episcopalatlanta.org
Web: www.episcopalatlanta.org

Assistant Bishop Rt Revd Keith B. Whitmore (*same address*)

BETHLEHEM (Province III)
Bishop Rt Revd Paul Victor Marshall, 333 Wyandotte St, Bethlehem, PA 18015, USA
Tel: 1 610 691 5655
Fax: 1 610 691 1682
email: bpoffice@diobeth.org
Web: www.diobeth.org

Assistant Bishop Rt Revd John P. Croneberger (*same address*)

CALIFORNIA (Province VIII)
Bishop Rt Revd Marc Handley Andrus, 1055 Taylor St, San Francisco, CA 94108, USA
Tel: 1 415 673 5015
Fax: 1 415 673 9268
email: bishopmarc@diocal.org
Web: www.diocal.org

CENTRAL ECUADOR (Province IX)
Interim Bishop Rt Revd Victor Scantlebury, calle Hernando Sarmiento N 39–54 Portete, Quito, Ecuador *Tel:* 593 2 245948
email: bpvictor@aol.com

CENTRAL FLORIDA (Province IV)
Bishop Rt Revd John Howe, Diocesan Office, 1017 E Robinson St, Orlando, Florida 32801, USA
Tel: 1 407 423 3567
Fax: 1 407 872 0006
email: jhowe@cfdiocese.org
Web: www.cfdiocese.org

CENTRAL GULF COAST (Province IV)
Bishop Rt Revd Philip Menzie Duncan II, 201 N Baylen St, Pensacola, Florida 32502, USA
Tel: 1 850 434 7337
Fax: 1 850 434 8577
email: staff@diocgc.org
Web: www.diocgc.org

CENTRAL NEW YORK (Province II)
Bishop Rt Revd Gladstone 'Skip' Adams, 310 Montgomery St, Suite 200, Syracuse, NY 13202–2093, USA *Tel:* 1 315 474 6596
Fax: 1 315 478 1632
email: bishop@cny.anglican.org
Web: www.cny.anglican.org

CENTRAL PENNSYLVANIA (Province III)
Bishop Rt Revd Nathan D. Baxter, 101 Pine St, Harrisburg, PA 17101, USA *Tel:* 1 717 236 5959
Fax: 1 717 236 6448
email: officemailbox@diocesecpa.org
Web: www.diocesecpa.org

CHICAGO (Province V)
Bishop Rt Revd Jeffery Lee, 65 E Huron St, Chicago, IL 60611, USA *Tel:* 1 312 751 4200
Fax: 1 312 787 5872
email: bishop@episcopalchicago.org
Web: www.epischicago.org

COLOMBIA (Province IX)
Bishop Rt Revd Francisco José Duque Gómez, Apartado Aereo 52964, Bogotá, DC Colombia
Tel: 57 1 288 3167
Fax: 57 1 288 3248
email: obispoduque@iglesiaepiscopal.org.co
Web: www.iglesiaepiscopal.org.co

COLORADO (Province VI)
Bishop Rt Revd Robert John O'Neill, 1300 Washington St, Denver, CO 80203–2008, USA
Tel: 1 303 837 1173
Fax: 1 303 837 1311
email: colorado@coloradodiocese.org
Web: www.coloradodiocese.org

CONNECTICUT (Province I)
Bishop Rt Revd Ian Theodore Douglas, 1335 Asylum Ave, Hartford, CT 06105–2295, USA
Tel: 1 860 233 4481
Fax: 1 860 523 1410
email: itdouglas@ctdiocese.org
Web: www.ctdiocese.org

Bishops Suffragan
Rt Revd Laura Ahrens (*same address*)
email: lahrens@ctdiocese.org

Rt Revd James Elliot Curry (*same address*)
email: jcurry@ctdiocese.org

DALLAS (Province VII)
Bishop Rt Revd James Monte Stanton, 1630 North Garrett Ave, Dallas, TX 75206, USA
Tel: 1 214 826 8310
Fax: 1 214 826 5968
email: jmsdallas@episcopal-dallas.org
Web: www.episcopal-dallas.org

Bishop Suffragan Rt Revd Paul Emil Lambert (*same address*) email; plambert@episcopal-dallas.org

DELAWARE (Province III)
Bishop Rt Revd Wayne Parker Wright, 2020 North Tatnall St, Wilmington, DE 19802, USA
Tel: 1 302 656 5441
Fax: 1 302 656 7342
email: bishop@dioceseofdelaware.net
Web: www.dioceseofdelaware.net

DOMINICAN REPUBLIC (Province IX)
Bishop Rt Revd Julio Cesar Holguin, c/o Iglesia Episcopal Domincana DMG 13602, 100 Airport Ave, Venice, FL 34282, USA *Tel:* 1 809 688 6016
Fax: 1 809 688 6344
email: iglepidom@verizon.net.do
Web: www.episcopaldominican.org

EAST CAROLINA (Province IV)
Bishop Rt Revd Clifton Daniel III, 705 Doctors Dr, Kinston, NC 28501, USA *Tel:* 1 252 522 0885
Fax: 1 252 523 5272
email: cdaniel@diocese-eastcarolina.org
Web: www.diocese-eastcarolina.org

EAST TENNESSEE (Province IV)
Bishop Rt Revd George Dibrell Young III, 814 Episcopal School Way, Knoxville, Tennessee 37932, USA *Tel:* 1 865 966 2110
Fax: 1 865 966 2535
email: gyoung@etdiocese.net
Web: www.etdiocese.net

EASTERN MICHIGAN (Province V)
Bishop Rt Revd S. Todd Ousley, Diocesan Office, 924 N Niagara St, Saginaw, Michigan 48602, USA
Tel: 1 989 752 6020
Fax: 1 989 752 6120
email: diocese@eastmich.org
Web: www.eastmich.org

EASTERN OREGON (Province VIII)
Bishop Rt Revd Bavi E. Rivera, 601 Union St, The Dalles, Oregon 97058, USA
Tel: 1 541 298 4477
Fax: 1 541 296 0939
email: diocese@episdioeo.org
Web: www.episdioeo.org

EASTON (Province III)
Bishop Rt Revd James J. Shand, 314 North St, Easton, MD 21601, USA *Tel:* 1 410 822 1919
Fax: 1 410 763 8259
email: diocese@dioceseofeaston.org
Web: www.dioceseofeaston.org

EAU CLAIRE (Province V)
Provisional Bishop Rt Revd Edwin Leidel, 510 So. Farwell St, Eau Claire, WI 54701
Tel: 1 715 835 3331
Fax: 1 715 835 9212
email: jstout@dioec.org
Web: www.dioec.com

EL CAMINO REAL (Province VIII)
Bishop Rt Revd Mary Gray-Reeves, 1092 Noche Buena St, Seaside, CA 93955, USA
Tel: 1 831 394 4465
Fax: 1 831 394 7133
email: bishopmary@edecr.org
Web: www.edecr.org

EUROPE, CONVOCATION OF EPISCOPAL CHURCHES IN
Bishop in Charge Rt Revd Pierre Welté Whalon, American Cathedral of the Holy Trinity, 23 Avenue George V, 75008 Paris, France
Tel: 33 1 53 23 84 06
Fax: 33 1 49 52 96 85
email: bishops@tec-europe.org
Web: www.tec-europe.org

FLORIDA (Province IV)
Bishop Rt Revd Samuel Johnson Howard, 325 Market St, Jacksonville, FL 32202, USA
Tel: 1 904 356 1328
Fax: 1 904 355 1934
email: diocese@diocesefl.org
Web: www.diocesefl.org

FOND DU LAC (Province V)
Bishop Rt Revd Russell Edward Jacobus, 1051 N. Lynndale Dr., Suite 1B, Appleton, WI 54914, USA
Tel: 1 920 830 8866
Fax: 1 920 830 8761
email: diofdl@diofdl.org
Web: www.diofdl.org

FORT WORTH (Province VII)
Provisional Bishop Rt Revd C. Wallis Ohl, 3550 Southwest Loop 820, Fort Worth, Texas 76133, USA *Tel:* 1 817 921 4533
Fax: 1 817 926 8278
email: bishop@episcopaldiocesefortworth.org
Web: www.episcopaldiocesefortworth.org

GEORGIA (Province IV)
Bishop Rt Revd Scott Anson Benhase, 611 E Bay St, Savannah, GA 31401–1296, USA
Tel: 1 912 236 4279
Fax: 1 912 236 2007
email: bishop@gaepiscopal.org
Web: www.gaepiscopal.org

HAITI (Province II)
Bishop Rt Revd Jean-Zaché Duracin, Église Épiscopale d'Haiti, Boite Postale 1309, Port-au-Prince, Haiti *Tel:* 509 257 1624
Fax: 509 257 3412
email: epihaiti@egliseepiscopaledhaiti.org
Web: egliseepiscopaledhaiti.org

HAWAII (Province VIII)
Bishop Rt Revd Robert L. Fitzpatrick, Diocesan Office, 229 Queen Emma Sq, Honolulu, HI 96813, USA *Tel:* 1 808 536 8166
Fax: 1 808 538 7194
email: bishopsecretary@episcopalhawaii.org
Web: www.episcopalhawaii.org

HONDURAS (Province IX)
Bishop Rt Revd Lloyd E. Allen, Colonia Trejo 23 Av 21 Calle,San Pedro Sula, Honduras 21105
Tel: 504 556 6155/6268
Fax: 504 566 6467
email: Honduras@anglicano.hn

IDAHO (Province VIII)
Bishop Rt Revd Brian James Thom, 1858 W. Judith Lane, Boise, ID 83705 *Tel:* 1 208 345 4440
Fax: 1 208 345 9735
email: bthom@idahodiocese.org
Web: episcopalidaho.org

INDIANAPOLIS (Province V)
Bishop Rt Revd Catherine Elizabeth Maples Waynick, 1100 W 42nd St, Indianapolis, IN 46208, USA *Tel:* 1 317 926 5454
Fax: 1 317 926 5456
email: bishop@indydio.org
Web: www.indydio.org

IOWA (Province VI)
Bishop Rt Revd Alan Scarfe, 225 37th St, Des Moines, IA 50312–4305, USA *Tel:* 1 515 277 6165
Fax: 1 515 277 0273
email: Ascarfe@iowaepiscopal.org
Web: www.iowaepiscopal.org

KANSAS (Province VII)
Bishop Rt Revd Dean Eliott Wolfe, Bethany Place, 835 SW Polk St, Topeka, KS 66612–1688, USA
Tel: 1 785 235 9255
Fax: 1 785 235 2449
email: dwolfe@episcopal-ks.org
Web: www.episcopal-ks.org

KENTUCKY (Province IV)
Bishop Rt Revd Terry Allen White, 425 S Second St, Louisville, KY 40202, USA
Tel: 1 502 584 7148
Fax: 1 502 587 8123
email: bishopwhite@episopalky.org
Web: www.episcopalky.org

LEXINGTON (Province IV)
Interim Bishop Rt Revd Chilton A. R. Knudsen, 203 E. Fourth St, Lexington, KY 40508, USA
Tel: 1 859 252 6527
Fax: 1 859 231 9077
email: chiltonknudson@diolex.org
Web: www.diolex.org

LITORAL ECUADOR (Province IX)
Bishop Rt Revd Alfredo Morante-Espana, Box 0901–5250Calle Amarillis Fuentes entre Av IV Trujillo y Calle D. Barrio Centenaro, Guayaquil-Ecuador
Tel: 593 4 443 050
Fax: 593 4 443 088
email: iglesia_litoral@hotmail.com

LONG ISLAND (Province II)
Bishop Rt Revd Lawrence C Provenzano, 36 Cathedral Ave, Garden City, NY 11530–0510
Tel: 1 516 248 4800
Fax: 1 516 248 1616
email: lprovenzano@dioceseli.org
Web: www.dioceselongisland.org

LOS ANGELES (Province VIII)
Bishop Rt Revd Joseph Jon Bruno, 940 Echo Park Ave, Box 512164, Los Angeles, CA 90051, USA
Tel: 1 213 482 2040
Fax: 1 213 482 5340
email: bishop@ladiocese.org
Web: www.ladiocese.org

Bishops Suffragan
Rt Revd Diane M. Jardine Bruce (*same address*)
email: djbsuffragan@ladiocese.org
Rt Revd Mary Douglas Glasspool (*same address*)
email: mdgsuffragan@ladiocese.org

LOUISIANA (Province IV)
Bishop Rt Revd Morris K. Thompson, 205 N 4th St, Baton Rouge, LA 70821–5026, USA
Tel: 1 225 706 6634
Fax: 225 706 6653
email: mthompson@edola.org
Web: www.edola.org

MAINE (Province I)
Bishop Rt Revd Stephen T. Lane, Loring House, 143 State St, Portland, ME 04101–3799, USA
Tel: 1 207 772 1953
Fax: 1 207 773 0095
email: slane@episcopalmaine.org
Web: www.episcopalmaine.org

MARYLAND (Province III)
Bishop Rt Revd Eugene Taylor Sutton, 4 East University Parkway, Baltimore, MD 21218, USA
Tel: 1 410 467 1399
Fax: 1 410 554 6387
email: esutton@and-md.org
Web: www.episcopalmaine.org

Assistant Bishop Rt Revd Joe Goodwin Burnett (*same address*)
email: jburnett@episcoplamaryland.org

MASSACHUSETTS (Province I)
Bishop Rt Revd M. Thomas Shaw SSJE, 138 Tremont St, Boston, MA 02111–1318, USA
Tel: 1 617 482 5800
Fax: 1 617 482 8431
email: jdrapeau@diomass.org
Web: www.diomass.org

Bishops Suffragan
Rt Revd Roy F. (Bud) Cederholm, Jr (*same address*) *email:* dianep@diomass.org

Rt Revd Gayle E. Harris (*same address*)
email: SHP@diomass.org

MICHIGAN (Province V)
Bishop Rt Revd Wendell Nathaniel Gibbs Jr, 4800 Woodward Ave, Detroit, MI 48201, USA
Tel: 1 313 833 4000
Fax: 1 313 831 0259
email: Wgibbs@edomi.org
Web: www.edomi.org

MILWAUKEE (Province V)
Bishop Rt Revd Steven Andrew Miller, 804 E Juneau Ave, Milwaukee, WI 53202–2798
Tel: 1 414 272 3028
Fax: 1 414 272 7790
email: bishop11@diomil.org
Web: www.diomil.org

MINNESOTA (Province VI)
Bishop Rt Revd Brian N. Prior, 1730 Clifton Place, Suite 201, Minneapolis, MN 55403-3242, USA
Tel: 1 612 871 5311
Fax: 1 612 871 0552
email: episcopal.centre@episcopalmn.org
Web: www.episcopalmn.org

MISSISSIPPI (Province IV)
Bishop Rt Revd Duncan Montgomery Gray III, 118 N Congress St, PO Box 23107, Jackson, MS 39225–3107, USA
Tel: 1 601 948 5954
Fax: 1 601 354 3401
email: pjones@dioms.org
Web: www.dioms.org

MISSOURI (Province V)
Bishop Rt Revd George Wayne Smith, 1210 Locust St, St Louis, MO 63103, USA
Tel: 1 314 231 1220
Fax: 1 314 231 3373
email: bishop@diocesemo.org
Web: www.diocesemo.org

MONTANA (Province VI)
Bishop Rt Revd C. Franklin Brookhart, 515 North Park Ave, Helena, MT 59601–8135, USA
Tel: 1 406 442 2230
Fax: 1 406 442 2238
email: cfbmt@qwestoffice.net
Web: www.mtepispcopal.org

NAVAJOLAND AREA MISSION (Province VIII)
Bishop Rt Revd Rt Revd David Earle Bailey, 1225 Mission Avenue,, Farmington, NM 87499–0720, USA
Tel: 1 505 327 7549
Fax: 1 505 327 6904
email: dbaileyecn@cox.net
Web: www.episcopal-navajo.org

NEBRASKA (Province VI)
Bishop J. Scott Barker,, 109 N 18th St, Omaha, NE 68102, USA *Tel:* 1 402 341 5373
Fax: 1 402 341 8683
email: sbarker@episcopal-ne.org
Web: www.episcopal-ne.org

NEVADA (Province VIII)
Bishop Rt Revd Dan T. Edwards, 6135 S Harrison Drive, Suite 1B, Las Vegas, NV 89120–4076, USA
Tel: 1 702 737 9190
Fax: 1 702 737 6488
email: bishop@nvdiocese.org
Web: www.episcopalnevada.org

NEW HAMPSHIRE (Province I)
Bishop Rt Revd A. Robert Hirschfeld, 63 Green St, Concord, NH 03301, USA
Tel: 1 603 224 1914
Fax: 1 603 225 7884
email: pbibber@nhepiscopal.org
Web: www.nhepiscopal.org

NEW JERSEY (Province II)
Bishop Rt Revd George Edward Councell, 808 West State Street, Trenton, NJ 08618–5326, USA
Tel: 1 609 394 5281
Fax: 1 609 394 9546
email: gcouncell@newjersey.anglican.org
Web: www.newjersey.anglican.org

NEW YORK (Province II)
Bishop Rt Revd Mark Sean Sisk, Synod House, 1047 Amsterdam Ave, New York, NY 10025, USA *Tel:* 1 212 316 7400
Fax: 1 212 316 7405
email: bpsisk@dioceseny.org
Web: www.dioceseny.org

Assistant Bishop Rt Revd Andrew Donnan Smith
email: bpsmith@dioceseny.org

NEWARK (Province II)
Bishop Rt Revd Mark Beckwith, 31 Mulberry St, Newark, NJ 07102, USA *Tel:* 1 923 430 9900
Fax: 1 923 622 3503
email: mbeckwith@dioceseofnewark.org
Web: www.dioceseofnewark.org

NORTH CAROLINA (Province IV)
Bishop Rt Revd Michael Bruce Curry, 200 West Morgan St, Suite 300, Raleigh, NC 27601, USA
Tel: 1 919 834 7474
Fax: 1 919 834 7546
email: michael.curry@episdionc.org
Web: www.episdionc.org

Assistant Bishop William O. Gregg
email: william.gregg@episdionc.org

Assisting Bishop Alfred (Chip) Marble Jr
email: chip.marble@episdionc.org

NORTH DAKOTA (Province VI)
Bishop Rt Revd Michael G. Smith, 3600 S. 25th St, Fargo, ND 58104–6861, USA *Tel:* 1 701 235 6688
Fax: 1 701 232 3077
email: BpNodak@aol.com
Web: www.episcopal-nd.org

NORTHERN CALIFORNIA (Province VIII)
Bishop Rt Revd Barry Leigh Beisner, , 1318 27th St, Sacramento, CA 95816 *Tel:* 1 916 442 6918
Fax: 1 916 442 6927
email: barry@norcalepiscopal.org
Web: norcalepiscopal.org

NORTHERN INDIANA (Province V)
Bishop Rt Revd Edward Stuart Little II, 117 N Lafayette Blvd, South Bend, Indiana 46601, USA
Tel: 1 574 233 6489
Fax: 1 574 287 7914
email: bishop@ednin.org/info@ednin.org
Web: www.ednin.org

NORTHERN MICHIGAN (Province V)
Bishop Rt Revd Rayford J. Ray, 131 E Ridge St, Marquette, MI 49855, USA *Tel:* 1 906 228 7160
Fax: 1 906 228 7171
email: rayfordray@chartermi.net
Web: www.upepiscopal.org

NORTHWEST TEXAS (Province VII)
Bishop Rt Revd James Scott Mayer, The Hulsey Episcopal Center, 1802 Broadway, Lubbock, TX 79401, USA *Tel:* 1 806 763 1370
Fax: 1 806 472 0641
email: diocese@nwtdiocese.org
Web: www.nwtdiocese.org

NORTHWESTERN PENNSYLVANIA (Province III)
Bishop Rt Revd Sean W. Rowe, 145 W 6th St, Erie, PA 16501, USA *Tel:* 1 814 456 4203
Fax: 1 814 454 8703
email: dionwpa@dionwpa.org
Web: www.dionwpa.org

OHIO (Province V)
Bishop Rt Revd Mark Hollingsworth Jr, 2230 Euclid Ave, Cleveland, OH 44115–2499, USA
Tel: 1 216 771 4815
Fax: 1 216 623 0735
email: mh@dohio.org
Web: www.dohio.org

Assisting Bishops
Rt Revd David L. Bowman (*same address*)
Rt Revd William Dailey Persell (*same address*)
Rt Revd Arthur B. Williams Jr
email: wperseel@dohio.org

OKLAHOMA (Province VII)
Bishop Rt Revd Edward Joseph Konieczny, 924 N Robinson, Oklahoma City, OK 73102, USA
Tel: 1 405 232 4820
Fax: 1 405 232 4912
email: bishoped@epiok.org
Web: www.epiok.org

OLYMPIA (Province VIII)
Bishop Rt Revd Gregory H. Rickel, 1551 10th Avenue, Seattle, WA 98102, USA
Tel: 1 206 325 4200
Fax: 1 206 325 4631
email: grickel@ecww.org
Web: www.ecww.org

OREGON (Province VIII)
Bishop Michael Joseph Hanley, 11800 S.W. Military Lane, Portland, OR 97219, USA
Tel: 1 503 636 5613
Fax: 1 503 636 5616
email: bishop@episcopaldioceseoregon.org
Web: www.episcopaldioceseoregon.org

PENNSYLVANIA (Province III)
Bishop Rt Revd Charles Ellsworth Bennison Jr, 240 South Fourth St, Philadelphia, PA 19106, USA
Tel: 1 215 627 6434
Fax: 1 215 627 2323
email: mail@diopa.org
Web: www.diopa.org

Assisting Bishop Rodney Rae Michel
email: rodmitre@aol.com

PITTSBURGH (Province III)
Provisional Bishop Rt Revd Kenneth L. Price, 4099 William Penn Hwy, Suite 502, Monroeville, PA 15146, USA *Tel:* 1 412 721 0853
email: office @episcopalpgh.org
Web: ibwww.epsicopalpgh.org

PUERTO RICO (Province IX)
Bishop Rt Revd David Andres Alvarez, PO Box 902, St Just, PR 00978–0902, Puerto Rico
Tel: 1 787 761 9800
Fax: 1 787 761 0320
email: iep@episcopalpr.org
Web: www.episcopalpr.org

QUINCY (Province V)
Provisional Bishop Rt Revd John Clark Buchanan, c/o St Paul's Cathedral, 3601 N North St, Peoria, IL 61604–1517, USA *Tel:* 1 309 685 8673
Fax: 1 309 685 8682
email: bishopbuchanan@hotmail.com
Web: www.thedioceseofquincyonline.com

RHODE ISLAND (Province I)
Bishop Rt Revd Geralyn Wolf, 275 N Main St, Providence, RI 02903–1298, USA
Tel: 1 401 274 4500
Fax: 1 401 331 9430
email: bishop@episcopalri.org
Web: www.episcopalri.org

RIO GRANDE (Province VII)
Bishop Rt Revd Michael Louis Vono, 4304 Carlisle Blvd NE, Albuquerque, NM 87107–4811, USA *Tel:* 1 505 881 0636
Fax: 1 505 883 9048
email: bpmichael@dioceserg.org
Web: www.dioceserg.org

ROCHESTER (Province II)
Bishop Rt Revd Prince Grenville Singh, 935 East Ave, Rochester, NY 14607, USA
Tel: 1 585 473 2977
Fax: 1 585 473 3195
email: prince@rochesterepiscopaldiocese.org
Web: rochesterepiscopaldiocese.org

SAN DIEGO (Province VIII)
Bishop Rt Revd James Robert Mathes, 2728 Sixth St, San Diego, CA 92103, USA
Tel: 1 619 291 5947
Fax: 1 619 291 8362
email: bishopmathes@edsd.org
Web: www.edsd.org

SAN JOAQUIN (Province VIII)
Provisional Bishop Rt Revd Chester L. Talton, 1528 Oakdale Road, Modesto, CA 95355, USA
Tel: 1 209 576 0104
Fax: 1 209 576 0114
email: bishop@diosanjoaquin.org
Web: www.diosanjoaquin.org

SOUTH CAROLINA (Province IV)
Bishop Rt Revd Mark Joseph Lawrence, 126 Coming St, Charleston, SC 29403, USA
Tel: 1 843 722 4075
Fax: 1 843 723 7628
email: bsnyder@dioceseofsc.org
Web: www.dioceseofsc.org

SOUTH DAKOTA (Province VI)
Bishop Rt Revd John T. Tarrant, 500 S Main Avenue, Sioux Falls, South Dakota 57104–6814, USA *Tel:* 1 605 338 9751
Fax: 1 605 336 6243
email: bishop.diocese@midconetwork.com
Web: www.diocesesd.org

SOUTHEAST FLORIDA (Province IV)
Bishop Rt Revd Leopold Frade, 525 NE 15 St, Miami, FL 33132, USA *Tel:* 1 305 373 0881
Fax: 1 305 375 8054
email: bishopfrade@aol.com
Web: www.diosef.org

SOUTHERN OHIO (Province V)
Bishop Rt Revd Thomas E. Breidenthal, 412 Sycamore St, Cincinnati, OH 45202, USA
Tel: 1 513 421 0311
Fax: 1 513 421 0315
email: tbreidenthal@diosohio.org
Web: www.diosohio.org

Bishop Suffragan Rt Revd Kenneth L. Price, 125 Broad St, Columbus, OH 43215–3649
Tel: 1 800 582 1712
Fax: 1 614 461 0315

SOUTHERN VIRGINIA (Province III)
Bishop Rt Revd Herman 'Holly' Hollerith IV, 600 Talbot Hall Rd, Norfolk, VA 23505–4301, USA
Tel: 1 757 423 8287
Fax: 1 757 440 5354
email: bishop@diosova.org
Web: www.diosova.org

SOUTHWEST FLORIDA (Province IV)
Bishop Rt Revd Dabney T. Smith, 7313 Merchant Ct, Sarasota, FL 34240–8437, USA
Tel: 1 941 556 0315
Fax: 1 941 556 0321
email: jnothum @episcopalswfla.org
Web: www.episcopalswfla.org

SOUTHWESTERN VIRGINIA (Province III)
Bishop Frank Neff Powell, 1002 First Street SW, Roanoke, VA 24016, USA *Tel:* 1 540 342 6797
Fax: 1 540 343 9114
email: npowell @dioswva.org
Web: www.dioswva.org

SPOKANE (Province VIII)
Bishop Rt Revd James Edward Waggoner Jr, 245 E 13th Ave, Spokane, WA 99202–1114, USA
Tel: 1 509 624 3191
Fax: 1 509 747 0049
email: jimw@spokanediocese.org
Web: www.spokanediocese.org

SPRINGFIELD (Province V)
Bishop Rt Revd Daniel Hayden Martins, 821 S 2nd St, Springfield, IL 62704, USA
Tel: 1 217 525 1876
Fax: 1 217 525 1877
email: bishop@episcopalspringfield.org
Web: www.episcopalspringfield.org

TAIWAN (Province VIII)
Bishop Rt Revd David J. H. Lai, Friendship House, 7 Lane 105, Hangchow South Rd, Sec. 1, Taipei, Taiwan 10060, Republic of China
Tel: 886 2 2341 1265
Fax: 886 2 2396 2014
email: skhtpe@ms12.hinet.net
Web: www.episcopaldiotaiwan@blogspot.com

TENNESSEE (Province IV)
Bishop Rt Revd John C. Bauerschmidt, 50 Vantage Way, Suite 107, Nashville, TN 37228, USA
Tel: 1 615 251 3322
Fax: 1 615 251 8010
email: info@episcopaldiocese-tn.org
Web: www.episcopaldiocese-tn.org

TEXAS (Province VII)
Bishop Rt Revd C. Andrew Doyle, 1225 Texas Ave, Houston, TX 77002–3504, USA
Tel: 1 713 520 6444
Fax: 1 713 520 5723
email: adoyle@epicenter.org
Web: www.epicenter.org

Suffragan Bishop Dena A. Harrison, 510 Rathervue Pl, PO Box 2247, Austin, TX 78768–2247
Tel: 1 512 478 0580
Fax: 1 512 478 5615
*email:*dharrison@epicenter.org

UPPER SOUTH CAROLINA (Province IV)
Bishop Rt Revd W. Andrew Waldo, 1115 Marion St, Columbia, SC 29201, USA
Tel: 1 803 771 7800
Fax: 1 803 799 5119
email: bishopwaldo@edusc.org
Web: www.edusc.org

UTAH (Province VIII)
Bishop Rt Revd Scott B. Hayashi, 75 South 200 East, Salt Lake City, UT 84110–3090, USA
Tel: 1 801 322 4131
Fax: 1 801 322 5096
email: shayashi@episcopal-ut.org
Web: www.episcopal-ut.org

VENEZUELA (Province IX)
Bishop Rt Revd Orlando Guerrero, Avenida Caroni 100, Colinas de Bello Monte, Caracas 1042-A, Venezuela
Tel: 58 212 753 0723
Fax: 58 212 751 3180
email: obispoguerrero@iglesianglicanavzla.org
Web: www.iglesianglicanavzla.org

VERMONT (Province I)
Bishop Rt Revd Thomas Clark Ely, 5 Rock Point Road, Burlington, VT 05408–2735, USA
Tel: 1 802 863 3431
Fax: 1 802 860 1562
email: adminasst @dioceseofvermont.org
Web: www.dioceseofvermont.org

VIRGIN ISLANDS (Province II)
Bishop Rt Revd Rt Revd Ambrose Gumbs, 13 Commandant Gade, Charlotte Amalie, VI 00801, USA
Tel: 1 340 776 1797
Fax: 1 340 777 8485
email: bpambrosegumbs@yahoo.com
Web: www.episcopalvi.com

VIRGINIA (Province III)
Bishop Rt Revd Shannon S. Johnston, 110 W Franklin St, Richmond, VA 23220
Tel: 1 804 643 8451
Fax: 1 804 644 6928
email: sjohnston@thediocese.net
Web: www.thediocese.net

Assistant Bishop
Rt Revd Edwin F. (Ted) Gulick, 110 W Franklin St, Richmond, VA 23220
email: tgulick@thediocese.net

WASHINGTON DC (Province III)
Bishop Mariann Edgar Budde, Episcopal Church House, Mount St Alban, Washington, DC 20016–5094, USA
Tel: 1 202 537 6555
Fax: 1 202 364 6605
email: mebudde @edow.org
Web: www.edow.org

WEST MISSOURI (Province VII)
Bishop Rt Revd Martin Scott Field, 420 W 14th St, Kansas City, MO 64105–3227, USA
Tel: 1 816 471 6161
Fax: 1 816 471 0379
email: bishopfield@diowestmol.org
Web: www.diowestmo.org

WEST TENNESSEE (Province IV)
Bishop Rt Revd Don Edward Johnson, 692 Poplar Ave, Memphis, TN 38105, USA
Tel: 1 901 526 0023
Fax: 1 901 526 1555
email: bishopjohnson@episwtn.org
Web: www.episwtn.org

WEST TEXAS (Province VII)
Bishop Rt Revd Gary R. Lillibridge, 111 Torcido Dr, San Antonio, TX 78209, USA
Tel: 1 210 824 5387
Fax: 1 210 824 2164
email: gary.lillibridge@dwtx.org
Web: www.dwtx.org

Bishop Suffragan Rt Revd David Reed (*same address*) *email:* email: david.reed@dwtx.org

WEST VIRGINIA (Province III)
Bishop Rt Revd W. Michie Klusmeyer, 1608 Virginia St East, Charleston, WV 25311–2114, USA *Tel:* 1 304 344 3597
Fax: 1 304 343 3295
email: mklusmeyer@wvdiocese.org
Web: www.wvdiocese.org

WESTERN KANSAS (Province VII)
Bishop Rt Revd Michael P. Milliken, 2 Hyde Park Dr, Hutchinson, KS 67502 *Tel:* 1 785 825 1626
Fax: 785 825 0974
email: tec.wks2011@gmail.com
Web: www.diowks.org

WESTERN LOUISIANA (Province VII)
Bishop Rt Revd D. Bruce MacPherson, 335 Main St, Pineville,LA 71360, USA
Tel: 1 318 422 1304
Fax: 1 318 442 8712
email: bishop@diocesewla.org
Web: www.diocesewla.org

WESTERN MASSACHUSETTS (Province I)
Bishop Rt Revd Gordon P. Scruton, 37 Chestnut St, Springfield, MA 01103, USA
Tel: 1 413 737 4786
Fax: 1 413 746 9873
email: diocese@diocesewma.org
Web: www.diocesewma.org

WESTERN MICHIGAN (Province V)
Bishop Rt Revd Robert R. Gepert, Episcopal Center, 535 Burdick St, Suite 1, Kalamazoo, MI 49007, USA *Tel:* 1 269 381 2710
Fax: 1 269 381 7067
email: rrgsupport@edwm.org
Web: www.edwm.org

WESTERN NEW YORK (Province II)
Bishop Rt Revd R. William Franklin, 114 Delaware Ave, Buffalo, NY 14209, USA
Tel: 1 716 881 0660
Fax: 1 716 881 1724
email: rwfranklin@episcopalwny.org
Web: www.episcopalwny.org

WESTERN NORTH CAROLINA (Province IV)
Bishop Rt Revd Granville Porter Taylor, 900B Centre Park Drive, Asheville, NC 28805, USA
Tel: 1 828 225 6656
Fax: 1 828 225 6657
email: bishop@diocesewnc.org
Web: www.diocesewnc.org

WYOMING (Province VI)
Bishop Rt Revd John S. Smylie, 123 S. Durbin St, Casper WY 82601, USA *Tel:* 1 307 225 6656
Fax: 1 307 577 9939
email: bishopsmylie@wyomingdiocese.org
Web: www.wyoming diocese.org

The Church in Wales

Members 66,720
The Church in Wales has been an independent province since its disestablishment and separation from the Church of England in 1920. It is practically coterminous with Wales and is the largest denomination in the country. The major policy-forming body is the Governing Body and the Church's inherited assets, including buildings, are held in trust by the Representative Body.

Archbishop Most Revd Barry Cennydd Morgan (*Bishop of Llandaff*) *Tel:* 029 2056 2400
Fax: 029 2056 8410
email: archbishop@churchinwales.org.uk

Provincial Secretary and Archbishop's Registrar Mr John Shirley, 39 Cathedral Rd, Cardiff CF11 9XF
Tel: 029 2034 8218
Fax: 029 2038 7835
email: information@churchinwales.org.uk
Web: www.churchinwales.org.uk

Archbishop's Media Officer Anna Morrell (*same address*) *Tel:* 029 2034 8208

THEOLOGICAL COLLEGE
St Michael's Theological College, 54 Cardiff Road, Llandaff, Cardiff CF5 2YJ (*Warden and Principal* Revd Canon Dr Peter H. Sedgwick)
Tel: 029 2056 3379
Fax: 029 2083 8008
email: info@stmichaels.ac.uk

BANGOR
Bishop Rt Revd Andrew Thomas Griffith John, Ty'r Esgob, Ffordd Garth Uchaf, Bangor, Gwynedd LL57 2SS *Tel:* 01248 362895
Fax: 01248 372454
email: bishop.bangor@churchinwales.org.uk
Web: www.churchinwales.org.uk/bangor

CATHEDRAL CHURCH OF ST DEINIOL, Bangor, Gwynedd
Dean The Very Reverend Alun John Hawkins, The Deanery, Cathedral Precinct, Bangor LL57 1LH *Tel:* 01248 362840

LLANDAFF
Bishop Most Revd Dr Barry Cennydd Morgan (*Archbishop of the Province*), Llys Esgob, The Cathedral Green, Llandaff, Cardiff CF5 2YE
Tel: 029 2056 2400
Fax: 029 2056 8410
email: archbishop@churchinwales.org.uk
Web: www.churchinwales.org.uk/llandaff

Assistant Bishop of Llandaff, Rt Revd David Jeffrey Wilbourne, Llys Esgob, The Cathedral Green, Cardiff CF5 2YE *Tel:* 029 20 562400
Fax: 029 2057 7129
email: asstbishop@churchinwales.org.uk

CATHEDRAL CHURCH OF ST PETER AND ST PAUL, Llandaff, Cardiff
Dean Very Revd John Lewis, The Deanery, The Cathedral Green, Llandaff, Cardiff CF5 2YF
Tel: 029 2056 1545

MONMOUTH
Bishop Rt Revd Dominic Walker OGS, Bishopstow, 91a Stow Hill, Newport NP20 4EA
Tel: 01633 263510
Fax: 01633 259946
email: bishop.monmouth@churchinwales.org.uk
Web: www.churchinwales.org.uk/monmouth

CATHEDRAL CHURCH OF ST WOOLOS, Newport
Dean Very Revd Dr Richard Fenwick, The Deanery, Stow Hill, Newport NP20 4ED
Tel: 01633 263338

ST ASAPH
Bishop Rt Revd Gregory Kenneth Cameron, Esgobty, Upper Denbigh Road, St Asaph LL17 0TW *Tel:* 01745 583503
Fax: 01745 584301
email: bishop.stasaph@churchinwales.org.uk
Web: www.churchinwales.org.uk/asaph

CATHEDRAL CHURCH OF ST ASAPH, St Asaph, Denbighshire
Dean Very Revd Christopher Potter, The Deanery, Upper Denbigh Road, St Asaph LL17 0RL *Tel:* 01745 583597
email: chris_potter@btinternet.com

ST DAVIDS
Bishop Rt Revd J. Wyn Evans, Llys Esgob, Abergwili, Carmarthen SA31 2JG
Tel: 01267 236597
Fax: 01267 243381
email: bishop.stdavids@churchinwales.org.uk
Web: www.churchinwales.org.uk/david

CATHEDRAL CHURCH OF ST DAVID AND ST ANDREW, St Davids, Pembrokeshire
Dean Very Revd David Jonathan Rees Lean, The Deanery, St Davids, Haverfordwest SA62 6RH *Tel:* 01437 720456
Fax: 01437 721885

SWANSEA AND BRECON
Bishop Rt Revd John David Edward Davies, Ely Tower, Castle Square, Brecon LD3 9DJ
Tel: 01874 622008
Fax: 01874 610927
email: bishop.swanbrec @churchinwales.org.uk
Web: www.churchinwales.org.uk/swanbrec

CATHEDRAL CHURCH OF ST JOHN THE EVANGELIST, Brecon, Powys
Dean Very Revd Geoffrey Osborne Marshall, The Deanery, Cathedral Close, Brecon LD3 9DP
Tel: 01874 623344
email: admin@breconcathedral.org.uk

ANGLICAN AND PORVOO COMMUNIONS

The Church of the Province of West Africa

Members 1,220,000
Church work began in Ghana as early as 1752 and in the Gambia, Guinea, Liberia and Sierra Leone in the nineteenth century. The Province of West Africa was founded in 1951 and was divided to form the Province of Nigeria and the Province of West Africa in 1979. The Church exists in an atmosphere of civil strife and Christians remain a minority.

Archbishop and Primate of the Province of West Africa Most Revd Dr Justice Ofei Akrofi (*Bishop of Accra*)

Dean of the Province of West Africa Rt Revd Albert D. Gomez (*Bishop of Guinea*)

Episcopal Secretary of the Province of West Africa Rt Revd Matthias K. Medadues-Badohu (*Bishop of Ho*)

Provincial Secretary Revd Canon Anthony M. Eiwuley, PO Box Lt 226, Lartebiokorshie, Accra, Ghana *Tel:* 233 302 257 370
233 27 720 1538 (Mobile)
email: cpwa@4u.com.gh/ morkeiwuley@gmail.com

Provincial Treasurer Mr Samuel Atuobi Twum (*same address*) *Tel:* 233 21 506 208
233 20 201 7969 (Mobile)
email: atlantichousing@yahoo.co.uk

THEOLOGICAL COLLEGES
Ghana
Trinity College (Ecumenical), PO Box 48, Legon, Ghana

St Nicholas Anglican Theological College, PO Box A 162, Cape Coast, Ghana

Liberia
Cuttington University College, Suacoco, PO Box 10–0277, 1000 Monrovia 10, Liberia

Sierra Leone
Theological Hall and Church Training Centre, PO Box 128, Freetown, Sierra Leone

ACCRA
Bishop Most Revd Dr Justice Ofei Akrofi, Bishopscourt, PO Box 8, Accra, Ghana
Tel: 233 302 662 292
Fax: 233 302 668 822
email: cpwa@4u.com.gh/ bishopakrofi@yahoo.com
Web: www.acceaanglican.org

Coadjutor Bishop Rt Revd Dr Daniel S. M. Torto (*same address*) *Tel:* 233 277 496 479 (Mobile)
email: dantorto@yahoo.com

BO
Bishop Rt Revd Emmanuel Josie Samuel Tucker, PO Box 21, Bo, Southern Province, Sierra Leone
Tel: 232 32 648
Fax: 232 32 605
232 76 677 862 (Mobile)
email: bomission@justice.com/ ejstucker@gmail.com

CAMEROON
Bishop Rt. Revd. Thomas-Babyngton Elango Dibo, BP 15705, New Bell, Douala, Cameroon
Tel: 237 755 58276
email: revdibo2@yahoo.com

CAPE COAST
Bishop Rt Revd Daniel S. A. Allotey, Bishopscourt, PO Box A 233, Adisadel Estates, Cape Coast, Ghana *Tel:* 233 3321 23 502
233 275 418 915 (Mobile)
Fax: 233 42 32 637
email: danallotey@priest.com

DUNKWA-ON-OFFIN
Bishop Rt Revd Edmund K. Dawson-Ahmoah, PO Box DW42, Dunkwa-on-Offin
233 24 464 4764 (Mobile)
email: papacy11@yahoo.co.uk

FREETOWN
Bishop Rt Revd Julius Olotu Prince Lynch, Bishop's Court, PO Box 537, Freetown, Sierra Leone *Tel:* 232 22 251 307
232 76 620 690 (Mobile)
email: bertajuls@yahoo.co.uk

GAMBIA
Bishop Rt Revd Dr Tilewa Johnson, Bishopscourt, PO Box 51, Banjul, The Gambia, West Africa *Tel:* 220 228 405
220 905 227 (Mobile)
email: stilewaj@hotmail.com
Web: www.gambiadiocese.com

GUINEA
Bishop Rt Revd Albert D. Gomez, BP 187, Conakry, Guinea *Tel:* 224 451 323
email: galbertdgomez@yahoo.fr

Coadjutor Bishop Rt Revd Jacques Boston (*same address*) *Tel:* 224 63 58 79 38 (Mobile)
email: bostonjacques@yahoo.com

HO
Bishop Rt Revd Matthias K. Mededues-Badohu, Bishopslodge, PO Box MA 300, Ho, Volta Region, Ghana *Tel:* 233 3620 26644 / 233 3620 28606
233 208 162 246 (Mobile)
email: matthoda@ucomgh.com/ matthiaskwab@googlemail.com

KOFORIDUA
Bishop Rt Revd Francis B. Quashie, PO Box 980, Koforidua, Ghana *Tel:* 233 3420 22 329
Fax: 233 81 22 060
email: fbquashie@yahoo.com

KUMASI
Bishop Rt Revd Daniel Yinka Sarfo, Bishop's House, PO Box 144, Kumasi, Ghana
Tel and *Fax:* 233 51 24 117
233 277 890 411 (Mobile)
email: anglicandioceseofkumasi@yahoo.com / dysarfo2000@yahoo.co.uk

Suffragan Bishop Rt Revd Dr Cyril K. Ben-Smith (*same address*) *Tel:* 233 2477 4308 (Mobile)
email: bishop. mampong@yahoo.co.uk

LIBERIA
Bishop Rt Revd Jonathan B. B. Hart, PO Box 10–0277, 1000 Monrovia 10, Liberia
Tel: 231 224 760
231 651 6343 (Mobile)
Fax: 231 227 519
email: jbbhart@yahoo.com / bishopecl12@yahoo.com
Web: www.liberia.anglican.org

SEKONDI
Bishop Rt Revd Col John Kwamina Otoo, PO Box 85, Sekondi, Ghana *Tel:* 233 3120 46832
233 208 200887 (Mobile)
email: angdiocesek@yahoo.co.uk

SUNYANI
Bishop Rt Revd Dr. Festus Yeboah-Asuamah, PO Box 23, Sunyani, Ghana *Tel:* 233 3520 23213
233 208 121 670 (Mobile)
Fax: 233 61 712300
email: fyasuamah@yahoo.com

TAMALE
Bishop Rt Revd (Hon) Dr Jacob K. Ayeebo, PO Box 110, Tamale, Ghana *Tel:* 233 3720 26639
233 243 419 864 (Mobile)
Fax: 233 3729 22906
email: bishopea2000@yahoo.com

WIAWSO
Bishop Rt Revd Abraham Kobina Ackah, PO Box 4, Sefwi, Wiawso, Ghana
Tel: 233 274 005 952 (Mobile)
email: bishopackah@yahoo.com

The Church in the Province of the West Indies

Members 770,000
The West Indies became a self-governing province of the worldwide Anglican Communion in 1883 because of the Church of England missions in territories that became British colonies. It is made up of two mainland dioceses, Belize and Guyana, and six island dioceses including the Bahamas and Turks and Caicos Islands, Barbados, Jamaica and the Cayman Islands, North Eastern Caribbean and Aruba, Trinidad and Tobago, and the Windward Islands. Great emphasis is being placed on training personnel for an indigenous ministry as the island locations and scattered settlements make pastoral care difficult and costly.

Archbishop of the Province Most Revd Dr John Walder Dunlop Holder *Fax:* 1 246 426 0871

Provincial Secretary Mrs Elenor Lawrence, Provincial Secretariat, Bamford House, Society Hill, St John, Barbados, West Indies
Tel: 1246 423 0842/3/8
Fax: 1 246 423 0855
email: bamford@sunbeach.net

THEOLOGICAL SEMINARIES
Codrington College, St John, Barbados (*Principal* Revd Dr Ian Rock)

United Theological College of the West Indies, PO Box 136, Golding Ave, Kingston 7, Jamaica (*Anglican Warden* Revd Garth Minott)

BARBADOS
Bishop Rt Revd Dr John Walder Dunlop Holder (*Archbishop of the Province*), Mandeville House, Collymore Rock, St Michael, Barbados
Tel: 1 246 426 2761/2
Fax: 1 246 426 0871
email: jwdh@sunbeach.net
Web: www.anglican.bb

BELIZE
Bishop Rt Revd Philip S. Wright, #25 Bishops Thorpe, PO Box 535, Southern Foreshore, Belize City, Belize, Central America *Tel:* 501 2 73 029
Fax: 501 2 76 898
email: bzediocese@btl.net
Web: www.belize.anglican.org

GUYANA
Bishop Rt Revd Cornell Moss, The Diocesan Office, PO Box 10949, 49 Barrack St, Georgetown, Guyana, West Indies *Tel:* 592 22 64 775
Fax: 592 22 76 091
email: dioofguy@networksgy.com

JAMAICA AND CAYMAN ISLANDS
Bishop Rt Revd Dr Howard Gregory, 2 Caledonia Ave, Kingston 5, Jamaica *Tel:* 1 876 920 2712
Fax: 1 876 960 1774
email: bishop.jamaica@anglicandiocese.com
Web: www.anglicandiocesejamaica.com
Bishops Suffragan
Rt Revd Robert McLean Thompson (*Bishop of Kingston*), 3 Duke Street, Kingston, Jamaica, West Indies *Tel:* 876 924 9044
Fax: 876 948 5362
email: bishop.kingston@anglicandiocese.com

Vacancy (*Bishop of Mandeville*), Bishop's Residence, 3 Cotton Tree Road, PO Box 84, Mandeville, Jamaica, West Indies *Tel:* 1 876 625 6818
Fax: 1 876 625 6819

Vacancy (*Bishop of Montego Bay*), PO Box 346, Montego Bay, Jamaica, West Indies
Tel: 1 876 952 4963
Fax: 1 876 971 8838

THE BAHAMAS AND THE TURKS AND CAICOS ISLANDS
Bishop Rt Revd Laish Z. Boyd, Church House, PO Box N-7107, Nassau, Bahamas
Tel: 1 242 322 3015/6/7
Fax: 1 242 322 7943
email: bishopboyd@bahamasanglican.org

Assistant Bishop Most Revd Drexel Wellington Gomez (*New Providence*) (*same address*)

NORTH EASTERN CARIBBEAN AND ARUBA
Bishop Rt Revd Leroy Errol Brooks, St Mary's Rectory, PO Box 180, The Valley, Anguilla
Tel: 1 264 497 2235
Fax: 1 264 497 8555
email: brookx@anguillanet.com

TRINIDAD AND TOBAGO
Bishop Rt Revd Claude Berkley, Hayes Court, 21 Maraval Road, Port of Spain, Trinidad, Trinidad and Tobago, West Indies
Tel: 1 868 622 7387
Fax: 1 868 628 1319
email: diocesett@tstt.net.tt

WINDWARD ISLANDS
Bishop Rt Revd C. Leopold Friday, Bishop's Court, Montrose, PO Box 502, St Vincent, West Indies
Tel: 1 784 456 1895
Fax: 1 784 456 2591
email: diocesewi@vincysurf.com

Other Churches and Extra-Provincial Dioceses

BERMUDA
(Anglican Church of Bermuda)
This extra-provincial diocese is under the metropolitical jurisdiction of the Archbishop of Canterbury.

Bishop Vacancy
Tel: 1 441 293 1787
email: see Diocesan Office

Diocesan Office, PO Box HM 769, Hamilton HM CX, Bermuda
Tel: 1 441 292 6987
Fax: 1 441 292 5421
email: diocoff@ibl.bm
Web: www.anglican.bm

Archdeacon Ven Andrew Doughty, Warwick Rectory, PO Box WK 530, Warwick, WK BX, Bermuda

THE CHURCH OF CEYLON (SRI LANKA)
Members 52,500
The work of the Anglican Church began in Sri Lanka (Ceylon) with the arrival of the British in 1796 and the appointment of the 1st Colonial Chaplain to minister to the British military and civil officials in the colony. Anglican missions in Sri Lanka commenced as far back as 1818 with the arrival of the Church Missionary Society and in 1840, the Society for the Propagation of the Gospel. The Diocese of Colombo was established in 1845 by Letters Patent. The Diocese of Colombo was disestablished in 1886 and was placed under the metropolitical care of the Metropolitan of India in Calcutta. In 1930 the Diocese became part of the newly formed Province of India, Pakistan (from 1947), Burma and Ceylon. In 1950 the Diocese of Colombo was bifurcated and the Diocese of Kurunegala was formed. The Province was dissolved in 1970 with the formation of the Churches of North India and Pakistan and the Province of Myanmar (Burma). Since then the Dioceses of Colombo and Kurunegala have been identified in the Anglican Communion as two extra-provincial Dioceses. In 1993, with the Church of Ceylon (Incorporation) Act passed by the Parliament of Sri Lanka, the Church of Ceylon was legally recognized and classified as a 'National Church' within the Communion. A new Church of Ceylon Constitution was adopted which now governs the Anglican Church in Sri Lanka and has a General Assembly and a Presiding Bishop. The Incorporated Trustees of the Church of Ceylon have responsibility for the financial management of the various properties and Trust funds owned and set up by the Dioceses over the past 165 years. The Dioceses are managed by the Bishop, Archdeacons and the respective Standing Committees.

Both Dioceses have new Bishops. Rt Revd Shantha Francis (consecrated 2010) is the Bishop of Kurunegala and is presently the Presiding Bishop of the Church of Ceylon, while Rt Revd Dhiloraj R. Canagasabey (consecrated 2011) is the new Bishop of Colombo.

Clergy, full-time workers and members of the laity are trained at the Ecumenical Theological College of Lanka, Pilimatalawa and the Cathedral Institute for Education and Formation, Colombo. On the ecumenical journey, both Dioceses are members of the National Christian Council of Sri Lanka and have cordial working relationships with the Roman Catholic Church, newer Evangelical and Pentecostal churches and other major faith groups prevailing in Sri Lanka. Through a few (11) government approved private Church Schools, the Dioceses are involved in primary and secondary secular education.

The challenges we face include the training and the empowerment of the people of God for mission and witness in the context of poverty, ethnic conflict and a multi-faith environment. The Church in Sri Lanka, in addition to its parochial and evangelistic ministries, is also now engaged in reconstruction in areas affected by the bitter ethnic war that ended in 2009 and in caring and providing relief and rehabilitation for internally displaced persons (IDPs).

THEOLOGICAL COLLEGE
Theological College of Lanka, Pilimatalawa, nr Kandy

COLOMBO
Bishop Rt Revd Dhiloraj R. Canagasabey, 368/3A Bauddhaloka Mawatha, Colombo 7
Tel: 94 1 684 810
Fax: 94 1 684 811
email: anglican@slttalk.net
Secretary Mrs Mary Thanja Pereis (*same address*)
email: sec.diocese.tr@gmail.com

KURUNEGALA

Bishop Rt Revd Shautha Francis, Bishop's House, Cathedral Close, Kurunegala *Tel:* 94 37 22 191
Fax: 94 37 26 806
email: bishopkg@sltnet.lk

Secretary Mrs Barbara Praesoody, Diocesan Office, 154, D. Senanayake Veediya, Kandy
Tel and *Fax:* 94 081 2222016
email: diokg@sltnet.lk

General Assembly of the Church of Ceylon Presiding Bishop: Rt Revd Shantha Francis; Vice Presiding Bishop: Rt Revd Dhiloraj R. Canagasabey; Secretary: Mrs Barbara Praesoody

EPISCOPAL CHURCH OF CUBA
(Iglesia Episcopal de Cuba)

Members 10,000

The Episcopal Church of Cuba is under a Metropolitan Council in matters of faith and order. Council members include the Primate of Canada, the Archbishop of the West Indies, and the Presiding Bishop of the Episcopal Church of the United States of America or a Bishop appointed by him.

Diocesan Bishop Rt Revd Griselda Delgado Del Carpio, Calle 6, 273, Vedado, La Habana 4, CP 10400, Cuba *Tel:* 537 32 11 20

THEOLOGICAL COLLEGE

Seminario Evangelico de Teologica, Matanzas Aptdo. 149, Matanzas (Interdenominational, run in cooperation with the Presbyterian Church)

CHURCH PAPER

Heraldo Episcopal Published three times a year. Contains diocesan, provincial and world news, homiletics, devotional and historical articles.

FALKLAND ISLANDS

In 1977 the Archbishop of Canterbury resumed episcopal jurisdiction over the Falkland Islands and South Georgia which had been relinquished in 1974 to the Church of the Southern Cone of America. In 2006 he appointed Bishop Stephen Venner, the Bishop of Dover, as his commissary, with the title Bishop for the Falkland Islands. The whole parish covers the Falkland Islands, South Georgia, and the South Sandwich Islands and British Antarctic Territory. Christ Church Cathedral is the most southerly cathedral in the world.

Bishop for the Falkland Islands Rt Revd Dr Stephen Venner (*Bishop to HM Forces*), 83 Hathaway Court, Rochester ME1 1QY *Tel:* 01634 838787
email: stephen@venner.org.uk

Rector Revd Dr Richard Hines, The Deanery, PO Box 160, Stanley, Falkland Islands, South Atlantic FIQQ 1ZZ *Tel:* 00 500 21100
Fax: 00 500 21100
email: christchurch@horizon.co.fk

Associate Minister Revd Kathy Biles (c/o *same address*) *email:* k.biles@horizon.co.fk

LUSITANIAN CHURCH
(Portuguese Episcopal Church)

Members 5,000

Founded in 1880 by a group of local Roman Catholic priests and lay people as a reaction to a number of dogmas from the first Vatican Council. The Church consisted of Roman Catholic priests who formed congregations in and around Lisbon using a translation of the 1662 English Prayer Book. Its own first Prayer Book of Common Prayer was issued in 1884. A Lusitanian bishop was consecrated in 1958 and in the early 1960s many provinces of the Anglican Communion established full communion with the Church in Portugal. Full integration occurred in 1980 when the Church became an extra-provincial diocese under the metropolitical authority of the Archbishop of Canterbury. It takes seriously its role in the emerging Europe and has a commitment to helping the poor. It has a strong mission emphasis for the many unchurched people in the country, specially by its two diaconal institutions providing services and help to children and the elderly. The Church and its leaders cooperate fully with the Diocese in Europe (Church of England) and the Convocation of American Churches in Europe, assisting in each other's congregation and being a united Anglican voice in an increasingly secular Europe. In 1998 the diocesan synod of the Lusitanian Church approved and accepted the Porvoo Declaration, expressing its desire to be involved in the life of the Porvoo Communion and to cooperate, with interchangeable ministries, with the congregations of the Porvoo Churches in Portugal.

Bishop Rt Revd Dr Fernando da Luz Soares, Secretaria Diocesana, Apartado 392, P-4431-905 Vila Nova de Gaia, Portugal *Tel:* 351 22 375 4018
Fax: 351 22 375 2016
email: centrodiocesano@igreja-lusitana.org
Web: www.igreja-lusitana.org

Treasurer Senhor António Vaz Pinto dos Santos, Tesouraria Diocesana (*same address*)

SPANISH EPISCOPAL REFORMED CHURCH

Members 5,000

Parishes: 32 self supported, plus a similar number of congregations.

The Spanish Church covers the whole country and is divided into three archdiaconates, with three archdeacons:

Archdiaconate I: Catalonia, Valencia and Balearic islands

Archdiaconate II: Andalusia and Canary islands

Archdiaconate III: Central and Northern Spain

Under the leadership of some former Roman Catholic priests, in 1868 the Spanish Reformed Episcopal Church was established in Gibraltar

ANGLICAN AND PORVOO COMMUNIONS

and was for some years under the pastoral care of the Church of Ireland. The first Bishop was appointed in 1880 and consecrated in 1894 by the Bishop of Meath along with two other Bishops, and the Church of Ireland accepted metropolitan authority. The same year the Church adopted the Mozarabic Liturgy, which was the liturgy of the early Spanish Church. The Church was fully integrated into the Anglican Communion in 1980 under the metropolitical authority of the Archbishop of Canterbury. It has a strong evangelistic and mission commitment and it is organized into departments: youth, women, ecumenism, Christian education, mission and evangelization. The Church also has a very important social programme for immigrants, which was established in many parishes by helping with clothes and food for over 26,000 people per year. The history of the Church has been one of persecution and difficulties, especially during Franco's dictatorship, but it is firm in its cooperation with the Diocese in Europe and the Convocation of American Churches in Europe for a stronger Anglican presence throughout Europe.

Bishop Rt Revd Carlos López Lozano (*Bishop of Madrid*), Spanish Reformed Episcopal Church, Calle Beneficencia 18, 28004 Madrid
Tel: 34 91 445 2560
Fax: 34 91 594 4572
email: eclesiae@arrakis.es
Web: www.anglicanos.org

Treasurer Señor Jesus Diaz Barragan (*same address*)

Regional Councils

COUNCIL OF THE ANGLICAN PROVINCES OF AFRICA

The Council of Anglican Provinces of Africa (CAPA) was established in 1979 in Chilema, Malawi, by Anglican Primates in Africa who saw the need to form a coordinating body that would help to bring the Anglican Communion in Africa together and to articulate issues affecting the Church. The organization was set up with the following aims and objectives:

- to help the Anglican churches in Africa develop beneficial relationships between themselves and with the wider Anglican Communion;
- to provide a forum for the Church in Africa to share experiences, consult and support each other;
- to confer about common responsibilities on the African continent;
- to establish opportunities for collaboration and joint activities;
- to maintain and develop relationships between the Anglican Church in Africa, partners, other denominations, fellowships, national and regional councils.

Today CAPA works with 12 Anglican provinces in Africa and the Diocese of Egypt. These provinces include Nigeria, West Africa, Sudan, Kenya, Uganda, Tanzania, Congo, Rwanda, Burundi, Central Africa, Southern Africa and Indian Ocean.

Chairman Most Revd Ian Ernest (*Primate of Indian Ocean*)

General Secretary The Rev Canon Grace Kaiso, PO Box 10329, 00100 Nairobi, Kenya

Tel: 254 20 3873 283/700
Fax: 254 20 3870 876
email: Generalsec@capa-hq.org
Web: www.capa-hq.org

Administrative Officer Mrs Elizabeth Gichovi (*same address*) *email:* info@capa-hq.org

HIV/AIDS TB & Malaria Programme Coordinator Mr Emmanuel Olatunji (*same address*)
email: olatunji@capa-hq.org/otunuel@yahoo.com

THE COUNCIL OF THE CHURCHES OF EAST ASIA

This Council, whose history began in 1954, has gone through an evolution. With most of the dioceses forming into provinces, the Council is now a fellowship for common action. Its membership includes dioceses in the Province of South East Asia, the Church of Korea, the Philippine Episcopal Church, Hong Kong Sheng Kung Hui, the Diocese of Taiwan (which is associated with the Episcopal Church of the USA), the Province of Myanmar, Nippon Sei Ko Kai (the Holy Catholic Church in Japan), the Philippine Independent Church and the Anglican Church of Australia who are members as a national Church or province.

Chairman Most Revd Dr Paul Kwong, Hong Kong Sheng Kung Hui, Provincial office: 16/F, Tung Wai Commercial Building, No.109–111 Gloucester Road, Wanchai, HK
Tel: 852 2526 5355
Fax: 852 2521 2199
email: Office1@hkskh.org
www.hkskh.org

UNITED CHURCHES IN FULL COMMUNION

CHURCHES RESULTING FROM THE UNION OF ANGLICANS WITH CHRISTIANS OF OTHER TRADITIONS

The population of the countries of South Asia is over 1,000 million and these Churches cover the whole area. The total Christian population is around 22–3 million and Christians of many different traditions, ranging from ancient oriental to pentecostal, are to be found here. The region is undergoing rapid social, economic and political change. There is also a resurgence of some of the great world religions. Although there is a great deal of industrialization and there have been 'green revolutions' in the agricultural sector in many countries, there is still a tremendous inequality in the distribution of wealth and income. In spite of the relatively small numbers of Christians, the Churches have grown steadily and have been responsible for many initiatives in education, medical work and community development. Their influence is out of all proportion to their size. The Church of England continues to relate to these Churches mainly through its mission agencies: CMS, USPG, SPCK and Crosslinks. In addition, the Oxford Mission, the Dublin University Mission to Chota Nagpur and the Religious Communities are doing valuable work. Support in money and personnel also comes from Churches in Canada, from CMS in Australia and New Zealand, from the USA, Holland, Germany, Scandinavia, Japan and Singapore. The Churches themselves are involved in the training and sending of mission personnel both inside and outside India, including the sending of mission partners to the UK. Mission partners from the Church of England work under the authority of the local church or institution to which they have been sent. The Church of North India, the Church of South India and Mar Thoma Syrian Church of Malenkara are in full communion with each other and are members of a joint council to further and deepen their unity. Since 1988, these Churches have become full members of the Lambeth Conference and the Anglican Consultative Council. Their moderators also attend the meetings of Anglican Primates.

The Church of Bangladesh

Members 15,623
Congregations/Pastorates 72
Bangladesh was part of the State of Pakistan which was partitioned from India in 1947. After the civil war between East and West Pakistan ended in 1971, East Pakistan became Bangladesh. The Church of Bangladesh is one of the United Churches, formed by a union of Anglicans with Christians of other traditions.

Moderator Rt Revd Paul S. Sakar (*Bishop of Kushtia*)

General Secretary Mr Augustin Dipok Karmokar, St Thomas' Church, 54 Johnson Road, Dhaka – 1100
Tel: 880 2 711 6546
Fax: 880 2 712 1632
email: cbdacdio@bangla.net

Treasurer Mr Joel Mondal (*same address*)

THEOLOGICAL COLLEGE
St Andrew's Theological College, 54/1 Barobag, Mirpur 2, Dhaka – 1216, Bangladesh (*Principal* Revd Sourav Folia) *Tel:* 880 2 802 0876

DHAKA
Bishop Rt Revd Michael S. Baroi (*Bishop of Dhaka and Moderator of the Church of Bangladesh*), St Thomas's Church, 54 Johnson Rd, Dhaka – 1100
Tel: 880 2 711 6546
Fax: 880 2 712 1632
email: cbdacdio@bangla.net

KUSHTIA
Bishop Rt Revd Paul S. Sarkar, 94 N.S. Road, Thanapara, Kushtia *Tel* and *Fax:* 880 71 54618
email: cob@citechco.net

The Church of North India

Members 1,250,000

The Church was inaugurated in 1970 after many years of preparation. It includes the Anglican Church, the United Church of Northern India (Congregationalist and Presbyterian), the Methodist Church (British and Australian Conferences), the Council of Baptist Churches in Northern India, the Church of the Brethren in India, and the Disciples of Christ. Along with the Church of South India, the Church of Pakistan and the Church of Bangladesh, it is one of the four United Churches.

Moderator Most Revd Joel V. Mal (*Bishop of Chandigarh*)

Deputy Moderator The Rt Revd Purely Lyngdoh (*Bishop of North East India*)

General Secretary and Acting Treasurer Revd Dr Enos Das Pradhan, CNI Bhavan, 16 Pandit Pant Marg, New Delhi 110 001 *Tel:* 91 11 2371 6513
email: gscni@ndb.vsnl.net.in/enos@cnisynod.org
Web: www.cnisynod.org

Treasurer Mr Kosala (*same address*)
email: cnitr@cnisynod.org

CHURCH PAPER

The North India Church Review The official monthly magazine of the CNI. Contains articles, reports, diocesan news, world news and letters.
Editor/Editorial Office (*same address*)

AGRA

Bishop Rt Revd S. R. Cutting, Bishop's House, 4/116-B Church Rd, Civil Lines, Agra 282 002, UP
Tel: 91 562 2854 845
Fax: 91 562 2520 074
email: doacni@sancharnet.in

AMRITSAR

Bishop Rt Revd Pradeep Kumar Samantaroy, 26 R. B. Prakash Chand Rd, Opp Police Ground, Amritsar 143 001, Punjab
Tel and Fax: 91 183 222 2910
email: bunu13@rediffmail.com
Web: www.amritsardiocese.org

ANDAMAN AND NICOBAR ISLANDS

Bishop Rt Revd Christopher Paul, Bishop's House, 21 Church Lane, Goal Ghar, Port Blair 744 101, Andaman and Nicobar Islands
Tel and *Fax:* 91 3192 231 362
email: cniportblair@yahoo.co.in

BARRACKPORE

Bishop Rt Revd Brojen Malakar, Bishop's Lodge, 86 Middle Rd, Barrackpore, Kolkata 700120, West Bengal *Tel:* 91 33 2592 0147
Fax: 91 33 2593 1852

BHOPAL

Bishop Rt Revd Laxman L. Maida, Bishop's House, 57, Rseidency Area, Behind Narmada Water Tank, Indore 452 001 (MP)
Tel: 91 731 270 0232
91 98270 34737 (Mobile)
email: bhopal_diocese@rediffmail.com

CHANDIGARH

Bishop Most Revd Joel Vidyasagar Mal (*Moderator CNI*), Bishop's House, Mission Compound, Brown Rd, Ludhiana 141 001, Punjab
Tel and *Fax:* 91 161 222 5707
email: bishopdoc@yahoo.com/joelvmal@yahoo.com

CHOTA NAGPUR

Bishop Rt Revd B. B. Baskey, Bishop's Lodge, PO Box 1, Church Rd, Ranchi 834 001, Jharkhand
Tel and Fax: 91 651 235 1184
email: rch_cndta@sancharnet.in

CUTTACK

Bishop Rt Revd Dr Samson Das, Bishop's House, Mission Rd, Cuttack 753 001, Orissa
Tel: 91 671 230 0102
email: diocese@vsnl.net

DELHI

Bishop Rt Revd Sunil Singh, Bishop's House, 1 Church Lane, Off North Ave, New Delhi 110 001
Tel: 91 11 2371 7471
email: stmartin@dels.vsnl.net.in

DURGAPUR

Bishop Rt Revd Probal Kanto Dutta, Bishop's House, St Michael's Church Compound, Aldrin Path, Bidhan Nagar, Dugapur 713 212
Tel: 91 343 253 4552
email: probal_dutta@yahoo.com

EASTERN HIMALAYA

Bishop Rt Revd Dr Naresh Ambala, Bishop's Lodge, PO Box 4, Darjeeling 734 101, W Bengal
Tel: 91 354 225 8183
email: bpambala@yahoo.com

GUJARAT

Bishop Rt Revd Vinodkumar Mathushellah Malaviya, Bishop's House, I.P. Mission Compound, Ellisbridge, Ahmedabad 380 006, Gujarat *Tel* and *Fax:* 91 79 2656 1950
email: gujdio@yahoo.co.in

JABALPUR

Bishop Rt Revd Prem Chand Singh, Bishop's House, 2131 Napier Town, Jabalpur 482 001, MP
Tel: 91 761 2622 109
email: bishoppcsingh@yahoo.co.in

KOLHAPUR
Bishop Rt Revd Bathuel Ramchandra Tiwade, Bishop's House, EP School Compound, Kolhapur 416 001, MS
Tel and *Fax:* 91 231 2654 832
email: kdccni@vsnl.com

KOLKATA
Bishop Rt Revd Ashok Biwas, Bishop's House, 51 Chowringhee Rd, Calcutta 700 071, WB
Tel: 91 33 6534 7770
Fax: 91 33 2822 6340
email: samrajubh@vsnl.net

LUCKNOW
Bishop Rt Revd Anil Stephen, Bishop's House, 25/11 Mahatma Gandhi Marg, Allahabad 211 011, UP
Tel: 91 532 242 7053
Fax: 91 532 256 0713

MARATHWADA
Bishop Rt Revd M. U. Kasab, Bungalow 28 / A, Mission Compound, Cantonment, Aurangabad 431 002, MS
Tel and *Fax:* 91 240 237 3136
email: revmukasab@yahoo.co.in

MUMBAI
Bishop Rt Revd Prakash Dinkar Patole, 19 Hazarimal Somani Marg, Fort Mumbai 400 001
Tel: 91 22 2206 0248
email: bishopbomcni@rediffmail.com

NAGPUR
Bishop Rt Rev Paul Dupare, Cathedral House, Opp. Indian Coffee House, Sadar, Nagpur 440 001, MS
Tel: 91 712 562 1737
Fax: 91 712 309 7310
email: bishop@nagpur.dot.org.in

NASIK
Bishop Rt Revd Pradip Lemuel Kamble, Bishop's House, 1 Outram Rd, Tarakpur, Ahmednagar 414 001, MS
Tel: 91 241 241 1806
Fax: 91 241 242 2314
email: bishopofnasik@rediffmail.com

NORTH EAST INDIA
Bishop Rt Revd Purely Lyngdoh (*Deputy Moderator, CNI*), Bishop's Kuti, Shillong, Meghalaya 793 001
Tel: 91 364 2223 155
Fax: 91 364 2501 178
email: bishopnei15@hotmail.com

PATNA
Bishop Rt Revd Philip Phembuar Marandih, Bishop's House, Christ Church Compound, Bhagalpur 812 001, Bihar
Tel: 91 641 2400 033/2300 714
Fax: 91 641 2300 714
email: cnipatna@rediffmail.com

PHULBANI
Bishop Rt Revd Bijay Kumar Nayak, Bishop's House, Mission Compound, Gudripori, G-udaigiri, Phulbani 762 100, Kandhamal, Orissa 762 001
Tel: 91 6847 260569
email: bp.bkn@rediffmail.com

PUNE
Bishop Rt Revd Vijay Bapurao Sathe, Pune Diocesan Office, 1 Stevely Road (General Bhagat Marg), Red Bungalow, Pune 411 001, MS
Tel: 91 20 2633 4374
email: punediocese@yahoo.co.in

RAJASTHAN
Bishop Rt Revd Collin Theodore, 2/10 CNI Social Centre, Civil Lines, Opp. Bus Stand, Jaipur Rd, Ajmer 305 001
Tel: 91 145 2420 633
Fax: 91 145 2621 627

SAMBALPUR
Bishop Rt Revd Christ Kiron Das, Mission Compound, Bolangir 767 001, Orissa
Tel and *Fax:* 91 6652 230625
email: bishop_ckdas@rediffmail.com

The Church of Pakistan

Members approx 1,000,000
One of four United Churches in the Anglican Communion, the Church of Pakistan comprises the Anglican Church of Pakistan, the dioceses of Lahore and Karachi, two conferences of the United Methodist Church, the Scottish Presbyterian Church in Pakistan, and the Pakistan Lutheran Church.

Moderator Rt Revd Samuel Robert Azariah (*Bishop of Raiwind*)

Deputy Moderator Rt Revd Sadiq Daniel (*Bishop of Karachi*)

General Secretary Revd Nasim Fayyaz, 17 Waris Road, Lahore
Tel: 92 423 588950

Treasurer Mr Wilson Massey, Cathedral Close, The Mall, Lahore
Tel: 92 423 7233560

FAISALABAD
Bishop Rt Revd John Samuel, Bishop's House, PO Box 27, Mission Rd, Gojra, Distt Toba Tek Sing
Tel: 92 46 351 4689
92 300 655 0074 (Mobile)
email: jsamuel@brain.net.pk

HYDERABAD
Moderator's Commissary Rt Revd Ifran Jamil (*Coadjutor Bishop of Lahore Diocese*) 27 Liaquat Rd, Civil Lines, Hyderabad 71000, Sind
Tel: 92 51 289 0420
email: rev_ijamil@hotmail.com

KARACHI
Bishop Rt Revd Saddiq Daniel (*Deputy Moderator, COP*), Holy Trinity Cathedral, Fatima Jinnah Rd, Karachi 75530 *Tel:* 92 521 6843
email: sadiqdaniel@hotmail.com

LAHORE
Bishop Rt Revd Dr Alexander John Malik (*Moderator, COP*), Bishopsbourne, Cathedral Close, The Mall, Lahore 54000 *Tel:* 92 42 723 3560 (Office)
92 42 7120 766 (Home)
Fax: 92 42 722 1270
email: bishop_Lahore@hotmail.com

MULTAN
Bishop Rt Revd Leo Rodrick Paul, 113 Qasim Rd, PO Box 204, Multan Cantt *Tel:* 92 61 458 3694
email: bishop_mdcop@bain.net.pk

PESHAWAR
Bishop Rt Revd Humphrey Sarfaraz Peters, Diocesan Centre, 1 Sir Syed Rd, Peshawar Cantt 2500 *Tel:* 92 91 527 9094
Fax: 92 91 5277499
email: bishopdop@hotmail.com

RAIWIND
Bishop Rt Revd Samuel Azariah, 17 Warris Rd, PO Box 2319, Lahore 54000 *Tel:* 92 42 758 8950
Fax: 92 42 757 7255
email: sammyazariah49@yahoo.com

SIALKOT
Bishop Rt Revd Samuel Pervez, Lal Kothi, Barah Patthar, Sialkot 2, Punjab *Tel:* 92 432 264 895
Fax: 92 432 264 828/92 300 8615 828
email: chs_sialkot@yahoo.com

ARABIAN GULF
Bishop for Rt Revd Azad Marshall (*Area Bishop within the Diocese of Cyprus*), PO Box 688, Lahore, Punjab 54000, Pakistan *Tel:* 92 42 542 0452
email: bishop@saintthomascenter.org

The Church of South India

Members 4,000,000
The Church was inaugurated in 1947 by the union of the South India United Church (itself a union of Congregational and Presbyterian/Reformed traditions), the southern Anglican dioceses of the Church of India, and Burma, and the Methodist Church in South India. It is one of the four United Churches in the Anglican Communion.

Moderator Most Revd Dr J. W. Gladstone (*Bishop in South Kerala*)

Deputy Moderator Rt Revd Dr A. Christopher Asir (*Bishop in Madurai-Ramnad*)

General Secretary Revd Moses Jayakumar, CSI Centre 5 Whites Rd, Royapettah, Chennai 600 014, India *Tel:* 91 44 2852 1566/4166 (office)
2852 3763 (home)
email: csi@vsnl.com

Honorary Treasurer Mr T. Devasahayam FCA, Tsoudury Nilayam, 2–5–211, Nakkalaguta, Hanamkonda, 506 001, Andhra Pradesh
Tel: 91 44 2852 4166 (Office)
91 870 225 2938 (Home)
Fax: 91 44 2858 4163
email: csisnd_tr@satyam.net.in

OFFICIAL MAGAZINE
CSI Life English Monthly Magazine. Contains articles, reports and news from the dioceses. *Editor:* The General Secretary CSI; *Managing Editor:* Rev. R. Mohanraj, Director, Dept of Communication, 5 Whites Road, Royapettah, Chennai 600 014; Yearly subscription Rs.150/- (£25 in UK, $30 in USA, $ 35 in Australia, $35 in New Zealand, sent by Air Mail).

CHENNAI (*formerly* **MADRAS**)
Bishop in Rt Revd Dr V. Devasahayam, Diocesan Office, PO Box 4914, 226 Cathedral Rd, Chennai 600 086, Tamil Nadu
Tel: 91 44 2811 3929/3933/7629
Fax: 91 44 2811 0608
email: bishopdeva@hotmail.com
Web: www.csimadrasdiocese.org

COIMBATORE
Bishop in Rt Revd Dr Manikam Dorai, Diocesan Office, 256 Race Course Rd, Coimbatore 641 018, Tamil Nadu *Tel:* 91 422 221 3605
Fax: 91 442 200 0400
email: bishopdorai@presidency.com

DORNAKAL
Bishop in Rt Revd Dr B. S. Devamani, Bishop's Office S. C. RLY, Cathedral Compound,

Dornakal 506 381, Warangal Dist., Andhra Pradesh *Tel:* 91 8719 227 752 (Home)
227 535 (Office)
email: bshpindk@yahoo.co.in

EAST KERALA
Bishop in Rt Revd Dr K. G. Daniel, Bishop's House, Melukavumattom, Kottayam 686 652, Kerala State *Tel:* 91 4822 291 044 (Home)
91 4822 220 001 (Office)
Fax: 91 4822 291 044
email: bishopkgdaniel@rediffmail.com

JAFFNA
Bishop in Rt Revd Daniel S. Thiagarajah, Bishop's office in Colombo, 36 5/2 Sinsapa Road, Colombo 6, Sri Lanka *Tel:* 94 60 21495 0795 (Office)
Fax: 94 11 250 5805
email: dsthiagarajah@yahoo.com

KANYAKUMARI
Bishop in Rt Revd G. Devakadasham, CSI Diocesan Office, 71A Dennis St, Nagercoil 629 001, Tamil Nadu *Tel:* 91 4652 231 539
Fax: 91 4652 226 560
email: csikkd@vsnl.in

KARIMNAGAR
Bishop in Rt Revd Dr P. Surya Prakash, Bishop's House, 2–8–95 CVRN Road, PO Box 40, Makarampura post, Karimnagar 505 001, Andhra Pradesh *Tel:* 91 878 22 62229
email: suryaprakash@yahoo.com/bishopsuryaprakash@yahoo.com

KARNATAKA CENTRAL
Bishop in Rt Revd S. Vasanthkumar, Diocesan Office, 20 Third Cross, CSI Compound, Bangalore 560 027, Karnataka
Tel: 91 80 2222 3766/4941
email: csikcd@vsnl.com

KARNATAKA NORTH
Bishop in Rt Revd J. Prabhakara Rao, Bishop's House, All Saints' Church Compound, Dharwad 580 008, Karnataka *Tel:* 91 836 244 7733
Fax: 91 836 274 5461
email: bishopprabhakar@yahoo.co.in

KARNATAKA SOUTH
Bishop in Rt Revd Devaraj Bangera, Bishop's House, Balmatta, Mangalore 575 001, Karnataka
Tel: 91 824 243 2657/242 1802
Fax: 91 824 242 1802
email: bishopbangera@rediffmail.com

KRISHNA-GODAVARI
Bishop in Rt Revd Dr G. Dyvasirvadam, CSI St Andrew's Cathedral Compound, Main Rd, Machilipatnam 521 002, AP *Tel:* 91 8672 220 623
email: bishopkrishna@yahoo.com

MADHYA KERALA
Bishop in Rt Revd Thomas Samuel, CSI Bishop's House, Cathedral Rd, Kottayam 686 018, Kerala
Tel: 91 481 2566 536
Fax: 91 481 566 531
email: csimkdbishop@sancharnet.in/csimkdbishop@bsnl.in/bishopthomassamuel@yahoo.com

MADURAI-RAMNAD
Bishop in Rt Revd Dr A. Christopher Asir (*Deputy Moderator, CSI*), 5 Bhulabai Desai Rd, Chockikulam, Madurai 625 002, Tamil Nadu
Tel: 91 452 256 3196/0541
Fax: 91 452 256 0864
email: bishop@csidmr.net

MEDAK
Bishop in Rt Revd Kanak Prasad, Bishop's Annexe, 145, MacIntyre Road, Secunderabad, Andhra Pradesh 500 003 *Tel:* 94 40 2783 3151
Fax: 94 40 2784 4215

NANDYAL
Bishop in Rt Revd Dr P. J. Lawrence, Bishop's House, Nandyal RS 518 502, Kurnool Dist., Andhra Pradesh *Tel:* 91 8514 222 477
Fax: 91 8514 242 255
email: lawrencejoba@yahoo.com

NORTH KERALA
Bishop in Rt Revd Dr K. P. Kuruvilla, PO Box 104, Shoranur 679 121, Kerala *Tel:* 91 466 2224 454
Fax: 91 466 2222 545
email: csinkd@md5.vsnl.net

RAYALASEEMA
Bishop in Rt Revd K. B. Yesuvaraprasad, Bishop's House, CSI Compound, Gooty 515 401, Ananthapur Dist, AP *Tel:* 91 8662 325 320
Fax: 91 8562 275 200

SOUTH KERALA
Bishop in Rt Revd J. W. Gladstone (*Moderator, CSI*), Bishop's House, LMS Compound, Trivandrum 695 033, Kerala State
Tel: 91 471 231 5490
Fax: 91 471 231 6439
email: bishopgladstone@yahoo.com

THOOTHUKUDI-NAZARETH
Bishop in Charge Rt Revd J. A. D. Jebachandran, Bishop's House, 111/32T, Polpettai Extension, State Bank Colony, Thoothukudi 628 002, Tamil Nadu *Tel:* 91 461 2345 430
Fax: 91 431 2346 911
email: bishoptnd@dataone.in
Web: http://csitnd.org

TIRUNELVELI
Bishop in Rt Revd Dr S. Jeyapaul David, Bishopstowe, PO Box 118, 16, North High

Ground Rd, Tirunelveli 627 002, Tamil Nadu *Tel:* 91 462 257 8744
Fax: 91 462 257 4525
email: bishop@csitirunelveli.org
Web: www.csitirunelveli.org

TRICHY-TANJORE
Bishop in Rt Revd Dr G. Paul Vasanthakumar, PO Box 31, 17 VOC Rd, Cantonment, Tiruchiarapalli 620 017, Tamil Nadu *Tel:* 91 431 2771 254
Fax: 91 431 2418 485
email: csittd@tr.net.in

VELLORE
Bishop in Rt Revd Dr Yesurathnam William, CSI Diocesan Office, 1/A Officer's Lane, Vellore 632 001, Tamil Nadu *Tel:* 91 416 2232 160
Fax: 91 416 2223 835
email: bishopwilliam@sify.com

THE HOLY CATHOLIC CHURCH IN CHINA

(Chung Hua Sheng Kung Hui)

The Chung Hua Sheng Kung Hui was an important denomination in China and its history dates back to the mid-nineteenth century. Today the CHSKU, as a separate denomination, no longer exists in the People's Republic of China, except for Hong Kong which returned to Chinese sovereignty on 1 July 1997. Under the formula 'one country – two systems' Hong Kong keeps its autonomy for 50 years, including its religious regulations. The same applies to Macao which was returned by Portugal to China at the end of 1999. On the Chinese mainland the denominational Protestant Churches entered into a post-denominational phase under the Three Self Patriotic Movement/China Christian Council in 1953. A united Church is still in the process of being formed and Christians of Anglican inspiration have very much been a part of this process. The most prominent of these, Bishop K. H. Ting, has now retired from active leadership of the China Christian Council and the Nanjing Union Theological Seminary.

Although the CHSKU is no longer in existence, many former Anglicans still share a strong spiritual affinity with other Anglican Churches on matters of belief and liturgical tradition. As the Chinese Protestant Church develops its own ecclesiology and forms of worship, the Anglican traditions are contributing to a richer synthesis.

Relations between the Church in China and the Churches in Britain are facilitated by the China Desk of Churches Together in Britain and Ireland (CTBI). It provides advice to government, churches and media, and publishes the *China Study Journal*, a documentary review of Chinese religions and government policy. The China Desk is a continuation of the ecumenical China Study Project which was established in 1972 by the leading missionary societies, including Anglican organizations such as the CMS, USPG and the Archbishop's China Appeal Fund.

The Friends of the Church in China, an ecumenical association which works closely with the China Desk of CTBI, takes a more grass-roots approach in relation to Christians in China. It publishes a popular newsletter on China and organizes visits to Chinese churches.

Contact: CBTI China Desk, 39 Eccleston Square, London SW1V 1BX.

Friends of the Church in China, c/o Seagulls, Pinmill, Chelmondiston, Ipswich IP9 1JN. Its Chairman is Canon Simon Brown.

OTHER CHURCHES IN COMMUNION WITH THE CHURCH OF ENGLAND

Old Catholic Churches of the Union of Utrecht

The Old Catholic Churches are a family of nationally organized churches which bound themselves together in the Union of Utrecht in 1889. Most of them owe their origin to Roman Catholics who were unable to accept the decrees of the First Vatican Council in 1870 and left the communion of that Church. The Archbishopric of Utrecht, however (from which the other Old Catholic Churches derived their episcopal orders), has been independent of Rome since the eighteenth century following a complex dispute involving papal and capitular rights of nomination and accusations of Jansenism (until 1910 in the Netherlands only). The Latin Mass continued in use, though all the Old Catholic Churches now worship in the vernacular. Their rites stand within the Western tradition, with various 'Eastern' features.

By the acceptance of the Bonn Agreement on 20 and 22 January 1932, the Convocation of Canterbury established full communion with the Old Catholic Churches by means of the following resolutions:

'That this House approves of the following statements agreed on between the representatives of the Old Catholic Churches and the Churches of the Anglican Communion at a Conference held at Bonn on 2 July 1931:

1. Each Communion recognises the catholicity and independence of the other and maintains its own.
2. Each Communion agrees to admit members of the other Communion to participate in the sacraments.
3. Intercommunion does not require from either Communion the acceptance of all doctrinal opinion, sacramental devotion, or liturgical practice characteristic of the other, but implies that each believes the other to hold all the essentials of the Christian Faith.

'And this House agrees to the establishment of Intercommunion between the Church of England and the Old Catholics on these terms.'

An Anglican–Old Catholic International Coordinating Council was established in 1998.

AUSTRIA
Bishop Rt Revd John Ekemezie Okoro, Schottenring 17/ 1/3/12, A–1010 Vienna
email: b.dilekci@altkatholiken.at
Web: www.altkatholiken.at

CROATIA
Bishop Vacancy, *under the care of Rt Revd Bernhard Heitz* (*Bishop Emeritus of Austria*), Etrichstraße 40 / 2/ 12, 1110 Vienna *email:* bischof.heitz@altkatholiken.at

CZECH REPUBLIC
Bishop Rt Revd Dušan Hejbal, Na Bateriich 27, CZ–162 00 Prague 6 *email:* stkat@starokatolici.cz
Web: www.starokatolici.cz

FRANCE
Bishop Delegate Most Revd Joris Vercammen (*Archbishop of Utrecht*)
Mission de France, 15 rue de Douai, 75009 Paris, France *email:* bishof@christkath.ch
Web: www.vieux-catholique-alsace.com

GERMANY
Bishop Rt Revd Dr Matthias Ring, Gregor–Mendel-Strasse 28, 53115 Bonn, Germany
email: ordinariat@alt-katholisch.de
Web: www.alt-katholisch.de

ITALY
Mission in Italy Revd Petr Živný, Viale Caterina da Forli, 58, 1–201146, Milano, Italy *Tel:* 39 2 48 70 94 43 *email:* altkatholischekircheitalien@ guarigione-liberazione-org
Web: www.chiesaveterocattolica.org

NETHERLANDS
Archbishop Most Revd Dr Joris Vercammen (*Archbishop of Utrecht and President of the International Bishops' Conference*), Kon Wilhelminalaan, 3, NL–3818 HN Amersfoort
email: buro@okkn.nl
Web: www.okkn.nl/welkom

POLAND (The Polish National Catholic Church)
Prime Bishop Most Revd Wiktor Wysoczanski, ul. Wilcza 31/16c, PL–002–544 Warsaw
email: polskokatolicki@pnet.pl
Web: www.polskokatolicki.pl

SWEDEN AND DENMARK
Bishop Delegate Rt Revd Dirk Jan Schoon, Ruysdaelstraat 37, NL–1070 XA Amsterdam, Netherlands *email:* bvh@okkn.nl

SWITZERLAND
Bishop Rt Revd Harald Rein, Willadingweg 39, CH–3006 Bern *email:* bischof@christkath.ch
Web: www.christkath.ch

Philippine Independent Church

The Philippine Independent Church is in part the result of the Philippine revolution against Spain in 1896 for religious emancipation and Filipino identity. It was formally established in 1902, declaring its independence from the Roman Catholic Church but seeking to remain loyal to the Catholic Faith. It now derives its succession from the Protestant Episcopal Church in the United States of America (and therefore from Anglican sources), with which full communion was established in September 1961. It has a membership of approximately seven million followers, 34 dioceses with 50 bishops, 600 regular church buildings and 2,000 village chapels served by about 600 priests.

Following the report of a Commission appointed by the Archbishop of Canterbury, full communion on the basis of the Bonn Agreement was established between the Church of England and the Philippine Independent Church in 1963 by the Convocations of Canterbury and York. It is in full communion with all the member Churches in the Anglican Communion.

The Philippine Independent Church is very active in its ecumenical relations. It is the most senior member in the National Council of the Churches in the Philippines, a member of the Council of Churches in East Asia, a member of the Christian Churches in Asia, and an active member of the World Council of Churches.

Supreme Bishop (*Obisbo Maximo*) Most Revd Tomas A. Millamena, 1500 Taft Avenue, Ermita, Manila, Philippines 2801.
Tel: 63 2 523 72 42
Fax: 63 2 521 39 32
email: ifiphil@hotmail.com

Mar Thoma Syrian Church of Malabar

The Christian community in South India is very ancient and is believed by its members to have been founded by the Apostle Thomas (Mar Thoma). Over the centuries contact with Christian bodies from outside India has led to the fragmentation of the original community into a number of jurisdictions. During the latter part of the nineteenth century the Christians of the West Syrian (Syrian Orthodox) tradition divided into two over the issue of the removal of non-biblical features from teaching and worship of the Church. The influence of Anglican missionaries of the Church Missionary Society who had been working in Malabar since the beginning of the nineteenth century accelerated the new stance in the Church. The larger section (which itself has subsequently divided into the Indian Orthodox and Jacobite Churches) chose closer links with Antioch and remained 'unreformed'; the smaller group, which eventually adopted the name of Mar Thoma Syrian Church of Malabar, undertook a conservative revision of its rites, removing elements (such as the invocation of saints and prayers for the dead) that were not scriptural practices but had given room for misunderstanding of the gospel. The general form of Mar Thoma worship remains eastern. Its episcopal succession derives from the Patriarchate of Antioch.

The former CIPBC (Church of India, Pakistan, Burma and Ceylon) had partial intercommunion with the Mar Thoma Church from 1937 until 1961 when a Concordat of Full Communion was established. The Mar Thoma Syrian Church of Malabar is now in full communion with the Churches of South India and North India. The union of these three churches is now known as the Communion of Churches in India (CCI), which fosters cooperation in mission, theological training, and formulations and involvement in social issues. The Mar Thoma Church has stated its desire to preserve its eastern traditions and is not willing to merge with the two Western United Churches. A number of Anglican Provinces are in full communion with the Mar Thoma Church, the Church of England having become so in 1974.

The Malabar Independent Syrian Church of Thozhiyoor occupies a unique position in the complex history of the Church in South India. At various times in the past its bishops have consecrated bishops for both the Orthodox and Mar Thoma Churches when the episcopal succession in those churches has died out. The MISC is fully Orthodox in rite and faith. It is in communion with the Mar Thoma Church and its current practice is to extend eucharistic hospitality to Christians of other traditions. The former Metropolitan was an ecumenical participant at the 1998 Lambeth Conference.

THE MAR THOMA SYRIAN CHURCH OF MALABAR

Metropolitan Most Revd Dr Philipose Mar Chrysostom Mar Thoma, Poolatheen, Tiruvalla 689 101, Kerala, South India

Tel: 91 469 263 0313
Fax: 91 469 260 2626
email: pulathen@md3.vsnl.net.in

Sabha Secretary Revd Dr Cherian Thomas, Mar Thoma Church Headquarters, Sabha Office, SCS Campus, Tiruvalla 689 101, Kerala, South India

Tel: 91 469 263 0449
Fax: 91 469 263 0327
email: marthoma@vsnl.com

THE MALABAR INDEPENDENT SYRIAN CHURCH

Most Revd Cyril Mar Basilios, St George's Cathedral, Thozhiyoor, Thrissur Dt 680 520, Kerala, South India

Maps of the Churches and Provinces of the Anglican Communion

MAPS	1	The Church of **England**; The Church of **Ireland** The **Scottish** Episcopal Church; The Church in **Wales**
	2	Anglican Church of **Australia** The Anglican Church of **Papua New Guinea**
	3	The Church of the Province of **Melanesia** Anglican Church in **Aotearoa, New Zealand and Polynesia**
	4 & 5	The Protestant Episcopal Church in the **United States of America** The Anglican Church of the **Central American Region** The Episcopal Anglican Church of **Brazil**; The Episcopal Church of **Cuba**; The Church in the Province of the **West Indies**; The Anglican Church of **Mexico** The Anglican Church of the **Southern Cone of America**
	6	The Anglican Church of **Canada**
	7	The Church of the Province of **Central Africa** The Church of the Province of the **Indian Ocean** The Anglican Church of **Southern Africa**
	8	The Anglican Church of **Kenya** The Anglican Church of **Tanzania**
	9	The Anglican Church of the Province of **Burundi** The Church of the Province of **Rwanda** The Church of the Province of **Uganda**
	10	The Church of the Province of the **Sudan** The Church of the Province of **Congo**
	11	The Church of **Nigeria** (Anglican Communion)
	12	The Anglican Communion in **Japan** The Episcopal Church in **Jerusalem and the Middle East** The Church of the Province of **West Africa**
	13	The Church of **North India**; The Church of **South India** The Church of **Pakistan**; The Church of Ceylon (**Sri Lanka**) The Church of **Bangladesh**
	14	The Anglican Church in **Korea**; The Church of the Province of **Myanmar** (Burma) The Episcopal Church in the **Philippines** The Province of the Anglican Church in **South East Asia** **Hong Kong Sheng Kung Hui**

The maps of the Anglican Communion which follow have been supplied by Nicola Lawrence of The Mothers' Union. She will be happy to hear of any changes which need to be made.

MAP 1

The Scottish Episcopal Church
1 Moray, Ross and Caithness
2 Argyll and the Isles
3 St Andrews, Dunkeld and Dunblane
4 Aberdeen and Orkney
5 Brechin
6 Glasgow and Galloway
7 Edinburgh

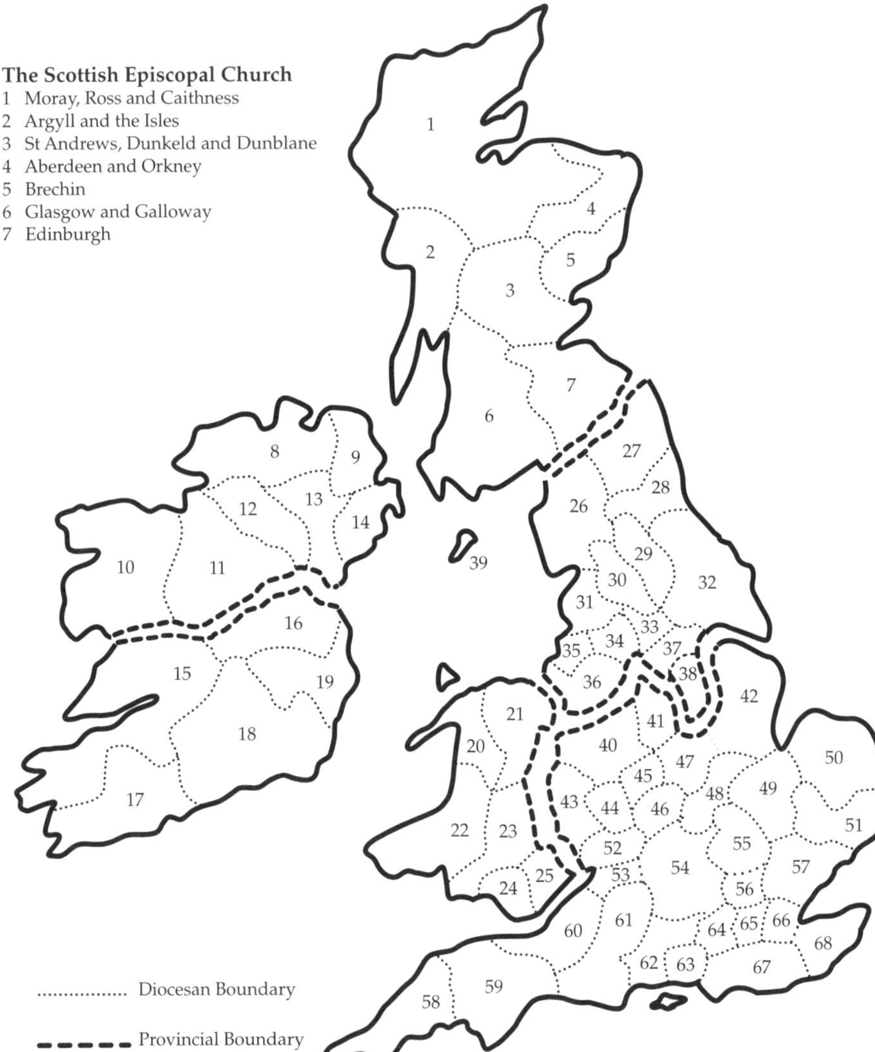

The Isles of Scilly are included in the Diocese of Truro

The Channel Islands are annexed to the Diocese of Winchester

The Church of Ireland

Province of Armagh

8 Derry and Raphoe
9 Connor
10 Tuam, Killala and Achonry
11 Kilmore, Elphin and Ardagh
12 Clogher
13 Armagh
14 Down and Dromore

Province of Dublin

15 Limerick and Killaloe
16 Meath and Kildare
17 Cork, Cloyne and Ross
18 Cashel and Ossory
19 Dublin and Glendalough

The Church in Wales

20 Bangor
21 St Asaph
22 St Davids
23 Swansea and Brecon
24 Llandaff
25 Monmouth

The Church of England

Province of York

26 Carlisle
27 Newcastle
28 Durham
29 Ripon and Leeds
30 Bradford
31 Blackburn
32 York
33 Wakefield
34 Manchester
35 Liverpool
36 Chester
37 Sheffield
38 Southwell and Nottingham
39 Sodor and Man

Province of Canterbury

40 Lichfield
41 Derby
42 Lincoln
43 Hereford
44 Worcester
45 Birmingham
46 Coventry
47 Leicester
48 Peterborough
49 Ely
50 Norwich
51 St Edmundsbury and Ipswich
52 Gloucester
53 Bristol
54 Oxford
55 St Albans
56 London
57 Chelmsford
58 Truro
59 Exeter
60 Bath and Wells
61 Salisbury
62 Winchester
63 Portsmouth
64 Guildford
65 Southwark
66 Rochester
67 Chichester
68 Canterbury
Diocese in Europe

Extra-Provincial Dioceses

Bermuda
Lusitanian Church
Spanish Episcopal Reformed Church
The Church of Ceylon
Falkland Islands

MAP 2

The Anglican Church of Australia

Province of Western Australia
1 North West Australia
2 Perth
3 Bunbury

Province of South Australia
4 Willochra
5 Adelaide
6 The Murray

Province of Queensland
7 The Northern Territory
8 North Queensland
9 Rockhampton
10 Brisbane

Province of New South Wales
11 Riverina
12 Bathurst
13 Armidale
14 Grafton
15 Newcastle
16 Sydney
17 Canberra and Goulburn

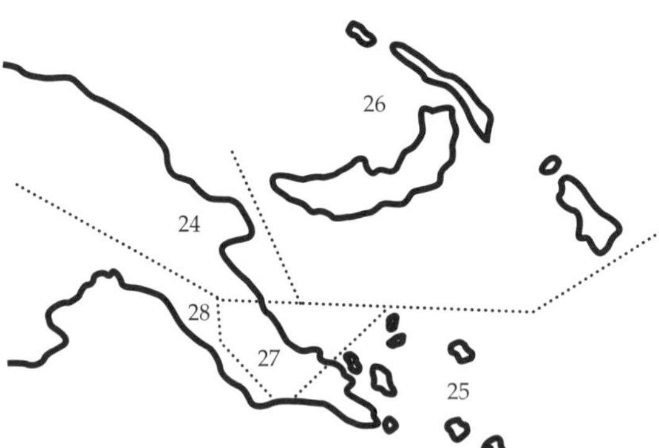

Province of Victoria
18 Ballarat
19 Bendigo
20 Wangaratta
21 Melbourne
22 Gippsland

23 Tasmania *(extra-provincial)*

The Anglican Church of Papua New Guinea

24 Aipo Rongo
25 Dogura
26 New Guinea Islands
27 Popondota
28 Port Moresby

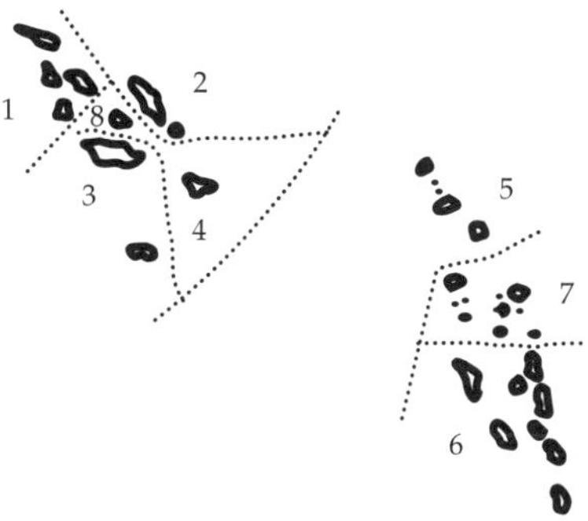

The Church of the Province of Melanesia
1 Ysabel
2 Malaita
3 Central Melanesia
4 Hanuato'o
5 Temotu
6 Vanuatu and New Caledonia
7 Banks and Torres
8 Central Solomons

The Anglican Church in Aotearoa, New Zealand and Polynesia
9 Auckland
10 Waikato
11 Waiapu
12 Wellington
13 Nelson
14 Christchurch
15 Dunedin
16 Polynesia

Bishopric of Aotearoa
A Hui Amorangi ki te Tai Tokerau
B Hui Amorangi ki te Manawa o te Wheke
C Hui Amorangi ki te Tairawhiti
D Hui Amorangi ki te Upoko o te Ika
E Hui Amorangi ki te Waipounamu

-·-·-·-·-·-·-·- Bishopric of Aotearoa

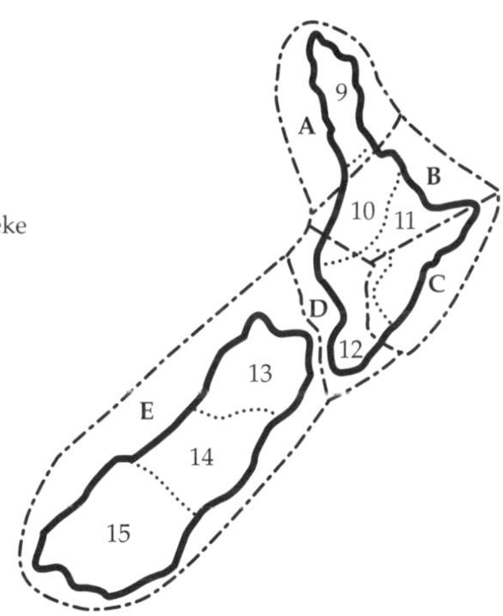

The Episcopal Church in the United States of America

Province I
1 Connecticut
2 Maine
3 Massachusetts
4 New Hampshire
5 Rhode Island
6 Vermont
7 Western Massachusetts

Province II
8 Albany
9 Central New York
10 Long Island
11 New Jersey
12 New York
13 Newark
14 Rochester
15 Western New York
Haiti *(see Map 5)*
Virgin Islands *(see Map 5)*
Convocation of American Churches in Europe

Province III
16 Bethlehem
17 Central Pennsylvania
18 Delaware
19 Easton
20 Maryland
21 Northwestern Pennsylvania
22 Pennsylvania
23 Pittsburgh
24 Southern Virginia
25 Southwestern Virginia
26 Virginia
27 Washington
28 West Virginia

Province IV
29 Alabama
30 Atlanta
31 Central Florida
32 Central Gulf Coast
33 East Carolina
34 East Tennessee
35 Florida
36 Georgia
37 Kentucky
38 Lexington
39 Louisiana
40 Mississippi
41 North Carolina
42 South Carolina
43 Southeast Florida
44 Southwest Florida
45 Tennessee
46 Upper South Carolina
47 West Tennessee
48 Western North Carolina

Province V
49 Chicago
50 Eau Claire
51 Fond du Lac
52 Indianapolis
53 Michigan
54 Milwaukee
55 Missouri
56 Northern Indiana
57 Northern Michigan
58 Ohio
59 Quincy
60 Southern Ohio
61 Springfield
62 Western Michigan
63 Eastern Michigan

Province VI
64 Colorado
65 Iowa
66 Minnesota
67 Montana
68 Nebraska
69 North Dakota
70 South Dakota
71 Wyoming

Province VII
72 Arkansas
73 Dallas
74 Fort Worth
75 Kansas
76 Northwest Texas
77 Oklahoma
78 Rio Grande
79 Texas
80 West Missouri
81 West Texas
82 Western Kansas
83 Western Louisiana

Province VIII
84 Arizona
85 California
86 Eastern Oregon
87 El Camino Real
88 Idaho
89 Los Angeles
90 Navajoland Area Mission
91 Nevada
92 Northern California
93 Olympia
94 Oregon
95 San Diego
96 San Joaquin
97 Spokane
98 Utah
Hawaii
Alaska *(see Map 6)*
Taiwan *(see Map 14)*
Micronesia

MAP 4

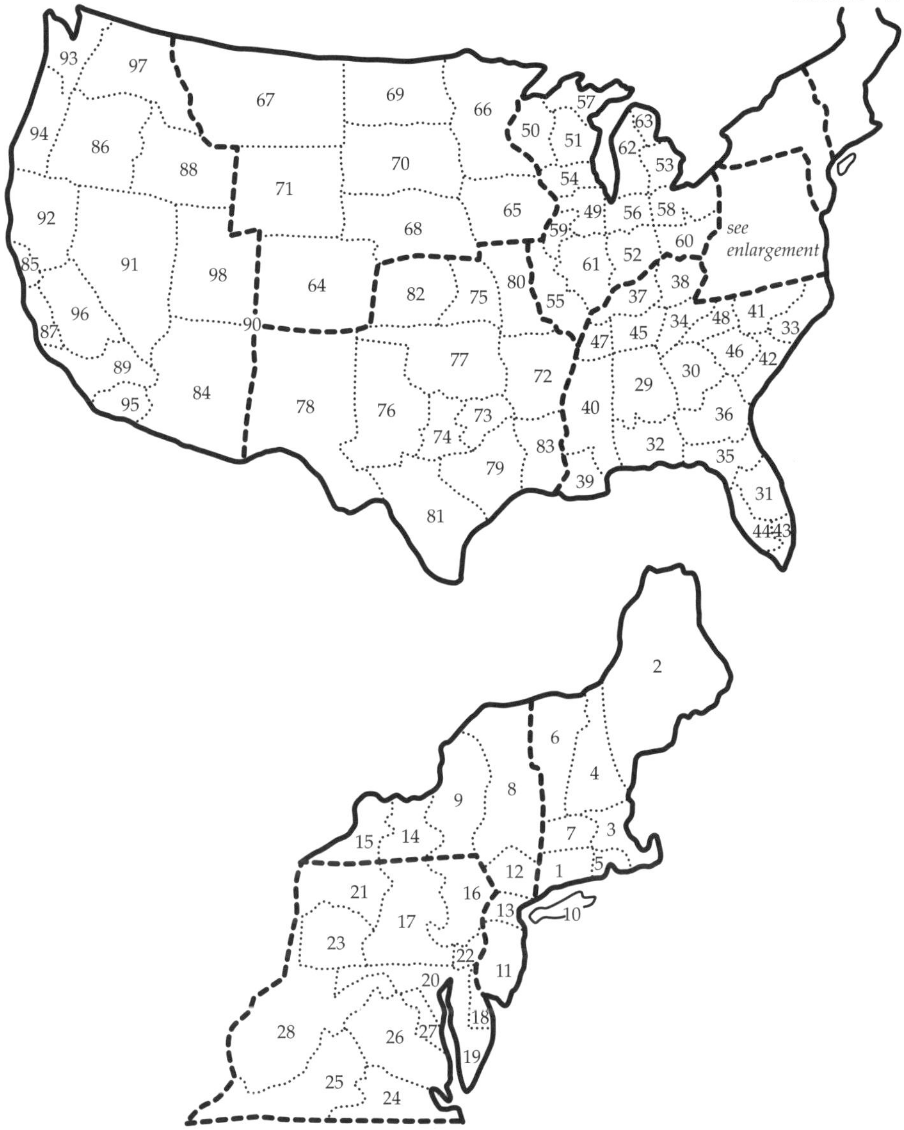

ANGLICAN AND PORVOO COMMUNIONS

MAP 5

The Church in the Province of the West Indies
32 Belize
33 Jamaica and the Cayman Islands
34 North Eastern Caribbean & Aruba
35 Windward Islands
36 Barbados
37 Trinidad and Tobago
38 Guyana
46 Suriname (part of the Diocese of Guyana)
47 Cayenne (part of the Diocese of Guyana)
39 The Bahamas and the Turks and Caicos Islands

Province IX
2 Honduras
6 Litoral Ecuador
7 Central Ecuador
8 Colombia
9 Dominican Republic
11 Puerto Rico
12 Venezuela

The Anglican Church of Mexico
13 Western Mexico
14 Northern Mexico
15 Mexico
16 Cuernavaca
17 Southeastern Mexico

The Anglican Church of the Central American Region
1 Guatemala
3 El Salvador
4 Nicaragua
5 Panama
10 Costa Rica

The Episcopal Anglican Church of Brazil
18 Rio de Janeiro
19 Recife
20 Southern Brazil
21 São Paulo
22 Southwestern Brazil
23 Brasilia
24 Pelotas
44 Curitiba
45 Amazon
48 Missionary District of Oesle-Brasil

Anglican Church of the Southern Cone of America
25 Argentina
26 Chile
27 Northern Argentina
28 Paraguay
29 Peru
30 Uruguay
31 Bolivia

The Episcopal Church of Cuba
(Autonomous diocese)
40 Cuba

41 Bermuda (*extra-provincial to Canterbury*)
42 Haiti (Province II ECUSA – *see Map 4*)
43 Virgin Islands (Province II ECUSA – *see Map 4*)

MAP 6

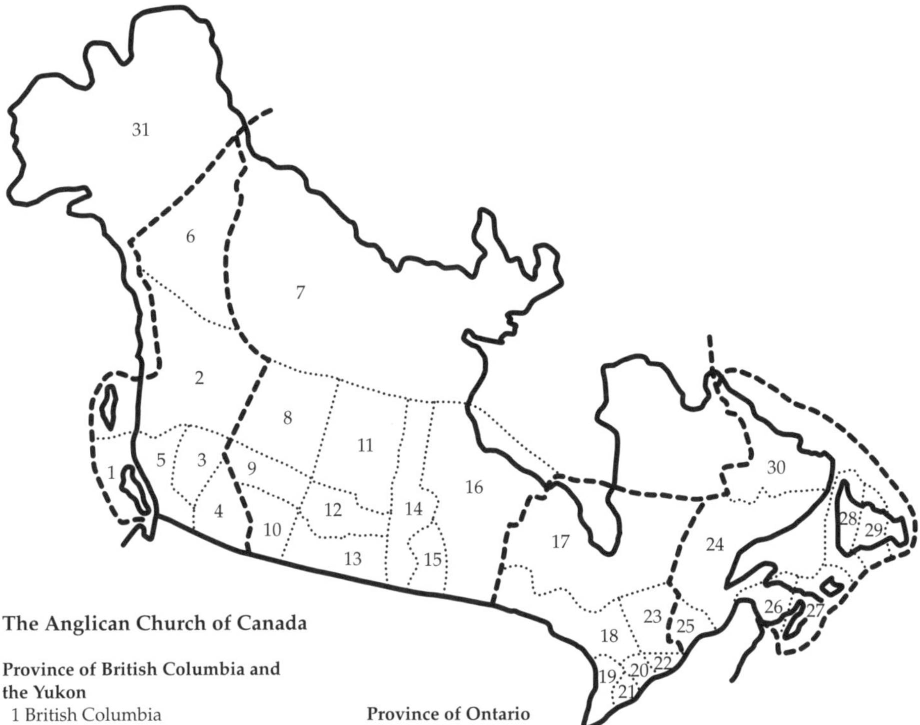

The Anglican Church of Canada

Province of British Columbia and the Yukon

1 British Columbia
2 Caledonia
3 Anglican Parishes of the Central Interior
4 Kootenay
5 New Westminster
6 Yukon

Province of Rupert's Land

7 The Arctic
8 Athabasca
9 Edmonton
10 Calgary
11 Saskatchewan
12 Saskatoon
13 Qu'Appelle
14 Brandon
15 Rupert's Land
16 Keewatin

Province of Ontario

17 Moosonee
18 Algoma
19 Huron
20 Toronto
21 Niagara
22 Ontario
23 Ottawa

Province of Canada

24 Quebec
25 Montreal
26 Fredericton
27 Nova Scotia and Prince Edward Island
28 Western Newfoundland
29 Central Newfoundland
30 Eastern Newfoundland and Labrador

31 Alaska *(in Province VIII of ECUSA)*

MAP 7

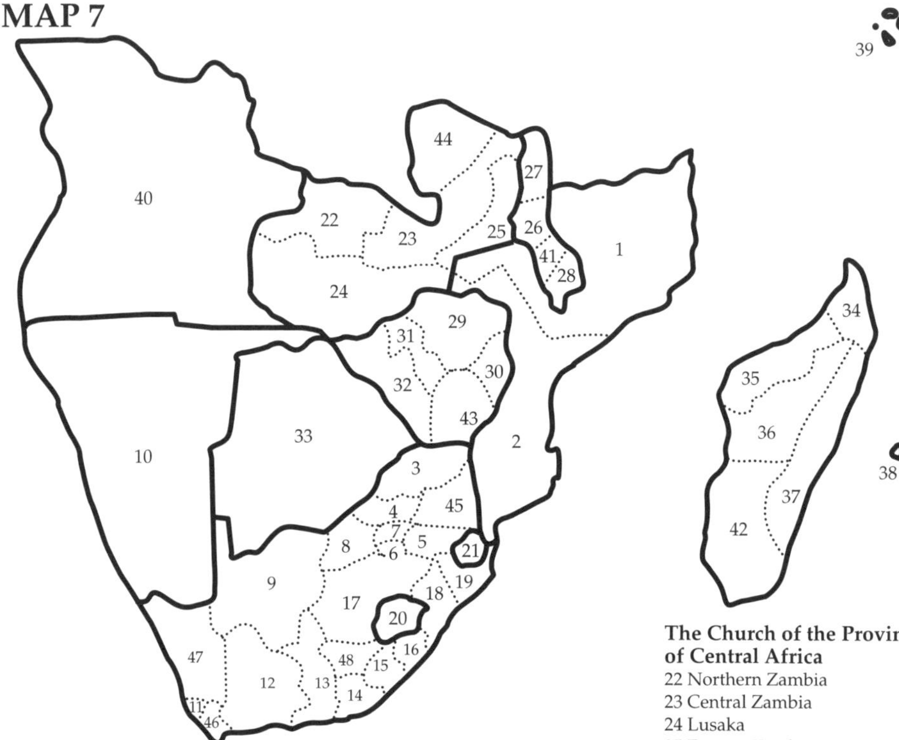

The Church of the Province of Central Africa

22 Northern Zambia
23 Central Zambia
24 Lusaka
25 Eastern Zambia
26 Lake Malawi
27 Northern Malawi
28 Southern Malawi
29 Harare
30 Manicaland
31 Central Zimbabwe
32 Matabeleland
33 Botswana
41 Upper Shire
43 Masvingo
44 Luapula

The Church of the Province of Southern Africa

1 Niassa
2 Lebombo
3 St Mark the Evangelist
4 Pretoria
5 Highveld
6 Christ the King
7 Johannesburg
8 Matlosane
9 Kimberley and Kuruman
10 Namibia
11 Cape Town
12 George
13 Port Elizabeth
14 Grahamstown
15 Mthatha
16 Umzimvubu
17 Free State
18 Natal
19 Zululand
20 Lesotho
21 Swaziland
40 Angola
45 Mpumalanga
46 False Bay
47 Saldanha Bay
48 Ukhahlamba

St Helena

The Church of the Province of the Indian Ocean

34 Antsiranana
35 Mahajanga
36 Antananarivo
37 Toamasina
38 Mauritius
39 Seychelles
42 Fianarantsoa

MAP 8

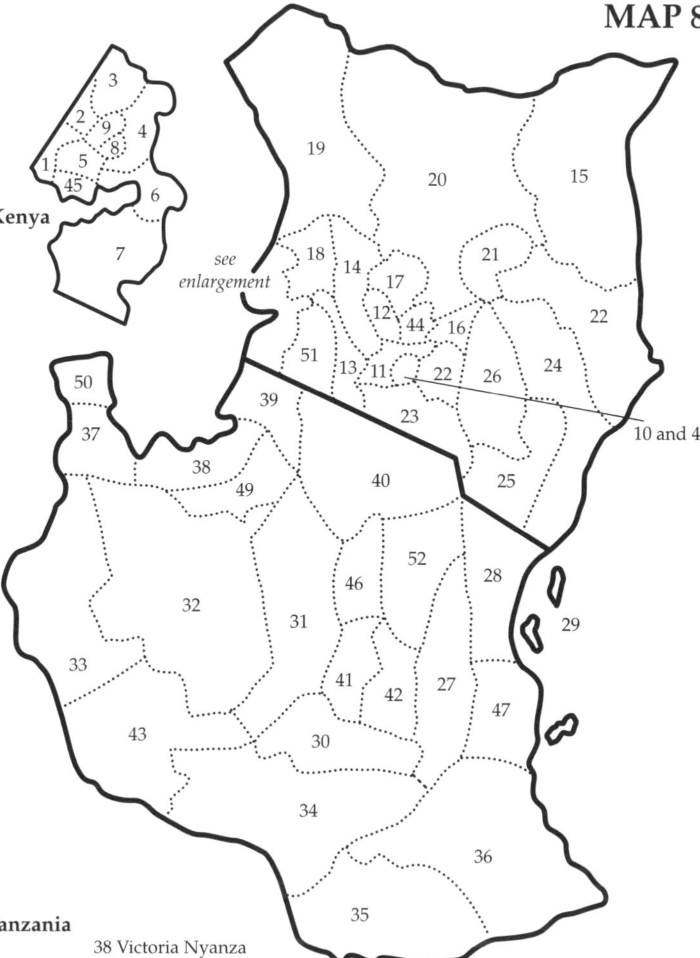

Anglican Church of Kenya

1 Nambale
2 Bungoma
3 Katakwa
4 Maseno North
5 Maseno West
6 Maseno South
7 Southern Nyanza
8 Butere
9 Mumias
10 Nairobi
11 Mount Kenya South
12 Mount Kenya West
13 Nakuru
14 Nyahururu
15 Embu
16 Mbeere
17 Mount Kenya Central
18 Eldoret
19 Kitale
20 Kirinyaga
21 Meru
22 Machakos
23 Kajiado
24 Mombasa
25 Taita Taveta
26 Kitui
44 Thika
45 Bondo
48 All Saints Cathedral
51 Kericho

Anglican Church of Tanzania

27 Morogoro
28 Tanga
29 Zanzibar
30 Ruaha
31 Rift Valley
32 Tabora
33 Western Tanganyika
34 South West Tanganyika
35 Ruvuma
36 Masasi
37 Kagera
38 Victoria Nyanza
39 Mara
40 Mount Kilimanjaro
41 Central Tanganyika
42 Mpwapwa
43 Southern Highlands
46 Kondoa
47 Dar-es-Salaam
49 Shinyanga
50 Lweru
52 Kiteto

MAP 9

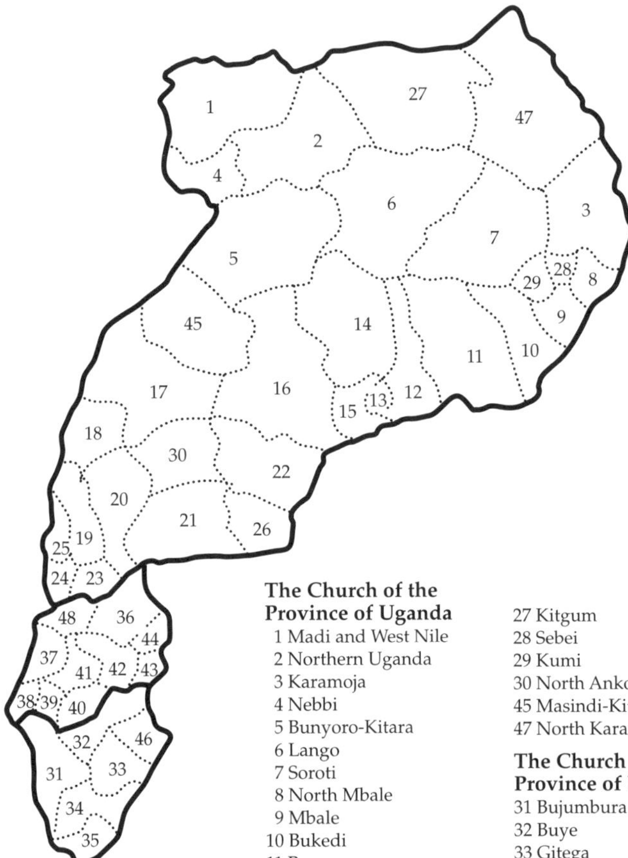

The Church of the Province of Uganda

1 Madi and West Nile
2 Northern Uganda
3 Karamoja
4 Nebbi
5 Bunyoro-Kitara
6 Lango
7 Soroti
8 North Mbale
9 Mbale
10 Bukedi
11 Busoga
12 Mukono
13 Kampala
14 Luweero
15 Namirembe
16 Mityana
17 Ruwenzori
18 South Ruwenzori
19 North Kigezi
20 West Ankole
21 Ankole
22 West Buganda
23 Kigezi
24 Muhabura
25 Kinkizi
26 Central Buganda
27 Kitgum
28 Sebei
29 Kumi
30 North Ankole
45 Masindi-Kitara
47 North Karamoja

The Church of the Province of Burundi

31 Bujumbura
32 Buye
33 Gitega
34 Matana
35 Makamba
46 Muyinga

The Church of the Province of Rwanda

36 Byumba
37 Shyira
38 Cyangugu
39 Kigeme
40 Butare
41 Shyogwe
42 Kigali
43 Kibungo
44 Gahini
48 Kivu

MAP 10

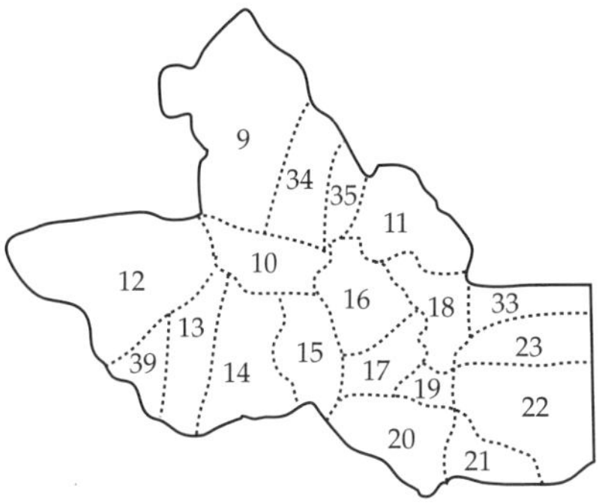

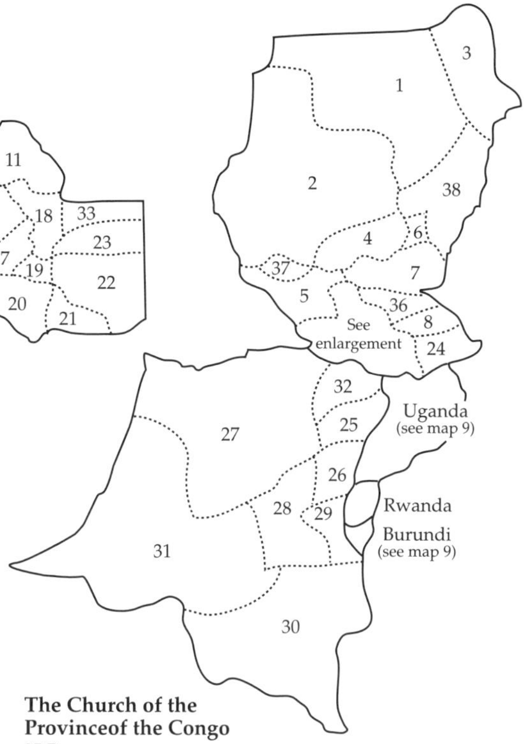

The Church of the Province of Sudan

1 Khartoum
2 El Obeid
3 Port Sudan
4 Kadugli and Nuba Mountains
5 Wau
6 Renk
7 Malakal
8 Bor
9 Rumbek
10 Cueibet
11 Yirol
12 Ezzo
13 Yambio
14 Ibba
15 Maridi
16 Mundri
17 Lui
18 Rokon
19 Lainya
20 Yei
21 Kajo-Keji
22 Rejaf
23 Juba
24 Torit
33 Terekeka
34 Pacong
35 Akot
36 Twic East
37 Aweil
38 Wad Medani
39 Nzara

The Church of the Provinceof the Congo

25 Boga
26 Nord-Kivu
27 Kisangani
28 Kindu
29 Bukavu
30 Katanga (formerly Shaba)
31 Kinshasa
32 Aru

The Church of Nigeria (Anglican Communion) *(see map overleaf)*

Province of Abuja
7 Minna
9 Abuja
10 Kafanchan
13 Makurdi
48 Lokoja
57 Oturkpo
66 Bida
70 Gwagwalada
71 Lafia
Idah
Kubwa
Zonkwa
Ijumu
Kutigi
Kwoi
Okene
Kotangora

Province of Bendel
19 Benin
26 Asaba
36 Warri
45 Sabongidda-Ora
74 Oleh
75 Ughelli
76 Esan
78 Ikka
Western Izon
Akoko-Edo
Ndokwa

Province of Ibadan
8 Kwara
14 Ibadan
15 Osun
16 Ilesa
30 Ife
46 Oke-Osun
61 Ibadan-North
62 Ibadan-South
64 Offa
65 Igbomina
Ajayi Crowther
New Bussa
Ogbomoso
Oke-Ogun
Oyo
Ekiti Kwara
Ife East
Jebba
Omu-Aran

MAP 11

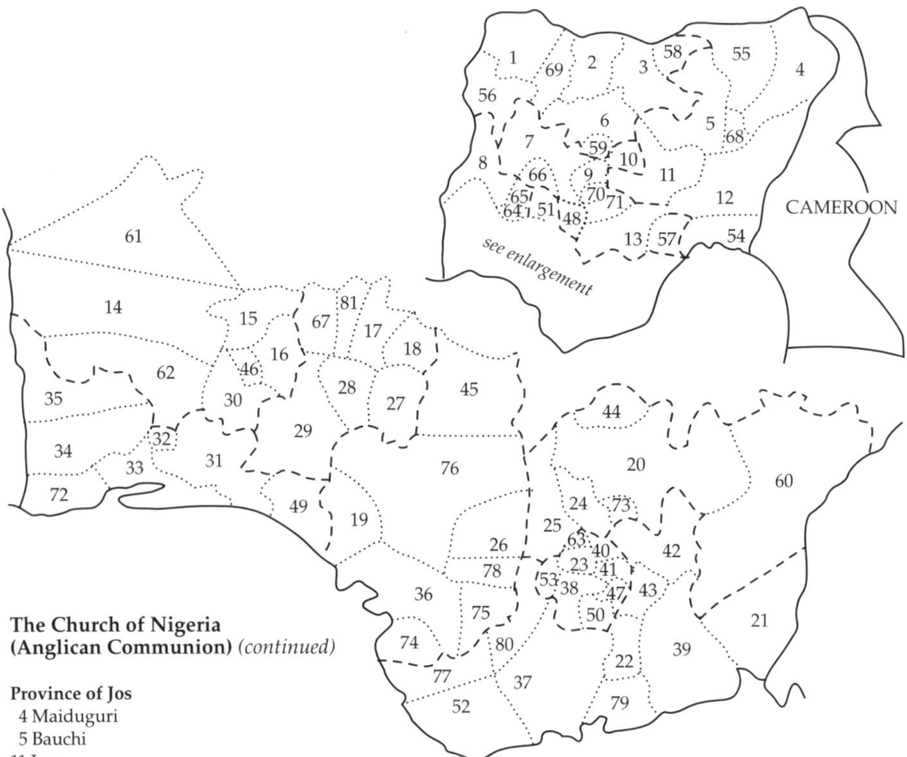

The Church of Nigeria (Anglican Communion) *(continued)*

Province of Jos
4 Maiduguri
5 Bauchi
11 Jos
12 Yola
54 Jalingo
55 Damaturu
68 Gombe
Langtang
Bukuru
Pankshin

Province of Kaduna
1 Sokoto
2 Katsina
3 Kano
6 Kaduna
56 Kebbi
58 Dutse
59 Wusasa
69 Gusau
Bari
Zaria

Province of Lagos
31 Ijebu
32 Remo
33 Lagos
34 Yewa
35 Egba
49 Diocese On The Coast
72 Lagos West
Badagary
Ijebu - North
Lagos Mainland
Awori
Egba West
Ifo

Province of The Niger
20 Enugu
24 Awka
25 On the Niger
44 Nsukka
53 Nnewi
60 Abakaliki
73 Oji River
Aguata
Ngbo
Afikpo
Awgu-Aninri
Enugu North
Ihiala
Ikwo
Mbammili
Niger West
Nike
Ogbaru

Province of Niger Delta
21 Calabar
22 Aba
37 The Niger Delta
39 Uyo
42 Ukwa
43 Umuahia
52 Niger Delta North
77 Niger Delta West
79 Okrika
80 Ahoada
Arochukwu Ohafi
Ikwuano
Isuikwuato
Ogoni
Aba Ngwa North
Etche
Ikwerre
Isiala Ngwa
Isiala Ngwa South
Northern Izon
Ogbia

Province of Ondo
17 Ekiti Oke
18 Akoko
27 Owo
28 Akure
29 Ondo
51 Kabba
67 Ekiti West
81 Ekiti

Province of Owerri
23 Orlu
38 Owerri
40 Okigwe North
41 Okigwe South
47 Mbaise
50 Egbu
63 Ideato
Ohaji-Egbema
Oru
On the Lake

A large number of new dioceses have been created in the Church of Nigeria. These are listed above (unnumbered) but unfortunately at the time of going to press it was not possible to confirm the geographical position of these dioceses and so they are not yet represented on the map.

MAP 12

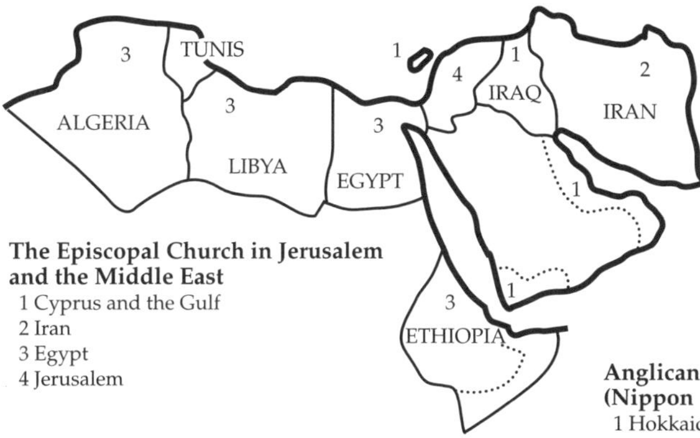

The Episcopal Church in Jerusalem and the Middle East

1 Cyprus and the Gulf
2 Iran
3 Egypt
4 Jerusalem

The Church of the Province of West Africa

1 The Gambia
2 Guinea
3 Liberia
4 Freetown
5 Bo
6 Tamale
7 Kumasi
8 Koforidua
9 Accra
10 Cape Coast
11 Sekondi
12 Sunyani
13 Ho
14 Wiawso
Cameroon (*see Map 11*)

Anglican Communion in Japan (Nippon Sei Ko Kai)

1 Hokkaido
2 Tohoku
3 Kita Kanto
4 Tokyo
5 Yokohama
6 Chubu (Mid Japan)
7 Kyoto
8 Osaka
9 Kobe
10 Kyushu
Okinawa (*see Map 14*)

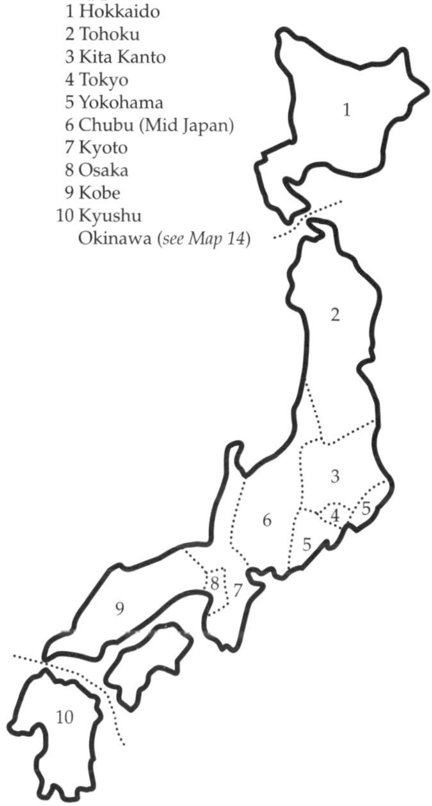

MAP 13

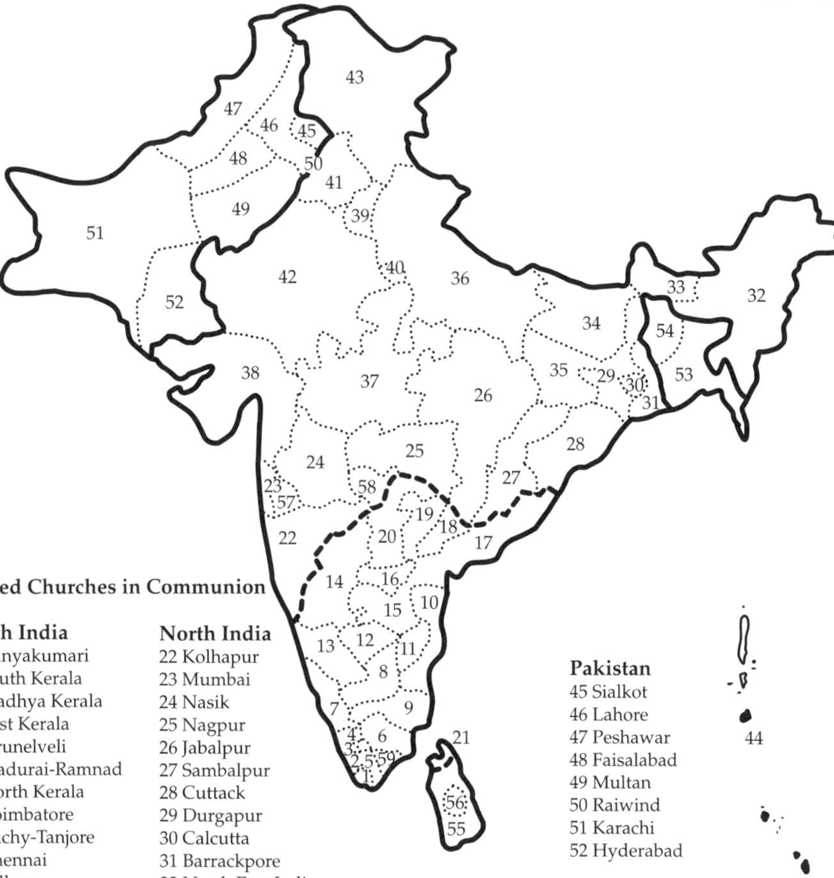

United Churches in Communion

South India
1 Kanyakumari
2 South Kerala
3 Madhya Kerala
4 East Kerala
5 Tirunelveli
6 Madurai-Ramnad
7 North Kerala
8 Coimbatore
9 Trichy-Tanjore
10 Chennai
11 Vellore
12 Karnataka Central
13 Karnataka South
14 Karnataka North
15 Rayalaseema
16 Nandyal
17 Krishna-Godavari
18 Dornakal
19 Karimnagar
20 Medak
21 Jaffna
59 Thoothukudi-Nazareth

North India
22 Kolhapur
23 Mumbai
24 Nasik
25 Nagpur
26 Jabalpur
27 Sambalpur
28 Cuttack
29 Durgapur
30 Calcutta
31 Barrackpore
32 North East India
33 Eastern Himalayas
34 Patna
35 Chota Nagpur
36 Lucknow
37 Bhopal
38 Gujarat
39 Delhi
40 Agra
41 Chandigarh
42 Rajasthan
43 Amritsar
44 Andaman and Nicobar Islands
57 Pune
58 Marathwada

Pakistan
45 Sialkot
46 Lahore
47 Peshawar
48 Faisalabad
49 Multan
50 Raiwind
51 Karachi
52 Hyderabad

Bangladesh
53 Dhaka
54 Kushtia

The Church of Ceylon (Sri Lanka)
55 Colombo
56 Kuranagala

MAP 14

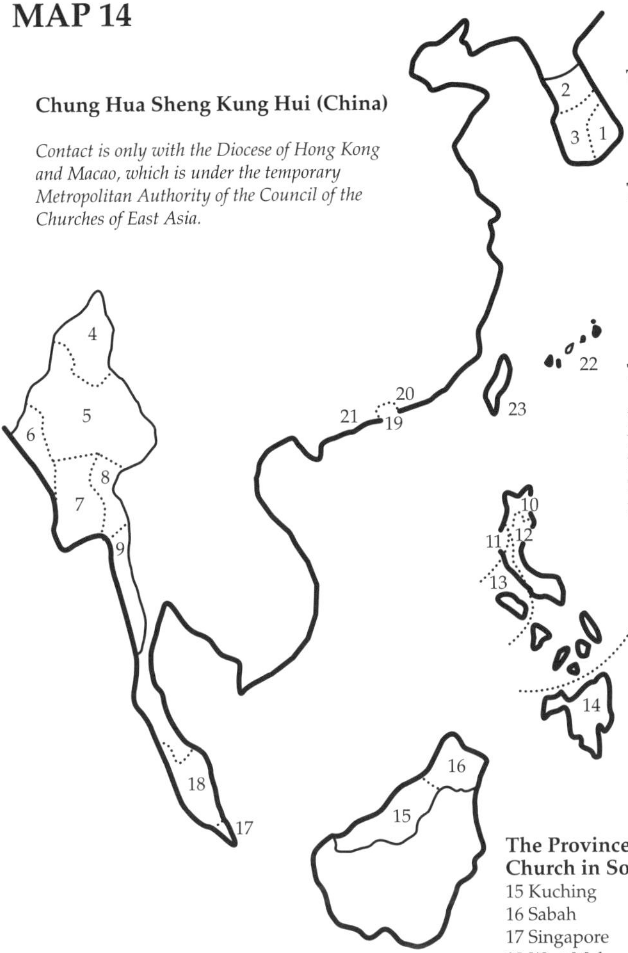

Chung Hua Sheng Kung Hui (China)

Contact is only with the Diocese of Hong Kong and Macao, which is under the temporary Metropolitan Authority of the Council of the Churches of East Asia.

The Anglican Church of Korea
1 Pusan
2 Seoul
3 Taejon

The Province of Myanmar
4 Myitkyina
5 Mandalay
6 Sittwe
7 Yangon
8 Toungoo
9 Hpa-an

The Episcopal Church in the Philippines
10 Northern Luzon
11 North Central Philippines
12 Northern Philippines
13 Central Philippines
14 Southern Philippines

The Province of the Anglican Church in South East Asia
15 Kuching
16 Sabah
17 Singapore
18 West Malaysia

22 Okinawa
(Diocese in the Anglican Communion in Japan)

23 Taiwan
(Diocese in Province VIII of ECUSA)

Hong Kong Sheng Kung Hui
(Hong Kong Anglican Church)
19 Hong Kong Island
20 Eastern Kowloon
21 Western Kowloon

THE COMMUNION OF PORVOO CHURCHES

In October 1992 representatives of the four British and Irish Anglican Churches, the five Nordic Lutheran Churches and the three Baltic Lutheran Churches met in Finland for the fourth and final plenary session of their formal Conversations, which had commenced in 1989. They agreed *The Porvoo Common Statement*, named after Porvoo Cathedral, in which they had celebrated the Eucharist together.

The Common Statement recommended that the participating churches jointly make the Porvoo Declaration, bringing them into communion with each other. This involves common membership, a single, interchangeable ministry and structures to enable the Churches to consult each other on significant matters of faith and order, life and work. The implementation of the commitments contained in the Declaration is coordinated by the Porvoo Agreement Contact Group. The Porvoo Panel of the Church of England was established in 2000 to monitor and develop the implementation of the Porvoo commitments in dioceses and sector ministries.

In 1994 and 1995 the Declaration was approved by the four Anglican Churches, four of the Nordic Lutheran Churches and two of the Baltic Lutheran Churches. The General Synod's final approval of the Declaration in July 1995, following a reference to the diocesan synods, was by overwhelming majorities in each House. The Declaration was signed in the autumn of 1996 at services in Trondheim (Norway), Tallinn (Estonia) and Westminster Abbey.

In 1980 the Lusitanian Church (Portuguese Episcopal Church) became an extra-provincial diocese under the metropolitical authority of the Archbishop of Canterbury and in 1998 the diocesan synod of the Lusitanian Church approved and accepted the Porvoo Declaration. Furthermore in 1980 the Spanish Reformed Episcopal Church fully integrated into the Anglican Communion also coming under the metropolitical authority of the Archbishop of Canterbury. Both churches by virtue of coming under the Archbishop of Canterbury's metropolitical authority and accepting the Porvoo Declaration were integrated into the Porvoo Communion (see also page 398).

The Evangelical Lutheran Chuch in Denmark decided to sign the Porvoo Declaration in December 2009. The Evangelical–Lutheran Church of Latvia has not yet reached its decision.

Along with the Evangelical Lutheran Church of Latvia, the Porvoo Communion is represented by two additional Churches with observer status. They are the Lutheran Church in Great Britain and the Latvian Evangelical Lutheran Church Abroad. The Porvoo Contact Group took the decision to invite both these Churches at its meeting in Madrid in October 2010.

The Nordic Lutheran Churches are the historic national Churches of their respective countries. At the Reformation, when they adhered to Lutheranism, they continued to be episcopally ordered, retaining the historic sees. In Sweden and Finland the succession of the laying on of hands at episcopal consecration was unbroken, whereas in Denmark, Norway and Iceland this was not the case. The Estonian and Latvian Lutheran Churches are similarly their countries' historic national Churches, which became Lutheran at the Reformation. Only in the northern part of Estonia was episcopacy retained, and there only until 1710, but it was restored in both Estonia and Latvia in the twentieth century, the bishops being consecrated in the historic succession. The Lithuanian Lutheran Church, which is now a small minority Church, adopted episcopacy in historic succession in 1976.

The Porvoo Agreement supersedes earlier separate agreements dating from the 1920s, 1930s and 1950s with the Churches concerned (except the Lithuanian Lutheran Church). These provided for mutual eucharistic hospitality and (with the Swedish, Finnish, Estonian and Latvian Churches) mutual participation in episcopal consecrations. Because of the Soviet occupation of the Baltic States, however, it was only in 1989 and 1992 respectively that it was possible for an Anglican bishop to participate in a Latvian and an Estonian consecration for the first time.

The Porvoo Declaration commits the signatory Churches 'to regard baptized members of all of our Churches as members of our own'. It also means that clergy ordained by bishops of the signatory Churches are placed in the same position with regard to ministry in the Church of England as those ordained by Anglican bishops overseas.

Further information can be found on the Porvoo website: www.porvoochurches.org, or is available from the European Secretary at the Council for Christian Unity at Church House, Westminster.

The Porvoo Agreement Contact Group

Co-Chairmen

Rt Revd Martin Wharton (*Bishop of Newcastle*)
email: bishop@newcastle.anglican.org

Rt Revd Peter Skov-Jacobsen (*Bishop of Copenhagen*) *email:* KMKBH@KM.DK

Co-Secretaries
Ms Beate Fagerli (Nordic and Baltic Churches)
email: beate.fagerli@kirken.no
Revd Dr Leslie Nathaniel (Church of England Council for Christian Unity – *see* page 175)
email: leslie.nathaniel@churchofengland.org

The Porvoo Panel
Chairman Rt Revd David Hamid (*Diocese in Europe*)

Porvoo Chaplains in England
Denmark
Revd Else Hviid, 4 St. Katharine's Precinct, Regent's Park, London NW1 4HH
Tel: 020 7935 1723

Estonia
Very Revd Lagle Heinla, Estonian House, 18 Chepstow Villas, London W11 2RB
Tel: 020 7229 6700

Finland
Revd Teemu Hälli, The Finnish Church in London, 33 Albion Street, London SE16 7JG
Tel: 020 7237 1261

Iceland
Chaplaincy being carried out by visits at regular intervals from Revd Adda Björnsdottie

Norway
Revd Torbjørn Holt, 1 St Olav's Square, Albion Street, London SE16 7JB
Tel: 020 7740 3900
Revd Thomas Wagle (*same address*)

Revd Ingrid Ims, Student Chaplain (*same address*)
Very Revd Michael Persson, 6 Harcourt Street, London W1H 2BD *Tel:* 020 7723 5681

Revd Anders Rune

Churches in the Communion of Porvoo Churches

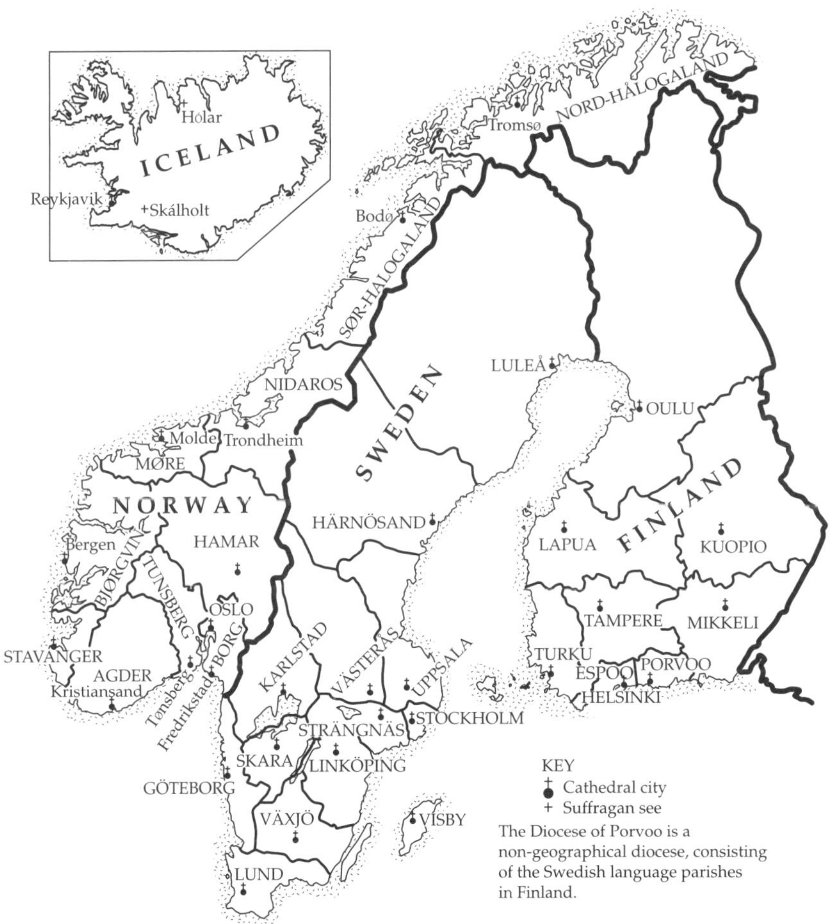

Note: An updated version reflecting all recent changes in the Porvoo Communion is in preparation

NORDIC LUTHERAN CHURCHES

The Evangelical Lutheran Church in Denmark

The Evangelical Lutheran Church in Denmark (ELCD) is the national church in Denmark, with approx. 2000 congregations divided into 10 dioceses, each presided over by a bishop. A bishop is elected by parish council members and pastors in the respective diocese. The role of the bishop is to oversee ministers and congregations in the diocese. The bishop of Copenhagen holds a specific position of honour as *primus inter pares*. There is no office of archbishop. Since 1948 the office has consequently been open to both men and women. In 2010 80.9 per cent of the Danish population (numbering 5.2 million) were members of the ELCD. A vast majority enter into membership as children when they are baptised.

In Denmark there is a strong relationship between the national church and the state. The ELCD is regarded as 'the church of the people' as well as an official national church since the institution of the Danish Constitution of 1849 in which it is particularly mentioned. Every parish council has had its own rights to decide on activities in its local context and to select the pastor of the parish. Thus the local congregation is the cornerstone of the church structure. The queen or king of Denmark is the supreme authority when it comes to organization, liturgy etc. whereas the national parliament (Folketinget) is the *de facto* deciding body with regard to church legislation. Thus, the ELCD is not regulated by a synod, a national church council, as is seen in most other Lutheran churches. The main part of the church budget comes from a membership fee collected by the national tax authorities and ear-marked grants from the state budget. In this way the state contributes to the administration of the church.

The ELCD signed the Porvoo Declaration at a ceremony in Copenhagen Cathedral on 3 October 2010.

General Secretary
Dr Joergen Skov Sorenson, Council on International Relations of the Evangelical Lutheran Church in Denmark, Peter Bangs Vej 1 D, DK-2000 Frederiksberg *Tel:* 45 33 11 44 88
Fax: 45 33 11 95 88
email: interchurch@interchurch.kd
Web: www.interchurch.dk

Bishop of Copenhagen Rt Revd Peter Skov-Jakobsen, Nørregade 11, DK-1165 Copenhagen K
Tel: 45 33 47 65 00
Fax: 45 33 14 39 69
email: kmkbh@km.dk
Web: www.folkekirken.dk/
www.lutheranchurch.dk

The Evangelical Lutheran Church of Finland

The first bishop in the Finnish Church was St Henrik, the Apostle of Finland. According to tradition, St Henrik was an Englishman who accompanied King Erik II of Sweden on a military expedition to south-western Finland in 1155 and was martyred there the following year. From the middle of the thirteenth century until 1809 Finland was part of Sweden, and until the Reformation it formed a single diocese (Turku) in the Province of Uppsala.

In 1554 the Swedish king appointed the Finnish Lutheran Reformer Mikael Agricola (d. 1557) as Bishop of Turku, at the same time founding a second Finnish see, Viipuri (eventually transferred to Tampere). In addition to translating the New Testament and parts of the Old into Finnish, Mikael Agricola compiled the first catechism, liturgy and ritual in Finnish. He is regarded as the father of Finnish as a written language.

A wave of revivals, beginning in the eighteenth century, gave rise in the nineteenth to four mass movements. These remained within the Church of Finland and are still influential on its life today.

In 1809 Finland was annexed by Russia. As a result, the Finnish Church became entirely independent of the Church of Sweden, and from 1817 the Bishop of Turku was styled Archbishop. Finland finally gained its independence in 1917.

Today, roughly 80 per cent of Finns are members of the Evangelical Lutheran Church of Finland, while only 4 per cent are members of other Churches. The ELCF is a 'folk church' (as is the Orthodox Church). The framework for its life is set by the Ecclesiastical Act. Amendments to this state law can only be proposed by the Synod, and Parliament can accept or reject but not amend such proposals. The Church is governed by the Synod, the Church Council and the Bishops' Conference. Although the Archbishop is only *primus inter pares* of the Finnish bishops, he is the President of the Synod and chairs both the Bishops' Conference and the Church Council.

The Church is organized in nine dioceses, one of which consists of the Swedish-speaking parishes (Porvoo). The diocese of Helsinki has recently divided into two, giving rise to the new see of Espoo.

Porvoo Agreement Contact Executive Secretary for Theology Tomi Karttunen, Department for International Relations, Satamakatu 11, Box 185, FI-00161 Helsinki *Tel:* 358 9 1802 290
Fax: 358 9 1802 230
email: tomi.karttunen@evl.fi
Web: www.evl.fi/english/index.html

ESPOO
Bishop Rt Revd Dr Mikko Heikka, Diocesan Chapter, PO Box 203, FI-02771 Espoo
Tel: 358 9 8050 8832
Fax: 358 9 8050 8848
email: mikko.heikka@evl.fi

HELSINKI
Bishop Rt Revd Irja Askola, Diocesan Chapter, PO Box 142, FI-00121 Helsinki *Tel:* 358 9 2340 3010
Fax: 358 9 2340 3050
email: irja.askola@evl.fi
Web: www.helsinginhiippakunta.evl.fi/information_in_english/

KUOPIO
Bishop Rt Revd Dr Wille Riekkinen, Diocesan Chapter, PO Box 42, FI-70101 Kuopio *Tel:* 358 17 288 8414
Fax: 358 17 288 8420
email: wille.riekkinen@evl.fi

LAPUA
Bishop Rt Revd Dr Simo Peura, Diocesan Chapter, PO Box 60, FI-62101 Lapua *Tel:* 358 6 4339 325
Fax: 358 6 4339 320
email: simo.peura@evl.fi

MIKKELI
Bishop Rt Revd Dr Seppo Häkkinen, Diocesan Chapter, PO Box 122, FI-50101 Mikkeli
Tel: 358 15 3216 011
Fax: 358 15 3216 016
email: seppo.hakkinen@evl.fi

OULU
Bishop Rt Revd Dr Samuel Salmi, Diocesan Chapter, PO Box 85, FI-90101 Oulu *Tel:* 358 8 311 4654
Fax: 358 8 311 0659
email: samuel.salmi@evl.fi

PORVOO
(The Diocese of Porvoo (Borgå) is a non-geographical Swedish-language diocese.)

Bishop Rt Revd Dr Björn Vikström, Diocesan Chapter, PO Box 30, FI-06101 Borgå
Tel: 358 19 529 7716
Fax: 358 19 585 705
email: bjorn.vikstrom@evl.fi
Web: http://borgastift.planeetta.com

TAMPERE
Bishop Rt Revd Dr Matti Repo, Diocesan Chapter, Eteläpuisto 2C, FI-33200 Tampere
Tel: 358 3 238 1130
Fax: 358 3 238 1150
email: matti.repo@evl.fi
Web: www.tampereenhiippakunta.fi/in_english

TURKU
Archbishop of Turku and Finland Rt Revd Kari Mäkinen, Diocesan Chapter, PO Box 60, FI-20501 Turku *Tel:* 358 2 279 7031
Fax: 358 2 279 7002
email: Arkkipiispa@evl.fi

Bishop of Turku Rt Revd Kaarlo Kalliala (*same address*) *Tel:* 358 2 279 7033
Fax: 358 2 2797 001
email: kaarlo.kalliala@evl.fi

The Evangelical Lutheran Church of Iceland

Christianity was adopted at Thingvellir by decree of the legislature in the year 1000. The ancient Icelandic sees of Skálholt and Hólar were founded in 1055 and 1106, respectively. Having previously been under the jurisdiction of Bremen and Lund, from 1153 Iceland belonged to the Province of Nidaros (Trondheim). Part of the Kingdom of Norway from 1262, Iceland eventually came under Danish rule. The Lutheran Reformation was introduced in 1541. From this time onwards until 1908 (with one exception in the late eighteenth century), Icelandic bishops were consecrated by the Bishops of Sealand (Copenhagen).

The two Icelandic sees were united in 1801, but in 1909 they were revived as suffragan sees. Iceland gained its independence from Denmark in 1918, becoming a republic in 1944.

A new Church law came into effect on 1 January 1998, granting the Church considerable autonomy from the state. The Church Assembly is the highest organ of the Church. Today, around 80 per cent of the Icelandic population are members of the Church of Iceland.

Porvoo Agreement Contact: Revd Steinunn A. Bjornsdottir, Laugavegi 31, 150 Reykjavík
Tel: 354 528 4000
Fax: 354 528 4098
email: Steinunn.bjornsdottir@kirkjan.is

The Church of Iceland comprises a single diocese, with two suffragan bishops in the ancient sees of Hólar and Skálholt.

Bishop of Iceland Rt Revd Agnes M. Sigurdardottir, Laugavegi 31, 150 Reykjavík *Tel:* 354 528 4000
Fax: 354 528 4098
email: agnes.m.sigurdardottir@kirkjan.is

Bishop of Skálholt Rt Revd Kristjan Valur Ingolfsson, Skálholt, Biskupshús, Skálholti, 801 Selfoss *Tel:* 354 486 8972
Fax: 354 486 8975
email: kristjan.valur.ingolfsson@kirkjan.is

Bishop of Hólar Rt Revd Solveig Lára Gudmundsdottir, Biskupssetur, Hólar, 551 Saudárkrókur *Tel:* 354 453 6300
Fax: 354 453 6301
email: srslara@ismennt.is

Contact for ecumenical affairs Ms Steinunn A. Björnsdóttir, Ecumenical Secretary, Bishop's office, Laugavegur 31, 150 Reykjavík, Iceland
Tel: 354 528 4000
Fax: 354 528 4098
email: steinunn.bjornsdottir@kirkjan.is

The Church of Norway

From around AD 1000 Christianity was brought to Norway by missionaries both from the British Isles and from Germany. Central to the Christianizing of Norway was King Olav Haraldsson. After his death in 1030 he was venerated as St Olave, and his shrine in Nidaros Cathedral (Trondheim) was a centre of pilgrimage. Episcopal sees were established in Nidaros, Bergen, Oslo (by 1100), and in Stavanger (1125) and Hamar (1153). Part of the Province of Lund from 1103, Norway became a separate province when Nidaros was raised to an archiepiscopal see in 1153. In addition to the five Norwegian sees, the Province of Nidaros also included six further dioceses covering Iceland, the Faeroes, Greenland, the Shetland and Orkney Islands, the Hebrides and the Isle of Man. Under Olav IV (1380–87) Norway was united with Denmark.

The Norwegian Reformation of 1537 was imposed by the new King of Denmark, Christian III, with little evidence of popular enthusiasm. New bishops ('superintendents') were ordained to the sees of Nidaros, Bergen and Stavanger by Johannes Bugenhagen, the Superintendent of Wittenberg, in 1537, and Bugenhagen's Danish Church Order was extended to Norway in 1539. Of the pre-Reformation bishops, Bishop Hans Rev of Oslo alone accepted the Reformation, and returned to his see (to which that of Hamar had been united) as Superintendent in 1541. The diocesan structure had been retained, with four of the five historic sees, and the term 'bishop' soon replaced its Latin synonym 'superintendent', but until recent years neither Bishop Rev nor any other bishop consecrated in the historic succession of the laying on of hands participated in the consecration of future bishops. Nidaros ceased to be an archiepiscopal see.

In the eighteenth and nineteenth centuries, pietist movements became influential, but they remained within the Church of Norway, the membership of which still amounts to 77 per cent of the population.

The Church of Norway has an 116-member General Synod, consisting of the members of the eleven diocesan councils (including the bishops), three members representing clergy, laity and lay employees, the moderators of the Sami Church Council and the Council on Ecumenical and International Relations, and three non-voting representatives of the theological faculties. Its executive is the 15-member National Council, which has a lay chair person. Related central bodies include the Bishops' Conference, the Council on Ecumenical and International Relations, the Sámi Church Council. and a doctrinal commission.

On 21st May 2012, the Norwegian Parliament passed a constitutional amendment that granted the Church of Norway increased autonomy.

The Parliament's recent decisions loosen historical ties between institutions of State and the majority Lutheran Church, which date back to the sixteenth century. One major consequence is that the responsibility for the appointment of bishops of Church of Norway shifted from the state to the church. A 500-year state-church tradition of the King/the Government appointing bishops has ended. The next bishop appointment will be made by the board of the National Council (15 members elected by the General Synod.)

The 116-member General Synod comprising bishops, pastors and lay church members adopted the new order for appointing bishops on 12–17 April this year.

Porvoo Agreement Contact Revd Dr Beate Fagerli, Council on Ecumenical and International Relations, PB 799 – Sentrum, N-0106 Oslo
Tel: 47 23 08 12 74
Fax: 47 23 08 12 01
email: beate.fagerli@kirken.no

AGDER
Presiding Bishop Rt Revd Helga Haugland Byfuglien, Diocesan Centre, Archbishop's House, N-7013 Trondheim/ *Tel:* 47 73 53 91 00
Or:
Church of Norway Bishop's Conference, PB 799 – Sentrum, N-0106 Oslo, *Tel:* 47 23 08 13 90
Fax: 47 23 08 12 01
email: bispemotet@kirken.no
Bishop Vacancy, Diocesan Centre, PB 208, 4662 Krisitansand S *Tel:* 47 38 10 52 20
Fax: 47 38 10 51 21

BJØRGVIN
Bishop Rt Revd Halvor Nordhaug, Diocesan Centre, Strandgt. 198, PB. 1960 Nordnes, 5018 Bergen *Tel:* 47 55 30 64 70
Fax: 47 55 30 64 85
email: bjoergvin.biskop@kirken.no

BORG
Bishop Rt Revd Atle Sommerfeldt, Diocesan Centre, Bjarne Aas gt 9, PB 403, N-1601 Fredrikstad *Tel:* 47 69 30 79 00
Fax: 47 69 30 79 01
email: borg.bdr@kirken.no

HAMAR
Bishop Rt Revd Solveig Fiske, Diocesan Centre, Folkestadgate 52, PB 172, N-2302 Hamar
Tel: 47 62 55 03 50
Fax: 47 62 55 03 51
email: hamar.bdr@kirken.no

MØRE
Bishop Rt Revd Ingeborg Synøve Midtømme, Diocesan Centre, Moldetrappa 1, N-6415 Molde
Tel: 47 71 25 06 70
Fax: 47 71 25 06 71
email: moere.bdr@kirken.no

NIDAROS
Bishop Rt Revd Tor Singsaas, Diocesan Centre, Archbishop's House, N-7013 Trondheim
Tel: 47 73 53 91 00
Fax: 47 73 53 91 11
email: nidaros.bdr@kirken.no

NORD-HÅLOGALAND
Bishop Rt Revd Per Oskar Kjølaas, Diocesan Centre, Conrad Holmboesvei 20, PB 790, N-9258 Tromsø *Tel:* 47 77 60 39 60/61
Fax: 47 77 60 39 70
email: nord-haalogaland.bdr@kirken.no

OSLO
Bishop Rt Revd Ole Chr. M. Kvarme, Diocesan Centre, St Halvards plass 3, PB 9307, Gronland, N-0135 Oslo *Tel:* 47 23 30 11 60
Fax: 47 23 30 11 99
email: oslo.bdr@kirken.no

SØR-HÅLOGALAND
Bishop Rt Revd Tor Berger Jørgensen, Diocesan Centre, Tolder Holmersvei 11, N-8003 Bodø
Tel: 47 75 54 85 50
Fax: 47 75 54 85 60
email: soer-haalogaland.bdr@kirken.no

STAVANGER
Bishop Rt Revd Erling J. Pettersen, Diocesan Centre, Domkirkeplasson 2, PB 629, N-4003 Stavanger *Tel:* 47 51 84 62 70
Fax: 47 51 84 62 71
email: stavanger.bdr@kirken.no

TUNSBERG
Bishop Rt Revd Laila Riksaasen Dahl,Diocesan Centre, Håkon 5.s gt, PB 1253, N-3105
Tel: 47 33 35 43 00
Fax: 47 33 35 43 01
email: tunsberg.bdr@kirken.no

The Church of Sweden

The first to preach the gospel in Sweden was St Ansgar (801–65), the first Archbishop of Hamburg-Bremen, but it was in the eleventh century that the systematic conversion of Sweden was begun, largely by missionaries from England. From 1104 the new Swedish dioceses formed part of the Nordic Province of Lund (which was Danish until 1658), but only until 1164, when Uppsala was raised to an archiepiscopal see. The most celebrated figure of the medieval Swedish Church is St Birgitta of Vadstena (1303–73), foundress of the Brigittine Order.

Under the Lutheran Reformers Olaus Petri (1493–1552) and his brother Laurentius (d. 1573), who became the first Lutheran archbishop in 1531, the Swedish Reformation was gradual, and moderate in character. The Augsburg Confession was adopted in 1593.

The eighteenth and nineteenth centuries saw both latitudinarian and pietist movements, and in the early twentieth century a strong high-church movement developed. Archbishop Nathan Söderblom (1866–1931), one of the leading figures of the Ecumenical Movement, used the concept of 'evangelical catholicity' to describe the Church of Sweden's position. The Conference of Bishops of the Anglican Communion adopted a resolution of altar and pulpit fellowship with the Church of Sweden in 1920. In 1997 Christina Odenberg became the Church of Sweden's first woman bishop, when she was appointed Bishop of Lund.

The Church of Sweden is governed by a General Synod with 251 members and a 15-member Central Board (chaired by the archbishop), together with the Bishops' Conference.

The bishops attend the Synod, but are not members of it, although they have all the rights of members except the right to vote. They are *ex-officio* members of the Synod Committee on Church Doctrine.

A separation of Church and State was effected in the year 2000, a year which also was marked by the 1000-year celebration of Christian faith in Sweden at the well of Husaby in the Diocese of Skara.

Porvoo Agreement Contact Revd Jenny Sjögreen, Ecumenical Officer, Church of Sweden, S-751 70 Uppsala *Tel:* 46 18 16 95 20
Fax: 46 18 16 95 38
email: jenny.sjogreen@svenskakyrkan.se

Archbishop's Chaplain Revd Lars Åstrand, S-751 70 Uppsala *Tel:* 46 76 622 5815
Fax: 46 18 16 96 25
email: lars.astrand@svenskakyrkan.se

(**Note:** *The dioceses here are arranged alphabetically. The order traditionally used in Sweden reflects the chronological seniority of the Swedish dioceses.*)

GÖTEBORG
Bishop Rt Revd Dr Per Eckerdal, Stiftskansliet, Box 11937, SE-404 39 Göteborg
Tel: 46 31 771 30 00
Fax: 46 31 771 30 30
email: per.eckerdal@svenskakyrkan.se

HÄRNÖSAND
Bishop Rt Revd Dr Tuulikki Koivunen Bylund), Stiftskansliet, Box 94, SE-871 22 Härnösand
Tel: 46 611 254 00
Fax: 46 611 134 75
email: tuulikki.bylund@svenskakyrkan.se

KARLSTAD
Bishop Rt Revd Esbjörn Hagberg, Stiftskansliet, Box 186, SE-651 05 Karlstad *Tel:* 46 54 17 24 00
Fax: 46 54 17 24 70
email: esbjorn.hagberg@svenskakyrkan.se

LINKÖPING
Bishop Rt Revd Martin Modéus, Stiftskansliet, Box 1367, SE-581 31 Linköping *Tel:* 46 13 24 26 00
Fax: 46 13 14 90 95
email: biskopen.linkoping@svenskakyrkan.se

LULEÅ
Bishop Rt Revd Hans Stiglund, Stiftskansliet, Stationsgatan 40, SE-972 32 Luleå
Tel: 46 920 26 47 00
Fax: 46 920 26 47 21
email: hans.stiglund@svenskakyrkan.se

LUND
Bishop Rt Revd Dr Antje Jackelén, Stiftskansliet, Box 32, SE-221 00 Lund *Tel:* 46 46 35 87 00
Fax: 46 46 18 49 48
email: antje.jackelen@svenskakyrkan.se

SKARA
Bishop Rt Revd Åke Bonnier, Malmgatan 14, SE-532 32 Skara *Tel:* 46 511 262 00
Fax: 46 511 262 70
email: ake.bonnier@svenskakyrkan.se

STOCKHOLM
Bishop Rt Revd Eva Brunne, Stiftskansliet, Box 16306, SE-103 25 Stockholm
Tel: 46 8 508 940 00
Fax: 46 8 24 75 75
email: eva.brunne@svenskakyrkan.se

STRÄNGNÄS
Bishop Rt Revd Dr Hans-Erik Nordin, Stiftskansliet, Box 84, SE-645 22 Strängnäs
Tel: 46 152 234 00
Fax: 46 152 234 56
email: hans-erik.nordin@svenskakyrkan.se

UPPSALA
Archbishop Most Revd Dr Anders Wejryd, SE-751 70 Uppsala *Tel:* 46 18 16 95 00
Fax: 46 18 16 96 25
email: archbishop@svenskakyrkan.se

Bishop Rt Revd Dr Ragnar Persenius, Box 1314, SE-751 43 Uppsala *Tel:* 46 18 68 07 00
Fax: 46 18 12 87 62
email: ragnar.persenius@svenskakyrkan.se

VÄSTERÅS
Bishop Rt Revd Thomas Söderberg, Stiftskansliet, V Kyrkogatan 9, SE-722 15 Västerås
Tel: 46 21 17 85 00
Fax: 46 21 12 93 10
email: thomas.soderberg@svenskakyrkan.se

VÄXJÖ
Bishop Rt Rev Jan-Olof Johansson, Box 527, SE-351 06 Växjö *Tel:* 46 470 77 38 00
Fax: 46 470 72 95 50
email: biskop.vaxjostift@svenskakyrkan.se

VISBY
Bishop Rt Revd Sven-Bernhard Fast, Stiftskansliet, Box 1334, SE-621 24 Visby
Tel: 46 498 40 49 00
Fax: 46 498 21 01 03
email: sven-bernhard.fast@svenskakyrkan.se

Further information about the history of the Nordic Lutheran Churches and of their relations with the Church of England can be found in Lars Österlin, *Churches of Northern Europe in Profile. A Thousand Years of Anglo-Nordic Relations* (Norwich, 1995).

BALTIC LUTHERAN CHURCHES

The Estonian Evangelical–Lutheran Church

The conversion of Estonia to Christianity began at the end of the tenth century, and the first known bishop was consecrated in 1165. The mission was prosecuted by the Brethren of the Sword, an order founded in 1202 which merged with the Teutonic Order in 1237. In 1219 the Danes conquered the northern area and founded the capital Reval (Tallinn), which became an episcopal see within the Province of Lund. Further sees were established at Dorpat (Tartu) in 1224 and Hapsal (Saare-Lääne) in 1227, within the Province of Riga, the capital of Livonia, which included the southern part of modern Estonia. In some areas secular authority was in the hands of the bishops, while in others the Teutonic Order held sway. The entire area was very much under German dominance.

The Lutheran movement reached Estonia in 1523, and as early as the following year an assembly in Reval decided to adhere to the Reformation. Later in the century, however, the twin provinces of Estonia and Livonia became divided between neighbouring powers. Most of Estonia placed itself under Swedish rule in 1561, but Denmark ruled the island of Oesel (Saarema) from 1560 to 1645 and Livonia was annexed by Poland from 1561 to 1621. In Swedish Estonia, the Church was governed by a bishop and consistory, but Danish ecclesiastical law was introduced in Oesel, while Livonia came under the influence of the Counter-Reformation. Superintendents, rather than bishops, were appointed for these areas after they came under Swedish rule (in 1621 and 1645).

In 1710 both provinces came under Russian rule. In Estonia the office of bishop was replaced with that of superintendent. The consistories were chaired by laymen. In 1832 the Lutheran Churches of all three Baltic provinces were united with Russia's German-speaking Lutheran Church into a Russian Lutheran Church, with a General Consistory in St Petersburg. Each province (and – until 1890 – Reval, Oesel and Riga separately) had its own general superintendent and consistory. The University of Dorpat (Tartu), originally founded in 1632, was refounded in 1802. As the only Protestant theological faculty in the Russian Empire, it was of great importance. Throughout the period up to 1918 the clergy were German, like the ruling elite. The Moravian Church, which was active in Estonia and Livonia from 1736, enjoyed considerable influence over the Estonian peasantry, and by 1854 there were 276 Moravian prayer halls. However, the Moravian authorities blocked the development of this movement into a separate Moravian Church, and the Moravians' adherents remained within the Lutheran Church.

In 1918 Estonia and the Estonian northern part of Livonia became an independent state. The Church too became independent. It remained united, having both German and Estonian clergy and members. The office of bishop was immediately restored, the first bishop being consecrated in 1921 by the Archbishop of Uppsala and a Finnish bishop.

Estonia's independent existence lasted little more than 20 years, however. In 1940 it was occupied by the Red Army. German occupation followed, but Soviet rule was restored in 1944. Archbishop Kópp, who had remained unconsecrated because the war prevented bishops from other countries travelling to Estonia, went into exile with 70 other clergy and tens of thousands of church members. As a result of this the Estonian Evangelical–Lutheran Church Abroad was born. Of the clergy who remained, one-third were eventually deported to Siberia. Not until 1968 was it possible for an archbishop to be consecrated, although the first post-war Archbishop had already been elected in 1949.

In 1988, Estonia began to move towards independence, which was achieved in 1991. This was accompanied by a remarkable blossoming of church life. The Theological Faculty at Tartu, which had been dissolved by the Soviet authorities, was reopened. The Theological Institute of the EELC in Tallinn, which was set up after the war, also continues its work.

The Estonian Evangelical–Lutheran Church still forms one diocese, headed by an Archbishop and a Suffragan Bishop. It is governed by a General Synod, the executive organ of which is the six-member Consistory.

Porvoo Agreement Contact Very Revd Veiko Vihuri, Karja kirikla, 94201 Pärsama, Saaremaa
Tel: 372 45 73 65
email: veiko.vihuri@eelk.ee

Archbishop of Estonia Most Revd Andres Põder, Consistory of the EELC, Kirikuplats 3, 10130 Tallinn
Tel: 372 6 27 73 50
Fax: 372 6 27 73 52
email: konsistoorium@eelk.ee
Web www.eelk.ee

ANGLICAN AND PORVOO COMMUNIONS

The Evangelical Lutheran Church of Lithuania

Not until 1387 was an episcopal see established in Vilnius, following the baptism the previous year of Grand Duke Jogaila (whose coronation as King of Poland inaugurated a union lasting until 1795), and it was 1418 before the inhabitants of German-dominated Samogitia (covering much of present-day Lithuania) were forced to accept baptism.

A Lutheran congregation was founded in Vilnius as early as 1521, but persecution forced the Lithuanian Reformer Martin Mazvydas to flee to Königsberg. In time the Lithuanian nobility established the Reformed faith on their estates, while the numerous German merchants and craftsmen established Lutheran congregations in the towns from the 1550s. Until the early nineteenth century, the Lutheran Church continued to be a German and urban minority Church.

Sigismund Vasa (1587–1632) successfully restored Roman Catholicism as the religion of the people, and subsequent anti-Protestant policies meant that by 1775, when religious freedom was granted, just 30 Reformed and five Lutheran congregations remained (except those in Prussian-ruled Tauragė/Tauroggen).

In 1795 most of Lithuania was ceded to Russia, and Lithuania's Lutheran congregations were placed under the Consistory of Courland (now southern Latvia). Immigration of Lutheran Letts, Germans and Lithuanians from East Prussia produced new Lutheran congregations, especially in the countryside. The pastors (only nine in 1918) were all Germans.

At independence in 1918, Lithuania's population included 75,000 Lutherans, of whom roughly 30,000 were Germans, 30,000 Lithuanians and 15,000 Letts. In 1920 separate synods had to be formed for the three linguistic groups, and for much of the inter-war period tension between them paralysed the Lutheran Church. By 1939, however, there were 55 congregations with 33 pastors. To these should be added the separate Lutheran Church of the Prussian *Memelgebiet*, which Lithuania annexed in 1923. By 1939 this had 135,000 members (the majority German) in 32 parishes, served by 39 pastors.

Lithuanian Lutheranism was soon to be decimated. In 1941, following the 1940 Soviet annexation of Lithuania, most of the German population, together with a large number of Lithuanian Lutherans, emigrated to Germany. In Memelland and the Vilnius area, both reintegrated into Lithuania and thus the Soviet Union in 1945, the picture was even more stark. All but 30,000 inhabitants fled, while the pastor of the historic Lutheran church in Vilnius emigrated with his entire congregation.

A provisional Lutheran Consistory found itself responsible for 20,000 Lithuanians and Letts in Lithuania proper, together with just 15,000 Lithuanians in Klaipėda (Memelland). There were no pastors in Klaipėda and only six in the rest of the country, three of whom were soon banished to Siberia. After Stalin's death in 1953 and a first post-war synod in 1955, the structures of church life were gradually restored, but several thousand more Protestants emigrated between 1957 and 1965. At a second synod in 1970, Jonas Kalvanas, the only pastor left who had studied theology at university (he was ordained in 1940), was elected to chair the Consistory. It was with his consecration as Bishop by the Archbishop of Estonia in 1976 that his church gained the historic episcopate. He was succeeded in 1995 by his son and namesake, whose early death in 2003 left the see vacant until the consecration in June 2004 of Bishop Mindaugas Sebutis.

In 2003 the Lutheran Church had 54 congregations, with about 20,000 communicant members and twenty-four clergy.

Porvoo Agreement Contact Revd Darius Petkunas, Simonaitytes 18–21, LT-5814 Klaipėda
Tel: 370 6 220 409
email: darius.petkunas@liuteronai.lt

Bishop of the Evangelical Lutheran Church of Lithuania Rt Revd Mindaugas Sebutis, Vokieciu 20, LT-01130 Vilnius *Tel* and *Fax:* 370 5 212 3792
email: sabutis@times.lt
Web: www.liuteronai.lt/index_ang.html

NON-SIGNATORY CHURCHES

The Evangelical Lutheran Church of Latvia

The Church of Latvia has not yet voted on the Porvoo Declaration.

Archbishop of Riga and Latvia Most Revd Janis Vanags, M.Pils 4, LV 1050, Riga
Tel: 371 6 225406
Fax: 371 6 225436
email: lelb@lelb.lv / archbishop@ lelb.lv

Porvoo Agreement Contact, Dr Sandra Gintere, Alksnaja iela 3, Riga, LV 1050, Latvia
email: sandra.gintere@ lelb.lv

There are also Anglican chaplaincies in most of the countries covered by the Porvoo Agreement. These belong to the Archdeaconry of Scandinavia and Germany within the Diocese in Europe. A leaflet giving details is available from the Diocesan Office of the Diocese in Europe, *see below*.

The *Directory of English-speaking Churches Abroad* (£4.00 as at 1 May 2009) lists English-speaking churches of Anglican and many other denominations in countries where English is not the first language, and is available from Intercontinental Church Society, 1 Athena Drive, Tachbrook Park, Warwick CV34 6NL
Tel: 01926 430 347
Fax: 01926 888 092
email: enquiries@ics-uk.org
Web: www.ics-uk.org

Credit card orders accepted by telephone or on the web site.

Continental Anglican churches are listed in the *Diocesan Directory* of the Diocese of Gibraltar in Europe, available from the Diocesan Office, 14 Tufton St, Westminster, London SW1P 3QZ *Tel:* 020 7976 8001
Fax: 020 7976 8002

PART 6

Ecumenical

PART 6 CONTENTS

ECUMENICAL

The Church of England is committed to the search for the full, visible unity of the Christian Church, and to the bodies which promote this at the local, intermediate, national, European and world levels. The Council for Christian Unity advises the General Synod and the Archbishops' Council on inter-church relations and acts as the principal channel of communication between the General Synod and the churches and ecumenical bodies, at the national and international levels. The CCU engages in informal ecumenical dialogue and implements any decisions of the General Synod regarding formal conversations.

ECUMENICAL CANONS
Canon B 43 (Of Relations with Other Churches) and Canon B 44 (Of Local Ecumenical Projects) make provision for sharing in worship and ministry with other churches. Full background information is given in *The Ecumenical Relations Code of Practice* (Church House, 1989). This paper, with its supplements, is now available electronically from http://www.churchofengland.org/about-us/work-other-churches/resources/the-ecumenical-canons.aspx or by contacting cu@churchofengland.org. A range of useful introductory resource papers is also available from the same address.

CHURCHES DESIGNATED UNDER THE ECUMENICAL RELATIONS MEASURE
The Church of England's legal office maintains the list of the churches that have been designated by the Archbishops of Canterbury and York as churches to which the Church of England (Ecumenical Relations) Measure, and thus Canons B 43 and B 44, apply. An up-to-date list is maintained on the Church of England web site at www.churchofengland.org/about-us/structure/churchlawlegis/canons/section-.b.aspx. The following are currently listed: The Baptist Union, the Methodist Church, the Moravian Church, the Roman Catholic Church in England and Wales, the United Reformed Church, the Congregational Federation, the International Ministerial Council of Great Britain, the Lutheran Council of Great Britain, the Greek Orthodox Archdiocese of Thyateira and Great Britain (Ecumenical Patriarchate), the Council of African and Afro-Caribbean Churches, the Free Church of England, the Southam Road Evangelical Church Banbury, Member Churches of the Evangelical Church in Germany (EKD), the Assemblies of God in Great Britain and Ireland, the New Testament Church of God, the Russian Patriarchal Church of Great Britain being the Orthodox Diocese of Sourozh (Moscow Patriarchate), the Independent Methodist Churches, the Church of the Augsburg Confession of Alsace and Lorraine, the Evangelical–Lutheran Church of France, the Council of Oriental Orthodox Churches of Great Britain and the Republic of Ireland.

Churches Together in England

Churches Together in England is in association with Churches Together in Britain and Ireland. Its basis is as follows:

> Churches Together in England unites in pilgrimage those Churches in England which, acknowledging God's revelation in Christ, confess the Lord Jesus Christ as God and Saviour according to the Scriptures, and, in obedience to God's will and in the power of the Holy Spirit, commit themselves:
> – to seek a deepening of their communion with Christ and with one another in the Church, which is his body; and
> – to fulfil their mission to proclaim the Gospel by common witness and service in the world to the glory of the one God, Father, Son and Holy Spirit.

The Presidents of Churches Together in England are: The Archbishop of Canterbury, the Archbishop of Westminster and Revd Michael Heaney; Bishop Jana Jerumba Grinberga; Archbishop Gregorios (Oecumenical Patriarchate, Archdiocese of Thyateira and GB, who meet together quarterly.

It has 36 Member Churches: Antiochian Orthodox Church, Apostolic Pastoral Association, Assemblies of God, Baptist Union of Great Britain, Cherubim and Seraphim Council of Churches, Church of England, Church of God of Prophecy, Church of Scotland (in England), Congregational Federation, Coptic Orthodox Church, Council for African and Caribbean Churches, Council of Oriental Orthodox Christian Churches, Free Church of England, Ichthus Christian Fellowship, Evangelische Synod Deutscher Sprache in Grossbritannien, Independent Methodist Churches, International Ministerial Council of Great Britain, Joint Council for Anglo-Caribbean Churches,

ECUMENICAL

Lutheran Council of Great Britain, Mar Thoma Church, Methodist Church, Moravian Church, New Testament Assembly, New Testament Church of God, Oecumenical Patriarchate (Archdiocese of Thyateira and GB), Pioneer, Redeemed Christian Church of God, Religious Society of Friends, Roman Catholic Church, Russian Orthodox Church, Salvation Army, Seventh Day Adventists, Transatlantic and Pacific Alliance of Churches, United Reformed Church, Wesleyan Holiness Church.

The Religious Society of Friends has membership under a clause designed for 'any Church or Association of Churches which on principle has no credal statements in its tradition'.

All substantive decisions are taken by these Member Churches.

Churches Together in England encourages its Member Churches to work together nationally, and provides various means for this purpose. There is an *Enabling Group*, which meets two times a year. Its Convenor is Bishop Christopher Foster and its Deputy Convenor Ruth Gee. There is a *Forum* of 300 members, which meets every three years. Its Moderator is Janet Scott and its Deputy Moderator Bishop Doye Agama.

There are 16 *Coordinating Groups* (*see below*).

There are also a large number of informal or as yet not formally recognized groups and networks.

Churches Together in England encourages its Member Churches to work together locally. To enable this most counties and metropolitan areas have established ecumenical councils and officers, whose task is to foster and encourage all sorts of ecumenical work locally within their areas. The main task of the two Field Officers (*see below*) is to support those working in counties and metropolitan areas.

Churches Together in England publishes an ecumenical e-news monthly, with a paper version, *CTE Digest*, available quarterly.

General Secretary Revd Dr David Cornick, Churches Together in England, 27 Tavistock Square, London WC1H 9HH *Tel:* 020 7529 8133
Web: www.churches-together.net

Field Officer South Revd John Bradley (*same address*)

Free Churches General Secretary Tbc (*same address*)

Finance Officer Mr Stephen Cutler (*same address*)

Executive Officer and Secretary of Health Care Chaplaincy Steering Committee Revd Debbie Hodge (*same address*)

Free Church Education Officer Miss Sarah Lane (*same address*)

Field Officer North & Midlands Jenny Bond (*same address*) *Tel:* 07805 380699

Minority Ethnic Christian Affairs Secretary Bishop Joe Aldred, 269 Kingsbury Rd, Birmingham B24 8RD *Tel:* 0777 563 2288
email: joe.aldred@cte.org.uk

COORDINATING GROUPS

GROUP FOR LOCAL UNITY
Secretary Revd John Bradley (*CTE address see above*) *Tel:* 020 7529 8144
email: john.bradley@cte.org.uk

GROUP FOR EVANGELIZATION
Secretary Captain Jim Currin (*address see above*)
Tel: 024 7626 1895
email: jim.currin@cte.org.uk

CHURCHES JOINT EDUCATION POLICY COMMITTEE
Miss Sarah Lane Cawte (*CTE address see above*)
Tel: 020 7529 8130
email: sarah.lane@cte.org.uk

CHURCHES CRIMINAL JUSTICE FORUM
Secretary Stuart Dew, Catholic Bishops' Conference of England and Wales, 39 Eccleston Square, London SW1V 1BX *Tel:* 020 7901 4878
email: dews@cbcew.org.uk

CHURCHES COMMITTEE FOR HOSPITAL CHAPLAINCY
Secretary Revd Debbie Hodge (*CTE address as above*) *Tel:* 020 7529 8136
email: debbie.hodge@cte.org.uk

CHURCHES COMMUNITY WORK ALLIANCE
Secretary Nils Chittenden, St Chad's College, North Bailey, Durham DH1 3RH
Tel: 0191 374 7342
email: nilsc@ccwa.org.uk

PRISON CHAPLAINCY HEADQUARTERS TEAM
Secretary Revd Bob Wilson, Prison Chaplaincy (*CTE address as above*) *Tel:* 020 7217 8048
email: chaplaincy@prisons-chap-hq.demon.co.uk

ECUMENICAL STRATEGY GROUP FOR MINISTERIAL TRAINING
Secretary Tony Milner, Catholic Bishops' Conference of England and Wales, 39 Eccleston Square, London SW1V 1BX
email: tony.milner@dabnet.org

THEOLOGY AND UNITY GROUP
Secretary Revd Dr David Cornick (*CTE address see above*) *Tel:* 020 7529 8133
email: david.cornick@cte.org.uk

CHURCHES RURAL GROUP
Convenor Canon Andrew Bowden, Arthur Rank Centre, The National Agricultural Centre, Stoneleigh Park, Warks. CV8 2LZ *Tel:* 024 7685 3060
email: info@arthurrankcentre.org.uk

CHURCHES TOGETHER FOR HEALING
Secretary Revd Elsie Howell, 60 Andrew Allan Rd, Rockwell Green, Wellington, Som. TA21 9DY *Tel:* 01823 664529
email: revelsie@howell.freeserve.co.uk

INDEM (Group for Mission in Industry and the Economy)
Mr David Wrighton, INDEM, 34 Chalvington Rd, Chandlers Ford, Eastleigh, Hants. SO53 3DX
Tel: 023 8026 1146
email: wrcgdgshim@cs.com

There are also four *Agencies*:

CHURCHES' MEDIA COUNCIL
(Formerly Churches' Advisory Council for Local Broadcasting)
Administrator Patricia Flynn, Christian Enquiry Agency, Freepost WC2947, South Croydon CR2 8UZ *Tel:* 020 8144 7177
email: cea@deogloria.co.uk

CHRISTIAN ENQUIRY AGENCY
Administrator Patricia Flynn, Christian Enquiry Agency, Freepost WC2947, South Croydon CR2 8UZ *Tel:* 020 8144 7177
email: cea@deogloria.co.uk

CHRISTIAN AID
PO Box 100, London SE1 7RL *Tel:* 020 7620 4444
email: info@christian-aid.org

CAFOD
Director Mr Chris Bain, 2 Romero Close, Stockwell Rd, London SW9 9TY *Tel:* 020 7733 7900
email: hqcafod@cafod.org.uk

The following are *Bodies in Association* with Churches Together in England: Action by Christians Against Torture, Association of Centres of Adult Theological Education, Association of Inter-Church Families, Bible Society, Christian Council on Ageing, Christian Council on Approaches to Defence and Disarmament, Christian Education, Christians Aware, Church Action on Poverty, Churches Alert to Sex Trafficking Across Europe (CHASTE), Churches Community Work Alliance (CCWA), Churches East–West Europe Relations Network (CEWERN), Churches for All, College of Preachers, Community of Aidan and Hilda, Corrymeela Community, Ecumenical Council for Corporate Responsibility, Ecumenical Society of the Blessed Virgin Mary, Faith in Europe, Feed the Minds, Fellowship of St Alban and St Sergius, Fellowship of Reconciliation, Focolare Movement, Housing Justice, Industrial Mission Association, International Ecumenical Fellowship, Iona Community, Irish School of Ecumenics, L'Arche, Living Stones, MODEM, Oikocredit, Retreat Association, Society for Ecumenical Studies, Student Christian Movement, William Temple Foundation, Women's World Day of Prayer, Young Men's Christian Association, Y Care International.

For addresses, *see* page 449 (under CTBI) or the **List of Organizations** (pages 261–265).

ECUMENICAL

Intermediate County Bodies and Area Ecumenical Councils

Bedfordshire
Churches Together in Bedfordshire
Andrew Gale
41 Springfield Way, Cranfield
Bedfordshire MK43 0JN
Tel: 01234 752 434
email: 1@andrewgale.me.uk

Berkshire
Churches Together in Berkshire
Vacancy
14 Hertford Close
Woose Hill
Wokingham
Berkshire RG41 3BH
Tel: 0118 977 6437
email: ctberks@sky.com

Birmingham (*see also* **West Midlands**)
Birmingham Churches Together
Revd Dr Colin Marsh
St George's Community Hub
Great Hampton Row
Newtown, Birmingham B19 3JG
Tel: 0121 236 3966
email: office@birminghamchurches.org.uk

Black Country (*see also* **Staffordshire**)
Black Country Churches Engaged (BCCE)
Philip Webb
52 South Avenue
Chellaston
Derbyshire DE73 6RS
Tel: 01332 705 078
email: dovedale.revs078@btinternet.com

Bristol, Greater
Churches Together in Greater Bristol
Jon Doble
162 Pennywell Lane
Bristol BS5 0TX
Tel: 0117 956 5447
email: jon@ccisr.org.uk

Buckinghamshire
Churches Together in Buckinghamshire (Except Milton Keynes)
Revd Mary Cotes
61 Green Lane
Wolverton
Bucks MK12 5HW
Tel: 01908 226 886
email: CTinBucks@aol.com

Cambridgeshire
Cambridgeshire Ecumenical Council
Mrs Priscilla Barlow
Silverlands, Church St
Litlington
Royston
Herts SG8 0QB
Tel: 01763 852841
email: priscilla.barlow@easynet.co.uk

Cheshire
Churches Together in Cheshire
David Betts
Tel: 01270 750 431
email: ceo.ctic@gmail.com

Cornwall
Churches Together in Cornwall
David Smith
Chyreene Warra
Rosehill
Marazion
Cornwall TR17 0HB
Tel: 01736 719 432
email: ses.dhs@hotmail.co.uk

Coventry *See* **Warwickshire**

Cumbria
Churches Together in Cumbria
Helen Boothroyd
email: htctic@tiscali.co.uk
Ruth Harvey
Croslands
Beacon Street
Penrith CA11 7TZ
Tel: 074 0363 8339
email: rctic@phoencoop.coop

Derbyshire and Nottinghamshire
Churches Together in Derbyshire & Nottinghamshire
Marcus Nolan
email: derbyshirecuf@gmail.com

Devon
Churches Together in Devon
Sabrina Groeschel
69 Betjeman Close
Sidmouth
Devon EX10 9FG
Tel: 01395 579 795
email: Sabrina_groeschel@yahoo.co.uk

Dorset
Churches Together in Dorset
Mrs Val Potter
22 D'Urberville Close
Dorchester
Dorset DT1 2JT
Tel: 01305 264416
email: ctdorset@clara.net

Durham *see* **North-East England**
Bill Offler
42 John Street North
Meadowfield
Durham DH7 8RS
Tel: 0191 378 2883
email: william.offler@virgin.net

Essex and London, East
Churches Together in Essex & East London CLG

Gloucestershire
Gloucestershire Churches Together
Revd Dr Alison Evans
Britannia Cottage
High Street
Kings Stanley
Stonehouse
GL10 3JD
Tel: 01453 824034
email: malcolm.alison@btinternet.com

Guernsey
Churches Together in Guernsey
Mr Roy Sarre
Le Campère
Les Villets
Forest
Guernsey
Channel Islands
GY8 0HP
Tel: 01481 265004

Hampshire and Isle of Wight
Churches Together in Hampshire & the Island
Andrew Wood
4 The Chase
Thornbury Wood
Chandler's Ford
Eastleigh
Hants SO53 5AZ
email: Andrew.wood4@btopenworld.com

Herefordshire
Churches Together in Herefordshire

Pippa Hadfield
email: pippa@ctih.org.uk

Hertfordshire
Churches Together in Hertfordshire

Major Gerald Peacock
83 Cromer Way
Luton
Bedfordshire
LU2 7EE
Tel: 01582 492993
email: geraldpeacock39@btinternet.com

Isle of Man
Churches Together in Man

Mrs Mavis Matthewman
Tarnalforn
12 Ballagarey Rd
Glen Vine
Isle of Man
IM4 4EA
Tel: 01624 851692

Isle of Wight *see* **Hampshire**

Jersey
Christians Together in Jersey

Martin Dryden
Monte Urbe House
La Rue de la Blinerie
St Clements
Jersey JE2 6QT
email: martin@mont-ube.net

Kent
Churches Together in Kent

Harvey Richardson
email: harvey.s.richardson@gmail.com

Lancashire
Churches Together in Lancashire

Revd Debbie Peatman (Ecumenical Development Officer)
Rectory, Church Walk, Morecambe
LA4 5PR
Tel: 07806 643 097
email: debbie.peatman@ctlancashire.org.uk
Revd Steven Hughes (Inter Faith Officer)
69 Liverpool Old Rd
Much Hoole
Preston Lancs
PR4 4RB
Tel: 01772 612267
email: steven.hughes@ctlancashire.org.uk

Leicestershire
Churches Together in Leicestershire

Vic Allsop
c/o 14 Church Lane
Hoby
Melton Mowbray
Leicestershire
LE14 3DR
Tel: 01664 434 697
email: ctil@fsmail.net

Lincolnshire
Churches Together in All Lincolnshire

Simon Dean (administrator)
c/o Church House
The Old Palace
Lincoln
LN2 1PU
Tel: 01522 504070
email: office@ctal.org.uk

London, East *see* **Essex**
East London Church Leaders Group

Revd Lee Batson
Vicarage, Church Rd
Boreham, Chelmsford
CM3 3EG
Tel: 01245 451087
email: lbatsom@chelmsford.anglican.org

London, North *see* **North Thames**

London, North Thames
Churches Together North Thames

Revd Bernie Collins
Ickenham United Reformed Church
Swakeleys Road
Ickenham
Uxbridge UB10 8BE
Tel: 07982 186 301
email: Revbcollins@aol.com

London, South
Churches Together in South London

John Richardson
c/o St John's Vicarage
Secker Street
London SE1 9UF
Tel: 01462 422502
email: john@ctslondon.org.uk

London, West
Churchlink West London

Fr William Taylor
25 Ladbroke Grove
London W11 3PD
Tel: 020 7727 3439
email: vicar@stjohnsnottinghill.com

Manchester, Greater
Greater Manchester Churches Together

Elaine Rowlinson
St Peter's House
Precinct Centre
Oxford Road
Manchester
M13 9GH
Tel: 0161 273 5508
Fax: 0161 272 7172
email: gmct@manchester.ac.uk

Merseyside
Churches Together in the Merseyside Region

Revd Ian Smith
Quaker Meeting House
22 School Lane
Liverpool L1 3BT
Tel: 0151 709 0125
email: office@ctmr.org.uk

Milton Keynes
Mission Partnership of the Milton Keynes Christian Council

Penny Warburton
c/o Christian Foundation
The Square
Aylesbury Street
Wolverton
MK12 5HX
Tel: 01908 311310
email: missionpartnership@talktalk.net

Norfolk
Norfolk and Waveney Churches Together

Simon Wilson
The Rectory
Guist Road
Foulsham
Norfolk NR20 5RZ
Tel: 01352 683 275
email: simon.wilson@anglican.org

North-East England
North East Christian Churches Together (NECCT)

Bill Offler
42 John Street North
Meadowfield
Durham DH7 8RS
Tel: 0191 378 2883
email: william.offler@virgin.net

Nottinghamshire (*see* **Derbyshire**)

Oxfordshire
Churches Together in Oxfordshire

Peter Smith (New appointment)
c/o Cowley Road Methodist Church
Jeune Street
Oxford OX4 1BN
Tel: 01865 723801

Peterborough (*see* **Shire and Soke**)

Shire and Soke
Churches Together in Northamptonshire & Peterborough

Gill Crow (Northamptonshire)
email: gillcrow@shireandsoke.org.uk
Philip Hutchinson (Peterborough)
email: philiphutchinson@shireandsoke.org.uk

Shropshire (Except Telford)
Churches Together in Shropshire

Mr Ged Cliffe
Fern Villa
Four Crosses
Llanymynech
Powys SY22 6PR
Tel: 01691 831374
email: gedcliffe@tiscali.co.uk

Somerset
Somerset Churches Together in Somerset

Gabrielle Grace
3 Champford Mews
Wellington
TA21 8JW
Tel: 07811 108 218
email: sctogether@honecoop.coop

Staffordshire
Churches Linked Across Staffs & the Potteries (CLASP) (*as* **Black Country**)

Mike Topliss
Tel: 01922 475 932
email: jmtopliss@talktalk.net

Suffolk
Churches Together in Suffolk

Julie Mansfield
Applegarth
Wilmslow Avenue
Woodbridge
Suffolk
IP12 4HW
Tel: 01394 384370
email: ctsuffolkjmmansfield@homecall.co.uk

Surrey
Churches Together in Surrey

Revd Susan Loveday
10 Abbey Gardens
Chertsey
Surrey KT16 8RQ
Tel: 01932 566920
email: sue.loveday.ctsurrey@lineone.net

Sussex Churches Together in Sussex	Mr Ian Chisnall 85 Hollingbury Rise Brighton BN1 7HH Tel: 07976 811654 (Mobile) *email:* ianpchisnall@aol.com
Swindon Swindon Churches Together	Revd Lee Rayfield *Tel:* 01793 523 810 *email:* bishop.swindon@bristoldiocese.org
Telford Telford Christian Council	Andy Smith Meeting Point House Southwater Square Town Centre Telford TF3 4HS *Tel:* 01952 291904 *email:* rebeccahiggs@staytelford.co.uk
Warwickshire Churches Together in Coventry & Warwickshire	Kay Dyer 6 Sycamore Close Stratford-upon-Avon CV37 0DZ *Tel:* 01789 298299 *email:* ctcw@fish.co.uk
Waveney *see* **Norfolk**	
Wiltshire Wiltshire Churches Together	Liz Overthrow *email:* roy.overthrow@btinternet.com
Worcestershire Churches Together in Worcestershire	Revd David Ryan 4 Daty Croft Home Meadow Worcester WR4 0JB *Tel:* 01905 616109 *email:* dpryangb@aol.com
Yorkshire, East and Hull Kingston upon Hull & East Yorkshire Churches Together	Mrs Cathy Crumpton Key Churches Together Methodist Central Hall King Edward St Hull HU1 3SQ *Tel:* 01482 328196 *email:* cathy@keyct.karoo.co.uk
Yorkshire, North York Moors North York Moors Churches Together	Barbara Burke York & Hull District Office 28 The Green Acomb, York YO26 5LR *Tel:* 01904 786 275 *email:* admin@yorkhullmethodist.org.uk
Yorkshire, South Churches Together in South Yorkshire	Erica Dunmow CTSY Office C/O SCEC Montgomery Hall Surrey Street Sheffield S1 2LG *email:* emdo@ctsy.yahoo.co.uk
Yorkshire, Vale of York ENVOY (Ecumenical Network in the Vale of York)	Nigel Currey 17 Mayfield Drive Brayton Selby North Yorkshire YO8 9JZ *Tel:* 01347 838593 *email:* ncurrey1@talktalk.net
Yorkshire, West West Yorkshire Ecumenical Council	Clive Barrett Hinsley Hall 62 Headingley Lane Leeds LS6 2BX *Tel:* 0113 261 8053 *Fax:* 0113 261 8054 *email:* office@wyec.co.uk

Churches Together in Britain and Ireland

Office 39 Ecclestone Square, London SW1V 1BX
Tel: 08456 806851
Fax: 08456 806852
email: gensec@ctbi.org.uk
Web: www.ctbi.org.uk

Churches Together in Britain and Ireland (CTBI) is an umbrella body through which the Churches co-operate on common issues. It works closely with the other 'Churches Together' bodies, which focus separately on England, Wales, Scotland and Ireland. Together they have an important role to witness to the essential unity of the Christian movement. CTBI's core tasks are providing 'structured ecumenical space' for meeting and encounter, facilitating shared study on common issues and fostering relationships – among the Churches and between the Churches and the wider world.

Churches Together in Britain and Ireland (formerly the Council of Churches for Britain and Ireland and the direct successor of the British Council of Churches) was established by its member Churches to enable them to work together for the advancement of the Christian religion, the relief of poverty, the advancement of education and any other charitable purpose. It seeks to further these objects by providing opportunities for representatives of the Churches from the four nations to meet together and to share some of their resources in the pursuance of jointly agreed activities.

Following a review of its work, Churches Together in Britain and Ireland has become an agency serving the churches through the four National Ecumenical Instruments. As a separate charitable company, limited by guarantee, CTBI now relates to the churches, as members, through the ecumenical structures of the nations. It is now more relational and its focus is on working agreed common themes across the different work areas described below. The current themes are:

- environment/climate change
- migration and the movements of people
- culture, identity and the public space

Our principal activities and Networks are:

- Witnessing to and working towards the visible unity of the Christian Churches and providing opportunities for representatives of the Churches to meet and to plan their work together. A **Senior Representatives Forum**, attended by delegates from all member churches and bodies in association, is held in the spring of each year. An annual **Networking Conference** brings together the various Networks which comprise members of the member Chruches, Agencies and Bodies in Association.
- Working on the Churches' behalf on issues of racial justice through the **Churches Racial Justice Network** (formerly known as CCRJ, the Churches' Commission for Racial Justice). The Racial Justice Network is a major vehicle for the Churches' engagement with the complex work of racial justice throughout Ireland, Scotland, Wales and England. Central to the work is the Racial Justice Fund, which supports a wide range of grassroots organizations. These funded groups are invited into a dynamic partnership designed to build their capacity for effective action and to provide first rate information and experience for use in education, lobbying and campaigning. **Racial Justice Sunday,** celebrated ecumenically on the second Sunday in September, gives an opportunity for vital educational work with churches and congregations and raises the media profile of the work of racial justice. Other projects include Capacity Building for Black Churches, the Bail Circle and the Peers project. The recent publication of *Migration Principles*, which in turn is building on the work of *Asylum Principles*, seeks to promote an active discussion and programme around the complex issue of migration. Working with other departments within CTBI, the Racial Justice team are taking forward Migration as a major theme.
- Through the **Churches Network for Mission (CNM),** seeking to serve and assist churches, agencies and the four national ecumenical instruments in our common task of participating in God's mission in the world. GMN is a key point of contact with world ecumenical mission bodies, particularly the World Council of Churches and the Council of European Churches. GMN's current projects include:
  - Preparation for and follow up to the **Edinburgh 2010 Mission Conference**
  - **Mission Theology Advisory Group,** offering expertise from around the four nations in Mission theology. Publications and web resources are being produced to support the ongoing work of the churches' mission in new contexts.
  - **China** – the China Desk provides a dedicated expert centre maintaining a wide range of relationships in China and undertaking research and analysis on Chinese affairs. It co-ordinates the work of the China Forum which acts as a bridge to Chinese Christians, both Catholic and Protestant, with partnership maintained through a variety of on-going projects.
- Through the **Churches Inter Religious Network,** working with the Churches to

engage effectively in relations and dialogue with other faiths in Britain and Ireland. The Network is a point of reference for the Churches which facilitates an exchange of information and experience among Christians about inter faith relations, whilst enabling critical reflection on the religiously and socially plural society of the four nations. In Scotland, it works through the Churches' Agency for Inter Faith Relations in Scotland. The Network seeks to fulfil its aims by responding to requests by the Churches on inter faith issues, monitoring inter faith relations in the four nations, nurturing links between Christians working in this field, pooling the theological resources of the Churches for ministry and witness in this area, and producing appropriate written or other material to help the Churches. In addition CTBI is a member body, on behalf of the Churches, of the Inter Faith Network for the United Kingdom, which provides a national forum for people from the main faith communities to meet, discuss and share.

- Through the **Churches International Student Network**, supporting international students by networking, education and communication among the Churches and between them, government and other agencies specializing in international students' affairs. The Network seeks to link the varied work of the many church agencies among students and supports the Churches in their response to the needs of international students. It initiated and maintains co-funding from the Foreign Office for denominational and ecumenical scholarships, administers World Council of Churches scholarships in Britain and Ireland and operates a hardship fund for international students for which it raises funding.
- Developing and publishing for the Churches **resources for study and prayer**. This includes printed and web based materials for the Week of Prayer for Christian Unity, which is observed each year from 18 to 25 January, as well as a Lent study programme.
- Through the **Church and Public Issues Network**, supporting and resourcing the Churches in their work on political, social and ethical issues, paying particular attention to:

  - public policy agendas of Westminster, and also Cardiff, Edinburgh, Belfast, Dublin and Brussels
  - the churches' engagement with contemporary social issues
  - moral/ethical issues, especially where there is a distinctive Christian contribution to be made

The Church and Society Forum takes a lead in networking those who work on church and society issues across the four nations, and in sharing and disseminating information and expertise. It represents the Churches jointly, where appropriate, to Government bodies, other agencies and elsewhere. It has one main residential meeting each year, with others as the need arises.

STAFF

Canon Robert Fyffe, *General Secretary*

Mr Stephen Cutler, *Director of Business and Finance*
Mrs Mary Gandy, *Resources Manager*
Lawrence Braschi, *China Desk Director*
Revd Peter Colwell, *Director of Programmes*
Mr Dave Chadwick, *Web Manager*

CTBI MEMBER CHURCHES AND BODIES OF CHURCHES

ANTIOCHIAN ORTHODOX CHURCH
Father George Hackney
Little Portion, Back Lane, Barnby, Newark NG24 2SD
Tel: 01636 626417
email: fathergeorge@macace.net

BAPTIST UNION OF GREAT BRITAIN
Revd Jonathan Edwards *General Secretary*
Baptist House, 129 Broadway, Didcot OX11 8RT
Tel: 01235 517700
Fax: 01235 517715
email: info@baptist.org.uk
Web: www.baptist.org.uk

CATHOLIC BISHOPS' CONFERENCE OF ENGLAND AND WALES
Fr Marcus Stock *General Secretary*
39 Eccleston Square, London SW1V 1BX
Tel: 020 7630 8220
Fax: 020 7901 4821
email: secretariat@cbcew.org.uk
Web: www.catholic-ew.org.uk

CATHOLIC BISHOPS' CONFERENCE OF SCOTLAND
Revd Paul Conroy *General Secretary*
64 Aitken St, Airdrie ML6 6LT *Tel:* 01236 764061
Fax: 01236 762489
email: GenSec@BpsConfScot.com
Web: www.scmo.org/_titles/bishops_conference.htm

CHURCH IN WALES
John Shirley *Provincial Secretary*
39 Cathedral Rd, Cardiff CF11 9XF
Tel: 029 2034 8200
Fax: 029 2038 7835
email: johnshirley@churchinwales.org.uk
Web: www.churchinwales.org.uk

CHURCH OF ENGLAND
Mr William Fittall *Secretary General of the General Synod and the Archbishops' Council*
Church House, Great Smith St, London SW1P 3AZ *Tel:* 020 7898 1000
Fax: 020 7898 1369
email: cofe.comms@c-of-e.org.uk
Web: www.cofe.anglican.org

CHURCH OF GOD OF PROPHECY
Bishop Wilton R. Powell *National Overseer*
6 Beacon Court, Birmingham Rd, Great Barr, Birmingham B43 6NN *Tel:* 0121 358 2231
Fax: 0121 358 8617
email: admin@cogop.org.uk
Web: www.cogop.org.uk

CHURCH OF IRELAND
Mrs Janet Maxwell *Head of Synod Services and Communications*
Church of Ireland House, Church Avenue, Rathmines, Dublin 6, RoI *Tel:* ++ 353 (0)1 4125621
Fax: ++ 353 (0)1 4978821
email: janet.maxwell@rcbdub.org
Web: www.ireland.anglican.org

CHURCH OF SCOTLAND
Revd John Chalmers *Principal Clerk (from July 2010)*
Principal Clerk's Office, 121 George St, Edinburgh EH2 4YN *Tel:* 0131 240 2240
Fax: 0131 240 2239
email: pracproc@cofscotland.org.uk
Web: www.churchofscotland.org.uk

CONGREGATIONAL FEDERATION
Revd Michael Heaney *General Secretary*
8 Castle Gate, Nottingham NG1 7AS
Tel: 0115 911 1460
Fax: 0115 911 1462
email: admin@congregational.org.uk
Web: www.congregational.org.uk

COPTIC ORTHODOX CHURCH
Bishop Angaelos
Coptic Orthodox Church Centre, Shephalbury Manor, Broadhall Way, Stevenage SG2 8RH
Tel: 01438 745232
Fax: 01438 313879
email: admin@CopticCentre.com
Web: www.CopticCentre.com

COUNCIL OF ORIENTAL ORTHODOX CHURCHES
Bishop Angaelos *President*
c/o Coptic Orthodox Church Centre (*as above*)
email: admin@CopticCentre.com

GERMAN-SPEAKING CONGREGATION
Mr Georg Staab
Council for German Church Work, 35 Craven Terrace, London W2 3EL *Tel:* 020 7706 8589
Fax: 020 7706 2870
email: office@ev-synode.org.uk
Web: www.ev-synode.org.uk

INDEPENDENT METHODIST CHURCHES
Mr William Gabb *General Secretary*
Independent Methodist Resource Centre & Registered Office
Fleet St, Pemberton, Wigan WN5 0DS
Tel: 01942 223526
Fax: 01942 227768
email: resourcecentre@imcgb.org.uk
Web: www.imcgb.org.uk

INTERNATIONAL MINISTERIAL COUNCIL OF GREAT BRITAIN (IMCGB)
Bishop Onye Obika
217 Langhedge Lane, London N18 2TG
Tel: 020 8345 5376
email: imcgb@aol.com
Web: www.imcgb.com

JOINT COUNCIL FOR ANGLO AND AFRICAN-CARIBBEAN CHURCHES
Revd Esme Beswick *President*
141 Railton Rd, London SE24 OLT
Tel and Fax: 020 7737 6542

LUTHERAN COUNCIL OF GREAT BRITAIN
Revd Thomas Bruch *General Secretary*
30 Thanet St, London WC1H 9QH
Tel: 020 7554 2900
Fax: 020 7383 3081
email: enquiries@lutheran.org.uk
Web: www.lutheran.org.uk

MAR THOMAS CHURCH
Dr Zac Varghese *Ecumenical Officer*
3 Rose Garden Close, Edgware, London HA8 7RF
Tel: 020 8951 5273
email: zacvarghese@aol.co.uk

METHODIST CHURCH
Revd Dr Martin Atkins *General Secretary*
25 Marylebone Rd, London NW1 5JR
Tel: 020 7467 5143
Fax: 020 7467 5226
email: generalsecretary@methodistchurch.org.uk
Web: www.methodist.org.uk

METHODIST CHURCH IN IRELAND
Revd Donald Ker *General Secretary*
1 Fountainville Ave, Belfast BT9 6AN
Tel: 028 9032 4554
Fax: 028 9023 9467
email: secretary@irishmethodist.org
Web: www.irishmethodist.org

MORAVIAN CHURCH
Jackie Morten
Moravian Church House, 5 Muswell Hill, London N10 3TJ *Tel:* 020 8883 3409
Fax: 020 8365 3371
email: office@moravian.org.uk
Web: www.moravian.org.uk

NEW TESTAMENT ASSEMBLY
Revd Nezlin Sterling *General Secretary*
5 Woodstock Ave, London W13 9UQ
Tel: 020 8579 3841
Fax: 020 8537 9253
email: njsterlnta@aol.com

NEW TESTAMENT CHURCH OF GOD
Bishop Donald Bolt
3 Cheyne Walk, Northampton NN1 5PT
Tel: 01604 643311
Fax: 01604 790254
email: bigmove@ntcg.org.uk
Web: www.ntcg.org.uk

OECUMENICAL PATRIARCHATE (ARCHDIOCESE OF THYATEIRA AND GREAT BRITAIN)
His Eminence Archbishop Gregorios
5 Craven Hill, London W2 3EN
Tel: 020 7723 4787
Fax: 020 7224 9301
email: thyateiragb@yahoo.com
Web: www.nostos.com/church/

PRESBYTERIAN CHURCH OF WALES
Revd Ifan Roberts *General Secretary*
Tabernacle Chapel, 81 Merthyr Road, Whitchurch, Cardiff CF14 1DD *Tel:* 029 2062 7465
Fax: 029 2061 6188
email: swyddfa.office@ebcpcw.org.uk
Web: www.ebcpcw.org.uk

RELIGIOUS SOCIETY OF FRIENDS
Gillian Ashmore *Chief Recording Clerk*
Friends House, 173 Euston Rd, London NW1 2BJ
Tel: 020 7663 1000
Fax: 020 7663 1001
email: enquiries@quaker.org.uk
Web: www.quaker.org.uk

RELIGIOUS SOCIETY OF FRIENDS IN IRELAND
Mr Ian Woods
40 Castle Grove, Swords, Co Dublin

RUSSIAN ORTHODOX CHURCH (ECUMENICAL PATRIARCHATE)
Mrs Gillian Crow
6 Maiden Place, London NW5 1HZ
email: gillian@crow.co.uk
Web www.exarchate-uk.org

SALVATION ARMY
Commissioner John Matear *Territorial Commander UK and RoI*
101 Newington Causeway, London SE1 6BN
Tel: 020 7367 4500
Fax: 020 7367 4728
email: info@salvationarmy.org.uk
Web: www.salvationarmy.org.uk

SCOTTISH EPISCOPAL CHURCH
Mr John Stuart *Secretary General for Synod Office*
21 Grosvenor Crescent, Edinburgh EH12 5EE
Tel: 0131 225 6357
Fax: 0131 346 7247
email: office@scotland.anglican.org
Web: www.scottishepiscopal.com

TRANS-ATLANTIC & PACIFIC ALLIANCE OF CHURCHES
Archbishop Paul Hackman *President*
281-283 Rye Lane, London SE15 4UA
Tel and Fax: 020 7639 4058
email: tapacglobal@aol.com

UNDEB YR ANNIBYNWYR CYMRAEG/UNION OF WELSH INDEPENDENTS
Revd Dr Geraint Tudor *General Secretary*
Tŷ John Penri, 5 Axis Court, Riverside Business Park, Swansea Vale, Swansea SA7 0AJ
Tel: 01792 795888
Fax: 01792 795376
email: Undeb@annibynwyr.org
Web: www.annibynwyr.org

UNITED FREE CHURCH OF SCOTLAND
Revd Andrew McMillan
11 Newton Place, Glasgow G3 7PR
Tel: 0141 332 3435
Fax: 0141 333 1973
email: office@ufcos.org.uk
Web: www.ufcos.org.uk

UNITED REFORMED CHURCH
Revd Roberta Rominger *General Secretary*
86 Tavistock Place, London WC1H 9RT
Tel: 020 7916 2020
Fax: 020 7916 2021
email: urc@urc.org.uk
Web: www.urc.org.uk

ASSOCIATE MEMBER

ROMAN CATHOLIC CHURCH OF IRELAND
Revd Aidan O'Boyle *Executive Secretary*
The Irish Episcopal Conference, Columba Centre, Maynooth, Co Kildare, Republic of Ireland
Tel: 00 353 1 505 3020
Fax: 00 353 1 629 2360
email: ex.sec@iecon.ie

BODIES IN ASSOCIATION

ACTION BY CHRISTIANS AGAINST TORTURE
Chas Raws, 38 The Mount, Heswello, Wirrall CH60 4RA
email: uk.acat@googlemail.com
Web: www.acatuk.org.uk

ASSOCIATION OF INTER-CHURCH FAMILIES
Mr Keith Lander (*Executive Officer*), 27 Tavistock Square, London WC1H 9HH
Tel: 020 7529 8131
Fax: 020 7529 8134
email: info@interchurchfamilies.org.uk
Web: www.interchurchfamilies.org.uk

BIBLE READING FELLOWSHIP
Richard Fisher, 15 The Chambers, Vineyard, Abingdon OX14 3FE *Tel:* 01865 319 700
email: enquiries@brf.org.uk
Web: www.brf.org.uk

BIBLE SOCIETY
James Catford (*Chief Executive*), Stonehill Green, Westlea, Swindon SN5 7DG *Tel:* 01793 418 100
Web: www.biblesociety.org.uk

CHRISTIAN COUNCIL ON AGEING
Mrs Christine Hodgson, 6 The Ridgeway, Market Harborough LE16 7HQ *Tel:* 01858 432771
email: info@ccoa.org.uk
Web: www.ccoa.org.uk

CHRISTIAN EDUCATION
Peter Fishpool (*Chief Executive*), 1020 Bristol Rd, Selly Oak, Birmingham B29 6LB
Tel: 0121 472 4242
Fax: 0121 472 7575
email: admin@christianeducation.org.uk
Web: www.christianeducation.org.uk

CHRISTIANS AWARE
Mrs Barbara Butler, 2 Saxby St, Leicester LE2 0ND
Tel and *Fax:* 0116 254 0770
email: barbarabutler@christiansaware.co.uk
Web: www.christiansaware.co.uk

CHURCH ACTION ON POVERTY
Mr Niall Cooper (*National Coordinator*), Dale House, 35 Dale St, Manchester M1 2HF
Tel: 0161 236 9321
Fax: 0161 237 5359
email: info@church-poverty.org.uk
Web: www.church-poverty.org.uk

CHURCHES' ALERT TO SEX TRAFFICKING ACROSS EUROPE
Angela Deavall (*Chief Executive*), PO Box 983, Cambridge CB3 8WY *Tel:* 0845 456 9335
email: contact@chaste.org.uk
Web: www.chaste.org.uk

COLLEGE OF PREACHERS
Ms Marfa Jones (*Administrator*), Chester House, Pages Lane, Muswell Hill, London N10 1PR
Tel: 020 8883 7850
email: administrator@collegeofpreachers.org.uk
Web: www.collegeofpreachers.org.uk

COMMUNITY OF AIDAN AND HILDA
Lindisfarne Retreat, The Open Gate, Holy Island, Berwick-upon-Tweed TD15 2SD
Tel: 01289 389222
email: ca-and-h@demon.co.uk
Web: www.aidanandhilda.org.uk

CORRYMEELA COMMUNITY
Corrymeela House, 8 Upper Crescent, Belfast BT7 1NT *Tel:* 028 9050 8080
Fax: 028 9050 8070
email: annemcdonagh@corrymeela.org
Web: www.corrymeela.org

ECUMENICAL COUNCIL FOR CORPORATE RESPONSIBILITY
Miles Litvinoff (*Coordinator*), PO Box 500, Oxford OX1 1ZL *Tel:* 020 8965 9682
email: info@eccr.org.uk
Web: www.eccr.org.uk

ECUMENICAL SOCIETY OF THE BLESSED VIRGIN MARY
Paul Paniccia, 1 Badgers Glade, Burghfield Common, Reading RG7 3RG

FAITH IN EUROPE
Dr Philip Walters (*General Secretary*), 81 Thorney Leys, Witney OX28 5BY *Tel:* 01993 771778
email: philip.walters@waltfam.freeserve.co.uk
Web: www.faithineurope.org.uk

FEED THE MINDS
Josephine Carlssen (*Director*), Park Place, 12 Lawn Lane, London SW8 1UD
Tel: 020 7592 3900
Fax: 020 7592 3939
email: info@feedtheminds.org.uk
Web: www.feedtheminds.org

FELLOWSHIP OF RECONCILIATION
Revd John Johansen-Berg (*Director*), St James' Church Centre, Beauchamp Lane, Oxford OX4 3LF *Tel:* 01865 748796
email: office@for.org.uk
Web: www.for.org.uk

FELLOWSHIP OF ST ALBAN AND ST SERGIUS
Revd Stephen Platt, 1 Canterbury Rd, Oxford OX2 6LU *Tel:* 01865 52991
Fax: 01865 316700
email: gensec@sobornost.org
Web: www.sobornost.org

FOCOLARE MOVEMENT
Celia Blackden, 11 Drummond Avenue, Leeds LS16 5JZ
email: celiablackden@yahoo.co.uk
Web: www.focolare.org.uk

HOUSING JUSTICE
Ms Alison Gelder (*Chief Executive*), 209 Old Marylebone Rd, London NW1 5QT
Tel: 020 7723 7273
Fax: 020 7723 5943
email: info@housingjustice.org.uk
Web: www.housingjustice.org.uk

INDUSTRIAL MISSION ASSOCIATION
Revd Stephen Hazlett, Northumbrian Industrial Mission, 14 The Oaks West, Sunderland SR2 8HZ
Tel: 07900 231360
Web: www.industrialmission.org.uk

INTERNATIONAL ECUMENICAL FELLOWSHIP
David Hardiman, 59 Old St, Headington, Oxford OX3 9HT *Tel:* 0191 4566 1643
email: davidhardiman@blueyonder.com
Web: www.uk-ief.co.uk

IONA COMMUNITY
Revd Peter Macdonald, 4th Floor, Savoy House, 140 Sauchiehall St, Glasgow G2 3DH
Tel: 0141 332 6343
Fax: 0141 332 1090
email: admin@iona.org.uk
Web: www.iona.org.uk

IRISH SCHOOL OF ECUMENICS
Prof Linda Hogan, 683 Antrim Rd, Belfast BT15 4EG *and* Bea House, Milltown Park, Dublin 6, RoI
Tel: +44 (0) 28 9077 5010
Fax: +44 (0) 28 9037 3986
email: lhogan2@tcd.ie
Web: www.tcd.ie/ise

L'ARCHE
Ms Lal Keenan, L'Arche Community, 15 Northwood High St, London SE27 9JU
Tel: 020 8670 6714
Fax: 020 8670 0818
email: info@larche.org.uk
Web: www.larche.org.uk

LIVING STONES
Dr Aziz Nour, 77 Exeter Rd, Southgate, London N14 5JU
Web: www.livingstonesonline.org.uk

MAGNET RESOURCES
Lynne Ling, PO Box 10378, Bishop's Stortford CM23 9FT *Tel:* 0844 7362524
Web: www.ourmagnet.co.uk

MODEM
Mr John Nelson (*National Secretary and Publications Editor*), 24 Rostron Crescent, Formby L37 2ET *Tel:* 01704 873973
Fax: 01704 871273
email: jrn24rcf2003@yahoo.co.uk
Web: www.modem.uk.com

OIKOCREDIT, ECUMENICAL DEVELOPMENT COOPERATIVE SOCIETY
Patrick Hynes, UK Support Office, PO Box 809, Garstang, Preston PR3 1TU
Web: www.oikocredit.org

OPERATION NOAH
Anne Pettifor, Grayston Centre, 28 Charles Square, London N1 6HT *Tel:* 0207 324 4761
email: admin@operationnoah.org
Web: www.operationnoah.org

PRISON FELLOWSHIP ENGLAND AND WALES
Tim Diaper, PO Box 945, Maldon, Essex CM9 4EW *Tel:* 01621 843232
Web: www.prisonfellowship.org

RETREAT ASSOCIATION
Alison MacTier, The Central Hall, 256 Bermondsey St, London SE1 3UJ *Tel:* 020 7357 7736
Fax: 020 7357 7724
email: info@retreats.org.uk
Web: www.retreats.org.uk

SOCIETY OF ECUMENICAL STUDIES
Revd Mark Woodruff (*Secretary*), 26 Daysbrook Rd, London SW2 3TD *Tel:* 020 8678 8195
email: ecumenicalstudies@btinternet.com
Web: www.ecumenicalstudies.org.uk

STUDENT CHRISTIAN MOVEMENT
Revd Martin Thompson, Unit 308F, The Big Peg, 120 Vyse St, Jewellery Quarter, Birmingham B18 6NF *Tel:* 0121 200 3355
email: co@movement.org.uk
Web: www.movement.org.uk

WOMEN'S WORLD DAY OF PRAYER MOVEMENT
Jean Hackett, National Office, Commercial Rd, Tunbridge Wells TN1 2RR *Tel:* 01892 541411
Fax: 01892 541745
email: office@wwdp-natcomm.org
Web: www.wwdp-natcomm.org

YOUNG MEN'S CHRISTIAN ASSOCIATION (YMCA)
Ms Helen Dennis (*Policy and Parliamentary Officer*), 53 Parker St, London WC2B 5PT
Tel: 0845 873 6633
email: enquiries@ymca.org.uk
Web: www.ymca.org.uk

Scotland, Wales and Ireland

ACTION OF CHURCHES TOGETHER IN SCOTLAND
7 Forrester Lodge, Inglewood House, Alloa FK10 2HU
Tel: 01259 216980
Fax: 01259 215964
email: ecumenical@acts-scotland.org

General Secretary Brother Stephen Smyth

Convenor of the Trustees and ACTS Members' Meeting Rev Dr. D. Douglas Galbraith

ACTS is the national ecumenical body for Scotland, the expression of the Churches' commitment to cooperation with one another in the service of Christ. ACTS works closely with its partners in England, Wales and Ireland. Its principal body is the Members' Meeting, composed of representatives from the member churches. The work of ACTS is forwarded by four Networks: Church and Society, Church Life, Mission, and Faith Studies. In addition to the core staff ACTS employs the Scottish Churches Racial Justice Officer.

Member Churches Church of Scotland, Congregational Federation, Methodist Church, Religious Society of Friends, Roman Catholic Church, Salvation Army, Scottish Episcopal Church, United Free Church, United Reformed Church.

CYTÛN: EGLWYSI YNGHYD YNG NGHYMRU
CHURCHES TOGETHER IN WALES
58 Richmond Rd, Cardiff, South Wales CF24 3UR
Tel (main office): 029 2046 4204
Web: www.cytun.org.uk

Chief Executive Revd Aled Edwards OBE
Tel: 029 2046 4375
*email:*aled@cytun.org.uk

Bilingual Office Administrator to Chief Executive Mrs Sasha Perriam
Tel: 029 2046 4204
email: post@cytun.org.uk

National Assembly Policy Officer Mr Geraint Hopkins
Tel: 029 2046 4378
email: geraint@cytun.org.uk

Faith Order and Witness Officer Rhian Linecar
Tel: 029 2046 4371
email: rhian@cytun.org.uk

Cytûn's Basis and Commitment:
Cytûn unites in pilgrimage those churches in Wales, which acknowledging God's revelation in Christ, confess the Lord Jesus Christ as God and Saviour according to the Scriptures, and in obedience to God's will and in the power of the Holy Spirit, commit ourselves.

To seek a deepening of their communion with Christ with one another and in the church which is his body, and to fulfil the mission to proclaim the gospel by common witness and service in the world, to the glory of the one God, Father, Son and Holy Spirit.

Member Denominations The Baptist Union of Wales, the Roman Catholic Church, the Church in Wales, the Congregational Federation, the Covenanted Baptist Churches, the German-speaking Lutheran Church, the Methodist Church, the Presbyterian Church of Wales, the Quakers, the Salvation Army, the Union of Welsh Independents, the United Reformed Church and the South Wales Baptist Association.

Aligned Groupings The Covenanted Churches in Wales, the Free Church Council of Wales.

Cytûn also works in close collaboration with the Commission of the Covenanted Church in Wales and the Free Church Council of Wales.

THE IRISH COUNCIL OF CHURCHES
Inter-Church Centre, 48 Elmwood Ave, Belfast BT9 6AZ
Tel: 028 9066 3145
Fax: 028 9066 4160
email: info@irishchurches.org
Web: www.irishchurches.org

President Most Revd Richard Clarke

Vice-President Revd Fr Godrey O'Donnell

Hon Treasurer Mr Robert Cochran

Executive Officer Mr Mervyn McCullagh

Administrator Mrs Karen Kelly

History From 1906 the Presbyterian and Methodist Churches had a joint committee for united efforts. In 1910 the General Assembly of the Presbyterian Church invited other evangelical Churches to set up similar joint committees with it. The Church of Ireland accepted and by 1911 the joint committee of these two Churches was in action. Following a recommendation of the 1920 Lambeth Conference, these joint committees developed in 1922 into the United Council of Christian Churches and Religious Communions in Ireland including six of the present member churches. In 1966 the United Council changed its name to the Irish Council of Churches. The Council employed its first full-time secretary in April 1972.

Aims The Irish Council of Churches is constituted by Christian Communions in Ireland willing to join in united efforts to promote the spiritual, physical, moral and social welfare of the people and the extension of the rule of Christ among all nations and over every region of life.

Member Churches (14) Antiochian Orthodox Church in Ireland, Greek Orthodox Church, Lifelink Network of Churches, Lutheran Church in Ireland, Methodist Church in Ireland, Irish District of the Moravian Church, Non-Subscribing Presbyterian Church of Ireland, Presbyterian Church in Ireland, Religious Society of Friends in Ireland, Rock of Ages Cherubim and Seraphim Church, Romanian Orthodox Church in Ireland, Russian Orthodox Church in Ireland, Salvation Army (Ireland Division).

Structure The Council consists of 83 members appointed by the member Churches, together with the Heads of the member Churches and up to ten co-opted members, the General Secretary, Treasurer and immediate Past President of the Council. There is an Annual Meeting and occasional gatherings. The member Churches appoint an Executive Committee, which meets quarterly and is responsible for the oversight of the work of the Council.

The Council continues to serve both jurisdictions (Northern Ireland and the Republic of Ireland) and comprises 14 member churches (see below). It is an associate member of Churches Together in Britain and Ireland and the Conference of European Churches and has links with the World Council of Churches.

(a) It is currently re-assessing its purpose and direction in the rapidly changing contexts both sides of the border; its ecumenical witness across the island and relationships between and beyond its member churches, and its international links through its Board of Overseas Affairs.
(b) It meets quarterly with the Roman Catholic Church in Ireland through the Irish Inter-Church Committee and every 18 months as the Irish Inter-Church Meeting. The last Meeting was held in Dublin in in October 2010, taking the focus of Baptism.
(c) The Inter-Church Committee on Social Issues (ICCSI), a forum of the Irish Inter-Church Committee, currently employs a Project Officer to working on a parish-based integration programme in the Republic.
(d) It is represented on various regional, national and CTBI bodies concerned with regional equality panels, inter-faith, international, mission, overseas aid, racial justice and TV and radio affairs, and the Week of Prayer for Christian Unity.
(e) It is currently serviced by 2 staff based in the Belfast office (Executive Officer and Adminstrator) and 1 part-time Ecumenical Officer based in Dublin.

More information about the Council's work can be obtained from www.irishchurches.org which includes the most recent Annual Report.

Meissen Agreement with the Evangelical Church in Germany

The Evangelical Church in Germany (Evangelische Kirche in Deutschland – EKD) is a Communion of 20 member churches (mostly *Landeskirchen* or territorial churches). Of these, seven are members of the United Evangelical Lutheran Church of Germany – VELKD (eight Lutheran churches were founding members of VELKD). One church in the EKD is purely Reformed, one is predominantly Reformed and twelve today form the Evangelical Church of the Union – UEK (seven churches were founding members of the UEK). One Church (the Evangelische Kirche in Mitteldeutschland) is a member of both VELKD and the UEK. In many of the United churches the Lutheran tradition predominates.

In November 1988 the General Synod welcomed the Meissen Common Statement, *On the Way to Visible Unity*, which called for a closer relationship between the Church of England and the German Evangelical Churches. The Meissen Declaration, which it recommended, was approved by the General Synod in July 1990 without dissent, and solemnly affirmed and proclaimed an Act of Synod on 29 January 1991. The Meissen Declaration makes provision for the Church of England and the Evangelical Church in Germany to live in closer fellowship with one another (though not yet with interchangeable ministries) and commits them to work towards the goal of full visible unity. The member churches of the EKD have been designated as churches to which the Ecumenical Canons apply (*see* **Ecumenical Canons**).

The Meissen Commission (the Sponsoring Body for the Church of England–EKD Relations) exists to oversee and encourage relationships (*see* Council for Christian Unity). Fuller information is contained in *The German Evangelical Churches* (CCU Occasional Paper No 1 £2.95 + 35p p&p) and *Anglo-German Ecumenical Links: An Information Pack* (£1 inc. p&p). The text of the Meissen Agreement can be found in *The Meissen Agreement: Texts* (CCU Occasional Paper No 2 £2.10 inc. p&p). These are all available from the Council for Christian Unity. Most of this material is downloadable from the CCU web site at www.cofe.anglican.org/info/ccu.

Co-Chairmen of the Meissen Commission Bishop Dr Friedrich Weber (*EKD*), Rt Revd Nicholas Baines (*Church of England*)

English Co-Secretary of the Meissen Commission Revd Dr Leslie Nathaniel, Council for Christian Unity, Church House, Great Smith St, London SW1P 3AZ *Tel:* 020 7898 1474

German Co-Secretary of the Meissen Commission OKR Christoph Ernst, EKD Kirchenamt, Postfach 21 02 20, D – 30402 Hannover, Germany
Tel: 00 49 511 2796 127
Fax: 00 49 511 2796 725
email: christoph.ernst@ekd.de
Web: www.ekd.de

The Reuilly Common Statement: Relations with the French Lutheran and Reformed Churches

Encouraged by the positive reception of the Meissen and Porvoo Agreements, the Anglican Churches of Britain and Ireland engaged in dialogue with the French Reformed and Lutheran Churches, with formal conversations beginning in 1994. These Churches had signalled their desire to enter into closer fellowship with Anglican Churches on the model of the Meissen Agreement, which the Church of England had concluded with the Evangelical Church in Germany (EKD).

The relations between the Anglican and French Churches are steeped in history. Contacts go back to the Middle Ages and took on a new character through the impetus of the Reformation. In later years, at times of turbulence and persecution, churches on both sides of the Channel welcomed those persecuted for their faith.

The conversations involved four participating churches from each side: the four Anglican Churches of the British Isles (the Church of England, the Church of Ireland, the Scottish Episcopal Church and the Church in Wales) and the four French Churches of the Lutheran and Reformed traditions (the Church of the Augsburg Confession of Alsace and Lorraine, the Evangelical Lutheran Church of France, the Reformed Church of Alsace and Lorraine and the Reformed Church of France).

The Reuilly Common Statement which forms the outcome of these conversations takes its name from a community of deaconesses, committed to prayer and meditation. The Statement was approved by the General Synod of the Church of England in November 1999, and the Statement was signed by the participatory Churches in Canterbury and Paris during the summer of 2001.

In common with other ecumenical statements, the Reuilly document first sets the scene, with the history and present context of the participants, and then moves on to current theological issues: the Church as Sign, Instrument and Foretaste of the Kingdom of God; the Church as Communion (*koinonia*); Growth towards Visible Unity; Agreement in Faith and the Apostolicity of the Church and its Ministry.

The Churches declare that they have found a high degree of unity and faith, and outline three areas of future work together: common efforts in witness and service; continuing theological work, particularly on questions of oversight, authority, eucharistic ministry and formally uniting ministries; the practical consequences of the Agreement: prayer, sharing of worship, partnership, and joint ventures across a range of areas.

Within France there have been conversations for greater unity and closer fellowship. The Evangelical Lutheran Church of France (EELF) and the Reformed Church of France (ERF) have continued discussions that will lead to the creation of a United Protestant Church of France by 2013. The joint Synods are to receive proposals for a United Protestant Church of France in 2013. The EELF and ERF's move toward unity follows a similar process by the Church of the Augsburg Confession of Alsace and Lorraine (ECAAL) and the Reformed Church of Alsace and Lorraine (ERAL), which in 2004 formed the Union of Protestant Churches in Alsace and Lorraine (UEPAL).

The implementation of the Agreement is coordinated by a Contact Group. The Anglican Co-Chairman is the Bishop of Colchester and the French Co-Chairman is Pasteur Geoffroy Goetz.

For information on current links and initiatives, contact:
Revd Dr Leslie Nathaniel, The Council for Christian Unity, Church House, Great Smith Street, London SW1P 3AZ

The full text of the Reuilly Declaration, together with background articles on the theological issues and the participating Churches, can be found in *Called to Witness and Service*, Church House Publishing (1999), ISBN 0 7151 5757 4.

Conference of European Churches

General Secretary Revd Dr Guy Liagre, PO Box 2100, 150 Route de Ferney, 1211 Geneva 2, Switzerland
Tel: 41 22 791 61 11
Fax: 41 22 791 62 27
email: cec@cec-kek.org
Web: ceceurope.org

Born in the era of the 'cold war' 53 years ago, CEC emerged into a fragmented and divided continent. Thus it was that Churches of Eastern and Western Europe felt one priority of their work to be promoting international understanding – building bridges. This CEC has consistently tried to do, always insisting that no 'iron curtain' exists among the Churches.

The supreme governing body of the Conference is the Assembly. Here all 120 member Churches are represented. The first Assembly was in 1959 and further Assemblies were held in 1960, 1962, 1964, 1967, 1971, 1974, 1979, 1986, 1992, 1997, 2003 and 2009.

CEC initiated the European Ecumenical Assembly 'Peace with Justice' held in Basel in May 1989, co-sponsored with the Council of European Bishops' Conferences (CCEE, Roman Catholic). A second European Ecumenical Assembly was held in Graz, Austria, in 1997 with the theme 'Reconciliation: Gift of God and Source of New Life'. In 2001, CEC and CCEE launched the 'Charta Oecumenica – guidelines for the growing cooperation among the Churches in Europe'. A third European Ecumenical Assembly was held in Sibiu, Romania, in 2007 with the theme 'The light of Christ shines upon all – Hope for renewal and unity in Europe'.

The 40-member Central Committee oversees the implementation of the decisions of the Assembly. A Presidium, drawn from the Central Committee, acts as the Executive Council of the Conference.

Since 1 January 1999 the European Ecumenical Commission on Church and Society (EECCS) with offices in Brussels and Strasbourg integrated with CEC, and, together with CEC's existing work, created the new Church and Society Commission of the CEC. A merger is also planned between CEC and the Brussels-based Churches' Commission for Migrants in Europe (CCME).

The Secretariat in Geneva and offices in Brussels and Strasbourg ensure the continuity of the activities.

World Council of Churches

The Church of England has taken its full share in the international ecumenical movement since the Edinburgh Conference of 1910. In 2009 the General Synod made a grant of £108,000 to the General Budget of the World Council of Churches.

Presidium Archbishop Dr Anastasios of Tirana and All Albania (Orthodox Autocephalous Church of Albania), Mr John Taroanui Doom (Maòhi Protestant Church, French Polynesia), Revd Dr Simon Dossou (Protestant Methodist Church in Benin), Revd Dr Soritua Nababan (Protestant Christian Batak Church (HKBP), Indonesia), Revd Dr Ofelia Ortega (Presbyterian-Reformed Church in Cuba), Patriarch Abune Paulos (Ethiopian Orthodox Tewahedo Church), Revd Dr Bernice Powell Jackson (United Church of Christ, USA), Dr Mary Tanner (Church of England)

Moderator of Central Committee Revd Dr Walter Altmann (Evangelical Church of the Lutheran Confession in Brazil)

Vice-Moderators
Metropolitan Prof Dr Gennadios of Sassima (Limouris) (Ecumenical Patriarchate of Constantinople)
Revd Dr Margaretha M. Hendriks-Ririmasse (Protestant Church in the Moluccas, Indonesia)

General Secretary Revd Dr Olav Fykse Tveit (Church of Norway)

Office PO Box 2100, 150 route de Ferney, 1211 Geneva 2, Switzerland
Tel: 00 41 22 791 61 11
Fax: 00 41 22 791 03 61
Web: www.oikoumene.com
Cable: Oikoumene Geneva
email: infowcc@wcc-coe.org

The World Council of Churches was brought into formal existence by a resolution of its first Assembly at Amsterdam in 1948.

Member Churches agree to the following basis:

> The World Council of Churches is a fellowship of churches which confess the Lord Jesus Christ as God and Saviour according to the Scriptures and therefore seek to fulfil together their common calling to the glory of the one God, Father, Son and Holy Spirit.

Extract from the Constitution

The primary purpose of the fellowship of churches in the WCC is to call one another to visible unity in one faith and in one eucharistic fellowship, expressed in worship and common life in Christ, through witness and service to the world, and to advance towards that unity in order that the world may believe.

In seeking *koinonia* in faith and life, witness and service, the churches through the Council will:

1. promote the prayerful search for forgiveness and reconciliation in a spirit of mutual accountability, the development of deeper relationships through theological dialogue, and the sharing of human, spiritual and material resources with one another;
2. facilitate common witness in each place and in all places, and support each other in their work for mission and evangelism;
3. express their commitment to *diakonia* in serving human need, breaking down barriers between people, promoting one human family in justice and peace, and upholding the integrity of creation, so that all may experience the fullness of life;
4. nurture the growth of an ecumenical consciousness through processes of education and a vision of life in community rooted in each particular cultural context;
5. assist each other in their relationships to and with people of other faith communities;
6. foster renewal and growth in unity, worship, mission and service.

In order to strengthen the one ecumenical movement, the Council will:

1. nurture relations with and among churches, especially within but also beyond its membership;
2. establish and maintain relations with national councils, regional conferences of churches, organizations of Christian World Communions and other ecumenical bodies;
3. support ecumenical initiatives at regional, national and local levels;
4. facilitate the creation of networks among ecumenical organizations;
5. work towards maintaining the coherence of the one ecumenical movement in its diverse manifestations.

The World Council shall offer counsel and provide opportunity for united action in matters of common interest.

It may take action on behalf of constituent churches only in such matters as one or more of them may commit to it and only on behalf of such churches.

The World Council shall not legislate for the churches; nor shall it act for them in any manner except as indicated or as may hereafter be specified by the constituent churches.

The WCC is governed by an Assembly of Member Churches, a Central Committee, and by an Executive Committee and other subordinate bodies as may be established. Assemblies are held every six to eight years and have been as follows:

1. AMSTERDAM, 1948 – theme: 'Man's Disorder and God's Design'
2. EVANSTON, 1954 – theme: 'Christ the Hope of the World'
3. NEW DELHI, 1961– theme: 'Jesus Christ, the Light of the World'
4. UPPSALA, 1968 – theme: 'Behold, I Make All Things New'
5. NAIROBI, 1975 – theme: 'Jesus Christ Frees and Unites'
6. VANCOUVER, 1983 – theme: 'Jesus Christ the Life of the World'
7. CANBERRA, 1991– theme: 'Come, Holy Spirit – Renew the Whole Creation'
8. HARARE 1998 – theme: 'Turn to God – Rejoice in Hope'
9. PORTO ALEGRE 2006 – theme: 'God, in your grace, transform the world'

The Central Committee elected by the Ninth Assembly includes two members of the Church of England: the Rt Revd Thomas Frederick Butler, Bishop of Southwark (now retired), and Dr Mary Tanner, one of the WCC presidents.

The WCC has 349 member churches, including 38 which are associated. Almost every Church of the Anglican Communion is included, together with most of the Orthodox Churches and all the main Protestant traditions. The Roman Catholic Church is not a member but has sent official observers to all main WCC meetings since 1960. It is a full member of the Faith and Order Commission of the WCC.

Regional Conferences

CONFERENCE OF EUROPEAN CHURCHES

See page 457.

PART 7

Who's Who

Abbreviations used in the biographies

AABM ..... Archbishops' Adviser for Bishops' Ministry
ABIST .... Associate, British Institute of Surgical Technology
ABM .... Advisory Board of Ministry (now Ministry Division)
AC .... Archbishops' Council
ACA ..... Associate, Institute of Chartered Accountants
ACC .... Anglican Consultative Council
ACCM .... Advisory Council for the Church's Ministry (now Ministry Division)
ACE .... Associateship of the College of Education Member, Association of Conference Executives
ACGI ... Associate, City and Guilds of London Institute
ACIB .... Associate, Chartered Institute of Bankers (formerly AIB)
ACII .... Associate, Chartered Insurance Institute
ACIS .. Associate, Institute of Chartered Secretaries and Administrators
ACMA .. Associate, Chartered Institute of Management Accountants (formerly ACWA)
ACORA ..... Archbishops' Commission on Rural Areas
ACP .... Associate, College of Preceptors
ACS .... Additional Curates Society
ACertCM .... Archbishop of Canterbury's Certificate in Church Music
AD .... Area Dean
ADipR .... Archbishop's Diploma for Readers
AHA .... Area Health Authority
AIA .... Associate, Institute of Actuaries
AKC .... Associate, King's College London
ALA .... Associate, Library Association
ALCD .... Associate, London College of Divinity
ALCM .... Associate, London College of Music
APR .... Association for Promoting Retreats
ARC .... Anglican-Roman Catholic
ARCIC .... Anglican-Roman Catholic International Commission
ARCM .... Associate, Royal College of Music
ARCO .... Associate, Royal College of Organists
ARCO(CHM) .... Associate, Royal College of Organists with Diploma in Choir Training
ARCS .... Associate, Royal College of Science
ARMIT .... Associate, Royal Melbourne Institute of Technology
ASWA ..... Anglican Society for the Welfare of Animals
ATCL ...... Associate, Trinity College of Music London
ATII .... Associate Member, Institute of Taxation
Aberd .... Aberdeen
Abp .... Archbishop
Aberw .... Aberystwyth
Acad .... Academy
AdDipEd .... Advanced Diploma in Education
Admin . Administration, Administrative, Administrator
Adn .... Archdeacon
Adnry .... Archdeaconry
Adv .... Adviser, Advisory
Agric .... Agricultural, Agriculture
Aid .... Aidan('s)
Alb .... Alban('s)
Andr .... Andrew('s), Andrews
Angl .... Anglican(s)
Ant .... Anthony('s)
Appt .... Appointment(s), appointed
Ascen .... Ascension
Assoc .... Associate, Association
Asst .... Assistant
Assur .... Assurance
Aug .... Augustine('s)
Auth .... Authority
b .... Born
B & W .... (Diocese of) Bath and Wells
BA .... Bachelor of Arts
BAGUPA .... Bishop's Advisory Group on UPAs
BBC .... British Broadcasting Corporation
BCC .... British Council of Churches (now see CCBI)
BCh or BChir Bachelor of Surgery (also see BS and ChB)
BD .... Bachelor of Divinity
BDS .... Bachelor of Dental Surgery
BEd .... Bachelor of Education
BFBS .... British and Foreign Bible Society
BLitt .... Bachelor of Letters
BM .... Board of Mission
BMU .... Board for Mission and Unity
Bmet .... Bachelor of Metallurgy
BMus .... Bachelor of Music (also see MusB or MusBac)
BNC .... Brasenose College
BPS .... British Pharmacological Society
BRF .... Bible Reading Fellowship
BS .... Bachelor of Science (also see BSc), Bachelor of Surgery (also see BCh, BChir and ChB)
BSR .... Board for Social Responsibility
BSc .... Bachelor of Science (also see BS)
BSocSc .... Bachelor of Social Science (also see BSSc)
BTh Btheol .... Bachelor of Theology (also see STB)
BVM&S . Bachelor of Veterinary Medicine and Surgery
BVSc .... Bachelor of Veterinary Science
BYFC .... British Youth for Christ
Bapt .... Baptist('s)
Barn .... Barnabas('s)
Bart .... Bartholomew('s)
Bd .... Board
Bedf .... Bedford
Bibl .... Biblical
Birm .... (Diocese of) Birmingham
Blackb .... (Diocese of) Blackburn
Boro .... Borough
Bp .... Bishop
Br .... British
Bradf .... (Diocese of) Bradford
Bris .... (Diocese of) Bristol
Bucks .... Buckingham(shire)
C .... Curate
C of E .... Church of England
C of I .... Church of Ireland
C-in-c .... Curate-in-charge
CA .... Church Army Member, Institute of Chartered Accountants of Scotland
CAB .... Citizens Advice Bureau
CAC .... Crown Appointments Commission (now Crown Nominations Commission)
CACLB .... Churches Advisory Council for Local Broadcasting (now Churches' Media Council)
CB .... Companion, Order of the Bath
CBE .... Commander, Order of the British Empire
CBF .... Central Board of Finance
CBI .... Confederation of British Industry
CCC .... Corpus Christi College, Council for the Care of Churches
CCCS Commonwealth and Continental Church Society
CCHH .... Churches Council for Health and Healing
CCLA .... Churches, Charities and Local Authorities
CCOM .... Churches' Commission on Mission
CCRJ .... Churches' Commission for Racial Justice
CCU .... Council for Christian Unity

WHO'S WHO

CCYW .... Certificate in Community Youth Work
CD .... Canadian Forces Decoration, Conventional District
CDC .... Clergy Discipline Commission
CEC .... Conference of European Churches
CECC .... Church of England Committee for Communications
CEDR .... Centre for Dispute Resolution
CEEC .... Church of England Evangelical Council
CEIG .... Christian Ethical Investment Group
CEM .... Christian Education Movement
CERT TH .... Certificate in Theology
CF .... Chaplain to the Forces
CFE .... College of Further Education
CHRISM .... Christians in Secular Ministry
CJGS ...... Community of the Companions of Jesus the Good Shepherd
CLASP .. Churches Linked Across Staffs & the Potteries
CME .... Continuing Ministerial Education
CMEAC ...... Committee for Minority Ethnic Anglican Concerns
CMS ... Church Mission Society, Church Music Society
CNC .... Crown Nominations Commission
CPA .... Chartered Patent Attorney
CPAS .... Church Pastoral Aid Society
CPC ...... Certificate of Professional Competence (Road Transport)
CQSW .... Certificate of Qualification in Social Work
CR .... Community of the Resurrection (Mirfield)
CRAC ... Central Religious Advisory Committee of the BBC and ITA
CRC .... Central Readers Council
CSC .... Community of the Servants of the Cross
CSEM .... Certificate in Special Education Management
CSO .... Central Statistical Office
CSR .... Council for Social Responsibility
CSWG .... Community of the Servants of the Will of God
CTBI .... Churches Together in Britain and Ireland
CTE .... Churches Together in England
CTH .... Certificate in Theology
CTM .... Certificate in Theology for Ministry
CU .... Church Union
CUF .... Church Urban Fund
CYCW ...... Certificate in Youth and Community Work
CYFA .... Church Youth Fellowships Association
Cam .... Cambridge
Cambs .... Cambridgeshire
Can .... Canon
Cant .... (Diocese of) Canterbury
Carl .... (Diocese of) Carlisle
Cath .... Catharine('s)/Catherine('s)
Cathl .... Cathedral
Cchem .... Certified/Chartered Chemist
CdipAF . Certified Diploma in Accounting and Finance
Cen .... Centre, Center, Central
Ceng .... Chartered Engineer
Cert CT .... Certificate in Ceramic Technology
CertEd .... Certificate of Education
CertMBiol .... Certificate of Microbiology
Ch .... Christ('s), Church(es)
Chair .... Chairman, Chairwoman
Chan .... Chancellor
Chapl .... Chaplain(s), Chaplaincy(ies)
ChB .... Bachelor of Surgery (also see BCh, BChir and BS)
Ch Ch .... Christ Church
Chelmsf .... (Diocese of) Chelmsford
Ches .... (Diocese of) Chester
Chich .... (Diocese of) Chichester
Chr .... Christian(s)
Chris .... Christopher('s)
Chu .... Churchill
Cl-in-c .... Cleric-in-charge
Clem .... Clement('s)
Cllr .... Councillor/Counsellor
Cmaths .... Chartered Mathematician
Co .... Company, County(ies)
Co-ord .... Coordinator, Coordinating
Coll .... College
Colleg .... Collegiate
Com .... Community
Commn .... Commission
Commr .... Commissioner
Comp .... Comprehensive
Conf .... Confederation, Conference
Consult .... Consultant/Consultancy
Corp .... Corporation
Coun .... Council
Conv .... Convocation
Cphys ... Chartered Physicist of the Institute of Physics
Cov .... (Diocese of) Coventry
Cstat .... Chartered Statistician
Ctee .... Committee
Cuth .... Cuthbert('s)
DAC Diocesan Advisory Committee, Diploma in Adult Counselling
DBE .... Diocesan Board of Education
DBF .... Diocesan Board of Finance
DCH .... Diploma in Child Health
DCL .... Doctor of Civil Law
DCO .... Diocesan Communications Officer
DD .... Doctor of Divinity
DDO .... Diocesan Director of Ordinands
DDS .... Doctor of Dental Surgery
DHSM .... Diploma in Health Service Management
DHSS .... Department of Health and Social Security
DIC .... Diploma of Membership of Imperial College London
DL .... Deputy Lieutenant
DLC .... Diploma of Loughborough College
DMS .... Diploma in Management Studies
DN .... Diploma in Nursing
DOE .... Department of the Environment
DPA .... Diploma in Public Administration
DPS .... Diploma in Pastoral Studies
DMin .... Doctor of Ministry
DPhil .... Doctor of Philosophy (also see PhD)
DProf .... Doctor in Professional Studies
DRACSC . Deployment, Remuneration and Conditions of Service Committee
DSPT .... Diploma in Social and Pastoral Theology
DSS ... Diploma in Social Studies Department of Social Security
DSc .... Doctor of Science (also see ScD)
DTI .... Department of Trade and Industry
DTS .... Diploma in Theological Studies
DTh .... Doctor of Theology (also see ThD)
DUniv .... Doctor of the University
Dav .... David('s)
Dep .... Deputy
Dept .... Department
Devel .... Development
Dio .... Diocese
Dioc .... Diocesan
Dip .... Diploma
DipAdEd .... Diploma in Advanced Education
DipBA .... Diploma in Business Administration
DipC .... Diploma in Counselling
DipChemEng .... Diploma in Chemical Engineering
DipEd .... Diploma in Education
DipHE .... Diploma in Higher Education
DipLA .... Diploma in Liturgy and Architecture
DipLRM .... Diploma in Leadership, Renewal and Mission Studies
DipMin .... Diploma in Ministry

DipN Diploma in Nursing
DipPallMed Diploma in Palliative Medicine
DipRJ Diploma in Retail Jewellery
DipSE Diploma in Special Education
DipSW Diploma in Social Work
DipSocSc Diploma in Social Sciences
DipTh Diploma in Theology
Dip UEM Diploma in Urban Estate Management
Dir Director
Distr District
Div Divinity, Division
Dn Deacon
Dny Deanery
Doct Doctrinal, Doctrine
Dom Domestic
Down Downing
Dr Doctor
Dss Deaconess
Dub Dublin
Dur (Diocese of) Durham
E East, Eastern
EAMTC East Anglian Ministerial Training Course
ECUSA Episcopal Church of the United States of America
EFAC Evangelical Fellowship in the Anglican Communion
EIG Ecclesiastical Insurance Group (now Ecclesiastical Insurance)
EJM(RC) Ecclesiastical Jurisdiction Measure (Revision Committee)
EKD Evangelische Kirche Deutschland
EPA European Patent Attorney
ERMC Eastern Region Ministry Course
Eccl Ecclesiastical
Ecum Ecumenical
Ed Editor, Editorial
Edin (Diocese of) Edinburgh
Edm Edmund('s)
Eds Edmundsbury
Educ Education
Educl Educational
Edw Edward('s)
Eliz Elizabeth('s)
Em Emmanuel('s)
Emer Emeritus
Eng Engineering
Environ Environmental
Engl English
Episc Episcopal Episcopalian
Eur (Diocese of) Gibraltar in Europe Europe, European
EurIng European Engineer
Eur Phys European Physicist
Ev Evangelist('s), Evangelists
Evang Evangelical, Evangelism
Ex (Diocese of) Exeter
Exam Examining
Exec Executive
FAC Fabric Advisory Committee
FASC Fellow, Academy of St Cecilia
FBA Fellow, British Academy
FBCS Fellow, British Computer Society
FCA Fellow, Institute of Chartered Accountants
FCAA Fellow, Cyprus Association of Actuaries
FCCA Fellow, Chartered Association of Certified Accountants (formerly FACCA)
FCEM Fellow, College of Emergency Medicine
FCIM Fellow, Chartered Institute of Marketing (formerly FInstM)
FC INST M Fellow, Chartered Institute of Marketing
FCIOB Fellow, Chartered Institute of Building
FCIPD Fellow, Chartered Institute of Personnel and Development (formerly FIPD)
FCP Fellow, College of Preceptors
FDSRCS Fellow in Dental Surgery, Royal College of Surgeons of England
FE Further Education
FGMS Fellow, Guild of Musicians and Singers
F&GP Finance and General Purposes
FIA Fellow, Institute of Actuaries
FIBMS Fellow, Institute of Biomedical Sciences
FIHT Fellow of the Institution of Highways and Transportation
FIMA Fellow, Institute of Mathematics and its Applications
FIMgt Fellow, Institute of Management
FJMU Fellow, Liverpool John Moores University
FKC Fellow, King's College London
FLAME Family Life and Marriage Education
FOAG Faith and Order Advisory Group
FPMI Fellow, Pensions Management Institute
FRAI Fellow, Royal Anthropological Institute
FRAeS Fellow, Royal Aeronautical Society
FRAS Fellow, Royal Astronomical Society
FRCO Fellow, Royal College of Organists
FRCOG Fellow, Royal College of Obstetricians and Gynaecologists
FRCOphth Fellow, Royal College of Ophthalmologists
FRCS Fellow, Royal College of Physicians and Surgeons of England
FRCSE or FRCSEd Fellow, Royal College of Surgeons of Edinburgh
FRHistS Fellow, Royal Historical Society
FRICS Fellow, Royal Institution of Chartered Surveyors (formerly FLAS and FSI)
FRIPHH Fellow, Royal Institute of Public Health and Hygiene
FRGS Fellow, Royal Geographical Society
FRS Fellow, Royal Society
FRSA Fellow, Royal Society of Arts
FRSC Fellow, Royal Society of Chemistry (formerly FRIC)
FRSL Fellow, Royal Society of Literature
FRSM Fellow, Royal Society of Medicine
FSA Fellow, Society of Antiquaries
FSCA Fellow, Royal Society of Company and Commercial Accountants
FTII Fellow, Institute of Taxation
Fell(s) Fellow(s), Fellowship
Fest Festival
Fin Financial
Fitzw Fitzwilliam
Foundn Foundation
Fran Francis(')
G&C Gonville and Caius
GAD Government Actuary's Department
GEC General Electric Company
GLC Greater London Council
GOE General Ordination Examination
GP General Practitioner
GS General Synod
Gabr Gabriel('s)
Gd Good
Gen General
Geo George('s)
Gib Gibraltar
Glas (Diocese of) Glasgow and Galloway, Glasgow
Glos Gloucestershire
Glouc (Diocese of) Gloucester
Gov Governor
Grp Group
Gr Grammar
Greg Gregorian
Gt Great
Guildf (Diocese of) Guildford
H Holy
H&FE Higher and Further Education

HA .... Health Authority
HCC .... Hospital Chaplaincies Council
HDipEd .... Higher Diploma in Education
HE .... Higher Education
HM .... Her (or His) Majesty('s)
HMP .... Her Majesty's Prison(s)
HNC .... Higher National Certificate
HND .... Higher National Diploma
HRH .... Her/His Royal Highness
Hatf .... Hatfield
Hd .... Head
Heref .... (Diocese of) Hereford
Hertf .... Hertford
Herts .... Hertfordshire
Hist .... History
Ho .... House
Hon .... Honorary, Honourable
Hosp(s) .... Hospital(s)
IARCCUM ... International Anglican – Roman Catholic Commission on Unity and Mission
IBA .... Independent Broadcasting Authority
ICI .... Imperial Chemical Industries
ICS .... Intercontinental Church Society
IDC .... Inter-Diocesan Certificate
IMEC .... Initial Ministerial Education Committee
IOM .... Isle of Man
IPR .... Insitute of Public Relations
ITV .... Independent Television
Imp .... Imperial
Inc, Incorp .... Incorporated
Incumb .... Incumbent
Ind .... Industry, Industrial
Info .... Information
Insp .... Inspector, Inspectorate
Inst .... Institute, Institution
Intercon .... Intercontinental
Internat .... International
Ips .... Ipswich
JP .... Justice of the Peace
Jas .... James('s)
Jasp .... Jasper('s)
Jes .... Jesus
Jo .... John('s)
Jos .... Joseph('s)
Jt or jt .... Joint
Jun .... Junior
K .... King('s)
KA .... Knight of St Andrew, Order of Barbados
KCVO ..... Knight Commander, Royal Victorian Order
KHS .... Knight of the Holy Sepulchre
Kath .... Katharine('s), Katherine('s)
LDSRCS(Eng) .... Licentiate in Dental Surgery of the Royal College of Surgeons (of England)
LEA .... Local Education Authority
LEP .... Local Ecumenical Project
LICeram .... Licenciate, Institute of Ceramics
LLAM ...... Licentiate, London Academy of Music and Dramatic Art
LLB .... Bachelor of Laws
LLD .... Doctor of Laws
LLM .... Master of Laws
LMH .... Lady Margaret Hall
LNSM ... Local Non-stipendiary Minister (or Ministry)
LRAM .... Licentiate, Royal Academy of Music
LRCP .... Licentiate, Royal College of Physicians
LRPS .... Licentiate, Royal Photographic Society
LRSC .... Licentiate, Royal Society of Chemistry
LSE . London School of Economics and Political Science
LTCL ...... Licentiate, Trinity College of Music, London
LTh .... Licentiate in Theology (also see LST)
LVO .... Lieutenant, Royal Victorian Order
Lab .... Laboratory
Lamp .... Lampeter
Lanc .... Lancaster
Lancs .... Lancashire
Laur .... Laurence('s)
Lawr .... Lawrence('s)
Lect .... Lecturer
Leic .... (Diocese of) Leicester
Leics .... Leicestershire
Leon .... Leonard('s)
Legis .... Legislative
Lib .... Librarian, Library
Lic .... Licence, Licensed, Licentiate
Lich .... (Diocese of) Lichfield
Linc .... (Diocese of) Lincoln
Lincs .... Lincolnshire
Liturg .... Liturgical
Liv .... (Diocese of) Liverpool
Llan .... (Diocese of) Llandaff
Lon .... (Diocese of) London
Loughb .... Loughborough
Lt .... Little
Ltd .... Limited
M .... Member
M&AA .... Michael and All Angels
MA .... Master of Arts
MB,BS &MB,ChB .... Conjoint degree of Bachelor of Medicine, Bachelor of Surgery
MBC .... Metropolitan (or Municipal) Borough Council
MBCS .... Member, British Computer Society
MBE .... Member, Order of the British Empire
MCIH .... Corporate Member, Chartered Institute of Housing
MCIJ .... Member, Chartered Institute of Journalists
MCIM .... Member, Chartered Institute of Marketing (formerly MInstM)
MCIPD . Member, Chartered Institute of Personnel and Development (formerly MIPD)
MCLIP .... Member, Chartered Institute of Library and Information Professionals
MCS .... Master of Christian Studies
MCSP .... Member, Chartered Society of Physiotherapy
MCST .... Member, College of Speech Therapists
MCT ..... Member, Association of Corporate Treasurers
MDCT ..... Manager's Diploma in Ceramic Technology
MDiv .... Master of Divinity
MEd .... Master of Education
MIBC .... Member, Institute of Business Counsellors
MICE .... Member, Institution of Civil Engineers (formerly AMICE)
MIChemE .. Member, Institution of Chemical Engineers
MIEE .... Member, Institution of Electrical Engineers (formerly AMIEE MIERE)
MIMA . Member, Institute of Management Accountants
MIMgt .... Member, Institute of Management
MIOT .... Member, Institute of Operating Theatre Technicians
MIPD .... Member, Institute of Personnel and Development (now see MCIPD)
MIPR .... Member, Institute of Public Relations
MIStructE ... Member, Institution of Structural Engineers
MInstD .... Member, Institute of Directors
MInstGA .... Member, Institute of Group Analysis
MInstP .... Member, Institute of Physics
MLitt .... Master of Letters
MOD .... Ministry of Defence
MOW .... Movement for the Ordination of Women
MP .... Member of Parliament
MPA .... Mission and Public Affairs
MPhil .... Master of Philosophy
MRCGP .... Member, Royal College of General Practitioners
MRCS .... Member, Royal College of Surgeons
MRCVS .... Member, Royal College of Veterinary Surgeons

MRSC .... Member, Royal Society of Chemistry
MSc .... Master of Science
MTech .... Master of Technology
MTh or MTheol .... Master of Theology (also see STM and ThM)
MU .... Mothers' Union
Magd .... Magdalen('s)/Magdalene('s)
Man .... (Diocese of) Manchester
Man Dir .... Managing Director
Mansf .... Mansfield
Marg .... Margaret('s)
Mart .... Martin('s)
Marlboro .... Marlborough
Matt .... Matthew('s)
Mert .... Merton
Meth .... Methodist
Metrop .... Metropolitan
Mgr .... Manager
Mgt .... Management
Mich .... Michael('s), Michael and All Angels
Mil .... Military
Min .... Minister, Ministries, Ministry, Minor
Minl .... Ministerial
Miss .... Mission('s), Missionary
Missr .... Missioner
Mod .... Moderator
Movt .... Movement
Mss .... Manuscripts
Mt .... Mount
Mus .... Music
MusB or MusBac .... Bachelor of Music (also see BMus)
N .... North
NACRO .... National Association for the Care and Rehabilitation of Offenders
NAHT .... National Association of Headteachers
NCA .... National Certificate in Agriculture
NCIs .... National Church Institutions
NDA .... National Diploma in Agriculture
NDD .... National Diploma in Design
NEOC ..... North East Oecumenical Course North East Ordination Course
NHS .... National Health Service
NNEB .... National Nursery Examination Board
NSM .... Non-stipendiary Minister (or Ministry)
NSW .... New South Wales (Australia)
NT .... New Testament
NTMTC .... North Thames Ministerial Training Course
NW .... North West/Northwestern
NZ .... New Zealand
Nat .... National
Newc .... (Diocese of) Newcastle
Nic .... Nicholas('s)/Nicolas('s)
Nn .... Northern
Norf .... Norfolk
Norw .... (Diocese of) Norwich
Northn .... Northampton
Nottm .... Nottingham
Notts .... Nottinghamshire
Nuff .... Nuffield
OAM .... Order of Australia Medal
OBE .... Officer, Order of the British Empire
OCF .... Officiating Chaplain to the Forces
OGS .... Oratory of the Good Shepherd
OLM .... Ordained Local Minister (or Ministry)
ONC .... Ordinary National Certificate
OStJ ... Officer, Most Venerable Order of the Hospital of St John of Jerusalem
OT .... Old Testament
OTC .... Open Theology College
OU, Open Univ .... Open University
Ord .... Ordinand(s), Ordination
Ox .... (Diocese of) Oxford
Oxon .... Oxfordshire
P .... Patron(s), Priest
P in O .... Priest in Ordinary
P-in-c .... Priest-in-charge
PACTA .... Professional Associate, Clinical Theology Association
PCC .... Parochial Church Council
PGCE .... Postgraduate Certificate in Education
PNG .... Papua New Guinea
POT .... Post Ordination Training
PPS .... Parliamentary Private Secretary
PR .... Public Relations
PRCC .. Policy and Resources Coordinating Committee
PRO .... Public Relations Officer
PV .... Priest Vicar
PWM .... Partnership for World Mission
Par .... Parish(es)
Parl .... Parliamentary
Pastl .... Pastoral
Patr .... Patrick('s), Patronage
Pemb .... Pembroke(shire)
Perm .... Permission
Pet .... Peter('s)
Peterb .... (Diocese of) Peterborough
Peterho .... Peterhouse
PhD .... Doctor of Philosophy (also see DPhil)
Phil .... Phil(l)ip('s)
Pk .... Park
plc .... public limited company
Poly .... Polytechnic
Portsm .... (Diocese of) Portsmouth
Prchr .... Preacher
Preb .... Prebendary
Prec .... Precentor
Prep .... Preparatory
Pres .... President
Prin .... Principal
Pris .... Prison(s)
Priv .... Private
Prof .... Professor, Professorial
Prov .... Provost, Provisions
Ptnr .... Partner
Pty .... Party
pt .... part-time
QC .... Queen's Counsel
QHC .... Queen's Honorary Chaplain
Qu .... Queen('s), Queens'
R .... Rector, Royal
RAMC .... Royal Army Medical Corps
RCHME . Royal Commission on Historical Monuments of England
RAF .... Royal Air Force
RC .... Roman Catholic
RCO .... Royal College of Organists
RD .... Royal Navy Reserve Decoration, Rural Dean
RE .... Religious Education
RGN .... Registered General Nurse
RHM .... Rank Hovis McDougall
RIBA .... (Member) Royal Institute of British Architects (formerly ARIBA)
RICS .... Royal Institute of Chartered Surveyors
RM .... Registered Midwife
RMA or RMC .... Royal Military Academy (formerly College), Sandhurst
RMN .... Registered Mental Nurse
RN .... Royal Navy
RSA .... Royal Society of Arts, Republic of South Africa
RSCM .... Royal School of Church Music
RSIN .... Rural Stress Information Network
Raph .... Raphael('s)
Rdr(s) .... Reader(s)
Red .... Redundant
Relig .... Religious
Relns .... Relations

Rep(s) .... Representative(s)
Res .... Residential, Residentiary
Resp .... Responsibility
Resurr .... Resurrection
Rev .... Review
Revd .... Reverend
Rich .... Richard('s)
Ripon .... Ripon and Leeds
Roch .... (Diocese of) Rochester
Rsch .... Research
Rt .... Right
Rtd or rtd .... Retired
S .... South, Southern
S&Man .... (Diocese of) Sodor and Man
SAMS .... South American Mission Society
SAOMC .... St Albans and Oxford Ministry Course
SASRA .... Soldiers' and Airmen's Scripture Readers Association
SBL .... Society of Biblical Literature
SCM .... State Certified Midwife, Student Christian Movement
SDMTS .... Southern Dioceses Ministerial Training Scheme
SE .... South East
SEITE ... South East Institute for Theological Education
SOAS .... School of Oriental and African Studies
SOSc .... Society of Ordained Scientists
SPCK ...... Society for Promoting Christian Knowledge
SPI .... Society of Practitioners of Insolvency
SRN .... State Registered Nurse
SRP .... State Registered Physiotherapist
SS .... Saints/Saints', Sidney Sussex
SSC ..... Secretarial Studies Certificate, Societas Sanctae Crucis (Society of the Holy Cross)
SSF .... Society of St Francis
SSM .... Society of the Sacred Mission
SST .... Society for the Study of Theology
STB .... Bachelor of Theology (also see BTh)
STETS ... Southern Theological Education and Training Scheme
STh .... Scholar in Theology (also see ThSchol)
STL .... Reader (or Professor) of Sacred Theology
STM ..... Master of Theology (also see MTh or MTheol and ThM)
SU .... Scripture Union
SW .... South West
Sacr .... Sacrist, Sacristan
Salis .... Salisbury
Sarum .... (Diocese of) Salisbury
Sav .... Saviour('s)
ScD .... Doctor of Science (also see DSc)
Sch(s) .... School(s)
Sec(s) .... Secretary(ies)
Secdry .... Secondary
Selw .... Selwyn
Sem .... Seminary
Sen .... Senior
Sheff .... (Diocese of) Sheffield
Shep .... Shepherd
Shrops .... Shropshire
So .... Souls, Souls'
Soc .... Social, Society
Som .... Somerset
Southn .... Southampton
Sq .... Square
St .... Saint
St Alb .... (Diocese of) St Albans
St And .... (Diocese of) St Andrews, Dunkeld and Dunblane
St As .... (Diocese of) St Asaph
St D .... (Diocese of) St Davids
St E&I .... (Diocese of) St Edmundsbury and Ipswich
Ste .... Sainte
Steph .... Stephen('s)
Stg .... Standing
Strg .... Steering
Suff .... Suffragan
Supt .... Superintendent
S'wark .... Southwark
S'well .... Southwell
Syn .... Synod
TCert .... Teacher's Certificate
TEFL .... Teacher of English as a Foreign Language
TETC .. Theological Education and Training Committee
TM .... Team Minister (or Ministry)
TR .... Team Rector
TV .... Team Vicar, Television
Tchr .... Teacher
Tdip .... Teacher's Diploma
Tech .... Technical, Technology
Techn .... Technician
Th, Theol .... Theological
ThD .... Doctorate in Theology (also see DTh)
ThM ..... Master of Theology (also see MTh or MTheol and STM)
Thos .... Thomas('s)
Tm .... Team
Tr .... Trainer
Treas .... Treasurer('s)
Trg .... Training
Trin .... Trinity
UCCF .. Universities and Colleges Christian Fellowship of Evangelical Unions (formerly IVF)
UCE .... University of Central England
UCL .... University College London
UEA .... University of East Anglia
UMIST ... University of Manchester Institute of Science and Technology
UPA .... Urban Priority Area (or Areas)
URC .... United Reformed Church
USCL .... United Society for Christian Literature
USPG .... United Society for the Propagation of the Gospel (formerly SPG, UMCA, and CMD)
UWE .... University of the West of England
UWIST .... University of Wales Institute of Science and Technology
Univ .... University
V .... Vicar, Virgin('s)
VRSC .... Vocations, Recruitment and Selection Committee
Vc .... Vice
Ven .... Venerable
Vis .... Visiting
Voc .... Vocational, Vocations
Vol .... Voluntary
W .... West, Western
w .... with
WATCH .... Women and the Church
WCC .... World Council of Churches
WEA .... Workers' Educational Association
WEMTC .. West of England Ministerial Training Course
Wadh .... Wadham
Wakef .... (Diocese of) Wakefield
Warw .... Warwickshire
Westf .... Westfield
Westmr .... Westminster
Wilf .... Wilfred('s), Wilfrid('s)
Wilts .... Wiltshire
Winch .... (Diocese of) Winchester
Wkg .... Working
Worc .... (Diocese of) Worcester
Wrdn .... Warden
YMCA .... Young Men's Christian Association

WHO'S WHO

A Directory of General Synod members, together with those suffragan bishops, deans and archdeacons who are not members of General Synod, and principal staff members of the General Synod, the Archbishops' Council, the Church Commissioners, the Pensions Board and Lambeth Palace, and Church Commissioners who are not members of General Synod. General Synod members are distinguished by the date of their membership, printed at the end of their entry, following the letters GS. Current membership of the General Synod is denoted by the lack of a closing date. The information contained here is supplied by the individuals concerned and no warranty is given as to its accuracy.

ADCOCK, Mrs Isabel Ruth, LLB
47 East Street Tollesbury Maldon Essex CM9 8QD [CHELMSFORD] *b* 1949 *educ* Gillingham Sch; Mid-Essex Tech Coll; Inns of Court Sch; *CV* Barrister 1975–81; 6th Form Tchr 1996–99; Tchr 1999–2000; Lect Legal Practice 2000; Legal Aid Cttee 2000–05
GS 2000–05, 2010 *Tel:* 01621 860326
email: Adcocki@hotmail.co.uk

AINSWORTH, Revd Janina Helen Margaret, BEd, MA
Church House Great Smith Street London SW1P 3AZ [CHIEF EDUCATION OFFICER, GENERAL SECRETARY, EDUCATION DIVISION AND NATIONAL SOCIETY] *b* 1950 *educ* Nottm High Sch for Girls; Homerton Coll Cam; Univ of Lanc; Ripon Coll Cuddesdon; *CV* Tchr-in-c RE Manor School Arbury Cambs 1974–74; Tchr-in-c RE Greaves Sch Lan 1975–79; Pt Lect St Mar Coll Lanc 1979–82; Educ Liaison Work Tameside Coun for Racial Equality 1983–84;RE Adv Man DBE 1986–98; Dioc Dir of Educ Man Dioc 1998–2007; deacon 2005, p 2006, NSM E Man Dioc 2005–07; Chief Educ Officer and Gen Sec Nat Soc from 2007; Assistant Priest St George in the East with St Paul. London, from 2012
Tel: 020 7898 1500
Fax: 020 7898 1520
email: janina.ainsworth@churchofengland.org

ALBAN JONES, Revd Timothy Morris, BA, MBE
The Vicarage Cross Green Soham, Ely Cambridgeshire, CB7 5DU [ELY] *b* 1964 *educ* Wycliffe Coll; Warwich Univ; Ripon Coll Cuddesdon; *CV* Asst C, Tupsley 1988–93;Chapl of St Michael's Hospice, Hereford 1990–92; TV Ross Team Ministry 1993–2000; Chapl with Deaf People 1994–2000; Dioc Voc Adv 1995–1999; V Soham and Wicken from 2000; POT Tutor from 2006; M Dioc Voc Panel from 2007; M Dioc Board of Patronage from 2009; Rural Dean of Fordham and Quy from 2010; Selection Off Board of Readers from 2010
GS 2010– *Tel:* 01353720423
email: vicar@soham.org.uk

ALDERTON-FORD, Revd Jonathan Laurence, B Th
Church Office Christ Church Moreton Hall Symonds Rd Bury St Edmunds IP32 7EW [ST EDMUNDSBURY AND IPSWICH] *b* 1957 *educ* Denes High Sch Lowestoft; Nottm Univ; St Jo Coll Nottm; *CV* C St Faith Gaywood Norw 1985–87; C St Andr Herne Bay 1987–90; Min Ch Ch LEP Moreton Hall from 1990; Chair Mid Anglia New Wine Network; Chair Passion Play for Bury St Edm; Elected M Dioc Commn from 2008; Trustee Premier Christian Radio; Can St Eds Cath from 2008
GS 1999– *Tel:* 01284 769956 (Home)
01284 725391 (Office)
Fax: 01284 725391
email: minister@ccmh.org.uk

ALEXANDER, Mrs April Rosemary, BA, Cert Ed
59 High Street Bletchingley Redhill Surrey RH1 4PB [SOUTHWARK] *b* 1943 *educ* R Masonic Sch Rickmansworth; Open Univ; Homerton Coll Cam; *CV* Various teaching posts 1964–84; Financial Services Industry 1984–92; Financial Services Authority (formerly Securities and Investments Bd) 1992–99; Exec Dir Occupational Pensions Regulatory Authority 1999–2005; Head of Trustee Educ, The Pensions Regulator 2005–07; Consult The Pensions Regulator and Pensions Ind 2007; Lay Chair Dioc Syn 1996–2006; M DRACSC; M GS Legis Cttee; M Ch Commn Bd of Govs 2009; M Audt Cttee of Ch Commns; M Steering Cttee Clergy Terms of Service 2007; M Rev Cttee Bps & Ps (Consecration and Ord of Women) Measure 2009
GS 2000– *Tel:* 01883 743421 07867 977823
email: april@abalexander.co.uk

ALI, Canon Linda, BA, MA
51 Thief Lane York YO10 3HQ [YORK] *b* 1943 *educ* Bp Anstey Gr Sch Trinidad; Univ of York; *CV* Trade Marks Co-ord, Colgate Palmolive Eur 1970–89; Trade Marks Mgr, Unilever Plc UK 1989–97; Researcher/writer, Nat Archives, Lon from 2002; M York Forum for Racial Concerns; M CMEAC from 2006; Chair of Trustees USPG: Anglicans in World Mission from 2009; M Derwent Dny Syn; M Soc Resp Coun, N Yorks
GS 2005– *Tel:* 01904 413698
07966 363721 (Mobile)
email: linda@jj26.fsnet.co.uk

ALLAIN-CHAPMAN, Dr Thomas Joseph, BA, MA, Ph D
Church House Great Smith St London SW1P 3AZ [PUBLISHING MANAGER, ARCHBISHOPS' COUNCIL] *b* 1969 *educ* Mount St Mary's Coll Sheff; K Coll Lon; *CV* freelance writer and ed 1994–95; Ed, HarperCollins Relig 1995–97; Asst Commissioning Ed,

WHO'S WHO

Collins Educ 1997–2000, Commissioning Ed 2000, Publishing Mgr 2000–05; Head of Publishing, Church Ho Publishing 2005–09; Dir ROOTS for Churches Ltd from 2006; Publishing Mgr AC from 2009 *Tel:* 020 7898 1450
Fax: 020 7898 1449
email: thomas.allain-chapman@churchofengland.org

ALLCHIN, Revd Maureen Ann, MA, Cert Ed
4 Northfields Bulkington Devizes SN10 1SE [SALISBURY] *b* 1950 *educ* Northfields Sch Lon; Liv Univ Inst of Educ; Sussex Univ; Salis and Wells Th Coll; *CV* Tchr and Sen Mistress, Steyning Gr Sch 1979–92; C (NSM), Chich Dioc 1991–93; C Storrington, Chich 1993–95; TV Bridport Tm, Salis Dioc 1995–2005; Bp's Lic from 2005; Dioc Selector for Rdr Min 1997–2000; Staff Tutor for CM Devel 1999–2005; Bd of Min portfolio holder for CMD 2000–03, for Interim Min 2005–07; Bp's Coun from 2006; P-in-c Canalside Benefice, Sarum 2006–08; Bp's Lic 2008–09; Interim Min 2009–10; P-in-C Holy Trinity, Trowbridge 2009–10, Bp's Lic from 2010
GS 2005–10 *Tel:* 01380 828931
email: maureen@mallchin.co.uk

ALLEN, Mrs (Penelope) Penny, Teaching Cert
12 Cranbrook Grove Perton Wolverhampton WV6 7RY [LICHFIELD] *b* 1950 *educ* Kibworth Beauchamp Gr; Oadby Beauchamp Upper Sch; Leic City Coll of Ed; *CV* Tchr, Leic 1971–74; Tchr Staffordshire 1974–77; Supply tcher 1985–88; Head of dept 1988–2009; M South Staffs District Counc 1989–91; M Perton Parish Counc from 1987; M Lichf Dioc; Lay Chair Trysull Deanery; M Ecum Ch Coun Perton
GS 2010– *Tel:* 01902 756125
email: mrspennyallen@yahoo.co.uk

ALLEN, Mr Timothy Edward, MA
Bell House Quay St Orford Woodbridge IP12 2NU [ST EDMUNDSBURY AND IPSWICH] *b* 1944 *educ* Framlingham Coll;Trin Coll Cam; *CV* Bank of England 1966–86; M Haringey Coun Lon 1972–78; Sec to Securities and Investments Bd 1986–97; Sec to Bd of Fin Services Authority 1997–98; M Dioc Syn; M Bp's Coun/DBF; M Agenda Plan and Business Cttee; Chair DAC; M Coun St Eds Cathl; M CNC St E and I vacancy 2006–07; M CCC 2006–08; M CBC from 2008; Chair CBC Sculpture and Furnishings Ctee; M Cathl and Ch Bldgs Div Grp; M Fees Advisory Commn 2001–12; M Min Div Fin Panel; Chair Revision Cttee on draft Stipends (Cessation of Special Payments) Measure 2004; Chair Revision Cttee on draft Pastl (Amendment) Measure 2004; M Revision Cttee draft Diocs, Pastl and Mission Measure 2006; Chair Revision Cttee on Draft Eccl Fees (Amendment) Measure 2009; Lay Elder Par of Orford from 2001; M Cathl Fabric Comm from 2011; Lay Canon of St Eds Cathl from 2011
GS 2000– *Tel:* 01394 450789
email: tim@bellhouseorford.com

ALLISTER, Rt Revd Donald Spargo, MA, DTh (Hon)
Bishop's Lodging The Palace Peterborough PE1 1YA [BISHOP OF PETERBOROUGH] *b* 1952 *educ* Birkenhead Sch; Peterho Cam; Trinity Th Coll Bris; *CV* C St Geo Hyde, Ches 1976–79; C St Nic Sevenoaks, Roch 1979–83; V Ch Ch Birkenhead, Ches 1983–89; Chaplain Arrowe Park Hosp 1983–85; R St Mary Cheadle, Ches 1989–2002; RD Cheadle 1999–2002; Adn of Chester 2002–10; Bp of Peterborough from 2010; CCU from 2006; Abps' Coun Fin Cttee from 2011
GS 2005– *Tel:* 01733 562492
Fax: 01733 890077
email: bishop@peterborough-diocese.org.uk

ALLSOPP, Ven Christine, BSc
Westbrook 11 The Drive Northampton NN1 4RZ [ARCHDEACON OF NORTHAMPTON; PETERBOROUGH] *b* 1947 *educ* St Alb Girls' Gr Sch; Univ of Aston; Salis and Wells (SDMTS); *CV* C St Pet Caversham and St Marg Mapledurham 1989–94; TV Bracknell Tm Min 1994–98; TR Bourne Valley 1998–2005; RD Alderbury 1999–2005; Non-res Can Salis Cathl 2002–05; Chair Dioc Ho of Clergy 2000–04; M Bd of Min 1998–2004; Non-res Can Peterb Cathl from 2005; Chair Peterb DBE from 2005
GS 2005– *Tel:* 01604 714015
Fax: 01604 792016
email: archdeacon.northampton@peterborough-diocese.org.uk

ALLSOPP, Dr Dennis, BSc PhD CBiol FSB MCLIP
Westbrook 11 The Drive Northampton NN1 4RZ [PETERBOROUGH] *b* 1946 *educ* Rotherham Gr Sch; Aston Univ; *CV* Rsrch Fellow, Info & Service Mgr, Biodeterioration Info Centre, Bio Sc Dept, Aston Univ 1970–83; Industrial Mycologist & Head of Genetic Resources & Industrial Services Division, Commonwealth Mycological Institute 1983–94; CAB International Biodiversity Co-ord 1994–96; Private Consult Bio, from 1996; M Provincial Panel for the Province of Cant, Clergy Discipline Measure, from 2009; Eucharistic Asst Peterb from 2006; M House of Laity, GS from 2010; M Parochial Ch Counc 1971–2005; Lay Pstrl Asst Salis Dioc, 2000–05; M Sarum Archdnry Prop Cttee 1998–2004; Churchwarden, Birm & Lon, 1970–1989; Deanery Prison Link Rep Reading Prison, Ox, 1980
GS 2010– *Tel:* 01604 792354
Fax: 01604 792016
email: dennis.allsopp@yahoo.com

ANGUS, Dr Christopher John, MA, PhD
Burtholme East Lanercost Brampton Cumbria CA8 2HH [CARLISLE] *b* 1949 *educ* Hampton Sch; Trin

Hall, Cam Univ; Newcastle Univ; *CV* Senior Systems Analyst, ICL 1970–75; Consult, Mancos 1975–78; Application Develop Manager, CAD-Centre, Cam 1978–83; Tech Dir, Prosys Technology 1983–89; Dir, Angus Assoc 1989–2000; Software Architect, Shell 2002–03; Chief Architect, Kalido 2003; M Bp's Counc 2006; M Adnry Mapping Cttee from 2001
GS 2010– *Tel:* 016977 41504
email: chris.angus@btinternet.com

ANNAS, Rt Revd Geoff
Ash Garth Broughton Crescent Barlaston Stoke-on-Trent ST12 9DD [AREA BISHOP OF STAFFORD] *b* 1953 *CV* Area Bp of Stafford from 2010
Tel: 01782 373308
email: bishop.stafford@lichfield.anglican.org

APPLEBY, Revd Jane Elizabeth, BSc, MSc, BA, BA
Battle Hill Vicarage Berwick Drive Wallsend NE28 9ED [NEWCASTLE] *b* 1958 *educ* Bris Univ; Newcastle Poly; Cranmer Hall, Dur; *CV* Planner, London Transport 1984–5; OU Tutor Mathematics 1991–94; Home Educator 1994–2001; AC Holy Cross, Fenham 2003–06; TV, Ch of the Good Shepherd LEP, Battle Hill, Wallsend from 2006; Dioc Ecum Officer from 2012
GS 2010– *Tel:* 01912627518
email: janeteappleby@yahoo.com
Web: www.cogswallsend.btck.co.uk

APPLEGATE, Ven John, Ph D
Southern North West Training Partnership Aiken Hall, University of Chester Crab Lane, Padgate Warrington WA2 0DB [MANCHESTER] *educ* Bris Univ; Trin Coll Bris; *CV* C Collyhurst, Man 1984–87; C Broughton 1987–94; C Higher Broughton 1987–92; C St Clem w St Matthias Lower Broughton 1987–92; C St Jas w St Clem and St Matthias Broughton 1992–94; R Broughton 1994–96; TR Broughton 1996–2002; AD Salford 1997–2002; Hon Rsch Fell and p-t Lect Man Univ from 2000; Adn of Bolton 2002–08; Course Prin Southern Northwest Trg Ptnrship from 2008
GS 2002– *Tel:* 01925 534303
email: snwtpprincipal@chester.ac.uk

ARDRON, Mrs (Yvonne) Shayne, BSc
93 Letchworth Road Leicester LE3 6FN [LEICESTER] *b* 1966 *educ* Laurence Jackson Sch; Prior Pursglove Coll; Leicester Polytech; *CV* Quality Control Tester 1988-95; Lay Rdr from 2005
GS 2010– *Tel:*
email: shayne.ardron@btinternet.com

ARMITSTEAD, Col Edward Bradley Lawrence, CBE
Pendomer House Pendomer Yeovil BA22 9PB [BATH AND WELLS] *b* 1946 *educ* Shrewsbury Sch; R Military Academy Sandhurst; Defence Services Staff Coll India; *CV* Army Officer 1967–2001, Rtd from 2001; Preacher and Tchr; M Coun SASRA until 2012; Vice President SASRA from 2012; Rdr; Chair Oak Hill Th Coll Coun
GS 2000– *Tel:* 01935 862785
email: e.armitstead@btinternet.com

ARMSTRONG, Very Revd Christopher John, Cert Ed, B Th
The Deanery Preston New Rd Blackburn BB2 6PS [DEAN OF BLACKBURN] *b* 1947 *educ* Dunstable Gr Sch; Dur Univ; Kelham Th Coll; Nottm Univ; *CV* Tchr Dunstable 1969–72; Asst C All SS Maidstone 1975–79; Chapl Coll of St Hild & St Bede Dur 1979–85; Dom Chapl to Abp of York and DDO 1985–91; Incumb St Mart Scarboro 1991–2001; Dean of Blackburn from 2001
GS 2003–05
Tel: 01254 52502 01254 503090 (Office)
Fax: 01254 689666
email: dean@blackburncathedral.co.uk
Web: www.blackburncathedral.com

ARORA, Revd Arun, LLB, BA, Solicitor of the Supreme Court of England and Wales
Church House Great Smith Street London SW1P 3AZ [DIRECTOR OF COMMUNICATIONS, ARCHBISHOPS' COUNCIL] *b* 1971 *educ* King Edward VI Five Ways Sch, Birm; Univ of Birm; Cranmer Hall Dur; *CV* Dioc Dir Communications, Birm 2000–04; Asst C St Mark's Harrogate 2006–10; Dir Communications Abp York 2006–09; Team Ldr, Wolverhampton Pioneer Ministries 2010–12; Dir Communications Abp's Coun from 2012
Tel: 020 7898 1462 07984 334564
email: arun.arora@churchofengland.org

ASHCROFT, Ven Mark David, BA, MA
14 Moorgate Avenue Withington Manchester M20 1HE [ARCHDEACON OF MANCHESTER] *b* 1954 *educ* Rugby; Worc Coll Ox; Fitzwilliam Coll Cam; Ridley Hall; *CV* Asst C Burnage St Margaret 1982–85; Tutor St Paul Sch of Divinity Kapsabet Kenya 1986–90; Prin St Paul Theol Coll Kapsabet Kenya 1990–95; R Ch Ch Harpurhey, Man 1996–2009; AD N Man 2000–2006; Adn of Man from 2009
Tel: 0161 448 1976
Fax: 0161 445 9458
email: Archdeaconmanchester@manchester.anglican.org

ASHE, Ven (Francis) John, B Met, Cert Th
Hollytree House Whitwell Rd Sparham Norwich NR9 5PN [ARCHDEACON OF LYNN; NORWICH] *b* 1953 *educ* Ch Hosp; Sheff Univ; Ridley Hall Cam; *CV* C Ashtead, Guild 1979–82; P-in-c St Faith Plumstead, Cape Town 1982–87; R Wisley-w-Pyrford, Guild 1987–93; V Godalming, Guild 1993–2001; RD Godalming 1996–2002; TR Godalming 2001–09; M Bp's Coun; Bp's Adv BAP (Pastl) 2002–2009; Hon Can Guild Cathl 2003–2009; Warden of Rdrs, Norw from 2009; Adn of Lynn from 2009
GS 2003–2009 *Tel:* 01362 688032
email: archdeacon.lynn@norwich.anglican.org

WHO'S WHO

ASHENDEN, Canon Dr Gavin Roy Pelham, LLB, BA, MTH, D Phil
Sussex Place Horsebridge Common Ashurst Steyning W Sussex BN44 3AL [UNIVERSITIES, SOUTHERN] *b* 1954 *educ* K Sch Cant; Bris Univ; Oak Hill Coll; Heythrop Coll, Lon Univ; Sussex Univ; *CV* C St Jas Bermondsey 1980–82; TV St Ant Hamsey Green, Sanderstead, S'wark 1982–89; Univ Chapl and Sen Lect Sussex Univ from 1989; Dir Aid to Russian Christians 1982–94; M of Coun and Vc-Chair Keston College 1982–95; M CCU 1995–2000; Dioc Adv on new relig movements; Exam Chapl to Bp of Chich; Preb of Hampstead, Chich Cathl 2003, Bursalis Preb 2005; Patron Child Aid 2005; Chapl to HM the Queen from 2008; Presenter BBC Surrey & BBC Susex Faith & Ethics 2008–11; Presenter BBC Faith in England podcast from 2008
GS 1995–2000, 2004– *Tel:* 01273 877123
07879 493491 (Mobile)
Fax: 01273 678918
email: g.ashenden@sussex.ac.uk

ASHFORD, Archdeacon of. See DOWN, Ven Philip Roy

ASHTON, Mr David,
2 Manor Drive Battyeford Mirfield WF14 0ER [WAKEFIELD] *b* 1941 *educ* Warw Rd Junior Sch; Dewsbury and Batley Tech Sch; Kitson Eng Coll; *CV* Br Telecom Integrity Mgr; M GS Stg Orders Cttee; M Bp's Coun
GS 1972– *Tel:* 01924 497996
email: david_ashton@hotmail.com

ASHWIN, Mr John Basil Edward Hamilton, MA, PGCE, FRSA
31 Wellington Rd Chichester PO19 6BB [CHICHESTER] *b* 1937 *educ* St Olave's and St Saviour's Sch S'wark; Selwyn Coll Cam; Cam Inst of Educ; *CV* Tchr of Engl then Head of Engl Dept, Emanuel Sch SW Lon 1963–69; Head of Engl Dept then Sen Master, William Morris Sen High Sch, Walthamstow 1969–75; Head, St Dav and St Kath Comp Sch, Hornsey 1975-81; Head, Bp Luffa Sch, Chich 1981–2000; Chair W Sussex Secdry Heads 1995–98; rtd: pt External Adv and Threshold Assessor for schools, Cam Educ Associates; Accredited Section 23 Insp; Mod Rdrs' Trg Chich Dio; Lay Chair Chich Dny Syn; Vc-Chair Govs, Univ Coll Chich; Consult for Secdry Heads; Sec Open Syn Grp from 2011
GS 2002–
Tel: 01243 786501 07939 333858 (Mobile)
email: johnashwin@tiscali.co.uk

ASHWORTH, Mrs Lorna,
6 Ruston Gardens Southgate London N14 4PF [CHICHESTER] *b* 1970 *CV* Elected to GS 2005
GS 2005– *email:* lashworth70@gmail.com

ASTIN, Revd Moira Anne Elizabeth, MA, MA, Dip Min
The Vicarage Vicarage Gardens Scunthorpe DN15 7AZ [OXFORD] *b* 1965 *educ* City of Lon Sch for Girls; Sir William Perkins Sch; Clare Coll Cam; Wycliffe Hall Th Coll; *CV* C Newbury 1995–99; Min Dunston Park LEP and C Thatcham from 1999; TV Thatcham 2001–05; TV Southlake St James Woodley 2009–11; AD North Lincs from 2011; P-in-c St Lawrence, Frodingham from 2011; Ecum Cons Dioc Oxf from 2011; M Brd Miss, 2000–02; M Misson-shaped Ch 2002–04; M Legal Aid Comm 2005–10; M Fees Review Grp 2007–09; M Standing Cttee, Conv Cant & House of Clergy 2005–10; M Ox Miss & Pstrl Cttee 2003–10; M CTE Grp for Local Unity (C of E Rep) from 2009; M Meth-Ang Panel for Unity in Mission from 2010; M CDC from 2010
GS 2000– *Tel:* 01724 334873
email: moira.astin@ntlworld.com

ASTON, Archdeacon of. See RUSSELL, Ven Brian Kenneth

ASTON, Suffragan Bishop of. See WATSON, Rt Revd Andrew John

ATKIN, Canon Dr Susan Anne Jennifer, BA, MA, Ph D
3 St Bride Court Colchester CO4 0PQ [CHELMSFORD] *b* 1948 *educ* Qu Eliz Girls' Gr Sch Barnet; Reading Univ; *CV* Admin Trainee Min of Defence 1973–75; Admin Asst City Univ 1975–78; Asst Registrar City Univ 1978–83; Dep Registrar City Univ 1983–86; Dep Registrar York Univ 1986–90; Planning Officer Essex Univ 1990–99; Coun and Court Officer Essex Univ 2000–02; retired 2002; M Dioc Syn from 1995; M Bp's Coun from 1998; Bp's Selector from 2002; Dioc Lay Chair from 2003; Hon Lay Can Chelms Cathl from 2006
GS 1995–2010 *Tel:* 01206 854976 (Home)
email: susan_atkin@lineone.net

ATKINSON, Very Revd Peter Gordon, MA, FRSA
The Deanery 10 College Green Worcester WR1 2LH [DEAN OF WORCESTER] *b* 1952 *educ* Maidstone Gr Sch; St Jo Coll Ox; Westcott Ho Cam; *CV* C Clapham Old Town TM 1979–83; P-in-C Tatsfield 1983–90; R H Trin Bath 1990–91; Prin Chich Th Coll 1991–94; Bursalis Preb Chich Cathl 1991–97; R Lavant 1994–97; Chan Chich Cathl 1997–2007; Dean of Worcester from 2007; M Dioc Syn 2000–05; Master St Oswald's Hosp Worc from 2007
GS 2000–05 *Tel:* 01905 732909 (Office)
01905 732939 (Study)
Fax: 01905 732906
email: peteratkinson@worcestercathedral.org.uk

ATKINSON, Rt Revd Richard William Bryant, MA, MA, OBE
Bishop's Lodge Bedford Road Cardington Bedford MK44 3SS [BISHOP OF BEDFORD] *b* 1958 *educ* St Paul's Sch Lon; Magd Coll Cam; Cuddesdon Th

Coll; Birm Univ; *CV* C Abingdon w Shippon 1984–87; TV Sheff Manor Par 1987–91; Hon M of Staff Cuddesdon Th Coll 1987–92; TR Sheff Manor Par 1991–96; V All SS Rotherham 1996–2002; Hon Can Sheff Cathl 1998–2002; Adn of Leicester 2002–12; Bp of Bedford from 2012; M CTE and CTBI 1997–2002; Ch Commr 2001–08; M Cen Ch Fund Cttee 1997–2002; CUF Trustee 2003–08; Dep Chair Places for People 1997–2005; Chair Phoenix Enterprises (Rotherham) Ltd 1998–2002; Chair Braunstone New Deal for Communities Programme 2003–06; Chair St Phil Cen for Study and Engagement in Multi Faith Society; Chair Launde Abbey Mgt Cttee 2002–08; M Carnegie Trust UK Enquiry into the Future of Civil Society in Britain and Ireland 2007–10; M Presence and Engagement Task Gp; Co-Chair National Hindu Christian Forum from 2010; Near Neighbours Trustee from 2011
GS 1991–2012 *Tel:* 01234 831432
Fax: 01234 831484
email: bishopbedford@stlabans.anglican.org

ATWELL, Very Revd James Edgar, MA, Th M, BD
The Deanery The Close Winchester SO23 9LS [DEAN OF WINCHESTER] *b* 1946 *educ* Dauntsey's Sch; Ex Coll Ox; Harvard Univ; Cuddesdon Th Coll; *CV* C St Jo E Dulwich 1970–74; C Gt St Mary Cam 1974–77; Chapl Jes Coll Cam 1977–81; V Towcester w Easton Neston 1981–95; RD Towcester 1983–91; Prov of St Eds 1995–2000; Dean 2000–06; Dean of Winchester from 2006
Tel: 01962 853738 (Home)
01962 857205 (Office)
Fax: 01962 857264
email: the.dean@winchester-cathedral.org.uk

ATWELL, Rt Revd Robert Ronald, BA (Hons), M.Litt
Bishop's Lodge Back Lane Dunham Town, Altrincham Cheshire WA14 4SG [SUFFRAGAN BISHOP OF STOCKPORT; CHESTER] *b* 1954 *educ* Wanstead High Sch; St John's Coll Dur; Westcott Ho Cam; *CV* Asst C John Keble Ch Mill Hill 1978–81; Chapl Trinity Coll Cam 1981–87; Benedictine Monk Burford Priory 1987–98; V Par of St Mary-the-Virgin Primrose Hill 1998–2008; Bp Stockport from 2008; Chair Min Cttee Chester Dioc; Trustee SNWTP; M Working Grp on Discipline in relation to matters of Doctrine, Ritual and Ceremonial
Tel: 0161 928 5611
Fax: 0161 929 0692
email: bpstockport@chester.anglican.org

AUCKLAND, Archdeacon of. See BARKER, Ven Nicholas John Willoughby

AUSTEN, Mr Simon Neil, BSc, MA, DipMin
12 Brunstock Close Lowry Hill Carlisle CA3 0HL [CARLISLE] *b* 1967 *educ* City of Lon Freemen's Sch; Warwick Univ; Wycliffe Hall Th Coll; *CV* Science master, Monkton Combe Junior Sch, 1988–89; Lay Asst, St. Michael's Bath 1990–91; Asst C, Great Chesam TM Dioc Ox 1994–98; Chapl, Stowe Sch, Buckingham 1998–2002; V, St. John's w St. Peter's, Carlisle from 2002; M C of E Evang Counc from 2004; GS from 2010; Bd of Educ from 2011
GS 2010– *Tel:* 01228 810076 07761 009497
email: simon@hkchurch.org.uk
Web: www.hkchurch.org.uk

AYERS, Revd Paul Nicholas, MA
Vicarage Vicarage Drive Pudsey LS28 7RL [BRADFORD] *b* 1961 *educ* Bradf Gr Sch; St Pet Coll Ox; Trin Coll Bris; *CV* C St Jo Bapt Clayton 1985–88; C St Andr Keighley 1988–91; V St Cuth Wrose 1991–97; V St Lawr and St Paul Pudsey from 1997
GS 1995– *Tel:* 0113 256 4197
email: paul.ayers@tiscali.co.uk

BACK, Mr Robin Philip, AIB, FRSA
The Old Manse Church Lane Guestwick Norfolk NR20 5QJ [NORWICH] *b* 1946 *educ* Uppingham; Geneva Univ; *CV* Standard Chartered Bank in Middle East, India, Indonesia, Thailand and USA 1967–88; MD Backs Electronic Publishing Ltd from 1989; Prime Wdn, Worshipful Co of Dyers of City of Lon 2002–03; M Bp's Coun from 2003; Lay Chair, Dioc Syn 2003–09; Lay Chair, Sparham Dny Syn 1996–2001; M DBF from 2003; Chair Friends of Scott Polar Research Inst, Univ of Cam 2007–10; Dir Wispire Ltd (diocesan trading company) from 2011
GS 2005–
Tel: 01362 683281 01362 683835 07802 244619
email: robin@bepl.co.uk

BAILEY, Ven David Charles, MA, M Sc, BA
14 Springside Rd Walmersley Bury BL9 5JE [ARCHDEACON OF BOLTON; MANCHESTER] *b* 1952 *educ* Bradf Gr Sch; Linc Coll Oxf; Nottm Univ; St Jo Coll Nottm; *CV* C St Jo Worksop 1980–83; C Edgware, P-in-c St Andr Broadfields 1983–87; V S Cave and Ellerker w Broomfleet 1987–97; RD Howden 1991–97; Hon Can York Minster 1998–2008; V Beverley Minster 1997–2008; Adn Bolton from 2008 *Tel:* 0161 761 6117
07944 518765 (Mobile)
email: archbolton@manchester.anglican.org

BAIN, Ven (John) Stuart, BA
St Nicholas' Vicarage Hedworth Lane Boldon Colliery NE35 9JA [ARCHDEACON OF SUNDERLAND; DURHAM] *b* 1955 *educ* Blaydon Sec Sch; Durham Univ; Westcott Ho Cam; *CV* C H Trin Washington 1980–84; C St Nic Dunston 1984–86; V St Oswald Shiney Row and St Aid Herrington 1986–92; P-in-c St Paul Spennymoor and Whitworth 1992–97; P-in-c St Jo Merrington 1994–97; AD Auckland 1996–2002; Hon Can Dur 1998; V St Paul Spennymoor, Whitworth and St Jo Merrington 1997–2002; Chair DFW Adoption from 1999; Asst P St Nic Hedworth 2002; P-in-c St Nic Hedworth from 2003; P-in-c St Geo E Boldon from 2009; P-in-C St

Nics Boldon from 2010; Adn of Sunderland from 2002 *Tel:* 0191 536 2300
Fax: 0191 519 3369
email: Archdeacon.of.Sunderland@durham.anglican.org

BAINES, Rt Revd Nicholas, BA(Hons)
Bishopscroft Ashwell Road Bradford BD9 4AU [BISHOP OF BRADFORD] *b* 1957 *educ* Holt Comp Sch Liv; Bradf Univ; Trin Coll Bris; *CV* C St Thos Kendal 1987–91; C H Trin Leic 1991–92; V Rothley 1992–2000; RD Goscote 1995–2000; Adn of Lambeth 2000–03; Broadcaster; Dir EIG 2002–10; Bp of Croydon 2003–10; Angl Co-Chair Meissen Comm; Chair Sandford St Mart Trust from 2009; Bp of Bradf from 2011
GS 1995–2003, 2004–05, 2011–
Tel: 01274 545414 07974 194735
Fax: 01274 544831
email: bishop.nick@bradford.anglican.org
Web: nickbaines.wordpress.com

BAKER, Rt Revd Jonathan Mark Richard, MA, M Phil, Hon DD
c/o London Diocesan House, 36 Causton St, London SW1P 4AU [SUFFRAGAN BISHOP OF FULHAM; LONDON] *b* 1966 *educ* Merchant Taylors' Sch Northwood; St Jo Coll Ox; St Steph Ho Th Coll; *CV* C All SS Ascot Heath 1993–96; P-in-c St Mark and H Trin Reading 1996–99; V St Mark and H Trin Reading 1999–2002; Prin Pusey Ho, Ox from 2003; Bp of Ebbsfleet 2011–12; Bp of Fulham from 2012
GS 2000–11 *Tel:* 020 7932 1100
Fax: 020 7932 1112

BALDRY, Sir Tony BA, LLB, MA, MP
c/o Parliamentary Unit Church House Westminster SW1P 3AZ [SECOND CHURCH ESTATES COMMISSIONER] *b* 1950 *CV* Barrister at Lincoln's Inn from 1975 *Tel:* 0207 8981478
Web: www.churchofengland.org/our-views/the-church-in-parliament/second-church-estates-commissioner.aspx

BANKS, Rt Revd Norman, MA (Oxon); PGCE
The Vicarage Church Street Little Walsingham, Norfolk NR22 6BL [BISHOP OF RICHBOROUGH] *b* 1954 *educ* Walllsend Gr; Oriel Coll Ox; Ox Dept Educ; St Stephen's Ho; *CV* C Christ Church with St Ann Newcastle 1982–84; C-in-c St Ann 1984–87; P-in-c Christ Church with St Ann 1987–1990; V Tynemouth St Paul Cullercoats 1990–2000; V Walsingham, Houghton and the Barshams 200–11; RD Burnham and Walsingham 2008–11, Chapl to HM the Queen 2008–11; Chapl to High Sheriff of Norfolk 2010–11; Bp of Richborough from 2011; M Coun NE Ordination course 1993–200; ABM Selector 1993–2000; Inspector of Theol Colls and Courses 1995–2000
GS 1990–2000, 2010– *Tel:* 01328 821316
email: bishop@richborough.org.uk

BARBER, Mr John Stephen, BSc
16 Launceston Close Cherry Tree Gardens Oldham OL8 2XE [MANCHESTER] *b* 1971 *educ* The Blue Coat C o fE, Oldham; Oldham Coll, Bolton Univ; *CV* Joiner/Carpenter, Oldham MBC, 1988–96; Bldg Surveyor, Oldham MBC, 1997– 2004; Senior Renewal Surveyor, Tameside MBC from 2004
GS 2010– *Tel:* 0161 620 0668
email: johnsbarber@btinternet.com

BARBER, Revd Neil Andrew Austin, BA
St Giles' Vicarage 16 Browning Street Normanton Derby DE23 8DN [DERBY] *b* 1963 *educ* Ealing Coll of H Ed; Oakhill Coll; NTMTC; *CV* Systems Eng/Project Mgr, IBM UK, 1986–95; Lay Assoc Min, St Mary's Basingstoke, Winc 1995–98; C St Mary's Basingstoke, Winc 1998–2001; Incumb, St Giles' Normanton by Derby from 2001
GS 2010– *Tel:* 01332–767483
email: neil.barber@stgiles-derby.org.uk

BARKER, Ven Nicholas John Willoughby, MA
Holy Trinity Vicarage 45 Milbank Rd Darlington DL3 9NL [ARCHDEACON OF AUCKLAND] *b* 1949 *educ* Sedbergh Sch; Oriel Coll Ox; Trin Coll Bris; *CV* C St Mary Watford 1977–80; TV St Jas and Em Didsbury 1980–86; TR St Geo Kidderminster 1986–2007; RD Kidderminster 2001–07; Adn of Auckland from 2007; Hon Can Dur Cathl from 2007
GS 2005–07 *Tel:* 01325 480444
07912 269 364 (Mobile)
Fax: 01325 354027
email: archdeacon.of.auckland@durham.anglican.org

BARKER, Ven Timothy Reed, MA
Archdeacon's House 1A Northfield Rd Quarrington Sleaford NG34 8RT [ARCHDEACON OF LINCOLN; LINCOLN] *b* 1956 *educ* Man Gr Sch; Queen's Coll Cam; Westcott Ho; *CV* C Nantwich 1980–83; V Norton St Berteline and St Christopher 1983–88; V Runcorn All Saints 1988–94; Urban Officer Ches 1990–98; Bp of Chester's Chap 1994–98; P assoc, Ches Cath 1994–98; V Spalding St Mary and Nicholas 1998–2009; Rural Dean Elloe West 2000–09; M Linc Cathl Chap 2000–09; Can and Preb of Linc from 2003; Rural Dean Elloe East 2008–09; P-in-C Spalding St Paul 2007–09; M DRACS Cttee 2001–05; M CME Panel 2003–06; M Clergy Terms of Service Implementation Group 2005–07; M Marriage Law Working Party 2006; M Dioc Syn from 1999; Trustee Alcuin Club from 1990; Adn Linc from 2009
GS 2000–05; 2008- *Tel:* 01529 304348 (Office)
07590 950041 (Mobile)
email: archdeacon.lincoln@lincoln.anglican.org

BARKING, Area Bishop of. See HAWKINS, Rt Revd David John Leader

BARNEY, Mr Stephen George, B Sc, MBA
The Dower House 77 Brook St Wymeswold LE12 6TT [LEICESTER] *b* 1950 *educ* Cranfield Univ; *CV* Main

Bd Dir public companies rtd; Rdr; Chair DBF; Trustee Launde Abbey; Dir SMCP
GS 2005– *Tel:* 01509 881160
07767 320320 (Mobile)
email: stephen4747@live.co.uk

BARNSTAPLE, Archdeacon of. See GUNN-JOHNSON, Ven David Allan

BARRELL, Mrs Anneliese Gledhill, MCSP, Grad Dip Phys, DSA
47 Whitleigh Ave Crownhill Plymouth PL5 3AU [EXETER] *b* 1938 *educ* Burlington Sch Lon; Prince of Wales Gen Hosp Sch of Physiotherapy, Lon; *CV* Rtd NHS physiotherapy mgr; pt lect, Plymouth Coll FE; M Dioc Coun for Work with Children and Young People, Portfolio Holder for Children, Lay Chair Moorside Deanery Syn; chwdn St Francis Honicknowle, Foundation Gov Notre Dame RC Girls Sec Sch Plymouth, PR Adviser SW Reg Trefoil Guild
GS 2000–
Tel: 01752 777053 0754 167115 (Mobile)
email: annagb@blueyonder.co.uk

BARTON, Mrs Jennifer Diane,
The End Game 21 Holland Close Rogerstone Newport NP10 0AU [WORCESTER] *b* 1942 *educ* Challney Secondary Sch, Luton; *CV* Computer Punch Card Operator, 1958–65; Worc Ed Dept, Spec needs Children 1986–93; M Dioc Brd Ed 1996–2006; M Worc Dioc Syn from 1998; M Martley & Worc West Deanery Syn from 1995
GS 2010– *Tel:* 01633 891193
email: JDNOUMENA@AOL.COM

BASHFORTH, Revd Alan George, MA, B Th
Vicarage 6 Penwinnick Parc St Agnes TR5 0UQ [TRURO] *b* 1964 *educ* Humphrey Davy Gr Sch; Ox Univ; Ex Univ; Ripon Coll Cuddesdon; *CV* Police officer, S Yorks Police 1983–90; nursing auxiliary 1990–93; C Calstock, Truro 1996–98; C St Ives, Truro 1998–2001; V St Agnes and Mithian w. Mount Hawke from 2001; RD Powder from 2004; M Bp's Coun; M DBF; M Dioc Pastl Cttee; Chair Ho of Clergy from 2009
GS 2005– *Tel:* 01872 553391
email: onepaw@btinternet.com

BASINGSTOKE, Suffragan Bishop of. See HANCOCK, Rt Revd Peter

BASTON, Ven Caroline Jane, BSc, PGCE, Cert Theol
5 The Boltons Wootton Bridge Ryde Isle of Wight PO33 4PB [ARCHDEACON OF THE ISLE OF WIGHT; PORTSMOUTH] *b* 1956 *educ* Godolphin Sch Salis; Birm Univ; City of Birm Poly; Ripon Coll Cuddesdon; *CV* C St Chris Thornhill, Southn, Winch 1989–94; R All SS Winch w. St Andr Chilcomb w. St Pet Chesil 1995–2006; Dioc Communications Officer 1995–98; DDO 1999–2006; Hon Can Winch Cathl from 2000; Adn of Isle of Wight from 2006; M Dioc Syn, Miss and Soc Forum, Bp's Coun, DAC, DBE *Tel:* 01983 884432
email: adiow@portsmouth.anglican.org

BATH AND WELLS, Bishop of. See PRICE, Rt Revd Peter Bryan

BATH, Archdeacon of. See PIGGOTT, Ven Andy (Andrew John)

BAYES, Rt Revd Paul, BA, DipTheol
Bishopswood 3 Stobarts Close Knebworth SG3 6ND [SUFFRAGAN BISHOP OF HERTFORD] *b* 1953 *educ* Belle Vue Boys' Sch, Bradf; Univ Birm; Queen's Coll Birm; *CV* C Tynemouth Cullercoats St Paul Newc 1979–82; Chapl Qu Eliz Coll Lon 1982–87; Chapl Chelsea Coll 1985–87; TV High Wycombe Ox 1987–90; TR 1990–94; TR Totton Win 1995–04; AD Lyndhurst 2000–04; Nat Miss and Evang Adv Abps' Coun 2004–10; Hon Can Worc Cathl 2007–10; Bp of Hertford from 2010 *Tel:* 01438 817260
email: bishophertford@stalbans.anglican.org

BAYLIS, Revd Sally Anne, BA,MA, PGCE
Daybrook Vicarage 241 Oxclose Lane Daybrook Nottingham NG5 6FB [SOUTHWELL & NOTT] *b* 1955 *educ* Herts & Essex H Sch, Bishop's Stortford; Queen's Coll Lon Univ of Kent; St John's Coll Nott; *CV* Bookseller 1978–85; Freelance editor/translator 1990–2003; Secondary School Tchr 1993–2001; AC All Hallows Gedling 2003–07 P-in-C St Paul's w St Timothy's Daybrook from 2007; M Dioc Syn from 2005
GS 2010– *Tel:* 0115 9262686 07506441634
email: sally504@btinternet.com

BAYNES, Canon Matthew Thomas Crispin, MA
The Rectory Bredon Tewkesbury GL20 7LT [WORCESTER] *b* 1962 *educ* Orange Hill H Sch, Edgware; MIddx UEA; Cam Univ; Westcott Ho Th Coll; *CV* Nursing Auxillary, St Christopher's Hospice, Sydenham 1983–84; C Ch Ch, Southgate1987–90; Chapl Southgate Tech Coll 1987–90; P-in-C, All Saints' Berkhamsted 1990–95; Chapl St. Francis Hospice, Berkhamsted 1990–95; V Ch Ch Coseley,1995–99; Assoc Dioc Chapl Agriculture & Rural Life 2002–09; R, Bredon w Bredon's Norton 1999; Rural Dean of Pershore 2005–11; P-in-C Beckford Grp P 2009; Can Worc 2010; St Alb Dioc Syn; Worc Dioc Syn; Worc Dioc Brd Ed; Worc Dioc Pstrl Cttee
GS 2010– *Tel:* 01684 772237
email: mbaynes@toucansurf.com

BAYNES, Mr Simon Henry Crews, BSc, C Eng, FBCS
4 Pilgrim Close St Albans AL2 2JD [ST ALBANS] *b* 1958 *educ* Orange Hill Boys' Gr Sch, Edgware, Middx; Sheff Univ; *CV* Logica 1979–2009, Dir Simon Baynes Ltd from 2009; Client Dir, Capital Cranfield Trustees Ltd from 2009; M CofE Pensions Board from 2009; Chair, Pension Trustees, Logica from 1997; Trustee Cam Univ Press Sen

Staff Pension Scheme from 2008; M Nat Audit Office Panel of Pensions Experts from 2011; Trustee, Life Academy (The Pre-Retirement Assoc) from 2007; Chartered Eng from 1990; M St Alb Dioc Syn from 2003; M St Alb DBF from 2003; M Dny Syn from 2001; M St Alb Cathl Fin Cttee 1997–2007, 2010–; M Inter-Dioc Fin Forum from 2005; M Bp's Coun from 2007; M CNC (St Alb Vacancy-in-See) 2008–09; Founder and vice-chair St Alb Dioc Penal Affairs Grp from 2008
GS 2005– *Tel:* 01727 875524 (Home)
01727 875537 (Office)
07860 828711 (Mobile)
email: simon@simonbaynes.fsnet.co.uk

BEACH, Very Revd Mark Howard Francis, BA, MA, DMIN
The Deanery Priors Gate House The Precinct Rochester ME1 1SR [DEAN OF ROCHESTER] *b* 1962 *educ* Ellesmore Coll Shropshire; Univ of Kent; Univ of Nottm; St Stephen's Ho; K Coll Lon; *CV* C Beeston S'well 1987–90; C Hucknall 1990–93; R Gedling 1993–2001; R Netherfield 1996–2001; Bp's Chapl Wakef 2001–03; TR Rugby Cov 2003–12; Transforming Communities Officer Dioc Cov 2010–12; Chair Warwickshire Community and Voluntary Action; Dean of Roch from 2012
GS 2008– *Tel:* 01634 202183 07930 577248
Fax: 01634 401410
email: mark.beach@o2.co.uk

BEAKE, Ven Stuart Alexander, MA
Archdeacon's House Lime Grove West Clandon Guildford GU4 7UT [ARCHDEACON OF SURREY; GUILDFORD] *b* 1949 *educ* K Coll Sch Wimbledon; Em Coll Cam; Cuddesdon Coll Ox; *CV* C St Mary Hitchin 1974–79; TV St Mary Hemel Hempstead 1979–85; Dom Chapl to Bp of Southwell 1985–87; V Shottery St Andr 1987–2000; RD Fosse Dny 1992–99; DDO Cov Dioc 1995–2000; Hon Can Cov Cathl 1999–2000; Can Res and Sub-Dean Cov Cathl 2000–05; Adn of Surrey from 2005; Can Res Guildf Cathl from 2011
GS 1980–85 *Tel:* 01483 790352 (Office)
01483 211924 (Home)
Fax: 01483 790333 (Office)
01483 223397 (Home)
email: stuart.beake@cofeguildford.org.uk

BEAL, Dr John Frank, PhD, BDS, MFDS(RCSEng), HonMFPH, FRSPH
Oakroyd 4 North Park Road Leeds LS8 1JD [RIPON AND LEEDS] *educ* Finchley County Gr Sch; Royal Dental Hospital of London; *CV* House Surgeon, Royal Dental Hosp of Lon 1965–66; Lect in Dental Public Health, Birm Univ 1966–76; Senior Dental Officer, Avon Area Health Authority (Teaching) 1977–79; Area Dental Officer, Birm Area Health Authority (Teaching) 1979–83; Consult in Dental Public Health, Leeds Health Authority, 1983–2008;Regional Dental Officer, Yorkshire Regional Health Authority, 1990–2009; Locum Consult in Dental Public Health, Wakefield District Primary Care Trust from 2010; Hospital Chapls Counc 1995–2000; M Bp's Counc, Ripon Dioc from 1990; Vice-chair Brd of Miss and Unity, Ripon Dioc 1987–89
GS 1995–2005; 2010– *Tel:* 0113–2948795
email: johnfbeal@hotmail.co.uk

BECK, Miss Rachel Gillian, BA
12 Cecil Street Lincoln LN1 3AU [LINCOLN] *b* 1980 *educ* Wales High Sch; Bp Grosseteste Coll; *CV* Receptionist Sheff Dioc Ch Ho 1999–2000; Admin Rotherham Youth Service 2000–01; PA to Asst Dir of Educ, Rotherham 2001–02; Primary Tchr, Linc from 2005–11; Res Cons Dioc Linc from 2011
GS 2000– *Tel:* 07753634477
email: rgbeck@btinternet.com

BEDFORD, Archdeacon of. See HUGHES, Ven Paul Vernon

BEDFORD, Suffragan Bishop of. See ATKINSON, Rt Revd Richard

BEER, Ven John Stuart, MA Oxon, MA Cantab
St Botolph's Rectory 1a Summerfield Cambridge CB3 9HE [ARCHDEACON OF CAMBRIDGE; ELY] *b* 1944 *educ* Roundhay Sch Leeds; Pemb Coll Ox; Westcott Ho Th Coll; *CV* C St Jo Knaresborough 1971–74; Fell and Chapl Fitzw Coll and New Hall Cam 1974–80; R Toft w Caldecote and Childerley and Harwick 1980–87; V Grantchester 1987–97; DDO, Dir of POT and Rdr Trg 1987-97; Hon Can Ely Cathl from 1989; Chair Cathl Pilgrims Assoc Conference 1986–96; M Ethics Cttee Dunn Nutrition Unit 1985–2001; Adn of Huntingdon 1997–2004; acting Adn of Wisbech 2002–04; Co-DDO and Dir POT 1997–2002; Bye-Fell Fitzw Coll from 2001; M Bp's Coun; Chair Liturg Cttee; M Fin Cttee; Bps' Selection Adv from 2002; Adn of Ely 2004–07; Adn of Cambridge from 2007
GS 2003–2010 *Tel:* 01223 350424
Fax: 01223 360929
email: archdeacon.cambridge@ely.anglican.org

BELCHER, Dr William Peter Argent, BSc, PhD
39 Redgrove Park Cheltenham Gloucestershire GL51 6QY [GLOUCESTER] *b* 1949 *educ* Framlingham Coll, Suffolk; Leeds Univ; Cam Univ; *CV* Materials Eng in Nuclear Electricity Generating Industry, Nuclear Electric Plc 1988–95; British Energy Generation Ltd. 1995–2009; Chwrdn, Lay Chair of PCC; Leadership Team of St Mary w St Matthew Ch, Cheltenham 2002–08; Materials Eng in Nuclear Electricity Generating Industry, EDF-Energy 2009
GS 2010– *Tel:* 01242228690
email: williambelcher@btinternet.com

BELL, Rt Revd James Harold, MA, BA, Cert Theol
Thistledown Main St Exelby Bedale DL8 2HD [SUFFRAGAN BISHOP OF KNARESBOROUGH; RIPON AND LEEDS] *b* 1950 *educ* Appleby Gr Sch; St Jo Coll Dur; Wycliffe Hall Ox; *CV* Hon C St Mich at the Northgate, Ox 1975–76; Chapl and lect BNC Ox

1976–82, Fell 1979–82; R St Mary Northolt, Lon 1982–93; Area Dean Ealing 1991–93; Adv for Min, Willesden Area 1993–97; Dir of Min and Tr, Ripon Dioc 1997–99; Res Can Ripon Cathl 1997–99; Dir of Mission Ripon Dioc 1999–2004; Hon Can Ripon Cathl 1999–2004; Bp of Knaresborough from 2004; M Dioc Syn, DBF, DBE (ex officio), Dioc Coun for Mission, Chair Rural Affairs Gp of the GS; Dir Meth Chapel Aid; M Harrogate Coll Consult Cttee; Gov York St Jo Univ Coll; Yorks Mini Course Coun from 2011
GS 2010– *Tel:* 01677 423525
01677 424392
Fax: 01677 423525
email: bishop.knaresb@btinternet.com

BENFIELD, Revd Paul John, LLB, BTh, Barrister
St Nicholas Vicarage Highbury Ave Fleetwood FY7 7DJ [BLACKBURN] *b* 1956 *educ* Cam Gr Sch for Boys; Newc Univ; Coll of Law, Chancery Lane, Lon; Chich Th Coll; *CV* Chancery barrister 1978–86; C Shiremoor, Newc 1989–92; C Hexham, Newc 1992–93; TV All SS, St Anne, St Mich & St Thos Lewes, Chich 1993–97; R Pulborough, Chich 1997–2000; V St Nich Fleetwood, Blackb from 2000; M Legal Aid Commn from 2006; M Rev Cttee on Draft Vacancies in Suffragan Sees and Other Eccl Offices Meas; M Rev Cttee on Draft Crown Benefices (Par Representatives) Meas 2008; M Revd Cttee for Draft Pastl and Miss Meas 2009; M Steering Cttee for Draft Care of Caths Meas 2009; M Fleetwood Town Coun f2009–11; M Dioc Commn from 2010; M C of E Pensions Bd from 2011
GS 2005– *Tel:* 01253 874402
email: benfield@btinternet.com

BENNETT, Dr Anthony John, BEd, MA, PhD
1 Merriefield Close, Broadstone Dorset BH18 8DG [WINCHESTER] *b* 1950 *educ* Nottingham Coll; Univ of Essex; *CV* Tchr History & US Politics, Royal Hospital Sch, Ipswich 1974–89; Tchr of US Politics, Charterhouse, 1989–2009; Under Master, Charterhouse 1997–2004; Deputy Headmaster, Charterhouse 2004–09; Bournemouth Deanery Syn M from 2010
GS 2010– *Tel:* 01202 252523
email: ajb44@ymail.com

BENSON, Ven Paddy (George Patrick), MA, BD, MPhil
3 Hatterall Close Hereford HR1 1GA [ARCHDEACON OF HEREFORD] *b* 1949 *educ* Benrose Sch Derby, Leighton Park Sch Reading; Ch Ch Ox; Trin Coll Bris; All Nations Christian Coll Ware; St John's Coll Nottm; *CV* Dir Academic Studies St Andrew's Institute, Kabare, Kenya 1978–87; Acting Dir Communications, Dioc Mt Kenya East 1987–89; Asst C St Mary Upton, Chester 1991–5; V Christ Church Barnston, Chester 1995–2010; Adn of Hereford from 2011
Tel: 01432 265659 07946 565679
email: archdeacon.hereford.anglican.org

BENYON, Mr Thomas, DipTh, OBE
Rectory Farm House 2 Church St Bladon Oxon OX20 1RS [OXFORD] *b* 1942 *educ* Wellington Sch; RMA Sandhurst; Wycliffe Hall Ox; *CV* Lieut Scots Guards 1963–67; District Coun AVDC; Contested Heyton 1974; MP Abingdon 1979–83; Chair Milton Keynes Health Auth 1989–92; Dir Buckingham Health Auth 1992–94; Founder ZANE: Zimbabwe A National Emergency
GS 2005– *Tel:* 01993 811722
07831 859085
email: tom.benyon@btinternet.com

BERKSHIRE, Archdeacon of. See RUSSELL, Ven Norman Atkinson

BERRY, Professor Anthony John, B Sc, M Phil, Ph D, DIC
24 Leafield Rd Disley Stockport SK12 2JF [CHESTER] *b* 1939 *educ* Bath Univ; Imp Coll Lon; Seattle Univ; Man Univ; *CV* Aerodynamicist Br Aircraft Corp 1962; Aerodynamics Engineer The Boeing Co Seattle 1965–69; Rsch Fell 1971–73, Lect 1973–86, Sen Lect 1986–95 in Mgt Devel Man Univ; Prof Sheff Hallam Univ 1995–2002; Prof emeritus 2002; M Dioc Syn; Rdr
GS 1994– *Tel:* 01663 762393
07759 492318
email: anthonyberry@btinternet.com

BESSANT, Canon Simon, B Mus, MA
The Vicarage 25a Mortomley Lane High Green Sheffield S35 3HS [SHEFFIELD] *b* 1956 *educ* Francis Combe Comp Watford; Sheff Univ; St Jo Coll Nottm; *CV* C St Jo and St Jas Bootle 1981–84; C Em Holloway 1984–85, P-in-c 1985–81; Ecum Adv for Bp of Stepney 1990–91; V Ch of the Redeemer Blackburn 1991–98; RD of Blackburn 1997–98; Dioc Dir for Miss and Evang and Officer for Dioc Bd for Miss and Unity 1998–2007; Dioc Dir for CME 1–4 2002–05; V All Saints Ecclesall, Sheff from 2007; M Lon Dioc Bd of Educ 1989–91; M Blackb Dioc Bd of Min 1995–2002; M Blackb Dioc Liturg Cttee 1998–2007; Sec to Blackb Dioc, Lancs Coun of Mosques Dialogue Grp 1998–2007; initiator and M Churches Together in Lancs Inter-Faith Forum 1999–2007, Chair 1999–2003; initiator and M Lancs Inter-Faith Forum 2000–2007, Chair 2001–03; GS rep on NEOC Bd 2001–05; M MPA Coun 2003–05; M Presence and Engagement Strg Grp 2004–05; M Follow-up Grp, Strg Cttee and Rev Cttee, Rev of Diocs Pastl and Miss Measure 2004–06; Chair Wkg Party creating code of practice on Miss Initiatives under Diocs, Pastl and Miss Measure from 2006; M Bradf Chs for Dialogue and Diversity Adv Grp from 2006; M AC 2006–07; M C of E Appts Cttee 2006–07; Hon Can Blackb Cath 2006–07; Can Emer Blackb Cath from 2006
GS 2001–07, 2008–
Tel: 0114 418 2036 07957 211319
email: simon.bessant@stsaviours.info

BESWICK, Mr David Terence,
1 Vicarage Close Eccleshall Stafford ST21 6BX [LICHFIELD] *b* 1933 *educ* Tarporley C of E Sch; *CV* Chwdn, St Helen Tarporley 1972–77; chwdn, H Trin Eccleshall 1984–2003, lay chair PCC 2003–04, 2011–; lay chair Eccleshall Dny Syn from 2003; M Lich Dioc Syn from 2002, Pastl Cttee from 2004; M Lich Bp's Coun from 2004
GS 2005– *Tel:* 01785 850622
email: dabeswick@btinternet.com

BETTS, Ven Steven James, B Sc, Cert Th
Emmaus House 65 The Close Norwich NR1 4DH [ARCHDEACON OF NORFOLK: NORWICH] *b* 1964 *educ* Nottm Bluecoat Gr Sch; York Univ; Cuddesdon Th Coll; *CV* C Bearsted w Thurnham 1990–94; Chapl to Bp of Norw 1994–97; V Old Catton Norw 1997–2005; RD Norw N 2001–05; M Dioc Commn 2001–09; Chair Dioc Ho of Clergy from 2003; M Bp's Coun from 2003; M DBF Exec from 2003; Bp's Officer for Ord and Initial Trg from 2005; Hon Can Norw Cathl from 2008; M Par Fin Gp Dioc of Norw from 2009; Adn of Norfolk from 2012
GS 2000– *Tel:* 01603 729816 (Office)
email: steven.betts@norwich.anglican.org

BEVERLEY, Bishop of. See WEBSTER, Rt Revd Glyn

BIRKENHEAD, Suffragan Bishop of. See SINCLAIR, Rt Revd (Gordon) Keith

BIRMINGHAM, Archdeacon of. See OSBORNE, Ven Hayward John

BIRMINGHAM, Bishop of. See URQUHART, Rt Revd David Andrew

BIRMINGHAM, Dean of. See OGLE, Very Revd Catherine

BISHOP, Ven Ian Gregory, BA, BSc ARICS
57A Sandbach Road Congleton Cheshire CW12 4LH [ARCHDEACON OF MACCLESFIELD; CHESTER] *b* 1962 *educ* Devizes Sch; Portsm Poly; Oak Hill Th Coll; *CV* Surveyor Croydon Counc 1984–86; Estate Mgr Gatwick Airport 1986–88; C Ch Ch Purley S'wark 1991–95; R Tas Valley Team Ministry 1995–2001; R Middlewich & Byley 2001–10; Rural Dean of Middlewich 2004–10; Archdn of Macclesfield from 2011
GS 2010– *Tel:* 01260 272875 07715 102519
email: ian.bishop@chester.anglican.org

BISHOP, Mrs Pamela Elizabeth, BSc, PGCE
250 Nottingham Road Mansfield Notts NG18 4SH [SOUTHWELL & NOTT] *b* 1944 *educ* Staveley Netherthorpe Gr Sch; Nott Univ; *CV* Science Tchr, The Latymer Sch 1967–70; Head of Biology, The Brunts Sch, 1970–77; Deputy Head, The Manor Sch 1977–79; Lect Ed, Nott Univ 1989–2001; Independent Education Consult & Ofsted School Inspector from 2001; Dioc Chair Ho of Laity from 2008; M Bp's Counc from 2006; Deanery Lay Chair from 2007
GS 2010– *Tel:* 01623 633494
email: pandpbishop@btopenworld.com

BISSON, Mrs Jane Victoria, FSI, ACIS, MSc
Glenhaven La Rocque Grouville Jersey JE3 9BB [WINCHESTER [CHANNEL ISLANDS]] *b* 1949 *educ* Blancheland Coll; *CV* Legal Trustees (Jersey) Ltd 1988–91; Integro Trust Co 1991–94; Fin Services Commn 1994; Royal Bank of Scotland Internat 1994–2000; Mourant Internat Fin Admin, Legal and Risk Dept from 2005; Regional Mgr KYCOS Ltd, Jersey and Guernsey; M AC Audit Cttee; M Dioc Syn
GS 1995–
Tel: 01534 853162 07797 750896 (Mobile)
email: jane_bisson@googlemail.com

BLACKBURN, Rt Revd Richard Finn, BA, MA
34 Wilson Rd Botanical Gardens Sheffield S11 8RN [BISHOP OF WARRINGTON; LIVERPOOL] *b* 1952 *educ* Aysgarth Sch; Eastbourne Coll; St Jo Coll Dur; Hull Univ; Westcott Ho Th Coll; *CV* NatWest Bank 1976–81; C St Dunstan and All SS Stepney 1983–87; P-in-c St Jo Bapt Isleworth 1987–92; V St Mark Mosborough w Em Waterthorpe 1992–99; RD Attercliffe 1996–99; Hon Can Sheff Cathl 1998–99; Can Res Sheff Cathl 1999–2005; M Pensions Bd 2004–09, Vc-Chair from 2006; Adn of Sheff and Rotherham 1999–2009; Bp of Warrington from 2009
GS 2000–05
Tel: 0114 266 6009 (Home) 01709 309110 (Office)
07714 329638 (Mobile)
Fax: 01709 309107 (Office)
email: archdeacons.office@sheffield.anglican.org

BLACKBURN, Archdeacon of. See HAWLEY, Ven John Andrew

BLACKBURN, Bishop of, [NOT APPOINTED AT TIME OF GOING TO PRESS]

BLACKBURN, Dean of. See ARMSTRONG, Very Revd Christopher John

BLOOR, Mrs Anne Felicity
The Springs Carlton Lane Burton Overy, Leicester LE8 9DF [LEICESTER] *b* 1945 *educ* Malvern Girls Coll; *Tel:* 0116 259 2440
Fax: 0116 259 0119
email: bloor@burtonovery.freeserve.co.uk

BOARDMAN, Ven Jonathan Thomas, MA
Via del Babuino 153 00187 Rome Italy [ARCHDEACON OF ITALY AND MALTA; EUROPE] *b* 1963 *educ* Bolton Sch; Magd Coll Ox; Magd Coll Cam; Westcott Ho; *CV* C St Mary W Derby, Liv 1990–93; Prec St Alb Abbey 1993–96; TR Catford and Downham, S'wark 1996–99; RD E Lewisham 1998–99; Chapl All SS Rome from 1999; Sen tutor,

Angl Cen Rome from 2001; M S'wark Dioc Syn and Bp's Coun 1996–99; M Eur Dioc Syn and Bp's Coun 2004–07; Area Dean Italy and Malta from 2007; Can Dioc Cath Chapter from 2007; Adn Italy and Malta from 2009
GS 2005–09 *Tel:* +39 06 3600 1881
+39 349 655 8844 (Mobile)
Fax: +39 06 3600 1881
email: office@allsaintsrome.org

BOARDMAN, Preb Philippa Jane, MBE, MA
Vicarage St Stephen's Rd London E3 5JL [LONDON] *b* 1963 *educ* Haberdashers' Aske's Sch for Girls; Jes Coll Cam; Ridley Hall Th Coll; *CV* C St Mary and St Steph Walthamstow 1990–93; Asst Pr St Mary of Eton Hackney Wick 1993–96; P-in-c St Paul w St Mark Old Ford 1996–2003, V from 2003; Preb St Paul's Cathl from 2002
GS 1994– *Tel:* 020 8981 4655 020 8980 9020
Fax: 020 8981 5055
email: boardman261@btinternet.com
Web: www.stpauloldford.com

BODDINGTON, Ms Caroline Elizabeth, MA (Oxon), MCIPD
The Wash House Lambeth Palace London SE1 7JU [ARCHBISHOPS' SECRETARY FOR APPOINTMENTS] *b* 1964 *educ* Malvern Girls' Coll; Keble Coll Ox; *CV* BG Grp 1986–2003: HR Strategy and Devel Mgr 1997–99, Hd of Learning and Devel 2000, Hd of HR Operations 2001–03; Abps' Sec for Appts from 2004
GS nc12 *Tel:* 020 7898 1876
020 7898 1877
email: caroline.boddington@churchofengland.org

BODMIN, Archdeacon of. See ELKINGTON, Ven Audrey Anne

BOLTON, Archdeacon of. See BAILEY, Ven David Charles

BOLTON, Suffragan Bishop of. See EDMONDSON, Rt Revd Christopher Paul

BONNEY, Very Revd Mark Philip John MA(Cantab), MA(Oxon), PGCE
The Deanery The College Ely CB7 2DN [DEAN OF ELY] *b* 1957 *Educ* Northgate Gr Sch for Boys, Ipswich; St Catharine's Coll Camb; St Stephen's Ho; *CV* Asst C St Peter's Stockton-on-Tees 1985–88; Chaplain, St Albans Abbey 1988–90; Precentor, St Albans Abbey 1990–92; V Eaton Bray with Edlesborough 1992–96; R Great Berkhamsted 1996–2004; RD Berkhamsted 2002–04; Treas and Can Res Salisbury Cathl 2004–12; Dean of Ely from 2012; GS Rep RSCM 1998–2001, 2005–10; Chaplain to GS 2001–05; M Westcott Ho Coun 2002–05; M Lit Commn 2002–05; Ch Salisbury DAC 2007–12
GS 1990–2010 *Tel:* 01353 660316
07811 466517 (Mobile)
email: m.bonney@cathedral.ely.anglican.org

BOOKER, Revd Michael Paul Montague, BA, MA, PGCE
92 Swaynes Lane Comberton Cambridge CB23 7EF [ELY] *b* 1957 *educ* Cambridgeshire County High Sch; Jesus Coll, Ox; Bris Univ; Trin Coll, Bris; *CV* Tchr, Purley Boys' High Sch 1980–84; C, St Mary Bredin, Cant 1987–91; V, St Mary, Leamington Priors 1991–96; Dir of Miss & Pstrl Studies, Ridley Hall, Cam 1996–2005; P-in-C, Comberton and Toft 2005–10; TR, Lordsbridge Team Ministry from 2010; Chair Dioc Children's Counc 2006–2010
GS 2010– *Tel:* 01223 260095
email: mikebooker@lordsbridge.org

BOOTH, Mr John David Sebastian, MA, FRSA
Arundel Park West Sussex BN18 9NR [CHICHESTER] *b* 1958 *educ* Huish's Gr Sch Taunton; Mert Coll Ox; *CV* Vc Pres Merrill Lynch 1983–86; Sen Vc Pres Prudential Bache 1988–93; Man Dir Bankers Trust Internat 1993–96; Chair Luther Pendragon Ltd 1992–2006; Chair Link ICAP (subs. of ICAP plc) 1996–2011; Chair Maintel Holdings PLC from 1996; Integrated Asset Mgt PLC from 1998, Jazz FM from 2009; Imaginarium Film Holdings from 2011; Dir Herald Investment Mgmt Ltd; Oldfield and Partners Ltd; Staffcare Ltd; Touchbase Ltd; M AC Fin Cttee 1999–2010 and Investment Review Group 2009–11; Investment Ctte from 2011; M CAC; M DBF; Chair Pensions Measure Review Cttee 2001–2; M Dioc of Europe Measure Steering Ctte 2011–12; Guardian Nat Shrine of Our Lady of Walsingham; M Chancellor's Court, University of Oxford; M Chancellor's Forum, Univ of the Arts Lon; Hon Fellow Mert Coll Ox; Hon. Fellow and Vc Coun St Steph Ho, Ox; Gov Pusey Ho, Ox; M Canterbury Cathedral Campaign Board; Chair Queen Victoria Clergy Fund from 2011
GS 1999– *Tel:* 01798 831344
07767 474343 (Mobile)
email: j@johnbooth.com

BOOYS, Revd Canon Sue (Susan) Elizabeth, BA, Cert Th, PGCE, MA
Rectory Manor Farm Rd Dorchester-on-Thames Wallingford OX10 7HZ [OXFORD] *b* 1956 *educ* Harrow County Girls' Sch; Bristol Univ; Ox Min Course; Heythrop, Lon Univ; *CV* C Kidlington Tm Ox 1995–99; TV Dorchester Tm Ox from 1999, TR from 2005; M Bp's Coun; M GS Business Cttee; Gov Ripon Coll Cuddesdon from 2006; AD Aston and Cuddesdon from 2007
GS 2002– *Tel:* 01865 340007
07815 609602 (Mobile)
Fax: 01865 340007
email: rector@dorchester-abbey.org.uk

BOUGHTON, Revd Paul Henry, BSc, ACA
The Rectory The Ridgeway Fetcham Surrey KT22 9AZ [TRUSTEE MEMBER, CHURCH OF ENGLAND PENSIONS BOARD] *b* 1955 *educ* Guildford; Imp Coll Lon; Ridley Hall Cam; *CV* Coopers & Lybrand

(now PwC) 1977–81; various posts with SGS UK and Swiss head office leading to Chief Financial Officer SGS, UK 1981–9; Asst C Christ Church, Guildf 1991–96; R Fetcham from 1996; voluntary M local authority Standards Committee 2000–05, Vc-Chair 2005–12; M Dioc Worship Cttee from 2001; M Dioc Syn from 2009; Clergy rep C of E Pensions Bd from 2010; Pensions Bd rep on EIAG from 2012 *Tel:* 01372 375000
email: boughtonfamily@yahoo.com

BOURNE, Revd Nigel Irvine, MA(Oxon), MBA, BA
The Vicarage 2A Vicarage Lane Chalk Gravesend Kent DA12 4TF [TRUSTEE MEMBER, CHURCH OF ENGLAND PENSIONS BOARD] *educ* The Vyne Comprehensive School Basingstoke; Queen Mary's VI Form College Basingstoke; St John's Coll Ox; Trin Coll Bris; OU; *CV* Royal Naval Engineer Officer 1979–89; Royal Naval Reserve Engineer Officer 1989–92; C St Thomas Bedhampton 1992–4; C St John Newport IOW 1994–8, V St Mary Chalk from 1998; M Dioc Syn from 1998; M Fin Cttee Bp's Coun 2003–6; M C of E Pensions Bd from 2009; M of Pensions Bd Housing Cttee from 2009 *Tel:* 01474 567906
email: vicarofchalk@hotmail.com

BOURNEMOUTH, Archdeacon of. See ROUCH, Ven Peter Bradford

BOYD-LEE, Mr Paul Winston Michael, BA, Dip Th
Manor Barn Horsington Templecombe BA8 0ET [SALISBURY] *b* 1941 *educ* Brighton Coll; Open Univ; Ex Univ; *CV* Theatre Mgr Rank Organization 1963–66; Credit Controller Internat Factors Ltd 1966–72; Dir Bible Truth Publishers from 1972; a Dir of Ch Army 1999–2011; M Ch Army Investment and Remuneration Cttees; M AC from 2005; M Audit Cttee from 2006; M Ethical Investment Adv Gp
GS 1991– *Tel:* 01963 371137
07710 604777 (Mobile)
email: paulbl@btinternet.com

BOYLING, Very Revd Mark Christopher, MA
The Deanery Carlisle CA3 8TZ [DEAN OF CARLISLE] *b* 1952 *educ* K Jas Gr Sch Almondbury, W Yorks; Keble Coll Ox; Cuddesdon Th Coll; *CV* C St Mark Northwood, Kirkby 1977–79, TV 1979–85; Chapl to Bp of Liv 1985–89; V St Pet Formby, Liv 1989–94; Can Res and Prec Liv Cathl 1994–2004; Dean of Carlisle from 2004
GS 2010– *Tel:* 01228 523335
Fax: 01228 547049
email: dean@carlislecathedral.org.uk

BRACKLEY, Rt Revd Ian James, MA
Dayspring 13 Pilgrims Way Guildford GU4 8AD [SUFFRAGAN BISHOP OF DORKING; GUILDFORD] *b* 1947 *educ* Westcliff High Sch; Keble Coll Ox; Cuddesdon Th Coll; Ecum Inst Geneva; *CV* C St Mary Magd w St Fran Lockleaze Bris 1971–74; Asst Chapl Bryanston Sch 1974–77; Chapl 1977–80; V St Mary E Preston Chich 1980–88; RD Arundel and Bognor 1982–87; TR St Wilf Haywards Heath 1988–96; RD Cuckfield 1989–95; Bp of Dorking from 1996; M Ho of Bps CME Cttee 2001–12; M Bd of Ch Army 2002–11; M CCU 2006–10; Chair Bd of Govs of STETS from 1999; Commissary Bp for Portsm Dioc 2009-10
GS 1990–95, 2001, 2005–10 *Tel:* 01483 570829
Fax: 01483 567268
email: bishop.ian@cofeguildford.org.uk

BRADFORD, Archdeacon of. See LEE, Ven David John

BRADFORD, Bishop of. See BAINES, Rt Revd Nicholas

BRADFORD, Dean of, [NOT APPOINTED AT TIME OF GOING TO PRESS],

BRADLEY, Ven Peter David Douglas, B Th
Rectory 1A College Rd Up Holland Skelmersdale WN8 0PY [ARCHDEACON OF WARRINGTON; LIVERPOOL] *b* 1949 *educ* Brookfield Comp Sch; Nottm Univ; Ian Ramsey Coll; Linc Th Coll; *CV* C Up Holland 1979–83; V H Spirit Dovecot 1983–94; Sec Dioc Bd of Min 1983–88; Sec Grp for Urban Min and Leadership 1984–88; Asst Dir In-Service Trg 1988–89; Dir CME from 1989; TR St Tho Up Holland from 1994; M BM Mission at Home Cttee; M Dioc Bd of Min; Hon Can Liv Cathl from 2000; Adn of Warrington from 2001/2
GS 1990–2010 *Tel:* 01695 622936
Fax: 01695 625865
email: archdeacon@peterbradley.fsnet.co.uk

BRADLEY, Very Revd Peter Edward, MA
Sheffield Cathedral Church St Sheffield S1 1HA [DEAN OF SHEFFIELD] *b* 1964 *educ* R Belfast Academical Inst; Trin Hall Cam; Ripon Coll Cuddesdon; *CV* C St Mich & All A w St Edm Northampton 1988–90; Chapl Gonville & Caius Coll Cam 1990–95; TV St Mich Abingdon 1995–98; TV All SS High Wycombe 1998–2003, TR 2003; Dean of Sheffield from 2003; Fell Coll of Prchrs, Washington DC from 2006
Tel: 0114 275 3434 0114 263 6063
Fax: 0114 279 7412
email: dean@sheffield-cathedral.org.uk
2nd email: deanpeterbradley@gmail.com

BRADWELL, Area Bishop of. See WRAW, Rt Revd John

BRANDON, Revd Beatrice, MA, DMS, FRSA, FRSM
Clopton Manor Clopton Northants NN14 3DZ [ARCHBISHOPS' ADVISER FOR THE HEALING MINISTRY] *b* 1955 *educ* Heythrop Coll Lon; *CV* M Dioc Past Ctee 1992–2005; M Abps Millenium Adv Gp 1996–2000; Dioc Vacancy-in-See Ctee 1996–2003; M Folllow-up Steering Grp to Abps' Commn on the Reorganization of the National Institutions 1996–98; Chair Ho Laity and Lay Vc Chair Dioc

Syn Peterb 1997–2003; Convener Ho Bps Healing Min Strg Gp 2000–07; M Cathl Coun Peterb Cathl 2001–05; Chair Chs Together for Healing 2004–08; M Peterb Dioc Bd of Patronage from 2006; Trustee Abp York Youth Trust 2008–11; Abps' Adv for Healing Min from 2007
GS 1995–2005 *Tel:* 01832 720346
Fax: 01832 720446
email: beatrice@healingministry.org.uk

BRETT, Mr Justin Edward, MA, PGCE
Roedean School Brighton BN2 5RQ [CHICHESTER] *b* 1971 *educ* Cheltenham Coll; Ex Coll Ox; *CV* Tchr Caldicott Sch 1995–2001; Head of English and RS, Brockhurst Sch 2001–2002; Policy Exec West Berkshire Counc 2003–04; Tchr, St Gabriel's Sch 2004–08; Head of Classics, St Aubyns Sch from 2008; Lay Chair Newbury Deanery 2006–08
GS 2005– *Tel:* 07876 746074
email: justin.brett@yahoo.co.uk

BREWER, Mrs Rosalind Patricia Anne, BA, RGN
37 Greenstead Road Newby Scarborough YO12 6HN [YORK] *b* 1947 *CV* Qualified RGN 1968; Staff Nurse 1968–70; Night Sister 1972–78; Practice Nursing Sister 1982–90; Family Planning Sister 1984–2006; Senior Practice Nursing Sister/Mgr 1990–2006; Cytology Adv to Primary Care Trust 1995–2006; Nurse Tutor and Assessor 1998–2006; Dioc Prop Sub Cttee from 2010; Archbp's Counc from 2006; Patronage Brd from 2006; Vice Chair Dioc Pstrl & Miss Sub Cttee from 2004;York Dioc Syn from 2006; Lay Chair Scarborough Deanery Syn from 2005
GS 2010– *Tel:* 01723369731
email: ros.brewer@btinternet.com

BRIDEN, Rt Worshipful Timothy John, MA, LLB
Lamb Chambers Lamb Building Temple London EC4Y 7AS [VICAR-GENERAL OF CANTERBURY] *b* 1951 *educ* Ipswich Sch; Downing Coll Cam; *CV* Chancellor of Dioc of B&W from 1993; Chancellor of Dioc of Truro from 1998; Vicar-General of Canterbury from 2005; M Legal Adv Commn
GS 2005– *Tel:* 020 7797 8300
Fax: 020 7797 8308
email: info@lambchambers.co.uk

BRINDLEY, Very Revd David Charles, BD, M Th, M Phil, AKC
The Deanery 13 Pembroke Rd Portsmouth PO1 2NS [DEAN OF PORTSMOUTH] *b* 1953 *educ* Wednesfield Gr Sch; K Coll Lon; *CV* C Epping, Chelms 1976–79; Lect, Coll of St Paul and St Mary, Cheltenham 1979–82; V Quorn and Dir of Clergy Trg, Leic 1982–86; Prin W of Eng Minl Trg Course 1987–94; TR Warwick 1994–2002; Dean of Portsm from 2002; Chair Portsm DAC from 2003; Sec and Treas Assoc of Engl Cathls 2005–09
GS 1985–87, 2004–2005, 2011–
Tel: 023 9282 4400 (Home)
023 9234 7605 (Office)
Fax: 023 9229 5480
email: david.brindley@portsmouthcathedral.org.uk

BRISTOL, Archdeacon of, [NOT APPOINTED AT TIME OF GOING TO PRESS,

BRISTOL, Bishop of. See HILL, Rt Revd Michael Arthur

BRISTOL, Dean of, see HOYLE, Very Revd Dr David Michael,

BRITTON, Mr Andrew James Christie, BA, MSc
2 Shabden Park High Rd, Chipstead Coulsdon, Surrey CR5 3SF [ARCHBISHOPS' COUNCIL] *b* 1940 *educ* R Gr Sch, Newc-upon-Tyne; Oriel Coll Ox; Lon Sch of Economics; *CV* Economist HM Treasury 1968–82; Dir Nat Institute of Economic and Social Research 1982–95; Exec Sec Ch's Enquiry into Unemployment and the Future of Work 1995–97; Chair S'wark Dioc Bd of Fin 2000–2007; Chair Abps' Coun Fin Cttee from 2007
GS 2007– *Tel:* 01737 553 678

BRIXWORTH, Suffragan Bishop of. See HOLBROOK, Rt Revd John Edward

BROADBENT, Rt Revd Pete (Peter Alan), MA
173 Willesden Lane Brondesbury London NW6 7YN [AREA BISHOP OF WILLESDEN; LONDON] *b* 1952 *educ* Merchant Taylors Sch Northwood; Jes Coll Cam; St Jo Coll Nottm; *CV* C St Nic Dur City 1977–80; C Em Holloway 1980–83; Chapl to N Lon Poly and Hon C St Mary Islington 1983–89; Bp's Chapl for Miss in Stepney 1980–89; Councillor and Chair of Planning Lon Boro of Islington 1982–89; V Trin St Mich Harrow 1989–95; AD Harrow 1994; Adn of Northolt 1995–2001; Bp of Willesden from 2001; M Dioc Commn 1989–92; M Panel of Chairmen GS 1990–92, from 2009; M C of E Evang Coun 1984–95, from 2006; Chair Vacancy-in-See Cttee Regulation Wkg Pty 1991–93; M GS Stg Orders Cttee 1991–95; M Appts Sub-Cttee 1992–95; M CBF 1991–98; M GS Stg Cttee 1992–98; Chair GS Business Sub-Cttee 1996–98; Chair Elections Review Grp 1996–2000; Chair Lon Dioc Bd for Schs 1996–2006; Chair Memralife Gp (Spring Harvest/ICC); Chair Business Cttee 1999–2000; M AC 1999–2000; M City Parochial Foundn 1999–2003; M Urban Bps Panel from 2001; Trustee CUF 2002–11; Chair Coun St Jo Coll Nottm 2002–10; Pres W Lon YMCA from 2004; Chair Standards Cttee, Lon Boro Harrow 2006–2010; Chair Eden Greater Lon Network from 2010; Chair Bless Network from 2004; Vc Pres CPAS from 2009; Chair Dioc Strategic Policy Cttee from 2009; Acting Bp of Stepney 2010–11
GS 1985–2001; 2004– *Tel:* 020 8451 0189
07957 144674 (Mobile)
Fax: 020 8451 4606
email: bishop.willesden@btinternet.com

BROMILOW, Dr Ian Geoffrey, BSc, MSc, Phd
The Old School Hilton Blandford Forum Dorset DT11 0DB [SALISBURY] *b* 1956 *educ* Tower Coll, Rainhill & Scarisbrick Hall Sch, Southport; UCL; ICL; Bris Univ; *CV* Country Chair, Shell Companies in Jordan & Iraq, Amman, Jordan, 2006–09; Country Chair, Shell Iraq, Dubai,UAE, 2005–06; Mging Dir, Shell/BP Kenya Ltd and Shell Tanzania, Nairobi, Kenya 2002–05; Gen Mgr, Shell Uganda and Shell Rwanda, 2000–02; Head Consumer Lubricants, Shell International, London, 1998–2000; Brand Mgr, Shell International, London, 1995–98; Marketing and Sales Mgr, SASLUCO (Shell Joint Venture), Jeddah, Saudi Arabia, 1991–95; Base oil Supply, Demand & Trading, Shell International, 1989–91; Oil Market Analyst, Shell International London, 1986–89; Math, Shell Rsrch, Amsterdam, The Netherlands, 1982–86; Lay Minister Training; Mission and Stewardship Adv, Sarum; Gov, Dunbury Sch, Dorset
GS 2010– *Tel:* 01258880044
email: igbromilow@gmail.com

BROMLEY AND BEXLEY, Archdeacon of. See WRIGHT, Ven Paul

BROOKE, Revd David Martin, MA, PGCE
The Rectory Church Lane Redmarshall Stockton-on-Tees TS21 1ES [DURHAM] *b* 1958 *educ* Ferryhill Comp Sch; Selwyn Coll Cam; ULIE; SAOMC; *CV* Asst Master, Bedford Sch 1981–85; Marketing Mngr, Epson UK 1985–92; Marketing Mngr, Dell UK 1992–99; C Luton Lewsey St Hugh St Alb 1999–00; NSM Sunnyside w Bourne End 2000–02; C 2002–04 V Bishopton w Gt Stainton Dur from 2004; R Redmarshall from 2004; R Grindon, Stillington and Wolviston from 2004; P-in-c Billingham St Mary from 2010; AD Stockton from 2007
GS 2010– *Tel:* 01740 630810 07967 326085
email: david@revd.co.uk

BROOKFIELD, Mr Joseph Adam, BA, MSc
30 Alexandra St Preston PR1 4BL [BLACKBURN] *b* 1978 *educ* Bootham Sch York; Lanc Univ; Ox Media and Bus Sch; Bath Univ; *CV* Intern, United Nations Info Cen 2002; freelance rsch, Immigration Adv Service 2003–04; vol rsch asst, Choices Team, Refugee Action 2003–04; M Blackb Dioc Youth Cttee; admin asst Manch Salford Housing Market Renewal Pathfinder from 2004
GS 2004–2005; 2005–2010 *Tel:* 01772 889442
email: j.brookfield@yahoo.co.uk

BROWN, Ven Andrew,
St George's Vicarage 16 Devonshire Rd Douglas, Isle of Man IM2 3RB [ARCHDEACON OF THE ISLE OF MAN] *Tel:* 01624 675430
email: archdeacon@sodorandman.im

BROWN, Mr Andrew Charles, B Sc, FRICS
Church House Great Smith St London SW1P 3AZ [SECRETARY, CHURCH COMMISSIONERS] *b* 1957 *educ* Ashmole Comp Sch; S Bank Poly; *CV* Healey & Baker 1981–84; St Quintin 1984–94; Dep Sec and Chief Surveyor Ch Commrs 1994–2003, Sec from 2003; M Fin and Invest Ctee, Lionheart from 2007; M Allchurches Trust from 2008; Trustee and Chair the2:67project 2007–10; Trustee William Leech (Foundn) and Dir William Leech (Invest) from 2007 *Tel:* 020 7898 1785
Fax: 020 7898 1131
email: andrew.brown@churchofengland.org

BROWN, Revd Dr Malcolm Arthur, MA, PhD, FHEA
Church House Great Smith St London SW1P 3AZ [DIRECTOR, MISSION AND PUBLIC AFFAIRS DIVISION, ARCHBISHOPS' COUNCIL] *b* 1954 *educ* Eltham Coll; Oriel Coll Ox; Man Univ; Westcott Ho Cam; *CV* C Riverhead w. Dunton Green, Roch 1979–83; TV and Ind Missioner, Southn City Centre, Winch 1983–91; Exec Sec William Temple Foundn 1991–2000; Hon C St Paul Heaton Moor, Man 1993–2000; Prin EAMTC 2000–05; Prin ERMC 2005–07; Dir MPA from 2007; M BSR Ind and Economic Affairs Cttee 1987–91; M BSR Soc, Economic and Ind Affairs Cttee 1997–2002; Th Consult Rev of Diocs, Pastl and Related Measures 2001–04; M Min Div Th Educ and Trg Cttee 2003–07; M Min Div Fin Panel 2006–07; Licensed to Dioc of Ely from 2011 *Tel:* 020 7898 1468
email: malcolm.brown@churchofengland.org

BROWN, Mr Richard Alexander Hamilton,
Glebe House Ingleby Arncliffe Northallerton Yorkshire DL6 3JX [YORK] *b* 1974 *educ* Stokesley Sch; Univ of Humberside; YMC; *CV* Comp Dir from 2005; Elected GS 2010
GS 2010– *Tel:* 01609 882141
email: richard.brown@yorksj.ac.uk

BRUINVELS, Canon Peter Nigel Edward, LLB, FRSA, FCIM, MCIJ, MCIPR
14 High Meadow Close St Paul's Rd West Dorking RH4 2LG [GUILDFORD] *b* 1950 *educ* St Jo Sch Leatherhead; Lon Univ; Inns of Court Sch of Law; *CV* MP Leic E 1983–87; Party Candidate The Wrekin 1997; Prin Peter Bruinvels Associates, Media Mgt and Public Affairs Consults; M Dioc Syn and Dorking Dny Syn from 1974; Freeman of City of Lon 1980; M Dios Commn 1991–96; M Legislative Cttee 1991–96 and from 2000, Dep Chair from 2010; News Broadcaster, Political Commentator and Freelance Journalist; Ch Commr from 1992, Pastl Cttee from 1993, Gov Ch Cmmrs from 1992; Mgt Adv Cttee 1999–2009; Ofsted and Section 48 SIAS RE Sch Insp from 1994; M DSS Child Support and Soc Security Appeals Tribunal 1994–99; Man Ed Bruinvels News & Media, Press and Broadcasting Agents; M Dioc Bd of Educ from 1994; M GS Bd of Educ 1996–2006; Co-opted M Surrey LEA 1997–2007; Gov Univ of York St Jo 1999–2007; Dir Ch Army and Chair Remuneration Cttee 1999–2004;

Independent Lay Chair NHS Complaints Tribunal 1999–2004; M Clergy Discipline Review Grp from 1999; Chair Surrey Schs Organization Cttee 2000–07; Court Member Univ of Sussex 2000–08; M Dearing Implementation Grp from 2001; County Field Officer (Surrey) Royal Br Legion from 2002; Dir E Elmbridge and Mid Surrey Primary Care Trust 2002–07; M Mgt Adv Cttee 1999–2009; Lay Can Guildf Cathl from 2002; Vc-Pres and Chair Ho of Laity, Dioc Syn from 2003; Guild CNC from 2003; M SE Veterans and War Pensions Cttee from 2003; Chair Surrey Joint Services Charities Cttee from 2004; Chair Guildf Dioc Bd of Educ 2005–08; Hon Sec Surrey County Appeals Cttee form 2002; M Guildf Coll of Cans from 2002; M Cathls Fabric Commn for Eng from 2006; M Guildf Cathl Coun from 2006; Gov Whitelands Coll (Roehampton Univ) from 2007, Chair from 2009; Dep Chair Nominations & Governance Cttee (Ch Commissioners) from 2009
GS 1985– *Tel:* 01306 887082 (Home)
01372 386500 (Office)
07721 411688 (Mobile)
Fax: 01372 375843
email: canonpeterbruinvels@talk21.com

BRYANT, Rt Revd Mark Watts, BA
Bishop's House 25 Ivy Lane Gateshead NE9 6QD [SUFFRAGAN BISHOP OF JARROW; DURHAM] *b* 1949 *educ* St Jo Sch Leatherhead; St Jo Coll Dur; Cuddesdon Th Coll; *CV* C Addlestone 1975–79; C St Jo Studley, Trowbridge 1979–83, V 1983–88; Chapl Trowbridge CFE 1979–83; DDO and Dir Vocations and Tr, Cov 1988–96; Hon Can Cov Cathl 1993–2001; TR Cov Caludon 1996–2001; AD Cov E 1999–2001; Adn of Coventry 2001–07; Can Res Cov Cathl 2006–07; Bp of Jarrow from 2007
GS 1998–2008 *Tel:* 0191 491 0917
Fax: 0191 491 5116
email: bishop.of.jarrow@durham.anglican.org

BUCKINGHAM, Archdeacon of. See GORHAM, Ven Karen Marisa

BUCKINGHAM, Area Bishop of. See WILSON, Rt Revd Alan Thomas Lawrence

BUCKLER, Very Revd Philip John Warr, MA
The Deanery 11 Minster Yard Lincoln LN2 1PJ [DEAN OF LINCOLN] *b* 1949 *educ* Highgate Sch; St Pet Coll Ox; Cuddesdon Coll; *CV* C St Pet Bushey Heath 1972–75; Chapl Trin Coll Cam 1975–81; Sacr and Min Can St Paul's Cathl 1981–86; V Hampstead 1987–99; AD N Camden 1993–98; Can Res St Paul's Cathl 1999–2007, Treas 2000–07; Dean of Lincoln from 2007 *Tel:* 01522 561611
Fax: 01522 561603
email: dean@lincolncathedral.com

BULL, Prof John W, BSc, PhD, DSc, Eur Ing, C Eng, FICE, FIStructE, FCIHT, FIHE, FIWSC
Gable Ends 11 Glebe Mews Bedlington NE22 6LJ [NEWCASTLE] *b* 1944 *educ* Farnborough Gr Sch; Univ of chester; Cardiff Univ; *CV* Tchr ILEA 1966–68; Engineer/Chartered Engineer Dur Co Coun 1974–79; Newc Univ 1979–2010, Prof of Civil Eng, Brunel Univ from 2010; M Dioc Syn from 1988; M Bp's Coun from 1988; Vc Pres Dioc Syn 1994–2006; Chair Dioc Bd of Educ 1991–97; Lay Chair Bedlington Dny Syn 1990–97; Dioc Bd of Educ 2004–10; M Coun Nat Soc from 2007
GS 1995– *Tel:* 01895 267916 (Office)
07710 200416 (Mobile)
Fax: 01865 269782
email: John.Bull@brunel.ac.uk

BULL, Revd Dr Timothy Martin (Tim), MA, MA, PhD, PhD, FRSA
The Rectory Wick Road Langham, Colchester CO4 5PG [CHELMSFORD] *b* 1965 *educ* Bradf Gr Sch; Worcester Coll Ox; Univ Dur; Fitzwilliam Coll Camb; King's Coll Lon; Ridley Hall; *CV* M Lee Abbey Community 1987–89; Software Eng and Researcher, DSE Ltd 1989–95; Lect Computer Science Univ Dur1995–96; C Walcot 199–2003; Tutor Open Theol Coll 2001–07; P-in-C Langham with Boxted from 2003; Colchester Area CMD Officer from 2003; Colchester Area Team from 2003; Dioc Syn 2003–06, 2010–; Dioc Readers' Cttee from 2004; Dioc Vocations Working Grp 2007–09; Padre to colchester (308) Squadron ATC from 2008; GS 2010–
GS 2010– *Tel:* 01206 230666
email: RevDrTim@gmail.com

BULLOCK, Revd Canon Sarah Ruth, BA(Hons), BA(Hons) (Dunelm)
St Edmunds Rectory 1 Range Road Whalley Range Manchester M16 8FS [MANCHESTER] *b* 1964 *educ* Fallowfield C of E Sch; Univ of Surrey; Cranmer Hall, St. John's Coll, Dur; *CV* English Tchr, Cheadle Hulme Sch 1986–90; Asst Dioc Yth Off, Man 1986–90; AC St. Paul, Kersal Moor w St Andrew, Man, 1993–98; P-in-C St Edmund, Whalley Range 1998-2004; P-in-C St. James' w St. Clement, Moss Side, 1999–2004; R United Benefice of St. Edmund, Whalley Range & St. James' w St. Clement, Man from 2004; Hon Can Man Cathl 2007; Bps Adv Womans Min, Man 2009; Dean City & Borough Man 2010; M Man Urban Regen & Sem Grp Commiss Urban Life & Faith, 1999–2009; M Discipleship & Min Training Cttee, Man, 2003–06; M Bps Adv Grp Sexuality 2004; Chair Discipleship & Min Training Cttee, Man, 2005; Bps Adv Womens Min, Man 2009; M Man Syn & DBF 2009; M Bps Counc 2010; M Min Devlp Review T, Man, 2010
GS 2010– *Tel and Fax:* 0161 226 1291
email: REVSBULLOCK@aol.com

BURNLEY, Suffragan Bishop of. See GODDARD, Rt Revd John William

BURRAGE, Mr Paul, BSc, FCA
Church House Great Smith St London SW1P 3AZ [DIRECTOR OF ACCOUNTING SERVICES, NATIONAL

WHO'S WHO

CHURCH INSTITUTIONS] *b* 1952 *educ* Reading Sch; Sir William Borlase's Sch; Newcastle Univ; *CV* Fin Man to Fin Dir in various internat Freight Forwarding Companies 1979–91; Fin Dir Heating Oil and Petroleum Distributor 1991–92; Consult, Dir of Fin and Resources British Red Cross 1993–2004; Head of Fin Refugee Coun 2005–05; Chief Accountant NCIs 2005–07; (Acting) Dir of Fin Accounting NCIs 2008–09; Dir Accounting Services from 2009 *Tel:* 020 7898 1677
Fax: 020 7898 1770
email: paul.burrage@churchofengland.org

BURRIDGE, Revd Prof Richard Alan, MA, Ph D, PGCE, Dip Th, FKC
King's College London Strand London WC2R 2LS [UNIVERSITIES, LONDON] *b* 1955 *educ* Bris Cathl Sch; Univ Coll Ox; Nottm Univ; St Jo Coll Nottm; *CV* Classics Master and Ho Tutor Sevenoaks Sch 1978–82; C SS Pet and Paul Bromley 1985–87; Chapl and pt Lect in Depts of Th and Classics & Ancient History Univ of Ex 1987–94; Dean of K Coll Lon from 1994; M Academic Bd NTMTC 1994–2008; Chair Chr Evidence Soc from 1994; Chair Eric Symes Abbott Memorial Fund from 1994; M Studiorum Novi Testamenti Societas from 1995; M SST from 1995; M SBL from 1995; ABM External Moderator to SW Min Tr Course 1995–99; Chair Min Div Educ Validatory Panel 1998–2004; M Min Div TETC 1998–2004; M CECC; Commr to Bp of High Veld 1996–2009; GS Rep PIM Consultation to Province of W Africa 1997; Adv and Writer for Nat Millennium Experience Co and Greenwich Dome 1998–99; M Vote 1 Min Div Wkg Party 1999–2000; M Review Grp on Structure and Funding of Ordination Tr 2000–03; FKC 2002; Chair Bp of S'wark's Theol Grp 2004–2009; rep Abp of Cant and Angl Communion at Second World Congress for Pastl Care of Catholic Foreign Students, Rome, Dec 2005; M Academic Board St Mellitus College from 2008; M Ethical Investment Adv Gp (Ch Commns' rep) from 2008; Prof of Bibl Interpretation at K Coll Lon from 2008; Woods Fell (Visiting Prof) at Virginia Theol Seminary, Alexandria VA, USA 2009; Dep Chr Ethical Investment Adv Gp from 2010
GS 1994– *Tel:* 020 7848 2333
Fax: 020 7848 2344
email: richard.burridge@kcl.ac.uk

BURROWS, Mr Gerald David, B Sc, M Sc, T Cert
3 Hall Rd Fulwood Preston PR2 9QD [BLACKBURN] *b* 1942 *educ* Wellington Gr Sch; Univ Coll of N Wales, Bangor; *CV* Scientific Officer Rutherford High Energy Lab 1967–69; Lect Grimsby Coll of Tech 1969–71; Sen Lect Blackb Coll from 1971
GS 1990– *Tel:* 01772 719159
email: gerald.burrows@talk21.com

BURROWS, Ven Peter, BTh
c/o Diocesan Church House 95–99 Effingham Street Rotherham S65 1BL [SUFFRAGAN BISHOP OF DONCASTER; SHEFFIELD] *b* 1955 *educ* Spondon Ho Sec Sch; Derby Coll of FE; Sarum and Wells Th Coll; *CV* C Baildon 1983–87; R Broughton Astley 1993–93; P-in-c Stoney Stanton w Croft 1993–95; TR Broughton Astley and Croft w Stoney Stanton 1995–2000; RD Guthlaxton I 1994–2000; DDO and Par Development Officer 1996–2000; M Dioc Syn; M Vacancy-in-See Cttee; M DAC; Coord Dioc Tm Forum; M Bp's Coun; Hon Can Leic Cathl; Dep Dir Min from 2002; Dir Min 2003–05; Adn Leeds 2005–11; Hon Can Ripon Cathl 2005–11; Bp of Doncaster from 2012; Chair Min and Training Devel Grp; Chair One City Projects and Oastler Centre; Trustee Children's Internat Summer Villages; M Inst of Directors
GS 2010– *Tel:* 01709 309100
email: bishoppeter@bishopofdoncaster.org.uk

BURTON-JONES, Ven Simon David, MA (Hons); BTh; MA
The Archdeaconry Kings Orchard, The Precinct Rochester, Kent ME1 1TG [ARCHDEACON OF ROCHESTER] *b* 1962 *educ* Fleetwood High Sch; Emmanuel Coll Cam; St John's Coll Nottm; *CV* TC St Peter's Darwen w St Paul's Hoddlesdon 1993–96; C St Mark's Biggin Hill 1996–98; V St Mary's Bromley 1998–2005; R St Nic Chislehurst 2005–10; Adn of Roch from 2010 *Tel:* 01634 813533 (Home) 01634 560000 (Office)
email: simonburtonjones@btinternet.com
web: www.simonburton-jones.com

BUSH, Most Revd Roger Charles, BA
14 St Mary's Street Truro TR1 2AF [DEAN OF TRURO] *b* 1956 *educ* Fakenham Gr Sch; K Coll Lon; Coll of the Resurr, Mirfield; *CV* C Newbold, Derby 1986–90; TV Parish of the Resurr, Leic 1990–94; TR Redruth w. Lanner & Treleigh, Truro 1994–2004; Can Chan, Truro Cathl 2004–06; Adn of Cornwall 2006–12; Dean of Truro from 2012
GS 2004– *Tel:* 01872 276782
Fax: 01872 277788
email: dean@trurocathedral.org.uk

BUTCHER, Dr Jackie (Jacqueline Anne), MA, M Sc, Ph D
10 Vernon Rd Totley Rise Sheffield S17 3QE [SHEFFIELD] *b* 1965 *educ* Wootton Upper Sch; Newnham Coll Cam; Sussex Univ; Leic Univ; *CV* Rsch Associate 1992–95; full-time mother 1995–2000; M Dioc Bd Faith & Justice; Bp's Adv in World Development Issues
GS 2000– *Tel:* 0114 262 1293
email: ja_butcher@yahoo.co.uk

BUTLER, Rt Revd Paul Roger, BA (Jt Hons) English and History; BA Oxon Theol
Bishop's Manor Bishop's Drive Southwell NG25 0JR [BISHOP OF SOUTHWELL AND NOTTINGHAM] *b* 1955 *educ* Kingston Grammar Sch; Nottm Univ; Wycliffe Hall; *CV* C All Saints w Holy Trinity, Wandsworth 1983–87; Scripture Union Inner Lon

Evang 1987–92; Dep Head of Miss 1992–94; NSM St Paul's, East Ham (Chelmsford) 1988–94; P-in-C St Mary w St Stephen Walthamstow (Chelmsford) 1994–97; P-in-C St Luke, Walthamstow 1994–97; TR of Walthamstow 1997–2004; AD Waltham Forest 2000–04; Can St Paul's Byumba, Rwanda from 2001; Bp of Southampton 2004–2009; Bp of Southwell and Nottm from 2009; Chair of CMS 2008–10; Jt Chair Churches Safeguarding Advisory Committee from 2011; Pres Scripture Union from 2011Bp of Southwell and Nottingham from 2009
GS 2009– *Tel:* 01636 812112
email: bishop@southwell.anglican.org

BUTLER, Canon Simon, BSc, DTS, MA
St Mary's Vicarage 32 Vicarage Crescent London SW11 3LD [SOUTHWARK] *b* 1964 *educ* Bournemouth Sch; UEA; Britannia R Naval Coll; St Jo Coll Nottm; *CV* C Chandler's Ford, Winch 1992–94; C St Jos Worker Northolt, Lon 1994–97; V Immanuel and St Andr Streatham, S'wark 1997–2004; AD Streatham 2002–04; P-in-c and acting TR Sanderstead TM, S'wark from 2004, TR 2006–11; V St Mary Battersea from 2011; Chair S'wark Dioc Liturg Cttee; Vice-Chair SEITE Coun
GS 2005– *Tel:* 020 72288 141 07941 552407
email: simon.butler7@gmail.com

BUTTERFIELD, Ven David John, B Mus, Dip Th, DPS
Brimley Lodge 27 Molescroft Rd Beverley HU17 7DX [ARCHDEACON OF THE EAST RIDING; YORK] *b* 1952 *educ* Belle Vue Boys Gr Sch Bradf; R Holloway Coll Lon Univ; St Jo Coll Nottm; *CV* C Ch Ch Southport 1977–81; Min St Thos CD Aldridge 1981–91; V St Mich Lilleshall w. St Mary Sheriffhales 1991–2002; V St Mich Lilleshall w. St Jo Muxton and St Mary Sheriffhales 2002–07; M BM 1995–96; RD Edgmond 1997–98; RD Edgmond and Shifnal 1999–2006; M Bp's Coun (Lich) 1994–2006; Chair Dioc Syn Ho of Clergy 2003–06; Adn of E Riding from 2007
GS 1990–2005 *Tel and Fax:* 01482 881659
email: archdeacon.of.eastriding@yorkdiocese.org

BUTTERY, Revd Graeme, BA, MA
St Oswald's Clergy House Brougham Terrace Hartlepool TS24 8EY [DURHAM] *b* 1962 *educ* Dame Allan's Boys Sch Newc; York Univ; Newc Univ; St Steph Ho Th Coll; *CV* C Peterlee 1988–91; C Sunderland, TM 1991–92; TV Sunderland, TM 1992–94; V St Lawr the Martyr Horsley Hill 1994–2005; V St Oswald Hartlepool from 2005; Can Dur Cathl from 2010
GS 1995– *Tel:* 01429 273201
email: G_BUTTERY@sky.com

CAMBRIDGE, Archdeacon of. See BEER, Ven John Stuart

CAMPBELL, Dr (John) Graham, Ph D, B Sc, FCA
18 Eaglesfield Hartford Northwich CW8 1NQ [CHESTER] *b* 1942 *educ* Man Gr Sch, Birm Univ; *CV* Birm Univ Rsch Chemist ICI 1966–71; Student Accountant Worth & Co 1971–74; Audit Sen Spicer & Pegler 1974–76; Accountant then Commercial Mgr Br Nuclear Fuels plc 1976–2003; M Bp's Coun from 1998; M Dioc Fin and Cen Services Cttee from 1997; M Foxhill Dioc Conf Cen Coun from 1998; M C of E Pensions Bd from 2004; Treas C of E Evang Coun 2005–10
GS 2000– *Tel:* 01606 75849
email: j.graham.campbell@googlemail.com

CANTERBURY, Archbishop of. See WELBY, Most Revd and Rt Hon Justin Portal

CANTERBURY, Archdeacon of. See WATSON, Ven Sheila Anne

CANTERBURY, Dean of. See WILLIS, Very Revd Robert Andrew

CAPON, Canon Dr Peter Charles, B Sc, Ph D
137 Birchfields Rd Manchester M14 6PJ [MANCHESTER] *b* 1944 *educ* Kimbolton Sch; Southn Univ; Cam Univ; Man Univ; *CV* Sen Lect in Computer Science Man Univ 1976–2004; rtd; Rdr at H Trin Rusholme, Manch from 1991; Lay Chair Manch Dioc Syn from 2011; Hon Lay Canon Manch Cathl from 2012
GS 1995– *Tel:* 0161 225 5970
email: peter.capon@cs.man.ac.uk

CAREY, Mr Kevin, MA
112A High St Hurstpierpoint BN6 9PX [CHICHESTER] *b* 1951 *educ* Downing Coll Cam; Harvard Univ; K Coll Lon; *CV* Founder Dir 1997, Chair from 2009, humanITy; Chair Ofcom Com Radio Fund; Chair RNIB; Head eInclusion Consultancy, ATcare; Dir, Social Investment Business; Founder jesus4u; lic Rdr from 2004
GS 2005–2010 *Tel:* 01273 835113 (Home)
01273 834321 (Work)
email: humanity@atlas.co.uk

CARLISLE, Archdeacon of. See ROBERTS, Ven Kevin

CARLISLE, Bishop of. See NEWCOME, Rt Revd James William Scobie

CARLISLE, Dean of. See BOYLING, Very Revd Mark Christopher

CARTWRIGHT, Revd Paul, BA, PGCE, MifL
Priory House 24 Kirkland Gardens Monk Bretton Barnsley S71 2GD [WAKEFIELD] *b* 1971 *educ* Hemsworth H Sch; Leeds Met Univ; Univ of Huddersfield; Leeds Univ; Coll of the Resurrection, Mirfield; *CV* Police Officer, West Yorkshire Police, 1990–2006; Major Incident/Crime Family

Liasion Officer, West Yorkshire Police 2002–06; Equalities & Diversity Trainer, West Yorkshire Police 2003–06; Asst Convenor Wakef Fellowship of Vocation from 2008; Barnsley Deanery Vocations Off from 2010; AC St Helen's Church, Athersley 2008–10; AC St John the Evangelist, Carlton from 2010; Police Chapl to West Yorkshire Police from 2010; GS Rep on CMEAC from 2011
GS 2010– *Tel:* 01226 285209 07852 174303
email: fr.paul.cartwright@gmail.com

CASSIDY, Rt Revd George Henry, B Sc, M Phil
Bishop's Manor Southwell NG25 0JR [BISHOP OF SOUTHWELL AND NOTTINGHAM] *b* 1942 *educ* Belfast High Sch; Qu Univ Belfast; Univ Coll Lon; Oak Hill Th Coll; *CV* C Ch Ch Clifton Bris 1972–75; V St Edyth Sea Mills Bris 1975–82; V St Paul Portman Sq Lon 1982–87; Adn of Lon and Can Res St Paul's Cathl 1987–99; Bp of S'well and Nottm from 1999; entered Ho of Lords 2003
GS 1995– *Tel:* 01636 812112
Fax: 01636 815401
email: bishop@southwell.anglican.org

CASTLE, Rt Revd Dr Brian Colin, BA, MA, Ph D
Bishop's Lodge 48 St Botolph's Road Sevenoaks TN13 3AG [SUFFRAGAN BISHOP OF TONBRIDGE; ROCHESTER] *b* 1949 *educ* Wilson's Gr Sch, Camberwell; Univ Coll London; Cuddesdon Coll Ox; Univ of Ox; Univ of Birm; *CV* Asst C St Nic Sutton 1977; Asst C St Pet Limpsfield, S'wark 1977–81; P-in-c Chingola, Chililabombwe and Solwezi, N Zambia 1981–4; Vis Lect Ecum Inst, Bossey, Switzerland 1984–5; V N Petherton and Northmoor Green 1985–92; Vc Prin and Dir of Pastl Studies Ripon Coll Cuddesdon 1992–2001; Bp of Tonbridge and Hon Can Roch Cathl and f2002; Abps' Adv for Alternative Spiritualities and New Relig Movts; Co-chair Miss Thel Adv Grp; M Faith & Order Commn *Tel:* 01732 456070
Fax: 01732 741449
email: bishop.tonbridge@rochester.anglican.org

CAWDELL, Revd Simon Howard, BA, MA CTM
The Rectory 16 East Castle Street Bridgnorth Shropshire WV16 4AL [HEREFORD] *b* 1965 *educ* Kings Sch, Worcester; Univ Coll Dur; Kings Coll, Lon; Ridley Hall, Cam; *CV* Investment Analyst; Coast Securities Ltd, Lon 1987–91; C St. Philip, Cheam Common S'wark 1994–98; V Claverley & Tuck Hill 1998–2010; TR Bridgnorth & P-in-C Morville w Aston Ayre, Acton Round & Monkhopton w Upton Cresset from 2010; Rural Dean of Bridgnorth from 2009; Dioc Syn from 2000–06, from 2009; Dioc Brd Fin from 1999 (Exec M 2007–10), Vice Chair Benefice Bldgs Cttee 2001–7, Chair Dioc Investment Cttee 2007–10
GS 2010– *Tel:* 01746 761573
email: s.h.cawdell@btinternet.com
Web: www.bridgnorth-anglican.org/
www.fulcrum-anglican.org

CHANDLER, Ven Ian Nigel, BD, AKC, CMTh
St Mark's House 46a Cambridge Road Ford Plymouth PL2 1PU [ARCHDEACON OF PLYMOUTH] *b* 1965 *educ* Bishopsgarth Sch Stockton-on-Tees; Stockton Sixth Form Coll; K Coll Lon; Chich Th Coll; *CV* C All SS Hove 1992–96; Dom Chapl to Bp of Chich 1996–2000; V St Rich Haywards Heath from 2000; RD Cuckfield from 2004; M Dioc Syn from 2000; M Dioc Fin Cttee from 2004; Adn of Plymouth from 2010 *Tel:* 01752 202401
email: archdeacon.of.plymouth@
exeter.anglican.org

CHAPMAN, Prof Mark David, MA, DipTh, DPhil
1 Church Close Cuddesdon Oxford OX44 9HD [OXFORD] *b* 1960 *educ* St Bartholomew's Sch, Newbury; Trin Coll Ox; Munich Univ; OMC; *CV* Sir Henry Stephenson Fellow, Univ Sheffield 1989–91; NSM Dorchester Team Ministry, 1994–99; Lect Systematic Th Ripon Coll Cuddesdon from 1992; Vice-Prin, Ripon Coll Cuddesdon from 2001; Visiting Prof, Oxford Brookes Univ from 2009; Rdr Modern Th, Ox Univ from 2008; NSM Assoc P Wheatley Team Ministry w spec respons Cuddesdon, Garsington & Horspath from 1999
GS 2010–
Tel: 01865 874310 01865 877405 07790 524494
Fax: 01865 874310
email: MChapman@ripon-cuddesdon.ac.uk

CHAPMAN, Mrs Mary Madeline, BA; CHARTERED DIR; DIP CIM
22 Addison Grove London W4 1ER [ARCHBISHOPS' COUNCIL] *b* 1949 *educ* Sutton High Sch; Univ Bristol; *CV* Marketing Exec, British Tourist Authority; Div Dir Nicholas Kiwi; Marketing Dir L'Oreal UK;Dir Biotherm; Dir Helena Rubenstein; Dir Personnel Operations and Management Development L'Oreal UK 1990–93; Chief Exec Investors in People 1993–98; Chief Exec CMI 1998–2008; M Coun Girls' Day School Trust from 2004; Non-exec Dir Royal Mint from 2008; Commissioner National Lottery from 2008; Chair Inst Customer Service from 2009; M Coun Brunel Univ from 2009; M Min Coun
Tel: 020 8994 4934 07919 415994
email: mary@marychapman.org

CHAPMAN, Revd Sarah Jean, Dip COT, GME
Bitterne Park Vicarage 7 Thorold Rd Southampton SO18 1HZ [WINCHESTER] *b* 1955 *educ* Cheltenham Ladies' Coll; Lon Coll of Occupational Therapy; SDMTS; *CV* C (NSM) Rogate w. Terwick and Trotton w. Chithurst, Chich 1989–94; C (NSM) Easebourne, Chich 1994–96; Dioc Lic to Officiate, Portsm 1996–97; NSM St Phil Cosham; V St Mary Magd Sheet, Portsm 1997–2002; V Bitterne Park, Winch from 2002; M Winch Dioc Healing and Wholeness Cttee 2003–05; Bp's Exam Chapl from 2003; M VRSC from 2006
GS 2003–05; 2005–10 *Tel:* 023 8055 1560
email: revsarah@sargil.co.uk

CHARING CROSS, Archdeacon of. See JACOB, Ven William Mungo

CHARMAN, Canon Jane Ellen Elizabeth, MA
4 The Sidings Downton Salisbury SP5 3QZ [SALISBURY] *b* 1960 *educ* Newtead Wood Sch, Orpington; St John's Coll Dur; Selwyn Coll Cam; Westcott House Th Coll; *CV* C, St George's Tuffley w St Margaret's Whaddon, Glouc, 1985–90; Chapl, Clare Coll Cam, 1990–95; R Duxford St Peter & V St Mary & St John Hinxton & St Mary Magdalene Ickleton, Ely, 1995–2004; Rural Dean Shelford Deanery, Ely, 2003–04; Dir Lrning for Discipleship and Ministry, Salisbury, from 2004; Dioc Rep South Central Regional Training Partnership Management Brd from 2006; Chair South Central Regional Training Partnership CMD Co-ord Grp from 2006; Chair South Central Regional Training Partnership Pioneer Ministry Co-ord Grp from 2008; M National CMD panel from 2009; M STETS Brd of Studies from 2009; Bp's Advisor for selection of candidates for ordination from 2012
GS 2010– *Tel:* 01725 512620 07814 899657
email: jane.charman@salisbury.anglican.org

CHARTRES, Rt Revd and Rt Hon Richard John Carew, KCVO, DD, FSA
The Old Deanery Dean's Court London EC4V 5AA [BISHOP OF LONDON] *b* 1947 *educ* Hertf Gr Sch; Trin Coll Cam; Cuddesdon Th Coll; Linc Th Coll; *CV* C St Andr Bedford 1973–75; Bp's Dom Chapl 1975–80; Chapl to Abp of Cant 1980–84; P-in-c St Steph w St Jo Westmr 1984–85; V 1986–92; DDO 1985–92; Prof Div Gresham Coll 1986–92; Six Preacher Cant Cathl 1991–96; Bp of Stepney 1992–95; Bp of Lon from 1995; Dean of HM Chapels Royal and PC 1996; Chair Ch Heritage Forum; Ch Commrs from 1999; M Centr Cttee CEC; M Jt Liaison Grp between CEC and Coun of Eur Catholic Bps' Confs; Chair Ch Buildings Cttee from 2003; Acting Chair Ch Commrs Bd from 1999; Chair Shrink the Footprint from 2004
GS 1995– *Tel:* 020 7248 6233
Fax: 020 7248 9721
email: bishop@londin.clara.co.uk

CHAVE, Preb Brian Philip, BA (OU)
The Vicarage Vowles Close Hereford HR4 0DF [HEREFORD] *b* 1951 *educ* Winslade Sch Ex; Seale-Hayne Agric Coll Devon; Trinity Coll Bris; *CV* C Cullompton w Kentisbeare and Blackborough, Ex 1984–87; TV Oakmoor Tm Min, Ex 1987–93; C for Agric, Heref 1993–96; Comms Officer and Bp's Staff Officer (Dom Chapl), Heref 1997–2001; TV W Heref Tm Min from 2001; Vc Pres Heref Dioc Syn and Chair Ho of C; M Bp's Coun; Chair Bd of Govs Whitecross High Sch, Heref
GS 2008– *Tel:* 01432 273086 (Office)
email: brianchave@btinternet.com

CHEESEMAN, Mr James Reginald,
25 Lambarde Drive Sevenoaks TN13 3HX [ROCHESTER] *b* 1934 *educ* Sevenoaks Sch; Coll of St Mark and St Jo; *CV* Supply Staff Kent Educ Cttee 1954–55; Asst Tchr Midfield Prim Sch 1957–68; Dep Hdmaster Edgebury Prim Sch 1968–69; Chair Ho of Laity Roch Dioc Syn 1976–79; M GS Bd of Educ 1981–91; Hdmaster Pet Hills' Sch Rotherhithe 1969–97; Co-Chair Sevenoaks Dny Syn 1976–96; Sec Sevenoaks Dny Syn; Trustee Guild of All So; Treas Qu Victoria Clergy Fund from 1991; Lay Chair Forward In Faith Roch; Chair Dioc Bd of Patronage; Sec Kent Cricket Bd
GS 1975– *Tel:* 01732 455718

CHEETHAM, Rt Revd Richard Ian, MA, PGCE, Cert Theol, PhD
Kingston Episcopal Area Office 620 Kingston Road Raynes Park SW20 8DN [AREA BISHOP OF KINGSTON; SOUTHWARK] *b* 1955 *educ* Kingston Gr Sch; Ch Ch Coll Ox; Ripon Coll Cuddesdon; King;' Coll London; *CV* C H Cross Fenham 1987–90; V St Aug of Cant Limbury, Luton 1990–99; RD Luton 1995–98; Adn of St Alb 1999–2002; Bp of Kingston from 2002; Co-Chair Nat Chr Muslim Forum 2010–12; Anglican President Nat Chr Muslim Forum, 2012 onwards; M Roehampton Univ Coun 2006–12; ex-Chair C of E Continuing Ministerial Devel; Chair S'wark Dioc Bd of Educ; Chair British Regional Committee of St George's College Jerusalem 2013 onwards; Hon Research Fellow, King's Coll London; President YMCA (London South West), Patron Fircroft Trust
Tel: 020 8545 2443
email: bishop.richard@southwark.anglican.org

CHELMSFORD, Bishop of. See COTTRELL, Rt Revd Stephen Geoffrey

CHELMSFORD, Dean of. See JUDD, Very Revd Peter Somerset Margesson

CHELTENHAM, Archdeacon of. See SPRINGETT, Ven Robert

CHESSUN, Rt Revd Christopher Thomas James, MA
Trinity House 4 Chapel Court Borough High Street London SE1 1HW *b* 1956 *educ* Hampton Gr Sch; Univ Coll Ox; Westcott Ho Cam; *CV* Asst C St Mich and AA Sandhurst 1983–87; Sen C St Mary Portsea 1987–99; Chapl and Min Can St Paul's Cathl 1989–93; R Stepney, St Dunstan and All SS 1993–2001; AD Tower Hamlets 1997–2001; Adn of Northolt 2001–05; M Dioc Syn 2001–05; Bp of Woolwich 2005–11; Bp for Urban Life and Faith from 2010; Bp of S'wark from 2011
Tel: 020 7939 9420 (Office)
020 8769 3256 (Home)
Fax: 0843 2906 894
email: bishop.christopher@southwark.anglican.org

CHESTER, Revd Philip Anthony Edwin, LLB, Dip Th
St Matthew's House 20 Great Peter St London SW1P 2BU [LONDON] *b* 1955 *educ* Calday Grange; Birm Univ; St Jo Coll Dur; *CV* Asst P St Chad Shrewsbury 1980–85; Asst P St Martin-in-the-Fields Lon 1985–88; Chapl K Coll Lon 1988–95; PV Westmr Abbey from 1990; V St Matt Westmr from 1995
GS 2005–2010 *Tel:* 020 7222 3704
Fax: 020 7233 0255
email: office@stmw.org

CHESTER, Archdeacon of, see GILBERTSON, Ven Michael Robert

CHESTER, Bishop of. See FORSTER, Rt Revd Peter Robert

CHESTER, Dean of. See McPHATE, Very Revd Prof Gordon Ferguson

CHESTERFIELD, Archdeacon of. See WILSON, Ven Christine Louise

CHICHESTER, Archdeacon of. See McKITTRICK, Ven Douglas Henry

CHICHESTER, Bishop of. See WARNER, Rt Revd Martin Clive

CHICHESTER, Dean of. See FRAYLING, Very Revd Nicholas Arthur

CLACK, Mr Jeremy William James, MMATH, FIA
62 Whitemoor Road Kenilworth Warwickshire CV8 2BP [TRUSTEE MEMBER OF CHURCH OF ENGLAND PENSIONS BOARD] *b* 1981 *educ* King Edward VI Sch Southampton; Univ of Warwick; *CV* Actuarial consultant; Ch Commisioner from 2012: M C of E Pensions Bd from 2012 *Tel:* 07779 639381
email: jwjclack@gmail.com

CLARK, Rt Revd Jonathan Dunnett, BA, M Litt, MA
St Matthew's House 100 George Street Croydon Surrey CR0 1PE [AREA BISHOP OF CROYDON; SOUTHWARK] *b* 1961 *educ* Ex Univ; Bris Univ; Southn Univ; Trin Coll Bris; *CV* C Stanwix, Carl 1988–92; Chapl Bris Univ 1992–93; Dir of Studies S Diocs Minl Tr Scheme 1994–97; Chapl Lon Metrop Univ 1997–2003; Chapl Univ of N Lon 1997–2002; Chapl Lon Metrop Univ 2002–03; AD Islington 1999–2003; R St Mary Stoke Newington 2003–12; P-in-c Brownswood Park 2003–11; Area Bp Croydon from 2012
GS 2005–2010
Tel: 020 8256 9630 020 8686 1822
07968 845698 (Mobile)
Fax: 020 8256 9631
email: bishop.jonathan@southwark.anglican.org

CLARK, Revd Jonathan Jackson, MA
St George's Church Great George Street Leeds LS1 3BR [RIPON AND LEEDS] *b* 1957 *educ* St Peters Sch, York; Linc Coll, Ox; Ridley, Cam; *CV* C, St Lukes, Princess Drive, Liv 1984–87; C, St Johns and St Marks, Clacton-on-sea 1987–92; V, St Simon, Shepherds Bush, London 1993–2003; Area Dean, Hammersmith and Fulham 1996–2001; R St George's Leeds from 2003; Chair of St George's Crypt Trustees from 2005
GS 2010– *Tel:* 01132438498
email: jonathan.clark@stgeorgesleeds.org.uk

CLARKE, Very Revd John Martin, MA, BD
The Dean's Lodgings 25 The Liberty Wells BA5 2SZ [DEAN OF WELLS; BATH AND WELLS] *b* 1952 *educ* W Buckland Sch; Hertf Coll Ox; New Coll Edin; Edin Th Coll; *CV* C Ascen Kenton, Newc 1976–79; Prec St Ninian's Cathl, Perth 1979–82; Info Officer and Communications Adv to GS of Scottish Episcopal Ch 1982–87; Philip Usher Memorial Sch, Greece 1987–88; V St Mary Battersea 1989–96; Prin Ripon Coll Cuddesdon 1997–2004; Dean of Wells from 2004
Tel: 01749 670278
email: dean@wellscathedral.uk.net

CLARKE, Canon Prof Michael Gilbert, CBE, BA, MA, DLitt, DL
Millington House 15 Lansdowne Crescent Worcester WR3 8JE [WORCESTER] *b* 1944 *educ* Qu Eliz Gr Sch Wakef; Sussex Univ; *CV* Lect in Politics Edin Univ 1969–75; Dep Dir Policy Planning Lothian Regional Coun 1975–81; Dir Local Government Tr Bd 1981–90; Chief Exec Local Government Mgt Bd 1990–93; Hd of Sch of Public Policy Birm Univ 1993–98; Pro-Vc Chan Birm Univ from 1998, Vc-Prin 2003–08; Lay Can and Chapter Member Worc Cathl 2001–10; Canon Emeritus 2010; M Diocs Commn from 2008, Chair from 2011; M Panel of Chairs from 2009
GS 1990-93, 1995– *Tel:* 01905 617634
email: michael.clarkeinworcester@btinternet.com

CLEVELAND, Archdeacon of. See FERGUSON, Ven Paul John

COCHRANE, Revd Philip Andrew, BA
The Parish Office West Street Fareham PO16 0EL [PORTSMOUTH] *b* 1970 *educ* Coleraine Acd Insti; Reading Univ; Trin Coll Bris; *CV* Customer service & sales w Equitable Life & Clerical Medl, 1992–2001; Buckinghamshire County Councillor, 1997–2001; Pensions Consult & Head of Reward Consulting w Jardine Lloyd Thompson Benefit Solutions, 2002–2004; AC, Parish of Holy Trin w St Columba, Fareham 2007–09; Bp Portsm's Adv Porvoo, from 2008; TV Parish of Holy Trin w St Columba, Fareham from 2009; M Dioc Litt & Worship Adv Grp from 2008; M Dioc Syn from 2009; M Bp's Counc from 2010
GS 2010– *Tel:* 01329 318665
email: Philip@scfareham.org.uk

COCKETT, Ven Elwin Wesley, BA
86 Aldersbrook Rd Manor Park London E12 5DH [ARCHDEACON OF WEST HAM; CHELMSFORD] *b* 1959 *educ* St Paul's Cathl Choir Sch; Forest Sch, Snaresbrook; Aston Trg Scheme; Oak Hill Coll; *CV* C St Chad, Chadwell Heath 1991–94; C-in-c St Paul, Harold Hill 1994–95, P-in-c 1995–97, V 1997–2000; TR Billericay and Little Burstead TM 2000–07; RD Basildon 2004–07; Adn of West Ham from 2007; Club Chapl West Ham United Football Club 1992–2011 *Tel:* 020 8989 8557
Fax: 020 8530 1311
email: a.westham@chelmsford.anglican.org

COCKSWORTH, Rt Revd Dr Christopher John, BA (Hons), PhD, PGCE, Hon DD
Bishop's House 23 Davenport Rd Coventry CV5 6PW [BISHOP OF COVENTRY] *b* 1959 *educ* Forest Sch for boys, Horsham; Univ of Man; Didsbury Sch of Educ; St John's Coll, Nottm; *CV* Asst C Ch Ch Epsom 1988–92; Chapl Royal Holloway Univ of Lon 1992–96; Dir S Theol Educ and Training Scheme 1996–2001; Prin Ridley Hall Cam 2001–08; Bp Cov from 2008
GS 2008– *Tel:* 024 7667 2244
Fax: 024 7671 3271
email: bishcov@btconnect.com

COLCHESTER, Archdeacon of. See COOPER, Ven Annette Joy

COLCHESTER, Area Bishop of. See MORGAN, Rt Revd Christopher Heudebourck

COLES, Revd Stephen Richard, MA, BA
The Cardinal's Hat 25 Romilly Rd Finsbury Park London N4 2QY [LONDON] *b* 1949 *educ* Latymer Upper Sch Hammersmith; Univ Coll Ox; Trin Hall Cam; Leeds Univ; Coll of the Resurrection, Mirfield; *CV* C St Mary Stoke Newington 1981–84; Chapl K Coll Cam 1984–89; V St Thos Finsbury Park from 1989
GS 2000– *Tel:* 020 7359 5741
email: cardinal.jeoffry@btconnect.com

COLLARD, Mr Peter, B Sc
1 Hedben Drive Glossop Derbyshire SK13 8RS [DERBY] *b* 1951 *educ* Durham Chorister Sch; Durham Sch; Univ Edin; *CV* Bp's Coun Derby; Bd of Finance Derby; Parish Share Review Grp
Tel: 01457 861435
email: peter@glossop.org

COLLIER, Rt Worshipful Peter Neville, MA, QC
Leeds Crown Court The Courthouse 1 Oxford Row Leeds LS1 3BG [VICAR-GENERAL OF YORK] *b* 1948 *educ* Hymers Coll, Hull; Selw Coll Cam; *CV* Chan Wakef 1992–2006; Chan Linc 1998–2006; Lay Can, York Minster from 2001; Chair York Minster Coun from 2005; Chan York from 2006–; Sen Circuit Judge and Hon Recorder of Leeds from 2007; Legal Advisory Comm from 2008; V Gen Province of York from 2008
GS 2008– *Tel:* 0113 306 2800

COLLINS, Ven Gavin Andrew, MA; MA
Victoria Lodge 36 Osborn Road Fareham Hants [ARCHDEACON OF THE MEON; PORTSMOUTH] *b* 1966 *educ* Sackville Sch East Grinstead; Trinity Hall Camb; Coll Law Guildford; Trinity Coll Bristol; *CV* AC St Barnabas Cambridge1997–2002; V Christ Church Chorleywood 2002–11; RD Rickmansworth 2006–11; Hon Canon St Alb Cathl; 2009–11; Adn of the Meon from 2011
Tel: 01329 608895
email: gavin.collins@portsmouth.anglican.org

COMBES, Ven Roger Matthew, LLB
3 Danehurst Crescent Horsham RH13 5HS [ARCHDEACON OF HORSHAM; CHICHESTER] *b* 1947 *educ* Sherborne Sch; K Coll Lon; Ridley Hall Th Coll; *CV* C St Paul Onslow Sq Lon 1974–77; C H Trin Brompton Lon 1976–77; C H Sepulchre Cam 1977–86; R St Matt St Leonards-on-Sea 1986–2003; M Bp's Coun from 1998; RD Hastings 1998–2002; Adn of Horsham from 2003
GS 1995–2005 *Tel:* 01403 262710
email: archhorsham@diochi.org.uk

CONDICK, Mrs Margaret, B Sc, Cert Ed
34 Rectory Lane Kirton Ipswich IP10 0PY [ST EDMUNDSBURY AND IPSWICH] *b* 1944 *educ* Sutton High Sch GPDST; Manch Univ; *CV* Tchr of Physics, Stockport 1967–70; pt tchr of maths, Suffolk 1985–97; Communications Officer, Chs Together in Suffolk 1998–2000; County Ecum Officer for Suffolk 2000–09
GS 2003– *Tel:* 01394 448576
email: margaret.condick@btopenworld.com

CONDRY, Rt Revd Dr Edward Francis, BA, BLitt, DPhil, MBA, PGCE
White Lodge 22 Westbury Road Warminster Wilts BA12 0AW [SUFFRAGAN BISHOP OF RAMSBURY; SALISBURY] *b* 1953 *educ* Latymer Upper Sch Hammersmith; Univ of East Anglia; Exeter Coll, Ox; Univ of Nottm; Lincoln Theol Coll; OU; *CV* Asst C Weston Favell, Peterb 1982–85; V Bloxham, Milcombe and South Newington, Oxford 1985–1993; TR, Rugby TM, Coventry 1993–2002; Can Res Cant Cathl 2002–12; Can Librarian 2002–3; Dir CME Cant Dioc 2002–07; Can Librarian and Dir of Education 2006–12; Bp of Ramsbury from 2012
email: bishop.ramsbury@salisbury.anglican.org

CONNER, Rt Revd David John, MA; KCVO
The Deanery Windsor Castle Windsor SL4 1NJ [DEAN OF WINDSOR] *b* 1947 *educ* Ex Coll Ox; St Steph Ho Th Coll; *CV* Hon C Summertown Ox 1971–76; Asst Chapl St Edw Sch Ox 1971–73; Chapl 1973–80; TV Wolvercote w Summertown 1976–80; Chapl Win Coll 1980–87; V Gt St Mary w

WHO'S WHO

St Mich Cam 1987–94; RD Cam 1989–94; Bp of Lynn 1994–98; Dean of Windsor from 1998; Bp to HM Forces 2001–09 *Tel:* 01753 865561
Fax: 01753 819002
email: david.conner@stgeorges-windsor.org

CONWAY, Rt Revd Stephen David, MA, MA
Bishop's Croft Winterbourne Earls Salisbury SP4 6HJ [BISHOP OF ELY] *b* 1957 *educ* Abp Tenison's Gr Sch Lon; Keble Coll Ox; Selw Coll Cam; Westcott Ho; *CV* C St Mary Heworth 1986–89; C St Mich and AA Bishopwearmouth 1989–90; DDO 1989–94; Hon C St Marg Dur 1990–94; P-in-c then V St Mary Cockerton 1994–98; Sen Chapl to Bp of Dur and Dioc Communications Officer 1998–2002; Adn of Dur and Can Res Dur Cathl 2002–06; Area Bp of Ramsbury from 2006; M Bps' Insp of Th Colls and Courses 1997–2006; Chair of Mental Health Matters from 2004–2010; GS 1995–2000; Chair Dioc Learning, Discipleship and Min Coun from 2006; Warden of Lay Mins from 2006–2010; Trustee Affirming Catholicism 2001–08, Vc-Pres from 2008; Anglican Bishop for L'Arche from 2010; Bp of Ely from 2010
GS 1995–2000 *Tel:* 01380 729808
Fax: 01380 738096
email: sramsbury@salisbury.anglican.org

COOK, Revd Canon James Christopher Donald, MA (Oxon)
St Agne's Vicarage 1 Buckingham Avenue Liverpool L17 3BA [LIVERPOOL] *b* 1949 *educ* Bournemouth Sch; Ch Ch Ox; St Stephen's House Th Coll; *CV* Regimental Officer, 5th Royal Inniskilling Dragoon Guards, 1973–78; Asst C Witney, Oxon, 1980–83; Chapl to the Forces, 1983–2004; P-in-C, St Agnes & St Pancras, Toxteth Park, Liv, 2004–06; V, St Agnes & St Pancras, Toxteth Park, Liv from 2006
GS 2010– *Tel:* 0151 733 1742
email: leoclericus@aol.com

COOK, Revd John Richard Millward, BA
The Vicarage Station Road, Wargrave Reading Berkshire RG10 8EU [OXFORD] *b* 1961 *educ* Repton Sch; St Jo Coll Dur; Wycliffe Hall Th Coll; *CV* C St Peter's Farnborough 1989–92; C and Dir of Tr All Souls, Langham Place, London 1992–98; V of St John w St Andrew, Chelsea 1998–2008; V of St Mary, Wargrave w St Peter's, Knowl Hill, Ox Dico, from 2008
GS 1995–2007; 2010–
Tel: 01189402202 01189402300
Fax: 01189401470
email: johnrmcook@btconnect.com

COOPER, Ven Annette Joy, BA, CQSW, Dip RS
63 Powers Hall End Witham CM8 1NH [ARCHDEACON OF COLCHESTER; CHELMSFORD] *b* 1953 *educ* Lilley and Stone Newark Girls High Sch; Open Univ; Lon Univ Extra-mural Dept; S'wark Ord Course; *CV* Local Auth Social Worker; Asst Chapl Tunbridge Wells Health Auth 1988–91; NSM Dn St Pet Pembury 1988; Chapl Bassetlaw Hosp and Community Services NHS Trust 1991–96; Chapl to Center Parcs Sherwood Village 1996–99; Chapl to S'well Dioc MU 1996–99; P-in-c Edwinstowe 1996–2004; AD Worksop 1999–2004; Hon Can S'well Minster 2002–04; M Dioc Bd of Educ 1994–97; M Bp's Coun from 1999; Vc-Pres/Chair Dioc Ho of Clergy 2001–04; M GS Panel of Chairmen 2003–04, 2006–11; M Discipline Commn from 2003; Adn of Colchester from 2004; M Nat Stewardship Cttee from 2007; Dir Allchurches Trust from 2008' M Appts Ctte from 2011; M Abps' Coun Finance Ctte from 2011' M Clergy Discipline (Amendment) Measure Steering Ctte from 2011
GS 2000–2004; 2005–2010; 2010–
Tel: 01376 513130
Fax: 01376 500789
email: a.colchester@chelmsford.anglican.org

COOPER, Ms Susan Margaret, B Sc, FIA, DPS, FCAA
28 Headstone Lane Harrow HA2 6HG [LONDON] *b* 1947 *educ* Harrow Weald Co Gr Sch; Univ Coll of Wales Aberystwyth; Birm Univ; *CV* Legal and Gen Assurance Soc 1969–80; Corporate Business Actuary BUPA 1980–90; Consultant Actuary 1992–2002; Consulting Actuary, GAD 2002–12; Rdr St Jo Bapt Pinner from 1995; M Strg Cttee for Draft Stipends (Cessation of Special Payments) Measure 2003–04; M Br Regional Cttee St Geo Coll Jerusalem from 2003; Hon Sec CHRISM f2006–07, Hon Treas 2008–09; M Strg Ctee for Draft C of E Pensions (Amendment) Measure 2007–08; Appts Ctte from 2011; Ho of Laity Standing Cttee from 2011; Audit Cttee from 2011; Dir Bd of Reference for Healthrow Multifaith Chaplaincy
GS 2000– *Tel:* 020 8863 2094 (Home)
07780 708478
email: scooper@hedstone.demon.co.uk

CORNWALL, Archdeacon of, [NOT APPOINTED AT TIME OF GOING TO PRESS]

CORTEEN, Mrs Christine,
21 Hillside Road Wool Wareham Dorset BH20 6DY [SALISBURY] *b* 1956 *educ* Merchant Taylors' Sch, Liv; Liv Univ; *CV* Local Government Off from 1977; Income and Payments Man, Poole Borough Counc from 1990; Counc Miss, Sarum; St Aldhelm's Miss Fund, Sarum; Learning for Discipleship and Ministry, Sarum
GS 2010– *Tel:* 01929462642
email: c.corteen@poole.gov.uk

COTTON, Canon Robert Lloyd, MA, Dip Th
Holy Trinity Rectory 9 Eastgate Gardens Guildford GU1 4AZ [GUILDFORD] *b* 1958 *educ* Uppingham; Merton Coll Ox; Westcott Ho Cam; *CV* C St Mary Bromley 1983-85; C Bisley & W End 1987–89; P-in-c St Paul E Molesey 1989–96; Prin Guildf

Dioc Min Course 1989–96; R H Trin & St Mary Guildf from 1996; Chair Ho of Clergy 2004–11; Can Dioc of Highveld, S Africa from 2006; Can Guildford Cathl from 2010; Abp's Coun from 2010
GS 2004– *Tel:* 01483 575489 07710 757248
email: rector@holytrinityguildford.org.uk
Web: www.holytrinityguildford.org.uk/blog

COTTRELL, Rt Revd Stephen Geoffrey, BA
Bishopscourt Main Rd Margaretting Ingatestone Essex CM4 0HD [BISHOP OF CHELMSFORD] *b* 1958 *educ* Belfairs High Sch for Boys; Poly of Central Lon; St Steph Ho; *CV* C Ch Ch & St Paul Forest Hill, S'wark 1984–88; P-in-c St Wilf Parklands, Chich and Asst Dir of Pastl Studies, Chich Th Coll 1988–93; Dioc Missr, Wakef 1993–98; Springboard Missr 1998–2001; Can Pastor Peterb Cathl 2001–04; Bp of Reading 2004–10; Bp of Chelmsford from 2010
GS 2010– *Tel:* 01277 352001
Fax: 01277 355374
email: bishopscourt@chelmsford.anglican.org

COVENTRY, Archdeacon Missioner of. See RODHAM, Ven Morris

COVENTRY, Bishop of. See COCKSWORTH, Rt Revd Dr Christopher John

COVENTRY, Dean of. See WITCOMBE, Very Revd John Julian

COX, Revd Alison, BTh, MHort
St Mark's Vicarage 2 Church Square Railway Street Dukinfield SK16 4PX [CHESTER] *b* 1963 *educ* Westville Girls' Sch; Weymouth Gr Sch; Pershore Coll Horticulture; Ripon Coll Cuddesdon; *CV* Asst Garden Centre mgr; Journalist; C St Mary's & St Nicolas, Spalding 2003–07; P-in-c St Mark's Dukinfield from 2007
GS 2010– *Tel:* 0161 330 2783
email: alisoncox19@hotmail.com

COX, Canon Simon John, MA, MA, BSc, PhD
All Hallows Rectory 86 All Hallows Rd Bispham Blackpool FY2 0AY [BLACKBURN] *b* 1953 *educ* Roxeth Manor CSM, South Harrow; Montgomery of Alamein CSM Sch Winchester; Eastleigh Tech Coll; Q Mary Coll London; Univ Liverpool; Ridley Hall Cam; Selwyn Coll Cam; Univ Lancaster; *CV* C Livesey St Andrew 1982–85; C Cheadle Hulme St Andrew i/c Emmanuel 1985–89; V Disley St Mary 1989–94; R Bispham All Hallows from 1994; P-in-C Blackpool South Shore St Peter 2005–07; AD Blackpool from 2004; Hon Can Blackburn from 2008; Vc Chair Dioc Ho of Clergy; M Bp's Coun; Bd Finance Exec, Pastl & Miss Comm; Property Commn; Chair Dioc Patronage Bd; Vc Chair DEF; Moderatur Blackpool Churches Together; Chapl TS Penelope Sea Cadet Unit; District Chapl Sea Cadets
GS 2002–2005, 2009– *Tel and Fax:* 01253 351886
email: Drsjcox@yahoo.co.uk

COX, Cllr Timothy Daniel, HND (Computing), B Sc (Computing, Lancs), CCNA 1–3
16 Convent Crescent Blackpool FY3 7QF [BLACKBURN] *b* 1980 *educ* Poynton High Sch; Montgomery High Sch Blackpool; Blackpool Sixth Form Coll; Man Metropolitan Univ; Blackpool and Fylde Coll; Lancaster Univ; UCLAN; *CV* Costing draughtsman 2001–04; Blackpool Unitary Authority Cllr from 2007; Co Ditr Blackpool Coastal Housing from 2007; Vc-Chair SACRE from 2007; Vc-Chair Business, Culture and Communities Overview and Scrutiny Cttee from 2007; Religious Diversity Champion Blackpool Coun from 2008; Database Support (Lancs County Coun) from 2008; Officer and Battalion Treas Boys' Brigade; Literacy Gov Anchorsholme Primary Sch 2004–07; Gov Bispham Endowed C of E Primary Sch from 2007; Gov Montgomery Language Coll from 2007; Lay Communion Asst; Co Dir and Charity Trustee; M Bp's Coun
GS 2000–2010 *Tel:* 01253 535000
0161 397007
07747 794903 (Mobile)
email: tim@asmine.com

CRAVEN, Prof John Anthony George, MA Cantab, Hon D Sc
Fyning Cross Rogate Petersfield GU31 5EF [APPOINTED MEMBER, ARCHBISHOPS' COUNCIL] *b* 1949 *educ* Pinner Gr Sch; K Coll Cam; Kennedy Memorial Scholar, Massachusetts Inst of Tech; *CV* Univ of Kent (Cant) Lect in Mathematical Economics 1971, Sen Lect 1976; Reader in Economics 1980, Prof of Economics 1986; elected Dean of Social Sciences 1987, re-elected 1990; Pro Vc-Chan 1991, Dep Vc-Chan 1993; Vc-Chan Univ of Ports from 1997; 1977–96 in Cant Dioc, at various times M and Treas Eastry PCC, M Dny and Dioc Syns, M CUF Dioc Cttee, Chair St Mart Trust for Homeless in Deal and Dover; in Ports Dioc, Foundn Gov St Luke's C of E Vol Aided Sch from 2002, Chair from 2003; M Ports Cathl Coun from 2003; Lay Can Ports Cathl from 2006; Gov S Kent Coll of FE 1991–96; Gov Highbury Coll of FE 1997–2002
GS 2006– *Tel:* 01730 821392 (Home)
023 9284 3190 (Office)
Fax: 023 9284 3400
email: john.craven@port.ac.uk

CRAVEN, Archdeacon of. See SLATER, Ven Paul John

CRAY, Rt Revd Graham Alan, BA
The Rectory Church Road Harrietsham Maidstone Kent ME17 1AP [ARCHBISHOPS' MISSIONER] *b* 1947 *educ* Trinity Sch of John Whitgift, Croydon; Leeds Univ; St Jo Coll Nottm; *CV* C St Mark Gillingham, Roch 1971–75; N Co-ord Ch Pastl Aid Soc 1975–78; V St Mich-le-Belfrey 1978–92; Prin Ridley Hall Cam 1992–2000; Six Prchr of Cant Cathl 1997–2002; Bp of Maidstone 2001–2009; Arch-

bishops' Missioner from 2009; Leader Fresh Expressions Tm; Assistant Bp Cant Dioc; Assistant Bp York Dioc; Assistant Bp Roch Dioc
GS 1985–92 *Tel:* 01622 851170
email: graham.cray@freshexpressions.org.uk
Web: www.freshexpressions.org.uk

CREDITON, Suffragan Bishop of. See McKINNEL, Rt Revd Nicholas Howard Paul

CROFT, Rt Revd Dr Steven John Lindsey,
Bishopscroft Snaithing Lane Sheffield S10 3LG [BISHOP OF SHEFFIELD] *b* 1957 *educ* Heath Sch Halifax; Worc Coll Ox; Cranmer Hall, St Jo Coll Dur; *CV* C St Andrew Enfield 1983–1987; V St George's Ovenden 1987–1996; Warden Cranmer Hall 1996–2004; Abps' Missioner and Team Ldr of Fresh Expressions 2004–09; Bp of Sheffield from 2009; Abps' Counc from 2011; House of Bps' Standing Ctte from 2011; Min Coun form 2011
Tel: 0114 230170
Fax: 0114 2630110
email: bishop@sheffield.anglican.org

CROFT, Canon William Stuart, MA, BA, MTh
315 Thorpe Road Longthorpe Peterborough PE3 6LU [PETERBOROUGH] *b* 1953 *educ* King Edward VI Sch; Trin Hall, Cam; King's Coll Lon; Ripon Col lCuddesdon; *CV* AC, St James Friern Barnet 1981–83; Tutor Chich Th Coll 1983–92; V, St Margaret of Antioch Fernhurst 1992 -98; Prec Peterb Cathl 1998–2004; Dioc Dir Ord, Peterb, 1998–2002; P-in-C, St Botolph's, Longthorpe, Peterb from 2004; M Joint Implementation Comm Ang Meth Covenant from 2003
GS 2010– *Tel:* 01733 263016
email: williamsbill_croft@hotmail.com

CROW, Mr Timothy, LLB
Legal Office Church House Great Smith St London SW1P 3AZ [DEPUTY OFFICIAL SOLICITOR TO THE CHURCH COMMISSIONERS] *b* 1954 *educ* Barnard Castle Sch; Mid-Essex Technical Coll and Sch of Art; *CV* Solicitor in private practice, Sussex 1979–95; Official Solicitor's Dept, Church Commissioners 1995–2000; Legal Office of the NCIs from 2000; Deputy Official Solicitor to the Church Commissioners from 2000 *Tel:* 020 7898 1717
email: tim.crow@churchofengland.org

CROYDON, Archdeacon of [NOT APPOINTED AT TIME OF GOING TO PRESS]

CROYDON, Area Bishop of. See CLARK, Rt Revd Jonathan Dunnett

CUMBERLAND, Archdeacon of West. See HILL, Ven Colin

CUNLIFFE, Ven Dr Christopher John, MA, D Phil, MA, A R Hist S
Derby Church House Full St Derby DE1 3DR [ARCHDEACON OF DERBY] *b* 1955 *educ* Charterhouse; Ch Ch Ox; Trin Coll Cam; Westcott Ho Cam; *CV* C Chesterfield Par Ch 1983–85; Chapl and Jun Rsch Fell, Linc Coll Ox 1985–89; Chapl City Univ and Guildhall Sch of Music and Drama 1989–91; Selection Sec and Voc Officer, Adv Bd of Min 1991–96; Bp of Lon's Adv for Ord Min 1996–2003; Clerk, All SS Educ Trust 2004; Chapl to Bp of Bradwell 2004–06; Adn of Derby from 2006; Chair Derby Dioc Communications Cttee; Can Res Derby Cathl 2006–08 *Tel:* 01332 388676
Fax: 01332 292969
email: archderby@derby.anglican.org

CURRAN, Ven Patrick Martin Stanley, BA, B Th
British Embassy Jauresgasse 12 Vienna 1030 Austria [ARCHDEACON OF THE EASTERN ARCHDEACONRY; EUROPE] *b* 1956 *educ* Ostsee Gymnasium, Timmendorfer Strand, Germany; Univ of K Coll Halifax, Nova Scotia, Canada; Southampton Univ; Chich Th Coll; *CV* C Heavitree with Ex St Paul Ex 1984–87; Bp's Chapl to Students, Bradf 1987–93; Chapl Bonn with Cologne, Eur 1993–2000; Can Malta Cathl 2000; Chapl Ch Ch Vienna from 2000; Adn of the Eastern Archdeaconry from 2002
Tel: 00 43 1 7148900 00 43 1 7185902
Fax: 00 43 1 7148900
email: office@christchurchvienna.org

CURRIE, Canon Stuart William, MA, PGCE
St Stephen's Vicarage 1 Beech Avenue Worcester WR3 8PZ [WORCESTER] *b* 1953 *educ* Boteler Gr Sch, Warrington; Hertford Coll Ox; Univ Coll Dur; Fitzwilliam Coll Cam; Westcott Ho; *CV* C Ch Ch Reading 1985–89; V in Banbury TM 1989–94; V Barbourne St Stephen from 1994; Chair Worc Dioc Ho of Clergy; Chair Worc DBE
GS 2008– *Tel:* 01905 452169
email: sw.currie@virgin.net

CUTTING, Revd Alastair Murray, B Ed, MA, L Th, DPS
Henfield Vicarage Church Lane Henfield BN5 9NY [CHICHESTER] *b* 1960 *educ* Geo Watson's Coll Edin; Lushington Sch Ooty, S India; Watford Boy's Gr Sch; Westhill Coll Birm; St Jo Coll Nottm; Heythrop Coll Lon; *CV* C All SS Woodlands, Sheff 1987–88; C Wadsley, Sheff 1989–91; Chapl to Nave and Town Cen, Uxbridge, Lon 1991–96; V Copthorne, Chich 1996–2010; V Henfield, R Sharmanbury and Woodmancote from 2010; M Bp's Coun from 1998; Asst RD E Grinstead 2002–10; Chair Ho of Clergy Chich from 2009; Pro-Prolocutor Prov Cant from 2011
GS 2005– *Tel:* 01273 492017 (Home)
01273 495532 (Office)
07736 676106 (Mobile)
email: acutting@mac.com

DAILEY, Miss Prudence Mary Prior, MA
15 Northfield Rd Headington Oxford OX3 9EW [OXFORD] *b* 1965 *educ* Simon Langton Gr Sch for

Girls Cant; K Sch Cant; Mert Coll Ox; *CV* NHS Gen Mgt Trainee and various admin posts in NHS 1988–97; Ox City Coun 1992–96; Sen Business Systems Analyst, Toys 'R' Us 1998–2009; Chairman Prayer Book Soc
GS 2000– *Tel:* 01865 766023
07730 516620 (Mobile)
email: prudence.dailey@tiscali.co.uk
2nd email: prudence.dailey@gmail.com

DAKIN, Rt Revd Timothy John, BA, MTh
Wolvesey Winchester SO23 9ND [BISHOP OF WINCHESTER] *b* 1958 *educ* Priory Sch Shrewsbury; St Mary's Sch Nairobi; Henley Sixth Form Coll; St Mark's and St Jo Coll Plymouth; K Coll Lon; Ch Ch Ox; Carlile Coll Nairobi ; *CV* Prin Carlile Coll, Nairobi 1993–2000; Hon C Nairobi Cathedral 1994–2000; Gen Sec CMS 2000–11; Can Theol Cov Cathl 2001–11; Assoc P St James Ruscombe & St Mary's Twyford 2000–11; M MPA Coun; M PWM Panel, Bp of Winchester from 2011
GS 2005– *Tel:* 01962 854050
Fax: 01962 897088
email: bishop.tim@winchester.anglican.org
Web: www.winchester.anglican.org

DALES, Mr Martin Paul,
Priory Cottage Old Malton YO17 7HB [YORK] *b* 1955 *educ* St Dunstan's Coll; Bretton Hall; Open Univ; *CV* Dep Hd, Housemaster and Dir of Music various schs 1976–94; Freelance musician, tchr and composer from 1994; Organist and Choirmaster from 1976, All Saints, Thornton-le-Dale from 2007; freelance broadcaster from 1976, BBC Radio York from 1994; music publisher from 1981; Media Relations Officer RSCM NE Yorks Area (Sec 2000–02); media and PR Adv various inc FindClaudia.co.uk and DontDrainUs.org; Coun Malton Town Coun 1989–99, 2003– (Mayor 1991–92, 1996–97); Secretary, Ryedale Cameras in Action; Chairman Amotherby Sch Govs; M Dioc Syn from 1995; M Coun for Min and Trg 1998–2000; past M Abp's Coun; M Revision Cttee Draft Amending Canon No 22; past M Appts Cttee; past M Ho of Laity Stg Cttee; M CCU; past M CMEAC; past M CTE Forum and CTBI Assembly; past Chair Chs Together in S Ryedale; M EKD Delegation 2005;
GS 1995– *Tel:* 01653 600990
07764 985009 (Mobile)
Fax: 01653 600990
email: mpd@martindales.me.uk

DALLISTON, Very Revd Christopher Charles, MA
The Deanery 26 Mitchell Avenue Newcastle upon Tyne NE2 3LA [DEAN OF NEWCASTLE] *b* 1956 *educ* Diss Gr Sch; Peterhouse Cam; St Steph Ho Ox; *CV* C St Andr Halsead w H Trin and Greenstead Green 1984–87; Dom Chapl to Bp of Chelms 1987–91; V St Edm Forest Gate, Chelms 1991–95; V St Botolp w St Chris Boston 1995–2003; Dean of Newcastle from 2003 *Tel:* 0191 281 6554
0191 232 1939
email: dean@stnicnewcastle.co.uk

DALLOW, Revd Gillian Margaret, BA, M Ed, PGCE, CEM
26 Baron's Court Road Penylan Cardiff HCF23 9DF [SYNODICAL SECRETARY, CONVOCATION OF CANTERBURY] *b* 1945 *educ* Cathays High Sch Cardiff; Univ of N Wales Bangor; Bris Univ; Oak Hill Th Coll; W of Eng Univ; *CV* Tchr Mill St Sec Mod Sch Pontypridd 1968–70; Hd of RE Heref High Sch for Girls 1970–73; Hd of RE and Student Counselling Heref Sixth Form Coll 1973–74; Scripture Union Schs Worker S West and Wales 1974–79; Hd of RE Colston's Girls Sch Bris 1979–85; Dioc Educ Adv B & W 1985–91; Dir Tr Lon Bible Coll 1991–98; Adv for Children's Min and P-in-c St Giles Barlestone from 1999; Dioc Dir Under 25s Trg from 2002; Synodical Sec, Conv of Cant from 2006; M C of E Evang Coun from 2006; Sec Eggs (Evangs on GS) from 2009; Perm to Officiate: Dioc of Lon and Dioc of Llandaff; Chapl to Welsh Assembly Government from 2009; Assoc P St Mark's Gabalfa and St Philip's Community Ch Tremorfa Cardiff
GS 2000–05
Tel: 0292 0463754 07801 650187 (Mobile)
email: g.dallow@btinternet.com

DAVENPORT, Miss Laura Elizabeth, BA, MA
8 Ashfield Avenue Union Mills Isle of Man IM4 4LN [SODOR AND MAN] *b* 1988 *educ* Queen Elizabeth II High Sch, Isle of Man; Cam Univ; Dur Univ; *CV* Dioc Yth Adv, from 2010; Yth Lder, Braddan Ch, from 2010; Business Analyst, Barclays Wealth from 2010; Dioc Comm Forum, from 2010
GS 2010– *Tel:* 01624852167 07624467232
email: laura.elizabeth.davenport@gmail.com

DAVIES, Mr John, PSC, MBIFM, MCIM
Vicarage Cottages Baughurst Road Ramsdell Tadley RG26 5SH [WINCHESTER] *b* 1951 *educ* King Edward's Sch; RMA; Army Staff Coll; *CV* Regular Army 1969–89; Various commercial appointments 1989–2001; Managing Dir Park Row Consultancy Ltd; Lay Chair Basingstoke Deanery from 2008; Bp's Counc Winc since 2009; Fin Cttee Winc 2006–09
GS 2005– *Tel:* 01256 851309
email: johndavies@parkrow.fsnet.co.uk

DAVIES, Very Revd Dr John Harverd, MA, M Phil, PhD
Derby Cathedral Centre 18–19 Iron Gate Derby DE1 3GP [DEAN OF DERBY] *b* 1957 *educ* Brentwood Sch; Keble Coll Ox; Corpus Christi Coll Cam; Lancaster Univ; Westcott Ho; *CV* C Liv Par Ch 1984–87; C Peterb Par Ch and Minor Can Peterb Cathl

WHO'S WHO

1987–90; V St Marg Anfield, Liv 1990–94; Chapl, Fell and Dir of Studies in Theol, Keble Coll Ox 1994–99; V Melbourne and DDO Derby Dioc 1999–2009; Dean of Derby from 2010; M Derby Dioc Bd for Min; M Dioc Syn; M GS Theol Educ and Trg Cttee 2006–07; Chair Industrial Miss in Derbyshire from 2009 *Tel:* 01332 341201
Fax: 01332 203991
email: dean@derbycathedral.org

DAVIES, Rt Revd Mark, BA, Cert PS
The Hollies Manchester Rd Rochdale OL11 3QY [SUFFRAGAN BISHOP OF MIDDLETON; MANCHESTER] *b* 1962 *educ* Hanley High Sch; Stoke-on-Trent Sixth Form Coll; Univ Coll of Ripon and York St Jo; Mirfield Th Coll; *CV* C St Mary Barnsley 1989–92; P-in-c St Paul Old Town Barnsley 1992–95; R Hemsworth from 1995; Asst DDO from 1998; RD Pontefract from 2000; Hon Can Wakef Cathl 2002–06; Adn of Rochdale 2006–08; Bp of Middleton from 2008
GS 2000–06 *Tel:* 01706 358550
email: bishopmark@manchester.anglican.org

DAVIES, Revd Nigel Lawrence, BEd
St Oswald's Vicarage Burneside Kendal Cumbria LA9 6QX [CARLISLE] *b* 1955 *educ* Black Bull Lane Sch; Hutton Gr Sch; St Martin's Coll, Lancaster; Salis and Wells Th Coll; *CV* Dn 1987; P 1988; C St Luke w All Souls, Heywood, Man 1987–91; V Burneside, 1991–07; Tutor Past Studies CBDTI 1992–98; Editor Dioc News 1999–2002; Rural Dean Kendal 2003–08; P-in-C Crosscrake 2004–06; P-in-C Skelsmergh w Selside and Longsleddale, 2006–07; Hon Canon Carlisle Cathl from 06; TR, Beacon Team. Kendal Deanery, Dioc Carlisle from 2007
GS 2009– *Tel:* 01539 722015
email: canon.nigel@beaconteam.org.uk

DAVIES, Ven Tony (Vincent Anthony), FRSA
St Matthew's House 100 George St Croydon CR0 1PJ [ARCHDEACON OF CROYDON; SOUTHWARK] *b* 1946 *educ* Green Lane Sec Mod Sch Leic; Brasted Th Coll; St Mich Coll Llan; *CV* C St Jas Owton Manor Hartlepool 1973–76; C St Faith Wandsworth 1976–78, V 1978–81; V St Jo Walworth 1981–93; RD S'wark and Newington 1988–93; Adn of Croydon from 1994; Bp's Adv for Healthcare Chapl from 2000 *Tel:* 020 8688 2943 (Home)
020 8256 9630 (Office)
Fax: 020 8256 9631
email: tony.davies@southwark.anglican.org

DELAP, Revd Dana Lrkse, BA, MA, MATM, Dip SW
9 Wanless Terrace Durham DH1 1RU [NEWCASTLE] *b* 1965 *educ* Lancaster Girls' Gr Sch; St Jo Coll Dur; *CV* Pastl Asst St Pet Monkwearmouth 1997–99; Dioc Devel Officer for Common Worship 1998–2001; M Dioc Liturg Cttee; Liturg Commn 2001–11, Vice-chair 2009–11; substitute Chapl HMP Low Newton 2002–9; C Fenham St James & St Basil, Newcastle; M Newcastle Dioc Worship and Liturgy Task Grp
GS 2000–2010 *Tel:* 0191 384 3854
07952 096789 (Mobile)
email: Dana@delap.org.uk
Web: www.liturgy.org.uk

DERBY, Archdeacon of. See CUNLIFFE, Ven Dr Christopher John

DERBY, Bishop of. See REDFERN, Rt Revd Dr Alastair Llewellyn John

DERBY, Dean of. See DAVIES, Very Revd John Harverd

DOBBIE, Brigadier William Ian Cotter, OBE, BSc(Eng)
5 Richmond Court White Lodge Close Hitchen Hatch Lane, Sevenoaks Kent TN13 3BF [ROCHESTER] *b* 1939 *educ* Wellington Coll; Royal Military Acad Sandhurst; Royal Military Coll of Sc; Army Staff Coll; RAF Staff Coll; *CV* Reg Off 1958–1992; Dep Chief of Staff 3 Armoured Division 1986–88; Comd Engineer HQ BAOR 1988–92; Proj Dir and Adm St Nicholas, Sevenoaks 1992–95; Gen Sec Counc of Vol Welfare Work 1995; Chair Soldiers' and Airmens' Scrip Readers Assoc, 1991; Roch Dioc Bd Patronage
GS 2000–05; 2006–10; 2010– *Tel:* 01732465109
email: gensec@cvww.org.uk

DOBSON, Revd Christopher John, BA, MA
St John's Vicarage Mayfield Park Fishponds Bristol, BS16 3NW [BRISTOL] *b* 1962 *educ* Norwich Sch; Aberystwyth Univ; Wycliffe Hall Th Coll; *CV* Manager HMSO Dept, Norwich 1984–85; Youth Worker Shrewsbury House, Everton 1985–86; C, St Mark, Biggin Hill 1989–92; C, St James and St Philip, Tunbridge Wells 1992–95; R, Alls Souls, Mount Pleasant, Harare 1996–2000; V, St Andrew, Paddock Wood, 2000–08; Bp's Adv Links, Rochester 2004–08; Ecumen and Global Partnership Off Bris from 2008
GS 2010– *Tel:* 01179060105 07530821641
email: chris.dobson@bristoldiocese.org

DOCHERTY, Mrs Lucy Clare, BA
33 Southampton Road Fareham Hampshire PO16 7DZ [PORTSMOUTH] *b* 1955 *educ* Tavistock Sch; Nott Univ; *CV* Commercial Retail & marketing posts, 1977–83; Non-exec Dir & Chair NCT Publ Ltd, 1996–99; Lay Brd M Fareham Pri Care Grp, 1999–2002; Vice Chair National Assoc of Lay People in Pri Care, 2000–03; Chair Fareham & Gosport Pri Care Trust, 2002–06; Non exec Dir Hampshire Probation Trust from 2007; Elected Gov Portsmouth Hosp Foundn Trust from 2007; Chair Govrs 6th Form Coll from 2010; Counc M, Ch House from 2010; Chair House of Laity Ports from 2006; Chair Ports Counc Soc Respons from 2006; Exec M Churches Together in Hampshire,

2000–09; Chair Christians Together in Fareham, Member since 1996
GS 2007– *Tel:* 01329 233602
email: lucy@docherty1.co.uk

DOE, Rt Revd Michael David, BA, LLD (Hon)
405 West Carriage House Royal Carriage Mews Royal Arsenal Woolwich SE18 6GA [PREACHER, GRAY'S INN; HONORARY ASSISTANT BISHOP OF SOUTHWARK] *b* 1947 *educ* Brockenhurst Gr Sch; Dur Univ; Ripon Hall Th Coll; *CV* C St Pet St Helier 1972–76, Hon C 1976–81; Youth Sec BCC 1976–81; V Blackbird Leys LEP Ox 1981–89; RD Cowley 1987–89; Soc Resp Adv Portsm 1989–94; Can Res Portsm Cathl 1989–94; Bp of Swindon 1994–2004; Convenor CTE 1999–2003; Gen Sec USPG 2004–11; Assistant Bp S'wark from 2004; Preacher Hon Soc Gray's Inn from 2011
GS 1990–94, 2000–04 *Tel:* 020 3259 3841
email: michaeldd@btinternet.com
Web: www.graysinn.info/

DONCASTER, Archdeacon of. See WILCOCKSON, Ven Stephen Anthony

DONCASTER, Suffragan Bishop of, see BURROWS, Rt Revd Peter

DORBER, Very Revd Adrian John, BA, M Th
The Deanery 16 The Close Lichfield WS13 7LD [DEAN OF LICHFIELD] *b* 1952 *educ* St Jo Coll, Dur Univ; K Coll Lon; Westcott Ho Cam; *CV* C Easthampstead, Bracknell, Ox 1979–85; Dny Youth Officer 1982–85; P-in-c St Barn Emmer Green 1985–88; Chapl Portsm Poly 1988–92, Lect 1991–97, Sen Chapl, Public Orator Portsm Univ 1992–97; Hon Chapl Portsm Cathl 1992–97; P-in-c Brancepeth, Dur 1997–2001; Dir Min and Trg 1997–2005; Hon Can Dur Cathl 1997–2005; Dean of Lichfield from 2005; M Dioc Syn and Bp's Coun; M Ch Leaders' Oversight Grp, W Midlands Regional Trg Partnership; Trustee Found for Ch Leadership; M Exec Ctte Assoc English Cathls; Chair Cathedrals Research Project; Chair of Governors, Lichfield Cathl Sch
Tel: 01543 306294 (Home)
01543 306250 (Office)
Fax: 01543 306109
email: adrian.dorber@lichfield-cathedral.org
2nd email: bernice.alexander@lichfield-cathedral.org
Web: www.lichfield-cathedral.org

DORCHESTER, Area Bishop of. See FLETCHER, Rt Revd Colin William

DORKING, Archdeacon of. See HENDERSON, Ven Julian Tudor

DORKING, Suffragan Bishop of. See BRACKLEY, Rt Revd Ian James

DORMOR, Revd Duncan James, MA, MSc, BA
St John's College Cambridge CB2 1TP [UNIVERSITIES, CAMBRIDGE] *b* 1967 *educ* Sherborne Sch; Magd Coll Ox; Lon Sch of Hygiene and Tropical Medicine; Ripon Coll Cuddesdon; *CV* C Wolverhampton Cen Par, Lich 1995–98; Chapl, St Jo Coll Cam 1998–2002, Dean and Fell from 2002; affiliated lect, Faculty of Div, Cam Univ from 2004; M Coun of Westcott Ho from 2006; M MPA Coun from 2011; Pres, St Jo Coll Cam from 2011; English ARC from 2012
GS 2005– *Tel:* 01223 338633
email: djd28@cam.ac.uk

DORSET, Archdeacon of. See WAINE, Ven Stephen

DOTCHIN, Revd Andrew Steward, Dip Th (Hons), PG Pstl Th
Whitton Rectory 176 Fircroft Road Ipswich IP1 6PS [ST EDMUNDSBURY AND IPSWICH] *b* 1956 *educ* Royal Hosp Sch, Ipswich; Witwatersrand Technikon, Johannesburg; FedTheo Seminary, Imbali; Anglia Ruskin Univ; *CV* C and P-in-C, Parish of Standerton with Evander, Jo'burg 1985–87; Asst P St Martin's in the Veld, Rosebank, Jo'Burg 1987–88; R St John the Divine, Belgravia Jo'burg, 1989–94; Chapl St Martin's School, Rosettenville, Christ the King 1994–2000; TV: Blyth Valley Team Ministry, Dioc St E&I 2000–04; Editor Third Order Chronicle, Euro Province Third Order Soc St Francis, 2003–10; M House of Clergy, Syn Anglican C of SA 1980–2000; M Prov Elective Assembly Cttee of ACSA, 1993–2000; M ACSA Pub Cttee, 1998–2000; M Exee Cttee SU Independent Sch, 1997–2000; M Dioc HIV/AIDS Cttee, Dioc Jo'burg, 1990–94; R Parish of Whitton w Thurleston and Akenham, Dioc St E&I from 2004; M Dioc Syn from 2002; M Board of Education, Dioc St E&I 2006–present; M Dioc Board of Patronage, Dioc St E&I 2006–present; M Vacncy in See Committee, Dioc St E&I 2006–present; Dioc Chapl MU Dioc St E&I 2010–present; Chapl 188 (Ipswich) Squadron Air Training Corps, 2005–present
GS 2010– *Tel:* 01473 741 389 07814 949828
email: andrew.dotchin@ntlworld.com

DOVER, Bishop of. See WILLMOTT, Rt Revd Trevor

DOWN, Ven Philip Roy, MA, M Th, ARMIT, CCPE
The Archdeaconry Pett Lane Charing Ashford TN27 0DL [ARCHDEACON OF ASHFORD; CANTERBURY] *b* 1953 *educ* Lakeside and Watsonia High Sch, Victoria, Australia; R Melbourne Inst of Tech; Melbourne Coll of Div; Hull Univ; *CV* Parish P Brighton, Victoria (Uniting Ch in Australia) 1982–86; Scunthorpe Circuit (Br Meth Conf) 1986–89; C St Mary and St Jas Gt Grimsby, Linc 1989–91, TV 1991–95; R St Steph Cant 1995–2002; AD Cant 1999–2002; Adn of Maidstone from

WHO'S WHO

2002; M DAC; M Dioc Property and Pastl Cttees; Chair Dioc Bd of Min and Trg, Archbp's Coun, Dioc Syn
GS 2005– *Tel:* 01233 840291
Fax: 01233 840759
email: pdown@archdeacashford.org

DRAPER, Very Revd Dr Jonathan Lee, BA, BA(Hons), PhD
The Deanery 10 Cathedral Close Exeter EX1 1EZ [DEAN OF EXETER] *b* 1952 *educ* Plainfield High Sch, Plainfield NJ, USA; Gordon Coll USA; Univ Dur; Ripon Coll Cuddesdon; *CV* Asst C St John the Divine Brooklands, Manchester 1983–5; Lect Ripon Coll Cuddesdon 1985–92; V Putney, S'wark 1992–2000; Can Theologian York Minster 200–12; Dean of Exeter from 2012
Tel: 01392 285979
email: dean@exeter-cathedral.org.uk
Web: www.exeter-cathedral.org.uk

DRIVER, Ven Penny (Penelope May), MEd, CertEd, MA Adult Ed
The Vicarage Windermere Road Lindal in Cartmel Grange over Sands LA11 6LB [ARCHDEACON OF WESTMORLAND AND FURNESS; CARLISLE] *b* 1952 *educ* All SS Coll Tottenham; Nn Ord Course; Man Univ; *CV* Dioc Youth Adv Newc 1986–88; C St Geo Cullercoats 1987–88; Dioc Youth Chapl Ripon from 1988–96; Min Can Ripon Cathl from 1996; Dioc Adv for Women's Mind from 1991; Ass DDO 1996–98; M CNC from 2003; Adn Exeter 2006–11; Ad Westmorland and Furness from 2012 *Tel:* 01539 534717
email: archdeacon.south@carlislediocese.org.uk

DRIVER, Revd Canon Roger John, Dip HE, BA (Hons), MA
The Vicarage 70 Merton Road Bootle Liverpool L20 7AT [LIVERPOOL] *b* 1964 *educ* Broadwey Secondary Modern; Weymouth Tech Coll, Liverpool Hope Univ; Trin Coll, Bris; Salis & Wells Th Coll; *CV* AC, St Peter's Much-Woolton, Liv 1990–93; TV, St Paul's, Fazakerley, Liv 1993–2000; TR (designate), Bootle Team Ministry, Liv 2000–03; P-in-C, St Andrew's, Litherland; St Leonard's, Bootle; St Matthew's, Bootle, Liverpool 2000–03; TR, Bootle Team Ministry, Liv from 2003; Civic Link Officer, Sefton Borough from 2004; Area Dean, Bootle, Liv from 2007; Hon Canon, Liv Cathl from 2007; M Bp's Counc, Liv 2001–09
GS 2010– *Tel and Fax:* 0151 922 3316
email: rogerdriver@btinternet.com

DUDLEY, Archdeacon of. See TRETHEWEY, Ven Frederick Martyn

DUDLEY, Suffragan Bishop of. See WALKER, Rt Revd David Stuart

DUDLEY-SMITH, Revd James, BA, MA, BTh
The Rectory 41 The Park Yeovil BA20 1DG [BATH AND WELLS] *b* 1966 *educ* Fitzw Coll Cam; Wycliffe Hall Ox; *CV* C New Borough and Leigh Sarum 1997–2001; C Hove Bp Hannington Memorial Ch Chich 2001–06; R Yeovil w Kingston Pitney B and W from 2006
GS 2010– *Tel:* 01935475352
email: jamesds@tesco.net

DUNLOP, Mrs Jennifer Mary, LLB
180a Dowson Rd Hyde SK14 5BW [CHESTER] *b* 1951 *educ* Woking Gr Sch for Girls; Hull Univ; *CV* Solicitor Dukinfield 1975–81; M Dioc Syn from 1988; Family Solicitor in Salford from 1995; Lay Chair Mottram Dny Syn 1990–2000; Solicitor Salford 1995–2011
GS 2000– *Tel:* 0161 368 2149
email: jennydunlop2004@yahoo.co.uk

DUNNETT, Revd John Frederick, MA, MSc, BA, CQSW
39 Crescent Rd Warley Brentwood Essex CM14 5JR [CHELMSFORD] *b* 1958 *educ* K Edw Sch Edgbaston; Sidney Sussex Coll Cam; Worc Coll Ox; Trin Coll Bris; *CV* Rsch Asst and Press Officer to Bp of B&W 1987–88; C Kirkheaton Par Ch 1988–93; V St Luke Cranham Park 1993–2006; Gen Dir CPAS from 2006
GS 2005– *Tel:* 01277 221419
email: jd@johndunnett.co.uk

DUNWICH, Suffragan Bishop of. See YOUNG, Rt Revd Clive

DURHAM, Archdeacon of. See JAGGER, Ven Ian

DURHAM, Bishop of, [NOT APPOINTED AT TIME OF GOING TO PRESS]

DURHAM, Dean of. See SADGROVE, Very Revd Michael

DURLACHER, Mrs Mary Caroline,
Archendines Chappel Road Fordham Colchester CO6 3LT [CHELMSFORD] *b* 1951 *educ* Cranborne Chase Sch; Kent Univ; Moore Coll; *CV* Churchwarden, All Saints Fordham & Eight Ash Green 1999–2005; Foundn Gov, C o E All Saints Fordham Primary Sch from 2005
GS 2010– *Tel:* 01206 240 627
email: marydurlacher@hotmail.com

DYER, Mrs Kay, BA, Cert Ed
6 Sycamore Close Stratford-upon-Avon CV37 0DZ [COVENTRY] *b* 1949 *educ* Blakedown High Sch Leamington Spa; Open Univ; Wolverhampton Univ; *CV* County Ecum Officer, Cov and Warw from 2004; OU tutor from 2003; Chair Cov Dioc Youth Initiative 1997–2001; Children's Work Co-ord, St Andrew Shottery, Stratford-upon-Avon from 2005; Lay Rdr from 2011
GS 2005– *Tel:* 01789 298299
email: kay.dyer@ntlworld.com

DZIEGIEL, Mrs Julie Patricia, MA(Hons)
239 Chartridge Lane Chesham Bucks HP5 2SF [OXFORD] *b* 1963 *educ* Pynton County High Sch; Newham Coll, Cam; *CV* Arthur Andersen, Chartered Accountants, 1984–88; Chartered Accountant 1988–94; Accountant & Company Sec from 1994; Church Treasurer from 2002
GS 2010– *Tel:* 01494 773713
email: julie@stronglg.demon.co.uk

EAGLES, Ven Peter Andrew, BA; AKC; BA; MTh
MoD Chaplains (Army) Army Headquarters, Marlborough Lines Andover, Hants SP11 8HJ [ARCHDEACON FOR THE ARMY] *b* 1959 *educ* RGS Guildford; King's Coll Sch Slavonic Studies Lon; Uni Heidelberg; St Stephens Ho; *CV* Tchr and translator 1982–86; C St Martin's Ruislip 1989–92; R Army Chapls Dept from 1992; Asst Chaplain General from 2008; Dir Trg and CME from 2011;Adn for the Army from 2011
GS 2011–
Tel: 01264 381841 01264 381836 07766 726326
Fax: 01264 381824
email: peter.eagles330@mod.uk

EAST RIDING, Archdeacon of. See BUTTERFIELD, Ven David John

EASTERN ARCHDEACONRY (Europe). See CURRAN, Ven Patrick Martin Stanley

EBBSFLEET, Bishop of. [NOT APPOINTED AT TIME OF GOING TO PRESS]

EDMONDSON, Rt Revd Christopher Paul, BA, Dip Th, MA, MBII
Bishop's Lodge Walkden Rd Worsley Manchester M28 2WH [SUFFRAGAN BISHOP OF BOLTON; MANCHESTER] *b* 1950 *educ* Blandford Gr Sch Dorset; Univ of Durham; Cranmer Hall, St John's Coll Dur; *CV* C Kirkheaton Par Ch 1973–79; V Ovenden St George 1979–86; Bp's Adv on Evang 1981–86; Dioc Officer for Evang and P-in-C Bampton, Carl 1986–92; V Shipley St Peter, Bradf 1992–2002; Warden Lee Abbey 2002–08; Bp of Bolton from 2008; Bp's Coun Carl 1989–1992; Chair Bradf Dioc Pastl Cttee 1994–2002; M Bp's Coun Man from 2008; Chair Scargill Movt Coun from 2009; Chair Greater Man Fresh Expressions Area Strategy Tm from 2009; Chair SNWTP from 2011 *Tel:* 0161 790 8289
Fax: 0161 703 9157
email: bishopchris@manchester.anglican.org

EDMONDSON, Very Revd Dr John James William, BA, Cert Th, MA, PhD
The Deanery Caldbec Hill Battle TN33 0JY [DEAN OF BATTLE] *b* 1955 *educ* Strode's Sch, Egham; Dur Univ; Cranmer Hall, Dur; *CV* C Gee Cross, Ches 1983–86; C St Paul Camberley, Guildf 1986–88, TV 1988–90; Chapl Elmhurst Ballet Sch, Camberley 1986–90; V Foxton w. Gumley and Laughton and Lubenham, Leic 1990–94; R St Mark Bexhill, Chich 1994–2005; Chich Dioc Vocations Adv 1998–2002; Asst DDO, Chich 2002–05; Dean of Battle, V Battle, Chich from 2005; P-in-c Sedlescombe and Whatlington, Chich 2005–07
Tel and Fax: 01424 772693
email: dean@johnedmondson.org.uk

EDMONTON, Area Bishop of. See WHEATLEY, Rt Revd Peter William

EDWARDS, Canon (Diana) Clare, Bth
22 The Precincts Canterbury CT1 2EP [CANTERBURY] *b* 1956 *educ* Nott Univ; Linc Th Coll; *CV* S Wimbledon H Trin and St Peters S'wark 1986–90; Par Dn 1987–90; Par Dn Lingfield and Crowhurst 1990–94; C 1994–94; Chapl St Piers Hosp Sch Lingfield 1990–95; R Bletchingley S'wark 1995–2004; RD Godstone 1998–2004; Hon Can S'wark Cathl 2001–04; Dean of Women's Min 2003–04; Can Res Cant Cathl from 2004
GS 2010– *Tel:* 01227865227
email: canonclare@canterbury-cathedral.org

ELCOCK, Dr Martin, BA, MB, Ch B
The Cottage 3 Digbeth Lane Claverley Wolverhampton WV5 7BP [HEREFORD] *b* 1963 *educ* Oldbury Wells Comp Sch Bridgnorth; Bris Univ; Man Univ; *CV* GP; Chair Good Shepherd Trust (homelessness and social inclusion charity in W Midlands/Derbys); primary sch gov; M Hosp Chapls Counc 2006–10
GS 2000– *Tel:* 01746 710423
07971 784639 (Mobile)
email: m.elcock@o2.co.uk

ELKINGTON, Ven Audrey Anne, BA; PhD; MA
4 Park Drive Bodmin Cornwall PL31 2QF [ARCHDEACON OF BODMIN; TRURO] *b* 1957 *educ* King Edward's Sch Witley; St Catherine's Ox; UEA; Durham; St John's Nottm; EA Min Training Course; *CV* D St Mary Monkseaton 1988–91; C St Mary Ponteland 1991–93; AP St Mary Magdalene Prudhoe 1993–2002; Adv Women's Min 2001–11; Bp's Chapl and DDO 2002–11; Adn of Bodmin from 2011 *Tel:* 01208 892811 07766 822872
email: audrey@truro.anglican.org

ELLIS, Rt Revd Tim (Timothy William), D Phil, AKC
Saxonwell Rectory Church St Long Bennington Newark NG23 5ES [SUFFRAGAN BISHOP OF GRANTHAM; LINCOLN] *b* 1953 *educ* City Sch Sheff; K Coll Lon; York Univ; St Aug Cant; *CV* C St Jo Old Trafford 1976–80; V St Tho Pendleton 1980–87; Chapl Salford Coll of Tech 1980–87; V St Leon Norwood, Sheff 1987–2001; P-in-c St Hilda Shiregreen, Sheff 1994–97; Adn of Stow and Lindsey 2001–2006; Vc Chair CCC; FAC York Min, Sheff Cathl, Linc Cathl; Bp of Grantham from 2006
Tel: 01400 283344
Fax: 01400 283321
email: bishop.grantham@lincoln.anglican.org

ELY, Bishop of. See CONWAY, Rt Revd Stephen David

ELY, Dean of. See BONNEY, Very Revd Mark

ETHERINGTON, Revd Ferial Mary Gould, BA
The Vicarage Station Road Flookburgh Grange over Sands LA11 7JY [CARLISLE] *b* 1944 *educ* Liskeard Gr Sch; Coll Law; St Albans MTS; *CV* Legal Exec 1976–93; St Alb Child Protection Off 1997–2004; Selection Conf Secr and Co-ord Ordained Local Min, Min Div, Abps' Counc 1997–2004; Carlisle Dioc Ministerial Review Off 2004–11; House-for-Duty TV, Cartmel Peninsula from 2010; M Legal Aid Commn 1991–93; M Rural Affairs Grp in Synod from 2011
GS 1990–93; 2007–
Tel: 015395 58751 07708 958082
email: ferial.etherington@btinternet.com

EUROPE, Archdeacon in North-West, [NOT APPOINTED AT TIME OF GOING TO PRESS]

EUROPE, Bishop of Gibraltar in. See ROWELL, Rt Revd (Douglas) Geoffrey

EUROPE, Suffragan Bishop in. See HAMID, Rt Revd David

EVERITT, Ven Michael John, BD AKC
6 Eton Park Preston PR2 9NL [ARCHDEACON OF LANCASTER; BLACKBURN] *b* 1968 *Educ* Warriner Sch, Bloxham; Banbury Upper Sch; King's Coll Lon; Gregorian Univ Rome; Queen's Coll Birm; Venerable English Coll Rome; *CV* Asst C Cleveleys St Andrew 1992–95; South Africa 1995–98; Succentor Bloemfontein Cathl 1995–96, precentor 1996–98; Anglican Chaplain Nat Hosp Bloemfontein 1995–98; Anglican Chaplain and Lect in Theology, Univ of the Orange Free State 1996–98; Senior Coll Chaplain; St Martin's Coll Lancaster 1998–2002; Asst Dir of Ordinands, Blackburn Diocese 2000–02; R Standish St Wilfrid 2002–11; AD Chorley Deanery 2005–11; P-in-C Appley Bridge All Saints 2006–10; Hon Can Blackburn Cathl 2010–11; Adn of Lancaster from 2011 *Tel:* 01772 700331
email: michael.everitt@blackburn.anglican.org

EXETER, Archdeacon of. See FUTCHER, Ven Christopher

EXETER, Bishop of. See LANGRISH, Rt Revd Michael Laurence

EXETER, Dean of. See DRAPER, Very Revd Jonathan Lee

FARTHING, Revd Paul Andrew, BA, STM, Dip Min
Vicarage Rangemore St Burton-on-Trent DE14 2ED [LICHFIELD] *b* 1958 *educ* Wilsons Gr Sch Camberwell; Vanier Coll Montreal; McGill Univ Montreal; Montreal Dioc Th Coll; *CV* C St Phil Montreal W 1983–85; R St Jo Divine Verdun 1985–96; R St Jo Ev Montreal 1996–99; V St Aidan and St Paul and P-in-c St Modwen Burton-on-Trent from 1999; M Gen Syn Angl Ch of Canada 1989–95; M Doct and Worship Cttee Angl Ch of Canada 1989–92; M Lichf Dioc Syn from 2000; M DBF from 2000
GS 2000– *Tel:* 01283 544054
email: burton.benefice@gmail.com

FAULL, Very Revd Vivienne Frances, MA, BA, MBA
Church House 10–14 Ogleforth York YO1 7Jn [DEAN OF YORK] *b* 1955 *educ* Qu Sch Ches; St Hilda's Coll Ox; Nottm Univ; Open Univ Business Sch; St Jo Coll Nottm; *CV* Dss St Matt and St Jas Mossley Hill 1982–85; Chapl Clare Coll Cam 1985–90; Chapl Glouc Cathl 1990–94; Can Pastor Cov Cathl 1994–2000; Vc Prov Cov Cath 1995–2000; Prov of Leic 2000–02; Dean of Leic 2002–12; Chair AEC from 2009; Dean of York from 2012
GS 1987–90, 2004– *Tel:* 01904 557202
Fax: 01904 557204
email: dean@yorkminster.org
Web: www.yorkminster.org

FEIST, Canon Nicholas James, L Th
Middleton Rectory Mellalieu St Middleton Manchester M24 5DN [MANCHESTER] *b* 1945 *educ* Merchant Taylors Sch; Lon Coll of Law; St Jo Coll Nottm; *CV* Solicitor; C St Jas and Em Didsbury 1976–80; V St Thos Friarmere 1980–88; R St Leon Middleton 1988–94; TR Middleton and Thornham from 1994; Hon Can Man Cathl from 1998; AD Heywood and Middleton 1999–2007; M Dioc Syn; M Bp's Coun; Dioc Fin Cttee; GS Legal Aid Commn from 2001
GS 2000–2010 *Tel and Fax:* 0161 643 2693
email: nickjfeist@ntlworld.com

FELIX, Revd David Rhys, LLB, Cert Th
Vicarage Daresbury Warrington WA4 4AE [CHESTER] *b* 1955 *educ* Calday Grange County Gr Sch; Univ of Wales; Ripon Coll, Cuddesdon; *CV* C St Barn Bromborough 1986–89; V St Andr Grange, Runcorn 1989–99; Chapl Halton Gen Hosp 1995–99; P-in-c H Trin Runcorn 1996–99; RD Frodsham 1998–99; Ind Missr, Halton 1998–99; V All SS Daresbury from 1999; Sen Ind Missr Chester Dio 2000–08; M Dioc Adv Bd for Min 1988–90; M Dioc Adoption Services Cttee 1990–92; Dny Ord Chapl 1990–96; M Dioc Pastl Grp 1994–95; M Dioc Syn from 1994; Dir DBF and M Bp's Coun from 1995; M Dioc Bd of Educ and Schs Cttee 1997–2003; M Archidiaconal Pastl Cttee 1992–94 and from 1998; M Eccl Law Soc from 1987 and of Gen Cttee from 2002; M Dioc Cttee for Miss and Unity 2001–08; Hon Can Ches Cathl 2006; Trustee, Southern North West Training from 2010
GS 2002–
Tel: 01925 740348 07778 859935 (Mobile)
email: david.felix@btinternet.com

FERGUSON, Mrs Linda Ann, BA(Hons), ILM L7 Cert. Executive and Leadership Coaching
Church House Great Smith Street London SW1P 3PS *educ* Burnham Gr Sch; *CV* Inland Revenue 1985–2005; HM Revenue and Customs Sen Policy Adv 2005–08; Head of Complaints Policy 2008–2011; Sen Customer & Strategy Adv 2011–12; Dir Customer Insight and Strategy C of E Pensions Bd from 2012 *Tel:* 020 7898 1833
email: linda.ferguson@churchofengland.org

FERGUSON, Ven Paul John, MA, FRCO (CHM), PGCE
48 Langbaurgh Road Hutton Rudby Yarm TS15 0HL [ARCHDEACON OF CLEVELAND; YORK] *b* 1955 *educ* Birkenhead Sch; New Coll Ox; Westmr Coll Ox; K Coll Cam; Westcott Ho Th Coll; *CV* C St Mary Chester 1985–88; Chapl and Sacr Westmr Abbey 1988–92; Prec Westmr Abbey 1992–95; Prec and Res Can York Minster 1995–2001; Adn of Cleveland from 2001; Wrdn of Rdrs from 2004; Sec Ho Bps' Th Grp 1992–2001; M Porvoo Panel from 2009
GS 2010–
Tel: 01642 706095 07770 592746 (Mobile)
email: archdeacon.of.cleveland@yorkdiocese.org

FIDDES, Revd Prof Paul, MA, D Phil, DD
Regent's Park College Pusey St Oxford OX1 2LB [ECUMENICAL REPRESENTATIVE] *b* 1947 *educ* St Pet Coll, Ox; Regent's Park Coll, Ox; *CV* Principal, Regent's Park Coll, Ox; Prof of Systematic Theol, Ox Univ; Min of Bapt Union of Gt Britain
GS 2005– *Tel:* 01865 288134
Fax: 01865 288121
email: paul.fiddes@regents.ox.ac.uk

FIELDEN, Mr Christopher Cameron, MA
Holly Cottage 19 The Street Broughton Giffard Melksham SN12 8PW [SALISBURY] *b* 1939 *educ* Rossall; Lamp; *CV* Pres, Wines & Spirit Assoc of GB and NI from 1990; Chair, Circle of Wine Writers 2006–08
GS 2010– *Tel:* 01225 782509
email: winesource@btconnect.com

FINCH, Mrs Sarah Rosemary Ann, BA
97 Englefield Rd Canonbury London N1 3LJ [LONDON] *b* 1945 *educ* Godolphin Sch Sarum; Dur Univ; Ox Univ; *CV* Ed Barrie and Jenkins 1972–75; Trustee BFBS 1978–2005; Chair Exec Cttee BFBS 1991–94; Freelance Non-Fiction Ed from 1986; Gov Sir John Cass's Foundn Primary Sch (C of E) from 1996; M CEEC from 2000; Coun M Latimer Trust from 2003; M Revision Ctee, Common Worship Ordinal; elected M Appts Ctee from 2005; Coun M Oak Hill Theol Coll from 2006; M Angl Mainstream Strg Cttee from 2006; Trustee Latimer Trust from 2007; Dep Chair Latimer Trust Cttee from 2009; M Fin and Gen Purposes Cttee of Oak Hill Theo Coll from 2009
GS 2000– *Tel:* 020 7226 2803
Fax: 020 7704 2257
email: sarahrafinch@yahoo.co.uk

FISHER, Ms Alison, CQSW, CMI
[WAKEFIELD] *b* 1959 *educ* King Edward VI, Devon; Leeds Univ; Univ Coll Cardiff; *CV* Probation Officer 1981–90, Senior Probation Officer from 1990; Non Exec Dir Calderdale & Huddersfield Foundn Trust from 2005; Gen Tching Counc, Lay m from 2007; Diversity Mgr, West Yorkshire Probation Trust from 2008
GS 2010–
email: alison.fisher1@ntlworld.com

FITTALL, Mr William Robert, MA
Church House Great Smith St London SW1P 3AZ [SECRETARY GENERAL OF THE GENERAL SYNOD AND THE ARCHBISHOPS' COUNCIL] *b* 1953 *educ* Dover Gr Sch; Ch Ch Ox; *CV* Home Office 1975–80; Ecole Nat d'Administration Paris 1980–81; Home Office 1981–91; Prin Private Sec to N Ireland Sec 1992–93; Home Office 1993–95; Under Sec and Chief of Assessments Staff, Cabinet Office 1995–97; Dir Crime Reduction and Com Programmes, Home Office 1997–2000; Assoc Political Dir, N Ireland Office 2000–02; Sec Gen GS and AC from 2002 *Tel:* 020 7898 1360
07738 883712 (Mobile)
Fax: 020 7898 1369
email: william.fittall@churchofengland.org

FITZSIMONS, Canon Kathryn Anne, Cert Th, Cert Ed; MA
52 Newton Court Oakwood Leeds LS8 2PH [RIPON AND LEEDS] *b* 1957 *educ* Richmond Sch; Bedford Coll of HE; NEOC; Univ of Leeds; *CV* NSM C St Jo Bilton, Harrogate 1990–2002; Soc Resp Officer 1992–99; Dioc Urban Officer from 1999; Hon Can Ripon Cathl from 2004; Pres Diaconal Assoc of the C of E 2003–10; Officer, Mission Resourcing Team; M DBF GS 2004–5, 2005–10, 2010–
Tel: 0113 248 5011
email: kathrynfitzsimons@hotmail.com

FLACH, Canon Deborah Mary, Dip HE Theol, Dip Counselling
7 rue Leonard de Vinci 59700 Marcq en Baroeul France [EUROPE] *b* 1954 *educ* Beckenham Convent Sch; Trin Coll Bris; Salis and Wells Th Coll; *CV* C St Pet Chantilly, France 1994–96; C H Trin Maisons-Laffitte, France 1996–2004, Asst Chapl 2004–07; M Dioc Syn from 1994; Asst Dir of Ordinands (France) 1997–2010; P-in-c Ch Ch, Lille (Eur) from 2007; Chair House of Clergy from 2007; Bp's Counc from 2007
GS 2005– *Tel:* +333 28526636
email: chaplain@christchurchlille.com

FLETCHER, Rt Revd Colin William, MA, OBE
Arran House Sandy Lane Yarnton Oxford OX5 1PB [AREA BISHOP OF DORCHESTER; OXFORD] *b* 1950 *educ* Marlboro Coll; Tr Coll Ox; Wycliffe Hall Th Coll; *CV* C St Pet Shipley 1975–79; Tutor Wycliffe Hall and C St Andr Ox 1979–84; V H Tr Margate 1984–93; RD Thanet 1989–93; Dom Chapl to Abp

of Cant 1993–2000; Canon Dallas Cathl 1993–2000; Bp of Dorchester from 2000
Tel: 01865 208218
Fax: 01865 849003
email: bishopdorchester@oxford.anglican.org

FLETCHER, Mr Ian Jack, FCA
38 Heaton Grove Heaton Bradford BD9 4DZ [BRADFORD] *b* 1952 *educ* Woodhouse Grove Sch; *CV* Articled Clerk, 1970–74; Chartered Accountant from 1975; Director, D J Fletcher (Insurances) Ltd from 1973; Chair Bradf District Community Foundation; Dir Bradford Churches For Dialogue and Diversity; Dir Wellsprings Ltd; Chair Church in the World Dioc Syn Cttee; Chair Dioc Urban Plus Panel; Lay Canon Bradf Cathl 2001–08
GS 2010–
Tel: 01274 492839 01274 729178 07788 413716
Fax: 01274 725470
email: ijf@fgco.com

FLETCHER, Revd Jeremy James, MA
Minster Vicarage Highgate Beverley HU17 0DN [YORK] *b* 1960 *educ* Woodhouse Grove Sch Bradf; Univ Coll Dur; St John's Nott; *CV* Asst C All Saints Stranton, Hartlepool 1988–91; Assoc Min St Nicholas Nottm 1991–94; P-in-C Skegby and Stanton Hill 1994–2000; P-in-C Teversal 1996–2000; Chapl to Bp Southwell 2000–02; Precentor York Minster 2002–09; V Beverley Minster from 2009
GS 1995–2002, 2009– *Tel:* 01482 881434
email: jeremy@jjfletcher.co.uk

FLETCHER, Mr Philip John, CBE, MA
20 Calais St Camberwell London SE5 9LP [APPOINTED MEMBER, ARCHBISHOPS' COUNCIL] *b* 1946 *educ* Marlborough Coll; Trin Coll Ox; *CV* Dir Gen Cities and Countryside Dept of Environment to 1996; Receiver, Metropolitan Police District 1996–2000; Dir Gen Water Services (OFWAT) 2000–06; Chair OFWAT 2006–12; Member Ofqual (Qualifications and Examinations Regulator) Bd from 2010; Chair MPA Coun from 2012
GS 2007– *Tel:* 020 7733 2200
email: philipjfletcher@yahoo.co.uk

FOLLETT, Mr Samuel (Joseph),
Christ Church Vicarage 5 High Oaks St Albans AL3 6DJ [ST ALBANS] *b* 1990 *educ* St. George's Sch, Harpenden; Nott Univ; *CV* PA to CE, Church Army 2009–10; Dir, Simplicity from 2007; Elected to GS 2010
GS 2010– *Tel:* 07868 258303
email: sam@samfollett.co.uk
2nd email: sam.follett@gmail.com

FORD, Revd Dr Mandy (Amanda Kirstine), BA, BTh, MA, PhD
10 Parkside Close Leicester LE4 1EP [LEICESTER] *b* 1961 *educ* Cranborne Chase Sch, Wiltshire; Middlesex Univ; Ox Univ; Nott Univ; St Stephen's House Th Coll; Nottm Univ; *CV* Tchr, Maynard Sch, Exeter 1990–98; C, Parish of the Resurrection, Leic 2000–05; Church Urban Fund Link Officer 2004–09; V, Christ the King, Leic from 2005; V, St Luke's Leic from 2011; Asst AD, City of Leic from 2009; AD from 2011; M Abp's Counc Urban Strategy Consult Grp 2004–09; M Cathl Fabric Adv Cttee from 2005; Chair from 2008; Chair of the House of Clergy from 2009
GS 2010– *Tel:* 0116 235 2667
email: mandyford@btinternet.com

FORD, Rt Revd John Frank, MA
31 Riverside Walk Tamerton Foliot Plymouth PL5 4AQ [SUFFRAGAN BISHOP OF PLYMOUTH; EXETER] *b* 1952 *educ* Chich Th Coll; *CV* C Ch Ch Forest Hill 1979–82; V St Aug Lee 1982–91; V Lower Beeding 1991–94; Dom Chapl to Bp of Horsham 1991–94; Dioc Missr from 1994; Can and Preb Chich Cathl from 1997; Prec of Chich Cathl from 2000; Bp of Plymouth from 2005
GS 1999–2005 *Tel:* 01752 769836
email: bishop.of.plymouth@exeter.anglican.org

FOREMAN, Mrs (Antoinette Joan) Anne, CCYW
5 St Leonards Road Exeter Devon EX2 4LA [EXETER] *b* 1943 *educ* Teignmouth Gr Sch; Bradf & Ilkley Comm Coll; *CV* Yth & Comm Worker, Sutton 1983–85; Senior Yth & Comm Worker, Kingston 1985–88; Asst Prin Yth Off, Sutton 1988–91; National Yth Off Genl Syn Brd Ed 1991–95; Ch House; M GS Brd Miss 2001–03; Lay Chair Okehampton Deanery; 2007–12; M Dioc Syn; M Bps Counc; Vice Chair Dioc Miss & Pstrl Cttee; Chair Vacancy in See Cttee; Bps Adv from 2008; External Exam BEd Fieldwork Placements St. Martins Coll Lan 1992–94; M Adv Counc Comm & Yth Work Course Goldsmiths Coll 1991–94; Dir & Trustee Guildford YMCA 2002–05; M Counc Mngment Univ Coll St. Mark & St. John 2006–10
GS 1999–2005; 2010–
Tel: 01392 279859 01392 217020
email: anne@anneforeman.co.uk

FORSTER, Rt Revd Dr Peter Robert, MA, BD, Ph D
Bishop's House Abbey Square Chester CH1 2JD [BISHOP OF CHESTER] *b* 1950 *educ* Tudor Grange Gr Sch Solihull; Merton Coll Ox; Edin Univ; Edin Th Coll; *CV* C St Matt and St Jas Mossley Hill Liv 1980–82; Sen Tutor St Jo Coll Dur 1983–91; V Beverley Minster 1991–96; Bp of Ches from 1996; Ch Commr 1999–2004, from 2009
GS 1985–91,1996– *Tel:* 01244 350864
email: bpchester@chester.anglican.org

FORWARD, Miss Emma Joy, BA, PGCE
24 Whitchurch Ave Exeter EX2 5NT [EXETER] *b* 1984 *educ* St Pet C of E High Sch Ex; St Hugh's Coll Ox; *CV* Trainee tchr from 2005; full time tchr from 2006
GS 2005– *Tel:* 01392 251617
email: emmaforward@yahoo.co.uk

FOSTER, Rt Revd Christopher Richard James, BA, MA (ECON), MA, HonDLitt
Bishopsgrove 26 Osborn Rd Fareham PO16 7DQ [BISHOP OF PORTSMOUTH] *b* 1953 *educ* R Gr Sch Guildf; Dur Univ; Manch Univ; Trinity Hall Cam, Wescott Ho Cam; *CV* Lect in Economics Univ of Dur 1976–77; Asst C Tettenhall Regis TM Wolverhampton 1980–82; Chapl Wadham Col Ox and Asst P St Mary w St Cross and St Pet in the East Ox 1982–86; V Ch Ch Southgate 1986–94; CME Dir Edmonton Area 1988–94; Sub Dean and Res Can St Alb1994–2001; Bp of Hertford 2001–2010; Bp of Portsmouth from 2010 *Tel:* 01329 280247
Fax: 01329 231538
email: bishports@portsmouth.anglican.org

FRAIS, Revd Jonathan Jeremy, LLB BA DipTh
The Rectory 11 Coverdale Avenue Little Common East Sussex TN39 4TY [CHICHESTER] *b* 1965 *educ* Judd Gr Sch; Tonbridge Kingston Poly; Oak Hill Coll; *CV* AC Ch Ch, Orpington 1992–96; Asst Chapl, St Andrew's, Moscow 1996–99; Chapl, Ch Ch, Kyiv, Ukraine 1999–2005; R, St Mark's, Bexhill, from 2005; M Adv Grp Ch Soc 2007–10
GS 2000–05; 2010– *Tel and Fax:* 01424 843733
email: frais@tiscali.co.uk

FRANCE, Revd Stephen Mark, Bth (Oxon)
Rectory Rectory Close Burwash East Sussex, TN19 7BH [CHICHESTER] *b* 1966 *educ* Tapton School; Wycliffe Hall Th Coll;; *CV* Whitehall Civil Servant 1986–97; Ox Univ 1997–2000; C Newbold w Dunston, Derby 2000–03; Independant Lay Member of Derbyshire C C Standard's Cttee 2001–05; Dioc Duty Press Officer; P-in-C Derby 2003–05; P-in-C Chich 2005–06; Rector, Burwash, Chich from 2006; Rector, Society of Catholic Priests, Chich from 2008; M Chesterfield Daycentre for the Homeless Cttee 2001–03; M Dioc Syn Derby 2002–05; M Dioc Comm Cttee, Derby 2002–05; M Coun for Developing Discipleship and Ministry 2002–05; Derbyshire CC Emergency Chapl 2004–05; Gov Walter Evans Sch 2003–05; M Soc of Catholic Preists, Chich from 2005, Gov Burwash Sch from 2005; Chair Barnsley Trust from 2005; M Dioc Syn, Chich from 2005; M Dioc and Adnry Pastoral and Miss Cttees from 2006; M Bp's Coun, Chich from 2008; Emergency Chapl, Chich from 2010; Abps' Fin Cttee from 2011
GS 2010– *Tel:* 01435 882301
email: revfrance@tiscali.co.uk

FRANCE, Archdeacon of, [NOT APPOINTED AT TIME OF GOING TO PRESS]

FRANKLIN, Revd Canon Richard Heighway, BA, MPhil
Holy Trinity Vicarage 7 Glebe Close Weymouth Dorset DT4 9RL [SALISBURY] *b* 1954 *educ* Warwick Sch; Southampton Univ; Salis & Wells Th Coll; *CV* C Thame w Towersey 1978–81; Asst chapl Univ of Southampton 1981–83; Tutor & Dir of Studies Chich Th Coll 1983–89; P-in-C Stalbridge 1989–94; V Holy Trinity Weymouth from 1994; Ed journal 'Studies in Christian Ethics' 1987–91; M Dioc Brd of Ch & Soc 1996–2006; Euro Off Bp of Salisbury from 1998; Rural Dean of Weymouth 2004–2008
GS 2003–05; 2010– *Tel:* 01305 760354
email: richardfranklin@iname.com

FRAYLING, Very Revd Nicholas Arthur, BA, Hon LLD, FJMU
The Deanery Canon Lane Chichester PO19 1PX [DEAN OF CHICHESTER] *b* 1944 *educ* Repton; Ex Univ; Cuddesdon; *CV* Mgt trg retail trade 1962–64; prison welfare 1964–66 and part-time 1966–71; C St Jo Peckham 1971–74; V All SS Tooting Graveney 1974–83; Can Res and Prec Liv Cathl 1983–87; R Liv 1987–2002; Dean of Chich from 2002; Chair S'wark DAC 1980–83; M Liv Dioc Syn and Bishop's Coun *Tel:* 01243 812485 (Office)
01243 812494 (Home)
Fax: 01243 812499
email: dean@chichestercathedral.org.uk

FREEMAN, Mr John, BA, Ad Dip Ed Mgt, DMS, Cert Ed, JP
The Smiths' House 99 High St Barwell LE9 8DS [LEICESTER] *b* 1947 *educ* Hinckley Gr Sch; Open Univ; De Montfort Univ, Garnett Coll; Birm Coll of Food; *CV* Lect South Fields Coll Leic 1972–82; Dir Faculty of Arts, N Herts Coll 1982–99; Ptnr, The Grove Tavern, Lon 1999–2003; Mgt Consult, Leic Univ from 2005
GS 2005–2010 *Tel:* 01455 842548
email: j.freeman5@btinternet.com

FREEMAN, Mr John Jeremy Collier, Eur Ing, DLC, B Sc, MIChemE, C ENG
Stable Court 20a Leigh Way Weaverham Northwich CW8 3PR [CHESTER] *b* 1937 *educ* Embley Park Sch; Loughb Univ; *CV* Graduate Chemical Engineer ICI 1961–94 inc Asst to Gen Mgr Magadi Soda Co, Kenya 1975–77; Rtd 1994, now very active in vol sector; M Local Agenda 21 Forum; Par Coun from 1980; Sch Gov from 1980; M Dioc Fin and Central Services Cttee from 1994; M Exec Chs Together in Cheshire from 1995; Chair Dioc PWM Cttee; M Dioc CSR Cttee; Chr Aid activist; Sec Dioc Justice and Devel Educ Grp; M Bp's Coun; M Dioc Syn; Dioc World Devel Adv; M Core Grp Angl World Devel Advs; Treas Open Syn Grp; Companion of the Melanesian Brotherhood
GS 2000– *Tel:* 01606 852872
Fax: 01606 854140
email: jjcfreeman@talktalk.net

FREEMAN, Rt Revd Robert John, B Sc, MA
Holmcroft 13 Castle Road Kendal LA9 7AU [SUFFRAGAN BISHOP OF PENRITH; CARLISLE] *b* 1952 *educ* Cambs High Sch; St Jo Coll Dur; Fitzw Coll Cam; Ridley Hall Cam; *CV* C St Jo Blackpool 1977–81; TV St Winifred Chigwell 1981–85; V Ch of the Martyrs Leic 1985–99; RD Christianity S (Leic) 1994–98; Hon Can Leic 1994–2003; Nat Evang

WHO'S WHO

Adv, AC from 1999; Chair Agenda and Support Cttee of Grp for Evangelisation (CTE) 2000–03; Sec Miss, Evang and Renewal in Eng Cttee, Bd of Mission, AC 1999–2003; Chair rejesus.co.uk from 2000; Dir Just Fairtrade Ltd 2000–03; Adn of Halifax 2003–11; M Chs Regional Commn for Yorkshire and Humberside 2004; Chair Chr Enquiry Agency f2006–10; Trustee Simeon and Hyndman's 2007–10; Chair Wakefield Dioc Bd of Finance 2008–11, Bp of Penrith from 2011
GS 1997–99, 2008–11
Tel: 01539 727836 07584 684308
email: bishop.penrith@carlislediocese.org.uk
Web: www.rejesus.co.uk

FRENCH, Mr Philip Colin, MA, MMath, MIET
Arden Five Oak Green Rd Five Oak Green Tonbridge TN12 6TJ [ROCHESTER] *b* 1960 *educ* R Gr Sch Newc; Br Sch Brussels; Churchill Coll Cam; *CV* Rsch Asst, Univ Coll Lon 1984–87; Overseas Career Service Officer, Br Coun 1987–96; (First Sec (Educ & Science), Calcutta 1988–91); Sen Consult, Hewlett-Packard Ltd 1996–99; Tech Dir, Software.com, later Openwave Systems Inc 1999–2003; IT mgt posts in HM Prison Service and Nat Offender Mgt Service 2003–08; Chief Technology Officer, Min of Justice 2009–12; Non-exec dir and trustee, Edusery from 2011; Government Sector Businuess Development Dir, Steria from 2012; PCC treasurer, URC elder and church treasurer; Trustee, Hands of Compassion (supporting education in Zambia)
GS 1985–88, 2005– *Tel:* 01892 838713 (Home)
07952 273253 (Mobile)
email: philip.c.french@btinternet.com

FRITH, Rt Revd Richard Michael Cokayne, MA
Hullen House Woodfield Lane Hessle HU13 0ES [SUFFRAGAN BISHOP OF HULL; YORK] *b* 1949 *educ* Marlboro Coll; Fitzw Coll Cam; St Jo Coll Nottm; *CV* C Mortlake w E Sheen 1974–78; TV Thamesmead 1978–83; TR Keynsham 1983–92; Adn of Taunton 1992–98; Bp of Hull from 1998
GS 1995–98 *Tel:* 01482 649019
Fax: 01482 647449
email: richard@bishop.karoo.co.uk

FROST, Rt Revd Dr Jonathan Hugh, BD, MTh, DUniv, MSSTh, FRSA
Bishop's House St Mary's Church Close Wessex Lane Southampton SO18 2ST [SUFFRAGN BISHOP OF SOUTHAMPTON; WINCHESTER] *b* 1964 *educ* KCS Wimbledon; Aberdeen Univ; Nottm Univ; Surrey Univ; Ridley Hall Camb; *CV* C W Bridgford St Giles 1993–97; Police Chapl Trent Div, Notts Constabulary 1994–97; R Ash St Peter 1997–2002; Can Res Guildf Cath 2002–10; Angl Chapl Univ of Surrey 2002–10; Bp's Adv for Inter-Faith Relations 2007–10; Co-ord Chapl Univ of Surrey 2007–10; Tutor Christian Doctrine Local Min Course 1999–2010; Bp ofSouthampton from 2010
GS 2009–2010 *Tel:* 023 8067 2684
email: bishop.jonathan@winchester.anglican.org

FROUDE, Ven Christine Ann, Dip Theol; ACIB
1 Orchard Close Winterbourne Bristol BS36 1BF [ARCHDEACON OF MALMESBURY] *b* 1947 *educ* Llwyn Y Bryn Girls Gr Swansea; Salisbury and Wells; *CV* C St Mary Magdalene Stoke Bishop 1995–99; Chapl Univ Hosps Bristol NHS Found Children's Directorate 1999–2001; D of Women's Min 2001–11; Hon Can Bristol Cathl 2001–11; Adn Malmesbury from 2011; Dioc Pastl Management Ctte; Dioc Housing and Glebe Ctte; DAC; Dioc Miss and Pastl Ctte; Dioc Finance Ctte
Tel: 01454 778366
email: christine.froude@bristoldiocese.org

FROUDE, Canon David Colin, ACIB
1 Orchard Close Winterborne Bristol BS36 1BF [BRISTOL] *b* 1949 *educ* Colston's Sch, Bris; *CV* HSBC Bank (formerly Midland) 1967–2004 retiring as Senior Manager; Par Clerk, St Mary's, Shirehampton, Bris 2001–11; M Bris Cathl Coun from 2002; M Provincial Panel Clergy Discipline Measure from 2003; Chair Bris Dioc Brd Finance Ltd 2004–11; Chair Bris DBF Fin Cttee 2004–11; Chair Bris DBF Budget Cttee 2004–11; Chair Bris DBF Remuneration Cttee 2004–11; M Bris DBF Audit Cttee 2004–11; M Bris Dioc Syn Agenda Cttee 2004–11; M Bp's Coun 2004–11; Chair Trustees Bris DBF Staff Retirement Benefit Scheme 2004–11; SW Region DBF Chair, M 2004–11, Convenor 2006–11; C of E Consultative Grp of DBF Chairs and Dioc Secs, M 2006–11, Chair 2009–11; M C of E Nat Procurement Grp from 2007; M Bishop of Bristol Senior Staff 2007–11; M Bristol Dioc Strategic Policy Grp 2007–09; M C of E Pensions Bd from 2009; Lay Canon Bris Cathl from 2010; Chair C of E Pensions Bd Audit Cttee from 2011; Chair Strg Ctte Draft Dioc Eur Measure 2012
GS 2010– *Tel:* 01454 778366 07768 958704
email: davidfroude@lineone.net

FRY, Mrs Christine Ann, BA, PG Dip
25 St Leonards Avenue, Chineham Basingstoke RG24 8RD [WINCHESTER] *b* 1964 *educ* Arden Sch;. Solihull Sixth Form Coll; Southampton Univ; Middlesex Poly; *CV* Probation Service Off, Middlesex Probation Area,1986–88; Trainee Probation Off, Middlesex Probation Area, 1988–90; Probation Off, Hampshire Probation Area 1990–93; Youth and Comm Worker, St Mary's Ch, Eastrop, Basingstoke 1993–95; Court Welfare Off, Hampshire Probation Area 1995–98; Probation Off, Hampshire Probation Area, 1998–2001; Senior Probation Off, Hampshire Probation Area 2001–08; Area Mgr, Hampshire Proabtion Area 2008–09; Business Change Mgr, Hampshire Probation Trust from 2010
GS 1995–2000; 2010– *Tel:* 01256 474466
email: chrisfry01@yahoo.co.uk

FRY, Sir Roger Gordon, KBE, BD, AKC, D Litt, FRSA, CBE
Avda Pio XII 92 28036 Madrid Spain [EUROPE] *b* 1943 *educ* Portsm Gr Sch; Lon Univ; *CV* Chair

King's Grp from 1981; Chair Coun of Br Independent Schs in the Eur Com from 1996; Pres Coun of Br Internat Schs from 2011; Dir Independent Schs Coun 2008–11
GS 1990–95; 2005–2010 *Tel:* +34 91 3598800
Fax: +34 91 3592767
email: roger.fry@kingsgroup.org

FULHAM, Suffragan Bishop of. See BAKER, Rt Revd Jonathan Mark Richard

FULLARTON, Mr Derek, FRSA
Lambeth Palace London SE1 7JU [PATRONAGE SECRETARY TO THE ARCHBISHOP OF CANTERBURY] *b* 1952 *educ* Camphill Sch Paisley; Glasgow Univ; *CV* On staff of Ch Commrs from 1974; on secondment as Private Sec to the Sec-General of GS 1985–89; M Engl Cttee, Friends of Angl Cen in Rome from 1990; Sec Palace Trustees Wells 1992–99; Sec Lambeth Palace Library Trustees 1996–2006; Admin Sec Lambeth Palace 1999–2006; Dir Lambeth Projects (2000) Ltd; Trustee, Archbishop of Canterbury's Charitable Foundation (2012); Abp's Patronage Sec from 2006
Tel: 020 7898 1252
07525 492758 (Mobile)
email: derek.fullarton@lambethpalace.org.uk

FUTCHER, Ven Christopher David, BD, MTh, MA
Emmanuel House Station Road Ide Exeter EX2 9RS [ARCHDEACON OF EXETER] *b* 1958 *educ* Strode's Gr Sch, Egham, Surrey; Univ of Edin; Heythrop Coll Univ of Lon; King's Coll Lon; Westcott Ho; *CV* Asst C Borehamwood TM 1982–85; Asst C All Saints Pin Green Stevenage 1985–88; V All Saints Pin Green Stevenage 1988–96; V St Stephen's St Albans 1996–2000; R Harpenden 2000–12; Dioc Ecum Officer 2004–12; Adn of Exeter from 2012; M English ARC 1991–2001 *Tel:* 01392 425577
email: archdeacon.of.exeter@exeter.anglican.org

GARLICK, Preb Kay (Kathleen Beatrice), BA, Cert Ed
Birch Lodge Much Birch HR2 8HT [HEREFORD] *b* 1949 *educ* Prendergast Gr Sch Catford; Leeds Univ; Birm Univ; Glouc Sch for Min; *CV* Hon C Much Birch w Lt Birch, Much Dewchurch etc 1990–2003; Ecum Chapl Heref Sixth Form Coll 1996–2002; P-in-c Parishes of the Wormelow Hundred from 2003; Rector 2006–09; M AC from 2006; Chair GS Business Cttee from 2006; Cath Chapl Heref Cath from 2009; Chapl to HM the Queen from 2011
GS 1995–2010 *Tel:* 01981 540666
email: kaygarlick@hotmail.com

GARNETT, Ven David Christopher, BA, MA
The Vicarage Edensor Bakewell Derbys DE45 1PH [ARCHDEACON OF CHESTERFIELD; DERBY] *b* 1945 *educ* Giggleswick Sch; Nottm Univ; Fitzw Coll Cam; Westcott Ho Th Coll; *CV* C Cottingham 1969–72; Chapl, Fell and Tutor Selw Coll Cam 1972–77; Pastl Adv Newnham Coll Cam 1972–77; R Patterdale 1977–80; DDO Carlisle 1977–80; V Heald Green 1980–87; Chapl St Ann's Hospice 1980–87; R Christleton 1987–92; TR Ellesmere Port 1992–96; Adn of Chesterfield from 1996; Chair Bp's Th Adv Grp 1987–93; Chair Assoc of Ch Fells 1987–92; V Edensor and Beeley from 2007
GS 1990–96, 2000–05 *Tel:* 01246 582130
email: davidcgarnett@yahoo.co.uk

GAY, Canon Perran Russell, MA, BA, PGCE, FRGS
Cathedral Office 14 St Mary's Street, Truro TR1 2AF [TRURO] *b* 1959 *educ* Truro Sch; Cam Univ; Ex Univ; Ox Univ; Ripon Coll Cuddesdon; *CV* AC Bodmin w Lanhydrock & Lanivet 1987–90; Bp Truro's Domestic Chapl 90–94; Truro Dioc Ecum Offr 1990–93; Dir Ministerial Training, Truro 1993–2001; Can Chan, Truro Cathl 1994–2001; Can Prec, Truro Cathl from 2001; Dioc Lit Adv, Truro from 2001; Chapl Epiphany Ho, Truro from 2007; M Dioc Brd Ed 1988–90; M Dioc Decade of Evan Steering Cttee 1990–94; Exec M of Churches Together Cornwall 1990–94; M CTE Enabling Grp 1992–94; M Praxis Counc from 1996; County Chapl, Royal British Legion from 1998; Chair, Dioc Deaf Ministry Support Grp 1996–2001; Chair, Dioc Lit Cttee from 2001; M Dioc Formation Grp from 2004; Chair, Dioc Porvoo Link Cttee from 2009; M CFCE from 2011; Dir Assco English Cathls from 2011
GS 2010– *Tel:* 01872 245003
Fax: 01872 277788
email: perran@perrangay.com

GEORGE, Rt Worshipful Charles Richard, MA, QC
Francis Taylor Building Inner Temple London EC4Y 7BY [DEAN OF THE ARCHES AND AUDITOR] *b* 1945 *educ* Bradfield Coll Magdalen Coll Ox; Corpus Christi Coll Cam; *CV* Asst master Eton College 1967–72; Barrister, Francis Taylor Building, Inner Temple (formerly 2 Harcourt Buildings) from 1975; Chancellor Dioc of S'wark 1996–2009; M of Panel of Chairmen of Bps' Disciplinary Tribunals for Provinces of Canterbury and York 2007–09; M of Ho Coun, St Stephen's Ho, Ox from 1999; Visiting Lecturer in Environmental Law, KCL from 2006; Dean of the Arches, Auditor of the Chancery Court of York, Master of the Faculties from 2009
GS 2009– *Tel:* 020 7353 8415
Fax: 020 73537622
email: charles.george@ukgateway.net

GERMANY AND NORTHERN EUROPE, Archdeacon of. See LLOYD, Ven Jonathan Wilford

GIBBS, Revd Dr Jonathan Robert, MA PhD
The Rectory Village Road Heswall, Wirral, Merseyside CH60 0DZ [CHESTER] *b* 1961 *educ* The King's Sch; Chester Jesus Coll Ox; Jesus College, Cam; Ridley Hall, Cam; *CV* AC Stalybridge, Holy Trin

1989–92; Chapl, Basel, Switzerland w Freiburg, Germany 1992–98; R, Heswall from 1998; M Bp's Counc from 1999; M Fin & Central Services Cottee from 1999; Chair of House of Clergy, Dioc Syn from 2006; Chair Dioc Clergy Chairs Forum from 2011; M Standing Ctte Ho of Clergy from 2011; M Coun British Funeral Services from 2012; M Meissen Ctte from 2012
GS 1995–98; 2010– *Tel:* 01513423471
email: jgibbs@heswallparish.co.uk

GIBRALTAR IN EUROPE, Bishop of. See ROWELL, Rt Revd (Douglas) Geoffrey

GIBRALTAR, Archdeacon of. See SUTCH, Ven David

GIBRALTAR, Dean of. See PADDOCK, Very Revd Dr John

GIDDINGS, Dr Philip James, MA, D Phil
5 Clifton Park Rd Caversham Reading RG4 7PD [OXFORD] *b* 1946 *educ* Sir Thos Rich's Sch Glouc; Worc and Nuff Colls Ox; *CV* Lect in Public Admin Ex Univ 1970-72; Sen Lect Politics and Intl Relations, Reading Univ; Rdr; M Dioc Syn from 1974; M Bp's Coun 1979–2006; Lay Vc Pres Dioc Syn 1989–2000; M BSR 1991–96, Exec Cttee 1992–96; M CAC 1992–97; M GS Panel of Chairmen 1995–96; Vc Chair GS Ho of Laity 1995–2000, 2005–10; Chair, GS Ho of Laity from 2010; M AC from 1999; Chair Ch and World Div AC 1999–2002; M Crown Appts Commn Review Grp 1999–2001; Elected M AC from 2000; Chair Coun of MPA from 2003; Convenor, Angl Mainstream UK from 2003; Dep Chair GS Legislative Cttee 2005–10; M GS Appointments Ctte from 2010, M Coun Wycliffe Hall, Oxford from 2011
GS 1985– *Tel:* 0118 954 3892 (Home)
0118 378 8207 (Office)
Fax: 0118 975 3833
email: P.J.Giddings@reading.ac.uk

GILBERTSON, Ven Dr Michael Robert, MA, BA, PhD
Church House Lower Lane Aldford Chester CH3 6HP [ARCHDEACON OF CHESTER] *b* 1961 *educ* Stockport Grammar Sch; New Coll Ox; Cranmer Hall Dur; *CV* Dept of Trade and Industry 1982–1991; C St Matthew's Surbiton 1997–2000; V All Saints Stranton 2000–2010; AD of Hartlepool 2002–2010; Hon Can Durham Cathedral 2008–2010; Adn of Chester from 2010 *Tel:* 01244 681973 (Office)
01244 405253 (Home)
email: michael.gilbertson@chester.anglican.org

GILLEY, Revd Dr Margaret (Meg) Mary, MTheol, PhD
St Chad's Rectory Dunsmuir Grove Bensham Gateshead NE8 4QL [DURHAM] *b* 1954 *educ* Nelson Gr Sch; St And Univ; Dur Univ; NEOC; *CV* Primary Care Devel rsch, Sunderland Health Commn 1991–94; Programmes Mgr, Sunderland Health Auth 1994–96; Locality Dir, Co Durham Health Auth 1996–98; Chief Exec, Darlington Primary Care Grp 1998–2000; C St Jo Birtley 2000–03; V St Mark Stockton & St Jo Elton 2003–2009; Assoc P Lanchester Deanery 2009–11; R Bensham and Teams from 2011
GS 2005–
Tel: 0191 478 6338 07752 432366 (Mobile)
email: meg.gilley@durham.anglican.org

GILLIVER, Miss Joy Alison, MA Oxon, MA, PGCE
3 Wadhurst Rise Brighton BN2 5PW [CHICHESTER] *b* 1961 *educ* Bishop Stopford Sch, Enfield; Regent's Park Coll, Ox Univ; Selwyn Coll Cam, Heythrop Coll, LU; *CV* RE Tchr, Sch of S. Helen & S. Katharine, Abingdon. 1983 -95; Head of RE, Hemel Hempstead Sch. 1995–97; RE Tchr, The Queen's Sch, Bushey 1997–98;Ed consult Birm 1997–98; Comm Develp worker, Kingstanding, Birm 1998–99; Adv ed & training of adults, Chich 1999–2009; Adv for Discipleship and Min, Chich from 2009; M Chich Dioc Rdrs Cttee from 1999; Dir Training Rdrs from 1999; Gov Univ Chich; Trustee Mother Agnes Trust; M English ARC from 2012
GS 2010– *Tel:* 07884 180545
email: joy.gilliver37@freeserve.co.uk

GILLSON, Mr Ross Louis, LLB(Hons), Barrister (England and Wales), Advocate (Guernsey)
Church House Great Smith Street London SW1P 3AZ [ADMINISTRATIVE SECRETARY TO THE HOUSE OF BISHOPS] *b* 1984 *educ* Guernsey Gr Sch; Exeter Univ; Cardiff Univ; Universite de Caen; *CV* Legal practice Guernsey 2007–09; Investigations Officer, Solicitors Regulation Authority 2009–11; Administrative Sec to Ho of Bps from 2011; Honourable Soc of the Inner Temple
Tel: 020 7898 1375
email: ross.gillson@churchofengland.org

GLEDHILL, Rt Revd Jonathan Michael, BA, MA, BCTS, D Univ (Keele)
Bishop's House 22 The Close Lichfield WS13 7LG [BISHOP OF LICHFIELD] *b* 1949 *educ* Strode's Sch Egham; Keele Univ; Bris Univ; Trin Coll Bris; *CV* C All SS Marple 1975–78; P-in-c St Geo Folkestone 1978–83; V St Mary Bredin Cant 1983–96; Tutor/Lect Cant Sch of Min 1983–94; Tutor/Lect SE Inst for Th Educ 1994–96; RD Cant 1988–94; Hon Can Cant Cathl 1992–96; Bp of Southn 1996–2003; M Meissen Commn 1993–96; Chair Angl Old Catholic Internat Co-ordinating Council Coun from 1998; Chair Nat Coll of Evangelists 1998–2010; Bp of Lichfield from 2003; Keele Univ Hon Dr Univ 2007
GS 1995–96, 2003– *Tel:* 01543 306000
Fax: 01543 306009
email: bishop.lichfield@lichfield.anglican.org

GLOUCESTER, Archdeacon of. See SEARLE, Ven Jacqueline Ann

GLOUCESTER, Bishop of. See PERHAM, Rt Revd Michael Francis

GLOUCESTER, Dean of. See LAKE, Very Revd Stephen

GNANADOSS, Miss Vasantha Berla Kirubaibai, B Sc
242 Links Rd London SW17 9ER [SOUTHWARK] *b* 1951 *educ* Portsm Gr Sch; Birkbeck Coll Lon; *CV* Commissioner's Secretariat, Metropolitan Police Service
GS 1990– *Tel:* 020 8769 3515
020 7230 5017
07803 590610 (Mobile)
email: vasanthignanadoss@yahoo.co.uk

GODDARD, Canon Giles William, MA (Cantab); MA Systematic Theology; MA Creative and Life Writing
St John's Vicarage 1 Secker Street London SE1 8UF [SOUTHWARK] *b* 1962 *educ* Lancing Coll Sussx; Clare Coll Camb; King's Coll Lon; S'wark Ordination Course; Goldsmiths Coll Lon; *CV* Asst Buyer John Lewis Partnership 1984–87; Housing Corp 1987–88; Dir Development ASRA Housing Assoc 1988–91; Dir S'wark Dioc Housing Assoc 1991–95; C St Faith's North Dulwich 1995–98; R St Peter's Walworth 1998–2009; AD S'wark and Newington 2001–06; Hon Can S'wark Cathl from 2008; P-in-C St John's Waterloo; Appts Ctte; Chair Inclusive Church
GS 2010– *Tel:* 07762 373674
email: giles@stjohnswaterloo.org

GODDARD, Rt Revd John William, BA
Dean House 449 Padiham Rd Burnley BB12 6TE [SUFFRAGAN BISHOP OF BURNLEY; BLACKBURN] *b* 1947 *educ* St Chad's Coll Dur Univ; *CV* C S Bank 1970–74; C Cayton w Eastfield 1974–75; V Ascen Middlesbrough 1975–82; RD Middlesbrough 1981–87; V All SS Middlesbrough 1982–88; Can and Preb York Minster 1987–88; Can Emer York from 1988; Vc Prin Edin Th Coll 1988–92; TR Ribbleton 1992–2000; Bp of Burnley from 2000
GS 2008– *Tel:* 01282 470360
07779 786114 (Mobile)
Fax: 01282 470361
email: bishop.burnley@googlemail.com

GODDARD, Mrs Madelaine, BSc, SRD
35 Princes Drive Littleover Derby DE23 6DX [DERBY] *b* 1944 *educ* Lewis Sch for Girls; Lon Univ; *CV* Sen Dietitian, Bethnal Green 1967–69; District Dietitian, N Gwent HMC 1969–77; pt tchr, Derby High Sch from 1986; Dioc Pres MU; Tax Commr
GS 2003– *Tel:* 01332 348077
07817 043257 (Mobile)
email: goddard35@btinternet.com

GODDARD, Mrs Vivienne, BA, PGCE
39 Kearsley Ave Tarleton Preston PR4 6BP [BLACKBURN] *b* 1948 *educ* Roch Girls' Gr Sch; Dur Univ; *CV* RE Tchr, Cleveland Girls Grammar School 1970–74 Supply Tchr 1974–76; DirCleveland Lay Training & Foundn Scheme for York Dioc; RE Tchr Bydales School, Marske, 1984–88; Acting Head of Dept, 1988–92; Publishing Manager, Rutherford House, Edinburgh, 1994–95; RE Tchr 1996–97; Local Non-Stipendiary Ministry Officer, Blackb1998; OLM Officer, Blackb 2004; Bp's Officer for LM 1996–2007
GS 1980–88; 2000–
Tel: 01772 812532 07779 786141 (Mobile)
email: viviennegoddard@talktalk.net

GODFREY, Very Revd Nigel Philip, BA; MA; MBA; MSc; MRTPI
St German's Cathedral Office The Deanery Albany Road Peel Isle of Man IM5 1JS [DEAN OF SODOR AND MAN] *b* 1951 *educ* Ripon Coll Cuddesdon; Lon Guildhall Univ; K Coll Lon; *CV* Ripon Coll Cuddesdon 1977. C Kennington St Jo w St Jas S'wark 1979–89; Community of Ch the Servant 1984–93; V Brixton Road Ch Ch S'wark 1989–2001; Prin OLM Scheme 2001–07; Chapl S'wark Cathl 2002–07; V German S & M from 2007; P-in-c Patrick from 2011; Vice-Dean St German's Cathl from 2007; Dean St Germans Cathl from October 2011 *Tel:* 01624 844830
email: dean@sodorandman.im

GODSALL, Revd Andrew Paul, BA
12 Cathedral Close Exeter Devon EX1 1EZ [EXETER] *b* 1959 *educ* Tudor Grange Gr Sch; Birm Univ; Ripon Coll Cuddesdon; *CV* BBC Studio Mgr 1981–86; BBC Radio Pro 1984-86; AC, St John's Great Stanmore, 1988–91; Assoc V, All Saints Ealing Comm, 1991–94; V, All Saints Hillingdon, 1994–2001; DDO, Willesden Area, Lon, 1999–2001; Asst & Chapl Bp Ex, 2001–06; Dir, Counc Worship & Min, 2006; Can Chan, Ex Cathl, 2006; Chair, Willesden Area Litt Resources Grp, 1995–99; Sec, Patterns of Ministry Working party, Ex, 2002–03
GS 2010– *Tel:* 01392 294920
email: andrew.godsall@exeter.anglican.org

GOODER, Dr Paula Ruth, MA, D Phil
61 Linden Rd Bournville Birmingham B30 1JT [BIRMINGHAM] *b* 1969 *educ* Fallowfield C of E H Sch, Loreto Sixth Form Coll, Manch; Worc Coll Ox; Qu Coll Ox; *CV* Tutor in Biblical Studies, Ripon Coll Cuddesdon 1995–2001; Tutor in NT Studies, Qu Foundn 2001–2007; Freelance Writer and Lecturer Biblical Studies from 2007; Can Theol Birm Cathl from 2005–; Canon Theol Guildf Cathl from 2010; Lay Can Salis Cathl from 2010; Six Preacher Cant Cathl from 2012
GS 2005– *Tel:* 0121 744 0260
email: prgooder@gmail.com

GOODING, Canon Ian Eric, B Com, BSc, LTh, Dip PS, C Eng
Holly Tree Cottage 17 Bostocks Lane Sandiacre Derbyshire NG10 5NL [DERBY] *b* 1942 *educ* Nottm H

WHO'S WHO

Sch; Leeds Univ; St Jo Coll Nottm; *CV* Devel/ Production Engineer Turner & Newhall 1965–67, PA to Works Dir 1967–68, Systems Analyst 1968–70; Rdr, Manch Dioc 1968–70; C Wandsworth S'wark 1973–75; C with charge of All SS Wandsworth 1975–77; R Stanton-by-Dale w. Dale Abbey, Derby 1977–2012, R Risley, Derby 1994–2012; sen industrial chapl 1977–2012; RD Erewash 1997–2012; Hon Can Derby Cathl from2002; M DBF and Exec Coun DBF; M Bp's Coun; M Derbyshire Ecum Industrial Cttee; Bd M Erewash Local Strategic Ptnrship 2004–12; Chair Stanton-by-Dale Par Coun 2007–12; M C of E Pensions Bd from 2006; Chair Trustees Chr Broadcasting Coun from 1988
GS 2005–2010
Tel: 0115 8498726 07974 370330 (Mobile)
Fax: 0115 932 4584
email: ian.e.gooding@googlemail.com

GORHAM, Ven Karen Marisa, BA, FRSA
Rectory Stone Aylesbury HP17 8RZ [ARCHDEACON OF BUCKINGHAM; OXFORD] *b* 1964 *educ* Mayflower Sch, Billericay; Trin Th Coll Bris; *CV* C Northallerton w Kirby Sigston 1995–99; P-in-c St Paul Maidstone, Asst DDO and RD Maidstone 1999–2007; Hon Can Cant 2006–07; Adn of Buckingham from 2007
GS 2003–07, 2010
Tel: 01865 208264 01865 208266
email: archdbuc@oxford.anglican.org

GOUDIE, Dr Richard Angus, MB BChir MRCGP
197 Gilesgate Durham DH1 1QN [DURHAM] *b* 1951 *educ* Barnard Castle Sch; St John's Coll Cam; Kings Coll Hosp Lon; Newcastle GP Vocational Training Scheme; *CV* GP, Cartington Terrace Medical Grp, Newcastle 1982–1991; GP, Kepier Medical Practice, Tyne and Wear, 1991; PCC m St Nicholas Church Dur & Dur Deanery Syn m from 1996; M Dur Dioc Syn from 2006; M Dur Dioc Syn Miss Cttee 2006–10; M Dur Bps Counc 2010
GS 2010–
Tel: 0191 3840013
Fax: 0191 5849493
email: angus.goudie@virgin.net

GOVENDER, Very Revd Rogers Morgan, BTh, Dip Th
Manchester Cathedral Cathedral Yard, Victoria St Manchester M3 1SX [DEAN OF MANCHESTER] *b* 1960 *educ* Glenover High Sch, Durban, S Africa; Univ of Natal (Pietermaritzburg), S Africa; St Paul's Coll, Grahamstown, S Africa; *CV* C Ch Ch Overport, S Africa 1985–87; R St Mary Greyville, Durban, S Africa 1988–92; R St Matt Hayfields, Pietermaritzburg, S Africa 1993–99; Adn of Pietermaritzburg 1997–99; R St Thos Berea, Durban 1999–2000; P-in-c Ch Ch Didsbury, Man 2001–05; P-in-c St Chris Withington, Man 2003–05; AD Withington 2003–05; Dean of Man from 2006; M Dioc Syn; M Bp's Coun; M AC CMEAC from 2006; M AC Liturg Commn from 2006; Chair Dioc Pastl Cttee
GS 2008–2010
Tel: 0161 833 2220
0161 792 2801 (Home)
07983 978346 (Mobile)
Fax: 0161 839 6218
email: dean@manchestercathedral.org

GRANTHAM, Suffragan Bishop of. See ELLIS, Rt Revd Dr Tim (Timothy William)

GREEN, Ven John, QHC, BCS
RN Chaplaincy Service MP 1.2 Leach Building Whale Island Portsmouth PO2 8BY [CHAPLAIN OF THE FLEET AND ARCHDEACON FOR THE ROYAL NAVY; ARMED FORCES SYNOD] *b* 1953 *educ* SW Ham County Tech Sch; Hendon Coll of Science and Tech; NE Lon Poly; Linc Th Coll; *CV* Project Eng, Thorn Lighting 1974–77, Sen Eng 1977–80; C St Mich and All Angels, Watford 1983–86; C St Steph w. St Julian, St Alb 1986–91; Chapl RN from 1991; Chapl of the Fleet and Adn for RN from Mar 2006; Hon Can Portsmouth Cath from 2006
GS 2005–
Tel: 023 9262 5055
Fax: 023 9262 5134
email: john.green107@mod.uk

GREENER, Very Revd Jonathan Desmond Francis, MA
The Deanery 1 Cathedral Close Margaret St, Wakefield WF1 2DP [DEAN OF WAKEFIELD] *b* 1961 *educ* Reigate Gr Sch; Trin Coll Cam; Coll of Resurrection Mirfield; *CV* C H Trin w St Matt, Southwark 1991–94; Dom Chapl to Bp of Truro 1994–96; V Ch of Good Shepherd, Brighton 1996–2003; Adn of Pontefract 2003–07; Dean of Wakefield from 2007; Ch Commr from 2011
GS 2003–07
Tel: 01924 239308 (Home)
01924 373923 (Office)
Fax: 01924 215054
email: jonathan.greener@wakefield-cathedral.org.uk

GREENWOOD, Mr Adrian Douglas Crispin, MA, MCIH
91 Lynton Rd Bermondsey London SE1 5QT [SOUTHWARK] *b* 1951 *educ* Judd Sch Tonbridge; Jes Coll Cam; Coll of Law Lon; *CV* Chwrdn St James Bermondsey 1983–92, 1995–2004; Lay Chair St James Bermondsey 1982; Chief Exec Gateway Housing Assoc (formerly Bethnal Green and Victoria Park Housing Assoc Ltd) 1992–2010; Trustee Salmon Youth Centre Bermondsey 2000–10, Chair from 2010; Trustee Isle of Dogs Community Foundation 1998; M Dioc Syn 1994, Lay Chair 2006; M Tower Hamlets Local Strategic Ptnrship 2002–10; Lay Chair Bermondsey Dny Syn 2004; Chair S'wark Churches Care from 2011
GS 2000–
email: amgreenwood@tiscali.co.uk

GREENWOOD, Mr Nigel Desmond, M Phil, M Ed, C CHEM, FRSC, FIBMS, FRIPH
47 Broomfield Adel Leeds LS16 7AD [RIPON AND LEEDS] *b* 1944 *educ* Leeds Gr Sch; Leeds Univ; Leic

Univ; *CV* Leeds Public Health Dept 1962–68; Tobacco Rsch Coun 1968–69; United Leeds Hosps 1969–74; Wigston CFE 1974–77; Keighley Tech Coll 1978–80; Airedale and Wharfedale Coll 1981–95; Educ and Trg Consult 1995–99; Dir One City Projects 1999–2011; Chair Dioc Bd of Educ; Convenor W Yorks Faith in F.E. Gp; Hon Lay Can Ripon Cath from 2009; M Ripon Cathl Coun from 2012; Churchwarden St Chad's Far Headlingly, Leeds from 2012; Trustee Trinity Ch Repair Fund; Trustee Arts@Trinity; Trustee Education Developments Ltd
GS 1990– *Tel:* 0113 261 1438
07940 587618 (Mobile)
email: greenwoodnd@aol.com

GREGORY, Rt Revd Clive Malcolm, BA, MA
61 Richmond Rd Wolverhampton WV3 9JH [AREA BISHOP OF WOLVERHAMPTON; LICHFIELD] *b* 1961 *educ* Sevenoaks Sch; Lanc Univ; Qu Coll Cam; Westcott Ho Cam; *CV* C St Jo Bapt Margate 1988–92; Sen Chapl Univ of Warwick 1992–98; TR Coventry East 1998–2007; Hon MA, Univ of Warwick 1999; Assoc DDO Coventry 2001–07; Area Bp of Wolverhampton from 2007 *Tel:* 01902 824503
Fax: 01902 824504
email: bishop.wolverhampton@lichfield.anglican.org

GRIMSBY, Suffragan Bishop of. See ROSSDALE, Rt Revd David Douglas James

GRYLLS, Revd Catherine Anne, MA, MTh, PGCE
15 Raglan Road Edgbaston Birmingham B5 7RA [BIRMINGHAM] *b* 1970 *educ* John Hanson Sch, Andover; Marlborough Coll; Cam Univ, Birm Univ, Ox Univ; Ripon Coll Cuddesdon; *CV* Tm, S'wark Dioc Retreat House 1991–92; Maths and RE Teacher, Saltley Sch, Birmingham, 1993–95; Maths Teacher, Holyhead Sch, Birmingham, 1995–97; Asst C, St Peter's Hall Green Birm 2000–04; P-in-C St Paul Balsall Heath and P-in-C St Mary & St Ambrose Edgbaston, Birm 2004–05; P-in-C, Balsall Heath and Edgbaston (SS Mary & Ambrose), Birm 2006–08; Incumbent, Balsall Heath and Edgbaston, Birm from 2008
GS 2010– *Tel:* 0121 440 2196
email: gryllsc@btinternet.com

GUERNSEY, Dean of. See MELLOR, Very Revd (Kenneth) Paul

GUILDFORD, Bishop of. See HILL, Rt Revd Christopher John

GUILDFORD, Dean of, [NOT APPOINTED AT TIME OF GOING TO PRESS]

GUILLE, Very Revd John Arthur, MA, B Th, Cert Ed
The Residence 1 Vicars Court Southwell NG25 0HP [DEAN OF SOUTHWELL; SOUTHWELL AND NOTTINGHAM] *b* 1949 *educ* Guernsey Gr Sch; Ch Ch Coll Cant; Southn Univ; Sarum and Wells Th Coll; Univ Wales: Lampeter; *CV* C Chandlers Ford 1976–80; P-in-c St Jo Bournemouth 1980–83; P-in-c St Mich Bournemouth 1983–84; V St Jo w St Mich Bournemouth 1984–89; R St Andre de la Pommeraye Guernsey 1989–99; Vc Dean Guernsey 1996–99; Adn of Basingstoke 1999–2000; Can Res Win Cathl from 1999; Adn of Win 2000–07; M Dioc Syn from 1977; Vc-Dean Win Cathl 2006–07; Dean of S'well from 2007
GS 1990–2000 *Tel:* 01636 817282
email: dean@southwellminster.org.uk
Web: soutwellminster.org.uk

GUNN-JOHNSON, Ven David Allan, S Th, MA
Stage Cross Sanders Lane Bishop's Tawton Barnstaple EX32 0BE [ARCHDEACON OF BARNSTAPLE; EXETER] *b* 1949 *educ* Stratton Gr Sch Biggleswade; St Steph Ho Ox; *CV* C St Matt Oxhey, St Albans 1981–84; C Cheshunt, St Albans 1984–88; TR Colyton, Exeter 1988–2003; RD Honiton 1990–96; Preb Ex Cathl 1999–2003; M Dioc Coun for Worship and Min; Adn Barnstaple from 2003; Dioc Wrdn of Rdrs from 2004; Episc V for the Diaconate from 2009
Tel: 01271 375475 07921 150428 (Mobile)
Fax: 01271 377934
email: archdeacon.of.barnstaple@exeter.anglican.org

HACKNEY, Archdeacon of. See TREWEEK, Ven Rachel

HACKWOOD, Ven Paul, B Sc Dip Theol, MBA
The Archdeaconry 21 Church Rd Glenfield LE3 8DP [ARCHDEACON OF LOUGHBOROUGH; LEICESTER] *b* 1961 *educ* Darlaston Comp Sch; Bradf Coll; Huddersfield Univ; Birm Univ; Bradf Sch of Mgt; Qu Coll Birm; *CV* C All SS Horton Bradf 1989–93; C St Oswald Chapel Green 1991–93; Soc Resp Adv St Alb Dioc 1993–97; V St Marg Thornbury Bradf 1997–2005; Adn Loughborough from 2005; Trustee CUF, M Funding Cttee from 2004; M W Yorks Police Auth 2003–05 *Tel:* 0116 248 7421
0116 231 1632
Fax: 0116 253 2889
email: paul.hackwood@leccofe.org

HADDOCK, Mr Peter,
43 Woodland Way Morden SM4 4DS [SOUTHWARK]
CV Elected to GS 2005
GS 2005–
email: peterhaddock@rspence.plus.com

HALIFAX, Archdeacon of, DAWTREY, Ven Anne

HALL, Ms Elizabeth, BA Econ (Hons); MA; CQSW
25 Marylebone Road London NW1 5JR *b* 1958 *educ* Grange Comp Sch Bradford; Manchester Univ; Northumbria Univ; *CV* Probation Service 1981–92; Guardian ad Litem Service 1992–2001; NE Regional Dir Children & Family Court Adv and Support Service (Cafcass); 2001–08; Head of Safeguarding CafCass; Safeguarding Adviser

WHO'S WHO

(Child and Adult Protection) Church of England and Methodist Church of Britain from 2010
Tel: 020 7467 5194 07969 087868
email: elizabeth.hall@churchofengland.org
2nd email: halle@methodistchurch.org.uk

HALL, Canon John Michael, BA Hons, MA
49 Mount Rd Fleetwood FY7 6QZ [BLACKBURN] *b* 1962 *educ* St Michael's CE High Sch Chorley; Runshaw Sixth Form Coll Leyland; Leeds Univ; Lanc Univ; Mirfield Theol Coll; *CV* Can Bloemfontein from 2000; Can Blackb from 2009; Chair Ho of Clergy Blackb from 2003; V Fleetwood, St David and St Peter
GS 2000–05, 2008–2010 *Tel:* 01253 876176
email: johnbloem@aol.com

HALL, Very Revd John Robert, BA, Hon DD, Hon DTheol, FRSA, Hon FCollT
The Deanery Westminster London SW1P 3PA [DEAN OF WESTMINSTER] *b* 1949 *educ* St Dunstan's Coll Catford; St Chad's Coll Dur; Cuddesdon Th Coll; *CV* Head of RE Malet Lambert High Sch Hull 1971–73; C St Jo Divine Kennington 1975–78; P-in-c All SS S Wimbledon 1978–84; V St Pet Streatham 1984–92; Exam Chapl to Bp of S'wark 1988–92; M GS Bd of Educ 1991–92; Chair FCP 1990–93; Dioc Dir of Educ Blackb 1992–98; Fell Woodard Corp from 1992; M Gov Body, St Mart's Coll Lanc 1992–98; Hon Can Blackb Cathl 1992–94 and 1998–2000; Res Can Blackb Cathl 1994–98; Can Emer from 2000; M Nat Soc Coun 1997–98; Trustee St Gabr's Trust 1998–2006; M Gov Body Cant Ch Ch Univ Coll 1999–2006; Trustee Urban Learning Found 1999–2002; M Gen Teaching Coun 2000–04; Gen Sec Bd of Educ and Nat Soc 1998–2002; CEO, Educ Division and Gen Sec Nat Soc 2003–06; Hon Asst C St Alban S Norwood 2003–06; Gov St Dunstan's Coll 2003–11; Chair of Govs Westmr Sch from 2006; Hon Fell Cant Ch Ch Univ; Hon Fell Coll of Teachers from 2009; Hon Fell St Chad's Coll, Dur from 2009; Dean of Westmr from 2006; Dean of the Order of the Bath from 2006; Pro-Chancellor, Roehampton Univ from 2011
GS 1984–92 *Tel:* 020 7654 4801
020 7654 4803
07973 418859 (Mobile)
Fax: 020 7654 4883
email: john.hall@westminster-abbey.org

HALL, Mr Robin Michael, LLB, MCIPR
44 St Margaret's Square Adelaide Avenue London SE4 1YR [SOUTHWARK] *b* 1979 *educ* Emmanuel Gr Sch; Gorseinon Tertiary Coll; Univ Coll, Dur Univ; *CV* Comm Mgr, London Underground 2007–10; Head of Labour Grp Off, London Borough of Islington, 2003–07; Caseworker & Parliamentary Asst, Office of Oona King MP, 2001–03; Ed & Welfare Off, Dur SU 2000–01; Public Affairs Mgr, Transport for London, from 2010; GS from 2010
GS 2010– *Tel:* 07779241322
email: robinhall79@googlemail.com

HALLIDAY, Canon Malcolm Keith,
8 Malham Court Silsden Keighley BD20 0QB [BRADFORD] *b* 1944 *educ* Rutlish Sch, Merton; *CV* Inland Revenue 1963–1985; Bradf Dioc Sec 1985–2010; Bradf Dioc Dir Edu 1999–2003; Rdr from 1979; Lay Canon Bradf Cathl 1999–2010; Lay Canon Emer Bradf Cathl from 2010
GS 2010– *Tel:* 01535 656777 07949 605093
email: malcolm.halliday@btinternet.com

HAM, Archdeacon of West. See COCKETT, Ven Elwin Wesley

HAMID, Rt Revd David, B Sc, M Div, DD
14 Tufton St London SW1P 3QZ [SUFFRAGAN BISHOP IN EUROPE] *b* 1955 *educ* Nelson High Sch, Burlington, Canada; McMaster Univ Canada; Univ of Trin Coll, Toronto, Canada; *CV* C St Chris Burlington Canada 1981–83; R St Jo Burlington Canada 1983–87; Miss Co-ord for Latin America/ Caribbean, GS of Angl Ch of Canada 1987–96; Dir of Ecum Affairs and Studies, Angl Consultative Coun 1996–2002; Suff Bp in Europe from 2002; ex officio M FOAG (C of E) 1996–2002; Co-Sec ARCIC 1996–2002; Co-Sec Angl-Orthodox Theol Dialogue 1996–2002; Co-Sec Angl-Lutheran Internat Wkg Grp 1999–2002; Co-Sec Angl-RC Commn on Unity and Miss 2001–02; Co-Sec Angl-Baptist Internat Conversations 1999–2002; Co-Sec Angl-Old Catholic Internat Co-ord Coun 1998–2002; Co-Sec Angl-Oriental Orthodox Dialogue 2001–02; Sec Inter-Angl Theol and Doct Commn 2001–02; Sec Inter-Angl Stg Cttee on Ecum Relns 2000–02; Consult to Jt Wkg Grp of WCC and RC Church 2000–06; Consult to Angl-RC Commn on Unity and Miss 2002–12; M Angl-Old Catholic Internat Co-ord Coun from 2005; Co-Chair Ang-RC Commn on Unity and Mission from 2012; Chair Porvoo Panel; Abp of Cant's Link Bp for Common Word Dialogue w Muslims; Chair Ref Grp for Abp of Cant's EU rep
Tel: 020 7898 1160 07801 449113 (Mobile)
Fax: 020 7898 1166
email: david.hamid@churchofengland.org
web: www.eurobishop.blogspot.com
Web: www.eurobishop.blogspot.com

HAMMOND, Sir Anthony Hilgrove, KCB, QC, MA, LLM
The White Cottage Blackheath Guildford GU4 8RB [STANDING COUNSEL TO THE GENERAL SYNOD] *b* 1940 *educ* Malvern Coll; Em Coll Cam; *CV* Solicitor GLC 1965–68; Legal Asst Home Office 1968; Sen Legal Asst 1970; Asst Legal Adv 1974; Prin Asst Legal Adv 1980; Legal Adv and Dep Under-Sec of State and Legal Adv Nn Ireland Office 1988; Solicitor and Dir Gen Legal Services DTI 1992; Treasury Solicitor HM Procurator Gen and Hd of Government Legal Service 1997–2000; Stg Counsel to the GS from 2000; M Legal Adv Commn
Tel: 01483 892607 / 01726 833156 (Home)
020 7898 1799 (Office)
Fax: 01483 890667 01726 833156

HAMMOND, Mr Robert Ian, BA, MA, AIWS, FRSA
22 South Primrose Hill Chelmsford CM1 2RG [CHELMSFORD] *b* 1966 *educ* Hylands Sch Chelmsf; Open Univ; Heythrop Coll, Lon Univ; *CV* NatWest Bank 1985–87; HM Customs and Excise 1987–2005; HM Revenue and Customs from 2005, Senior Prin–Strategic Organisation Design Manager; Freelance Wine and Spirit Educator and Judge from 2009; Chelms Dioc Syn from 1996; M Bp's Coun from 2003; M Chelms Cathl Coun from 2003; M MPA Coun 2006–11; M Dioc Bd of Patr 2007–010; M Dioc Pastl Ctee 2007–2010; M C of E (Eccl Fees) Measure: Steering Ctee 2008–2010; M Dioceses Commn from 2011; Chair of Govs Cathl Sch Chelmsf
GS 2000– *Tel:* 01245 269105
07711 672308 (Mobile)
email: rihammond@me.com

HAMPSTEAD, Archdeacon of. See MILLER, Ven Luke Jonathan

HANCOCK, Rt Revd Peter, MA, BA
Bishop's Lodge Colden Lane Old Alresford SO24 9DY [SUFFRAGAN BISHOP OF BASINGSTOKE; WINCHESTER] *b* 1955 *educ* Price's Sch Fareham; Selw Coll Cam; Oak Hill Th Coll; St Jo Coll Nottm; *CV* C Ch Ch Portsdown 1980–83; C Radipole and Melcombe Regis TM 1983–87; V St Wilf Cowplain 1987–99; RD Havant 1993–98; Hon Can Portsm Cathl 1997–99; Adn of The Meon 1999–2010; Bp of Basingstoke from 2010; Acting Warden of Rdrs 1999–2000; Acting RD Gosport 2002–03; Dir of Mission 1999–2006; Chair CPAS Trustees 2004–2010
GS 2005–2010 *Tel:* 01962 737330 (Office)
email: bishop.peter@winchester.anglican.org

HANCOCK, Mr Paul, BDS, MSc, Dip HSM, MHSM, FRSH
Mamre 3 Arncliffe Drive Burtonwood Warrington WA5 4NB [LIVERPOOL] *b* 1946 *educ* K Edw VI Sch Lich; Man Univ; *CV* Gen dental practitioner 1968–74; Com Dental Officer 1974; Sen Dental Officer 1974–93; Asst District Dental Officer 1993–97; Asst Dir Dental Services 1997–99; Asst Clinical Dir Dental Services from 1999; M Liv Dioc Syn 1997–2003; M Bd of Miss and Unity 1998–2003; Lay Swanwick Conference Cttee Sec and Treas 1998–2003; Par Treas from 2004; M Dny Syn from 2005; M Dioc Syn from 2008
GS 2005– *Tel:* 01925 292559
Fax: 01925 295988
email: hancockpa1@aol.com

HAND, Revd Nigel Arthur, Lth Th
Birmingham Cathedral Colmore Row Birmingham B3 2QB [BIRMINGHAM] *b* 1954 *educ* St John's Th Coll, Nott; *CV* Asst C St Luke 1984–88; Asst C and TV Walton 1988–97; Asst C Selly Park 1997–2004; Adn Moseley 2004–07; P-in-C Selly Park 2004–08; Canon Residentiary and Canon Missioner, Birm Cathl from 2008
GS 2010– *Tel:* 01212621856
Fax: 01212621860
email: canonmissioner@birminghamcathedral.com

HANSON, Dr Charles Goring, MA, PhD
Longlands House Ashgate Lane Wetheral Carlise, CA4 8HE [CARLISE] *b* 1934 *educ* Felsted Sch, Essex; Trin Hall Cam; *CV* Lect and Senior Lect Economic, Univ of Newcastle upon Tyne, 1962–95; Retired
GS 2010– *Tel:* 01228560337
email: charleshansonecon@yahoo.co.uk

HARBORD, Canon (Paul) Geoffrey, MA, LLM
4 Clarke Drive Sheffield S10 2NS [SHEFFIELD] *b* 1956 *educ* Thornbridge Gr Sch Sheff; Keble Coll Ox; Chich Th Coll; Cardiff Univ; *CV* C Rawmarsh w Parkgate 1983–86; C St Geo Doncaster 1986–90; P-in-c St Edm Sprotbrough 1990–95; V Masbrough 1995–2003; JP from 1999; M Legal Aid Commn; M DAC; M Dioc Worship and Liturg Cttee; Dom Chapl to Bp of Sheff from 2003; M Coun Coll of Resurrection, Mirfield; M CDC 2003–06; Hon Can Sheff Cathl 2007
GS 2000– *Tel:* 0114 266 1932 0114 230 2170
Fax: 0114 263 0110
email: geoffrey@bishopofsheffield.org.uk

HARDING, Mr Nick (Nicholas) Andrew, B Ed
8 Belmont Close Mansfield Woodhouse NG19 9GD [SOUTHWELL AND NOTTINGHAM] *b* 1964 *educ* St Philip's RC Coll Birm; Ex Univ; *CV* Primary sch tchr 1985–88; Dir ICIS Trust 1989–94; Educ Officer, S'well Minster 1995–2002; S'well Dioc Children's Officer from 2002; M GS Bd of Educ Children's Panel; M Dioc Liturg Cttee, Bd of Educ, Lay Min Grp; magistrate
GS 2005–
Tel: 01636 817234 (Work)
07827 291694 (Mobile)
Fax: 01623 622272
email: nick@southwell.anglican.org

HARDMAN, Ven Christine Elizabeth, B Sc (Econ), M Th
129A Honor Oak Park Forest Hill London SE23 3LD *b* 1951 *educ* Qu Eliz Girls' Gr Sch Barnet; City of Lon Poly; Westmr Coll Ox; St Alb Dioc Minl Trg Scheme; *CV* Dss St Jo Bapt Markyate 1984–87; C 1987–88; Course Dir St Alb Minl Trg Scheme 1988–96; V H Trin Stevenage from 1996; RD Stevenage from 1999; Adn of Lewisham and Greenwich 2001–12; M Dioc Syn; M Bp's Coun; Prolocutor Lower Ho Conv Cant from 2011; M AC from 2011; M Appts Cttee from 2011; M LAC from 2011
GS 1998–2001, 2004– *Tel:* 020 8699 8207 (Home)
020 7939 9400 (Office)
Fax: 020 7939 9465
email: christine.hardman@southwark.anglican.org

WHO'S WHO

HARGREAVES-SMITH, Mr Aiden Richard, MA, LLM, FRSA
23 Battlebridge Court Wharfdale Rd London N1 9UA [LONDON] *b* 1968 *educ* Batley Gr Sch; Man Univ; Europeenne de Formation Professionnelle, Paris; Univ of Westminster; Man Metropolitan Univ; Coll of Law; *CV* Civil Service 1992–95; Tutor St Anselm Hall 1991–93, Sen Tutor 1993–98, M SCR from 1991; Trainee Solicitor Winckworth and Pemberton 1998–2000; Solicitor Winckworth Sherwood from 2000, Partner from 2007, Head Eccl, Educ and Charities Dep from 2010; Registrar Dioc in Eur and Bp's Legal Sec from 2009; Assoc Fell, Soc for Advanced Legal Studies from 1998; M Eccl Law Soc from 2002, M Gen Cttee from 2005; M Charity Law Assoc; M Soc for the Maintenance of the Faith from 2002; M Coun Qu Victoria Clergy Fund from 2003; Gov Pusey Ho, Ox from 2003; M Sen Appts Review Grp; Assoc M Ecum Coun for Corporate Responsibility from 2005; M C of E Appts Cttee from 2005; M Fees Adv Commn (appt by Pres of Law Soc) from 2005; M Stg Cttee Ho of Laity; M CNC; M Pastl Measure Appeals Panel
GS 2000– *Tel:* 020 7833 9182 (Home)
020 7593 5064 (Office
email: arhs1@tiscali.co.uk

HARLEY, Ven Michael, AKC, Cert Ed, S Th, M Phil
22 St John's Street Winchester Hants SO23 0HF [ARCHDEACON OF WINCHESTER] *b* 1950 *educ* Qu Eliz Gr Sch Crediton; K Coll Lon; Ch Ch Coll Cant; St Aug Coll Cant; Lambeth; Univ of Kent at Cant; *CV* C St William Walderslade, Roch 1975–78; C-in-charge St Barn Weeke, Winch 1978–81; V Pear Tree, Southn 1981–86; V Hurstbourne Tarrant 1986–99; V Chandler's Ford 1999–2009; Winch Dioc Rural Officer 1991–97; RD Andover 1994–99; Chair Winch Dioc Ho of Clergy 2005–09; STETS tutor 2003–06; Hon Can Winch Cath from 2007; Par P St Faith Winch, Master St Cross Winch 2009–11; Adn Winch from 2009
GS 2005– *Tel:* 01962 869442
email: michael.harley@winchester.anglican.org

HARLOW, Archdeacon of. See WEBSTER, Ven Martin Duncan

HARPER, Revd Canon (Rosemary Elizabeth) Rosie, BA, MA LRAM, DipRAM
The Rectory Church Street Amersham Bucks HP7 0DB [OXFORD] *b* 1955 *educ* Blyth G Sch; Birm Univ; Royal Academy of Music, Lon; Heythrop Coll; NTMTC; *CV* Singer & lect vocal studies; Chapl High Sheriff of Buckingham 2009–10; Acting P-in-c St Leonard's Chesham Bois, 2002–03; AC St Mary's w Coleshill, Amersham, 1990–2002; V Great Missenden w Ballinger & Little Hampden 2003; Chapl Bp Buckingham 2005; Bp's Counc 2006; Dioc Brd Patronage 2006; Hon Can Ch Ch from 2011
GS 2010– *Tel:* 01494728988 07743679651
email: rosieswiss@yahoo.com

HARRISON, Prof Glynn, MD, FRCPsych
2 Harley Place Clifton Bristol BS8 3JT [BRISTOL] *b* 1949 *educ* Havelock Sch Grimsby; Dundee Univ; *CV* Consult psychiatrist, Nottm 1982–94; Foundation Chair of Com Mental Health, Nottm Univ 1994–97; Norah Cooke Hurle Prof of Mental Health, Bris Univ 1997–2009; Hon Consult Psychiatrist, AWP Trust, Bath 1997–2009; Prof Emeritus of Psychiatry, Bris Univ from 2009; Pres Internat Federation of Psychiatric Epidemiology from 2007; M CNC from 2007
GS 2005–
email: glynn.harrison9@gmail.com

HARRISON, Dr Jamie (James Herbert), MB, BS, FRCGP, MA
5 Dunelm Court South St Durham DH1 4QX [DURHAM] *b* 1953 *educ* Stockport Gr Sch; Magd Coll Ox; K Coll Hosp Medical Sch Lon; *CV* GP Durham City from 1990; Pres SCR St Jo Coll Dur; Rdr; Lay Chair, Dur Dioc Syn; Dep GP Dean Dir, Northern Deanery, North East SHA
GS 1995– *Tel:* 0191 384 8643
Fax: 0191 386 5934
email: dunelm5@btinternet.com

HART, Mr Peter David, Cert. Ed
10 Ashbank Place Crewe Cheshire CW1 3FR [CHESTER] *b* 1949 *educ* Crewe Grammar Sch; Madeley Coll of Edu; *CV* Primary Sch Teacher 1971–2004; Lay Chair Nantwich Deanery Syn; M Archdiaconal Miss and Pastoral Cttee; Lay Chair Foward in Faith Ches Dioc
GS 2010– *Tel:* 01270216248 07857500115
email: peter.hart03@talktalk.net

HASLAM, Mrs (Agnes) Lois, Dip Ad Ed, Cert Ed
3 Poplar Close Gatley Cheadle Cheshire SK8 4LU [CHESTER] *b* 1938 *educ* Whalley Range High Sch Man; Man Univ; Totley Hall Coll of Educ; *CV* Tchr St Marg C of E Secdry Sch Man 1959–60; tchr Cheadle Adult Educ Cen 1961–70, 1972–75, Prin 1975–84; tchr Gatley Playgroup 1970–72; Stockport Boro Co-ord for Adult Basic Educ 1984–95; retd 1995; Lay Chair Stockport Dny Syn; Dioc Selector for Ordinands; Spiritual Dir; past M Melanesian Wkg Grp; M Dioc Bd of Educ, Adult Educ and Lay Trg, Cathls Meas 1999 Transitional Coun, Round Tables Future of Educ and Trg; Nat Bp's Selector for 4 years
GS 2005– *Tel and Fax:* 0161 428 2164
email: loishaslam@btinternet.com

HAWKINS, Revd Canon Clive, MA, Dip Th, DHSM
Eastrop Rectory 2A Wallis Rd Basingstoke RG21 3DW [WINCHESTER] *b* 1953 *educ* Simon Langton Gr Sch for Boys, Cant; St Pet Coll Ox; Trin Th Coll Bris; *CV* C Ch Ch Winch 1982–86; R St Mary Eastrop, Basingstoke from 1986; AD Basingstoke 2000–08; M Bp's Coun, Dioc Stg Cttee, Dioc Syn, N Area Team 2000–08, N Area Pastl Cttee 2000–08; M Strg Cttee Eccl Offices (Terms of Service) Measure; CNC

GS 2005– *Tel:* 01256 830021 (Home)
01256 464249 (Church)
Fax: 01256 330305
email: clive.hawkins@stmarys-basingstoke.org.uk

HAWKINS, Rt Revd David John Leader, B Th, L Th, ALCD
Barking Lodge 35 Verulam Ave Walthamstow London E17 8ES [AREA BISHOP OF BARKING; CHELMSFORD] *b* 1949 *educ* Wrekin Coll Shrops; Nottm Univ; Lon Coll of Div; St Jo Coll Nottm; *CV* C St Andr Bebington 1973–76; Wrdn Bida Bible Trg Cen, Nigeria 1976–82; Can Emer Kaduna, Nigeria 1982; P-in-c St Matt with St Luke Ox 1983–86; V St Geo Leeds 1986–99, TR 1999–2002; Exec Trustee, St Geo's Crypt 1986–2002; Chair Dioc Communications Cttee, Ripon and Leeds 1998–2002; Chapl Yorks Country Cricket Club 1986–2002; Chair of Trustees Leeds Faith in Schs 1993–2002; Dir Ashlar Ho 1986–2002; Area Bp of Barking from 2003; Dioc Hd Bp Miss and Par Devel from 2004; Dioc Hd Bp Youth and Children from 2004; Apb's Hd Bp on Black Majority Ch from 2006; Pres Bardsey Bird and Field Observatory from 2007; Chair Lon Global Day of Prayer 2007 *Tel:* 020 8509 7377
Fax: 020 8521 4097
email: b.barking@chelmsford.anglican.org

HAWKINS, Revd (Patricia Sally) Pat, MA, BPhil, BTh, CQSW
The Vicarage Lymer Road Oxley Wolverhampton WV10 6AA [LICHFIELD] *b* 1959 *educ* Wygeston Girls Gr Sch, Leic; Lady Margaret Hall, Ox; Exeter Univ;St. Stephen's House Th Coll; *CV* Residential Social worker w adolescents 1980–83; LA Social Worker, Devon 1985–86; M Comm of St. Francis 1986–99; C, P of Stafford 2001–04; Incumbent, P of Oxley 2004; Area Dean, Wolverhampton 2008; M Lichf Dioc Syn 2003–4, from 2006; Preb Lichfield Cathl from 2009; RD Wulfrun from 2011
GS 2010– *Tel:* 01902 783342
email: pathawkins@btinternet.com

HAWLEY, Ven John Andrew, BD, AKC, Cert Theol
19 Clarence Park Blackburn BB2 7FA [ARCHDEACON OF BLACKBURN] *b* 1950 *educ* Ecclesfield Gr Sch; K Coll Lon; Wycliffe Hall Th Coll; *CV* C H Trin Hull 1974–77; C Bradf Cathl 1977–80; V All SS Woodlands, Doncaster 1980–91; TR Dewsbury 1991–2002; Chair Mission Doncaster 1985–2001; M Bp's Coun 1985–91; Vc Chair Wakef Dioc BMU 1991–96; M Action Partners Coun 1992–99; Chair Wakef Dioc Communications 1996–2002; Chair Wakef Dioc Red Chs Uses 1999–2002; Chair Wakef Dioc Ho of Clergy 2000–02; M Pastl Measure Review Grp from 2001; M Misc Provisions Measure Revision Grp from 2000; Adn of Blackburn from 2002; Acting Adn of Lanc from 2010; Vice Chair Abps' Coun Working Grp on House for Duty 2010–12
GS 1996–2002
Tel: 01254 262571 01254 503074 (Secretary)
07980 945035 (Mobile)
Fax: 01254 667309
email: archdeacon.blackburn@gmail.com

HEALD, Mrs Veronica Mary,
9 West Street Geddington Kettering Northants NN14 1BD [PETERBOROUGH] *b* 1949 *educ* Barnsley Girs High Sch; Barnsley Tech Coll; *CV* NHS Sec from 2009; Elected GS 2010
GS 2010– *Tel:* 01536744276
email: v.heald@talktalk.net

HENDERSON, Ven Janet, BA, RGN
Hoppus House Smith Lane, Hutton Conyers Ripon HG4 5DX [ARCHDEACON OF RICHMOND; RIPON AND LEEDS] *b* 1957 *educ* Ardwyn Gr Sch, Aberw; Dur Univ; Addenbrooke's Sch of Nursing, Cam; Cranmer Hall Dur; *CV* C SS Pet and Paul Wisbech 1988–90; Par Deacon, Bestwood TM Nottm 1990–93; Lect, St Jo Coll Nottm 1993–97; Lect, Cam Theol Federation 1997–2001; P-in-c St Patr Nuthall and Dean of Women's Min, S'well and Nottm Dioc 2001–07; Res Can Ripon Cathl 2007–11; Adn of Richmond from 2007
Tel: 01765 601316
email: janeth@riponleeds-diocese.org.uk

HENDERSON, Ven Julian Tudor, MA
The Old Cricketers Portsmouth Rd Ripley Woking GU23 6ER [ARCHDEACON OF DORKING; GUILDFORD] *b* 1954 *educ* Radley Coll; Keble Coll Ox; Ridley Hall Cam; *CV* C St Mary Islington 1979–83; V Em and St Mary in the Castle, Hastings 1983–92; V H Trin Claygate 1992–2005; RD 1996–2001; Chair Dioc Evangelical Fellowship 1997–2001; Hon Can Guild Cathl 2002; Tutor Dioc Min Course from 2003; Adn of Dorking from 2005; Chair Intercontinental Ch Soc from 2011; Chair Bus Ctte from 2012
GS 2004– *Tel:* 01483 479300 (Office)
01483 479568 (Home)
email: julian.henderson@cofeguildford.org.uk

HEPPLESTON, Mr Michael,
Turnpike House 1 Turnpike Newchurch Lancashire BB4 9DU [MANCHESTER] *b* 1957 *CV* Man Dioc Syn; Man Min & Pstrl Cttee; Organist and Mus Dir St Michael & All Angels Peek Green; Regional Operations Mgr, Media on the Move from 2005
GS 2010– *Tel:* 01706 220349
email: mheppleston@mediaotm.com

HERBERT, Revd Clare Marguerite, BA, MTh, CQSW
37 Sydenham Hill London SE26 6SH [LONDON] *b* 1954 *educ* Okehampton Sch; St Hild's Coll, Dur Univ; New Coll, Edinb Univ; Social Work Dept, Bris Univ; Linc Th Coll; *CV* Parish Worker and Asst Univ Chapl, St Paul's Univ Ch, Bris 1981–85; Child and Family Social Worker, North Bris,

WHO'S WHO

1986–89; Paediatric Renal Social Worker, Southmead Hosp, Bris 1989–92; Pastoral Care Adv, Lay Ministry Dept Lon Dioc, 1992–95; C, St Martin-in-the-Fields, 1995–98; R, St Anne w St Thomas and St Peter Soho, 1998–2007; National Coord of Inclusive Church, 2007–10; Lect Inclusive Th at St Martin-in-the-Fields, from 2010; Bp's Staff and Area Counc of the Two Cities Area of the Lon Dioc, 2000–05; Dean of Women for the Two Cities Area.
GS 2010
Tel: 0208 761 3616 0207 766 1143 07504 577210
Fax: 0207 839 5163
email: herbert.clare@googlemail.com

HEREFORD, Archdeacon of. See BENSON, Ven Paddy

HEREFORD, Bishop of. See PRIDDIS, Rt Revd Anthony Martin

HEREFORD, Dean of. See TAVINOR, Very Revd Michael Edward

HERTFORD, Archdeacon of. See JONES, Ven Trevor Pryce

HERTFORD, Suffragan Bishop of. See BAYES, Rt Revd Paul

HESKETT, Mr Robert William, B Sc, FRICS
5 Strand London WC2N 5AF [CHURCH COMMISSIONER] *b* 1953 *educ* St Edw Sch Ox; Univ of S Bank; *CV* With Land Securities plc from 1978, currently Portfolio Dir for Lon; Dep Chair Assets Cttee and Chair Property Grp; Ch Commr from 1998
Tel: 020 7024 3857
Fax: 020 7024 3770
email: robert.heskett@landsecurities.com

HIBBERT, Revd Richard Charles, BA
Christ Church Vicarage 115 Denmark St Bedford MK40 3TJ [ST ALBANS] *b* 1962 *educ* Merchant Taylors' Sch Northwood; Trin Coll Bris; *CV* C St Mary Luton 1996–2000; V Ch Ch Bedford from 2000; asst RD Bedford 2004–2010; RD Bedford from 2010; M CEEC 2006–2010; M MPA Coun from 2010
GS 2005– *Tel and Fax:* 01234 359342
email: vicar@ccbedford.org
Web: www.ccbedford.org

HILL, Rt Revd Christopher John, BD, AKC, M Th
Willow Grange Woking Rd Guildford GU4 7QS [BISHOP OF GUILDFORD] *b* 1945 *educ* Sebright Sch Worcs; K Coll Lon; *CV* C Tividale Lich 1969–73; C Codsall 1973–74; Abp's Asst Chapl on Foreign Relations 1974–81; Abp's Sec for Ecum Affairs 1981–89; Angl Sec ARCIC I and II 1974–91; Hon Can Cant Cathl 1982–89; Chapl to HM The Queen 1987–96; Can Res and Prec St Paul's Cathl 1989–96; M C of E-German Chs Conversations 1987–89; C of E Nordic-Baltic Conversations 1989–93; Vc Chair Eccl Law Soc 1993–2002, Chair from 2002; Chair Cathl Precs Conf 1994–96; Co-Chair C of E-French Protestant Conversations 1993–98; M Legal Adv Cttee from 1991; Co-Chair Lon Soc Jews and Chrs 1991–96; M CCU 1991–96, Chair from 2008; Bp of Stafford 1996–2004; M FOAG 1997–2008, Vc Chair from 1998 (now known as Faith and Order Commission - FAOC); Co-Chair Meissen Th Conversations from 1998; Vc-Chair Ho of Bps' Wkg Pty on Women in the Episcopate 2000–04; M Wkg Pty on Review of Bps' legal costs, Fees Adv Commn 2003; M Liturg Commn 2003–05; M Ordinal Revision Grp from 2004; M CDC from 2004; Chair Wkg Pty on Women Bps 2005–06; M Ho of Bps Theol Grp from 2005; Clerk of the Closet from 2005; Bp of Guildford from 2004; Chair CCU from 2008; Chair Bps' Eur Grp from 2008; M King's Coll Lon Coun from 2009; Vc Pres Coun of European Ch from 2009; M Ho of Lords (Lords Spiritual) from 2010; M ARCIC III from 2011
GS 2000– *Tel:* 01483 590500
Fax: 01483 590501
email: bishop.christopher@cofeguildford.org.uk

HILL, Rt Revd Michael Arthur,
58a High St Winterbourne Bristol BS36 1JQ [BISHOP OF BRISTOL] *b* 1949 *educ* Wilmslow Gr Sch; NW Cheshire CFE; Man Coll of Commerce; Ridley Hall Cam; Fitzw Coll Cam; *CV* C St Mary Magd Addiscombe 1977–80; C St Paul Slough 1980–83; P-in-c St Leon Chesham Bois 1983–90, R 1990–92; RD Amersham 1989–92; Adn of Berks 1992–98; Bp of Buckingham 1998–2003; Bp of Bristol from 2003
GS 1995–98, 2003– *Tel:* 01454 777728
07808 290908 (Mobile)
Fax: 01454 777814
email: bishop@bristoldiocese.org

HILL, Ven Peter, BSc, PGCE, MTh
4 Victoria Crescent Sherwood Nottingham NG5 4DA [ARCHDEACON OF NOTTINGHAM; SOUTHWELL AND NOTTINGHAM] *b* 1950 *educ* Man Univ; Nottm Univ; Wycliffe Hall, Ox; *CV* Schoolteacher 1973–81; C Porchester, S'well 1983–86; V Huthwaite 1986–95; P-in-c Calverton 1995–2004; RD S'well 1997–2001; Chair Dioc Bd of Educ 2001–04; Dioc Chief Exec 2004–07; Hon Can S'well Minster from 2001; Adn of Nottingham from 2007; M Dearing Commn Church Schools 1999–2001; M Conv Comm on Guidelines for the Professional Conduct of the Clergy 2000–03; Faiths Advocate Nottingham City Strategic Partnership from 2010; Vc Dioc Commn from 2011
GS 1993–2004, 2010– *Tel:* 0115 985 8641 (Home)
01636 817206 (Office)
07771 778182
Fax: 01636 815882 (Office)
email: archdeacon-nottm@southwell.anglican.org

HILLS, Mr Nicholas Paul, BA
Church House Westminster London SW1P 3AZ [ADMINISTRATIVE SECRETARY, CENTRAL SECRETARIAT] *b* 1964 *educ* Sir Joseph Williamson's Mathematical Sch, Roch; Leic Univ; *CV* 1987–99 Teacher; on staff of Abps' Coun from 1999; Fin Div from 1999; Central Secretariat from 2002; Sec Appts Cttee; Sec Ho of Laity and Ho of Laity Stg Cttee; Asst Sec Abps' Coun *Tel:* 020 7898 1363
Fax: 020 7989 1369
email: nicholas.hills@churchofengland.org

HIND, Mr Timothy Charles, MA, FCII
Plowman's Corner The Square Westbury-sub-Mendip Wells BA5 1HJ [BATH AND WELLS] *b* 1950 *educ* Watford Boys Gr Sch; St Jo Coll Cam; *CV* Various posts at Sun Life (now AXA) from 1972; Quality Mgr, AXA UK; Chartered Insurer; M Bp's Coun; Chair Dioc Vacancy-in-See Cttee 1996–98; M Dioc Bd of Educ 1995–97; M Bd of Educ (Schs and Colls) 1995–97; M C of E Pensions Bd 1996–2010; M C of E Pensions Bd Investment and Fin Cttee 1996–97; M ABM 1998; M DRACSC 1999–2008; Lay Vc-Chair Dioc Syn from 1999–2009; Lay Chair Axbridge Dny Syn 1984–91; M Dioc Bd of Patr 1986–94; Vc-Chair Bd of Govs Kings of Wessex Com Sch 1996–99; Churchwarden St Jo Bapt Axbridge 2001–05; Sec OSG 2001–04; Chair OSG 2004–11; Vc Chair C of E Pensions Bd from 2010; Vc Ho of Laity from 2011; Legis Cttee from 2011; Standing Orders Cttee from 2011
GS 1995–2000, 2001– *Tel:* 01749 870356 (Home)
07977 917434 (Mobile, Office)
07977 580374 (Mobile)
email: tim@hind.org.uk

HINE, Mr Peter Geoffrey, BA
Chapel Howe Sour Nook Sebergham Carlisle CA5 7DY [CARLISLE] *b* 1949 *educ* Wallasey Tech Gr Sch; Dur Univ; *CV* Various posts w Financial Services sector 1972–98; Vol ch and ed worker 1998–2002; Trustee C of E Pension Scheme 1998–2001; Trustee and Dir Worldshare from1999; Finance Resources Off Dioc Carlisle from 2002
GS 2010– *Tel:* 01228 815401 07584 684297
Fax: 01228 815400
email: ghine@carlislediocese.org.uk

HM FORCES, Bishop to. See VENNER, Rt Revd Stephen Squires

HOBBS, Revd Christopher John Pearson, BA, BD, Dip.Ed., AKC
St Thomas's Vicarage 2 Sheringham Ave Southgate London N14 4UE [LONDON] *b* 1960 *educ* St Andrew's Cathl Sch, Sydney; Sydney Univ; King's Coll Lon; Wycliffe Hall Th Coll; *CV* Tchr, Hill House International Junior Sch 1983–86; C, Christ Church Barnet 1991–94; Asst Minister, Jesmond Parish Church 1994–97; V St Thomas's Oakwood from 1997
GS 2010– *Tel and Fax:* 02083601749
email: christopher.hobbs@blueyonder.co.uk

HOBBS, Revd Maureen Patricia, BSc, Dip Bus Admin, CTM
Vicarage 20 Dartmouth Ave Pattingham WV6 7DP [LICHFIELD] *b* 1954 *educ* Wanstead High Sc Lon; Surrey Univ; Warwick Univ; Westcott Ho Cam; *CV* Asst linguist specialist, GCHQ 1976–78; recruitment and mgt consult 1978–95; C St Chad w. St Mary, Shrewsbury 1997–2001; R Baschurch and Weston Lullingfield w. Hordley from 2001; P-in-C Pattingham w Patshull from 2009; RD Tryshull from 2009; Min Dev Adv for Wolverhampton Episcopal Area; Dioc Adv for Women in Min 2003–11
GS 2005–10; 2010–
Tel: 01902 700257 07812 805371 (Mobile)
email: hobbsmaureen@yahoo.co.uk

HODGSON, Mr Charles Christopher, BSc, NCA
The Smithy East Worlington Crediton EX17 4SY [EXETER] *b* 1945 *educ* St Peter's, Weston-super-Mare; Wellington Coll, Berks; Bristol; *CV* Rtd Eng; hill farmer; M Bp's Dioc Coun Ex; Coun for Church and Society, Ex; Dioc Rural Support Grp, Ex; M Inter Dioc Finance Forum; M GS Rural Affairs Grp
GS 2010– *Tel:* 01884 861571 0796064023
email: catherine-charles.hodgson@virgin.net

HOLBROOK, Rt Revd John Edward, MA
Orchard Acre 11 North Street Mears Ashby Northampton NN6 0DW [SUFFRAGAN BISHOP OF BRIXWORTH; PETERBOROUGH] *b* 1962 *educ* Bris Cathl Sch; St Pet Coll Ox; Ridley Hall Cam; *CV* C Barnes St Mary S'wark 86–89; C Bletchley 1989–93; C N Bletchley CD 1989–93; V Adderbury w Milton 1993–2002; RD Deddington 2000–02; R Wimborne Minster 2002–11; P-in-c Witchampton, Stanbridge and Long Crichel etc 2002–11; P-in-c Horton, Chalbury, Hinton Martel and Holt St Jas 2006–11; RD Wimborne 2004–11; Chapl S and E Dorset Primary Care Trust 2002–11; Can and Preb Sarum Cathl 2006–11; Suff Bp of Brixworth Pet from 2011; Can Pet Cathl from 2011
Tel: 01733 562492 01604 812318
email: bishop.brixworth@peterborough-diocese.org.uk

HOLGATE, Mr Robert Geoffrey, BA, FCA
66 Purnells Way Knowle Solihull B93 9EE [BIRMINGHAM] *b* 1952 *educ* Lawrence Sheriff Sch, Rugby; Leeds Univ;; *CV* C Accountant trainee 1973–76; Audit Asst 1976–78; Tax Asst and Manager 1978–89; Senior Tax Manager KPMG from 1989; Dioc Birm Bp's Counc 1998–2010; Fin Subcttee 1998–2010; Vice Chair Dioc Brd Fin 2001–10; Acting Chair Dioc Brd Fin 2008–09; M Inter Dioc Fin Forum 2008–10; M Dioc Vacancy in See Cttee from 2000
GS 2010– *Tel:* 0121 232 3406 01564 776573
email: rands.holgate@btinternet.com

HOLLINGHURST, Revd Anne Elizabeth, BA(Hons); MSt
23 Hall Place Gardens St Albans AL1 3SB [ST ALBANS] *b* 1964 *educ* Range High Sch and Sixth Form, Formby; Univ Bristol; Univ Camb; *CV* Youth worker St Stephen Hyson Green & St Leodegarius Old Basford 1990–93; AC St Saviour Nottingham 1996–99; Chapl Derby Cathl 1999–2005; Chapl Bp of Manchester 2005–10; Res Can Manchester Cath 2005–10; V St Peter's St Albans from 2010; Dioc Syn
GS 2011– *Tel:* 01727 851464
email: annehollinghurst@hotmail.co.uk

HOLMES, Mrs Madeleine Ratcliffe,
Le Peladis Rte Pommier 24350 Lisle Dordogne France [EUROPE] *b* 1942 *educ* Knutsford Secondary Sch; Wimslow Eve Class; St John's, Nottm; *CV* Fashion Model 1976–80; Admin/Direct Mail copywriting and PRPerferap Ltd, High Wycombe 1980–86; Sales & Production Co-ord Communications Direct High Wycombe, 1985–86; PA and PR customers of Software House, Actiontech Ltd, High Wycombe, 1987; PA to Dir Gen Royal Institute of Public Administration 1989–91; Odgers & Co London PA to Management Consult 1989–97; Rder 2006; Dioc Synod Rep 2006–09; Contribtr Chapl Bp's Coun 2006–09; Local Radio Programme for Chapl 2007–12; Archdeaconry subcttee 'Building Together in France' 2007; Prayer Chain Coord Chapl from 2008; Dioc Environment Off from 2010; M MPA Team
GS 2010– *Tel:* 00335 53 04 85 44
email: madeleine@peladis.plus.com
2nd email: madeleine.holmes13@gmail.com

HOLTAM, Rt Revd Nicholas Roderick, BA; MA; Hon DCL; BD; FKC
South Canonry 71 The Close Salisbury, Wilts SP1 2ER [BISHOP OF SALISBURY] *b* 1954 *educ* Latymer Gr Sch Edmonton; Collingwood Coll, Dur; King's Coll Lon; Westcott H Camb; *CV* AC St Dunstan and All Saints Stepney 1979–83; Tutor Linc Theol Coll 1983–87; V Christ and St John's with St Luke's Isle of Dogs 1988–95; V St Martin-in-the-Fields 1995–2011; Bp of Salisbury from 2011; Dioc Syn Linc 1986–87; Stepney Area Syn 1988–95; Chair Tower Hamlets Dny Com for Social Responsibility 1990–91; ABM/Min Div Educ Selector 1992–2001; Tower Hamlets Dny Syn Standing Cttee 1993–95; Stepney Area Bp's Coun 1993–95; Westminster (St Margaret's) Dny Syn 1995–2011; Dioc Bps' Coun 2007–11; Dioc Syn Lon 2008–11 *Tel:* 01722 334031
Fax: 01722 4113112
email: bishop.salisbury@salisbury.anglican.org

HORSHAM, Archdeacon of. See COMBES, Ven Roger Matthew

HORSHAM, Area Bishop of. See SOWERBY, Rt Revd Mark

HOUGHTON, Revd James Robert, AKC, Cert Ed
St Michael's Vicarage 15 Long Acre Close Eastbourne BN21 1UF [CHICHESTER] *b* 1944 *educ* Highgate Sch; K Coll Lon; St Luke's, Ex; *CV* C St Chad E Herrington, Sunderland, Dur 1968–70; Asst Youth Chapl, Bris 1970–72; C St Lawr Heavitree, Ex 1973–78; Mgr Yiewsley and W Drayton Com Cen and Hon C St Mart W Drayton, Lon 1978–80; Chapl and Head of Relig Studies Grey Coat Hosp, Westmr, Lon 1980–88; Chapl and Head of Relig Studies Stonar Sch, Melksham, Salis 1988–96; Chapl and Head of Relig Studies Sch of St Mary and St Anne, Abbots Bromley, Lich 1996–99; R Buxted and Hadlow Down, Chich 1999–2002; V St Mich and All Angels, Eastbourne, Chich from 2002
GS 2005– *Tel:* 01323 645740
email: fatherjamie@btopenworld.com

HOULDING, Preb David Nigel Christopher, AKC, DD(hc)
All Hallows' House 52 Courthope Rd London NW3 2LD [LONDON] *b* 1953 *educ* K Sch Cant; K Coll Lon; St Aug Coll Cant; *CV* Lay Chapl Chr Medical Coll Vellore, S India 1976–77; C All SS Hillingdon 1977–81; C St Alb Holborn w St Pet Saffron Hill 1981–85; V St Steph w All Hallows Hampstead from 1985; Preb St Paul's Cath from 2004; Pro-Prolocutor Conv of Cant form 1998; Chair Dioc Ho of Clergy and Vc-Chair Dioc Syn from 2000; AD of N Camden 2001–03; Master SSC from 1997; M Dioc Syn from 1991; M Bp's Coun from 1997; M Edmonton Coun; M Dioc Liturg Grp; M Coun ACS; M Coun of St Steph Ho, Ox from 2001; Ldr, Cath Grp in GS 2000 07; M Adv Panel for Vocations 1997–2002; M Weekday Lectionary and Rules to Order the Service Revision Cttees 1999; M CCRJ 2000–01; M GS Appts Cttee from 2001; M CAC Perry Review Strg Grp 2002–03; M Conv Wkg Grp on Clergy Code of Practice 2000–03; M Clergy Employment Review Grp 2003–05 and Follow-up Grp from 2005; M Meth Cov Impl Grp from 2003; Chair C of E Appts Cttee from 2004, reappointed 2006, 2009; M AC 2004–05, re-elected 2007; Fell Nashotah Ho from 2005; M CCU from 2006; M strg ctee, Clergy Terms of Service; Pres Ch Union from 2012
GS 1995– *Tel:* 020 7267 7833
020 7267 6317(Office)
07710 403294 (Mobile)
Fax: 020 7267 6317 (Office)
email: fr.houlding@lineone.net

HOWARD, Father Andrew, BA, MA
45 Lothian Rd Middlesbrough TS4 2HS [YORK] *b* 1963 *educ* Allestree Woodlands Sch Derby; High Peak Coll of FE Buxton; Man Poly; Man Univ; Leeds Univ; Coll of the Resurr Mirfield; *CV* Asst C Worksop Priory 1997–2001; V St Timothy of Ephesus, Hemlington 2001–05; Chapl Univ of Teesside, Assoc P St Jo and St Columba Middlesbrough from 2005
GS 2009– *Tel:* 01642 242926 07740 932758
email: a.howard@tees.ac.uk

HOWE, Ven George Alexander, BA
1 St John's Gate Threlkald Keswick CA12 4TZ b 1905 *educ* Liv Inst High Sch; St Jo Coll Dur; Westcott Ho Th Coll; *CV* C St Cuth Peterlee 1975–79; C St Mary Norton-on-Tees 1979–81; V Hart w Elwich Hall 1981–85; R Sedgefield 1988–91; RD Sedgefield 1988–91; V H Trin Kendal 1991–2000; RD Kendal 1994–99; Adn of Westmorland and Furness 2000–11; Dioc Ecum Offic 2001–11; Chair Ch and Com Fund from 2007; M CCU from 2006; M Meth/Angl Panel for Unity in Miss from 2010; Bps' Chaplain and Chief of Staff from 2011; DDO from 2011; Adn Emer from 2011
Tel: 07879 452763
email: george.howe@carlislediocese.org.uk

HOYLE, Very Revd Dr David Michael, MA, PhD
Bristol Cathedral College Green Bristol BS1 5TJ [DEAN OF BRISTOL] *b* 1957 *educ* Watford Boys Grammar Sch; Corpus Christi Coll Cam; Ripon Coll Cuddesdon; *CV* Asst C Good Shepherd Cam1986–1988; Chapl and Fell Magdalene College Cam1988–1991; Dean and Fell Magadalene Coll Cam 1991–1995; Dir of Studies Magadalene Coll Cam from 1995; V Ch Ch Southgate 1995–2002; Dir POT Edmonton Area 2000–2002; Dir of Mini Dioc of Glos and Can Res Glos Cathl 2002–2010; Dean of Bristol Cathl from 2010; Secretary Ho of Bps Theol Gp 2002–2007
Tel: 0117 926 4879
Fax: 0117 925 3678
email: dean@bristol-cathedral.co.uk

HUBBARD, Ven Julian Richard Hawes, MA (Cantab, Oxon)
Church House Westminster London SW1P 3AZ [DIRECTOR OR MINISTRY, ARCHBISHOPS' COUNCIL] *b* 1955 *educ* K Edw VI Gr Sch Chelms; Em Coll Cam; Wycliffe Hall Ox; *CV* C St Dionis Parsons Green Lon 1981–84; Chapl Jesus Coll Ox 1984–89; Tutor Wycliffe Hall Ox 1984–89; Selection Sec ACCM 1989–91; Sen Selection Sec ABM 1991–93; V St Thos on the Bourne Guildf 1993–99; RD Farnham 1996–99; Guidf Dioc FE Officer 1993–97; Dir Minl Trg Guidf Dioc 1999–2005; Res Can Guidf Cathl 1999–2005; Adn Oxf and Res Can Ch Ch from 2005; Dir of Min, AC from 2011
Tel: 020 7898 1390
email: julian.hubbard@churchofengland.org

HUDSON-WILKIN, Revd Rose Josephine, B Phil Ed
Vicarage Livermere Rd London E8 4EZ [LONDON] *b* 1961 *educ* Montego Bay High Sch for Girls, Jamaica; Birm Univ; Queens Th Coll Birm; *CV* C St Matt, Wolverhampton 1991–95; Assoc Priest Ch of Good Shepherd, W Bromwich 1995–98; Dioc Officer for Black Angl Concerns 1995–98; V H Trin Dalston and All SS Haggerston from 1998; Chair CMEAC; Bp's Senior Selector
GS 1995–98; 2003–2010 *Tel:* 020 7254 5062
07882 459289 (Mobile)
Fax: 020 7249 7028
email: revdrose@aol.com

HUGHES, Ven Paul Vernon, Dip UEM, Cert Theol Oxon
17 Lansdowne Rd Luton LU3 1EE [ARCHDEACON OF BEDFORD; ST ALBANS] *b* 1953 *educ* Pocklington Sch, E Yorks; Poly Cen Lon; Ripon Coll Cuddesdon; *CV* Res Property Surveyor, Chestertons 1974–79; C Chipping Barnet w Arkley 1982–86; TV Dunstable Tm Min 1986–93; V Boxmoor 1993–2003; RD Hemel Hempstead 1996–2003; Adn of Bedford from 2003; M DBF Cttees, DAC, Dioc Pastl and Miss Cttee, Closed Chs Uses Cttee, Bd for Ch and Soc, New Devel Areas, Bp's Staff, Bp's Staff Deployment Grp *Tel:* 01582 730722
Fax: 01582 877354
email: archdbedf@stalbans.anglican.org

HULL, Suffragan Bishop of. See FRITH, Rt Revd Richard Michael Cokayne

HUMPHREYS, Mrs Jennifer Ann, BA
34 Riverside Banwell North Somerset BS29 6EE [BATH AND WELLS] *b* 1951 *educ* Wesley Coll Bristol; *CV* World Mission Adviser Bath and Wells from 1998
GS 2010– *Tel:* 01934 822052 01749 670777
email: rodjen@humphreys.eclipse.co.uk
2nd email:
jenny.humphreys@bathwells.anglican.org

HUMPHREYS, Ms Jacqueline Louise, MA, LLM
St John's Chambers 101 Victoria St Bristol BS1 6PU [BRISTOL] *b* 1970 *educ* Churchill Comp Sch; Worc Coll Ox; Inns of Court Sch of Law; Cardiff Univ; *CV* Barrister from 1994; M Family Law Bar Assoc from 1998; M Eccles Law Soc from 1999; M Legis Cttee from 2000; M Legal Adv Commn from 2000; M Rules Cttee from 2004, M Legal Aid Cttee from 2006
GS 2000– *Tel:* 0117 921 3456
Fax: 0117 929 4821
email: jacqueline.humphreys@stjohnschambers.co.uk

HUNGERFORD, Miss Priscilla Mary Louise, MBE
Pamber Place Pamber End Tadley, Hants RG26 5QJ [WINCHESTER] *b* 1944 *educ* St Catherine's Bramley; La Colline. Vevey. Switzerland; *CV* Parliament Office, Ho of Lords 1967–2005; Hon Steward Westminster Abbey from 1991; Chwdn St James's church Bramley from 2008
GS 2009–2010, 2010– *Tel:* 01256 850934

HUNTINGDON AND WISBECH, Archdeacon of. See McCURDY, Ven Hugh Kyle

HUNTINGDON, Suffragan Bishop of. See THOMSON, Rt Revd David

HURLEY, Mr Robert Michael, BA
Nursery House 38 Furlong Road Bourne End Bucks SL8 5AA [OXFORD] *b* 1987 *educ* John Hampden Gr

Sch; Sir William Borlase's Gr Sch; Nott Univ; *CV* Info Analyst, Enfield Pri Care Trust; Senior Comm Analyst, North West Lon Hosp NHS Trust
GS 2008– *Tel:* 01628 524214 07845 564464
email: rmh@rmhurley.com

HUTCHINSON-CERVANTES, Revd Canon Ian Charles, BSc, MSc, MA, GDip Th
St George's Anglican Church Calle Nunez de Balboa 43 28001 Madrid Spain 28001 [EUROPE] *b* 1962 *educ* St Thomas' Sch, Malaysia; St Paul's Coll NZ; Amazon Valley Acad, Brazil; Cant Univ NZ; Reading Univ; Cam Univ; Cardiff Univ; Westcott House Th Coll; *CV* Asst C, St Mary the V, Ox, 1989–92; LT St Marys Pro-Cathl, Dioc Venezuela 1993; P-in-c St Andrews w St Barnabbas, Dioc Belize, 1993–97; Miss Personnel Prog Off & Regional Dask Off Latin America and Caribbean, USPG 1997–2004; Chapl St George's Ch, Madrid, Dioc Euro from 2004; Bp's Nom USPG Counc; Bp's Rep PWM; Dioc Obs IERE Syn; Hon Can St John the Baptist, Dioc Argentina 2002; Hon Can Cathl of the Redeemer, Pelotas, Brazil from 2006; Can Cathl Holy Trinity, Gib from 2010
GS 2010– *Tel:* +34915765109
email: chaplain@stgeorgesmadrid.com

INESON, Revd Dr Emma Gwynneth, BA, MPhil, PhD
11 Glentworth Rd Redland Bristol BS6 7EG [BRISTOL] *b* 1969 *educ* Bryntirion Comp Schl, Bridgend, Wales; Birm Univ; Trin Coll Bris; *CV* Tching Asst Eng Lang, Birm Univ, 1993–97; Asst C, Dore, Sheffield 2000–03; Chapl, Lee Abbey Devon 2003–06; Tutor Prac Th, Trin Coll Bris from 2007; NS Assit C and Assoc Min from 2010, St Matthew and St Nathanael, Kingsdown, Bris from 2006; M Bris Dioc Remun Cttee from 2008
GS 2010– *Tel:* 0117 968 2803 0117 962 4186
email: inesone@trinity-bris.ac.uk

INGE, Rt Revd Dr John Geoffrey, BSc, PGCE, MA, PhD, Hon DLitt
Bishop's Office The Old Palace Deansway Worcester WR1 2JE [BISHOP OF WORCESTER] *b* 1955 *educ* Kent Coll Cant; Dur Univ; Keble Coll Ox; Coll of the Resurrection Mirfield; *CV* Asst Chapl Lancing Coll 1984–86; Jun Chapl Harrow Sch 1986–89, Sen Chap 1989–90; V Wallsend St Luke, Newc 1990–96; Res Can Ely Cathl 1996–2003, Vice Dean 1999–2003; Bp of Huntingdon 2003–07; M Coun Ridley Hall from 2004; Trustee, Common Purpose from 2005, Trust Protector from 2011; Bp of Worcester from 2007; Visitor, Com of the Holy Name from 2007; Visitor Mucknell Com from 2009; Chair Coll of Evangelists from 2010; M Faith and Order Commn from 2010; Hon DLitt Univ Worc 2011; Chair Coun Abp's Examination in Theology from 2012 *Tel:* 01905 731599
Fax: 01905 739382
email: bishop.worcester@cofe-worcester.org.uk

IPGRAVE, Rt Revd Michael Geoffrey, PhD, MA, OBE
37 South Road London SE23 2UJ [BISHOP OF WOOLWICH; SOUTHWARK] *b* 1958 *educ* Magd Coll Sch, Brackley; Oriel Coll Ox; St Chad's Coll Dur; SOAS, Lon Univ; Ripon Coll Cuddesdon; *CV* Dn 1982; P 1983 (Peterb); C All SS Oakham w. Hambleton and Egleton, and Braunston w. Brooke, Peterb 1982–85; Asst P The Resurrection, Chiba, Yokohama, Japan 1985–87; TV The Ascension, Leic 1987–90; TV The Holy Spirit, Leic 1990–94; P-in-c St Mary de Castro, Leic 1994–95; TR The Holy Spirit, Leic 1995–99; Dioc Adv on Inter Faith Relns 1990–99; Bp's Chapl 1990–99; Hon Asst P The Presentation, Leic 1999–2004; Hon Can Leic Cathl 1994–2004; Inter Faith Relns Adv, AC 1999–2004; Sec Chs Commn on Inter Faith Relns 1999–2004; Adn of Southwark2004–12; Can Miss S'wark Cathl 2010–12; Bp of Woolwich from 2012 *Tel:* 020 7939 9407
email: bishop.michael@southwark.anglican.org

IRELAND, Revd Mark Campbell, M Theol, MA
35 Crescent Rd Wellington Telford TF1 3DW [LICHFIELD] *b* 1960 *educ* Bromsgrove High Sch; Oban High Sch; St Jo Sch Marlborough; St Andr Univ; Wycliffe Hall Ox; Cliff Coll, Sheff Univ; *CV* Tchr, Murree Chr Sch, Pakistan 1981–82; C St Gabriel Blackb 1984–87; C Lancaster Priory 1987–89; Chapl HM Prison, Lancaster 1987–89; V Baxenden, Accrington 1989–97; Dioc Missr, Lich 1998–2007; TV St Matt Walsall 1998–2007; Tm Leader, Miss Div, Lich Dioc 2002–06; M Bp's Coun 2000–03; V All SS Wellington w. St Cath Eyton from 2007; M Abps' Coun from 2011
GS 1995–98; 2005– *Tel:* 01952 641251 (Home)
01952 248554 (Office)
email: markcireland@gmail.com

ISLE OF MAN, Archdeacon of. See BROWN, Ven Andrew

ISLE OF WIGHT, Archdeacon of the. See BASTON, Ven Caroline Jane

ISON, Very Revd David John, BA, PhD, DPS
The Deanery 9 Amen Court London EC4M 7BU [DEAN OF ST PAUL'S] *b* 1954 *educ* Brentwood Sch; Leic Univ; Nottm Univ; K Coll Lon; St Jo Coll Nottm ; *CV* C St Nic w. St Luke Deptford, S'wark 1979–85; Tutor, Ch Army Trg Coll 1985–88; V St Phil Potters Green, Cov 1988–93; Dioc Officer for CME, Ex 1993–2005; Res Can Ex 1995–2005; Dean of Bradf 2005–11; Dean of St Paul's from 2012
GS 1990–93, 2010– *Tel:* 020 7236 2827
email: thedean@stpaulscathedral.org.uk

ITALY AND MALTA, Archdeacon of. See BOARDMAN, Ven Jonathan Thomas

JACKSON, Revd Richard Charles, MA, MSc, DipHE
The Vicarage Cowfold Road Bolney, Haywards Heath East Sussex RH17 5QR [CHICHESTER] *b* 1961 *educ*

Latymer Upper Sch; Ch Ch, Ox; Cranfield Univ; Trin Coll Bris; *CV* Rural Dean of Horsham, 2004–09; Archdnry Warden of Rdrs 1999–2004; V Rudgwick 1998–2009; C All Saints, Lindfield 1994–98; Senior Agronomist, Cleanacres Ltd 1985–92; Dioc Adv Miss & Renewal from 2009; Dioc Rdrs Cttee 1999–2004
GS 2010– *Tel:* 01444 881301 01273 421021
email: richard.jackson@diochi.org.uk

JACOB, Ven William Mungo, LLB, MA, Ph D
15a Gower Street London WC1E 6HW [ARCHDEACON OF CHARING CROSS; LONDON] *b* 1944 *educ* K Edw VII Sch King's Lynn; Hull Univ; Linacre Coll Ox; Edin Univ; Ex Univ; St Steph Ho Th Coll; *CV* C Wymondham 1970–73; Asst Chapl Ex Univ 1973–75; Dir of Pastl Studies Sarum and Wells Th Coll 1975–80; Vc-Prin 1977–80; Sec Cttee for Th Educ ACCM 1980–86; Warden Linc Th Coll 1986–96; Adn at The Old Deanery 1996–2000; Adn of Charing Cross from 1996; R St Giles-in-the-Fields from 2000
GS 1999–2000 *Tel:* 020 7636 4646 (Home)
020 7323 1992 (Office)
Fax: 020 7323 4102 (Office)
email: archdeacon.charingcross@london.anglican.org

JAGGER, Ven Ian, MA, MA
15 The College Durham DH1 3EQ [ARCHDEACON OF DURHAM] *b* 1955 *educ* Huddersfield New Coll; K Coll Cam; St Jo Coll Dur; *CV* C St Mary Virgin Twickenham Lon 1982–85; P-in-c Willen, Milton Keynes Ox 1985–87; TV Willen, Stantonbury LEP 1987–94; Chapl Willen Hospice 1985–94; Dir Milton Keynes Chr Trg Scheme 1986–94; TR Fareham H Trin Portsm 1994–98; Ecum Officer Portsm Dio 1994–96; RD Fareham 1996–98; Can Res Portsm Cathl and Dioc Missr 1998–2001; Adn of Auckland 2001–06; Adn of Durham and Can Res Dur Cathl from 2006
GS 2002– *Tel:* 0191 384 7534
Fax: 0191 386 6915
email: archdeacon.of.durham@durham.anglican.org

JAGO, Mr Derek, ONC
21 Clarence Gdns Bishop Auckland DL14 7RB [DURHAM] *b* 1949 *educ* Willington Sec Sch; Bp Auckland Coll; New Coll Dur; Gateshead Coll; *CV* Rdr to pars of Witton Park, Etherley and Escomb from 1999; pt Broadcaster; LibDem District Coun Wear Valley; M Auckland Dny Syn
GS 1998– *Tel and Fax:* 01388 458358
email: Derek_Jago@btclick.com

JAMES, Rt Revd Graham Richard, BA
Bishop's House Norwich NR3 1SB [BISHOP OF NORWICH] *b* 1951 *educ* Northampton Gr Sch; Lanc Univ; Cuddesdon Th Coll; *CV* C Christ Carpenter Peterb 1975–78; C Digswell 1978–82; TR Digswell 1982–83; Selection Sec and Sec for CME ACCM 1983–85; Sen Selection Sec 1985–87; Chapl to Abp of Cant 1987–93; Bp of St Germans 1993–99; Bp of Norw from 1999; M Bd of Countryside Agency 2001–06; Chair Rural Bps Panel 2001–06; Chair CRAC, BBC and Ofcom 2004–08; M AC from 2006; Chair Min Div from 2006; Chair Stg Conf on Relig and Belief, BBC 2009–11; M HoL Selection Cttee on Communications from 2011
GS 1995– *Tel:* 01603 629001
Fax: 01603 761613
email: bishop@norwich.anglican.org
Web: www.norwich.anglican.org

JAMES, Mr Philip John, B SocSc
Church House Great Smith St London SW1P 3AZ [HEAD OF (RESOURCE) STRATEGY AND DEVELOPMENT UNIT, CHURCH COMMISSIONERS AND ARCHBISHOPS' COUNCIL] *b* 1967 *educ* Bris Gr Sch; Birm Univ; *CV* On staff of Ch Commrs from 1988; Hd of Policy Unit from 1999; Head of (Resource) Strategy and Development Unit, Ch Commrs and AC from 2009 *Tel:* 020 7898 1671
email: philip.james@churchofengland.org

JARROW, Suffragan Bishop of. See BRYANT, Rt Revd Mark Watts

JEANS, Ven Alan Paul, B Th, MIAS, MIBC, MA
Herbert House 118 Lower Rd Salisbury SP2 9NW [ARCHDEACON OF SARUM; SALISBURY] *b* 1958 *educ* Bournemouth Sch; Dorset Inst of HE; Southn Univ; Sarum and Wells Th Coll; Univ Wales Lamp; *CV* C Parkstone Team 1989–93; P-in-c Bp Cannings, All Cannings and Etchilhampton 1993–98; Dioc Adv for Par Develt 1998–2005; M DAC; Adn of Sarum from 2003; Asst DDO 2005–07; RD Alderbury 2005–07; DDO from 2007
GS 2000–05, 2010– *Tel:* 01722 336290 (Home)
01380 729808 (Office)
Fax: 01380 738096
email: adsarum@salisbury.anglican.org

JENKINS, Ven Dr David Harold, MA, PhD
Sudbury Lodge Stanningfield Road Bury St Edmunds IP30 0TL [ARCHDEACON OF SUDBURY] *b* 1961 *educ* Belfast Royal Academy; Sidney Sussex Coll Cam; Ripon Coll Cuddesdon; Univ Wales: Lampeter; *CV* Asst C Good Shepherd Cambridge 1989–1991; Asst C St Peter's Earley Reading 1991–1994; V St Michael & All Angels Blackpool 1994–1999; V St John Baptist Broughton Preston 1999–2004; DDE Dioc of Carlisle 2004–2010; Residentiary Can Carlisle Cathl 2004–2010; Adn of Sudbury from 2010 *Tel:* 01284 386942
email: archdeacon.david@stedmundsbury.anglican.org

JENKINS, Canon Gary John, BA, PGCE, BA, MTh
4 Carlton Road Redhill Surrey RH1 2BX [SOUTHWARK] *b* 1959 *educ* Sir Walter St John's School, Battersea University of York Oak Hill; *CV* C St Luke's, West Norwood 1989–94; V St Peter's, St Helier, 1994–2001; V, Holy Trin, Redhill from 2001; M Bps S'wark Th Issues Grp, 2005–10; M

S'wark Dioc Syn, from 2001; AD Reigate from 2012
GS 2010– *Tel:* 01737 779917
email: gary@htredhill.com

JEPSON, Dr Rachel Margaret Elizabeth, B Ed (Hons), MA, PhD, TEFL, FIMA
56a Upland Rd Selly Park Birmingham B29 7JS [BIRMINGHAM] *b* 1967 *educ* Edgbaston CE Coll for Girls; Univ Coll of St Mart Lanc; Univ of Glos w Trin Coll Bris; St Jo Coll Dur; *CV* Tchr Grove Sch Handsworth 1993–98; Res Tutor St Jo Coll Dur 1998–2002; M Dioc Bd of Educ to 2006; GS Rep, CTE Forum and CTBI Assembly; Appt M Revision Cttee Care of Cathls Measure 2002; Appt M Additional Collects Revision Cttee 2003; M Birm Dioc Bp's Coun; M Birm Stg Adv Coun for Relig Educ; Tchr (Phase Leader, RE Co-ord), Rookery Sch, Handsworth from 2007; Appt Revision Cttee C of E (Misc Provisions) Meas 2008; Vc-Chair PCC St Martin-in-the-Bull Ring Birm Par Ch 2008–11; Appt M Governing Body Queen's Found Birm 2012
GS 2000– *Tel:* 0121 472 2064
email: rachel.jepson@tiscali.co.uk

JERSEY, Dean of. See KEY, Very Revd Robert Frederick

JESSIMAN, Revd Timothy Edward, MA
61 Hart Plain Avenue Waterlooville Hampshire PO8 8RG [PORTSMOUTH] *b* 1958 *educ* Portsm Tech High Sch; Trent Poly; Ox Poly; Portsm Univ; York St John Univ; Oak Hill Th Coll; *CV* Chapl North Devon NHS 1995–2000; Chapl Grenville Sch 1996–99; TV St Peter's in the Torridge Estuary Team Ministry Ex 1995–2000; Minster The Beacon Church Ecum Ch Plant 1999–2000; M Ex Dioc Sy 1996–2000; V Hart Plain Ch, Joint Methodist and Anglican Local Ecum Partnership from 2000; M Dioc Syn; M Dioc Miss & Soc Forum; M Dioc Evan Working Grp; Dioc 'Back to Church Sunday' Co-ord; M Urban Min Grp; M Fresh Expressions Southern Regional Training Partnership
GS 2010– *Tel:* 02392264551
email: tim.jessiman@ntlworld.com

JOHN, Very Revd Jeffrey Philip Hywel, MA, D Phil
The Deanery Sumpter Yard St Albans AL1 1BY [DEAN OF ST ALBANS] *b* 1953 *educ* Tonyrefail Gr Sch; Hertf Coll Ox; BNC Ox; Magd Coll Ox; St Steph Ho; *CV* C St Aug Penarth 1978–80; Asst Chapl Magd Coll Ox 1980–82; Chapl and lect BNC Ox 1982–84; Fell and Dean of Divinity Magd Coll Ox 1984–91; V H Trin Eltham 1991–97; Dir of Trg S'wark Dioc and Can Theol and Chanc S'wark Cathl 1997–2004; M GS Stg Cttee 1996–2000; M GS Appts Cttee 1995–2000; M S'wark Dioc Syn, Bp's Coun 1997–2004; Dean of St Alb from 2004 *Tel:* 01727 890202
Fax: 01727 890227
email: dean@stalbanscathedral.org

JOHNS, Mrs Sue (Susan Margaret), HNC, M Phil
8 Dragonfly Lane Norwich NR4 7JR [NORWICH] *b* 1955 *educ* Thorpe Gr Sch; Norw City Coll; Leeds Univ; *CV* Analytical Chemist, Public Analyst's Lab 1973–80; Housewife and Mother; Food Scientist MAFF CSL Food Science Lab Norw 1991–98; Joint Food Safety and Standards Grp 1998–2000; Food Standards Agency 2000–09, Health & Safety Exec, currently Priv Sec to Chair and Bd Sec
GS 1990– *Tel:* 020 7227 3822
Fax: 01603 507609 (Home)
email: sue1326@hotmail.com

JOHNSTON, Mrs Mary Geraldine, BA, AKC, CMCIPD
56 Fairlawn Grove Chiswick London W4 5EH [LONDON] *b* 1939 *educ* Barking Abbey Sch; K Coll Lon; *CV* Personnel Dept ICI 1961–66; Personnel Admin and Employee Relations Singer Co New York 1966–68; American Express New York 1968–70; Asst Personnel Mgr and Staff Devel Mgr Guinness Overseas 1970–80; M Lon and S'wark Dioc Jt Prisons and Penal Concerns Grp 1995–2008; M Coun Corp Church Ho 1999–2008; M Revision Comm Clergy Terms of Service; Dir Affirming Catholicism; Convenor of Affirming Catholics in Synod; M CNC
GS 1995– *Tel:* 020 8995 6427
email: marygjohnston@btinternet.com

JONES, Mr David Arthur,
Church Farm Cottage West Milton Bridport DT6 3SA [SALISBURY] *b* 1936 *educ* Abingdon; RMA Sandhurst; RAF & Army Command & Staff Coll; *CV* Army officer 1959–85 (Colonel); Assoc Dir Oxfam 1985–93; Assoc Dir Internat Alert 1994–97; vol Cov Dio rep for CUF and Dioc Devel Fund; retired; Insp of Th Colls; Lyme Bay Dny Info Officer; M MPA Coun of AC from 2006
GS 1995–2001; 2003–10 *Tel:* 01308 485304
email: david@nerissajmes.plus.com

JONES, Canon Joyce Rosemary, MA
Oakfield 206 Barnsley Road, Denby Dale Huddersfield HD8 8TS [WAKEFIELD] *b* 1954 *educ* King Edward VI H Sch birm; Cam Univ; Newnham Coll; NOC; *CV* AC All Saints Pontefract 1997–2000; Vocations Adv, Asst Chapl Kirkwood Hospice & AC Cumberworth Denby and Denby Dale 2000–0; P-in-cShelley and Shepley from 2001; Bp's Adv for Prayer and Spirituality 2005–11; RD Kirkburton from 2011
GS 2010– *Tel:* 01484 862350
Fax: 01484 862350
email: joycerjones@aol.com

JONES, Rt Revd James Stuart, BA, PGCE, DD
Bishop's Lodge Woolton Park Liverpool L25 6DT [BISHOP OF LIVERPOOL] *b* 1948 *educ* Duke of York's Military Sch Dover; Ex Univ; Wycliffe Hall Th Coll; *CV* C Ch Ch Clifton 1982–90; V Em S Croy-

don 1990–94; Bp of Hull 1994–98; Bp of Liv from 1998
GS 1995– *Tel:* 0151 421 0831
Fax: 0151 428 3055
email: bishopslodge@liverpool.anglican.org
Web: www.liverpool.anglican.org

JONES, Ven Philip Hugh, Dip Chr Theol & Min, Solicitor
27 The Avenue Lewes BN7 1QT [ARCHDEACON OF LEWES AND HASTINGS; CHICHESTER] *b* 1951 *educ* Leys Sch Cam; Chich Theol Coll; *CV* C St Mary V Horsham 1994–97; V H Innocents Southwater 1997–2005; RD Horsham 2002–05; Adn of Lewes & Hastings from 2005 *Tel:* 01273 479530
Fax: 01273 476529
email: archlandh@diochi.org.uk

JONES, Revd Rhiannon Elizabeth, BA, MA, MA
23 Hallewell Road Birmingham B16 0LP [BIRMINGHAM] *b* 1972 *educ* Ox High Sch; Ex Univ; Lon Sch of Theol; Ridley Hall, Cam; *CV* Co-ord of Jubilee Cen, Cam 1995–98; C Huntingdon Team Min 2000–04; R Fulbourn, Great Wilbraham, Little Wilbraham and Six Mile Bottom 2004–10; Transforming Church Co-ord, Birm from 2010; M Ely Bp's Coun 2005–10; M Lit Com 2006-11
GS 2005–2010 *Tel:* 0121 454 5040 07595 880584
email: rhiannonejones@me.com

JONES, Revd Sharon Ann, BA, CERT TH
St Andrew's Vicarage Arm Road Dearnley OL15 8NJ [MANCHESTER] *b* 1960 *educ* St Kath Coll Liv; Cranmer Hall Dur; *CV* DSS 1985 D 1987 P 1994. Rubery Birm 1985–89; Par Dn 1987–89; C-in-c Chelmsley Wood St Aug CD 1989–92; Perm to Offic Newc 1992–93; Chapl HM Pris Acklington 1993–97; Chapl HM YOI Castington 1997–2000; Chapl HM Pris Forest Bank 2000–06; P-in-c Dearnley Man from 2006; AD Salford 2003–06; AD Rochdale 2006–09
GS 2010– *Tel:* 01706 378466 07738 96627
email: sharon@dearnleyvicarage.plus.com

JONES, Ven Trevor Pryce, B Ed, B Th, LL M, Cert Ed, ACP
Glebe House St Mary's Lane Hertingfordbury Hertford SG14 2LE [ARCHDEACON OF HERTFORD; ST ALBAN'S] *b* 1948 *educ* Dial Stone Sch Stockport; St Luke's Coll Ex; Southn Univ; Sarum and Wells Th Coll; Univ of Wales, Cardiff Law Sch; St Jo Coll Dur; *CV* C St Geo Glouc 1976–79; Warden Bp Mascall Centre Ludlow and M Heref Dioc Educ Tm 1979–84; DCO 1981–96; Sec Heref-Nurnberg Eur Ecum Partnership 1982–87; M Bp's Coun 1987–87; M Dioc Ecum Cttee 1985–87, Chair 1996–97; TR Heref S Wye TM 1984–97; OCF 1985–97; Preb Heref Cathl 1993–97; M Dioc Pastl/Minl Cttee 1996–97; Adn of Hertford from 1997; Hon Can St Alb Cathl 1997; Chair St Alb and Ox Min Course 1998–2007; Chair Reach Out Projects Mgt Coun from 1998, Reach Out Plus from 2010; Bp's Selector 2001–08; Chair Rural Strategy Grp from 2001; Vc-Chair ERMC from 2004; Chair Hockerill Educ Foundn 2005; M Legal Adv Commn 2006–10
GS 2000–05; 2005–10 *Tel:* 01992 581629
Fax: 01992 535349
email: archdhert@stalbans.anglican.org

JUDD, Very Revd Peter Somerset Margesson, MA, DL
The Dean's House 3 Harlings Grove Waterloo Lane Chelmsford CM1 1YQ [DEAN OF CHELMSFORD] *b* 1949 *educ* Charterhouse Sch; Trin Hall Cam; Cuddesdon Th Coll; *CV* C St Phil w St Steph Salford 1974–76; Chapl Clare Coll Cam 1976–81; Acting Dean Clare Coll 1980–81; TV Burnham w Dropmore, Hitcham and Taplow 1981–88; V St Mary V Iffley 1988–97; RD Cowley 1995–97; R and Prov of Chelmsf from 1997, Dean from 2000
GS 2003–05 *Tel:* 01245 354318 (Home)
01245 294492 (Office)
07740 456844 (Mobile)
Fax: 01245 294499
email: dean@chelmsfordcathedral.org.uk
Web: www.chelmsfordcathedral.org

JUDKINS, Mrs Mary, BA, PGCE, MA
Old Vicarage 3 Church Lane East Ardsley Wakefield WF3 2LJ [WAKEFIELD] *b* 1951 *educ* Leominster Gr Sch; Bris Univ; St Mary's Coll Cheltenham; Open Univ; *CV* Tchr in Bris and E Grinstead 1984–94; Supply Tchr; Homemaker/Mother; Lay Chair Dioc Syn; GS Rep SAMS 1995–2005; M CCU; M CMEAC 2000–05; delegate WCC 9th Assembly 2006; vol co-ord N Kirklees Chr Faith Cen, Dewsbury Minster from 2005; Educ Officer Interfaith Kirklees (Schools) from 2007
GS 1995– *Tel:* 01924 826802
email: elephantmj@aol.com

JUKES, Very Revd Keith Michael, BA
Minster House Bedern Bank Ripon HG4 1PE [DEAN OF RIPON; RIPON AND LEEDS] *b* 1954 *educ* Leeds Univ; Linc Th Coll; *CV* C H Trin Wordsley, Lich 1978–81; C Wolverhampton 1981–83; C-in-c Stoneydelph St Martin CD 1983–90; TR Glascote and Stoneydelph 1990–91; RD Tamworth 1990–91; TR Cannock and V Hatherton 1991–97; Preb Lich Cathl 1996–97; P-in-c Selby Abbey, York 1997–99, V 1999–2007; Dean of Ripon from 2007 *Tel:* 01765 602609
01765 603462
07890 956004 (Mobile)
Fax: 01765 690398
email: deankeith@riponcathedral.org.uk

KAJUMBA, Ven Daniel Steven Kimbugwe, BA, HND, Dip Th, Dip IMBM, LAMDA
84 Higher Drive Purley CR8 2HJ [ARCHDEACON OF REIGATE; SOUTHWARK] *b* 1952 *educ* Christian Life Coll; Bournemouth Univ; Open Univ; S'wark Ord Course; Lond Univ; *CV* C St Alb Goldington 1985–87; pt Chapl Bedford Prison; Uganda 1987–98: Man Dir Transocean; Gen Man Rio Holdings

Internat; Kingdom of Buganda Sec Gen, Cabinet Min PR, Functions and Protocol, Min Foreign Affairs; TV St Fran Horley 1999–2001; Adn of Reigate from 2001; M Dioc Syn; M Bp's Coun; M Business Cttee; M Fin Cttee; M Exec and Glebe Cttee; M Stipends and Budget Cttee; M Parsonages and Property Maintenance Cttee; M Fairer Shares Cttee; M Sites/Advisory and Red Churches Uses Cttee; M CMEAC; M Croydon Area Coun *Tel:* 020 8660 9276 (Home) 020 8681 5496 (Work) 07949 594460 (Mobile) *Fax:* 020 8660 9276 (Home) 020 8686 2074 (Work)
email: daniel.kajumba@southwark.anglican.org

KEARON, Canon Kenneth Arthur, BA, MA, M Phil, DD
Anglican Communion Office St Andrew's House 16 Tavistock Crescent London W11 1AP [SECRETARY GENERAL, ANGLICAN COMMUNION] *b* 1953 *educ* Mountjoy Sch Dub; Trin Coll Dub; Cam Univ; Irish Sch of Ecumenics; *CV* Dn 1981; P 1982; C All SS Raheny and St Jo Coolock, Dioc of Dublin and Glendalough 1981–84; Dean of Residence Trin Coll Dub 1984–91; R Tullow, Dub 1991–99; Dir Irish Sch of Ecumenics 1999–2004; M Chapter of Ch Ch Cathl, Dub from 1995, Chan 2002–04; Sec Gen Angl Communion from 2005; Hon Can St Paul's Cathl Lon, St Geo Cathl Jerusalem, Ch Ch Cathl Cant *Tel:* 020 7313 3905 *Fax:* 020 7313 3999
email: kenneth.kearon@anglicancommunion.org

KELLY, Mr Declan Gerard, MSc, BSc, MCLIP
Church House Great Smith St London SW1P 3AZ [DIRECTOR OF LIBRARIES, ARCHIVES AND IT, CHURCH COMMISSIONERS] *b* 1960 *educ* St Hugh's Coll Nottm; Qu Mary Coll Lon; Sheffield Univ; *CV* Rsch Centre Mgr, BBC World Service 1993–97; Intake and Acquisitions Mgr, BBC Archives 1997–99, Rsch Services Mgr 2000–03, Output Services Mgr 2003–05; Dir of Libraries, Archives and IT, Ch Commrs from 2005 *Tel:* 020 7898 1432
email: declan.kelly@churchofengland.org
Web: www.lambethpalacelibrary.org

KEMP, Mr David Stephen,
11 Ham Shades Lane Whitstable Kent CT5 1NT [CANTERBURY] *b* 1947 *educ* Simon Langton Gr Sch, Cant; *CV* Sec Herne Bay Bldg Soc 1978–86; Dep CEO, Kent Reliance Bldg Soc 1986–90; Dioc Sec, Cant 1990–2007; Gov Cant Ch Ch Univ 2006; Chair Cant Dioc Child Protection Management Gp from 2007
GS 2010– *Tel:* 01227 272470
email: kemps11@btinternet.com

KENNY, Miss Bernadette, LLB (Hones), Barrister
29 Great Smith Street London SW1P 3PS [CEO, CHURCH OF ENGLAND PENSIONS BOARD] *educ* Chichester High Sch for Girls; Univ Man; Inns of Court Sch of Law; *CV* Lord Chancellor's Dept 1980–1991; Dep Circuit Adm SE Circuit 1991–93; Head of Agency Team, Court Service 1993–94, Head of Personnel and Training, 1994–99, Dir Operational Policy 1999–2002; Dir Dept Constitutional Affairs 2002–04; CEO Royal Parks 2005; Dir Gen Personal Tax, HM Revenue and Customs 2005–11; CEO Church of England Pensions Bd from 2011 *Tel:* 020 8898 1807
email: bernadette.kenny@churchofengland.org

KENSINGTON, Area Bishop of. See WILLIAMS, Rt Revd Paul Gavin

KENT, Mr Ian David,
Brightmanshayes Petrockstowe Okehampton EX20 3EY [EXETER] *b* 1980 *educ* Gt Torrington Sch; Plymouth Coll of Art and Design; *CV* Printer from 1996; M Dioc Syn from 2000
GS 2000–2010 *Tel and Fax:* 01409 281281
email: ian.kent@brightmanshayes.freeserve.co.uk

KEY, Very Revd Robert Frederick, BA, DPS
The Deanery David Place St Helier Jersey JE2 4TE [DEAN OF JERSEY; WINCHESTER] *b* 1952 *educ* Alleyn's Sch Dulwich; Bris Univ; Oak Hill Th Coll; *CV* C St Ebbe Ox 1976–80; Min St Patr Wallington 1980–85; V Eynsham and Cassington 1985–91; V St Andr Ox 1991–2001; M Coun Wycliffe Hall 1985–2010; M Coll of Evangelists; Gen Dir CPAS 2001–05; Canon Preacher dioc Rio Grande from 2004; Dean of Jersey from 2005
GS 1995–2005, 2010–
Tel and Fax: 01534 720001 07700 711952
email: robert_f_key@yahoo.com

KEY, Mr Simon Robert, MA, Cert Ed, FSA
4 Old St Salisbury SP2 8JL [SALISBURY] *b* 1945 *educ* Salis Cathl Sch; Sherborne Sch; Clare Coll Cam; *CV* Master, Loretto Sch Edin 1967–69; Harrow Sch 1969-83; Min for Local Government and Inner Cities 1990–92, for Nat Heritage 1992–93, for Transport 1993–94; Shadow Min for Defence 1997–99, for Internat Devel 1999–2001, for Science 2003–05; MP for Salis 1983–2010; M Salis Dioc Syn from 2003; M Coun of Salis Cathl from 2002; Fellow Soc of Antiquaries from 2006; Lay Can Salis Cath from 2008; M Eccl Cttee of Parliament 2005–10; M Defence Select Cttee 2005–10; Chair, Salisbury Magna Carta 2015 Project from 2011; Chair, Ho of Laity, Sarum from 2011
GS 2005– *Tel:* 01722 326622 07770 940782
email: srobertkey@hotmail.com

KIDDLE, Canon John, MA, MTh
19 Stanbury Avenue Watford Herts WD17 3HW [ST ALBANS] *b* 1958 *educ* Monkton Combe Sch; Queens' Coll Cam; Heythrop Coll UL; Ridley Hall, Cam; *CV* AC, Ormskirk Parish Church, 1982–86; V, St Gabriel's Church Huyton Quarry, 1986–91; V, St Luke's Church Watford, 1991–08; Rural Dean of Watford, 1999–04Hon Can St Alb Cathl 2005–10; Off Miss and Devlp, St Alb from 2008; Residentiary Can St Alb Cathl from 2010; Dir Miss St Alb from 2011; M Dioc Syn 1986–89;

Sec Brd Miss and Unity 1986–89; M Dioc Syn 1997–00; M Dioc Pstrl Cttee 1997–00; M Bedford Deanery Review 1999–00; Chair Luton Deanery Review Grp 2003–04; Chair Dioc Vision for Action Grp 2004–06; Exec Off Brd Ch and Soc from 2008
GS 2010–
Tel: 01923 460083, 01727 818146 07590 636966
email: john.kiddle@stalbans.anglican.org

KILLWICK, Canon Simon David Andrew, BD, AKC, Cert Th
Christ Church Rectory Monton St Moss Side Manchester M14 4GP [MANCHESTER] *b* 1956 *educ* Westmr Sch; K Coll Lon; St Steph Ho Th Coll; *CV* C St Mark Worsley 1981–84; TV St Mary Ellenbrook 1984–97; P-in-c Ch Ch Moss Side from 1997, R from 2006; Exam Chapl to Bp of Man 2002–07; Hon Can Manch from 2004; AD Hulme 2007–12
GS 1998– *Tel:* 0161 226 2476
email: frskillwick@btinternet.com

KINGS, Rt Revd Graham Ralph, MA, DipTh, PhD
Sherborne House Tower Hill Iwerne Minster Blandford Forum DT11 8NH [SUFFRAGAN BISHOP OF SHERBORNE; SALISBURY] *b* 1953 *educ* Buckhurst Hill County Sch; RMA Sandhurst; Hertford Coll Ox; Ridley Hall Cam; Selwyn Coll Cam; *CV* Asst C St Mark Harlesden 1980–84; CMS Mission Partner Kenya 1985–91; Dir Studies and Vc Prin St Andrew's Coll Kabare 1985–91; Hon Can St Andrew's Cath Kerugoya Kenya 1991; Overseas Advr Henry Martyn Trust Cam 1992–95; Lect Mission Stud 1992–2000; Dir Henry Martyn Centre for Mission studies in World Christianity 1995–2000, Cambridge Theological Federation; V St Mary Islington 2000–09; M MTAG 1996–2005; Trustee Anvil 1998–2004; M Lit Comm from 2002; Manager Ang Comm Network for Inter faith Concerns from 2007; Theol Sec Fulcrum from 2003; Area Bp of Sherborne from 2009
Tel: 01202 659427
Fax: 01202 691418
email: gsherborne@salisbury.anglican.org

KINGSTON, Area Bishop of. See CHEETHAM, Rt Revd Richard Ian

KINSON, Mrs Wendy Elizabeth, BA
The Old Laundry Maer Newcastle ST5 5EF [LICHFIELD] *b* 1953 *educ* Bp Blackhall Sch Ex; Sussex Univ; *CV* CAB Adv from 1993; Child care worker from 2000; Chair Dioc Syn Ho of Laity from 2003
GS 1995–2010 *Tel:* 01782 680613

KIRK, Revd Gavin John, BTh, MA
The Precentory Minster Yard Lincoln LN2 1PX [LINCOLN] *b* 1961 *CV* Asst C, Seaford-cum-Sutton 1986–89; Succentor Rochester Cathl 1989–91; Head of Classics and Asst Chapl, The King's Schl, Rochester, 1991–98; Can Res & Precentor Portsmouth Cathl 1998–2003; Canon Residentiary & Precentor, Lincoln Cathl from 2003; Chair Portsmouth Bp's Adv Grp for Worship 1998–2003; Trustee NTMTS 2001–03; Warden Com Holy Cross from 2006; Chair Lincoln Dioc Lit Cttee from 2008; Ch Bp's Advisory Grp for Prayer and Spirituality from 2011
GS 2003–10 *Tel:* 01452 524167
email: dean@gloucestercathedral.org.uk
Web: www.gloucestercathedral.org.uk

KNARESBOROUGH, Suffragan Bishop of. See BELL, Rt Revd James Harold

LAKE, Very Revd Stephen, BTh
The Deanery, 1 Millers Green, Gloucester GL1 2BP [DEAN OF GLOUCESTER] *b* 1963 *educ* Homefield Sch Dorset; Chich Th Coll; *CV* C Sherborne Abbey 1988–92; V Branksome St Aldhelm 1992–2001; RD Poole 2000–01; Can Res and Sub Dean, St Albans Cathl 2001–11; Dean of Gloucester from 2011; Trustee, Scout Assoc
GS 2003–10 *Tel:* 01452 524167
email: dean@gloucestercathedral.org.uk
Web: www.gloucestercathedral.org.uk

LAMBETH, Archdeacon of. See SKILTON, Ven Christopher John

LANCASTER, Archdeacon of. See EVERITT, Ven Michael John

LANCASTER, Suffragan Bishop of. See PEARSON, Rt Revd Geoffrey Seagrave

LANGRISH, Rt Revd Michael Laurence, B Soc Sc, BA, MA, Hon DD (Birm), Hon DD (Ex)
The Palace Exeter EX1 1HY [BISHOP OF EXETER] *b* 1946 *educ* K Edw Sch Southn; Birm Univ; Fitzw Coll Cam; Ridley Hall Th Coll; *CV* C Stratford-upon-Avon 1973–76; Chapl Rugby Sch 1976–81; V Offchurch and DDO 1981–87; Exam Chapl to Bp of Cov 1982–89; Chair ACCM Vocations Cttee 1984–91; TR Rugby 1987–93; Chair Ho of Clergy Dioc Syn 1988–93; Hon Can Cov Cathl 1990–93, Bp of Birkenhead 1993–2000; M BAGUPA 1996–98; M Urban Bps' Panel 1996–2000; M BSR Community and Urban Affairs Cttee 1998–2001; Bp of Exeter from 2000; Chair Rural Affairs Cttee, M BM 2001–06; M Ch Commrs Bishoprics and Cathls Cttee 2002–06; Chair Melanesian Mission 2002–09; M Bd of Chr Aid 2003–11; Chair Toyne Follow-up Grp 2004–06; M Ho of Lords from 2005; Chair Diocs Pastl and Miss Measure Grp 2006–08; Chair Rural Strategy Grp 2006–09; Chair Ch Legislation Adv Cttee from 2009
GS 1985–93, 1999– *Tel:* 01392 272362
Fax: 01392 430923
email: bishop.of.exeter@exeter.anglican.org

LANGSTAFF, Rt Revd James Henry, MA (Oxon), BA (Nottm)
Bishopscourt St Margaret's Street Rochester ME1 1TS [BISHOP OF ROCHESTER] *b* 1956 *educ* Cheltenham

Coll; Ox Univ; Nottm Univ; St Jo Coll Nottm; *CV* C St Pet Farnborough, Guildf 1981–86, P-in-c 1985–86; P-in-c St Matt Duddeston & St Clem Nechells, Birm 1986, V 1987–96; RD Birm City 1995–96; Chapl to Bp of Birm 1996–2000; R H Trin Sutton Coldfield, Birm 2000–04; Area Dean of Sutton Coldfield 2002–04; Bp of Lynn 2004–10; Bp of Rochester from 2010; Chair Flagship Housing Grp 2006–10; M E of England Regional Assembly 2007;10 Chair Housing Justice from 2008
GS 2010– *Tel:* 01634 842721 07551 007560
email: bishop.rochester@rochester.anglican.org

LASH, Very Revd Archimandrite Ephrem, MA, STB
18 Tuffnell Park Mansions London N7 6HS [ECUMENICAL REPRESENTATIVE (ORTHODOX CHURCHES)] *b* 1930 *educ* Downside Sch; St Jo Coll Ox; Seminaire St Sulpice, Paris; Ecole Pratique des Hautes Etudes (Diplom) Paris; *CV* Lect in Bibl and Patristic Studies Univ of Newc 1978–84; rtd
GS 1995– *Tel:* 0203 218 8007
07932 191789 (Mobile)
email: ephrem@chorlton.com

LAW-JONES, Revd Peter Deniston, MA, PGCE
The Vicarage St Thomas Road Lytham St Annes FY8 1JL [BLACKBURN] *b* 1955 *educ* Greenhill Sch, Rochdale; Newcastle Univ; Man Univ; Lanc University; Linc Th Coll; *CV* Teacher, John Leggott 6th Form Coll 1981–84; Asst C St Lawrence Chorley 1987–91; V St Francis Feniscliffe 1991–96; Hon. Tutor Lancashire and Cumbria Th Partnership 1999–2009; V St Thomas St Annes on the Sea from 1996; Area Dean of Kirkham from 2009; M DiocPastoral and Miss Cttee from 2009; M Bp's Counc from 2009; M Dioc Bd Miss from 2009
GS 2010– *Tel:* 01253 723750
email: peter.lawjones@tesco.net

LEAFE, Mrs Susannah Mary, BSc PGCE
6 Troy Court Daglands Road Fowey PL23 1JX [TRURO] *b* 1971 *educ* Wimbledon H Sch; Bris Univ; Nott Univ; *CV* Head of Geography, Clifton H Sch 1996–2008; Tchr Geography, Queen Elizabeth's Hosp 2008; FLAME coord, Truro Dioc 2009–10; Women's Ministry Facilitator, Fowey Parish Ch from 2008
GS 2010– *Tel:* 07753690120
email: dands.leafe@blueyonder.co.uk

LEATHARD, Prof Helen Louise, B Sc, Ph D, F B Pharmacol S, MA
29 Coronation Way Lancaster LA1 2TQ [BLACKBURN] *b* 1947 *educ* Kirkby Stephen Gr Sch Westmorland; Chelsea Coll Lon; K Coll Hosp Medical Sch; St Mart Coll Lancaster; *CV* Rsch Fell K Coll Hosp Medical Sch 1974–76; Lect in Pharmacology; Charing Cross and Westmr Medical Sch 1977–92; Sen Lect in Physiology St Martin's Coll Lanc 1992–94; Rdr in Pharmacology and Human Physiology St Martin's Coll Lanc (now Univ of Cumbria) 1994–2001; Prof of Healing Science and Pharmacology from 2001, Prof Emerita, in retirement 2010; M Dioc Syn; Guild of St Raph Coun; Editor Chrism; M Order of St Luke from 2003; Consult Cen for Study of Theol and Health; M Tunstall Dny Syn; Rdr
GS 2000– *Tel:* 01524 849495 (Home)
email: helenleathard@btinternet.com

LEE, Ven David John, B Sc, MA, PhD, Dip Theol, Dip Miss Studies
47 Kirkgate Shipley W Yorkshire BD18 3EH [ARCHDEACON OF BRADFORD] *b* 1946 *educ* Wolverhampton Gr Sch; Bris Univ; All Nations Chr Coll; Lon Univ; Cam Univ; Birm Univ; Ridley Hall, Cam; *CV* Sch Master, Lesotho 1967–68; Sch Master, Walsall 1968–77; C St Marg Putney, S'wark 1977–80; Lect in NT and Theol, Bp Tucker Coll Uganda 1980–86; Lect in Biblical Studies and Missiology, Selly Oak Colls, Tutor Crowther Hall, Selly Oak 1986–91; R Middleton and Wishaw 1991–96; Dir for Miss and Res Can Birm Cathl 1996–2004; Adn of Bradford from 2004; sometime involvement with Angl Ch Planting Initiatives, Nat Coun for Chr Unity (Local Unity Panel), Grace Houses, Birm (internat student work), Chaplaincy Plus, Birm (work-based chaplaincy and mission), Samuel White Charities, Middleton (almshouse trust); Bradf Chs for Dialogue and Diversity (miss educ); Gov Imm C of E Com Coll, Idle, Bradf
GS 2005 *Tel:* 01274 200698
07711 671351 (Mobile)
Fax: 01274 200698
email: david.lee@bradford.anglican.org

LEE, Revd John, B Sc, M Sc, MInstGA, FRSM
The Wash House Lambeth Palace London SE1 7JU [CLERGY APPOINTMENTS ADVISER] *b* 1947 *educ* St Dunstan's Coll Catford; Univ Coll Swansea; Inst of Grp Analysis Lon; Ripon Hall Th Coll; *CV* Experimental Officer R Australian Navy Rsch Laboratory Sydney 1971–73; pt Nursing Auxiliary Chu Hosp Ox 1973–75; C Cockett 1975–78; P-in-c St Teilo Cockett 1976–78; Pr/Counsellor St Botoloph Aldgate 1978–84; Hon Psychotherapist Dept of Psychological Medicine St Bart's Hosp Lon 1980–86; Course Consultant St Alb Minl Tr Scheme 1980–85; P-in-c Chiddingstone w Chiddingstone Causeway 1984–89; R 1989–98; Tutor in Individual and Grp Psychotherapy Dept of Psychological Medicine St Bart's Medical Sch 1987–92; Staff Consult Richmond Fell 1989–98; Psychotherapist and Grp Analyst in private practice 1987–98; Clergy Appointments Adv from 1998; Chapl to HM the Queen from 2010
Tel: 020 7898 1898
Fax: 020 7898 1899
email: admin.caa@churchofengland.org

LEE, Revd (John Charles) Hugh Mellanby, MA, M Tech, FRSA
12 Walton St Oxford OX1 2HG [OXFORD] *b* 1944

educ Marlboro Coll; Trin Hall Cam; Brunel Univ; Ox NSM Course; *CV* Operational Rsch Scientist Nat Coal Bd 1966–76; Coal Supply Tm Leader Internat Energy Agency 1976–84; Dep Hd of Economics Br Coal 1984–91; Dir Coal and Electricity Consulting WEFA Energy 1992–95; NSM Amersham-on-the-Hill 1981–88; NSM St Aldate Ox 1988–93; NSM Wheatley 1993–95; pt Work and Economic Life Missr Berks, Bucks and Oxon 1995–2002; NSM House for Duty P-in-c, St Mich at the North Gate, Ox and City R 2002–09; pt Consult Energy Economist from 1995; Treas and Trustee Chs Media Trust 1994–2001; Dir EBICO from 1998, Chair from 2003; Moderator CHRISM 1998–2001 and 2009–12; married Anne Mellanby 1967; children Kate born 1971, Alexander born 1973; founding trustee Ox Industrial Chapl from 1998; M DRASCS 2004–06; M Conv Cant Standing Ctte from 2011
GS 2000– *Tel:* 01865 316245 07879 426625
email: hugh.lee@btinternet.com

LEEDS, Archdeacon of. See HOOPER, Ven Paul

LEICESTER, Archdeacon of. See STRATFORD, VenTimothy Richard

LEICESTER, Bishop of. See STEVENS, Rt Revd Timothy John

LEICESTER, Dean of, [NOT APPOINTED AT TIME OF GOING TO PRESS]

LENNOX, Mr Lionel Patrick Madill, LLB
Provincial and Diocesan Registry Stamford House Piccadilly York YO1 9PP [REGISTRAR OF PROVINCE AND DIOCESE OF YORK; REGISTRAR OF CONVOCATION OF YORK; REGISTRAR OF TRIBUNALS FOR PROVINCE OF YORK] *educ* St Jo Sch Leatherhead; Birm Univ; Leeds Metropolitan Univ; *CV* Solicitor from 1973; In private practice 1973–80; Asst Legal Adv GS 1981–87; Sec Abp of Cant's Grp on Affinity 1982–84; Sec Bp of Lon's Grp on Blasphemy 1981–87; Sec Legal Adv Commn 1986–89; Registrar Province and Dioc York, Legal Secretary to the Archbp of York, Registrar York Conv and Eccl Notary from 1987 and Ptnr Denison Till (York) Solicitors from 1987; M Legal Adv Commn from 1987; Notary Public from 1992; M Eccll Rule Cttee from 1992; Registrar of Tribunals from 2006; Trustee Yorks Hist Chs Trust; Trustee St Leon Hospice York 2000–09; City of York Under Sheriff 2006–07; Pres Yorkshire Law Soc 2007–08
Tel: 01904 623487
01904 611411
Fax: 01904 561470

LEWES AND HASTINGS, Archdeacon of. See JONES, Ven Philip Hugh

LEWES, Area Bishop of, [NOT APPOINTED AT TIME OF GOING TO PRESS]

LEWIS, Very Revd Christopher Andrew, MA, Ph D
The Deanery Christ Church Oxford OX1 1DP [DEAN OF CHRIST CHURCH, OXFORD] *b* 1944 *educ* Marlboro Coll; Bris Univ; CCC Cam; Westcott Ho Th Coll; Episc Th Sch Cam Mass; *CV* Royal Navy 1961–66; C Barnard Castle 1973–76; Tutor Ripon Coll Cuddesdon 1976–81; Dir Ox Inst for Ch and Soc 1976–79; P-in-c Aston Rowant and Crowell 1978–81; Vc Prin Ripon Coll Cuddesdon 1981–82; V Spalding 1982–87; Can Res Cant Cathl 1987–94; Dir Minl Tr Cant dio 1989–94; Sen Insp Theol Colls and Courses from 1991; Dean of St Alb 1994–2003; Chair Inspections Wkg Pty, Ho of Bp's Cttee for Min 1996–2003; TETC 1996–2003; Chair Assoc of Engl Cathls 2000–09; Dean Ch Ch Ox from 2003
GS 1985–88, 1995–2005 *Tel:* 01865 276161
Fax: 01865 276238
email: rachel.perham@chch.ox.ac.uk

LEWIS, Revd Edward John, JP, BA, B Ed, MA, FRSA, M Inst D
Church House Great Smith St London SW1P 3AZ [CHIEF EXECUTIVE AND DIRECTOR OF TRAINING, HOSPITAL CHAPLAINCIES COUNCIL] *b* 1958 *educ* Penlan Sch Swansea; Univ of Wales; Chich Th Col; Univ of Surrey; *CV* C Llangiwg 1983–85; Sen C Morriston and Asst Chapl Morriston Hosp 1985–87; V Tregaron, Strata Florida and Ystradmeurig and Chapl Tregaron Hosp 1987–89; Sen Chapl Walsall Hosps NHS Trust, Walsall Com Trust and District Chapl Walsall HA 1989–2000; Asst RD Walsall 1995–2000; Sec and Dir Tr HCC from 2000; Visiting Lect, St Mary's Univ Coll Twickenham from 2003; Chair City of Westmr Magistrates' Trg Ctee from 2007; Chaplain to HMQ from 2008
Tel: 020 7898 1892 07957 529646
Fax: 020 7898 1891
email: edward.lewis@churchofengland.org

LEWIS, Mr Paul, BA, Postgrad Dip (Environmental Planning)
Church House Great Smith St London SW1P 3AZ [PASTORAL AND CLOSED CHURCHES SECRETARY, BISHOPRICS AND CATHEDRALS SECRETARY, CHURCH COMMISSIONERS] *b* 1952 *educ* Cantonian High Sch, Cardiff; Liv Univ; *CV* Asst Planner Chorley Borough Coun 1974–85; Appeals Officer Monmouth Borough Coun 1985–91; Asst Borough Planning Officer Hastings Borough Coun 1991–95, Borough Planning Officer/Chief Planner 1995–2004; Pastl and Closed Chs Sec Ch Commrs from 2004; Bishoprics and Cathls Sec Ch Commrs from 2009
Tel: 020 7898 1741 07894 930474
Fax: 020 7898 1873
email: paul.lewis@churchofengland.org

LEWISHAM AND GREENWICH, Archdeacon of, [NOT APPOINTED AT TIME OF GOING TO PRESS]

LICHFIELD, Archdeacon of. See LILEY, Ven Christopher Frank

LICHFIELD, Bishop of. See GLEDHILL, Rt Revd Jonathan Michael

LICHFIELD, Dean of. See DORBER, Very Revd Adrian John

LILEY, Ven Christopher Frank, B Ed
24 The Close Lichfield WS13 7LD [ARCHDEACON OF LICHFIELD] *b* 1947 *educ* Bp Lonsdale Coll of Educ, Derby; Linc Th Coll; *CV* C Kingswinford 1974–79; TV Ch Ch Stafford 1979–84; V Norton, Letchworth 1984–96; RD Hitchin 1990–96; P-in-c St Alkmund Shrewsbury 1996–2001; V St Chad w St Mary Shrewsbury 1996–2001; Adn of Lich from 2001; Chair Bd of Min to 2002 *Tel:* 01543 306145
01543 306146
Fax: 01543 306147
email: archdeacon.lichfield@lichfield.anglican.org

LILLEY, Canon Christopher Howard, Dip CM, FTII
The Chrysalis 12 Hillside Ave Sutton on Sea Mablethorpe LN12 2JH [LINCOLN] *b* 1951 *educ* K Sch Grantham; St Jo Coll Nottm; *CV* Hon C Skegness and Winthorpe 1985–93; C Gt Limber w Brocklesby 1993–96; P-in-c Middle Rasen Grp 1996–97; R Middle Rasen Grp 1997–2002; V Scawby with Redbourne and Hibaldstow and P-in-c Waddingham, Snitterby and Bishop Norton 2002–2010; RD Yarborough 2002–2009; M Bp's Coun 2001–2009; Dioc Ecum Officer 2001–2009; Ch Commr 1997–98; M AC Fin Cttee 1999–2001 and 2004–07; M Ch Commrs Bishoprics and Cathls Cttee 1999–2006; P-in-c Kirton w. Lindsey and Grayingham 2006–2010; M CCU 2007–11; Miss Enabler (NSM) Mablethorpe and Sutton on Sea Gps of Par from 2010; Acting Dioc Warden of Rdrs from 2011
GS 1996– *Tel:* 01507 440039
email: c.lilley@btinternet.com

LINCOLN, Archdeacon of. See BARKER, Ven Timothy Reed

LINCOLN, Bishop of. See LOWSON, Rt Revd Christopher

LINCOLN, Dean of. See BUCKLER, Very Revd Philip John Warr

LINDISFARNE, Archdeacon of. See ROBINSON, Ven Peter John Alan

LINDSEY, Archdeacon of Stow and. See SINCLAIR, Ven Jane Elizabeth Margaret

LIVERPOOL, Archdeacon of. See PANTER, Ven Ricky (Richard) James Graham

LIVERPOOL, Bishop of. See JONES, Rt Revd James Stuart

LIVERPOOL, Dean of. See WILCOX, Very Revd Pete (Peter Jonathan)

LLOYD, Ven Jonathan Wilford, B Sc, MA, Dip Applied Social Studies, CQSW
Tuborgvej 82 2900 Hellerup Copenhagen Denmark [ARCHDEACON OF GERMANY AND NORTHERN EUROPE] *b* 1956 *educ* Lancing Coll; Surrey Univ; City of Lon Poly; Goldsmiths Coll Lon Univ; North Lon Poly; S'wark Ord Course; *CV* PA to Bp of Namibia-in-Exile 1975–78; Rsch IDAF 1978–80; Com Wkr Lewisham 1980–81; Soc Wkr Lon Boro of S'wark 1982–84; Family Soc Wkr and Practice Tchr, Newham FWA 1984–86; Prin Soc Wkr St Chris Hospice Lond 1986–91; Help the Hospices Intl Fell (Sloan Kettering Meml Hosp, New York) 1991; Peace Monitor Kwa Zulu Natal (EMPSA) 1993; hon C St Bart Sydenham 1990–93, hon P-in-c 1993–94; Dir of Soc Resp, S'wark dioc 1991–95; M Lambeth Millennium Gp 1996–99; Priest V S'wark Cathl 1991–97; Chair Lond and S'wark Diocs Prisons and Criminal Justice Gp 1992–96; Bp's Officer for Ch and Society, S'wark 1995–97; M S'wark Dioc Miss Team 1995–97; M Bd of Dirs S Lon Industrial Miss 1991–95; S'wark Dioc Eur Link Officer 1991–97; Univ Chapl and Ecum Chaplaincy Team Leader, Univ of Bath 1997–2004; M Dioc Bd of Ed 1998–2003; Trustee Dorothy Ho Hospice Care 1998–2001; Chair Conf of Eur Univ Chapls 1998–2002; P-in-c Charlcombe w. Bath St Steph 2004–09; Co-Vc-Chair B & W Dioc Coun for Miss 2004–06; Non-Exec Dir R United Hosp Bath NHS Trust 2002–09; Chair B & W Dioc Soc Resp Grp 2004–09; M Bp's Coun 2008–09; M Inter-Dioc Fin Forum 2006–09; Chapl St Alban Copenhagen with Aarhus (Dioc in Eur) from 2009; Adn Germany and N Eur from 2010; Hon Can Holy Trin Pro-Cath Brussels from 2010
GS 1995–97, 2005–09 *Tel:* 00 45 39 62 77 36
email: jlloyd.uk@btinternet.com

LLOYD, Canon Nigel James Clifford, MA, BTh, STh
St John's Vicarage 5 Macaulay Road Broadstone Poole BH18 8AR [SALISBURY] *b* 1951 *educ* Lancing Coll; Nottm Univ; Linc Th Coll; Sarum Coll; *CV* C Sherborne Abbey 1981–84; R Lytchett Matravers 1984–92; TR Lower Parkstone 1992–12; V Broadstone from 2012; Area Ecum Officer 1994–99; Dioc Ecum Officer 1999–2001; Asst RD Poole 2000–01, RD 2001–09; non-res Can and Preb of Salis Cathl from 2002; M CCU 2001–05; M Bp's Coun 2000–05; Bd M Lewis Manning Hospice from 2005; Surrogate from 2010; Bd M Poole Mission Communities from 2011
GS 2000– *Tel:* 01202 694109 (Home)
07940 348776 (Mobile)
email: canon.nigel@gmail.com

LONDON (ST PAUL'S), Dean of. See ISON, Very Revd David John

LONDON, Archdeacon of. See MEARA, Ven David Gwynne

LONDON, Bishop of. See CHARTRES, Rt Revd and Rt Hon Richard John Carew

LORDING, Mrs Rosemary Kathleen, BA
93 Kings Acre Rd Hereford HR4 0RQ [HEREFORD] *b* 1947 *educ* Eliz Newcomen Sch, Lon; Mid Essex Tech Coll, Chelms; Herefordshire Coll of Tech; *CV* Catering mgt 1968–73; Personnel and trg mgr, retail 1988–96; Gen Mgr, Three Counties Trg 1996–99; Trg and Devel Mgr, Herefordshire Primary Care Trust 1999–2001; voluntary worker; M Bp's Coun, Dioc Policy and Resources Cttee, DBF Revenue Cttee; additional M Heref Cathl Chapter; Chair Ho of Laity Heref Dioc; Can Heref Cathl from 2010
GS 2004– *Tel:* 01432 340050
email: rk.lording@virgin.net

LOUGHBOROUGH, Archdeacon of. See NEWMAN, Ven David Maurice Frederick

LOVEGROVE, Mr Philip Albert, LLB, LLM, OBE
Chenies Lodge 24 Chenies Avenue Little Chaldont Bucks HP6 6PP [ST ALBANS] *b* 1937 *educ* Pet Symonds Sch Win; K Coll Lon; *CV* Investment Banker and Fin Consult from 1962; M Ch Assembly 1965–70; Ch Commr 1983–98; Chair St Alb DBF 1970–2004; M Bp's Coun 1970–2004; M GS Stg Cttee 1980–85 and 1990–98; Lay Can St Alb Cathl 1998–2004
GS 1977–2010 *Tel:* 07767 458097 (Mobile)
Fax: 020 7448 4765 (Office)
email: annelovegrove1@btinternet.com

LOWMAN, Ven David Walter, BD, AKC
The Archdeacon's Lodge 136 Broomfield Road Chelmsford CM1 1RN [ARCHDEACON OF SOUTHEND; CHELMSFORD] *b* 1948 *educ* Crewkerne Gr Sch; K Coll Lon; St Aug Coll Cant; *CV* Civil Servant 1966–70; C Notting Hill TM 1975–78; C St Aug w St Jo Kilburn 1978–81; Selection Sec and Voc Adv ACCM 1981–86; TR Wickford and Runwell 1986–93; DDO, Lay Min Adv and NSM Officer 1993–2001, Hon Can Chelmsf Cathl from 1993; M Dioc Syn from 1986; Vc Chair St Mellitus Coll 2008; Gov Brentwood Sch; Sen Selector, Bps' Selection Confs; M Marriage Law Reform Group
GS 1995–2005 *Tel:* 01245 258257
Fax: 01245 250845
email: a.southend@chelmsford.anglican.org

LOWSON, Rt Revd Christopher, M Th, STM, LLM, AKC
Bishop's Office The Old Palace Minster Yard Lincoln LN2 1PU [BISHOP OF LINCOLN] *b* 1953 *educ* Newc Cathl Sch; Consett Gr Sch; K Coll Lon; St Aug Coll Cant; Pacific Sch of Religion Berkeley California (WCC Scholar); Heythrop Coll Lon; Cardiff Law Sch; *CV* C St Mary Richmond 1977–82; P-in-c H Trin Eltham 1982–83, V 1983–91; Chapl Avery Hill Coll 1982–85; Chapl Thames Poly 1985–91; V Petersfield and R Buriton 1991–99; RD Petersfield 1995–99; Vis Lect Portsm Univ 1998–2006; Adn of Portsm Jan-Nov 1999; Adn of Portsdown 1999–2006; Chair Bd of Min; Bp of Portsm's Adv to Hosp Chaplaincy; Dioc Rep on Inter-Diocesan Fin Forum 1999–2006; Dir of Min, AC 2006–11; PV Westmr Abbey 2006–11; Bp of Lincoln from 2011
GS 2000–05, 2011–
Tel: 01522 534701 01522 504050
email: bishop.lincoln@lincoln.anglican.org
Web: www.lincoln.anglican.org

LUDLOW, Archdeacon of. See MAGOWAN, Rt Revd Alistair James

LUDLOW, Suffragan Bishop of. See MAGOWAN, Rt Revd Alistair James

LUNN, Councillor Robin Christopher, BA
Little Hambledon 10 Malthouse Crescent Inkberrow WR7 4EF [WORCESTER] *b* 1968 *educ* Ditcham Park Sch; Univ of Kent; *CV* Business Devel Mgr from 2005; County Councillor for Redditch N from 2005
GS 2004– *Tel:* 01386 792073
07785 305849 (Mobile)
Fax: 01386 791531
email: robin.lunn@axawinterthur.co.uk

LYNAS, Revd Stephen Brian, B Th, MBE, PGCE
Bishops' Office The Palace Wells Somerset BA5 2PD [BATH AND WELLS] *b* 1952 *educ* Borden Gr Sch, Kent; St Jo Coll Nottm; Trin Hall Cam; *CV* C Penn, Lich 1978–81; Relig Progr Org BBC Radio Stoke-on-Trent 1981–84; C Hanley 1981–82; C Edensor 1982–84; Relig Progr Producer BBC Bris 1985–88; Relig Progr Sen Producer BBC S and W Eng 1988–91; Hd Relig Progr TV South 1991–92; Com and Relig Affairs Ed Westcountry TV from 1992; Abps' Officer for Millennium 1996–2001; P Resources Adv, B&W Dioc 2001–07; Sen Chapl and Adv to Bps of B & W and Taunton from 2007
GS 2005– *Tel:* 01749 672341
Fax: 01749 679355
email: chaplain@bathwells.anglican.org

LYNN, Archdeacon of. See ASHE, Ven (Francis) John

LYNN, Suffragan Bishop of. See MEYRICK, Rt Revd Jonathan

LYON, Mrs Rosemary Jane, BA, MA, PGCE
13 New Acres Newburgh Wigan WN8 7TU [BLACKBURN] *b* 1962 *educ* Ormskirk Grammar Sch; St Aidan's Coll Dur Univ; York Univ; Lon Univ; *CV* Teacher Cardinal Vaugh Mem Sch 1985–88; Vol Pastoral Asst Dioc Argentina 1988–89; Cowley High Sch 1989–90; Chester Catholic High Sch 1990–92; Tarporley County Sch 1992–93; Ormskirk Grammar Sch 1993–94; Maricourt Catholic High Sch from 2002; St Mary's Catholic Pri Sch

from 2010; M W Dev Gp Blackb; Elected to GS 2010
GS 2010– *Tel:* 01257464541
email: rosie.jl46@yahoo.co.uk

MACCLESFIELD, Archdeacon of. See BISHOP, Ven Ian Gregory

MacLEAY, Revd Angus Murdo, MA, M Phil
Rectory Rectory Lane Sevenoaks TN13 1JA [ROCHESTER] *b* 1959 *educ* The Vyne Basingstoke; Qu Mary's Sixth Form Coll Basingstoke; Univ Coll Ox; Wycliffe Hall Ox; *CV* C H Trin Platt, Man 1988–92; V St Jo Houghton w. St Pet Kingmoor, Carl 1992–2001; R St Nich Sevenoaks from 2001; M Angl-Meth Formal Conversations 1998–2001; M Dioc Syn; M Revision Cttee for Consecration and Ordination of Women Measure; M ho of Bps' Code of Practice Working Grp Concerning Women Bishops
GS 1995–2001; 2005– *Tel:* 01732 740340
Fax: 01732 742810
email: office@stnicholas-sevenoaks.org

MAGOWAN, Rt Revd Alistair James, B Sc, Dip HE, M Th (Oxon)
Bishop's House Corvedale Road Craven Arms SY7 9BT [SUFFRAGAN BISHOP OF LUDLOW AND ARCHDEACON OF LUDLOW; HEREFORD] *b* 1955 *educ* K Sch Worc; Leeds Univ; Trin Coll Bris; Westmr Coll Ox; *CV* C St Jo Bapt Owlerton 1981–84; C St Nic Dur 1984–89; Chapl St Aid Coll Dur 1984–89; V St Jo Bapt Egham 1989–2000; RD Runnymede 1993–2000; Chair Guidf Dioc Bd of Educ 1996–2000; Adn of Dorset 2000–09; Suff Bp of Ludlow from 2009; Adn of Ludlow from 2009; Chair Salis DBE 2004–09
GS 1995–2000, 2004–10 *Tel:* 01588 673571
email: bishopofludlow@btinternet.com

MAIDSTONE, Archdeacon of, TAYLOR, Ven Stephen

MAIDSTONE, Suffragan Bishop of. [NOT APPOINTED AT TIME OF GOING TO PRESS]

MALCOURONNE, Mr Keith Robert, MA, FCA, CF
20 Riverside Rd Staines TW18 2LE [GUILDFORD] *b* 1959 *educ* Sutton Manor Gr Sch; New Coll Ox; *CV* Chair Insight Management & Systems Consultants Ltd from 2005; Dir Globus Energy plc from 2007; Fin Dir The Specialist Washing Company Ltd from 2007; Managing ptnr, Bolton Colby Chartered Accountants 1993–2005; Fin ptnr BC technologies LLP from 2000; Man Dir Heathrow Corporate Consulting Ltd from 2005; Dir and Chair Bd Fin and Audit Ctee, World Vision UK; Chartered Accountant, corporate financier and bus consult from 1983; Nat Chair of Crusaders 1991–97; Chair Berega Relief Equipment and Devel Trust from 2001; Treas Ox Cen for Miss Studies; Vc-Chair AC Audit Cttee from 2006; Chair Fin and Audit Ctee Urban Saints; M Guildf Dioc Bp's Coun and DBF exec, Dioc Audit Cttee; Lay Chair Runnymede Dny
GS 2005– *Tel:* 01784 455501
07990 511905 (Mobile)
email: keith@bc-group.co.uk

MALLARD, Canon Zahida, Dip Mgt Studies, PG Dip Diversity Mgt
17 The Crescent Crossflatts Bingley BD16 2EU [BRADFORD] *b* 1968 *educ* Westborough High Sch Dewsbury; Dewsbury and Batley Tech and Art Coll; Wulfrun Coll Wolverhampton; Wolverhampton Poly; Bradf Univ; Queen's Birm Th Coll; *CV* Welfare Rights Officer Bradf Coun from 1992, Welfare Rights Manager 2000–09, Interpreting and Translation Service Manager 2006, Development Officer: Equalities and Diversity 2009; M DBE; M Dioc Bd for Ch in Society; Dioc Link Person to CMEAC; M MPA Coun; M Bradf Com Legal Services Advice Partnership Bd; Common Purpose Graduate; Bp's Counc Bradf from 2003; Brd Edu 2006–09; Lay Canon from 2010; Trustee Bd of Social Aid and Bradf Hate Crime Alliance
GS 2000– *Tel:* 01274 562640 (Home)
01274 435174 (Office)
07931 761202 (Mobile)
email: zahidamallard@yahoo.co.uk

MALLETT, Revd Dr Marlene Rosemarie, BA, PhD
St John's Vicarage 49 Wiltshire Road London SW9 7NE [SOUTHWARK] *b* 1959 *educ* Foxford Comp Sch; Sussex Univ; Warwick Univ; SEITE; *CV* AC Ch Ch North Brixton 2004–07; C Exec Off, Brent Mental Health Consortium 200204; Rsrch Sociologist, Med Rsrch Counc 1991–2002; Academic Co-ord, Centre for Caribbean Med, Guys, Kings & St. Thomas' Med Sch, 2001–02; Hon. Lect, Dept. of Legal, Political & Social Sciences, South Bank Univ 1995–97; Rsrch Fellow Institute of Social & Economic Rsrch, Univ of the West Indies, Cave Hill Campus, 1989–90; Rsrch Consult, Swedish International Development Agency, Addis Ababa 1988; Project Admin Rsrch Co-op Adv Grp, 1987–88; Rsrch Consult Women & Development Project, Commonwealth Secr HQ, 1986–87; Rsrch Asst, Institute of Development Studies, 1985–86; Rsrch Admin, Institute of Development Studies, 1983–85; Rsrcher/Admin Eastern & Southern African Universities Rsrch Project, ESAURP, Univ of Dar es Salaam, 1982–83; P-in-C St. John the Evan, Angell Town from 2007; M Dioc Syn from 2005; Convenor of Kingston Area Minority Ethnic Anglican Concerns Cttee 2006; M Dioc Minority Ethnic Anglican Concerns Cttee 2006; M Kingston Area Forum 2007; M Dioc Litt Cttee from 2008; M Liturgical Commn from 2011; M S'wark Cathl Chapter from 2012
GS 2010– *Tel:* 0207 733 0585
email: rosemarie.mallett@gmail.com

MALMESBURY, Archdeacon of. See FROUDE, Ven Christine Ann

MAN, Archdeacon of. See SMITH, Ven Brian

MANCHESTER, Archdeacon of. See ASHCROFT, Ven Mark

MANCHESTER, Bishop of. See McCULLOCH, Rt Revd Nigel Simeon

MANCHESTER, Dean of. See GOVENDER, Very Revd Rogers Morgan

MANDELBROTE, Mr Giles Howard, MA, FSA
Lambeth Palace Library London SE1 7JU [LIBRARIAN AND ARCHIVIST, LAMBETH PALACE LIBRARY] *b* 1961 *educ* Eton Coll; St John's Coll Ox; *CV* Editor Quiller Press (publishers) 1989–92; Curatorial Officer, Royal Commission on Historical Manuscripts 1992–95; Curator, British Collections 1501–1800, British Library 1995–2010; Librarian and Archivist, Lambeth Palace Library from 2010 *Tel:* 020 7898 1266
Fax: 020 7898 7932
email: giles.mandelbrote@churchofengland.org
Web: www.lambethpalacelibrary.org

MANSELL, Ven Clive Neville Ross, LLB, Dip HE
3 The Ridings Blackhurst Lane Tunbridge Wells TN2 4RU [ARCHDEACON OF TONBRIDGE; ROCHESTER] *b* 1953 *educ* City of Lon Sch; Leic Univ; Coll of Law; Trin Coll Bris; *CV* Solicitor (no longer practising); C Gt Malvern Priory 1982–85; Min Can Ripon Cathl 1985–89; R Kirklington w Burneston, Wath and Pickhill 1989–2002; AD Wensley 1998–2002; Archdeacon of Tonbridge from 2002; M Revision Cttee on the Draft Churchwardens Measure; M Legal Aid Commn from 1996; Ch Commr from 1997–2008 (M Ch Commissioners' Assets Cttee, Red Chs Cttee); M Revision Cttee on Draft Amending Canon No 22; M Revision Cttee on Draft C of E (Misc Provisions) Measure and Draft Amending Canon No 23; Chair Strg Cttee C of E Pensions (Amendment) Measure; M Strg Cttee, Common Worship Ordinal, Chair Dioc Bd of Educ; M Dioc Bd of Patronage; M Dioc Rural Adv Grp; Chair Ch in Society; M Bp's Coun; formerly Chair of Dioc Bd for Mission, Ecumenism and Parish Devt, M Eccl Law Soc; Dep Prolocutor N Province/Prov of York 2001–02; M Appeal Panel for Internal Syn Elections and Elections of Convocations; M of Appeal Panel constituted under Schedule 4 of the 1983 Pastoral Measure; M GS Panel of Chairmen(2003–2010,;Ch Revision Cttee on Draft Bps and Ps (Consecration and Ord of Women) Measure; M Nat Adns Forum 2003–2010; Chair of Adns on GS; Simeon's Trustee 2003–08; Foundation Fell Univ of Gloucestershire
GS 1995– *Tel:* 01892 520660
email: archdeacon.tonbridge@rochester.anglican.org

MANTLE, Dr Richard John, DMus (Hon) FRSA
Cleveland House Barrowby Lane Kirkby Overblow Yorkshire HG3 1HQ [RIPON AND LEEDS] *b* 1947 *educ* Tiffin Sch; Ealing Coll of Higher Ed; *CV* Deputy Managing Dir, ENO 1979–85; Managing Dir Scottish Opera 1985–91; Gen Dir Edmonton Opera Canada, 1991–94; Guardian of the Holy House, Shrine of Our Lady of Walsingham from 1999; Treasurer, College of Guardians, Dir WCTA Ltd; Gen Dir Opera North from 1994; Dir and Trustee, Nat Opera Studio from 1995; M Coun Coll of the Resurrection Mirfield from 2010; M Abps' Coun Fin Ctte from 2011; M Advisory Bd, Music Dept Univ York from 2012
GS 2010– *Tel:* 01423 81592
email: richard.mantle@operanorth.co.uk

MARSHALL, Dr Edmund Ian, MA, Ph D
37 Roundwood Lane Harpenden Herts AL5 3BP [ST ALBANS] *b* 1940 *educ* Humberstone Foundn Sch Clee; Magd Coll Ox; Liv Univ; *CV* Univ Lect Liv and Hull 1962–66; Mathematician in Industry 1967–71; MP Goole 1971–83; Lect in Management Science Bradf Univ 1984–2000; Vc-Pres Meth Conf 1992–93; M Dioc Syn from 1996; M Bp's Coun 1997–2007; M Dioc Pastl Cttee 1998–2007; Bp's Adv for Ecum Affairs Wakef 1998–2007; Chair Wakef Cathl Com Cttee 2000–07; Rdr 1994–2007; M Wakef Cathl Chap 2003–07; M CCU 2006–11; Chair Rev Ctee for Diocs Pastl and Miss Measure 2006; Reader St Alb Dioc from 2008
GS 2000– *Tel:* 01582 461236
email: edmund.marshall@btinternet.com

MARSHALL, Mr Lee, BSc, MBA
Church House Great Smith Street London SW1P 3PS [CHIEF OF STAFF, CHURCH OF ENGLAND PENSIONS BOARD] *b* 1961 *educ* Tunbridge Wells Gr Sch for Boys; Univ of Lancaster; Univ Manchester (Business Sch); *CV* On staff of Ch Commissioners from 1983, holding various posts including Assset Accountant; SAP Project Business Change Mgr; Chief of Staff, C of E Pensions Bd from 2009
Tel: 020 7898 1681
email: lee.marshall@churchofengland.org

MARTIN, Mrs (Bridget Elizabeth) Anne, BEd, MMus, MPhil, LTCL
8 Woodberry Close Chiddingfold GU8 4SF [GUILDFORD] *b* 1949 *educ* Whyteleafe Gr Sch; Homerton Coll Cam; Lon Univ Inst of Educ; Surrey Univ; Trin Coll of Music; *CV* Primary sch music specialist in state (inc ch schs) and private sectors in Suffolk, Cambs and Germany 1972–79; lect in music, Basford Hall FE Coll Nottm 1982–84; head of music, St Ives Prep Sch, Haslemere 1988–96; rsch Renaissance music Surrey Univ 1996–98; music tchr, Tormead Sch Guildf 1998–2001; Head of Music, St Teresa's Prep Sch; M Godalming Dny Syn 2005 and Guildf DBE from 2006; Guildf Bp's Coun 2009; M Rural Affairs GP from 2011; long-serving M of ch choir; involved with Chr Aid locally for 20 yrs; Musical dir Annual festival of

Soc of Recorder Players 2012; currently self-employed specialist recorder tchr, accompanist, arranger, writer, adjudicator and conductor
GS 2005– *Tel:* 01428 683854 07789 992979
email: be_anne_martin@hotmail.com

MASON, Canon Dr John Philip, MA PhD CChem FRSC
3 Flaxyards Eaton Lane Tarporley CW6 9GL [CHESTER] *b* 1959 *educ* King George V Sch; Ch Coll Cam; Birm Univ; *CV* Rsrch Scientist, Harwell Laboratory 1980–85; Rsrch & Business Mgr, AEA Technology 1986–94; Programme/Business Mgr, Laboratory of the Government Chemist (LGC) 1994–2002; Dir LGC Grp Holdings plc 2002–06; Dioc Sec, Chester 2006–10
GS 2010– *Tel:* 01829 733971
email: johnpmason@gmail.com

MAURICE, Rt Revd Peter David, BA, Dip Th
The Palace Wells BA5 2PD [SUFFRAGAN BISHOP OF TAUNTON; BATH AND WELLS] *b* 1951 *educ* Purley Gr Sch; St Chad's Coll Dur; Mirfield Th Coll; Westmr Coll Ox; *CV* C St Paul Wimbledon Park 1975–79; TV All SS East Sheen 1979–85; V H Trin Rotherhithe 1985–96; RD Bermondsey 1991–96; V All SS Tooting 1996–2003; Adn of Wells 2003–06; Bp of Taunton from 2006 *Tel:* 01749 672341
Fax: 01749 679355
email: bishop.taunton@bathwells.anglican.org

McCULLOCH, Rt Revd Nigel Simeon, MA; Hon DCL
Bishopscourt Bury New Rd Manchester M7 4LE [BISHOP OF MANCHESTER] *b* 1942 *educ* Liv Coll; Selw Coll Cam; Cuddesdon Th Coll; *CV* C Ellesmere Port 1966–70; Chapl Ch Coll Cam 1970–73; Dir of Th Studies Ch Coll Cam 1970–75; Dioc Missr Norw Dioc 1973–78; R SS Thos & Edm Sarum 1978–86; Adn of Sarum 1979–86; Chair ABM Finance Cttee 1987–92; Bp of Taunton 1986–92; Bp of Wakef 1992–2002; Chair Dec of Evang Stg Grp 1989–98; Chair Communications Cttee 1993–98; Lord High Almoner 1997–2012; Chair BM Miss, Evang and Renewal Cttee 1998–99; Chair Statistics Rev Grp 1998–2000; Chair Sandford St Mart Trust and Relig in Broadcasting Grp 1999–2008; Bp of Manchester from 2002; M Ho of Lords Select Cttees on BBC and Communications 2005–10; Chair Coun of Chr and Jews from 2007; Chair Women in the Episcopate Legislation Grp 2006–09; Chair Steering Grp for Women in the Episcopate Legis Revision 2009–12
GS 1990– *Tel:* 0161 792 2096 (Office)
Fax: 0161 792 6826
email: bishop@bishopscourt.manchester.anglican.org

McCURDY, Ven Hugh Kyle, BA(Hons)
Whitgift House The College Ely CB7 4DL [ARCHDEACON OF HUNTINGDON AND WISBECH; ELY] *b* 1958 *educ* Geo Abbot Sch Guild; Portsm Poly; Cardiff Univ; Trin Coll Bris; *CV* C St Jo Egham 1985–88; C St Jo Woking 1988–91; V St Andr Histon 1991–2005; P-in-c St Andr Impington 1998–2005; RD N Stowe 1994–2005; Adn of Huntingdon and Wisbech from 2005; M DAC, Pastl Cttee, Bp's Coun; Acting Dir of Miss; Trustee Cambridgeshire ACRE; Gov Wisbech Grammar Sch; M Cam Theol Federation Coun; M Coun Ridley Hall Th Coll; M CPAS Coun of Reference
GS 2010–
Tel: 01353 658404 01353 652709 (Office)
email: archdeacon.handw@ely.anglican.org

McDONALD, Very Revd Alan Douglas, LLB, BD, MTH, DLitt, DD
1 Cairnhill Gardens St Andrews Fife KY16 8QY [CHURCH OF SCOTLAND] *b* 1951 *educ* Glas Academy; Strathclyde Univ; Edin Univ; St Andrews Univ; New Coll Edin; *CV* Comm Min, Edin 1979–83; P Min Holburn Central, Aberdeen 1983–98; P Min St Leonards, St Andrews from 1998; Convener Ch and Nation Cttee 2000–04; Moderator Gen Ass C of S from 2006
GS 2010– *Tel:* 01334472793
email: alan.d.mcdonald@talk21.com

McDONOUGH, Canon Philip Michael James, BSc
28 Washbrook Close Barton-le-Clay MK45 4LF [ST ALBANS] *b* 1939 *educ* Wandsworth Tech Coll Lon; Imp Coll Lon; *CV* Asst Chapl Luton and Dunstable Hosp 1996–2004; Rdr from 1985; Sec St Alb Dioc Rdrs Assoc 1995–2004; M CRC Exec 1999–2004; M AC Min Div VRSC 2000–05; M C of E Hosp Chapl Coun, Coun St Alb Cathl 2001–09; Lay Chair Ampthill Dny Syn 2002–10; Hon Can St Alb Cathl 2002–09, Emeritus 2009; Associate Sec CRC 2004–05; Trustee Br Red Cross Soc Staff Pension Fund from 2006; M St Alb Bd for Christian Dev from 2007; Lay Chair Ampthill & Shefford Dny Syn 2011
GS 2000–2005; 2005–2010; 2010–
Tel: 01582 881772 07759 444879
email: canonpmcdonough@btinternet.com

McFARLANE, Ven Janet (Jan) Elizabeth, B Med Sci, BA, Dip Min Std
31 Bracondale Norwich NR1 2AT [ARCHDEACON OF NORWICH AND DIRECTOR OF COMMUNICATIONS] *b* 1964 *educ* Blythe Bridge High Sch Stoke-on-Trent; Sheff Univ; Dur Univ; Cranmer Hall Dur; *CV* Speech therapist 1987–90; C Stafford TM, Lich 1993–96; Chapl and Min Can, Ely Cathl 1996–99; Norw Dioc Communications Officer 1999–2009; Chapl to Bp of Norw 2001–09; Hon PV Nor Cath 2000–09; M Bp's Coun, Dioc Syn; Adn Norwich from 2009; Dioc Dir of Communications from 2009
GS 2005– *Tel:* 01603 620007
email: archdeacon.norwich@norwich.anglican.org

McGINLEY, Revd John Charles, BSocSci, BA
5 Ratcliffe Road Leicester LE2 3TE [LEICESTER] *b* 1969 *educ* Hewett Comp Sch, Norwich; Birm

Univ; Trinity Coll Bris; *CV* Asst Buyer, Harrods Ltd, 1990–93; Asst C Holy Trinity w St Paul, Hounslow 1996–2000; TV Holy Trinity w St John, Hinckley 2000–05; TR Holy Trinity w St John, Hinckley 2005–09; V Holy Trinity Leic from 2009; GS 2010– *Tel:* 0116 2548981 0116 2448867
email: vicar@holytrinityleicester.org

McGREGOR, Revd Alexander Scott, MA
Legal Office Church House Great Smith St London SW1P 3AZ [DEPUTY LEGAL ADVISER TO THE ARCHBISHOPS' COUNCIL AND THE GENERAL SYNOD] *b* 1972 *educ* John Lyon Sch Harrow; Ch Ch Ox; Coll of Law; Inns of Court Sch of Law; St Albans and Ox Min Course; *CV* Barrister in independent practice 1996–2005; Legal Adviser in the Legal Office of the NCIs 2006–08; Deputy Legal Adviser to the Archbishops' Coun and the GS from 2009; M The Honourable Soc of Lincoln's Inn from 1994; M Dacorum Boro Coun 1999–2007; Assistant C (NSM) St Mary Harrow 2006–09; Assistant C (NSM) St Barnabas Pimlico and St Mary Bourne Street from 2009; Deputy Chancellor Dioc of Ox from 2007 *Tel:* 020 7898 1748
email: alexander.mcgregor@churchofengland.org

McINTYRE, Revd Eva, MA (Oxon)
The Vicarage Church Avenue Stourport on Severn DY13 9DD [WORCESTER] *b* 1960 *educ* Parkstone Grammar Schor Girls; Worcester Coll Ox; St Stephen's Ho; Birm Sch of Acting; *CV* Dss St James Devizes 1984–6; Dn Oakdale team Ministry 1986–8; Producer Religious Programmes BBC Radio Leeds 1988–90; Producer BBC 1990–1; Area Co-ordinator Christian Aid 1992–8; Freelance writer; R Bangor Monachorum and Worthenbury, Church in Wales 1998–2003; Co-ordinating Chaplain HMP Brockhill 2003–06; V Stourport on Severn and Wilden from 2006; Co-ordinator of Mental Health Matters from 2011; member of CMDDP (cttee of the Abps' Coun) from 2011
Tel: 01299 822041
email: evacymru@btinternet.com
Web: www.mentalhealthmatters-cofe.org

McISAAC, Mrs Debrah, BA, LLB/D. Jur. Law Soc of Eng & Wales
Parsonage Farm House White Way Pitton Wiltshire SP5 1DT [SALISBURY] *b* 1953 *educ* Marian High Sch,Saskatchewan; Canada Univ of Saskatchewan; Osgoode Hall, York Univ, Canada; Wycliffe Hall; Ripon Coll Cuddesdon; *CV* Adv, Off of the Ombudsman, Province of Saskatchewan, 1973; Spec Adv, Minister of Justice, Ottawa, 1975; Barrister and Solicitor, Edmonton, Alberta, Canada admitted 1976; Barrister and Solicitor, Law So of Upper Canada admitted 1983; Solicitor,Law Soc of England and Wales admitted 1985; Solicitor Durrant Piesse, Lon 1985–86; Solicitor, Freshfields, Lon 1986–88; Dir Prof Devlp, Lovells, Lon, 1989–2000; Chief Monitor,Training Contracts, Law Soc of Eng & Wales, 2000–06; Principal, D Ball Consulting 2000–10; Legal Ed and Training Grp; Treasurer,1994–96; Chair, 1996–98; Lord Chancellor's Adv Cttee Ed & Conduct Standing Conf, 1994–99; Advocacy Sub-cttee of Law Soc's Training Cttee, 1998–2008; Counc of the Law Soc of Eng & Wales; Counc M, 2005–08; Chair, Ed & Training Cttee, 2005–08; M, Regulatory Affairs Grp, 2005–07; M, Regulatory Affairs Brd, 2007–08; M Dioc Syn Sarum from 2009; M Sarum Archdeaconary Miss &Pstrl Cttee from 2010; Lay Chair, Alderbury Dny Syn form 2010; Alderbury Deanery Standing & Pstrl Cttee, from 2005
GS 2010–
Tel: 01722 712758/0207 373 8742/07879 662188
email: db@dball.com

McKINNEL, Rt Revd Nicholas Howard Paul
MA (Cantab); MA (Oxon)
32 The Avenue Tiverton Devon EX16 4HW [SUFFRAGAN BISHOP OF CREDITON; EXETER] *b* 1954 *Educ* Marlborough Coll; Queens' Coll Cam; Wycliffe Hall Ox; *CV* C St Mary's, West Kensington 1980–83; Angl Chaplain Liverpool Univ 1983–87; R Hatherleigh, Meeth, Exbourne and Jacobstowe 1987–94; TR St Andrew's Plymouth and St Paul's, Stonhouse 1994–2012; Bp of Crediton from 2012
Tel: 01884 250002
email: bishop.of.crediton@exeter.anglican.org

McKITTRICK, Ven Douglas Henry, BTh
2 Yorklands Dyke Rd Avenue Hove BN3 6RW [ARCHDEACON OF CHICHESTER] *b* 1953 *educ* John Marley Comp Sch, Newcastle-upon-Tyne; St Steph Ho Ox; *CV* C St Paul Deptford, S'wark 1977–80; C St Jo Tuebrook, Liv 1980–81; TV St Steph Grove St, Liv 1981–89; V St Agnes Toxteth Pk, Liv 1989–97; V St Pet with Chapel Royal Brighton, Chich from 1997; RD of Brighton from 1998; Can and Preb of Chich Cathl from 1998; Archdeacon of Chichester from 2002; M DAC, Bd of Educ, DBF, Pastl Cttee, Parsonages Cttee; Bp's Adv Hosp Chaplaincy; Coun M Additional Curates Soc 2005; M Hosp Chapl Coun 2006; Bp's Adv on Ecumenism; M Eccl Law Soc; M Nikaean Club
GS 2004– *Tel:* 01273 505330 (Home)
01273 421021 (Office)
Fax: 01273 421041
email: archchichester@diochi.org.uk

McLEAN, Revd (Margaret Anne) Maggie, MA
Battyeford Vicarage 107A Stocks Bank Road Mirfield WF14 9QT [WAKEFIELD] *b* 1962 *educ* Greenhead Gr Sch; Birm Univ; Heythrop Coll; Cranmer Hall Dur; *CV* C All Saints Church, Bedford 1991–94; Chapl St Albans High Sch for Girls 1994–98; Assoc P St Alb Abbey; Asst Social Responsibility Adv 1998–99; Anglican Chapl, Univ of Huddersfield 1999–2002; P-in-C St Philip and St James, Scholes and St Luke and Whitechapel, Cleckheaton 2002–09; P-in-C Christ the King,

Battyeford from 2009; DiocTraining Off; Canon Wakefield Cathl from 2011
GS 2010– *Tel:* 01924493277 07791 880691
email: m.a.mclean@btinternet.com

McMULLEN, Canon Christine Elizabeth, BA, Dip Ad Ed, MA
Farm Cottage Montpelier Place Buxton SK17 7EJ [DERBY] *b* 1943 *educ* Homelands Sch Derby; R Holloway Coll Lon; Nott Univ; Derby Univ; *CV* Rdr from 1986; Chair Buxton Dny from 2005; Lay Can Derby Cathl from 2010; Dir Pastl Studies, Nn Ord Course 1994, Vice Prin 1995–2009; M Lit Comm from 2011
GS 1990– *Tel:* 01298 73997
email: christine.mcmullen@hotmail.com

McPHATE, Very Revd Prof Gordon Ferguson, BA, MA, M Th, M Sc, MB, Ch B, MD, FRCP
The Deanery 7 Abbey St Chester CH1 2JF [DEAN OF CHESTER] *b* 1950 *educ* Perth Gr Sch; Cam Univ; Aberd Univ; Edin Univ; Surrey Univ; Westcott Ho Cam; *CV* Lect in Physiology, Guy's Hosp Lon 1979–84; Hon C Sanderstead, S'wark 1978–80; Hon PV and Sacrist, S'wark Cathl 1980–86; Registrar in Chemical Pathology, Guildf Hosps 1984–86; Lect and Sen Lect in Pathology, Univ of St Andr 1986–2002; Hon Angl Chapl, Univ of St Andr 1986–2002; Consult Chemical Pathologist, Fife Hosps 1993–2002; Dean of Chester from 2002; Vis Prof of Theol, Univ of Chester from 2003
GS 2004–05 *Tel:* 01244 500971
email: dean@chestercathedral.com

McPHERSON, Mrs Katherine, MBA, BA
59 Mycenae Rd London SE3 7SE [APPOINTED MEMBER, ARCHBISHOPS' COUNCIL] *b* 1964 *educ* P. L. Meth Girls' Sch Singapore; Temasek Jun Coll Singapore; Nat Univ of Singapore; Univ of Kent; *CV* Exec Consult, Ernst and Young Singapore 1987–92; Sen Mgr, Ernst and Young Lon 1992–95; Lon Hd of Sales and Marketing (Media & Resources), Ernst and Young 1996–98; Nat Hd of Sales and Marketing (Telecoms, Media & Entertainment), Ernst and Young 1998–99; Project Dir (secondment), BBC Mar-Nov 1999; Managing Consult, Cap Gemini Ernst and Young 1999–2001; Operations Dir, YMCA Lambeth, Lewisham and S'wark 2001–2002; Dir Business Devel and Marketing, EMEA, White and Case 2002–04; Apptd M AC 2003–09; Head of Bus Devel, Corporate Div, Herbert Smith 2004–05; Head of Bus Devel, Europe, Herbert Smith 2005–07; Head Winning Business, Global Markets, KPMG 2007–10; Dir Global Markets, KMPG from 2010
GS 2003–10 *Tel:* 020 8858 1856 (Home)
07984 046149 (Mobile)
email: mcpherson.katherine@gmail.com *2nd email:* mcpehrson.katherine@gmail.com

MEARA, Ven David Gwynne, MA, S.Th, FSA
Rectory St Brides Church Fleet St London EC4Y 8AU [ARCHDEACON OF LONDON] *b* 1947 *educ* Merchant Taylor's Sch Northwood; Oriel Coll Ox; Cuddesdon Theol Coll; *CV* C Ch Ch Reading 1973–77; Chapl Univ of Reading 1977–82; V Basildon Aldworth and Ashampstead 1982–94; RD Bradfield 1990–94; R Buckinham 1994–2000; AD Buckingham 1994–2000; Chair Ox Dioc Adv Gp on Miss 1990–2000; R St Bride's Fleet St from 2000; Adn of Lon from 2009; Hon Can Ch Ch Ox; M Lon DAC from 2009; M Dioc Syn from 2009
Tel: 020 7427 0133
020 7236 7891
Fax: 020 7583 4867
email: archdeacon.london@london.anglican.org

MELLOR, Very Revd (Kenneth) Paul, BA, MA
The Deanery Cornet St St Peter Port Guernsey GY1 1BZ [DEAN OF GUERNSEY; WINCHESTER] *b* 1949 *educ* Ashfield Sch, Kirkby-in-Ashfield; Southn Univ; Leeds Univ; Mirfield Th Coll; Cuddesdon Th Coll; *CV* C St Mary V Cottingham 1973–76; C All SS Ascot 1976–80; V St Mary Magd Tilehurst 1980–85; V Menheniot 1985–94; RD E Wivelshire 1990–94; Hon Can Truro Cathl 1990–94; Chair Dioc Bd of Miss and Unity 1990–95; CFCE 1996–2000; Can Treas Truro Cathl 1994–2003; Dean of Guernsey from 2003
GS 1994–2003; 2005– *Tel:* 01481 720036
07720 506863 (Mobile)
Fax: 01481 722948
email: kpaulmellor@cwgsy.net

MEON, Archdeacon of The. See COLLINS, Ven Gavin Andrew

MESSHAM, Canon Barbara Lynn, Cert Ed
18 Vicarage Gate Guildford Surrey GU2 7QJ [GUILDFORD] *b* 1952 *educ* Christ's Hosp Girls' High Sch; Nott Univ; Bretton Hall Coll; STETS; *CV* Maths Tchr, 1975–96; AC St Thomas-on-the-Bourne, Farnham 1999–2003; V, All Saints' Church, Guildford from 2003; Rural Dean of Guildford 2006–11; Hon Can Guild Cathl from 2010; M Guild Dioc Syn
GS 2010– *Tel:* 01483 572006
email: barbara@messhams.co.uk

MEYRICK, Rt Revd (Cyril) Jonathan, MA (Oxon), DEd(Hon)
The Old Vicarage Castle Acre King's Lynn PE32 2AA [SUFFRAGAN BISHOP OF LYNN; NORWICH] *b* 1952 *educ* Lancing Coll; St Jo Coll Ox; Salis & Well Th Coll; *CV* C Bicester, Ox 1976–78; Bp's Chapl, Ox 1978–81; OT tutor, Codrington Coll, Barbados 1981–84; TV Burnham Team, Ox 1984–90; TR Tisbury, Salis 1990–98; RD Chalke, Sarum 1997–98; Res Can Roch 1998–2005; acting Dean of Roch 2002–04; Dean of Exeter 2005–2011; Chair Coun for Miss & Unity 2005–2011; Bp of Lynn from 2011
Tel: 01760 755553 01760 755085
email: bishop.lynn@norwich.anglican.org
Web: www.norwich.agnlican.org

MIDDLESEX, Archdeacon of. See WELCH, Ven Stephan John

MIDDLETON, Suffragan Bishop of. See DAVIES, Rt Revd Mark

MILLAR, Revd Dr Sandra, BA; MA; PhD; DipTh; DipMin
18 Overbury Road Gloucester GL1 4EA [GLOUCESTER] *b* 1957 *educ* Rugby High Sch for Girls; Univ Coll, Cardiff; Warwick Univ; Ripon Coll, Cuddesdon; *CV* Product mgr, Boots Company, 1979–84; Product mgr, Coop 1984–88; Sales/Marketing Mgr, Windsor Foods 1989–91; Sales/Marketing Mgr, SU 1991–93; National Dir Kings Kids England 1994–98; AC, Chipping Barnet w Arkley 2000–03; TV, Dorchester Team and tutor at Ripon Coll Cuddesdon 2003–07; Children's Off, Glouc from 2007; Brd for Christian Devlp, St Alb 2000–03; Dioc Syn, St. Alb 2000–03; Gov of SAOMC 2001–06; M Miss Initiatives Grp, from 2007; M Bps Worship, Prayer and Spirituality Grp from 2007
GS 2010– *Tel:* 01452 835554 07976 823986
email: smillar@glosdioc.org.uk

MILLER, Ven Geoff (Geoffrey Vincent), BEd, MA
80 Moorside North Fenham Newcastle-upon-Tyne NE4 9DU [ARCHDEACON OF NORTHUMBERLAND; NEWCASTLE] *b* 1956 *educ* Sharston High Sch, Manch; Dur Univ; St Jo Coll Nottm; Newc Univ; *CV* C Jarrow 1983–86; TV St Aidan Billingham 1986–92; Dioc Urban Devel Officer 1991–99; Com Chapl Stockton-on-Tees 1992–94; P-in-c St Cuth Darlington 1994–96, V 1996–99; Dioc Urban Officer and Res Can Newc Cathl 1999–2005; Adn of Northumberland from 2005; M DAC; M Dioc Pastl Cttee; M Fin, Pastl, Parsonages cttees and Strat Dev Grp Bp's Coun; M Dioc Safeguarding Cttee; M Shepherd's Dene, Sons of Clergy, Ch Inst, Hosp of God at Greatham, Lord Crewe Trust; Chair Br Cttee of French Protestant Industrial Miss; Trustee News Coun Volunatry Service; Chair Strategic Dev Grp Bp's Coun, Chair Shepherd's Dene Trustees; Special Trustee Newc Healthcare Charity; Newc Fairness Commn 2012 *Tel:* 0191 273 8245
Fax: 0191 226 0286
email: g.miller@newcastle.anglican.org

MILLER, Ms Loraine, BA (Hons)
Church House Great Smith Street London SW1P 3PS [HEAD OF HOUSING, CHURCH OF ENGLAND PENSIONS BOARD] *b* 1957 *educ* The Skinners' Company's Sch for Girls; Queen Mary Coll; *CV* Nat Trng Mgr, English Ch Housing Grp 1984–89; Supported Housing Bus Mgr, English Ch Housing Grp 1989–2007; Dep Housing Mgr C of E Pensions Bd 2007–09; Head of Housing, C of E Pensions Bd from 2009
Tel: 020 7898 1852
email: loraine.miller@churchofengland.org

MILLER, Ven Luke Jonathan, MA (Cantab); MA (Oxon)
The Archeaconry House 39 Bounds Green Road Wood Green, London N22 8HE [ARCHDEACON OF HAMPSTEAD; LONDON] *b* 1966 *educ* Haileybury Sch; Sidney Sussex Coll Camb; St Stephen's Ho; *CV* AC St Matthew Oxhey 1991–94; AC St Mary the Virgin Tottenham 1994–95; V St Mary the Virgin Tottenham 1995–2011; AD East Haringay 2005–11; Acting Adn Hampstead 2009–10; Adn Hampstead from 2011; Dioc Syn 1998–2005, 2009–; M Edmonton Area Coun from 2005; M Dioc Strategic Planning Com from 2008; M Stephen's Ho Coun from 2008 and Chair Fin and Gen Purposes Ctte from 2008; Chair Area Fin Ctte from 2011; DAC; M St Stephen's Ho *Tel:* 020 7932 1190
email: archdeacon.hampstead@london.anglican.org

MILLS, Mr David John, MBE
51 Greenways Over Kellet Carnforth LA6 1DE [CARLISLE] *b* 1937 *CV* Senior Probation Officer (Rtd); Rdr; Bp's Adv CDC; M Dioc Bd of Educ
GS 1985– *Tel:* 01524 732194
email: david.j.mills@btinternet.com

MONCKTON, Mrs Joanna Mary,
Horsebrook Hall Brewood Stafford ST19 9LP [LICHFIELD] *b* 1941 *educ* Oxton Ho Sch Kenton Exeter; *CV* High Sheriff of Staffordshire 1995–96; Dir Penk (Holdings) Ltd and Penk Ltd; Farm Partner; Housewife; Chairman Lichf Branch Prayer Book Soc 1982–2001; Shannon Trust rep for HMYOI Brinsford until 2010
GS 1990– *Tel:* 01902 850288
email: jmm@strettonestate.com

MORGAN, Rt Revd Christopher Heudebourck, Dip Th, BA, M Th
1 Fitzwalter Rd Lexden Colchester CO3 3SS [AREA BISHOP OF COLCHESTER; CHELMSFORD] *b* 1947 *educ* City of Bath Boys Sch; Lanc Univ; Heythrop Coll Lon; Kelham Th Coll; *CV* C Birstall 1973–76; Asst Chap Brussels 1976–80; P-in-c Redditch St Geo 1980–81; TV Redditch, The Ridge 1981–85; V Sonning 1985–96; Prin Berks Chr Tr Scheme 1985–89; Dir Pastl Studies St Alb and Ox Min Course 1992–95; Glouc Dioc Officer for Min 1996–2001; Dioc Can Res Glouc Cathl 1996–2001; Bp of Colchester from 2001 *Tel:* 01206 576648
Fax: 01206 763868
email: b.colchester@chelmsford.anglican.org

MORGAN, Mr David Geoffrey Llewelyn,
25 Newbiggen St Thaxted CM6 2QS [CHELMSFORD] *b* 1935 *educ* St Jo Sch Leatherhead; *CV* Rtd Solicitor; Company Dir; Chair Dioc Bd of Patr; M Dioc Fin Cttee from 1988; Trustee Victoria Clergy Fund from 1989; Chair Nat CU Coun from 1998; Gen Sec Guild of All Souls from 2003
GS 1990– *Tel:* 01371 830132
email: dgllm@btinternet.com

MORGAN, Ven Ian David John BA Hons LTCL
Glebe House The Street Ashfield cum Thorpe Stowmarket Suffolk IP14 6LX [ARCHDEACON OF SUFFOLK; ST EDMUNDSBURY] *b* 1957 *Educ* Wallingford Sch; Univ of Hull; Ripon Coll Cuddesdon; *CV* C Holy Trinity Hereford 1983–86; C St Nicolas and St Mary de Haura, Shoreham by Sea 1986–88); Presenter, Producer, Senior Producer BBC Network and Local Radio 1988–92; V All Hallows Ipswich 1992–95; R South West Ipswich Team Ministry 1995–12; CUF Link Officer from 2006; RD Ipswich 2008–12); Hon Canon, St Edmundsbury Cathedral from 2009; Adn of Suffolk from 2012 *Tel:* 01728 685497
email:
archdeacon.ian@stedmundsbury.anglican.org
Web: www.stedmundsbury.anglican.org

MORGAN, Mrs Susan Deirdre, BA (Hons), Chartered FCIPD, MHSM, FRSA
Church House Great Smith St London SW1P 3AZ [DIRECTOR OF HUMAN RESOURCES, ARCHBISHOPS' COUNCIL] *b* 1956 *educ* The Dame Alice Harpur Sch Bedford; N Lon Poly; *CV* Dir of Personnel Essex and Herts Health Services 1991–94; Dir Human Resources and Commercial Services Princess Alexandra Hosp NHS Trust Harlow 1994–97; Employers' rep on the Employment Tribunals for Engl and Wales from 1992; Personnel Dir CBF 1997–98; Dir of Human Resources to AC from 1998, serving all of the Nat Church Insts; M Race Panel of Employment Tribunals from 2002; Chair Staff Cttee, Chelmsf Dioc from 2005; M Staff Sttee WHCM Counselling and Support from 2009; M Nominations and Appts Cttee St John Ambulance 2011; M Remuneration Cttee Mission for Seafarers from 2012
Tel: 020 7898 1565 07983 588350
email: su.morgan@churchofengland.org

MORRIS, Revd Jane Elizabeth, BA, MSc, PGCE
156 Anson Road London NW2 6BH [LONDON] *b* 1960 *educ* Ealing Gr Sch; York Univ; NEOC; *CV* Tchr, Science at Tadcaster Gr Sch 1972–74; Head of Science at the Mount Sch, York 1974–92; Head of Science and Chapl, Queen Margaret's Sch, Escrick 1992–95; AC St Michael-le-Belfrey Church, York 1992–95; Assoc V St George's Church, Leeds 1995–2005; Brd of Studies, NEOC 1998–2002; Lder West Yorkshire New Wine Network 2003–05; M New Wine North Leadership 2003–05; V St Gabriel's Church, Cricklewood from 2005; Healing Ministry Adv in the Willesden Episcopal Area; M New Wine Leadership Team for Lon and the South East 2005–10; Resource Church Leader for the Alpha Course
GS 2010– *Tel:* 02084526305
email: jane.morris@st-gabriels.org

MORRIS, Ven Roger Anthony Brett, BSc (Hons), ARCS, MA (Cantab)
The Archdeacon's House Walkers Lane Whittington Worcester WR5 2RE [ARCHDEACON OF WORCESTER] *b* 1968 *educ* Chipping Sodbury Sch; Filton Tech Coll; Imperial Coll Lon; Trin Coll Cam; Ridley Hall Cam; *CV* Asst C of Northleach, W Hampnett and Farmington, Cold Aston, W Notgrove and Turkdean 1993–96; R of Sevenhampton w Charlton Abbotts, Hawling and Whittington, Dowdeswell w Andoversford, The Shiptons and Salperton, and Withington 1996–2003; Dir Par Devel and Evang, Cov 2003–08; Adn of Worc from 2008 *Tel:* 01905 773301 07590 696212
email: rmorris@cofe-worcester.org.uk

MOUNTFORD, Mr Roger Philip, BSc(Econ), MS(Management)
Hookstile House Byers Lane Godstone Surrey RH9 8JH [TRUSTEE MEMBER, CHURCH OF ENGLAND PENSIONS BOARD] *educ* Kingston Gr Sch; Lon Sch Econ; Stanford Bus Sch; *CV* Merchant banker 1971–2000, followed by various directorships; Gov Lon Sch Econ; M C of E Pensions Bd
Tel: 01342 893198 07799 662601
email: mountford.roger@btinternet.com

MUGGERIDGE, Miss Sally, BA(Hons), MBA, Cert Th, FCIPD, FIOD, FCIM Chartered Marketer
The Old Farm House Pike Road, Eythorne Dover Kent CT15 4DJ [CANTERBURY] *b* 1949 *educ* South Hampstead High Sch; Guildhall Sch Music and Drama; Westfield Coll, Lon Univ; Henley Management Coll; SE Inst Th Ed *CV* Marketing Director Mercury Communications Ltd. 1990–1992; Management Developm't Director, Cable & Wireless plc 1992–1996; HR Director, Cable & Wireless (Asia Pacific) 1996–1999; Development Director, Pearson plc 1999–2003; International President, The Malcolm Muggeridge Soc 2003; Dir Total Oil from 2010; Chief Executive Industry and Parliament Trust 2003–2010; Master, The Worshipful Company of Marketors; Freeman of the City of London 1995; Vc Pres Foundn Ch Leadership 2011; Trustee Tutu Foundn UK 2003; M Chartered Institute of Marketing Academic Senate 2005; M Counc, Kent Univ 2006–12; M Chartered Dir Cttee IOD 2007; Lay M Sandwich Deanery Syn and Cant Dioc Syn
GS 2010–
Tel: 01304 831964 020 7790 0511 07770 381911
email: sally@sallymuggeridge.com

MUNRO, Revd Dr Robert Speight, B Sc, BA, Dip Ap Th, PGCE, D Min
Rectory 1 Depleach Rd Cheadle SK8 1DZ [CHESTER] *b* 1963 *educ* William Hulme's Gr Sch Man; Bris Univ; All Souls Coll Lon; Man Univ; Oak Hill Th Coll; Refrmd Th Sem US; *CV* Teach Math and PE Hazel Grove HS 1987–1990; C St Jo Bapt Hartford 1993–97; R St Wilf Davenham 1997–2003; R St Mary Cheadle from 2003; M Bp's Coun from 2000
GS 2005– *Tel:* 0161 428 3440 0161 428 8050
Fax: 0161 428 3440 0161 428 8050
email: rob@munro.org.uk

NAGEL, Mrs Mary Philippa, B Ed
Aldwick Vicarage 25 Gossamer Lane Bognor Regis PO21 3AT [CHICHESTER] *b* 1954 *educ* Worthing High Sch; Lon Univ; *CV* Section 23 Insp of Schs until 2005
GS 1990– *Tel:* 01243 262049
email: mary@nagel.me.uk

NEIL-SMITH, Mr (Noel) Jonathan, MA
Church House Great Smith St London SW1P 3AZ [ADMINISTRATIVE SECRETARY, CENTRAL SECRETARIAT] *b* 1959 *educ* Marlboro Coll; St Jo Coll Cam; *CV* On staff of Ch Commrs from 1981; Bishoprics Officer 1994–96; Seconded to GS from 1997; Asst Sec Ho of Bps 1997–98; Sec Ho of Bps 1998–2011; Sec Diocs Comm from 2011; Sec Ho of Clergy from 2011; Hon Lay Can Guildf Cathl from 2002 *Tel:* 020 7898 1373
Fax: 020 7898 1369
email: jonathan.neil-smith@churchofengland.org

NEWARK, Archdeacon of. See PICKEN, Ven David

NEWCASTLE, Assistant Bishop of. See WHITE, Rt Revd Frank (Francis)

NEWCASTLE, Bishop of. See WHARTON, Rt Revd (John) Martin

NEWCASTLE, Dean of. See DALLISTON, Very Revd Christopher Charles

NEWCOMBE, Dr Lindsay Kathleen, BEng, PhD
Holy Trinity Vicarage 3 Bletchley Street London N1 7QG [LONDON] *b* 1980 *educ* Purbeck Sch, Wareham; UCL; *CV* Research Fell, Dept of Mech Eng, UCL 2001–06, PhD research in bioengineering 2006–09; Tech Specialist (Orthopaedics), BSI from 2009
GS 2010– *Tel:* 020 7253 4796
email: lindsaynewcombe@gmail.com

NEWCOME, Rt Revd James William Scobie, MA
Bishop's House Ambleside Road Keswick CA12 4DD [BISHOP OF CARLISLE] *b* 1953 *educ* Marlboro Coll; Trin Coll Ox; Selw Coll Cam; Ridley Hall Th Coll; *CV* C All SS Leavesden 1978–82; Min Bar Hill LEP Ely 1982–94; Tutor Ridley Hall Cam 1983–88; V Dry Drayton 1990–94; RD N Stowe 1993–94; DDO Ches 1994–2000; Res Can Ches Cathl 1994–2002; Dioc Dir of Min 1996–2002; Suff Bp of Penrith 2002–09; Bp Carlisle from 2009; M Bps CME Cttee; Chair Nat Stewardship Cttee; M SAGE Grp; Lead Bp on Healthcare; Dir Univ Cumbria; Lead Bishop for URC; Pres St John's Coll Dur
GS 2000–02 *Tel:* 01768 773430
email: bishop.carlisle@carlislediocese.org.uk

NEWEY, Mr (Sidney) Brian, MA
Chestnut Cottage The Green South Warborough OX10 7DN [OXFORD] *b* 1937 *educ* Burton-upon-Trent Gr Sch; Worc Coll Ox; *CV* With Br Rail from 1960, Gen Mgr W Region 1984–87; Dir Regional Railways 1987–90; Asst to Chief Exec Br Rail 1990–93; Consult in transport 1993–96; rtd; M AC Fin Cttee; M AC Audit Cttee; M DRACSC; M Nat Soc Investment Cttee; Chair Ox DBF and assoc cttees
GS 2005– *Tel:* 01865 858322
Fax: 01865 858043

NEWMAN, Rt Revd Adrian, B Sc, Dip Th, M Phil
63 Coborn Road London E3 2DB [AREA BISHOP OF STEPNEY; LONDON] *b* 1958 *educ* Rickmansworth Comp Sch; Bris Univ; Trin Coll Bris; *CV* C St Mark Forest Gate 1985–89; V Hillsborough and Wadsley Bridge, Sheff 1989–96; R St Mart in the Bull Ring, Birm 1996–2004; Dean of Roch 2005–11; Bp of Stepney from 2011; Hon Fell Cant Ch Ch Univ *Tel:* 0207 932 1140
email: bishop.stepney@london.anglican.org

NEWMAN, Ven David Maurice Frederick, BA, MA
St Martin's House 7 Peacock Lane Leicester LE1 5FX [ARCHDEACON OF LOUGHBOROUGH; LEICESTER] *b* 1954 *educ* The Leys Sch Cam; Hertf Coll Ox; St John's Nottm; *CV* Asst C Christ Church Orpington 1979–83; Asst C St Mary's Bushbury 1983–86; V All Saints Ockbrook and St Stephen's Borrowash 1986–1997; TR Emmanuel Loughborough and St Mary-in-Charnwood, Nanpanton 1997–2009; AD Akeley East deanery 1999–2006; Chair Ho Clergy Leic Dioc 2006–09; Adn of Loughborough from 2009
Tel: 0116 261 5321 07817 664189
email: dmfnewman@talktalk.net

NEWTON, Rt Revd Keith, BD, AKC, PGCE
Richborough House 6 Mellish Gardens Woodford Green IG8 0BH [SUFFRAGAN BISHOP OF RICHBOROUGH; PROVINCIAL EPISCOPAL VISITOR, CANTERBURY] *b* 1952 *educ* Alsop High Sch Liv; Lon Univ; K Coll, Ch Ch Coll Cant; St Aug Coll Cant; *CV* C St Mary Gt Ilford 1975–78; V St Matt Wimbledon TM 1978–85; R St Paul Blantyre, S Malawi 1985–86; Dean of Blantyre 1986–91; P-in-c H Nativity Knowle 1991–93, V 1993–2002; P-in-c All Hallows Easton 1997–2002; Bp of Richborough from 2002 *Tel:* 020 8505 7259
07976 585891 (Mobile)
Fax: 020 8504 3349
email: pev@btinternet.com

NEWTON, Canon Sandra Clare, MSc, BSc, BA
50 Broomgrove Road Sheffield South Yorkshire S10 2NA [TRUSTEE MEMBER, CHURCH OF ENGLAND PENSIONS BOARD] *b* 1951 *educ* Minchenden Gr Sch; Lon Sch Econ; OU; *CV* Hon Can Sheffield Cathl from 2006; Chair Sheffield Dioc Bd of Fin from 2008; Chair Museums Sheffield 2009–12; M C of E Pensions Bd from 2010; M Abp's Coun Fin Cttee from 2011 *Tel:* 0114 266 1079
email: sandracnewton@aol.com

NORFOLK, Archdeacon of. See BETTS, Ven Steven

NORTH, Rt Revd Philip John, MA
[SUFFRAGAN BISHOP OF WHITBY; YORK] *b* 1966 *educ* The Latymer Sch, Edmonton; York Uni; St Stephen's House, Ox; *CV* AC S Mary and S Peter, Sunderland 1992–96; V Holy Trin, Hartlepool 1996–2002; Area Dean of Hartlepool 2000–02; P Administrator of the Shrine of Our Lady of Walsingham 2002–08; T R of the Parish of Old St Pancras 2008–12; Bp of Whitby from 2012
GS 2010–12 *email:* philip.north@mac.com

NORTH-WEST EUROPE, Archdeacon in, [NOT APPOINTED AT TIME OF GOING TO PRESS]

NORTHAMPTON, Archdeacon of. See ALLSOPP, Ven Christine

NORTHOLT, Archdeacon of, [NOT APPOINTED AT TIME OF GOING TO PRESS]

NORTHUMBERLAND, Archdeacon of. See MILLER, Ven Geoff (Geoffrey Vincent)

NORWICH, Archdeacon of. See McFARLANE, Ven Janet Elizabeth

NORWICH, Bishop of. See JAMES, Rt Revd Graham Richard

NORWICH, Dean of. See SMITH, Very Revd Graham Charles Morell

NOTTINGHAM, Archdeacon of. See HILL, Ven Peter

NUNN, Very Revd Andrew Peter, BA, BA
Southwark Cathedral London Bridge London SE1 9DA [DEAN OF SOUTHWARK] *b* 1957 *educ* Guthlaxton Upper Sch Wigston, Leic; Leic Poly; Leeds Univ; Coll of Resurr Mirfield; *CV* C St Jas Manston, Ripon 1983–87; C Leeds Richmond Hill 1987–91, V 1991–95; Chapl Agnes Stewart C of E High Sch, Leeds 1987–95; Personal Asst to Bp of S'wark 1995–99; Vice-Provost, Prec and Can Res S'wark Cathl 1999–2000; Sub-Dean, Prec and Can Res S'wark Cathl 2000–11, Dean of S'wark from 2012; M Dioc Syn; CNC from 2011
GS 2005–10, 2010–
Tel: 020 7367 6727 07961 332051
Fax: 020 7367 6725
email: andrew.nunn@southwark.anglican.org
Web: www.southwarkcathedral.org

O'BRIEN, Mr Gerald Michael, B Sc, DMS
Chestnuts 14 Oakhill Rd Sevenoaks Kent TN13 1NP [ROCHESTER] *b* 1948 *educ* Dulwich Coll; Bris Univ; *CV* Promotions Sec, ICS 1994–97; Dir of Communications, Crosslinks 1997–2002; M CEEC 1988–92, from 1996; M CPAS Coun 1999–2004
GS 1980–85, 1987–
Tel: 01732 453894 07711 938517 (Mobile)
email: gmobrien@btinternet.com

O'HARA, Mr Ian Daniel, MBPsS, MITOL
139 Waterside Walk Grindle Rd Longford Coventry CV6 6DS [COVENTRY] *b* 1963 *educ* K Henry VIII Sch Cov; *CV* Recruitment and Trg Mgr, Choices Video 1995–2004; Hd of Learning and Devel, Courts Furnishers 2004–05; Learning and Devel Consult, Roadchef from 2005; Chair Cov Dioc Forward in Faith; M organizing cttee, annual Ebbsfleet children's and young people's eucharistic festival; M Bp's Coun
GS 2005–2010 *Tel:* 02476 361577
07775 420045 (Mobile)
email: ianoh@sky.com

OAKHAM, Archdeacon of. See STEELE, Ven Gordon

OGLE, Very Revd Catherine, BA, MPhil, MA, MA
38 Goodby Road Moseley Birmingham B13 8NJ [DEAN OF BIRMINGHAM] *b* 1961 *educ* Perse Sch for Girls, Cam; Univ of Leeds; Fitzwilliam Coll Cam; Westcott Ho Cam; Univ Leeds; *CV* AC St Mary Middleton, Leeds 1988–91; Relig Programmes Ed BBC Leeds 1991–95; NSM St Margaret & All Hallows, Leeds 1991–95; P-in-C Woolley w W Bretton 1995–2001; Ed Wakef Dioc Magazine 1995–2001; V Huddersfield 2001–2010; Dean of Birmingham from 2010; M Wakef Dioc Liturgy Gp, Communications Gp, Dioc Syn; M Coun Coll of the Resurrection, Mirfield 2008–10; Hon Can Wakef Cathl from 2008 *Tel:* 0121 262 1840
Fax: 0121 262 1860
email: dean@birminghamcathedral.com
Web: www.birminghamcathedral.org

OLDHAM, Mr Gavin David Redvers, MA (Cantab)
Ashfield House St Leonards Tring HP23 6NP [OXFORD; CHURCH COMMISSIONER] *b* 1949 *educ* Eton; Trin Coll Cam; *CV* Wedd Durlacher Mordaunt 1975–86, Partner 1984–86; Secretariat Barclays De Zoete Wedd (BZW) 1984–88; Chief Exec Barclayshare Ltd 1986–89, Chair 1989–90; Chair/Chief Exec The Share Cen Ltd from 1990; Chief Exec Share plc from 2000; Chair The Share Foundn from 2005; Ch Commr from 1999; M Fin Cttee AC from 2001; M Ethical Investment Adv Grp from 1999
GS 1995– *Tel:* 01494 758348 (Home)
01296 439100 (Office)
07767 337696 (Mobile)
Fax: 01296 414410
email: ceo@share.co.uk

OLIVER, Canon Thomas Gordon, L Th, B Th, Dip Ad Ed
The Rectory Shipley Hills Road Meopham Gravesend Kent DA13 0AD [ROCHESTER] *b* 1948 *educ* Whinney Hill Sec Mod Sch Dur; Dur Johnson Gr Tech Sch; Lon Coll of Div; St Jo Coll Nottm; *CV* C St Jo

the Divine Thorpe Edge 1972–76; C St Mark Woodthorpe 1976–80; V All SS Huthwaite 1980–85; Dir Pastl Studies St Jo Coll Nottm 1985–94; Dioc Dir of Tr 1994–99; Bp's Officer for Min and Trg from 1999; Hind Report' follow-up Task Forces for IME and CMD 2006–08; Continuing Min Ed Devlp Panel 2006–09; R Meopham and Nurstead from 2009
GS 1995– *Tel:* 01474 812068 07718 763518
Fax: 01474 812970
email: canongordon.oliver@gmail.com

OSBORNE, Mrs Emma Charlotte, MA
Lawn Farm Milton Lilbourne Pewsey SN9 5LQ [CHURCH COMMISSIONER] *b* 1964 *educ* Redland High Sch, Bris; Ch Ch Ox; *CV* County NatWest 1985–89; Lloyds Investment Mgrs 1989–91; Credit Suisse/CSFB 1991–97; Investment Mgr, Chubb Insurance from 1997 *Tel:* 01672 563459
020 7956 5362
email: emma.osborne@lawnfarm.co.uk

OSBORNE, Ven Hayward John, MA, PGCE
Birmingham Diocesan Office 175 Harborne Park Rd Birmingham B17 0BH [ARCHDEACON OF BIRMINGHAM] *b* 1948 *educ* Sevenoaks Sch; New Coll Ox; Westcott Ho Th Coll; *CV* C St Pet and St Paul Bromley 1973–77; C Halesowen 1977–80, TV 1980–83; TR St Barnabas Worc 1983–88; V St Mary Moseley 1988–2001; AD Moseley 1994–2001; Hon Can Birm Cathl from 2000; Adn of Birm from 2001
GS 1998– *Tel:* 0121 426 0441 (Office)
email: hs.osborne@btinternet.com

OSBORNE, Very Revd June, BA (Econ) Hons, M Phil, Cert Theol, DL
The Deanery 7 The Close Salisbury SP12EF [DEAN OF SALISBURY] *b* 1953 *educ* Whalley Range Gr Sch, Manch; Manch Univ; Birm Univ; St Jo Coll Nottm; Wycliffe Hall Ox; *CV* C St Mart-in-the-Bullring and Chapl, Birm Children's Hosp 1980–84; St Mark Old Ford 1984–89; St Paul w St Steph and St Mark Old Ford 1989–95; Can Treas Salis Cathl 1995–2004; Dean of Salis from 2004; M Bd of Soc Resp 1985–90; M Stg Cttee GS 1990–95; Sen Insp of Theol Educ 1994–2004; Chair DAC 2003–07; Deputy Lieut of Wilts from 2006
GS 1985–95; 2004–05
Tel: 01722 555110 07771 743760
Fax: 01722 555155
email: thedean@salcath.co.uk

OSBORNE, Revd Malcolm Eric (Max), DipTHm
All Saints Vicarage 32 Warrington St Newmarket CB8 8BA [ST EDMUNDSBURY AND IPSWICH] *b* 1964 *educ* St John's Nottm; *CV* P Cavendish Com Ch 1996–98; Min-in-Charge Triangle Ch Ipswich 1999–2002; Deanery Adv for Social Responsibility 1999–2002; St Lawrence Preacher 1999–2002; V All Saints Newmarket from 2002
GS 2003–5, 2008–10 *Tel:* 01638 662514
email: max9@btopenworld.com

OXFORD (CHRIST CHURCH), Dean of. See LEWIS, Very Revd Christopher Andrew

OXFORD, Archdeacon of, [NOT APPOINTED AT TIME OF GOING TO PRESS]

OXFORD, Bishop of. See PRITCHARD, Rt Revd John Lawrence

PACKER, Rt Revd John Richard, MA
Hollin House Weetwood Avenue Leeds LS16 5NG [BISHOP OF RIPON AND LEEDS] *b* 1946 *educ* Man Gr Sch; Keble Coll Ox; Ripon Hall Th Coll; *CV* C St Pet St Helier 1970–73; Dir Pastl Studies Ripon Hall 1973–75 and Ripon Coll Cuddesdon 1975–77; Chapl St Nic Abingdon 1973–77; V Wath upon Dearne w Adwick upon Dearne 1977–86; RD Wath 1983–86; R Sheff Manor 1986–91; RD Attercliffe 1990–1991; Adn of W Cumberland 1991–96; P-in-c Bridekirk 1995–96; Bp of Warrington 1996–2000; Bp of Ripon and Leeds from 2000; Ho of Lords from 2006
GS 1985–91, 1992–96, 2000–10, 2010–
Tel: 0113 224 2789 (Office)
0113 274 2395 (Home)
Fax: 0113 230 5471
email: bishop@riponleeds-diocese.org.uk

PADDOCK, Very Revd Dr John Alllan Barnes, BA, MA, PhD, PGCE, FRSA
The Deanery Bomb House Lane Gibraltar [DEAN OF GIBRALTAR; EUROPE] *b* 1951 *CV* Dean of Gibraltar from 2008 *Tel:* 00350 200 78377
Fax: 00350 78463
email: deangib@gibraltar.gi

PANTER, Ven Ricky (Richard) James Graham, Cert Ed, GOE
2a Monfa Rd Bootle L20 6BQ [ARCHDEACON OF LIVERPOOL] *b* 1948 *educ* Monkton Combe Sch Bath; Worc Coll of Educ; Oak Hill Th Coll; *CV* RE tchr, Chatham Tech High Sch for Boys 1970–71; primary tchr, Boscombe C of E Primary 1971–73; C H Trin Rusholme, Man 1976–80, Asst V St Cyprian w Ch Ch Toxteth 1980–85; V St Andr Clubmoor 1985–96; V St Jo and St Jas Orrell Hey, Bootle 1996–11; AD Bootle 1999–2002; Adn of Liverpool from 2002; M Dioc BMU Ecumenism Cttee 1985–90; M Dioc Pastl Cttee 1991–96
Tel: 0151 922 3758 (Home)
0151 705 2154 (Office)
07540 300842 (Mobile)
Fax: 0151 922 3758
email: ricky.panter@liverpool.anglican.org

PARSONS, Revd Canon Dr Michael William Semper, MA, DPhil
6 Spa Villas Montpellier Gloucester GL1 1LB [GLOUCESTER] *b* 1947 *educ* Hul GS; St Catherine's Coll, Ox; Selwyn Coll; Ridley Hall Cam; *CV* Prin Lect Th, Univ Glouc 2009–10; DDO and Dir C Training, Glouc 2000–04; DDO & P-in-C, Hempsted, Glouc 1996–2000; TR, Walbrook Epiphany,

Derby 1995–96; P-in-C, Derby St Augustine, Derby 1985–95; Vocations Adv, Derby 1987–96; SPCK Fellow, NEICE & Hon Lect Th, Univ Dur 1984–85; SPCK Viewdata Fellow, Dept Th, Univ Dur 1981–84; AC, Edmonton All Saints, Lon 1978–81; Univ Tching Fellow, Dept Physics, Univ Nott 1973–75; Lect Physics, St Catherine's Coll, Ox 1972–73; Prin, WEMTC 2004–11; Exec Dir, Ian Ramsey Centre, Th Fac, Ox Univ 1999; P-i-C St Oswald, Glos from 2011; Hon Can Glos Cathl form 2011
GS 2003–05; 2010– *Tel and Fax:* 01452 524550
email: mwsp@btinternet.com

PATERSON, Rt Revd Robert Mar Eskine, BA, MA, DipTh
Thie yn Aspick 4 The Falls Tromode Rd Douglas Isle of Man IM4 4PZ [BISHOP OF SODOR AND MAN] *b* 1949 *educ* King Henry VIII Sch, Cov; St John's Coll Dur Univ; Cranmer Hall Dur; *CV* C Harpurhey Man 1972–73; C Sketty Swansea 1973–78; R Llangattock and Llangynidr 1978–83; V Gabalfa Cardiff 1983–94; TR Cowbridge, Llandaff 1994–2000; Prin Officer Ch in Wales Coun for Miss and Min 2000–06; Chapl and Researcher to Abp of York 2006–08; Bp Sodor and Man from 2008; Vc Chair Liturg Commn; Vc Chair Fresh Expressions Bd; Chair Central Rders Coun; M Min Coun *Tel:* 01624 622108 07624 450633
email: bishop@sodorandman.im
Web: www.sodorandman.im

PAVER, Canon Elizabeth Caroline, FRSA
113 Warning Tongue Lane Bessacar Doncaster DN4 6TB [SHEFFIELD] *b* 1944 *educ* Doncaster Girls High Sch; St Mary's Coll Cheltenham; *CV* In Primary Educ 28 years; Hdtchr Crags Rd Nurs/Inf Sch 1976–80; Hdtchr Askern Nurs/Inf Sch Littlemoor 1980–86; Hdtchr Intake Nursery and First Sch Doncaster from 1986; M Nat Coun NAHT from 1991; Centenary Nat Pres 1997–97; NAHT Appointee to Gen Teaching Coun from 2000; past M Panel of Chairmen GS; Lay Chair Dioc Syn; M Bp's Coun; M Dioc Bd of Educ Tr Cttee; apptd M AC 1999–2002; Lay Can Sheff Cathl from 2000; Ch Commr from 2004
GS 1991– *Tel:* 01302 530706
Fax: 01302 360811
email: jr.paver@talktalk.net

PEARSON, Rt Revd Geoffrey Seagrave, BA
Shireshead Vicarage Whinney Brow Forton Preston PR3 0AE [SUFFRAGAN BISHOP OF LANCASTER; BLACKBURN] *b* 1951 *educ* St Jo Coll Dur; Cranmer Hall Dur; *CV* C Kirkheaton, Wakef 1974–77; C-in-c Redeemer, Blackb 1977–82, V 1982–85; Asst Home Sec GS Bd for Miss and Unity 1985–89; Hon C Forty Hill, Lon 1985–89; Exec Sec BCC Evang Cttee 1986–89; V Roby, Liv 1989–2006; AD Huyton 2002–06; Hon Can Liv Cathl 2003–06; Bp of Lancaster from 2006
Tel: 01524 799900 07809 618385 (Mobile)
Fax: 01524 799901
email: bishoplancaster@gmail.com

PENFOLD, Revd Susan, BA, MA, PhD
The Vicarage Church Lane Great Harwood BB6 7PU [BLACKBURN] *b* 1952 *educ* York Univ; Bris Univ; Selwyn Coll Cam Univ; Ridley Hall Th Coll; *CV* Rsrch Asst, Dept Biochemistry, Bris Univ, 1976–77; Travelling Sec, Universities and Colleges Christian Fellowship, 1977–81; Deaconess, Buckhurst Hill, Chelmsf 1984–87; C, Parish of Greenside, Dur 1987–90; C Cononley w Bradley, Bradf 1990–97; Assoc DDO, Bradf 1996–2001; Dioc Dir Ordinands and Dean of Ministry, Wakef 2001–08; Dir Ministry and Residentiary Canon, Blackb from 2008; M Coun Coll of the Resurrection, Mirfield, 2001–08; M Ministry Division FinPanel 2003–08; Assessor for the Lower House of the Convocation of York 2005–08, 2010
GS 2005–08; 2010–
Tel: 01254 503085 07753 987977
email: Sue.penfold@blackburn.anglican.org

PENRITH, Suffragan Bishop of. See FREEMAN, Rt Revd Robert John

PENTLAND, Ven Raymond Jackson, QHC, BA, MTh
Chaplaincy Services (RAF) HQ AIR CMD, Royal Air Force High Wycombe HP14 4UE [ARCHDEACON FOR THE ROYAL AIR FORCE] *b* 1957 *educ* Cowdenknowes High Sch Greenock; William Booth Memorial Coll; Open Univ; Ox Univ; St Jo Coll Nottm; *CV* C St Jude Mapperley, S'well 1988–90; Chapl RAF 1990–2005; Command Chapl 2005–06; Archdeacon for the RAF from 2006; Hon Can and Preb Linc Cathl from 2006; Chaplain-in-Chief RAF from 2009
GS 2005–
Tel: 01494 493801 01494 493802 07796 007620
email: ray.pentland929@mod.uk

PERHAM, Rt Revd Michael Francis, MA, FRSCM, Hon DPhil
2 College Green Gloucester GL1 2LR [BISHOP OF GLOUCESTER] *b* 1947 *educ* Hardye's Sch Dorchester; Keble Coll Ox; Cuddesdon Th Coll; *CV* C St Mary Addington 1976–81; Chapl to Bp of Win 1981–84; TR Oakdale, Poole 1984–92; Can Res and Prec Norw Cathl 1992–98; Vc Dean 1995–98; Prov of Derby 1998–2000; Dean of Derby 2000–04; M Liturg Commn 1986-2001; M Cathls Fabric Commn 1996–2001; M AC 1999–2004; Chair GS Business Cttee 2001–04; Bp of Gloucester from 2004; Chair SPCK 2003–11; Bp Protector Soc of St Francis from 2005; Chair Hosp Chapl Coun 2007–10; Vc-Chair MPA Coun 2007–10; Chair Govs of Ripon Coll Cuddesdon from 2009; Author
GS 1989–92, 1993–
Tel: 01452 410022 ext. 271 01452 524598
Fax: 01452 308324
email: bshpglos@glosdioc.org.uk

PERUMBALATH, Revd Dr John, MA, MTh, PhD
Vicarage Perry Street Northfleet Gravesend Kent DA11 8RD [ROCHESTER] *b* 1966 *educ* Calicut Univ;

Osmania Univ; North West Univ; Serampore Th Coll; *CV* Lect in New Testament, Serampore Coll 1993–95; V St James' Church, Calcutta 1995–2000; V St Thomas' Church, Calcutta 2000–01; Asst P St George's Church, Beckenham 2002–05; T Northfleet and Rosherville 2005–08; V All Saints Church, Gravesend from 2008; Dioc Urban Officer from 2008; M Bp's Coun from 2007; M Adv Coun for Ministry and Training 2007–10; Tutor, Coll of Preachers from 2008; Trustee USPG from 2009
GS 2010– *Tel:* 01474 534398
email: jperumbalath@btopenworld.com

PETERBOROUGH, Bishop of. See ALLISTER, Rt Revd Donald Spargo

PETERBOROUGH, Dean of. See TAYLOR, Very Revd Charles William

PHILPOTT, Preb Sam (Samuel), MBE
21, Plaistow Crescent Plymouth PL5 2EA [EXETER] *b* 1941 *educ* R Naval Hosp Sch Holbrook; Kelham Th Coll; *CV* C St Mark Swindon 1965–70; C St Martin Torquay 1970–73; TV All SS Exmouth 1973–76; V Shaldon 1976–78; P-in-c St Pet Plymouth 1978–80, V from 1980; RD Plymouth Devonport 1985–91 and 1995–2001; Preb of Ex Cathl from 1991; Acting P-in-c St Thomas N Keyham from 1997, P-in-c from 1999; P-in-c St Peter and the Holy Apostles 2009; Chair of Governors St Peter's C of E VA Primary Sch from 1978; Gov of All Saints C of E Academy Plymouth 2010; Chair Dioc Ho of Clergy 2000–09; M Bp's Coun; M Dioc Bd of Educ (Vc Chair of DBE); M Dioc Budget Assess Grp 2000–09; M DBF Stg Cttee 2000–09; M Dioc Vacancy-in-See Cttee; M Bp of Plymouth's Adv Grp for Plymouth city; M Drake Foundn Plymouth; Chair Community Ctte and Grants Cttee, Grass Roots Panel 2009–11; Dir and Chair Millfields Comm Economic Devel Trust Plymouth; Bp of Ebbsfleet's Coun of Priests; M Nat Coun and Exec Cttee Forward in Faith; Regional Dn Tamar, Forward in Faith; Trustee of Confraternity of the Blessed Sacrament
GS 1990– *Tel:* 01752 298502 07770 504415
Fax: 01752 222007
email: frphilpott@gmail.com

PICKEN, Ven David Anthony, BA(Hons), MA, PGCE
22 Rufford Road Edwinstowe Notts NG21 9HY [ARCHDEACON OF NEWARK; SOUTHWELL] *b* 1963 *educ* Kingsmead; Lon amd Nottm Univs; Ch Ch Cant; Lincoln Theol Coll; *CV* Asst C Worth TM 1990–3; TV St Clare's and Hospital Chapl 1993–97; TR Wordsley 1997–2004; AD Kingswinford 2001–04; TR High Wycombe 2004–11; AD Wycombe 2008–11; Adn of Newark from 2012; M Bp's Coun; Chair Liturgical Cttee; M DAC; M Fin Cttee; M Church closure working group; M Design Team for 2020 planning
Tel: 01636 817206 07917 690576
email: archdeacon-newark@southwell.anglican.org

PIGGOTT, Ven Andy (Andrew John), B Sc (Econ), Dip Th, PGCE
56 Grange Rd Saltford Bristol BS31 3AG [ARCHDEACON OF BATH; BATH AND WELLS] *b* 1951 *educ* Thornes Ho Gr Sch Wakef; Holly Lodge Gr Sch Smethwick; Q Mary Coll Lon; Nottm Univ; St Jo Coll Nottm; *CV* C St Phil w. St Jas Dorridge, Birm 1986–89; TV St Chad Kidderminster w. St Geo Team, Worc 1989–94; V St Lawr Biddulph, Lich 1994–99; CPAS Min & Vocations Adv 1999–2001, acting Gen Dir 2000–01, Patr Sec 2001–05; Adn of Bath from 2005; GS 2010–
GS 2010– *Tel:* 01225 873609
Fax: 01225 874610
email: adbath@bathwells.anglican.org

PILGRIM, Revd (Colin) Mark, BA, MA, CertEs
St Peter's Vicarage 17 The Drive Henleaze Bristol BS9 4LD [BRISTOL] *b* 1956 *educ* St John's Sch, Leatherhead; Kingston Poly; Geneva Univ; W of Eng Univ; Westcott House Th Coll; *CV* C, Chorlton-cum-Hardy, Man 1984–87; C, Ecum P Whitchurch, 1987–89; V, St Oswald's, Bedminster Down 1989–95; Dioc Child and Y Off, Bris 1995–2001; V, St Peter, Henleaze from 2001; Area Dean, Bris West Deanery from 2006; Chair Dioc Lit and Wor Cttee 2004–08; M Bp's Counc from 2010
GS 2009– *Tel:* 0117 962 0636
email: markpilgrimis@aol.com

PLATTEN, Rt Revd Stephen George, B Ed, Dip Theol, BD, D Litt
Bishop's Lodge Woodthorpe Lane Wakefield WF2 6JL [BISHOP OF WAKEFIELD] *b* 1947 *educ* Stationers' Company's Sch; Lon Univ Inst of Educ; Trin Coll Ox; Cuddesdon Th Coll; *CV* C Headington 1975–78; Chapl and Tutor Linc Th Coll 1978–82; DDO and Minl Tr and Can Res Portsm Cathl 1982–89; Sec for Ecum Affairs to Abp of Cant 1990–95; Dean of Norw 1995–2003; Bp of Wakefield from 2003; Chair SCM Cant Press from 2001; Chair Govs Angl Centre in Rome from 2002; Chair Liturg Commn from 2005; M Ho of Lords from 2009; Court Asst of Stationers' Co from 2011; Fell Guild Church Musicians from 2012
GS 1997– *Tel:* 01924 255349
Fax: 01924 250202
email: bishop@bishopofwakefield.org.uk

PLAYLE, Mrs Kathleen (Kathy),
136 Abbs Cross Lane Hornchurch Essex RM12 4XT [CHELMSFORD] *b* 1950 *Tel:* 01708 442211
email: kathyplayle@btconnect.com

PLYMING, Revd Dr Philip James John, BA, MA, PhDThe Vi
The Vicarage Church Road Claygate Esher KT10 0JP [GUILDFORD] *b* 1974 *educ* Oakmeeds Comm Sch; Haywards Heath VIth Form Coll; Cam Univ; Dur Univ; Edin Univ; Cranmer Hall Dur; *CV* C Ch Ch Chineham 2001–06; V, Holy Trin Claygate from

WHO'S WHO

2006; M Guildf Dioc Syn from 2007; M RACSC from 2011
GS 2009– *Tel:* 01372 463603
email: philipplyming@holytrinityclaygate.org.uk

PLYMOUTH, Archdeacon of. See CHANDLER, Ven Ian Nigel

PLYMOUTH, Suffragan Bishop of. See FORD, Rt Revd John Frank

PODMORE, Dr Colin John, MA, D Phil, F R Hist S
Church House Great Smith St London SW1P 3AZ [CLERK TO THE SYNOD] *b* 1960 *educ* Bodmin Gr Sch; Bodmin Sch; Keble Coll Ox; Selw Coll Cam; *CV* Tchr St Mich C of E High Sch Chorley 1983–85; Asst Sec BMU, CCU 1988–97; Dep Sec CCU 1998–99; Sec IFCG 1988–91; Co-Sec Meissen Commn 1991–99; Co-Sec Porvoo Contact Grp 1996–99; Cen Secretariat from 1999; Sec Liturg Publ Grp 1999–2002; Sec Liturg Commn 2002–09; Sec CAC Rev Grp 1999–2001; Sec Ho of Clergy 2002–11; Sec Diocs Commn 2002–11; Sec Liturg Commn 2002–9; Sen Appts Rev Grp 2005–7; Clerk to the Synod from 2011; Dir Central Secretariat and Dir Ecum Relations from 2011 *Tel:* 020 7898 1385
email: colin.podmore@churchofengland.org

POLL, Ven Martin George, BA(Hons); CTh
Navy Command HQ MP1–2 Leach Building, Whale Island Portsmouth, Hants PO2 8BY [ARCHDEACON FOR THE ROYAL NAVY] *b* 1961 *educ* Edmonton County Sch; Christ Church Coll Canterbury; Ripon Coll Cuddesdon; *CV* AC John Keble Mill Hill; Chapl RN from 1990 (HMS Raleigh, Commando Helicopter Force, Britannia RN Coll, HMS Invincible, HMS Illustrious; RNAS Yeovilton; HMS Neptune, Staff Chapl); Dir Naval Chaplaincy Service; Adn for the Royal Navy
Tel: 02392 625552
email: martinpoll791@mod.uk

PONTEFRACT, Archdeacon of. See TOWNLEY, Ven Peter Kenneth

PONTEFRACT, Suffragan Bishop of. See ROBINSON, Rt Revd Anthony William

PORTER, Rt Revd Anthony, MA (Oxon), MA (Cantab)
Dunham House 8 Westgate Southwell NG25 0JL [SUFFRAGAN BISHOP OF SHERWOOD; SOUTHWELL AND NOTTINGHAM] *b* 1952 *educ* Aire Boro Gr Sch; Don Valley High Sch; Gravesend Sch for Boys; Hertford Coll Ox; Ridley Hall Cam; *CV* C Edgware, Lon 1977–80; C St Mary Haughton, Manch 1980–83; P-in-c Ch Ch Bacup 1983–87, V 1987–91; R Rusholme 1991–2006; Bp of Sherwood from 2006; M Dioc Syn, Bp's Coun; M Coll of Evangs 2009 *Tel:* 01636 819133
email: bishopsherwood@southwell.anglican.org

PORTSDOWN, Archdeacon of. See READER, Ven Dr Trevor Alan John

PORTSMOUTH, Bishop of. See FOSTER, Rt Revd Christopher Richard James

PORTSMOUTH, Dean of. See BRINDLEY, Very Revd David Charles

POTTER, Ven Peter Maxwell, MA
St Ursula's Church Jubilaumsplatz 2 3000 Bern 6 Switzerland [ARCHDEACON OF SWITZERLAND; EUROPE] *b* 1946 *educ* County Grammar Sch Crewe; Univ Coll Swansea; Univ of British Columbia; Salisbury and Wells Theol Coll; *CV* C Bradford-on-Avon 1985–88; C Harnham 1988–91; P-in-c N Bradley, Southwick and Heywood 1991–96; V St Anne's Sale 1996–2000; R St Columba's Largs 2000–08; Chapl St Ursula's Berne w Neuchatel from 2008; Adn of Switzerland from 2009 *Tel:* 0041 31 351 0343
email: berne@anglican.ch

POUNDS, Mrs Sylvia Lyn, RGN, RDN
3 Woodlands Louth Lincolnshire LN11 0WS [LINCOLN] *b* 1950 *educ* Cheadle County Gr Sch; Trent Polytech; Coll of St Mark and St John Plymouth, Lincoln Sch of Th and Min Studies; *CV* Nursing and Nurse Management Posts 1976–1990; Dir of Nursing and Health Visiting 1990–92; Sector Manager Comm Health Care NHS 1992–94; Nurse Non-Exec Dir 1992–95; Gen Manager Adult and Older Peoples Mental Health 1994–2000; Dir Goole Development Trust 1997–98; Head of Specialist Child and Adolescent Mental Health, 2000 -10; Student of Theology from 2010
GS 2010– *Tel:* 07771 549947
email: spounds@btconnect.com

PRATT, Ven Richard David, MA (Oxon), BCS, PhD (Birmingham)
50 Stainburn Road Workington Cumbria CA14 1SN [ARCHDEACON OF WEST CUMBERLAND] *b* 1955 *educ* Ranelagh School, Bracknell; Lincoln Coll, Ox; Nottingham Univ; Lincoln Theol Coll; Birm Univ; *CV* C All Hallows Wellingborough 1984–87; TV Kingsthorpe 1987–92; V St Benedict's Hunsbury 1992–7, P-in-C St Cuthbert's Carlisle and DCO Carlisle Diocese 1997–2008; Adn West Cumbria from 2009
Tel: 01900 66190 07788 728508
email: archdeacon.west@carlislediocese.org.uk

PRATT, Revd Stephen Samuel, BA, DipH.E, BA, PGCE
The Rectory 203 St Michaels Road Chell Stoke on Trent ST6 6JT [LICHFIELD] *b* 1967 *educ* St Margarets Aigburth Liv; Univ Coll Chester, Keele Univ; Oak Hill Th Coll; *CV* Maths Tchr & Head of Year at St Edwards C of E, Romford 1989–98; C All Saints, Goodmayes 2000–03; TV Chell Team Ministry 2003–07; P-in-C St Michael Chell w Ch of the Saviour Chell Heath 2007–08; V St Michael Chell

w Ch of the Saviour Chell Heath from 2008; Chapl to TA Forces from 2005; Voc Advisor from 2008
GS 2010– *Tel:* 01782 838708 07951027290
email: stephen_pratt@sky.com

PRESLAND, Mr Andrew Roy, B Sc
58 Harborough Rd Rushden NN10 0LP [PETERBOROUGH] *b* 1966 *educ* Rushden Boys' Sch; Leic Univ; *CV* Asst Statistician, DOE 1989–95; Statistician DOE, later DETR 1995–99; Sen Lib Clerk (Statistics), Ho of Commons Lib (secondment) 1999–2001; Statistician, Office of Dep Prime Min (local govt finance) 2001–06, DCLG 2006–11 (strategy and performance), and from 2011 (homelessness statistics); Lay Chair, Higham Dny Syn; Treas E Northants Faith Gp from 2005; M Bp's Coun from 2006; M AC Fin Cttee 2006–11; M DBF 2006–08;
GS 2003– *Tel:* 01933 316927
email: andrewpresland@harboroughroad58.freeserve.co.uk

PRESTON, Dr John Philip Harry, BSc, PHD
Church House Great Smith St London SW1P 3AZ [NATIONAL STEWARDSHIP AND RESOURCES OFFICER, ARCHBISHOPS' COUNCIL] *b* 1965 *educ* Lakes Sch; Exmouth Sch; Lancs Univ; *CV* Marketing Mgr Procter and Gamble 1989–2000; Grp Marketing Dir S Staffordshire Grp 2000–02; Marketing, Sales and NPD Mgr, Freshway Foods 2002–05; Nat Stewardship and Resources Officer from 2005 *Tel:* 020 7898 1540
email: john.preston@churchofengland.org

PRICE, Rt Revd Peter Bryan, Cert Ed, DPS
The Palace Wells BA5 2PD [BISHOP OF BATH AND WELLS] *b* 1944 *educ* Glastonbury Sch Morden; Redland Coll of Educ Bris; Oak Hill Th Coll; Heythrop Coll Lon; *CV* Asst Tchr Ashton Park Sch Bris 1966–70; Sen Tutor Lindley Lodge Young People's Cen 1970; Head of RE Cordeaux High Sch Louth 1970–72; Com Chapl and C Ch Ch Portsdown 1974–78; Chapl Scargill Ho 1978–80; V St Mary Magd Addiscombe 1980–88; Can Chan S'wark Cathl 1988–91; Gen Sec USPG 1992–97; M Miss Agencies Wkg Grp 1992–93; M Angl Commn on Miss 1993–96; Bp of Kingston 1997–2002; M BM; M PWM; M Ch Commn on Miss; M Miss Th Adv Grp; M Gov Body SPCK; Chair S'wark Dioc Bd of Educ; Chair The Manna Soc 1997–2001; Chair Bp's Palace Trust from 2002; Bp of Bath and Wells from 2002; M Ho of Lords from 2008; Chair Angl Communion Pastl Visitors Programme from 2008
GS 2002– *Tel:* 01749 672341
Fax: 01749 679355
email: bishop@bathwells.anglican.org

PRIDDIS, Rt Revd Anthony Martin, MA, Dip Theol, FCEM
The Bishop's House Hereford HR4 9BN [BISHOP OF HEREFORD] *b* 1948 *educ* Watford Gr Sch; CCC Cam; New Coll Ox; Cuddesdon Th Coll; *CV* C New Addington 1972–75; Chapl Ch Ch Ox 1975–80; TV St Jo High Wycombe 1980–86; P-in-c Amersham 1986–90, R 1990–96; RD Amersham 1992–96; Hon Can Ch Ch Ox from 1995; Bp of Warwick 1996–2004; Bp of Hereford from 2004; Trustee Cov Relate 2001–03; Trustee FLAME Network 2001–06, Co-Chair 2003–06; Lay M Bd Coll of Emergency Medicine 2002–08; Central Safeguarding Liaison Grp from 2002; W Midlands Cultural Consortium 2002–05; Trustee Eveson Charitable Trust from 2004; Hon Fell Coll of Emergency Medicine from 2004; Chair Rural Bps' Panel 2006–9; Rural Affairs Group from 2009; House of Lords from 2009
GS 2004– *Tel:* 01432 271355
Fax: 01432 373346
email: bishop@hereford.anglican.org

PRITCHARD, Rt Revd John Lawrence, MA, MLitt
Diocesan Church House North Hinksey Lane Oxford OX2 0NB [BISHOP OF OXFORD] *b* 1948 *educ* Arnold Sch Blackpool; St Pet Coll Ox; Ridley Hall Th Coll; St Jo Coll Dur; *CV* C St Mart-in-the-Bull-Ring Birm 1972–76; Dioc Youth Officer B and W 1976–79; P-in-c St Geo Wilton 1980–88; Dir Pastl Studies Cranmer Hall, St Jo Coll Dur 1989–93; Warden Cranmer Hall 1993–96; Adn of Cant and Can Res Cant Cathl 1996–2001; Bp of Jarrow 2002–07; Bp of Oxford from 2007; Hon Fell St Peter's Coll Ox; Hon Fell St Jo Coll Dur; Chair Abps' Coun Bd of Educ and Nat Soc from 2011; Chair SPCK 2011; M Adv Coun on the Relations of Bishops and Religious Communities from 2007; Pres Guild of Health; M Coun St George's Ho Windsor
GS 1999–2002, 2007– *Tel:* 01865 208222 (Office)
Fax: 01865 790470
email: bishopoxon@oxford.anglican.org
Web: www.oxford.anglican.org

PROUD, Rt Revd Andrew John, BD; AKC;
Bishop's House Tidmarsh Lane Tidmarsh, Reading RG8 8HA [AREA BISHOP OF READING; OXFORD] *b* 1954 *educ* K Coll Lon; SOAS;.Linc Th Coll ; *CV* C Stansted Mountfitchet Chelmsf 1980–83; TV Borehamwood St Alb 1983–90; C Bp's Hatfield 1990–92; R E Barnet 92–2001; Chapl Adis Ababa St Matt Ethiopia 2002–07; Area Bp Ethiopia and Horn of Africa 2007–11; Area Bp of Reading from 2011 *Tel:* 0118 984 1216
Fax: 0118 984 1218
email: bishopreading@oxford.anglican.org

PWAISIHO, Rt Revd William Alaha, OBE, SECONDARY CERT, Dip Th
Rectory Church Lane Gawsworth Macclesfield SK11 9RJ [HONORARY ASSISTANT BISHOP OF CHESTER] *b* 1948 *educ* Alangaula Sch, Pawa and Selwyn Coll, Bp Patteson Theol Centre Kohimarama, Honiara, all in Solomon Islands; *CV* Chapl to Abp of Melanesia 1976–77; C Kohimarama Par Auckland NZ 1977–78; Chapl/Tutor Bp Patteson Theol Cen

WHO'S WHO

Kohimarama 1978–79; Dean St Barn Cathl Honiara 1980–81; Bp of Malaita Solomon Islands 1981–89; Gen Sec Melanesian DM 1990–95; Industrial Mgr and Chapl to Kumagai Gumi Ltd, Solomon Islands 1995–96; Asst Bp and C in Sale from 1997; Asst Bp and R Gawsworth from 1999; M Dioc Syn; M Ho Bps Dioc Minority Ethnic Cttee; Melanesian Miss Engl Cttee; M ChsTogether UK Pacific Forum; first missionary Bp from Melanesia to UK since 1849; first Pacific islander to hold office of Rector in UK and to be appointed Chapl to High Sheriff; awarded OBE 2004; M Cheshire Constabulary Ethnic Minority Independent Adv Grp; Hon Chapl to Crimebeat Eng and Wales; M Rotary Club of Macclesfield
GS 1997– *Tel and Fax:* 01260 223201
email: bishop.gawsworth@virgin.net

PYE, Mr Christopher Charles, BA, M Sc
140 Hinckley Rd St Helens WA11 9JY [LIVERPOOL] *b* 1946 *educ* Grange Park Sch St Helens; Open Univ; Manchester Univ; *CV* Technologist in Glass Industry from 1963; Rtd Occupational Hygiene Mgr; Lay Chair St Helens Dny Syn from 1986; Lay Chair Dioc Syn 1991–2003; Rdr
GS 1985–90, 1992– *Tel:* 01744 609506
email: chrispye@blueyonder.co.uk

RAMSBURY, Suffragan Bishop of. See CONDRY, Rt Revd Edward Francis

RAWLINGS, Ven John Edmund Frank, AKC
Blue Hills Bradley Rd Bovey Tracey Newton Abbot TQ13 9EU [ARCHDEACON OF TOTNES; EXETER] *b* 1947 *educ* Godalming Gr Sch; K Coll Lon; St Aug Coll Cant; *CV* C Rainham 1970–73; C Tattenham Corner w. Burgh Heath 1973–76; Chapl RN 1976–92; V Tavistock w. Gulworthy 1992–2006; RD Tavistock 1997–2002; Preb of Ex 1999–2006; Adn of Totnes from 2006; Chapl to Melanesian Brotherhood Companions from 2006
Tel: 01626 832064
Fax: 01626 834947
email: archdeacon.of.totnes@exeter.anglican.org

RAYFIELD, Rt Revd Dr Lee Stephen, B Sc (Hons), PhD, CTM
Mark House Field Rise Swindon SN1 4HP [SUFFRAGAN BISHOP OF SWINDON; BRISTOL] *b* 1955 *educ* Thos Bennett Comp Sch, Crawley; Crawley Coll of Tech; Southn Univ; St Mary's Hosp Medical Sch, Lon Univ; Ridley Hall, Cam; *CV* C All SS w. St Andr Woodford Wells, Chelmsf 1993–97; P-in-c St Pet w. St Mark Hosp Ch Furze Platt, Ox 1997–2004, V 2004–05; AD Maidenhead & Windsor, Ox 2000–05; Bp of Swindon from 2005; M UK Gene Therapy Adv Cttee 2000–09; M Soc of Ordained Scientists from 1995; M Fell of Par Evang from 1995; Coun M Evang Alliance from 2007; M Ho of Bps CME Cttee from 2007 (CMD Cttee from 2012); M Ethical Investment Adv Grp from 2007; M Human Embryology and Fertilisation Authority from 2012 *Tel:* 01793 538654
Fax: 01793 525181
email: bishop.swindon@bristoldiocese.org
Web: www.bristol.anglican.org/news/microblog

RAZZALL, Revd Charles Humphrey, MA
St Michael's Rectory 198 Ford Lane Crewe CW1 3TN [CHESTER] *b* 1905 *educ* St Paul's Sch, Lon; Worchester Coll Ox; Westcott House Th Coll; *CV* Asst C Catford and Downham T, 1979–83; V St Hilda w St Cyprian, Crofton Park 1983–87; TV Oldham 1987–2001; Area Dean Oldham 1992–99; Hon Can Man Cathl 1998–2001; R St Michael Coppenhall, Crewe from 2001
GS 1995–2000; 2010– *Tel:* 01270215151
email: razzall@angelfields.eclipse.co.uk

READ, Revd Charles William,
42 Heigham Road Norwich NR2 3AU [NORWICH] *b* 1960 *educ* King Edward VI Sch, Lichfield; Man Univ; Man Poly; St John's Coll, Nott; *CV* Head of RS, Audenshaw High School 1982–86; C, Oldham Team Ministry, 1988–90; C, St.Clement Urmston 1990–93; Goodshaw & Crawshawbooth 1993–94;P-in-C & TV Broughton Team Ministry 1994–99; Lect Lit & Doc, Cranmer Hall, Dur 1999–2006; Vice-Prin & Dir Studies Norwich Dioc Ministry Course from 2007; Eucharistic Prayers Steering Cttee 1998–2000; Thl Ed & Training Cttee 2005–06
GS 1997–2000; 2005–06; 2010–
Tel: 01603 729813
email: charlesread@norwich.anglican.org

READER, Ven Dr Trevor Alan John, B Sc, M Sc, Ph D, SOSc
5 Brading Ave Southsea PO4 9QJ [ARCHDEACON OF PORTSDOWN; PORTSMOUTH] *b* 1946 *educ* Haverfordwest Gr Sch; Portsm Poly; S Diocs Min Trg Scheme, Salis & Wells Th Coll; *CV* Rsch Asst biological sciences Ports Poly 1968–72, Sen Lect 1972–86; C St Mary, Alverstoke 1986–89; P-in-c, then V St Mary, Hook w Warsash 1989–98; P-in-c Blendworth, H Trin w Chalton St Mich & All Angels w Idsworth St Hubert and Ports Dioc Dir of NSM 1998–2003; Adn of Isle of Wight 2003–06; Adn of Portsdown from 2006; Chair Dioc Bd of Educ 2003–10; M DAC for Care of Chs; M Dioc Parsonages and Property Cttee; Bp's Liaison Officer for Prisons 2003–06; Bp's Adv to Hosp Chapl from 2006 *Tel:* 023 9243 2693
07826 846133 (Mobile)
Fax: 023 9229 8788
email: adportsdown@portsmouth.anglican.org

READING, Area Bishop of. See PROUD, Rt Revd Andrew John

REDFERN, Rt Revd Dr Alastair Llewellyn John, MA, MA, Ph D
The Bishop's House 6 King St Duffield Belper DE56 4EU [BISHOP OF DERBY] *b* 1948 *educ* Bicester Sch; Ch Ch Ox; Trin Coll Cam; Westcott Ho Th Coll;

Bris Univ; *CV* C Tettenhall 1976–79; Lect in Ch Hist, Dir of Pastl Studies and Vc-Prin Cuddesdon Th Coll 1979–87; C All SS Cuddesdon 1983–87; Can Res Bris Cathl 1987–97; Can Theologian and Dir of Tr 1987–97; Mod of Par Resource Tm 1995–97; M ABM Initial Minl Educ Cttee; Mod Abps Dip for Rdrs; Bp of Grantham 1997–2005; Dean of Stamford 1998–2005; Chair Fin Panel, Min Div; M Theol, Educ and Trg Cttee; M Bp's Cttee for Min; M Bp's CME Cttee; M Legal Aid Commn; Bp of Derby from 2005; M Ho of Bps Th Gp; Co-ch Intern Faith Network for the UK; M BD Trustees Christian Aid
GS 2005– *Tel:* 01332 840132
Fax: 01332 840397
email: bishop@bishopofderby.org

REED, Ven John Peter Cyril, BD, AKC, Cert Th (Oxon)
2 Monkton Heights West Monkton Taunton TA2 8LU [ARCHDEACON OF TAUNTON; BATH & WELLS] *b* 1951 *educ* Monkton Combe Sch; K Coll Lon; Cuddesdon Th Coll; *CV* Asst C Croydon Par Ch 1979–82; Prec St Alb 1982–86; R Timsbury and Priston 1986–93; Chapl for Rural Affairs Bath Adnry 1987–93; TR Ilminster and District TM 1993–99; Adn Taunton from 1999; Dioc Warden of Rdrs
Tel: 01823 413315
Fax: 01823 413384
email: adtaunton@bathwells.anglican.org

REES, Mrs Christina (Henking Muller), BA, MA, FRSA
Churchfield Pudding Lane Barley Royston Herts SG8 8JX [ST ALBANS] *b* 1953 *educ* Hampton Day Sch; Pomona Coll; Wheaton Graduate Sch; K Coll Lon; *CV* Researcher IBA 1980; Asst Public Relns Officer The Children's Society 1985–87; Writer from 1980; Broadcaster from 1990; Consultant and Trainer from 1995; Coach from 2003; M Strg Cttee and Initiation Services Revision Cttee 1996–98; M CECC 1996–98; M ABM 1996–98; Chair WATCH 1996–2010; Trustee, Li Tim-Oi Foundn from 1997; Elected M AC 1999–2000; Convenor, Church and Media Consultation 2000, 2005, 2010; Trustee, Chr Evidence Soc 2000–05; M Theol Educ and Trg Cttee 2000–05; GS rep, Bd Govs Ripon Coll Cuddesdon from 2000; co-opted Bd Govs Tr Coll Bris 2000–05; M CMEAC 1999–2004; Dir Churchfield Trust; M CRAC; Dip in Coaching (Coaching Futures/OCR) 2003; elected M AC from 2005; Trustee Chr Assoc of Business Execs; M Bus Cttee from 2011; Consultant, Ernst and Young from 2011
GS 1990–
Tel: 01763 848472 01763 848822 07768 151646
Fax: 01763 848774
email: christina@mediamaxima.com

REES, Canon (Vivian) John (Howard), MA, LLB, M Phil
16 Beaumont St Oxford OX1 2LZ [JOINT REGISTRAR, PROVINCE OF CANTERBURY] *b* 1951 *educ* Skinners' Sch Tunbridge Wells; Southn Univ; Ox Univ; Leeds Univ; Wycliffe Hall Th Coll; *CV* Solicitor and Eccl Notary (Admitted 1975); C Moor Allerton TM 1979–82; Chapl and Tutor Sierra Leone Th Hall, Freetown 1983–86; Ptnr Winckworth Sherwood Solicitors from 1986; Treas Eccl Law Soc from 1995; Jt Registrar Ox Dioc from 1998; Jt Registrar Prov of Cant from 2000; Registrar, Court of Arches from 200; Legal Adv ACC from 1998; Vc-Chair Legal Adv Commn from 2001; Provincial Can Cant Cathl from 2001; Registrar, Clergy Discipline Tribunals Prov of Cant from 2006
GS 1995–2000 *Tel:* 01865 297200 (Office)
01865 865875 (Home)
07973 327417 (Mobile)
Fax: 01865 726274
email: jrees@wslaw.co.uk *2nd email:* vjhrees@btinternet.com
Web: www.wslaw.co.uk

REID, Canon Jenny (Jennifer), BA
Healam 9 Poplars Rd Linthorpe Middlesbrough TS5 6RL [YORK] *b* 1943 *CV* University lecturer, rtd
GS 2000– *Tel:* 01642 823127 (Home)
01642 782095 (Office)
email: jennyreid@ntlworld.com

REIGATE, Archdeacon of. See KAJUMBA, Ven Daniel Steven Kimbugwe

RENSHAW, Canon Elizabeth, MBE, Adv Dip Bus Man & Admin Man
82 Ennisdale Drive West Kirby Wirral CH48 9UA [CHESTER] *educ* Bus Man 1991–2008; Proj Coordinator 2008–11; *CV* DBF Chairs rep, Eccls Fees Comm; Chair, Chester Dioc Bd Finance; Bp's Coun; Chair, Finance and Scrutiny, HR and Staffing Review Cttes; Lay Canon Chester Cathl; Cathl Council; Par Giving Adv; Secondary Sch Gov; Trustee Educational Trust
GS 2010– *Tel:* 0151 625 5044
email: betty.renshaw@gmail.com

REPTON, Suffragan Bishop of. See SOUTHERN, Rt Revd Humphrey Ivo John

RICE, Dr Philip, BSc MSc, PhD,MICE C.Eng, MEI
23 Christchurch Square Homerton London E9 7HU [LONDON] *b* 1949 *educ* Doncaster Gr Sch; LSE, UCL; *CV* Rsrch Fellow Transport Section, Imperial Coll 1978–85; Direct Entrant Economist Civil service, 1985; Economic Adv, Dept of Energy, Energy Forecasts and Oil Prices, 1985–91; Economic Adv, Inland Revenue, Statistics and Economics Division, Oil & Financial Sector and Capital Gains Tax 1991–98; Senior Economist, Inland Revenue, Team Leader, Direct Business Taxes & Anti-Avoidance, from 1998; Lay Chair of

Hackney Deanery, Lon Dioc 2000–06; M Bp's Counc Lon Dioc from 2006
GS 2010– *Tel:* 02089851914
email: phillip@christopherrice.orangehome.co.uk

RICHBOROUGH, Bishop of. See BANKS, Rt Revd Norman

RICHMOND, Revd Dr Patrick Henry, MA(Oxon), DPhil
161 Newmarket Road Norwich NR4 6SY [NORWICH] *b* 1969 *educ* Marlborough Coll, Wilts; Balliol Coll; Green Coll, Ox; Wycliffe Hall Th Coll; *CV* C, Church of the Martyrs, Leic 1997–2001; Chapl & Fellow, St Catharine's Coll, Cam 2001–06; Dean of Chapel, St Catharine's Coll, Cam 2006–07; V, Ch Ch, Eaton, Norwich from 2007
GS 2010– *Tel:* 01603 2508449 07982785765
email: phr@eatonparish.com
Web: www.eatonparish.com

RICHMOND, Archdeacon of. See HENDERSON, Ven Janet

RIPON AND LEEDS, Bishop of. See PACKER, Rt Revd John Richard

RIPON, Dean of. See JUKES, Very Revd Keith Michael

ROBERTS, Canon (John) Mark Arnott, AKC, PGCE
Rectory Knightrider St Sandwich CT13 9ER [CANTERBURY] *b* 1954 *educ* Caterham Sch; K Coll Lon Univ; Ch Ch Coll Cant; Chich Th Coll; *CV* C St Mary V, Ashford, Kent 1977–82; V and R St Mary's Bay, St Mary in the Marsh, Ivychurch 1982–91; R Sandwich from 1991; P-in-C Worth 2004–10; P-inC Eastry, Northbourn & Tilmanstone from 2010; Area Dean of Sandwich 2000–06; M Dioc Syn; Hon Can Cant Cathl from 2003; Chair Dioc Syn Ho of Clergy 2006–12
GS 2003– *Tel:* 01304 613138
email: revdmarkroberts@supanet.com

ROBERTS, Ven Kevin Thomas, MA, BA
2 The Abbey Carlisle CA3 8TZ [ARCHDEACON OF CARLISLE] *b* 1955 *educ* Guisborough Grammar Sch; Prior Pursglove Coll; Queens' Coll Cam; Univ Nottm; St John's Coll Nottm; *CV* C Beverley Minster 1983–86; C St James Woodley 1986–91; V Meole Brace 1991–2009; RD Shrewsbury 1998–2008; Preb Lichfield Cathl 2002–09; Res Can Carlisle Cathl from 2009; Adn Carlisle from 2009; Ox Dioc Syn 1988–91; Lich Dioc Syn 1992–2009; Bps Coun Lich 1997–2006; Lich Vacancy-in-See Comm 1998–2003; Chair Carlisle Bd of Educ from 2009 *Tel:* 01228 523026 (Home)
01228 522573 (Office)
07584 684300 (Mobile)
email: archdeacon.north@carlislediocese.org.uk

ROBERTS, Ven Stephen John, BD, MTh
2 Alma Rd Wandsworth London SW18 1AB [ARCHDEACON OF WANDSWORTH; SOUTHWARK] *b* 1958 *educ* Newcastle-under-Lyme High Sch; K Coll Lon; Westcott Ho Cam; Heythrop Coll Lon; *CV* C St Mary Riverhead w. St Jo Dunton Green, Roch 1983–86; C St Martin-in-the-Fields, S'wark 1986–89; V St Geo Camberwell and Wrdn Trin Coll Centre, S'wark 1989–2000; Sen DDO and Can Res, S'wark Cathl 2000–05; Adn of Wandsworth from 2005 *Tel:* 020 8874 8567 (Home)
020 8785 1985 (Work)
Fax: 020 8785 1981
email: stephen.roberts@southwark.anglican.org

ROBERTS, Revd Dr Vaughan Simon, BA, MA, PhD
The Rectory The Butts Warwick CV34 4SS [COVENTRY] *b* 1959 *educ* Montgomery of Alamein Comp Sch; Winch and Peter Symonds Coll; Univ Coll of N Wales, Bangor; Univ of Bath; McCormick Theol Sem, Chicago; Westcott Ho Cam; *CV* C St Thomas-on-the-Bourne Farnham 1985–89; Chapl Phyllis Tuckwell Hosp Farnham 1988–89; Univ Chapl Univ of Bath 1989–96; P-in-c Ch Ch Proprietory Chapel Bath 1992–96; Dir Ords and Vocations Adv Bath and Wells 1996–2003; P-in-c Chewton Mendip Benefice 1996–2003; M Coun for WEMTC 1998–2003; M Coun for STETS 1999–2003; TR Warwick and V Collegiate Ch of St Mary from 2003; M AAR from 2008
GS 2009–2010 *Tel and Fax:* 01926 492909
email: vaughan.roberts@btinternet.com

ROBILLIARD, Mr David John,
Le Petit Gree Torteval Guernsey GY8 0RD [WINCHESTER (CHANNEL ISLANDS)] *b* 1952 *educ* Guernsey Gr Sch for Boys; *CV* Clearing and Internat Banking 1969–82; HM Dep Greffier 1982–87; Prin Asst Chief Exec Guernsey Civil Service 1987–94; Hd of Constitutional Affairs States of Guernsey 1994–2007; Prin Officer States Assembly and Constitution Ctee from 2008; Dep Clerk Guernsey States of Deliberation from 2010; M Dioc Stg Cttee; & Bp's Coun Treas Guernsey Dny Syn; chwdn of Torteval
GS 1998– *Tel:* 01481 264344 (Home)
01481 749507 (Office)
07781 164344 (Mobile)
Fax: 01481 713884
email: villula@cwgsy.net

ROBINSON, Rt Revd Anthony William, Cert Ed
Pontefract House 181a Manygates Lane Wakefield WF2 7DR [SUFFRAGAN BISHOP OF PONTEFRACT; WAKEFIELD] *b* 1956 *educ* Bedf Modern Sch; Bedf Coll of HE; Sarum and Wells Th Coll; *CV* C St Paul Tottenham 1982–85; TV Resurr Leic 1985–89, TR 1989–97; RD Christianity N 1992–97; Hon Can Leic Cathl from 1994; M CBF 1995–97; M CMEAC

1996–97; Adn of Pontefract 1997–2003; Bishop of Pontefract from 2002
GS 1995–97, 2000–02 *Tel:* 01924 250781
Fax: 01924 240490
email: bishop.pontefract@wakefield.anglican.org

ROBINSON, Ven Peter John Alan, BA, MA, PhD
4 Acomb Close Morpeth NE61 2YH [ARCHDEACON OF LINDISFARNE; NEWCASTLE] *b* 1961 *educ* St Jo Coll Camb; St Jo Coll Durham; *CV* C North Shield 1995–99; Dir Urban Ministry and Theology Project, Newc East Deanery; P-in-c Byker St Martin 1999–2008; P-in-c Byker St Michael w St Lawrence 2001–08; Hon Can Newcastle Cathl 2007–08; Adn of Lindisfarne from 2008; Chair William Temple Foundation from 2009
Tel: 01670 503810 07786 642124
Fax: 01670 503 469
email: p.robinson@newcastle.anglican.org

ROCHDALE, Archdeacon of. See VANN, Cherry Elizabeth

ROCHESTER, Archdeacon of. See BURTON-JONES, Ven Simon David

ROCHESTER, Bishop of. See LANGSTAFF, Rt Revd James Henry

ROCHESTER, Dean of. See BEACH, Very Revd Mark Howard Francis

RODGERS, Mrs Sue (Susan Elizabeth),
13 Rowlands Ave Waterlooville PO7 7RT [PORTSMOUTH] *b* 1954 *educ* Haywards Heath Sec Sch; *CV* WRNS 1971–79; Night Staff St Mary's Hosp Portsm; Bereavement Cllr; Co-ord Bereavement Grp; Par Asst/Administrator St Wilf Cowplain until 2001; Lay Can Portsm Cath from 2008
GS 2000– *Tel:* 023 9225 3091
07974 570414 (Mobile)
Fax: 023 9223 3367
email: Sue@Rodgersuk.com

RODHAM, Ven Morris, MA, PGCE, BA, DipHE
3 The Gardens Thurlaston Rugby CV23 9LS [ARCHDEACON MISSIONER, DIOCESE OF COVENTRY] *b* 1959 *educ* RGS Newcastle; Durham Univ Hatfield College; Bristol Univ; Trinity Coll Bristol; *CV* Regular Army (Royal Artillery) 1978, 1981–84; Tchr Warwick Schl (Classics, CCF, Hockey) 1985–90; C St Mark's Leamington 1993–1997; V St Mary's Leamington 1997–2010; RD Warwick and Leamington 2006–10; Adn Missioner from 2010
Tel: 02476 521337
email: morris.rodham@covcofe.org

ROSE, Revd Susan Margaret, B Ed
The Vicarage Station Road Cheddar Somerset BS27 3AH [BATH AND WELLS] *b* 1959 *educ* Stoud Girls High Sch; Keswick Grammar Sch; Westminster Coll Higher Ed; SAOMC;; *CV* Teacher, 1981–98; C,North Petherton w Moorland, 1998–2000; Rector, The Alfred Jewel Benefice, 2000–09; P-in-C, Cheddar; Rodney Stoke w Draycott, 2009; Sec Cttee Ministerial Review, 2000–04; Design team Bps Course for Rdrs, 2003–05; Vocations Chapl 2004–06; Rural Dean 2006–09; M Dioc Patronage Brd, from 2009
GS 2010– *Tel:* 01934 740394
email: rev.suerose@virgin.net

ROSEMARY CHN, Sister, MA, MA, PGCE, Dip Pastl Th (APU)
Convent of the Holy Name Morley Rd Oakwood Derby DE21 4QZ [RELIGIOUS COMMUNITIES (SOUTH)] *b* 1944 *educ* Barr's Hill Sch Cov; Newnham Coll Cam; Hughes Hall Cam; St Mary's Coll Dur Univ; Westcott Ho Cam; *CV* Various teaching posts, 1967–76; Community of the Holy Name from 1976; Dn 1998; P 1999 (Derby Dioc); C St Osmund, Derby 1998–2001; Perm to officiate, Derby and S'well Diocs from 2001; Assoc P, Morley, Smalley and Loscoe (Derby) from 2010
GS 2003– *Tel:* 01332 671716
email: rosemarychn@yahoo.co.uk

ROSSDALE, Rt Revd David Douglas James, MA, M Sc
Bishop's House Church Lane Irby-on-Humber Grimsby DN37 7JR [SUFFRAGAN BISHOP OF GRIMSBY; LINCOLN] *b* 1953 *educ* St Jo Sch Leatherhead; K Coll Lon; Westmr Coll Ox; Roehampton Inst; Chich Th Coll; *CV* C St Laur Upminster 1981–86; V St Luke Moulsham 1986–90; V H Trin Cookham 1990–2000; AD Maidenhead 1994–2000; Hon Can Ch Ch Ox 1999–2000; Bp of Grimsby from 2000; Hon Can and Preb Lincoln from 2000 *Tel:* 01472 371715
Fax: 01472 371716
email: rossdale@btinternet.com

ROUCH, Ven Dr Peter Bradford, MA (Oxon); MA (Cantab); PhD
22 Bellflower Way Chandler's Ford Hampshire SO53 4HN [ARCHDEACON OF BOURNEMOUTH; WINCHESTER] *b* 1966 *educ* Sir Joseph Williamson's Mathematical Sch Rochester; Brasenose Coll Ox; Peterhouse Cam; Univ Manchester;
GS 310512 *Tel:* 02380 260955
email: peter.rouch@winchester.anglican.org

ROWELL, Rt Revd (Douglas) Geoffrey, MA, Ph D, D Phil, DD, Hon DD
Bishop's Lodge Worth Crawley RH10 7RT [BISHOP OF GIBRALTAR IN EUROPE] *b* 1943 *educ* Eggar's Gr Sch Alton; Win Coll; CCC Cam; Cuddesdon Th Coll; *CV* Asst Chapl and Hastings Rashdall Student New Coll Ox 1968–72; Hon C St Andr Headington 1968–72; Fell, Chapl and Tutor in Th Keble Coll Ox 1972–94, Emer Fell from 1994; Univ Lect in Th 1977–94; M Liturg Commn 1980–90; Gov Pusey Ho Ox 1979–1995, Pres 1995–2009, Gov from 2009; M Gov Body SPCK 1984–94 and from 1997; Hon Dir Abp's Exam in Th 1986–2001; Can and Preb Chich Cathl 1981–2001; M

WHO'S WHO

Angl-Oriental Orthodox Internat Forum from 1985, Angl Co-Chair from 1996; Conservator Mirfield Cert in Pastl Th 1987–93; M Coun Mgt St Steph Ho Th Coll from 1988, Chairman from 2004; M Doct Commn 1990–95, Consult 1996–99, M 1999–2004; Bp of Basingstoke 1994–2001; C of E Rep on CTBI 1995–2001; Vis Prof Univ Coll Chich (Sch of Religion and Theol) 1996–2003; Chair Chs Funerals Grp from 1997; M Inter Angl Stg Commn on Ecum Relns 2000–2008, Vc-Chairman from 2003; Hon Can Win Cathl 2000–2001; Ho Bps Theol Grp 1999–2011; M Clergy Discipline (Theol and Liturg) Wkg Pty 2000–03; M Ho of Bps' Wkg Pty on Women in the Episcopate 2000–04; Bp of Gib in Eur from 2001
GS 2001– *Tel:* 01293 883051
Fax: 01293 884479
email: bishop.europe@churchofengland.org

ROY, Mr Anirban, BA, CIMA Adv Dip
11 Longton Grove London SE26 6QQ [LONDON] *b* 1977 *educ* Tiffin Sch; Trin Coll, Cam; *CV* Head of Regulatory Compliance, Office of Comm Ofcom, 2007–10; Policy Manager, Ofcom 2004–07; Strategy Consult Solving International, 2002–04; Corporate Finance Consult, Arthur D. Little, 1999–2002; Principal, Ofcom from 2010
GS 2010– *Tel:* 07968 173 213
email: urbanroy@gmail.com

RUOFF, Mrs Alison Laura, SRN, SCM, DN
The White House 75 Crossbrook St Cheshunt EN8 8LU [LONDON] *b* 1942 *educ* Sutton Coldfield Girls High Sch; Nightingale Sch of Nursing, St Thos Hosp; Br Hosp for Mothers and Babies; Nursing Inst Worc; RCN; *CV* VSO India 1961–62; Night Sister St Thos Hosp 1966–67; Asst Dir of Nursing Internat Grenfell Assoc Newfoundland 1968–70; Admin Sister St Thos Hosp Grp 1970–72; Nursing Officer/Sen Nursing Officer Univ Coll Hosp 1972–74; Housewife and mother; JP 1979–2003; M Dioc Bp's Coun; CEEC Exec; Lay Chair Lon DEF; Trustee Barnabus Fund; speaker and broadcaster
GS 1995–
Tel: 01992 623113 07956 569323 (Mobile)
email: alison_ruoff@hotmail.com

RUSSELL, Ven Brian Kenneth, MA, PhD
26 George Rd Edgbarton Birmingham B15 1PJ [ARCHDEACON OF ASTON; BIRMINGHAM] *b* 1950 *educ* Bris Gr Sch; Trin Hall Cam; Birm Univ; Cuddesdon Ox; *CV* C St Matt Redhill 1976–79; P-in-c St Jo Kirk Merrington, Dur and Dir of Studies NEOC 1979–83; Dir of Studies and Lect in Chr Doct, Linc Theol Coll 1983–86; Sec Cttee for Theol Educ and Selection Sec, ACCM/ABM 1986–93; Bp's Dir for Min, Birm Dioc 1993–2005; sch gov; Hon Can Birm Cathl from 1999; M Vol and Continuing Educ Cttee, GS Bd of Educ 1994–99; Bp's Sen Selector from 1998; Bp's Sen Insp for Theol Colls and Courses from 2001; M Bps' Inspections Wkg Pty from 2003; Bp's Exam Chapl, Birm from 1996; Chair Birm Dioc Ministries Forum from 2005; Gov Q Foundn for Theol Educ, Birm from 1994; Adn of Aston from 2005
Tel: 0121 426 0428
0121 454 5525
Fax: 0121 428 1114
email: b.russell@birmingham.anglican.org

RUSSELL, Ven Norman Atkinson, MA, BD
Foxglove House Love Lane Donnington Newbury RG14 2JG [ARCHDEACON OF BERKSHIRE; OXFORD] *b* 1943 *educ* R Belfast Academical Inst; Chu Coll Cam; Lon Coll of Div; *CV* C Ch Ch w Em Clifton 1970–74; C Ch Ch Trent Park Enfield 1974–77; R Harwell w Chilton 1977–84; P-in-c Gerrards Cross 1984–88; P-in-c Fulmer 1985–88; R Gerrards Cross and Fulmer 1988–98; GS 2002–10; Hon Can Ch Ch Ox 1995–98; RD Amersham 1996–98; Adn of Berks from 1998; Prolocutor Lower Ho Conv of Cant 2005–10; M Abp's Coun 2005–10; M Appts Cttee 2006–10; M Ch Heritage Forum 2006–10; Vc-Chair Ecum Coun for Corporate Resp 1999–2002; M Clergy Terms of Service Implementation Grp/Panel 2005–10
GS 2002–2010
Tel: 01635 552820 07776 180991 (Mobile)
Fax: 01635 522165
email: archdber@oxford.anglican.org

RUSSELL, Mrs Victoria Christine, Cert Ed
Foxglove House Love Lane Donnington Newbury RG14 2JG [OXFORD] *b* 1948 *educ* Badminton Sch; Whitelands Coll of Ed; *CV* Tchr, 1970–76; Head of RE & Geography, Gateway School, Bucks, 1989–1996; Head of RE & Geography, Maltman's Green School, Bucks, 1996–2006; M Ox Healing Team
GS 2010– *Tel:* 01635 552 820 07765 951 021
Fax: 01635 522 165
email: vcrussell@googlemail.com

RUTHERFORD, Revd Rosalind Elizabeth, BA PGCE
45 Beaconsfield Road Basingstoke Hampshire RG21 3DG [WINCHESTER] *b* 1952 *educ* King's H Sch for Girls; Warwick St Hugh's Coll, Ox; Goldsmiths' Coll, UL; STETS; *CV* Field Officer, Third World First 1974–76; Toy Library Organiser, Manchester Youth and Community Service1976–77; Tchr, Parliament Hill Sch for Girls 1998–80;Tchr Burlington Danes Sch 1980–84; Adult Education tutor Reading Adult Coll 1987–2003; C St Peter's Earley 2003–06; TV Basingstoke Team Ministry from 2006
GS 2010– *Tel:* 01256 464616
email: vicar@allsaintsbasingstoke.org.uk

RYLANDS, Rt Revd Mark James, MA
Athlone House 68 London Road Shrewsbury SY2 6PG [AREA BISHOP OF SHREWSBURY] *b* 1961 *CV* Area Bp of Shrewsbury from 2009
Tel: 01743 235867
email: bishop.shrewsbury@lichfield.anglican.org

SADGROVE, Very Revd Michael, MA, FRSA, DL
The Deanery Durham DH1 3EQ [DEAN OF DURHAM] *b* 1950 *educ* Univ Coll Sch Lon; Ball Coll Ox; Trin Coll Bris; *CV* Lic to Offic Ox dio 1975–76; Lect OT Sarum & Wells Th Coll 1977–82; Vc-Prin 1980–82; V Alnwick 1982–87; Can Res, Prec and Vc-Provost Cov Cathl 1987–95; Provost of Sheff 1995–2000, Dean 2000–03; Dean of Durham from 2003; Chair Dur Univ Ethics Adv Cttee; M Dur Univ Coun; R St Chad's Coll Dur
Tel: 0191 384 7500 07828 516198
Fax: 0191 386 4267
email: michael.sadgrove@durhamcathedral.co.uk
Web: www.durhamcathedral.co.uk
Blog http://decanalwoolgatherer.blogspot.com
Twitter @sadgrovem

SALFORD, Archdeacon of, see SHARPLES, Ven David,

SALISBURY, Bishop of. See HOLTAM, Rt Revd Nicholas Roderick

SALISBURY, Dean of. See OSBORNE, Very Revd June

SALOP, Archdeacon of. See THOMAS, Ven Paul Wyndham

SARGENT, Lieutenant Commander Philippa Mary, MA, PGDip
31 Launceston Close Priddy's Hard Gosport PO12 4GE [REPRESENTATIVE, ARMED FORCES SYNOD] *b* 1968 *educ* Bennett Memorial Sch for Girls; Ox Univ; Portsm Univ; *CV* Naval Officer from 1991
GS 2005– *Tel:* 023 9258 3080
email: philippa.sargent@virgin.net

SARUM, Archdeacon of. See JEANS, Ven Alan Paul

SAXBY, Revd Canon Martin Peter, BA, DipTh
St Matthews Vicarage 7 Vicarage Road Rugby CV22 7AJ [COVENTRY] *b* 1952 *educ* Wandsworth Comp Sch; St. John's Coll, Dur; Cranmer Hall; *CV* AC St. Mary Magdalene, Peckham 1978–81; AC Ramsey w St Peter's Upwood & Ramsey St. Mary's 1981–84; Incumb Mattishall w Mattishall Burgh, Welborne and Yaxham 1984–90; Incumb St. Matthew's Rugby1990–2007; Incumb St. Matthew's & St. Oswald's Rugby 2008; Area Dean of Rugby 2005; M Bp's Counc from 2004; Joint Chair Dioc Miss Fund 2010–11; Chair Dioc Miss Links Cttee from 2011; Hon Can Coventry Catheral from 2011 GS 2010– *Tel:* 01788 330442
Fax: 07053 480 079
email: martinpa@m2o.org.uk

SCOTT, Mrs Angela Mary, MTh, Cert Ed
The Stead Willow Grove Chislehurst Kent BR7 5BU [ROCHESTER] *b* 1950 *educ* Portsmouth High Sch; Bedord Coll of Phys Ed; Spurgeon's Th Coll; *CV* Tchr, Stratford House Sch, Kent 1972–75; Home Maker 1975–99; Part-time Tchr, Marjory McClure Sch, Kent 1984–87; Supply Tching, Bromley 1987–92; Church Admin, 1992–98; Dioc Pastoral Asst from 2000; Dioc Tutor, 2000–08
GS 2000–05; 2010–
Tel: 020 8467 3589 07809 438737
email: a@5scotts.freeserve.co.uk

SCOWEN, Mr Clive Richard, LLB
69 Brooke Ave Harrow HA2 0ND [LONDON] *b* 1958 *educ* John Lyon Sch Harrow; Bris Univ; Inns of Court Sch of Law; *CV* Called to bar (Inner Temple) 1981; law reporter, Incorporated Coun of Law Reporting 1983–90; Dep Ed Weekly Law Reports 1990–2000; Joint Ed, Law Reports Consolidated Index from 2000; Man Ed, Weekly Law Reports 2006–07; Ed Law Reports and Weekly Law Reports from 2008; Councillor, Lon Boro of Harrow 1990–2002; Rdr from 1991; M Bris Univ Court from 1980; Dir Glencoe Trust Ltd; Dir Soul Survivor Harrow; Trustee, Charles Gardner Meml Fund; Trustee, Maseno Project Trust; M MPA Coun; M GS Stg Orders Cttee; M Lon Dioc Bp's Coun; Dir Lon Dioc Fund; M Willesden Area Coun; M Bp of Lon's Miss Fund Bd; M Harrow Dny Stg Cttee
GS 2005– *Tel:* 020 8422 1329
07771 780805 (Mobile)
email: clivescowen@onetel.com

SEARLE, Ven Jacqueline Ann, MA, BEd, Dip Th
2 College Green Gloucester GL1 2LY [ARCHDEACON OF GLOUCESTER] *b* 1960 *educ* Talbot Heath, Bournemouth; Whitelands Coll, Lon; Trin Coll Bris; *CV* Tchr 1982–90; C Ch Ch Roxeth 1992–94; C St Stephen's Ealing 1994–96; Tutor Applied Th & Dean of Women Trin Coll Bris 1996–2003; Dean of Women's Ministry Derby 2007–10; Incumb St Peter's, Littleover, Derby from 2003; RD Derby South 2010–12; Adn of Glos from 2012; Can Res Glos Cathl from 2012
GS 2010–12 *Tel:* 01452 835594
Fax: 01452 381528
email: archdglos@glosdioc.org.uk

SEDDON, Mr (William Trevor) Bill, BSc, ASIP
20 Carpenters Wood Drive Chorleywood Rickmansworth Herts WD3 5RJ [ST ALBANS] *b* 1952 *educ* Grove Park Boys' Gr Sch, Wrexham; UCL; *CV* Asst Investment Man, Central Fin Brd Methodist Ch, 1985–87; Investment Man, Dominion Insurance 1980–85; Asset Manager Paine Webber 1977–80; Asst Investment Man, White Weld 1975–77; Trainee Investment Man, Central Brd Fin C of E 1973–75; Investment M & CE, Central Fin Brd Methodist Ch and Epworth Investment Management Ltd from 1987.
GS 2010– *Tel:* 01923 285727
Fax: 0207 496 3631
email: bill.seddon@cfbmethodistchurch

SELBY, Suffragan Bishop of. See WALLACE, Rt Revd Martin William

WHO'S WHO

SELVARATNAM, Revd Christian Nathan, BSc, DipTheol
52 The Gallops York YO24 3NF [YORK] *b* 1968 *educ* Wolfreton Sch; Univ of Warwick; Cranmer Hall Th Coll; *CV* Holy Trin Ch, Coventry, Head Verger 1990–92; Copyzone Printers, Bishop's Stortford, Mgr & Graphic designer 1992–96; Comm Ch, Bishop's Stortford, Asst Pastor 1994–99; York City Ch, Senior pastor, 1999–2004; Alpha International, Dir of Alpha in the North of England from 2004; G2 (Fresh Expression of Church), P-in-C from 2008; St Michael le Belfrey, Head of Discipleship and New Initiatives from 2010
GS 2010– *Tel:* 01904 624190
email: christian.selvaratnam@gmail.com

SENTAMU, Most Revd and Rt Hon Dr John Tucker Mugabi, LLB, MA, Ph D, LLD (Hon), DD (Hon), FRSA, Privy Counsellor
Bishopthorpe Palace Bishopthorpe York YO23 2GE [ARCHBISHOP OF YORK] *b* 1949 *educ* Makerere Univ Kampala; Selw Coll Cam; Ridley Hall Th Coll; *CV* Asst Chapl Selw Coll Cam 1979; Chapl HM Remand Cen Latchmere Ho 1979–82; C St Andr Ham 1979–82; C St Paul Herne Hill 1982–83; P-in-c H Trin Tulse Hill; Par Priest St Matthias 1983–84; V H Trin and St Matthias Tulse Hill 1985–96; P-in-c St Sav Brixton 1987–89; Bp of Stepney 1996–2002; M NACRO Young Offenders Cttee 1986–95; M Abp's Adv Grp on UPAs 1986–92; M ABM Coun from 1985; M Stg Cttee GS Ho of Clergy 1985–96; M GS Stg Cttee 1988–96; M GS Policy Cttee 1990–96; Chair Dioc Ho of Clergy 1992–96; M Decade of Evang Strg Grp and Springboard Exec 1991–96; M Turnbull Proposals Strg Grp; M Strg Grp Women (Priests) Ordination Measure; Pro-Prolocutor Conv of Cant 1990–94; Chair CMEAC 1990–99; Prolocutor Conv of Cant 1994–96; M The Stephen Lawrence Judicial Inquiry 1997–99; Pres and Chair Lon Marriage Guidance Coun 2000–04; Chair Damilola Taylor Murder Review 2002; Fell Univ Coll Ch Ch Cant 2001; Fell Qu Mary Coll Univ of Lon 2001; Hon Dr OU 2001; D Phil (Hon) Univ of Glos 2002; DD (Hon) Univ of Birm 2003; Chair ECI NDC 2002–04; Chair NHS Sickle Cell and Thalassaemia Screening Programme from 2001; Bp of Birmingham 2002–05; Midlander of the Year 2003; Vc-Chair Commn on Urban Life and Faith; Pres Youth for Christ, Eng and Nat YMCA; Abp of York from 2005; LLD (Hon), Univ of Leic 2005; Hon Fell Selw Coll Cam 2005; Chan York St Jo Univ from 2006; Freeman City of Lon 2000; DD (Hon) Univ of Hull 2007; DL (Hon) Univ of Sheff 2007; Yorkshire Man of the Year 2007; Speaker of the Year 2007; Master Bencher (Hon) Gray's Inn 2007; Freeman City of Montego Bay 2007; Chan Univ of Cumbria from 2007; Hon Dr Birm City Univ 2008; DD (Hon) Univ of Cam 2008; DCL (Hon) Northumbria Univ 2008; DD (Hon) Univ of Nottm 2008; DD (Hon) Wycliffe Coll Toronto 2009; LLD (Hon) Teesside University 2009; DTheol (Hon) Univ of Chester 2009; Hon Dr Univ of York 2010; LLD (Hon) Univ of Leeds 2010; DD (Hon) Sewanee (University of the South) Tennessee 2010; DD (Hon) Univ of London 2010; York Tourism Awards 'York Ambassador' 2010; Sponsor York Fairness Commn from 2011
GS 1985–96; 2002– *Tel:* 01904 707021
Fax: 01904 709204
email: office@archbishopofyork.org
Web: www.archbishopofyork.org

SHAND, Mr John Alexander Ogilvie, MA, LlB (Cant), MA (Birm)
1 Old Barhouse Mews Hill Top Longdon Green, Rugeley Staffordshire, WS15 4GA [LICHFIELD] *b* 1942 *educ* Nottingham High Sch; Queen's Coll Cam; Centre for Reformation and Early Modern Studies Univ Birm; *CV* Barrister Midland and Ox Circuit, 1965–69, 1972–81; Tutor and Fellow Queen's Coll Cam 1969–72; Chair Ind Tribunal 1981–88; Circuit Judge 1988–2005; Chan Dioc of Lich and S'well
GS 2010– *Tel:* 01543492662
email: jaoshand@yahoo.co.uk

SHARPLES, Ven David,
2 The Walled Gardens Ewhurst Avenue Swinton M7 0FR [ARCHDEACON OF SALFORD; MANCHESTER] *b* 1958 *CV* Adn of Salford from 2010
Tel: 0161 794 2331
0161 708 9366
email: archdeaconsalford@manchester.anglican.org

SHEFFIELD AND ROTHERHAM, Archdeacon of. See SNOW, Ven Martyn James

SHEFFIELD, Bishop of. See CROFT, Rt Revd Dr Steven John Lindsey

SHEFFIELD, Dean of. See BRADLEY, Very Revd Peter Edward

SHELLEY, Dr (John Richard) Jack, MA, MB BChir, MRCGP
Shobrooke Park Crediton Devon EX17 1DG [EXETER] *b* 1943 *educ* King's Sch, Cam Univ; St Mary's Univ; Ex Univ; SWMTC Rdr Cert; *CV* Chair Devon Local Med Cttee 1999–2002; Partner South Molton Health Centre 1974–2003; Farmer 1974; Med Prac 1967; Rdr Ex 2009; M Ex Dioc Syn from 2002; M Counc Worship & Min Ex from 2003; Lay Chair Cadbury Deanery from 2005; Rdr from 2009
GS 2009– *Tel:* 01363775153 07971136901
email: jack@shobrookepark.com

SHERBORNE, Archdeacon of. See TAYLOR, Ven Paul Stanley

SHERBORNE, Suffragan Bishop of. See KINGS, Rt Revd Graham Ralph

SHERIFF, Canon Suzanne, BA
78 Station Rd Tadcaster LS24 9JR [YORK] *b* 1963 *educ* Dorchester Gr Sch for Girls; Trin Coll Bris; *CV* Par Dn St Nich Hull 1987–91; Par Dn/C St Aidan Hull 1991–96; TV Marfleet 1996–2000; TR Marfleet 2000–07; M York Dioc Syn; M Coll of Cans York Minster from 2001; V Tadcaster and Newton Kyme from 2007
GS 2005– *Tel:* 01937 833394
email: sue.sheriff@virgin.net

SHERWOOD, Suffragan Bishop of. See PORTER, Rt Revd Anthony

SHOREY, Mr Kenneth John, BA, Cert Ed
30 Pool Road Hartley Wintney Hook RG27 8RD [WINCHESTER] *b* 1947 *educ* Greenford Gr Sch; Borough Road Coll; OU; *CV* Headteacher, Court Moor Sch, Hampshire, 1987–2005; Chief Exec Positive Parenting Publ & Programmes, 2006–09; Project Dir Care for the Family, 2009–10; Sessional Consultant for Hampshire CC Children's Serv from 2005
GS 2010– *Tel:* 01252 843803 07931 511849
email: ken@shoreyfamily.co.uk

SHREWSBURY, Area Bishop of. See RYLANDS, Rt Revd Mark

SIMS, Ven Christopher Sidney,
1a Small Street Walsall W Midlands WS1 3PR [ARCHDEACON OF WALSALL] *b* 1949 *educ* Bramcote Hills Gr Sch; Chester Coll of Ed; Wycliffe Hall; *CV* AC St Jo the Evang Walmley 1977–80; V St Cyprian w St Chad Hay Mill Birm 1980–88; V St Michael Stanwix w St Mark Belah Carl 1988–96; RD Carl 1990–95; Hon Can Carl Cathl 1991–96; P-in-c Allhallows and Torpenhow, Boltongate w Ireby and Uldale, Bassenthwaite w Isel and Setmurthy 1996–2001; TR Binsey TM 2001–03; V Shrewsbury Abbey and St Peter Monkmoor 2003–09; RD Shrewsbury 2008–09; Adn of Walsall from 2009
GS 2010– *Tel:* 01922 707861, 01922 709092
07527 252752 (Mobile)
Fax: 01922 700951
email: archdeacon.walsall@lichfield.anglican.org

SINCLAIR, Rt Revd (Gordon) Keith, MA, BA
Bishop's Lodge 67 Bidston Rd Prenton CH43 6TR [SUFFRAGAN BISHOP OF BIRKENHEAD; CHESTER] *b* 1952 *educ* Trin Sch Croydon; Ch Ch Ox; Cranmer Hall Dur; *CV* C Ch Ch Summerfield 1984–88; pt Chapl, Children's Hosp Birm; V SS Pet & Paul Aston juxta Birm 1988–2001; AD Aston 2000–01; V H Trin Cov 2001–06; Bp of Birkenhead from 2007; M Bp's Coun and Dioc Syn, Ches; Trustee/Chair Ches DBE; Gov Bp's High Sch Ches; Trustee Historic Cheshire Chs Preservation Trust; Trustee Chs Together in Merseyside; Chair Gov Body for Bp's High Sch; Chair CPAS Coun of Reference; Trustee, Five Talents; Coun of Reference True Freedom Trust *Tel:* 0151 652 2741
Fax: 0151 651 2330
email: bpbirkenhead@chester.anglican.org

SINCLAIR, Ven Jane Elizabeth Margaret, MA, BA
Sanderlings Willingham Rd Market Rasen LN8 3RE [ARCHDEACON OF STOW AND LINDSEY; LINCOLN] *b* 1956 *educ* Westonbirt Sch Tetbury; St Hugh's Coll Ox; Nottm Univ; St Jo Coll Nottm; *CV* Dss St Paul w St Jo Herne Hill and St Sav Ruskin Park 1983–86; Lect in Liturg and Chapl St Jo Coll Nottm 1986–93; Can Res and Prec Sheff Cathl 1993–2003; M Liturg Commn 1986–2001; M Archbishops' Commn on Ch Music 1989–1992; M Cathl Fabric Commn for Eng 2001–10; V Rotherham Minster (All SS) 2003–07; Adn of Stow and Lindsey from 2007
GS 1995–2007 *Tel:* 01673 849896
07809 521995 (Mobile)
email: archdeacon.stowlindsey@lincoln.anglican.org

SINCLAIR, Revd John Robert,
The Vicarage High Street Newburn Newcastle NE15 8LQ [NEWCASTLE] *b* 1958 *educ* Walbottle High Sch; Oak Hill Th Coll; *CV* C Ponteland S Mary Newcastle 1992–96; V Longbenton St Mary Magdalene Newcastle 1996–2001; V Newburn St Michael & All Angels Newcastle from 2001; AD Newcastle West from 2007; Hon Can Newcastle Cathl from 2008; Chair House of Clergy from 2009; M Evang Task Group 2001; M Dioc Fin Strategy Grp 2009
GS 2010– *Tel:* 0191 2290 522 07746 743857
email: johnsinclair247@aol.com

SKILTON, Ven Christopher John, MA, Cert Theol, MA (Miss & Min)
7 Hoadly Rd London SW16 1AE [ARCHDEACON OF LAMBETH; SOUTHWARK] *b* 1955 *educ* Latymer Upper Sch Hammersmith; Magd Coll Cam; Wycliffe Hall Ox; *CV* C St Mary Ealing 1980–84; C Newborough w Leigh St Jo Wimborne 1984–88; TV St Paul Gt Baddow 1988–95; TR Sanderstead 1995–2003; RD Croydon S 2000–03; Adn of Lambeth from 2004 *Tel:* 020 8545 2440 (Office)
020 8769 4384 (Home)
07903 704506 (Mobile)
Fax: 020 8545 2441 (Office)
email: chris.skilton@southwark.anglican.org

SLACK, Mr Stephen, MA
Church House Great Smith Street London SW1P 3AZ [REGISTRAR AND CHIEF LEGAL ADVISER TO THE GENERAL SYNOD, JOINT REGISTRAR OF THE PROVINCES OF CANTERBURY AND YORK, CHIEF LEGAL ADVISER TO THE ARCHBISHOPS' COUNCIL AND OFFICIAL SOLICITOR TO THE CHURCH COMMISSIONERS] *b* 1954 *educ* Aylesbury Gr Sch; Ch Ch Ox; *CV* Solicitor in private practice 1979–84; Sen Lawyer Charity Commn Liv 1984–89; Hd Legal Section Charity Commn Taunton 1989–2001; Hd Legal Office and Chief Legal Adv to AC and GS from 2001, Registrar GS, Jt Registrar Provinces

WHO'S WHO

Cant and York, M Legal Adv Commn from 2001; Official Solicitor to Ch Commrs from 2009
Tel: 020 7898 1366
Fax: 020 7898 1718
020 7898 1721
email: stephen.slack@churchofengland.org

SLATER, Mr Colin Stuart, MBE
11 Muriel Rd Beeston Nottingham NG9 2HH [SOUTHWELL AND NOTTINGHAM] *b* 1934 *educ* Belle Vue Gr Sch Bradf; *CV* Chief PRO Notts Co Coun 1969–87, Severn Trent Water 1987–89, Notts Co Cricket Club 1989–95; Chair BBC Radio Nottm Adv Coun 1975–79; former Chair Soc of Co PROs and IPR Local Govt Grp; M Coun Inst of PR 1986–90; JP 1977–2004; Chair Nottingham Magistrates 2003 and 2004; Chair Notts Courts Bd 2005–07; Chair Notts-Derbys Courts Bd 2007–12; PR Consult and freelance broadcaster from 1995; M Bp's Coun, Fin Cttee; Vc-Chair Chr Stewardship Cttee of AC from 1999; M Coun St Jo (Nottm) Coll from 2006 and its Stg Ctee from 2008, Vc Chair from 2010; awarded Freedom of Borough of Broxtowe (Notts) 2010
GS 1990–
Tel and Fax: 0115 925 7532 07919 008788 (Mobile)
email: colinslater@mac.com

SLATER, Ven Paul John, MA, BA
Woodlands Netherghyll Lane Cononley Keighley BD20 8PB [ARCHDEACON OF CRAVEN; BRADFORD] *b* 1958 *educ* Bradf Gr Sch; Corpus Christi Ox; St Jo Coll Dur; *CV* C St Andr Keighley 1984–88; P-in-c St Jo Cullingworth 1988–93; Dir Lay Trg Foundn Course 1988–93; PA to Bp of Bradf 1993–95; Wrdn of Rdrs 1992–96; R St Mich Haworth 1995–2001; Bp's Officer for Min from 2001; Adn of Craven from 2005
Tel: 01535 635113 (home) 01535 650533 (office)
Fax: 01535 635113
email: paul.slater@bradford.anglican.org

SLATER, Mrs Susan Gay, Cert Ed, DGA
3 Church St Spalding PE11 2PB [LINCOLN] *b* 1944 *educ* Ox High Sch; Homerton Coll Cam; *CV* Admin trainee/Higher Exec Officer, DHSS 1967–74; domestic admin and voluntary work 1974–94; PA to Nat Dir Leprosy Mission England and Wales 1994–2005; rtd 2005; Gen Adv S Holland CAB from 2005; M Linc Dioc HR Cttee 2005–10; Sec Elloe W Dny Syn 2005–10; M Ch & Com Fund Cttee 2005–10; Chair S Holland Fairtrade Steering Gp 2008–10; Rdr in Training, Linc Theol Sch from 2010
GS 2005– *Tel:* 01775 768286
email: sueslater@d-lweb.net

SLOMAN, Mrs Anne, BA, OBE
All Saints Cottage Bale Rd Sharrington NR24 2PF [CHAIR, CHURCH BUILDINGS COUNCIL] *b* 1944 *educ* Farlington, Horsham; St Hilda's Coll Ox; *CV* BBC journalist 1967–2003; ed five gen election programmes 1974–92; asst ed Today Programme 1981–82; ed Special Current Affairs 1983–93; dep hd weekly TV and radio programmes 1994–96; M Coun RIIA 1992–2002; BBC's Chief Political Adv 1996–2003; OBE 2004; M McLean Wkg Pty, Clergy Terms of Service from 2003; M C of E Broadcasting Grp 2004–09; M Communications Panel from 2004; Trustee Norfolk Com Foundn from 2005; Vc-Chair Norfolk Com Foundn from 2006; Co-ord Ch Buildings Campaign 2006–09; Appt M Abp's Coun 2002–09; Chair Ch Buildings Coun from 2009
Tel: 01263 862291 (Norfolk) 020 7898 1010 (Office)
07717 772174 (Mobile)
Fax: 01263 862291 (Home)
email: annesloman@hotmail.com

SMITH, Rt Revd Dr Alan Gregory Clayton, BA, MA, Ph D, Hon DD (Birm)
Abbey Gate House Abbey Mill Lane St Albans AL3 4HD [BISHOP OF ST ALBANS] *b* 1957 *educ* Trowbridge High Sch for Boys; Birm Univ; Wycliffe Hall Th Coll; Univ of Wales, Bangor; *CV* C St Lawr Pudsey 1981–82, w St Paul 82–84; Chapl Lee Abbey 1984–90; Dioc Missr and Exec Sec Lichf Dioc BMU 1990–97; TV St Matt Walsall 1990–97; Adn of Stoke-upon-Trent 1997–2001; Canon of Lichfield Cathedral, 1997–2009; Bp of Shrewsbury 2001–09; Chair Shrops Strategic Ptnrship 2006–09; M Rural Bps Panel from 2006–09; Joint Chair Angl Meth Working Party on the Ecclesiology of Emerging Expressions of Ch from 2009; Bp of St Albans from 2009
GS 1999–2001, 2009– *Tel:* 01727 853305
Fax: 01727 846715
email: bishop@stalbans.anglican.org

SMITH, Ms Anna Louise,
69 Belgrave Road Liverpool L17 7AQ [REPRESENTATIVE OF THE CHURCH OF ENGLAND YOUTH COUNCIL] *b* 1905 *educ* Abp Blanch Sch, Liv, Hope Univ; *Tel:*
email: AnnaSmith73@hotmail.com

SMITH, Mr Christopher John Addison, BA, FCA
Lambeth Palace London SE1 7JU [CHIEF OF STAFF, LAMBETH PALACE] *b* 1949 *educ* St Pet Sch York; Univ of E Anglia; *CV* Price Waterhouse 1970–93, various trainee and mgmt posts 1970–89, Human Resources Ptnr 1989–93; Gen Sec Dioc of Lon 1993–99; Gen Mgr C. Hoare & Co. Bankers 1999–2003; M CBF, Exec, Staff Cttee, AC Fin Cttee 1995–2000; Chief of Staff, Lambeth Palace from 2003
GS 1995–2000 *Tel:* 020 7898 1200
email: chris.smith@lambethpalace.org.uk

SMITH, Very Revd Graham Charles Morell, BA
The Deanery The Close Norwich NR1 4 EG [DEAN OF NORWICH] *b* 1947 *educ* Whitgift Sch Croydon; Dur Univ; Westcott Ho Cam; *CV* C All SS Tooting Graveney, S'wark 1976–80; TV Thamesmead Ecum Par, S'wark 1980–87; TR Kidlington w.

Hampton Poyle, Ox 1987–97; R Leeds 1997–2004; Dean of Norwich from 2004 *Tel:* 01603 218308
Fax: 01603 766032
email: dean@cathedral.org.uk

SMITH, Mr Graham William, BSc, DMS
20 Parklands Wotton-under-Edge GL12 7LT [GLOUCESTER] *b* 1943 *educ* Mundella Gr Sch; Aston Univ; *CV* Principal Eng, Project Management Dept, Nat Power plc until 1992; Bursar and Clerk to Govs, Katharine Lady Berkeley's Sch 1993–96; rtd 1996; M Bp's Coun; M Dioc Syn; M IDFF; M Queen Victoria Clergy Fund; Trustee Bishop Monk Horfield Trust
GS 2005– *Tel:* 01453 842618
email: smithgra@supanet.com

SMITH, Ven Jonathan Peter,
6 Sopwell Lane St Albans Herts AL1 1RR [ARCHDEACON OF ST ALBANS] *b* 1955 *educ* Ipswich Sch; King's Coll London; Queens' Coll Cam; Westcott Ho Cam; *CV* Asst C All Saints' Gosforth 1980–82; Asst C Waltham Abbey 1982–85; Chapl The City Univ 1985–88; R Harrold and Carlton w Chellington 1988–97; V St John's Harpenden 1997–2008; Rural Dean Wheathampstead 1999–2008; Adn St Alb from 2008; St Alb Bp's Counc; St Alb Brd Patronage; St Alb Brd Fin; St Alb Miss & Pstrl Cttee; St Alb Brd Ed; St Alb Adv Cttee; St Alb Urban Forum; Residentiary Can Cathl and Abbey Ch of St Alb
GS 2010– *Tel:* 01727 818121
Fax: 01727 844469
email: archdstalbans@stalbans.anglican.org

SMITH, Mr Peter Reg, FRICS
48 The Mowbrays Framlingham Woodbridge IP3 9DL [ST EDMUNDSBURY AND IPSWICH] *b* 1946 *educ* K Edw VI Sch Southn; Coll of Estate Mgt; *CV* M Coun USPG 1991–2011; Chair Dioc Overseas Miss Grp 1997–2004; Chair Dioc Ho of Laity 1997–2000; M Bd of Miss 2001–03; M Bp's Coun and Pastl Cttee; M Vacancy-in-See Cttee; M Revision Cttee, Common Worship Ordinal; M Revision Cttee, Pastl (Amendment) Measure; M CFCE 2006–11; Lay Can St Eds Cathl 2005–11; Trustee, Queen Victoria Clergy Fund
GS 1993–
Tel: 01728 727489 07790 596502 (Mobile)
email: happyhackers@usa.net

SNOW, Ven Martyn James, BSc; BTh
34 Wilson Road Sheffiled S11 8Rn [ARCHDEACON OF SHEFFIELD AND ROTHERHAM] *b* 1968 *educ* Newcastle Royal Gr; Sheffield Univ; Wycliffe Hall Ox; *CV* C St Andrew's Brinsworth with St Mary's Catcliffe 1995–98; 1999–2001 CMS Mission Partner Dioc Guinea; 2001–10 V Christ Church Pitsmoor; Adn of Sheffield and Rotherham from 2010
Tel: 01709 309107 0772 9104792
email: archdeacons.office@sheffield.anglican.org

SODOR AND MAN, Bishop of. See PATERSON, Rt Revd Robert Mar Erskine

SODOR AND MAN, DEAN OF. See GODFREY, Very Revd Nigel Philip

SOUTHAMPTON, Suffragan Bishop of. See FROST, Rt Revd Jonathan

SOUTHEND, Archdeacon of. See LOWMAN, Ven David Walter

SOUTHERN, Rt Revd Humphrey Ivo John, MA
Repton House Church St, Lea Matlock DE4 5JP [SUFFRAGAN BISHOP OF REPTON; DERBY] *b* 1960 *educ* Harrow Sch; Ch Ch Ox; Ripon Coll Cuddesdon; *CV* C St Marg Rainham, Roch 1986–89; C Walton-on-the-Hill, Liv 1989–92; V Hale, TR Hale w. Badshot Lea, Guild 1992–99; Guild Dioc Ecum Officer 1993–99; TR Tisbury, TR Nadder Valley Tm Min, Sarum 1999–2007; RD Chalke 2000–07; Hon Can Salis Cathl 2006–07; Bp of Repton from 2007; M Guild Dioc Syn 1992–99; M Sarum Dioc Syn 2000–07; Chair Ho of Clergy, Sarum Dioc Syn 2004–07; M Sarum Dioc Pastl Cttee 2000–07; Chair Derby Dioc Pastl Cttee from 2007
Tel: 01629 534644
Fax: 01629 534003
email: bishop@repton.free-online.co.uk

SOUTHWARK, Archdeacon of, [NOT APPOINTED AT TIME OF GOING TO PRESS]

SOUTHWARK, Bishop of. See CHESSUN, Rt Revd Christopher

SOUTHWARK, Dean of. See NUNN, Very Revd Andrew Peter

SOUTHWELL AND NOTTINGHAM, Bishop of. See BUTLER, Rt Revd Paul Roger

SOUTHWELL AND NOTTINGHAM, Dean of. See GUILLE, Very Revd John Arthur

SOWERBY, Rt Revd Mark Crispin Rake, BD, AKC, MA
Bishop's House 21 Guildford Rd Horsham W Sussex RH12 1LU [AREA BISHOP OF HORSHAM; CHICHESTER] *b* 1963 *educ* Barnard Castle Sch; St Aidan & St Jo Fisher's United Sixth Form Harrogate; K Coll Lon; Lanc Univ, Coll of Resurrection, Mirfield; *CV* C Knaresborough 1987–90; C St Cuth Darwen w. St Steph Tockholes 1990–92; V St Mary Magd Accrington 1992–97; Chapl St Christopher's CE Hich Schl Accrington 1992–97; Chapl Accrington Victoria Hosp 1992–97; Asst DDO Blackb 1993–96; M Blackburn Dioc Syn; Selection Sec/Vocations Officer ABM/Min Div of AC 1997–2001; Sec Vocations Adv Sub-Cttee (ABM) then Voc Panel (Min Div); Staff M VRSC and Candidates Cttee/Panel 1997–2001; V St Wilf Harrogate 2001–04, TR from 2004; M Ripon Dioc Syn 2001–09; Asst DDO Ripon 2005–09; Dio Minl Rev Adv from 2008; M

Mirfield/NOC Jt Monitoring Body 2001–09; Bp's Insp of Colls and Courses; M Coun Coll of Ressurrection, Mirfield; Frere Trustee (Mirfield); M VRSC 2006–07; M Min Coun from 2008; TR St Wilfrid's Harrogate; M Ripon Dioc Dyn 2002–09; M Mirfield/NOC Jt Monitoring Body 2001–09; M Coun Coll of Resurrection Mirfield 2005–09; Area Bp of Horsham from 2009
GS 2005–09 *Tel:* 01403 211139 *Fax:* 01403 217349
email: bishop.horsham@diochi.org.uk

SPENCER, Mrs Caroline Sarah, BA, PGCE
Little Eggarton, Eggarton Lane Godmersham Canterbury CT4 7DY [CANTERBURY] *b* 1953 *educ* Wycombe Abbey Sch; St Hilda's Coll Ox; Lon Univ Inst of Educ; *CV* Asst Tchr Hist Sydenham High Sch 1976–80; pt Tutor Westmr Tutors Ltd 1981–84; Mother and Vol Worker for Ch and Com from 1980; M Dioc Abp's' Coun; Lay Member, Chapter of Cant Cathl; Chair, Dioc Licensed Ministries Framework; Chair Open Syn Grp
GS 1995–
Tel: 01227 731170 07947 045025 (Mobile)
email: caroline@eggarton.eclipse.co.uk

SPENCER, Dr Jonathan Page, CB, MA, DPhil
Little Eggarton, Eggarton Lane Godmersham Canterbury CT4 7DY [CHAIR, CHURCH OF ENGLAND PENSIONS BOARD] *b* 1949 *educ* Bournemouth Sch; Univ Camb; Univ Ox; *CV* DTI 1974–2002 (Principal Private Secretary 1982–3, Dir Insurance 1991–7, Dir Gen 1997–2002); LCD/DCA 2002–5 (Dir Gen Policy); Chair C of E Pensions Bd form 2009; Dep Chair, East Kent Hospitals Trust from 2007; M Gibraltar Fin Services Commn 2011; M Solicitors Regulatory Authority 2005–9; company director from 2006
GS 2009– *Tel:* 01227 731170
email: jspencer@eggarton.eclipse.co.uk

SPIERS, Canon Peter Hendry, BA, Cert Th
St Luke's Vicarage 71 Liverpool Rd Crosby Liverpool L23 5SE [LIVERPOOL] *b* 1961 *educ* Liv Coll; St Jo Coll Dur; Ridley Hall Th Coll; *CV* C St Luke Princess Drive 1986–90; TV St Pet Everton 1990–95; V St Geo Everton 1995–2005; P-in-c St Luke Crosby from 2005; AD Sefton from 2009
GS 2000– *Tel:* 0151 924 1737 07590 690780
email: pete@spiersfamily.eclipse.co.uk

SPRINGETT, Ven Robert, BTh, MA
Abbey Cottage Stables 1 Gloucester Rd Tewkesbury Gloucestershire GL20 5SS [ARCHDEACON OF CHELTENHAM] *b* 1962 *educ* Brentwood Sch; Nottm Univ; Kings Coll Lon; Lincoln Theol Coll; *CV* C St James Colchester 1989–92; C St Martin Basildon 1992–94; P-in-C South Ockendon and Belhus Park 1994–2001; AD Thurrock 1998–2001; R Wanstead 2001–10; Area Dean of Redbridge 2008–10; Adn of Cheltenham from 2010; M DAC Bd of Educ *Tel:* 01684 300067 (Home)
01452 835581 (Office)
07962 273544
email: archdchelt@glosdioc.org.uk

ST ALBANS, Archdeacon of. See SMITH, Ven Jonathan Peter

ST ALBANS, Bishop of. See SMITH, Rt Revd Alan Gregory Clayton

ST ALBANS, Dean of. See JOHN, Very Revd Jeffrey Philip Hywel

ST EDMUNDSBURY AND IPSWICH, Bishop of. See STOCK, Rt Revd (William) Nigel

ST EDMUNDSBURY, Dean of. See WARD, Very Revd Frances Elizabeth Fearn

ST GERMANS, Suffragan Bishop of. [NOT APPOINTED AT TIME OF GOING TO PRESS]

ST PAUL'S, Dean of. See ISON, Very Revd David John

STAFFORD, Area Bishop of. See ANNAS, Rt Revd Geoff

STEADMAN, Revd Mark John, LLB, MA
Trinity House 4 Chapel Court, Borough High Street London SE1 1HW [SOUTHWARK] *b* 1974 *educ* Horndean Comm Sch; Univ of Southampton; Inns of Court Sch of Law; Cam Univ; Westcott Ho Th Coll; *CV* AC S. Mary's Portsea 2002–05; P-in-C S. Philip with S. Mark Camberwell 2005–11; Area Dean Bermondsey 2008–11; Acting Area Dean Camberwell 2009–11; Chapl to Bp of Southwark from 2011; M Dioc IME Staff Team from 2005; M Legal Advisory Commn from 2011; M Porvoo Panel 2012
GS 2010– *Tel:* 0207 939 9420 07870 266553
Fax: 08432 906294
email: mark.steadman@southwark.anglican.org

STEELE, Ven Gordon John, MA
The Diocesan Office The Palace Peterborough PE1 1YB *b* 1965 *educ* Owen's Gr Sch Lon, Univ Kent, Worcester Coll Ox, Coll of the Resurrection, Mirfield; *CV* Diocesan Treasurer, Tanzania 1977–80; C St John the Baptist, Greenhill, Harrow 1984–88; part-time Chapl to Bp of Willesden 1987–92; TV, St Andrew's, Uxbridge 1988–94; V St Alban's, Northampton 1994–2001; V St John the Baptist, Peterb 2001–12; RD Peterb 2004–10; Hon Canof Peterb Cathl from 2004; Adn of Oakham from 2012 *Tel and Fax:* 01733 555271
email: archdeacon.oakham@peterborough-diocese.org.uk
Web: www.peterborough-diocese.org.uk

STEPNEY, Area Bishop of. See NEWMAN, Rt Revd Adrian

STEVENS, Mr Robin Michael, B Sc
3 Aldeburgh Way Chelmsford CM1 7PB [CHELMSFORD] *b* 1945 *educ* Chigwell Sch; Birm Univ; *CV* Eng Marconi Communication Systems 1967–79;

eng Thames Television 1979–91; Nat Stewardship Officer, AC 1992–2005; Chelmsf Borough councillor 2005–11; Dep Mayor Chelmsf 2010–11; Rdr from 1990
GS 2005– *Tel:* 01245 268042 07721 046991
email: rms@ukgateway.net

STEVENS, Rt Revd Timothy John, MA, DCL, DLitt
Bishop's Lodge 10 Springfield Rd Leicester LE2 3BD [BISHOP OF LEICESTER] *b* 1946 *educ* Chigwell Sch; Selw Coll Cam; Ripon Coll Cuddesdon; *CV* C E Ham TM 1976–79; TV St Alb Upton Park 1979–80; TR Canvey Island 1980–88; Bp of Chelmsf's Urban Officer 1988–91; Adn of West Ham 1991–95; Bp of Dunwich 1995–99; Bp of Leic from 1999; Chair Urban Bps Panel 2001–06; Chair Children's Soc 2004–10; M AC 2006–10; M Ho of Bps Standing Cttee 2006–10; Chair Westcott Ho Coun from 2007; Convenor of Lords Spiritual Ho of Lords from 2009
GS 1987–95, 1999– *Tel:* 0116 270 8985
07860 692258
Fax: 0116 270 3288
email: bishop.tim@leccofe.org

STOBART, Dr Cherida Dawn, BSc, BVSc, PhD, MRCVS
Fern Cottage 31 Pauls Causeway Congresbury North Somerset [BATH AND WELLS] *b* 1962 *educ* St Clare's Convent Sch, Glamorgan; Bryntirion Comp, Glamorgan; Bris Univ; Open Univ; Trin Coll, Bris; Vet Surgeon, Hereford, 1986–87;; *CV* Rsch Asst, Vet Med, Bris Univ 1987–88; PhD Vet Med Bris Univ 1988–1991; Post Doc Rsch Assoc, Vet Med Bris Univ 1992–93; Rsch Assoc, Social Med, 1994; Rsch Fell, Health Services Rsch, 1995–98; Rsch Manager, Med Rsch Coun (MRC) Health Services Rsch Unit, Bris Univ 1998–2000; Finance and HR Manager, MRC Health Services Rsch Unit, Bris Univl 2000–2007; MRC Clinical Trial Manager, Primary Care, Bris Uni from 2008
GS 2010– *Tel:* 01934 832188
email: cherida.hopper@bristol.ac.uk

STOBER, Revd (Brenda) Jacqueline, BSc, BA(Hons), PGCE
20 Eardisley Road Liverpool L18 0HS [LIVERPOOL] *b* 1957 *educ* Childwall Valley High Sch; Liv Univ; Lanc Univ; Leeds Univ; Northern Ordination Course; *CV* Biology tchr, Liv 1981–86; Day-care provider Canada 1992–98; Primary tchr, Sefton, 1999–2005; Special Needs tchr, Sefton, 2005–07; Stipendiary C, Emmanuel P Ch, Southport 2007–11; Stipendiary C Holy Trinity Wavertree, Liv from 2011
GS 2010– *Tel:* 0151 345 5695 07821 471269
email: jackstober@yahoo.co.uk

STOCK, Rt Revd (William) Nigel, BA, Dip Theol
Bishop's House 4 Park Rd Ipswich IP1 3ST [BISHOP OF ST EDMUNDSBURY AND IPSWICH] *b* 1950 *educ* Dur Sch; Dur Univ; Ripon Coll Cuddesdon; *CV* C St Pet Stockton 1976–79; P-in-c St Pet Taraka, PNG 1979–84; V St Mark Shiremoor 1985–91; TR N Shields 1991–98; RD Tynemouth 1992–98; Hon Can Newc Cathl 1997–98; Res Can Dur Cathl 1998–2000; Bp of Stockport 2000–07; Bp of St E & I from 2007; M Ho of Bps CME Cttee 2002–09; M Appts Cttee of C of E from 2003; Chair Local Unity Panel (CCU) 2007–09; M Min Coun from 2008; M Dioc Commn from 2008; Co-Chair Meth Angl Panel for Unity in Miss from 2009; Chair Melanesian Miss from 2009; M Ho of Lords from 2011
GS 2003– *Tel:* 01473 252829
Fax: 01473 232552
email: bishop.nigel@stedmundsbury.anglican.org
Web: www.stedmundsbury.anglican.org

STOCKPORT, Suffragan Bishop of. See ATWELL, Rt Revd Robert Ronald

STOKE-UPON-TRENT, Archdeacon of. See STONE, Ven Godfrey Owen

STOKOE, Father (Wayne) Jeffrey, Dip HE
17 Heaton Gardens Edlington DN12 1SY [SHEFFIELD] *b* 1956 *educ* Trin Ho Navigation Sch, Hull; Coll of the Resurrection, Mirfield; *CV* C St Catherine of Siena Sheff 1996–98; V St Jo the Baptist Edlington from 1999; Hon Chapl 103 (Doncaster) sqdrn ATC from 2003
GS 2009– *Tel:* 01709 858358
email: wjs@stokoej.freeserve.co.uk

STONE, Ven Godfrey Owen, MA, PGCE, Dip LRM
39 The Brackens Clayton Newcastle-under-Lyme ST5 4JL [ARCHDEACON OF STOKE-UPON-TRENT; LICHFIELD] *b* 1949 *educ* St Bart Gr Sch Newbury; Ex Coll Ox; Wycliffe Hall Ox; *CV* C Rushden with Newton Bromswold, Peterb 1981–87; Dir of Pastl Studies, Wycliffe Hall Ox 1987–92; TR Bucknall Tm Min, Lich 1992–2002; RD Stoke-upon-Trent 1998–2002; Adn of Stoke-upon-Trent from 2002
Tel: 01782 663066 07786 447115
Fax: 01782 711165
email: archdeacon.stoke@lichfield.anglican.org

STORKEY, Dr Elaine, BA, MA, DD, Ph D (Hon)
The Old School High St Coton Cambridgeshire CB23 7PL [ELY] *educ* Ossett Gr Sch; Univ Coll of Wales Abth; McMaster Univ Ontario; York Univ; *CV* Tutor in Philosophy Man Coll Ox 1967–68; Rsch Fell in Sociology Stirling Univ 1968–69; Tutor Open Univ 1976–80; Vis Lect Calvin Coll USA 1980–81; Covenant Coll USA 1981–82; Lect in Philosophy Oak Hill Th Coll 1982–87; Lect in Faculty of Social Science Open Univ 1987–91; Dir Inst for Contemporary Christianity 1992–98; Vis Lect in Theol K Coll Lon 1996–2001; Ext Mod Birkbeck Coll Lon from 1998; Scriptwriter for BBC OU; Assoc Ed 'Third Way' from 1984; Broadcaster BBC from 1987; M ACORA 1988–90; M Crown Appts Commn 1990; Vc-Pres UCCF 1987–93; M Abps' Commn on Cathl 1992–94; M Lausanne Wkg Pty on Th 1992–97; M CRAC

1993–98; Examiner Sociology of Religion Lon Univ from 1993; Trustee C of E Newspaper from 1994; Vc-Pres Cheltenham and Glouc Coll of HE from 1994; M Forum for the Future 1995–98; M Orthodox-Evang Dialogue WCC from 1996; New Coll Scholar Univ of NSW Sydney 1997; Pres Tear Fund from 1997; M Wkg Pty on Chr-Jewish Relns from 1998; Lambeth DD 1998; M John Ray Inst from 1999; Sen Rsch Fell Wycliffe Hall, Ox 2003–07; M CNC 2002–07; Visiting Prof Messiah Coll, Pennsylvania, USA summer 2005; Chair Fulcrum from 2006; columnist for Swedish newspaper 'Dagen' from 2006; Chair Ch Army Ord and Commn Review Gp 2007–08; Examiner Univ of Wales 2008
GS 1987–
Tel: 01954 212381 07969 354673 (Mobile)
email: elaine@storkey.com

STOW AND LINDSEY, Archdeacon of. See SINCLAIR, Ven Jane Elizabeth Margaret

STRAIN, Revd Christopher Malcolm, LLB, Solicitor, Cert Theol (Oxon)
St Luke's Vicarage 2 Birchwood Rd Parkstone Poole BH14 9NP [SALISBURY] *b* 1956 *educ* Aldwickbury Prep Sch; Bedford Sch; Southn Univ; Guildf Coll of Law; Wycliffe Hall; *CV* C St Jo w. Em Werrington, Peterb 1986–89; C-in-charge St Steph Broadwater, Worthing, Chich 1989–1994; TV Hampreston and Stapehill, Wimborne, Salis 1994–2000; V St Luke Parkstone from 2000; Sch gov; Chapl to Scouts and Cubs, Poole; Surrogate for Marriages; Chair Ch Together in Poole; Asst RD Poole from 2010
GS 2005– *Tel:* 01202 741030
email: cmstrain@tiscali.co.uk

STRATFORD, Ven Dr Timothy Richard, B Sc, PhD
St Martin's House 7 Peacock Lane Leicester LE1 5PZ [ARCHDEACON OF LEICESTER] *b* 1961 *educ* Knowsley Hey Comp Sch; York Univ; Wycliffe Hall Th Coll; Univ of Sheff; *CV* C Mossley Hill 1986–89; C St Helens St Helen 1989–91; Chapl to Bp of Liv 1991–94; V Gd Shep W Derby 1994–2003; TR Kirkby and TV St Chad Kirkby 2003–12; M Liturg Commn from 2006; Adn of Leicester from 2012
GS 2000– *Tel:* 0116 261 5317
Fax: 0116 261 5220
email: tim.stratford@leccofe.org

STROYAN, Rt Revd John Ronald Angus, M Theol, MA
Warwick House 139 Kenilworth Rd Coventry CV4 7AP [SUFFRAGAN BISHOP OF WARWICK; COVENTRY] *b* 1955 *educ* Harrow Sch; St Andr Univ; Q Coll Birm; Ecum Inst, Bossey, Switzerland; Univ of Wales; *CV* C St Pet Hillfields, Cov E Tm 1983–87; V St Matt w. St Chad Smethwick, Birm 1987–94; V Bloxham, Milcombe & S Newington, Ox 1994–2005; AD Deddington, Ox 2002–05; Bp of Warwick from 2005; Pres Com of the Cross of Nails UK from 2007; Sec W Midlands Regional Gp from 2008; M Rural Bps' Panel from 2009; Co-Moderator Chs Together in Cov and Warwickshire from 2009; M Internat Commn for Angl-Orthodox Theol Dialogue from 2009
Tel: 024 7641 2627
Fax: 024 7641 5254
email: bishop.warwick@CovCofE.org

STUART, Rt Revd Ian Campbell, MA, BA, Cert Ed, Dip Ed Admin
Pro Vice-Chancellor's Office Liverpool Hope University Hope Park Taggart Avenue Liverpool L16 9JD [ASSISTANT BISHOP, LIVERPOOL] *educ* New England Univ (NSW); Melbourne Univ; St Barn Coll of Min, Townsville; *CV* Australia 85–99; Asst Bp and Bp Administrator N Queensland 1992–99; Chapl Liv Hope 1999–2001; Asst Bp Liv from 1999; Provost Hope Park 2001–05; Asst Vc-Chan Liv Hope Univ from 2005 *Tel:* 0151 291 3547
Fax: 0151 291 3669
email: Stuarti@hope.ac.uk

STURGESS, Mrs Sheridan Jane, MA (Cantab) FCA
Holywell Pengover Road Liskeard Cornwall PL14 3NW [TRURO] *b* 1955 *educ* Kidderminster H Sch; Newnham Coll, Cam; *CV* Dioc Sec, Truro, 2002–10; Stewardship Adv, Truro 1997–2002; Parish Admin, St Martin's Ch, Liskeard 1994–97; Self-employed Chartered Accountant, Sheridan Sturgess & Co 1983–94; M Fin Cttee 2008–10 and 2011; M Ch & Comm Fund 2005–09; M Inter-Dioc Fin Forum 2002–10
GS 2010– *Tel:* 01579 346411 07793 805685
email: sheri.sturgess@gmail.com

SUDBURY, Archdeacon of, JENKINS, Ven Dr David Harold

SUFFOLK, Archdeacon of. See MORGAN, Ven Ian David John

SUGDEN, Canon Dr Christopher Michael Neville, MA, M Phil, PhD
36 North Hinksey Village Oxford OX2 0NA [OXFORD] *b* 1948 *educ* K Sch Roch; St Pet Coll Ox; Nottm Univ; Westmr Coll Ox; St Jo Coll Nottm; *CV* C St Geo Leeds 1974–77; relig programmes producer, BBC Radio Leeds 1977; Asst Presbyter St Jo Bangalore, Ch of S India 1978–83; Asst Dir Assoc for Theol Educ by Extension, India 1978–83; Assoc Dir EFICOR Education and Training Unit, India 1979–83; Registrar and Dir of Academic Affairs, Ox Cen for Miss Studies 1983–2001; Exec Dir OCMS 2001–04; Exec Sec Angl Mainstream Internat from 2004; Trustee/Chair of Trustees of Traidcraft 1986–2007; M MPA Coun 2006–10; Can St Luke's Cathl, Jos, Nigeria from 2001; Trustee and Sec Angl Internat Devel from 2008; Dir and Sec Fell of Confessing Angls UK and Ireland from 2009; Dir and Sec Oxford Centre for Religion and Public Life from 2009; Dir and Sec Oxford Centre for Training, Reseach, Advocacy and Dialogue from 2009; Dir and Sec St

Augustine's Soc from 2010; Hon Can St Anselm's Cathl, Sunyani, Ghana from 2010; Bp's Commissary for Diocs of NE Caribbean and Aruba, West Indies and Sunyani, Ghana, West Africa
GS 2005–2010, 2011–
Tel: 01865 883388 07808 297043
Fax: 01865 790932
email: sugdenmainstream@gmail.com
Web: www.anglican-mainstream.net

SULLIVAN, Ven Nicola Ann, BTh, SRN, RM
6 The Liberty Wells BA5 2SU [ARCHDEACON OF WELLS; BATH AND WELLS] *b* 1958 *educ* Ips Convent of Jesus and Mary; Mills Gr Sch, Framlingham; St Bart's Hosp; Bris Maternity Hosp; Wycliffe Hall Ox; *CV* C St Anne Earlham, Norw 1995–99; Assoc V Bath Abbey 1999–2002; Subdean Wells Cathl 2003–07; Bp's Chapl and Pastl Asst 2002–07; Adn of Wells and Res Can Wells Cathl from 2007; M Norw Dioc Syn 1997–99; M B & W Dioc Syn, Bp's Coun, DBF
Tel: 01749 685147
Fax: 01749 679755
email: adwells@bathwells.anglican.org

SUNDERLAND, Archdeacon of. See BAIN, Ven (John) Stuart

SURREY, Archdeacon of. See BEAKE, Ven Stuart Alexander

SUTCH, Ven (Christopher) David, AKC, TD
St Andrew's Chaplaincy, Oficina 1 Edf Jupiter, Avda Nuestro Padre Jesus Cautivo 74 Los Boliches Fuengirola 29640 [ARCHDEACON OF GIBRALTAR] *b* 1947 *educ* St John's Sch Leatherhead; King's Coll Lon; St Augustine's Theo Coll Cant; *CV* C Hartcliffe 1970–75; T V Dorcan 1975–79; V Alveston 1979–89; V Cainscross w Selsley 1999–2007; Chapl Costa Del Sol (East) 2007–08; Adn Gibraltar from 2008
Tel and Fax: 0034 952 580 600 0034 617 577 391
email: frdavid@standrews-cofe-spain.com

SUTCLIFFE, Mr Tom (James Thomas), MA
12 Polworth Rd Streatham London SW16 2EU [SOUTHWARK] *b* 1943 *educ* Prebendal Sch Chich; Hurstpierpoint Coll; Magd Coll Ox; *CV* Engl tchr Central Tutorial Sch for Young Musicians (now Purcell Sch) 1964–65; Countertenor lay-clerk Westmr Cathl 1966–70; Mgr Musica Reservata 1966–69; performer with Schola Polyphonica, Pro Cantione Antiqua, Musica Reservata, Concentus Musicus, Vienna and Darmstadt Opera 1966–70; Advertisement Mgr and Ed 'Music and Musicians' magazine 1968–73; Sub-ed, opera critic, dep arts ed, dep obits ed 'Guardian' 1973–96; Opera Critic 'Evening Standard' 1996–2002; Leverhulme Fell 1991, 2005; Hon Fell Rose Bruford Coll from 2006; M Exec Cttee Affirming Catholicism 1996–2002; Chair Music Section of Critics' Circle 1999–2009; Pres of Critic's Circle 2010–12; dramaturg in Brussels and Vienna from 1998; M Cathls Fabric Commn for Eng 2002–11; M Editorial Advisory Board of The Bridge (Southwark) since 1995; columnist in New Directions since 2010
GS 1990–
Tel: 020 8677 5849 020 86777939 07815 101314
Fax: 020 8677 7939
email: tomsutcliffe@email.msn.com

SUTTON, Mrs Debbie (Deborah Margaret), BSc, PG Dip Dietetics
2 Taswell Rd Southsea PO5 2RG [PORTSMOUTH] *b* 1957 *educ* Walthamstow Hall, Sevenoaks; Chelsea Coll, Lon Univ; *CV* Dietitian, Portsm Hosps NHS Trust 1981–98; Project Dietician from 2008
GS 2005–10, 2010– *Tel:* 023 9275 6926
email: deb2tas@hotmail.com

SWINDON, Suffragan Bishop of. See RAYFIELD, Rt Revd Dr Lee Stephen

SWINSON, Mrs Margaret Anne, MA, ACA, CTA
46 Glenmore Ave Liverpool L18 4QF [LIVERPOOL] *b* 1957 *educ* Alice Ottley Sch Worc; Liv Univ; *CV* Accountant (Tax Specialist); M (Vc-Chair) CCU from 2006; Mod CTBI from 2006; M ACC from 2012; GS Stg Cttee 1991–97; M BSR 1990–95; Chair Race and Com Relns Cttee 1990–95; Trustee CUF 1987–97; M CTBI; C of E Delegate to WCC Canberra 1991; M CBF 1996–98; M Bd of Miss 2001–03; M CCU from 2006; Mod CTBI from 2006
GS 1985– *Tel:* 0151 724 3533
email: maggie@swinsonfamily.net

SWITZERLAND, Archdeacon in. See POTTER, Ven Peter Maxwell

SYKES, Revd Clare Mary, BA
The Vicarage 28 Church Lane Bromyard Herefordshire HR7 4DZ [HEREFORD] *b* 1961 *educ* Beaconsfield Sch; St. John's Th Coll; WEMTC; *CV* M&S Mgmnt trainee 1980–83; Tear Fund, PA, 1983–87; The Benefice of Tupsley w Hampton Bp, Dioc Heref, Stipendiary AC, 1996–2001; The Benefice of Bromyard & Stoke Lacy, Self-Supporting Assoc Min from 2001; NHS Chapl Bromyard Comm Hosp from 2001; Rural Dean of Bromyard from 2005
GS 2010 *Tel:* 01885 482438
email: clare@thesykes.plus.com

SYKES, Mr John Nicholas, MA
Tower Place West London EC3R 5BU [CHURCH COMMISSIONER] *b* 1959 *educ* Bradford Gr Sch; Jes Coll Ox; *CV* Investment Consult; Baillie, Gifford & Co Ltd 1980–84; Baring Asset Mgt 1984–97; Sen Consult William M Mercer Investment from 1997; Ch Commr from 2001; M Assets Cttee and Securities Grp *Tel and Fax:* 020 7178 3268
email: nick.sykes@mercer.com

SYKES, Rt Revd Stephen Whitefield, MA, DD (Cam), Hon DD (Zurich), Hon DD (Virginia Theol Sem)
Ingleside Whinney Hill Durham DH1 3BE [HONORARY ASSISTANT BISHOP, DURHAM] *b* 1939 *educ* Bris

WHO'S WHO

Gr Sch; Monkton Combe Sch; St Jo Coll Cam; Harvard Univ; Ripon Hall Th Coll; *CV* Asst Lect Div Cam Univ 1964–68; Fell and Dean St Jo Coll Cam 1964–74; Lect 1968–74; Van Mildert Prof Dur Univ 1974–85; Can Res Dur Cathl 1974–85; Regius Prof Div Cam Univ 1985–90; Bp of Ely 1990–99; Prin St Jo Coll Dur 1999–2006; Prof Theol Dur Univ; Asst Bp Dur; Chair Doct Commn 1997–2005
GS 1990–99 *Tel:* 0191 384 6465
Fax: 0191 375 0637

TAN, Dr Chik Kaw, B Pharm, MSc, PhD, MRPharmS, PGCMedEd
12 Montfort Place Westlands Newcastle-under-Lyme ST5 2HE [LICHFIELD] *b* 1956 *educ* Anglo-Chinese Sch, Ipoh, Malaysia; Bath Univ; Aston Univ; Keele Univ; *CV* Pres Bath Univ Chr Union 1979–80; Adv Bris Chinese Chr Fellowship 1981–86; Prayer Grp leader, Newcastle-under-Lyme OMF Prayer Grp 1986–95; M OMF Internat 1996–2002; Assoc Pastor, Surabaya (Indonesia) Internat Chr Fellowship 2001–02; M Preaching Tm, St Jas Audley from 1987; Hon Sen Lect Keele Univ from 2005; M Newc Dny Syn; M Lich Dioc Syn; M N Staffs Local Rsch Ethics Cttee 2202–2008; GS 2008–2010
GS 2005– *Tel:* 01782 441604
email: ck11x@yahoo.ie

TANN, Prof Jennifer, BA; PhD
Thanet House High Street Chalford Stroud GL6 8DH [GLOUCESTER] *b* 1939 *educ* Badminton Sch; Man Univ; Leic Univ; *CV* Prof Innovation, Birm Univ, 1989–2008; Dir Continuing Ed, Univ Newcastle 1986–89; R Aston Univ 1974–86; Lec Aston Univ 1969–74; Prof Emerita, Birm Univ from 2008; Management Consultant, Caret Ltd from 1992
GS 2010– *Tel:* 01453 884142
email: innovation.jt@media-maker.com

TATTERSALL, Mr Geoffrey Frank, MA, QC
2 The Woodlands Lostock Bolton BL6 4JD [MANCHESTER] *b* 1947 *educ* Man Gr Sch; Ch Ch Ox; *CV* Barrister; Called to Bar Lincoln's Inn 1970; Bencher 1997; In practice Nn Circuit from 1970; Recorder Crown Court from 1989; QC from 1992; Called to Bar NSW 1992; SC from 1995; Judge of Appeal IOM from 1997; Deputy High Court Judge from 2003; Lay Chair Bolton Dny Syn 1993–2002; Chair Ho of Laity Dioc Syn 1994–2003; M Fees Adv Commn from 1995; M Strg Cttee Clergy Discipline Measure from 1996; M Bp's Coun; M DBF and Trust and Fin Cttee till 2004; Chair Stg Orders Cttee GS from 1999; Chan of Carl Dioc from 2003; Hon Lay Can Manch Cathl 2003; Chan Manch Dioc from 2004; Dep V-Gen S & Man 2004–08; External Reviewer of decisions of Dir of Fair Access from 2005; Chair Disciplinary Tribunals, Clergy Discipline Measure from 2006; Chair Revision Cttee, draft C of E Marriage Measure 2006–07; Chair Revision Cttee, draft Eccl Officer (Terms of Service) Measure 2007–08; M Strg and Revisions Cttee for draft C of E Bps and Ps (Consecration and Ord of Women) Measure from 2009; M Worshipful Co of Par Clerks from 2009; Par Clerk St George-in-the-East
GS 1995– *Tel:* 01204 846265
Fax: 01204 849863
email: gftqc@hotmail.co.uk

TAUNTON, Archdeacon of. See REED, Ven John Peter Cyril

TAUNTON, Suffragan Bishop of. See MAURICE, Rt Revd Peter David

TAVINOR, Very Revd Michael Edward, MA, MMus, MTh, ARCO, PGCE
The Deanery College Cloisters Cathedral Close Hereford HR1 2NG [DEAN OF HEREFORD] *b* 1953 *educ* Bishopshalt Sch Hillingdon, Middx; Univ Coll Dur; Em Coll Cam; K Coll Lon; Ripon Coll Cuddesdon; Univ Wales: Lampeter; *CV* C St Pet Ealing Lon 1982–85; Prec, Sacrist and Min Can Ely Cathl 1985–90; P-in-c Stuntney Ely 1987–90; V Tewkesbury with Walton Cardiff Glouc 1990–2002; V Twyning Glos 1999–2002; Hon Can Glouc Cathl 1997–2002; Dean of Hereford from 2002; M Dioc Syn from 2002; Pres Ch Music Soc 2005; Hon Fell Guild of Ch Musicians from 2006
Tel: 01432 374203
Fax: 01432 374220
email: dean@herefordcathedral.org

TAYLOR, Very Revd Charles William, BA, MA, Hon FGCM
The Deanery Minster Precincts Peterborough PE1 1XS [DEAN OF PETERBOROUGH] *b* 1953 *educ* St Paul's Cathl Choir Sch; Marlborough Coll; Selwyn Coll Cam; Cuddesdon Coll Ox; Ch Divinity Sch of Pacific, Graduate Theol Union, Berkeley, Calif USA; *CV* C Cen Wolverhampton TM 1976–79; Chapl Westmr Abbey (Minor Can) 1979–84; V Stanmore w. Oliver's Battery, Winch 1984–90; R N Stoneham & Bassett, Southn 1990–95; Can Res and Prec, Lich Cathl 1995–2007; Dean of Peterb from 2007; M Lich Dioc Liturg Cttee 1976–79; M Winch Dioc Liturg Cttee 1984–95; Chair Lich Dioc Worship Team 1995–2006; M Cathls Liturg and Music Cttee 1996–2007; Gov King's Sch Peterb, Oakham Sch, Uppingham Sch from 2007; M Peterb City Com Cohesion Bd from 2008; Dir Peterb Culture & Leisure Trust from 2010; Chair Cathedrals Plus from 2011
GS 310512 *Tel:* 01733 562780
email: charles.taylor@peterborough-cathedral.org.uk

TAYLOR, Ven Paul Stanley, B Ed, M Th
Aldhelm House Rectory Lane West Stafford Dorchester DT2 8AB [ARCHDEACON OF SHERBORNE; SALISBURY] *b* 1953 *educ* Lodge Farm Co Sec Sch; Redditch Co High Sch; Westmr Coll Ox; Westcott Ho Cam; *CV* C St Steph Bush Hill Park 1984–88; V St Andr Southgate 1988–97; Asst Dir POT

1987–94, Dir 1994–2000, 2002–04; V St Mary & Ch Ch Hendon 1997–2004; AD W Barnet 2000–04; Assoc Tutor NTMTC 2001–04; Adn of Sherborne from 2004 *Tel:* 01305 269074
07796 691203 (Mobile)
Fax: 01305 269074
email: adsherborne@salisbury.anglican.org

TERRETT, Group Captain Paul Everard, OBE, LLB
Idle Cottage Sharptor Liskeard PL14 5AT [TRURO] *b* 1934 *educ* Cotham Gr Sch; Bris Univ; *CV* Dny lay Chair from 1996; Can Emer Truro Cathl; Chair Truro DBF 2003–06, Vc-Chair from 2006; M Bp's Coun, DBF, Patr, Pastl and Glebe Ctees, DBE
GS 2005– *Tel:* 01579 362741
email: terretts@sharptor.co.uk

TEWKESBURY, Suffragan Bishop of. **See WENT, Rt Revd John Stewart**

THEODORESON, Mr Ian, FCA
Church House Great Smith St London SW1P 3AZ [CHIEF FINANCE OFFICER, NATIONAL CHURCH INSTITUTIONS] *educ* Sen Mgr Ernst & Young 1977–87; Fin Dir Save the Children 1987–95; Dir Corporate Resources Barnardo's 1995–2009; Chief Finance Officer, NCIs from 2009;
Tel: 020 7898 1795
email: ian.theodoreson@churchofengland.org

THETFORD, Suffragan Bishop of. **See WINTON, Rt Revd Alan Peter**

THOMAS, Ven Paul Wyndham, BA; MA; BA; Cert Theol
Archdeacon's House The Vicarage Tong, Shifnal TF11 8PW [ARCHDEACON OF SALOP] *b* 1955 *educ* Cardiff High Sch; Oriel Coll Ox; Wycliffe Hall Ox; *CV* C Llangynwyd with Maesteg 1979–85; TV Langport Area churches 1985–90; P-in-C Thorp Arch W Walton and Clergy Training Off Dioc York 1990–93 V Nether w Upper Poppleton 1993–2004; P-in-C Doxey and Par Dev Adv 2004–11; Adn of Salop from 2011; DAC; Bldngs and Benefices Cttee; Glebe Cttee; Bp's Coun; Dioc Syn
Tel: 01902 372622
Fax: 01902 374060
email: archdeacon.salop@lichfield.anglican.org

THOMAS, Revd Rod (Roderick Charles Howell), B Sc, Cert Th
St Matthew's Vicarage 3 Sherford Rd Elburton Plymouth PL9 8DQ [EXETER] *b* 1954 *educ* Ealing Gr Sch for Boys; LSE; Wycliffe Hall Th Coll ; *CV* Dir Employment Affairs CBI 1987–91; C St Paul Stonehouse Plymouth 1993–95; C St Andr Plymouth 1995–99; P-in-c St Matt Elburton 1999–2005, V from 2005; Chair Reform; M BM 2001–03; M Wkg Pty on Sen Ch Appts from 2005; M CPAS Coun of Reference from 2005
GS 2000– *Tel:* 01752 402771
email: rod.thomas@elburtonchurch.com

THOMAS-BETTS, Dr Anna, MBE, MA, Ph D
68 Halkingcroft Langley Slough SL3 7AY [OXFORD] *b* 1941 *educ* Christava Mahilalayam, Alwaye, S India; Madras Chr Coll, Madras Univ; Keele Univ; *CV* Lect in Physics Madras Chr Coll 1960–62; Post-Doctoral Rsch Asst Imp Coll Lon 1966–74; Lect in Geophysics Imp Coll Lon 1974–92, Sen Lect 1992–2001; Coll Tutor 1998–2010; M CCU 1991–96; M CBF 1996–99; M BSR 2000–02; M MPA from 2003; M Gov Body of Ripon Coll Cuddesdon from 2006; Chair Independent Monitoring Bd, Colnbrook Immigration Removal Cen f2004–09; Chair Forum of Chairs of Independent Monitoring Bds at Immigration Removal Cen 2007–08; Rep for immigration detention estate on Nat Coun IMBs from 2009
GS 1990– *Tel:* 01753 822013 (Home)
email: anna.t_b@btinternet.com

THOMPSON, Mr Roy, AIBD
May Rose Cottage Sheriff Hutton York YO60 6SS [YORK] *b* 1937 *educ* High Storrs Gr Sch Sheff; Sheff Coll of Art; Guildf Sch of Art; *CV* Construction Marketing Consult, CBC; Sec, Open Syn Grp; CRC YH Culture Task Grp; Trustee Chs Tourism Assoc
GS 2000–10 *Tel:* 01347 878644
07779 095273 (Mobile)
email: roythompson2@btinternet.com

THOMSON, Canon Celia Stephana Margaret, MA
3 Miller's Green Gloucester GL1 2BN [GLOUCESTER] *b* 1955 *educ* St Swithun's Winch 1967–71; Ox Univ; Salisbury and Wells Theol Coll; *CV* C St Barnabas Southfields, S'wark 1991–95; V Ch Ch W Wimbledon, S'wark 1995–2003; Tutor in Ethics, SEITE 1995–2000; Vocations Adv Lambeth Adnry 1995–2000; Bp's Adv from 2007; Can Pastor Glouc Cath from 2003; M CDC and Cathls Fabric Commn for England from 2011
GS 2008– *Tel:* 01452 415824
email: cthomson@gloucestercathedral.org.uk

THOMSON, Rt Revd David, MA, D Phil, FRSA, FSA, FRHistS
14 Lynn Road Ely CB6 1DA [SUFFRAGAN BISHOP OF HUNTINGDON; ELY] *b* 1952 *educ* K Edw VII Sch Sheffield; Keble Coll Ox; Selwyn Coll Cam; Westcott Ho Cam; *CV* C Maltby 1981–84; TV Banbury 1984–94; TR Cockermouth 1994–2002; Chair Dioc Children and Young People's Cttee; Bp's Adv for Healthcare Chapl, Team and Grp Mins and Deliverance Min; Archdeacon of Carlisle and Can Res Carl Cathl 2002–08; Bp Huntingdon from 2008; Hon Can Ely Cathl from 2008
Tel: 01353 662137
07771 864550 (Mobile)
Fax: 01353 669357
email: bishop.huntingdon@ely.anglican.org
Web: bpdt.wordpress.com

THORNTON, Rt Revd Tim (Timothy) Martin, BA, MA
Lis Escop Feock Truro TR3 6QQ [BISHOP OF TRURO] *b* 1957 *educ* Devonport High Sch for Boys; Southn Univ; St Steph Ho Ox; K Coll Lond; *CV* C Todmorden 1980–82; P-in-c Walsden 1982–85; Lect Univ of Wales (Cardiff) 1985–87; Chapl 1985–86; Sen Chapl 1986–87; Bp's Chapl Wakef 1987–91; DDO Wakef 1988–91; Bp's Chapl Lon 1991–94; Dep P in O 1992–2001; Prin N Thames Minl Tr Course 1994–98; V Kensington St Mary Abbots w S Geo, Gov St Mary Abbots C of E Primary Sch, Chair Campden Charities 1998–2001; AD Kensington 2000–01; K Coll Theol Trustee; Area Bp of Sherborne 2001–08; Trustee BRF; Bp Truro from 2009; Chair The Children's Society
Tel: 01872 862657
Fax: 01872 862037
email: bishop@truro.anglican.org

THRELFALL-HOLMES, Dr Miranda, MA (Cantab; BA; MA; PhD; Dip Min
6 St John's Road Durham DH1 4NU [NORTHERN UNIVERSITIES] *b* 1973 *educ* Boston High Sch; Christ's College Camb; Univ Coll Dur; Cranmer Hall; *CV* C St Gabriel's Heaton 2008–06; Chapl & Solway Fellow Univ Coll Dur from 2006, Acting Sen Tutor and Vice-Master 2011; Interim Prin Ustinov Coll Dur 2012; V St Mary Magdalene Belmont and St Laurence Pittington from 2012; AP St John's Neville's Cross 2007–12; Church of England rep on tripartite discussions with Church of Scotland and Episcopal Church of Scotland; M Exec Cttee Anglo-Nordic-Baltic theological Colloquium; Chair WATCH North-East
GS 2007–10, 2010–
Tel: 0191 386 7224 (Parish Office) 07736 365183
email: miranda.threlfall-holmes@durham.ac.uk
Web: MirandaThrelfallHolmes.blogspot.com

TICEHURST, Mrs Carol Ann,
35 South Park Lincoln LN5 8ER [LINCOLN] *b* 1938 *educ* Sincil Girls' Sch Lincoln; Lincoln Coll; *CV* Medical Sec; hdmaster's PA; Pres R Br Legion Lincs Women's Section and caseworker from 1998; M GS Catholic Grp; M Forward in Faith
GS 1995– *Tel:* 01522 580728
email: xxcaticehurst@virginmedia.com

TONBRIDGE, Archdeacon of. See MANSELL, Ven Clive Neville Ross

TONBRIDGE, Suffragan Bishop of. See CASTLE, Rt Revd Dr Brian Colin

TOOKE, Mr Stephen Edgar,
The Haven 21 Wisbech Road March Cambridgeshire PE15 8ED [ELY] *b* 1946 *educ* Queen's Sch; Isle of Ely Coll; *CV* Police Superintendent 1989–96; National Co-ord SPCK Worldwide 1996–99; Area Fundraising Mgr The Children's Soc 1999–2001; Lay Chair Ely Dioc Syn 1996– 2009; Rdr from 1997; Lay Chair Deanery Syn from 2002; M Ely Dioc Bp's Counc; M Vacancy in See Cttee and CNC. 2001 and 2010; M Coun for Min
GS 1995–2005; 2010– *Tel:* 01354652844
email: stooke@havenmarch.plus.com

TOTNES, Archdeacon of. See RAWLINGS, Ven John Edmund Frank

TOWNLEY, Ven Peter Kenneth, BA, DSPT
The Vicarage Kirkthorpe Wakefield WF1 5SZ [ARCHDEACON OF PONTEFRACT] *b* 1955 *educ* Moston Brook High Sch Man; Sheff Univ; Man Univ; Ridley Hall Th Coll; *CV* C Ch Ch Ashton-under-Lyne 1980–83; P-in-c St Hugh's CD Oldham 1983–88; R All SS Stretford 1988–96; V St Mary-le-Tower Ipswich 1996–2008; M Meissen Commn 1991–2001; RD of Ipswich from 2001; Hon Can from 2003; M Porvoo Panel from 2003; M Inter-dioc Fin Forum; Adn Pontefract from 2008; Chair Meissen Library Management Cttee in Durham
GS 1992–95, 2000–08 *Tel:* 01924 434459 (Office)
01924 896327 (Home)
Fax: 01924 364834 (Office)
01924 896327 (Home)
email: archdeacon.pontefract@wakefield.anglican.org

TOWNSEND, Mr James Edward, BA, PGCE
46 Tuscany House 19 Dickinson St Manchester M1 4LX [MANCHESTER] *b* 1987 *educ* Dean Close Sch; York Univ; *CV* Maths Tchr, Copley High Sch Stalybridge from 2009; GS 2010
GS 2010– *Tel:* 07816 779635
email: james@jamestownsend.org

TRETHEWEY, Ven Frederick Martyn, BA, Dip Th, S Th
15 Worcester Rd Droitwich WR9 8AA [ARCHDEACON OF DUDLEY; WORCESTER] *b* 1949 *educ* St Austell Gr Sch; Lon Univ; Oak Hill Th Coll; *CV* C Tollington Pk St Mark w St Anne 1978–82; C Whitehall Pk St Andr Hornsey Lane 1982–87; TV Hornsey Rise Whitehall Pk Tm 1987–88; V Brockmoor, Lich 1988–93; V Brockmoor, Worc 1993–2001; Chapl Russells Hall Hosp Dudley 1988–94; Chapl Dudley Grp of Hosps NHS Trust 1994–2001; RD Himley 1996–2001; Hon Can Worc Cathl 1999–2001; Adn Dudley from 2001; Rep Dudley Com Ptnrship 2001–05; Chair Black Country Chs Engaged Enabling Grp 2003–05
Tel: 01905 773301
Fax: 0871 8133257
email: ftrethewey@cofe-worcester.org.uk

TREWEEK (nee Montgomery), Ven Rachel, BA, BTh
St Andrew's House 35 St Andrew's Hill London EC4V 5DE [ARCHDEACON OF HACKNEY; LONDON] *b* 1963 *educ* Broxbourne Sch; Reading Univ; Wycliffe Hall Ox; *CV* Paediatric Speech and Language Therapist, Gospel Oak Health Cen, Hampstead Health Auth 1985–87; Speech and Language Therapist, Child Devel Team,

Hampstead Health Auth 1987–89; Clinical Mgr for Paediatric Speech and Language Therapists in Health Cens, Bloomsbury, Hampstead & Islington Health Auths 1989–91; C St Geo Tufnell Park, Lon 1994–97, Assoc V 1997–99; V St Jas the Less Bethnal Green, Lon 1999–2006; Adn of Northolt 2006–11; Adn of Hackney from 2011CME Officer, Stepney Area, Lon Dioc 1999–2001; Bp's Visitor, Stepney Area 2004–06; GS 2010–
GS 2010– *Tel:* 020 7932 1145
email: archdeacon.hackney@london.anglican.org

TROTT, Revd Stephen, BA, MA, LLM
Rectory 41 Humfrey Lane Boughton Northampton NN2 8RQ [PETERBOROUGH] *b* 1957 *educ* Bp Vesey's Gr Sch Sutton Coldfield; Hull Univ; Fitzw Coll Cam; Cardiff Univ; Westcott Ho Th Coll (Cam Federation of Th Colls); *CV* C Hessle 1984–87; C St Alb Hull 1987–88; R Pitsford w Boughton from 1988; Sec CME 1988–93; Vis Chapl Pitsford Sch from 1991, Gov and Dir from 2001; Surrogate for Marriage Licences from 2001; M Dioc Syn from 1990; M Vacancy-in-See Cttee from 1995; Clerical Vc-Pres Dioc Syn and Chair Dioc Ho of Clergy 2000–03; M Peterb Cathl Coun 2001–04; M of DBF and Bishop's Council from 2010; Chair Church Buildings Cttee from 2010; M Eccl Law Soc from 1988; M Legis Cttee 1995–2000, 2005–10; M Legal Adv Commn 1996–2006; M CCBI and CTE 1996–99; M Revision Cttee on Calendar, Lectionary and Collects 1996; Ch Commr from 1997, Bd of Govs from 1999; M Pastl Cttee 1998–2012; Closed Chs Cttee from 2004, Dep Chair from 2009; M Nominations and Governance Cttee from 2009–2012; M DRACSC 1999–2001; M Revision Cttee on Clergy Discipline Measure 1999–2000; GS Rep on Gov Body of SAOMC 2001–06; C of E Delegate to Conf of Eur Chs, Trondheim, 2003; M Pastl (Amendment) Measure Revision Cttee from 2004; M Follow-up Grp, Review of Diocs, Pastl & Related Measures from 2004; M Panel of Reference, Angl Communion from 2005; M Strg Cttee Diocs Pastl and Miss Measure 2005–06; Stg Cttee, Conv of Cant from 2006–2010; M Revision Cttee, Eccl Fees Meas 2011; Synodical Sec, Convocation of Cant from 2010; M Council of Christians and Jews from 2011
GS 1995– *Tel:* 01604 845655 07712 863000
email: revstrott@btinternet.com

TRURO, Bishop of. See THORNTON, Rt Revd Tim Martin

TRURO, Dean of. See BUSH, Very Revd Roger Charles

TUPLING, Revd Katie (Catherine Louise), B Theol, ODMTG
Vicarage Church Bank Hathersage, Hope Valley S32 1AJ [DERBY] *b* 1974 *educ* St Mary Redcliffe and Temple Sch Bris; Westhill Coll Birm; Wycliffe Hall Ox; *CV* Vol Chr Youth Worker, Bris 1992–93; Ch Com and Youth Worker, Birm 1997–98; Co-ord, After Sch Clubs, Birm 1997–98; Playleader, After Sch Club, Birm 1998–2001; C St Pet Belper 2003–07; P-in-c Hathersage, P-in-c Bamford w. Derwent from 2007, P-in-c Grindleford from 2008
GS 2005–2010 *Tel:* 01433 650215
email: revtup@tup-house.freeserve.co.uk

TURNER, Canon (Thelma) Ann, B Sc
Grote Steenweg 47/42 2600 Berchem Belgium [EUROPE] *b* 1948 *educ* Wintringham Gr Sch, Grimsby; Univ of Kent at Cant; *CV* Hd of Science, Upminster Comp Sch 1972–78; Scientific Engl trainer 1985–91; written communication trainer from 1991; M Adnry of NW Eur Stg Cttee; Vc-Chair Ho of Laity, Dioc in Eur; M Dioc Communications Cttee, Dioc OLM Wkg Party, Dioc PIM Consultation, Bp's Coun; Lay Can (Gibraltar) from 2009
GS 2005– *Tel:* 0032 3440 2581
0032 477 626 184 (Mobile)
email: ann@turner.be

URQUHART, Rt Revd David Andrew, BA(Hons); Hon DD
Bishop's Croft, Old Church Road Harborne Birmingham B17 0BG [BISHOP OF BIRMINGHAM] *b* 1952 *educ* Rugby Sch; Ealing Business Sch; Wycliffe Hall Th Coll; *CV* C St Nic Hull 1984–87; TV Drypool Hull 1987–92; V H Trin Cov 1992–2000; Bp of Birkenhead 2000–06; Chair CMS Trustees 1994–2007; Prelate of Order of St Mich and St Geo from 2005; Abp of Cant's Episcopal Link with China from 2006; Bp of Birm from 2006; Chair Ridley Hall Coun from 2010; Lords Spiritual from 2010
GS 2006– *Tel:* 0121 427 1163
email: bishop@birmingham.anglican.org
Web: www.birmingham.anglican.org

VANN, Ven Cherry Elizabeth, GRSM, ARCM, Dip RS, Cert in Counselling, Br Sign Lang Level 3
57 Melling Rd Oldham OL4 1PN [ARCHDEACON OF ROCHDALE; MANCHESTER] *b* 1958 *educ* Lutterworth Upper Sch; R Coll of Music; Westcott Ho; *CV* C St Mich, Flixton 1989–92; Chapl Bolton Coll of HE and FE and C Bolton Par Ch 1992–98; Chapl among Deaf People and TV E Farnworth and Kearsley 1998–2004; TR E. Farnworth & Kearsley 2004–08; Bp's Adv in Women's Min 2004–09; AD Farnworth 2005–08; Hon Can Man Cathl 2007; Adn Rochdale from 2008
GS 2003– *Tel:* 0161 678 1454
07803 139274 (Mobile)
email: archrochdale@manchester.anglican.org

VENNER, Rt Revd Stephen Squires, BA, MA, DD, DUni, DL
83 Hathaway Court The Esplanade Rochester ME1 1QY [BISHOP TO HM FORCES] *b* 1944 *educ* Hardye's Sch Dorchester; Birm Univ; Linacre Coll Ox; Lon Inst of Educ; St Steph Ho Th Coll; *CV* C St Pet Streatham 1968–71; Hon C St Marg Streatham Hill 1971–72; Hon C Ascen Balham 1972–74; V St Pet Clapham and Bp's Chapl to Overseas

WHO'S WHO

Students 1974–76; V St Jo Trowbridge 1976–82; V H Trin Weymouth 1982–94; M Dorset LEA 1982–94; Chair Dioc Bd of Educ Sarum 1989–94; RD Weymouth 1988–94; Non-Res Can Sarum Cathl 1989–94; Chair Ho of Clergy Dioc Syn 1993–94; M GS Bd of Educ from 1985, Chair VCE Cttee from 1997; Bp of Middleton 1994–99; Chair Dioc Bd of Educ 1994–99; Bp of Dover (Bp in Cant) 1999–2009; Co-Chair C of E/Moravian Contact Grp 1994-99; Pres Woodard Corp 1999–2002; Vc-Chair Gov Ch Ch Univ Coll Cant 2000–05; Vc-Chair C of E Bd of Educ 2001–09; Chapl to Lord Warden of the Cinque Ports 2004–09; Chair of Govs (Pro-Chan) Cant Ch Ch Univ 2005–09; Bp for the Falklands from 2006; Bp to HM Forces from 2009; Deputy Lieutenant of Kent from 2010; Hon Asst Bp Rochester from 2010; Hon Asst Bp Europe from 2011
GS 1985–94, 2000–09 *Tel:* 01634 838787 (Home)
07980 743628 (Mobile)
email: stephen@venner.org.uk

VINCE, Mr Jacob Peter, MA, DBA, MRICS
3 High St Horam Heathfield TN21 0EJ [CHICHESTER] *b* 1960 *educ* Latymer Upper Sch; Univ of Wales; City Univ; *CV* Dir and Charterer Surveyor from 1996; M Bp's Coun; Ch Commr; M Ch Buildings (Uses and Disposals) Cttee
GS 2005– *Tel:* 01453 812623
01435 813700
Fax: 01435 813732
email: jacob.vince@btconnect.com

VINCENT, Mr Adrian, BA, MA
16 Faris Barn Drive Woodham Surrey KT15 3DZ [GUILDFORD] *b* 1970 *educ* George Abbot Sch; Dur Univ; Kings' Coll Lon; *CV* ITT Lon and Edinb Insurance Grp 1993–95; Asst Grants Sec, Adv Brd Min 1995–97; Archbps' Commission on the Organisation of the C of E 1997–98; Statistics Unit, Archbps' Counc 1999–2000; Exec Off, House of Bps Dept of the Central Sec 2000–07; Policy Off, The Gen Counc of the Bar 2007–08; Head of Remuneration and Policy, The Gen Counc of the Bar from 2008
GS 2010– *Tel:* 01932 349335
email: avwebsite@hotmail.co.uk
Web: www.adrianvincent.org.uk

WAINE, Ven Stephen,
28 Merriefield Drive Broadstone BH18 8BP [ARCHDEACON OF DORSET] *b* 1959 *CV* Adn of Dorset from 2010 *Tel:* 01202 659427
Fax: 01202 691418
email: addorset@salisbury.anglican.org

WAKEFIELD, Bishop of. See PLATTEN, Rt Revd Stephen George

WAKEFIELD, Dean of. See GREENER, Very Revd Jonathan

WALKER, Canon Anthony (Tony) Charles St John, MA
St Saviour's Vicarage 31 Richmond Rd Retford DN22 6SJ [SOUTHWELL AND NOTTINGHAM] *b* 1955 *educ* Brentwood Sch; Tr Coll Ox; Wycliffe Hall Ox; *CV* C Bradf Cathl 1981–84; C St Ann w. Em Nottm 1984–88; V St Saviour Retford 1988–2001; P-in-c St Swithun E Retford 2001; TR Retford 2002–11; TR Retford Area Team Ministry from 2011; AD Retford 2000–09; Hon Can S'well Minster from 2004; Hon Can Southwell Minster 2004–11; Can Emeritus Southwell Minster from 2011; M Dioc Syn, Bp's Coun
GS 2004– *Tel and Fax:* 01777 703800
email: tony@tonywalker.f9.co.uk

WALKER, Rt Revd David Stuart, MA, FRSA
Bishop's House Bishops Walk Cradley Heath B64 7RH [SUFFRAGAN BISHOP OF DUDLEY; WORCESTER] *b* 1957 *educ* Man Gr Sch; K Coll Cam; Qu Th Coll Birm; *CV* C Handsworth 1983–86; TV Maltby 1986–91; Ind Chapl Maltby 1986–91; V Bramley and Ravenfield 1991–95; TR Bramley and Ravenfield w Hooton Roberts and Braithwell 1995–2000; Hon Can Sheff Cathl 2000; Bp of Dudley from 2000; M Adv Coun on Relns of Bps and Relig Coms from 2002, Chair from 2008; Chair Housing Justice 2003–07; Sec W Midlands Regional Bps Grp 2003–08; Chair Housing Assoc Charitable Trust 2004–10; M Bps' Urban Panel 2004–10; M NPIA Independent Adv Panel from 2009; M C of E Pensions Bd from 2006, Dep Vc Chair 2010–11, Vc Chair from 2011; M CMEAC from 2006; M CUF from 2008; M Equality and DIversity Bd Adv Gp (Homes and Cttees Agency) from 2009; Chair C of E Pensions Bd Housing Cttee from 2009; Chair Sandwell Homes from 2011
GS 2005– *Tel:* 0121 550 3407
Fax: 0121 550 7340
email: bishop.david@cofe-worcester.org.uk

WALKER, Mrs (Pauline) Debra, B Pharm, MRPharmS
Willow Lodge Church Lane Lydiate L31 4HL [LIVERPOOL] *b* 1960 *educ* Ormskirk Gr Sch; Bradf Univ; *CV* Pharmacist qualified 1982; Elected to GS 2010
GS 2010– *Tel:* 0151 520 2496
email: debrawalker@btinternet.com

WALKER, Revd Ruth Elizabeth, BA, PGCE
The Vicarage 5 Howard Close Bidford-on-Avon Warwickshire B50 4EL [COVENTRY] *b* 1958 *educ* Hayes Sch; St.John's Coll, Dur; Hughes Hall,Cam; St.John's Coll Nott; *CV* RE Tchr The Embrook School, Wokingham, Berks 1980–83; RE Tchr, Ranelagh School, Bracknell, Berks 1983–86; Parish Dn St. Mary's Princes Risborough w Ilmer, Ox 1988–90; AC & Congregational Chapl Bradf Cathl 1990–93; AC P of West Swindon & the Lydiards, Bris1993–94; NSM P of West Swindon & the Lydiards, Bris 1994–96; AC St. John the Baptist & St. Andrew Parks & Walcot, Bris 1996–98; Hon.Ce

PTO P of Ch Ch Swindon, Bris 1999; Assoc Minr Keresley w Coundon & C-in-C Keresley Village Comm Ch, Cov 1999–2010; Area Dean Cov North Deanery 2004–10; Assoc Min Heart of England Parishes, Cov 2010
GS 2010– *Tel and Fax:* 01789 772217
email: ruth@heartparishes.org.uk

WALKER, Mr Timothy Edward Hanson, CB, MA, D Phil, D Sc (Hon), FIET, FRSA
Church House Great Smith St London SW1P 3AZ [THIRD CHURCH ESTATES COMMISSIONER] *b* 1945 *educ* Tonbridge Sch; Brasenose Coll Ox; *CV* Dir Gen Immigration, Home Office 1995–98; Dep Chair HM Customs and Excise, 1998–2000; Dir Gen Health and Safety Exec 2000–05; Non Exec Dir Lon Strategic Health Auth, 2006–2009; Third Ch Estates Commr from 2006; Chair Ch Commrs Bishoprics and Caths, Pastl and Closed Chs Ctees; Trustee Prostate Cancer Charity from 2006; Chair Accountancy and Actuarial Discipline Bd from 2008; Dir Fin Reporting Coun from 2008
Tel: 020 7898 1624
email: timothy.walker@churchofengland.org

WALLACE, Rt Revd Martin William, BD, AKC
Bishop's House Barton-le-Street Malton YO17 6PL [SUFFRAGAN BISHOP OF SELBY; YORK] *b* 1948 *educ* Varndean Gr Sch for Boys Brighton; Tauntons Sch Southn; K Coll Lon; St Aug Coll Cant; *CV* C Attercliffe Sheff 1971–74; C New Malden 1974–77; V St Mark Forest Gate 1977–93; Chapl Forest Gate Hosp 1977–80; RD Newham 1982–91; P-in-c Em Forest Gate 1985–89; P-in-c All SS Forest Gate 1991–93; Dioc Urban Officer 1991–93; Hon Can Chelmsf Cathl 1989–97; P-in-c St Thos Bradwell and St Lawr 1993–97; Ind Chapl Maldon and Dengie 1993–97; Adn of Colchester 1997–2003; Suff Bp of Selby from 2003 *Tel:* 01653 627191
Fax: 01653 627193
email: bishselby@clara.net

WALLER, Revd David Arthur,
St Saviour's Vicarage 210 Markhouse Rd London E17 8EP [CHELMSFORD] *b* 1961 *educ* Leeds Univ; *CV* C Aldwick, Chich 1991–95; pt Chapl Bognor Regis War Memorial Hosp 1994–95; TV Crawley 1995–2000; V St Saviour Walthamstow from 2000; M Dioc Bd of Educ from 2000; Asst AD Waltham Forest from 2004
GS 2005–2010 *Tel:* 020 8520 2036
email: d.a.waller@btinternet.com

WALSALL, Archdeacon of. See SIMS, Ven Christopher Sidney

WANDSWORTH, Archdeacon of. See ROBERTS, Ven Stephen John

WARD, Very Revd Dr Frances Elizabeth Fearn, M Theol; PhD
Deanery The Great Churchyard Bury St Edmunds Suffolk IP33 1RS [DEAN OF ST EDMUNDSBURY] *b* 1959 *educ* King's Sch Ely; Univ of St Andrews; Royal Lon Hospital; Univ of Cam; Univ of Man; Univ of Bradf; Westcott Ho Cam; *CV* Par Deacon St Bartholomew, Westhoughton 1989–93; Tutor Practical Theol, Northern Coll (URC & Cong. Fed) 1993–98; Hon C St George, Unsworth 1998–99; V St Peter, Bury 1999–2005; Bp's Advisor on Women's Min 2002–04; Hon C St Stephen and all Martyrs' Leverbridge 2005–06; Residentiary Can Bradf Cathl 2006–2010; Dean of St Edmundsbury from 2010 *Tel:* 01284 748722
Fax: 01284 768655
email: dean@stedscathedral.org

WARD, Mr John Selwyn, LLB
[LONDON] *b* 1971 *educ* Abbey Gate Coll Ches; Bris Univ; Katholieke Universiteit Leuven; Coll of Law, Ches; *CV* Solicitor; trainee solicitor, S J Berwin, Lon 1994–96; Stagiaire, Directorate Gen for Competition, Eur Commn 1996–97; asst solicitor, S J Berwin, Brussels 1997; Sen Legal Adv, Office of Fair Trading 1997–2003; Sen Legal Adv, DEFRA 2003–07, and from 2010; Legal Sec to the Advocate Gen for Scotland 2007–10; M PCC Emm Ch W Hampstead from 1999; M N Camden Dny Syn from 2002; Convener GS Human Sexuality Grp from 2006;
GS 2005– *Tel:* 07734 080573 (Mobile)
email: jward.anglican@zen.co.uk

WARD, Revd Dr Kevin, MA, Ph D
Theology & Religious Studies University of Leeds Leeds LS2 9JT [UNIVERSITIES, NORTHERN] *b* 1947 *educ* Pudsey Gr Sch; Edin Univ; Trin Coll Cam; Bp Tucker Th Coll, Mukono, Uganda; *CV* CMS Miss Ptnr (Tutor Bp Tucker Th Coll, Ch of Uganda) 1975–91; Tutor Qu Coll Birm 1991; Par Min Halifax, Wakef Dio 1991–95; Sen Lect in African Studies, Sch of Th and Relig Studies, Leeds Univ from 1995; NSM St Mich Headingley, Ripon Dio; M Ripon Dioc Wkg Grp in Human Sexuality; Trustee CMS 2003–10; Newsletter Editor, Uganda Church Association from 1993
GS 2003–05; 2005– *Tel:* 0113 343 3641
email: trskw@leeds.ac.uk

WARNER, Mr David Hugh, Dip Ed, GOE
41 Ox Lane Harpenden AL5 4HF [ST ALBANS] *b* 1932 *educ* St Jo Sch Leatherhead; St Mark and St Jo Coll Chelsea; Cam Inst of Educ; St Alb Min Tr Scheme; *CV* Dep Head St Nic Harpenden C of E JMI Sch 1964–71; Head Wigginton C of E JMI Sch 1972–73; Head St Helen's Wheathampstead C of E JMI Sch 1974–93; Rtd
GS 1995– *Tel and Fax:* 01582 762379
email: dhwarner@tiscali.co.uk

WARNER, Rt Revd Martin Clive, BA, MA, PhD
The Palace Chichester West Sussex PO19 1PY [BISHOP OF CHICHESTER] *b* 1958 *educ* K Sch Roch; Maidstone Gr Sch; St Chad's Coll Dur; St Steph Ho; *CV* C St Pet Plymouth 1984–88; TV Resurr Leic 1988–93; P Admin Shrine of Our Lady of

WHO'S WHO

Walsingham 1993–2002; Can Pastor, St Paul's Cathl from 2003; Treasurer, St Paul's Cathl 2008–09; Bp of Whitby 2009–12; Bp of Chichester from 2012 *Tel:* 01243 782161
Fax: 01243 531332

WARREN, Dr Yvonne, MA, PhD, UKCP, BACP
Cornerston 6 Hillview Stratford Upon Avon Warwickshire CV37 9AY [COVENTRY] *b* 1938 *educ* Beford High Sch; *CV* Nurse 1957–61; Relate Supervisor 1980–95; Psychotherapist from 1996; Bp's Adv from 1990; Candidates Panel from 1994; R from 1996; Bp's Visitor 1990–2006; Lay Rep GS Ridley Hall Th Coll 2000–07; Act Dioc Adv Pastoral Care and Counselling until 2011; Abps' Assessor from 2011
GS 2000–05; 2005–07; 2010– *Tel:* 01789414255
email: ywarren@hotmail.co.uk

WARRINGTON, Archdeacon of. See BRADLEY, Ven Peter David Douglas

WARRINGTON, Suffragan Bishop of. See BLACKBURN, Rt Revd Richard Finn

WARWICK, Suffragan Bishop of. See STROYAN, Rt Revd John Ronald Angus

WATSON, Rt Revd Andrew John, MA
16 Coleshill St Sutton Coldfield W Midlands B72 1SH [SUFFRAGAN BISHOP OF ASTON; BIRMINGHAM] *b* 1961 *educ* Win Coll; CCC Cam; Ridley Hall Th Coll; *CV* C St Pet Ipsley 1987–90; C St Jo and St Pet Notting Hill 1990–95; V St Steph E Twickenham from 1995; M Bp's Coun; M MPA Coun from 2006; AD Hampton 2003–08; Bp of Aston from 2008; M Bd Queen's Foundation, Birminghamfrom 2011; M Bd Abps' College of Evangelists from 2011
GS 2000–08 *Tel:* 020 426 0406 (Office)
0121 354 6632 (Home)
email: bishopofaston@birmingham.anglican.org

WATSON, Ven Sheila Anne, MA, M Phil
29 The Precincts Canterbury CT1 2EP [ARCHDEACON OF CANTERBURY] *b* 1953 *educ* Ayr Acad; St And Univ; Corpus Christi Coll Ox; Coates Hall Th Coll Edin; *CV* Dss St Sav Bridge of Allan and St Jo Alloa, St And 1979–80; Dss St Mary Monkseaton Newc 1980–84; Officer for Miss and Min Kensington Episc Area Lon 1984–87; Hon C St Luke and Ch Ch Chelsea Lon 1987–96; Selection Sec ABM 1992–93, Senior Selection Sec 1993–96; Adv in CME Salis 1997–2002; Dioc Dir of Min Salis 1998–2002; Hon Can Salis 2000; Adn of Buckingham 2002–07; Adn of Canterbury from 2007 *Tel:* 01227 865238
Fax: 01227 785209
email: archdeacon@canterbury-cathedral.org

WEBSTER, Rt Revd Glyn Hamilton, SRN
c/o Bishopthorpe Palace, Bishopthorpe, York YO23 2GE [BISHOP OF BEVERLEY] *b* 1951 *educ* Darwen Sec Tech (Gr) Sch; St Jo Coll Dur; *CV* C All SS Huntington York 1977–81; V St Luke Ev York and Sen Chapl York District Hosp 1981–92; Sen Chapl York Health Services NHS Trust 1992–99; Can and Preb York Minster 1994–99; RD York 1997–2004; Can Res and Treas York Minster from 1999; Can Pastor from 2000; Prolocutor of York from 2000; M AC from 2000; Chair Dioc Ho of Clergy; Chan York Minster from 2004; Assoc DDO from 2005; M GS Business Cttee from 2005; M Hosp Chapl Coun from 2005; Bp of Beverley from 2012
GS 1995– *Tel:* 01904 707021/2
email: office@archbishopofyork.org

WEBSTER, Ven Martin Duncan, BSc, Dip Th
Glebe House Church Lane Sheering Bishops Stortford CM22 7NR [ARCHDEACON OF HARLOW; CHELMSFORD] *b* 1952 *educ* Dury Falls Sec Modern Sch; Abbs Cross Tech High Sch; Nottm Univ; Linc Th Coll; *CV* C St Pet and St Mich Thundersley, Chelmsf 1978–81; TV Canvey Island 1981–86; V All SS and St Giles Nazeing 1986–99; AD Harlow 1989–99; NSM Officer 1995–99; TR Waltham Abbey 1999–2009; Adn Harlow from 2009
GS 2005–2010 *Tel:* 01297 734524
email: a.harlow@chelmsford.anglican.org

WELBY, Rt Revd Justin Portal,
Lambeth Palace, London SE1 7JU [ARCHBISHOP OF CANTERBURY] *b* 1956 *educ* Eton Coll; Trin Coll Cam; St Jo Coll Dur; Cranmer Hall ; *CV* Mgr Project Finance, Soc Nationale Elf Aquitaine, Paris 1978–83; Treas Elf UK plc, Lon 1983–84; Grp Treas Enterprise Oil plc, Lon 1984–89; C All SS Chilvers Coton and St Mary V, Astley, Nuneaton, Cov 1992–95; R St Jas Southam and St Mich & All Angels Ufton, Cov 1995–2002; Dir of Internat Min and Res Can Cov Cathl 2002–05; Sub-Dean and Can for Reconciliation Min, Cov Cathl 2005–07; P-in-c H Trin Cov 2007; Dean of Liv 2007–11; Bp of Durham 2011–12; Abp of Canterbury from 2013 *Tel:* 020 7261 1200
Fax: 020 7261 9836

WELCH, Ven Stephan John, BA, DipTheol, MTh
98 Dukes Ave Chiswick London W4 2AF [ARCHDEACON OF MIDDLESEX; LONDON] *b* 1950 *educ* Luton Gr Sch; Luton Sixth Form Coll; Hull Univ; Birm Univ; Heythrop Coll, Lon Univ; Qu Coll Birm; *CV* C Ch Ch Waltham Cross, St Alb 1977–80; P-in-c and V St Mary Reculver & St Bart Herne Bay, Cant 1980–92; V St Mary Hurley & St Jas the Less Stubbings, Ox 1992–2000; V St Pet Hammersmith, Lon 2000–06; AD Hammersmith and Fulham 2001–06; Adn of Middlesex from 2006; Chair Lon Dioc Bd for Schs; M DAC, DBF, Bp's Coun
Tel: 020 8742 8308 07780 704059 (Mobile)
email: archdeacon.middlesex@
london.anglican.org

WELLS, Archdeacon of. See SULLIVAN, Ven Nicola Ann

WELLS, Dean of. See CLARKE, Very Revd John Martin

WENT, Rt Revd John Stewart, MA
Bishop's House Church Rd Staverton Cheltenham GL51 0TW [SUFFRAGAN BISHOP OF TEWKESBURY; GLOUCESTER] *b* 1944 *educ* Colchester R Gr Sch; Cam Univ; Oak Hill Th Coll; *CV* C Em Northwood 1969–75; V H Trin Margate 1975–83; Vc Prin Wycliffe Hall Ox 1983–89; Adn of Surrey 1989–96; Bp of Tewkesbury from 1996
GS 1990–95 *Tel:* 01242 680188
Fax: 01242 680233
email: bshptewk@glosdioc.org.uk

WEST CUMBERLAND, Archdeacon of. See PRATT, Ven Richard

WEST HAM, Archdeacon of. See COCKETT, Ven Elwin Wesley

WESTMINSTER, Dean of. See HALL, Very Revd John Robert

WESTMORLAND AND FURNESS, Archdeacon of. See DRIVER, Ven Penny (Penelope May)

WHARTON, Rt Revd (John) Martin, CBE MA
Bishop's House 29 Moor Rd South Newcastle-upon-Tyne NE3 1PA [BISHOP OF NEWCASTLE] *b* 1944 *educ* Ulverston Gr Sch; Dur Univ; Linacre Coll Ox; Ripon Hall Th Coll; *CV* C St Pet Birm 1972–75; C St Jo Bapt Croydon 1975–77; Dir of Pastl Studies Ripon Coll Cuddesdon 1977–83; Exec Sec Bd of Min and Tr Bradf Dio 1983–91; Can Res Bradf Cathl and Bp's Officer for Min and Tr 1992; Bp of Kingston-upon-Thames 1992–97; Bp of Newc from 1997
GS 1998– *Tel:* 0191 285 2220
Fax: 0191 284 6933
email: bishop@newcastle.anglican.org

WHEATLEY, Rt Revd Peter William, MA
27 Thurlow Rd London NW3 5PP [AREA BISHOP OF EDMONTON; LONDON] *b* 1947 *educ* Ipswich Sch; Qu Coll Ox; Pemb Coll Cam; Mirfield Th Coll; Ripon Hall Th Coll; *CV* C All SS Fulham 1973–78; V H Cross, Cromer St, St Pancras 1978–82; V St Jas W Hampstead, P-in-c St Mary w All So Kilburn 1982–95; Chair Chr Concern for S Africa 1992–95; Dir POT Edmonton Area 1985–95; M BSR Internat Affairs Cttee 1981–96; Adn of Hampstead 1995–99; Bp of Edmonton from 1999
GS 1975–95 *Tel:* 020 7435 5890
Fax: 020 7435 6049
email: bishop.edmonton@london.anglican.org

WHITBY, Suffragan Bishop of. See NORTH, Rt Revd Philip John

WHITE, Mr David Peter, AMusLCM, BSc, FCMA, DChA, CGMA
Church House Great Smith St London SW1P 3AZ [HEAD OF FINANCIAL POLICY AND PLANNING, FINANCE AND RESOURCES, NATIONAL CHURCH INSTITUTIONS] *b* 1966 *educ* Dartford Gr Sch; LSE; *CV* On staff of Church Commissioners since 1990, Head of Fin Planning, Ch Crs 2002–07, Head of Fin Policy and Planning, AC and Ch Crs 2007–11, Head of Fin Policy and Planning, National Church Instutions from 2011 *Tel:* 020 7898 1684
Fax: 020 7898 1131
email: david.white@churchofengland.org

WHITE, Rt Revd Frank (Francis), BSc, DipTh
Bishop's House 29 Moor Rd South Newcastle Upon Tyne NE3 1PA [ASSISTANT BISHOP OF NEWCASTLE] *b* 1949 *educ* St Cuth Gr Sch Newc; Consett Tech Coll; UWIST Cardiff; Univ Coll Cardiff; St Jo Coll Nottm; *CV* Dir Youth Action York 1971–73; Detached Youth Worker Man Catacombs Trust 1973–77; C St Nic Dur 1980–84; C St Mary and St Cuth Chester-le-Street 1984–87; Chapl to Dur HA Hosps 1987–89; V St Jo Ev Birtley 1989–97; RD Chester-le-Street 1993–97; Hon Can Dur Cathl 1997–2002; Adn of Sunderland 1997–2002; Bp of Brixworth from 2002–2010; Hon Can Peterb Cathl from 2002–2010; Fell Univ of Northampton from 2010; Asst Bp of Newc from 2010; Hon Can Newc Cathl from 2010
GS 1987–2000 *Tel:* 0191 285 2220
Fax: 0191 284 6933
email: bishopfrank@newcastle.anglican.org
Web: www.newcastle.anglican.org

WHITE, Mrs Margaret Joan, MBE, CQSW
The White House 6 Blayney Row Heddon Station Newcastle NE158QD [NEWCASTLE] *b* 1933 *educ* Skerry's Coll; Walbottle Gr Sch; Rutherford Coll of F Ed; Sunderland Poly; *CV* Shorthand Typist 1948–52; Sec Thos. Cook 1952–54; Secy Lon & Lanc Insurance Co. 1954–56; Sec Assoc Anaesthetists, Winnipeg, 1956–60; Sec Chipman Chemicals, Winnipeg 1960–61; Sec Med Rsrch Counc,Newcastle 1961–62; Sec Transport & Genl Workers' Union 1962–65; Sec Westlands Special Sch 1965–74; Ed Welfare Off, Newcastle LEA, 1974–92; Dioc Apptmt, AFIA Rep MU from 1990
GS 2010– *Tel:* 0191 2674569
email: heddonstation@btinternet.com

WHITE, Canon Bob (Robert Charles), MA, Cert Th
St Mary's Vicarage Fratton Rd Portsmouth PO1 5PA [PORTSMOUTH] *b* 1961 *educ* Portsmouth Gr Sch; Mansfield Coll Ox; St Steph Ho Ox; *CV* C St Jo Forton 1985–88; C St Mark North End with special responsibility for St Fran Hilsea 1988–92; V St Clare Warren Park 1992–2000; V St Fran Leigh Park 1994–2000; RD Havant 1998–2000; V St Mary Portsea from 2000; AD Portsmouth from

WHO'S WHO

2011; M Bp's Coun; Dioc Adv on Urban Ministry; CUF Link Officer; Chair Dioc Ho of Clergy
GS 1995–2000, 2004– *Tel:* 023 9282 2687
email: revrcwhite@aol.com

WHITEHEAD, Hazel, BD, AKC, MA, D. MIN
The Rectory 5 The Spinning Walk Shere Surrey GU5 9HN [GUILDFORD] *b* 1954 *educ* Fryerns Gr; King's Coll Lon; NTMTC, Lambeth; *CV* Tchr 1989–95; AC St Mary Oatlands 1993–1997; Prin Guild Dioc Min 1994–2005; Dioc Dir Min Training 2005; Archbp's CMD Assesor BAP Adv; Co-Chair South Central Regional Training Partnership from 2008; M TETC and EVP 1994–2004; Chair CAEIMT 2003–05
GS 2010–
Tel: 01483 709307 01483 202394 07824 556043
Fax: 01483 790333
email: hazel.whitehead@cofeguildford.org.uk

WHITTAM SMITH, Mr Andreas, MA, CBE
154 Campden Hill Rd London W8 7AS [FIRST CHURCH ESTATES COMMISSIONER] *b* 1937 *educ* Birkenhead Sch; Keble Coll Ox; *CV* Founder & Ed 'The Independent' 1986–94; Dir Independent Print Limited); Pres Br Bd of Film Classification 1997–2002; Chair Fin Ombudsman Service Ltd 1999–2003; Chair The Children's Mutual 2005–10;; Vc-Pres Nat Coun for One-Parent Families; Chair Ch Commrs Assets Cttee; M Ch Commrs Bd of Govs; M AC from 2002
GS 2002– *Tel:* 020 7221 8354
email: andreasws@mac.com

WHITWORTH, Mrs Ruth,
4 Cravenwood Close Weeley Heath Clacton-on-Sea CO16 9DG [CHELMSFORD] *b* 1952
GS 1990–99; 2005–10; 2010– *Tel:* 01255 426175
email: ruth@greenend.com

WIGHT, Archdeacon of the Isle of. See BASTON, Ven Caroline Jane

WILCOCKSON, Ven Stephen Anthony, MA(Oxon), BA
14 Armthorpe Lane Doncaster South Yorkshire DN2 5LZ [ARCHDEACON OF DONCASTER; SHEFFIELD] *b* 1951 *educ* Park High Sch Birkenhead; Nottm Univ; Ox Univ; Wycliffe Hall; *CV* C St Lawrence Pudsey 1976–78; Sen C All Saints w Holy Trinity Wandsworth 1978–81; V St Peter Rock Ferry 1981–86; V St Mark, Lache cum Saltney 1986–95; V St Paul, Howell Hill 1995–2009; RD Epsom 2000–07; Par Dev Officer Chester Dioc 2009–12; Adn of Doncaster from 2012; Dioc Syn; Miss and Pastl Cttee; Bp's Coun; DAC; Bd of Educ; Fin and Property Cttee; Safeguarding Cttee; Communications Grp *Tel:* 01302 325787 01709 309110
email: steve.wilcockson@sheffield.anglican.org

WILCOX, Very Revd Dr Pete (Peter Jonathan) BA, MA, DPhil
1 Cathedral Close Liverpool L1 7BR [DEAN OF LIVERPOOL] *b* 1961 *educ* Worksop Coll; St John's Coll Durham; Robinson Coll Cam; St John's Coll Ox; Ridley Hall Cam; *CV* C All Saints', Preston on Tees 1987–1990; Asst P St Margaret's with St Philip and St Giles Ox 1990–93; TV St Edmund's Chapel Gateshead and Dir Cranmer Hall Urban Mission Centre 1993–98; P-in-C St Paul's Church at the Crossing, Walsall 1998–2006; Can Chancellor Lichfield Cathl 2006–12; Dean of Liverpool from 2012 *Tel:* 0151 702 7220
email: dean@liverpoolcathedral.org.uk
Web: www.liverpoolcathedral.org.uk

WILLESDEN, Area Bishop of. See BROADBENT, Rt Revd Pete (Peter Alan)

WILLIAMS, Sister Anne, Dip EvS
Good Shepherd Clergy House Forest Rd Ford Estate Sunderland SR4 0DX [DURHAM] *b* 1946 *educ* A J Dawson Gr Sch Wellfield; Wilson Carlile Coll of Evang; *CV* Civil Servant 1964–70; Fin Office Admin 1971–93; Communications/PR Support for Third World charity 1993–96; Dep Bursar Dur High Sch for Girls 1996–2002; Vc-Chairman Forward in Faith from 1994; Ch Army Ev in trg 2003–04; Com Missioner from 2004; Miss Enabler pt-time 2004–09; Regional Devel Officer CLCGB from 2009
GS 1990– *Tel:* 0191 5656 870 (Home)
07715 178654 (Mobile)
email: sranneca@aol.com

WILLIAMS, Revd David Grant, BSc Soc Sci
Christ Church Vicarage Sleepers Hill Winchester SO22 4ND [WINCHESTER] *b* 1961 *educ* Newport Free Gr Sch; Bris Univ; Crowther Hall, Birm; Wycliffe Hall Th Coll; *CV* Deputy Headteacher (CMS Mission Partner), Kitui District, Kenya 1983–85; Lay Asst, Christ Ch Clifton, Bris 1985–1986; AC Ecclesall, Sheffield Dioc 1989–92; V Ch Ch Dore, Sheffield Dic 1992–2002; Area Dean, Eccesall Deanery, Sheffield Dioc 1997–2002; Chapl,Aldine House Secure Unit, Sheffield 1998–2002; V Ch Ch Winc from 2002; M Dioc Pstrl Cttee 1997–2002; Chair Dioc Stewardship Grp 2000–02; M Bps Counc & Dioc Standing Cttee from 2010;
GS 2010– *Tel:* 01962 862414
01962 854454 07889 547095
email: david.williams@ccwinch.org.uk

WILLIAMS, Rt Revd Paul Gavin, BA
Dial House Riverside Twickenham TW1 3DT [AREA BISHOP OF KENSINGTON; LONDON] *b* 1968 *educ* Court Fields Sch Wellington; Grey Coll Univ Dur; Wycliffe Hall Ox; *CV* C St James Muswell Hill 1992–95; Asst V Christ Ch Clifton 1996–99; R St James Gerrards Cross w Fulmer 1999–2009; Area Bp of Kensington from 2009; Chair Trustees CPAS from 2011 *Tel:* 020 8892 7781
email: bishop.kensington@london.anglican.org

WILLIS, Very Revd Robert Andrew, DL
The Deanery The Precincts Canterbury CT1 2EP [DEAN OF CANTERBURY] *b* 1947 *educ* Kingswood Gr Sch; Warw Univ; Worc Coll Ox; Cuddesdon Th Coll; *CV* C St Chad Shrewsbury 1972–75; V Choral Sarum Cathl 1975–78; TR Tisbury and RD Chalke 1978–89; V Sherborne 1987–92; RD Sherborne 1991–92; Dean of Heref 1992–2001; Dean of Cant from 2001; M PWM Cttee 1990–2001; M Cathls Fabric Commn from 1993; M Liturg Commn 1994–98; Chair Deans' Conf from 1999
GS 1985–92, 1994–
Tel: 01227 762862 01227 865200
Fax: 01227 865222
email: dean@canterbury-cathedral.org

WILLMOTT, Rt Revd Trevor, MA, Dip Theol
The Bishop's Office Old Palace Canterbury CT1 2EE [BISHOP OF DOVER AND BISHOP IN CANTERBURY] *b* 1950 *educ* Plymouth Coll; St Pet Coll Ox; Fitzw Coll Cam; Westcott Ho Th Coll; *CV* C St Geo Norton 1974–77; Asst Chapl Oslo w Trondheim 1978–79; Chapl Naples w Capri, Bari and Sorrento 1979–83; R Ecton and Wdn Peterb Dioc Retreat Ho 1983–89; DDO and Dir of POT 1986–97; Can Res and Prec Peterb Cathl 1989–97; Adn of Dur and Can Res Dur Cathl 1997–2002; Suff Bp of Basingstoke 2002–2010; Bp of Dover from 2010; M GS Business Sub-cttee from 2005; M Ho of Bps Stg Cttee from 2005; Trustee Foundn for Chr Leadership; M Rural Bps Panel from 2004; Patr Cross Borders YMCA from 2005; Trustee St Michael's Coll, Llandaff; Visitor to the Sisters of Bethany
GS 2000– *Tel:* 01227 459382 *Fax:* 01227 784985
email: trevor.willmott@bishcant.org

WILSON, Rt Revd Alan Thomas Lawrence, MA, D Phil
Sheridan Grimms Hill Great Missenden HP16 9BG [AREA BISHOP OF BUCKINGHAM; OXFORD] *b* 1955 *educ* St Jo Coll Cam; Ball Col Ox; Wycliffe Hall Ox; *CV* Hon C Eynsham, Ox 1979–81, C 1981–82; C Caversham and Mapledurham 1982–89; V St Jo Caversham 1989–92; Angl substitute Chapl, HMP Reading, 1990–1992; R Sandhurst 1992–2003; RD Sonning 1998–2003; Area Bp of Buckingham from 2003; M Coun, Wycombe Abbey Sch from 2008; Chair Ox Dioc Bd of Educ from 2010; Univ of Buckingham Visiting Prof in Theol from 2010
Tel: 01494 862173
07525 655756 (Mobile)
Fax: 01494 890508
email: bishopbucks@oxford.anglican.org

WILSON, Mr Brian Kenneth, MA FIA
84 Albert Road Epsom Surrey KT17 4EL [SOUTHWARK] *b* 1947 *educ* Lewes Co Sch for Boys; Univ Oxford; *CV* Sch Master, Dulwich Coll 1971–74; Sch Master, King's Sch Cant 1974–76; Asst Actuary, Bacon & Woodrow 1976–83; Partner, Bacon & Woodrow 1983–2002; Prin, Hewitt Assoc 2002–10; Prin, Aon Hewitt 2010; rtd 2010; M C of E Pensions Bd from 2011; M Remuneration and Conditions of Service Cttee of AC from 2011
GS 2010– *Tel:* 01372 740155
email: brian.k.wilson@btinternet.com

WILSON, Ven Christine Louise, Dip Th
The Old Vicarage Baslow Derbyshire DE45 1RY [ARCHDEACON OF CHESTERFIELD; DERBY] *b* 1958 *educ* Margaret Hardy Sch, Brighton; SDMTS; *CV* C Henfield w. Shermanbury and Woodmancate, Chich 1997–2002; TV Hove 2002–08; V Goring by Sea 2008–10; Adn Chesterfield from 2010; Chich Dioc Overseas Cttee 2007–09; Adv Cttee, Derby from 2010; Bd of Finance, Derby from 2010; Bd of Edu, Derby from 2010; Pastoral Cttee, Derby from 2010; Parsonages Cttee, Derby from 2010; Chair Peak Centre from 2010; Glebe Ctte, Derby from 2010
GS 2010– *Tel:* 01246 583023
email: archchesterfield@derby.anglican.org

WILSON, Mr John, MIH, MIF
49 Oakhurst Lichfield WS14 9AL [LICHFIELD] *b* 1946 *educ* Polytechnic of North London; *CV* HM Forces 1961–76; Deputy Area School Meals Advisor, Cambridgeshire County Council 1977–78; Regional Sales and marketing Manager, Bateman Catering 1978 -83; Dir of Training, Mantislight Ltd, 1983–87; Dir Operations, Deansbury Ltd, 1987–92; Charity Management Consult, Charity Support Services, 1992–97; National Fundraising and Marketing Advisor, Age Concern England, 1997–2001; Charity Management Consult, Charity Support Services, 2001–06; Chief Exec, Line Line, 2006–10; M Dioc Syn from 1989; M Dioc Pastoral Cttee from 2000; M Bp's Coun from 2000; M Brd of Partonage from 2003; Dioc Chair of Ho of Laity from 2009; Lay Chair of Lichf Deanery from 1987; Treasurer Church House Deaneries Group (The National Deaneries Network) from 2003; Chair Board of Directors/ Trustees Link Line Community Services from 2010; Managing Director Church Jobs Ltd (www.churchjobfinder.co.uk) from 2010
GS 2005– *Tel:* 01543 268678 07785 334077
Fax: 01543 411685
email: charity.services@btclick.com

WILSON-RUDD, Miss Fay (Felicity),
3 Old School Place North Grove Wells BA5 2TD [BATH AND WELLS] *b* 1941 *educ* Filton High Sch; *CV* Asst Stewardship Adv St Alb Dio 1981–84; Resources Adv B & W 1984–2001; pt Chapl Co-ord Somerset NHS Ptnrship and Soc Care Trust from 1999
GS 1993– *Tel and Fax:* 01749 677286 (Home)
07712 581903 (Mobile)
email: faywilsonrudd@msn.com

WILTS, Archdeacon of, [NOT APPOINTED AT TIME OF GOING TO PRESS]

WINCHESTER, Archdeacon of. **See HARLEY, Ven Michael**

WINCHESTER, Bishop of. See DAKIN, Rt Revd Timothy John

WINCHESTER, Dean of. See ATWELL, Very Revd James Edgar

WINDSOR, Dean of. See CONNER, Rt Revd David John

WINSTANLEY, Rt Revd Alan Leslie, B Th
The Rectory Shirwell Barnstaple EX31 4JU [HONORARY ASSISTANT BISHOP OF EXETER] *b* 1949 *educ* Leigh Boys' Gr Sch, Lancs; St Jo Coll Nottm; *CV* C St Andr Livesey, Blackb 1972–75; C St Mary Gt Sankey Liv 1975–78; V Penketh Liv 1978–81; SAMS Miss Lima, Peru 1982–85, Arequipa 1986–87; Bp of Peru and Bolivia 1988–93; V Eastham and Hon Asst Bp of Chester 1994–2003; V St Jo Ev, Whittle-le-Woods and Hon Asst Bp of Blackburn 2003–12; R in the Shirwell Team and Hon Asst Bp of Exeter from 2012 *Tel:* 01271 250436
Fax: 01271 850436
email: alan.winstanley123@btinternet.com

WINTER, Revd Canon Dr Dagmar, Dr Theol
Vicarage Kirkwhelpington Newcastle upon Tyne NE19 2RT [NEWCASTLE] *b* 1963 *educ* Gesamtschule Oberursel; Erlangen Univ; Aberd Univ; Heidelberg Univ; Herborn Th Coll; *CV* C St Mark Bromley 1996–99; Assoc V and Dny Trg Officer Hexham Abbey 1999–2006; P-in-c Kirkwhelpington w Kirkharle & Kirkheaton, and Cambo and Dioc Officer for Rural Affairs from 2006; AD of Morpeth from 2010; Hon Can Newc Cathl from 2011
GS 2005–
email: dagmar.winter@btinternet.com

WINTON, Rt Revd Alan Peter, BA, PhD
The Red House 53 Norwich Rd Stoke Holy Cross Norwich NR14 8AB [BISHOP OF THETFORD] *b* 1958 *educ* Chislehurst and Sidcup Gr Sch; Trin Coll Bristol; Univ Sheff; Linc Theol Coll; *CV* Asst C Christ Ch Southgate 1991–95; P-in-C St Paul's Walden w Preston 1995–99; CME Officer Dioc St Albans 1995–99; R Welwyn w Ayot St Peter 1999–2005, TR Welwyn 2005–09; Bp of Thetford from 2009; Chair Discipleship and Min Forum Dioc Norw; Chair Norw Dioc Ministry Course Governing Body *Tel:* 01508 491014
Fax: 01508 492105
email: bishop.thetford@norwich.anglican.org

WISBECH, Archdeacon of, [NOT APPOINTED AT TIME OF GOING TO PRESS]

WITCOMBE, Very Revd John Julian, MA, MPhil
1 Hill Top Coventry CV1 5AB [DEAN OF COVENTRY] *b* 1959 *educ* Bramcote Hills Gr Sch; Nott High Sch; Emman Colle, Cam; Nott Univ; St. John's Coll, Nott; *CV* C, St John's Birtley, Dur 1984–87; C-in-C, St. Barnabas' Inham Nook, S'well 1987–91; V, St. Luke's Lodge Moor, Sheff, 1991–95; TR, Uxbridge, Lon, 1995–98; Dean, St John's Coll Nott, 1998–2005; Off Min & Dir of Ordinands, Glouc, 2005–2010; Dir, Dept of Disicipleship and Ministry, Glouc 2010–12; Res Can Glouc Cathl 2010–12; Dean of Coventry from 2012
GS 2010– *Tel:* 024 7652 1223
Web: www.coventrycathedral.org.uk

WITTS, Mrs Susan Anne, BA
20 Amber Drive Chorley PR6 0LA [BLACKBURN] *b* 1958 *educ* Mather Colll Man; Edge Hill Univ; Church Coll Cert Sch Work St Martin's Lanc; *CV* Primary Sch Tchr 1979–2005; Asst Dir Children's Work, Bd Edu; Blackb Dioc from 2005; Dioc Blackb bd Edu Liturg Ctee; Elected to GS 2010
GS 2010– *Tel:* 01254 503070
email: susan.witts@blackburn.anglican.org

WOLSTENHOLME, Canon Carol, OBE, FCIPD
12 Ashleigh Crescent Denton Newcastle upon Tyne NE5 2AE [NEWCASTLE] *b* 1943 *educ* Rutherford High Sch Newc; *CV* Dept Work and Pensions Human Resources 1960-2003; Mgt Consult from 2000; Reader 2006; Cathl Coun 2006; Chair Newc Dioc Miss and Pastl Ctee from 2006; M Newc Dioc Strategical Devel Gp from 2007; Bp's Coun from 2007; Chair Deaneries Dev Task Grp 2009; Trustee Lindisfarne Reg Trg Partnership 2012
GS 2009– *Tel:* 0191 2745144
email: cawol43@aol.com

WOLVERHAMPTON, Area Bishop of. See GREGORY, Rt Revd Clive Malcolm

WOLVERSON, Revd Marc Ali Morad, BA, Dip Min
Vicarage 85 Buxton Rd High Lane Stockport SK6 8DS [CHESTER] *b* 1968 *educ* St Louis Country Day Sch, USA; Loyola Univ, USA; Kansas Univ, USA; Ripon Coll Cuddesdon; *CV* C St Mary Nantwich 1996–99; Asst R and sch Chapl, St Luke's Episcopal Ch and Sch, Baton Rouge, Louisiana 1999–2000; Assoc V St Mich and All Angels Bramhall 2000–04; V St Thos High Lane from 2004; M Ches Dioc Syn; Dioc Spiritual Dir, Cursillo
GS 2005 *Tel:* 01663 762627
email: frmarc@onetel.com

WOOD, Canon Frances Mary, BA(Hons)
8 Butts Lane Egglescliffe Stockton-on-Tees TS16 9BT [DURHAM] *b* 1946 *educ* Harrogate Gr Sch; Univ Reading; *Tel:* 01642 782113 07742 732019
email: fran.wood3@virginmedia.com

WOOD, Canon (Nicholas) Martin, AKC, MTh
101 London Road Bowers Gifford Basildon Essex SS13 2DU [CHELMSFORD] *b* 1951 *educ* Brentwood Sch; Mid Essex Tech Coll; Kings Coll Lon; St Augustine's Coll, Cant; Univ of Wales Lampeter; *CV* C East Ham Team Ministry 1975–78; C in C, St. Luke, Leyton 1978–81; V Rush Green 1981–91; Chapl Barking Coll 1981–91; TR Elland 1991–2005; Rural Dean of Brighouse & Elland 1996–

2005; Hon can Wakef Cathl 2001–05; P Develp Adv Bradwell Episcopal Area of Chelms from 2005; Hon can Chelms Cathl from 2008; Chelms Dioc Brd Miss 1983–84; Chelms Dioc Pstrl support & develp grp 1985–88; Wakef Dioc Syn 1991–05; Wakef Bp's Counc 1997–2005; Wakef Dioc Brd Min & Training sub cttee 1991–94; Wakef Dioc clergy ed and training grp 1994–98; Wakef Min Scheme Counc & ed sub grp 1996–2005; Wakef Min Adv Grp 1994–2005; Chair Wakef Dioc Family Life grp FLAME 1998–2005; Chelms Miss and P Develop Adv Grp from 2005; Chelms Dioc Syn from 2009; Chair Ho of Clergy Dioc Syn Chelmsf from 2010; Chapl to Bp of Bradwell and Parish Dev Adv (Bradwell Area) 2011–12; Miss and Min Adv (Bradwell Area) from 2012
GS 2010– *Tel:* 01268 552219 07814 909976
email: mwood@chelmsford.anglican.org
Web: www.chelmsford.anglican.org/mwood

WOOLWICH, Area Bishop of. See IPGRAVE, Rt Revd Michael Geoffrey

WORCESTER, Archdeacon of. See MORRIS, Ven Roger Anthony Brett

WORCESTER, Bishop of. See INGE, Rt Revd Dr John Geoffrey

WORCESTER, Dean of. See ATKINSON, Very Revd Peter Gordon

WRAW, Rt Revd John Michael, BA
Bishop's House Orsett Rd Horndon-on-the-Hill SS17 8NS [AREA BISHOP OF BRADWELL; CHELMSFORD] *b* 1959 *educ* K Sch Chester; Lincoln Coll Ox; Fitzwilliam Coll Cam; Ridley Hall Cam; *CV* C St Pet Bromyard, Heref 1985–88; TV Sheff Manor Team 1988–92; V Clifton St Jas, Sheff 1992–2001; P-in-c Wickersley St Alb, Sheff 2001–04; Adn of Wilts 2004–12; Bp of Bradwell from 2012
Tel: 01375 673806
Fax: 01375 674222
email: email: b.bradwell@chelmsford.anglican.org

WRIGHT, Ven Dr Paul, BD, MTh, DMin, AKC
The Archdeaconry The Glebe Chislehurst BR7 5PX [ARCHDEACON OF BROMLEY AND BEXLEY; ROCHESTER] *b* 1954 *educ* Crayford Sch; K Coll Lon; Heythrop Coll Lon; Ripon Coll, Cuddesdon; Lampeter Univ of Wales; *CV* C St Geo Beckenham, Roch 1979–83; C St Mary w St Matthias & St Jo, S'wark 1983–85; Chapl Ch Sch Richmond, S'wark 1983–85; V St Aug Gillingham, Roch 1985–90; R St Paulinus Crayford, Roch 1990–99; RD Erith 1993–97; Hon Can Roch Cathl 1998–2003; V St Jo Evang Sidcup, Roch 1999–2003; Adn of Bromley and Bexley from 2003; M Bp's Coun; M Dioc Bd of Patr; Chair Adv Bd for Miss and Unity; M Eccl Law Soc; Bp's Insp of Theol Colls
Tel and Fax: 020 8467 8743 07985 902601 (Mobile)
email: archdeacon.bromley@rochester.anglican.org

WYNNE, Mrs Alison,
88 Balcarres Rd Leyland PR25 3ED [BLACKBURN] *b* 1961 *educ* Pleckgate High Sch, Blackb; *CV* Wages clerk, MOD 1979–83; Computer Programmer, MOD 1983–86; Computer Applications Programmer, Lancs Constabulary 1986–87; IT Systems Programmer, Lancs Constabulary 1987–89; Chr outreach worker from 2001; Orthopaedic support worker Lancashire Teaching Hospitals from 2009; Ch Min Asst from 2012
GS 2005– *Tel:* 01772 454209
07719 727527 (Mobile)
email: alison@wynne.org.uk

WYTHE, Mr John Michael, BSc, FRICS
Woodpeckers Ashwood Rd Woking GU22 7JN [CHURCH COMMISSIONER] *b* 1956 *educ* Woking Gr Sch for Boys; Reading Univ; *CV* Dir and Head of Fund Management at Prudential Property Investment Managers until 2010; Ch Commissioner from 2007; M Assets Cttee; current bd, cttee and Trustee roles with Norges Bank, PrudentialIM&G, CBRE Global Investors, DTZ Investment Management, The Portman Estate, Pollen Estate and Sue Ryder *Tel:* 01483 726710
email: jm.wythe@gmail.com

YEOMAN, Revd Ruth Jane, MA, BSc, MSc
Vicarage 12 Fairfax Gardens Menston Ilkley LS29 6ET [BRADFORD] *b* 1960 *educ* Nottm Bluecoat Sch; Sheff Univ; Ripon Coll Cuddesdon; *CV* C St Pet and St Paul Coleshill w. Maxstoke, Birm 1991–95; Asst P St Phil and St Jas Hodge Hill and Adv for Children's Work, Birm Dioc 1995–2000; Houseleader, L'Arch Lambeth Com 2001–02; V St Jo Divine Menston w. Woodhead from 2003; Assoc DDO Bradf from 2006; NADAWM representative Bradf from 2009
GS 2005–
Tel: 01943 877739 07752 912646 (Mobile)
email: ruthjyeoman@hotmail.com

YORK, Archbishop of. See SENTAMU, Most Revd and Rt Hon Dr John Tucker Mugabi

YORK, Archdeacon of, [NOT APPOINTED AT TIME OF GOING TO PRESS]

YORK, Dean of. See FAULL, Very Revd Vivienne Frances

YOUNG, Rt Revd Clive, BA
28 Westerfield Rd Ipswich IP4 2UJ [SUFFRAGAN BISHOP OF DUNWICH; ST EDMUNDSBURY AND IPSWICH] *b* 1948 *educ* K Edw VI Gr Sch Chelmsf; Dur Univ; Ridley Hall Cam; *CV* C Neasden cum Kingsbury 1972–75; C St Paul Hammersmith 1975–79; P-in-c St Paul w St Steph Old Ford 1979–82; V 1982–92; AD Tower Hamlets 1988–92; Adn of Hackney 1992–99; V St Andr Holborn 1992–99; Bp of Dunwich from 1999 *Tel:* 01473 222276
Fax: 01473 210303
email: bishop.clive@stedmundsbury.anglican.org 912646 (Mobile)
email: ruthjyeoman@hotmail.com

WHO'S WHO

INDEX

Note: Names of dioceses appear in *italics*; page references in **bold** type indicate maps. Names beginning 'St' are filed as if spelled 'Saint'. Hyphens and apostrophes are ignored for filing purposes.